PREFACE

This book contains core materials for the study of European Union Law. We have attempted to edit the material to focus on both constitutional provisions and the key areas of substantive law. Inevitably cuts have had to be made in the selection of material. Extracts from both the current consolidated version of the constitutional treaties and the revised (pending ratification) consolidated version of the constitutive treaties are included. This has added to the length of the book for this edition only. The fate of the revised (Treaty of Lisbon) version will be determined during the forthcoming academic year. In this book, the consolidated texts of the EU treaties as amended by the Treaty of Lisbon are reproduced from www.fco.gov.uk (Crown Copyright 2008).

These materials are free from annotations, thus are suitable not only for private study but also for examinations. For more detailed study, however, recourse should be had to the full (unedited) text of the instruments, most of which can be located through links from the website of the European Union: http://europa.eu and from http://eur-lex.europa.eu.

The materials are accurate, to the best of our knowledge, as of April 2008.

Nicole Busby
Rhona Smith

Contents

PRIMARY CONSTITUTIONAL LEGISLATION

CONSOLIDATED VERSION OF THE TREATY
ESTABLISHING THE EUROPEAN COMMUNITY

[THE CONTRACTING PARTIES]

DETERMINED to lay the foundations of an ever closer union among the peoples of Europe,

RESOLVED to ensure the economic and social progress of their countries by common action to eliminate the barriers which divide Europe,

AFFIRMING as the essential objective of their efforts the constant improvements of the living and working conditions of their peoples,

RECOGNISING that the removal of existing obstacles calls for concerted action in order to guarantee steady expansion, balanced trade and fair competition,

ANXIOUS to strengthen the unity of their economies and to ensure their harmonious development by reducing the differences existing between the various regions and the backwardness of the less favoured regions,

DESIRING to contribute, by means of a common commercial policy, to the progressive abolition of restrictions on international trade,

INTENDING to confirm the solidarity which binds Europe and the overseas countries and desiring to ensure the development of their prosperity, in accordance with the principles of the Charter of the United Nations,

RESOLVED by thus pooling their resources to preserve and strengthen peace and liberty, and calling upon the other peoples of Europe who share their ideal to join in their efforts,

DETERMINED to promote the development of the highest possible level of knowledge for their peoples through a wide access to education and through its continuous updating,

HAVE DECIDED to create a EUROPEAN COMMUNITY and … have agreed as follows.

PART ONE
PRINCIPLES

Article 1

By this Treaty, the HIGH CONTRACTING PARTIES establish among themselves a EUROPEAN COMMUNITY.

Article 2

The Community shall have as its task, by establishing a common market and an economic and monetary union and by implementing common policies or activities referred to in Articles 3 and 4, to promote throughout the Community a harmonious, balanced and sustainable development of economic activities, a high level of employment and of social protection, equality between men and women, sustainable and non-inflationary growth, a high degree of competitiveness and convergence of economic performance, a high level of protection and improvement of the quality of the environment, the raising of the standard of living and quality of life, and economic and social cohesion and solidarity among Member States.

Article 3

1. For the purposes set out in Article 2, the activities of the Community shall include, as provided in this Treaty and in accordance with the timetable set out therein:
    (a) the prohibition, as between Member States, of customs duties and quantitative restrictions on the import and export of goods, and of all other measures having equivalent effect;
    (b) a common commercial policy;
    (c) an internal market characterised by the abolition, as between Member States, of obstacles to the free movement of goods, persons, services and capital;
    (d) measures concerning the entry and movement of persons as provided for in Title IV;
    (e) a common policy in the sphere of agriculture and fisheries;
    (f) a common policy in the sphere of transport;
    (g) a system ensuring that competition in the internal market is not distorted;

(h)   the approximation of the laws of Member States to the extent required for the functioning of the common market;

(i)   the promotion of coordination between employment policies of the Member States with a view to enhancing their effectiveness by developing a coordinated strategy for employment;

(j)   a policy in the social sphere comprising a European Social Fund;

(k)   the strengthening of economic and social cohesion;

(l)   a policy in the sphere of the environment;

(m)   the strengthening of the competitiveness of Community industry;

(n)   the promotion of research and technological development;

(o)   encouragement for the establishment and development of trans-European networks;

(p)   a contribution to the attainment of a high level of health protection;

(q)   a contribution to education and training of quality and to the flowering of the cultures of the Member States;

(r)   a policy in the sphere of development cooperation;

(s)   the association of the overseas countries and territories in order to increase trade and promote jointly economic and social development;

(t)   a contribution to the strengthening of consumer protection;

(u)   measures in the spheres of energy, civil protection and tourism.

2.   In all the activities referred to in this Article, the Community shall aim to eliminate inequalities, and to promote equality, between men and women.

Article 4

1.   For the purposes set out in Article 2, the activities of the Member States and the Community shall include, as provided in this Treaty and in accordance with the timetable set out therein, the adoption of an economic policy which is based on the close coordination of Member States' economic policies, on the internal market and on the definition of common objectives, and conducted in accordance with the principle of an open market economy with free competition.

2.   Concurrently with the foregoing, and as provided in this Treaty and in accordance with the timetable and the procedures set out therein, these activities shall include the irrevocable fixing of exchange rates leading to the introduction of a single currency, the ecu, and the definition and conduct of a single monetary policy and exchange-rate policy the primary objective of both of which shall be to maintain price stability and, without prejudice to this objective, to support the general economic policies in the Community, in accordance with the principle of an open market economy with free competition.

3.   These activities of the Member States and the Community shall entail compliance with the following guiding principles: stable prices, sound public finances and monetary conditions and a sustainable balance of payments.

Article 5

The Community shall act within the limits of the powers conferred upon it by this Treaty and of the objectives assigned to it therein.

In areas which do not fall within its exclusive competence, the Community shall take action, in accordance with the principle of subsidiarity, only if and in so far as the objectives of the proposed action cannot be sufficiently achieved by the Member States and can therefore, by reason of the scale or effects of the proposed action, be better achieved by the Community.

Any action by the Community shall not go beyond what is necessary to achieve the objectives of this Treaty.

Article 6

Environmental protection requirements must be integrated into the definition and implementation of the Community policies and activities referred to in Article 3, in particular with a view to promoting sustainable development.

Article 7

1.   The tasks entrusted to the Community shall be carried out by the following institutions:

> — a EUROPEAN PARLIAMENT,
> — a COUNCIL,
> — a COMMISSION,
> — a COURT OF JUSTICE,
> — a COURT OF AUDITORS.
> Each institution shall act within the limits of the powers conferred upon it by this Treaty.

2. The Council and the Commission shall be assisted by an Economic and Social Committee and a Committee of the Regions acting in an advisory capacity.

Article 8

A European system of central banks (hereinafter referred to as 'ESCB') and a European Central Bank (hereinafter referred to as 'ECB') shall be established in accordance with the procedures laid down in this Treaty; they shall act within the limits of the powers conferred upon them by this Treaty and by the Statute of the ESCB and of the ECB (hereinafter referred to as 'Statute of the ESCB') annexed thereto.

Article 9

A European Investment Bank is hereby established, which shall act within the limits of the powers conferred upon it by this Treaty and the Statute annexed thereto.

Article 10

Member States shall take all appropriate measures, whether general or particular, to ensure fulfilment of the obligations arising out of this Treaty or resulting from action taken by the institutions of the Community. They shall facilitate the achievement of the Community's tasks.

They shall abstain from any measure which could jeopardise the attainment of the objectives of this Treaty.

Article 11

1. Member States which intend to establish enhanced cooperation between themselves in one of the areas referred to in this Treaty shall address a request to the Commission, which may submit a proposal to the Council to that effect. In the event of the Commission not submitting a proposal, it shall inform the Member States concerned of the reasons for not doing so.

2. Authorisation to establish enhanced cooperation as referred to in paragraph 1 shall be granted, in compliance with Articles 43 to 45 of the Treaty on European Union, by the Council, acting by a qualified majority on a proposal from the Commission and after consulting the European Parliament. When enhanced cooperation relates to an area covered by the procedure referred to in Article 251 of this Treaty, the assent of the European Parliament shall be required.

   A member of the Council may request that the matter be referred to the European Council. After that matter has been raised before the European Council, the Council may act in accordance with the first subparagraph of this paragraph.

3. The acts and decisions necessary for the implementation of enhanced cooperation activities shall be subject to all the relevant provisions of this Treaty, save as otherwise provided in this Article and in Articles 43 to 45 of the Treaty on European Union.

Article 11a

Any Member State which wishes to participate in enhanced cooperation established in accordance with Article 11 shall notify its intention to the Council and to the Commission, which shall give an opinion to the Council within three months of the date of receipt of that notification. Within four months of the date of receipt of that notification, the Commission shall take a decision on it, and on such specific arrangements as it may deem necessary.

Article 12

Within the scope of application of this Treaty, and without prejudice to any special provisions contained therein, any discrimination on grounds of nationality shall be prohibited.

The Council, acting in accordance with the procedure referred to in Article 251, may adopt rules designed to prohibit such discrimination.

Article 13

1. Without prejudice to the other provisions of this Treaty and within the limits of the powers conferred by it upon the Community, the Council, acting unanimously on a proposal from the Commission and after consulting the European Parliament, may take appropriate action to combat discrimination based on sex, racial or ethnic origin, religion or belief, disability, age or sexual orientation.

2. By way of derogation from paragraph 1, when the Council adopts Community incentive measures, excluding any harmonisation of the laws and regulations of the Member States, to support action taken by the Member States in order to contribute to the achievement of the objectives referred to in paragraph 1, it shall act in accordance with the procedure referred to in Article 251.

Article 14

1. The Community shall adopt measures with the aim of progressively establishing the internal market over a period expiring on 31 December 1992, in accordance with the provisions of this Article and of Articles 15, 26, 47(2), 49, 80, 93 and 95 and without prejudice to the other provisions of this Treaty.

2. The internal market shall comprise an area without internal frontiers in which the free movement of goods, persons, services and capital is ensured in accordance with the provisions of this Treaty.

3. The Council, acting by a qualified majority on a proposal from the Commission, shall determine the guidelines and conditions necessary to ensure balanced progress in all the sectors concerned.

Article 15

When drawing up its proposals with a view to achieving the objectives set out in Article 14, the Commission shall take into account the extent of the effort that certain economies showing differences in development will have to sustain during the period of establishment of the internal market and it may propose appropriate provisions.

If these provisions take the form of derogations, they must be of a temporary nature and must cause the least possible disturbance to the functioning of the common market.

Article 16

Without prejudice to Articles 73, 86 and 87, and given the place occupied by services of general economic interest in the shared values of the Union as well as their role in promoting social and territorial cohesion, the Community and the Member States, each within their respective powers and within the scope of application of this Treaty, shall take care that such services operate on the basis of principles and conditions which enable them to fulfil their missions.

PART TWO

CITIZENSHIP OF THE UNION

Article 17

1. Citizenship of the Union is hereby established. Every person holding the nationality of a Member State shall be a citizen of the Union. Citizenship of the Union shall complement and not replace national citizenship.

2. Citizens of the Union shall enjoy the rights conferred by this Treaty and shall be subject to the duties imposed thereby.

Article 18

1. Every citizen of the Union shall have the right to move and reside freely within the territory of the Member States, subject to the limitations and conditions laid down in this Treaty and by the measures adopted to give it effect.

2. If action by the Community should prove necessary to attain this objective and this Treaty has not provided the necessary powers, the Council may adopt provisions with a view to facilitating the exercise of the rights referred to in paragraph 1. The Council shall act in accordance with the procedure referred to in Article 251.

3. Paragraph 2 shall not apply to provisions on passports, identity cards, residence permits or any other such document or to provisions on social security or social protection.

Article 19

1. Every citizen of the Union residing in a Member State of which he is not a national shall have the right to vote and to stand as a candidate at municipal elections in the Member State in which he resides, under the same conditions as nationals of that State. This right shall be exercised subject to detailed arrangements adopted by the Council, acting unanimously on a proposal from the Commission and after consulting the European Parliament; these arrangements may provide for derogations where warranted by problems specific to a Member State.

2. Without prejudice to Article 190(4) and to the provisions adopted for its implementation, every citizen of the Union residing in a Member State of which he is not a national shall have the right to vote and to stand as a candidate in elections to the European Parliament in the Member State in which he resides, under the same conditions as nationals of that State. This right shall be exercised subject to detailed arrangements adopted by the Council, acting unanimously on a proposal from the Commission and after consulting the European Parliament; these arrangements may provide for derogations where warranted by problems specific to a Member State.

Article 20

Every citizen of the Union shall, in the territory of a third country in which the Member State of which he is a national is not represented, be entitled to protection by the diplomatic or consular authorities of any Member State, on the same conditions as the nationals of that State. Member States shall establish the necessary rules among themselves and start the international negotiations required to secure this protection.

Article 21

Every citizen of the Union shall have the right to petition the European Parliament in accordance with Article 194.

Every citizen of the Union may apply to the Ombudsman established in accordance with Article 195.

Every citizen of the Union may write to any of the institutions or bodies referred to in this Article or in Article 7 in one of the languages mentioned in Article 314 and have an answer in the same language.

Article 22

The Commission shall report to the European Parliament, to the Council and to the Economic and Social Committee every three years on the application of the provisions of this part. This report shall take account of the development of the Union.

On this basis, and without prejudice to the other provisions of this Treaty, the Council, acting unanimously on a proposal from the Commission and after consulting the European Parliament, may adopt provisions to strengthen or to add to the rights laid down in this part, which it shall recommend to the Member States for adoption in accordance with their respective constitutional requirements.

PART THREE
COMMUNITY POLICIES

TITLE I
FREE MOVEMENT OF GOODS

Article 23

1. The Community shall be based upon a customs union which shall cover all trade in goods and which shall involve the prohibition between Member States of customs duties on imports and exports and of all charges having equivalent effect, and the adoption of a common customs tariff in their relations with third countries.

2.   The provisions of Article 25 and of Chapter 2 of this title shall apply to products originating in Member States and to products coming from third countries which are in free circulation in Member States.

Article 24

Products coming from a third country shall be considered to be in free circulation in a Member State if the import formalities have been complied with and any customs duties or charges having equivalent effect which are payable have been levied in that Member State, and if they have not benefited from a total or partial drawback of such duties or charges.

CHAPTER 1
THE CUSTOMS UNION

Article 25

Customs duties on imports and exports and charges having equivalent effect shall be prohibited between Member States. This prohibition shall also apply to customs duties of a fiscal nature.

Article 26

Common Customs Tariff duties shall be fixed by the Council acting by a qualified majority on a proposal from the Commission.

Article 27

In carrying out the tasks entrusted to it under this chapter the Commission shall be guided by:
- (a)   the need to promote trade between Member States and third countries;
- (b)   developments in conditions of competition within the Community in so far as they lead to an improvement in the competitive capacity of undertakings;
- (c)   the requirements of the Community as regards the supply of raw materials and semi-finished goods; in this connection the Commission shall take care to avoid distorting conditions of competition between Member States in respect of finished goods;
- (d)   the need to avoid serious disturbances in the economies of Member States and to ensure rational development of production and an expansion of consumption within the Community.

CHAPTER 2
PROHIBITION OF QUANTITATIVE RESTRICTIONS BETWEEN MEMBER STATES

Article 28

Quantitative restrictions on imports and all measures having equivalent effect shall be prohibited between Member States.

Article 29

Quantitative restrictions on exports, and all measures having equivalent effect, shall be prohibited between Member States.

Article 30

The provisions of Articles 28 and 29 shall not preclude prohibitions or restrictions on imports, exports or goods in transit justified on grounds of public morality, public policy or public security; the protection of health and life of humans, animals or plants; the protection of national treasures possessing artistic, historic or archaeological value; or the protection of industrial and commercial property. Such prohibitions or restrictions shall not, however, constitute a means of arbitrary discrimination or a disguised restriction on trade between Member States.

Article 31

1.   Member States shall adjust any State monopolies of a commercial character so as to ensure that no discrimination regarding the conditions under which goods are procured and marketed exists between nationals of Member States.

The provisions of this Article shall apply to any body through which a Member State, in law or in fact, either directly or indirectly supervises, determines or appreciably influences imports or exports between Member States. These provisions shall likewise apply to monopolies delegated by the State to others.

2.   Member States shall refrain from introducing any new measure which is contrary to the principles laid down in paragraph 1 or which restricts the scope of the articles dealing with the prohibition of customs duties and quantitative restrictions between Member States.

3.   If a State monopoly of a commercial character has rules which are designed to make it easier to dispose of agricultural products or obtain for them the best return, steps should be taken in applying the rules contained in this article to ensure equivalent safeguards for the employment and standard of living of the producers concerned.

TITLE III
FREE MOVEMENT OF PERSONS, SERVICES AND CAPITAL

CHAPTER 1
WORKERS

Article 39

1.   Freedom of movement for workers shall be secured within the Community.

2.   Such freedom of movement shall entail the abolition of any discrimination based on nationality between workers of the Member States as regards employment, remuneration and other conditions of work and employment.

3.   It shall entail the right, subject to limitations justified on grounds of public policy, public security or public health:

(a)   to accept offers of employment actually made;

(b)   to move freely within the territory of Member States for this purpose;

(c)   to stay in a Member State for the purpose of employment in accordance with the provisions governing the employment of nationals of that State laid down by law, regulation or administrative action;

(d)   to remain in the territory of a Member State after having been employed in that State, subject to conditions which shall be embodied in implementing regulations to be drawn up by the Commission.

,4.   The provisions of this article shall not apply to employment in the public service.

Article 40

The Council shall, acting in accordance with the procedure referred to in Article 251 and after consulting the Economic and Social Committee, issue directives or make regulations setting out the measures required to bring about freedom of movement for workers, as defined in Article 39, in particular:

(a)   by ensuring close cooperation between national employment services;

(b)   by abolishing those administrative procedures and practices and those qualifying periods in respect of eligibility for available employment, whether resulting from national legislation or from agreements previously concluded between Member States, the maintenance of which would form an obstacle to liberalisation of the movement of workers;

(c)   by abolishing all such qualifying periods and other restrictions provided for either under national legislation or under agreements previously concluded between Member States as imposed on workers of other Member States conditions regarding the free choice of employment other than those imposed on workers of the State concerned;

(d)   by setting up appropriate machinery to bring offers of employment into touch with applications for employment and to facilitate the achievement of a balance between supply and demand in the employment market in such a way as to avoid serious threats to the standard of living and level of employment in the various regions and industries.

Article 41

Member States shall, within the framework of a joint programme, encourage the exchange of young workers.

Article 42

The Council shall, acting in accordance with the procedure referred to in Article 251, adopt such measures in the field of social security as are necessary to provide freedom of movement for workers; to this end, it shall make arrangements to secure for migrant workers and their dependants:

(a)   aggregation, for the purpose of acquiring and retaining the right to benefit and of calculating the amount of benefit, of all periods taken into account under the laws of the several countries;

(b)   payment of benefits to persons resident in the territories of Member States. The Council shall act unanimously throughout the procedure referred to in Article 251.

CHAPTER 2

RIGHT OF ESTABLISHMENT

Article 43

Within the framework of the provisions set out below, restrictions on the freedom of establishment of nationals of a Member State in the territory of another Member State shall be prohibited. Such prohibition shall also apply to restrictions on the setting-up of agencies, branches or subsidiaries by nationals of any Member State established in the territory of any Member State.

Freedom of establishment shall include the right to take up and pursue activities as self-employed persons and to set up and manage undertakings, in particular companies or firms within the meaning of the second paragraph of Article 48, under the conditions laid down for its own nationals by the law of the country where such establishment is effected, subject to the provisions of the chapter relating to capital.

Article 44

1.   In order to attain freedom of establishment as regards a particular activity, the Council, acting in accordance with the procedure referred to in Article 251 and after consulting the Economic and Social Committee, shall act by means of directives.

2.   The Council and the Commission shall carry out the duties devolving upon them under the preceding provisions, in particular:

(a)   by according, as a general rule, priority treatment to activities where freedom of establishment makes a particularly valuable contribution to the development of production and trade;

(b)   by ensuring close cooperation between the competent authorities in the Member States in order to ascertain the particular situation within the Community of the various activities concerned;

(c)   by abolishing those administrative procedures and practices, whether resulting from national legislation or from agreements previously concluded between Member States, the maintenance of which would form an obstacle to freedom of establishment;

(d)   by ensuring that workers of one Member State employed in the territory of another Member State may remain in that territory for the purpose of taking up activities therein as self-employed persons, where they satisfy the conditions which they would be required to satisfy if they were entering that State at the time when they intended to take up such activities;

(e)   by enabling a national of one Member State to acquire and use land and buildings situated in the territory of another Member State, in so far as this does not conflict with the principles laid down in Article 33(2);

(f)   by effecting the progressive abolition of restrictions on freedom of establishment in every branch of activity under consideration, both as regards the conditions for setting up agencies, branches or subsidiaries in the territory of a Member State and as regards the subsidiaries in the territory of a Member State and as regards the conditions governing the entry of personnel belonging to the main establishment into managerial or supervisory posts in such agencies, branches or subsidiaries;

(g)   by coordinating to the necessary extent the safeguards which, for the protection of the interests of members and other, are required by Member States of companies or firms within the meaning of the second paragraph of Article 48 with a view to making such safeguards equivalent throughout the Community;

(h)   by satisfying themselves that the conditions of establishment are not distorted by aids granted by Member States.

Article 45

The provisions of this chapter shall not apply, so far as any given Member State is concerned, to activities which in that State are connected, even occasionally, with the exercise of official authority.

The Council may, acting by a qualified majority on a proposal from the Commission, rule that the provisions of this chapter shall not apply to certain activities.

Article 46

1.   The provisions of this chapter and measures taken in pursuance thereof shall not prejudice the applicability of provisions laid down by law, regulation or administrative action providing for special treatment for foreign nationals on grounds of public policy, public security or public health.

2.   The Council shall, acting in accordance with the procedure referred to in Article 251, issue directives for the coordination of the abovementioned provisions.

Article 47

1.   In order to make it easier for persons to take up and pursue activities as self-employed persons, the Council shall, acting in accordance with the procedure referred to in Article 251, issue directives for the mutual recognition of diplomas, certificates and other evidence of formal qualifications.

2.   For the same purpose, the Council shall, acting in accordance with the procedure referred to in Article 251, issue directives for the coordination of the provisions laid down by law, regulation or administrative action in Member States concerning the taking-up and pursuit of activities as self-employed persons. The Council, acting unanimously throughout the procedure referred to in Article 251, shall decide on directives the implementation of which involves in at least one Member State amendment of the existing principles laid down by law governing the professions with respect to training and conditions of access for natural persons. In other cases the Council shall act by qualified majority.

3.   In the case of the medical and allied and pharmaceutical professions, the progressive abolition of restrictions shall be dependent upon coordination of the conditions for their exercise in the various Member States.

Article 48

Companies or firms formed in accordance with the law of a Member State and having their registered office, central administration or principal place of business within the Community shall, for the purposes of this Chapter, be treated in the same way as natural persons who are nationals of Member States.

'Companies or firms' means companies or firms constituted under civil or commercial law, including cooperative societies, and other legal persons governed by public or private law, save for those which are non-profit-making.

CHAPTER 3

SERVICES

Article 49

Within the framework of the provisions set out below, restrictions on freedom to provide services within the Community shall be prohibited in respect of nationals of Member States who are established in a State of the Community other than that of the person for whom the services are intended.

The Council may, acting by a qualified majority on a proposal from the Commission, extend the provisions of the Chapter to nationals of a third country who provide services and who are established within the Community.

Article 50

Services shall be considered to be 'services' within the meaning of this Treaty where they are normally provided for remuneration, in so far as they are not governed by the provisions relating to freedom of movement for goods, capital and persons.

'Services' shall in particular include:

    (a)   activities of an industrial character;

    (b)   activities of a commercial character;

    (c)   activities of craftsmen;

    (d)   activities of the professions.

Without prejudice to the provisions of the chapter relating to the right of establishment, the person providing a service may, in order to do so, temporarily pursue his activity in the State where the service is provided, under the same conditions as are imposed by that State on its own nationals.

Article 51

1. Freedom to provide services in the field of transport shall be governed by the provisions of the title relating to transport.

2. The liberalisation of banking and insurance services connected with movements of capital shall be effected in step with the liberalisation of movement of capital.

Article 52

1. In order to achieve the liberalisation of a specific service, the Council shall, on a proposal from the Commission and after consulting the Economic and Social Committee and the European Parliament, issue directives acting by a qualified majority.

2. As regards the directives referred to in paragraph 1, priority shall as a general rule be given to those services which directly affect production costs or the liberalisation of which helps to promote trade in goods.

Article 53

The Member States declare their readiness to undertake the liberalisation of services beyond the extent required by the directives issued pursuant to Article 52(1), if their general economic situation and the situation of the economic sector concerned so permit.

To this end, the Commission shall make recommendations to the Member States concerned.

Article 54

As long as restrictions on freedom to provide services have not been abolished, each Member State shall apply such restrictions without distinction on grounds of nationality or residence to all persons providing services within the meaning of the first paragraph of Article 49.

Article 55

The provisions of Articles 45 to 48 shall apply to the matters covered by this chapter.

CHAPTER 4

CAPITAL AND PAYMENTS

Article 56

1. Within the framework of the provisions set out in this chapter, all restrictions on the movement of capital between Member States and between Member States and third countries shall be prohibited.

2. Within the framework of the provisions set out in this chapter, all restrictions on payments between Member States and between Member States and third countries shall be prohibited.

Article 57

1. The provisions of Article 56 shall be without prejudice to the application to third countries of any restrictions which exist on 31 December 1993 under national or Community law adopted in respect of the movement of capital to or from third countries involving direct investment — including in real estate — establishment, the provision of financial services or the admission of securities to capital markets. In respect of restrictions exisating under national law in Bulgaria, Estonia and Hungary, the relevant date shall be 21 December 1999.

2.   Whilst endeavouring to achieve the objective of free movement of capital between Member States and third countries to the greatest extent possible and without prejudice to the other chapters of this Treaty, the Council may, acting by a qualified majority on a proposal from the Commission, adopt measures on the movement of capital to or from third countries involving direct investment — including investment in real estate — establishment, the provision of financial services or the admission of securities to capital markets. Unanimity shall be required for measures under this paragraph which constitute a step back in Community law as regards the liberalisation of the movement of capital to or from third countries.

Article 58

1.   The provisions of Article 56 shall be without prejudice to the right of Member States:
   (a)   to apply the relevant provisions of their tax law which distinguish between taxpayers who are not in the same situation with regard to their place of residence or with regard to the place where their capital is invested;
   (b)   to take all requisite measures to prevent infringements of national law and regulations, in particular in the field of taxation and the prudential supervision of financial institutions, or to lay down procedures for the declaration of capital movements for purposes of administrative or statistical information, or to take measures which are justified on grounds of public policy or public security.
2.   The provisions of this chapter shall be without prejudice to the applicability of restrictions on the right of establishment which are compatible with this Treaty.
3.   The measures and procedures referred to in paragraphs 1 and 2 shall not constitute a means of arbitrary discrimination or a disguised restriction on the free movement of capital and payments as defined in Article 56.

Article 59

Where, in exceptional circumstances, movements of capital to or from third countries cause, or threaten to cause, serious difficulties for the operation of economic and monetary union, the Council, acting by a qualified majority on a proposal from the Commission and after consulting the ECB, may take safeguard measures with regard to third countries for a period not exceeding six months if such measures are strictly necessary.

Article 60

1.   If, in the cases envisaged in Article 301, action by the Community is deemed necessary, the Council may, in accordance with the procedure provided for in Article 301, take the necessary urgent measures on the movement of capital and on payments as regards the third countries concerned.
2.   Without prejudice to Article 297 and as long as the Council has not taken measures pursuant to paragraph 1, a Member State may, for serious political reasons and on grounds of urgency, take unilateral measures against a third country with regard to capital movements and payments. The Commission and the other Member States shall be informed of such measures by the date of their entry into force at the latest.
   The Council may, acting by a qualified majority on a proposal from the Commission, decide that the Member State concerned shall amend or abolish such measures. The President of the Council shall inform the European Parliament of any such decision taken by the Council.

TITLE IV
VISAS, ASYLUM, IMMIGRATION AND OTHER POLICIES RELATED TO FREE
MOVEMENT OF PERSONS

Article 61

In order to establish progressively an area of freedom, security and justice, the Council shall adopt:
   (a)   within a period of five years after the entry into force of the Treaty of Amsterdam, measures aimed at ensuring the free movement of persons in accordance with Article 14, in conjunction with directly related flanking measures with respect to external border controls, asylum and immigration, in accordance with the provisions of Article

62(2) and (3) and Article 63(1)(a) and (2)(a), and measures to prevent and combat crime in accordance with the provisions of Article 31(e) of the Treaty on European Union;

(b)   other measures in the fields of asylum, immigration and safeguarding the rights of nationals of third countries, in accordance with the provisions of Article 63;

(c)   measures in the field of judicial cooperation in civil matters as provided for in Article 65;

(d)   appropriate measures to encourage and strengthen administrative cooperation, as provided for in Article 66;

(e)   measures in the field of police and judicial cooperation in criminal matters aimed at a high level of security by preventing and combating crime within the Union in accordance with the provisions of the Treaty on European Union.

Article 62

The Council, acting in accordance with the procedure referred to in Article 67, shall, within a period of five years after the entry into force of the Treaty of Amsterdam, adopt:

1.   measures with a view to ensuring, in compliance with Article 14, the absence of any controls on persons, be they citizens of the Union or nationals of third countries, when crossing internal borders;

2.   measures on the crossing of the external borders of the Member States which shall establish:

(a)   standards and procedures to be followed by Member States in carrying out checks on persons at such borders;

(b)   rules on visas for intended stays of no more than three months, including:

(i)   the list of third countries whose nationals must be in possession of visas when crossing the external borders and those whose nationals are exempt from that requirement;

(ii)   the procedures and conditions for issuing visas by Member States;

(iii)   a uniform format for visas;

(iv)   rules on a uniform visa;

3.   measures setting out the conditions under which nationals of third countries shall have the freedom to travel within the territory of the Member States during a period of no more than three months.

Article 63

The Council, acting in accordance with the procedure referred to in Article 67, shall, within a period of five years after the entry into force of the Treaty of Amsterdam, adopt:

1.   measures on asylum, in accordance with the Geneva Convention of 28 July 1951 and the Protocol of 31 January 1967 relating to the status of refugees and other relevant treaties, within the following areas:

(a)   criteria and mechanisms for determining which Member State is responsible for considering an application for asylum submitted by a national of a third country in one of the Member States,

(b)   minimum standards on the reception of asylum seekers in Member States,

(c)   minimum standards with respect to the qualification of nationals of third countries as refugees,

(d)   minimum standards on procedures in Member States for granting or withdrawing refugee status;

2.   measures on refugees and displaced persons within the following areas:

(a)   minimum standards for giving temporary protection to displaced persons from third countries who cannot return to their country of origin and for persons who otherwise need international protection,

(b)   promoting a balance of effort between Member States in receiving and bearing the consequences of receiving refugees and displaced persons;

3.   measures on immigration policy within the following areas:

(a)   conditions of entry and residence, and standards on procedures for the issue by Member States of long-term visas and residence permits, including those for the purpose of family reunion,

(b)   illegal immigration and illegal residence, including repatriation of illegal residents;

4.   measures defining the rights and conditions under which nationals of third countries who are legally resident in a Member State may reside in other Member States.

Measures adopted by the Council pursuant to points 3 and 4 shall not prevent any Member State from maintaining or introducing in the areas concerned national provisions which are compatible with this Treaty and with international agreements.

Measures to be adopted pursuant to points 2(b), 3(a) and 4 shall not be subject to the five-year period referred to above.

Article 64

1.   This title shall not affect the exercise of the responsibilities incumbent upon Member States with regard to the maintenance of law and order and the safeguarding of internal security.

2.   In the event of one or more Member States being confronted with an emergency situation characterised by a sudden inflow of nationals of third countries and without prejudice to paragraph 1, the Council may, acting by qualified majority on a proposal from the Commission, adopt provisional measures of a duration not exceeding six months for the benefit of the Member States concerned.

Article 65

Measures in the field of judicial cooperation in civil matters having cross-border implications, to be taken in accordance with Article 67 and in so far as necessary for the proper functioning of the internal market, shall include:

(a)   improving and simplifying:
    — the system for cross-border service of judicial and extrajudicial documents,
    — cooperation in the taking of evidence,
    — the recognition and enforcement of decisions in civil and commercial cases, including decisions in extrajudicial cases;

(b)   promoting the compatibility of the rules applicable in the Member States concerning the conflict of laws and of jurisdiction;

(c)   eliminating obstacles to the good functioning of civil proceedings, if necessary by promoting the compatibility of the rules on civil procedure applicable in the Member States.

Article 66

The Council, acting in accordance with the procedure referred to in Article 67, shall take measures to ensure cooperation between the relevant departments of the administrations of the Member States in the areas covered by this title, as well as between those departments and the Commission.

Article 67

1.   During a transitional period of five years following the entry into force of the Treaty of Amsterdam, the Council shall act unanimously on a proposal from the Commission or on the initiative of a Member State and after consulting the European Parliament.

2.   After this period of five years:
    — the Council shall act on proposals from the Commission; the Commission shall examine any request made by a Member State that it submit a proposal to the Council,
    — the Council, acting unanimously after consulting the European Parliament, shall take a decision with a view to providing for all or parts of the areas covered by this title to be governed by the procedure referred to in Article 251 and adapting the provisions relating to the powers of the Court of Justice.

3.   By derogation from paragraphs 1 and 2, measures referred to in Article 62(2)(b) (i) and (iii) shall, from the entry into force of the Treaty of Amsterdam, be adopted by the Council acting by a qualified majority on a proposal from the Commission and after consulting the European Parliament.

4.   By derogation from paragraph 2, measures referred to in Article 62(2)(b) (ii) and (iv) shall, after a period of five years following the entry into force of the Treaty of Amsterdam, be adopted by the Council acting in accordance with the procedure referred to in Article 251.

5.   By derogation from paragraph 1, the Council shall adopt, in accordance with the procedure referred to in Article 251:

— the measures provided for in Article 63(1) and (2)(a) provided that the Council has previously adopted, in accordance with paragraph 1 of this article, Community legislation defining the common rules and basic principles governing these issues,

— the measures provided for in Article 65 with the exception of aspects relating to family law.

Article 68

1.   Article 234 shall apply to this title under the following circumstances and conditions: where a question on the interpretation of this title or on the validity or interpretation of acts of the institutions of the Community based on this title is raised in a case pending before a court or a tribunal of a Member State against whose decisions there is no judicial remedy under national law, that court or tribunal shall, if it considers that a decision on the question is necessary to enable it to give judgment, request the Court of Justice to give a ruling thereon.

2.   In any event, the Court of Justice shall not have jurisdiction to rule on any measure or decision taken pursuant to Article 62(1) relating to the maintenance of law and order and the safeguarding of internal security.

3.   The Council, the Commission or a Member State may request the Court of Justice to give a ruling on a question of interpretation of this title or of acts of the institutions of the Community based on this title. The ruling given by the Court of Justice in response to such a request shall not apply to judgments of courts or tribunals of the Member States which have become *res judicata*.

Article 69

The application of this title shall be subject to the provisions of the Protocol on the position of the United Kingdom and Ireland and to the Protocol on the position of Denmark and without prejudice to the Protocol on the application of certain aspects of Article 14 of the Treaty establishing the European Community to the United Kingdom and to Ireland.

TITLE VI

COMMON RULES ON COMPETITION, TAXATION AND APPROXIMATION OF LAWS

CHAPTER 1

RULES ON COMPETITION

SECTION 1

RULES APPLYING TO UNDERTAKINGS

Article 81

1.   The following shall be prohibited as incompatible with the common market: all agreements between undertakings, decisions by associations of undertakings and concerted practices which may affect trade between Member States and which have as their object or effect the prevention, restriction or distortion of competition within the common market, and in particular those which:

(a)   directly or indirectly fix purchase or selling prices or any other trading conditions;

(b)   limit or control production, markets, technical development, or investment;

(c)   share markets or sources of supply;

(d)   apply dissimilar conditions to equivalent transactions with other trading parties, thereby placing them at a competitive disadvantage;

(e)   make the conclusion of contracts subject to acceptance by the other parties of supplementary obligations which, by their nature or according to commercial usage, have no connection with the subject of such contracts.

2.   Any agreements or decisions prohibited pursuant to this article shall be automatically void.

3.   The provisions of paragraph 1 may, however, be declared inapplicable in the case of:

— any agreement or category of agreements between undertakings,

— any decision or category of decisions by associations of undertakings,

— any concerted practice or category of concerted practices, which contributes to improving the production or distribution of goods or to promoting technical or economic progress, while allowing consumers a fair share of the resulting benefit, and which does not:

(a) impose on the undertakings concerned restrictions which are not indispensable to the attainment of these objectives;

(b) afford such undertakings the possibility of eliminating competition in respect of a substantial part of the products in question.

Article 82

Any abuse by one or more undertakings of a dominant position within the common market or in a substantial part of it shall be prohibited as incompatible with the common market in so far as it may affect trade between Member States.

Such abuse may, in particular, consist in:

(a) directly or indirectly imposing unfair purchase or selling prices or other unfair trading conditions;

(b) limiting production, markets or technical development to the prejudice of consumers;

(c) applying dissimilar conditions to equivalent transactions with other trading parties, thereby placing them at a competitive disadvantage;

(d) making the conclusion of contracts subject to acceptance by the other parties of supplementary obligations which, by their nature or according to commercial usage, have no connection with the subject of such contracts.

Article 83

1. The appropriate regulations or directives to give effect to the principles set out in Articles 81 and 82 shall be laid down by the Council, acting by a qualified majority on a proposal from the Commission and after consulting the European Parliament.

2. The regulations or directives referred to in paragraph 1 shall be designed in particular:

(a) to ensure compliance with the prohibitions laid down in Article 81(1) and in Article 82 by making provision for fines and periodic penalty payments;

(b) to lay down detailed rules for the application of Article 81(3), taking into account the need to ensure effective supervision on the one hand, and to simplify administration to the greatest possible extent on the other;

(c) to define, if need be, in the various branches of the economy, the scope of the provisions of Articles 81 and 82;

(d) to define the respective functions of the Commission and of the Court of Justice in applying the provisions laid down in this paragraph;

(e) to determine the relationship between national laws and the provisions contained in this section or adopted pursuant to this article.

Article 84

Until the entry into force of the provisions adopted in pursuance of Article 83, the authorities in Member States shall rule on the admissibility of agreements, decisions and concerted practices and on abuse of a dominant position in the common market in accordance with the law of their country and with the provisions of Article 81, in particular paragraph 3, and of Article 82.

Article 85

1. Without prejudice to Article 84, the Commission shall ensure the application of the principles laid down in Articles 81 and 82. On application by a Member State or on its own initiative, and in cooperation with the competent authorities in the Member States, which shall give it their assistance, the Commission shall investigate cases of suspected infringement of these principles. If it finds that there has been an infringement, it shall propose appropriate measures to bring it to an end.

2. If the infringement is not brought to an end, the Commission shall record such infringement of the principles in a reasoned decision. The Commission may publish its decision and authorise Member States to take the measures, the conditions and details of which it shall determine, needed to remedy the situation.

Article 86

    1.   In the case of public undertakings and undertakings to which Member States grant special or exclusive rights, Member States shall neither enact nor maintain in force any measure contrary to the rules contained in this Treaty, in particular to those rules provided for in Article 12 and Articles 81 to 89.

    2.   Undertakings entrusted with the operation of services of general economic interest or having the character of a revenue-producing monopoly shall be subject to the rules contained in this Treaty, in particular to the rules on competition, in so far as the application of such rules does not obstruct the performance, in law or in fact, of the particular tasks assigned to them. The development of trade must not be affected to such an extent as would be contrary to the interests of the Community.

    3.   The Commission shall ensure the application of the provisions of this Article and shall, where necessary, address appropriate directives or decisions to Member States.

SECTION 2

AIDS GRANTED BY STATES

Article 87

    1.   Save as otherwise provided in this Treaty, any aid granted by a Member State or through State resources in any form whatsoever which distorts or threatens to distort competition by favouring certain undertakings or the production of certain goods shall, in so far as it affects trade between Member States, be incompatible with the common market.

    2.   The following shall be compatible with the common market:

        (a)   aid having a social character, granted to individual consumers, provided that such aid is granted without discrimination related to the origin of the products concerned;

        (b)   aid to make good the damage caused by natural disasters or exceptional occurrences;

        (c)   aid granted to the economy of certain areas of the Federal Republic of Germany affected by the division of Germany, in so far as such aid is required in order to compensate for the economic disadvantages caused by that division.

    3.   The following may be considered to be compatible with the common market:

        (a)   aid to promote the economic development of areas where the standard of living is abnormally low or where there is serious underemployment;

        (b)   aid to promote the execution of an important project of common European interest or to remedy a serious disturbance in the economy of a Member State;

        (c)   aid to facilitate the development of certain economic activities or of certain economic areas, where such aid does not adversely affect trading conditions to an extent contrary to the common interest;

        (d)   aid to promote culture and heritage conservation where such aid does not affect trading conditions and competition in the Community to an extent that is contrary to the common interest;

        (e)   such other categories of aid as may be specified by decision of the Council acting by a qualified majority on a proposal from the Commission.

Article 88

    1.   The Commission shall, in cooperation with Member States, keep under constant review all systems of aid existing in those States. It shall propose to the latter any appropriate measures required by the progressive development or by the functioning of the common market.

    2.   If, after giving notice to the parties concerned to submit their comments, the Commission finds that aid granted by a State or through State resources is not compatible with the common market having regard to Article 87, or that such aid is being misused, it shall decide that the State concerned shall abolish or alter such aid within a period of time to be determined by the Commission. If the State concerned does not comply with this decision within the prescribed time, the Commission or any other interested State may, in derogation from the provisions of Articles 226 and 227, refer the matter to the Court of Justice direct.

        On application by a Member State, the Council may, acting unanimously, decide that aid which that State is granting or intends to grant shall be considered to be compatible with the common market, in derogation from the provisions of Article 87 or from the regulations provided for in Article 89, if such a decision is justified by exceptional circumstances. If, as regards the aid in question, the Commission has already initiated the procedure provided for in the first subparagraph of this paragraph, the fact that the State concerned has made its application to the Council shall have the effect of suspending that procedure until the Council has made its attitude known.

If, however, the Council has not made its attitude known within three months of the said application being made, the Commission shall give its decision on the case.

3.   The Commission shall be informed, in sufficient time to enable it to submit its comments, of any plans to grant or alter aid. If it considers that any such plan is not compatible with the common market having regard to Article 87, it shall without delay initiate the procedure provided for in paragraph 2. The Member State concerned shall not put its proposed measures into effect until this procedure has resulted in a final decision.

Article 89

The Council, acting by a qualified majority on a proposal from the Commission and after consulting the European Parliament, may make any appropriate regulations for the application of Articles 87 and 88 and may in particular determine the conditions in which Article 88(3) shall apply and the categories of aid exempted from this procedure.

CHAPTER 2

TAX PROVISIONS

Article 90

No Member State shall impose, directly or indirectly, on the products of other Member States any internal taxation of any kind in excess of that imposed directly or indirectly on similar domestic products.

Furthermore, no Member State shall impose on the products of other Member States any internal taxation of such a nature as to afford indirect protection to other products.

Article 91

Where products are exported to the territory of any Member State, any repayment of internal taxation shall not exceed the internal taxation imposed on them whether directly or indirectly.

Article 92

In the case of charges other than turnover taxes, excise duties and other forms of indirect taxation, remissions and repayments in respect of exports to other Member States may not be granted and countervailing charges in respect of imports from Member States may not be imposed unless the measures contemplated have been previously approved for a limited period by the Council acting by a qualified majority on a proposal from the Commission.

Article 93

The Council shall, acting unanimously on a proposal from the Commission and after consulting the European Parliament and the Economic and Social Committee, adopt provisions for the harmonisation of legislation concerning turnover taxes, excise duties and other forms of indirect taxation to the extent that such harmonisation is necessary to ensure the establishment and the functioning of the internal market within the time limit laid down in Article 14.

CHAPTER 3

APPROXIMATION OF LAWS

Article 94

The Council shall, acting unanimously on a proposal from the Commission and after consulting the European Parliament and the Economic and Social Committee, issue directives for the approximation of such laws, regulations or administrative provisions of the Member States as directly affect the establishment or functioning of the common market.

Article 95

1. By way of derogation from Article 94 and save where otherwise provided in this Treaty, the following provisions shall apply for the achievement of the objectives set out in Article 14. The Council shall, acting in accordance with the procedure referred to in Article 251 and after consulting the Economic and Social Committee, adopt the measures for the approximation of the provisions laid down by law, regulation or administrative action in Member States which have as their object the establishment and functioning of the internal market.

2. Paragraph 1 shall not apply to fiscal provisions, to those relating to the free movement of persons nor to those relating to the rights and interests of employed persons.

3. The Commission, in its proposals envisaged in paragraph 1 concerning health, safety, environmental protection and consumer protection, will take as a base a high level of protection, taking account in particular of any new development based on scientific facts. Within their respective powers, the European Parliament and the Council will also seek to achieve this objective.

4. If, after the adoption by the Council or by the Commission of a harmonisation measure, a Member State deems it necessary to maintain national provisions on grounds of major needs referred to in Article 30, or relating to the protection of the environment or the working environment, it shall notify the Commission of these provisions as well as the grounds for maintaining them.

5. Moreover, without prejudice to paragraph 4, if, after the adoption by the Council or by the Commission of a harmonisation measure, a Member State deems it necessary to introduce national provisions based on new scientific evidence relating to the protection of the environment or the working environment on grounds of a problem specific to that Member State arising after the adoption of the harmonisation measure, it shall notify the Commission of the envisaged provisions as well as the grounds for introducing them.

6. The Commission shall, within six months of the notifications as referred to in paragraphs 4 and 5, approve or reject the national provisions involved after having verified whether or not they are a means of arbitrary discrimination or a disguised restriction on trade between Member States and whether or not they shall constitute an obstacle to the functioning of the internal market.

   In the absence of a decision by the Commission within this period the national provisions referred to in paragraphs 4 and 5 shall be deemed to have been approved.

   When justified by the complexity of the matter and in the absence of danger for human health, the Commission may notify the Member State concerned that the period referred to in this paragraph may be extended for a further period of up to six months.

7. When, pursuant to paragraph 6, a Member State is authorised to maintain or introduce national provisions derogating from a harmonisation measure, the Commission shall immediately examine whether to propose an adaptation to that measure.

8. When a Member State raises a specific problem on public health in a field which has been the subject of prior harmonisation measures, it shall bring it to the attention of the Commission which shall immediately examine whether to propose appropriate measures to the Council.

9. By way of derogation from the procedure laid down in Articles 226 and 227, the Commission and any Member State may bring the matter directly before the Court of Justice if it considers that another Member State is making improper use of the powers provided for in this Article.

10. The harmonisation measures referred to above shall, in appropriate cases, include a safeguard clause authorising the Member States to take, for one or more of the non-economic reasons referred to in Article 30, provisional measures subject to a Community control procedure.

Article 96

Where the Commission finds that a difference between the provisions laid down by law, regulation or administrative action in Member States is distorting the conditions of competition in the common market and that the resultant distortion needs to be eliminated, it shall consult the Member States concerned.

If such consultation does not result in an agreement eliminating the distortion in question, the Council shall, on a proposal from the Commission, acting by a qualified majority, issue the necessary directives. The Commission and the Council may take any other appropriate measures provided for in this Treaty.

Article 97

1. Where there is a reason to fear that the adoption or amendment of a provision laid down by law, regulation or administrative action may cause distortion within the meaning of Article 96, a Member State desiring to proceed therewith shall consult the Commission. After consulting the Member States, the Commission shall recommend to the States concerned such measures as may be appropriate to avoid the distortion in question.

2. If a State desiring to introduce or amend its own provisions does not comply with the recommendation addressed to it by the Commission, other Member States shall not be required, pursuant to Article 96, to amend their own provisions in order to eliminate such distortion. If the Member State which has ignored the recommendation of the Commission causes distortion detrimental only to itself, the provisions of Article 96 shall not apply.

TITLE VII
ECONOMIC AND MONETARY POLICY

CHAPTER 1
ECONOMIC POLICY

Article 98

Member States shall conduct their economic policies with a view to contributing to the achievement of the objectives of the Community, as defined in Article 2, and in the context of the broad guidelines referred to in Article 99(2). The Member States and the Community shall act in accordance with the principle of an open market economy with free competition, favouring an efficient allocation of resources, and in compliance with the principles set out in Article 4.

Article 99

1. Member States shall regard their economic policies as a matter of common concern and shall coordinate them within the Council, in accordance with the provisions of Article 98.

2. The Council shall, acting by a qualified majority on a recommendation from the Commission, formulate a draft for the broad guidelines of the economic policies of the Member States and of the Community, and shall report its findings to the European Council.

   The European Council shall, acting on the basis of the report from the Council, discuss a conclusion on the broad guidelines of the economic policies of the Member States and of the Community.

   On the basis of this conclusion, the Council shall, acting by a qualified majority, adopt a recommendation setting out these broad guidelines. The Council shall inform the European Parliament of its recommendation.

3. In order to ensure closer coordination of economic policies and sustained convergence of the economic performances of the Member States, the Council shall, on the basis of reports submitted by the Commission, monitor economic developments in each of the Member States and in the Community as well as the consistency of economic policies with the broad guidelines referred to in paragraph 2, and regularly carry out an overall assessment.

   For the purpose of this multilateral surveillance, Member States shall forward information to the Commission about important measures taken by them in the field of their economic policy and such other information as they deem necessary.

4. Where it is established, under the procedure referred to in paragraph 3, that the economic policies of a Member State are not consistent with the broad guidelines referred to in paragraph 2 or that they risk jeopardising the proper functioning of economic and monetary union, the Council may, acting by a qualified majority on a recommendation from the Commission, make the necessary recommendations to the Member State concerned. The Council may, acting by a qualified majority on a proposal from the Commission, decide to make its recommendations public.

The President of the Council and the Commission shall report to the European Parliament on the results of multilateral surveillance. The President of the Council may be invited to appear before the competent committee of the European Parliament if the Council has made its recommendations public.

5. The Council, acting in accordance with the procedure referred to in Article 252, may adopt detailed rules for the multilateral surveillance procedure referred to in paragraphs 3 and 4 of this Article.

Article 100

1. Without prejudice to any other procedures provided for in this Treaty, the Council, acting by a qualified majority on a proposal from the Commission, may decide upon the measures appropriate to the economic situation, in particular if severe difficulties arise in the supply of certain products.

2. Where a Member State is in difficulties or is seriously threatened with severe difficulties caused by natural disasters or exceptional occurrences beyond its control, the Council, acting by a qualified majority on a proposal from the Commission, may grant, under certain conditions, Community financial assistance to the Member State concerned. The President of the Council shall inform the European Parliament of the decision taken.

Article 101

1. Overdraft facilities or any other type of credit facility with the ECB or with the central banks of the Member States (hereinafter referred to as 'national central banks') in favour of Community institutions or bodies, central governments, regional, local or other public authorities, other bodies governed by public law, or public undertakings of Member States shall be prohibited, as shall the purchase directly from them by the ECB or national central banks of debt instruments.

2. Paragraph 1 shall not apply to publicly owned credit institutions which, in the context of the supply of reserves by central banks, shall be given the same treatment by national central banks and the ECB as private credit institutions.

Article 102

1. Any measure, not based on prudential considerations, establishing privileged access by Community institutions or bodies, central governments, regional, local or other public authorities, other bodies governed by public law, or public undertakings of Member States to financial institutions, shall be prohibited.

2. The Council, acting in accordance with the procedure referred to in Article 252, shall, before 1 January 1994, specify definitions for the application of the prohibition referred to in paragraph 1.

Article 103

1. The Community shall not be liable for or assume the commitments of central governments, regional, local or other public authorities, other bodies governed by public law, or public undertakings of any Member State, without prejudice to mutual financial guarantees for the joint execution of a specific project. A Member State shall not be liable for or assume the commitments of central governments, regional, local or other public authorities, other bodies governed by public law, or public undertakings of another Member State, without prejudice to mutual financial guarantees for the joint execution of a specific project.

2. If necessary, the Council, acting in accordance with the procedure referred to in Article 252, may specify definitions for the application of the prohibition referred to in Article 101 and in this Article.

Article 104

1. Member States shall avoid excessive government deficits.

2. The Commission shall monitor the development of the budgetary situation and of the stock of government debt in the Member States with a view to identifying gross errors. In particular it shall examine compliance with budgetary discipline on the basis of the following two criteria:

(a)   whether the ratio of the planned or actual government deficit to gross domestic product exceeds a reference value, unless:

— either the ratio has declined substantially and continuously and reached a level that comes close to the reference value,

— or, alternatively, the excess over the reference value is only exceptional and temporary and the ratio remains close to the reference value;

(b)   whether the ratio of government debt to gross domestic product exceeds a reference value, unless the ratio is sufficiently diminishing and approaching the reference value at a satisfactory pace.

The reference values are specified in the Protocol on the excessive deficit procedure annexed to this Treaty.

3.   If a Member State does not fulfil the requirements under one or both of these criteria, the Commission shall prepare a report. The report of the Commission shall also take into account whether the government deficit exceeds government investment expenditure and take into account all other relevant factors, including the medium-term economic and budgetary position of the Member State.

The Commission may also prepare a report if, notwithstanding the fulfilment of the requirements under the criteria, it is of the opinion that there is a risk of an excessive deficit in a Member State.

4.   The Committee provided for in Article 114 shall formulate an opinion on the report of the Commission.

5.   If the Commission considers that an excessive deficit in a Member State exists or may occur, the Commission shall address an opinion to the Council.

6.   The Council shall, acting by a qualified majority on a recommendation from the Commission, and having considered any observations which the Member State concerned may wish to make, decide after an overall assessment whether an excessive deficit exists.

7.   Where the existence of an excessive deficit is decided according to paragraph 6, the Council shall make recommendations to the Member State concerned with a view to bringing that situation to an end within a given period. Subject to the provisions of paragraph 8, these recommendations shall not be made public.

8.   Where it establishes that there has been no effective action in response to its recommendations within the period laid down, the Council may make its recommendations public.

9.   If a Member State persists in failing to put into practice the recommendations of the Council, the Council may decide to give notice to the Member State to take, within a specified time limit, measures for the deficit reduction which is judged necessary by the Council in order to remedy the situation.

In such a case, the Council may request the Member State concerned to submit reports in accordance with a specific timetable in order to examine the adjustment efforts of that Member State.

10.   The rights to bring actions provided for in Articles 226 and 227 may not be exercised within the framework of paragraphs 1 to 9 of this Article.

11.   As long as a Member State fails to comply with a decision taken in accordance with paragraph 9, the Council may decide to apply or, as the case may be, intensify one or more of the following measures:

— to require the Member State concerned to publish additional information, to be specified by the Council, before issuing bonds and securities,

— to invite the European Investment Bank to reconsider its lending policy towards the Member State concerned,

— to require the Member State concerned to make a non-interest-bearing deposit of an appropriate size with the Community until the excessive deficit has, in the view of the Council, been corrected,

— to impose fines of an appropriate size.

The President of the Council shall inform the European Parliament of the decisions taken.

12. The Council shall abrogate some or all of its decisions referred to in paragraphs 6 to 9 and 11 to the extent that the excessive deficit in the Member State concerned has, in the view of the Council, been corrected. If the Council has previously made public recommendations, it shall, as soon as the decision under paragraph 8 has been abrogated, make a public statement that an excessive deficit in the Member State concerned no longer exists.

13. When taking the decisions referred to in paragraphs 7 to 9, 11 and 12, the Council shall act on a recommendation from the Commission by a majority of two thirds of the votes of its members weighted in accordance with Article 205(2), excluding the votes of the representative of the Member State concerned.

14. Further provisions relating to the implementation of the procedure described in this article are set out in the Protocol on the excessive deficit procedure annexed to this Treaty.

    The Council shall, acting unanimously on a proposal from the Commission and after consulting the European Parliament and the ECB, adopt the appropriate provisions which shall then replace the said Protocol.

    Subject to the other provisions of this paragraph, the Council shall, before 1 January 1994, acting by a qualified majority on a proposal from the Commission and after consulting the European Parliament, lay down detailed rules and definitions for the application of the provisions of the said Protocol.

CHAPTER 2
MONETARY POLICY

Article 105

1. The primary objective of the ESCB shall be to maintain price stability. Without prejudice to the objective of price stability, the ESCB shall support the general economic policies in the Community with a view to contributing to the achievement of the objectives of the Community as laid down in Article 2. The ESCB shall act in accordance with the principle of an open market economy with free competition, favouring an efficient allocation of resources, and in compliance with the principles set out in Article 4.

2. The basic tasks to be carried out through the ESCB shall be:
   — to define and implement the monetary policy of the Community,
   — to conduct foreign-exchange operations consistent with the provisions of Article 111,
   — to hold and manage the official foreign reserves of the Member States,
   — to promote the smooth operation of payment systems.

3. The third indent of paragraph 2 shall be without prejudice to the holding and management by the governments of Member States of foreign-exchange working balances.

4. The ECB shall be consulted:
   — on any proposed Community act in its fields of competence,
   — by national authorities regarding any draft legislative provision in its fields of competence, but within the limits and under the conditions set out by the Council in accordance with the procedure laid down in Article 107(6). The ECB may submit opinions to the appropriate Community institutions or bodies or to national authorities on matters in its fields of competence.

5. The ESCB shall contribute to the smooth conduct of policies pursued by the competent authorities relating to the prudential supervision of credit institutions and the stability of the financial system.

6. The Council may, acting unanimously on a proposal from the Commission and after consulting the ECB and after receiving the assent of the European Parliament, confer upon the ECB specific tasks concerning policies relating to the prudential supervision of credit institutions and other financial institutions with the exception of insurance undertakings.

Article 106

1. The ECB shall have the exclusive right to authorise the issue of banknotes within the Community. The ECB and the national central banks may issue such notes. The banknotes issued by the ECB and the national central banks shall be the only such notes to have the status of legal tender within the Community.

2.   Member States may issue coins subject to approval by the ECB of the volume of the issue. The Council may, acting in accordance with the procedure referred to in Article 252 and after consulting the ECB, adopt measures to harmonise the denominations and technical specifications of all coins intended for circulation to the extent necessary to permit their smooth circulation within the Community.

Article 107

1.   The ESCB shall be composed of the ECB and of the national central banks.
2.   The ECB shall have legal personality.
3.   The ESCB shall be governed by the decision-making bodies of the ECB which shall be the Governing Council and the Executive Board.
4.   The Statute of the ESCB is laid down in a Protocol annexed to this Treaty.
5.   Articles 5.1, 5.2, 5.3, 17, 18, 19.1, 22, 23, 24, 26, 32.2, 32.3, 32.4, 32.6, 33.1(a) and 36 of the Statute of the ESCB may be amended by the Council, acting either by a qualified majority on a recommendation from the ECB and after consulting the Commission or unanimously on a proposal from the Commission and after consulting the ECB. In either case, the assent of the European Parliament shall be required.
6.   The Council, acting by a qualified majority either on a proposal from the Commission and after consulting the European Parliament and the ECB or on a recommendation from the ECB and after consulting the European Parliament and the Commission, shall adopt the provisions referred to in Articles 4, 5.4, 19.2, 20, 28.1, 29.2, 30.4 and 34.3 of the Statute of the ESCB.

Article 108

When exercising the powers and carrying out the tasks and duties conferred upon them by this Treaty and the Statute of the ESCB, neither the ECB, nor a national central bank, nor any member of their decision-making bodies shall seek or take instructions from Community institutions or bodies, from any government of a Member State or from any other body. The Community institutions and bodies and the governments of the Member States undertake to respect this principle and not to seek to influence the members of the decision-making bodies of the ECB or of the national central banks in the performance of their tasks.

Article 109

Each Member State shall ensure, at the latest at the date of the establishment of the ESCB, that its national legislation including the statutes of its national central bank is compatible with this Treaty and the Statute of the ESCB.

Article 110

1.   In order to carry out the tasks entrusted to the ESCB, the ECB shall, in accordance with the provisions of this Treaty and under the conditions laid down in the Statute of the ESCB:
        — make regulations to the extent necessary to implement the tasks defined in Article 3.1, first indent, Articles 19.1, 22 and 25.2 of the Statute of the ESCB and in cases which shall be laid down in the acts of the Council referred to in Article 107(6),
        — take decisions necessary for carrying out the tasks entrusted to the ESCB under this Treaty and the Statute of the ESCB,
        — make recommendations and deliver opinions.
2.   A regulation shall have general application. It shall be binding in its entirety and directly applicable in all Member States.
       Recommendations and opinions shall have no binding force.
       A decision shall be binding in its entirety upon those to whom it is addressed.
       Articles 253, 254 and 256 shall apply to regulations and decisions adopted by the ECB.
       The ECB may decide to publish its decisions, recommendations and opinions.
3.   Within the limits and under the conditions adopted by the Council under the procedure laid down in Article 107(6), the ECB shall be entitled to impose fines or periodic penalty payments on undertakings for failure to comply with obligations under its regulations and decisions.

Article 111

1. By way of derogation from Article 300, the Council may, acting unanimously on a recommendation from the ECB or from the Commission, and after consulting the ECB in an endeavour to reach a consensus consistent with the objective of price stability, after consulting the European Parliament, in accordance with the procedure in paragraph 3 for determining the arrangements, conclude formal agreements on an exchange-rate system for the ecu in relation to non-Community currencies. The Council may, acting by a qualified majority on a recommendation from the ECB or from the Commission, and after consulting the ECB in an endeavour to reach a consensus consistent with the objective of price stability, adopt, adjust or abandon the central rates of the ecu within the exchange-rate system. The President of the Council shall inform the European Parliament of the adoption, adjustment or abandonment of the ecu central rates.

2. In the absence of an exchange-rate system in relation to one or more non-Community currencies as referred to in paragraph 1, the Council, acting by a qualified majority either on a recommendation from the Commission and after consulting the ECB or on a recommendation from the ECB, may formulate general orientations for exchange-rate policy in relation to these currencies. These general orientations shall be without prejudice to the primary objective of the ESCB to maintain price stability.

3. By way of derogation from Article 300, where agreements concerning monetary or foreign-exchange regime matters need to be negotiated by the Community with one or more States or international organisations, the Council, acting by a qualified majority on a recommendation from the Commission and after consulting the ECB, shall decide the arrangements for the negotiation and for the conclusion of such agreements. These arrangements shall ensure that the Community expresses a single position. The Commission shall be fully associated with the negotiations. Agreements concluded in accordance with this paragraph shall be binding on the institutions of the Community, on the ECB and on Member States.

4. Subject to paragraph 1, the Council, acting by a qualified majority on a proposal from the Commission and after consulting the ECB, shall decide on the position of the Community at international level as regards issues of particular relevance to economic and monetary union and on its representation, in compliance with the allocation of powers laid down in Articles 99 and 105.

5. Without prejudice to Community competence and Community agreements as regards economic and monetary union, Member States may negotiate in international bodies and conclude international agreements.

CHAPTER 3

INSTITUTIONAL PROVISIONS

Article 112

1. The Governing Council of the ECB shall comprise the members of the Executive Board of the ECB and the Governors of the national central banks.

2. (a) The Executive Board shall comprise the President, the Vice-President and four other members.

   (b) The President, the Vice-President and the other members of the Executive Board shall be appointed from among persons of recognised standing and professional experience in monetary or banking matters by common accord of the governments of the Member States at the level of Heads of State or Government, on a recommendation from the Council, after it has consulted the European Parliament and the Governing Council of the ECB.

   Their term of office shall be eight years and shall not be renewable.

   Only nationals of Member States may be members of the Executive Board.

Article 113

1. The President of the Council and a member of the Commission may participate, without having the right to vote, in meetings of the Governing Council of the ECB. The President of the Council may submit a motion for deliberation to the Governing Council of the ECB.

2. The President of the ECB shall be invited to participate in Council meetings when the Council is discussing matters relating to the objectives and tasks of the ESCB.

3. The ECB shall address an annual report on the activities of the ESCB and on the monetary policy of both the previous and current year to the European Parliament, the Council and the Commission, and also to the European Council. The President of the ECB shall present this report to the Council and to the European Parliament, which may hold a general debate on that basis.

The President of the ECB and the other members of the Executive Board may, at the request of the European Parliament or on their own initiative, be heard by the competent committees of the European Parliament.

Article 114

1. In order to promote coordination of the policies of Member States to the full extent needed for the functioning of the internal market, a Monetary Committee with advisory status is hereby set up.

It shall have the following tasks:

— to keep under review the monetary and financial situation of the Member States and of the Community and the general payments system of the Member States and to report regularly thereon to the Council and to the Commission,

— to deliver opinions at the request of the Council or of the Commission, or on its own initiative for submission to those institutions,

— without prejudice to Article 207, to contribute to the preparation of the work of the Council referred to in Articles 59, 60, 99(2), (3), (4) and (5), 100, 102, 103, 104, 116(2), 117(6), 119, 120, 121(2) and 122(1),

— to examine, at least once a year, the situation regarding the movement of capital and the freedom of payments, as they result from the application of this Treaty and of measures adopted by the Council; the examination shall cover all measures relating to capital movements and payments; the Committee shall report to the Commission and to the Council on the outcome of this examination.

The Member States and the Commission shall each appoint two members of the Monetary Committee.

2. At the start of the third stage, an Economic and Financial Committee shall be set up. The Monetary Committee provided for in paragraph 1 shall be dissolved.

The Economic and Financial Committee shall have the following tasks:

— to deliver opinions at the request of the Council or of the Commission, or on its own initiative for submission to those institutions,

— to keep under review the economic and financial situation of the Member States and of the Community and to report regularly thereon to the Council and to the Commission, in particular on financial relations with third countries and international institutions, — without prejudice to Article 207, to contribute to the preparation of the work of the Council referred to in Articles 59, 60, 99(2), (3), (4) and (5), 100, 102, 103, 104, 105(6), 106(2), 107(5) and (6), 111, 119, 120(2) and (3), 122(2), 123(4) and (5), and to carry out other advisory and preparatory tasks assigned to it by the Council,

— to examine, at least once a year, the situation regarding the movement of capital and the freedom of payments, as they result from the application of this Treaty and of measures adopted by the Council; the examination shall cover all measures relating to capital movements and payments; the Committee shall report to the Commission and to the Council on the outcome of this examination.

The Member States, the Commission and the ECB shall each appoint no more than two members of the Committee.

3. The Council shall, acting by a qualified majority on a proposal from the Commission and after consulting the ECB and the Committee referred to in this Article, lay down detailed provisions concerning the composition of the Economic and Financial Committee. The President of the Council shall inform the European Parliament of such a decision.

4.   In addition to the tasks set out in paragraph 2, if and as long as there are Member States with a derogation as referred to in Articles 122 and 123, the Committee shall keep under review the monetary and financial situation and the general payments system of those Member States and report regularly thereon to the Council and to the Commission.

Article 115

For matters within the scope of Articles 99(4), 104 with the exception of paragraph 14, 111, 121, 122 and 123(4) and (5), the Council or a Member State may request the Commission to make a recommendation or a proposal, as appropriate. The Commission shall examine this request and submit its conclusions to the Council without delay.

TITLE VIII

EMPLOYMENT

Article 125

Member States and the Community shall, in accordance with this title, work towards developing a coordinated strategy for employment and particularly for promoting a skilled, trained and adaptable workforce and labour markets responsive to economic change with a view to achieving the objectives defined in Article 2 of the Treaty on European Union and in Article 2 of this Treaty.

Article 126

1.   Member States, through their employment policies, shall contribute to the achievement of the objectives referred to in Article 125 in a way consistent with the broad guidelines of the economic policies of the Member States and of the Community adopted pursuant to Article 99(2).

2.   Member States, having regard to national practices related to the responsibilities of management and labour, shall regard promoting employment as a matter of common concern and shall coordinate their action in this respect within the Council, in accordance with the provisions of Article 128.

Article 127

1.   The Community shall contribute to a high level of employment by encouraging cooperation between Member States and by supporting and, if necessary, complementing their action. In doing so, the competences of the Member States shall be respected.

2.   The objective of a high level of employment shall be taken into consideration in the formulation and implementation of Community policies and activities.

Article 128

1.   The European Council shall each year consider the employment situation in the Community and adopt conclusions thereon, on the basis of a joint annual report by the Council and the Commission.

2.   On the basis of the conclusions of the European Council, the Council, acting by a qualified majority on a proposal from the Commission and after consulting the European Parliament, the Economic and Social Committee, the Committee of the Regions and the Employment Committee referred to in Article 130, shall each year draw up guidelines which the Member States shall take into account in their employment policies. These guidelines shall be consistent with the broad guidelines adopted pursuant to Article 99(2).

3.   Each Member State shall provide the Council and the Commission with an annual report on the principal measures taken to implement its employment policy in the light of the guidelines for employment as referred to in paragraph 2.

4.   The Council, on the basis of the reports referred to in paragraph 3 and having received the views of the Employment Committee, shall each year carry out an examination of the implementation of the employment policies of the Member States in the light of the guidelines for employment. The Council, acting by a qualified majority on a recommendation from the Commission, may, if it considers it appropriate in the light of that examination, make recommendations to Member States.

5.   On the basis of the results of that examination, the Council and the Commission shall make a joint annual report to the European Council on the employment situation in the Community and on the implementation of the guidelines for employment.

Article 129

The Council, acting in accordance with the procedure referred to in Article 251 and after consulting the Economic and Social Committee and the Committee of the Regions, may adopt incentive measures designed to encourage cooperation between Member States and to support their action in the field of employment through initiatives aimed at developing exchanges of information and best practices, providing comparative analysis and advice as well as promoting innovative approaches and evaluating experiences, in particular by recourse to pilot projects.

Those measures shall not include harmonisation of the laws and regulations of the Member States.

Article 130

The Council, after consulting the European Parliament, shall establish an Employment Committee with advisory status to promote coordination between Member States on employment and labour market policies. The tasks of the Committee shall be:

— to monitor the employment situation and employment policies in the Member States and the Community,

— without prejudice to Article 207, to formulate opinions at the request of either the Council or the Commission or on its own initiative, and to contribute to the preparation of the Council proceedings referred to in Article 128.

In fulfilling its mandate, the Committee shall consult management and labour.

Each Member State and the Commission shall appoint two members of the Committee.

TITLE IX

COMMON COMMERCIAL POLICY

Article 131

By establishing a customs union between themselves Member States aim to contribute, in the common interest, to the harmonious development of world trade, the progressive abolition of restrictions on international trade and the lowering of customs barriers.

The common commercial policy shall take into account the favourable effect which the abolition of customs duties between Member States may have on the increase in the competitive strength of undertakings in those States.

Article 132

1.   Without prejudice to obligations undertaken by them within the framework of other international organisations, Member States shall progressively harmonise the systems whereby they grant aid for exports to third countries, to the extent necessary to ensure that competition between undertakings of the Community is not distorted.

On a proposal from the Commission, the Council shall, acting by a qualified majority, issue any directives needed for this purpose.

2.   The preceding provisions shall not apply to such a drawback of customs duties or charges having equivalent effect nor to such a repayment of indirect taxation including turnover taxes, excise duties and other indirect taxes as is allowed when goods are exported from a Member State to a third country, in so far as such a drawback or repayment does not exceed the amount imposed, directly or indirectly, on the products exported.

Article 133

1.   The common commercial policy shall be based on uniform principles, particularly in regard to changes in tariff rates, the conclusion of tariff and trade agreements, the achievement of uniformity in measures of liberalisation, export policy and measures to protect trade such as those to be taken in the event of dumping or subsidies.

2.   The Commission shall submit proposals to the Council for implementing the common commercial policy.

3.   Where agreements with one or more States or international organisations need to be negotiated, the Commission shall make recommendations to the Council, which shall authorise the Commission to open the necessary negotiations. The Council and the Commission shall be responsible for ensuring that the agreements negotiated are compatible with internal Community policies and rules.

The Commission shall conduct these negotiations in consultation with a special committee appointed by the Council to assist the Commission in this task and within the framework of such directives as the Council may issue to it. The Commission shall report regularly to the special committee on the progress of negotiations.

The relevant provisions of Article 300 shall apply.

4.   In exercising the powers conferred upon it by this Article, the Council shall act by a qualified majority.

5.   Paragraphs 1 to 4 shall also apply to the negotiation and conclusion of agreements in the fields of trade in services and the commercial aspects of intellectual property, in so far as those agreements are not covered by the said paragraphs and without prejudice to paragraph 6.

By way of derogation from paragraph 4, the Council shall act unanimously when negotiating and concluding an agreement in one of the fields referred to in the first subparagraph, where that agreement includes provisions for which unanimity is required for the adoption of internal rules or where it relates to a field in which the Community has not yet exercised the powers conferred upon it by this Treaty by adopting internal rules.

The Council shall act unanimously with respect to the negotiation and conclusion of a horizontal agreement insofar as it also concerns the preceding subparagraph or the second subparagraph of paragraph 6.

This paragraph shall not affect the right of the Member States to maintain and conclude agreements with third countries or international organisations in so far as such agreements comply with Community law and other relevant international agreements.

6.   An agreement may not be concluded by the Council if it includes provisions which would go beyond the Community's internal powers, in particular by leading to harmonisation of the laws or regulations of the Member States in an area for which this Treaty rules out such harmonisation.

In this regard, by way of derogation from the first subparagraph of paragraph 5, agreements relating to trade in cultural and audiovisual services, educational services, and social and human health services, shall fall within the shared competence of the Community and its Member States. Consequently, in addition to a Community decision taken in accordance with the relevant provisions of Article 300, the negotiation of such agreements shall require the common accord of the Member States. Agreements thus negotiated shall be concluded jointly by the Community and the Member States.

The negotiation and conclusion of international agreements in the field of transport shall continue to be governed by the provisions of Title V and Article 300.

7.   Without prejudice to the first subparagraph of paragraph 6, the Council, acting unanimously on a proposal from the Commission and after consulting the European Parliament, may extend the application of paragraphs 1 to 4 to international negotiations and agreements on intellectual property in so far as they are not covered by paragraph 5.

Article 134

In order to ensure that the execution of measures of commercial policy taken in accordance with this Treaty by any Member State is not obstructed by deflection of trade, or where differences between such measures lead to economic difficulties in one or more Member States, the Commission shall recommend the methods for the requisite cooperation between Member States. Failing this, the Commission may authorise Member States to take the necessary protective measures, the conditions and details of which it shall determine.

In case of urgency, Member States shall request authorisation to take the necessary measures themselves from the Commission, which shall take a decision as soon as possible; the Member States concerned shall then notify the measures to the other Member States. The Commission may decide at any time that the Member States concerned shall amend or abolish the measures in question.

In the selection of such measures, priority shall be given to those which cause the least disturbance of the functioning of the common market.

TITLE X
CUSTOMS COOPERATION

Article 135

Within the scope of application of this Treaty, the Council, acting in accordance with the procedure referred to in Article 251, shall take measures in order to strengthen customs cooperation between Member States and between the latter and the Commission. These measures shall not concern the application of national criminal law or the national administration of justice.

TITLE XI
SOCIAL POLICY, EDUCATION, VOCATIONAL TRAINING AND YOUTH

CHAPTER 1
SOCIAL PROVISIONS

Article 136

The Community and the Member States, having in mind fundamental social rights such as those set out in the European Social Charter signed at Turin on 18 October 1961 and in the 1989 Community Charter of the Fundamental Social Rights of Workers, shall have as their objectives the promotion of employment, improved living and working conditions, so as to make possible their harmonisation while the improvement is being maintained, proper social protection, dialogue between management and labour, the development of human resources with a view to lasting high employment and the combating of exclusion.

To this end the Community and the Member States shall implement measures which take account of the diverse forms of national practices, in particular in the field of contractual relations, and the need to maintain the competitiveness of the Community economy.

They believe that such a development will ensue not only from the functioning of the common market, which will favour the harmonisation of social systems, but also from the procedures provided for in this Treaty and from the approximation of provisions laid down by law, regulation or administrative action.

Article 137

1. With a view to achieving the objectives of Article 136, the Community shall support and complement the activities of the Member States in the following fields:
    (a) improvement in particular of the working environment to protect workers' health and safety;
    (b) working conditions;
    (c) social security and social protection of workers;
    (d) protection of workers where their employment contract is terminated;
    (e) the information and consultation of workers;
    (f) representation and collective defence of the interests of workers and employers, including co-determination, subject to paragraph 5;
    (g) conditions of employment for third-country nationals legally residing in Community territory;
    (h) the integration of persons excluded from the labour market, without prejudice to Article 150;
    (i) equality between men and women with regard to labour market opportunities and treatment at work;
    (j) the combating of social exclusion;
    (k) the modernisation of social protection systems without prejudice to point (c).
2. To this end, the Council:

(a)   may adopt measures designed to encourage cooperation between Member States through initiatives aimed at improving knowledge, developing exchanges of information and best practices, promoting innovative approaches and evaluating experiences, excluding any harmonisation of the laws and regulations of the Member States;

(b)   may adopt, in the fields referred to in paragraph 1(a) to (i), by means of directives, minimum requirements for gradual implementation, having regard to the conditions and technical rules obtaining in each of the Member States. Such directives shall avoid imposing administrative, financial and legal constraints in a way which would hold back the creation and development of small and medium-sized undertakings.

The Council shall act in accordance with the procedure referred to in Article 251 after consulting the Economic and Social Committee and the Committee of the Regions, except in the fields referred to in paragraph 1(c), (d), (f) and (g) of this article, where the Council shall act unanimously on a proposal from the Commission, after consulting the European Parliament and the said Committees. The Council, acting unanimously on a proposal from the Commission, after consulting the European Parliament, may decide to render the procedure referred to in Article 251 applicable to paragraph 1(d), (f) and (g) of this article.

3.   A Member State may entrust management and labour, at their joint request, with the implementation of directives adopted pursuant to paragraph 2.

In this case, it shall ensure that, no later than the date on which a directive must be transposed in accordance with Article 249, management and labour have introduced the necessary measures by agreement, the Member State concerned being required to take any necessary measure enabling it at any time to be in a position to guarantee the results imposed by that directive.

4.   The provisions adopted pursuant to this article:

— shall not affect the right of Member States to define the fundamental principles of their social security systems and must not significantly affect the financial equilibrium thereof,

— shall not prevent any Member State from maintaining or introducing more stringent protective measures compatible with this Treaty.

5.   The provisions of this article shall not apply to pay, the right of association, the right to strike or the right to impose lock-outs.

Article 138

1.   The Commission shall have the task of promoting the consultation of management and labour at Community level and shall take any relevant measure to facilitate their dialogue by ensuring balanced support for the parties.

2.   To this end, before submitting proposals in the social policy field, the Commission shall consult management and labour on the possible direction of Community action.

3.   If, after such consultation, the Commission considers Community action advisable, it shall consult management and labour on the content of the envisaged proposal. Management and labour shall forward to the Commission an opinion or, where appropriate, a recommendation.

4.   On the occasion of such consultation, management and labour may inform the Commission of their wish to initiate the process provided for in Article 139. The duration of the procedure shall not exceed nine months, unless the management and labour concerned and the Commission decide jointly to extend it.

Article 139

1.   Should management and labour so desire, the dialogue between them at Community level may lead to contractual relations, including agreements.

2.   Agreements concluded at Community level shall be implemented either in accordance with the procedures and practices specific to management and labour and the Member States or, in matters covered by Article 137, at the joint request of the signatory parties, by a Council decision on a proposal from the Commission.

The Council shall act by qualified majority, except where the agreement in question contains one or more provisions relating to one of the areas for which unanimity is required pursuant to Article 137(2). In that case, it shall act unanimously.

Article 140

With a view to achieving the objectives of Article 136 and without prejudice to the other provisions of this Treaty, the Commission shall encourage cooperation between the Member States and facilitate the coordination of their action in all social policy fields under this chapter, particularly in matters relating to:

— employment,
— labour law and working conditions,
— basic and advanced vocational training,
— social security,
— prevention of occupational accidents and diseases,
— occupational hygiene,
— the right of association and collective bargaining between employers and workers.

To this end, the Commission shall act in close contact with Member States by making studies, delivering opinions and arranging consultations both on problems arising at national level and on those of concern to international organisations.

Before delivering the opinions provided for in this article, the Commission shall consult the Economic and Social Committee.

Article 141

1. Each Member State shall ensure that the principle of equal pay for male and female workers for equal work or work of equal value is applied.

2. For the purpose of this article, 'pay' means the ordinary basic or minimum wage or salary and any other consideration, whether in cash or in kind, which the worker receives directly or indirectly, in respect of his employment, from his employer. Equal pay without discrimination based on sex means:
   (a) that pay for the same work at piece rates shall be calculated on the basis of the same unit of measurement;
   (b) that pay for work at time rates shall be the same for the same job.

3. The Council, acting in accordance with the procedure referred to in Article 251, and after consulting the Economic and Social Committee, shall adopt measures to ensure the application of the principle of equal opportunities and equal treatment of men and women in matters of employment and occupation, including the principle of equal pay for equal work or work of equal value.

4. With a view to ensuring full equality in practice between men and women in working life, the principle of equal treatment shall not prevent any Member State from maintaining or adopting measures providing for specific advantages in order to make it easier for the underrepresented sex to pursue a vocational activity or to prevent or compensate for disadvantages in professional careers.

Article 142

Member States shall endeavour to maintain the existing equivalence between paid holiday schemes.

Article 143

The Commission shall draw up a report each year on progress in achieving the objectives of Article 136, including the demographic situation in the Community. It shall forward the report to the European Parliament, the Council and the Economic and Social Committee.

The European Parliament may invite the Commission to draw up reports on particular problems concerning the social situation.

Article 144

The Council, after consulting the European Parliament, shall establish a Social Protection Committee with advisory status to promote cooperation on social protection policies between Member States and with the Commission. The tasks of the Committee shall be:

— to monitor the social situation and the development of social protection policies in the Member States and the Community,

— to promote exchanges of information, experience and good practice between Member States and with the Commission,

— without prejudice to Article 207, to prepare reports, formulate opinions or undertake other work within its fields of competence, at the request of either the Council or the Commission or on its own initiative.

In fulfilling its mandate, the Committee shall establish appropriate contacts with management and labour.

Each Member State and the Commission shall appoint two members of the Committee.

Article 145

The Commission shall include a separate chapter on social developments within the Community in its annual report to the European Parliament.

The European Parliament may invite the Commission to draw up reports on any particular problems concerning social conditions.

CHAPTER 3

EDUCATION, VOCATIONAL TRAINING AND YOUTH

Article 149

1. The Community shall contribute to the development of quality education by encouraging cooperation between Member States and, if necessary, by supporting and supplementing their action, while fully respecting the responsibility of the Member States for the content of teaching and the organisation of education systems and their cultural and linguistic diversity.

2. Community action shall be aimed at:

    — developing the European dimension in education, particularly through the teaching and dissemination of the languages of the Member States,

    — encouraging mobility of students and teachers, by encouraging inter alia, the academic recognition of diplomas and periods of study,

    — promoting cooperation between educational establishments,

    — developing exchanges of information and experience on issues common to the education systems of the Member States,

    — encouraging the development of youth exchanges and of exchanges of socioeducational instructors,

    — encouraging the development of distance education.

3. The Community and the Member States shall foster cooperation with third countries and the competent international organisations in the field of education, in particular the Council of Europe.

4. In order to contribute to the achievement of the objectives referred to in this Article, the Council:

    — acting in accordance with the procedure referred to in Article 251, after consulting the Economic and Social Committee and the Committee of the Regions, shall adopt incentive measures, excluding any harmonisation of the laws and regulations of the Member States,

    — acting by a qualified majority on a proposal from the Commission, shall adopt recommendations.

Article 150

1. The Community shall implement a vocational training policy which shall support and supplement the action of the Member States, while fully respecting the responsibility of the Member States for the content and organisation of vocational training.

2. Community action shall aim to:

    — facilitate adaptation to industrial changes, in particular through vocational training and retraining,

    — improve initial and continuing vocational training in order to facilitate vocational integration and reintegration into the labour market,

— facilitate access to vocational training and encourage mobility of instructors and trainees and particularly young people,

— stimulate cooperation on training between educational or training establishments and firms,

— develop exchanges of information and experience on issues common to the training systems of the Member States.

3. The Community and the Member States shall foster cooperation with third countries and the competent international organisations in the sphere of vocational training.

4. The Council, acting in accordance with the procedure referred to in Article 251 and after consulting the Economic and Social Committee and the Committee of the Regions, shall adopt measures to contribute to the achievement of the objectives referred to in this article, excluding any harmonisation of the laws and regulations of the Member States.

TITLE XII
CULTURE

Article 151

1. The Community shall contribute to the flowering of the cultures of the Member States, while respecting their national and regional diversity and at the same time bringing the common cultural heritage to the fore.

2. Action by the Community shall be aimed at encouraging cooperation between Member States and, if necessary, supporting and supplementing their action in the following areas:

— improvement of the knowledge and dissemination of the culture and history of the European peoples,

— conservation and safeguarding of cultural heritage of European significance,

— non-commercial cultural exchanges,

— artistic and literary creation, including in the audiovisual sector.

3. The Community and the Member States shall foster cooperation with third countries and the competent international organisations in the sphere of culture, in particular the Council of Europe.

4. The Community shall take cultural aspects into account in its action under other provisions of this Treaty, in particular in order to respect and to promote the diversity of its cultures.

5. In order to contribute to the achievement of the objectives referred to in this Article, the Council:

— acting in accordance with the procedure referred to in Article 251 and after consulting the Committee of the Regions, shall adopt incentive measures, excluding any harmonisation of the laws and regulations of the Member States. The Council shall act unanimously throughout the procedure referred to in Article 251,

— acting unanimously on a proposal from the Commission, shall adopt recommendations.

TITLE XIII
PUBLIC HEALTH

Article 152

1. A high level of human health protection shall be ensured in the definition and implementation of all Community policies and activities.

Community action, which shall complement national policies, shall be directed towards improving public health, preventing human illness and diseases, and obviating sources of danger to human health. Such action shall cover the fight against the major health scourges, by promoting research into their causes, their transmission and their prevention, as well as health information and education.

The Community shall complement the Member States' action in reducing drugs-related health damage, including information and prevention.

2. The Community shall encourage cooperation between the Member States in the areas referred to in this Article and, if necessary, lend support to their action.

Member States shall, in liaison with the Commission, coordinate among themselves their policies and programmes in the areas referred to in paragraph 1. The Commission may, in close contact with the Member States, take any useful initiative to promote such coordination.

3. The Community and the Member States shall foster cooperation with third countries and the competent international organisations in the sphere of public health.

4. The Council, acting in accordance with the procedure referred to in Article 251 and after consulting the Economic and Social Committee and the Committee of the Regions, shall contribute to the achievement of the objectives referred to in this article through adopting:

    (a) measures setting high standards of quality and safety of organs and substances of human origin, blood and blood derivatives; these measures shall not prevent any Member State from maintaining or introducing more stringent protective measures;

    (b) by way of derogation from Article 37, measures in the veterinary and phytosanitary fields which have as their direct objective the protection of public health;

    (c) incentive measures designed to protect and improve human health, excluding any harmonisation of the laws and regulations of the Member States.

    The Council, acting by a qualified majority on a proposal from the Commission, may also adopt recommendations for the purposes set out in this article.

5. Community action in the field of public health shall fully respect the responsibilities of the Member States for the organisation and delivery of health services and medical care. In particular, measures referred to in paragraph 4(a) shall not affect national provisions on the donation or medical use of organs and blood.

TITLE XIV
CONSUMER PROTECTION

Article 153

1. In order to promote the interests of consumers and to ensure a high level of consumer protection, the Community shall contribute to protecting the health, safety and economic interests of consumers, as well as to promoting their right to information, education and to organise themselves in order to safeguard their interests.

2. Consumer protection requirements shall be taken into account in defining and implementing other Community policies and activities.

3. The Community shall contribute to the attainment of the objectives referred to in paragraph 1 through:

    (a) measures adopted pursuant to Article 95 in the context of the completion of the internal market;

    (b) measures which support, supplement and monitor the policy pursued by the Member States.

4. The Council, acting in accordance with the procedure referred to in Article 251 and after consulting the Economic and Social Committee, shall adopt the measures referred to in paragraph 3(b).

5. Measures adopted pursuant to paragraph 4 shall not prevent any Member State from maintaining or introducing more stringent protective measures. Such measures must be compatible with this Treaty. The Commission shall be notified of them.

TITLE XIX
ENVIRONMENT

Article 174

1. Community policy on the environment shall contribute to pursuit of the following objectives:
    — preserving, protecting and improving the quality of the environment,
    — protecting human health,
    — prudent and rational utilisation of natural resources,
    — promoting measures at international level to deal with regional or worldwide environmental problems.

2. Community policy on the environment shall aim at a high level of protection taking into account the diversity of situations in the various regions of the Community. It shall be based on the precautionary principle and on the principles that preventive action should be taken, that environmental damage should as a priority be rectified at source and that the polluter should pay.

    In this context, harmonisation measures answering environmental protection requirements shall include, where appropriate, a safeguard clause allowing Member States to take provisional measures, for non-economic environmental reasons, subject to a Community inspection procedure.

3. In preparing its policy on the environment, the Community shall take account of:
    — available scientific and technical data,
    — environmental conditions in the various regions of the Community,
    — the potential benefits and costs of action or lack of action,
    — the economic and social development of the Community as a whole and the balanced development of its regions.

4. Within their respective spheres of competence, the Community and the Member States shall cooperate with third countries and with the competent international organisations. The arrangements for Community cooperation may be the subject of agreements between the Community and the third parties concerned, which shall be negotiated and concluded in accordance with Article 300.

    The previous subparagraph shall be without prejudice to Member States' competence to negotiate in international bodies and to conclude international agreements.

Article 175

1. The Council, acting in accordance with the procedure referred to in Article 251 and after consulting the Economic and Social Committee and the Committee of the Regions, shall decide what action is to be taken by the Community in order to achieve the objectives referred to in Article 174.

2. By way of derogation from the decision-making procedure provided for in paragraph 1 and without prejudice to Article 95, the Council, acting unanimously on a proposal from the Commission and after consulting the European Parliament, the Economic and Social Committee and the Committee of the Regions, shall adopt:
    (a) provisions primarily of a fiscal nature;
    (b) measures affecting:
         — town and country planning,
         — quantitative management of water resources or affecting, directly or indirectly, the availability of those resources,
         — land use, with the exception of waste management;
    (c) measures significantly affecting a Member State's choice between different energy sources and the general structure of its energy supply.

    The Council may, under the conditions laid down in the first subparagraph, define those matters referred to in this paragraph on which decisions are to be taken by a qualified majority.

3. In other areas, general action programmes setting out priority objectives to be attained shall be adopted by the Council, acting in accordance with the procedure referred to in Article 251 and after consulting the Economic and Social Committee and the Committee of the Regions.

    The Council, acting under the terms of paragraph 1 or paragraph 2 according to the case, shall adopt the measures necessary for the implementation of these programmes.

4. Without prejudice to certain measures of a Community nature, the Member States shall finance and implement the environment policy.

5. Without prejudice to the principle that the polluter should pay, if a measure based on the provisions of paragraph 1 involves costs deemed disproportionate for the public authorities of a Member State, the Council shall, in the act adopting that measure, lay down appropriate provisions in the form of:

— temporary derogations, and/or

— financial support from the Cohesion Fund set up pursuant to Article 161.

Article 176

The protective measures adopted pursuant to Article 175 shall not prevent any Member State from maintaining or introducing more stringent protective measures. Such measures must be compatible with this Treaty. They shall be notified to the Commission.

TITLE XX

DEVELOPMENT COOPERATION

Article 177

1. Community policy in the sphere of development cooperation, which shall be complementary to the policies pursued by the Member States, shall foster:
    — the sustainable economic and social development of the developing countries, and more particularly the most disadvantaged among them,
    — the smooth and gradual integration of the developing countries into the world economy,
    — the campaign against poverty in the developing countries.
2. Community policy in this area shall contribute to the general objective of developing and consolidating democracy and the rule of law, and to that of respecting human rights and fundamental freedoms.
3. The Community and the Member States shall comply with the commitments and take account of the objectives they have approved in the context of the United Nations and other competent international organisations.

Article 178

The Community shall take account of the objectives referred to in Article 177 in the policies that it implements which are likely to affect developing countries.

Article 179

1. Without prejudice to the other provisions of this Treaty, the Council, acting in accordance with the procedure referred to in Article 251, shall adopt the measures necessary to further the objectives referred to in Article 177. Such measures may take the form of multiannual programmes.
2. The European Investment Bank shall contribute, under the terms laid down in its Statute, to the implementation of the measures referred to in paragraph 1.
3. The provisions of this Article shall not affect cooperation with the African, Caribbean and Pacific countries in the framework of the ACP-EC Convention.

Article 180

1. The Community and the Member States shall coordinate their policies on development cooperation and shall consult each other on their aid programmes, including in international organisations and during international conferences. They may undertake joint action. Member States shall contribute if necessary to the implementation of Community aid programmes.
2. The Commission may take any useful initiative to promote the coordination referred to in paragraph 1.

Article 181

Within their respective spheres of competence, the Community and the Member States shall cooperate with third countries and with the competent international organisations. The arrangements for Community cooperation may be the subject of agreements between the Community and the third parties concerned, which shall be negotiated and concluded in accordance with Article 300.

The previous paragraph shall be without prejudice to Member States' competence to negotiate in international bodies and to conclude international agreements.

TITLE XXI
ECONOMIC, FINANCIAL AND TECHNICAL COOPERATION WITH THIRD COUNTRIES

Article 181a

1. Without prejudice to the other provisions of this Treaty, and in particular those of Title XX, the Community shall carry out, within its spheres of competence, economic, financial and technical cooperation measures with third countries. Such measures shall be complementary to those carried out by the Member States and consistent with the development policy of the Community.

   Community policy in this area shall contribute to the general objective of developing and consolidating democracy and the rule of law, and to the objective of respecting human rights and fundamental freedoms.

2. The Council, acting by a qualified majority on a proposal from the Commission and after consulting the European Parliament, shall adopt the measures necessary for the implementation of paragraph 1. The Council shall act unanimously for the association agreements referred to in Article 310 and for the agreements to be concluded with the States which are candidates for accession to the Union.

3. Within their respective spheres of competence, the Community and the Member States shall cooperate with third countries and the competent international organisations. The arrangements for Community cooperation may be the subject of agreements between the Community and the third parties concerned, which shall be negotiated and concluded in accordance with Article 300.

   The first subparagraph shall be without prejudice to the Member States' competence to negotiate in international bodies and to conclude international agreements.

PART FIVE
INSTITUTIONS OF THE COMMUNITY

TITLE I
PROVISIONS GOVERNING THE INSTITUTIONS

CHAPTER 1
THE INSTITUTIONS

SECTION 1
THE EUROPEAN PARLIAMENT

Article 189

The European Parliament, which shall consist of representatives of the peoples of the States brought together in the Community, shall exercise the powers conferred upon it by this Treaty.

The number of Members of the European Parliament shall not exceed 736.

Editor's Note: The final number is dependent on the Nice Declaration on Enlargement or the Draft Constitution. In terms of the Protocol concerning the conditions and arrangements for admission of the republic of Bulgaria and Romania to the European Union, Art 21, Bulgaria will have 18 MEPs and Romania 35 until 2009.

Article 190

1. The representatives in the European Parliament of the peoples of the States brought together in the Community shall be elected by direct universal suffrage.

2. The number of representatives elected in each Member State shall be as follows:

Belgium	24
Czech Republic	24
Denmark	14
Germany	99
Estonia	6
Greece	24
Spain	54

France	78
Ireland	13
Italy	78
Cyprus	6
Latvia	9
Lithuania	13
Luxembourg	6
Hungary	24
Malta	5
Netherlands	27
Austria	18
Poland	54
Portugal	24
Slovenia	7
Slovakia	14
Finland	14
Sweden	19
United Kingdom	78

In the event of amendments to this paragraph, the number of representatives elected in each Member State must ensure appropriate representation of the peoples of the States brought together in the Community.

3.   Representatives shall be elected for a term of five years.

4.   The European Parliament shall draw up a proposal for elections by direct universal suffrage in accordance with a uniform procedure in all Member States or in accordance with principles common to all Member States.

The Council shall, acting unanimously after obtaining the assent of the European Parliament, which shall act by a majority of its component members, lay down the appropriate provisions, which it shall recommend to Member States for adoption in accordance with their respective constitutional requirements.

5.   The European Parliament, after seeking an opinion from the Commission and with the approval of the Council acting by a qualified majority, shall lay down the regulations and general conditions governing the performance of the duties of its Members. All rules or conditions relating to the taxation of Members or former Members shall require unanimity within the Council.

Editor's Note: *With effect from the start of the 2009–14 term, Art 190(2), first subparagraph, shall be replaced by the following:*

2.   *The number of representatives elected in each Member State shall be as follows:*

Belgium	*22*
Bulgaria	*17*
Czech Republic	*22*
Denmark	*13*
Germany	*99*
Estonia	*6*
Greece	*22*
Spain	*50*
France	*72*
Ireland	*12*
Italy	*72*
Cyprus	*6*
Latvia	*8*
Lithuania	*12*
Luxembourg	*6*

Hungary	*22*
Malta	*5*
Netherlands	*25*
Austria	*17*
Poland	*50*
Portugal	*22*
Romania	*33*
Slovenia	*7*
Slovakia	*13*
Finland	*13*
Sweden	*18*
United Kingdom	*72*

Article 191

Political parties at European level are important as a factor for integration within the Union. They contribute to forming a European awareness and to expressing the political will of the citizens of the Union.

The Council, acting in accordance with the procedure referred to in Article 251, shall lay down the regulations governing political parties at European level and in particular the rules regarding their funding.

Article 192

In so far as provided in this Treaty, the European Parliament shall participate in the process leading up to the adoption of Community acts by exercising its powers under the procedures laid down in Articles 251 and 252 and by giving its assent or delivering advisory opinions.

The European Parliament may, acting by a majority of its Members, request the Commission to submit any appropriate proposal on matters on which it considers that a Community act is required for the purpose of implementing this Treaty.

Article 193

In the course of its duties, the European Parliament may, at the request of a quarter of its Members, set up a temporary Committee of Inquiry to investigate, without prejudice to the powers conferred by this Treaty on other institutions or bodies, alleged contraventions or maladministration in the implementation of Community law, except where the alleged facts are being examined before a court and while the case is still subject to legal proceedings.

The temporary Committee of Inquiry shall cease to exist on the submission of its report.

The detailed provisions governing the exercise of the right of inquiry shall be determined by common accord of the European Parliament, the Council and the Commission.

Article 194

Any citizen of the Union, and any natural or legal person residing or having its registered office in a Member State, shall have the right to address, individually or in association with other citizens or persons, a petition to the European Parliament on a matter which comes within the Community's fields of activity and which affects him, her or it directly.

Article 195

1. The European Parliament shall appoint an Ombudsman empowered to receive complaints from any citizen of the Union or any natural or legal person residing or having its registered office in a Member State concerning instances of maladministration in the activities of the Community institutions or bodies, with the exception of the Court of Justice and the Court of First Instance acting in their judicial role.

    In accordance with his duties, the Ombudsman shall conduct inquiries for which he finds grounds, either on his own initiative or on the basis of complaints submitted to him direct or through a Member of the European Parliament, except where the alleged facts are or have been the subject of legal proceedings. Where the Ombudsman establishes an instance of maladministration, he shall refer the matter to the institution concerned, which shall have a period of three months in which to inform him of its views. The Ombudsman shall then forward a report to the European Parliament and the institution concerned. The person lodging the complaint shall be informed of the outcome of such inquiries.

The Ombudsman shall submit an annual report to the European Parliament on the outcome of his inquiries.

2.   The Ombudsman shall be appointed after each election of the European Parliament for the duration of its term of office. The Ombudsman shall be eligible for reappointment.

The Ombudsman may be dismissed by the Court of Justice at the request of the European Parliament if he no longer fulfils the conditions required for the performance of his duties or if he is guilty of serious misconduct.

3.   The Ombudsman shall be completely independent in the performance of his duties. In the performance of those duties he shall neither seek nor take instructions from any body. The Ombudsman may not, during his term of office, engage in any other occupation, whether gainful or not.

4.   The European Parliament shall, after seeking an opinion from the Commission and with the approval of the Council acting by a qualified majority, lay down the regulations and general conditions governing the performance of the Ombudsman's duties.

Article 196

The European Parliament shall hold an annual session. It shall meet, without requiring to be convened, on the second Tuesday in March.

The European Parliament may meet in extraordinary session at the request of a majority of its Members or at the request of the Council or of the Commission.

Article 197

The European Parliament shall elect its President and its officers from among its Members.

Members of the Commission may attend all meetings and shall, at their request, be heard on behalf of the Commission.

The Commission shall reply orally or in writing to questions put to it by the European Parliament or by its Members.

The Council shall be heard by the European Parliament in accordance with the conditions laid down by the Council in its Rules of Procedure.

Article 198

Save as otherwise provided in this Treaty, the European Parliament shall act by an absolute majority of the votes cast.

The Rules of Procedure shall determine the quorum.

Article 199

The European Parliament shall adopt its Rules of Procedure, acting by a majority of its Members.

The proceedings of the European Parliament shall be published in the manner laid down in its Rules of Procedure.

Article 200

The European Parliament shall discuss in open session the annual general report submitted to it by the Commission.

Article 201

If a motion of censure on the activities of the Commission is tabled before it, the European Parliament shall not vote thereon until at least three days after the motion has been tabled and only by open vote.

If the motion of censure is carried by a two-thirds majority of the votes cast, representing a majority of the Members of the European Parliament, the Members of the Commission shall resign as a body. They shall continue to deal with current business until they are replaced in accordance with Article 214. In this case, the term of office of the Members of the Commission appointed to replace them shall expire on the date on which the term of office of the Members of the Commission obliged to resign as a body would have expired.

SECTION 2
THE COUNCIL

Article 202

To ensure that the objectives set out in this Treaty are attained the Council shall, in accordance with the provisions of this Treaty:

— ensure coordination of the general economic policies of the Member States,

— have power to take decisions,

— confer on the Commission, in the acts which the Council adopts, powers for the implementation of the rules which the Council lays down. The Council may impose certain requirements in respect of the exercise of these powers. The Council may also reserve the right, in specific cases, to exercise directly implementing powers itself. The procedures referred to above must be consonant with principles and rules to be laid down in advance by the Council, acting unanimously on a proposal from the Commission and after obtaining the opinion of the European Parliament.

Article 203

The Council shall consist of a representative of each Member State at ministerial level, authorised to commit the government of that Member State.

The office of President shall be held in turn by each Member State in the Council for a term of six months in the order decided by the Council acting unanimously.

Article 204

The Council shall meet when convened by its President on his own initiative or at the request of one of its Members or of the Commission.

Article 205

1. Save as otherwise provided in this Treaty, the Council shall act by a majority of its Members.
2. Where the Council is required to act by a qualified majority, the votes of its Members shall be weighted as follows:

Belgium	12
Bulgaria	10
Czech Republic	12
Denmark	7
Germany	29
Estonia	4
Greece	12
Spain	27
France	29
Ireland	7
Italy	29
Cyprus	4
Latvia	4
Lithuania	7
Luxembourg	4
Hungary	12
Malta	3
Netherlands	13
Austria	10
Poland	27
Portugal	12
Romania	14
Slovenia	4
Slovakia	7
Finland	7
Sweden	10
United Kingdom	29

Acts of the Council shall require for their adoption at least 255 votes in favour cast by a majority of the members where this Treaty requires them to be adopted on a proposal from the Commission.

In other cases, for their adoption acts of the Council shall require at least 255 votes in favour, cast by at least two-thirds of the members.

3.   Abstentions by Members present in person or represented shall not prevent the adoption by the Council of acts which require unanimity.

4.   When a decision is to be adopted by the Council by a qualified majority, a member of the Council may request verification that the Member States constituting the qualified majority represent at least 62% of the total population of the Union. If that condition is shown not to have been met, the decision in question shall not be adopted.

Article 206

Where a vote is taken, any Member of the Council may also act on behalf of not more than one other member.

Article 207

1.   A committee consisting of the Permanent Representatives of the Member States shall be responsible for preparing the work of the Council and for carrying out the tasks assigned to it by the Council. The Committee may adopt procedural decisions in cases provided for in the Council's Rules of Procedure.

2.   The Council shall be assisted by a General Secretariat, under the responsibility of a Secretary-General, High Representative for the common foreign and security policy, who shall be assisted by a Deputy Secretary-General responsible for the running of the General Secretariat. The Secretary-General and the Deputy Secretary-General shall be appointed by the Council acting by a qualified majority.

The Council shall decide on the organisation of the General Secretariat.

3.   The Council shall adopt its Rules of Procedure.

For the purpose of applying Article 255(3), the Council shall elaborate in these Rules the conditions under which the public shall have access to Council documents. For the purpose of this paragraph, the Council shall define the cases in which it is to be regarded as acting in its legislative capacity, with a view to allowing greater access to documents in those cases, while at the same time preserving the effectiveness of its decision-making process. In any event, when the Council acts in its legislative capacity, the results of votes and explanations of vote as well as statements in the minutes shall be made public.

Article 208

The Council may request the Commission to undertake any studies the Council considers desirable for the attainment of the common objectives, and to submit to it any appropriate proposals.

Article 209

The Council shall, after receiving an opinion from the Commission, determine the rules governing the committees provided for in this Treaty.

Article 210

The Council shall, acting by a qualified majority, determine the salaries, allowances and pensions of the President and Members of the Commission, and of the President, Judges, Advocates-General and Registrar of the Court of Justice and of the Members and Registrar of the Court of First Instance. It shall also, again by a qualified majority, determine any payment to be made instead of remuneration.

SECTION 3

THE COMMISSION

Article 211

In order to ensure the proper functioning and development of the common market, the Commission shall:

- ensure that the provisions of this Treaty and the measures taken by the institutions pursuant thereto are applied,
- formulate recommendations or deliver opinions on matters dealt with in this Treaty, if it expressly so provides or if the Commission considers it necessary,
- have its own power of decision and participate in the shaping of measures taken by the Council and by the European Parliament in the manner provided for in this Treaty,
- exercise the powers conferred on it by the Council for the implementation of the rules laid down by the latter.

Article 212

The Commission shall publish annually, not later than one month before the opening of the session of the European Parliament, a general report on the activities of the Community.

Article 213

1. The Commission shall consist of 20 Members, who shall be chosen on the grounds of their general competence and whose independence is beyond doubt.

    The number of Members of the Commission may be altered by the Council, acting unanimously.

    Only nationals of Member States may be Members of the Commission.

    The Commission must include at least one national of each of the Member States, but may not include more than two Members having the nationality of the same State.

2. The Members of the Commission shall, in the general interest of the Community, be completely independent in the performance of their duties.

    In the performance of these duties, they shall neither seek nor take instructions from any government or from any other body. They shall refrain from any action incompatible with their duties. Each Member State undertakes to respect this principle and not to seek to influence the Members of the Commission in the performance of their tasks.

    The Members of the Commission may not, during their term of office, engage in any other occupation, whether gainful or not. When entering upon their duties they shall give a solemn undertaking that, both during and after their term of office, they will respect the obligations arising therefrom and in particular their duty to behave with integrity and discretion as regards the acceptance, after they have ceased to hold office, of certain appointments or benefits. In the event of any breach of these obligations, the Court of Justice may, on application by the Council or the Commission, rule that the Member concerned be, according to the circumstances, either compulsorily retired in accordance with Article 216 or deprived of his right to a pension or other benefits in its stead.

Editor's Note: The 2003 Accession Treaty provides, in Art 45, that each new Member State will have a Commissioner. The Treaty is not formally changed.

Article 214

1. The Members of the Commission shall be appointed, in accordance with the procedure referred to in paragraph 2, for a period of five years, subject, if need be, to Article 201. Their term of office shall be renewable.

2. The Council, meeting in the composition of Heads of State or Government and acting by a qualified majority, shall nominate the person it intends to appoint as President of the Commission; the nomination shall be approved by the European Parliament.

    The Council, acting by a qualified majority and by common accord with the nominee for President, shall adopt the list of the other persons whom it intends to appoint as Members of the Commission, drawn up in accordance with the proposals made by each Member State.

    The President and the other Members of the Commission thus nominated shall be subject as a body to a vote of approval by the European Parliament. After approval by the European Parliament, the President and the other Members of the Commission shall be appointed by the Council, acting by a qualified majority.

Editor's Note: The 2003 Accession Treaty, Art 45, addresses transitional interim arrangements for the new Commissioners.

Article 215

Apart from normal replacement, or death, the duties of a Member of the Commission shall end when he resigns or is compulsorily retired.

A vacancy caused by resignation, compulsory retirement or death shall be filled for the remainder of the Member's term of office by a new Member appointed by the Council, acting by a qualified majority. The Council may, acting unanimously, decide that such a vacancy need not be filled.

In the event of resignation, compulsory retirement or death, the President shall be replaced for the remainder of his term of office. The procedure laid down in Article 214(2) shall be applicable for the replacement of the President.

Save in the case of compulsory retirement under Article 216, Members of the Commission shall remain in office until they have been replaced or until the Council has decided that the vacancy need not be filled, as provided for in the second paragraph of this Article.

Article 216

If any Member of the Commission no longer fulfils the conditions required for the performance of his duties or if he has been guilty of serious misconduct, the Court of Justice may, on application by the Council or the Commission, compulsorily retire him.

Article 217

1. The Commission shall work under the political guidance of its President, who shall decide on its internal organisation in order to ensure that it acts consistently, efficiently and on the basis of collegiality.
2. The responsibilities incumbent upon the Commission shall be structured and allocated among its Members by its President. The President may reshuffle the allocation of those responsibilities during the Commission's term of office. The Members of the Commission shall carry out the duties devolved upon them by the President under his authority.
3. After obtaining the approval of the College, the President shall appoint Vice-Presidents from among its Members.
4. A Member of the Commission shall resign if the President so requests, after obtaining the approval of the College.

Article 218

1. The Council and the Commission shall consult each other and shall settle by common accord their methods of cooperation.
2. The Commission shall adopt its Rules of Procedure so as to ensure that both it and its departments operate in accordance with the provisions of this Treaty. It shall ensure that these Rules are published.

Article 219

The Commission shall act by a majority of the number of Members provided for in Article 213.

A meeting of the Commission shall be valid only if the number of Members laid down in its Rules of Procedure is present.

SECTION 4
THE COURT OF JUSTICE

Article 220

The Court of Justice and the Court of First Instance, each within its jurisdiction, shall ensure that in the interpretation and application of this Treaty the law is observed.

In addition, judicial panels may be attached to the Court of First Instance under the conditions laid down in Article 225a in order to exercise, in certain specific areas, the judicial competence laid down in this Treaty.

Article 221

The Court of Justice shall consist of one judge per Member State.

The Court of Justice shall sit in chambers or in a Grand Chamber, in accordance with the rules laid down for that purpose in the Statute of the Court of Justice.

When provided for in the Statute, the Court of Justice may also sit as a full Court.

Article 222

The Court of Justice shall be assisted by eight Advocates-General. Should the Court of Justice so request, the Council, acting unanimously, may increase the number of Advocates-General.

It shall be the duty of the Advocate-General, acting with complete impartiality and independence, to make, in open court, reasoned submissions on cases which, in accordance with the Statute of the Court of Justice, require his involvement.

Article 223

The Judges and Advocates-General of the Court of Justice shall be chosen from persons whose independence is beyond doubt and who possess the qualifications required for appointment to the highest judicial offices in their respective countries or who are jurisconsults of recognised competence; they shall be appointed by common accord of the governments of the Member States for a term of six years.

Every three years there shall be a partial replacement of the Judges and Advocates-General, in accordance with the conditions laid down in the Statute of the Court of Justice.

The Judges shall elect the President of the Court of Justice from among their number for a term of three years. He may be re-elected.

Retiring Judges and Advocates-General may be reappointed.

The Court of Justice shall appoint its Registrar and lay down the rules governing his service.

The Court of Justice shall establish its Rules of Procedure. Those Rules shall require the approval of the Council, acting by a qualified majority.

Article 224

The Court of First Instance shall comprise at least one judge per Member State. The number of Judges shall be determined by the Statute of the Court of Justice. The Statute may provide for the Court of First Instance to be assisted by Advocates-General.

The members of the Court of First Instance shall be chosen from persons whose independence is beyond doubt and who possess the ability required for appointment to high judicial office. They shall be appointed by common accord of the governments of the Member States for a term of six years. The membership shall be partially renewed every three years. Retiring members shall be eligible for reappointment.

The Judges shall elect the President of the Court of First Instance from among their number for a term of three years. He may be re-elected.

The Court of First Instance shall appoint its Registrar and lay down the rules governing his service.

The Court of First Instance shall establish its Rules of Procedure in agreement with the Court of Justice. Those Rules shall require the approval of the Council, acting by a qualified majority.

Unless the Statute of the Court of Justice provides otherwise, the provisions of this Treaty relating to the Court of Justice shall apply to the Court of First Instance.

Article 225

1. The Court of First Instance shall have jurisdiction to hear and determine at first instance actions or proceedings referred to in Articles 230, 232, 235, 236 and 238, with the exception of those assigned to a judicial panel and those reserved in the Statute for the Court of Justice. The Statute may provide for the Court of First Instance to have jurisdiction for other classes of action or proceeding.

    Decisions given by the Court of First Instance under this paragraph may be subject to a right of appeal to the Court of Justice on points of law only, under the conditions and within the limits laid down by the Statute.

2. The Court of First Instance shall have jurisdiction to hear and determine actions or proceedings brought against decisions of the judicial panels set up under Article 225a.

    Decisions given by the Court of First Instance under this paragraph may exceptionally be subject to review by the Court of Justice, under the conditions and within the limits laid down by the Statute, where there is a serious risk of the unity or consistency of Community law being affected.

3. The Court of First Instance shall have jurisdiction to hear and determine questions referred for a preliminary ruling under Article 234, in specific areas laid down by the Statute.

Where the Court of First Instance considers that the case requires a decision of principle likely to affect the unity or consistency of Community law, it may refer the case to the Court of Justice for a ruling.

Decisions given by the Court of First Instance on questions referred for a preliminary ruling may exceptionally be subject to review by the Court of Justice, under the conditions and within the limits laid down by the Statute, where there is a serious risk of the unity or consistency of Community law being affected.

Article 225a

The Council, acting unanimously on a proposal from the Commission and after consulting the European Parliament and the Court of Justice or at the request of the Court of Justice and after consulting the European Parliament and the Commission, may create judicial panels to hear and determine at first instance certain classes of action or proceeding brought in specific areas.

The decision establishing a judicial panel shall lay down the rules on the organisation of the panel and the extent of the jurisdiction conferred upon it.

Decisions given by judicial panels may be subject to a right of appeal on points of law only or, when provided for in the decision establishing the panel, a right of appeal also on matters of fact, before the Court of First Instance.

The members of the judicial panels shall be chosen from persons whose independence is beyond doubt and who possess the ability required for appointment to judicial office. They shall be appointed by the Council, acting unanimously.

The judicial panels shall establish their Rules of Procedure in agreement with the Court of Justice. Those Rules shall require the approval of the Council, acting by a qualified majority.

Unless the decision establishing the judicial panel provides otherwise, the provisions of this Treaty relating to the Court of Justice and the provisions of the Statute of the Court of Justice shall apply to the judicial panels.

Article 226

If the Commission considers that a Member State has failed to fulfil an obligation under this Treaty, it shall deliver a reasoned opinion on the matter after giving the State concerned the opportunity to submit its observations.

If the State concerned does not comply with the opinion within the period laid down by the Commission, the latter may bring the matter before the Court of Justice.

Article 227

A Member State which considers that another Member State has failed to fulfil an obligation under this Treaty may bring the matter before the Court of Justice.

Before a Member State brings an action against another Member State for an alleged infringement of an obligation under this Treaty, it shall bring the matter before the Commission.

The Commission shall deliver a reasoned opinion after each of the States concerned has been given the opportunity to submit its own case and its observations on the other party's case both orally and in writing.

If the Commission has not delivered an opinion within three months of the date on which the matter was brought before it, the absence of such opinion shall not prevent the matter from being brought before the Court of Justice.

Article 228

1.   If the Court of Justice finds that a Member State has failed to fulfil an obligation under this Treaty, the State shall be required to take the necessary measures to comply with the judgment of the Court of Justice.

2.   If the Commission considers that the Member State concerned has not taken such measures it shall, after giving that State the opportunity to submit its observations, issue a reasoned opinion specifying the points on which the Member State concerned has not complied with the judgment of the Court of Justice.

     If the Member State concerned fails to take the necessary measures to comply with the Court's judgment within the time limit laid down by the Commission, the latter may bring the case before the Court of Justice. In so doing it shall specify the amount of the lump sum or penalty payment to be paid by the Member State concerned which it considers appropriate in the circumstances.

If the Court of Justice finds that the Member State concerned has not complied with its judgment it may impose a lump sum or penalty payment on it.

This procedure shall be without prejudice to Article 227.

Article 229

Regulations adopted jointly by the European Parliament and the Council, and by the Council, pursuant to the provisions of this Treaty, may give the Court of Justice unlimited jurisdiction with regard to the penalties provided for in such regulations.

Article 229a

Without prejudice to the other provisions of this Treaty, the Council, acting unanimously on a proposal from the Commission and after consulting the European Parliament, may adopt provisions to confer jurisdiction, to the extent that it shall determine, on the Court of Justice in disputes relating to the application of acts adopted on the basis of this Treaty which create Community industrial property rights. The Council shall recommend those provisions to the Member States for adoption in accordance with their respective constitutional requirements.

Article 230

The Court of Justice shall review the legality of acts adopted jointly by the European Parliament and the Council, of acts of the Council, of the Commission and of the ECB, other than recommendations and opinions, and of acts of the European Parliament intended to produce legal effects vis-à-vis third parties.

It shall for this purpose have jurisdiction in actions brought by a Member State, the European Parliament, the Council or the Commission on grounds of lack of competence, infringement of an essential procedural requirement, infringement of this Treaty or of any rule of law relating to its application, or misuse of powers.

The Court of Justice shall have jurisdiction under the same conditions in actions brought by the Court of Auditors and by the ECB for the purpose of protecting their prerogatives.

Any natural or legal person may, under the same conditions, institute proceedings against a decision addressed to that person or against a decision which, although in the form of a regulation or a decision addressed to another person, is of direct and individual concern to the former.

The proceedings provided for in this article shall be instituted within two months of the publication of the measure, or of its notification to the plaintiff, or, in the absence thereof, of the day on which it came to the knowledge of the latter, as the case may be.

Article 231

If the action is well founded, the Court of Justice shall declare the act concerned to be void. In the case of a regulation, however, the Court of Justice shall, if it considers this necessary, state which of the effects of the regulation which it has declared void shall be considered as definitive.

Article 232

Should the European Parliament, the Council or the Commission, in infringement of this Treaty, fail to act, the Member States and the other institutions of the Community may bring an action before the Court of Justice to have the infringement established.

The action shall be admissible only if the institution concerned has first been called upon to act. If, within two months of being so called upon, the institution concerned has not defined its position, the action may be brought within a further period of two months.

Any natural or legal person may, under the conditions laid down in the preceding paragraphs, complain to the Court of Justice that an institution of the Community has failed to address to that person any act other than a recommendation or an opinion.

The Court of Justice shall have jurisdiction, under the same conditions, in actions or proceedings brought by the ECB in the areas falling within the latter's field of competence and in actions or proceedings brought against the latter.

Article 233

The institution or institutions whose act has been declared void or whose failure to act has been declared contrary to this Treaty shall be required to take the necessary measures to comply with the judgment of the Court of Justice.

This obligation shall not affect any obligation which may result from the application of the second paragraph of Article 288.

This article shall also apply to the ECB.

Article 234

The Court of Justice shall have jurisdiction to give preliminary rulings concerning:

(a)   the interpretation of this Treaty;

(b)   the validity and interpretation of acts of the institutions of the Community and of the ECB;

(c)   the interpretation of the statutes of bodies established by an act of the Council, where those statutes so provide.

Where such a question is raised before any court or tribunal of a Member State, that court or tribunal may, if it considers that a decision on the question is necessary to enable it to give judgment, request the Court of Justice to give a ruling thereon.

Where any such question is raised in a case pending before a court or tribunal of a Member State against whose decisions there is no judicial remedy under national law, that court or tribunal shall bring the matter before the Court of Justice.

Article 235

The Court of Justice shall have jurisdiction in disputes relating to compensation for damage provided for in the second paragraph of Article 288.

Article 236

The Court of Justice shall have jurisdiction in any dispute between the Community and its servants within the limits and under the conditions laid down in the Staff Regulations or the Conditions of employment.

Article 237

The Court of Justice shall, within the limits hereinafter laid down, have jurisdiction in disputes concerning:

(a)   the fulfilment by Member States of obligations under the Statute of the European Investment Bank. In this connection, the Board of Directors of the Bank shall enjoy the powers conferred upon the Commission by Article 226;

(b)   measures adopted by the Board of Governors of the European Investment Bank. In this connection, any Member State, the Commission or the Board of Directors of the Bank may institute proceedings under the conditions laid down in Article 230;

(c)   measures adopted by the Board of Directors of the European Investment Bank. Proceedings against such measures may be instituted only by Member States or by the Commission, under the conditions laid down in Article 230, and solely on the grounds of non-compliance with the procedure provided for in Article 21(2), (5), (6) and (7) of the Statute of the Bank;

(d)   the fulfilment by national central banks of obligations under this Treaty and the Statute of the ESCB. In this connection the powers of the Council of the ECB in respect of national central banks shall be the same as those conferred upon the Commission in respect of Member States by Article 226. If the Court of Justice finds that a national central bank has failed to fulfil an obligation under this Treaty, that bank shall be required to take the necessary measures to comply with the judgment of the Court of Justice.

Article 238

The Court of Justice shall have jurisdiction to give judgment pursuant to any arbitration clause contained in a contract concluded by or on behalf of the Community, whether that contract be governed by public or private law.

Article 239

The Court of Justice shall have jurisdiction in any dispute between Member States which relates to the subject matter of this Treaty if the dispute is submitted to it under a special agreement between the parties.

Article 240

Save where jurisdiction is conferred on the Court of Justice by this Treaty, disputes to which the Community is a party shall not on that ground be excluded from the jurisdiction of the courts or tribunals of the Member States.

Article 241

Notwithstanding the expiry of the period laid down in the fifth paragraph of Article 230, any party may, in proceedings in which a regulation adopted jointly by the European Parliament and the Council, or a regulation of the Council, of the Commission, or of the ECB is at issue, plead the grounds specified in the second paragraph of Article 230 in order to invoke before the Court of Justice the inapplicability of that regulation.

Article 242

Actions brought before the Court of Justice shall not have suspensory effect. The Court of Justice may, however, if it considers that circumstances so require, order that application of the contested act be suspended.

Article 243

The Court of Justice may in any cases before it prescribe any necessary interim measures.

Article 244

The judgments of the Court of Justice shall be enforceable under the conditions laid down in Article 256.

Article 245

The Statute of the Court of Justice shall be laid down in a separate Protocol.

The Council, acting unanimously at the request of the Court of Justice and after consulting the European Parliament and the Commission, or at the request of the Commission and after consulting the European Parliament and the Court of Justice, may amend the provisions of the Statute, with the exception of Title I.

SECTION 5

THE COURT OF AUDITORS

Article 246

The Court of Auditors shall carry out the audit.

Article 247

1. The Court of Auditors shall consist of one national from each Member State.
2. The Members of the Court of Auditors shall be chosen from among persons who belong or have belonged in their respective countries to external audit bodies or who are especially qualified for this office. Their independence must be beyond doubt.
3. The Members of the Court of Auditors shall be appointed for a term of six years. The Council, acting by a qualified majority after consulting the European Parliament, shall adopt the list of Members drawn up in accordance with the proposals made by each Member State. The term of office of the Members of the Court of Auditors shall be renewable.

    They shall elect the President of the Court of Auditors from among their number for a term of three years. The President may be re-elected.
4. The Members of the Court of Auditors shall, in the general interest of the Community, be completely independent in the performance of their duties.

    In the performance of these duties, they shall neither seek nor take instructions from any government or from any other body. They shall refrain from any action incompatible with their duties.

5.   The Members of the Court of Auditors may not, during their term of office, engage in any other occupation, whether gainful or not. When entering upon their duties they shall give a solemn undertaking that, both during and after their term of office, they will respect the obligations arising therefrom and in particular their duty to behave with integrity and discretion as regards the acceptance, after they have ceased to hold office, of certain appointments or benefits.

6.   Apart from normal replacement, or death, the duties of a Member of the Court of Auditors shall end when he resigns, or is compulsorily retired by a ruling of the Court of Justice pursuant to paragraph 7.

The vacancy thus caused shall be filled for the remainder of the Member's term of office.

Save in the case of compulsory retirement, Members of the Court of Auditors shall remain in office until they have been replaced.

7.   A Member of the Court of Auditors may be deprived of his office or of his right to a pension or other benefits in its stead only if the Court of Justice, at the request of the Court of Auditors, finds that he no longer fulfils the requisite conditions or meets the obligations arising from his office.

8.   The Council, acting by a qualified majority, shall determine the conditions of employment of the President and the Members of the Court of Auditors and in particular their salaries, allowances and pensions. It shall also, by the same majority, determine any payment to be made instead of remuneration.

9.   The provisions of the Protocol on the privileges and immunities of the European Communities applicable to the Judges of the Court of Justice shall also apply to the Members of the Court of Auditors.

Article 248

1.   The Court of Auditors shall examine the accounts of all revenue and expenditure of the Community. It shall also examine the accounts of all revenue and expenditure of all bodies set up by the Community in so far as the relevant constituent instrument does not preclude such examination.

The Court of Auditors shall provide the European Parliament and the Council with a statement of assurance as to the reliability of the accounts and the legality and regularity of the underlying transactions which shall be published in the Official Journal of the European Union. This statement may be supplemented by specific assessments for each major area of Community activity.

2.   The Court of Auditors shall examine whether all revenue has been received and all expenditure incurred in a lawful and regular manner and whether the financial management has been sound. In doing so, it shall report in particular on any cases of irregularity.

The audit of revenue shall be carried out on the basis both of the amounts established as due and the amounts actually paid to the Community.

The audit of expenditure shall be carried out on the basis both of commitments undertaken and payments made.

These audits may be carried out before the closure of accounts for the financial year in question.

3.   The audit shall be based on records and, if necessary, performed on the spot in the other institutions of the Community, on the premises of any body which manages revenue or expenditure on behalf of the Community and in the Member States, including on the premises of any natural or legal person in receipt of payments from the budget. In the Member States the audit shall be carried out in liaison with national audit bodies or, if these do not have the necessary powers, with the competent national departments. The Court of Auditors and the national audit bodies of the Member States shall cooperate in a spirit of trust while maintaining their independence. These bodies or departments shall inform the Court of Auditors whether they intend to take part in the audit.

The other institutions of the Community, any bodies managing revenue or expenditure on behalf of the Community, any natural or legal person in receipt of payments from the budget, and the national audit bodies or, if these do not have the necessary powers, the competent national departments, shall forward to the Court of Auditors, at its request, any document or information necessary to carry out its task.

In respect of the European Investment Bank's activity in managing Community expenditure and revenue, the Court's rights of access to information held by the Bank shall be governed by an agreement between the Court, the Bank and the Commission. In the absence of an agreement, the Court shall nevertheless have access to information necessary for the audit of Community expenditure and revenue managed by the Bank.

4.   The Court of Auditors shall draw up an annual report after the close of each financial year. It shall be forwarded to the other institutions of the Community and shall be published, together with the replies of these institutions to the observations of the Court of Auditors, in the *Official Journal of the European Union*. The Court of Auditors may also, at any time, submit observations, particularly in the form of special reports, on specific questions and deliver opinions at the request of one of the other institutions of the Community. It shall adopt its annual reports, special reports or opinions by a majority of its Members. However, it may establish internal chambers in order to adopt certain categories of reports or opinions under the conditions laid down by its Rules of Procedure. It shall assist the European Parliament and the Council in exercising their powers of control over the implementation of the budget. The Court of Auditors shall draw up its Rules of Procedure. Those rules shall require the approval of the Council, acting by a qualified majority.

CHAPTER 2
PROVISIONS COMMON TO SEVERAL INSTITUTIONS

Article 249

In order to carry out their task and in accordance with the provisions of this Treaty, the European Parliament acting jointly with the Council, the Council and the Commission shall make regulations and issue directives, take decisions, make recommendations or deliver opinions.

A regulation shall have general application. It shall be binding in its entirety and directly applicable in all Member States.

A directive shall be binding, as to the result to be achieved, upon each Member State to which it is addressed, but shall leave to the national authorities the choice of form and methods.

A decision shall be binding in its entirety upon those to whom it is addressed.

Recommendations and opinions shall have no binding force.

Article 250

1.   Where, in pursuance of this Treaty, the Council acts on a proposal from the Commission, unanimity shall be required for an act constituting an amendment to that proposal, subject to Article 251(4) and (5).

2.   As long as the Council has not acted, the Commission may alter its proposal at any time during the procedures leading to the adoption of a Community act.

Article 251

1.   Where reference is made in this Treaty to this Article for the adoption of an act, the following procedure shall apply.

2.   The Commission shall submit a proposal to the European Parliament and the Council.

The Council, acting by a qualified majority after obtaining the opinion of the European Parliament:

— if it approves all the amendments contained in the European Parliament's opinion, may adopt the proposed act thus amended,

— if the European Parliament does not propose any amendments, may adopt the proposed act,

— shall otherwise adopt a common position and communicate it to the European Parliament. The Council shall inform the European Parliament fully of the reasons which led it to adopt its common position. The Commission shall inform the European Parliament fully of its position.

If, within three months of such communication, the European Parliament:

      (a)   approves the common position or has not taken a decision, the act in question shall be deemed to have been adopted in accordance with that common position;

      (b)   rejects, by an absolute majority of its component members, the common position, the proposed act shall be deemed not to have been adopted;

      (c)   proposes amendments to the common position by an absolute majority of its component members, the amended text shall be forwarded to the Council and to the Commission, which shall deliver an opinion on those amendments.

3.   If, within three months of the matter being referred to it, the Council, acting by a qualified majority, approves all the amendments of the European Parliament, the act in question shall be deemed to have been adopted in the form of the common position thus amended; however, the Council shall act unanimously on the amendments on which the Commission has delivered a negative opinion. If the Council does not approve all the amendments, the President of the Council, in agreement with the President of the European Parliament, shall within six weeks convene a meeting of the Conciliation Committee.

4.   The Conciliation Committee, which shall be composed of the Members of the Council or their representatives and an equal number of representatives of the European Parliament, shall have the task of reaching agreement on a joint text, by a qualified majority of the Members of the Council or their representatives and by a majority of the representatives of the European Parliament. The Commission shall take part in the Conciliation Committee's proceedings and shall take all the necessary initiatives with a view to reconciling the positions of the European Parliament and the Council. In fulfilling this task, the Conciliation Committee shall address the common position on the basis of the amendments proposed by the European Parliament.

5.   If, within six weeks of its being convened, the Conciliation Committee approves a joint text, the European Parliament, acting by an absolute majority of the votes cast, and the Council, acting by a qualified majority, shall each have a period of six weeks from that approval in which to adopt the act in question in accordance with the joint text. If either of the two institutions fails to approve the proposed act within that period, it shall be deemed not to have been adopted.

6.   Where the Conciliation Committee does not approve a joint text, the proposed act shall be deemed not to have been adopted.

7.   The periods of three months and six weeks referred to in this Article shall be extended by a maximum of one month and two weeks respectively at the initiative of the European Parliament or the Council.

Article 252

Where reference is made in this Treaty to this Article for the adoption of an act, the following procedure shall apply.

      (a)   The Council, acting by a qualified majority on a proposal from the Commission and after obtaining the opinion of the European Parliament, shall adopt a common position.

      (b)   The Council's common position shall be communicated to the European Parliament. The Council and the Commission shall inform the European Parliament fully of the reasons which led the Council to adopt its common position and also of the Commission's position.

           If, within three months of such communication, the European Parliament approves this common position or has not taken a decision within that period, the Council shall definitively adopt the act in question in accordance with the common position.

      (c)   The European Parliament may, within the period of three months referred to in point (b), by an absolute majority of its component Members, propose amendments to the Council's common position. The European Parliament may also, by the same majority, reject the Council's common position. The result of the proceedings shall be transmitted to the Council and the Commission.

           If the European Parliament has rejected the Council's common position, unanimity shall be required for the Council to act on a second reading.

(d)   The Commission shall, within a period of one month, re-examine the proposal on the basis of which the Council adopted its common position, by taking into account the amendments proposed by the European Parliament.

The Commission shall forward to the Council, at the same time as its re-examined proposal, the amendments of the European Parliament which it has not accepted, and shall express its opinion on them. The Council may adopt these amendments unanimously.

(e)   The Council, acting by a qualified majority, shall adopt the proposal as re-examined by the Commission.

Unanimity shall be required for the Council to amend the proposal as re-examined by the Commission.

(f)   In the cases referred to in points (c), (d) and (e), the Council shall be required to act within a period of three months. If no decision is taken within this period, the Commission proposal shall be deemed not to have been adopted.

(g)   The periods referred to in points (b) and (f) may be extended by a maximum of one month by common accord between the Council and the European Parliament.

Article 253

Regulations, directives and decisions adopted jointly by the European Parliament and the Council, and such acts adopted by the Council or the Commission, shall state the reasons on which they are based and shall refer to any proposals or opinions which were required to be obtained pursuant to this Treaty.

Article 254

1.   Regulations, directives and decisions adopted in accordance with the procedure referred to in Article 251 shall be signed by the President of the European Parliament and by the President of the Council and published in the Official Journal of the European Union. They shall enter into force on the date specified in them or, in the absence thereof, on the 20th day following that of their publication.

2.   Regulations of the Council and of the Commission, as well as directives of those institutions which are addressed to all Member States, shall be published in the Official Journal of the European Union. They shall enter into force on the date specified in them or, in the absence thereof, on the 20th day following that of their publication.

3.   Other directives, and decisions, shall be notified to those to whom they are addressed and shall take effect upon such notification.

Article 255

1.   Any citizen of the Union, and any natural or legal person residing or having its registered office in a Member State, shall have a right of access to European Parliament, Council and Commission documents, subject to the principles and the conditions to be defined in accordance with paragraphs 2 and 3.

2.   General principles and limits on grounds of public or private interest governing this right of access to documents shall be determined by the Council, acting in accordance with the procedure referred to in Article 251 within two years of the entry into force of the Treaty of Amsterdam.

3.   Each institution referred to above shall elaborate in its own Rules of Procedure specific provisions regarding access to its documents.

Article 256

Decisions of the Council or of the Commission which impose a pecuniary obligation on persons other than States, shall be enforceable.

Enforcement shall be governed by the rules of civil procedure in force in the State in the territory of which it is carried out. The order for its enforcement shall be appended to the decision, without other formality than verification of the authenticity of the decision, by the national authority which the government of each Member State shall designate for this purpose and shall make known to the Commission and to the Court of Justice.

When these formalities have been completed on application by the party concerned, the latter may proceed to enforcement in accordance with the national law, by bringing the matter directly before the competent authority.

Enforcement may be suspended only by a decision of the Court of Justice. However, the courts of the country concerned shall have jurisdiction over complaints that enforcement is being carried out in an irregular manner.

CHAPTER 3

THE ECONOMIC AND SOCIAL COMMITTEE

Article 257

An Economic and Social Committee is hereby established. It shall have advisory status.

The Committee shall consist of representatives of the various economic and social components of organised civil society, and in particular representatives of producers, farmers, carriers, workers, dealers, craftsmen, professional occupations, consumers and the general interest.

Article 258

The number of members of the Committee shall be as follows:

Belgium	12
Bulgaria	12
Czech Republic	12
Denmark	9
Germany	24
Estonia	7
Greece	12
Spain	21
France	24
Ireland	9
Italy	24
Cyprus	6
Latvia	7
Lithuania	9
Luxembourg	6
Hungary	12
Malta	5
Netherlands	12
Austria	12
Poland	21
Portugal	12
Romania	15
Slovenia	7
Slovakia	9
Finland	9
Sweden	12
United Kingdom	24

The members of the Committee may not be bound by any mandatory instructions. They shall be completely independent in the performance of their duties, in the general interest of the Community.

The Council, acting by a qualified majority, shall determine the allowances of members of the Committee.

Article 259

1.   The members of the Committee shall be appointed for four years, on proposals from the Member States. The Council, acting by a qualified majority, shall adopt the list of members

drawn up in accordance with the proposals made by each Member State. The term of office of the members of the Committee shall be renewable.

2.   The Council shall consult the Commission. It may obtain the opinion of European bodies which are representative of the various economic and social sectors to which the activities of the Community are of concern.

Article 260

The Committee shall elect its chairman and officers from among its members for a term of two years.

It shall adopt its Rules of Procedure.

The Committee shall be convened by its chairman at the request of the Council or of the Commission. It may also meet on its own initiative.

Article 261

The Committee shall include specialised sections for the principal fields covered by this Treaty. These specialised sections shall operate within the general terms of reference of the Committee. They may not be consulted independently of the Committee.

Subcommittees may also be established within the Committee to prepare on specific questions or in specific fields, draft opinions to be submitted to the Committee for its consideration.

The Rules of Procedure shall lay down the methods of composition and the terms of reference of the specialised sections and of the subcommittees.

Article 262

The Committee must be consulted by the Council or by the Commission where this Treaty so provides. The Committee may be consulted by these institutions in all cases in which they consider it appropriate. It may issue an opinion on its own initiative in cases in which it considers such action appropriate.

The Council or the Commission shall, if it considers it necessary, set the Committee, for the submission of its opinion, a time limit which may not be less than one month from the date on which the chairman receives notification to this effect. Upon expiry of the time limit, the absence of an opinion shall not prevent further action.

The opinion of the Committee and that of the specialised section, together with a record of the proceedings, shall be forwarded to the Council and to the Commission.

The Committee may be consulted by the European Parliament.

CHAPTER 4

THE COMMITTEE OF THE REGIONS

Article 263

A committee, hereinafter referred to as 'the Committee of the Regions', consisting of representatives of regional and local bodies who either hold a regional or local authority electoral mandate or are politically accountable to an elected assembly, is hereby established with advisory status.

The number of members of the Committee shall be as follows:

Belgium	12
Bulgaria	12
Czech Republic	12
Denmark	9
Germany	24
Estonia	7
Greece	12
Spain	21
France	24
Ireland	9
Italy	24
Cyprus	6

Latvia	7
Lithuania	9
Luxembourg	6
Hungary	12
Malta	5
Netherlands	12
Austria	12
Poland	21
Portugal	12
Romania	15
Slovenia	7
Slovakia	9
Finland	9
Sweden	12
United Kingdom	24

The members of the Committee and an equal number of alternate members shall be appointed for four years, on proposals from the respective Member States. Their term of office shall be renewable. The Council, acting by a qualified majority, shall adopt the list of members and alternate members drawn up in accordance with the proposals made by each Member State. When the mandate referred to in the first paragraph on the basis of which they were proposed comes to an end, the term of office of members of the Committee shall terminate automatically and they shall then be replaced for the remainder of the said term of office in accordance with the same procedure. No member of the Committee shall at the same time be a Member of the European Parliament.

The members of the Committee may not be bound by any mandatory instructions. They shall be completely independent in the performance of their duties, in the general interest of the Community.

Article 264

The Committee of the Regions shall elect its chairman and officers from among its members for a term of two years.

It shall adopt its Rules of Procedure.

The Committee shall be convened by its chairman at the request of the Council or of the Commission. It may also meet on its own initiative.

Article 265

The Committee of the Regions shall be consulted by the Council or by the Commission where this Treaty so provides and in all other cases, in particular those which concern cross-border cooperation, in which one of these two institutions considers it appropriate.

The Council or the Commission shall, if it considers it necessary, set the Committee, for the submission of its opinion, a time limit which may not be less than one month from the date on which the chairman receives notification to this effect. Upon expiry of the time limit, the absence of an opinion shall not prevent further action.

Where the Economic and Social Committee is consulted pursuant to Article 262, the Committee of the Regions shall be informed by the Council or the Commission of the request for an opinion. Where it considers that specific regional interests are involved, the Committee of the Regions may issue an opinion on the matter.

The Committee of the Regions may be consulted by the European Parliament.

It may issue an opinion on its own initiative in cases in which it considers such action appropriate.

The opinion of the Committee, together with a record of the proceedings, shall be forwarded to the Council and to the Commission.

CHAPTER 5

THE EUROPEAN INVESTMENT BANK

Article 266

The European Investment Bank shall have legal personality.

The members of the European Investment Bank shall be the Member States.

The Statute of the European Investment Bank is laid down in a Protocol annexed to this Treaty. The Council acting unanimously, at the request of the European Investment Bank and after consulting the European Parliament and the Commission, or at the request of the Commission and after consulting the European Parliament and the European Investment Bank, may amend Articles 4, 11 and 12 and Article 18(5) of the Statute of the Bank.

Article 267

The task of the European Investment Bank shall be to contribute, by having recourse to the capital market and utilising its own resources, to the balanced and steady development of the common market in the interest of the Community. For this purpose the Bank shall, operating on a non-profit-making basis, grant loans and give guarantees which facilitate the financing of the following projects in all sectors of the economy:

(a)   projects for developing less-developed regions;

(b)   projects for modernising or converting undertakings or for developing fresh activities called for by the progressive establishment of the common market, where these projects are of such a size or nature that they cannot be entirely financed by the various means available in the individual Member States;

(c)   projects of common interest to several Member States which are of such a size or nature that they cannot be entirely financed by the various means available in the individual Member States.

In carrying out its task, the Bank shall facilitate the financing of investment programmes in conjunction with assistance from the Structural Funds and other Community Financial Instruments.

TITLE II
FINANCIAL PROVISIONS

Article 268

All items of revenue and expenditure of the Community, including those relating to the European Social Fund, shall be included in estimates to be drawn up for each financial year and shall be shown in the budget.

Administrative expenditure occasioned for the institutions by the provisions of the Treaty on European Union relating to common foreign and security policy and to cooperation in the fields of justice and home affairs shall be charged to the budget. The operational expenditure occasioned by the implementation of the said provisions may, under the conditions referred to therein, be charged to the budget.

The revenue and expenditure shown in the budget shall be in balance.

Article 269

Without prejudice to other revenue, the budget shall be financed wholly from own resources.

The Council, acting unanimously on a proposal from the Commission and after consulting the European Parliament, shall lay down provisions relating to the system of own resources of the Community, which it shall recommend to the Member States for adoption in accordance with their respective constitutional requirements.

Article 270

With a view to maintaining budgetary discipline, the Commission shall not make any proposal for a Community act, or alter its proposals, or adopt any implementing measure which is likely to have appreciable implications for the budget without providing the assurance that that proposal or that measure is capable of being financed within the limit of the Community's own resources arising under provisions laid down by the Council pursuant to Article 269.

Article 271

The expenditure shown in the budget shall be authorised for one financial year, unless the regulations made pursuant to Article 279 provide otherwise.

In accordance with conditions to be laid down pursuant to Article 279, any appropriations, other than those relating to staff expenditure, that are unexpended at the end of the financial year may be carried forward to the next financial year only.

Appropriations shall be classified under different chapters grouping items of expenditure according to their nature or purpose and subdivided, as far as may be necessary, in accordance with the regulations made pursuant to Article 279.

The expenditure of the European Parliament, the Council, the Commission and the Court of Justice shall be set out in separate parts of the budget, without prejudice to special arrangements for certain common items of expenditure.

Article 272

1. The financial year shall run from 1 January to 31 December.

2. Each institution of the Community shall, before 1 July, draw up estimates of its expenditure. The Commission shall consolidate these estimates in a preliminary draft budget. It shall attach thereto an opinion which may contain different estimates.

   The preliminary draft budget shall contain an estimate of revenue and an estimate of expenditure.

3. The Commission shall place the preliminary draft budget before the Council not later than 1 September of the year preceding that in which the budget is to be implemented.

   The Council shall consult the Commission and, where appropriate, the other institutions concerned whenever it intends to depart from the preliminary draft budget.

   The Council, acting by a qualified majority, shall establish the draft budget and forward it to the European Parliament.

4. The draft budget shall be placed before the European Parliament not later than 5 October of the year preceding that in which the budget is to be implemented.

   The European Parliament shall have the right to amend the draft budget, acting by a majority of its Members, and to propose to the Council, acting by an absolute majority of the votes cast, modifications to the draft budget relating to expenditure necessarily resulting from this Treaty or from acts adopted in accordance therewith.

   If, within 45 days of the draft budget being placed before it, the European Parliament has given its approval, the budget shall stand as finally adopted. If within this period the European Parliament has not amended the draft budget nor proposed any modifications thereto, the budget shall be deemed to be finally adopted.

   If within this period the European Parliament has adopted amendments or proposed modifications, the draft budget together with the amendments or proposed modifications shall be forwarded to the Council.

5. After discussing the draft budget with the Commission and, where appropriate, with the other institutions concerned, the Council shall act under the following conditions:

   (a) the Council may, acting by a qualified majority, modify any of the amendments adopted by the European Parliament;

   (b) with regard to the proposed modifications:

   — where a modification proposed by the European Parliament does not have the effect of increasing the total amount of the expenditure of an institution, owing in particular to the fact that the increase in expenditure which it would involve would be expressly compensated by one or more proposed modifications correspondingly reducing expenditure, the Council may, acting by a qualified majority, reject the proposed modification. In the absence of a decision to reject it, the proposed modification shall stand as accepted,

   — where a modification proposed by the European Parliament has the effect of increasing the total amount of the expenditure of an institution, the Council may, acting by a qualified majority, accept this proposed modification. In the absence of a decision to accept it, the proposed modification shall stand as rejected,

   — where, pursuant to one of the two preceding subparagraphs, the Council has rejected a proposed modification, it may, acting by a qualified majority, either retain the amount shown in the draft budget or fix another amount.

The draft budget shall be modified on the basis of the proposed modifications accepted by the Council.

If, within 15 days of the draft being placed before it, the Council has not modified any of the amendments adopted by the European Parliament and if the modifications proposed by the latter have been accepted, the budget shall be deemed to be finally adopted. The Council shall inform the European Parliament that it has not modified any of the amendments and that the proposed modifications have been accepted.

If within this period the Council has modified one or more of the amendments adopted by the European Parliament or if the modifications proposed by the latter have been rejected or modified, the modified draft budget shall again be forwarded to the European Parliament. The Council shall inform the European Parliament of the results of its deliberations.

6. Within 15 days of the draft budget being placed before it, the European Parliament, which shall have been notified of the action taken on its proposed modifications, may, acting by a majority of its Members and three fifths of the votes cast, amend or reject the modifications to its amendments made by the Council and shall adopt the budget accordingly. If within this period the European Parliament has not acted, the budget shall be deemed to be finally adopted.

7. When the procedure provided for in this Article has been completed, the President of the European Parliament shall declare that the budget has been finally adopted.

8. However, the European Parliament, acting by a majority of its Members and two thirds of the votes cast, may, if there are important reasons, reject the draft budget and ask for a new draft to be submitted to it.

9. A maximum rate of increase in relation to the expenditure of the same type to be incurred during the current year shall be fixed annually for the total expenditure other than that necessarily resulting from this Treaty or from acts adopted in accordance therewith.

The Commission shall, after consulting the Economic Policy Committee, declare what this maximum rate is as it results from:

— the trend, in terms of volume, of the gross national product within the Community,

— the average variation in the budgets of the Member States, and

— the trend of the cost of living during the preceding financial year.

The maximum rate shall be communicated, before 1 May, to all the institutions of the Community. The latter shall be required to conform to this during the budgetary procedure, subject to the provisions of the fourth and fifth subparagraphs of this paragraph.

If, in respect of expenditure other than that necessarily resulting from this Treaty or from acts adopted in accordance therewith, the actual rate of increase in the draft budget established by the Council is over half the maximum rate, the European Parliament may, exercising its right of amendment, further increase the total amount of that expenditure to a limit not exceeding half the maximum rate.

Where the European Parliament, the Council or the Commission consider that the activities of the Communities require that the rate determined according to the procedure laid down in this paragraph should be exceeded, another rate may be fixed by agreement between the Council, acting by a qualified majority, and the European Parliament, acting by a majority of its Members and three fifths of the votes cast.

10. Each institution shall exercise the powers conferred upon it by this article, with due regard for the provisions of the Treaty and for acts adopted in accordance therewith, in particular those relating to the Communities' own resources and to the balance between revenue and expenditure.

Article 273

If, at the beginning of a financial year, the budget has not yet been voted, a sum equivalent to not more than one twelfth of the budget appropriations for the preceding financial year may be spent each month in respect of any chapter or other subdivision of the budget in accordance with the provisions of the Regulations made pursuant to Article 279; this arrangement shall not, however, have the effect of placing at the disposal of the Commission appropriations in excess of one twelfth of those provided for in the draft budget in course of preparation.

The Council may, acting by a qualified majority, provided that the other conditions laid down in the first subparagraph are observed, authorise expenditure in excess of one twelfth.

If the decision relates to expenditure which does not necessarily result from this Treaty or from acts adopted in accordance therewith, the Council shall forward it immediately to the European Parliament; within 30 days the European Parliament, acting by a majority of its Members and three fifths of the votes cast, may adopt a different decision on the expenditure in excess of the one twelfth referred to in the first subparagraph. This part of the decision of the Council shall be suspended until the European Parliament has taken its decision. If within the said period the European Parliament has not taken a decision which differs from the decision of the Council, the latter shall be deemed to be finally adopted.

The decisions referred to in the second and third subparagraphs shall lay down the necessary measures relating to resources to ensure application of this Article.

Article 274

The Commission shall implement the budget, in accordance with the provisions of the regulations made pursuant to Article 279, on its own responsibility and within the limits of the appropriations, having regard to the principles of sound financial management. Member States shall cooperate with the Commission to ensure that the appropriations are used in accordance with the principles of sound financial management.

The regulations shall lay down detailed rules for each institution concerning its part in effecting its own expenditure.

Within the budget, the Commission may, subject to the limits and conditions laid down in the regulations made pursuant to Article 279, transfer appropriations from one chapter to another or from one subdivision to another.

Article 275

The Commission shall submit annually to the Council and to the European Parliament the accounts of the preceding financial year relating to the implementation of the budget. The Commission shall also forward to them a financial statement of the assets and liabilities of the Community.

Article 276

1. The European Parliament, acting on a recommendation from the Council which shall act by a qualified majority, shall give a discharge to the Commission in respect of the implementation of the budget. To this end, the Council and the European Parliament in turn shall examine the accounts and the financial statement referred to in Article 275, the annual report by the Court of Auditors together with the replies of the institutions under audit to the observations of the Court of Auditors, the statement of assurance referred to in Article 248(1), second subparagraph and any relevant special reports by the Court of Auditors.

2. Before giving a discharge to the Commission, or for any other purpose in connection with the exercise of its powers over the implementation of the budget, the European Parliament may ask to hear the Commission give evidence with regard to the execution of expenditure or the operation of financial control systems. The Commission shall submit any necessary information to the European Parliament at the latter's request.

3. The Commission shall take all appropriate steps to act on the observations in the decisions giving discharge and on other observations by the European Parliament relating to the execution of expenditure, as well as on comments accompanying the recommendations on discharge adopted by the Council.

    At the request of the European Parliament or the Council, the Commission shall report on the measures taken in the light of these observations and comments and in particular on the instructions given to the departments which are responsible for the implementation of the budget. These reports shall also be forwarded to the Court of Auditors.

Article 277

The budget shall be drawn up in the unit of account determined in accordance with the provisions of the regulations made pursuant to Article 279.

Article 278

The Commission may, provided it notifies the competent authorities of the Member States concerned, transfer into the currency of one of the Member States its holdings in the currency of another Member State, to the extent necessary to enable them to be used for purposes which come within the scope of this Treaty. The Commission shall as far as possible avoid making such transfers if it possesses cash or liquid assets in the currencies which it needs.

The Commission shall deal with each Member State through the authority designated by the State concerned. In carrying out financial operations the Commission shall employ the services of the bank of issue of the Member State concerned or of any other financial institution approved by that State.

Article 279

1. The Council, acting unanimously on a proposal from the Commission and after consulting the European Parliament and obtaining the opinion of the Court of Auditors, shall:
    (a) make Financial Regulations specifying in particular the procedure to be adopted for establishing and implementing the budget and for presenting and auditing accounts;
    (b) lay down rules concerning the responsibility of financial controllers, authorising officers and accounting officers, and concerning appropriate arrangements for inspection.
    From 1 January 2007, the Council shall act by a qualified majority on a proposal from the Commission and after consulting the European Parliament and obtaining the opinion of the Court of Auditors.
2. The Council, acting unanimously on a proposal from the Commission and after consulting the European Parliament and obtaining the opinion of the Court of Auditors, shall determine the methods and procedure whereby the budget revenue provided under the arrangements relating to the Community's own resources shall be made available to the Commission, and determine the measures to be applied, if need be, to meet cash requirements.

Article 280

1. The Community and the Member States shall counter fraud and any other illegal activities affecting the financial interests of the Community through measures to be taken in accordance with this article, which shall act as a deterrent and be such as to afford effective protection in the Member States.
2. Member States shall take the same measures to counter fraud affecting the financial interests of the Community as they take to counter fraud affecting their own financial interests.
3. Without prejudice to other provisions of this Treaty, the Member States shall coordinate their action aimed at protecting the financial interests of the Community against fraud. To this end they shall organise, together with the Commission, close and regular cooperation between the competent authorities.
4. The Council, acting in accordance with the procedure referred to in Article 251, after consulting the Court of Auditors, shall adopt the necessary measures in the fields of the prevention of and fight against fraud affecting the financial interests of the Community with a view to affording effective and equivalent protection in the Member States. These measures shall not concern the application of national criminal law or the national administration of justice.
5. The Commission, in cooperation with Member States, shall each year submit to the European Parliament and to the Council a report on the measures taken for the implementation of this article.

PART SIX
GENERAL AND FINAL PROVISIONS

Article 281

The Community shall have legal personality.

Article 282

In each of the Member States, the Community shall enjoy the most extensive legal capacity accorded to legal persons under their laws; it may, in particular, acquire or dispose of movable and immovable property and may be a party to legal proceedings. To this end, the Community shall be represented by the Commission.

Article 283

The Council shall, acting by a qualified majority on a proposal from the Commission and after consulting the other institutions concerned, lay down the Staff Regulations of officials of the European Communities and the Conditions of employment of other servants of those Communities.

Article 284

The Commission may, within the limits and under conditions laid down by the Council in accordance with the provisions of this Treaty, collect any information and carry out any checks required for the performance of the tasks entrusted to it.

Article 285

1. Without prejudice to Article 5 of the Protocol on the Statute of the European System of Central Banks and of the European Central Bank, the Council, acting in accordance with the procedure referred to in Article 251, shall adopt measures for the production of statistics where necessary for the performance of the activities of the Community.
2. The production of Community statistics shall conform to impartiality, reliability, objectivity, scientific independence, cost-effectiveness and statistical confidentiality; it shall not entail excessive burdens on economic operators.

Article 286

1. From 1 January 1999, Community acts on the protection of individuals with regard to the processing of personal data and the free movement of such data shall apply to the institutions and bodies set up by, or on the basis of, this Treaty.
2. Before the date referred to in paragraph 1, the Council, acting in accordance with the procedure referred to in Article 251, shall establish an independent supervisory body responsible for monitoring the application of such Community acts to Community institutions and bodies and shall adopt any other relevant provisions as appropriate.

Article 287

The members of the institutions of the Community, the members of committees, and the officials and other servants of the Community shall be required, even after their duties have ceased, not to disclose information of the kind covered by the obligation of professional secrecy, in particular information about undertakings, their business relations or their cost components.

Article 288

The contractual liability of the Community shall be governed by the law applicable to the contract in question.

In the case of non-contractual liability, the Community shall, in accordance with the general principles common to the laws of the Member States, make good any damage caused by its institutions or by its servants in the performance of their duties.

The preceding paragraph shall apply under the same conditions to damage caused by the ECB or by its servants in the performance of their duties.

The personal liability of its servants towards the Community shall be governed by the provisions laid down in their Staff Regulations or in the Conditions of employment applicable to them.

Article 289

The seat of the institutions of the Community shall be determined by common accord of the governments of the Member States.

Article 290

The rules governing the languages of the institutions of the Community shall, without prejudice to the provisions contained in the Statute of the Court of Justice, be determined by the Council, acting unanimously.

Article 291

The Community shall enjoy in the territories of the Member States such privileges and immunities as are necessary for the performance of its tasks, under the conditions laid down in the Protocol of 8 April 1965 on the privileges and immunities of the European Communities. The same shall apply to the European Central Bank, the European Monetary Institute, and the European Investment Bank.

Article 292

Member States undertake not to submit a dispute concerning the interpretation or application of this Treaty to any method of settlement other than those provided for therein.

Article 293

Member States shall, so far as is necessary, enter into negotiations with each other with a view to securing for the benefit of their nationals:
— the protection of persons and the enjoyment and protection of rights under the same conditions as those accorded by each State to its own nationals,
— the abolition of double taxation within the Community,
— the mutual recognition of companies or firms within the meaning of the second paragraph of Article 48, the retention of legal personality in the event of transfer of their seat from one country to another, and the possibility of mergers between companies or firms governed by the laws of different countries,
— the simplification of formalities governing the reciprocal recognition and enforcement of judgments of courts or tribunals and of arbitration awards.

Article 294

Member States shall accord nationals of the other Member States the same treatment as their own nationals as regards participation in the capital of companies or firms within the meaning of Article 48, without prejudice to the application of the other provisions of this Treaty.

Article 295

This Treaty shall in no way prejudice the rules in Member States governing the system of property ownership.

Article 296

1. The provisions of this Treaty shall not preclude the application of the following rules:
    (a) no Member State shall be obliged to supply information the disclosure of which it considers contrary to the essential interests of its security;
    (b) any Member State may take such measures as it considers necessary for the protection of the essential interests of its security which are connected with the production of or trade in arms, munitions and war material; such measures shall not adversely affect the conditions of competition in the common market regarding products which are not intended for specifically military purposes.
2. The Council may, acting unanimously on a proposal from the Commission, make changes to the list, which it drew up on 15 April 1958, of the products to which the provisions of paragraph 1(b) apply.

Article 297

Member States shall consult each other with a view to taking together the steps needed to prevent the functioning of the common market being affected by measures which a Member State may be called upon to take in the event of serious internal disturbances affecting the maintenance of law and order, in the event of war, serious international tension constituting a threat of war, or in order to carry out obligations it has accepted for the purpose of maintaining peace and international security.

Article 298

If measures taken in the circumstances referred to in Articles 296 and 297 have the effect of distorting the conditions of competition in the common market, the Commission shall, together with the State concerned, examine how these measures can be adjusted to the rules laid down in the Treaty.

By way of derogation from the procedure laid down in Articles 226 and 227, the Commission or any Member State may bring the matter directly before the Court of Justice if it considers that another Member State is making improper use of the powers provided for in Articles 296 and 297. The Court of Justice shall give its ruling in camera.

Article 299

1. This Treaty shall apply to the Kingdom of Belgium, the Republic of Bulgaria, the Czech Republic, the Kingdom of Denmark, the Federal Republic of Germany, the Republic of Estonia, the Hellenic Republic, the Kingdom of Spain, the French Republic, Ireland, the Italian Republic, the Republic of Cyprus, the Republic of Latvia, the Republic of Lithuania, the Grand Duchy of Luxembourg, the Republic of Hungary, the Republic of Malta, the Kingdom of the Netherlands, the Republic of Austria, the Republic of Poland, the Portuguese Republic, Romania, the Republic of Slovenia, the Slovak Republic, the Republic of Finland, the Kingdom of Sweden and the United Kingdom of Great Britain and Northern Ireland.

2. The provisions of this Treaty shall apply to the French overseas departments, the Azores, Madeira and the Canary Islands.

    However, taking account of the structural social and economic situation of the French overseas departments, the Azores, Madeira and the Canary Islands, which is compounded by their remoteness, insularity, small size, difficult topography and climate, economic dependence on a few products, the permanence and combination of which severely restrain their development, the Council, acting by a qualified majority on a proposal from the Commission and after consulting the European Parliament, shall adopt specific measures aimed, in particular, at laying down the conditions of application of the present Treaty to those regions, including common policies. The Council shall, when adopting the relevant measures referred to in the second subparagraph, take into account areas such as customs and trade policies, fiscal policy, free zones, agriculture and fisheries policies, conditions for supply of raw materials and essential consumer goods, State aids and conditions of access to structural funds and to horizontal Community programmes.

    The Council shall adopt the measures referred to in the second subparagraph taking into account the special characteristics and constraints of the outermost regions without undermining the integrity and the coherence of the Community legal order, including the internal market and common policies.

3. The special arrangements for association set out in part four of this Treaty shall apply to the overseas countries and territories listed in Annex II to this Treaty.

    This Treaty shall not apply to those overseas countries and territories having special relations with the United Kingdom of Great Britain and Northern Ireland which are not included in the aforementioned list.

4. The provisions of this Treaty shall apply to the European territories for whose external relations a Member State is responsible.

5. The provisions of this Treaty shall apply to the Åland Islands in accordance with the provisions set out in Protocol 2 to the Act concerning the conditions of accession of the Republic of Austria, the Republic of Finland and the Kingdom of Sweden.

6. Notwithstanding the preceding paragraphs:

    (a) this Treaty shall not apply to the Faeroe Islands;

    (b) this Treaty shall not apply to the sovereign base areas of the United Kingdom of Great Britain and Northern Ireland in Cyprus;

    (c) this Treaty shall apply to the Channel Islands and the Isle of Man only to the extent necessary to ensure the implementation of the arrangements for those islands set out in the Treaty concerning the accession of new Member States to the European Economic Community and to the European Atomic Energy Community signed on 22 January 1972.

Article 300

1. Where this Treaty provides for the conclusion of agreements between the Community and one or more States or international organisations, the Commission shall make recommendations to the Council, which shall authorise the Commission to open the necessary negotiations. The Commission shall conduct these negotiations in consultation with special committees appointed by the Council to assist it in this task and within the framework of such directives as the Council may issue to it.

   In exercising the powers conferred upon it by this paragraph, the Council shall act by a qualified majority, except in the cases where the first subparagraph of paragraph 2 provides that the Council shall act unanimously.

2. Subject to the powers vested in the Commission in this field, the signing, which may be accompanied by a decision on provisional application before entry into force, and the conclusion of the agreements shall be decided on by the Council, acting by a qualified majority on a proposal from the Commission. The Council shall act unanimously when the agreement covers a field for which unanimity is required for the adoption of internal rules and for the agreements referred to in Article 310.

   By way of derogation from the rules laid down in paragraph 3, the same procedures shall apply for a decision to suspend the application of an agreement, and for the purpose of establishing the positions to be adopted on behalf of the Community in a body set up by an agreement, when that body is called upon to adopt decisions having legal effects, with the exception of decisions supplementing or amending the institutional framework of the agreement.

   The European Parliament shall be immediately and fully informed of any decision under this paragraph concerning the provisional application or the suspension of agreements, or the establishment of the Community position in a body set up by an agreement.

3. The Council shall conclude agreements after consulting the European Parliament, except for the agreements referred to in Article 133(3), including cases where the agreement covers a field for which the procedure referred to in Article 251 or that referred to in Article 252 is required for the adoption of internal rules. The European Parliament shall deliver its opinion within a time limit which the Council may lay down according to the urgency of the matter. In the absence of an opinion within that time limit, the Council may act.

   By way of derogation from the previous subparagraph, agreements referred to in Article 310, other agreements establishing a specific institutional framework by organising cooperation procedures, agreements having important budgetary implications for the Community and agreements entailing amendment of an act adopted under the procedure referred to in Article 251 shall be concluded after the assent of the European Parliament has been obtained.

   The Council and the European Parliament may, in an urgent situation, agree upon a time limit for the assent.

4. When concluding an agreement, the Council may, by way of derogation from paragraph 2, authorise the Commission to approve modifications on behalf of the Community where the agreement provides for them to be adopted by a simplified procedure or by a body set up by the agreement; it may attach specific conditions to such authorisation.

5. When the Council envisages concluding an agreement which calls for amendments to this Treaty, the amendments must first be adopted in accordance with the procedure laid down in Article 48 of the Treaty on European Union.

6. The European Parliament, the Council, the Commission or a Member State may obtain the opinion of the Court of Justice as to whether an agreement envisaged is compatible with the provisions of this Treaty. Where the opinion of the Court of Justice is adverse, the agreement may enter into force only in accordance with Article 48 of the Treaty on European Union.

7. Agreements concluded under the conditions set out in this Article shall be binding on the institutions of the Community and on Member States.

Article 301

Where it is provided, in a common position or in a joint action adopted according to the provisions of the Treaty on European Union relating to the common foreign and security policy, for an action by the Community to interrupt or to reduce, in part or completely, economic relations with one or more third countries, the Council shall take the necessary urgent measures. The Council shall act by a qualified majority on a proposal from the Commission.

Article 302

It shall be for the Commission to ensure the maintenance of all appropriate relations with the organs of the United Nations and of its specialised agencies.

The Commission shall also maintain such relations as are appropriate with all international organisations.

Article 303

The Community shall establish all appropriate forms of cooperation with the Council of Europe.

Article 304

The Community shall establish close cooperation with the Organisation for Economic Cooperation and Development, the details of which shall be determined by common accord.

Article 305

1.   The provisions of this Treaty shall not affect the provisions of the Treaty establishing the European Coal and Steel Community, in particular as regards the rights and obligations of Member States, the powers of the institutions of that Community and the rules laid down by that Treaty for the functioning of the common market in coal and steel.

2.   The provisions of this Treaty shall not derogate from those of the Treaty establishing the European Atomic Energy Community.

Article 306

The provisions of this Treaty shall not preclude the existence or completion of regional unions between Belgium and Luxembourg, or between Belgium, Luxembourg and the Netherlands, to the extent that the objectives of these regional unions are not attained by application of this Treaty.

Article 307

The rights and obligations arising from agreements concluded before 1 January 1958 or, for acceding States, before the date of their accession, between one or more Member States on the one hand, and one or more third countries on the other, shall not be affected by the provisions of this Treaty.

To the extent that such agreements are not compatible with this Treaty, the Member State or States concerned shall take all appropriate steps to eliminate the incompatibilities established. Member States shall, where necessary, assist each other to this end and shall, where appropriate, adopt a common attitude.

In applying the agreements referred to in the first paragraph, Member States shall take into account the fact that the advantages accorded under this Treaty by each Member State form an integral part of the establishment of the Community and are thereby inseparably linked with the creation of common institutions, the conferring of powers upon them and the granting of the same advantages by all the other Member States.

Article 308

If action by the Community should prove necessary to attain, in the course of the operation of the common market, one of the objectives of the Community, and this Treaty has not provided the necessary powers, the Council shall, acting unanimously on a proposal from the Commission and after consulting the European Parliament, take the appropriate measures.

Article 309

1.   Where a decision has been taken to suspend the voting rights of the representative of the government of a Member State in accordance with Article 7(3) of the Treaty on European Union, these voting rights shall also be suspended with regard to this Treaty.

2.   Moreover, where the existence of a serious and persistent breach by a Member State of principles mentioned in Article 6(1) of the Treaty on European Union has been determined in accordance with Article 7(2) of that Treaty, the Council, acting by a qualified majority, may decide to suspend certain of the rights deriving from the application of this Treaty to the

Member State in question. In doing so, the Council shall take into account the possible consequences of such a suspension on the rights and obligations of natural and legal persons. The obligations of the Member State in question under this Treaty shall in any case continue to be binding on that State.

3.   The Council, acting by a qualified majority, may decide subsequently to vary or revoke measures taken in accordance with paragraph 2 in response to changes in the situation which led to their being imposed.

4.   When taking decisions referred to in paragraphs 2 and 3, the Council shall act without taking into account the votes of the representative of the government of the Member State in question. By way of derogation from Article 205(2) a qualified majority shall be defined as the same proportion of the weighted votes of the members of the Council concerned as laid down in Article 205(2).

This paragraph shall also apply in the event of voting rights being suspended in accordance with paragraph 1. In such cases, a decision requiring unanimity shall be taken without the vote of the representative of the government of the Member State in question.

Article 310

The Community may conclude with one or more States or international organisations agreements establishing an association involving reciprocal rights and obligations, common action and special procedure.

Article 311

The protocols annexed to this Treaty by common accord of the Member States shall form an integral part thereof.

Article 312

This Treaty is concluded for an unlimited period.

CONSOLIDATED VERSION OF THE TREATY ON EUROPEAN UNION

RESOLVED to mark a new stage in the process of European integration undertaken with the establishment of the European Communities,

RECALLING the historic importance of the ending of the division of the European continent and the need to create firm bases for the construction of the future Europe,

CONFIRMING their attachment to the principles of liberty, democracy and respect for human rights and fundamental freedoms and of the rule of law,

CONFIRMING their attachment to fundamental social rights as defined in the European Social Charter signed at Turin on 18 October 1961 and in the 1989 Community Charter of the Fundamental Social Rights of Workers,

DESIRING to deepen the solidarity between their peoples while respecting their history, their culture and their traditions,

DESIRING to enhance further the democratic and efficient functioning of the institutions so as to enable them better to carry out, within a single institutional framework, the tasks entrusted to them,

RESOLVED to achieve the strengthening and the convergence of their economies and to establish an economic and monetary union including, in accordance with the provisions of this Treaty, a single and stable currency,

DETERMINED to promote economic and social progress for their peoples, taking into account the principle of sustainable development and within the context of the accomplishment of the internal market and of reinforced cohesion and environmental protection, and to implement policies ensuring that advances in economic integration are accompanied by parallel progress in other fields,

RESOLVED to establish a citizenship common to nationals of their countries,

RESOLVED to implement a common foreign and security policy including the progressive framing of a common defence policy, which might lead to a common defence in accordance with the provisions of Article 17, thereby reinforcing the European identity and its independence in order to promote peace, security and progress in Europe and in the world,

RESOLVED to facilitate the free movement of persons, while ensuring the safety and security of their peoples, by establishing an area of freedom, security and justice, in accordance with the provisions of this Treaty,

RESOLVED to continue the process of creating an ever closer union among the peoples of Europe, in which decisions are taken as closely as possible to the citizen in accordance with the principle of subsidiarity,

IN VIEW of further steps to be taken in order to advance European integration,

HAVE DECIDED to establish a European Union ...

TITLE I
COMMON PROVISIONS

Article 1

By this Treaty, the HIGH CONTRACTING PARTIES establish among themselves a EUROPEAN UNION, hereinafter called 'the Union'.

This Treaty marks a new stage in the process of creating an ever closer union among the peoples of Europe, in which decisions are taken as openly as possible and as closely as possible to the citizen. The Union shall be founded on the European Communities, supplemented by the policies and forms of cooperation established by this Treaty. Its task shall be to organise, in a manner demonstrating consistency and solidarity, relations between the Member States and between their peoples.

Article 2

The Union shall set itself the following objectives:

— to promote economic and social progress and a high level of employment and to achieve balanced and sustainable development, in particular through the creation of an area without internal frontiers, through the strengthening of economic and social cohesion and through the establishment of economic and monetary union, ultimately including a single currency in accordance with the provisions of this Treaty,

— to assert its identity on the international scene, in particular through the implementation of a common foreign and security policy including the progressive framing of a common defence policy, which might lead to a common defence, in accordance with the provisions of Article 17,

— to strengthen the protection of the rights and interests of the nationals of its Member States through the introduction of a citizenship of the Union,

— to maintain and develop the Union as an area of freedom, security and justice, in which the free movement of persons is assured in conjunction with appropriate measures with respect to external border controls, asylum, immigration and the prevention and combating of crime,

— to maintain in full the *acquis communautaire* and build on it with a view to considering to what extent the policies and forms of cooperation introduced by this Treaty may need to be revised with the aim of ensuring the effectiveness of the mechanisms and the institutions of the Community.

The objectives of the Union shall be achieved as provided in this Treaty and in accordance with the conditions and the timetable set out therein while respecting the principle of subsidiarity as defined in Article 5 of the Treaty establishing the European Community.

Article 3

The Union shall be served by a single institutional framework which shall ensure the consistency and the continuity of the activities carried out in order to attain its objectives while respecting and building upon the *acquis communautaire*.

The Union shall in particular ensure the consistency of its external activities as a whole in the context of its external relations, security, economic and development policies. The Council and the Commission shall be responsible for ensuring such consistency and shall cooperate to this end. They shall ensure the implementation of these policies, each in accordance with its respective powers.

Article 4

The European Council shall provide the Union with the necessary impetus for its development and shall define the general political guidelines thereof.

The European Council shall bring together the Heads of State or Government of the Member States and the President of the Commission. They shall be assisted by the Ministers for Foreign Affairs of the Member States and by a Member of the Commission. The European Council shall meet at least twice a year, under the chairmanship of the Head of State or Government of the Member State which holds the Presidency of the Council.

The European Council shall submit to the European Parliament a report after each of its meetings and a yearly written report on the progress achieved by the Union.

Article 5

The European Parliament, the Council, the Commission, the Court of Justice and the Court of Auditors shall exercise their powers under the conditions and for the purposes provided for, on the one hand, by the provisions of the Treaties establishing the European Communities and of the subsequent Treaties and Acts modifying and supplementing them and, on the other hand, by the other provisions of this Treaty.

Article 6

1. The Union is founded on the principles of liberty, democracy, respect for human rights and fundamental freedoms, and the rule of law, principles which are common to the Member States.
2. The Union shall respect fundamental rights, as guaranteed by the European Convention for the Protection of Human Rights and Fundamental Freedoms signed in Rome on 4 November 1950 and as they result from the constitutional traditions common to the Member States, as general principles of Community law.
3. The Union shall respect the national identities of its Member States.
4. The Union shall provide itself with the means necessary to attain its objectives and carry through its policies.

Article 7

1. On a reasoned proposal by one third of the Member States, by the European Parliament or by the Commission, the Council, acting by a majority of four fifths of its members after obtaining the assent of the European Parliament, may determine that there is a clear risk of a serious breach by a Member State of principles mentioned in Article 6(1), and address appropriate recommendations to that State. Before making such a determination, the Council shall hear the Member State in question and, acting in accordance with the same procedure, may call on independent persons to submit within a reasonable time limit a report on the situation in the Member State in question.

   The Council shall regularly verify that the grounds on which such a determination was made continue to apply.
2. The Council, meeting in the composition of the Heads of State or Government and acting by unanimity on a proposal by one third of the Member States or by the Commission and after obtaining the assent of the European Parliament, may determine the existence of a serious and persistent breach by a Member State of principles mentioned in Article 6(1), after inviting the government of the Member State in question to submit its observations.
3. Where a determination under paragraph 2 has been made, the Council, acting by a qualified majority, may decide to suspend certain of the rights deriving from the application of this Treaty to the Member State in question, including the voting rights of the representative of the government of that Member State in the Council. In doing so, the Council shall take into account the possible consequences of such a suspension on the rights and obligations of natural and legal persons.

   The obligations of the Member State in question under this Treaty shall in any case continue to be binding on that State.
4. The Council, acting by a qualified majority, may decide subsequently to vary or revoke measures taken under paragraph 3 in response to changes in the situation which led to their being imposed.

5.   For the purposes of this Article, the Council shall act without taking into account the vote of the representative of the government of the Member State in question. Abstentions by members present in person or represented shall not prevent the adoption of decisions referred to in paragraph 2. A qualified majority shall be defined as the same proportion of the weighted votes of the members of the Council concerned as laid down in Article 205(2) of the Treaty establishing the European Community.

This paragraph shall also apply in the event of voting rights being suspended pursuant to paragraph 3.

6.   For the purposes of paragraphs 1 and 2, the European Parliament shall act by a two-thirds majority of the votes cast, representing a majority of its Members.

TITLE V

PROVISIONS ON A COMMON FOREIGN AND SECURITY POLICY

Article 11

1.   The Union shall define and implement a common foreign and security policy covering all areas of foreign and security policy, the objectives of which shall be:
   — to safeguard the common values, fundamental interests, independence and integrity of the Union in conformity with the principles of the United Nations Charter,
   — to strengthen the security of the Union in all ways,
   — to preserve peace and strengthen international security, in accordance with the principles of the United Nations Charter, as well as the principles of the Helsinki Final Act and the objectives of the Paris Charter, including those on external borders,
   — to promote international cooperation,
   — to develop and consolidate democracy and the rule of law, and respect for human rights and fundamental freedoms.

2.   The Member States shall support the Union's external and security policy actively and unreservedly in a spirit of loyalty and mutual solidarity.

The Member States shall work together to enhance and develop their mutual political solidarity. They shall refrain from any action which is contrary to the interests of the Union or likely to impair its effectiveness as a cohesive force in international relations.

The Council shall ensure that these principles are complied with.

Article 12

The Union shall pursue the objectives set out in Article 11 by:
— defining the principles of and general guidelines for the common foreign and security policy,
— deciding on common strategies,
— adopting joint actions,
— adopting common positions,
— strengthening systematic cooperation between Member States in the conduct of policy.

Article 15

The Council shall adopt common positions. Common positions shall define the approach of the Union to a particular matter of a geographical or thematic nature. Member States shall ensure that their national policies conform to the common positions.

Article 16

Member States shall inform and consult one another within the Council on any matter of foreign and security policy of general interest in order to ensure that the Union's influence is exerted as effectively as possible by means of concerted and convergent action.

Article 17

1.   The common foreign and security policy shall include all questions relating to the security of the Union, including the progressive framing of a common defence policy, which might lead to a common defence, should the European Council so decide. It shall in that case recommend to the Member States the adoption of such a decision in accordance with their respective constitutional requirements.

The policy of the Union in accordance with this Article shall not prejudice the specific character of the security and defence policy of certain Member States and shall respect the obligations of certain Member States, which see their common defence realised in the North Atlantic Treaty Organisation (NATO), under the North Atlantic Treaty and be compatible with the common security and defence policy established within that framework.

The progressive framing of a common defence policy will be supported, as Member States consider appropriate,by cooperation between them in the field of armaments.

2. Questions referred to in this Article shall include humanitarian and rescue tasks, peacekeeping tasks and tasks of combat forces in crisis management, including peacemaking.

3. Decisions having defence implications dealt with under this Article shall be taken without prejudice to the policies and obligations referred to in paragraph 1, second subparagraph.

4. The provisions of this Article shall not prevent the development of closer cooperation between two or more Member States on a bilateral level, in the framework of the Western European Union (WEU) and NATO, provided such cooperation does not run counter to or impede that provided for in this title.

5. With a view to furthering the objectives of this Article, the provisions of this Article will be reviewed in accordance with Article 48.

Article 18

1. The Presidency shall represent the Union in matters coming within the common foreign and security policy.

2. The Presidency shall be responsible for the implementation of decisions taken under this title; in that capacity it shall in principle express the position of the Union in international organisations and international conferences.

3. The Presidency shall be assisted by the Secretary-General of the Council who shall exercise the function of High Representative for the common foreign and security policy.

4. The Commission shall be fully associated in the tasks referred to in paragraphs 1 and 2. The Presidency shall be assisted in those tasks if need be by the next Member State to hold the Presidency.

5. The Council may, whenever it deems it necessary, appoint a special representative with a mandate in relation to particular policy issues.

Article 19

1. Member States shall coordinate their action in international organisations and at international conferences. They shall uphold the common positions in such forums.

In international organisations and at international conferences where not all the Member States participate, those which do take part shall uphold the common positions.

2. Without prejudice to paragraph 1 and Article 14(3), Member States represented in international organisations or international conferences where not all the Member States participate shall keep the latter informed of any matter of common interest.

Member States which are also members of the United Nations Security Council will concert and keep the other Member States fully informed. Member States which are permanent members of the Security Council will, in the execution of their functions, ensure the defence of the positions and the interests of the Union, without prejudice to their responsibilities under the provisions of the United Nations Charter.

Article 20

The diplomatic and consular missions of the Member States and the Commission delegations in third countries and international conferences, and their representations to international organisations, shall cooperate in ensuring that the common positions and joint actions adopted by the Council are complied with and implemented.

They shall step up cooperation by exchanging information, carrying out joint assessments and contributing to the implementation of the provisions referred to in Article 20 of the Treaty establishing the European Community.

Article 21

The Presidency shall consult the European Parliament on the main aspects and the basic choices of the common foreign and security policy and shall ensure that the views of the European Parliament are duly taken into consideration. The European Parliament shall be kept regularly informed by the Presidency and the Commission of the development of the Union's foreign and security policy.

The European Parliament may ask questions of the Council or make recommendations to it. It shall hold an annual debate on progress in implementing the common foreign and security policy.

Article 22

1. Any Member State or the Commission may refer to the Council any question relating to the common foreign and security policy and may submit proposals to the Council.
2. In cases requiring a rapid decision, the Presidency, of its own motion, or at the request of the Commission or a Member State, shall convene an extraordinary Council meeting within 48 hours or, in an emergency, within a shorter period.

Article 23

1. Decisions under this title shall be taken by the Council acting unanimously. Abstentions by members present in person or represented shall not prevent the adoption of such decisions.

Article 24

1. When it is necessary to conclude an agreement with one or more States or international organisations in implementation of this title, the Council may authorise the Presidency, assisted by the Commission as appropriate, to open negotiations to that effect. Such agreements shall be concluded by the Council on a recommendation from the Presidency.
2. The Council shall act unanimously when the agreement covers an issue for which unanimity is required for the adoption of internal decisions.
3. When the agreement is envisaged in order to implement a joint action or common position, the Council shall act by a qualified majority in accordance with Article 23(2).
4. The provisions of this Article shall also apply to matters falling under Title VI. When the agreement covers an issue for which a qualified majority is required for the adoption of internal decisions or measures, the Council shall act by a qualified majority in accordance with Article 34 (3).
5. No agreement shall be binding on a Member State whose representative in the Council states that it has to comply with the requirements of its own constitutional procedure; the other members of the Council may agree that the agreement shall nevertheless apply provisionally.
6. Agreements concluded under the conditions set out by this Article shall be binding on the institutions of the Union.

Article 25

Without prejudice to Article 207 of the Treaty establishing the European Community, a Political and Security Committee shall monitor the international situation in the areas covered by the common foreign and security policy and contribute to the definition of policies by delivering opinions to the Council at the request of the Council or on its own initiative. It shall also monitor the implementation of agreed policies, without prejudice to the responsibility of the Presidency and the Commission.

Within the scope of this title, this Committee shall exercise, under the responsibility of the Council, political control and strategic direction of crisis management operations.

The Council may authorise the Committee, for the purpose and for the duration of a crisis management operation, as determined by the Council, to take the relevant decisions concerning the political control and strategic direction of the operation, without prejudice to Article 47.

Article 26

The Secretary-General of the Council, High Representative for the common foreign and security policy, shall assist the Council in matters coming within the scope of the common foreign and security policy, in particular through contributing to the formulation, preparation and implementation of policy decisions, and, when appropriate and acting on behalf of the Council at the request of the Presidency, through conducting political dialogue with third parties.

Article 27

The Commission shall be fully associated with the work carried out in the common foreign and security policy field.

TITLE VI
PROVISIONS ON POLICE AND JUDICIAL COOPERATION IN CRIMINAL MATTERS

Article 29

Without prejudice to the powers of the European Community, the Union's objective shall be to provide citizens with a high level of safety within an area of freedom, security and justice by developing common action among the Member States in the fields of police and judicial cooperation in criminal matters and by preventing and combating racism and xenophobia.

That objective shall be achieved by preventing and combating crime, organised or otherwise, in particular terrorism, trafficking in persons and offences against children, illicit drug trafficking and illicit arms trafficking, corruption and fraud, through:

— closer cooperation between police forces, customs authorities and other competent authorities in the Member States, both directly and through the European Police Office (Europol), in accordance with the provisions of Articles 30 and 32,

— closer cooperation between judicial and other competent authorities of the Member States including cooperation through the European Judicial Cooperation Unit ('Eurojust'), in accordance with the provisions of Articles 31 and 32,

— approximation, where necessary, of rules on criminal matters in the Member States, in accordance with the provisions of Article 31(e).

Article 30

1. Common action in the field of police cooperation shall include:

    (a) operational cooperation between the competent authorities, including the police, customs and other specialised law enforcement services of the Member States in relation to the prevention, detection and investigation of criminal offences;

    (b) the collection, storage, processing, analysis and exchange of relevant information, including information held by law enforcement services on reports on suspicious financial transactions, in particular through Europol, subject to appropriate provisions on the protection of personal data;

    (c) cooperation and joint initiatives in training, the exchange of liaison officers, secondments, the use of equipment, and forensic research;

    (d) the common evaluation of particular investigative techniques in relation to the detection of serious forms of organised crime.

2. The Council shall promote cooperation through Europol and shall in particular, within a period of five years after the date of entry into force of the Treaty of Amsterdam:

    (a) enable Europol to facilitate and support the preparation, and to encourage the coordination and carrying out, of specific investigative actions by the competent authorities of the Member States, including operational actions of joint teams comprising representatives of Europol in a support capacity;

    (b) adopt measures allowing Europol to ask the competent authorities of the Member States to conduct and coordinate their investigations in specific cases and to develop specific expertise which may be put at the disposal of Member States to assist them in investigating cases of organised crime;

    (c) promote liaison arrangements between prosecuting/investigating officials specialising in the fight against organised crime in close cooperation with Europol;

    (d) establish a research, documentation and statistical network on cross-border crime.

Article 31

1. Common action on judicial cooperation in criminal matters shall include:

    (a)   facilitating and accelerating cooperation between competent ministries and judicial or equivalent authorities of the Member States, including, where appropriate, cooperation through Eurojust, in relation to proceedings and the enforcement of decisions;

    (b)   facilitating extradition between Member States;

    (c)   ensuring compatibility in rules applicable in the Member States, as may be necessary to improve such cooperation;

    (d)   preventing conflicts of jurisdiction between Member States;

    (e)   progressively adopting measures establishing minimum rules relating to the constituent elements of criminal acts and to penalties in the fields of organised crime, terrorism and illicit drug trafficking.

2.   The Council shall encourage cooperation through Eurojust by:

    (a)   enabling Eurojust to facilitate proper coordination between Member States' national prosecuting authorities;

    (b)   promoting support by Eurojust for criminal investigations in cases of serious crossborder crime, particularly in the case of organised crime, taking account, in particular, of analyses carried out by Europol;

    (c)   facilitating close cooperation between Eurojust and the European Judicial Network, particularly, in order to facilitate the execution of letters rogatory and the implementation of extradition requests.

Article 32

The Council shall lay down the conditions and limitations under which the competent authorities referred to in Articles 30 and 31 may operate in the territory of another Member State in liaison and in agreement with the authorities of that State.

Article 33

This title shall not affect the exercise of the responsibilities incumbent upon Member States with regard to the maintenance of law and order and the safeguarding of internal security.

Article 34

1.   In the areas referred to in this title, Member States shall inform and consult one another within the Council with a view to coordinating their action. To that end, they shall establish collaboration between the relevant departments of their administrations.

2.   The Council shall take measures and promote cooperation, using the appropriate form and procedures as set out in this title, contributing to the pursuit of the objectives of the Union. To that end, acting unanimously on the initiative of any Member State or of the Commission, the Council may:

    (a)   adopt common positions defining the approach of the Union to a particular matter;

    (b)   adopt framework decisions for the purpose of approximation of the laws and regulations of the Member States. Framework decisions shall be binding upon the Member States as to the result to be achieved but shall leave to the national authorities the choice of form and methods. They shall not entail direct effect;

    (c)   adopt decisions for any other purpose consistent with the objectives of this title, excluding any approximation of the laws and regulations of the Member States. These decisions shall be binding and shall not entail direct effect; the Council, acting by a qualified majority, shall adopt measures necessary to implement those decisions at the level of the Union;

    (d)   establish conventions which it shall recommend to the Member States for adoption in accordance with their respective constitutional requirements. Member States shall begin the procedures applicable within a time limit to be set by the Council.

Unless they provide otherwise, conventions shall, once adopted by at least half of the Member States, enter into force for those Member States. Measures implementing conventions shall be adopted within the Council by a majority of two thirds of the Contracting Parties.

3.   Where the Council is required to act by a qualified majority, the votes of its members shall be weighted as laid down in Article 205(2) of the Treaty establishing the European Community,

and for their adoption acts of the Council shall require at least 255 votes in favour, cast by at least two thirds of the members. When a decision is to be adopted by the Council by a qualified majority, a member of the Council may request verification that the Member States constituting the qualified majority represent at least 62% of the total population of the Union. If that condition is shown not to have been met, the decision in question shall not be adopted.

4. For procedural questions, the Council shall act by a majority of its members.

Article 35

1. The Court of Justice of the European Communities shall have jurisdiction, subject to the conditions laid down in this Article, to give preliminary rulings on the validity and interpretation of framework decisions and decisions, on the interpretation of conventions established under this title and on the validity and interpretation of the measures implementing them.

2. By a declaration made at the time of signature of the Treaty of Amsterdam or at any time thereafter, any Member State shall be able to accept the jurisdiction of the Court of Justice to give preliminary rulings as specified in paragraph 1.

3. A Member State making a declaration pursuant to paragraph 2 shall specify that either:

   (a) any court or tribunal of that State against whose decisions there is no judicial remedy under national law may request the Court of Justice to give a preliminary ruling on a question raised in a case pending before it and concerning the validity or interpretation of an act referred to in paragraph 1 if that court or tribunal considers that a decision on the question is necessary to enable it to give judgment; or

   (b) any court or tribunal of that State may request the Court of Justice to give a preliminary ruling on a question raised in a case pending before it and concerning the validity or interpretation of an act referred to in paragraph 1 if that court or tribunal considers that a decision on the question is necessary to enable it to give judgment.

4. Any Member State, whether or not it has made a declaration pursuant to paragraph 2, shall be entitled to submit statements of case or written observations to the Court in cases which arise under paragraph 1.

5. The Court of Justice shall have no jurisdiction to review the validity or proportionality of operations carried out by the police or other law enforcement services of a Member State or the exercise of the responsibilities incumbent upon Member States with regard to the maintenance of law and order and the safeguarding of internal security.

6. The Court of Justice shall have jurisdiction to review the legality of framework decisions and decisions in actions brought by a Member State or the Commission on grounds of lack of competence, infringement of an essential procedural requirement, infringement of this Treaty or of any rule of law relating to its application, or misuse of powers. The proceedings provided for in this paragraph shall be instituted within two months of the publication of the measure.

7. The Court of Justice shall have jurisdiction to rule on any dispute between Member States regarding the interpretation or the application of acts adopted under Article 34(2) whenever such dispute cannot be settled by the Council within six months of its being referred to the Council by one of its members. The Court shall also have jurisdiction to rule on any dispute between Member States and the Commission regarding the interpretation or the application of conventions established under Article 34(2)(d).

Article 36

1. A Coordinating Committee shall be set up consisting of senior officials. In addition to its coordinating role, it shall be the task of the Committee to:
   — give opinions for the attention of the Council, either at the Council's request or on its own initiative,
   — contribute, without prejudice to Article 207 of the Treaty establishing the European Community, to the preparation of the Council's discussions in the areas referred to in Article 29.

2.   The Commission shall be fully associated with the work in the areas referred to in this title.

Article 37

Within international organisations and at international conferences in which they take part, Member States shall defend the common positions adopted under the provisions of this title.

Articles 18 and 19 shall apply as appropriate to matters falling under this title.

Article 38

Agreements referred to in Article 24 may cover matters falling under this title.

Article 39

1.   The Council shall consult the European Parliament before adopting any measure referred to in Article 34(2)(b), (c) and (d). The European Parliament shall deliver its opinion within a time limit which the Council may lay down, which shall not be less than three months. In the absence of an opinion within that time limit, the Council may act.

2.   The Presidency and the Commission shall regularly inform the European Parliament of discussions in the areas covered by this title.

3.   The European Parliament may ask questions of the Council or make recommendations to it. Each year, it shall hold a debate on the progress made in the areas referred to in this title.

Article 40

1.   Enhanced cooperation in any of the areas referred to in this title shall have the aim of enabling the Union to develop more rapidly into an area of freedom, security and justice, while respecting the powers of the European Community and the objectives laid down in this title.

2.   Articles 29 to 39 and Articles 40a to 41 shall apply to the enhanced cooperation provided for by this Article, save as otherwise provided in Article 40a and in Articles 43 to 45.

3.   The provisions of the Treaty establishing the European Community concerning the powers of the Court of Justice and the exercise of those powers shall apply to this Article and to Articles 40a and 40b.

Article 40a

1.   Member States which intend to establish enhanced cooperation between themselves under Article 40 shall address a request to the Commission, which may submit a proposal to the Council to that effect. In the event of the Commission not submitting a proposal, it shall inform the Member States concerned of the reasons for not doing so. Those Member States may then submit an initiative to the Council designed to obtain authorisation for the enhanced cooperation concerned.

2.   The authorisation referred to in paragraph 1 shall be granted, in compliance with Articles 43 to 45, by the Council, acting by a qualified majority, on a proposal from the Commission or on the initiative of at least eight Member States, and after consulting the European Parliament. The votes of the members of the Council shall be weighted in accordance with Article 205(2) of the Treaty establishing the European Community.

A member of the Council may request that the matter be referred to the European Council. After that matter has been raised before the European Council, the Council may act in accordance with the first subparagraph of this paragraph.

Article 40b

Any Member State which wishes to participate in enhanced cooperation established in accordance with Article 40a shall notify its intention to the Council and to the Commission, which shall give an opinion to the Council within three months of the date of receipt of that notification, possibly accompanied by a recommendation for such specific arrangements as it may deem necessary for that Member State to become a party to the cooperation in question. The Council shall take a decision on the request within four months of the date of receipt of that notification. The decision shall be deemed to be taken unless the Council, acting by a qualified majority within the same period, decides to hold it in abeyance; in that case, the Council shall state the reasons for its decision and set a deadline for re-examining it.

For the purposes of this Article, the Council shall act under the conditions set out in Article 44(1).

TITLE VII
PROVISIONS ON ENHANCED COOPERATION

Article 43

Member States which intend to establish enhanced cooperation between themselves may make use of the institutions, procedures and mechanisms laid down by this Treaty and by the Treaty establishing the European Community provided that the proposed cooperation:

(a) is aimed at furthering the objectives of the Union and of the Community, at protecting and serving their interests and at reinforcing their process of integration;

(b) respects the said Treaties and the single institutional framework of the Union;

(c) respects the *acquis communautaire* and the measures adopted under the other provisions of the said Treaties;

(d) remains within the limits of the powers of the Union or of the Community and does not concern the areas which fall within the exclusive competence of the Community;

(e) does not undermine the internal market as defined in Article 14(2) of the Treaty establishing the European Community, or the economic and social cohesion established in accordance with Title XVII of that Treaty;

(f) does not constitute a barrier to or discrimination in trade between the Member States and does not distort competition between them;

(g) involves a minimum of eight Member States;

(h) respects the competences, rights and obligations of those Member States which do not participate therein;

(i) does not affect the provisions of the Protocol integrating the Schengen acquis into the framework of the European Union;

(j) is open to all the Member States, in accordance with Article 43b.

Article 43a

Enhanced cooperation may be undertaken only as a last resort, when it has been established within the Council that the objectives of such cooperation cannot be attained within a reasonable period by applying the relevant provisions of the Treaties.

Article 45

The Council and the Commission shall ensure the consistency of activities undertaken on the basis of this title and the consistency of such activities with the policies of the Union and the Community, and shall cooperate to that end.

TITLE VIII
FINAL PROVISIONS

Article 47

Subject to the provisions amending the Treaty establishing the European Economic Community with a view to establishing the European Community, the Treaty establishing the European Coal and Steel Community and the Treaty establishing the European Atomic Energy Community, and to these final provisions, nothing in this Treaty shall affect the Treaties establishing the European Communities or the subsequent Treaties and Acts modifying or supplementing them.

Article 48

The government of any Member State or the Commission may submit to the Council proposals for the amendment of the Treaties on which the Union is founded.

If the Council, after consulting the European Parliament and, where appropriate, the Commission, delivers an opinion in favour of calling a conference of representatives of the governments of the Member States, the conference shall be convened by the President of the Council for the purpose of determining by common accord the amendments to be made to those Treaties. The European Central Bank shall also be consulted in the case of institutional changes in the monetary area. The amendments shall enter into force after being ratified by all the Member States in accordance with their respective constitutional requirements.

Article 51

This Treaty is concluded for an unlimited period.

Article 52

2.   This Treaty shall enter into force on 1 January 1993, provided that all the Instruments of ratification have been deposited, or, failing that, on the first day of the month following the deposit of the Instrument of ratification by the last signatory State to take this step.

PROTOCOL ON THE POSITION OF THE UNITED KINGDOM AND IRELAND

THE HIGH CONTRACTING PARTIES,

DESIRING to settle certain questions relating to the United Kingdom and Ireland,

HAVING REGARD to the Protocol on the application of certain aspects of Article 7a of the Treaty establishing the European Community to the United Kingdom and to Ireland,

HAVE AGREED UPON the following provisions which shall be annexed to the Treaty establishing the European Community and to the Treaty on European Union,

Article 1

Subject to Article 3, the United Kingdom and Ireland shall not take part in the adoption by the Council of proposed measures pursuant to Title IIIa of the Treaty establishing the European Community. By way of derogation from Article 148(2) of the Treaty establishing the European Community, a qualified majority shall be defined as the same proportion of the weighted votes of the members of the Council concerned as laid down in the said Article 148(2). The unanimity of the members of the Council, with the exception of the representatives of the governments of the United Kingdom and Ireland, shall be necessary for decisions of the Council which must be adopted unanimously.

Article 2

In consequence of Article 1 and subject to Articles 3, 4 and 6, none of the provisions of Title IIIa of the Treaty establishing the European Community, no measure adopted pursuant to that Title, no provision of any international agreement concluded by the Community pursuant to that Title, and no decision of the Court of Justice interpreting any such provision or measure shall be binding upon or applicable in the United Kingdom or Ireland; and no such provision, measure or decision shall in any way affect the competences, rights and obligations of those States; and no such provision, measure or decision shall in any way affect the *acquis communautaire* nor form part of Community law as they apply to the United Kingdom or Ireland.

Article 3

1.   The United Kingdom or Ireland may notify the President of the Council in writing, within three months after a proposal or initiative has been presented to the Council pursuant to Title IIIa of the Treaty establishing the European Community, that it wishes to take part in the adoption and application of any such proposed measure, whereupon that State shall be entitled to do so. By way of derogation from Article 148(2) of the Treaty establishing the European Community, a qualified majority shall be defined as the same proportion of the weighted votes of the members of the Council concerned as laid down in the said Article 148(2).

The unanimity of the members of the Council, with the exception of a member which has not made such a notification, shall be necessary for decisions of the Council which must be adopted unanimously. A measure adopted under this paragraph shall be binding upon all Member States which took part in its adoption.

2.   If after a reasonable period of time a measure referred to in paragraph 1 cannot be adopted with the United Kingdom or Ireland taking part, the Council may adopt such measure in accordance with Article 1 without the participation of the United Kingdom or Ireland. In that case Article 2 applies.

Article 4

The United Kingdom or Ireland may at any time after the adoption of a measure by the Council pursuant to Title IIIa of the Treaty establishing the European Community notify its intention to the Council and to the Commission that it wishes to accept that measure. In that case, the procedure provided for in Article 5a(3) of the Treaty establishing the European Community shall apply *mutatis mutandis*.

Article 5

A Member State which is not bound by a measure adopted pursuant to Title IIIa of the Treaty establishing the European Community shall bear no financial consequences of that measure other than administrative costs entailed for the institutions.

Article 6

Where, in cases referred to in this Protocol, the United Kingdom or Ireland is bound by a measure adopted by the Council pursuant to Title IIIa of the Treaty establishing the European Community, the relevant provisions of that Treaty, including Article 73p, shall apply to that State in relation to that measure.

Article 7

Articles 3 and 4 shall be without prejudice to the Protocol integrating the Schengen acquis into the framework of the European Union.

Article 8

Ireland may notify the President of the Council in writing that it no longer wishes to be covered by the terms of this Protocol. In that case, the normal treaty provisions will apply to Ireland.

which contributes to improving the production or distribution of goods or to promoting technical or economic progress, while allowing consumers a fair share of the resulting benefit, and which does not:
(a)   impose on the undertakings concerned restrictions which are not indispensable to the attainment of these objectives;
(b)   afford such undertakings the possibility of eliminating competition in respect of a substantial part of the products in question.

TREATY OF AMSTERDAM

ANNEX

Tables of equivalences referred to in Article 12 of the Treaty of Amsterdam

A. Treaty on European Union

Previous numbering	New numbering	Previous numbering	New numbering
TITLE I	TITLE I	Article J.17	Article 27
Article A	Article 1	Article J.18	Article 28
Article B	Article 2	TITLE VI	TITLE VI
Article C	Article 3	Article K.1	Article 29
Article D	Article 4	Article K.2	Article 30
Article E	Article 5	Article K.3	Article 31
Article F	Article 6	Article K.4	Article 32
Article F.1	Article 7	Article K.5	Article 33
TITLE II	TITLE II	Article K.6	Article 34
Article G	Article 8	Article K.7	Article 35
TITLE III	TITLE III	Article K.8	Article 36
Article H	Article 9	Article K.9	Article 37
TITLE IV	TITLE IV	Article K.10	Article 38
Article I	Article 10	Article K.11	Article 39
TITLE V	TITLE V	Article K.12	Article 40
Article J.1	Article 11	Article K.13	Article 41
Article J.2	Article 12	Article K.14	Article 42
Article J.3	Article 13	TITLE VIa	TITLE VII
Article J.4	Article 14	Article K.15	Article 43
Article J.5	Article 15	Article K.16	Article 44
Article J.6	Article 16	Article K.17	Article 45
Article J.7	Article 17	TITLE VII	TITLE VIII
Article J.8	Article 18	Article L	Article 46
Article J.9	Article 19	Article M	Article 47
Article J.10	Article 20	Article N	Article 48
Article J.11	Article 21	Article O	Article 49
Article J.12	Article 22	Article P	Article 50
Article J.13	Article 23	Article Q	Article 51
Article J.14	Article 24	Article R	Article 52
Article J.15	Article 25	Article S	Article 53
Article J.16	Article 26		

B. Treaty establishing the European Community

Previous numbering	New numbering	Previous numbering	New numbering
PART ONE	PART ONE	Article 42	Article 36
Article 1	Article 1	Article 43	Article 37
Article 2	Article 2	Article 46	Article 38
Article 3	Article 3	TITLE III	TITLE III
Article 3a	Article 4	CHAPTER 1	CHAPTER 1
Article 3b	Article 5	Article 48	Article 39
Article 3c	Article 6	Article 49	Article 40
Article 4	Article 7	Article 50	Article 41
Article 4a	Article 8	Article 51	Article 42
Article 4b	Article 9	CHAPTER 2	CHAPTER 2
Article 5	Article 10	Article 52	Article 43
Article 5a	Article 11	Article 54	Article 44
Article 6	Article 12	Article 55	Article 45
Article 6a	Article 13	Article 56	Article 46
Article 7a	Article 14	Article 57	Article 47
Article 7c	Article 15	Article 58	Article 48
Article 7d	Article 16	CHAPTER 3	CHAPTER 3
PART TWO	PART TWO	Article 59	Article 49
Article 8	Article 17	Article 60	Article 50
Article 8a	Article 18	Article 61	Article 51
Article 8b	Article 19	Article 63	Article 52
Article 8c	Article 20	Article 64	Article 53
Article 8d	Article 21	Article 65	Article 54
Article 8e	Article 22	Article 66	Article 55
PART THREE	PART THREE	CHAPTER 4	CHAPTER 4
TITLE I	TITLE I	Article 73b	Article 56
Article 9	Article 23	Article 73c	Article 57
Article 10	Article 24	Article 73d	Article 58
CHAPTER 1	CHAPTER 1	Article 73f	Article 59
Article 12	Article 25	Article 73g	Article 60
Article 28	Article 26	TITLE IIIa	TITLE IV
Article 29	Article 27	Article 73i	Article 61
CHAPTER 2	CHAPTER	Article 73j	Article 62
Article 30	Article 28	Article 73k	Article 63
Article 34	Article 29	Article 73l	Article 64
Article 36	Article 30	Article 73m	Article 65
Article 37	Article 31	Article 73n	Article 66
TITLE II	TITLE II	Article 73o	Article 67
Article 38	Article 32	Article 73p	Article 68
Article 39	Article 33	Article 73q	Article 69
Article 40	Article 34	TITLE IV	TITLE V
Article 41	Article 35	Article 74	Article 70

Previous numbering	New numbering	Previous numbering	New numbering
Article 75	Article 71	Article 105a	Article 106
Article 76	Article 72	Article 106	Article 107
Article 77	Article 73	Article 107	Article 108
Article 78	Article 74	Article 108	Article 109
Article 79	Article 75	Article 108a	Article 110
Article 80	Article 76	Article 109	Article 111
Article 81	Article 77	CHAPTER 3	CHAPTER 3
Article 82	Article 78	Article 109a	Article 112
Article 83	Article 79	Article 109b	Article 113
Article 84	Article 80	Article 109c	Article 114
TITLE V	TITLE VI	Article 109d	Article 115
CHAPTER 1	CHAPTER 1	CHAPTER 4	CHAPTER 4
SECTION 1	SECTION 1	Article 109e	Article 116
Article 85	Article 81	Article 109f	Article 117
Article 86	Article 82	Article 109g	Article 118
Article 87	Article 83	Article 109h	Article 119
Article 88	Article 84	Article 109i	Article 120
Article 89	Article 85	Article 109j	Article 121
Article 90	Article 86	Article 109k	Article 122
SECTION 3	SECTION 2	Article 109l	Article 123
Article 92	Article 87	Article 109m	Article 124
Article 93	Article 88	TITLE VIa	TITLE VIII
Article 94	Article 89	Article 109n	Article 125
CHAPTER 2	CHAPTER 2	Article 109o	Article 126
Article 95	Article 90	Article 109p	Article 127
Article 96	Article 91	Article 109q	Article 128
Article 98	Article 92	Article 109r	Article 129
Article 99	Article 93	Article 109s	Article 130
CHAPTER 3	CHAPTER 3	TITLE VII	TITLE IX
Article 100	Article 94	Article 110	Article 131
Article 100a	Article 95	Article 112	Article 132
Article 101	Article 96	Article 113	Article 133
Article 102	Article 97	Article 115	Article 134
TITLE VI	TITLE VII	TITLE VIIa	TITLE X
CHAPTER 1	CHAPTER 1	Article 116	Article 135
Article 102a	Article 98	TITLE VIII	TITLE XI
Article 103	Article 99	CHAPTER 1	CHAPTER 1
Article 103a	Article 100	Article 117	Article 136
Article 104	Article 101	Article 118	Article 137
Article 104a	Article 102	Article 118a	Article 138
Article 104b	Article 103	Article 118b	Article 139
Article 104c	Article 104	Article 118c	Article 140
CHAPTER 2	CHAPTER 2	Article 119	Article 141
Article 105	Article 105	Article 119a	Article 142

Previous numbering	New numbering	Previous numbering	New numbering
Article 120	Article 143	TITLE XVII	TITLE XX
Article 121	Article 144	Article 130u	Article 177
Article 122	Article 145	Article 130v	Article 178
CHAPTER 2	CHAPTER 2	Article 130w	Article 179
Article 123	Article 146	Article 130x	Article 180
Article 124	Article 147	Article 130y	Article 181
Article 125	Article 148	PART FOUR	PART FOUR
CHAPTER 3	CHAPTER 3	Article 131	Article 182
Article 126	Article 149	Article 132	Article 183
Article 127	Article 150	Article 133	Article 184
TITLE IX	TITLE XII	Article 134	Article 185
Article 128	Article 151	Article 135	Article 186
TITLE X	TITLE XIII	Article 136	Article 187
Article 129	Article 152	Article 136a	Article 188
TITLE XI	TITLE XIV	PART FIVE	PART FIVE
Article 129a	Article 153	TITLE I	TITLE I
TITLE XII	TITLE XV	CHAPTER 1	CHAPTER 1
Article 129b	Article 154	SECTION 1	SECTION 1
Article 129c	Article 155	Article 137	Article 189
Article 129d	Article 156	Article 138	Article 190
TITLE XIII	TITLE XVI	Article 138a	Article 191
Article 130	Article 157	Article 138b	Article 192
TITLE XIV	TITLE XVII	Article 138c	Article 193
Article 130a	Article 158	Article 138d	Article 194
Article 130b	Article 159	Article 138e	Article 195
Article 130c	Article 160	Article 139	Article 196
Article 130d	Article 161	Article 140	Article 197
Article 130e	Article 162	Article 141	Article 198
TITLE XV	TITLE XVIII	Article 142	Article 199
Article 130f	Article 163	Article 143	Article 200
Article 130g	Article 164	Article 144	Article 201
Article 130h	Article 165	SECTION 2	SECTION 2
Article 130i	Article 166	Article 145	Article 202
Article 130j	Article 167	Article 146	Article 203
Article 130k	Article 168	Article 147	Article 204
Article 130l	Article 169	Article 148	Article 205
Article 130m	Article 170	Article 150	Article 206
Article 130n	Article 171	Article 151	Article 207
Article 130o	Article 172	Article 152	Article 208
Article 130p	Article 173	Article 153	Article 209
TITLE XVI	TITLE XIX	Article 154	Article 210
Article 130r	Article 174	SECTION 3	SECTION 3
Article 130s	Article 175	Article 155	Article 211
Article 130t	Article 176	Article 156	Article 212

Previous numbering	New numbering	Previous numbering	New numbering
Article 157	Article 213	Article 191	Article 254
Article 158	Article 214	Article 191a	Article 255
Article 159	Article 215	Article 192	Article 256
Article 160	Article 216	CHAPTER 3	CHAPTER 3
Article 161	Article 217	Article 193	Article 257
Article 162	Article 218	Article 194	Article 258
Article 163	Article 219	Article 195	Article 259
SECTION 4	SECTION 4	Article 196	Article 260
Article 164	Article 220	Article 197	Article 261
Article 165	Article 221	Article 198	Article 262
Article 166	Article 222	CHAPTER 4	CHAPTER 4
Article 167	Article 223	Article 198a	Article 263
Article 168	Article 224	Article 198b	Article 264
Article 168a	Article 225	Article 198c	Article 265
Article 169	Article 226	CHAPTER 5	CHAPTER 5
Article 170	Article 227	Article 198d	Article 266
Article 171	Article 228	Article 198e	Article 267
Article 172	Article 229	TITLE II	TITLE II
Article 173	Article 230	Article 199	Article 268
Article 174	Article 231	Article 201	Article 269
Article 175	Article 232	Article 201a	Article 270
Article 176	Article 233	Article 202	Article 271
Article 177	Article 234	Article 203	Article 272
Article 178	Article 235	Article 204	Article 273
Article 179	Article 236	Article 205	Article 274
Article 180	Article 237	Article 205a	Article 275
Article 181	Article 238	Article 206	Article 276
Article 182	Article 239	Article 207	Article 277
Article 183	Article 240	Article 208	Article 278
Article 184	Article 241	Article 209	Article 279
Article 185	Article 242	Article 209a	Article 280
Article 186	Article 243	PART SIX	PART SIX
Article 187	Article 244	Article 210	Article 281
Article 188	Article 245	Article 211	Article 282
SECTION 5	SECTION 5	Article 212	Article 283
Article 188a	Article 246	Article 213	Article 284
Article 188b	Article 247	Article 213a	Article 285
Article 188c	Article 248	Article 213b	Article 286
CHAPTER 2	CHAPTER 2	Article 214	Article 287
Article 189	Article 249	Article 215	Article 288
Article 189a	Article 250	Article 216	Article 289
Article 189b	Article 251	Article 217	Article 290
Article 189c	Article 252	Article 218	Article 291
Article 190	Article 253	Article 219	Article 292

Previous numbering	New numbering	Previous numbering	New numbering
Article 220	Article 293	Article 230	Article 303
Article 221	Article 294	Article 231	Article 304
Article 222	Article 295	Article 232	Article 305
Article 223	Article 296	Article 233	Article 306
Article 224	Article 297	Article 234	Article 307
Article 225	Article 298	Article 235	Article 308
Article 227	Article 299	Article 236	Article 309
Article 228	Article 300	Article 238	Article 310
Article 228a	Article 301	Article 239	Article 311
Article 229	Article 302	Article 240	Article 312

CONSOLIDATED TEXTS OF THE EU TREATIES AS AMENDED BY THE TREATY OF LISBON
Cm 7310
CONSOLIDATED VERSION
OF THE TREATY ON EUROPEAN UNION

[THE CONTRACTING PARTIES]

RESOLVED to mark a new stage in the process of European integration undertaken with the establishment of the European Communities,

DRAWING INSPIRATION from the cultural, religious and humanist inheritance of Europe, from which have developed the universal values of the inviolable and inalienable rights of the human person, freedom, democracy, equality and the rule of law,

RECALLING the historic importance of the ending of the division of the European continent and the need to create firm bases for the construction of the future Europe,

CONFIRMING their attachment to the principles of liberty, democracy and respect for human rights and fundamental freedoms and of the rule of law,

CONFIRMING their attachment to fundamental social rights as defined in the European Social Charter signed at Turin on 18 October 1961 and in the 1989 Community Charter of the Fundamental Social Rights of Workers,

DESIRING to deepen the solidarity between their peoples while respecting their history, their culture and their traditions,

DESIRING to enhance further the democratic and efficient functioning of the institutions so as to enable them better to carry out, within a single institutional framework, the tasks entrusted to them,

RESOLVED to achieve the strengthening and the convergence of their economies and to establish an economic and monetary union including, in accordance with the provisions of this Treaty and of the Treaty on the Functioning of the European Union, a single and stable currency,

DETERMINED to promote economic and social progress for their peoples, taking into account the principle of sustainable development and within the context of the accomplishment of the internal market and of reinforced cohesion and environmental protection, and to implement policies ensuring that advances in economic integration are accompanied by parallel progress in other fields,

RESOLVED to establish a citizenship common to nationals of their countries,

RESOLVED to implement a common foreign and security policy including the progressive framing of a common defence policy, which might lead to a common defence in accordance with the provisions of Article 42, thereby reinforcing the European identity and its independence in order to promote peace, security and progress in Europe and in the world,

RESOLVED to facilitate the free movement of persons, while ensuring the safety and security of their peoples, by establishing an area of freedom, security and justice, in accordance with the provisions of this Treaty and of the Treaty on the Functioning of the European Union,

RESOLVED to continue the process of creating an ever closer union among the peoples of Europe, in which decisions are taken as closely as possible to the citizen in accordance with the principle of subsidiarity,

IN VIEW of further steps to be taken in order to advance European integration,

HAVE DECIDED to establish a European Union and to this end … have agreed as follows.

TITLE I

COMMON PROVISIONS

Article 1

By this Treaty, the HIGH CONTRACTING PARTIES establish among themselves a EUROPEAN UNION, hereinafter called 'the Union' on which the Member States confer competences to attain objectives they have in common.

This Treaty marks a new stage in the process of creating an ever closer union among the peoples of Europe, in which decisions are taken as openly as possible and as closely as possible to the citizen. The Union shall be founded on the present Treaty and on the Treaty on the Functioning of the European Union (hereinafter referred to as 'the Treaties'). Those two Treaties shall have the same legal value. The Union shall replace and succeed the European Community.

Article 2

The Union is founded on the values of respect for human dignity, freedom, democracy, equality, the rule of law and respect for human rights, including the rights of persons belonging to minorities. These values are common to the Member States in a society in which pluralism, non-discrimination, tolerance, justice, solidarity and equality between women and men prevail.

Article 3

1. The Union's aim is to promote peace, its values and the well-being of its peoples.
2. The Union shall offer its citizens an area of freedom, security and justice without internal frontiers, in which the free movement of persons is ensured in conjunction with appropriate measures with respect to external border controls, asylum, immigration and the prevention and combating of crime.
3. The Union shall establish an internal market. It shall work for the sustainable development of Europe based on balanced economic growth and price stability, a highly competitive social market economy, aiming at full employment and social progress, and a high level of protection and improvement of the quality of the environment. It shall promote scientific and technological advance.

    It shall combat social exclusion and discrimination, and shall promote social justice and protection, equality between women and men, solidarity between generations and protection of the rights of the child.

    It shall promote economic, social and territorial cohesion, and solidarity among Member States.

    It shall respect its rich cultural and linguistic diversity, and shall ensure that Europe's cultural heritage is safeguarded and enhanced.
4. The Union shall establish an economic and monetary union whose currency is the euro.
5. In its relations with the wider world, the Union shall uphold and promote its values and contribute to the protection if its citizens. It shall contribute to peace, security, the sustainable development of the Earth, solidarity and mutual respect among peoples, free and fair trade, eradication of poverty and the protection of human rights, in particular the rights of the child, as well as to the strict observance and the development of international law , including respect for the principles of the United Nations Charter.
6. The Union shall pursue its objectives by appropriate means commensurate with the competences which are conferred upon it in the Treaties.

Article 4

1. In accordance with Article 5, competences not conferred upon the Union in the Treaties remain with the Member States.
2. The Union shall respect the equality of Member States before the Treaties as well as their national identities, inherent in their fundamental structures, political and constitutional, inclusive of regional and local self-government. it shall respect their essential State functions,

including ensuring the territorial integrity of the State, maintaining law and order and safeguarding national security. In particular, national security remains the sole responsibility of each Member State.

3. Pursuant to the principle of sincere cooperation, the Union and the Member States shall, in full mutual respect, assist each other in carrying out tasks which flow from the Treaties.

The Member States shall take any appropriate measure, general or particular, to ensure fulfilment of the obligations arising out of the Treaties or resulting from the acts of the institutions of the Union.

The Member States shall facilitate the achievement of the Union's tasks and refrain from any measure which could jeopardise the attainment of the Union's objectives.

Article 5

1. The limits of Union competences are governed by the principle of conferral. The use of Union competences is governed by the principles of subsidiarity and proportionality.

2. Under the principle of conferral, the Union shall act only within the limits of the competences conferred upon it by the Member States in the Treaties to attain the objectives set out therein. Competences not conferred upon the Union in the Treaties remain with the Member States.

3. Under the principle of subsidiarity, in areas which do not fall within its exclusive competence, the Union shall act only if and insofar as the objectives of the proposed action cannot be sufficiently achieved by the Member States, either at central level or at regional and local level, but can rather, by reason of the scale or effects of the proposed action, be better achieved at Union level.

The institutions of the Union shall apply the principle of subsidiarity as laid down in the Protocol on the application of the principles of subsidiarity and proportionality. National Parliaments ensure compliance with the principle of subsidiarity in accordance with the procedure set out in that Protocol.

4. Under the principle of proportionality, the content and form of Union action shall not exceed what is necessary to achieve the objectives of the Treaties.

The institutions of the Union shall apply the principle of proportionality as laid down in the Protocol on the application of the principles of subsidiarity and proportionality.

Article 6

1. The Union recognises the rights, freedoms and principles set out in the Charter of Fundamental Rights of the European Union of 7 December 2000, as adapted at Strasbourg, on 12 December 2007, which shall have the same legal value as the Treaties.

The provisions of the Charter shall not extend in any way the competences of the Union as defined in the Treaties.

The rights, freedoms and principles in the Charter shall be interpreted in accordance with the general provisions in Title VII of the Charter governing its interpretation and application and with due regard to the explanations referred to in the Charter, that set out the sources of those provisions.

2. The Union shall accede to the European Convention for the Protection of Human Rights and Fundamental Freedoms. Such accession shall not affect the Union's competences as defined in the Treaties.

3. Fundamental rights, as guaranteed by the European Convention for the Protection of Human Rights and Fundamental Freedoms and as they result from the constitutional traditions common to the Member States, shall constitute general principles of the Union's law.

Article 7

1. On a reasoned proposal by one third of the Member States, by the European Parliament or by the European Commission, the Council, acting by a majority of four fifths of its members after obtaining the consent of the European Parliament, may determine that there is a clear risk of a serious breach by a Member State of the values referred to in Article 2. Before making such a determination, the Council shall hear the Member State in question and may address recommendations to it, acting in accordance with the same procedure.

        The Council shall regularly verify that the grounds on which such a determination was made continue to apply.

2.   The European Council, acting by unanimity on a proposal by one third of the Member States or by the Commission and after obtaining the consent of the European Parliament, may determine the existence of a serious and persistent breach by a Member State of the values referred to in Article 2, after inviting the Member State in question to submit its observations.

3.   Where a determination under paragraph 2 has been made, the Council, acting by a qualified majority, may decide to suspend certain of the rights deriving from the application of the Treaties to the Member State in question, including the voting rights of the representative of the government of that Member State in the Council. In doing so, the Council shall take into account the possible consequences of such a suspension on the rights and obligations of natural and legal persons.

        The obligations of the Member State in question under this Treaty shall in any case continue to be binding on that State.

4.   The Council, acting by a qualified majority, may decide subsequently to vary or revoke measures taken under paragraph 3 in response to changes in the situation which led to their being imposed.

5.   The voting arrangements applying to the European Parliament, the European Council and the Council for the purposes of this Article are laid down in Article 354 of the Treaty on the Functioning of the European Union.

Article 8

1.   The Union shall develop a special relationship with neighbouring countries, aiming to establish an area of prosperity and good neighbourliness, founded on the values of the Union and characterised by close and peaceful relations based on cooperation.

2.   For the purposes of paragraph 1, the Union may conclude specific agreements with the countries concerned. These agreements may contain reciprocal rights and obligations as well as the possibility of undertaking activities jointly. Their implementation shall be the subject of periodic consultation.

TITLE II

PROVISIONS ON DEMOCRATIC PRINCIPLES

Article 9

In all its activities, the Union shall observe the principle of the equality of its citizens, who shall receive equal attention from its institutions, bodies, offices and agencies. Every national of a Member State shall be a citizen of the Union. Citizenship of the Union shall be additional to national citizenship and shall not replace it.

Article 10

1.   The functioning of the Union shall be founded on representative democracy.

2.   Citizens are directly represented at Union level in the European Parliament.

        Member States are represented in the European Council by their Heads of State or Government and in the Council by their governments, themselves democratically accountable either to their national Parliaments, or to their citizens.

3.   Every citizen shall have the right to participate in the democratic life of the Union. Decisions shall be taken as openly and as closely as possible to the citizen.

4.   Political parties at European level contribute to forming European political awareness and to expressing the will of citizens of the Union.

Article 11

1.   The institutions shall, by appropriate means, give citizens and representative associations the opportunity to make known and publicly exchange their views in all areas of Union action.

2.   The institutions shall maintain an open, transparent and regular dialogue with representative associations and civil society.

3.   The European Commission shall carry out broad consultations with parties concerned in order to ensure that the Union's actions are coherent and transparent.

4.   Not less than one million citizens who are nationals of a significant number of Member States may take the initiative of inviting the European Commission, within the framework of its powers, to submit any appropriate proposal on matters where citizens consider that a legal act of the Union is required for the purpose of implementing the Treaties.

The procedures and conditions required for such a citizens' initiative shall be determined in accordance with the first paragraph of Article 24 of the Treaty on the Functioning of the European Union.

Article 12

National Parliaments contribute actively to the good functioning of the Union:

(a)   through being informed by the institutions of the Union and having draft legislative acts of the Union forwarded to them in accordance with the Protocol on the role of national Parliaments in the European Union;

(b)   by seeing to it that the principle of subsidiarity is respected in accordance with the procedures provided for in the Protocol on the application of the principles of subsidiarity and proportionality;

(c)   by taking part, within the framework of the area of freedom, security and justice, in the evaluation mechanisms for the implementation of the Union policies in that area, in accordance with Article 70 of the Treaty on the Functioning of the European Union, and through being involved in the political monitoring of Europol and the evaluation of Eurojust's activities in accordance with Articles 88 and 85 of that Treaty;

(d)   by taking part in the revision procedures of the Treaties, in accordance with Article 48 of this Treaty;

(e)   by being notified of applications for accession to the Union, in accordance with Article 49 of this Treaty;

(f)   by taking part in the interparliamentary cooperation between national Parliaments and with the European Parliament, in accordance with the Protocol on the role of national Parliaments in the European Union.

TITLE III
PROVISIONS ON THE INSTITUTIONS

Article 13

1.   The Union shall have an institutional framework which shall aim to promote its values, advance its objectives, serve its interests, those of its citizens and those of the Member States, and ensure the consistency, effectiveness and continuity of its policies and actions.

This institutional framework comprises:
— The European Parliament,
— The European Council,
— The Council,
— The European Commission (hereinafter referred to as 'the Commission'),
— The Court of Justice of the European Union,
— The European Central Bank,
— The Court of Auditors.

2.   Each institution shall act within the limits of the powers conferred on it in the Treaties, and in conformity with the procedures, conditions and objectives set out in them. The institutions shall practise mutual sincere cooperation.

3.   The provisions relating to the European Central Bank and the Court of Auditors and detailed provisions on the other institutions are set out in the Treaty on the Functioning of the European Union.

4.   The European Parliament, the Council and the Commission shall be assisted by an Economic and Social Committee and a Committee of the Regions acting in an advisory capacity.

Article 14

1.   The European Parliament shall, jointly with the Council, exercise legislative and budgetary functions. It shall exercise functions of political control and consultation as laid down in the Treaties. It shall elect the President of the Commission.

2. The European Parliament shall be composed of representatives of the Union's citizens. They shall not exceed seven hundred and fifty in number, plus the President. Representation of citizens shall be degressively proportional, with a minimum threshold of six members per Member State. No Member State shall be allocated more than ninety-six seats.

The European Council shall adopt by unanimity, on the initiative of the European Parliament and with its consent, a decision establishing the composition of the European Parliament, respecting the principles referred to in the first subparagraph.

3. The members of the European Parliament shall be elected for a term of five years by direct universal suffrage in a free and secret ballot.

4. The European Parliament shall elect its President and its officers from among its members.

Article 15

1. The European Council shall provide the Union with the necessary impetus for its development and shall define the general political directions and priorities thereof. It shall not exercise legislative functions.

2. The European Council shall consist of the Heads of State or Government of the Member States, together with its President and the President of the Commission. The High Representative of the Union for Foreign Affairs and Security Policy shall take part in its work.

3. The European Council shall meet twice every six months, convened by its President. When the agenda so requires, the members of the European Council may decide each to be assisted by a minister and, in the case of the President of the Commission, by a member of the Commission. When the situation so requires, the President shall convene a special meeting of the European Council.

4. Except where the Treaties provide otherwise, decisions of the European Council shall be taken by consensus.

5. The European Council shall elect its President, by a qualified majority, for a term of two and a half years, renewable once. In the event of an impediment or serious misconduct, the European Council can end the President's term of office in accordance with the same procedure.

6. The President of the European Council:
   (a) shall chair it and drive forward its work;
   (b) shall ensure the preparation and continuity of the work of the European Council in cooperation with the President of the Commission, and on the basis of the work of the General Affairs Council;
   (c) shall endeavour to facilitate cohesion and consensus within the European Council;
   (d) shall present a report to the European Parliament after each of the meetings of the European Council.

   The President of the European Council shall, at his or her level and in that capacity, ensure the external representation of the Union on issues concerning its common foreign and security policy, without prejudice to the powers of the High Representative of the Union for Foreign Affairs and Security Policy.

   The President of the European Council shall not hold a national office.

Article 16

1. The Council shall, jointly with the European Parliament, exercise legislative and budgetary functions. It shall carry out policy-making and coordinating functions as laid down in the Treaties.

2. The Council shall consist of a representative of each Member State at ministerial level, who may commit the government of the Member State in question and cast its vote.

3. The Council shall act by a qualified majority except where the Treaties provide otherwise.

4. As from 1 November 2014, a qualified majority shall be defined as at least 55% of the members of the Council, comprising at least fifteen of them and representing Member States comprising at least 65% of the population of the Union.

   A blocking minority must include at least four Council members, failing which the qualified majority shall be deemed attained.

The other arrangements governing the qualified majority are laid down in Article 238(2) of the Treaty on the Functioning of the European Union.

5. The transitional provisions relating to the definition of the qualified majority which shall be applicable until 31 October 2014 and those which shall be applicable from 1 November 2014 to 31 March 2017 are laid down in the Protocol on transitional provisions.

6. The Council shall meet in different configurations, the list of which shall be adopted in accordance with Article 236 of the Treaty on the Functioning of the European Union.

The General Affairs Council shall ensure consistency in the work of the different Council configurations. It shall prepare and ensure the follow-up to meetings of the European Council, in liaison with the President of the European Council and the Commission.

The Foreign Affairs Council shall elaborate the Union's external action on the basis of strategic guidelines laid down by the European Council and ensure that the Union's action is consistent.

7. A Committee of Permanent Representatives of the Governments of the Member States shall be responsible for preparing the work of the Council.

8. The Council shall meet in public when it deliberates and votes on a draft legislative act. To this end, each Council meeting shall be divided into two parts, dealing respectively with deliberations on Union legislative acts and on non-legislative activities.

9. The Presidency of Council configurations, other than that of Foreign Affairs, shall be held by Member State representatives in the Council on the basis of equal rotation, in accordance with the conditions established in accordance with Article 236 of the Treaty on the Functioning of the European Union.

Article 17

1. The Commission shall promote the general interest of the Union and take appropriate initiatives to that end. It shall ensure the application of the Treaties, and of measures adopted by the institutions pursuant to the Treaties. It shall oversee the application of Union law under the control of the Court of Justice of the European Union. It shall execute the budget and manage programmes. It shall exercise coordinating, executive and management functions, as laid down in the Treaties. With the exception of the common foreign and security policy, and other cases provided for in the Treaties, it shall ensure the Union's external representation. It shall initiate the Union's annual and multiannual programming with a view to achieving interinstitutional agreements.

2. Union legislative acts may only be adopted on the basis of a Commission proposal, except where the Treaties provide otherwise. Other acts shall be adopted on the basis of a Commission proposal where the Treaties so provide.

3. The Commission's term of office shall be five years.

The members of the Commission shall be chosen on the ground of their general competence and European commitment from persons whose independence is beyond doubt.

In carrying out its responsibilities, the Commission shall be completely independent. Without prejudice to Article 18(2), the members of the Commission shall neither seek nor take instructions from any Government or other institution, body, office or entity. They shall refrain from any action incompatible with their duties or the performance of their tasks.

4. The Commission appointed between the date of entry into force of the Treaty of Lisbon and 31 October 2014, shall consist of one national of each Member State, including its President and the High Representative of the Union for Foreign Affairs and Security Policy who shall be one of its Vice-Presidents.

5. As from 1 November 2014, the Commission shall consist of a number of members, including its President and the High Representative of the Union for Foreign Affairs and Security Policy, corresponding to two thirds of the number of Member States, unless the European Council, acting unanimously, decides to alter this number.

The members of the Commission shall be selected from among the nationals of the Member States on the basis of a system of strictly equal rotation between the Member States, reflecting the demographic and geographical range of all the Member States. This system shall be established unanimously by the European Council in accordance with Article 244 of the Treaty on the Functioning of the European Union.

6. The President of the Commission shall:
   (a) lay down guidelines within which the Commission is to work;
   (b) decide on the internal organisation of the Commission, ensuring that it acts consistently, efficiently and as a collegiate body;
   (c) appoint Vice-Presidents, other than the High Representative of the Union for Foreign Affairs and Security Policy, from among the members of the Commission.

   A member of the Commission shall resign if the President so requests. The High Representative of the Union for Foreign Affairs and Security Policy shall resign, in accordance with the procedure set out in Article 18(1), if the President so requests.

7. Taking into account the elections to the European Parliament and after having held the appropriate consultations, the European Council, acting by a qualified majority, shall propose to the European Parliament a candidate for President of the Commission. This candidate shall be elected by the European Parliament by a majority of its component members. If he does not obtain the required majority, the European Council, acting by a qualified majority, shall within one month propose a new candidate who shall be elected by the European Parliament following the same procedure.

   The Council, by common accord with the President-elect, shall adopt the list of the other persons whom it proposes for appointment as members of the Commission. They shall be selected, on the basis of the suggestions made by Member States, in accordance with the criteria set out in paragraph 3, second subparagraph, and paragraph 5, second subparagraph.

   The President, the High Representative of the Union for Foreign Affairs and Security Policy and the other members of the Commission shall be subject as a body to a vote of consent by the European Parliament. On the basis of this consent the Commission shall be appointed by the European Council, acting by a qualified majority.

8. The Commission, as a body, shall be responsible to the European Parliament. In accordance with Article 234 of the Treaty on the Functioning of the European Union, the European Parliament may vote on a motion of censure of the Commission. If such a motion is carried, the members of the Commission shall resign as a body and the High Representative of the Union for Foreign Affairs and Security Policy shall resign from the duties that he carries out in the Commission.

Article 18

1. The European Council, acting by a qualified majority, with the agreement of the President of the Commission, shall appoint the High Representative of the Union for Foreign Affairs and Security Policy. The European Council may end his term of office by the same procedure.

2. The High Representative shall conduct the Union's common foreign and security policy. He shall contribute by his proposals to the development of that policy, which he shall carry out as mandated by the Council. The same shall apply to the common security and defence policy.

3. The High Representative shall preside over the Foreign Affairs Council.

4. The High Representative shall be one of the Vice-Presidents of the Commission. He shall ensure the consistency of the Union's external action. He shall be responsible within the Commission for responsibilities incumbent on it in external relations and for coordinating other aspects of the Union's external action. In exercising these responsibilities within the Commission, and only for these responsibilities, the High Representative shall be bound by Commission procedures to the extent that this is consistent with paragraphs 2 and 3.

Article 19

1. The Court of Justice of the European Union shall include the Court of Justice, the General Court and specialised courts. It shall ensure that in the interpretation and application of the Treaties the law is observed.

Member States shall provide remedies sufficient to ensure effective legal protection in the fields covered by Union law.

2. The Court of Justice shall consist of one judge from each Member State. It shall be assisted by Advocates-General.

The General Court shall include at least one judge per Member State.

The Judges and the Advocates-General of the Court of Justice and the Judges of the General Court shall be chosen from persons whose independence is beyond doubt and who satisfy the conditions set out in Articles 253 and 254 of the Treaty on the Functioning of the European Union. They shall be appointed by common accord of the governments of the Member States for six years. Retiring Judges and Advocates General may be reappointed.

3. The Court of Justice of the European Union shall, in accordance with the Treaties:

(a) rule on actions brought by a Member State, an institution or a natural or legal person;

(b) give preliminary rulings, at the request of courts or tribunals of the Member States, on the interpretation of Union law or the validity of acts adopted by the institutions;

(c) rule in other cases provided for in the Treaties.

TITLE IV
PROVISIONS ON ENHANCED CO-OPERATION

Article 20

1. Member States which wish to establish enhanced cooperation between themselves within the framework of the Union's non-exclusive competences may make use of its institutions and exercise those competences by applying the relevant provisions of the Treaties, subject to the limits and in accordance with the detailed arrangements laid down in this Article and in Articles 326 to 334 of the Treaty on the Functioning of the European Union.

Enhanced cooperation shall aim to further the objectives of the Union, protect its interests and reinforce its integration process. Such cooperation shall be open at any time to all Member States, in accordance with Article 328 of the Treaty on the Functioning of the European Union.

2. The decision authorising enhanced cooperation shall be adopted by the Council as a last resort, when it has established that the objectives of such cooperation cannot be attained within a reasonable period by the Union as a whole, and provided that at least nine Member States participate in it. The Council shall act in accordance with the procedure laid down in Article 329 of the Treaty on the Functioning of the European Union.

3. All members of the Council may participate in its deliberations, but only members of the Council representing the Member States participating in enhanced cooperation shall take part in the vote. The voting rules are set out in Article 330 of the Treaty on the Functioning of the European Union.

4. Acts adopted in the framework of enhanced cooperation shall bind only participating Member States. They shall not be regarded as part of the acquis which has to be accepted by candidate States for accession to the Union.

TITLE V
GENERAL PROVISIONS ON THE UNION'S EXTERNAL ACTION AND SPECIFIC PROVISIONS ON THE COMMON FOREIGN AND SECURITY POLICY

CHAPTER I
PROVISIONS HAVING GENERAL APPLICATION

Article 21

1. The Union's action on the international scene shall be guided by the principles which have inspired its own creation, development and enlargement, and which it seeks to advance in the wider world: democracy, the rule of law, the universality and indivisibility of human rights and fundamental freedoms, respect for human dignity, the principles of equality and solidarity, and respect for the principles of the United Nations Charter and international law.

The Union shall seek to develop relations and build partnerships with third countries, and international, regional or global organisations which share the principles referred to in the first subparagraph. It shall promote multilateral solutions to common problems, in particular in the framework of the United Nations.

2. The Union shall define and pursue common policies and actions, and shall work for a high degree of cooperation in all fields of international relations, in order to:

(a) safeguard its values, fundamental interests, security, independence and integrity;

(b) consolidate and support democracy, the rule of law, human rights and the principles of international law;

(c) preserve peace, prevent conflicts and strengthen international security, in accordance with the purposes and principles of the United Nations Charter, with the principles of the Helsinki Final Act and with the aims of the Charter of Paris, including those relating to external borders;

(d) foster the sustainable economic, social and environmental development of developing countries, with the primary aim of eradicating poverty;

(e) encourage the integration of all countries into the world economy, including through the progressive abolition of restrictions on international trade;

(f) help develop international measures to preserve and improve the quality of the environment and the sustainable management of global natural resources, in order to ensure sustainable development;

(g) assist populations, countries and regions confronting natural or man-made disasters; and

(h) promote an international system based on stronger multilateral cooperation and good global governance.

3. The Union shall respect the principles and pursue the objectives set out in paragraphs 1 and 2 in the development and implementation of the different areas of the Union's external action covered by this Title and by Part Five of the Treaty on the Functioning of the European Union, and of the external aspects of its other policies.

The Union shall ensure consistency between the different areas of its external action and between these and its other policies. The Council and the Commission, assisted by the High Representative of the Union for Foreign Affairs and Security Policy, shall ensure that consistency and shall cooperate to that effect.

CHAPTER 2
SPECIFIC PROVISIONS CONCERNING THE COMMON FOREIGN AND SECURITY POLICY

SECTION 1
COMMON PROVISIONS

Article 23

The Union's action on the international scene, pursuant to this Chapter, shall be guided by the principles, shall pursue the objectives of, and be conducted in accordance with, the general provisions laid down in Chapter 1.

Article 24

1. The Union's competence in matters of common foreign and security policy shall cover all areas of foreign policy and all questions relating to the Union's security, including the progressive framing of a common defence policy that might lead to a common defence.

The common foreign and security policy is subject to specific rules and procedures. It shall be defined and implemented by the European Council and the Council acting unanimously, except where the Treaties provide otherwise. The adoption of legislative acts shall be excluded. The common foreign and security policy shall be put into effect by the High Representative of the Union for Foreign Affairs and Security Policy and by Member States, in accordance with the Treaties. The specific role of the European Parliament and of the

Commission in this area is defined by the Treaties. The Court of Justice of the European Union shall not have jurisdiction with respect to these provisions, with the exception of its jurisdiction to monitor compliance with Article 40 of this Treaty and to review the legality of certain decisions as provided for by the second paragraph of Article 275 of the Treaty on the Functioning of the European Union.

2. Within the framework of the principles and objectives of its external action, the Union shall conduct, define and implement a common foreign and security policy, based on the development of mutual political solidarity among Member States, the identification of questions of general interest and the achievement of an ever increasing degree of convergence of Member States' actions.

3. The Member States shall support the Union's external and security policy actively and unreservedly in a spirit of loyalty and mutual solidarity and shall comply with the Union's action in this area.

    The Member States shall work together to enhance and develop their mutual political solidarity. They shall refrain from any action which is contrary to the interests of the Union or likely to impair its effectiveness as a cohesive force in international relations.

    The Council and the High Representative shall ensure compliance with these principles.

Article 25

The Union shall conduct the common foreign and security policy by:

(a) defining the general guidelines,

(b) adopting decisions defining:

   (i)   actions to be undertaken by the Union;

   (ii)   positions to be taken by the Union;

   (iii) arrangements for the implementation of the decisions referred to in points (i) and (ii);

   and by

(c) strengthening systematic cooperation between Member States in the conduct of policy.

Article 28

1. Where the international situation requires operational action by the Union, the Council shall adopt the necessary decisions. They shall lay down their objectives, scope, the means to be made available to the Union, if necessary their duration, and the conditions for their implementation.

    If there is a change in circumstances having a substantial effect on a question subject to such a decision, the Council shall review the principles and objectives of that decision and take the necessary decisions.

2. Decisions referred to in paragraph 1 shall commit the Member States in the positions they adopt and in the conduct of their activity.

3. Whenever there is any plan to adopt a national position or take national action pursuant to a decision as referred to in paragraph I, information shall be provided by the Member State concerned in time to allow, if necessary, for prior consultations within the Council. The obligation to provide prior information shall not apply to measures which are merely a national transposition of Council decisions.

4. In cases of imperative need arising from changes in the situation and failing a review of the Council decision as referred to in paragraph 1, Member States may take the necessary measures as a matter of urgency having regard to the general objectives of that decision. The Member State concerned shall inform the Council immediately of any such measures.

5. Should there be any major difficulties in implementing a decision as referred to in this Article, a Member State shall refer them to the Council which shall discuss them and seek appropriate solutions. Such solutions shall not run counter to the objectives of the decision referred to in paragraph 1 or impair its effectiveness.

Article 29

The Council shall adopt decisions which shall define the approach of the Union to a particular matter of a geographical or thematic nature. Member States shall ensure that their national policies conform to the Union's positions.

Article 30

1. Any Member State, the High Representative of the Union for Foreign Affairs and Security Policy, or the High Representative with the Commission's support, may refer any question relating to the common foreign and security policy to the Council and may submit to it initiatives or proposals as appropriate.

2. In cases requiring a rapid decision, the High Representative, of his own motion, or at the request of a Member State, shall convene an extraordinary Council meeting within 48 hours or, in an emergency, within a shorter period.

Article 31

1. Decisions under this Chapter shall be taken by the European Council and the Council acting unanimously, except where this Chapter provides otherwise. The adoption of legislative acts shall be excluded.

Article 37

The Union may conclude agreements with one or more States or international organisations in implementation of this Chapter.

Article 38

Without prejudice to Article 240 of the Treaty on the Functioning of the European Union, a Political and Security Committee shall monitor the international situation in the areas covered by the common foreign and security policy and contribute to the definition of policies by delivering opinions to the Council at the request of the Council or of the High Representative of the Union for Foreign Affairs and Security Policy or on its own initiative. It shall also monitor the implementation of agreed policies, without prejudice to the powers of the High Representative.

Within the scope of this Chapter, the Political and Security Committee shall exercise, under the responsibility of the Council and of the High Representative, the political control and strategic direction of crisis management operations referred to in Article 43.

The Council may authorise the Committee, for the purpose and for the duration of a crisis management operation, as determined by the Council, to take the relevant decisions concerning the political control and strategic direction of the operation.

Article 39

In accordance with Article 16 of the Treaty on the Functioning of the European Union and by way of derogation from paragraph 2 thereof, the Council shall adopt a decision laying down the rules relating to the protection of individuals with regard to the processing of personal data by the Member States when carrying out activities which fall within the scope of this Chapter, and the rules relating to the free movement of such data. Compliance with these rules shall be subject to the control of independent authorities.

SECTION 2
PROVISIONS ON THE COMMON SECURITY AND DEFENCE POLICY

Article 42

1. The common security and defence policy shall be an integral part of the common foreign and security policy. It shall provide the Union with an operational capacity drawing on civilian and military assets. The Union may use them on missions outside the Union for peace-keeping, conflict prevention and strengthening international security in accordance with the principles of the United Nations Charter. The performance of these tasks shall be undertaken using capabilities provided by the Member States.

2. The common security and defence policy shall include the progressive framing of a common Union defence policy. This will lead to a common defence, when the European Council,

acting unanimously, so decides. It shall in that case recommend to the Member States the adoption of such a decision in accordance with their respective constitutional requirements.

The policy of the Union in accordance with this Section shall not prejudice the specific character of the security and defence policy of certain Member States and shall respect the obligations of certain Member States, which see their common defence realised in the North Atlantic Treaty Organisation (NATO), under the North Atlantic Treaty and be compatible with the common security and defence policy established within that framework.

3. Member States shall make civilian and military capabilities available to the Union for the implementation of the common security and defence policy, to contribute to the objectives defined by the Council. Those Member States which together establish multinational forces may also make them available to the common security and defence policy.

Member States shall undertake progressively to improve their military capabilities. An Agency in the field of defence capabilities development, research, acquisition and armaments (hereinafter referred to as 'the European Defence Agency') shall identify operational requirements, shall promote measures to satisfy those requirements, shall contribute to identifying and, where appropriate, implementing any measure needed to strengthen the industrial and technological base of the defence sector, shall participate in defining a European capabilities and armaments policy, and shall assist the Council in evaluating the improvement of military capabilities.

4. Decisions relating to the common security and defence policy, including those initiating a mission as referred to in this Article, shall be adopted by the Council acting unanimously on a proposal from the High Representative of the Union for Foreign Affairs and Security Policy or an initiative from a Member State. The High Representative may propose the use of both national resources and Union instruments, together with the Commission where appropriate.

5. The Council may entrust the execution of a task, within the Union framework, to a group of Member States in order to protect the Union's values and serve its interests. The execution of such a task shall be governed by Article 44.

6. Those Member States whose military capabilities fulfil higher criteria and which have made more binding commitments to one another in this area with a view to the most demanding missions shall establish permanent structured cooperation within the Union framework. Such cooperation shall be governed by Article 46. It shall not affect the provisions of Article 43.

7. If a Member State is the victim of armed aggression on its territory, the other Member States shall have towards it an obligation of aid and assistance by all the means in their power, in accordance with Article 51 of the United Nations Charter. This shall not prejudice the specific character of the security and defence policy of certain Member States.

Commitments and cooperation in this area shall be consistent with commitments under the North Atlantic Treaty Organisation, which, for those States which are members of it, remains the foundation of their collective defence and the forum for its implementation.

Article 43

1. The tasks referred to in Article 42(1), in the course of which the Union may use civilian and military means, shall include joint disarmament operations, humanitarian and rescue tasks, military advice and assistance tasks, conflict prevention and peacekeeping tasks, tasks of combat forces in crisis management, including peace-making and post-conflict stabilisation. All these tasks may contribute to the fight against terrorism, including by supporting third countries in combating terrorism in their territories.

2. The Council shall adopt decisions relating to the tasks referred to in paragraph 1, defining their objectives and scope and the general conditions for their implementation. The High Representative of the Union for Foreign Affairs and Security Policy, acting under the authority of the Council and in close and constant contact with the Political and Security Committee, shall ensure coordination of the civilian and military aspects of such tasks.

Article 45

1. The European Defence Agency referred to in Article 42(3), subject to the authority of the Council, shall have as its task to:

    (a) contribute to identifying the Member States' military capability objectives and evaluating observance of the capability commitments given by the Member States;

    (b) promote harmonisation of operational needs and adoption of effective, compatible procurement methods;

    (c) propose multilateral projects to fulfil the objectives in terms of military capabilities, ensure coordination of the programmes implemented by the Member States and management of specific cooperation programmes;

    (d) support defence technology research, and coordinate and plan joint research activities and the study of technical solutions meeting future operational needs;

    (e) contribute to identifying and, if necessary, implementing any useful measure for strengthening the industrial and technological base of the defence sector and for improving the effectiveness of military expenditure.

2. The European Defence Agency shall be open to all Member States wishing to be part of it. The Council, acting by a qualified majority, shall adopt a decision defining the Agency's statute, seat and operational rules. That decision should take account of the level of effective participation in the Agency's activities. Specific groups shall be set up within the Agency bringing together Member States engaged in joint projects. The Agency shall carry out its tasks in liaison with the Commission where necessary.

TITLE VI

FINAL PROVISIONS

Article 47

The Union shall have legal personality.

CONSOLIDATED VERSION OF THE
TREATY ON THE FUNCTIONING OF THE EUROPEAN UNION

[THE CONTRACTING PARTIES]

DETERMINED to lay the foundations of an ever closer union among the peoples of Europe,

RESOLVED to ensure the economic and social progress of their States by common action to eliminate the barriers which divide Europe,

AFFIRMING as the essential objective of their efforts the constant improvements of the living and working conditions of their peoples,

RECOGNISING that the removal of existing obstacles calls for concerted action in order to guarantee steady expansion, balanced trade and fair competition,

ANXIOUS to strengthen the unity of their economies and to ensure their harmonious development by reducing the differences existing between the various regions and the backwardness of the less favoured regions,

DESIRING to contribute, by means of a common commercial policy, to the progressive abolition of restrictions on international trade,

INTENDING to confirm the solidarity which binds Europe and the overseas countries and desiring to ensure the development of their prosperity, in accordance with the principles of the Charter of the United Nations,

RESOLVED by thus pooling their resources to preserve and strengthen peace and liberty, and calling upon the other peoples of Europe who share their ideal to join in their efforts,

DETERMINED to promote the development of the highest possible level of knowledge for their peoples through a wide access to education and through its continuous updating,

and to this end ... have agreed as follows.

PART ONE

PRINCIPLES

Article 1

1. This Treaty organises the functioning of the Union and determines the areas of, delimitation of, and arrangements for exercising its competences.
2. This Treaty and the Treaty on European Union constitute the Treaties on which the Union is founded. These two Treaties, which have the same legal value, shall be referred to as 'the Treaties'.

TITLE I

CATEGORIES AND AREAS OF UNION COMPETENCE

Article 2

1. When the Treaties confer on the Union exclusive competence in a specific area, only the Union may legislate and adopt legally binding acts, the Member States being able to do so themselves only if so empowered by the Union or for the implementation of acts of the Union.
2. When the Treaties confer on the Union a competence shared with the Member States in a specific area, the Union and the Member States may legislate and adopt legally binding acts in that area. The Member States shall exercise their competence to the extent that the Union has not exercised its competence. The Member States shall exercise their competence again to the extent that the Union has decided to cease exercising its competence.
3. The Member States shall coordinate their economic and employment policies within arrangements as determined by this Treaty, which the Union shall have competence to provide.
4. The Union shall have competence, in accordance with the provisions of the Treaty on European Union, to define and implement a common foreign and security policy, including the progressive framing of a common defence policy.
5. In certain areas and under the conditions laid down in the Treaties, the Union shall have competence to carry out actions to support, coordinate or supplement the actions of the Member States, without thereby superseding their competence in these areas.

   Legally binding acts of the Union adopted on the basis of the provisions in the Treaties relating to these areas shall not entail harmonisation of Member States' laws or regulations.
6. The scope of and arrangements for exercising the Union's competences shall be determined by the provisions of the Treaties relating to each area.

Article 3

1. The Union shall have exclusive competence in the following areas:
   (a) customs union;
   (b) the establishing of the competition rules necessary for the functioning of the internal market;
   (c) monetary policy for the Member States whose currency is the euro;
   (d) the conservation of marine biological resources under the common fisheries policy;
   (e) common commercial policy.
2. The Union shall also have exclusive competence for the conclusion of an international agreement when its conclusion is provided for in a legislative act of the Union or is necessary to enable the Union to exercise its internal competence, or insofar as its conclusion may affect common rules or alter their scope.

Article 4

1. The Union shall share competence with the Member States where the Treaties confer on it a competence which does not relate to the areas referred to in Articles 3 and 6.
2. Shared competence between the Union and the Member States applies in the following principal areas:
   (a) internal market;
   (b) social policy, for the aspects defined in this Treaty;

      (c)   economic, social and territorial cohesion;

      (d)   agriculture and fisheries, excluding the conservation of marine biological resources;

      (e)   environment;

      (f)   consumer protection;

      (g)   transport;

      (h)   trans-European networks;

      (i)   energy;

      (j)   area of freedom, security and justice;

      (k)   common safety concerns in public health matters, for the aspects defined in this Treaty.

3.   In the areas of research, technological development and space, the Union shall have competence to carry out activities, in particular to define and implement programmes; however, the exercise of that competence shall not result in Member States being prevented from exercising theirs.

4.   In the areas of development cooperation and humanitarian aid, the Union shall have competence to carry out activities and conduct a common policy; however, the exercise of that competence shall not result in Member States being prevented from exercising theirs.

Article 5

1.   The Member States shall coordinate their economic policies within the Union. To this end, the Council shall adopt measures, in particular broad guidelines for these policies.

      Specific provisions shall apply to those Member States whose currency is the euro.

2.   The Union shall take measures to ensure coordination of the employment policies of the Member States, in particular by defining guidelines for these policies.

3.   The Union may take initiatives to ensure coordination of Member States' social policies.

Article 6

The Union shall have competence to carry out actions to support, coordinate or supplement the actions of the Member States. The areas of such action shall, at European level, be:

      (a)   protection and improvement of human health;

      (b)   industry;

      (c)   culture;

      (d)   tourism;

      (e)   education, vocational training, youth and sport;

      (f)   civil protection;

      (g)   administrative cooperation.

TITLE II
PROVISIONS HAVING GENERAL APPLICATION

Article 7

The Union shall ensure consistency between its policies and activities, taking all of its objectives into account and in accordance with the principle of conferral of powers.

Article 8

In all its activities, the Union shall aim to eliminate inequalities, and to promote equality, between men and women.

Article 9

In defining and implementing its policies and actions, the Union shall take into account requirements linked to the promotion of a high level of employment, the guarantee of adequate social protection, the fight against social exclusion, and a high level of education, training and protection of human health.

Article 10

In defining and implementing its policies and activities, the Union shall aim to combat discrimination based on sex, racial or ethnic origin, religion or belief, disability, age or sexual orientation.

Article 11

Environmental protection requirements must be integrated into the definition and implementation of the Union policies and activities, in particular with a view to promoting sustainable development.

Article 12

Consumer protection requirements shall be taken into account in defining and implementing other Union policies and activities.

Article 13

In formulating and implementing the Union's agriculture, fisheries, transport, internal market, research and technological development and space policies, the Union and the Member States shall, since animals are sentient beings, pay full regard to the welfare requirements of animals, while respecting the legislative or administrative provisions and customs of the Member States relating in particular to religious rites, cultural traditions and regional heritage.

Article 14

Without prejudice to Article 4 of the Treaty on European Union or to Articles 93, 106 and 107 of this Treaty, and given the place occupied by services of general economic interest in the shared values of the Union as well as their role in promoting social and territorial cohesion, the Union and the Member States, each within their respective powers and within the scope of application of the Treaties, shall take care that such services operate on the basis of principles and conditions, particularly economic and financial conditions, which enable them to fulfil their missions. The European Parliament and the Council, acting by means of regulations in accordance with the ordinary legislative procedure, shall establish these principles and set these conditions without prejudice to the competence of Member States, in compliance with the Treaties, to provide, to commission and to fund such services.

Article 15

1.   In order to promote good governance and ensure the participation of civil society, the institutions, bodies, offices and agencies of the Union shall conduct their work as openly as possible.
2.   The European Parliament shall meet in public, as shall the Council when considering and voting on a draft legislative act.
3.   Any citizen of the Union, and any natural or legal person residing or having its registered office in a Member State, shall have a right of access to documents of the Union institutions, bodies, offices and agencies, whatever their medium, subject to the principles and the conditions to be defined in accordance with this paragraph.

     General principles and limits on grounds of public or private interest governing this right of access to documents shall be determined by the European Parliament and the Council, acting by means of regulations in accordance with the ordinary legislative procedure.

     Each institution, body, office or agency shall ensure that its proceedings are transparent and shall elaborate in its own Rules of Procedure specific provisions regarding access to its documents, in accordance with the regulations referred to in the second subparagraph.

     The Court of Justice of the European Union, the European Central Bank and the European Investment Bank shall be subject to this paragraph only when exercising their administrative tasks.

     The European Parliament and the Council shall ensure publication of the documents relating to the legislative procedures under the terms laid down by the regulation referred to in the second subparagraph.

Article 16

1.   Everyone has the right to the protection of personal data concerning them.
2.   The European Parliament and the Council, acting in accordance with the ordinary legislative procedure, shall lay down the rules relating to the protection of individuals with regard to the processing of personal data by Union institutions, bodies, offices and agencies, and by the Member States when carrying out activities which fall within the scope of Union law, and the

rules relating to the free movement of such data. Compliance with these rules shall be subject to the control of independent authorities.

The rules adopted on the basis of this article shall be without prejudice to the specific rules laid down in Article 39 of the Treaty on European Union.

Article 17

1. The Union respects and does not prejudice the status under national law of churches and religious associations or communities in the Member States.
2. The Union equally respects the status under national law of philosophical and non-confessional organisations.
3. Recognising their identity and their specific contribution, the Union shall maintain an open, transparent and regular dialogue with these churches and organisations.

PART TWO
NON-DISCRIMINATION AND CITIZENSHIP OF THE UNION

Article 18

Within the scope of application of the Treaties, and without prejudice to any special provisions contained therein, any discrimination on grounds of nationality shall be prohibited.

The European Parliament and the Council, acting in accordance with the ordinary legislative procedure, may adopt rules designed to prohibit such discrimination.

Article 19

1. Without prejudice to the other provisions of the Treaties and within the limits of the powers conferred by them upon the Union, the Council, acting unanimously in accordance with a special legislative procedure and after obtaining the consent of the European Parliament, may take appropriate action to combat discrimination based on sex, racial or ethnic origin, religion or belief, disability, age or sexual orientation.
2. By way of derogation from paragraph 1, the European Parliament and the Council, acting in accordance with the ordinary legislative procedure, may adopt the basic principles of the Union's incentive measures, excluding any harmonisation of the laws and regulations of the Member States, to support action taken by the Member States in order to contribute to the achievement of the objectives referred to in paragraph 1.

Article 20

1. Citizenship of the Union is hereby established. Every person holding the nationality of a Member State shall be a citizen of the Union. Citizenship of the Union shall be additional to and not replace national citizenship.
2. Citizens of the Union shall enjoy the rights and be subject to the duties provided for in the Treaties. They shall have, *inter alia*:
   (a) the right to move and reside freely within the territory of the Member States;
   (b) the right to vote and to stand as candidates in elections to the European Parliament and in municipal elections in their Member State of residence, under the same conditions as nationals of that State;
   (c) the right to enjoy, in the territory of a third country in which the Member State of which they are nationals is not represented, the protection of the diplomatic and consular authorities of any Member State on the same conditions as the nationals of that State;
   (d) the right to petition the European Parliament, to apply to the European Ombudsman, and to address the institutions and advisory bodies of the Union in any of the Treaty languages and to obtain a reply in the same language.

   These rights shall be exercised in accordance with the conditions and limits defined by the Treaties and by the measures adopted thereunder.

Article 21

1. Every citizen of the Union shall have the right to move and reside freely within the territory of the Member States, subject to the limitations and conditions laid down in the Treaties and by the measures adopted to give them effect.

2. If action by the Union should prove necessary to attain this objective and the Treaties have not provided the necessary powers, the European Parliament and the Council, acting in accordance with the ordinary legislative procedure, may adopt provisions with a view to facilitating the exercise of the rights referred to in paragraph 1.

3. For the same purposes as those referred to in paragraph 1 and if the Treaties have not provided the necessary powers, the Council, acting in accordance with a special legislative procedure, may adopt measures concerning social security or social protection. The Council shall act unanimously after consulting the European Parliament.

Article 22

1. Every citizen of the Union residing in a Member State of which he is not a national shall have the right to vote and to stand as a candidate at municipal elections in the Member State in which he resides, under the same conditions as nationals of that State. This right shall be exercised subject to detailed arrangements adopted by the Council, acting unanimously in accordance with a special legislative procedure and after consulting the European Parliament; these arrangements may provide for derogations where warranted by problems specific to a Member State.

2. Without prejudice to Article 223(1) and to the provisions adopted for its implementation, every citizen of the Union residing in a Member State of which he is not a national shall have the right to vote and to stand as a candidate in elections to the European Parliament in the Member State in which he resides, under the same conditions as nationals of that State. This right shall be exercised subject to detailed arrangements adopted by the Council, acting unanimously in accordance with a special legislative procedure and after consulting the European Parliament; these arrangements may provide for derogations where warranted by problems specific to a Member State.

Article 23

Every citizen of the Union shall, in the territory of a third country in which the Member State of which he is a national is not represented, be entitled to protection by the diplomatic or consular authorities of any Member State, on the same conditions as the nationals of that State. Member States shall adopt the necessary provisions and start the international negotiations required to secure this protection.

The Council, acting in accordance with a special legislative procedure and after consulting the European Parliament, may adopt directives establishing the coordination and cooperation measures necessary to facilitate such protection.

Article 24

The European Parliament and the Council, acting by means of regulations in accordance with the ordinary legislative procedure, shall adopt the provisions for the procedures and conditions required for a citizens' initiative within the meaning of Article 11 of the Treaty on European Union, including the minimum number of Member States from which such citizens must come.

Every citizen of the Union shall have the right to petition the European Parliament in accordance with Article 227.

Every citizen of the Union may apply to the Ombudsman established in accordance with Article 228.

Every citizen of the Union may write to any of the institutions or bodies referred to in this Article or in Article 13 of the Treaty on European Union in one of the languages mentioned in Article 55(1) of the Treaty on European Union and have an answer in the same language.

PART THREE
UNION POLICIES AND INTERNAL ACTIONS

TITLE I
THE INTERNAL MARKET

Article 26

1. The Union shall adopt measures with the aim of establishing or ensuring the functioning of the internal market, in accordance with the relevant provisions of the Treaties.

2.   The internal market shall comprise an area without internal frontiers in which the free movement of goods, persons, services and capital is ensured in accordance with the provisions of the Treaties.

3.   The Council, on a proposal from the Commission, shall determine the guidelines and conditions necessary to ensure balanced progress in all the sectors concerned.

Article 27

When drawing up its proposals with a view to achieving the objectives set out in Article 26, the Commission shall take into account the extent of the effort that certain economies showing differences in development will have to sustain for the establishment of the internal market and it may propose appropriate provisions.

If these provisions take the form of derogations, they must be of a temporary nature and must cause the least possible disturbance to the functioning of the internal market.

TITLE II

FREE MOVEMENT OF GOODS

Article 28

1.   The Union shall comprise a customs union which shall cover all trade in goods and which shall involve the prohibition between Member States of customs duties on imports and exports and of all charges having equivalent effect, and the adoption of a common customs tariff in their relations with third countries.

2.   The provisions of Article 30 and of Chapter 2 of this Title shall apply to products originating in Member States and to products coming from third countries which are in free circulation in Member States.

Article 29

Products coming from a third country shall be considered to be in free circulation in a Member State if the import formalities have been complied with and any customs duties or charges having equivalent effect which are payable have been levied in that Member State, and if they have not benefited from a total or partial drawback of such duties or charges.

CHAPTER 1

THE CUSTOMS UNION

Article 30

Customs duties on imports and exports and charges having equivalent effect shall be prohibited between Member States. This prohibition shall also apply to customs duties of a fiscal nature.

Article 31

Common Customs Tariff duties shall be fixed by the Council on a proposal from the Commission.

Article 32

In carrying out the tasks entrusted to it under this chapter the Commission shall be guided by:

(a)   the need to promote trade between Member States and third countries;

(b)   developments in conditions of competition within the Union in so far as they lead to an improvement in the competitive capacity of undertakings;

(c)   the requirements of the Union as regards the supply of raw materials and semifinished goods; in this connection the Commission shall take care to avoid distorting conditions of competition between Member States in respect of finished goods;

(d)   the need to avoid serious disturbances in the economies of Member States and to ensure rational development of production and an expansion of consumption within the Union.

CHAPTER 2

CUSTOMS COOPERATION

Article 33

Within the scope of application of the Treaties, the European Parliament and the Council, acting in accordance with the ordinary legislative procedure, shall take measures in order to strengthen customs cooperation between Member States and between the latter and the Commission.

CHAPTER 3
PROHIBITION OF QUANTITATIVE RESTRICTIONS BETWEEN MEMBER STATES

Article 34

Quantitative restrictions on imports and all measures having equivalent effect shall be prohibited between Member States.

Article 35

Quantitative restrictions on exports, and all measures having equivalent effect, shall be prohibited between Member States.

Article 36

The provisions of Articles 34 and 35 shall not preclude prohibitions or restrictions on imports, exports or goods in transit justified on grounds of public morality, public policy or public security; the protection of health and life of humans, animals or plants; the protection of national treasures possessing artistic, historic or archaeological value; or the protection of industrial and commercial property. Such prohibitions or restrictions shall not, however, constitute a means of arbitrary discrimination or a disguised restriction on trade between Member States.

Article 37

1. Member States shall adjust any State monopolies of a commercial character so as to ensure that no discrimination regarding the conditions under which goods are procured and marketed exists between nationals of Member States.
    The provisions of this Article shall apply to any body through which a Member State, in law or in fact, either directly or indirectly supervises, determines or appreciably influences imports or exports between Member States. These provisions shall likewise apply to monopolies delegated by the State to others.
2. Member States shall refrain from introducing any new measure which is contrary to the principles laid down in paragraph 1 or which restricts the scope of the articles dealing with the prohibition of customs duties and quantitative restrictions between Member States.
3. If a State monopoly of a commercial character has rules which are designed to make it easier to dispose of agricultural products or obtain for them the best return, steps should be taken in applying the rules contained in this article to ensure equivalent safeguards for the employment and standard of living of the producers concerned.

TITLE III
AGRICULTURE AND FISHERIES

Article 38

1. The Union shall define and implement a common agriculture and fisheries policy.
    The internal market shall extend to agriculture, fisheries and trade in agricultural products. 'Agricultural products' means the products of the soil, of stock farming and of fisheries and products of first-stage processing directly related to these products. References to the common agricultural policy or to agriculture, and the use of the term 'agricultural', shall be understood as also referring to fisheries, having regard to the specific characteristics of this sector.
2. Save as otherwise provided in Articles 39 to 44, the rules laid down for the establishment and functioning of the internal market shall apply to agricultural products.
3. The products subject to the provisions of Articles 39 to 44 are listed in Annex I.
4. The operation and development of the internal market for agricultural products must be accompanied by the establishment of a common agricultural policy.

Article 39

1. The objectives of the common agricultural policy shall be:
    (a) to increase agricultural productivity by promoting technical progress and by ensuring the rational development of agricultural production and the optimum utilisation of the factors of production, in particular labour;

(b)   thus to ensure a fair standard of living for the agricultural community, in particular by increasing the individual earnings of persons engaged in agriculture;
(c)   to stabilise markets;
(d)   to assure the availability of supplies;
(e)   to ensure that supplies reach consumers at reasonable prices.

2.   In working out the common agricultural policy and the special methods for its application, account shall be taken of:

(a)   the particular nature of agricultural activity, which results from the social structure of agriculture and from structural and natural disparities between the various agricultural regions;
(b)   the need to effect the appropriate adjustments by degrees;
(c)   the fact that in the Member States agriculture constitutes a sector closely linked with the economy as a whole.

Article 40

1.   In order to attain the objectives set out in Article 39, a common organisation of agricultural markets shall be established.

This organisation shall take one of the following forms, depending on the product concerned:

(a)   common rules on competition;
(b)   compulsory coordination of the various national market organisations;
(c)   a European market organisation.

2.   The common organisation established in accordance with paragraph 1 may include all measures required to attain the objectives set out in Article 39, in particular regulation of prices, aids for the production and marketing of the various products, storage and carryover arrangements and common machinery for stabilising imports or exports.

The common organisation shall be limited to pursuit of the objectives set out in Article 39 and shall exclude any discrimination between producers or consumers within the Union.

Any common price policy shall be based on common criteria and uniform methods of calculation.

3.   In order to enable the common organisation referred to in paragraph 1 to attain its objectives, one or more agricultural guidance and guarantee funds may be set up.

Article 41

To enable the objectives set out in Article 39 to be attained, provision may be made within the framework of the common agricultural policy for measures such as:

(a)   an effective coordination of efforts in the spheres of vocational training, of research and of the dissemination of agricultural knowledge; this may include joint financing of projects or institutions;
(b)   joint measures to promote consumption of certain products.

Article 42

The provisions of the Chapter relating to rules on competition shall apply to production of and trade in agricultural products only to the extent determined by the European Parliament and the Council within the framework of Article 43(2) and in accordance with the procedure laid down therein, account being taken of the objectives set out in Article 39.

The Council, on a proposal from the Commission, may authorise the granting of aid:

(a)   for the protection of enterprises handicapped by structural or natural conditions;
(b)   within the framework of economic development programmes.

Article 43

1.   The Commission shall submit proposals for working out and implementing the common agricultural policy, including the replacement of the national organisations by one of the forms of common organisation provided for in Article 40(1), and for implementing the measures specified in this title.

These proposals shall take account of the interdependence of the agricultural matters mentioned in this title.

Article 44

Where in a Member State a product is subject to a national market organisation or to internal rules having equivalent effect which affect the competitive position of similar production in another Member State, a countervailing charge shall be applied by Member States to imports of this product coming from the Member State where such organisation or rules exist, unless that State applies a countervailing charge on export.

The Commission shall fix the amount of these charges at the level required to redress the balance; it may also authorise other measures, the conditions and details of which it shall determine.

TITLE IV
FREE MOVEMENT OF PERSONS, SERVICES AND CAPITAL

CHAPTER 1
WORKERS

Article 45

1. Freedom of movement for workers shall be secured within the Union.
2. Such freedom of movement shall entail the abolition of any discrimination based on nationality between workers of the Member States as regards employment, remuneration and other conditions of work and employment.
3. It shall entail the right, subject to limitations justified on grounds of public policy, public security or public health:
   (a) to accept offers of employment actually made;
   (b) to move freely within the territory of Member States for this purpose;
   (c) to stay in a Member State for the purpose of employment in accordance with the provisions governing the employment of nationals of that State laid down by law, regulation or administrative action;
   (d) to remain in the territory of a Member State after having been employed in that State, subject to conditions which shall be embodied in regulations to be drawn up by the Commission.
4. The provisions of this article shall not apply to employment in the public service.

Article 46

The European Parliament and the Council shall, acting in accordance with the ordinary legislative procedure and after consulting the Economic and Social Committee, issue directives or make regulations setting out the measures required to bring about freedom of movement for workers, as defined in Article 45, in particular:
   (a) by ensuring close cooperation between national employment services;
   (b) by abolishing those administrative procedures and practices and those qualifying periods in respect of eligibility for available employment, whether resulting from national legislation or from agreements previously concluded between Member States, the maintenance of which would form an obstacle to liberalisation of the movement of workers;
   (c) by abolishing all such qualifying periods and other restrictions provided for either under national legislation or under agreements previously concluded between Member States as imposed on workers of other Member States conditions regarding the free choice of employment other than those imposed on workers of the State concerned;
   (d) by setting up appropriate machinery to bring offers of employment into touch with applications for employment and to facilitate the achievement of a balance between supply and demand in the employment market in such a way as to avoid serious threats to the standard of living and level of employment in the various regions and industries.

Article 47

Member States shall, within the framework of a joint programme, encourage the exchange of young workers.

Article 48

The European Parliament and the Council, acting in accordance with the ordinary legislative procedure, shall adopt such measures in the field of social security as are necessary to provide freedom of movement for workers; to this end, it shall make arrangements to secure for employed and self-employed migrant workers and their dependants:

(a)   aggregation, for the purpose of acquiring and retaining the right to benefit and of calculating the amount of benefit, of all periods taken into account under the laws of the several countries;

(b)   payment of benefits to persons resident in the territories of Member States.

Where a member of the Council declares that a draft legislative act referred to in the first subparagraph would affect important aspects of its social security system, including its scope, cost or financial structure, or would affect the financial balance of that system, it may request that the matter be referred to the European Council. In that case, the ordinary legislative procedure shall be suspended. After discussion, the European Council shall, within four months of this suspension, either:

(a)   refer the draft back to the Council, which shall terminate the suspension of the ordinary legislative procedure, or

(b)   take no action or request the Commission to submit a new proposal; in that case, the act originally proposed shall be deemed not to have been adopted.

CHAPTER 2

RIGHT OF ESTABLISHMENT

Article 49

Within the framework of the provisions set out below, restrictions on the freedom of establishment of nationals of a Member State in the territory of another Member State shall be prohibited. Such prohibition shall also apply to restrictions on the setting-up of agencies, branches or subsidiaries by nationals of any Member State established in the territory of any Member State.

Freedom of establishment shall include the right to take up and pursue activities as self-employed persons and to set up and manage undertakings, in particular companies or firms within the meaning of the second paragraph of Article 54, under the conditions laid down for its own nationals by the law of the country where such establishment is effected, subject to the provisions of the Chapter relating to capital.

Article 50

1.   In order to attain freedom of establishment as regards a particular activity, the European Parliament and the Council, acting in accordance with the ordinary legislative procedure and after consulting the Economic and Social Committee, shall act by means of directives.

2.   The European Parliament, the Council and the Commission shall carry out the duties devolving upon them under the preceding provisions, in particular:

(a)   by according, as a general rule, priority treatment to activities where freedom of establishment makes a particularly valuable contribution to the development of production and trade;

(b)   by ensuring close cooperation between the competent authorities in the Member States in order to ascertain the particular situation within the Union of the various activities concerned;

(c)   by abolishing those administrative procedures and practices, whether resulting from national legislation or from agreements previously concluded between Member States, the maintenance of which would form an obstacle to freedom of establishment;

(d)   by ensuring that workers of one Member State employed in the territory of another Member State may remain in that territory for the purpose of taking up activities therein as self-employed persons, where they satisfy the conditions which they would be required to satisfy if they were entering that State at the time when they intended to take up such activities;

(e)   by enabling a national of one Member State to acquire and use land and buildings situated in the territory of another Member State, in so far as this does not conflict with the principles laid down in Article 39(2);

(f)   by effecting the progressive abolition of restrictions on freedom of establishment in every branch of activity under consideration, both as regards the conditions for setting up agencies, branches or subsidiaries in the territory of a Member State and as regards the subsidiaries in the territory of a Member State and as regards the conditions governing the entry of personnel belonging to the main establishment into managerial or supervisory posts in such agencies, branches or subsidiaries;

(g)   by coordinating to the necessary extent the safeguards which, for the protection of the interests of members and other, are required by Member States of companies or firms within the meaning of the second paragraph of Article 54 with a view to making such safeguards equivalent throughout the Union;

(h)   by satisfying themselves that the conditions of establishment are not distorted by aids granted by Member States.

Article 51

The provisions of this Chapter shall not apply, so far as any given Member State is concerned, to activities which in that State are connected, even occasionally, with the exercise of official authority. The European Parliament and the Council, acting in accordance with the ordinary legislative procedure, may rule that the provisions of this Chapter shall not apply to certain activities.

Article 52

1.   The provisions of this Chapter and measures taken in pursuance thereof shall not prejudice the applicability of provisions laid down by law, regulation or administrative action providing for special treatment for foreign nationals on grounds of public policy, public security or public health.

2.   The European Parliament and the Council, acting in accordance with the ordinary legislative procedure, shall issue directives for the coordination of the abovementioned provisions.

Article 53

1.   In order to make it easier for persons to take up and pursue activities as selfemployed persons, the European Parliament and the Council, acting in accordance with the ordinary legislative procedure, shall issue directives for the mutual recognition of diplomas, certificates and other evidence of formal qualifications and for the coordination of the provisions laid down by law, regulation or administrative action in Member States concerning the taking-up and pursuit of activities as self-employed persons.

2.   In the case of the medical and allied and pharmaceutical professions, the progressive abolition of restrictions shall be dependent upon coordination of the conditions for their exercise in the various Member States.

Article 54

Companies or firms formed in accordance with the law of a Member State and having their registered office, central administration or principal place of business within the Union shall, for the purposes of this Chapter, be treated in the same way as natural persons who are nationals of Member States.

'Companies or firms' means companies or firms constituted under civil or commercial law, including cooperative societies, and other legal persons governed by public or private law, save for those which are non-profit-making.

Article 55

Member States shall accord nationals of the other Member States the same treatment as their own nationals as regards participation in the capital of companies or firms within the meaning of Article 54, without prejudice to the application of the other provisions of the Treaties.

CHAPTER 3
SERVICES

Article 56

Within the framework of the provisions set out below, restrictions on freedom to provide services within the Union shall be prohibited in respect of nationals of Member States who are established in a Member State other than that of the person for whom the services are intended.

The European Parliament and the Council, acting in the accordance with the ordinary legislative procedure, may extend the provisions of the Chapter to nationals of a third country who provide services and who are established within the Union.

Article 57

Services shall be considered to be 'services' within the meaning of the Treaties where they are normally provided for remuneration, in so far as they are not governed by the provisions relating to freedom of movement for goods, capital and persons.

'Services' shall in particular include:

  (a)   activities of an industrial character;
  (b)   activities of a commercial character;
  (c)   activities of craftsmen;
  (d)   activities of the professions.

Without prejudice to the provisions of the Chapter relating to the right of establishment, the person providing a service may, in order to do so, temporarily pursue his activity in the Member State where the service is provided, under the same conditions as are imposed by that State on its own nationals.

Article 58

1.   Freedom to provide services in the field of transport shall be governed by the provisions of the title relating to transport.

2.   The liberalisation of banking and insurance services connected with movements of capital shall be effected in step with the liberalisation of movement of capital.

Article 59

1.   In order to achieve the liberalisation of a specific service, the European Parliament and the Council, acting in accordance with the ordinary legislative procedure and after consulting the Economic and Social Committee, shall issue directives.

2.   As regards the directives referred to in paragraph 1, priority shall as a general rule be given to those services which directly affect production costs or the liberalisation of which helps to promote trade in goods.

Article 60

The Member States shall endeavour to undertake the liberalisation of services beyond the extent required by the directives issued pursuant to Article 59(1), if their general economic situation and the situation of the economic sector concerned so permit.

To this end, the Commission shall make recommendations to the Member States concerned.

Article 61

As long as restrictions on freedom to provide services have not been abolished, each Member State shall apply such restrictions without distinction on grounds of nationality or residence to all persons providing services within the meaning of the first paragraph of Article 56.

Article 62

The provisions of Articles 51 to 54 shall apply to the matters covered by this Chapter.

CHAPTER 4
CAPITAL AND PAYMENTS

Article 63

1.   Within the framework of the provisions set out in this Chapter, all restrictions on the movement of capital between Member States and between Member States and third countries shall be prohibited.

2.   Within the framework of the provisions set out in this Chapter, all restrictions on payments between Member States and between Member States and third countries shall be prohibited.

Article 64
1.   The provisions of Article 63 shall be without prejudice to the application to third countries of any restrictions which exist on 31 December 1993 under national or Union law adopted in respect of the movement of capital to or from third countries involving direct investment - including in real estate establishment, the provision of financial services or the admission of securities to capital markets. In respect of restrictions existing under national law in Bulgaria, Estonia and Hungary, the relevant date shall be 31 December 1999.
2.   Whilst endeavouring to achieve the objective of free movement of capital between Member States and third countries to the greatest extent possible and without prejudice to the other Chapters of the Treaties, the European Parliament and the Council, acting in accordance with the ordinary legislative procedure, shall adopt the measures on the movement of capital to or from third countries involving direct investment — including investment in real estate — establishment, the provision of financial services or the admission of securities to capital markets.
3.   Notwithstanding paragraph 2, only the Council, acting in accordance with a special legislative procedure, may unanimously, and after consulting the European Parliament, adopt measures which constitute a step backwards in Union law as regards the liberalisation of the movement of capital to or from third countries.

Article 65
1.   The provisions of Article 63 shall be without prejudice to the right of Member States:
     (a)   to apply the relevant provisions of their tax law which distinguish between taxpayers who are not in the same situation with regard to their place of residence or with regard to the place where their capital is invested;
     (b)   to take all requisite measures to prevent infringements of national law and regulations, in particular in the field of taxation and the prudential supervision of financial institutions, or to lay down procedures for the declaration of capital movements for purposes of administrative or statistical information, or to take measures which are justified on grounds of public policy or public security.
2.   The provisions of this Chapter shall be without prejudice to the applicability of restrictions on the right of establishment which are compatible with the Treaties.
3.   The measures and procedures referred to in paragraphs 1 and 2 shall not constitute a means of arbitrary discrimination or a disguised restriction on the free movement of capital and payments as defined in Article 63.
4.   In the absence of measures pursuant to Article 64(3), the Commission or, in the absence of a Commission decision within three months from the request of the Member State concerned, the Council, may adopt a decision stating that restrictive tax measures adopted by a Member State concerning one or more third countries are to be considered compatible with the Treaties insofar as they are justified by one of the objectives of the Union and compatible with the proper functioning of the internal market. The Council shall act unanimously on application by a Member State.

Article 66
Where, in exceptional circumstances, movements of capital to or from third countries cause, or threaten to cause, serious difficulties for the operation of economic and monetary union, the Council, on a proposal from the Commission and after consulting the European Central Bank, may take safeguard measures with regard to third countries for a period not exceeding six months if such measures are strictly necessary.

TITLE V
AREA OF FREEDOM, SECURITY AND JUSTICE

CHAPTER 1
GENERAL PROVISIONS

Article 67

1. The Union shall constitute an area of freedom, security and justice with respect for fundamental rights and the different legal systems and traditions of the Member States.
2. It shall ensure the absence of internal border controls for persons and shall frame a common policy on asylum, immigration and external border control, based on solidarity between Member States, which is fair towards third-country nationals. For the purpose of this Title, stateless persons shall be treated as third-country nationals.
3. The Union shall endeavour to ensure a high level of security through measures to prevent and combat crime, racism and xenophobia, and through measures for coordination and cooperation between police and judicial authorities and other competent authorities, as well as through the mutual recognition of judgments in criminal matters and, if necessary, through the approximation of criminal laws.
4. The Union shall facilitate access to justice, in particular through the principle of mutual recognition of judicial and extrajudicial decisions in civil matters.

Article 68

The European Council shall define the strategic guidelines for legislative and operational planning within the area of freedom, security and justice.

Article 69

National Parliaments ensure that the proposals and legislative initiatives submitted under Chapters 4 and 5 comply with the principle of subsidiarity, in accordance with the arrangements laid down by the Protocol on the application of the principles of subsidiarity and proportionality.

Article 75

Where necessary to achieve the objectives set out in Article 67, as regards preventing and combating terrorism and related activities, the European Parliament and the Council, acting by means of regulations in accordance with the ordinary legislative procedure, shall define a framework for administrative measures with regard to capital movements and payments, such as the freezing of funds, financial assets or economic gains belonging to, or owned or held by, natural or legal persons, groups or non-State entities.

The Council, on a proposal from the Commission, shall adopt measures to implement the framework referred to in the first paragraph.

The acts referred to in this Article shall include necessary provisions on legal safeguards.

CHAPTER 2
POLICIES ON BORDER CHECKS, ASYLUM AND IMMIGRATION

Article 77

1. The Union shall develop a policy with a view to:
    (a) ensuring the absence of any controls on persons, whatever their nationality, when crossing internal borders;
    (b) carrying out checks on persons and efficient monitoring of the crossing of external borders;
    (c) the gradual introduction of an integrated management system for external borders.
2. For the purposes of paragraph I, the European Parliament and the Council, acting in accordance with the ordinary legislative procedure, shall adopt measures concerning:
    (a) the common policy on visas and other short-stay residence permits;
    (b) the checks to which persons crossing external borders are subject;
    (c) the conditions under which nationals of third countries shall have the freedom to travel within the Union for a short period;

(d)   any measure necessary for the gradual establishment of an integrated management system for external borders;

(e)   the absence of any controls on persons, whatever their nationality, when crossing internal borders.

3.   If action by the Union should prove necessary to facilitate the exercise of the right referred to in Article 20(2)(a), and if the Treaties have not provided the necessary powers, the Council, acting in accordance with a special legislative procedure, may adopt provisions concerning passports, identity cards, residence permits or any other such document. The Council shall act unanimously after consulting the European Parliament.

4.   This Article shall not affect the competence of the Member States concerning the geographical demarcation of their borders, in accordance with international law.

Article 78

1.   The Union shall develop a common policy on asylum. subsidiary protection and temporary protection with a view to offering appropriate status to any third-country national requiring international protection and ensuring compliance with the principle of *non-refoulement*. This policy must be in accordance with the Geneva Convention of 28 July 1951 and the Protocol of 31 January 1967 relating to the status of refugees, and other relevant treaties.

2.   For the purposes of paragraph 1. the European Parliament and the Council, acting in accordance with the ordinary legislative procedure. shall adopt measures for a common European asylum system comprising:

(a)   a uniform status of asylum for nationals of third countries, valid throughout the Union;

(b)   a uniform status of subsidiary protection for nationals of third countries who, without obtaining European asylum, are in need of international protection;

(c)   a common system of temporary protection for displaced persons in the event of a massive inflow;

(d)   common procedures for the granting and withdrawing of uniform asylum or subsidiary protection status;

(e)   criteria and mechanisms for determining which Member State is responsible for considering an application for asylum or subsidiary protection;

(f)   standards concerning the conditions for the reception of applicants for asylum or subsidiary protection;

(g)   partnership and cooperation with third countries for the purpose of managing inflows of people applying for asylum or subsidiary or temporary protection.

3.   In the event of one or more Member States being confronted with an emergency situation characterised by a sudden inflow of nationals of third countries, the Council, on a proposal from the Commission, may adopt provisional measures for the benefit of the Member State(s) concerned. It shall act after consulting the European Parliament.

Article 79

1.   The Union shall develop a common immigration policy aimed at ensuring, at all stages, the efficient management of migration flows, fair treatment of third-country nationals residing legally in Member States, and the prevention of, and enhanced measures to combat, illegal immigration and trafficking in human beings.

2.   For the purposes of paragraph 1, the European Parliament and the Council, acting in accordance with the ordinary legislative procedure, shall adopt measures in the following areas:

(a)   the conditions of entry and residence, and standards on the issue by Member States of long-term visas and residence permits, including those for the purpose of family reunification;

(b)   the definition of the rights of third-country nationals residing legally in a Member State, including the conditions governing freedom of movement and of residence in other Member States;

(c)   illegal immigration and unauthorised residence, including removal and repatriation of persons residing without authorisation;

(d)   combating trafficking in persons, in particular women and children.

3.   The Union may conclude agreements with third countries for the readmission to their countries of origin or provenance of third-country nationals who do not or who no longer fulfil the conditions for entry, presence or residence in the territory of one of the Member States.

4.   The European Parliament and the Council, acting in accordance with the ordinary legislative procedure, may establish measures to provide incentives and support for the action of Member States with a view to promoting the integration of third-country nationals residing legally in their territories, excluding any harmonisation of the laws and regulations of the Member States.

5.   This Article shall not affect the right of Member States to determine volumes of admission of third-country nationals coming from third countries to their territory in order to seek work, whether employed or self-employed.

CHAPTER 3
JUDICIAL COOPERATION IN CIVIL MATTERS

Article 81

1.   The Union shall develop judicial cooperation in civil matters having cross-border implications, based on the principle of mutual recognition of judgments and of decisions in extrajudicial cases. Such cooperation may include the adoption of measures for the approximation of the laws and regulations of the Member States.

2.   For the purposes of paragraph 1, the European Parliament and the Council, acting in accordance with the ordinary legislative procedure, shall adopt measures, particularly when necessary for the proper functioning of the internal market, aimed at ensuring:
    (a)   the mutual recognition and enforcement between Member States of judgments and of decisions in extrajudicial cases;
    (b)   the cross-border service of judicial and extrajudicial documents;
    (c)   the compatibility of the rules applicable in the Member States concerning conflict of laws and of jurisdiction;
    (d)   cooperation in the taking of evidence;
    (e)   effective access to justice;
    (f)   the elimination of obstacles to the proper functioning of civil proceedings, if necessary by promoting the compatibility of the rules on civil procedure applicable in the Member States;
    (g)   the development of alternative methods of dispute settlement;
    (h)   support for the training of the judiciary and judicial staff.

3.   Notwithstanding paragraph 2, measures concerning family law with cross-border implications shall be established by the Council, acting in accordance with a special legislative procedure. The Council shall act unanimously after consulting the European Parliament.

    The Council, on a proposal from the Commission, may adopt a decision determining those aspects of family law with cross-border implications which may be the subject of acts adopted by the ordinary legislative procedure. The Council shall act unanimously after consulting the European Parliament.

    The proposal referred to in the second subparagraph shall be notified to the national Parliaments. If a national Parliament makes known its opposition within six months of the date of such notification, the decision shall not be adopted. In the absence of opposition, the Council may adopt the decision.

CHAPTER 4
JUDICIAL COOPERATION IN CRIMINAL MATTERS

Article 82

1.   Judicial cooperation in criminal matters in the Union shall be based on the principle of mutual recognition of judgments and judicial decisions and shall include the approximation of

the laws and regulations of the Member States in the areas referred to in paragraph 2 and in Article 83.

The European Parliament and the Council, acting in accordance with the ordinary legislative procedure, shall adopt measures to:

(a)   lay down rules and procedures for ensuring recognition throughout the Union of all forms of judgments and judicial decisions;

(b)   prevent and settle conflicts of jurisdiction between Member States;

(c)   support the training of the judiciary and judicial staff;

(d)   facilitate cooperation between judicial or equivalent authorities of the Member States in relation to proceedings in criminal matters and the enforcement of decisions.

2.   To the extent necessary to facilitate mutual recognition of judgments and judicial decisions and police and judicial cooperation in criminal matters having a crossborder dimension, the European Parliament and the Council may, by means of directives adopted in accordance with the ordinary legislative procedure, establish minimum rules. Such rules shall take into account the differences between the legal traditions and systems of the Member States.

They shall concern:

(a)   mutual admissibility of evidence between Member States;

(b)   the rights of individuals in criminal procedure;

(c)   the rights of victims of crime;

(d)   any other specific aspects of criminal procedure which the Council has identified in advance by a decision; for the adoption of such a decision, the Council shall act unanimously after obtaining the consent of the European Parliament.

Adoption of the minimum rules referred to in this paragraph shall not prevent Member States from maintaining or introducing a higher level of protection for individuals.

3.   Where a member of the Council considers that a draft directive as referred to in paragraph 2 would affect fundamental aspects of its criminal justice system, it may request that the draft directive be referred to the European Council. In that case, the ordinary legislative procedure shall be suspended. After discussion, and in case of a consensus, the European Council shall, within four months of this suspension, refer the draft back to the Council, which shall terminate the suspension of the ordinary legislative procedure.

Within the same timeframe, in case of disagreement, and if at least nine Member States wish to establish enhanced cooperation on the basis of the draft directive concerned, they shall notify the European Parliament, the Council and the Commission accordingly. In such a case, the authorisation to proceed with enhanced cooperation referred to in Article 20(2) of the Treaty on European Union and Article 329(1) of this Treaty shall be deemed to be granted and the provisions on enhanced cooperation shall apply.

CHAPTER 5
POLICE COOPERATION

Article 87

1.   The Union shall establish police cooperation involving all the Member States' competent authorities, including police, customs and other specialised law enforcement services in relation to the prevention, detection and investigation of criminal offences.

Article 88

1.   Europol's mission shall be to support and strengthen action by the Member States' police authorities and other law enforcement services and their mutual cooperation in preventing and combating serious crime affecting two or more Member States, terrorism and forms of crime which affect a common interest covered by a Union policy.

TITLE VII
COMMON RULES ON COMPETITION, TAXATION AND APPROXIMATION OF LAWS

CHAPTER 1
RULES ON COMPETITION

SECTION I
RULES APPLYING TO UNDERTAKINGS

Article 101

1. The following shall be prohibited as incompatible with the internal market: all agreements between undertakings, decisions by associations of undertakings and concerted practices which may affect trade between Member States and which have as their object or effect the prevention, restriction or distortion of competition within the internal market, and in particular those which:

   (a) directly or indirectly fix purchase or selling prices or any other trading conditions;
   (b) limit or control production, markets, technical development, or investment;
   (c) share markets or sources of supply;
   (d) apply dissimilar conditions to equivalent transactions with other trading parties, thereby placing them at a competitive disadvantage;
   (e) make the conclusion of contracts subject to acceptance by the other parties of supplementary obligations which, by their nature or according to commercial usage, have no connection with the subject of such contracts.

2. Any agreements or decisions prohibited pursuant to this Article shall be automatically void.

3. The provisions of paragraph 1 may, however, be declared inapplicable in the case of:
   — any agreement or category of agreements between undertakings,
   — any decision or category of decisions by associations of undertakings,
   — any concerted practice or category of concerted practices,

   which contributes to improving the production or distribution of goods or to promoting technical or economic progress, while allowing consumers a fair share of the resulting benefit, and which does not:

   (a) impose on the undertakings concerned restrictions which are not indispensable to the attainment of these objectives;
   (b) afford such undertakings the possibility of eliminating competition in respect of a substantial part of the products in question.

Article 102

Any abuse by one or more undertakings of a dominant position within the internal market or in a substantial part of it shall be prohibited as incompatible with the internal market in so far as it may affect trade between Member States.

Such abuse may, in particular, consist in:

   (a) directly or indirectly imposing unfair purchase or selling prices or other unfair trading conditions;
   (b) limiting production, markets or technical development to the prejudice of consumers;
   (c) applying dissimilar conditions to equivalent transactions with other trading parties, thereby placing them at a competitive disadvantage;
   (d) making the conclusion of contracts subject to acceptance by the other parties of supplementary obligations which, by their nature or according to commercial usage, have no connection with the subject of such contracts.

Article 103

1. The appropriate regulations or directives to give effect to the principles set out in Articles 101 and 102 shall be laid down by the Council, on a proposal from the Commission and after consulting the European Parliament.

2. The regulations or directives referred to in paragraph 1 shall be designed in particular:

   (a) to ensure compliance with the prohibitions laid down in Article 101(1) and in Article 102 by making provision for fines and periodic penalty payments;

(b)   to lay down detailed rules for the application of Article 101(3), taking into account the need to ensure effective supervision on the one hand, and to simplify administration to the greatest possible extent on the other;

(c)   to define, if need be, in the various branches of the economy, the scope of the provisions of Articles 101 and 102;

(d)   to define the respective functions of the Commission and of the Court of Justice of the European Union in applying the provisions laid down in this paragraph;

(e)   to determine the relationship between national laws and the provisions contained in this Section or adopted pursuant to this Article.

Article 104

Until the entry into force of the provisions adopted in pursuance of Article 103, the authorities in Member States shall rule on the admissibility of agreements, decisions and concerted practices and on abuse of a dominant position in the internal market in accordance with the law of their country and with the provisions of Article 101, in particular paragraph 3, and of Article 102.

Article 105

1.   Without prejudice to Article 104, the Commission shall ensure the application of the principles laid down in Articles 101 and 102. On application by a Member State or on its own initiative, and in cooperation with the competent authorities in the Member States, which shall give it their assistance, the Commission shall investigate cases of suspected infringement of these principles. If it finds that there has been an infringement, it shall propose appropriate measures to bring it to an end.

2.   If the infringement is not brought to an end, the Commission shall record such infringement of the principles in a reasoned decision. The Commission may publish its decision and authorise Member States to take the measures, the conditions and details of which it shall determine, needed to remedy the situation.

3.   The Commission may adopt regulations relating to the categories of agreement in respect of which the Council has adopted a regulation or a directive pursuant to Article 103(2)(b).

Article 106

1.   In the case of public undertakings and undertakings to which Member States grant special or exclusive rights, Member States shall neither enact nor maintain in force any measure contrary to the rules contained in the Treaties, in particular to those rules provided for in Article 18 and Articles 101 to 109.

2.   Undertakings entrusted with the operation of services of general economic interest or having the character of a revenue-producing monopoly shall be subject to the rules contained in the Treaties, in particular to the rules on competition, in so far as the application of such rules does not obstruct the performance, in law or in fact, of the particular tasks assigned to them. The development of trade must not be affected to such an extent as would be contrary to the interests of the Union.

3.   The Commission shall ensure the application of the provisions of this Article and shall, where necessary, address appropriate directives or decisions to Member States.

SECTION 2
AIDS GRANTED BY STATES

Article 107

1.   Save as otherwise provided in the Treaties, any aid granted by a Member State or through State resources in any form whatsoever which distorts or threatens to distort competition by favouring certain undertakings or the production of certain goods shall, in so far as it affects trade between Member States, be incompatible with the internal market.

2.   The following shall be compatible with the internal market:

(a)   aid having a social character, granted to individual consumers, provided that such aid is granted without discrimination related to the origin of the products concerned;

(b)   aid to make good the damage caused by natural disasters or exceptional occurrences;

      (c)   aid granted to the economy of certain areas of the Federal Republic of Germany affected by the division of Germany, in so far as such aid is required in order to compensate for the economic disadvantages caused by that division. Five years after the entry into force of the Treaty of Lisbon, the Council, acting on a proposal from the Commission, may adopt a decision repealing this point.

   3.   The following may be considered to be compatible with the internal market:

      (a)   aid to promote the economic development of areas where the standard of living is abnormally low or where there is serious underemployment, and of the regions referred to in Article 349, in view of their structural, economic and social situation;

      (b)   aid to promote the execution of an important project of common European interest or to remedy a serious disturbance in the economy of a Member State;

      (c)   aid to facilitate the development of certain economic activities or of certain economic areas, where such aid does not adversely affect trading conditions to an extent contrary to the common interest;

      (d)   aid to promote culture and heritage conservation where such aid does not affect trading conditions and competition in the Union to an extent that is contrary to the common interest;

      (e)   such other categories of aid as may be specified by decision of the Council on a proposal from the Commission.

Article 108

   1.   The Commission shall, in cooperation with Member States, keep under constant review all systems of aid existing in those States. It shall propose to the latter any appropriate measures required by the progressive development or by the functioning of the internal market.

   2.   If, after giving notice to the parties concerned to submit their comments, the Commission finds that aid granted by a State or through State resources is not compatible with the internal market having regard to Article 107, or that such aid is being misused, it shall decide that the State concerned shall abolish or alter such aid within a period of time to be determined by the Commission.

      If the State concerned does not comply with this decision within the prescribed time, the Commission or any other interested State may, in derogation from the provisions of Articles 258 and 259, refer the matter to the Court of Justice of the European Union direct.

      On application by a Member State, the Council may, acting unanimously, decide that aid which that State is granting or intends to grant shall be considered to be compatible with the internal market, in derogation from the provisions of Article 107 or from the regulations provided for in Article 109, if such a decision is justified by exceptional circumstances. If, as regards the aid in question, the Commission has already initiated the procedure provided for in the first subparagraph of this paragraph, the fact that the State concerned has made its application to the Council shall have the effect of suspending that procedure until the Council has made its attitude known.

      If, however, the Council has not made its attitude known within three months of the said application being made, the Commission shall give its decision on the case.

   3.   The Commission shall be informed, in sufficient time to enable it to submit its comments, of any plans to grant or alter aid. If it considers that any such plan is not compatible with the internal market having regard to Article 107, it shall without delay initiate the procedure provided for in paragraph 2. The Member State concerned shall not put its proposed measures into effect until this procedure has resulted in a final decision.

   4.   The Commission may adopt regulations relating to the categories of State aid that the Council has, pursuant to Article 109, determined may be exempted from the procedure provided for by paragraph 3 of this Article.

Article 109

The Council, on a proposal from the Commission and after consulting the European Parliament, may make any appropriate regulations for the application of Articles 107 and 108 and may in particular determine the conditions in which Article 108(3) shall apply and the categories of aid exempted from this procedure.

CHAPTER 2
TAX PROVISIONS

Article 110

No Member State shall impose, directly or indirectly, on the products of other Member States any internal taxation of any kind in excess of that imposed directly or indirectly on similar domestic products.

Furthermore, no Member State shall impose on the products of other Member States any internal taxation of such a nature as to afford indirect protection to other products.

Article 111

Where products are exported to the territory of any Member State, any repayment of internal taxation shall not exceed the internal taxation imposed on them whether directly or indirectly.

Article 112

In the case of charges other than turnover taxes, excise duties and other forms of indirect taxation, remissions and repayments in respect of exports to other Member States may not be granted and countervailing charges in respect of imports from Member States may not be imposed unless the measures contemplated have been previously approved for a limited period by the Council on a proposal from the Commission.

Article 113

The Council shall, acting unanimously in accordance with a special legislative procedure and after consulting the European Parliament and the Economic and Social Committee, adopt provisions for the harmonisation of legislation concerning turnover taxes, excise duties and other forms of indirect taxation to the extent that such harmonisation is necessary to ensure the establishment and the functioning of the internal market and to avoid distortion of competition.

CHAPTER 3
APPROXIMATION OF LAWS

Article 114

1. Save where otherwise provided in the Treaties, the following provisions shall apply for the achievement of the objectives set out in Article 26. The European Parliament and the Council shall, acting in accordance with the ordinary legislative procedure and after consulting the Economic and Social Committee, adopt the measures for the approximation of the provisions laid down by law, regulation or administrative action in Member States which have as their object the establishment and functioning of the internal market.

2. Paragraph 1 shall not apply to fiscal provisions, to those relating to the free movement of persons nor to those relating to the rights and interests of employed persons.

3. The Commission, in its proposals envisaged in paragraph 1 concerning health, safety, environmental protection and consumer protection, will take as a base a high level of protection, taking account in particular of any new development based on scientific facts. Within their respective powers, the European Parliament and the Council will also seek to achieve this objective.

4. If, after the adoption of a harmonisation measure by the European Parliament and the Council, by the Council or by the Commission, a Member State deems it necessary to maintain national provisions on grounds of major needs referred to in Article 36, or relating to the protection of the environment or the working environment, it shall notify the Commission of these provisions as well as the grounds for maintaining them.

5. Moreover, without prejudice to paragraph 4, if, after the adoption of a harmonisation measure by the European Parliament and the Council, by the Council or by the Commission, a Member State deems it necessary to introduce national provisions based on new scientific evidence relating to the protection of the environment or the working environment on grounds of a problem specific to that Member State arising after the adoption of the harmonisation

measure, it shall notify the Commission of the envisaged provisions as well as the grounds for introducing them.

6. The Commission shall, within six months of the notifications as referred to in paragraphs 4 and 5, approve or reject the national provisions involved after having verified whether or not they are a means of arbitrary discrimination or a disguised restriction on trade between Member States and whether or not they shall constitute an obstacle to the functioning of the internal market.

In the absence of a decision by the Commission within this period the national provisions referred to in paragraphs 4 and 5 shall be deemed to have been approved.

When justified by the complexity of the matter and in the absence of danger for human health, the Commission may notify the Member State concerned that the period referred to in this paragraph may be extended for a further period of up to six months.

7. When, pursuant to paragraph 6, a Member State is authorised to maintain or introduce national provisions derogating from a harmonisation measure, the Commission shall immediately examine whether to propose an adaptation to that measure.

8. When a Member State raises a specific problem on public health in a field which has been the subject of prior harmonisation measures, it shall bring it to the attention of the Commission which shall immediately examine whether to propose appropriate measures to the Council.

9. By way of derogation from the procedure laid down in Articles 258 and 259, the Commission and any Member State may bring the matter directly before the Court of Justice of the European Union if it considers that another Member State is making improper use of the powers provided for in this Article.

10. The harmonisation measures referred to above shall, in appropriate cases, include a safeguard clause authorising the Member States to take, for one or more of the non-economic reasons referred to in Article 36, provisional measures subject to a Union control procedure.

Article 115

Without prejudice to Article 114, the Council shall, acting unanimously in accordance with a special legislative procedure and after consulting the European Parliament and the Economic and Social Committee, issue directives for the approximation of such laws, regulations or administrative provisions of the Member States as directly affect the establishment or functioning of the internal market.

Article 116

Where the Commission finds that a difference between the provisions laid down by law, regulation or administrative action in Member States is distorting the conditions of competition in the internal market and that the resultant distortion needs to be eliminated, it shall consult the Member States concerned.

If such consultation does not result in an agreement eliminating the distortion in question, the European, Parliament and the Council, acting in accordance with the ordinary legislative procedure, shall issue the necessary directives. Any other appropriate measures provided for in the Treaties may be adopted.

Article 117

1. Where there is a reason to fear that the adoption or amendment of a provision laid down by law, regulation or administrative action may cause distortion within the meaning of Article 116, a Member State desiring to proceed therewith shall consult the Commission. After consulting the Member States, the Commission shall recommend to the States concerned such measures as may be appropriate to avoid the distortion in question.

2. If a State desiring to introduce or amend its own provisions does not comply with the recommendation addressed to it by the Commission, other Member States shall not be required, pursuant to Article 116, to amend their own provisions in order to eliminate such distortion. If the Member State which has ignored the recommendation of the Commission causes distortion detrimental only to itself, the provisions of Article 116 shall not apply.

Article 118

In the context of the establishment and functioning of the internal market, the European Parliament and the Council, acting in accordance with the ordinary legislative procedure, shall establish measures for the creation of European intellectual property rights to provide uniform protection of intellectual property rights throughout the Union and for the setting up of centralised Union-wide authorisation, coordination and supervision arrangements.

The Council, acting in accordance with a special legislative procedure, shall by means of regulations establish language arrangements for the European intellectual property rights. The Council shall act unanimously after consulting the European Parliament.

TITLE VIII
ECONOMIC AND MONETARY POLICY

CHAPTER 1
ECONOMIC POLICY

Article 119

1. For the purposes set out in Article 3 of the Treaty on European Union, the activities of the Member States and the Union shall include, as provided in the Treaties, the adoption of an economic policy which is based on the close coordination of Member States' economic policies, on the internal market and on the definition of common objectives, and conducted in accordance with the principle of an open market economy with free competition.

2. Concurrently with the foregoing, and as provided in the Treaties and in accordance with the procedures set out therein, these activities shall include a single currency, the euro, and the definition and conduct of a single monetary policy and exchange-rate policy the primary objective of both of which shall be to maintain price stability and, without prejudice to this objective, to support the general economic policies in the Union, in accordance with the principle of an open market economy with free competition.

3. These activities of the Member States and the Union shall entail compliance with the following guiding principles: stable prices, sound public finances and monetary conditions and a sustainable balance of payments.

CHAPTER 2
MONETARY POLICY

Article 127

1. The primary objective of the European System of Central Banks, hereinafter referred to as 'ESCB', shall be to maintain price stability. Without prejudice to the objective of price stability, the ESCB shall support the general economic policies in the Union with a view to contributing to the achievement of the objectives of the Union as laid down in Article 3 of the Treaty on European Union. The ESCB shall act in accordance with the principle of an open market economy with free competition, favouring an efficient allocation of resources, and in compliance with the principles set out in Article 119.

2. The basic tasks to be carried out through the ESCB shall be:
   — to define and implement the monetary policy of the Union,
   — to conduct foreign-exchange operations consistent with the provisions of Article 219;
   — to hold and manage the official foreign reserves of the Member States,
   — to promote the smooth operation of payment systems.

Article 128

1. The European Central Bank shall have the exclusive right to authorise the issue of euro banknotes within the Union. The European Central Bank and the national central banks may issue such notes. The banknotes issued by the European Central Bank and the national central banks shall be the only such notes to have the status of legal tender within the Union.

2. Member States may issue euro coins subject to approval by the European Central Bank of the volume of the issue. The Council, on a proposal from the Commission and after consulting the European Parliament and the European Central Bank, may, adopt measures to harmonise the

denominations and technical specifications of all coins intended for circulation to the extent necessary to permit their smooth circulation within the Union.

CHAPTER 3
INSTITUTIONAL PROVISIONS

Article 134

1. In order to promote coordination of the policies of Member States to the full extent needed for the functioning of the internal market, an Economic and Financial Committee is hereby set up.
2. The Economic and Financial Committee shall have the following tasks:
   - to deliver opinions at the request of the Council or Commission, or on its own initiative for submission to those institutions,
   - to keep under review the economic and financial situation of the Member States and of the Union and to report regularly thereon to the Council and to the Commission, in particular on financial relations with third countries and international institutions,
   - without prejudice to Article 240, to contribute to the preparation of the work of the Council referred to in Articles 66, 75, 121(2), (3), (4) and (6), 122, 124, 125, 126, 127(6), 128(2), 129(3) and (4), 219, 138(1), 143, 144(2) and (3), and 140(2) and (3), and to carry out other advisory and preparatory tasks assigned to it by the Council,
   - to examine, at least once a year, the situation regarding the movement of capital and the freedom of payments, as they result from the application of the Treaties and of measures adopted by the Council; the examination shall cover all measures relating to capital movements and payments; the Committee shall report to the Commission and to the Council on the outcome of this examination.

   The Member States, the Commission and the European Central Bank shall each appoint no more than two members of the Committee.
3. The Council shall, on a proposal from the Commission and after consulting the European Central Bank and the Committee referred to in this Article, lay down detailed provisions concerning the composition of the Economic and Financial Committee. The President of the Council shall inform the European Parliament of such a decision.
4. In addition to the tasks set out in paragraph 2, if and as long as there are Member States with a derogation as referred to in Article 139, the Committee shall keep under review the monetary and financial situation and the general payments system of those Member States and report regularly thereon to the Council and to the Commission.

TITLE IX
EMPLOYMENT

Article 145

Member States and the Union shall, in accordance with this title, work towards developing a coordinated strategy for employment and particularly for promoting a skilled, trained and adaptable workforce and labour markets responsive to economic change with a view to achieving the objectives defined in Article 3 of the Treaty on European Union.

TITLE X
SOCIAL POLICY

Article 151

The Union and the Member States, having in mind fundamental social rights such as those set out in the European Social Charter signed at Turin on 21 October 1961 and in the 1989 Community Charter of the Fundamental Social Rights of Workers, shall have as their objectives the promotion of employment, improved living and working conditions, so as to make possible their harmonisation while the improvement is being maintained, proper social protection, dialogue between management and labour, the development of human resources with a view to lasting high employment and the combating of exclusion.

To this end the Union and the Member States shall implement measures which take account of the diverse forms of national practices, in particular in the field of contractual relations, and the need to maintain the competitiveness of the Union economy.

They believe that such a development will ensue not only from the functioning of the internal market, which will favour the harmonisation of social systems, but also from the procedures provided for in the Treaties and from the approximation of provisions laid down by law, regulation or administrative action.

Article 152

The Union recognises and promotes the role of the social partners at its level, taking into account the diversity of national systems. It shall facilitate dialogue between the social partners, respecting their autonomy.

The Tripartite Social Summit for Growth and Employment shall contribute to social dialogue.

Article 153

1. With a view to achieving the objectives of Article 151, the Union shall support and complement the activities of the Member States in the following fields:
   (a) improvement in particular of the working environment to protect workers' health and safety;
   (b) working conditions;
   (c) social security and social protection of workers;
   (d) protection of workers where their employment contract is terminated;
   (e) the information and consultation of workers;
   (f) representation and collective defence of the interests of workers and employers, including co-determination, subject to paragraph 5;
   (g) conditions of employment for third-country nationals legally residing in Union territory;
   (h) the integration of persons excluded from the labour market, without prejudice to Article 166;
   (i) equality between men and women with regard to labour market opportunities and treatment at work;
   (j) the combating of social exclusion;
   (k) the modernisation of social protection systems without prejudice to point (c).

2. To this end, the European Parliament and the Council:
   (a) may adopt measures designed to encourage cooperation between Member States through initiatives aimed at improving knowledge, developing exchanges of information and best practices, promoting innovative approaches and evaluating experiences, excluding any harmonisation of the laws and regulations of the Member States;
   (b) may adopt, in the fields referred to in paragraph 1(a) to (i), by means of directives, minimum requirements for gradual implementation, having regard to the conditions and technical rules obtaining in each of the Member States. Such directives shall avoid imposing administrative, financial and legal constraints in a way which would hold back the creation and development of small and medium-sized undertakings.

   The European Parliament and the Council shall act in accordance with the ordinary legislative procedure after consulting the Economic and Social Committee and the Committee of the Regions.

   In the fields referred to in paragraph 1(c), (d), (f) and (g), the Council shall act unanimously, in accordance with a special legislative procedure, after consulting the European Parliament and the said Committees.

   The Council, acting unanimously on a proposal from the Commission, after consulting the European Parliament, may decide to render the ordinary legislative procedure applicable to paragraph 1(d), (f) and (g).

3. A Member State may entrust management and labour, at their joint request, with the implementation of directives adopted pursuant to paragraph 2, or, where appropriate, with the implementation of a Council decision adopted in accordance with Article 155.

   In this case, it shall ensure that, no later than the date on which a directive or a decision must be transposed or implemented, management and labour have introduced the necessary measures by agreement, the Member State concerned being required to take any necessary measure enabling it at any time to be in a position to guarantee the results imposed by that directive or that decision.

4.   The provisions adopted pursuant to this Article:
   — shall not affect the right of Member States to define the fundamental principles of their social security systems and must not significantly affect the financial equilibrium thereof,
   — shall not prevent any Member State from maintaining or introducing more stringent protective measures compatible with the Treaties.

5.   The provisions of this Article shall not apply to pay, the right of association, the right to strike or the right to impose lock-outs.

Article 154

1.   The Commission shall have the task of promoting the consultation of management and labour at Union level and shall take any relevant measure to facilitate their dialogue by ensuring balanced support for the parties.

2.   To this end, before submitting proposals in the social policy field, the Commission shall consult management and labour on the possible direction of Union action.

3.   If, after such consultation, the Commission considers Union action advisable, it shall consult management and labour on the content of the envisaged proposal. Management and labour shall forward to the Commission an opinion or, where appropriate, a recommendation.

4.   On the occasion of such consultations set out in paragraphs 2 and 3, management and labour may inform the Commission of their wish to initiate the process provided for in Article 155. The duration of this process shall not exceed nine months, unless the management and labour concerned and the Commission decide jointly to extend it.

Article 155

1.   Should management and labour so desire, the dialogue between them at Union level may lead to contractual relations, including agreements.

2.   Agreements concluded at Union level shall be implemented either in accordance with the procedures and practices specific to management and labour and the Member States or, in matters covered by Article 153, at the joint request of the signatory parties, by a Council decision on a proposal from the Commission. The European Parliament shall be informed.
   The Council shall act unanimously where the agreement in question contains one or more provisions relating to one of the areas for which unanimity is required pursuant to Article 153(2).

Article 156

With a view to achieving the objectives of Article 151 and without prejudice to the other provisions of the Treaties, the Commission shall encourage cooperation between the Member States and facilitate the coordination of their action in all social policy fields under this Chapter, particularly in matters relating to:

— employment,
— labour law and working conditions,
— basic and advanced vocational training,
— social security,
— prevention of occupational accidents and diseases, occupational hygiene,
— the right of association and collective bargaining between employers and workers.

To this end, the Commission shall act in close contact with Member States by making studies, delivering opinions and arranging consultations both on problems arising at national level and on those of concern to international organisations, in particular initiatives aiming at the establishment of guidelines and indicators, the organisation of exchange of best practice, and the preparation of the necessary elements for periodic monitoring and evaluation. The European Parliament shall be kept fully informed.

Before delivering the opinions provided for in this Article, the Commission shall consult the Economic and Social Committee.

Article 157

1.   Each Member State shall ensure that the principle of equal pay for male and female workers for equal work or work of equal value is applied.

2.   For the purpose of this article, 'pay' means the ordinary basic or minimum wage or salary and any other consideration, whether in cash or in kind, which the worker receives directly or indirectly, in respect of his employment, from his employer.

Equal pay without discrimination based on sex means:

(a)   that pay for the same work at piece rates shall be calculated on the basis of the same unit of measurement;

(b)   that pay for work at time rates shall be the same for the same job.

3.   The European Parliament and the Council, acting in accordance with the ordinary legislative procedure, and after consulting the Economic and Social Committee, shall adopt measures to ensure the application of the principle of equal opportunities and equal treatment of men and women in matters of employment and occupation, including the principle of equal pay for equal work or work of equal value.

4.   With a view to ensuring full equality in practice between men and women in working life, the principle of equal treatment shall not prevent any Member State from maintaining or adopting measures providing for specific advantages in order to make it easier for the underrepresented sex to pursue a vocational activity or to prevent or compensate for disadvantages in professional careers.

Article 158

Member States shall endeavour to maintain the existing equivalence between paid holiday schemes.

Article 159

The Commission shall draw up a report each year on progress in achieving the objectives of Article 151, including the demographic situation in the Union. It shall forward the report to the European Parliament, the Council and the Economic and Social Committee.

Article 160

The Council, acting by a simple majority after consulting the European Parliament, shall establish a Social Protection Committee with advisory status to promote cooperation on social protection policies between Member States and with the Commission. The tasks of the Committee shall be:

— to monitor the social situation and the development of social protection policies in the Member States and the Union,

— to promote exchanges of information, experience and good practice between Member States and with the Commission,

— without prejudice to Article 240, to prepare reports, formulate opinions or undertake other work within its fields of competence, at the request of either the Councilor the Commission or on its own initiative.

In fulfilling its mandate, the Committee shall establish appropriate contacts with management and labour.

Each Member State and the Commission shall appoint two members of the Committee.

Article 161

The Commission shall include a separate chapter on social developments within the Union in its annual report to the European Parliament.

The European Parliament may invite the Commission to draw up reports on any particular problems concerning social conditions.

TITLE XI

THE EUROPEAN SOCIAL FUND

Article 162

In order to improve employment opportunities for workers in the internal market and to contribute thereby to raising the standard of living, a European Social Fund is hereby established in accordance with the provisions set out below; it shall aim to render the employment of workers easier and to increase their geographical and occupational mobility within the Union, and to facilitate their adaptation to industrial changes and to changes in production systems, in particular through vocational training and retraining.

TITLE XII
EDUCATION, VOCATIONAL TRAINING, YOUTH AND SPORT

Article 165

1. The Union shall contribute to the development of quality education by encouraging cooperation between Member States and, if necessary, by supporting and supplementing their action, while fully respecting the responsibility of the Member States for the content of teaching and the organisation of education systems and their cultural and linguistic diversity. The Union shall contribute to the promotion of European sporting issues, while taking account of the specific nature of sport, its structures based on voluntary activity and its social and educational function.

2. Union action shall be aimed at:
   — developing the European dimension in education, particularly through the teaching and dissemination of the languages of the Member States,
   — encouraging mobility of students and teachers, by encouraging *inter alia*, the academic recognition of diplomas and periods of study,
   — promoting cooperation between educational establishments,
   — developing exchanges of information and experience on issues common to the education systems of the Member States,
   — encouraging the development of youth exchanges and of exchanges of socioeducational instructors, and encouraging the participation of young people in democratic life in Europe,
   — encouraging the development of distance education.
   — developing the European dimension in sport, by promoting fairness and openness in sporting competitions and cooperation between bodies responsible for sports, and by protecting the physical and moral integrity of sportsmen and sportswomen, especially the youngest sportsmen and sportswomen.

3. The Union and the Member States shall foster cooperation with third countries and the competent international organisations in the field of education and sport, in particular the Council of Europe.

4. In order to contribute to the achievement of the objectives referred to in this Article:
   — the European Parliament and the Council, acting in accordance with the ordinary legislative procedure, after consulting the Economic and Social Committee and the Committee of the Regions, shall adopt incentive measures, excluding any harmonisation of the laws and regulations of the Member States,
   — the Council, on a proposal from the Commission, shall adopt recommendations.

Article 166

1. The Union shall implement a vocational training policy which shall support and supplement the action of the Member States, while fully respecting the responsibility of the Member States for the content and organisation of vocational training.

2. Union action shall aim to:
   — facilitate adaptation to industrial changes, in particular through vocational training and retraining,
   — improve initial and continuing vocational training in order to facilitate vocational integration and reintegration into the labour market,
   — facilitate access to vocational training and encourage mobility of instructors and trainees and particularly young people,
   — stimulate cooperation on training between educational or training establishments and firms,

     — develop exchanges of information and experience on issues common to the training systems of the Member States.

3.   The Union and the Member States shall foster cooperation with third countries and the competent international organisations in the sphere of vocational training.

4.   The European Parliament and the Council, acting in accordance with the ordinary legislative procedure and after consulting the Economic and Social Committee and the Committee of the Regions, shall adopt measures to contribute to the achievement of the objectives referred to in this Article, excluding any harmonisation of the laws and regulations of the Member States, and the Council, on a proposal from the Commission, shall adopt recommendations.

TITLE XIII

CULTURE

Article 167

1.   The Union shall contribute to the flowering of the cultures of the Member States, while respecting their national and regional diversity and at the same time bringing the common cultural heritage to the fore.

2.   Action by the Union shall be aimed at encouraging cooperation between Member States and, if necessary, supporting and supplementing their action in the following areas:

    — improvement of the knowledge and dissemination of the culture and history of the European peoples,

    — conservation and safeguarding of cultural heritage of European significance,

    — non-commercial cultural exchanges,

    — artistic and literary creation, including in the audiovisual sector.

3.   The Union and the Member States shall foster cooperation with third countries and the competent international organisations in the sphere of culture, in particular the Council of Europe.

4.   The Union shall take cultural aspects into account in its action under other provisions of the Treaties, in particular in order to respect and to promote the diversity of its cultures.

5.   In order to contribute to the achievement of the objectives referred to in this Article:

    — the European Parliament and the Council acting in accordance with the ordinary legislative procedure and after consulting the Committee of the Regions, shall adopt incentive measures, excluding any harmonisation of the laws and regulations of the Member States.

    — the Council, on a proposal from the Commission, shall adopt recommendations.

TITLE XIV

PUBLIC HEALTH

Article 168

1.   A high level of human health protection shall be ensured in the definition and implementation of all the Union's policies and activities.

Union action, which shall complement national policies, shall be directed towards improving public health, preventing human illness and diseases, and obviating sources of danger to physical and mental health. Such action shall cover the fight against the major health scourges, by promoting research into their causes, their transmission and their prevention, as well as health information and education, and monitoring, early warning of and combating serious cross-border threats to health.

The Union shall complement the Member States' action in reducing drugs-related health damage, including information and prevention.

2.   The Union shall encourage cooperation between the Member States in the areas referred to in this Article and, if necessary, lend support to their action. It shall in particular encourage cooperation between the Member States to improve the complementarity of their health services in cross-border areas.

Member States shall, in liaison with the Commission, coordinate among themselves their policies and programmes in the areas referred to in paragraph 1. The Commission may, in close contact with the Member States, take any useful initiative to promote such coordination, in particular initiatives aiming at the establishment of guidelines and indicators, the organisation of exchange of best practice, and the preparation of the necessary elements for periodic monitoring and evaluation. The European Parliament shall be kept fully informed.

3.   The Union and the Member States shall foster cooperation with third countries and the competent international organisations in the sphere of public health.

4.   By way of derogation from Article 2(5) and Article 6(a) and in accordance with Article 4(2)(k), the European Parliament and the Council, acting in accordance with the ordinary legislative procedure and after consulting the Economic and Social Committee and the Committee of the Regions, shall contribute to the achievement of the objectives referred to in this Article through adopting, in order to meet common safety concerns:

(a)   measures setting high standards of quality and safety of organs and substances of human origin, blood and blood derivatives; these measures shall not prevent any Member State from maintaining or introducing more stringent protective measures;

(b)   measures in the veterinary and phytosanitary fields which have as their direct objective the protection of public health;

(c)   measures setting high standards of quality and safety for medicinal products and devices for medical use.

5.   The European Parliament and the Council, acting in accordance with the ordinary legislative procedure and after consulting the Economic and Social Committee and the Committee of the Regions, may also adopt incentive measures designed to protect and improve human health and in particular to combat the major cross-border health scourges, measures concerning monitoring, early warning of and combating serious cross-border threats to health, and measures which have as their direct objective the protection of public health regarding tobacco and the abuse of alcohol, excluding any harmonisation of the laws and regulations of the Member States.

6.   The Council, on a proposal from the Commission, may also adopt recommendations for the purposes set out in this Article.

7.   Union action shall respect the responsibilities of the Member States for the definition of their health policy and for the organisation and delivery of health services and medical care. The responsibilities of the Member States shall include the management of health services and medical care and the allocation of the resources assigned to them. The measures referred to in paragraph 4(a) shall not affect national provisions on the donation or medical use of organs and blood.

TITLE XV

CONSUMER PROTECTION

Article 169

1.   In order to promote the interests of consumers and to ensure a high level of consumer protection, the Union shall contribute to protecting the health, safety and economic interests of consumers, as well as to promoting their right to information, education and to organise themselves in order to safeguard their interests.

2.   The Union shall contribute to the attainment of the objectives referred to in paragraph 1 through:

(a)   measures adopted pursuant to Article 114 in the context of the completion of the internal market;

(b)   measures which support, supplement and monitor the policy pursued by the Member States.

3.   The European Parliament and the Council, acting in accordance with the ordinary legislative procedure and after consulting the Economic and Social Committee, shall adopt the measures referred to in paragraph 2(b).

4.   Measures adopted pursuant to paragraph 3 shall not prevent any Member State from maintaining or introducing more stringent protective measures. Such measures must be compatible with the Treaties. The Commission shall be notified of them.

TITLE XVIII
ECONOMIC, SOCIAL AND TERRITORIAL COHESION

Article 174

In order to promote its overall harmonious development, the Union shall develop and pursue its actions leading to the strengthening of its economic, social and territorial cohesion.

In particular, the Union shall aim at reducing disparities between the levels of development of the various regions and the backwardness of the least favoured regions.

Among the regions concerned, particular attention shall be paid to rural areas, areas affected by industrial transition, and regions which suffer from severe and permanent natural or demographic handicaps such as the northernmost regions with very low population density and island, cross-border and mountain regions.

TITLE XX
ENVIRONMENT

Article 191

1. Union policy on the environment shall contribute to pursuit of the following objectives:
   — preserving, protecting and improving the quality of the environment,
   — protecting human health,
   — prudent and rational utilisation of natural resources,
   — promoting measures at international level to deal with regional or worldwide environmental problems, and in particular combating climate change.
2. Union policy on the environment shall aim at a high level of protection taking into account the diversity of situations in the various regions of the Union. It shall be based on the precautionary principle and on the principles that preventive action should be taken, that environmental damage should as a priority be rectified at source and that the polluter should pay.

   In this context, harmonisation measures answering environmental protection requirements shall include, where appropriate, a safeguard clause allowing Member States to take provisional measures, for non-economic environmental reasons, subject to a procedure of inspection by the Union.
3. In preparing its policy on the environment, the Union shall take account of:
   — available scientific and technical data,
   — environmental conditions in the various regions of the Union,
   — the potential benefits and costs of action or lack of action,
   — the economic and social development of the Union as a whole and the balanced development of its regions.
4. Within their respective spheres of competence, the Union and the Member States shall cooperate with third countries and with the competent international organisations. The arrangements for Union cooperation may be the subject of agreements between the Union and the third parties concerned.

   The previous subparagraph shall be without prejudice to Member States' competence to negotiate in international bodies and to conclude international agreements.

Article 192

1. The European Parliament and the Council, acting in accordance with the ordinary legislative procedure and after consulting the Economic and Social Committee and the Committee of the Regions, shall decide what action is to be taken by the Union in order to achieve the objectives referred to in Article 191.

TITLE XXI
ENERGY

Article 194

1. In the context of the establishment and functioning of the internal market and with regard for the need to preserve and improve the environment, the Union's policy on energy shall aim, in a spirit of solidarity between Member States, to:

(a)   ensure the functioning of the energy market;
(b)   ensure security of energy supply in the Union; and
(c)   promote energy efficiency and energy saving and the development of new and renewable forms of energy; and
(d)   promote the interconnection of energy networks.

TITLE XXII
TOURISM

Article 195

1.   The Union shall complement the action of the Member States in the tourism sector, in particular by promoting the competitiveness of Union undertakings in that sector.
      To that end, Union action shall be aimed at:
      (a)   encouraging the creation of a favourable environment for the development of undertakings in this sector;
      (b)   promoting cooperation between the Member States, particularly by the exchange of good practice.
2.   The European Parliament and the Council, acting in accordance with the ordinary legislative procedure, shall establish specific measures to complement actions within the Member States to achieve the objectives referred to in this Article, excluding any harmonisation of the laws and regulations of the Member States.

TITLE XXIII
CIVIL PROTECTION

Article 196

1.   The Union shall encourage cooperation between Member States in order to improve the effectiveness of systems for preventing and protecting against natural or man-made disasters. The Union's action shall aim to:
      (a)   support and complement Member States' action at national, regional and local level in risk prevention, in preparing their civil-protection personnel and in responding to natural or man-made disasters within the Union;
      (b)   promote swift, effective operational cooperation within the Union between national civil-protection services;
      (c)   promote consistency in international civil-protection work.
2.   The European Parliament and Council, acting in accordance with the ordinary legislative procedure shall establish the measures necessary to help achieve the objectives referred to in paragraph 1, excluding any harmonisation of the laws and regulations of the Member States.

TITLE XXIV
ADMINISTRATIVE CO-OPERATION

Article 197

1.   Effective implementation of Union law by the Member States, which is essential for the proper functioning of the Union, shall be regarded as a matter of common interest.
2.   The Union may support the efforts of Member States to improve their administrative capacity to implement Union law. Such action may include facilitating the exchange of information and of civil servants as well as supporting training schemes. No Member State shall be obliged to avail itself of such support. The European Parliament and the Council, acting by means of regulations in accordance with the ordinary legislative procedure, shall establish the necessary measures to this end, excluding any harmonisation of the laws and regulations of the Member States.
3.   This Article shall be without prejudice to the obligations of the Member States to implement Union law or to the prerogatives and duties of the Commission. It shall also be without prejudice to other provisions of the Treaties providing for administrative cooperation among the Member States and between them and the Union.

PART FIVE
EXTERNAL ACTION BY THE UNION

TITLE I
GENERAL PROVISIONS ON THE UNION'S EXTERNAL ACTION

Article 205

The Union's action on the international scene, pursuant to this Part, shall be guided by the principles, pursue the objectives and be conducted in accordance with the general provisions laid down in Chapter 1 of Title V of the Treaty on European Union.

TITLE II
COMMON COMMERCIAL POLICY

Article 206

By establishing a customs union in accordance with Articles 28 to 32, the Union shall contribute, in the common interest, to the harmonious development of world trade, the progressive abolition of restrictions on international trade and on foreign direct investment, and the lowering of customs and other barriers.

Article 207

1. The common commercial policy shall be based on uniform principles, particularly with regard to changes in tariff rates, the conclusion of tariff and trade agreements relating to trade in goods and services, and the commercial aspects of intellectual property, foreign direct investment, the achievement of uniformity in measures of liberalisation, export policy and measures to protect trade such as those to be taken in the event of dumping or subsidies. The common commercial policy shall be conducted in the context of the principles and objectives of the Union's external action.

2. The European Parliament and the Council, acting by means of regulations in accordance with the ordinary legislative procedure, shall adopt the measures defining the framework for implementing the common commercial policy.

3. Where agreements with one or more third countries or international organisations need to be negotiated and concluded, Article 218 shall apply, subject to the special provisions of this Article.

    The Commission shall make recommendations to the Council, which shall authorise it to open the necessary negotiations. The Council and the Commission shall be responsible for ensuring that the agreements negotiated are compatible with internal Union policies and rules.

    The Commission shall conduct these negotiations in consultation with a special committee appointed by the Council to assist the Commission in this task and within the framework of such directives as the Council may issue to it. The Commission shall report regularly to the special committee and to the European Parliament on the progress of negotiations.

4. For the negotiation and conclusion of the agreements referred to in paragraph 3, the Council shall act by a qualified majority.

    For the negotiation and conclusion of agreements in the fields of trade in services and the commercial aspects of intellectual property, as well as foreign direct investment, the Council shall act unanimously where such agreements include provisions for which unanimity is required for the adoption of internal rules.

    The Council shall also act unanimously for the negotiation and conclusion of agreements:

    (a) in the field of trade in cultural and audiovisual services, where these agreements risk prejudicing the Union's cultural and linguistic diversity;

    (b) in the field of trade in social, education and health services, where these agreements risk seriously disturbing the national organisation of such services and prejudicing the responsibility of Member States to deliver them.

5. The negotiation and conclusion of international agreements in the field of transport shall be subject to Title VI of Part Three and to Article 218.

6. The exercise of the competences conferred by this Article in the field of the common commercial policy shall not affect the delimitation of competences between the Union and the

Member States, and shall not lead to harmonisation of legislative or regulatory provisions of the Member States insofar as the Treaties exclude such harmonisation.

TITLE III
COOPERATION WITH THIRD COUNTRIES AND HUMANITARIAN AID

CHAPTER 1
DEVELOPMENT COOPERATION

Article 208

1. Union policy in the field of development cooperation shall be conducted within the framework of the principles and objectives of the Union's external action. The Union's development cooperation policy and that of the Member States complement and reinforce each other.

    The Union's development cooperation policy shall have as its primary objective the reduction and, in the long term, the eradication of poverty. The Union shall take account of the objectives of development cooperation in the policies that it implements which are likely to affect developing countries.

2. The Union and the Member States shall comply with the commitments and take account of the objectives they have approved in the context of the United Nations and other competent international organisations.

Article 209

1. The European Parliament and the Council, acting in accordance with the ordinary legislative procedure, shall adopt the measures necessary for the implementation of development cooperation policy, which may relate to multiannual cooperation programmes with developing countries or programmes with a thematic approach.

2. The Union may conclude with third countries and competent international organisations any agreement helping to achieve the objectives referred to in Article 21 of the Treaty on European Union and in Article 208 of this Treaty.

    The first subparagraph shall be without prejudice to Member States' competence to negotiate in international bodies and to conclude agreements.

3. The European Investment Bank shall contribute, under the terms laid down in its Statute, to the implementation of the measures referred to in paragraph 1.

Article 210

1. In order to promote the complementarity and efficiency of their action, the Union and the Member States shall coordinate their policies on development cooperation and shall consult each other on their aid programmes, including in international organisations and during international conferences. They may undertake joint action. Member States shall contribute if necessary to the implementation of Union aid programmes.

2. The Commission may take any useful initiative to promote the coordination referred to in paragraph 1.

Article 211

Within their respective spheres of competence, the Union and the Member States shall cooperate with third countries and with the competent international organisations.

CHAPTER 2
ECONOMIC, FINANCIAL AND TECHNICAL COOPERATION WITH THIRD COUNTRIES

Article 212

1. Without prejudice to the other provisions of the Treaties, and in particular Articles 208 to 211, the Union shall carry out economic, financial and technical cooperation measures, including assistance, in particular financial assistance, with third countries other than developing countries. Such measures shall be consistent with the development policy of the Union and shall be carried out within the framework of the principles and objectives of its external action. The Union's measures and those of the Member States shall complement and reinforce each other.

2. The European Parliament and the Council, acting in accordance with the ordinary legislative procedure, shall adopt the measures necessary for the implementation of paragraph 1.

3. Within their respective spheres of competence, the Union and the Member States shall cooperate with third countries and the competent international organisations. The arrangements for Union cooperation may be the subject of agreements between the Union and the third parties concerned.

    The first subparagraph shall be without prejudice to the Member States' competence to negotiate in international bodies and to conclude international agreements.

Article 213

When the situation in a third country requires urgent financial assistance from the Union, the Council shall adopt the necessary decisions on a proposal from the Commission.

CHAPTER 3

HUMANITARIAN AID

Article 214

1. The Union's operations in the field of humanitarian aid shall be conducted within the framework of the principles and objectives of the external action of the Union. Such operations shall be intended to provide ad hoc assistance and relief and protection for people in third countries who are victims of natural or man-made disasters, in order to meet the humanitarian needs resulting from these different situations. The Union's operations and those of the Member States shall complement and reinforce each other.
2. Humanitarian aid operations shall be conducted in compliance with the principles of international law and with the principles of impartiality, neutrality and nondiscrimination.
3. The European Parliament and the Council, acting in accordance with the ordinary legislative procedure, shall establish the measures defining the framework within which the Union's humanitarian aid operations shall be implemented.
4. The Union may conclude with third countries and competent international organisations any agreement helping to achieve the objectives referred to in paragraph 1 and in Article 21 of the Treaty on European Union.

    The first subparagraph shall be without prejudice to Member States' competence to negotiate in international bodies and to conclude agreements.
5. In order to establish a framework for joint contributions from young Europeans to the humanitarian aid operations of the Union, a European Voluntary Humanitarian Aid Corps shall be set up. The European Parliament and the Council, acting by means of regulations in accordance with the ordinary legislative procedure, shall determine the rules and procedures for the operation of the Corps.
6. The Commission may take any useful initiative to promote coordination between actions of the Union and those of the Member States, in order to enhance the efficiency and complementarity of Union and national humanitarian aid measures.
7. The Union shall ensure that its humanitarian aid operations are coordinated and consistent with those of international organisations and bodies, in particular those forming part of the United Nations system.

TITLE IV

RESTRICTIVE MEASURES

Article 215

1. Where a decision, adopted in accordance with Chapter 2 of Title V of the Treaty on European Union, provides for the interruption or reduction, in part or completely, of economic and financial relations with one or more third countries, the Council, acting by a qualified majority on a joint proposal from the High Representative of the Union for Foreign Affairs and Security Policy and the Commission, shall adopt the necessary measures. It shall inform the European Parliament thereof.

2. Where a decision adopted in accordance with Chapter 2 of Title V of the Treaty on European Union so provides, the Council may adopt restrictive measures under the procedure referred to in paragraph 1 against natural or legal persons and groups or non-State entities.

3. The acts referred to in this Article shall include necessary provisions on legal safeguards.

TITLE V
INTERNATIONAL AGREEMENTS

Article 216

1. The Union may conclude an agreement with one or more third countries or international organisations where the Treaties so provides or where the conclusion of an agreement is necessary in order to achieve, within the framework of the Union's policies, one of the objectives referred to in the Treaties, or is provided for in a legally binding act of the Union or is likely to affect common rules or alter their scope.

2. Agreements concluded by the Union are binding on the institutions of the Union and on its Member States.

Article 217

The Union may conclude with one or more third countries or international organisations agreements establishing an association involving reciprocal rights and obligations, common action and special procedure.

Article 218

1. Without prejudice to the specific provisions laid down in Article 207, agreements between the Union and third countries or international organisations shall be negotiated and concluded in accordance with the following procedure.

2. The Council shall authorise the opening of negotiations, adopt negotiating directives, authorise the signing of agreements and conclude them.

3. The Commission, or the High Representative of the Union for Foreign Affairs and Security Policy where the agreement envisaged relates exclusively or principally to the common foreign and security policy, shall submit recommendations to the Council, which shall adopt a decision authorising the opening of negotiations and, depending on the subject of the agreement envisaged, nominating the Union's negotiator or the head of the Union's negotiating team.

4. The Council may address directives to the negotiator and designate a special committee in consultation with which the negotiations must be conducted.

5. The Council, on a proposal by the negotiator, shall adopt a decision authorising the signing of the agreement and, if necessary, its provisional application before entry into force.

6. The Council, on a proposal by the negotiator, shall adopt a decision concluding the agreement. Except where agreements relate exclusively to the common foreign and security policy, the Council shall adopt the decision concluding the agreement:

   (a) after obtaining the consent of the European Parliament in the following cases:

      (i) association agreements;

      (ii) agreement on Union accession to the European Convention for the Protection of Human Rights and Fundamental Freedoms;

      (iii) agreements establishing a specific institutional framework by organising cooperation procedures;

      (iv) agreements with important budgetary implications for the Union;

      (v) agreements covering fields to which either the ordinary legislative procedure applies, or the special legislative procedure where consent by the European Parliament is required.

   The European Parliament and the Council may, in an urgent situation, agree upon a time-limit for consent.

   (b) after consulting the European Parliament in other cases. The European Parliament shall deliver its opinion within a time-limit which the Council may set depending on the urgency of the matter. In the absence of an opinion within that time-limit, the Council may act.

7. When concluding an agreement, the Council may, by way of derogation from paragraphs 5, 6 and 9, authorise the negotiator to approve on the Union's behalf modifications to the agreement where it provides for them to be adopted by a simplified procedure or by a body set up by the agreement. The Council may attach specific conditions to such authorisation.

8. The Council shall act by a qualified majority throughout the procedure.

However, it shall act unanimously when the agreement covers a field for which unanimity is required for the adoption of an act of the Union as well as for association agreements and the agreements referred to in Article 212 with the States which are candidates for accession. The Council shall act unanimously for the agreement on accession of the Union to the European Convention for the Protection of Human Rights and Fundamental Freedoms; the decision concluding this agreement shall enter into force after it has been approved by the Member States in accordance with their respective constitutional requirements.

9. The Council, on a proposal from the Commission or the High Representative of the Union for Foreign Affairs and Security Policy, shall adopt a decision suspending application of an agreement and establishing the positions to be adopted on the Union's behalf in a body set up by an agreement, when that body is called upon to adopt acts having legal effects, with the exception of acts supplementing or amending the institutional framework of the agreement.

10. The European Parliament shall be immediately and fully informed at all stages of the procedure.

11. A Member State, the European Parliament, the Councilor the Commission may obtain the opinion of the Court of Justice as to whether an agreement envisaged is compatible with the Treaties. Where the opinion of the Court is adverse, the agreement envisaged may not enter into force unless it is amended or the Treaties are revised.

Article 219

1. By way of derogation from Article 218(1), the Council, either on a recommendation from the European Central Bank or on a recommendation from the Commission and after consulting the European Central Bank, in an endeavour to reach a consensus consistent with the objective of price stability, may conclude formal agreements on an exchange-rate system for the euro in relation to currencies of third States. The Council shall act unanimously after consulting the European Parliament and in accordance with the procedure provided for in paragraph 3.

The Council may, either on a recommendation from the European Central Bank or on a recommendation from the Commission, and after consulting the European Central Bank, in an endeavour to reach a consensus consistent with the objective of price stability, adopt, adjust or abandon the central rates of the euro within the exchange rate system. The President of the Council shall inform the European Parliament of the adoption, adjustment or abandonment of the euro central rates.

2. In the absence of an exchange-rate system in relation to one or more currencies of third States as referred to in paragraph 1, the Council, acting either on a recommendation from the Commission and after consulting the European Central Bank or on a recommendation from the European Central Bank, may formulate general orientations for exchange-rate policy in relation to these currencies. These general orientations shall be without prejudice to the primary objective of the ESCB to maintain price stability.

3. By way of derogation from Article 218, where agreements concerning monetary or foreign exchange regime matters need to be negotiated by the Union with one or more third States or international organisations, the Council, acting on a recommendation from the Commission and after consulting the European Central Bank, shall decide the arrangements for the negotiation and for the conclusion of such agreements. These arrangements shall ensure that the Union expresses a single position. The Commission shall be fully associated with the negotiations.

4. Without prejudice to Union competence and Union agreements as regards economic and monetary union, Member States may negotiate in international bodies and conclude international agreements.

TITLE VI
THE UNION'S RELATIONS WITH INTERNATIONAL ORGANISATIONS
AND THIRD COUNTRIES AND UNION DELEGATIONS

Article 220

1.   The Union shall establish all appropriate forms of cooperation with the organs of the United Nations and its specialised agencies, the Council of Europe, the Organisation for Security and Cooperation in Europe and the Organisation for Economic Cooperation and Development.
     The Union shall also maintain such relations as are appropriate with other international organisations.

2.   The High Representative of the Union for Foreign Affairs and Security Policy shall be instructed to implement this Article.

Article 221

1.   Union delegations in third countries and at international organisations shall represent the Union.

2.   Union delegations shall be placed under the authority of the High Representative of the Union for Foreign Affairs and Security Policy. They shall act in close cooperation with Member States' diplomatic and consular missions.

TITLE VII
SOLIDARITY CLAUSE

Article 222

1.   The Union and its Member States shall act jointly in a spirit of solidarity if a Member State is the object of a terrorist attack or the victim of a natural or man-made disaster. The Union shall mobilise all the instruments at its disposal, including the military resources made available by the Member States, to:
     (a)   — prevent the terrorist threat in the territory of the Member States;
            — protect democratic institutions and the civilian population from any terrorist attack;
            — assist a Member State in its territory, at the request of its political authorities, in the event of a terrorist attack;
     (b)   assist a Member State in its territory, at the request of its political authorities, in the event of a natural or man-made disaster.

2.   Should a Member State be the object of a terrorist attack or the victim of a natural or man-made disaster, the other Member States shall assist it at the request of its political authorities. To that end, the Member States shall coordinate between themselves in the Council.

3.   The arrangements for the implementation by the Union of this solidarity clause shall be defined by a decision adopted by the Council acting on a joint proposal by the Commission and the High Representative of the Union for Foreign Affairs and Security Policy. The Council shall act in accordance with Article 31 (1) of the Treaty on European Union where this decision has defence implications. The European Parliament shall be informed.
     For the purposes of this paragraph and without prejudice to Article 240, the Council shall be assisted by the Political and Security Committee with the support of the structures developed in the context of the common security and defence policy and by the Committee referred to in Article 71; the two committees shall, if necessary, submit joint opinions.

4.   The European Council shall regularly assess the threats facing the Union in order to enable the Union and its Member States to take effective action.

PART SIX
INSTITUTIONAL AND FINANCIAL PROVISIONS

TITLE I
PROVISIONS GOVERNING THE INSTITUTIONS

CHAPTER 1
THE INSTITUTIONS

SECTION 1
THE EUROPEAN PARLIAMENT

Article 223

1. The European Parliament shall draw up a proposal to lay down the provisions necessary for the election of its members by direct universal suffrage in accordance with a uniform procedure in all Member States or in accordance with principles common to all Member States.
    The Council, acting unanimously in accordance with a special legislative procedure and after obtaining the consent of the European Parliament, which shall act by a majority of its component members, shall lay down the necessary provisions. These provisions shall enter into force following their approval by the Member States in accordance with their respective constitutional requirements.
2. The European Parliament, acting by means of regulations on its own initiative in accordance with a special legislative procedure, after seeking an opinion from the Commission and with the approval of the Council, shall lay down the regulations and general conditions governing the performance of the duties of its Members. All rules or conditions relating to the taxation of Members or former Members shall require unanimity within the Council.

Article 224

The European Parliament and the Council, acting in accordance with the ordinary legislative procedure, by means of regulations, shall lay down the regulations governing political parties at European level referred to in Article 10(4) of the Treaty on European Union and in particular the rules regarding their funding.

Article 225

The European Parliament may, acting by a majority of its component members, request the Commission to submit any appropriate proposal on matters on which it considers that a Union act is required for the purpose of implementing the Treaties. If the Commission does not submit a proposal, it shall inform the European Parliament of the reasons.

Article 226

In the course of its duties, the European Parliament may, at the request of a quarter of its component Members, set up a temporary Committee of Inquiry to investigate, without prejudice to the powers conferred by the Treaties on other institutions or bodies, alleged contraventions or maladministration in the implementation of Union law, except where the alleged facts are being examined before a court and while the case is still subject to legal proceedings.
The temporary Committee of Inquiry shall cease to exist on the submission of its report.
The detailed provisions governing the exercise of the right of inquiry shall be determined by the European Parliament, acting by means of regulations on its own initiative in accordance with a special legislative procedure, after obtaining the consent of the Council and the Commission.

Article 227

Any citizen of the Union, and any natural or legal person residing or having its registered office in a Member State, shall have the right to address, individually or in association with other citizens or persons, a petition to the European Parliament on a matter which comes within the Union's fields of activity and which affects him, her or it directly.

Article 228

1. A European Ombudsman, elected by the European Parliament, shall be empowered to receive complaints from any citizen of the Union or any natural or legal person residing or having its

registered office in a Member State concerning instances of maladministration in the activities of the Union institutions, bodies, offices or agencies, with the exception of the Court of Justice of the European Union acting in its judicial role. He or she shall examine such complaints and report on them.

In accordance with his duties, the Ombudsman shall conduct inquiries for which he finds grounds, either on his own initiative or on the basis of complaints submitted to him direct or through a Member of the European Parliament, except where the alleged facts are or have been the subject of legal proceedings. Where the Ombudsman establishes an instance of maladministration, he shall refer the matter to the institution, body, office or agency concerned, which shall have a period of three months in which to inform him of its views. The Ombudsman shall then forward a report to the European Parliament and the institution, body, office or agency concerned. The person lodging the complaint shall be informed of the outcome of such inquiries.

The Ombudsman shall submit an annual report to the European Parliament on the outcome of his inquiries.

2.   The Ombudsman shall be elected after each election of the European Parliament for the duration of its term of office. The Ombudsman shall be eligible for reappointment.

The Ombudsman may be dismissed by the Court of Justice at the request of the European Parliament if he no longer fulfils the conditions required for the performance of his duties or if he is guilty of serious misconduct.

3.   The Ombudsman shall be completely independent in the performance of his duties. In the performance of those duties he shall neither seek nor take instructions from any Government, institution, body, office or entity. The Ombudsman may not, during his term of office, engage in any other occupation, whether gainful or not.

4.   The European Parliament acting by means of regulations on its own initiative in accordance with a special legislative procedure shall, after seeking an opinion from the Commission and with the approval of the Council, lay down the regulations and general conditions governing the performance of the Ombudsman's duties.

Article 229

The European Parliament shall hold an annual session. It shall meet, without requiring to be convened, on the second Tuesday in March.

The European Parliament may meet in extraordinary part-session at the request of a majority of its component members or at the request of the Councilor of the Commission.

Article 230

The Commission may attend all the meetings and shall, at its request, be heard.

The Commission shall reply orally or in writing to questions put to it by the European Parliament or by its Members.

The European Council and the Council shall be heard by the European Parliament in accordance with the conditions laid down in the Rules of Procedure of the European Council and those of the Council.

Article 231

Save as otherwise provided in the Treaties, the European Parliament shall act by a majority of the votes cast.

The Rules of Procedure shall determine the quorum.

Article 232

The European Parliament shall adopt its Rules of Procedure, acting by a majority of its Members. The proceedings of the European Parliament shall be published in the manner laid down in the Treaties and its Rules of Procedure.

Article 233

The European Parliament shall discuss in open session the annual general report submitted to it by the Commission.

Article 234

If a motion of censure on the activities of the Commission is tabled before it, the European Parliament shall not vote thereon until at least three days after the motion has been tabled and only by open vote.

If the motion of censure is carried by a two-thirds majority of the votes cast, representing a majority of the component members of the European Parliament, the members of the Commission shall resign as a body and the High Representative of the Union for Foreign Affairs and Security Policy shall resign from duties that he or she carries out in the Commission. They shall remain in office and continue to deal with current business until they are replaced in accordance with Article 17 of the Treaty on European Union. In this case, the term of office of the members of the Commission appointed to replace them shall expire on the date on which the term of office of the members of the Commission obliged to resign as a body would have expired.

SECTION 2

THE EUROPEAN COUNCIL

Article 235

1. Where a vote is taken, any member of the European Council may also act on behalf of not more than one other member.

   Article 16(4) of the Treaty on European Union and Article 238(2) of this Treaty shall apply to the European Council when it is acting by a qualified majority. Where the European Council decides by vote, its President and the President of the Commission shall not take part in the vote.

   Abstentions by members present in person or represented shall not prevent the adoption by the European Council of acts which require unanimity.

2. The President of the European Parliament may be invited to be heard by the European Council.

3. The European Council shall act by a simple majority for procedural questions and for the adoption of its Rules of Procedure.

4. The European Council shall be assisted by the General Secretariat of the Council.

Article 236

The European Council shall adopt by a qualified majority:

    (a)   a decision establishing the list of Council configurations, other than those of the General Affairs Council and of the Foreign Affairs Council, in accordance with Article 16(6) of the Treaty on European Union;

    (b)   a decision on the Presidency of Council configurations, other than that of Foreign Affairs, in accordance with Article 16(9) of the Treaty on European Union.

SECTION 3

THE COUNCIL

Article 237

The Council shall meet when convened by its President on his own initiative or at the request of one of its Members or of the Commission.

Article 238

1. Where it is required to act by a simple majority, the Council shall act by a majority of its component members.

2. By way of derogation from Article 16(4) of the Treaty on European Union, as from 1 November 2014 and subject to the provisions laid down in the Protocol on transitional provisions, where the Council does not act on a proposal from the Commission or from the High Representative of the Union for Foreign Affairs and Security Policy, the qualified majority shall be defined as at least 72% of the members of the Council, representing Member States comprising at least 65% of the population of the Union.

3. As from 1 November 2014 and subject to the provisions laid down in the Protocol on transitional provisions, in cases where, under the Treaties, not all the members of the Council participate in voting, a qualified majority shall be defined as follows:

(a)   A qualified majority shall be defined as at least 55% of the members of the Council representing the participating Member States, comprising at least 65% of the population of these States.

A blocking minority must include at least the minimum number of Council members representing more than 35% of the population of the participating Member States, plus one member, failing which the qualified majority shall be deemed attained;

(b)   By way of derogation from point (a), when the Council does not act on a proposal from the Commission or from the High Representative of the Union for Foreign Affairs and Security Policy, the qualified majority shall be defined as at least 72% of the members of the Council representing Member States comprising at least 65% of the population of these States.

4.   Abstentions by Members present in person or represented shall not prevent the adoption by the Council of acts which require unanimity.

Article 239

Where a vote is taken, any Member of the Council may also act on behalf of not more than one other member.

Article 240

1.   A committee consisting of the Permanent Representatives of the Governments of the Member States shall be responsible for preparing the work of the Council and for carrying out the tasks assigned to it by the latter. The Committee may adopt procedural decisions in cases provided for in the Council's Rules of Procedure.

2.   The Council shall be assisted by a General Secretariat, under the responsibility of a Secretary-General appointed by the Council.

The Council shall decide on the organisation of the General Secretariat by a simple majority.

3.   The Council shall act by a simple majority regarding procedural matters and for the adoption of its Rules of Procedure.

Article 241

The Council, acting by a simple majority, may request the Commission to undertake any studies the Council considers desirable for the attainment of the common objectives, and to submit to it any appropriate proposals. If the Commission does not submit a proposal, it shall inform the Council of the reasons.

Article 242

The Council acting by a simple majority shall, after consulting the Commission, determine the rules governing the committees provided for in the Treaties.

Article 243

The Council shall determine the salaries, allowances and pensions of the President of the European Council, the President of the Commission, the High Representative of the Union for Foreign Affairs and Security Policy, the members of the Commission, the Presidents, members and Registrars of the Court of Justice of the European Union, and the Secretary-General of the Council. It shall also determine any payment to be made instead of remuneration.

SECTION 4

THE COMMISSION

Article 244

In accordance with Article 17(5) of the Treaty on European Union, the members of the Commission shall be chosen on the basis of a system of rotation established unanimously by the European Council and on the basis of the following principles:

(a)   Member States shall be treated on a strictly equal footing as regards determination of the sequence of, and the time spent by, their nationals as members of the Commission; consequently, the difference between the total number of terms of office held by nationals of any given pair of Member States may never be more than one;

(b)   subject to point (a), each successive Commission shall be so composed as to reflect satisfactorily the demographic and geographical range of all the Member States.

Article 245

The Members of the Commission shall refrain from any action incompatible with their duties. Member States shall respect their independence and shall not seek to influence them in the performance of their tasks.

The Members of the Commission may not, during their term of office, engage in any other occupation, whether gainful or not. When entering upon their duties they shall give a solemn undertaking that, both during and after their term of office, they will respect the obligations arising therefrom and in particular their duty to behave with integrity and discretion as regards the acceptance, after they have ceased to hold office, of certain appointments or benefits. In the event of any breach of these obligations, the Court of Justice may, on application by the Council acting by a simple majority or the Commission, rule that the Member concerned be, according to the circumstances, either compulsorily retired in accordance with Article 247 or deprived of his right to a pension or other benefits in its stead.

Article 246

Apart from normal replacement, or death, the duties of a Member of the Commission shall end when he resigns or is compulsorily retired.

A vacancy caused by resignation, compulsory retirement or death shall be filled for the remainder of the member's term of office by a new member of the same nationality appointed by the Council, by common accord with the President of the Commission, after consulting the European Parliament and in accordance with the criteria set out in the second subparagraph of Article 17(3) of the Treaty on European Union.

The Council may, acting unanimously on a proposal from the President of the Commission, decide that such a vacancy need not be filled, in particular when the remainder of the member's term of office is short.

In the event of resignation, compulsory retirement or death, the President shall be replaced for the remainder of his term of office. The procedure laid down in Article 17(7), first subparagraph, of the Treaty on European Union shall be applicable for the replacement of the President.

In the event of resignation, compulsory retirement or death, the High Representative of the Union for Foreign Affairs and Security Policy shall be replaced, for the remainder of his or her term of office, in accordance with Article 18(1) of the Treaty on European Union.

In the case of the resignation of all the members of the Commission, they shall remain in office and continue to deal with current business until they have been replaced, for the remainder of their term of office, in accordance with Article 17 of the Treaty on European Union.

Article 247

If any Member of the Commission no longer fulfils the conditions required for the performance of his duties or if he has been guilty of serious misconduct, the Court of Justice may, on application by the Council acting by a simple majority or the Commission, compulsorily retire him.

Article 248

Without prejudice to Article 18(4) of the Treaty on European Union, the responsibilities incumbent upon the Commission shall be structured and allocated among its members by its President, in accordance with Article 17(6) of that Treaty. The President may reshuffle the allocation of those responsibilities during the Commission's term of office. The Members of the Commission shall carry out the duties devolved upon them by the President under his authority.

Article 249

1.   The Commission shall adopt its Rules of Procedure so as to ensure that both it and its departments operate. It shall ensure that these Rules are published.
2.   The Commission shall publish annually, not later than one month before the opening of the session of the European Parliament, a general report on the activities of the Union.

Article 250

The Commission shall act by a majority of its members.

Its Rules of Procedure shall determine the quorum.

SECTION 5
THE COURT OF JUSTICE OF THE EUROPEAN UNION

Article 251

The Court of Justice shall sit in chambers or in a Grand Chamber, in accordance with the rules laid down for that purpose in the Statute ofthe Court of Justice ofthe European Union.

When provided for in the Statute, the Court of Justice may also sit as a full Court.

Article 252

The Court of Justice shall be assisted by eight Advocates-General. Should the Court of Justice so request, the Council, acting unanimously, may increase the number of Advocates-General.

It shall be the duty of the Advocate-General, acting with complete impartiality and independence, to make, in open court, reasoned submissions on cases which, in accordance with the Statute of the Court of Justice of the European Union, require his involvement.

Article 253

The Judges and Advocates-General of the Court of Justice shall be chosen from persons whose independence is beyond doubt and who possess the qualifications required for appointment to the highest judicial offices in their respective countries or who are jurisconsults of recognised competence; they shall be appointed by common accord of the governments of the Member States for a term of six years, after consultation ofthe panel provided for in Article 255.

Every three years there shall be a partial replacement of the Judges and AdvocatesGeneral, in accordance with the conditions laid down in the Statute of the Court of Justice of the European Union.

The Judges shall elect the President of the Court of Justice from among their number for a term of three years. He may be re-elected.

Retiring Judges and Advocates-General may be reappointed.

The Court of Justice shall appoint its Registrar and lay down the rules governing his service.

The Court of Justice shall establish its Rules of Procedure. Those Rules shall require the approval of the Council.

Article 254

The number of Judges of the Court shall be determined by the Statute of the Court of Justice of the European Union. The Statute may provide for the General Court to be assisted by Advocates-General.

The members of the General Court shall be chosen from persons whose independence is beyond doubt and who possess the ability required for appointment to high judicial office. They shall be appointed by common accord of the governments of the Member States for a term of six years, after consultation of the panel provided for in Article 255. The membership shall be partially renewed every three years. Retiring members shall be eligible for reappointment.

The Judges shall elect the President of the General Court from among their number for a term of three years. He may be re-elected.

The General Court shall appoint its Registrar and lay down the rules governing his servIce.

The General Court shall establish its Rules of Procedure in agreement with the Court of Justice. Those Rules shall require the approval of the Council.

Unless the Statute of the Court of Justice of the European Union provides otherwise, the provisions of the Treaties relating to the Court of Justice shall apply to the General Court.

Article 255

A panel shall be set up in order to give an opinion on candidates' suitability to perform the duties of Judge and Advocate-General of the Court of Justice and the General Court before the governments of the Member States make the appointments referred to in Articles 253 and 254.

The panel shall comprise seven persons chosen from among former members of the Court of Justice and the General Court, members of national supreme courts and lawyers of recognised competence, one of whom shall be proposed by the European Parliament. The Council shall adopt a decision establishing the panel's operating rules and a decision appointing its members. It shall act on the initiative of the President of the Court of Justice.

Article 256

1. The General Court shall have jurisdiction to hear and determine at first instance actions or proceedings referred to in Articles 263, 265, 268, 270 and 272, with the exception of those assigned to a specialised court set up under Article 257 and those reserved in the Statute for the Court of Justice. The Statute may provide for the General Court to have jurisdiction for other classes of action or proceeding.

    Decisions given by the General Court under this paragraph may be subject to a right of appeal to the Court of Justice on points of law only, under the conditions and within the limits laid down by the Statute.

2. The General Court shall have jurisdiction to hear and determine actions or proceedings brought against decisions of the specialised courts.

    Decisions given by the General Court under this paragraph may exceptionally be subject to review by the Court of Justice, under the conditions and within the limits laid down by the Statute, where there is a serious risk of the unity or consistency of Union law being affected.

3. The General Court shall have jurisdiction to hear and determine questions referred for a preliminary ruling under Article 267, in specific areas laid down by the Statute.

    Where the General Court considers that the case requires a decision of principle likely to affect the unity or consistency of Union law, it may refer the case to the Court of Justice for a ruling.

    Decisions given by the General Court on questions referred for a preliminary ruling may exceptionally be subject to review by the Court of Justice, under the conditions and within the limits laid down by the Statute, where there is a serious risk of the unity or consistency of Union law being affected.

Article 257

The European Parliament and the Council, acting in accordance with the ordinary legislative procedure, may establish specialised courts attached to the General Court to hear and determine at first instance certain classes of action or proceeding brought in specific areas. The European Parliament and the Council shall act by means of regulations either on a proposal from the Commission after consultation of the Court of Justice or at the request of the Court of Justice after consultation of the Commission.

The regulation establishing a specialised court shall lay down the rules on the organisation of the court and the extent of the jurisdiction conferred upon it.

Decisions given by specialised courts may be subject to a right of appeal on points of law only or, when provided for in the regulation establishing the specialised court, a right of appeal also on matters of fact, before the General Court.

The members of the specialised courts shall be chosen from persons whose independence is beyond doubt and who possess the ability required for appointment to judicial office. They shall be appointed by the Council, acting unanimously.

The specialised courts shall establish their Rules of Procedure in agreement with the Court of Justice. Those Rules shall require the approval of the Council.

Unless the regulation establishing the specialised court provides otherwise, the provisions of the Treaties relating to the Court of Justice of the European Union and the provisions of the Statute of the Court of Justice of the European Union shall apply to the specialised courts. Title I of the Statute and Article 64 thereof shall in any case apply to the specialised courts.

Article 258

If the Commission considers that a Member State has failed to fulfil an obligation under the Treaties, it shall deliver a reasoned opinion on the matter after giving the State concerned the opportunity to submit its observations.

If the State concerned does not comply with the opinion within the period laid down by the Commission, the latter may bring the matter before the Court of Justice of the European Union.

Article 259

A Member State which considers that another Member State has failed to fulfil an obligation under the Treaties may bring the matter before the Court of Justice of the European Union.

Before a Member State brings an action against another Member State for an alleged infringement of an obligation under the Treaties, it shall bring the matter before the Commission.

The Commission shall deliver a reasoned opinion after each of the States concerned has been given the opportunity to submit its own case and its observations on the other party's case both orally and in writing.

If the Commission has not delivered an opinion within three months of the date on which the matter was brought before it, the absence of such opinion shall not prevent the matter from being brought before the Court.

Article 260

1. If the Court of Justice of the European Union finds that a Member State has failed to fulfil an obligation under the Treaties, the State shall be required to take the necessary measures to comply with the judgment of the Court.

2. If the Commission considers that the Member State concerned has not taken the necessary measures to comply with the judgment of the Court, it may bring the case before the Court after giving that State the opportunity to submit its observations. It shall specify the amount of the lump sum or penalty payment to be paid by the Member State concerned which it considers appropriate in the circumstances.

    If the Court finds that the Member State concerned has not complied with its judgment it may impose a lump sum or penalty payment on it.

    This procedure shall be without prejudice to Article 259.

3. When the Commission brings a case before the Court pursuant to Article 258 on the grounds that the Member State concerned has failed to fulfil its obligation to notify measures transposing a directive adopted under a legislative procedure, it may, when it deems appropriate, specify the amount of the lump sum or penalty payment to be paid by the Member State concerned which it considers appropriate in the circumstances.

    If the Court finds that there is an infringement it may impose a lump sum or penalty payment on the Member State concerned not exceeding the amount specified by the Commission. The payment obligation shall take effect on the date set by the Court in its judgment.

Article 261

Regulations adopted jointly by the European Parliament and the Council, and by the Council, pursuant to the provisions of the Treaties, may give the Court of Justice of the European Union unlimited jurisdiction with regard to the penalties provided for in such regulations.

Article 262

Without prejudice to the other provisions of the Treaties, the Council, acting unanimously in accordance with a special legislative procedure and after consulting the European Parliament, may adopt provisions to confer jurisdiction, to the extent that it shall determine, on the Court of Justice of the European Union in disputes relating to the application of acts adopted on the basis of the Treaties which create European intellectual property rights. These provisions shall enter into force after their approval by the Member States in accordance with their respective constitutional requirements.

Article 263

The Court of Justice of the European Union shall review the legality of legislative acts, of acts of the Council, of the Commission and of the European Central Bank, other than recommendations and opinions, and of acts of the European Parliament and of the European Council intended to produce legal effects vis-à-vis third parties. It shall also review the legality of acts of bodies, offices or agencies of the Union intended to produce legal effects vis-à-vis third parties.

It shall for this purpose have jurisdiction in actions brought by a Member State, the European Parliament, the Council or the Commission on grounds of lack of competence, infringement of an essential procedural requirement, infringement of the Treaties or of any rule of law relating to their application, or misuse of powers.

The Court shall have jurisdiction under the same conditions in actions brought by the Court of Auditors, by the European Central Bank and by the Committee of the Regions for the purpose of protecting their prerogatives.

Any natural or legal person may, under the conditions referred to in the first and second subparagraphs, institute proceedings against an act addressed to that person or which is of direct and individual concern to them, and against a regulatory act which is of direct concern to them and does not entail implementing measures.

Acts setting up bodies, offices and agencies of the Union may lay down specific conditions and arrangements concerning actions brought by natural or legal persons against acts of these bodies, offices or agencies intended to produce legal effects in relation to them.

The proceedings provided for in this Article shall be instituted within two months of the publication of the measure, or of its notification to the plaintiff, or, in the absence thereof, of the day on which it came to the knowledge of the latter, as the case may be.

Article 264

If the action is well founded, the Court of Justice of the European Union shall declare the act concerned to be void.

However, the Court shall, if it considers this necessary, state which of the effects of the act which it has declared void shall be considered as definitive.

Article 265

Should the European Parliament, the European Council, the Council, the Commission or the European Central Bank, in infringement of the Treaties, fail to act, the Member States and the other institutions of the Union may bring an action before the Court of Justice to have the infringement established. This Article shall apply, under the same conditions, to bodies, offices and agencies of the Union which fail to act.

The action shall be admissible only if the institution, body, office or agency concerned has first been called upon to act. If, within two months of being so called upon, the institution, body, office or agency concerned has not defined its position, the action may be brought within a further period of two months.

Any natural or legal person may, under the conditions laid down in the preceding paragraphs, complain to the Court that an institution, body, office or agency of the Union has failed to address to that person any act other than a recommendation or an opinion.

Article 266

The institution, body, office or agency whose act has been declared void or whose failure to act has been declared contrary to the Treaties shall be required to take the necessary measures to comply with the judgment of the Court of Justice.

This obligation shall not affect any obligation which may result from the application of the second paragraph of Article 340.

Article 267

The Court of Justice of the European Union shall have jurisdiction to give preliminary rulings concerning:

    (a)   the interpretation of the Treaties;

    (b)   the validity and interpretation of acts of the institutions, bodies, offices or agencies of the Union;

Where such a question is raised before any court or tribunal of a Member State, that court or tribunal may, if it considers that a decision on the question is necessary to enable it to give judgment, request the Court to give a ruling thereon.

Where any such question is raised in a case pending before a court or tribunal of a Member State against whose decisions there is no judicial remedy under national law, that court or tribunal shall bring the matter before the Court.

If such a question is raised in a case pending before a court or tribunal of a Member State with regard to a person in custody, the Court of Justice of the European Union shall act with the minimum of delay.

Article 268

The Court of Justice of the European Union shall have jurisdiction in disputes relating to compensation for damage provided for in the second and third paragraphs of Article 340.

Article 269

The Court of Justice shall have jurisdiction to decide on the legality of an act adopted by the European Councilor by the Council pursuant to Article 7 of the Treaty on European Union solely at the request of the Member State concerned by a determination of the European Council or of the Council and in respect solely of the procedural stipulations contained in that Article.

Such a request must be made within one month from the date of such determination. The Court shall rule within one month from the date of the request.

Article 270

The Court of Justice of the European Union shall have jurisdiction in any dispute between the Union and its servants within the limits and under the conditions laid down in the Staff Regulations of Officials and the Conditions of Employment of other servants of the Union.

Article 271

The Court of Justice of the European Union shall, within the limits hereinafter laid down, have jurisdiction in disputes concerning:

(a)   the fulfilment by Member States of obligations under the Statute of the European Investment Bank. In this connection, the Board of Directors of the Bank shall enjoy the powers conferred upon the Commission by Article 258;

(b)   measures adopted by the Board of Governors of the European Investment Bank. In this connection, any Member State, the Commission or the Board of Directors of the Bank may institute proceedings under the conditions laid down in Article 263;

(c)   measures adopted by the Board of Directors of the European Investment Bank. Proceedings against such measures may be instituted only by Member States or by the Commission, under the conditions laid down in Article 263, and solely on the grounds of non-compliance with the procedure provided for in Article 19(2), (5), (6) and (7) of the Statute of the Bank;

(d)   the fulfilment by national central banks of obligations under the Treaties and the Statute of the ESCB and of the ECB. In this connection the powers of the Governing Council of the European Central Bank in respect of national central banks shall be the same as those conferred upon the Commission in respect of Member States by Article 258. If the Court finds that a national central bank has failed to fulfil an obligation under the Treaties, that bank shall be required to take the necessary measures to comply with the judgment of the Court.

Article 272

The Court of Justice of the European Union shall have jurisdiction to give judgment pursuant to any arbitration clause contained in a contract concluded by or on behalf of the Union, whether that contract be governed by public or private law.

Article 273

The Court of Justice shall have jurisdiction in any dispute between Member States which relates to the subject matter of the Treaties if the dispute is submitted to it under a special agreement between the parties.

Article 274

Save where jurisdiction is conferred on the Court of Justice of the European Union by the Treaties, disputes to which the Union is a party shall not on that ground be excluded from the jurisdiction of the courts or tribunals of the Member States.

Article 275

The Court of Justice of the European Union shall not have jurisdiction with respect to the provisions relating to the common foreign and security policy nor with respect to acts adopted on the basis of those provisions.

However, the Court shall have jurisdiction to monitor compliance with Article 40 of the Treaty on European Union and to rule on proceedings, brought in accordance with the conditions laid down in the fourth paragraph of Article 263 of this Treaty, reviewing the legality of decisions providing for restrictive measures against natural or legal persons adopted by the Council on the basis of Chapter 2 of Title V of the Treaty on European Union.

Article 276

In exercising its powers regarding the provisions of Chapters 4 and 5 of Title V of Part Three relating to the area of freedom, security and justice, the Court of Justice of the European Union shall have no jurisdiction to review the validity or proportionality of operations carried out by the police or other law-enforcement services of a Member State or the exercise of the responsibilities incumbent upon Member States with regard to the maintenance of law and order and the safeguarding of internal security.

Article 277

Notwithstanding the expiry of the period laid down in Article 263, fifth paragraph, any party may, in proceedings in which an act of general application adopted by an institution, body, office or agency of the Union is at issue, plead the grounds specified in Article 263, second paragraph, in order to invoke before the Court of Justice of the European Union the inapplicability of that act.

Article 278

Actions brought before the Court of Justice of the European Union shall not have suspensory effect. The Court may, however, if it considers that circumstances so require, order that application of the contested act be suspended.

Article 279

The Court of Justice of the European Union may in any cases before it prescribe any necessary interim measures.

Article 280

The judgments of the Court of Justice of the European Union shall be enforceable under the conditions laid down in Article 299.

Article 281

The Statute of the Court of Justice of the European Union shall be laid down in a separate Protocol. The European Parliament and the Council, acting in accordance with the ordinary legislative procedure, may amend the provisions of the Statute, with the exception of Title I and Article 64. The European Parliament and the Council shall act either at the request of the Court of Justice and after consultation of the Commission, or on a proposal from the Commission and after consultation of the Court of Justice.

SECTION 6

THE EUROPEAN CENTRAL BANK

Article 282

1. The European Central Bank, together with the national central banks, shall constitute the European System of Central Banks (ESCB). The European Central Bank, together with the national central banks of the Member States whose currency is the euro, which constitute the Eurosystem, shall conduct the monetary policy of the Union.
2. The ESCB shall be governed by the decision-making bodies of the European Central Bank. The primary objective of the ESCB shall be to maintain price stability. Without prejudice to that objective, it shall support the general economic policies in the Union in order to contribute to the achievement of the latter's objectives.
3. The European Central Bank shall have legal personality. It alone may authorise the issue of the euro. It shall be independent in the exercise of its powers and in the management of its finances. The institutions, bodies, offices and agencies of the Union and the governments of the Member States shall respect that independence.

4. The European Central Bank shall adopt such measures as are necessary to carry out its tasks in accordance with Articles 127 to 133, with Article 138, and with the conditions laid down in the Statute of the ECSB and of the ECB. In accordance with these same Articles, those Member States whose currency is not the euro, and their central banks, shall retain their powers in monetary matters.

5. Within the areas falling within its responsibilities, the European Central Bank shall be consulted on all proposed Union acts, and all proposals for regulation at national level, and may give an opinion.

THE COURT OF AUDITORS

Article 285

The Court of Auditors shall carry out the Union's audit.

It shall consist of one national of each Member State. Its members shall be completely independent in the performance of their duties, in the Union's general interest.

Article 286

1. The Members of the Court of Auditors shall be chosen from among persons who belong or have belonged in their respective States to external audit bodies or who are especially qualified for this office. Their independence must be beyond doubt.

2. The Members of the Court of Auditors shall be appointed for a term of six years. The Council, after consulting the European Parliament, shall adopt the list of Members drawn up in accordance with the proposals made by each Member State. The term of office of the Members of the Court of Auditors shall be renewable.

    They shall elect the President of the Court of Auditors from among their number for a term of three years. The President may be re-elected.

3. In the performance of these duties, the Members of the Court of Auditors shall neither seek nor take instructions from any government or from any other body. The Members of the Court of Auditors shall refrain from any action incompatible with their duties.

4. The Members of the Court of Auditors may shall not, during their term of office, engage in any other occupation, whether gainful or not. When entering upon their duties they shall give a solemn undertaking that, both during and after their term of office, they will respect the obligations arising therefrom and in particular their duty to behave with integrity and discretion as regards the acceptance, after they have ceased to hold office, of certain appointments or benefits.

5. Apart from normal replacement, or death, the duties of a Member of the Court of Auditors shall end when he resigns, or is compulsorily retired by a ruling of the Court of Justice pursuant to paragraph 6.

    The vacancy thus caused shall be filled for the remainder of the Member's term of office.

    Save in the case of compulsory retirement, Members of the Court of Auditors shall remain in office until they have been replaced.

6. A Member of the Court of Auditors may be deprived of his office or of his right to a pension or other benefits in its stead only if the Court of Justice, at the request of the Court of Auditors, finds that he no longer fulfils the requisite conditions or meets the obligations arising from his office.

7. The Council shall determine the conditions of employment of the President and the Members of the Court of Auditors and in particular their salaries, allowances and pensions. It shall also, determine any payment to be made instead of remuneration.

8. The provisions of the Protocol on the privileges and immunities of the European Union applicable to the Judges of the Court of Justice of the European Union shall also apply to the Members of the Court of Auditors.

Article 287

1. The Court of Auditors shall examine the accounts of all revenue and expenditure of the Union. It shall also examine the accounts of all revenue and expenditure of all bodies, offices or agencies set up by the Union in so far as the relevant constituent instrument does not preclude such examination.

The Court of Auditors shall provide the European Parliament and the Council with a statement of assurance as to the reliability of the accounts and the legality and regularity of the underlying transactions which shall be published in the *Official Journal of the European Union*. This statement may be supplemented by specific assessments for each major area of Union activity.

2. The Court of Auditors shall examine whether all revenue has been received and all expenditure incurred in a lawful and regular manner and whether the financial management has been sound. In doing so, it shall report in particular on any cases of irregularity.

The audit of revenue shall be carried out on the basis both of the amounts established as due and the amounts actually paid to the Union.

The audit of expenditure shall be carried out on the basis both of commitments undertaken and payments made.

These audits may be carried out before the closure of accounts for the financial year in question.

3. The audit shall be based on records and, if necessary, performed on the spot in the other institutions, on the premises of any body, office or agency which manages revenue or expenditure on behalf of the Union and in the Member States, including on the premises of any natural or legal person in receipt of payments from the budget. In the Member States the audit shall be carried out in liaison with national audit bodies or, if these do not have the necessary powers, with the competent national departments. The Court of Auditors and the national audit bodies of the Member States shall cooperate in a spirit of trust while maintaining their independence. These bodies or departments shall inform the Court of Auditors whether they intend to take part in the audit.

The other institutions of the Union, any bodies, offices or agencies managing revenue or expenditure on behalf of the Union, any natural or legal person in receipt of payments from the budget, and the national audit bodies or, if these do not have the necessary powers, the competent national departments, shall forward to the Court of Auditors, at its request, any document or information necessary to carry out its task.

In respect of the European Investment Bank's activity in managing Union expenditure and revenue, the Court's rights of access to information held by the Bank shall be governed by an agreement between the Court, the Bank and the Commission. In the absence of an agreement, the Court shall nevertheless have access to information necessary for the audit of Union expenditure and revenue managed by the Bank.

4. The Court of Auditors shall draw up an annual report after the close of each financial year. It shall be forwarded to the other institutions of the Union and shall be published, together with the replies of these institutions to the observations of the Court of Auditors, in the *Official Journal of the European Union*.

The Court of Auditors may also, at any time, submit observations, particularly in the form of special reports, on specific questions and deliver opinions at the request of one of the other institutions of the Union.

It shall adopt its annual reports, special reports or opinions by a majority of its component Members. However, it may establish internal chambers in order to adopt certain categories of reports or opinions under the conditions laid down by its Rules of Procedure.

It shall assist the European Parliament and the Council in exercising their powers of control over the implementation of the budget.

The Court of Auditors shall draw up its Rules of Procedure. Those rules shall require the approval of the Council.

CHAPTER 2
LEGAL ACTS OF THE UNION, ADOPTION PROCEDURES AND OTHER PROVISIONS
SECTION 1
THE LEGAL ACTS OF THE UNION

Article 288

To exercise the Union's competences, the institutions shall adopt regulations, directives, decisions, recommendations and opinions.

A regulation shall have general application. It shall be binding in its entirety and directly applicable in all Member States.

A directive shall be binding, as to the result to be achieved, upon each Member State to which it is addressed, but shall leave to the national authorities the choice of form and methods.

A decision shall be binding in its entirety. A decision which specifies those to whom it is addressed shall be binding only on them.

Recommendations and opinions shall have no binding force.

Article 289

1. The ordinary legislative procedure shall consist in the joint adoption by the European Parliament and the Council of a regulation, directive or decision on a proposal from the Commission. This procedure is defined in Article 294.
2. In the specific cases provided for by the Treaties, the adoption of a regulation, directive or decision by the European Parliament with the participation of the Council, or by the latter with the participation of the European Parliament, shall constitute a special legislative procedure.
3. Legal acts adopted by legislative procedure shall constitute legislative acts.
4. In the specific cases provided for by the Treaties, legislative acts may be adopted on the initiative of a group of Member States or of the European Parliament, on the recommendation of the European Central Bank or at the request of the Court of Justice or the European Investment Bank.

Article 290

1. A legislative act may delegate to the Commission the power to adopt non-legislative acts to supplement or amend certain non-essential elements of the legislative act.
    The objectives, content, scope and duration of the delegation of power shall be explicitly defined in the legislative acts. The essential elements of an area shall be reserved for the legislative act and accordingly shall not be the subject of a delegation of power.
2. Legislative acts shall explicitly lay down the conditions to which the delegation is subject; these conditions may be as follows:
    (a) the European Parliament or the Council may decide to revoke the delegation;
    (b) the delegated act may enter into force only if no objection has been expressed by the European Parliament or the Council within a period set by the legislative act.
    For the purposes of (a) and (b), the European Parliament shall act by a majority of its component members, and the Council by a qualified majority.
3. The adjective 'delegated' shall be inserted in the title of delegated acts.

Article 291

1. Member States shall adopt all measures of national law necessary to implement legally binding Union acts.
2. Where uniform conditions for implementing legally binding Union acts are needed, those acts shall confer implementing powers on the Commission, or, in duly justified specific cases and in the cases provided for in Articles 24 and 26 of the Treaty on European Union, on the Council.
3. For the purposes of paragraph 2, the European Parliament and the Council, acting by means of regulations in accordance with the ordinary legislative procedure, shall lay down in advance the rules and general principles concerning mechanisms for control by Member States of the Commission's exercise of implementing powers.
4. The word 'implementing' shall be inserted in the title of implementing acts.

Article 292

The Council shall adopt recommendations. It shall act on a proposal from the Commission in all cases where the Treaties provide that it shall adopt acts on a proposal from the Commission. It shall act unanimously in those areas in which unanimity is required for the adoption of a Union act. The Commission, and the European Central Bank in the specific cases provided for in the Treaties, shall adopt recommendations.

SECTION 2
PROCEDURES FOR THE ADOPTION OF ACTS AND OTHER PROVISIONS

Article 293

1. Where, pursuant to the Treaties, the Council acts on a proposal from the Commission, it may amend that proposal only by acting unanimously, except in the cases referred to in paragraphs 10 and 13 of Articles 294, in Articles 310, 312 and 314 and in the second paragraph of Article 315.
2. As long as the Council has not acted, the Commission may alter its proposal at any time during the procedures leading to the adoption of a Union act.

Article 294

1. Where reference is made in the Treaties to the ordinary legislative procedure for the adoption of an act, the following procedure shall apply.
2. The Commission shall submit a proposal to the European Parliament and the Council.

First reading

3. The European Parliament shall adopt its position at first reading and communicate it to the Council.
4. If the Council approves the European Parliament's position, the act concerned shall be adopted in the wording which corresponds to the position of the European Parliament.
5. If the Council does not approve the European Parliament's position, it shall adopt its position at first reading and communicate it to the European Parliament.
6. The Council shall inform the European Parliament fully of the reasons which led it to adopt its position at first reading. The Commission shall inform the European Parliament fully of its position.

Second reading

7. If, within three months of such communication, the European Parliament:
   (a) approves the Council's position at first reading or has not taken a decision, the act concerned shall be deemed to have been adopted in the wording which corresponds to the position of the Council;
   (b) rejects, by a majority of its component members, the Council's position at first reading, the proposed act shall be deemed not to have been adopted;
   (c) proposes, by a majority of its component members, amendments to the Council's position at first reading, the text thus amended shall be forwarded to the Council and to the Commission, which shall deliver an opinion on those amendments.
8. If, within three months of receiving the European Parliament's amendments, the Council, acting by a qualified majority:
   (a) approves all those amendments, the act in question shall be deemed to have been adopted;
   (b) does not approve all the amendments, the President of the Council, in agreement with the President of the European Parliament, shall within six weeks convene a meeting of the Conciliation Committee.
9. The Council shall act unanimously on the amendments on which the Commission has delivered a negative opinion.

Conciliation

10. The Conciliation Committee, which shall be composed of the members of the Councilor their representatives and an equal number of members representing the European Parliament, shall have the task of reaching agreement on a joint text, by a qualified majority of the members of the Councilor their representatives and by a majority of the members representing the European Parliament within six weeks of its being convened, on the basis of the positions of the European Parliament and the Council at second reading.

11. The Commission shall take part in the Conciliation Committee's proceedings and shall take all necessary initiatives with a view to reconciling the positions of the European Parliament and the Council.

12. If, within six weeks of its being convened, the Conciliation Committee does not approve the joint text, the proposed act shall be deemed not to have been adopted.

Third reading

13. If, within that period, the Conciliation Committee approves a joint text, the European Parliament, acting by a majority of the votes cast, and the Council, acting by a qualified majority, shall each have a period of six weeks from that approval in which to adopt the act in question in accordance with the joint text. If they fail to do so, the proposed act shall be deemed not to have been adopted.

14. The periods of three months and six weeks referred to in this Article shall be extended by a maximum of one month and two weeks respectively at the initiative of the European Parliament or the Council.

Special provisions

15. Where, in the cases provided for in the Treaties, a legislative act is submitted to the ordinary legislative procedure on the initiative of a group of Member States, on a recommendation by the European Central Bank, or at the request of the Court of Justice, paragraph 2, the second sentence of paragraph 6, and paragraph 9 shall not apply.

    In such cases, the European Parliament and the Council shall communicate the proposed act to the Commission with their positions at first and second readings. The European Parliament or the Council may request the opinion of the Commission throughout the procedure, which the Commission may also deliver on its own initiative. It may also, if it deems it necessary, take part in the Conciliation Committee in accordance with paragraph 11.

Article 295

The European Parliament, the Council and the Commission shall consult each other and by common agreement make arrangements for their cooperation. To that end, they may, in compliance with the Treaties, conclude interinstitutional agreements which may be of a binding nature.

Article 296

1. Where the Treaties do not specify the type of act to be adopted, the institutions shall select it on a case-by-case basis, in compliance with the applicable procedures and with the principle of proportionality.

2. Legal acts shall state the reasons on which they are based and shall refer to any proposals, initiatives, recommendations, requests or opinions required by the Treaties.

3. When considering draft legislative acts, the European Parliament and the Council shall refrain from adopting acts not provided for by the relevant legislative procedure in the area in question.

Article 297

1. Legislative acts adopted under the ordinary legislative procedure shall be signed by the President of the European Parliament and by the President of the Council.

   Legislative acts adopted under a special legislative procedure shall be signed by the President of the institution which adopted them.

   Legislative acts shall be published in the *Official Journal of the European Union*. They shall enter into force on the date specified in them or, in the absence thereof, on the twentieth day following that of their publication.

2. Non-legislative acts adopted in the form of regulations, directives or decisions which do not specify to whom they are addressed, shall be signed by the President of the institution which adopted them.

Regulations and directives which are addressed to all Member States, as well as decisions which do not specify to whom they are addressed, shall be published in the *Official Journal of the European Union*. They shall enter into force on the date specified in them or, in the absence thereof, on the twentieth day following that of their publication.

Other directives, and decisions which specify to whom they are addressed, shall be notified to those to whom they are addressed and shall take effect upon such notification.

Article 298

1. In carrying out their missions, the institutions, bodies, offices and agencies of the Union shall have the support of an open, efficient and independent European administration.
2. In compliance with the Staff Regulations and Conditions of Employment adopted on the basis of Article 336, the European Parliament and the Council, acting by means of regulations in accordance with the ordinary legislative procedure, shall establish provisions to that end.

Article 299

Acts of the Council, of the Commission or of the European Central Bank which impose a pecuniary obligation on persons other than States, shall be enforceable.

Enforcement shall be governed by the rules of civil procedure in force in the State in the territory of which it is carried out. The order for its enforcement shall be appended to the decision, without other formality than verification of the authenticity of the decision, by the national authority which the government of each Member State shall designate for this purpose and shall make known to the Commission and to the Court of Justice of the European Union.

When these formalities have been completed on application by the party concerned, the latter may proceed to enforcement in accordance with the national law, by bringing the matter directly before the competent authority.

Enforcement may be suspended only by a decision of the Court. However, the courts of the country concerned shall have jurisdiction over complaints that enforcement is being carried out in an irregular manner.

CHAPTER 3
THE UNION'S ADVISORY BODIES

Article 300

1. The European Parliament, the Council and the Commission shall be assisted by an Economic and Social Committee and a Committee of the Regions, exercising advisory functions.
2. The Economic and Social Committee shall consist of representatives of organisations of employers, of the employed, and of other parties representative of civil society, notably in socio-economic, civic, professional and cultural areas.
3. The Committee of the Regions shall consist of representatives of regional and local bodies who either hold a regional or local authority electoral mandate or are politically accountable to an elected assembly.
4. The members of the Economic and Social Committee and the Committee of the Regions shall not be bound by any mandatory instructions. They shall be completely independent in the performance of their duties, in the Union's general interest.
5. The rules referred to in paragraphs 2 and 3 governing the nature of their composition shall be reviewed at regular intervals by the Council to take account of economic, social and demographic developments within the Union. The Council, on a proposal from the Commission, shall adopt decisions to that end.

SECTION 1
THE ECONOMIC AND SOCIAL COMMITTEE

Article 301

The number of members of the Economic and Social Committee shall not exceed 350.

The Council, acting unanimously on a proposal from the Commission, shall adopt a decision determining the Committee's composition.

Article 302

1. The members of the Committee shall be appointed for five years The Council" shall adopt the list of members drawn up in accordance with the proposals made by each Member State. The term of office of the members of the Committee shall be renewable.

2. The Council shall act after consulting the Commission. It may obtain the opinion of European bodies which are representative of the various economic and social sectors and of civil society to which the Union's activities are of concern.

Article 303

The Committee shall elect its chairman and officers from among its members for a term of two and a half years.

It shall adopt its Rules of Procedure.

The Committee shall be convened by its chairman at the request of the European Parliament, the Council or of the Commission. It may also meet on its own initiative.

Article 304

The Committee shall be consulted by the European Parliament, by the Councilor by the Commission where the Treaties so provide. The Committee may be consulted by these institutions in all cases in which they consider it appropriate. It may issue an opinion on its own initiative in cases in which it considers such action appropriate.

The European Parliament, the Councilor the Commission shall, if it considers it necessary, set the Committee, for the submission of its opinion, a time limit which may not be less than one month from the date on which the chairman receives notification to this effect. Upon expiry of the time limit, the absence of an opinion shall not prevent further action.

The opinion of the Committee, together with a record of the proceedings, shall be forwarded to the European Parliament, to the Council and to the Commission.

SECTION 2

THE COMMITTEE OF THE REGIONS

Article 305

The number of members of the Committee of the Regions shall not exceed 350.

The Council, acting unanimously on a proposal from the Commission, shall adopt a decision determining the Committee's composition.

The members of the Committee and an equal number of alternate members shall be appointed for five years. Their term of office shall be renewable. The Council shall adopt the list of members and alternate members drawn up in accordance with the proposals made by each Member State. When the mandate referred to in Article 300(3) on the basis of which they were proposed comes to an end, the term of office of members of the Committee shall terminate automatically and they shall then be replaced for the remainder of the said term of office in accordance with the same procedure. No member of the Committee shall at the same time be a Member of the European Parliament.

Article 306

The Committee of the Regions shall elect its chairman and officers from among its members for a term of two and a half years.

It shall adopt its Rules of Procedure.

The Committee shall be convened by its chairman at the request of the European Parliament, the Councilor of the Commission. It may also meet on its own initiative.

Article 307

The Committee of the Regions shall be consulted by the European Parliament, by the Council or by the Commission where the Treaties so provide and in all other cases, in particular those which concern cross-border cooperation, in which one of these institutions considers it appropriate.

The European Parliament, the Councilor the Commission shall, if it considers it necessary, set the Committee, for the submission of its opinion, a time limit which may not be less than one month from the date on which the chairman receives notification to this effect. Upon expiry of the time limit, the absence of an opinion shall not prevent further action.

Where the Economic and Social Committee is consulted, the Committee of the Regions shall be informed by the European Parliament, the Council or the Commission of the request for an opinion. Where it considers that specific regional interests are involved, the Committee of the Regions may issue an opinion on the matter.

It may issue an opinion on its own initiative in cases in which it considers such action appropriate.

The opinion of the Committee, together with a record of the proceedings, shall be forwarded to the European Parliament, the Council and to the Commission.

CHAPTER 4
THE EUROPEAN INVESTMENT BANK

Article 308

The European Investment Bank shall have legal personality.

The members of the European Investment Bank shall be the Member States.

The Statute of the European Investment Bank is laid down in a Protocol annexed to the Treaties. The Council acting unanimously in accordance with a special legislative procedure, at the request of the European Investment Bank and after consulting the European Parliament and the Commission, or on a proposal from the Commission and after consulting the European Parliament and the European Investment Bank, may amend the Statute of the Bank.

TITLE II
FINANCIAL PROVISIONS

Article 310

1. All items of revenue and expenditure of the Union shall be included in estimates to be drawn up for each financial year and shall be shown in the budget.

   The Union's annual budget shall be established by the European Parliament and the Council in accordance with Article 314.

   The revenue and expenditure shown in the budget shall be in balance.

2. The expenditure shown in the budget shall be authorised for the annual budgetary period in accordance with the regulation referred to in Article 322.

3. The implementation of expenditure shown in the budget shall require the prior adoption of a legally binding act of the Union providing a legal basis for its action and for the implementation of the corresponding expenditure in accordance with the regulation referred to in Article 322, except in cases for which that law provides.

4. With a view to maintaining budgetary discipline, the Union shall not adopt any act which is likely to have appreciable implications for the budget without providing an assurance that the expenditure arising from such an act is capable of being financed within the limit of the Union's own resources and in compliance with the multiannual financial framework referred to in Article 312.

5. The budget shall be implemented in accordance with the principle of sound financial management. Member States shall cooperate with the Union to ensure that the appropriations entered in the budget are used in accordance with this principle.

6. The Union and the Member States, in accordance with Article 325, shall counter fraud and any other illegal activities affecting the financial interests of the Union.

CHAPTER 1
THE UNION'S OWN RESOURCES

Article 311

The Union shall provide itself with the means necessary to attain its objectives and carry through its policies.

Without prejudice to other revenue, the budget shall be financed wholly from own resources.

The Council, acting in accordance with a special legislative procedure, shall unanimously and after consulting the European Parliament adopt a decision laying down the provisions relating to the system of own resources of the Union. In this context it may establish new categories of own resources or abolish an existing category. That decision shall not enter into force until it is approved by the Member States in accordance with their respective constitutional requirements.

The Council, acting by means of regulations in accordance with a special legislative procedure, shall lay down implementing measures of the Union's own resources system insofar as this is provided for in the decision adopted on the basis of the third paragraph. The Council shall act after obtaining the consent of the European Parliament.

CHAPTER 2
THE MULTIANNUAL FINANCIAL FRAMEWORK

Article 312

1. The multiannual financial framework shall ensure that Union expenditure develops in an orderly manner and within the limits of its own resources.

   It shall be established for a period of at least five years.

   The annual budget of the Union shall comply with the multiannual financial framework.

2. The Council, acting in accordance with a special legislative procedure, shall adopt a regulation laying down the multi annual financial framework. The Council shall act unanimously after obtaining the consent of the European Parliament, which shall be given by a majority of its component members.

   The European Council may, unanimously, adopt a decision authorising the Council to act by a qualified majority when adopting the regulation of the Council referred to in the first subparagraph.

3. The financial framework shall determine the amounts of the annual ceilings on commitment appropriations by category of expenditure and of the annual ceiling on payment appropriations. The categories of expenditure, limited in number, shall correspond to the Union's major sectors of activity.

   The financial framework shall lay down any other provisions required for the annual budgetary procedure to run smoothly.

4. Where no Council regulation determining a new financial framework has been adopted by the end of the previous financial framework, the ceilings and other provisions corresponding to the last year of that framework shall be extended until such time as that act is adopted.

5. Throughout the procedure leading to the adoption of the financial framework, the European Parliament, the Council and the Commission shall take any measure necessary to facilitate its adoption.

CHAPTER 3
THE UNION'S ANNUAL BUDGET

Article 313

The financial year shall run from 1 January to 31 December.

Article 314

The European Parliament and the Council, acting in accordance with a special legislative procedure, shall establish the Union's annual budget in accordance with the following provisions.

1. With the exception of the European Central Bank, each institution shall, before 1 July, draw up estimates of its expenditure for the following financial year. The Commission shall consolidate these estimates in a draft budget. which may contain different estimates.

   The draft budget shall contain an estimate of revenue and an estimate of expenditure.

2. The Commission shall submit a proposal containing the draft budget to the European Parliament and to the Council not later than 1 September of the year preceding that in which the budget is to be implemented.

   The Commission may amend the draft budget during the procedure until such time as the Conciliation Committee, referred to in paragraph 5, is convened.

3. The Council shall adopt its position on the draft budget and forward it to the European Parliament not later than 1 October of the year preceding that in which the budget is to be

implemented. The Council shall inform the European Parliament in full of the reasons which led it to adopt its position.

4.   If, within forty-two days of such communication, the European Parliament:

    (a)   approves the position of the Council, the budget shall be adopted;

    (b)   has not taken a decision, the budget shall be deemed to have been adopted;

    (c)   adopts amendments by a majority of its component members, the amended draft shall be forwarded to the Council and to the Commission. The President of the European Parliament, in agreement with the President of the Council, shall immediately convene a meeting of the Conciliation Committee. However, if within ten days of the draft being forwarded the Council informs the European Parliament that it has approved all its amendments, the Conciliation Committee shall not meet.

5.   The Conciliation Committee, which shall be composed of the members of the Council or their representatives and an equal number of members representing the European Parliament, shall have the task of reaching agreement on a joint text, by a qualified majority of the members of the Council or their representatives and by a majority of the representatives of the European Parliament within twenty-one days of its being convened, on the basis of the positions of the European Parliament and the Council.

The Commission shall take part in the Conciliation Committee's proceedings and shall take all the necessary initiatives with a view to reconciling the positions of the European Parliament and the Council.

6.   If, within the twenty-one days referred to in paragraph 5, the Conciliation Committee agrees on a joint text, the European Parliament and the Council shall each have a period of fourteen days from the date of that agreement in which to approve the joint text.

7.   If, within the period of fourteen days referred to in paragraph 6:

    (a)   the European Parliament and the Council both approve the joint text or fail to take a decision, or if one of these institutions approves the joint text while the other one fails to take a decision, the budget shall be deemed to be definitively adopted in accordance with the joint text, or

    (b)   the European Parliament, acting by a majority of its component members, and the Council both reject the joint text, or if one of these institutions rejects the joint text while the other one fails to take a decision, a new draft budget shall be submitted by the Commission, or

    (c)   the European Parliament, acting by a majority of its component members, rejects the joint text while the Council approves it, a new draft budget shall be submitted by the Commission, or

    (d)   the European Parliament approves the joint text whilst the Council rejects it, the European Parliament may, within fourteen days from the date of the rejection by the Council and acting by a majority of its component members and three-fifths of the votes cast, decide to confirm all or some of the amendments referred to in paragraph 4(c). Where a European Parliament amendment is not confirmed, the position agreed in the Conciliation Committee on the budget heading which is the subject of the amendment shall be retained. The budget shall be deemed to be definitively adopted on this basis.

8.   If, within the twenty-one days referred to in paragraph 5, the Conciliation Committee does not agree on a joint text, a new draft budget shall be submitted by the Commission.

9.   When the procedure provided for in this Article has been completed, the President of the European Parliament shall declare that the budget has been definitively adopted.

10.   Each institution shall exercise the powers conferred upon it under this Article in compliance with the Treaties and the acts adopted thereunder, with particular regard to the Union's own resources and the balance between revenue and expenditure.

Article 315

If, at the beginning of a financial year, the budget has not yet been definitively adopted, a sum equivalent to not more than one twelfth of the budget appropriations for the preceding financial year may be spent each month in respect of any chapter of the budget in accordance with the provisions of the Regulations made pursuant to Article 322; that sum shall not, however, exceed one twelfth of the appropriations provided for in the same chapter of the draft budget.

The Council on a proposal by the Commission may, provided that the other conditions laid down in the first paragraph are observed, authorise expenditure in excess of one twelfth, in accordance with the regulations made pursuant to Article 322. The Council shall forward the decision immediately to the European Parliament.

The decision referred to in the second subparagraph shall lay down the necessary measures relating to resources to ensure application of this Article, in accordance with the acts referred to in Article 311.

It shall enter into force thirty days following its adoption if the European Parliament, acting by a majority of its component members, has not decided to reduce this expenditure within that time-limit.

Article 316

In accordance with conditions to be laid down pursuant to Article 322, any appropriations, other than those relating to staff expenditure, that are unexpended at the end of the financial year may be carried forward to the next financial year only.

Appropriations shall be classified under different chapters grouping items of expenditure according to their nature or purpose and subdivided, in accordance with the regulations made pursuant to Article 322.

The expenditure of the European Parliament, the European Council and the Council, the Commission and the Court of Justice of the European Union shall be set out in separate parts of the budget, without prejudice to special arrangements for certain common items of expenditure.

CHAPTER 5
COMMON PROVISIONS

Article 320

The multiannual financial framework and the annual budget shall be drawn up in euro.

Article 321

The Commission may, provided it notifies the competent authorities of the Member States concerned, transfer into the currency of one of the Member States its holdings in the currency of another Member State, to the extent necessary to enable them to be used for purposes which come within the scope of the Treaties. The Commission shall as far as possible avoid making such transfers if it possesses cash or liquid assets in the currencies which it needs,

The Commission shall deal with each Member State through the authority designated by the State concerned, In carrying out financial operations the Commission shall employ the services of the bank of issue of the Member State concerned or of any other financial institution approved by that State,

Article 322

1. The European Parliament and the Council, acting in accordance with the ordinary legislative procedure, and after consulting the Court of Auditors shall adopt by means of regulations:
    (a) the financial rules which determine in particular the procedure to be adopted for establishing and implementing the budget and for presenting and auditing accounts;
    (b) rules providing for checks on the responsibility of financial actors, in particular authorising officers and accounting officers.
2. The Council, acting on a proposal from the Commission and after consulting the European Parliament and the Court of Auditors, shall determine methods and procedure whereby the budget revenue provided under the arrangements relating to the Union's own resources shall be made available to the Commission, and determine the measures to be applied, if need be, to meet cash requirements.

Article 323

The European Parliament, the Council and the Commission shall ensure that the financial means are made available to allow the Union to fulfil its legal obligations in respect of third parties.

Article 324

Regular meetings between the Presidents of the European Parliament, the Council and the Commission shall be convened, on the initiative of the Commission, under the budgetary procedures referred to in this Chapter, The Presidents shall take all the necessary steps to promote consultation and the reconciliation of the positions of the institutions over which they preside in order to facilitate the implementation of this Title.

CHAPTER 6
COMBATTING FRAUD

Article 325

1. The Union and the Member States shall counter fraud and any other illegal activities affecting the financial interests of the Union through measures to be taken in accordance with this Article, which shall act as a deterrent and be such as to afford effective protection in the Member States, and in all the Union's institutions, bodies, offices and agencies.

TITLE III
ENHANCED COOPERATION

Article 326

Any enhanced cooperation shall comply with the Treaties and Union law.

Such cooperation shall not undermine the internal market or economic, social and territorial cohesion, It shall not constitute a barrier to or discrimination in trade between Member States, nor shall it distort competition between them.

Article 327

Any enhanced cooperation shall respect the competences, rights and obligations of those Member States which do not participate in it. Those Member States shall not impede its implementation by the participating Member States.

PART SEVEN
GENERAL AND FINAL PROVISIONS

Article 335

In each of the Member States, the Union shall enjoy the most extensive legal capacity accorded to legal persons under their laws; it may, in particular, acquire or dispose of movable and immovable property and may be a party to legal proceedings. To this end, the Union shall be represented by the Commission. However, the Union shall be represented by each of the institutions, by virtue of their administrative autonomy, in matters relating to their respective operation.

Article 336

The European Parliament and the Council shall, acting by means of regulations in accordance with the ordinary legislative procedure on a proposal from the Commission and after consulting the other institutions concerned, lay down the Staff Regulations of officials of the European Union and the Conditions of employment of other servants of the Union.

Article 337

The Commission may, within the limits and under conditions laid down by the Council, acting by a simple majority in accordance with the provisions of the Treaties, collect any information and carry out any checks required for the performance of the tasks entrusted to it.

Article 338

1. Without prejudice to Article 5 of the Protocol on the Statute of the European System of Central Banks and of the European Central Bank, the European Parliament and the Council, acting in accordance with the ordinary legislative procedure, shall adopt measures for the production of statistics where necessary for the performance of the activities of the Union.
2. The production of Union statistics shall conform to impartiality, reliability, objectivity, scientific independence, cost-effectiveness and statistical confidentiality; it shall not entail excessive burdens on economic operators.

Article 339

The members of the institutions of the Union, the members of committees, and the officials and other servants of the Union shall be required, even after their duties have ceased, not to disclose information of the kind covered by the obligation of professional secrecy, in particular information about undertakings, their business relations or their cost components.

Article 340

The contractual liability of the Union shall be governed by the law applicable to the contract in question.

In the case of non-contractual liability, the Union shall, in accordance with the general principles common to the laws of the Member States, make good any damage caused by its institutions or by its servants in the performance of their duties.

Notwithstanding the second paragraph, the European Central Bank shall, in accordance with the general principles common to the laws of the Member States, make good any damage caused by it or by its servants in the performance of their duties.

The personal liability of its servants towards the Union shall be governed by the provisions laid down in their Staff Regulations or in the Conditions of employment applicable to them.

Article 341

The seat of the institutions of the Union shall be determined by common accord of the governments of the Member States.

Article 342

The rules governing the languages of the institutions of the Union shall, without prejudice to the provisions contained in the Statute of the Court of Justice, be determined by the Council, acting unanimously by means of regulations.

Article 343

The Union shall enjoy in the territories of the Member States such privileges and immunities as are necessary for the performance of its tasks, under the conditions laid down in the Protocol of 8 April 1965 on the privileges and immunities of the European Union. The same shall apply to the European Central Bank and the European Investment Bank.

Article 344

Member States undertake not to submit a dispute concerning the interpretation or application of the Treaties to any method of settlement other than those provided for therein.

Article 345

The Treaties shall in no way prejudice the rules in Member States governing the system of property ownership.

Article 346

1. The provisions of the Treaties shall not preclude the application of the following rules:
    (a) no Member State shall be obliged to supply information the disclosure of which it considers contrary to the essential interests of its security;
    (b) any Member State may take such measures as it considers necessary for the protection of the essential interests of its security which are connected with the production of or trade in arms, munitions and war material; such measures shall not adversely affect the conditions of competition in the internal market regarding products which are not intended for specifically military purposes.
2. The Council may, acting unanimously on a proposal from the Commission, make changes to the list, which it drew up on 15 April 1958, of the products to which the provisions of paragraph 1(b) apply.

Article 347

Member States shall consult each other with a view to taking together the steps needed to prevent the functioning of the internal market being affected by measures which a Member State may be called upon to take in the event of serious internal disturbances affecting the maintenance of law and order, in the event of war, serious international tension constituting a threat of war, or in order to carry out obligations it has accepted for the purpose of maintaining peace and international security.

Article 348

If measures taken in the circumstances referred to in Articles 346 and 347 have the effect of distorting the conditions of competition in the internal market, the Commission shall, together with the State concerned, examine how these measures can be adjusted to the rules laid down in the Treaties.

By way of derogation from the procedure laid down in Articles 258 and 259, the Commission or any Member State may bring the matter directly before the Court of Justice if it considers that another Member State is making improper use of the powers provided for in Articles 346 and 347. The Court of Justice shall give its ruling in camera.

Article 349

Taking account of the structural social and economic situation of Guadeloupe, French Guiana, Martinique, Reunion, Saint Barthélemy, Saint Martin, the Azores, Madeira and the Canary Islands, which is compounded by their remoteness, insularity, small size, difficult topography and climate, economic dependence on a few products, the permanence and combination of which severely restrain their development, the Council, on a proposal from the Commission and after consulting the European Parliament, shall adopt specific measures aimed, in particular, at laying down the conditions of application of the Treaties to those regions, including common policies. Where the specific measures in question are adopted by the Council in accordance with a special legislative procedure, it shall also act on a proposal from the Commission and after consulting the European Parliament.

The measures referred to in the first paragraph concern in particular areas such as customs and trade policies, fiscal policy, free zones, agriculture and fisheries policies, conditions for supply of raw materials and essential consumer goods, State aids and conditions of access to structural funds and to horizontal Union programmes.

The Council shall adopt the measures referred to in the first subparagraph taking into account the special characteristics and constraints of the outermost regions without undermining the integrity and the coherence of the Union legal order, including the internal market and common policies.

Article 350

The provisions of the Treaties shall not preclude the existence or completion of regional unions between Belgium and Luxembourg, or between Belgium, Luxembourg and the Netherlands, to the extent that the objectives of these regional unions are not attained by application of the Treaties.

Article 351

The rights and obligations arising from agreements concluded before 1 January 1958 or, for acceding States, before the date of their accession, between one or more Member States on the one hand, and one or more third countries on the other, shall not be affected by the provisions of the Treaties.

To the extent that such agreements are not compatible with the Treaties, the Member State or States concerned shall take all appropriate steps to eliminate the incompatibilities established. Member States shall, where necessary, assist each other to this end and shall, where appropriate, adopt a common attitude.

In applying the agreements referred to in the first paragraph, Member States shall take into account the fact that the advantages accorded under the Treaties by each Member State form an integral part of the establishment of the Union and are thereby inseparably linked with the creation of common institutions, the conferring of powers upon them and the granting of the same advantages by all the other Member States.

Article 352

1. If action by the Union should prove necessary, within the framework of the policies defined by the Treaties, to attain one of the objectives set out in the Treaties, and the Treaties have not provided the necessary powers, the Council, acting unanimously on a proposal from the

European Commission and after obtaining the consent of the European Parliament, shall adopt the appropriate measures. Where the measures in question are adopted by the Council in accordance with a special legislative procedure, it shall also act unanimously on a proposal from the Commission and after obtaining the consent of the European Parliament.

2.   Using the procedure for monitoring the subsidiarity principle referred to in Article 5(3) of the Treaty on European Union, the Commission shall draw national Parliaments' attention to proposals based on this Article.

3.   Measures based on this Article shall not entail harmonisation of Member States' laws or regulations in cases where the Treaties exclude such harmonisation.

4.   This Article cannot serve as a basis for attaining objectives pertaining to the common foreign and security policy and any acts adopted pursuant to this Article shall respect the limits set out in Article 40, second paragraph, of the Treaty on European Union.

STATUTE OF THE COURT OF JUSTICE

Editor's Note: This is the current version. A new Statute appears in the protocol to the consolidated (Treaty of Lisbon) treaty.

Article 1

The Court of Justice shall be constituted and shall function in accordance with the provisions of the Treaty on European Union (EU Treaty), of the Treaty establishing the European Community (EC Treaty), of the Treaty establishing the European Atomic Energy Community (EAEC Treaty) and of this Statute.

TITLE 1
JUDGES AND ADVOCATES GENERAL

Article 2

Before taking up his duties each Judge shall, in open court, take an oath to perform his duties impartially and conscientiously and to preserve the secrecy of the deliberations of the Court.

Article 3

The Judges shall be immune from legal proceedings. After they have ceased to hold office, they shall continue to enjoy immunity in respect of acts performed by them in their official capacity, including words spoken or written.

The Court, sitting as a full Court, may waive the immunity.

Where immunity has been waived and criminal proceedings are instituted against a Judge, he shall be tried, in any of the Member States, only by the court competent to judge the members of the highest national judiciary.

Articles 12 to 15 and Article 18 of the Protocol on the privileges and immunities of the European Communities shall apply to the Judges, Advocates General, Registrar and Assistant Rapporteurs of the Court, without prejudice to the provisions relating to immunity from legal proceedings of Judges which are set out in the preceding paragraphs.

Article 4

The Judges may not hold any political or administrative office.

They may not engage in any occupation, whether gainful or not, unless exemption is exceptionally granted by the Council.

When taking up their duties, they shall give a solemn undertaking that, both during and after their term of office, they will respect the obligations arising therefrom, in particular the duty to behave with integrity and discretion as regards the acceptance, after they have ceased to hold office, of certain appointments or benefits.

Any doubt on this point shall be settled by decision of the Court.

Article 5

Apart from normal replacement, or death, the duties of a Judge shall end when he resigns.

Where a Judge resigns, his letter of resignation shall be addressed to the President of the Court for transmission to the President of the Council. Upon this notification a vacancy shall arise on the bench.

Save where Article 6 applies, a Judge shall continue to hold office until his successor takes up his duties.

Article 6

A Judge may be deprived of his office or of his right to a pension or other benefits in its stead only if, in the unanimous opinion of the Judges and Advocates General of the Court, he no longer fulfils the requisite conditions or meets the obligations arising from his office. The Judge concerned shall not take part in any such deliberations.

The Registrar of the Court shall communicate the decision of the Court to the Presidents of the European Parliament and of the Commission and shall notify it to the President of the Council.

In the case of a decision depriving a Judge of his office, a vacancy shall arise on the bench upon this latter notification.

Article 7

A Judge who is to replace a member of the Court whose term of office has not expired shall be appointed for the remainder of his predecessor's term.

Article 8

The provisions of Articles 2 to 7 shall apply to the Advocates General.

TITLE II

ORGANISATION

Article 9

When every three years, the Judges are partially replaced, fourteen and thirteen Judges shall be replaced alternately.

When, every three years, the Advocates General are partially replaced, four Advocates General shall be replaced on each occasion.

Article 10

The Registrar shall take an oath before the Court to perform his duties impartially and conscientiously and to preserve the secrecy of the deliberations of the Court.

Article 11

The Court shall arrange for replacement of the Registrar on occasions when he is prevented from attending the Court.

Article 12

Officials and other servants shall be attached to the Court to enable it to function. They shall be responsible to the Registrar under the authority of the President.

Article 13

On a proposal from the Court, the Council may, acting unanimously, provide for the appointment of Assistant Rapporteurs and lay down the rules governing their service. The Assistant Rapporteurs may be required, under conditions laid down in the Rules of Procedure, to participate in preparatory inquiries in cases pending before the Court and to cooperate with the Judge who acts as Rapporteur. The Assistant Rapporteurs shall be chosen from persons whose independence is beyond doubt and who possess the necessary legal qualifications; they shall be appointed by the Council. They shall take an oath before the Court to perform their duties impartially and conscientiously and to preserve the secrecy of the deliberations of the Court.

Article 14

The Judges, the Advocates General and the Registrar shall be required to reside at the place where the Court has its seat.

Article 15

The Court shall remain permanently in session. The duration of the judicial vacations shall be determined by the Court with due regard to the needs of its business.

Article 16

The Court shall form chambers consisting of three and five Judges. The Judges shall elect the Presidents of the chambers from among their number. The Presidents of the chambers of five Judges shall be elected for three years. They may be re-elected once.

The Grand Chamber shall consist of thirteen Judges. It shall be presided over by the President of the Court. The Presidents of the chambers of five Judges and other Judges appointed in accordance with the conditions laid down in the Rules of Procedure shall also form part of the Grand Chamber. The Court shall sit in a Grand Chamber when a Member State or an institution of the Communities that is party to the proceedings so requests.

The Court shall sit as a full Court where cases are brought before it pursuant to Article 195(2), Article 213(2), Article 216 or Article 247(7) of the EC Treaty or Article 107d(2), Article 126(2), Article 129 or Article 160b(7) of the EAEC Treaty.

Moreover, where it considers that a case before it is of exceptional importance, the Court may decide, after hearing the Advocate General, to refer the case to the full Court.

Article 17

Decisions of the Court shall be valid only when an uneven number of its members is sitting in the deliberations.

Decisions of the chambers consisting of either three or five Judges shall be valid only if they are taken by three Judges.

Decisions of the Grand Chamber shall be valid only if nine Judges are sitting.

Decisions of the full Court shall be valid only if fifteen Judges are sitting.

In the event of one of the Judges of a chamber being prevented from attending, a Judge of another chamber may be called upon to sit in accordance with conditions laid down in the Rules of Procedure

Article 18

No Judge or Advocate General may take part in the disposal of any case in which he has previously taken part as agent or adviser or has acted for one of the parties, or in which he has been called upon to pronounce as a member of a court or tribunal, of a commission of inquiry or in any other capacity.

If, for some special reason, any Judge or Advocate General considers that he should not take part in the judgment or examination of a particular case, he shall so inform the President. If, for some special reason, the President considers that any Judge or Advocate General should not sit or make submissions in a particular case, he shall notify him accordingly.

Any difficulty arising as to the application of this Article shall be settled by decision of the Court.

A party may not apply for a change in the composition of the Court or of one of its chambers on the grounds of either the nationality of a Judge or the absence from the Court or from the chamber of a Judge of the nationality of that party.

TITLE III
PROCEDURE

Article 19

The Member States and the institutions of the Communities shall be represented before the Court by an agent appointed for each case; the agent may be assisted by an adviser or by a lawyer.

The States, other than the Member States, which are parties to the Agreement on the European Economic Area and also the EFTA Surveillance Authority referred to in that Agreement shall be represented in same manner.

Other parties must be represented by a lawyer.

Only a lawyer authorised to practise before a court of a Member State or of another State which is a party to the Agreement on the European Economic Area may represent or assist a party before the Court.

Such agents, advisers and lawyers shall, when they appear before the Court, enjoy the rights and immunities necessary to the independent exercise of their duties, under conditions laid down in the Rules of Procedure.

As regards such advisers and lawyers who appear before it, the Court shall have the powers normally accorded to courts of law, under conditions laid down in the Rules of Procedure.

University teachers being nationals of a Member State whose law accords them a right of audience shall have the same rights before the Court as are accorded by this Article to lawyers.

Article 20

The procedure before the Court shall consist of two parts: written and oral.

The written procedure shall consist of the communication to the parties and to the institutions of the Communities whose decisions are in dispute, of applications, statements of case, defences and observations, and of replies, if any, as well as of all papers and documents in support or of certified copies of them. Communications shall be made by the Registrar in the order and within the time laid down in the Rules of Procedure.

The oral procedure shall consist of the reading of the report presented by a Judge acting as Rapporteur, the hearing by the Court of agents, advisers and lawyers and of the submissions of the Advocate General, as well as the hearing, if any, of witnesses and experts.

Where it considers that the case raises no new point of law, the Court may decide, after hearing the Advocate General, that the case shall be determined without a submission from the Advocate General.

Article 21

A case shall be brought before the Court by a written application addressed to the Registrar. The application shall contain the applicant's name and permanent address and the description of the signatory, the name of the party or names of the parties against whom the application is made, the subject-matter of the dispute, the form of order sought and a brief statement of the pleas in law on which the application is based.

The application shall be accompanied, where appropriate, by the measure the annulment of which is sought or, in the circumstances referred to in Article 232 of the EC Treaty and Article 148 of the EAEC Treaty, by documentary evidence of the date on which an institution was, in accordance with those Articles, requested to act. If the documents are not submitted with the application, the Registrar shall ask the party concerned to produce them within a reasonable period, but in that event the rights of the party shall not lapse even if such documents are produced after the time-limit for bringing proceedings.

Article 22

A case governed by Article 18 of the EAEC Treaty shall be brought before the Court by an appeal addressed to the Registrar. The appeal shall contain the name and permanent address of the applicant and the description of the signatory, a reference to the decision against which the appeal is brought, the names of the respondents, the subject-matter of the dispute, the submissions and a brief statement of the grounds on which the appeal is based.

The appeal shall be accompanied by a certified copy of the decision of the Arbitration Committee which is contested.

If the Court rejects the appeal, the decision of the Arbitration Committee shall become final.

If the Court annuls the decision of the Arbitration Committee, the matter may be reopened, where appropriate, on the initiative of one of the parties in the case, before the Arbitration Committee. The latter shall conform to any decisions on points of law given by the Court.

Article 23

In the cases governed by Article 35(1) of the EU Treaty, by Article 234 of the EC Treaty and by Article 150 of the EAEC Treaty, the decision of the court or tribunal of a Member State which suspends its proceedings and refers a case to the Court shall be notified to the Court by the court or tribunal concerned. The decision shall then be notified by the Registrar of the Court to the parties, to the Member States and to the Commission, and also to the Council or to the European Central Bank if the act the validity or interpretation of which is in dispute originates from one of them, and to the European Parliament and the Council if the act the validity or interpretation of which is in dispute was adopted jointly by those two institutions.

Within two months of this notification, the parties, the Member States, the Commission and, where appropriate, the European Parliament, the Council and the European Central Bank, shall be entitled to submit statements of case or written observations to the Court.

In the cases governed by Article 234 of the EC Treaty, the decision of the national court or tribunal shall, moreover, be notified by the Registrar of the Court to the States, other than the Member States, which are parties to the Agreement on the European Economic Area and also to the EFTA Surveillance Authority referred to in that Agreement which may, within two months of notification, where one of the fields of application of that Agreement is concerned, submit statements of case or written observations to the Court.

Where an agreement relating to a specific subject-matter, concluded by the Council and one or more non-member States provides that those States are to be entitled to submit statements of case or written observations where a court or tribunal of a Member State refers to the Court of Justice for a preliminary ruling a question falling within the scope of the agreement, the decision of the national court or tribunal containing that question shall also be notified to the non-member States concerned. Within two months from such notification, those States may lodge at the Court statements of case or written observations.

Article 24

The Court may require the parties to produce all documents and to supply all information which the Court considers desirable. Formal note shall be taken of any refusal.

The Court may also require the Member States and institutions not being parties to the case to supply all information which the Court considers necessary for the proceedings.

Article 25

The Court may at any time entrust any individual, body, authority, committee or other organisation it chooses with the task of giving an expert opinion.

Article 26

Witnesses may be heard under conditions laid down in the Rules of Procedure.

Article 27

With respect to defaulting witnesses the Court shall have the powers generally granted to courts and tribunals and may impose pecuniary penalties under conditions laid down in the Rules of Procedure.

Article 28

Witnesses and experts may be heard on oath taken in the form laid down in the Rules of Procedure or in the manner laid down by the law of the country of the witness or expert.

Article 29

The Court may order that a witness or expert be heard by the judicial authority of his place of permanent residence.

The order shall be sent for implementation to the competent judicial authority under conditions laid down in the Rules of Procedure. The documents drawn up in compliance with the letters rogatory shall be returned to the Court under the same conditions.

The Court shall defray the expenses, without prejudice to the right to charge them, where appropriate, to the parties.

Article 30

A Member State shall treat any violation of an oath by a witness or expert in the same manner as if the offence had been committed before one of its courts with jurisdiction in civil proceedings. At the instance of the Court, the Member State concerned shall prosecute the offender before its competent court.

Article 31

The hearing in court shall be public, unless the Court, of its own motion or on application by the parties, decides otherwise for serious reasons.

Article 32

During the hearings the Court may examine the experts, the witnesses and the parties themselves. The latter, however, may address the Court only through their representatives.

Article 33

Minutes shall be made of each hearing and signed by the President and the Registrar.

Article 34

The case list shall be established by the President.

Article 35

The deliberations of the Court shall be and shall remain secret.

Article 36

Judgments shall state the reasons on which they are based. They shall contain the names of the Judges who took part in the deliberations.

Article 37

Judgments shall be signed by the President and the Registrar. They shall be read in open court.

Article 38

The Court shall adjudicate upon costs.

Article 39

The President of the Court may, by way of summary procedure, which may, in so far as necessary, differ from some of the rules contained in this Statute and which shall be laid down in the Rules of Procedure, adjudicate upon applications to suspend execution, as provided for in Article 242 of the EC Treaty and Article 157 of the EAEC Treaty, or to prescribe interim measures in pursuance of Article 243 of the EC Treaty or Article 158 of the EAEC Treaty, or to suspend enforcement in accordance with the fourth paragraph of Article 256 of the EC Treaty or the third paragraph of Article 164 of the EAEC Treaty.

Should the President be prevented from attending, his place shall be taken by another Judge under conditions laid down in the Rules of Procedure.

The ruling of the President or of the Judge replacing him shall be provisional and shall in no way prejudice the decision of the Court on the substance of the case.

Article 40

Member States and institutions of the Communities may intervene in cases before the Court.

The same right shall be open to any other person establishing an interest in the result of any case submitted to the Court, save in cases between Member States, between institutions of the Communities or between Member States and institutions of the Communities.

Without prejudice to the second paragraph, the States, other than the Member States, which are parties to the Agreement on the European Economic Area, and also the EFTA Surveillance Authority referred to in that Agreement, may intervene in cases before the Court where one of the fields of application that Agreement is concerned.

An application to intervene shall be limited to supporting the form of order sought by one of the parties.

Article 41

Where the defending party, after having been duly summoned, fails to file written submissions in defence, judgment shall be given against that party by default. An objection may be lodged against the judgment within one month of it being notified. The objection shall not have the effect of staying enforcement of the judgment by default unless the Court decides otherwise.

Article 42

Member States, institutions of the Communities and any other natural or legal persons may, in cases and under conditions to be determined by the Rules of Procedure, institute third-party proceedings to contest a judgment rendered without their being heard, where the judgment is prejudicial to their rights.

Article 43

If the meaning or scope of a judgment is in doubt, the Court shall construe it on application by any party or any institution of the Communities establishing an interest therein.

Article 44

An application for revision of a judgment may be made to the Court only on discovery of a fact which is of such a nature as to be a decisive factor, and which, when the judgment was given, was unknown to the Court and to the party claiming the revision.

The revision shall be opened by a judgment of the Court expressly recording the existence of a new fact, recognising that it is of such a character as to lay the case open to revision and declaring the application admissible on this ground.

No application for revision may be made after the lapse of 10 years from the date of the judgment.

Article 45

Periods of grace based on considerations of distance shall be determined by the Rules of Procedure. No right shall be prejudiced in consequence of the expiry of a time-limit if the party concerned proves the existence of unforeseeable circumstances or of force majeure.

Article 46

Proceedings against the Communities in matters arising from non-contractual liability shall be barred after a period of five years from the occurrence of the event giving rise thereto. The period of limitation shall be interrupted if proceedings are instituted before the Court or if prior to such proceedings an application is made by the aggrieved party to the relevant institution of the Communities. In the latter event the proceedings must be instituted within the period of two months provided for in Article 230 of the EC Treaty and Article 146 of the EAEC Treaty; the provisions of the second paragraph of Article 232 of the EC Treaty and the second paragraph of Article 148 of the EAEC Treaty, respectively, shall apply where appropriate.

TITLE IV

THE COURT OF FIRST INSTANCE OF THE EUROPEAN COMMUNITIES

Article 47

Articles 2 to 8, Articles 14 and 15, the first, second, fourth and fifth paragraphs of Article 17 and Article 18 shall apply to the Court of First Instance and its members. The oath referred to in Article 2 shall be taken before the Court of Justice and the decisions referred to in Articles 3, 4 and 6 shall be adopted by that Court after hearing the Court of First Instance.

The fourth paragraph of Article 3 and Articles 10, 11 and 14 shall apply to the Registrar of the Court of First Instance mutatis mutandis.

Article 48

The Court of First Instance shall consist of twenty-seven Judges.

Article 49

The members of the Court of First Instance may be called upon to perform the task of an Advocate General.

It shall be the duty of the Advocate General, acting with complete impartiality and independence, to make, in open court, reasoned submissions on certain cases brought before the Court of First Instance in order to assist the Court of First Instance in the performance of its task.

The criteria for selecting such cases, as well as the procedures for designating the Advocates General, shall be laid down in the Rules of Procedure of the Court of First Instance.

A member called upon to perform the task of Advocate General in a case may not take part in the judgment of the case.

Article 50

The Court of First Instance shall sit in chambers of three or five Judges. The Judges shall elect the Presidents of the chambers from among their number. The Presidents of the chambers of five Judges shall be elected for three years. They may be re-elected once.

The composition of the chambers and the assignment of cases to them shall be governed by the Rules of Procedure. In certain cases governed by the Rules of Procedure, the Court of First Instance may sit as a full court or be constituted by a single Judge.

The Rules of Procedure may also provide that the Court of First Instance may sit in a Grand Chamber in cases and under the conditions specified therein.

Article 51

By way of derogation from the rule laid down in Article 225(1) of the EC Treaty and Article 140a(1) of the EAEC Treaty, jurisdiction shall be reserved to the Court of Justice in the actions referred to in Articles 230 and 232 of the EC Treaty and in Articles 146 and 148 of the EAEC Treaty when they are brought by a Member State:

(a) against an act of or failure to act by the European Parliament or the Council, or by those institutions acting jointly, except for:

— decisions taken by the Council under the third subparagraph of Article 88(2) of the EC Treaty;

— acts of the Council adopted pursuant to a Council regulation concerning measures to protect trade within the meaning of Article 133 of the EC Treaty;

— acts of the Council by which it exercises implementing powers in accordance with the third indent of Article 202 of the EC Treaty;

(b) against an act of or failure to act by the Commission under Article 11a of the EC Treaty.

Jurisdiction shall also be reserved to the Court of Justice in the actions referred to in the same articles when they are brought by an institution of the Communities or the European Central Bank against an act of or failure to act by the European Parliament, the Council, both those institutions acting jointly, the Commission, or brought by an institution of the Communities against an act of or failure to act by the European Central Bank.

Article 52

The President of the Court of Justice and the President of the Court of First Instance shall determine, by common accord, the conditions under which officials and other servants attached to the Court of Justice shall render their services to the Court of First Instance to enable it to function. Certain officials or other servants shall be responsible to the Registrar of the Court of First Instance under the authority of the President of the Court of First Instance.

Article 53

The procedure before the Court of First Instance shall be governed by Title III.

Such further and more detailed provisions as may be necessary shall be laid down in its Rules of Procedure. The Rules of Procedure may derogate from the fourth paragraph of Article 40 and from Article 41 in order to take account of the specific features of litigation in the field of intellectual property.

Notwithstanding the fourth paragraph of Article 20, the Advocate General may make his reasoned submissions in writing.

Article 54

Where an application or other procedural document addressed to the Court of First Instance is lodged by mistake with the Registrar of the Court of Justice, it shall be transmitted immediately by that Registrar to the Registrar of the Court of First Instance; likewise, where an application or other procedural document addressed to the Court of Justice is lodged by mistake with the Registrar of the Court of First Instance, it shall be transmitted immediately by that Registrar to the Registrar of the Court of Justice.

Where the Court of First Instance finds that it does not have jurisdiction to hear and determine an action in respect of which the Court of Justice has jurisdiction, it shall refer that action to the Court of Justice; likewise, where the Court of Justice finds that an action falls within the jurisdiction of the Court of First Instance, it shall refer that action to the Court of First Instance, whereupon that Court may not decline jurisdiction.

Where the Court of Justice and the Court of First Instance are seised of cases in which the same relief is sought, the same issue of interpretation is raised or the validity of the same act is called in question, the Court of First Instance may, after hearing the parties, stay the proceedings before it until such time as the Court of Justice has delivered judgment. In the same circumstances, the Court of Justice may also decide to stay the proceedings before it; in that event, the proceedings before the Court of First Instance shall continue.

Where a Member State and an institution of the Communities are challenging the same act, the Court of First Instance shall decline jurisdiction so that the Court of Justice may rule on those applications.

Article 55

Final decisions of the Court of First Instance, decisions disposing of the substantive issues in part only or disposing of a procedural issue concerning a plea of lack of competence or inadmissibility, shall be notified by the Registrar of the Court of First Instance to all parties as well as all Member States and the institutions of the Communities even if they did not intervene in the case before the Court of First Instance.

Article 56

An appeal may be brought before the Court of Justice, within two months of the notification of the decision appealed against, against final decisions of the Court of First Instance and decisions of that Court disposing of the substantive issues in part only or disposing of a procedural issue concerning a plea of lack of competence or inadmissibility.

Such an appeal may be brought by any party which has been unsuccessful, in whole or in part, in its submissions. However, interveners other than the Member States and the institutions of the Communities may bring such an appeal only where the decision of the Court of First Instance directly affects them.

With the exception of cases relating to disputes between the Communities and their servants, an appeal may also be brought by Member States and institutions of the Communities which did not intervene in the proceedings before the Court of First Instance. Such Member States and institutions shall be in the same position as Member States or institutions which intervened at first instance.

Article 57

Any person whose application to intervene has been dismissed by the Court of First Instance may appeal to the Court of Justice within two weeks from the notification of the decision dismissing the application.

The parties to the proceedings may appeal to the Court of Justice against any decision of the Court of First Instance made pursuant to Article 242 or Article 243 or the fourth paragraph of Article 256 of the EC Treaty or Article 157 or Article 158 or the third paragraph of Article 164 of the EAEC Treaty within two months from their notification.

The appeal referred to in the first two paragraphs of this Article shall be heard and determined under the procedure referred to in Article 39.

Article 58

An appeal to the Court of Justice shall be limited to points of law. It shall lie on the grounds of lack of competence of the Court of First Instance, a breach of procedure before it which adversely affects the interests of the appellant as well as the infringement of Community law by the Court of First Instance.

No appeal shall lie regarding only the amount of the costs or the party ordered to pay them.

Article 59

Where an appeal is brought against a decision of the Court of First Instance, the procedure before the Court of Justice shall consist of a written part and an oral part. In accordance with conditions laid down in the Rules of Procedure, the Court of Justice, having heard the Advocate and the parties, may dispense with the oral procedure.

Article 60

Without prejudice to Articles 242 and 243 of the EC Treaty or Articles 157 and 158 of the EAEC Treaty, an appeal shall not have suspensory effect.

By way of derogation from Article 244 of the EC Treaty and Article 159 of the EAEC Treaty, decisions of the Court of First Instance declaring a regulation to be void shall take effect only as from the date of expiry of the period referred to in the first paragraph of Article 56 of this Statute or, if an appeal shall have been brought within that period, as from the date of dismissal of the appeal, without prejudice, however, to the right of a party to apply to the Court of Justice, pursuant to Articles 242 and 243 of the EC Treaty or Articles 157 and 158 of the EAEC Treaty, for the suspension of the effects of the regulation which has been declared void or for the prescription of any other interim measure.

Article 61

If the appeal is well founded, the Court of Justice shall quash the decision of the Court of First Instance. It may itself give final judgment in the matter, where the state of the proceedings so permits, or refer the case back to the Court of First Instance for judgment.

Where a case is referred back to the Court of First Instance, that Court shall be bound by the decision of the Court of Justice on points of law.

When an appeal brought by a Member State or an institution of the Communities, which did not intervene in the proceedings before the Court of First Instance, is well founded, the Court of Justice may, if it considers this necessary, state which of the effects of the decision of the Court of First Instance which has been quashed shall be considered as definitive in respect of the parties to the litigation.

Article 62

In the cases provided for in Article 225(2) and (3) of the EC Treaty and Article 140a(2) and (3) of the EAEC Treaty, where the First Advocate General considers that there is a serious risk of the unity or consistency of Community law being affected, he may propose that the Court of Justice review the decision of the Court of First Instance.

The proposal must be made within one month of delivery of the decision by the Court of First Instance. Within one month of receiving the proposal made by the First Advocate General, the Court of Justice shall decide whether or not the decision should be reviewed.

TITLE IVa
JUDICIAL PANELS

Article 62a

The provisions relating to the jurisdiction, composition, organisation and procedure of the judicial panels established under Articles 225a of the EC Treaty and 140b of the EAEC Treaty are set out in an Annex to this Statute.

TITLE V
FINAL PROVISIONS

Article 63

The Rules of Procedure of the Court of Justice and of the Court of First Instance shall contain any provisions necessary for applying and, where required, supplementing this Statute.

Article 64

Until the rules governing the language arrangements applicable at the Court of Justice and the Court of First Instance have been adopted in this Statute, the provisions of the Rules of Procedure of the Court of Justice and of the Rules of Procedure of the Court of First Instance governing language arrangements shall continue to apply. Those provisions may only be amended or repealed in accordance with the procedure laid down for amending this Statute.

ANNEX I
THE EUROPEAN UNION CIVIL SERVICE TRIBUNAL

Article 1

The European Union Civil Service Tribunal (hereafter the Civil Service Tribunal) shall exercise at first instance jurisdiction in disputes between the Communities and their servants referred to in Article 236 of the EC Treaty and Article 152 of the EAEC Treaty, including disputes between all bodies or agencies and their servants in respect of which jurisdiction is conferred on the Court of justice.

Article 2

The Civil Service Tribunal shall consist of seven judges. Should the Court of justice so request, the Council, acting by a qualified majority, may increase the number of judges.

The judges shall be appointed for a period of six years. Retiring judges may be reappointed.

Any vacancy shall be filled by the appointment of a new judge for a period of six years.

Article 3

1. The judges shall be appointed by the Council, acting in accordance with the fourth paragraph of Article 225a of the EC Treaty and the fourth paragraph of Article 140b of the EAEC Treaty, after consulting the committee provided for by this Article. When appointing judges, the Council shall ensure a balanced composition of the Tribunal on as broad a geographical basis as possible from among nationals of the Member States and with respect to the national legal systems represented.

2. Any person who is a Union citizen and fulfils the conditions laid down in the fourth paragraph of Article 225a of the EC Treaty and the fourth paragraph of Article 140b of the EAEC Treaty may submit an application. The Council, acting by a qualified majority on a recommendation from the Court, shall determine the conditions and the arrangements governing the submission and processing of such applications.

3. A committee shall be set up comprising seven persons chosen from among former members of the Court of justice and the Court of First instance and lawyers of recognised competence. The committee's membership and operating rules shall be determined by the Council, acting by a qualified majority on a recommendation by the President of the Court of justice.

4. The committee shall give an opinion on candidates' suitability to perform the duties of judge at the Civil Service Tribunal. The committee shall append to its opinion a list of candidates having the most suitable high-level experience. Such list shall contain the names of at least twice as many candidates as there are judges to be appointed by the Council.

Article 4

1. The judges shall elect the President of the Civil Service Tribunal from among their number for a term of three years. He may be re-elected.

2. The Civil Service Tribunal shall sit in chambers of three judges. It may, in certain cases determined by its rules of procedure, sit in full court or in a chamber of five judges or of a single judge.

3. The President of the Civil Service Tribunal shall preside over the full court and the chamber of five judges. The Presidents of the chambers of three judges shall be designated as provided in paragraph 1. If the President of the Civil Service Tribunal is assigned to a chamber of three judges, he shall preside over that chamber.

4. The jurisdiction of and quorum for the full court as well as the composition of the chambers and the assignment of cases to them shall be governed by the rules of procedure.

Article 5

Articles 2 to 6, 14, 15, the first, second and fifth paragraphs of Article 17, and Article 18 of the Statute of the Court of justice shall apply to the Civil Service Tribunal and its members.

The oath referred to in Article 2 of the Statute shall be taken before the Court of justice, and the decisions referred to in Articles 3, 4 and 6 thereof shall be adopted by the Court of justice after consulting the Civil Service Tribunal.

Article 6

1. The Civil Service Tribunal shall be supported by the departments of the Court of justice and of the Court of First Instance. The President of the Court of justice or, in appropriate cases, the President of the Court of First Instance, shall determine by common accord with the President of the Civil Service Tribunal the conditions under which officials and other servants attached to the Court of justice or the Court of First Instance shall render their services to the Civil Service Tribunal to enable it to function. Certain officials or other servants shall be responsible

to the Registrar of the Civil Service Tribunal under the authority of the President of that Tribunal.

2. The Civil Service Tribunal shall appoint its Registrar and lay down the rules governing his service. The fourth paragraph of Article 3 and Articles 10, 11 and 14 of the Statute of the Court of justice shall apply to the Registrar of the Tribunal.

Article 7

1. The procedure before the Civil Service Tribunal shall be governed by Title 111 of the Statute of the Court of justice, with the exception of Articles 22 and 23. Such further and more detailed provisions as may be necessary shall be laid down in the rules of procedure.

2. The provisions concerning the Court of First Instance's language arrangements shall apply to the Civil Service Tribunal.

3. The written stage of the procedure shall comprise the presentation of the application and of the statement of defence, unless the Civil Service Tribunal decides that a second exchange of written pleadings is necessary. Where there is such second exchange, the Civil Service Tribunal may, with the agreement of the parties, decide to proceed to judgment without an oral procedure.

4. At all stages of the procedure, including the time when the application is filed, the Civil Service Tribunal may examine the possibilities of an amicable settlement of the dispute and may try to facilitate such settlement.

5. The Civil Service Tribunal shall rule on the costs of a case. Subject to the specific provisions of the Rules of Procedure, the unsuccessful party shall be ordered to pay the costs should the court so decide.

Article 8

1. Where an application or other procedural document addressed to the Civil Service Tribunal is lodged by mistake with the Registrar of the Court of justice or Court of First Instance, it shall be transmitted immediately by that Registrar to the Registrar of the Civil Service Tribunal. Likenise, where an application or other procedural document addressed to the Court of justice or to the Court of First Instance is lodged by mistake with the Registrar of the Civil Service Tribunal, it shall be transmitted immediately by that Registrar to the Registrar of the Court of justice or Court of First Instance.

2. Where the Civil Service Tribunal finds that it does not have jurisdiction to hear and determine an action in respect of which the Court of justice or the Court of First Instance has jurisdiction, it shall refer that action to the Court of justice or to the Court of First Instance. Likewise, where the Court of justice or the Court of First Instance finds that an action falls within the jurisdiction of the Civil Service Tribunal, the Court seised shall refer that action to the Civil Service Tribunal, whereupon that Tribunal may not decline jurisdiction.

3. Where the Civil Service Tribunal and the Court of First Instance are seised of cases in which the same issue of interpretation is raised or the validity of the same act is called in question, the Civil Service Tribunal, after hearing the parties, may stay the proceedings until the judgment of the Court of First Instance has been delivered.

Where the Civil Service Tribunal and the Court of First Instance are seised of cases in which the same relief is sought, the Civil Service Tribunal shall decline jurisdiction so that the Court of First Instance may act on those cases.

Article 9

An appeal may be brought before the Court of First Instance, within two months of notification of the decision appealed against, against final decisions of the Civil Service Tribunal and decisions of that Tribunal disposing of the substantive issues in part only or disposing of a procedural issue concerning a plea of lack of jurisdiction or inadmissibility.

Such an appeal may be brought by any party which has been unsuccessful, in whole or in part, in its submissions. However, interveners other than the Member States and the institutions of the Communities may bring such an appeal only where the decision of the Civil Service Tribunal directly affects them.

Article 10

1. Any person whose application to intervene has been dismissed by the Civil Service Tribunal may appeal to the Court of First Instance within two weeks of notification of the decision dismissing the application.

2. The parties to the proceedings may appeal to the Court of First Instance against any decision of the Civil Service Tribunal made pursuant to Article 242 or Article 243 or the fourth paragraph of Article 256 of the EC Treaty or Article 157 or Article 158 or the third paragraph of Article 164 of the EAEC Treaty within two months of its notification.

3. The President of the Court of First Instance may, by way of summary procedure, which may, insofar as necessary, differ from some of the rules contained in this Annex and which shall be laid down in the rules of procedure of the Court of First Instance, adjudicate upon appeals brought in accordance with paragraphs 1 and 2.

Article 11

1. An appeal to the Court of First Instance shall be limited to points of law. it shall lie on the grounds of lack of jurisdiction of the Civil Service Tribunal, a breach of procedure before it which adversely affects the interests of the appellant as well as the infringement of Community law by the Tribunal.

2. No appeal shall lie regarding only the amount of the costs or the party ordered to pay them.

Article 12

1. Without prejudice to Articles 242 and 243 of the EC Treaty or Articles 157 and 158 of the EAEC Treaty, an appeal before the Court of First Instance shall not have suspensory effect.

2. Where an appeal is brought against a decision of the Civil Service Tribunal, the procedure before the Court of First Instance shall consist of a written part and an oral part. In accordance with conditions laid down in the rules of procedure, the Court of First Instance, having beard the parties, may dispense with the oral procedure.

Article 13

1. If the appeal is well founded, the Court of First Instance shall quash the decision of the Civil Service Tribunal and itself give judgment in the matter. It shall refer the case back to the Civil Service Tribunal for judgment where the state of the proceedings does not permit a decision by the Court.

2. Where a case is referred back to the Civil Service Tribunal, the Tribunal shall be bound by the decision of the Court of First Instance on points of law.

RULES OF PROCEDURE OF THE COURT OF JUSTICE

MAY 2004

This edition has no legal force and the preambles have therefore been omitted.

INTERPRETATION

Article 1

In these Rules:

— "Union Treaty" means the Treaty on European Union,

— "EC Treaty" means the Treaty establishing the European Community,

— "EAEC Treaty" means the Treaty establishing the European Atomic Energy Community,

— "Statute" means the Protocol on the Statute of the Court of Justice,

— "EEA Agreement" means the Agreement on the European Economic Area. For the purposes of these Rules:

— "institutions" means the institutions of the Communities and bodies which are established by the Treaties, or by an act adopted in implementation thereof, and which may be parties before the Court,

— "EFTA Surveillance Authority" means the surveillance authority referred to in the EEA Agreement.

TITLE 1
ORGANISATION OF THE COURT

CHAPTER 1
JUDGES AND ADVOCATES GENERAL

Article 2

The term of office of a Judge shall begin on the date laid down in his instrument of appointment. In the absence of any provisions regarding the date, the term shall begin on the date of the instrument.

Article 3

1. Before taking up his duties, a Judge shall at the first public sitting of the Court which he attends after his appointment take the following oath:

   "I swear that I will perform my duties impartially and conscientiously; I swear that I will preserve the secrecy of the deliberations of the Court".

2. Immediately after taking the oath, a Judge shall sign a declaration by which he solemnly undertakes that, both during and after his term of office, he will respect the obligations arising therefrom, and in particular the duty to behave with integrity and discretion as regards the acceptance, after he has ceased to hold office, of certain appointments and benefits.

Article 4

When the Court is called upon to decide whether a Judge no longer fulfils the requisite conditions or no longer meets the obligations arising from his office, the President shall invite the Judge concerned to make representations to the Court, in closed session and in the absence of the Registrar.

Article 5

Articles 2, 3 and 4 of these Rules shall apply to Advocates General.

Article 6

Judges and Advocates General shall rank equally in precedence according to their seniority in office.

Where there is equal seniority in office, precedence shall be determined by age.

Retiring Judges and Advocates General who are reappointed shall retain their former precedence.

CHAPTER 2
PRESIDENCY OF THE COURT AND CONSTITUTION OF THE CHAMBERS

Article 7

1. The Judges shall, immediately after the partial replacement provided for in Article 223 of the EC Treaty, and Article 139 of the EAEC Treaty, elect one of their number as President of the Court for a term of three years.

2. If the office of the President of the Court falls vacant before the normal date of expiry thereof, the Court shall elect a successor for the remainder of the term.

3. The elections provided for in this Article shall be by secret ballot. If a Judge obtains an absolute majority he shall be elected. If no Judge obtains an absolute majority, a second ballot shall be held and the Judge obtaining the most votes shall be elected. Where two or more Judges obtain an equal number of votes the oldest of them shall be deemed elected.

Article 8

The President shall direct the judicial business and the administration of the Court; he shall preside at hearings and deliberations.

Article 9

1. The Court shall set up Chambers of five and three Judges in accordance with Article 16 of the Statute and shall decide which Judges shall be attached to them.

   The assignment of Judges to Chambers shall be published in the *Official Journal of the European Union*.

2. As soon as an application initiating proceedings has been lodged, the President shall assign the case to one of the Chambers of three Judges for any preparatory inquiries and shall designate a Judge from that Chamber to act as Rapporteur.

3. For cases assigned to a formation of the Court in accordance with Article 44(3), the word 'Court' in these Rules shall mean that formation.

4. In cases assigned to a Chamber of five or three Judges, the powers of the President of the Court shall be exercised by the President of the Chamber.

Article 10

1. The Judges shall, immediately after the election of the President of the Court, elect the Presidents of the Chambers of five Judges for a term of three years.

    The Judges shall elect the Presidents of the Chambers of three Judges for a term of one year.

    The Court shall appoint for a period of one year the First Advocate General. The provisions of Article 7(2) and (3) shall apply.

    The elections and appointment made in pursuance of this paragraph shall be published in the *Official Journal of the European Union*.

2. The First Advocate General shall assign each case to an Advocate General as soon as the Judge-Rapporteur has been designated by the President. He shall take the necessary steps if an Advocate General is absent or prevented from acting.

Article 11

When the President of the Court is absent or is prevented from attending or when the office of President is vacant, the functions of President shall be exercised by a President of a Chamber of five Judges according to the order of precedence laid down in Article 6 of these Rules.

When the President of the Court and the Presidents of the Chambers of five Judges are all prevented from attending at the same time, or their posts are vacant at the same time, the functions of President shall be exercised by one of the Presidents of the Chambers of three Judges according to the order of precedence laid down in Article 6 of these Rules.

If the President of the Court and all the Presidents of Chambers are all prevented from attending at the same time, or their posts are vacant at the same time, the functions of President shall be exercised by one of the other Judges according to the order of precedence laid down in Article 6 of these Rules.

CHAPTER 2a

FORMATIONS OF THE COURT

Article 11a

The Court shall sit in the following formations:

— the full Court, composed of all the Judges;

— the Grand Chamber, composed of 13 Judges in accordance with Article 11b,

— Chambers composed of five or three Judges in accordance with Article 11c.

Article 11b

1. For each case the Grand Chamber shall be composed of the President of the Court, the Presidents of the Chambers of five Judges, the Judge-Rapporteur and the number of Judges necessary to reach 13. The last mentioned Judges shall be designated from the list referred to in paragraph 2, following the order laid down therein, the starting-point moving on by one name at each general meeting of the Court.

2. After the election of the President of the Court and of the Presidents of the Chambers of five Judges, a list of the other Judges shall be drawn up for the purposes of determining the composition of the Grand Chamber. That list shall follow the order laid down in Article 6 of these Rules, alternating with the reverse order: the first Judge on that list shall be the first according to the order laid down in that Article, the second Judge shall be the last according to that order, the third Judge shall be the second according to that order, the fourth Judge the penultimate according to that order, and so on.

    The list shall be published in the *Official Journal of the European Union*.

Article 11c

1. The Chambers of five Judges and three Judges shall, for each case, be composed of the President of the Chamber, the Judge-Rapporteur and the number of Judges required to attain the number of five and three Judges respectively. Those last-mentioned Judges shall be designated from the lists referred to in paragraph 2 and following the order laid down in them, the starting-point being moved on by one name at each general meeting of the Court.

2. For the composition of the Chambers of five Judges, after the election of the Presidents of those Chambers lists shall be drawn up including all the Judges attached to the Chamber concerned, with the exception of its President. The lists shall be drawn up in the same way as the list referred to in Article 11b(2).

   For the composition of the Chambers of three Judges, after the election of the Presidents of those Chambers lists shall be drawn up including all the Judges attached to the Chamber concerned, with the exception of its President. The lists shall be drawn up according to the order laid down in Article 6 of these Rules.

   The lists referred to in this paragraph shall be published in the *Official Journal of the European Union*.

Article 11d

Where the Court considers that several cases must be heard and determined together by one and the same formation of the Court, the composition of that formation shall be that fixed for the case in respect of which the preliminary report was first examined.

Article 11e

When a member of the formation determining a case is prevented from attending, he shall be replaced by a Judge according to the order of the lists referred to in Article 11b(2) or 11c(2).

When the President of the Court is prevented from attending, the functions of the President of the Grand Chamber shall be exercised in accordance with the provisions of Article 11.

When the President of a Chamber of five Judges is prevented from attending, the functions of President of the Chamber shall be exercised by a President of a Chamber of three Judges, where necessary according to the order laid down in Article 6 of these Rules or, if that Chamber does not include a President of a Chamber of three Judges, by one of the other Judges according to the order laid down in Article 6.

When the President of a Chamber of three Judges is prevented from attending, the functions of President of the Chamber shall be exercised by a Judge of that Chamber according to the order laid down in Article 6 of these Rules.

CHAPTER 3

REGISTRY

Section 1 — The Registrar and Assistant Registrars

Article 12

1. The Court shall appoint the Registrar. Two weeks before the date fixed for making the appointment, the President shall inform the Members of the Court of the applications which have been made for the post.

2. An application shall be accompanied by full details of the candidate's age, nationality, university degrees, knowledge of any languages, present and past occupations and experience, if any, in judicial and international fields.

3. The appointment shall be made following the procedure laid down in Article 7(3) of these Rules.

4. The Registrar shall be appointed for a term of six years. He may be reappointed.

5. The Registrar shall take the oath in accordance with Article 3 of these Rules.

6. The Registrar may be deprived of his office only if he no longer fulfils the requisite conditions or no longer meets the obligations arising from his office; the Court shall take its decision after giving the Registrar an opportunity to make representations.

7. If the office of Registrar falls vacant before the normal date of expiry of the term thereof, the Court shall appoint a new Registrar for a term of six years.

Article 13

The Court may, following the procedure laid down in respect of the Registrar, appoint one or more Assistant Registrars to assist the Registrar and to take his place in so far as the Instructions to the Registrar referred to in Article 15 of these Rules allow.

Article 14

Where the Registrar and the Assistant Registrars are absent or prevented from attending or their posts are vacant, the President shall designate an official or other servant to carry out temporarily the duties of Registrar.

Article 15

Instructions to the Registrar shall be adopted by the Court acting on a proposal from the President.

Article 16

1. There shall be kept in the Registry, under the control of the Registrar, a register initialled by the President, in which all pleadings and supporting documents shall be entered in the order in which they are lodged.
2. When a document has been registered, the Registrar shall make a note to that effect on the original and, if a party so requests, on any copy submitted for the purpose.
3. Entries in the register and the notes provided for in the preceding paragraph shall be authentic.
4. Rules for keeping the register shall be prescribed by the Instructions to the Registrar referred to in Article 15 of these Rules.
5. Persons having an interest may consult the register at the Registry and may obtain copies or extracts on payment of a charge on a scale fixed by the Court on a proposal from the Registrar. The parties to a case may on payment of the appropriate charge also obtain copies of pleadings and authenticated copies of judgments and orders.
6. Notice shall be given in the Official Journal of the European Union of the date of registration of an application initiating proceedings, the names and addresses of the parties, the subject-matter of the proceedings, the form of order sought by the applicant and a summary of the pleas in law and of the main supporting arguments.
7. Where the Council or the Commission is not a party to a case, the Court shall send to it copies of the application and of the defence, without the annexes thereto, to enable it to assess whether the inapplicability of one of its acts is being invoked under Article 241 of the EC Treaty, or Article 156 of the EAEC Treaty. Copies of that act shall likewise be sent to the European Parliament, to enable it to assess whether the inapplicability of an act adopted jointly by that institution and by the Council is being invoked under Article 241 of the EC Treaty.

Article 17

1. The Registrar shall be responsible, under the authority of the President, for the acceptance, transmission and custody of documents and for effecting service as provided for by these Rules.
2. The Registrar shall assist the Court, the President and the Presidents of Chambers and the Judges in all their official functions.

Article 18

The Registrar shall have custody of the seals. He shall be responsible for the records and be in charge of the publications of the Court.

Article 19

Subject to Articles 4 and 27 of these Rules, the Registrar shall attend the sittings of the Court and of the Chambers.

Section 2 — Other departments

Article 20

1. The officials and other servants of the Court shall be appointed in accordance with the provisions of the Staff Regulations.

2.   Before taking up his duties, an official shall take the following oath before the President, in the presence of the Registrar:
      "I swear that I will perform loyally, discreetly and conscientiously the duties assigned to me by the Court of Justice of the European Communities."

Article 21

The organisation of the departments of the Court shall be laid down, and may be modified, by the Court on a proposal from the Registrar.

Article 22

The Court shall set up a translating service staffed by experts with adequate legal training and a thorough knowledge of several official languages of the Court.

Article 23

The Registrar shall be responsible, under the authority of the President, for the administration of the Court, its financial management and its accounts; he shall be assisted in this by an administrator.

CHAPTER 4
ASSISTANT RAPPORTEURS

Article 24

1.   Where the Court is of the opinion that the consideration of and preparatory inquiries in cases before it so require, it shall, pursuant to Article 13 of the Statute, propose the appointment of Assistant Rapporteurs.
2.   Assistant Rapporteurs shall in particular assist the President in connection with applications for the adoption of interim measures and assist the Judge-Rapporteurs in their work.
3.   In the performance of their duties the Assistant Rapporteurs shall be responsible to the President of the Court, the President of a Chamber or a Judge-Rapporteur, as the case may be.
4.   Before taking up his duties, an Assistant Rapporteur shall take before the Court the oath set out in Article 3 of these Rules.

CHAPTER 5
THE WORKING OF THE COURT

Article 25

1.   The dates and times of the sittings of the Grand Chamber and of the full Court shall be fixed by the President.
2.   The dates and times of the sittings of the Chambers of five and three Judges shall be fixed by their respective Presidents.
3.   The Court may choose to hold one or more sittings in a place other than that in which the Court has its seat.

Article 26

1.   Where, by reason of a Judge being absent or prevented from attending, there is an even number of Judges, the most junior Judge within the meaning of Article 6 of these Rules shall abstain from taking part in the deliberations unless he is the Judge-Rapporteur. In that case the Judge immediately senior to him shall abstain from taking part in the deliberations.
2.   If after the Grand Chamber or full Court has been convened it is found that the quorum referred to in the third or fourth paragraph of Article 17 of the Statute has not been attained, the President shall adjourn the sitting until there is a quorum.
3.   If in any Chamber of five or three Judges the quorum referred to in the second paragraph of Article 17 of the Statute has not been attained and it is not possible to replace the Judges prevented from attending in accordance with Article 11e, the President of that Chamber shall so inform the President of the Court who shall designate another Judge to complete the Chamber.

Article 27

1.   The Court shall deliberate in closed session.

2. Only those Judges who were present at the oral proceedings and the Assistant Rapporteur, if any, entrusted with the consideration of the case may take part in the deliberations.

3. Every Judge taking part in the deliberations shall state his opinion and the reasons for it.

4. Any Judge may require that any questions be formulated in the language of his choice and communicated in writing to the Court before being put to the vote.

5. The conclusions reached by the majority of the Judges after final discussion shall determine the decision of the Court. Votes shall be cast in reverse order to the order of precedence laid down in Article 6 of these Rules.

6. Differences of view on the substance, wording or order of questions or on the interpretation of the voting shall be settled by decision of the Court.

7. Where the deliberations of the Court concern questions of its own administration, the Advocates General shall take part and have a vote. The Registrar shall be present, unless the Court decides to the contrary.

10. Where the Court sits without the Registrar being present it shall, if necessary, instruct the most junior Judge within the meaning of Article 6 of these Rules to draw up minutes. The minutes shall be signed by that Judge and by the President.

Article 28

1. Subject to any special decision of the Court, its vacations shall be as follows:
   — from 18 December to 10 January,
   — from the Sunday before Easter to the second Sunday after Easter,
   — from 15 July to 15 September.
   During the vacations, the functions of President shall be exercised at the place where the Court has its seat either by the President himself, keeping in touch with the Registrar, or by a President of Chamber or other Judge invited by the President to take his place.

2. In a case of urgency, the President may convene the Judges and the Advocates General during the vacations.

3. The Court shall observe the official holidays of the place where it has its seat.

4. The Court may, in proper circumstances, grant leave of absence to any Judge or Advocate General.

CHAPTER 6
LANGUAGES

Article 29

1. The language of a case shall be Danish, Dutch, English, Finnish, French, German, Greek, Irish, Italian, Portuguese, Spanish or Swedish.

2. The language of a case shall be chosen by the applicant, except that:
   (a) where the defendant is a Member State or a natural or legal person having the nationality of a Member State, the language of the case shall be the official language of that State; where that State has more than one official language, the applicant may choose between them;
   (b) at the joint request of the parties, the use of another of the languages mentioned in paragraph 1 for all or part of the proceedings may be authorised;
   (c) at the request of one of the parties, and after the opposite party and the Advocate General have been heard, the use of another of the languages mentioned in paragraph 1 as the language of the case for all or part of the proceedings may be authorised by way of derogation from subparagraphs (a) and (b); such a request may not be submitted by an institution of the European Communities.
   In cases to which Article 103 of these Rules applies, the language of the case shall be the language of the national court or tribunal which refers the matter to the Court. At the duly substantiated request of one of the parties to the main proceedings, and after the opposite party and the Advocate General have been heard, the use of another of the languages mentioned in paragraph 1 may be authorised for the oral procedure.

Requests as above may be decided on by the President; the latter may, and where he wishes to accede to a request without the agreement of all the parties, must, refer the request to the Court.

Editor's Note: The language of a case is now any of the 20 official languages of the Union.

3. The language of the case shall in particular be used in the written and oral pleadings of the parties and in supporting documents, and also in the minutes and decisions of the Court.

Any supporting documents expressed in another language must be accompanied by a translation into the language of the case.

In the case of lengthy documents, translations may be confined to extracts. However, the Court may, of its own motion or at the request of a party, at any time call for a complete or fuller translation.

Notwithstanding the foregoing provisions, a Member State shall be entitled to use its official language when intervening in a case before the Court or when taking part in any reference of a kind mentioned in Article 103. This provision shall apply both to written statements and to oral addresses. The Registrar shall cause any such statement or address to be translated into the language of the case.

The States, other than the Member States, which are parties to the EEA Agreement, and also the EFTA Surveillance Authority, may be authorised to use one of the languages mentioned in paragraph 1, other than the language of the case, when they intervene in a case before the Court or participate in preliminary ruling proceedings envisaged by Article 23 of the Statute. This provision shall apply both to written statements and oral addresses. The Registrar shall cause any such statement or address to be translated into the language of the case.

Non-member States taking part in proceedings for a preliminary ruling pursuant to the fourth paragraph of Article 23 of the Statute may be authorised to use one of the languages mentioned in paragraph (1) of this Article other than the language of the case. This provision shall apply both to written statements and to oral statements. The Registrar shall cause any such statement or address to be translated into the language of the case.

4. Where a witness or expert states that he is unable adequately to express himself in one of the languages referred to in paragraph (1) of this Article, the Court may authorise him to give his evidence in another language. The Registrar shall arrange for translation into the language of the case.

5. The President of the Court and the Presidents of Chambers in conducting oral proceedings, the Judge-Rapporteur both in his preliminary report and in his report for the hearing, Judges and Advocates General in putting questions and Advocates General in delivering their opinions may use one of the languages referred to in paragraph 1 of this Article other than the language of the case. The Registrar shall arrange for translation into the language of the case.

Article 30

1. The Registrar shall, at the request of any Judge, of the Advocate General or of a party, arrange for anything said or written in the course of the proceedings before the Court to be translated into the languages he chooses from those referred to in Article 29(1).

2. Publications of the Court shall be issued in the languages referred to in Article 1 of Council Regulation No 1.

Article 31

The texts of documents drawn up in the language of the case or in any other language authorised by the Court pursuant to Article 29 of these Rules shall be authentic.

CHAPTER 7
RIGHTS AND OBLIGATIONS OF AGENTS, ADVISERS AND LAWYERS

Article 32

1. Agents, advisers and lawyers appearing before the Court or before any judicial authority to which the Court has addressed letters rogatory, shall enjoy immunity in respect of words spoken or written by them concerning the case or the parties.

2. Agents, advisers and lawyers shall enjoy the following further privileges and facilities:
    (a) papers and documents relating to the proceedings shall be exempt from both search and seizure; in the event of a dispute the customs officials or police may seal those papers and documents; they shall then be immediately forwarded to the Court for inspection in the presence of the Registrar and of the person concerned;
    (b) agents, advisers and lawyers shall be entitled to such allocation of foreign currency as may be necessary for the performance of their duties;
    (c) agents, advisers and lawyers shall be entitled to travel in the course of duty without hindrance.

Article 33

In order to qualify for the privileges, immunities and facilities specified in Article 32, persons entitled to them shall furnish proof of their status as follows:
    (a) agents shall produce an official document issued by the party for whom they act, and shall forward without delay a copy thereof to the Registrar;
    (b) advisers and lawyers shall produce a certificate signed by the Registrar. The validity of this certificate shall be limited to a specified period, which may be extended or curtailed according to the length of the proceedings.

Article 34

The privileges, immunities and facilities specified in Article 32 of these Rules are granted exclusively in the interests of the proper conduct of proceedings.

The Court may waive the immunity where it considers that the proper conduct of proceedings will not be hindered thereby.

Article 35

1. Any adviser or lawyer whose conduct towards the Court, a Judge, an Advocate General or the Registrar is incompatible with the dignity of the Court, or who uses his rights for purposes other than those for which they were granted, may at any time be excluded from the proceedings by an order of the Court, after the Advocate General has been heard; the person concerned shall be given an opportunity to defend himself.
2. Where an adviser or lawyer is excluded from the proceedings, the proceedings shall be suspended for a period fixed by the President in order to allow the party concerned to appoint another adviser or lawyer.
3. Decisions taken under this Article may be rescinded.
    The order shall have immediate effect.

Article 36

The provisions of this Chapter shall apply to university teachers who have a right of audience before the Court in accordance with Article 19 of the Statute.

TITLE II
PROCEDURE

CHAPTER 1
WRITTEN PROCEDURE

Article 37

1. The original of every pleading must be signed by the party's agent or lawyer.
    The original, accompanied by all annexes referred to therein, shall be lodged together with five copies for the Court and a copy for every other party to the proceedings. Copies shall be certified by the party lodging them.
2. Institutions shall in addition produce, within time-limits laid down by the Court, translations of all pleadings into the other languages provided for by Article 1 of Council Regulation No 1. The second subparagraph of paragraph 1 of this Article shall apply.
3. All pleadings shall bear a date. In the reckoning of time-limits for taking steps in proceedings, only the date of lodgment at the Registry shall be taken into account.

4. To every pleading there shall be annexed a file containing the documents relied on in support of it, together with a schedule listing them.

5. Where in view of the length of a document only extracts from it are annexed to the pleading, the whole document or a full copy of it shall be lodged at the Registry.

6. Without prejudice to the provisions of paragraphs 1 to 5, the date on which a copy of the signed original of a pleading, including the schedule of documents referred to in paragraph 4, is received at the Registry by telefax or other technical means of communication available to the Court shall be deemed to be the date of lodgment for the purposes of compliance with the time-limits for taking steps in proceedings, provided that the signed original of the pleading, accompanied by the annexes and copies referred to in the second subparagraph of paragraph 1 above, is lodged at the Registry no later than 10 days thereafter.

Article 38

1. An application of the kind referred to in Article 21 of the Statute shall state:
   (a) the name and address of the applicant;
   (b) the designation of the party against whom the application is made;
   (c) the subject-matter of the proceedings and a summary of the pleas in law on which the application is based;
   (d) the form of order sought by the applicant;
   (e) where appropriate, the nature of any evidence offered in support.

2. For the purpose of the proceedings, the application shall state an address for service in the place where the Court has its seat and the name of the person who is authorised and has expressed willingness to accept service.

   In addition to, or instead of, specifying an address for service as referred to in the first subparagraph, the application may state that the lawyer or agent agrees that service is to be effected on him by telefax or other technical means of communication.

   If the application does not comply with the requirements referred to in the first and second subparagraphs, all service on the party concerned for the purpose of the proceedings shall be effected, for so long as the defect has not been cured, by registered letter addressed to the agent or lawyer of that party. By way of derogation from Article 79(1), service shall then be deemed to be duly effected by the lodging of the registered letter at the post office of the place where the Court has its seat.

3. The lawyer acting for a party must lodge at the Registry a certificate that he is authorised to practise before a court of a Member State or of another State which is a party to the EEA Agreement.

4. The application shall be accompanied, where appropriate, by the documents specified in the second paragraph of Article 21 of the Statute.

5. An application made by a legal person governed by private law shall be accompanied by:
   (a) the instrument or instruments constituting or regulating that legal person or a recent extract from the register of companies, firms or associations or any other proof of its existence in law;
   (b) proof that the authority granted to the applicant's lawyer has been properly conferred on him by someone authorised for the purpose.

6. An application submitted under Articles 238 and 239 of the EC Treaty and Articles 153 and 154 of the EAEC Treaty shall be accompanied by a copy of the arbitration clause contained in the contract governed by private or public law entered into by the Communities or on their behalf, or, as the case may be, by a copy of the special agreement concluded between the Member States concerned.

11. If an application does not comply with the requirements set out in paragraphs 3 to 6 of this Article, the Registrar shall prescribe a reasonable period within which the applicant is to comply with them whether by putting the application itself in order or by producing any of the abovementioned documents. If the applicant fails to put the application in order or to produce the required documents within the time prescribed, the Court shall, after hearing the Advocate

General, decide whether the non-compliance with these conditions renders the application formally inadmissible.

Article 39

The application shall be served on the defendant. In a case where Article 38(7) applies, service shall be effected as soon as the application has been put in order or the Court has declared it admissible notwithstanding the failure to observe the formal requirements set out in that Article.

Article 40

1. Within one month after service on him of the application, the defendant shall lodge a defence, stating:
    (a) the name and address of the defendant;
    (b) the arguments of fact and law relied on;
    (c) the form of order sought by the defendant;
    (d) the nature of any evidence offered by him.
    The provisions of Article 38(2) to (5) of these Rules shall apply to the defence.
2. The time-limit laid down in paragraph 1 of this Article may be extended by the President on a reasoned application by the defendant.

Article 41

1. The application initiating the proceedings and the defence may be supplemented by a reply from the applicant and by a rejoinder from the defendant.
2. The President shall fix the time-limits within which these pleadings are to be lodged.

Article 42

1. In reply or rejoinder a party may offer further evidence. The party must, however, give reasons for the delay in offering it.
2. No new plea in law may be introduced in the course of proceedings unless it is based on matters of law or of fact which come to light in the course of the procedure.
    If in the course of the procedure one of the parties puts forward a new plea in law which is so based, the President may, even after the expiry of the normal procedural time-limits, acting on a report of the Judge-Rapporteur and after hearing the Advocate General, allow the other party time to answer on that plea.
    The decision on the admissibility of the plea shall be reserved for the final judgment.

Article 43

The Court may, at any time, after hearing the parties and the Advocate General, if the assignment referred to in Article 10(2) has taken place, order that two or more cases concerning the same subject-matter shall, on account of the connection between them, be joined for the purposes of the written or oral procedure or of the final judgment. The cases may subsequently be disjoined. The President may refer these matters to the Court.

CHAPTER 1a
THE PRELIMINARY REPORT
AND ASSIGNMENT OF CASES TO FORMATIONS

Article 44

1. The President shall fix a date on which the Judge-Rapporteur is to present his preliminary report to the general meeting of the Court, either:
    (a) after the rejoinder has been lodged, or
    (b) where no reply or no rejoinder has been lodged within the time-limit fixed in accordance with Article 41(2), or
    (c) where the party concerned has waived his right to lodge a reply or rejoinder, or
    (d) where the expedited procedure referred to in Article 62a is to be applied, when the President fixes a date for the hearing.
2. The preliminary report shall contain recommendations as to whether a preparatory inquiry or any other preparatory step should be undertaken and as to the formation to which the case should be assigned. It shall also contain the Judge-Rapporteur's recommendation, if any, as to

whether to dispense with a hearing as provided for in Article 44a and as to whether to dispense with an Opinion of the Advocate General pursuant to the fifth subparagraph of Article 20 of the Statute.

The Court shall decide, after hearing the Advocate General, what action to take upon the recommendations of the Judge-Rapporteur.

3.   The Court shall assign to the Chambers of five and three Judges any case brought before it in so far as the difficulty or importance of the case or particular circumstances are not such as to require that it should be assigned to the Grand Chamber.

However, a case may not be assigned to a Chamber of five or three Judges if a Member State or an institution of the Communities, being a party to the proceedings, has requested that the case be decided by the Grand Chamber. For the purposes of this provision, "party to the proceedings" means any Member State or any institution which is a party to or an intervener in the proceedings or which has submitted written observations in any reference of a kind mentioned in Article 103. A request such as that referred to in this subparagraph may not be made in proceedings between the Communities and their servants.

The Court shall sit as a full Court where cases are brought before it pursuant to the provisions referred to in the fourth paragraph of Article 16 of the Statute. It may assign a case to the full Court where, in accordance with the fifth paragraph of Article 16 of the Statute, it considers that the case is of exceptional importance.

4.   The formation to which a case has been assigned may, at any stage of the proceedings, refer the case back to the Court in order that it may be reassigned to a formation composed of a greater number of Judges.

Where a preparatory inquiry has been opened, the formation determining the case may, if it does not undertake it itself, assign the inquiry to the Chamber referred to in Article 9(2) of these Rules.

Where the oral procedure is opened without an inquiry, the President of the formation determining the case shall fix the opening date.

Article 44b

Without prejudice to any special provisions laid down in these Rules, the procedure before the Court shall also include an oral part. However, after the pleadings referred to in Article 40(1) and, as the case may be, in Article 41(1) have been lodged, the Court, acting on a report from the Judge-Rapporteur and after hearing the Advocate General, and if none of the parties has submitted an application setting out the reasons for which he wishes to be heard, may decide otherwise. The application shall be submitted within a period of one month from notification to the party of the close of the written procedure. That period may be extended by the President.

CHAPTER 2

PREPARATORY INQUIRIES AND OTHER PREPARATORY MEASURES

Section 1 — Measures of inquiry

Article 45

1.   The Court, after hearing the Advocate General, shall prescribe the measures of inquiry that it considers appropriate by means of an order setting out the facts to be proved. Before the Court decides on the measures of inquiry referred to in paragraph 2(c), (d) and (e) the parties shall be heard.

The order shall be served on the parties.

2.   Without prejudice to Articles 24 and 25 of the Statute, the following measures of inquiry may be adopted:

(a)   the personal appearance of the parties;

(b)   a request for information and production of documents;

(c)   oral testimony;

(d)   the commissioning of an expert's report;

(e)   an inspection of the place or thing in question.

3.   The measures of inquiry which the Court has ordered may be conducted by the Court itself, or be assigned to the Judge-Rapporteur.

The Advocate General shall take part in the measures of inquiry.

4. Evidence may be submitted in rebuttal and previous evidence may be amplified.

Article 46

1. A Chamber to which a preparatory inquiry has been assigned may exercise the powers vested in the Court by Articles 45 and 47 to 53 of these Rules; the powers vested in the President of the Court may be exercised by the President of the Chamber.

2. Articles 56 and 57 of these Rules shall apply to proceedings before the Chamber.

3. The parties shall be entitled to attend the measures of inquiry.

Section 2 — The summoning and examination of witnesses and experts

Article 47

1. The Court may, either of its own motion or on application by a party, and after hearing the Advocate General, order that certain facts be proved by witnesses. The order of the Court shall set out the facts to be established.

   The Court may summon a witness of its own motion or on application by a party or at the instance of the Advocate General.

   An application by a party for the examination of a witness shall state precisely about what facts and for what reasons the witness should be examined.

2. The witness shall be summoned by an order of the Court containing the following information:

   (a) the surname, forenames, description and address of the witness;

   (b) an indication of the facts about which the witness is to be examined;

   (c) where appropriate, particulars of the arrangements made by the Court for reimbursement of expenses incurred by the witness, and of the penalties which may be imposed on defaulting witnesses.

   The order shall be served on the parties and the witnesses.

3. The Court may make the summoning of a witness for whose examination a party has applied conditional upon the deposit with the cashier of the Court of a sum sufficient to cover the taxed costs thereof; the Court shall fix the amount of the payment.

   The cashier shall advance the funds necessary in connection with the examination of any witness summoned by the Court of its own motion.

4. After the identity of the witness has been established, the President shall inform him that he will be required to vouch the truth of his evidence in the manner laid down in these Rules.

   The witness shall give his evidence to the Court, the parties having been given notice to attend. After the witness has given his main evidence the President may, at the request of a party or of his own motion, put questions to him.

   The other Judges and the Advocate General may do likewise.

   Subject to the control of the President, questions may be put to witnesses by the representatives of the parties.

5. After giving his evidence, the witness shall take the following oath:

   "I swear that I have spoken the truth, the whole truth and nothing but the truth."

   The Court may, after hearing the parties, exempt a witness from taking the oath.

6. The Registrar shall draw up minutes in which the evidence of each witness is reproduced.

   The minutes shall be signed by the President or by the Judge-Rapporteur responsible for conducting the examination of the witness, and by the Registrar. Before the minutes are thus signed, witnesses must be given an opportunity to check the content of the minutes and to sign them.

   The minutes shall constitute an official record.

Article 48

1. Witnesses who have been duly summoned shall obey the summons and attend for examination.

2. If a witness who has been duly summoned fails to appear before the Court, the Court may impose upon him a pecuniary penalty not exceeding EUR 5 000 and may order that a further summons be served on the witness at his own expense.

The same penalty may be imposed upon a witness who, without good reason, refuses to give evidence or to take the oath or where appropriate to make a solemn affirmation equivalent thereto.

3. If the witness proffers a valid excuse to the Court, the pecuniary penalty imposed on him may be cancelled. The pecuniary penalty imposed may be reduced at the request of the witness where he establishes that it is disproportionate to his income.

4. Penalties imposed and other measures ordered under this Article shall be enforced in accordance with Articles 244 and 256 of the EC Treaty and Articles 159 and 164 of the EAEC Treaty.

Article 49

1. The Court may order that an expert's report be obtained. The order appointing the expert shall define his task and set a time-limit within which he is to make his report.

2. The expert shall receive a copy of the order, together with all the documents necessary for carrying out his task. He shall be under the supervision of the Judge-Rapporteur, who may be present during his investigation and who shall be kept informed of his progress in carrying out his task.

   The Court may request the parties or one of them to lodge security for the costs of the expert's report.

3. At the request of the expert, the Court may order the examination of witnesses. Their examination shall be carried out in accordance with Article 47 of these Rules.

4. The expert may give his opinion only on points which have been expressly referred to him.

5. After the expert has made his report, the Court may order that he be examined, the parties having been given notice to attend.

   Subject to the control of the President, questions may be put to the expert by the representatives of the parties.

6. After making his report, the expert shall take the following oath before the Court:

   "I swear that I have conscientiously and impartially carried out my task."

   The Court may, after hearing the parties, exempt the expert from taking the oath.

Article 50

1. If one of the parties objects to a witness or to an expert on the ground that he is not a competent or proper person to act as witness or expert or for any other reason, or if a witness or expert refuses to give evidence, to take the oath or to make a solemn affirmation equivalent thereto, the matter shall be resolved by the Court.

2. An objection to a witness or to an expert shall be raised within two weeks after service of the order summoning the witness or appointing the expert; the statement of objection must set out the grounds of objection and indicate the nature of any evidence offered.

Article 51

1. Witnesses and experts shall be entitled to reimbursement of their travel and subsistence expenses. The cashier of the Court may make a payment to them towards these expenses in advance.

2. Witnesses shall be entitled to compensation for loss of earnings, and experts to fees for their services. The cashier of the Court shall pay witnesses and experts their compensation or fees after they have carried out their respective duties or tasks.

Article 52

The Court may, on application by a party or of its own motion, issue letters rogatory for the examination of witnesses or experts, as provided for in the supplementary rules mentioned in Article 125 of these Rules.

Article 53

1. The Registrar shall draw up minutes of every hearing. The minutes shall be signed by the President and by the Registrar and shall constitute an official record.

2.   The parties may inspect the minutes and any expert's report at the Registry and obtain copies at their own expense.

Section 3 — Closure of the preparatory inquiry

Article 54

Unless the Court prescribes a period within which the parties may lodge written observations, the President shall fix the date for the opening of the oral procedure after the preparatory inquiry has been completed.

Where a period had been prescribed for the lodging of written observations, the President shall fix the date for the opening of the oral procedure after that period has expired.

Section 4 — Preparatory Measures

Article 54a

The Judge-Rapporteur and the Advocate General may request the parties to submit within a specified period all such information relating to the facts, and all such documents or other particulars, as they may consider relevant. The information and/or documents provided shall be communicated to the other parties.

CHAPTER 3
ORAL PROCEDURE

Article 55

1.   Subject to the priority of decisions provided for in Article 85 of these Rules, the Court shall deal with the cases before it in the order in which the preparatory inquiries in them have been completed. Where the preparatory inquiries in several cases are completed simultaneously, the order in which they are to be dealt with shall be determined by the dates of entry in the register of the applications initiating them respectively.

2.   The President may in special circumstances order that a case be given priority over others.

      The President may in special circumstances, after hearing the parties and the Advocate General, either on his own initiative or at the request of one of the parties, defer a case to be dealt with at a later date. On a joint application by the parties the President may order that a case be deferred.

Article 56

1.   The proceedings shall be opened and directed by the President, who shall be responsible for the proper conduct of the hearing.

2.   The oral proceedings in cases heard *in camera* shall not be published.

Article 57

The President may in the course of the hearing put questions to the agents, advisers or lawyers of the parties.

The other Judges and the Advocate General may do likewise.

Article 58

A party may address the Court only through his agent, adviser or lawyer.

Article 59

1.   The Advocate General shall deliver his opinion orally at the end of the oral procedure.

2.   After the Advocate General has delivered his opinion, the President shall declare the oral procedure closed.

Article 60

The Court may at any time, in accordance with Article 45(1), after hearing the Advocate General, order any measure of inquiry to be taken or that a previous inquiry be repeated or expanded. The Court may direct the Chamber or the Judge-Rapporteur to carry out the measures so ordered.

Article 61

The Court may after hearing the Advocate General order the reopening of the oral procedure.

Article 62

1. The Registrar shall draw up minutes of every hearing. The minutes shall be signed by the President and by the Registrar and shall constitute an official record.
2. The parties may inspect the minutes at the Registry and obtain copies at their own expense.

CHAPTER 3a
EXPEDITED PROCEDURES

Article 62a

1. On application by the applicant or the defendant, the President may exceptionally decide, on the basis of a recommendation by the Judge-Rapporteur and after hearing the other party and the Advocate General, that a case is to be determined pursuant to an expedited procedure derogating from the provisions of these Rules, where the particular urgency of the case requires the Court to give its ruling with the minimum of delay.

   An application for a case to be decided under an expedited procedure shall be made by a separate document lodged at the same time as the application initiating the proceedings or the defence, as the case may be.
2. Under the expedited procedure, the originating application and the defence may be supplemented by a reply and a rejoinder only if the President considers this to be necessary.

   An intervener may lodge a statement in intervention only if the President considers this to be necessary.
3. Once the defence has been lodged or, if the decision to adjudicate under an expedited procedure is not made until after that pleading has been lodged, once that decision has been taken, the President shall fix a date for the hearing, which shall be communicated forthwith to the parties. He may postpone the date of the hearing where the organisation of measures of inquiry or of other preparatory measures so requires.

   Without prejudice to Article 42, the parties may supplement their arguments and offer further evidence in the course of the oral procedure. They must, however, give reasons for the delay in offering such further evidence.
4. The Court shall give its ruling after hearing the Advocate General.

CHAPTER 4
JUDGMENTS

Article 63

The judgment shall contain:
— a statement that it is the judgment of the Court,
— the date of its delivery,
— the names of the President and of the Judges taking part in it,
— the name of the Advocate General,
— the name of the Registrar,
— the description of the parties,
— the names of the agents, advisers and lawyers of the parties,
— a statement of the forms of order sought by the parties,
— a statement that the Advocate General has been heard,
— a summary of the facts,
— the grounds for the decision,
— the operative part of the judgment, including the decision as to costs.

Article 64

1. The judgment shall be delivered in open court; the parties shall be given notice to attend to hear it.
2. The original of the judgment, signed by the President, by the Judges who took part in the deliberations and by the Registrar, shall be sealed and deposited at the Registry; the parties shall be served with certified copies of the judgment.
3. The Registrar shall record on the original of the judgment the date on which it was delivered.

Article 65

The judgment shall be binding from the date of its delivery.

Article 66

1. Without prejudice to the provisions relating to the interpretation of judgments the Court may, of its own motion or on application by a party made within two weeks after the delivery of a judgment, rectify clerical mistakes, errors in calculation and obvious slips in it.
2. The parties, whom the Registrar shall duly notify, may lodge written observations within a period prescribed by the President.
3. The Court shall take its decision in closed session after hearing the Advocate General.
4. The original of the rectification order shall be annexed to the original of the rectified judgment. A note of this order shall be made in the margin of the original of the rectified judgment.

Article 67

If the Court should omit to give a decision on a specific head of claim or on costs, any party may within a month after service of the judgment apply to the Court to supplement its judgment.

The application shall be served on the opposite party and the President shall prescribe a period within which that party may lodge written observations.

After these observations have been lodged, the Court shall, after hearing the Advocate General, decide both on the admissibility and on the substance of the application.

Article 68

The Registrar shall arrange for the publication of reports of cases before the Court.

CHAPTER 5

COSTS

Article 69

1. A decision as to costs shall be given in the final judgment or in the order which closes the proceedings.
2. The unsuccessful party shall be ordered to pay the costs if they have been applied for in the successful party's pleadings.

    Where there are several unsuccessful parties the Court shall decide how the costs are to be shared.
3. Where each party succeeds on some and fails on other heads, or where the circumstances are exceptional, the Court may order that the costs be shared or that the parties bear their own costs.

    The Court may order a party, even if successful, to pay costs which the Court considers that party to have unreasonably or vexatiously caused the opposite party to incur.
4. The Member States and institutions which intervene in the proceedings shall bear their own costs.

    The States, other than the Member States, which are parties to the EEA Agreement, and also the EFTA Surveillance Authority, shall bear their own costs if they intervene in the proceedings.

    The Court may order an intervener other than those mentioned in the preceding subparagraphs to bear his own costs.
5. A party who discontinues or withdraws from proceedings shall be ordered to pay the costs if they have been applied for in the other party's observations on the discontinuance. However, upon application by the party who discontinues or withdraws from proceedings, the costs shall be borne by the other party if this appears justified by the conduct of that party.

    Where the parties have come to an agreement on costs, the decision as to costs shall be in accordance with that agreement.

    If costs are not claimed, the parties shall bear their own costs.
6. Where a case does not proceed to judgment the costs shall be in the discretion of the Court.

Article 70

Without prejudice to the second subparagraph of Article 69(3) of these Rules, in proceedings between the Communities and their servants the institutions shall bear their own costs.

Article 71

Costs necessarily incurred by a party in enforcing a judgment or order of the Court shall be refunded by the opposite party on the scale in force in the State where the enforcement takes place.

Article 72

Proceedings before the Court shall be free of charge, except that:

   (a)   where a party has caused the Court to incur avoidable costs the Court may, after hearing the Advocate General, order that party to refund them;

   (b)   where copying or translation work is carried out at the request of a party, the cost shall, in so far as the Registrar considers it excessive, be paid for by that party on the scale of charges referred to in Article 16(5) of these Rules.

Article 73

Without prejudice to the preceding Article, the following shall be regarded as recoverable costs:

   (a)   sums payable to witnesses and experts under Article 51 of these Rules;

   (b)   expenses necessarily incurred by the parties for the purpose of the proceedings, in particular the travel and subsistence expenses and the remuneration of agents, advisers or lawyers.

Article 74

   1.   If there is a dispute concerning the costs to be recovered, the Chamber referred to in Article 9(2) of these Rules to which the case has been assigned shall, on application by the party concerned and after hearing the opposite party and the Advocate General, make an order, from which no appeal shall lie.

   2.   The parties may, for the purposes of enforcement, apply for an authenticated copy of the order.

Article 75

   1.   Sums due from the cashier of the Court shall be paid in the currency of the country where the Court has its seat.

   At the request of the person entitled to any sum, it shall be paid in the currency of the country where the expenses to be refunded were incurred or where the steps in respect of which payment is due were taken.

   2.   Other debtors shall make payment in the currency of their country of origin.

   3.   Conversions of currency shall be made at the official rates of exchange ruling on the day of payment in the country where the Court has its seat.

CHAPTER 6

LEGAL AID

Article 76

   1.   A party who is wholly or in part unable to meet the costs of the proceedings may at any time apply for legal aid.

   The application shall be accompanied by evidence of the applicant's need of assistance, and in particular by a document from the competent authority certifying his lack of means.

   2.   If the application is made prior to proceedings which the applicant wishes to commence, it shall briefly state the subject of such proceedings.

   The application need not be made through a lawyer.

   3.   The President shall designate a Judge to act as Rapporteur. The Chamber of three Judges to which the latter belongs shall, after considering the written observations of the opposite party and after hearing the Advocate General, decide whether legal aid should be granted in full or in part, or whether it should be refused. The Chamber shall consider whether there is manifestly no cause of action.

   The Chamber shall make an order without giving reasons, and no appeal shall lie therefrom.

4. The Chamber may at any time, either of its own motion or on application, withdraw legal aid if the circumstances which led to its being granted alter during the proceedings.

5. Where legal aid is granted, the cashier of the Court shall advance the funds necessary to meet the expenses.

In its decision as to costs the Court may order the payment to the cashier of the Court of the whole or any part of amounts advanced as legal aid.

The Registrar shall take steps to obtain the recovery of these sums from the party ordered to pay them.

CHAPTER 7
DISCONTINUANCE

Article 77

If, before the Court has given its decision, the parties reach a settlement of their dispute and intimate to the Court the abandonment of their claims, the President shall order the case to be removed from the register and shall give a decision as to costs in accordance with Article 69(5), having regard to any proposals made by the parties on the matter.

This provision shall not apply to proceedings under Articles 230 and 232 of the EC Treaty and Articles 146 and 148 of the EAEC Treaty.

Article 78

If the applicant informs the Court in writing that he wishes to discontinue the proceedings, the President shall order the case to be removed from the register and shall give a decision as to costs in accordance with Article 69(5).

CHAPTER 8
SERVICE

Article 79

1. Where these Rules require that a document be served on a person, the Registrar shall ensure that service is effected at that person's address for service either by the dispatch of a copy of the document by registered post with a form for acknowledgement of receipt or by personal delivery of the copy against a receipt.

The Registrar shall prepare and certify the copies of documents to be served, save where the parties themselves supply the copies in accordance with Article 37(1) of these Rules.

2. Where, in accordance with the second subparagraph of Article 38(2), the addressee has agreed that service is to be effected on him by telefax or other technical means of communication, any procedural document other than a judgment or order of the Court may be served by the transmission of a copy of the document by such means.

Where, for technical reasons or on account of the nature or length of the document, such transmission is impossible or impracticable, the document shall be served, if the addressee has failed to state an address for service, at his address in accordance with the procedures laid down in paragraph 1 of this article. The addressee shall be so advised by telefax or other technical means of communication. Service shall then be deemed to have been effected on the addressee by registered post on the tenth day following the lodging of the registered letter at the post office of the place where the Court has its seat, unless it is shown by the acknowledgement of receipt that the letter was received on a different date or the addressee informs the Registrar, within three weeks of being advised by telefax or other technical means of communication, that the document to be served has not reached him.

CHAPTER 9
TIME-LIMITS

Article 80

1. Any period of time prescribed by the Union Treaty, the EC Treaty and the EAEC Treaty, the Statute of the Court or these Rules for the taking of any procedural step shall be reckoned as follows:

(a) where a period expressed in days, weeks, months or years is to be calculated from the moment at which an event occurs or an action takes place, the day during which that event occurs or that action takes place shall not be counted as falling within the period in question;

(b) a period expressed in weeks, months or in years shall end with the expiry of whichever day in the last week, month or year is the same day of the week, or falls on the same date, as the day during which the event or action from which the period is to be calculated occurred or took place. If, in a period expressed in months or in years, the day on which it should expire does not occur in the last month, the period shall end with the expiry of the last day of that month;

(c) where a period is expressed in months and days, it shall first be reckoned in whole months, then in days;

(d) periods shall include official holidays, Sundays and Saturdays;

(e) periods shall not be suspended during the judicial vacations.

2. If the period would otherwise end on a Saturday, Sunday or an official holiday, it shall be extended until the end of the first following working day.

A list of official holidays drawn up by the Court shall be published in the *Official Journal of the European Union*.

Article 81

1. Where the period of time allowed for initiating proceedings against a measure adopted by an institution runs from the publication of that measure, that period shall be calculated, for the purposes of Article 80(1)(a), from the end of the 14th day after publication thereof in the *Official Journal of the European Union*.

2. The prescribed time-limits shall be extended on account of distance by a single period of 10 days.

Article 82

Any time-limit prescribed pursuant to these Rules may be extended by whoever prescribed it.

The President and the Presidents of Chambers may delegate to the Registrar power of signature for the purpose of fixing time-limits which, pursuant to these Rules, it falls to them to prescribe or of extending such time-limits.

CHAPTER 10
STAY OF PROCEEDINGS

Article 82a

1. The proceedings may be stayed:

(a) in the circumstances specified in the third paragraph of Article 54 of the Statute, by order of the Court, made after hearing the Advocate General;

(b) in all other cases, by decision of the President adopted after hearing the Advocate General and, save in the case of references for a preliminary ruling as referred to in Article 103, the parties.

The proceedings may be resumed by order or decision, following the same procedure.

The orders or decisions referred to in this paragraph shall be served on the parties.

2. The stay of proceedings shall take effect on the date indicated in the order or decision of stay or, in the absence of such indication, on the date of that order or decision.

While proceedings are stayed time shall cease to run for the purposes of prescribed time-limits for all parties.

3. Where the order or decision of stay does not fix the length of stay, it shall end on the date indicated in the order or decision of resumption or, in the absence of such indication, on the date of the order or decision of resumption.

From the date of resumption time shall begin to run afresh for the purposes of the time-limits.

TITLE III
SPECIAL FORMS OF PROCEDURE

CHAPTER 1
SUSPENSION OF OPERATION OR ENFORCEMENT AND OTHER INTERIM MEASURES

Article 83

1. An application to suspend the operation of any measure adopted by an institution, made pursuant to Article 242 of the EC Treaty or Article 157 of the EAEC Treaty, shall be admissible only if the applicant is challenging that measure in proceedings before the Court. An application for the adoption of any other interim measure referred to in Article 243 of the EC Treaty or Article 158 of the EAEC Treaty shall be admissible only if it is made by a party to a case before the Court and relates to that case.

2. An application of a kind referred to in paragraph 1 of this Article shall state the subject-matter of the proceedings, the circumstances giving rise to urgency and the pleas of fact and law establishing a prima facie case for the interim measures applied for.

3. The application shall be made by a separate document and in accordance with the provisions of Articles 37 and 38 of these Rules.

Article 84

1. The application shall be served on the opposite party, and the President shall prescribe a short period within which that party may submit written or oral observations.

2. The President may order a preparatory inquiry.
   The President may grant the application even before the observations of the opposite party have been submitted. This decision may be varied or cancelled even without any application being made by any party.

Article 85

The President shall either decide on the application himself or refer it to the Court.

If the President is absent or prevented from attending, Article 11 of these Rules shall apply.

Where the application is referred to it, the Court shall postpone all other cases, and shall give a decision after hearing the Advocate General. Article 84 shall apply.

Article 86

1. The decision on the application shall take the form of a reasoned order, from which no appeal shall lie. The order shall be served on the parties forthwith.

2. The enforcement of the order may be made conditional on the lodging by the applicant of security, of an amount and nature to be fixed in the light of the circumstances.

3. Unless the order fixes the date on which the interim measure is to lapse, the measure shall lapse when final judgment is delivered.

4. The order shall have only an interim effect, and shall be without prejudice to the decision of the Court on the substance of the case.

Article 87

On application by a party, the order may at any time be varied or cancelled on account of a change in circumstances.

Article 88

Rejection of an application for an interim measure shall not bar the party who made it from making a further application on the basis of new facts.

Article 89

The provisions of this Chapter shall apply to applications to suspend the enforcement of a decision of the Court or of any measure adopted by another institution, submitted pursuant to Articles 244 and 256 of the EC Treaty or Articles 159 and 164 of the EAEC Treaty.

The order granting the application shall fix, where appropriate, a date on which the interim measure is to lapse.

Article 90

 1. An application of a kind referred to in the third and fourth paragraphs of Article 81 of the EAEC Treaty shall contain:

  (a) the names and addresses of the persons or undertakings to be inspected;

  (b) an indication of what is to be inspected and of the purpose of the inspection.

 2. The President shall give his decision in the form of an order. Article 86 of these Rules shall apply.

  If the President is absent or prevented from attending, Article 11 of these Rules shall apply.

CHAPTER 2
PRELIMINARY ISSUES

Article 91

 1. A party applying to the Court for a decision on a preliminary objection or other preliminary plea not going to the substance of the case shall make the application by a separate document. The application must state the pleas of fact and law relied on and the form of order sought by the applicant; any supporting documents must be annexed to it.

 2. As soon as the application has been lodged, the President shall prescribe a period within which the opposite party may lodge a document containing a statement of the form of order sought by that party and its pleas in law.

 3. Unless the Court decides otherwise, the remainder of the proceedings shall be oral.

 4. The Court shall, after hearing the Advocate General, decide on the application or reserve its decision for the final judgment.

  If the Court refuses the application or reserves its decision, the President shall prescribe new time-limits for the further steps in the proceedings.

Article 92

 1. Where it is clear that the Court has no jurisdiction to take cognisance of an action or where the action is manifestly inadmissible, the Court may, by reasoned order, after hearing the Advocate General and without taking further steps in the proceedings, give a decision on the action.

 2. The Court may at any time of its own motion consider whether there exists any absolute bar to proceeding with a case or declare, after hearing the parties, that the action has become devoid of purpose and that there is no need to adjudicate on it; it shall give its decision in accordance with Article 91(3) and (4) of these Rules.

CHAPTER 3
INTERVENTION

Article 93

 1. An application to intervene must be made within six weeks of the publication of the notice referred to in Article 16(6) of these Rules.

  The application shall contain:

  (a) the description of the case;

  (b) the description of the parties;

  (c) the name and address of the intervener;

  (d) the intervener's address for service at the place where the Court has its seat;

  (e) the form of order sought, by one or more of the parties, in support of which the intervener is applying for leave to intervene;

  (f) a statement of the circumstances establishing the right to intervene, where the application is submitted pursuant to the second or third paragraph of Article 40 of the Statute.

  The intervener shall be represented in accordance with Article 19 of the Statute.

  Articles 37 and 38 of these Rules shall apply.

 2. The application shall be served on the parties.

  The President shall give the parties an opportunity to submit their written or oral observations before deciding on the application.

The President shall decide on the application by order or shall refer the application to the Court.

3. If the President allows the intervention, the intervener shall receive a copy of every document served on the parties. The President may, however, on application by one of the parties, omit secret or confidential documents.

4. The intervener must accept the case as he finds it at the time of his intervention.

5. The President shall prescribe a period within which the intervener may submit a statement in intervention.

    The statement in intervention shall contain:

    (a) a statement of the form of order sought by the intervener in support of or opposing, in whole or in part, the form of order sought by one of the parties;

    (b) the pleas in law and arguments relied on by the intervener;

    (c) where appropriate, the nature of any evidence offered.

6. After the statement in intervention has been lodged, the President shall, where necessary, prescribe a time-limit within which the parties may reply to that statement.

7. Consideration may be given to an application to intervene which is made after the expiry of the period prescribed in paragraph 1 but before the decision to open the oral procedure provided for in Article 44(3). In that event, if the President allows the intervention, the intervener may, on the basis of the Report for the Hearing communicated to him, submit his observations during the oral procedure, if that procedure takes place.

CHAPTER 4
JUDGMENTS BY DEFAULT AND APPLICATIONS TO SET THEM ASIDE

Article 94

1. If a defendant on whom an application initiating proceedings has been duly served fails to lodge a defence to the application in the proper form within the time prescribed, the applicant may apply for judgment by default.

    The application shall be served on the defendant. The Court may decide to open the oral procedure on the application.

2. Before giving judgment by default the Court shall, after hearing the Advocate General, consider whether the application initiating proceedings is admissible, whether the appropriate formalities have been complied with, and whether the application appears well founded. The Court may order a preparatory inquiry.

3. A judgment by default shall be enforceable. The Court may, however, grant a stay of execution until the Court has given its decision on any application under paragraph 4 to set aside the judgment, or it may make execution subject to the provision of security of an amount and nature to be fixed in the light of the circumstances; this security shall be released if no such application is made or if the application fails.

4. Application may be made to set aside a judgment by default.

    The application to set aside the judgment must be made within one month from the date of service of the judgment and must be lodged in the form prescribed by Articles 37 and 38 of these Rules.

5. After the application has been served, the President shall prescribe a period within which the other party may submit his written observations.

    The proceedings shall be conducted in accordance with Article 44 et seq. of these Rules.

6. The Court shall decide by way of a judgment which may not be set aside.

    The original of this judgment shall be annexed to the original of the judgment by default. A note of the judgment on the application to set aside shall be made in the margin of the original of the judgment by default.

CHAPTER 6
EXCEPTIONAL REVIEW PROCEDURES

Section 1 — Third-party proceedings

Article 97

1. Articles 37 and 38 of these Rules shall apply to an application initiating third-party proceedings. In addition such an application shall:

   (a) specify the judgment contested;

   (b) state how that judgment is prejudicial to the rights of the third party;

   (c) indicate the reasons for which the third party was unable to take part in the original case.

   The application must be made against all the parties to the original case.

   Where the judgment has been published in the Official Journal of the European Union, the application must be lodged within two months of the publication.

2. The Court may, on application by the third party, order a stay of execution of the judgment. The provisions of Title III, Chapter I, of these Rules shall apply.

3. The contested judgment shall be varied on the points on which the submissions of the third party are upheld.

   The original of the judgment in the third-party proceedings shall be annexed to the original of the contested judgment. A note of the judgment in the third-party proceedings shall be made in the margin of the original of the contested judgment.

Section 2 — Revision

Article 98

An application for revision of a judgment shall be made within three months of the date on which the facts on which the application is based came to the applicant's knowledge.

Article 99

1. Articles 37 and 38 of these Rules shall apply to an application for revision. In addition such an application shall:

   (a) specify the judgment contested;

   (b) indicate the points on which the judgment is contested;

   (c) set out the facts on which the application is based;

   (d) indicate the nature of the evidence to show that there are facts justifying revision of the judgment, and that the time-limit laid down in Article 98 has been observed.

2. The application must be made against all parties to the case in which the contested judgment was given.

Article 100

1. Without prejudice to its decision on the substance, the Court, in closed session, shall, after hearing the Advocate General and having regard to the written observations of the parties, give in the form of a judgment its decision on the admissibility of the application.

2. If the Court finds the application admissible, it shall proceed to consider the substance of the application and shall give its decision in the form of a judgment in accordance with these Rules.

3. The original of the revising judgment shall be annexed to the original of the judgment revised. A note of the revising judgment shall be made in the margin of the original of the judgment revised.

CHAPTER 7
APPEALS AGAINST DECISIONS OF THE ARBITRATION COMMITTEE

Article 101

1. An application initiating an appeal under the second paragraph of Article 18 of the EAEC Treaty shall state:

    (a)   the name and address of the applicant;

    (b)   the description of the signatory;

    (c)   a reference to the arbitration committee's decision against which the appeal is made;

    (d)   the description of the parties;

    (e)   a summary of the facts;

    (f)   the pleas in law of and the form of order sought by the applicant.

2.   Articles 37(3) and (4) and 38(2), (3) and (5) of these Rules shall apply.

       A certified copy of the contested decision shall be annexed to the application.

3.   As soon as the application has been lodged, the Registrar of the Court shall request the arbitration committee registry to transmit to the Court the papers in the case.

4.   Articles 39, 40 and 55 et seq. of these Rules shall apply to these proceedings.

5.   The Court shall give its decision in the form of a judgment. Where the Court sets aside the decision of the arbitration committee it may refer the case back to the committee.

CHAPTER 8
INTERPRETATION OF JUDGMENTS

Article 102

1.   An application for interpretation of a judgment shall be made in accordance with Articles 37 and 38 of these Rules. In addition it shall specify:

    (a)   the judgment in question;

    (b)   the passages of which interpretation is sought.

       The application must be made against all the parties to the case in which the judgment was given.

2.   The Court shall give its decision in the form of a judgment after having given the parties an opportunity to submit their observations and after hearing the Advocate General.

       The original of the interpreting judgment shall be annexed to the original of the judgment interpreted. A note of the interpreting judgment shall be made in the margin of the original of the judgment interpreted.

CHAPTER 9
PRELIMINARY RULINGS AND OTHER REFERENCES FOR INTERPRETATION

Article 103

1.   In cases governed by Article 23 of the Statute, the procedure shall be governed by the provisions of these Rules, subject to adaptations necessitated by the nature of the reference for a preliminary ruling.

2.   The provisions of paragraph 1 shall apply to the references for a preliminary ruling provided for in the Protocol concerning the interpretation by the Court of Justice of the Convention of 29 February 1968 on the mutual recognition of companies and legal persons and the Protocol concerning the interpretation by the Court of Justice of the Convention of 27 September 1968 on jurisdiction and the enforcement of judgments in civil and commercial matters, signed at Luxembourg on 3 June 1971, and to the references provided for by Article 4 of the latter Protocol.

       The provisions of paragraph 1 shall apply also to references for interpretation provided for by other existing or future agreements.

Article 104

1.   The decisions of national courts or tribunals referred to in Article 103 shall be communicated to the Member States in the original version, accompanied by a translation into the official language of the State to which they are addressed.

       In the cases governed by the third paragraph of Article 23 of the Statute, the decisions of national courts or tribunals shall be notified to the States, other than the Member States, which are parties to the EEA Agreement, and also to the EFTA Surveillance Authority, in the original version, accompanied by a translation into one of the languages mentioned in Article 29(1), to be chosen by the addressee of the notification.

Where a non-member State has the right to take part in proceedings for a preliminary ruling pursuant to the fourth paragraph of Article 23 of the Statute, the original version of the decision of the national court or tribunal shall be communicated to it together with a translation into one of the languages mentioned in Article 29(1), to be chosen by the non-member State concerned.

2. As regards the representation and attendance of the parties to the main proceedings in the preliminary ruling procedure the Court shall take account of the rules of procedure of the national court or tribunal which made the reference.

3. Where a question referred to the Court for a preliminary ruling is identical to a question on which the Court has already ruled, where the answer to such a question may be clearly deduced from existing case-law or where the answer to the question admits of no reasonable doubt, the Court may, after informing the court or tribunal which referred the question to it, hearing any observations submitted by the persons referred to in Article 23 of the Statute and hearing the Advocate General, give its decision by reasoned order in which, if appropriate, reference is made to its previous judgment or to the relevant case-law.

4. Without prejudice to paragraph (3) of this Article, the procedure before the Court in the case of a reference for a preliminary ruling shall also include an oral part. However, after the statements of case or written observations referred to Article 23 of the Statute have been submitted, the Court, acting on a report from the Judge-Rapporteur, after informing the persons who under the aforementioned provisions are entitled to submit such statements or observations, may, after hearing the Advocate General, decide otherwise, provided that none of those persons has submitted an application setting out the reasons for which he wishes to be heard. The application shall be submitted within a period of one month from service on the party or person of the written statements of case or written observations which have been lodged. That period may be extended by the President.

5. The Court may, after hearing the Advocate General, request clarification from the national court.

6. It shall be for the national court or tribunal to decide as to the costs of the reference.
   In special circumstances the Court may grant, by way of legal aid, assistance for the purpose of facilitating the representation or attendance of a party.

Article 104a

At the request of the national court, the President may exceptionally decide, on a proposal from the Judge-Rapporteur and after hearing the Advocate General, to apply an accelerated procedure derogating from the provisions of these Rules to a reference for a preliminary ruling, where the circumstances referred to establish that a ruling on the question put to the Court is a matter of exceptional urgency.

In that event, the President may immediately fix the date for the hearing, which shall be notified to the parties in the main proceedings and to the other persons referred to in Article 23 of the Statute when the decision making the reference is served.

The parties and other interested persons referred to in the preceding paragraph may lodge statements of case or written observations within a period prescribed by the President, which shall not be less than 15 days. The President may request the parties and other interested persons to restrict the matters addressed in their statement of case or written observations to the essential points of law raised by the question referred.

The statements of case or written observations, if any, shall be notified to the parties and to the other persons referred to above prior to the hearing.

The Court shall rule after hearing the Advocate General.

CHAPTER 10
SPECIAL PROCEDURES UNDER ARTICLES 103 TO 105 OF THE EAEC TREATY

Article 105

1. Four certified copies shall be lodged of an application under the third paragraph of Article 103 of the EAEC Treaty. The Commission shall be served with a copy.

2. The application shall be accompanied by the draft of the agreement or contract in question, by the observations of the Commission addressed to the State concerned and by all other supporting documents.

    The Commission shall submit its observations to the Court within a period of 10 days, which may be extended by the President after the State concerned has been heard.

    A certified copy of the observations shall be served on that State.

3. As soon as the application has been lodged the President shall designate a Judge to act as Rapporteur. The First Advocate General shall assign the case to an Advocate General as soon as the Judge-Rapporteur has been designated.

4. The decision shall be taken in closed session after the Advocate General has been heard.

    The agents and advisers of the State concerned and of the Commission shall be heard if they so request.

Article 106

1. In cases provided for in the last paragraph of Article 104 and the last paragraph of Article 105 of the EAEC Treaty, the provisions of Article 37 et seq. of these Rules shall apply.

2. The application shall be served on the State to which the respondent person or undertaking belongs.

CHAPTER 11

OPINIONS

Article 107

1. A request by the European Parliament for an opinion pursuant to Article 300 of the EC Treaty shall be served on the Council, on the Commission and on the Member States. Such a request by the Council shall be served on the Commission and on the European Parliament. Such a request by the Commission shall be served on the Council, on the European Parliament and on the Member States. Such a request by a Member State shall be served on the Council, on the Commission, on the European Parliament and on the other Member States.

    The President shall prescribe a period within which the institutions and Member States which have been served with a request may submit their written observations.

2. The Opinion may deal not only with the question whether the envisaged agreement is compatible which the provisions of the EC Treaty but also with the question whether the Community or any Community institution has the power to enter into that agreement.

Article 108

1. As soon as the request for an Opinion has been lodged, the President shall designate a Judge to act as Rapporteur.

2. The Court sitting in closed session shall, after hearing the Advocates General, deliver a reasoned Opinion.

3. The Opinion, signed by the President, by the Judges who took part in the deliberations and by the Registrar, shall be served on the Council, the Commission, the European Parliament and the Member States.

CHAPTER 12

REQUESTS FOR INTERPRETATION UNDER ARTICLE 68 OF THE EC TREATY

Article 109a

1. A request for a ruling on a question of interpretation under Article 68(3) of the EC Treaty shall be served on the Commission and the Member States if the request is submitted by the Council, on the Council and the Member States if the request is submitted by the Commission and on the Council, the Commission and the other Member States if the request is submitted by a Member State.

    The President shall prescribe a time-limit within which the institutions and the Member States on which the request has been served are to submit their written observations.

2. As soon as the request referred to in paragraph 1 has been submitted, the President shall designate the Judge-Rapporteur. The First Advocate General shall thereupon assign the request to an Advocate General.

3. The Court shall, after the Advocate General has delivered his Opinion, give its decision on the request by way of judgment.

   The procedure relating to the request shall include an oral part where a Member State or one of the institutions referred to in paragraph 1 so requests.

CHAPTER 13
SETTLEMENT OF THE DISPUTES REFERRED TO IN ARTICLE 35 OF THE UNION TREATY

Article 109b

1. In the case of disputes between Member States as referred to in Article 35(7) of the Union Treaty, the matter shall be brought before the Court by an application by a party to the dispute. The application shall be served on the other Member States and on the Commission.

   In the case of disputes between Member States and the Commission as referred to in Article 35(7) of the Union Treaty, the matter shall be brought before the Court by an application by a party to the dispute. The application shall be served on the other Member States, the Council and the Commission if it was made by a Member State. The application shall be served on the Member States and on the Council if it was made by the Commission.

   The President shall prescribe a time-limit within which the institutions and the Member States on which the application has been served are to submit their written observations.

2. As soon as the application referred to in paragraph 1 has been submitted, the President shall designate the Judge-Rapporteur. The First Advocate General shall thereupon assign the application to an Advocate General.

3. The Court shall, after the Advocate General has delivered his Opinion, give its ruling on the dispute by way of judgment. The procedure relating to the application shall include an oral part where a Member State or one of the institutions referred to in paragraph 1 so requests.

4. The same procedure shall apply where an agreement concluded between the Member States confers jurisdiction on the Court to rule on a dispute between Member States or between Member States and an institution.

TITLE IV
APPEALS AGAINST DECISIONS OF THE COURT OF FIRST INSTANCE

Article 110

Without prejudice to the arrangements laid down in Article 29(2)(b) and (c) and the fourth subparagraph of Article 29(3) of these Rules, in appeals against decisions of the Court of First Instance as referred to in Articles 56 and 57 of the Statute, the language of the case shall be the language of the decision of the Court of First Instance against which the appeal is brought.

Article 111

1. An appeal shall be brought by lodging an application at the Registry of the Court of Justice or of the Court of First Instance.

2. The Registry of the Court of First Instance shall immediately transmit to the Registry of the Court of Justice the papers in the case at first instance and, where necessary, the appeal.

Article 112

1. An appeal shall contain:
   (a) the name and address of the appellant;
   (b) the names of the other parties to the proceedings before the Court of First Instance;
   (c) the pleas in law and legal arguments relied on;
   (d) the form or order sought by the appellant.
   Article 37 and Article 38(2) and (3) of these Rules shall apply to appeals.

2. The decision of the Court of First Instance appealed against shall be attached to the appeal. The appeal shall state the date on which the decision appealed against was notified to the appellant.

3. If an appeal does not comply with Article 38(3) or with paragraph 2 of this Article, Article 38(7) of these Rules shall apply.

Article 113

1. An appeal may seek:
   — to set aside, in whole or in part, the decision of the Court of First Instance;
   — the same form of order, in whole or in part, as that sought at first instance and shall not seek a different form of order.
2. The subject-matter of the proceedings before the Court of First Instance may not be changed in the appeal.

Article 114

Notice of the appeal shall be served on all the parties to the proceedings before the Court of First Instance. Article 39 of these Rules shall apply.

Article 115

1. Any party to the proceedings before the Court of First Instance may lodge a response within two months after service on him of notice of the appeal. The time-limit for lodging a response shall not be extended.
2. A response shall contain:
   (a) the name and address of the party lodging it;
   (b) the date on which notice of the appeal was served on him;
   (c) the pleas in law and legal arguments relied on;
   (d) the form of order sought by the respondent.
   Article 37 and Article 38(2) and (3) of these Rules shall apply.

Article 116

1. A response may seek:
   — to dismiss, in whole or in part, the appeal or to set aside, in whole or in part, the decision of the Court of First Instance;
   — the same form of order, in whole or in part, as that sought at first instance and shall not seek a different form of order.
2. The subject-matter of the proceedings before the Court of First Instance may not be changed in the response.

Article 117

1. The appeal and the response may be supplemented by a reply and a rejoinder where the President, on application made by the appellant within seven days of service of the response, considers such further pleading necessary and expressly allows the submission of a reply in order to enable the appellant to put forward his point of view or in order to provide a basis for the decision on the appeal. The President shall prescribe the date by which the reply is to be submitted and, upon service of that pleading, the date by which the rejoinder is to be submitted.
2. Where the response seeks to set aside, in whole or in part, the decision of the Court of First Instance on a plea in law which was not raised in the appeal, the appellant or any other party may submit a reply on that plea alone within two months of the service of the response in question. Paragraph 1 shall apply to any further pleading following such a reply.

Article 118

Subject to the following provisions, Articles 42(2), 43, 44, 55 to 90, 93, 95 to 100 and 102 of these Rules shall apply to the procedure before the Court of Justice on appeal from a decision of the Court of First Instance.

Article 119

Where the appeal is, in whole or in part, clearly inadmissible or clearly unfounded, the Court may at any time, acting on a report from the Judge-Rapporteur and after hearing the Advocate General, by reasoned order dismiss the appeal in whole or in part.

Article 120

After the submission of pleadings as provided for in Article 115(1) and, if any, Article 117(1) and (2) of these Rules, the Court, acting on a report from the Judge-Rapporteur and after hearing the Advocate General and the parties, may decide to dispense with the oral part of the procedure unless one of the parties submits an application setting out the reasons for which he wishes to be heard. The application shall be submitted within a period of one month from notification to the party of the close of the written procedure. That period may be extended by the President.

Article 121

The report referred to in Article 44(2) shall be presented to the Court after the pleadings provided for in Article 115(1) and where appropriate Article 117(1) and (2) of these Rules have been lodged. Where no such pleadings are lodged, the same procedure shall apply after the expiry of the period prescribed for lodging them.

Article 122

Where the appeal is unfounded or where the appeal is well founded and the Court itself gives final judgment in the case, the Court shall make a decision as to costs.

In proceedings between the Communities and their servants:

— Article 70 of these Rules shall apply only to appeals brought by institutions;
— by way of derogation from Article 69(2) of these Rules, the Court may, in appeals brought by officials or other servants of an institution, order the parties to share the costs where equity so requires.

If the appeal is withdrawn Article 69(5) shall apply.

When an appeal brought by a Member State or an institution which did not intervene in the proceedings before the Court of First Instance is well founded, the Court of Justice may order that the parties share the costs or that the successful appellant pay the costs which the appeal has caused an unsuccessful party to incur.

Article 123

An application to intervene made to the Court in appeal proceedings shall be lodged before the expiry of a period of one month running from the publication referred to in Article 16(6).

TITLE V
PROCEDURES PROVIDED FOR BY THE EEA AGREEMENT

Article 123a

1.   In the case governed by Article 111(3) of the EEA Agreement, the matter shall be brought before the Court by a request submitted by the Contracting Parties to the dispute. The request shall be served on the other Contracting Parties, on the Commission, on the EFTA Surveillance Authority and, where appropriate, on the other persons to whom a reference for a preliminary ruling raising the same question of interpretation of Community legislation would be notified.

     The President shall prescribe a period within which the Contracting Parties and the other persons on whom the request has been served may submit written observations.

     The request shall be made in one of the languages mentioned in Article 29(1). Paragraphs 3 to 5 of that Article shall apply. The provisions of Article 104(1) shall apply *mutatis mutandis*.

2.   As soon as the request referred to in paragraph 1 of this Article has been submitted, the President shall appoint a Judge-Rapporteur. The First Advocate General shall, immediately afterwards, assign the request to an Advocate General.

     The Court shall, after hearing the Advocate General, give a reasoned decision on the request in closed session.

3.   The decision of the Court, signed by the President, by the Judges who took part in the deliberations and by the Registrar, shall be served on the Contracting Parties and on the other persons referred to in paragraph 1.

Article 123b

In the case governed by Article 1 of Protocol 34 to the EEA Agreement, the request of a court or tribunal of an EFTA State shall be served on the parties to the case, on the Contracting Parties, on the Commission, on the EFTA Surveillance Authority and, where appropriate, on the other persons to whom a reference for a preliminary ruling raising the same question of interpretation of Community legislation would be notified.

If the request is not submitted in one of the languages mentioned in Article 29(1), it shall be accompanied by a translation into one of those languages.

Within two months of this notification, the parties to the case, the Contracting Parties and the other persons referred to in the first paragraph shall be entitled to submit statements of case or written observations.

The procedure shall be governed by the provisions of these Rules, subject to the adaptations called for by the nature of the request.

Miscellaneous provisions

Article 124

1. The President shall instruct any person who is required to take an oath before the Court, as witness or expert, to tell the truth or to carry out his task conscientiously and impartially, as the case may be, and shall warn him of the criminal liability provided for in his national law in the event of any breach of this duty.

2. The witness shall take the oath either in accordance with the first subparagraph of Article 47(5) of these Rules or in the manner laid down by his national law.

   Where his national law provides the opportunity to make, in judicial proceedings, a solemn affirmation equivalent to an oath as well as or instead of taking an oath, the witness may make such an affirmation under the conditions and in the form prescribed in his national law.

   Where his national law provides neither for taking an oath nor for making a solemn affirmation, the procedure described in paragraph 1 shall be followed.

3. Paragraph 2 shall apply *mutatis mutandis* to experts, a reference to the first subparagraph of Article 49(6) replacing in this case the reference to the first subparagraph of Article 47(5) of these Rules.

Article 125

Subject to the provisions of Article 223 of the EC Treaty and Article 139 of the EAEC Treaty and after consultation with the Governments concerned, the Court shall adopt supplementary rules concerning its practice in relation to:

   (a)   letters rogatory;
   (b)   applications for legal aid;
   (c)   reports of perjury by witnesses or experts, delivered pursuant to Article 30 of the Statute.

Article 125a

The Court may issue practice directions relating in particular to the preparation and conduct of the hearings before it and to the lodging of written statements of case or written observations.

Article 126

These Rules replace the Rules of Procedure of the Court of Justice of the European Communities adopted on 4 December 1974 (OJ L 350 of 28 December 1974, p. 1), as last amended on 15 May 1991.

Article 127

These Rules, which are authentic in the languages mentioned in Article 29(1) of these Rules, shall be published in the *Official Journal of the European Union* and shall enter into force on the first day of the second month following their publication.

ANNEX
DECISION ON OFFICIAL HOLIDAYS

THE COURT OF JUSTICE OF THE EUROPEAN COMMUNITIES,
having regard to Article 80(2) of the Rules of Procedure, which requires the Court to draw up a list of official holidays;
DECIDES:

Article 1

For the purposes of Article 80(2) of the Rules of Procedure the following shall be official holidays:
— New Year's Day;
— Easter Monday;
— 1 May;
— Ascension Day;
— Whit Monday;
— 23 June;
— 15 August;
— 1 November;
— 25 December;
— 26 December.
The official holidays referred to in the first paragraph hereof shall be those observed at the place where the Court of Justice has its seat.

Article 2

Article 80(2) of the Rules of Procedure shall apply only to the official holidays mentioned in Article 1 of this Decision.

Article 3

This Decision, which shall be annexed to the Rules of Procedure, shall enter into force on the day of their publication in the *Official Journal of the European Union*.

COMMUNITY CHARTER OF THE FUNDAMENTAL SOCIAL RIGHTS OF WORKERS

Having regard to the Resolutions of the European Parliament of 15 March 1989, 14 September 1989 and 22 November 1989, and to the Opinion of the Economic and Social Committee of 22 February 1989;

Whereas the completion of the internal market is the most effective means of creating employment and ensuring maximum well-being in the Community; whereas employment development and creation must be given first priority in the completion of the internal market; whereas it is for the Community to take up the challenges of the future with regard to economic competitiveness, taking into account, in particular, regional inbalances;

Whereas the social consensus contributes to the strengthening of the competitiveness of undertakings, of the economy as a whole and to the creation of employment; whereas in this respect it is an essential condition for ensuring sustained economic development;

Whereas the completion of the internal market must favour the approximation of improvements in living and working conditions, as well as economic and social cohesion within the European Community while avoiding distortions of competition;

Whereas the completion of the internal market must offer improvements in the social field for workers of the European Community, especially in terms of freedom of movement, living and working conditions, health and safety at work, social protection, education and training;

Whereas, in order to ensure equal treatment, it is important to combat every form of discrimination, including discrimination on grounds of sex, colour, race, opinions and beliefs, and whereas, in a spirit of solidarity, it is important to combat social exclusion;

Whereas it is for Member States to guarantee the workers from non-member countries and members of their families who are legally resident in a Member State of the European Community are able to enjoy, as regards their living and working conditions, treatment comparable to that enjoyed by workers who are nationals of the Member State concerned;

Whereas inspiration should be drawn from the Conventions of the International Labour Organisation and from the European Social Charter of Council of Europe;

Whereas the Treaty, as amended by the Single European Act, contains provisions laying down the powers of the Community relating inter alia to the freedom of movement of workers (Articles 7, 48 to 51), the right of establishment (Articles 52 to 58), the social field under the conditions laid down in Articles 117 to 122–in particular as regards the improvement of health and safety in the working environment (Article 118a), the development of the dialogue between management and labour at European level (Article 118b), equal pay for men and women for equal work (Article 119) – the general principles for implementing a common vocational training policy (Article 128), economic and social cohesion (Article 130a to 130e) and, more generally, the approximation of legislation (Articles 100, 100a and 235); whereas the implementation of the Charter must not entail an extension of the Community's powers as defined by the Treaties;

Whereas the aim of the present Charter is on the one hand to consolidate the progress made in the social field, through action by the Member States, the two sides of industry and the Community;

Whereas its aim is on the other hand to declare solemnly that the implementation of the Single European Act must take full account of the social dimension of the Community and that it is necessary in this context to ensure at appropriate levels the development of the social rights of workers of the European Community, especially employed workers and self-employed persons;

Whereas, in accordance with the conclusions of the Madrid European Council, the respective roles of Community rules, national legislation and collective agreements must be clearly established;

Whereas, by virtue of the principle of subsidiarity, responsibility for the initiatives to be taken with regard to the implementation of these social rights lies with the Member States or their constituent parts and, within the limits of its powers, with the European Community; whereas such implementation may take the form of laws, collective agreements or existing practices at the various appropriate levels and whereas it requires in many spheres the active involvement of the two sides of industry;

Whereas the solemn proclamation of fundamental social rights at European Community level may not, when implemented, provide grounds for any retrogression compared with the situation currently existing in each Member State;

Have adopted the following Declaration constituting the 'Community Charter of the Fundamental Social Rights of Workers':

TITLE I FUNDAMENTAL SOCIAL RIGHTS OF WORKERS

Freedom of movement
1. Every worker of the European Community shall have the right to freedom of movement throughout the territory of the Community, subject to restrictions justified on grounds of public order, public safety or public health.
2. The right to freedom of movement shall enable any worker to engage in any occupation or profession in the Community in accordance with the principles of equal treatment as regards access to employment, working conditions and social protection in the host country.
3. The right of freedom of movement shall also imply:
    — harmonisation of conditions of residence in all Member States, particularly those concerning family reunification;
    — elimination of obstacles arising from the non-recognition of diplomas or equivalent occupational qualifications;
    — improvement of the living and working conditions of frontier workers.

Employment and remuneration
4. Every individual shall be free to choose and engage in an occupation according to the regulations governing each occupation.
5. All employment shall be fairly remunerated.
    To this end, in accordance with arrangements applying in each country:
    — workers shall be assured of an equitable wage, i.e., a wage sufficient to enable them to have a decent standard of living;

— workers subject to terms of employment other than an open-ended full-time contract shall benefit from an equitable reference wage;

— wages may be withheld, seized or transferred only in accordance with national law; such provisions should entail measures enabling the worker concerned to continue to enjoy the necessary means of subsistence for him or herself and his or her family.

6. Every individual must be able to have access to public placement services free of charge.

Improvement of living and working conditions

7. The completion of the internal market must lead to an improvement in the living and working conditions of workers in the European Community. This process must result from an approximation of these conditions while the improvement is being maintained, as regards in particular the duration and organisation of working time and forms of employment other than open-ended contracts, such as fixed-term contracts, part-time working, temporary work and seasonal work.

    The improvement must cover, where necessary, the development of certain aspects of employment regulations such as procedures for collective redundancies and those regarding bankruptcies.

8. Every worker of the European Community shall have a right to a weekly rest period and to annual paid leave, the duration of which must be progressively harmonised in accordance with national practices.

9. The conditions of employment of every worker of the European Community shall be stipulated in laws, a collective agreement or a contract of employment, according to arrangements applying in each country.

Social protection

According to the arrangements applying in each country:

10. Every worker of the European Community shall have a right to adequate social protection and shall, whatever his status and whatever the size of the undertaking in which he is employed, enjoy an adequate level of social security benefits.

    Persons who have been unable either to enter or re-enter the labour market and have no means of subsistence must be able to receive sufficient resources and social assistance in keeping with their particular situation.

Freedom of association and collective bargaining

11. Employers and workers of the European Community shall have the right of association in order to constitute professional organisations or trade unions of their choice for the defence of their economic and social interests.

    Every employer and every worker shall have the freedom to join or not to join such organisations without any personal or occupational damage being thereby suffered by him.

12. Employers or employers' organisations, on the one hand, and workers' organisations, on the other, shall have the right to negotiate and conclude collective agreements under the conditions laid down by national legislation and practice.

    The dialogue between the two sides of industry at European level which must be developed, may, if the parties deem it desirable, result in contractual relations in particular at inter-occupational and sectoral level.

13. The right to resort to collective action in the event of a conflict of interests shall include the right to strike, subject to the obligations arising under national regulations and collective agreements.

    In order to facilitate the settlement of industrial disputes the establishment and utilisation at the appropriate levels of conciliation, mediation and arbitration procedures should be encouraged in accordance with national practice.

14. The internal legal order of the Member States shall determine under which conditions and to what extent the rights provided for in Articles 11 to 13 apply to the armed forces, the police and the civil service.

Vocational training

15. Every worker of the European Community must be able to have access to vocational training and to benefit therefrom throughout his working life. In the conditions governing access to such training there may be no discrimination on grounds of nationality.

    The competent public authorities, undertakings or the two sides of industry, each within their own sphere of competence, should set up continuing and permanent training systems enabling every person to undergo retraining more especially through leave for training purposes, to improve his skills or to acquire new skills, particularly in the light of technical developments.

Equal treatment for men and women

16. Equal treatment for men and women must be assured. Equal opportunities for men and women must be developed.

    To this end, action should be intensified to ensure the implementation of the principle of equality between men and women as regards in particular access to employment, remuneration, working conditions, social protection, education, vocational training and career development.

    Measures should also be developed enabling men and women to reconcile their occupational and family obligations.

Information, consultation and participation for workers

17. Information, consultation and participation for workers must be developed along appropriate lines, taking account of the practices in force in the various Member States.

    This shall apply especially in companies or groups of companies having establishments or companies in two or more Member States of the European Community.

18. Such information, consultation and participation must be implemented in due time, particularly in the following cases:

    — when technological changes which, from the point of view of working conditions and work organisation, have major implications for the work-force, are introduced into undertakings;

    — in connection with restructuring operations in undertakings or in cases of mergers having an impact on the employment of workers;

    — in cases of collective redundancy procedures;

    — when transfrontier workers in particular are affected by employment policies pursued by the undertaking where they are employed.

Health protection and safety at the workplace

19. Every worker must enjoy satisfactory health and safety conditions in his working environment. Appropriate measures must be taken in order to achieve further harmonisation of conditions in this area while maintaining the improvements made.

    These measures shall take account, in particular, of the need for the training, information, consultation and balanced participation of workers as regards the risks incurred and the steps taken to eliminate or reduce them.

    The provisions regarding implementation of the internal market shall help to ensure such protection.

Protection of children and adolescents

20. Without prejudice to such rules as may be more favourable to young people, in particular those ensuring their preparation for work through vocational training, and subject to derogations limited to certain light work, the minimum employment age must not be lower than the minimum school-leaving age and, in any case, not lower than 15 years.

21. Young people who are in gainful employment must receive equitable remuneration in accordance with national practice.

22. Appropriate measures must be taken to adjust labour regulations applicable to young workers so that their specific development and vocational training and access to employment needs are met. The duration of work must, in particular, be limited – without it being possible to circumvent this limitation through recourse to overtime – and night work prohibited in the

case of workers of under 18 years of age, save in the case of certain jobs laid down in national legislation or regulations.

23. Following the end of compulsory education, young people must be entitled to receive initial vocational training of a sufficient duration to enable them to adapt to the requirements of their future working life; for young workers, such training should take place during working hours.

Elderly persons

According to the arrangements applying in each country:

24. Every worker of the European Community must, at the time of retirement, be able to enjoy resources affording him or her a decent standard of living.

25. Any person who has reached retirement age but who is not entitled to a pension or who does not have other means of subsistence, must be entitled to sufficient resources and to medical and social assistance specifically suited to his needs.

Disabled persons

26. All disabled persons, whatever the origin and nature of their disablement, must be entitled to additional concrete measures aimed at improving their social and professional integration. These measures must concern, in particular, according to the capacities of the beneficiaries, vocational training, ergonomics, accessibility, mobility, means of transport and housing.

TITLE II IMPLEMENTATION OF THE CHARTER

27. It is more particularly the responsibility of the Member States, in accordance with national practices, notably through legislative measures or collective agreements, to guarantee the fundamental social rights in this Charter and to implement the social measures indispensable to the smooth operation of the internal market as part of a strategy of economic and social cohesion.

28. The European Council invites the Commission to submit as soon as possible initiatives which fall within its powers, as provided for in the Treaties, with a view to the adoption of legal instruments for the effective implementation, as and when the internal market is completed, of those rights which come within the Community's area of competence.

29. The Commission shall establish each year, during the last three months, a report on the application of the Charter by the Member States and by the European Community.

30. The report of the Commission shall be forwarded to the European Council, the European Parliament and the Economic and Social Committee.

CHARTER OF FUNDAMENTAL RIGHTS

PREAMBLE

The peoples of Europe, in creating an ever closer union among them, are resolved to share a peaceful future based on common values.

Conscious of its spiritual and moral heritage, the Union is founded on the indivisible, universal values of human dignity, freedom, equality and solidarity; it is based on the principles of democracy and the rule of law. It places the individual at the heart of its activities, by establishing the citizenship of the Union and by creating an area of freedom, security and justice.

The Union contributes to the preservation and to the development of these common values while respecting the diversity of the cultures and traditions of the peoples of Europe as well as the national identities of the Member States and the organisation of their public authorities at national, regional and local levels; it seeks to promote balanced and sustainable development and ensures free movement of persons, goods, services and capital, and the freedom of establishment.

To this end, it is necessary to strengthen the protection of fundamental rights in the light of changes in society, social progress and scientific and technological developments by making those rights more visible in a Charter.

This Charter reaffirms, with due regard for the powers and tasks of the Community and the Union and the principle of subsidiarity, the rights as they result, in particular, from the constitutional traditions and international obligations common to the Member States, the Treaty on European Union, the

Community Treaties, the European Convention for the Protection of Human Rights and Fundamental Freedoms, the Social Charters adopted by the Community and by the Council of Europe and the case law of the Court of Justice of the European Communities and of the European Court of Human Rights.

Enjoyment of these rights entails responsibilities and duties with regard to other persons, to the human community and to future generations.

The Union therefore recognises the rights, freedoms and principles set out hereafter.

CHAPTER I
DIGNITY

Article 1   Human dignity

Human dignity is inviolable. It must be respected and protected.

Article 2   Right to life

1. Everyone has the right to life.
2. No one shall be condemned to the death penalty, or executed.

Article 3   Right to the integrity of the person

1. Everyone has the right to respect for his or her physical and mental integrity.
2. In the fields of medicine and biology, the following must be respected in particular:
   - the free and informed consent of the person concerned, according to the procedures laid down by law,
   - the prohibition of eugenic practices, in particular those aiming at the selection of persons,
   - the prohibition on making the human body and its parts as such a source of financial gain,
   - the prohibition of the reproductive cloning of human beings.

Article 4   Prohibition of torture and inhuman or degrading treatment or punishment

No one shall be subjected to torture or to inhuman or degrading treatment or punishment.

Article 5   Prohibition of slavery and forced labour

1. No one shall be held in slavery or servitude.
2. No one shall be required to perform forced or compulsory labour.
3. Trafficking in human beings is prohibited.

CHAPTER II
FREEDOMS

Article 6   Right to liberty and security

Everyone has the right to liberty and security of person.

Article 7   Respect for private and family life

Everyone has the right to respect for his or her private and family life, home and communications.

Article 8   Protection of personal data

1. Everyone has the right to the protection of personal data concerning him or her.
2. Such data must be processed fairly for specified purposes and on the basis of the consent of the person concerned or some other legitimate basis laid down by law. Everyone has the right of access to data which has been collected concerning him or her, and the right to have it rectified.
3. Compliance with these rules shall be subject to control by an independent authority.

Article 9   Right to marry and right to found a family

The right to marry and the right to found a family shall be guaranteed in accordance with the national laws governing the exercise of these rights.

Article 10 Freedom of thought, conscience and religion

1. Everyone has the right to freedom of thought, conscience and religion. This right includes freedom to change religion or belief and freedom, either alone or in community with others and in public or in private, to manifest religion or belief, in worship, teaching, practice and observance.
2. The right to conscientious objection is recognised, in accordance with the national laws governing the exercise of this right.

Article 11 Freedom of expression and information

1. Everyone has the right to freedom of expression. This right shall include freedom to hold opinions and to receive and impart information and ideas without interference by public authority and regardless of frontiers.
2. The freedom and pluralism of the media shall be respected.

Article 12 Freedom of assembly and of association

1. Everyone has the right to freedom of peaceful assembly and to freedom of association at all levels, in particular in political, trade union and civic matters, which implies the right of everyone to form and to join trade unions for the protection of his or her interests.
2. Political parties at Union level contribute to expressing the political will of the citizens of the Union.

Article 13 Freedom of the arts and sciences

The arts and scientific research shall be free of constraint. Academic freedom shall be respected.

Article 14 Right to education

1. Everyone has the right to education and to have access to vocational and continuing training.
2. This right includes the possibility to receive free compulsory education.
3. The freedom to found educational establishments with due respect for democratic principles and the right of parents to ensure the education and teaching of their children in conformity with their religious, philosophical and pedagogical convictions shall be respected, in accordance with the national laws governing the exercise of such freedom and right.

Article 15 Freedom to choose an occupation and right to engage in work

1. Everyone has the right to engage in work and to pursue a freely chosen or accepted occupation.
2. Every citizen of the Union has the freedom to seek employment, to work, to exercise the right of establishment and to provide services in any Member State.
3. Nationals of third countries who are authorised to work in the territories of the Member States are entitled to working conditions equivalent to those of citizens of the Union.

Article 16 Freedom to conduct a business

The freedom to conduct a business in accordance with Community law and national laws and practices is recognised.

Article 17 Right to property

1. Everyone has the right to own, use, dispose of and bequeath his or her lawfully acquired possessions. No one may be deprived of his or her possessions, except in the public interest and in the cases and under the conditions provided for by law, subject to fair compensation being paid in good time for their loss. The use of property may be regulated by law insofar as is necessary for the general interest.
2. Intellectual property shall be protected.

Article 18 Right to asylum

The right to asylum shall be guaranteed with due respect for the rules of the Geneva Convention of 28 July 1951 and the Protocol of 31 January 1967 relating to the status of refugees and in accordance with the Treaty establishing the European Community.

Article 19 Protection in the event of removal, expulsion or extradition
1. Collective expulsions are prohibited.
2. No one may be removed, expelled or extradited to a State where there is a serious risk that he or she would be subjected to the death penalty, torture or other inhuman or degrading treatment or punishment.

CHAPTER III
EQUALITY

Article 20 Equality before the law
Everyone is equal before the law.

Article 21 Non-discrimination
1. Any discrimination based on any ground such as sex, race, colour, ethnic or social origin, genetic features, language, religion or belief, political or any other opinion, membership of a national minority, property, birth, disability, age or sexual orientation shall be prohibited.
2. Within the scope of application of the Treaty establishing the European Community and of the Treaty on European Union, and without prejudice to the special provisions of those Treaties, any discrimination on grounds of nationality shall be prohibited.

Article 22 Cultural, religious and linguistic diversity
The Union shall respect cultural, religious and linguistic diversity.

Article 23 Equality between men and women
Equality between men and women must be ensured in all areas, including employment, work and pay.

The principle of equality shall not prevent the maintenance or adoption of measures providing for specific advantages in favour of the under-represented sex.

Article 24 The rights of the child
1. Children shall have the right to such protection and care as is necessary for their wellbeing. They may express their views freely. Such views shall be taken into consideration on matters which concern them in accordance with their age and maturity.
2. In all actions relating to children, whether taken by public authorities or private institutions, the child's best interests must be a primary consideration.
3. Every child shall have the right to maintain on a regular basis a personal relationship and direct contact with both his or her parents, unless that is contrary to his or her interests.

Article 25 The rights of the elderly
The Union recognises and respects the rights of the elderly to lead a life of dignity and independence and to participate in social and cultural life.

Article 26 Integration of persons with disabilities
The Union recognises and respects the right of persons with disabilities to benefit from measures designed to ensure their independence, social and occupational integration and participation in the life of the community.

CHAPTER IV
SOLIDARITY

Article 27 Workers' right to information and consultation within the undertaking
Workers or their representatives must, at the appropriate levels, be guaranteed information and consultation in good time in the cases and under the conditions provided for by Community law and national laws and practices.

Article 28 Right of collective bargaining and action
Workers and employers, or their respective organisations, have, in accordance with Community law and national laws and practices, the right to negotiate and conclude collective agreements at the appropriate levels and, in cases of conflicts of interest, to take collective action to defend their interests, including strike action.

Article 29 Right of access to placement services

Everyone has the right of access to a free placement service.

Article 30 Protection in the event of unjustified dismissal

Every worker has the right to protection against unjustified dismissal, in accordance with Community law and national laws and practices.

Article 31 Fair and just working conditions

1. Every worker has the right to working conditions which respect his or her health, safety and dignity.
2. Every worker has the right to limitation of maximum working hours, to daily and weekly rest periods and to an annual period of paid leave.

Article 32 Prohibition of child labour and protection of young people at work

The employment of children is prohibited. The minimum age of admission to employment may not be lower than the minimum school leaving age, without prejudice to such rules as may be more favourable to young people and except for limited derogations.

Young people admitted to work must have working conditions appropriate to their age and be protected against economic exploitation and any work likely to harm their safety, health or physical, mental, moral or social development or to interfere with their education.

Article 33 Family and professional life

1. The family shall enjoy legal, economic and social protection.
2. To reconcile family and professional life, everyone shall have the right to protection from dismissal for a reason connected with maternity and the right to paid maternity leave and to parental leave following the birth or adoption of a child.

Article 34 Social security and social assistance

1. The Union recognises and respects the entitlement to social security benefits and social services providing protection in cases such as maternity, illness, industrial accidents, dependency or old age, and in the case of loss of employment, in accordance with the procedures laid down by Community law and national laws and practices.
2. Everyone residing and moving legally within the European Union is entitled to social security benefits and social advantages in accordance with Community law and national laws and practices.
3. In order to combat social exclusion and poverty, the Union recognises and respects the right to social and housing assistance so as to ensure a decent existence for all those who lack sufficient resources, in accordance with the procedures laid down by Community law and national laws and practices.

Article 35 Health care

Everyone has the right of access to preventive health care and the right to benefit from medical treatment under the conditions established by national laws and practices. A high level of human health protection shall be ensured in the definition and implementation of all Union policies and activities.

Article 36 Access to services of general economic interest

The Union recognises and respects access to services of general economic interest as provided for in national laws and practices, in accordance with the Treaty establishing the European Community, in order to promote the social and territorial cohesion of the Union.

Article 37 Environmental protection

A high level of environmental protection and the improvement of the quality of the environment must be integrated into the polices of the Union and ensured in accordance with the principle of sustainable development.

Article 38 Consumer Protection

Union policies shall ensure a high level of consumer protection.

CHAPTER V
CITIZEN'S RIGHTS

Article 39 Right to vote and to stand as a candidate at elections to the European Parliament

1.   Every citizen of the Union has the right to vote and to stand as a candidate at elections to the European Parliament in the Member State in which he or she resides, under the same conditions as nationals of that State.
2.   Members of the European Parliament shall be elected by direct universal suffrage in a free and secret ballot.

Article 40 Right to vote and to stand as a candidate at municipal elections

Every citizen of the Union has the right to vote and to stand as a candidate at municipal elections in the Member State in which he or she resides under the same conditions as nationals of that State.

Article 41 Right to good administration

1.   Every person has the right to have his or her affairs handled impartially, fairly and within a reasonable time by the institutions and bodies of the Union.
2.   This right includes:
     •   the right of every person to be heard, before any individual measure which would affect him or her adversely is taken;
     •   the right of every person to have access to his or her file, while respecting the legitimate interests of confidentiality and of professional and business secrecy;
     •   the obligation of the administration to give reasons for its decisions.
3.   Every person has the right to have the Community make good any damage caused by its institutions or by its servants in the performance of their duties, in accordance with the general principles common to the laws of the Member States.
4.   Every person may write to the institutions of the Union in one of the languages of the Treaties and must have an answer in the same language.

Article 42 Right of access to documents

Any citizen of the Union, and any natural or legal person residing or having its registered office in a Member State, has a right of access to European Parliament, Council and Commission documents.

Article 43 Ombudsman

Any citizen of the Union and any natural or legal person residing or having its registered office in a Member State has the right to refer to the Ombudsman of the Union cases of maladministration in the activities of the Community institutions or bodies, with the exception of the Court of Justice and the Court of First Instance acting in their judicial role.

Article 44 Right to petition

Any citizen of the Union and any natural or legal person residing or having its registered office in a Member State has the right to petition the European Parliament.

Article 45 Freedom of movement and of residence

1.   Every citizen of the Union has the right to move and reside freely within the territory of the Member States.
2.   Freedom of movement and residence may be granted, in accordance with the Treaty establishing the European Community, to nationals of third countries legally resident in the territory of a Member State.

Article 46 Diplomatic and consular protection

Every citizen of the Union shall, in the territory of a third country in which the Member State of which he or she is a national is not represented, be entitled to protection by the diplomatic or consular authorities of any Member State, on the same conditions as the nationals of that Member State.

CHAPTER VI

JUSTICE

Article 47 Right to an effective remedy and to a fair trial

Everyone whose rights and freedoms guaranteed by the law of the Union are violated has the right to an effective remedy before a tribunal in compliance with the conditions laid down in this Article. Everyone is entitled to a fair and public hearing within a reasonable time by an independent and impartial tribunal previously established by law. Everyone shall have the possibility of being advised, defended and represented.

Legal aid shall be made available to those who lack sufficient resources insofar as such aid is necessary to ensure effective access to justice.

Article 48 Presumption of innocence and right of defence

1. Everyone who has been charged shall be presumed innocent until proved guilty according to law.
2. Respect for the rights of the defence of anyone who has been charged shall be guaranteed.

Article 49 Principles of legality and proportionality of criminal offences and penalties

1. No one shall be held guilty of any criminal offence on account of any act or omission which did not constitute a criminal offence under national law or international law at the time when it was committed. Nor shall a heavier penalty be imposed than that which was applicable at the time the criminal offence was committed. If, subsequent to the commission of a criminal offence, the law provides for a lighter penalty, that penalty shall be applicable.
2. This Article shall not prejudice the trial and punishment of any person for any act or omission which, at the time when it was committed, was criminal according to the general principles recognised by the community of nations.
3. The severity of penalties must not be disproportionate to the criminal offence.

Article 50 Right not to be tried or punished twice in criminal proceedings for the same criminal offence

No one shall be liable to be tried or punished again in criminal proceedings for an offence for which he or she has already been finally acquitted or convicted within the Union in accordance with the law.

CHAPTER VII

GENERAL PROVISIONS

Article 51 Scope

1. The provisions of this Charter are addressed to the institutions and bodies of the Union with due regard for the principle of subsidiarity and to the Member States only when they are implementing Union law. They shall therefore respect the rights, observe the principles and promote the application thereof in accordance with their respective powers.
2. This Charter does not establish any new power or task for the Community or the Union, or modify powers and tasks defined by the Treaties.

Article 52 Scope of guaranteed rights

1. Any limitation on the exercise of the rights and freedoms recognised by this Charter must be provided for by law and respect the essence of those rights and freedoms. Subject to the principle of proportionality, limitations may be made only if they are necessary and genuinely meet objectives of general interest recognised by the Union or the need to protect the rights and freedoms of others.
2. Rights recognised by this Charter which are based on the Community Treaties or the Treaty on European Union shall be exercised under the conditions and within the limits defined by those Treaties.
3. Insofar as this Charter contains rights which correspond to rights guaranteed by the Convention for the Protection of Human Rights and Fundamental Freedoms, the meaning and scope of those rights shall be the same as those laid down by the said Convention. This provision shall not prevent Union law providing more extensive protection.

Article 53 Level of protection

Nothing in this Charter shall be interpreted as restricting or adversely affecting human rights and fundamental freedoms as recognised, in their respective fields of application, by Union law and international law and by international agreements to which the Union, the Community or all the Member States are party, including the European Convention for the Protection of Human Rights and Fundamental Freedoms, and by the Member States' constitutions.

Article 54 Prohibition of abuse of rights

Nothing in this Charter shall be interpreted as implying any right to engage in any activity or to perform any act aimed at the destruction of any of the rights and freedoms recognised in this Charter or at their limitation to a greater extent than is provided for herein.

COMPETITION LAW

COMMISSION REGULATION (EC) No 2790/1999 of 22 DECEMBER 1999 on the application of Article 81(3) of the Treaty to categories of vertical agreements and concerted practices
[1999] OJ L336/21

...

Whereas:

...

(2) Experience acquired to date makes it possible to define a category of vertical agreements which can be regarded as normally satisfying the conditions laid down in Article 81(3).

(3) This category includes vertical agreements for the purchase or sale of goods or services where these agreements are concluded between non-competing undertakings, between certain competitors or by certain associations of retailers of goods; it also includes vertical agreements containing ancillary provisions on the assignment or use of intellectual property rights; for the purposes of this Regulation, the term 'vertical agreements' includes the corresponding concerted practices.

(4) For the application of Article 81(3) by regulation, it is not necessary to define those vertical agreements which are capable of falling within Article 81(1); in the individual assessment of agreements under Article 81(1), account has to be taken of several factors, and in particular the market structure on the supply and purchase side.

(5) The benefit of the block exemption should be limited to vertical agreements for which it can be assumed with sufficient certainty that they satisfy the conditions of Article 81(3).

(6) Vertical agreements of the category defined in this Regulation can improve economic efficiency within a chain of production or distribution by facilitating better coordination between the participating undertakings; in particular, they can lead to a reduction in the transaction and distribution costs of the parties and to an optimisation of their sales and investment levels.

(7) The likelihood that such efficiency-enhancing effects will outweigh any anti-competitive effects due to restrictions contained in vertical agreements depends on the degree of market power of the undertakings concerned and, therefore, on the extent to which those undertakings face competition from other suppliers of goods or services regarded by the buyer as interchangeable or substitutable for one another, by reason of the products' characteristics, their prices and their intended use.

(8) It can be presumed that, where the share of the relevant market accounted for by the supplier does not exceed 30%, vertical agreements which do not contain certain types of severely anti-competitive restraints generally lead to an improvement in production or distribution and allow consumers a fair share of the resulting benefits; in the case of vertical agreements containing exclusive supply obligations, it is the market share of the buyer which is relevant in determining the overall effects of such vertical agreements on the market.

(9) Above the market share threshold of 30%, there can be no presumption that vertical agreements falling within the scope of Article 81(1) will usually give rise to objective advantages of such a character and size as to compensate for the disadvantages which they create for competition.

(10) This Regulation should not exempt vertical agreements containing restrictions which are not indispensable to the attainment of the positive effects mentioned above; in particular, vertical agreements containing certain types of severely anti-competitive restraints such as minimum and fixed resale-prices, as well as certain types of territorial protection, should be excluded from the benefit of the block exemption established by this Regulation irrespective of the market share of the undertakings concerned.

(11) In order to ensure access to or to prevent collusion on the relevant market, certain conditions are to be attached to the block exemption; to this end, the exemption of non-compete obligations should be limited to obligations which do not exceed a definite duration; for the same reasons, any direct or indirect obligation causing the members of a selective distribution

system not to sell the brands of particular competing suppliers should be excluded from the benefit of this Regulation.

(12) The market-share limitation, the non-exemption of certain vertical agreements and the conditions provided for in this Regulation normally ensure that the agreements to which the block exemption applies do not enable the participating undertakings to eliminate competition in respect of a substantial part of the products in question.

(13) In particular cases in which the agreements falling under this Regulation nevertheless have effects incompatible with Article 81(3), the Commission may withdraw the benefit of the block exemption; this may occur in particular where the buyer has significant market power in the relevant market in which it resells the goods or provides the services or where parallel networks of vertical agreements have similar effects which significantly restrict access to a relevant market or competition therein; such cumulative effects may for example arise in the case of selective distribution or non-compete obligations.

(14) Regulation No 19/65/EEC empowers the competent authorities of Member States to withdraw the benefit of the block exemption in respect of vertical agreements having effects incompatible with the conditions laid down in Article 81(3), where such effects are felt in their respective territory, or in a part thereof, and where such territory has the characteristics of a distinct geographic market; Member States should ensure that the exercise of this power of withdrawal does not prejudice the uniform application throughout the common market of the Community competition rules or the full effect of the measures adopted in implementation of those rules.

(15) In order to strengthen supervision of parallel networks of vertical agreements which have similar restrictive effects and which cover more than 50% of a given market, the Commission may declare this Regulation inapplicable to vertical agreements containing specific restraints relating to the market concerned, thereby restoring the full application of Article 81 to such agreements.

(16) This Regulation is without prejudice to the application of Article 82.

(17) In accordance with the principle of the primacy of Community law, no measure taken pursuant to national laws on competition should prejudice the uniform application throughout the common market of the Community competition rules or the full effect of any measures adopted in implementation of those rules, including this Regulation,

HAS ADOPTED THIS REGULATION:

Article 1

For the purposes of this Regulation:

(a) 'competing undertakings' means actual or potential suppliers in the same product market; the, product market includes goods or services which are regarded by the buyer as interchangeable with or substitutable for the contract goods or services, by reason of the products' characteristics, their prices and their intended use;

(b) 'non-compete obligation' means any direct or indirect obligation causing the buyer not to manufacture, purchase, sell or resell goods or services which compete with the contract goods or services, or any direct or indirect obligation on the buyer to purchase from the supplier or from another undertaking designated by the supplier more than 80% of the buyer's total purchases of the contract goods or services and their substitutes on the relevant market, calculated on the basis of the value of its purchases in the preceding calendar year;

(c) 'exclusive supply obligation' means any direct or indirect obligation causing the supplier to sell the goods or services specified in the agreement only to one buyer inside the Community for the purposes of a specific use or for resale;

(d) 'Selective distribution system' means a distribution system where the supplier undertakes to sell the contract goods or services, either directly or indirectly, only to distributors selected on the basis of specified criteria and where these distributors undertake not to sell such goods or services to unauthorised distributors;

(e) 'intellectual property rights' includes industrial property rights, copyright and neighbouring rights;

(f) 'know-how' means a package of non-patented practical information, resulting from experience and testing by the supplier, which is secret, substantial and identified: in this context, 'secret' means that the know-how, as a body or in the precise configuration and assembly of its components, is not generally known or easily accessible; 'substantial' means that the know-how includes information which is indispensable to the buyer for the use, sale or resale of the contract goods or services; 'identified' means that the know-how must be described in a sufficiently comprehensive manner so as to make it possible to verify that it fulfils the criteria of secrecy and substantiality;

(g) 'buyer' includes an undertaking which, under an agreement falling within Article 81(1) of the Treaty, sells goods or services on behalf of another undertaking.

Article 2

1. Pursuant to Article 81(3) of the Treaty and subject to the provisions of this Regulation, it is hereby declared that Article 81(1) shall not apply to agreements or concerted practices entered into between two or more undertakings each of which operates, for the purposes of the agreement, at a different level of the production or distribution chain, and relating to the conditions under which the parties may purchase, sell or resell certain goods or services ('vertical agreements').

   This exemption shall apply to the extent that such agreements contain restrictions of competition falling within the scope of Article 81(1) ('vertical restraints').

2. The exemption provided for in paragraph 1 shall apply to vertical agreements entered into between an association of undertakings and its members, or between such an association and its suppliers, only if all its members are retailers of goods and if no individual member of the association, together with its connected undertakings, has a total annual turnover exceeding EUR 50 million; vertical agreements entered into by such associations shall be covered by this Regulation without prejudice to the application of Article 81 to horizontal agreements concluded between the members of the association or decisions adopted by the association.

3. The exemption provided for in paragraph 1 shall apply to vertical agreements containing provisions which relate to the assignment to the buyer or use by the buyer of intellectual property rights, provided that those provisions do not constitute the primary object of such agreements and are directly related to the use, sale or resale of goods or services by the buyer or its customers. The exemption applies on condition that, in relation to the contract goods or services, those provisions do not contain restrictions of competition having the same object or effect as vertical restraints which are not exempted under this Regulation.

4. The exemption provided for in paragraph 1 shall not apply to vertical agreements entered into between competing undertakings; however, it shall apply where competing undertakings enter into a non-reciprocal vertical agreement and:

   (a) the buyer has a total annual turnover not exceeding EUR 100 million, or

   (b) the supplier is a manufacturer and a distributor of goods, while the buyer is a distributor not manufacturing goods competing with the contract goods, or

   (c) the supplier is a provider of services at several levels of trade, while the buyer does not provide competing services at the level of trade where it purchases the contract services.

5. This Regulation shall not apply to vertical agreements the subject matter of which falls within the scope of any other block exemption regulation.

Article 3

1. Subject to paragraph 2 of this Article, the exemption provided for in Article 2 shall apply on condition that the market share held by the supplier does not exceed 30% of the relevant market on which it sells the contract goods or services.

2. In the case of vertical agreements containing exclusive supply obligations, the exemption provided for in Article 2 shall apply on condition that the market share held by the buyer does not exceed 30% of the relevant market on which it purchases the contract goods or services.

Article 4

The exemption provided for in Article 2 shall not apply to vertical agreements which, directly or indirectly, in isolation or in combination with other factors under the control of the parties, have as their object:

    (a)   the restriction of the buyer's ability to determine its sale price, without prejudice to the possibility of the supplier's imposing a maximum sale price or recommending a sale price, provided that they do not amount to a fixed or minimum sale price as a result of pressure from, or incentives offered by, any of the parties;

    (b)   the restriction of the territory into which, or of the customers to whom, the buyer may sell the contract goods or services, except:

        — the restriction of active sales into the exclusive territory or to an exclusive customer group reserved to the supplier or allocated by the supplier to another buyer, where such a restriction does not limit sales by the customers of the buyer,

        — the restriction of sales to end users by a buyer operating at the wholesale level of trade,

        — the restriction of sales to unauthorised distributors by the members of a selective distribution system, and

        — the restriction of the buyer's ability to sell components, supplied for the purposes of incorporation, to customers who would use them to manufacture the same type of goods as those produced by the supplier;

    (c)   the restriction of active or passive sales to end users by members of a selective distribution system operating at the retail level of trade, without prejudice to the possibility of prohibiting a member of the system from operating out of an unauthorised place of establishment;

    (d)   the restriction of cross-supplies between distributors within a selective distribution system, including between distributors operating at different level of trade;

    (e)   the restriction agreed between a supplier of components and a buyer who incorporates those components, which limits the supplier to selling the components as spare parts to end-users or to repairers or other service providers not entrusted by the buyer with the repair or servicing of its goods.

Article 5

The exemption provided for in Article 2 shall not apply to any of the following obligations contained in vertical agreements:

    (a)   any direct or indirect non-compete obligation, the duration of which is indefinite or exceeds five years. A non-compete obligation which is tacitly renewable beyond a period of five years is to be deemed to have been concluded for an indefinite duration. However, the time limitation of five years shall not apply where the contract goods or services are sold by the buyer from premises and land owned by the supplier or leased by the supplier from third parties not connected with the buyer, provided that the duration of the non-compete obligation does not exceed the period of occupancy of the premises and land by the buyer;

    (b)   any direct or indirect obligation causing the buyer, after termination of the agreement, not to manufacture, purchase, sell or resell goods or services, unless such obligation:

        — relates to goods or services which compete with the contract goods or services, and

        — is limited to the premises and land from which the buyer has operated during the contract period, and

        — is indispensable to protect know-how transferred by the supplier to the buyer,

    and provided that the duration of such non-compete obligation is limited to a period of one year after termination of the agreement; this obligation is without prejudice to the possibility of imposing a restriction which is unlimited in time on the use and disclosure of know-how which has not entered the public domain;

    (c)   any direct or indirect obligation causing the members of a selective distribution system not to sell the brands of particular competing suppliers.

Article 6

The Commission may withdraw the benefit of this Regulation, pursuant to Article 7(1) of Regulation No 19/65/EEC, where it finds in any particular case that vertical agreements to which this Regulation applies nevertheless have effects which are incompatible with the conditions laid down in Article 81(3) of the Treaty, and in particular where access to the relevant market or competition therein is significantly restricted by the cumulative effect of parallel networks of similar vertical restraints implemented by competing suppliers or buyers.

Article 7

Where in any particular case vertical agreements to which the exemption provided for in Article 2 applies have effects incompatible with the conditions laid down in Article 81(3) of the Treaty in the territory of a Member State, or in a part thereof, which has all the characteristics of a distinct geographic market, the competent authority of that Member State may withdraw the benefit of application of this Regulation in respect of that territory, under the same conditions as provided in Article 6.

Article 8

1. Pursuant to Article 1 a of Regulation No 19/65/EEC, the Commission may by regulation declare that, where parallel networks of similar vertical restraints cover more than 50% of a relevant market, this Regulation shall not apply to vertical agreements containing specific restraints relating to that market.

2. A regulation pursuant to paragraph 1 shall not become applicable earlier than six months following its adoption.

Article 9

1. The market share of 30% provided for in Article 3(1) shall be calculated on the basis of the market sales value of the contract goods or services and other goods or services sold by the supplier, which are regarded as interchangeable or substitutable by the buyer, by reason of the products' characteristics, their prices and their intended use; if market sales value data are not available, estimates based on other reliable market information, including market sales volumes, may be used to establish the market share of the undertaking concerned. For the purposes of Article 3(2), it is either the market purchase value or estimates thereof which shall be used to calculate the market share.

2. For the purposes of applying the market share, threshold provided for in Article 3 the following rules shall apply:

    (a) the market share shall be calculated on the basis of data relating to the preceding calendar year;

    (b) the market share shall include any goods or services supplied to integrated distributors for the purposes of sale;

    (c) if the market share is initially not more than 30% but subsequently rises above that level without exceeding 35%, the exemption provided for in Article 2 shall continue to apply for a period of two consecutive calendar years following the year in which the 30% market share threshold was first exceeded;

    (d) if the market share is initially not more than 30% but subsequently rises above 35%, the exemption provided for in Article 2 shall continue to apply for one calendar year following the year in which the level of 35% was first exceeded;

    (e) the benefit of points (c) and (d) may not be combined so as to exceed a period of two calendar years.

Article 10

1. For the purpose of calculating total annual turnover within the meaning of Article 2(2) and (4), the turnover achieved during the previous financial year by the relevant party to the vertical agreement and the turnover achieved by its connected undertakings in respect of all goods and services, excluding all taxes and other duties, shall be added together. For this purpose, no account shall be taken of dealings between the party to the vertical agreement and its connected undertakings or between its connected undertakings.

2. The exemption provided for in Article 2 shall remain applicable where, for any period of two consecutive financial years, the total annual turnover threshold is exceeded by no more than 10%.

Article 11

1. For the purposes of this Regulation, the terms 'undertaking', 'supplier' and 'buyer' shall include their respective connected undertakings.

2. 'Connected undertakings' are:
   (a) undertakings in which a party to the agreement, directly or indirectly:
       — has the power to exercise more than half the voting rights, or
       — has the power to appoint more than half the members of the supervisory board, board of management or bodies legally representing the undertaking, or
       — has the right to manage the undertaking's affairs;
   (b) undertakings which directly or indirectly have, over a party to the agreement, the rights or powers listed in (a);
   (c) undertakings in which an undertaking referred to in (b) has, directly or indirectly, the rights or powers listed in (a);
   (d) undertakings in which a party to the agreement together with one or more of the undertakings referred to in (a), (b) or (c), or in which two or more of the latter undertakings, jointly have the rights or powers listed in (a);
   (e) undertakings in which the rights or the powers listed in (a) are jointly held by:
       — parties to the agreement or their respective connected undertakings referred to in (a) to (d), or
       — one or more of the parties to the agreement or one or more of their connected undertakings referred to in (a) to (d) and one or more third parties.

3. For the purposes of Article 3, the market share held by the undertakings referred to in paragraph 2(e) of this Article shall be apportioned equally to each undertaking having the rights or the powers listed in paragraph 2(a).

Article 12

1. The exemptions provided for in Commission Regulations (EEC) No 1983/83(4), (EEC) No 1984/83(5) and (EEC) No 4087/88(6) shall continue to apply until 31 May 2000.

2. The prohibition laid down in Article 81(1) of the EC Treaty shall not apply during the period from 1 June 2000 to 31 December 2001 in respect of agreements already in force on 31 May 2000 which do not satisfy the conditions for exemption provided for in this Regulation but which satisfy the conditions for exemption provided for in Regulations (EEC) No 1983/83, (EEC) No 1984/83 or (EEC) No 4087/88.

Article 13

This Regulation shall enter into force on 1 January 2000.

COUNCIL REGULATION (EC) No 1/2003
on the implementation of the rules on competition laid down in Articles 81 and 82 of the Treaty
[2003] OJ L1/1

THE COUNCIL OF THE EUROPEAN UNION,

Having regard to the Treaty establishing the European Community, and in particular Article 83 thereof,

HAS ADOPTED THIS REGULATION:

CHAPTER I
PRINCIPLES

Article 1   Application of Articles 81 and 82 of the Treaty

1. Agreements, decisions and concerted practices caught by Article 81(1) of the Treaty which do not satisfy the conditions of Article 81(3) of the Treaty shall be prohibited, no prior decision to that effect being required.

2. Agreements, decisions and concerted practices caught by Article 81(1) of the Treaty which satisfy the conditions of Article 81(3) of the Treaty shall not be prohibited, no prior decision to that effect being required.

3. The abuse of a dominant position referred to in Article 82 of the Treaty shall be prohibited, no prior decision to that effect being required.

Article 2   Burden of proof

In any national or Community proceedings for the application of Articles 81 and 82 of the Treaty, the burden of proving an infringement of Article 81(1) or of Article 82 of the Treaty shall rest on the party or the authority alleging the infringement. The undertaking or association of undertakings claiming the benefit of Article 81(3) of the Treaty shall bear the burden of proving that the conditions of that paragraph are fulfilled.

Article 3   Relationship between Articles 81 and 82 of the Treaty and national competition laws

1. Where the competition authorities of the Member States or national courts apply national competition law to agreements, decisions by associations of undertakings or concerted practices within the meaning of Article 81(1) of the Treaty which may affect trade between Member States within the meaning of that provision, they shall also apply Article 81 of the Treaty to such agreements, decisions or concerted practices. Where the competition authorities of the Member States or national courts apply national competition law to any abuse prohibited by Article 82 of the Treaty, they shall also apply Article 82 of the Treaty.

2. The application of national competition law may not lead to the prohibition of agreements, decisions by associations of undertakings or concerted practices which may affect trade between Member States but which do not restrict competition within the meaning of Article 81(1) of the Treaty, or which fulfil the conditions of Article 81(3) of the Treaty or which are covered by a Regulation for the application of Article 81(3) of the Treaty. Member States shall not under this Regulation be precluded from adopting and applying on their territory stricter national laws which prohibit or sanction unilateral conduct engaged in by undertakings.

3. Without prejudice to general principles and other provisions of Community law, paragraphs 1 and 2 do not apply when the competition authorities and the courts of the Member States apply national merger control laws nor do they preclude the application of provisions of national law that predominantly pursue an objective different from that pursued by Articles 81 and 82 of the Treaty.

CHAPTER II

POWERS

Article 4   Powers of the Commission

For the purpose of applying Articles 81 and 82 of the Treaty, the Commission shall have the powers provided for by this Regulation.

Article 5   Powers of the competition authorities of the Member States

The competition authorities of the Member States shall have the power to apply Articles 81 and 82 of the Treaty in individual cases. For this purpose, acting on their own initiative or on a complaint, they may take the following decisions:
— requiring that an infringement be brought to an end,
— ordering interim measures,
— accepting commitments,
— imposing fines, periodic penalty payments or any other penalty provided for in their national law.

Where on the basis of the information in their possession the conditions for prohibition are not met they may likewise decide that there are no grounds for action on their part.

Article 6   Powers of the national courts

National courts shall have the power to apply Articles 81 and 82 of the Treaty.

CHAPTER III

COMMISSION DECISIONS

Article 7   Finding and termination of infringement

1.   Where the Commission, acting on a complaint or on its own initiative, finds that there is an infringement of Article 81 or of Article 82 of the Treaty, it may by decision require the undertakings and associations of undertakings concerned to bring such infringement to an end. For this purpose, it may impose on them any behavioural or structural remedies which are proportionate to the infringement committed and necessary to bring the infringement effectively to an end. Structural remedies can only be imposed either where there is no equally effective behavioural remedy or where any equally effective behavioural remedy would be more burdensome for the undertaking concerned than the structural remedy. If the Commission has a legitimate interest in doing so, it may also find that an infringement has been committed in the past.

2.   Those entitled to lodge a complaint for the purposes of paragraph 1 are natural or legal persons who can show a legitimate interest and Member States.

Article 8   Interim measures

1.   In cases of urgency due to the risk of serious and irreparable damage to competition, the Commission, acting on its own initiative may by decision, on the basis of a prima facie finding of infringement, order interim measures.

2.   A decision under paragraph 1 shall apply for a specified period of time and may be renewed in so far this is necessary and appropriate.

Article 9   Commitments

1.   Where the Commission intends to adopt a decision requiring that an infringement be brought to an end and the undertakings concerned offer commitments to meet the concerns expressed to them by the Commission in its preliminary assessment, the Commission may by decision make those commitments binding on the undertakings. Such a decision may be adopted for a specified period and shall conclude that there are no longer grounds for action by the Commission.

2.   The Commission may, upon request or on its own initiative, reopen the proceedings:

   (a)   where there has been a material change in any of the facts on which the decision was based;

   (b)   where the undertakings concerned act contrary to their commitments; or

   (c)   where the decision was based on incomplete, incorrect or misleading information provided by the parties.

Article 10   Finding of inapplicability

Where the Community public interest relating to the application of Articles 81 and 82 of the Treaty so requires, the Commission, acting on its own initiative, may by decision find that Article 81 of the Treaty is not applicable to an agreement, a decision by an association of undertakings or a concerted practice, either because the conditions of Article 81(1) of the Treaty are not fulfilled, or because the conditions of Article 81(3) of the Treaty are satisfied.

The Commission may likewise make such a finding with reference to Article 82 of the Treaty.

CHAPTER IV

COOPERATION

Article 11   Cooperation between the Commission and the competition authorities of the Member States

1.   The Commission and the competition authorities of the Member States shall apply the Community competition rules in close cooperation.

2.   The Commission shall transmit to the competition authorities of the Member States copies of the most important documents it has collected with a view to applying Articles 7, 8, 9, 10 and Article 29(1). At the request of the competition authority of a Member State, the Commission shall provide it with a copy of other existing documents necessary for the assessment of the case.

3. The competition authorities of the Member States shall, when acting under Article 81 or Article 82 of the Treaty, inform the Commission in writing before or without delay after commencing the first formal investigative measure. This information may also be made available to the competition authorities of the other Member States.

4. No later than 30 days before the adoption of a decision requiring that an infringement be brought to an end, accepting commitments or withdrawing the benefit of a block exemption Regulation, the competition authorities of the Member States shall inform the Commission. To that effect, they shall provide the Commission with a summary of the case, the envisaged decision or, in the absence thereof, any other document indicating the proposed course of action. This information may also be made available to the competition authorities of the other Member States. At the request of the Commission, the acting competition authority shall make available to the Commission other documents it holds which are necessary for the assessment of the case. The information supplied to the Commission may be made available to the competition authorities of the other Member States. National competition authorities may also exchange between themselves information necessary for the assessment of a case that they are dealing with under Article 81 or Article 82 of the Treaty.

5. The competition authorities of the Member States may consult the Commission on any case involving the application of Community law.

6. The initiation by the Commission of proceedings for the adoption of a decision under Chapter III shall relieve the competition authorities of the Member States of their competence to apply Articles 81 and 82 of the Treaty. If a competition authority of a Member State is already acting on a case, the Commission shall only initiate proceedings after consulting with that national competition authority.

Article 12   Exchange of information

1. For the purpose of applying Articles 81 and 82 of the Treaty the Commission and the competition authorities of the Member States shall have the power to provide one another with and use in evidence any matter of fact or of law, including confidential information.

2. Information exchanged shall only be used in evidence for the purpose of applying Article 81 or Article 82 of the Treaty and in respect of the subject-matter for which it was collected by the transmitting authority. However, where national competition law is applied in the same case and in parallel to Community competition law and does not lead to a different outcome, information exchanged under this Article may also be used for the application of national competition law.

3. Information exchanged pursuant to paragraph 1 can only be used in evidence to impose sanctions on natural persons where:
    — the law of the transmitting authority foresees sanctions of a similar kind in relation to an infringement of Article 81 or Article 82 of the Treaty or, in the absence thereof,
    — the information has been collected in a way which respects the same level of protection of the rights of defence of natural persons as provided for under the national rules of the receiving authority. However, in this case, the information exchanged cannot be used by the receiving authority to impose custodial sanctions.

Article 13   Suspension or termination of proceedings

1. Where competition authorities of two or more Member States have received a complaint or are acting on their own initiative under Article 81 or Article 82 of the Treaty against the same agreement, decision of an association or practice, the fact that one authority is dealing with the case shall be sufficient grounds for the others to suspend the proceedings before them or to reject the complaint. The Commission may likewise reject a complaint on the ground that a competition authority of a Member State is dealing with the case.

2. Where a competition authority of a Member State or the Commission has received a complaint against an agreement, decision of an association or practice which has already been dealt with by another competition authority, it may reject it.

Article 14   Advisory Committee

1. The Commission shall consult an Advisory Committee on Restrictive Practices and Dominant Positions prior to the taking of any decision under Articles 7, 8, 9, 10, 23, Article 24(2) and Article 29(1).

2. For the discussion of individual cases, the Advisory Committee shall be composed of representatives of the competition authorities of the Member States. For meetings in which issues other than individual cases are being discussed, an additional Member State representative competent in competition matters may be appointed. Representatives may, if unable to attend, be replaced by other representatives.

3. The consultation may take place at a meeting convened and chaired by the Commission, held not earlier than 14 days after dispatch of the notice convening it, together with a summary of the case, an indication of the most important documents and a preliminary draft decision. In respect of decisions pursuant to Article 8, the meeting may be held seven days after the dispatch of the operative part of a draft decision. Where the Commission dispatches a notice convening the meeting which gives a shorter period of notice than those specified above, the meeting may take place on the proposed date in the absence of an objection by any Member State. The Advisory Committee shall deliver a written opinion on the Commission's preliminary draft decision. It may deliver an opinion even if some members are absent and are not represented. At the request of one or several members, the positions stated in the opinion shall be reasoned.

4. Consultation may also take place by written procedure. However, if any Member State so requests, the Commission shall convene a meeting. In case of written procedure, the Commission shall determine a time-limit of not less than 14 days within which the Member States are to put forward their observations for circulation to all other Member States. In case of decisions to be taken pursuant to Article 8, the time-limit of 14 days is replaced by seven days. Where the Commission determines a time-limit for the written procedure which is shorter than those specified above, the proposed time-limit shall be applicable in the absence of an objection by any Member State.

5. The Commission shall take the utmost account of the opinion delivered by the Advisory Committee. It shall inform the Committee of the manner in which its opinion has been taken into account.

6. Where the Advisory Committee delivers a written opinion, this opinion shall be appended to the draft decision. If the Advisory Committee recommends publication of the opinion, the Commission shall carry out such publication taking into account the legitimate interest of undertakings in the protection of their business secrets.

7. At the request of a competition authority of a Member State, the Commission shall include on the agenda of the Advisory Committee cases that are being dealt with by a competition authority of a Member State under Article 81 or Article 82 of the Treaty. The Commission may also do so on its own initiative. In either case, the Commission shall inform the competition authority concerned.

   A request may in particular be made by a competition authority of a Member State in respect of a case where the Commission intends to initiate proceedings with the effect of Article 11(6). The Advisory Committee shall not issue opinions on cases dealt with by competition authorities of the Member States. The Advisory Committee may also discuss general issues of Community competition law.

Article 15   Cooperation with national courts

1. In proceedings for the application of Article 81 or Article 82 of the Treaty, courts of the Member States may ask the Commission to transmit to them information in its possession or its opinion on questions concerning the application of the Community competition rules.

2. Member States shall forward to the Commission a copy of any written judgment of national courts deciding on the application of Article 81 or Article 82 of the Treaty. Such copy shall be forwarded without delay after the full written judgment is notified to the parties.

3. Competition authorities of the Member States, acting on their own initiative, may submit written observations to the national courts of their Member State on issues relating to the

application of Article 81 or Article 82 of the Treaty. With the permission of the court in question, they may also submit oral observations to the national courts of their Member State. Where the coherent application of Article 81 or Article 82 of the Treaty so requires, the Commission, acting on its own initiative, may submit written observations to courts of the Member States. With the permission of the court in question, it may also make oral observations.

For the purpose of the preparation of their observations only, the competition authorities of the Member States and the Commission may request the relevant court of the Member State to transmit or ensure the transmission to them of any documents necessary for the assessment of the case.

4. This Article is without prejudice to wider powers to make observations before courts conferred on competition authorities of the Member States under the law of their Member State.

Article 16 Uniform application of Community competition law

1. When national courts rule on agreements, decisions or practices under Article 81 or Article 82 of the Treaty which are already the subject of a Commission decision, they cannot take decisions running counter to the decision adopted by the Commission. They must also avoid giving decisions which would conflict with a decision contemplated by the Commission in proceedings it has initiated. To that effect, the national court may assess whether it is necessary to stay its proceedings. This obligation is without prejudice to the rights and obligations under Article 234 of the Treaty.

2. When competition authorities of the Member States rule on agreements, decisions or practices under Article 81 or Article 82 of the Treaty which are already the subject of a Commission decision, they cannot take decisions which would run counter to the decision adopted by the Commission.

CHAPTER V
POWERS OF INVESTIGATION

Article 17 Investigations into sectors of the economy and into types of agreements

1. Where the trend of trade between Member States, the rigidity of prices or other circumstances suggest that competition may be restricted or distorted within the common market, the Commission may conduct its inquiry into a particular sector of the economy or into a particular type of agreements across various sectors. In the course of that inquiry, the Commission may request the undertakings or associations of undertakings concerned to supply the information necessary for giving effect to Articles 81 and 82 of the Treaty and may carry out any inspections necessary for that purpose.

The Commission may in particular request the undertakings or associations of undertakings concerned to communicate to it all agreements, decisions and concerted practices.

The Commission may publish a report on the results of its inquiry into particular sectors of the economy or particular types of agreements across various sectors and invite comments from interested parties.

2. Articles 14, 18, 19, 20, 22, 23 and 24 shall apply *mutatis mutandis*.

Article 18 Requests for information

1. In order to carry out the duties assigned to it by this Regulation, the Commission may, by simple request or by decision, require undertakings and associations of undertakings to provide all necessary information.

2. When sending a simple request for information to an undertaking or association of undertakings, the Commission shall state the legal basis and the purpose of the request, specify what information is required and fix the time-limit within which the information is to be provided, and the penalties provided for in Article 23 for supplying incorrect or misleading information.

3. Where the Commission requires undertakings and associations of undertakings to supply information by decision, it shall state the legal basis and the purpose of the request, specify

what information is required and fix the time-limit within which it is to be provided. It shall also indicate the penalties provided for in Article 23 and indicate or impose the penalties provided for in Article 24. It shall further indicate the right to have the decision reviewed by the Court of Justice.

4.   The owners of the undertakings or their representatives and, in the case of legal persons, companies or firms, or associations having no legal personality, the persons authorised to represent them by law or by their constitution shall supply the information requested on behalf of the undertaking or the association of undertakings concerned. Lawyers duly authorised to act may supply the information on behalf of their clients. The latter shall remain fully responsible if the information supplied is incomplete, incorrect or misleading.

5.   The Commission shall without delay forward a copy of the simple request or of the decision to the competition authority of the Member State in whose territory the seat of the undertaking or association of undertakings is situated and the competition authority of the Member State whose territory is affected.

6.   At the request of the Commission the governments and competition authorities of the Member States shall provide the Commission with all necessary information to carry out the duties assigned to it by this Regulation.

Article 19   Power to take statements

1.   In order to carry out the duties assigned to it by this Regulation, the Commission may interview any natural or legal person who consents to be interviewed for the purpose of collecting information relating to the subject-matter of an investigation.

2.   Where an interview pursuant to paragraph 1 is conducted in the premises of an undertaking, the Commission shall inform the competition authority of the Member State in whose territory the interview takes place. If so requested by the competition authority of that Member State, its officials may assist the officials and other accompanying persons authorised by the Commission to conduct the interview.

Article 20   The Commission's powers of inspection

1.   In order to carry out the duties assigned to it by this Regulation, the Commission may conduct all necessary inspections of undertakings and associations of undertakings.

2.   The officials and other accompanying persons authorised by the Commission to conduct an inspection are empowered:

    (a)   to enter any premises, land and means of transport of undertakings and associations of undertakings;

    (b)   to examine the books and other records related to the business, irrespective of the medium on which they are stored;

    (c)   to take or obtain in any form copies of or extracts from such books or records;

    (d)   to seal any business premises and books or records for the period and to the extent necessary for the inspection;

    (e)   to ask any representative or member of staff of the undertaking or association of undertakings for explanations on facts or documents relating to the subject-matter and purpose of the inspection and to record the answers.

3.   The officials and other accompanying persons authorised by the Commission to conduct an inspection shall exercise their powers upon production of a written authorisation specifying the subject matter and purpose of the inspection and the penalties provided for in Article 23 in case the production of the required books or other records related to the business is incomplete or where the answers to questions asked under paragraph 2 of the present Article are incorrect or misleading. In good time before the inspection, the Commission shall give notice of the inspection to the competition authority of the Member State in whose territory it is to be conducted.

4.   Undertakings and associations of undertakings are required to submit to inspections ordered by decision of the Commission. The decision shall specify the subject matter and purpose of the inspection, appoint the date on which it is to begin and indicate the penalties provided for in Articles 23 and 24 and the right to have the decision reviewed by the Court of Justice. The

Commission shall take such decisions after consulting the competition authority of the Member State in whose territory the inspection is to be conducted.

5.   Officials of as well as those authorised or appointed by the competition authority of the Member State in whose territory the inspection is to be conducted shall, at the request of that authority or of the Commission, actively assist the officials and other accompanying persons authorised by the Commission. To this end, they shall enjoy the powers specified in paragraph 2.

6.   Where the officials and other accompanying persons authorised by the Commission find that an undertaking opposes an inspection ordered pursuant to this Article, the Member State concerned shall afford them the necessary assistance, requesting where appropriate the assistance of the police or of an equivalent enforcement authority, so as to enable them to conduct their inspection.

7.   If the assistance provided for in paragraph 6 requires authorisation from a judicial authority according to national rules, such authorisation shall be applied for. Such authorisation may also be applied for as a precautionary measure.

8.   Where authorisation as referred to in paragraph 7 is applied for, the national judicial authority shall control that the Commission decision is authentic and that the coercive measures envisaged are neither arbitrary nor excessive having regard to the subject matter of the inspection. In its control of the proportionality of the coercive measures, the national judicial authority may ask the Commission, directly or through the Member State competition authority, for detailed explanations in particular on the grounds the Commission has for suspecting infringement of Articles 81 and 82 of the Treaty, as well as on the seriousness of the suspected infringement and on the nature of the involvement of the undertaking concerned. However, the national judicial authority may not call into question the necessity for the inspection nor demand that it be provided with the information in the Commission's file. The lawfulness of the Commission decision shall be subject to review only by the Court of Justice.

Article 21 Inspection of other premises

1.   If a reasonable suspicion exists that books or other records related to the business and to the subject-matter of the inspection, which may be relevant to prove a serious violation of Article 81 or Article 82 of the Treaty, are being kept in any other premises, land and means of transport, including the homes of directors, managers and other members of staff of the undertakings and associations of undertakings concerned, the Commission can by decision order an inspection to be conducted in such other premises, land and means of transport.

2.   The decision shall specify the subject matter and purpose of the inspection, appoint the date on which it is to begin and indicate the right to have the decision reviewed by the Court of Justice. It shall in particular state the reasons that have led the Commission to conclude that a suspicion in the sense of paragraph 1 exists. The Commission shall take such decisions after consulting the competition authority of the Member State in whose territory the inspection is to be conducted.

3.   A decision adopted pursuant to paragraph 1 cannot be executed without prior authorisation from the national judicial authority of the Member State concerned. The national judicial authority shall control that the Commission decision is authentic and that the coercive measures envisaged are neither arbitrary nor excessive having regard in particular to the seriousness of the suspected infringement, to the importance of the evidence sought, to the involvement of the undertaking concerned and to the reasonable likelihood that business books and records relating to the subject matter of the inspection are kept in the premises for which the authorisation is requested. The national judicial authority may ask the Commission, directly or through the Member State competition authority, for detailed explanations on those elements which are necessary to allow its control of the proportionality of the coercive measures envisaged.

However, the national judicial authority may not call into question the necessity for the inspection nor demand that it be provided with information in the Commission's file. The lawfulness of the Commission decision shall be subject to review only by the Court of Justice.

4. The officials and other accompanying persons authorised by the Commission to conduct an inspection ordered in accordance with paragraph 1 of this Article shall have the powers set out in Article 20(2)(a), (b) and (c). Article 20(5) and (6) shall apply *mutatis mutandis*.

Article 22 Investigations by competition authorities of Member States

1. The competition authority of a Member State may in its own territory carry out any inspection or other fact-finding measure under its national law on behalf and for the account of the competition authority of another Member State in order to establish whether there has been an infringement of Article 81 or Article 82 of the Treaty. Any exchange and use of the information collected shall be carried out in accordance with Article 12.

2. At the request of the Commission, the competition authorities of the Member States shall undertake the inspections which the Commission considers to be necessary under Article 20(1) or which it has ordered by decision pursuant to Article 20(4). The officials of the competition authorities of the Member States who are responsible for conducting these inspections as well as those authorised or appointed by them shall exercise their powers in accordance with their national law.

    If so requested by the Commission or by the competition authority of the Member State in whose territory the inspection is to be conducted, officials and other accompanying persons authorised by the Commission may assist the officials of the authority concerned.

CHAPTER VI
PENALTIES

Article 23 Fines

1. The Commission may by decision impose on undertakings and associations of undertakings fines not exceeding 1% of the total turnover in the preceding business year where, intentionally or negligently:

    (a) they supply incorrect or misleading information in response to a request made pursuant to Article 17 or Article 18(2);

    (b) in response to a request made by decision adopted pursuant to Article 17 or Article 18(3), they supply incorrect, incomplete or misleading information or do not supply information within the required time-limit;

    (c) they produce the required books or other records related to the business in incomplete form during inspections under Article 20 or refuse to submit to inspections ordered by a decision adopted pursuant to Article 20(4);

    (d) in response to a question asked in accordance with Article 20(2)(e),
        — they give an incorrect or misleading answer,
        — they fail to rectify within a time-limit set by the Commission an incorrect, incomplete or misleading answer given by a member of staff, or
        — they fail or refuse to provide a complete answer on facts relating to the subject-matter and purpose of an inspection ordered by a decision adopted pursuant to Article 20(4);

    (e) seals affixed in accordance with Article 20(2)(d) by officials or other accompanying persons authorised by the Commission have been broken.

2. The Commission may by decision impose fines on undertakings and associations of undertakings where, either intentionally or negligently:

    (a) they infringe Article 81 or Article 82 of the Treaty; or

    (b) they contravene a decision ordering interim measures under Article 8; or

    (c) they fail to comply with a commitment made binding by a decision pursuant to Article 9.

    For each undertaking and association of undertakings participating in the infringement, the fine shall not exceed 10% of its total turnover in the preceding business year.

    Where the infringement of an association relates to the activities of its members, the fine shall not exceed 10% of the sum of the total turnover of each member active on the market affected by the infringement of the association.

3. In fixing the amount of the fine, regard shall be had both to the gravity and to the duration of the infringement.

4. When a fine is imposed on an association of undertakings taking account of the turnover of its members and the association is not solvent, the association is obliged to call for contributions from its members to cover the amount of the fine.

    Where such contributions have not been made to the association within a time-limit fixed by the Commission, the Commission may require payment of the fine directly by any of the undertakings whose representatives were members of the decision-making bodies concerned of the association.

    After the Commission has required payment under the second subparagraph, where necessary to ensure full payment of the fine, the Commission may require payment of the balance by any of the members of the association which were active on the market on which the infringement occurred.

    However, the Commission shall not require payment under the second or the third subparagraph from undertakings which show that they have not implemented the infringing decision of the association and either were not aware of its existence or have actively distanced themselves from it before the Commission started investigating the case.

    The financial liability of each undertaking in respect of the payment of the fine shall not exceed 10% of its total turnover in the preceding business year.

5. Decisions taken pursuant to paragraphs 1 and 2 shall not be of a criminal law nature.

Article 24 Periodic penalty payments

1. The Commission may, by decision, impose on undertakings or associations of undertakings periodic penalty payments not exceeding 5% of the average daily turnover in the preceding business year per day and calculated from the date appointed by the decision, in order to compel them:

    (a) to put an end to an infringement of Article 81 or Article 82 of the Treaty, in accordance with a decision taken pursuant to Article 7;

    (b) to comply with a decision ordering interim measures taken pursuant to Article 8;

    (c) to comply with a commitment made binding by a decision pursuant to Article 9;

    (d) to supply complete and correct information which it has requested by decision taken pursuant to Article 17 or Article 18(3);

    (e) to submit to an inspection which it has ordered by decision taken pursuant to Article 20(4).

2. Where the undertakings or associations of undertakings have satisfied the obligation which the periodic penalty payment was intended to enforce, the Commission may fix the definitive amount of the periodic penalty payment at a figure lower than that which would arise under the original decision. Article 23(4) shall apply correspondingly.

CHAPTER VII

LIMITATION PERIODS

Article 25 Limitation periods for the imposition of penalties

1. The powers conferred on the Commission by Articles 23 and 24 shall be subject to the following limitation periods:

    (a) three years in the case of infringements of provisions concerning requests for information or the conduct of inspections;

    (b) five years in the case of all other infringements.

2. Time shall begin to run on the day on which the infringement is committed. However, in the case of continuing or repeated infringements, time shall begin to run on the day on which the infringement ceases.

3. Any action taken by the Commission or by the competition authority of a Member State for the purpose of the investigation or proceedings in respect of an infringement shall interrupt the limitation period for the imposition of fines or periodic penalty payments. The limitation period shall be interrupted with effect from the date on which the action is notified to at least one undertaking or association of undertakings which has participated in the infringement. Actions which interrupt the running of the period shall include in particular the following:

(a) written requests for information by the Commission or by the competition authority of a Member State;

(b) written authorisations to conduct inspections issued to its officials by the Commission or by the competition authority of a Member State;

(c) the initiation of proceedings by the Commission or by the competition authority of a Member State;

(d) notification of the statement of objections of the Commission or of the competition authority of a Member State.

4. The interruption of the limitation period shall apply for all the undertakings or associations of undertakings which have participated in the infringement.

5. Each interruption shall start time running afresh. However, the limitation period shall expire at the latest on the day on which a period equal to twice the limitation period has elapsed without the Commission having imposed a fine or a periodic penalty payment. That period shall be extended by the time during which limitation is suspended pursuant to paragraph 6.

6. The limitation period for the imposition of fines or periodic penalty payments shall be suspended for as long as the decision of the Commission is the subject of proceedings pending before the Court of Justice.

Article 26 Limitation period for the enforcement of penalties

1. The power of the Commission to enforce decisions taken pursuant to Articles 23 and 24 shall be subject to a limitation period of five years.

2. Time shall begin to run on the day on which the decision becomes final.

3. The limitation period for the enforcement of penalties shall be interrupted:

(a) by notification of a decision varying the original amount of the fine or periodic penalty payment or refusing an application for variation;

(b) by any action of the Commission or of a Member State, acting at the request of the Commission, designed to enforce payment of the fine or periodic penalty payment.

4. Each interruption shall start time running afresh.

5. The limitation period for the enforcement of penalties shall be suspended for so long as:

(a) time to pay is allowed;

(b) enforcement of payment is suspended pursuant to a decision of the Court of Justice.

CHAPTER VIII
HEARINGS AND PROFESSIONAL SECRECY

Article 27 Hearing of the parties, complainants and others

1. Before taking decisions as provided for in Articles 7, 8, 23 and Article 24(2), the Commission shall give the undertakings or associations of undertakings which are the subject of the proceedings conducted by the Commission the opportunity of being heard on the matters to which the Commission has taken objection. The Commission shall base its decisions only on objections on which the parties concerned have been able to comment. Complainants shall be associated closely with the proceedings.

2. The rights of defence of the parties concerned shall be fully respected in the proceedings. They shall be entitled to have access to the Commission's file, subject to the legitimate interest of undertakings in the protection of their business secrets. The right of access to the file shall not extend to confidential information and internal documents of the Commission or the competition authorities of the Member States. In particular, the right of access shall not extend to correspondence between the Commission and the competition authorities of the Member States, or between the latter, including documents drawn up pursuant to Articles 11 and 14. Nothing in this paragraph shall prevent the Commission from disclosing and using information necessary to prove an infringement.

3. If the Commission considers it necessary, it may also hear other natural or legal persons. Applications to be heard on the part of such persons shall, where they show a sufficient interest, be granted. The competition authorities of the Member States may also ask the Commission to hear other natural or legal persons.

4.   Where the Commission intends to adopt a decision pursuant to Article 9 or Article 10, it shall publish a concise summary of the case and the main content of the commitments or of the proposed course of action. Interested third parties may submit their observations within a time limit which is fixed by the Commission in its publication and which may not be less than one month. Publication shall have regard to the legitimate interest of undertakings in the protection of their business secrets.

Article 28 Professional secrecy

1.   Without prejudice to Articles 12 and 15, information collected pursuant to Articles 17 to 22 shall be used only for the purpose for which it was acquired.

2.   Without prejudice to the exchange and to the use of information foreseen in Articles 11, 12, 14, 15 and 27, the Commission and the competition authorities of the Member States, their officials, servants and other persons working under the supervision of these authorities as well as officials and civil servants of other authorities of the Member States shall not disclose information acquired or exchanged by them pursuant to this Regulation and of the kind covered by the obligation of professional secrecy. This obligation also applies to all representatives and experts of Member States attending meetings of the Advisory Committee pursuant to Article 14.

CHAPTER IX
EXEMPTION REGULATIONS

Article 29 Withdrawal in individual cases

1.   Where the Commission, empowered by a Council Regulation, such as Regulations 19/65/EEC, (EEC) No 2821/71, (EEC) No 3976/ 87, (EEC) No 1534/91 or (EEC) No 479/92, to apply Article 81(3) of the Treaty by regulation, has declared Article 81(1) of the Treaty inapplicable to certain categories of agreements, decisions by associations of undertakings or concerted practices, it may, acting on its own initiative or on a complaint, withdraw the benefit of such an exemption Regulation when it finds that in any particular case an agreement, decision or concerted practice to which the exemption Regulation applies has certain effects which are incompatible with Article 81(3) of the Treaty.

2.   Where, in any particular case, agreements, decisions by associations of undertakings or concerted practices to which a Commission Regulation referred to in paragraph 1 applies have effects which are incompatible with Article 81(3) of the Treaty in the territory of a Member State, or in a part thereof, which has all the characteristics of a distinct geographic market, the competition authority of that Member State may withdraw the benefit of the Regulation in question in respect of that territory.

CHAPTER X
GENERAL PROVISIONS

Article 30 Publication of decisions

1.   The Commission shall publish the decisions, which it takes pursuant to Articles 7 to 10, 23 and 24.

2.   The publication shall state the names of the parties and the main content of the decision, including any penalties imposed. It shall have regard to the legitimate interest of undertakings in the protection of their business secrets.

Article 31 Review by the Court of Justice

The Court of Justice shall have unlimited jurisdiction to review decisions whereby the Commission has fixed a fine or periodic penalty payment. It may cancel, reduce or increase the fine or periodic penalty payment imposed.

Article 32 Exclusions

This Regulation shall not apply to:

(a)   international tramp vessel services as defined in Article 1(3)(a) of Regulation (EEC) No 4056/86;

(b)   a maritime transport service that takes place exclusively between ports in one and the same Member State as foreseen in Article 1(2) of Regulation (EEC) No 4056/86.

Article 33 Implementing provisions

1. The Commission shall be authorised to take such measures as may be appropriate in order to apply this Regulation. The measures may concern, *inter alia*:

    (a) the form, content and other details of complaints lodged pursuant to Article 7 and the procedure for rejecting complaints;

    (b) the practical arrangements for the exchange of information and consultations provided for in Article 11;

    (c) the practical arrangements for the hearings provided for in Article 27.

2. Before the adoption of any measures pursuant to paragraph 1, the Commission shall publish a draft thereof and invite all interested parties to submit their comments within the time-limit it lays down, which may not be less than one month. Before publishing a draft measure and before adopting it, the Commission shall consult the Advisory Committee on Restrictive Practices and Dominant Positions.

Article 44 Report on the application of the present Regulation

Five years from the date of application of this Regulation, the Commission shall report to the European Parliament and the Council on the functioning of this Regulation, in particular on the application of Article 11(6) and Article 17.

On the basis of this report, the Commission shall assess whether it is appropriate to propose to the Council a revision of this Regulation.

Article 45 Entry into force

This Regulation shall enter into force on the 20th day following that of its publication in the Official Journal of the European Communities.

It shall apply from 1 May 2004.

This Regulation shall be binding in its entirety and directly applicable in all Member States.

REGULATION No 17
first regulation implementing Articles 81 and 82 of the Treaty
[1962] OJ L13/204

Article 8 Duration and revocation of decisions under Article 85(3)

...

3. The Commission may revoke or amend its decision or prohibit specified acts by the parties:

    (a) where there has been a change in any of the facts which were basic to the making of the decision;

    (b) where the parties commit a breach of any obligation attached to the decision;

    (c) where the decision is based on incorrect information or was induced by deceit;

    (d) where the parties abuse the exemption from the provisions of Article 85(1) of the Treaty granted to them by the decision.

    In cases to which subparagraphs (b), (c) or (d) apply, the decision may be revoked with retroactive effect.

COUNCIL REGULATION (EC) No 139/2004 of 20 JANUARY 2004
on the control of concentrations between undertakings (the EC Merger Regulation)
[2004] OJ L24/1

THE COUNCIL OF THE EUROPEAN UNION,

Having regard to the Treaty establishing the European Community, and in particular Articles 83 and 308 thereof,

Whereas:

(1) Council Regulation (EEC) No 4064/89 of 21 December 1989 on the control of concentrations between undertakings has been substantially amended. Since further amendments are to be made, it should be recast in the interest of clarity.

HAS ADOPTED THIS REGULATION:

Article 1   Scope

1. Without prejudice to Article 4(5) and Article 22, this Regulation shall apply to all concentrations with a Community dimension as defined in this Article.

2. A concentration has a Community dimension where:

   (a) the combined aggregate worldwide turnover of all the undertakings concerned is more than EUR 5000 million; and

   (b) the aggregate Community-wide turnover of each of at least two of the undertakings concerned is more than EUR 250 million,

   unless each of the undertakings concerned achieves more than two-thirds of its aggregate Community-wide turnover within one and the same Member State.

3. A concentration that does not meet the thresholds laid down in paragraph 2 has a Community dimension where:

   (a) the combined aggregate worldwide turnover of all the undertakings concerned is more than EUR 2 500 million;

   (b) in each of at least three Member States, the combined aggregate turnover of all the undertakings concerned is more than EUR 100 million;

   (c) in each of at least three Member States included for the purpose of point (b), the aggregate turnover of each of at least two of the undertakings concerned is more than EUR 25 million; and

   (d) the aggregate Community-wide turnover of each of at least two of the undertakings concerned is more than EUR 100 million,

   unless each of the undertakings concerned achieves more than two-thirds of its aggregate Community-wide turnover within one and the same Member State.

4. On the basis of statistical data that may be regularly provided by the Member States, the Commission shall report to the Council on the operation of the thresholds and criteria set out in paragraphs 2 and 3 by 1 July 2009 and may present proposals pursuant to paragraph 5.

5. Following the report referred to in paragraph 4 and on a proposal from the Commission, the Council, acting by a qualified majority, may revise the thresholds and criteria mentioned in paragraph 3.

Article 2   Appraisal of concentrations

1. Concentrations within the scope of this Regulation shall be appraised in accordance with the objectives of this Regulation and the following provisions with a view to establishing whether or not they are compatible with the common market.

   In making this appraisal, the Commission shall take into account:

   (a) the need to maintain and develop effective competition within the common market in view of, among other things, the structure of all the markets concerned and the actual or potential competition from undertakings located either within or out with the Community;

   (b) the market position of the undertakings concerned and their economic and financial power, the alternatives available to suppliers and users, their access to supplies or markets, any legal or other barriers to entry, supply and demand trends for the relevant goods and services, the interests of the intermediate and ultimate consumers, and the development of technical and economic progress provided that it is to consumers' advantage and does not form an obstacle to competition.

2. A concentration which would not significantly impede effective competition in the common market or in a substantial part of it, in particular as a result of the creation or strengthening of a dominant position, shall be declared compatible with the common market.

3. A concentration which would significantly impede effective competition, in the common market or in a substantial part of it, in particular as a result of the creation or strengthening of a dominant position, shall be declared incompatible with the common market.

4.   To the extent that the creation of a joint venture constituting a concentration pursuant to Article 3 has as its object or effect the coordination of the competitive behaviour of undertakings that remain independent, such coordination shall be appraised in accordance with the criteria of Article 81(1) and (3) of the Treaty, with a view to establishing whether or not the operation is compatible with the common market.

5.   In making this appraisal, the Commission shall take into account in particular:
—   whether two or more parent companies retain, to a significant extent, activities in the same market as the joint venture or in a market which is downstream or upstream from that of the joint venture or in a neighbouring market closely related to this market,
—   whether the coordination which is the direct consequence of the creation of the joint venture affords the undertakings concerned the possibility of eliminating competition in respect of a substantial part of the products or services in question.

Article 3   Definition of concentration

1.   A concentration shall be deemed to arise where a change of control on a lasting basis results from:
(a)   the merger of two or more previously independent undertakings or parts of undertakings, or
(b)   the acquisition, by one or more persons already controlling at least one undertaking, or by one or more undertakings, whether by purchase of securities or assets, by contract or by any other means, of direct or indirect control of the whole or parts of one or more other undertakings.

2.   Control shall be constituted by rights, contracts or any other means which, either separately or in combination and having regard to the considerations of fact or law involved, confer the possibility of exercising decisive influence on an undertaking, in particular by:
(a)   ownership or the right to use all or part of the assets of an undertaking;
(b)   rights or contracts which confer decisive influence on the composition, voting or decisions of the organs of an undertaking.

3.   Control is acquired by persons or undertakings which:
(a)   are holders of the rights or entitled to rights under the contracts concerned; or
(b)   while not being holders of such rights or entitled to rights under such contracts, have the power to exercise the rights deriving therefrom.

4.   The creation of a joint venture performing on a lasting basis all the functions of an autonomous economic entity shall constitute a concentration within the meaning of paragraph 1(b).

5.   A concentration shall not be deemed to arise where:
(a)   credit institutions or other financial institutions or insurance companies, the normal activities of which include transactions and dealing in securities for their own account or for the account of others, hold on a temporary basis securities which they have acquired in an undertaking with a view to reselling them, provided that they do not exercise voting rights in respect of those securities with a view to determining the competitive behaviour of that undertaking or provided that they exercise such voting rights only with a view to preparing the disposal of all or part of that undertaking or of its assets or the disposal of those securities and that any such disposal takes place within one year of the date of acquisition; that period may be extended by the Commission on request where such institutions or companies can show that the disposal was not reasonably possible within the period set;
(b)   control is acquired by an office-holder according to the law of a Member State relating to liquidation, winding up, insolvency, cessation of payments, compositions or analogous proceedings;
(c)   the operations referred to in paragraph 1(b) are carried out by the financial holding companies referred to in Article 5(3) of Fourth Council Directive 78/660/EEC of 25 July 1978 based on Article 54(3)(g) of the Treaty on the annual accounts of certain types of companies provided however that the voting rights in respect of the holding are exercised, in particular in relation to the appointment of members of the management

and supervisory bodies of the undertakings in which they have holdings, only to maintain the full value of those investments and not to determine directly or indirectly the competitive conduct of those undertakings.

Article 4   **Prior notification of concentrations and pre-notification referral at the request of the notifying parties**

1.   Concentrations with a Community dimension defined in this Regulation shall be notified to the Commission prior to their implementation and following the conclusion of the agreement, the announcement of the public bid, or the acquisition of a controlling interest.

   Notification may also be made where the undertakings concerned demonstrate to the Commission a good faith intention to conclude an agreement or, in the case of a public bid, where they have publicly announced an intention to make such a bid, provided that the intended agreement or bid would result in a concentration with a Community dimension.

   For the purposes of this Regulation, the term 'notified concentration' shall also cover intended concentrations notified pursuant to the second subparagraph. For the purposes of paragraphs 4 and 5 of this Article, the term 'concentration' includes intended concentrations within the meaning of the second subparagraph.

2.   A concentration which consists of a merger within the meaning of Article 3(1)(a) or in the acquisition of joint control within the meaning of Article 3(1)(b) shall be notified jointly by the parties to the merger or by those acquiring joint control as the case may be. In all other cases, the notification shall be effected by the person or undertaking acquiring control of the whole or parts of one or more undertakings.

3.   Where the Commission finds that a notified concentration falls within the scope of this Regulation, it shall publish the fact of the notification, at the same time indicating the names of the undertakings concerned, their country of origin, the nature of the concentration and the economic sectors involved. The Commission shall take account of the legitimate interest of undertakings in the protection of their business secrets.

4.   Prior to the notification of a concentration within the meaning of paragraph 1, the persons or undertakings referred to in paragraph 2 may inform the Commission, by means of a reasoned submission, that the concentration may significantly affect competition in a market within a Member State which presents all the characteristics of a distinct market and should therefore be examined, in whole or in part, by that Member State.

   The Commission shall transmit this submission to all Member States without delay. The Member State referred to in the reasoned submission shall, within 15 working days of receiving the submission, express its agreement or disagreement as regards the request to refer the case. Where that Member State takes no such decision within this period, it shall be deemed to have agreed.

   Unless that Member State disagrees, the Commission, where it considers that such a distinct market exists, and that competition in that market may be significantly affected by the concentration, may decide to refer the whole or part of the case to the competent authorities of that Member State with a view to the application of that State's national competition law.

   The decision whether or not to refer the case in accordance with the third subparagraph shall be taken within 25 working days starting from the receipt of the reasoned submission by the Commission. The Commission shall inform the other Member States and the persons or undertakings concerned of its decision. If the Commission does not take a decision within this period, it shall be deemed to have adopted a decision to refer the case in accordance with the submission made by the persons or undertakings concerned.

   If the Commission decides, or is deemed to have decided, pursuant to the third and fourth subparagraphs, to refer the whole of the case, no notification shall be made pursuant to paragraph 1 and national competition law shall apply. Article 9(6) to (9) shall apply *mutatis mutandis*.

5.   With regard to a concentration as defined in Article 3 which does not have a Community dimension within the meaning of Article 1 and which is capable of being reviewed under the national competition laws of at least three Member States, the persons or undertakings

referred to in paragraph 2 may, before any notification to the competent authorities, inform the Commission by means of a reasoned submission that the concentration should be examined by the Commission.

The Commission shall transmit this submission to all Member States without delay.

Any Member State competent to examine the concentration under its national competition law may, within 15 working days of receiving the reasoned submission, express its disagreement as regards the request to refer the case.

Where at least one such Member State has expressed its disagreement in accordance with the third subparagraph within the period of 15 working days, the case shall not be referred. The Commission shall, without delay, inform all Member States and the persons or undertakings concerned of any such expression of disagreement.

Where no Member State has expressed its disagreement in accordance with the third subparagraph within the period of 15 working days, the concentration shall be deemed to have a Community dimension and shall be notified to the Commission in accordance with paragraphs 1 and 2. In such situations, no Member State shall apply its national competition law to the concentration.

6.   The Commission shall report to the Council on the operation of paragraphs 4 and 5 by 1 July 2009. Following this report and on a proposal from the Commission, the Council, acting by a qualified majority, may revise paragraphs 4 and 5.

Article 5   Calculation of turnover

1.   Aggregate turnover within the meaning of this Regulation shall comprise the amounts derived by the undertakings concerned in the preceding financial year from the sale of products and the provision of services falling within the undertakings' ordinary activities after deduction of sales rebates and of value added tax and other taxes directly related to turnover. The aggregate turnover of an undertaking concerned shall not include the sale of products or the provision of services between any of the undertakings referred to in paragraph 4.

Turnover, in the Community or in a Member State, shall comprise products sold and services provided to undertakings or consumers, in the Community or in that Member State as the case may be.

2.   By way of derogation from paragraph 1, where the concentration consists of the acquisition of parts, whether or not constituted as legal entities, of one or more undertakings, only the turnover relating to the parts which are the subject of the concentration shall be taken into account with regard to the seller or sellers.

However, two or more transactions within the meaning of the first subparagraph which take place within a two-year period between the same persons or undertakings shall be treated as one and the same concentration arising on the date of the last transaction.

3.   In place of turnover the following shall be used:

(a)   for credit institutions and other financial institutions, the sum of the following income items as defined in Council Directive 86/635/EEC, after deduction of value added tax and other taxes directly related to those items, where appropriate:

(i)   interest income and similar income;

(ii)   income from securities:

— income from shares and other variable yield securities,

— income from participating interests,

— income from shares in affiliated undertakings;

(iii)   commissions receivable;

(iv)   net profit on financial operations;

(v)   other operating income.

The turnover of a credit or financial institution in the Community or in a Member State shall comprise the income items, as defined above, which are received by the branch or division of that institution established in the Community or in the Member State in question, as the case may be;

(b)   for insurance undertakings, the value of gross premiums written which shall comprise all amounts received and receivable in respect of insurance contracts issued by or on behalf of the insurance undertakings, including also outgoing reinsurance premiums, and after deduction of taxes and parafiscal contributions or levies charged by reference to the amounts of individual premiums or the total volume of premiums; as regards Article 1(2)(b) and (3)(b), (c) and (d) and the final part of Article 1(2) and (3), gross premiums received from Community residents and from residents of one Member State respectively shall be taken into account.

4. Without prejudice to paragraph 2, the aggregate turnover of an undertaking concerned within the meaning of this Regulation shall be calculated by adding together the respective turnovers of the following:

  (a)   the undertaking concerned;

  (b)   those undertakings in which the undertaking concerned, directly or indirectly:

      (i)   owns more than half the capital or business assets, or

      (ii)   has the power to exercise more than half the voting rights, or

      (iii) has the power to appoint more than half the members of the supervisory board, the administrative board or bodies legally representing the undertakings, or

      (iv) has the right to manage the undertakings' affairs;

  (c)   those undertakings which have in the undertaking concerned the rights or powers listed in (b);

  (d)   those undertakings in which an undertaking as referred to in (c) has the rights or powers listed in (b);

  (e)   those undertakings in which two or more undertakings as referred to in (a) to (d) jointly have the rights or powers listed in (b).

5. Where undertakings concerned by the concentration jointly have the rights or powers listed in paragraph 4(b), in calculating the aggregate turnover of the undertakings concerned for the purposes of this Regulation:

  (a)   no account shall be taken of the turnover resulting from the sale of products or the provision of services between the joint undertaking and each of the undertakings concerned or any other undertaking connected with any one of them, as set out in paragraph 4(b) to (e);

  (b)   account shall be taken of the turnover resulting from the sale of products and the provision of services between the joint undertaking and any third undertakings. This turnover shall be apportioned equally amongst the undertakings concerned.

Article 6   Examination of the notification and initiation of proceedings

1. The Commission shall examine the notification as soon as it is received.

  (a)   Where it concludes that the concentration notified does not fall within the scope of this Regulation, it shall record that finding by means of a decision.

  (b)   Where it finds that the concentration notified, although falling within the scope of this Regulation, does not raise serious doubts as to its compatibility with the common market, it shall decide not to oppose it and shall declare that it is compatible with the common market.

      A decision declaring a concentration compatible shall be deemed to cover restrictions directly related and necessary to the implementation of the concentration.

  (c)   Without prejudice to paragraph 2, where the Commission finds that the concentration notified falls within the scope of this Regulation and raises serious doubts as to its compatibility with the common market, it shall decide to initiate proceedings. Without prejudice to Article 9, such proceedings shall be closed by means of a decision as provided for in Article 8(1) to (4), unless the undertakings concerned have demonstrated to the satisfaction of the Commission that they have abandoned the concentration.

2. Where the Commission finds that, following modification by the undertakings concerned, a notified concentration no longer raises serious doubts within the meaning of paragraph 1(c), it shall declare the concentration compatible with the common market pursuant to paragraph 1(b).

The Commission may attach to its decision under paragraph 1(b) conditions and obligations intended to ensure that the undertakings concerned comply with the commitments they have entered into vis-à-vis the Commission with a view to rendering the concentration compatible with the common market.

3.   The Commission may revoke the decision it took pursuant to paragraph 1(a) or (b) where:

  (a)   the decision is based on incorrect information for which one of the undertakings is responsible or where it has been obtained by deceit, or

  (b)   the undertakings concerned commit a breach of an obligation attached to the decision.

4.   In the cases referred to in paragraph 3, the Commission may take a decision under paragraph 1, without being bound by the time limits referred to in Article 10(1).

5.   The Commission shall notify its decision to the undertakings concerned and the competent authorities of the Member States without delay.

Article 7   Suspension of concentrations

1.   A concentration with a Community dimension as defined in Article 1, or which is to be examined by the Commission pursuant to Article 4(5), shall not be implemented either before its notification or until it has been declared compatible with the common market pursuant to a decision under Articles 6(1)(b), 8(1) or 8(2), or on the basis of a presumption according to Article 10(6).

2.   Paragraph 1 shall not prevent the implementation of a public bid or of a series of transactions in securities including those convertible into other securities admitted to trading on a market such as a stock exchange, by which control within the meaning of Article 3 is acquired from various sellers, provided that:

  (a)   the concentration is notified to the Commission pursuant to Article 4 without delay; and

  (b)   the acquirer does not exercise the voting rights attached to the securities in question or does so only to maintain the full value of its investments based on a derogation granted by the Commission under paragraph 3.

3.   The Commission may, on request, grant a derogation from the obligations imposed in paragraphs 1 or 2. The request to grant a derogation must be reasoned. In deciding on the request, the Commission shall take into account *inter alia* the effects of the suspension on one or more undertakings concerned by the concentration or on a third party and the threat to competition posed by the concentration. Such a derogation may be made subject to conditions and obligations in order to ensure conditions of effective competition. A derogation may be applied for and granted at any time, be it before notification or after the transaction.

4.   The validity of any transaction carried out in contravention of paragraph 1 shall be dependent on a decision pursuant to Article 6(1)(b) or Article 8(1), (2) or (3) or on a presumption pursuant to Article 10(6).

This Article shall, however, have no effect on the validity of transactions in securities including those convertible into other securities admitted to trading on a market such as a stock exchange, unless the buyer and seller knew or ought to have known that the transaction was carried out in contravention of paragraph 1.

Article 8   Powers of decision of the Commission

1.   Where the Commission finds that a notified concentration fulfils the criterion laid down in Article 2(2) and, in the cases referred to in Article 2(4), the criteria laid down in Article 81(3) of the Treaty, it shall issue a decision declaring the concentration compatible with the common market.

A decision declaring a concentration compatible shall be deemed to cover restrictions directly related and necessary to the implementation of the concentration.

2.   Where the Commission finds that, following modification by the undertakings concerned, a notified concentration fulfils the criterion laid down in Article 2(2) and, in the cases referred to in Article 2(4), the criteria laid down in Article 81(3) of the Treaty, it shall issue a decision declaring the concentration compatible with the common market.

The Commission may attach to its decision conditions and obligations intended to ensure that the undertakings concerned comply with the commitments they have entered into vis-à-vis the Commission with a view to rendering the concentration compatible with the common market. A decision declaring a concentration compatible shall be deemed to cover restrictions directly related and necessary to the implementation of the concentration.

3. Where the Commission finds that a concentration fulfils the criterion defined in Article 2(3) or, in the cases referred to in Article 2(4), does not fulfil the criteria laid down in Article 81(3) of the Treaty, it shall issue a decision declaring that the concentration is incompatible with the common market.

4. Where the Commission finds that a concentration:
   (a) has already been implemented and that concentration has been declared incompatible with the common market, or
   (b) has been implemented in contravention of a condition attached to a decision taken under paragraph 2, which has found that, in the absence of the condition, the concentration would fulfil the criterion laid down in Article 2(3) or, in the cases referred to in Article 2(4), would not fulfil the criteria laid down in Article 81(3) of the Treaty, the Commission may:
   — require the undertakings concerned to dissolve the concentration, in particular through the dissolution of the merger or the disposal of all the shares or assets acquired, so as to restore the situation prevailing prior to the implementation of the concentration; in circumstances where restoration of the situation prevailing before the implementation of the concentration is not possible through dissolution of the concentration, the Commission may take any other measure appropriate to achieve such restoration as far as possible,
   — order any other appropriate measure to ensure that the undertakings concerned dissolve the concentration or take other restorative measures as required in its decision.

   In cases falling within point (a) of the first subparagraph, the measures referred to in that subparagraph may be imposed either in a decision pursuant to paragraph 3 or by separate decision.

5. The Commission may take interim measures appropriate to restore or maintain conditions of effective competition where a concentration:
   (a) has been implemented in contravention of Article 7, and a decision as to the compatibility of the concentration with the common market has not yet been taken;
   (b) has been implemented in contravention of a condition attached to a decision under Article 6(1)(b) or paragraph 2 of this Article;
   (c) has already been implemented and is declared incompatible with the common market.

6. The Commission may revoke the decision it has taken pursuant to paragraphs 1 or 2 where:
   (a) the declaration of compatibility is based on incorrect information for which one of the undertakings is responsible or where it has been obtained by deceit; or
   (b) the undertakings concerned commit a breach of an obligation attached to the decision.

7. The Commission may take a decision pursuant to paragraphs 1 to 3 without being bound by the time limits referred to in Article 10(3), in cases where:
   (a) it finds that a concentration has been implemented
       (i) in contravention of a condition attached to a decision under Article 6(1)(b), or
       (ii) in contravention of a condition attached to a decision taken under paragraph 2 and in accordance with Article 10(2), which has found that, in the absence of the condition, the concentration would raise serious doubts as to its compatibility with the common market; or
   (b) a decision has been revoked pursuant to paragraph 6.

8. The Commission shall notify its decision to the undertakings concerned and the competent authorities of the Member States without delay.

Article 9   **Referral to the competent authorities of the Member States**

1. The Commission may, by means of a decision notified without delay to the undertakings concerned and the competent authorities of the other Member States, refer a notified concentration to the competent authorities of the Member State concerned in the following circumstances.

2. Within 15 working days of the date of receipt of the copy of the notification, a Member State, on its own initiative or upon the invitation of the Commission, may inform the Commission, which shall inform the undertakings concerned, that:

    (a)   a concentration threatens to affect significantly competition in a market within that Member State, which presents all the characteristics of a distinct market, or

    (b)   a concentration affects competition in a market within that Member State, which presents all the characteristics of a distinct market and which does not constitute a substantial part of the common market.

3. If the Commission considers that, having regard to the market for the products or services in question and the geographical reference market within the meaning of paragraph 7, there is such a distinct market and that such a threat exists, either:

    (a)   it shall itself deal with the case in accordance with this Regulation; or

    (b)   it shall refer the whole or part of the case to the competent authorities of the Member State concerned with a view to the application of that State's national competition law.

    If, however, the Commission considers that such a distinct market or threat does not exist, it shall adopt a decision to that effect which it shall address to the Member State concerned, and shall itself deal with the case in accordance with this Regulation.

    In cases where a Member State informs the Commission pursuant to paragraph 2(b) that a concentration affects competition in a distinct market within its territory that does not form a substantial part of the common market, the Commission shall refer the whole or part of the case relating to the distinct market concerned, if it considers that such a distinct market is affected.

4. A decision to refer or not to refer pursuant to paragraph 3 shall be taken:

    (a)   as a general rule within the period provided for in Article 10(1), second subparagraph, where the Commission, pursuant to Article 6(1)(b), has not initiated proceedings; or

    (b)   within 65 working days at most of the notification of the concentration concerned where the Commission has initiated proceedings under Article 6(1)(c), without taking the preparatory steps in order to adopt the necessary measures under Article 8(2), (3) or (4) to maintain or restore effective competition on the market concerned.

5. If within the 65 working days referred to in paragraph 4(b) the Commission, despite a reminder from the Member State concerned, has not taken a decision on referral in accordance with paragraph 3 nor has taken the preparatory steps referred to in paragraph 4(b), it shall be deemed to have taken a decision to refer the case to the Member State concerned in accordance with paragraph 3(b).

6. The competent authority of the Member State concerned shall decide upon the case without undue delay.

    Within 45 working days after the Commission's referral, the competent authority of the Member State concerned shall inform the undertakings concerned of the result of the preliminary competition assessment and what further action, if any, it proposes to take. The Member State concerned may exceptionally suspend this time limit where necessary information has not been provided to it by the undertakings concerned as provided for by its national competition law.

    Where a notification is requested under national law, the period of 45 working days shall begin on the working day following that of the receipt of a complete notification by the competent authority of that Member State.

7. The geographical reference market shall consist of the area in which the undertakings concerned are involved in the supply and demand of products or services, in which the conditions of competition are sufficiently homogeneous and which can be distinguished from neighbouring areas because, in particular, conditions of competition are appreciably different

in those areas. This assessment should take account in particular of the nature and characteristics of the products or services concerned, of the existence of entry barriers or of consumer preferences, of appreciable differences of the undertakings' market shares between the area concerned and neighbouring areas or of substantial price differences.

8. In applying the provisions of this Article, the Member State concerned may take only the measures strictly necessary to safeguard or restore effective competition on the market concerned.

9. In accordance with the relevant provisions of the Treaty, any Member State may appeal to the Court of Justice, and in particular request the application of Article 243 of the Treaty, for the purpose of applying its national competition law.

Article 10 Time limits for initiating proceedings and for decisions

1. Without prejudice to Article 6(4), the decisions referred to in Article 6(1) shall be taken within 25 working days at most. That period shall begin on the working day following that of the receipt of a notification or, if the information to be supplied with the notification is incomplete, on the working day following that of the receipt of the complete information.

   That period shall be increased to 35 working days where the Commission receives a request from a Member State in accordance with Article 9(2) or where, the undertakings concerned offer commitments pursuant to Article 6(2) with a view to rendering the concentration compatible with the common market.

2. Decisions pursuant to Article 8(1) or (2) concerning notified concentrations shall be taken as soon as it appears that the serious doubts referred to in Article 6(1)(c) have been removed, particularly as a result of modifications made by the undertakings concerned, and at the latest by the time limit laid down in paragraph 3.

3. Without prejudice to Article 8(7), decisions pursuant to Article 8(1) to (3) concerning notified concentrations shall be taken within not more than 90 working days of the date on which the proceedings are initiated. That period shall be increased to 105 working days where the undertakings concerned offer commitments pursuant to Article 8(2), second subparagraph, with a view to rendering the concentration compatible with the common market, unless these commitments have been offered less than 55 working days after the initiation of proceedings.

   The periods set by the first subparagraph shall likewise be extended if the notifying parties make a request to that effect not later than 15 working days after the initiation of proceedings pursuant to Article 6(1)(c). The notifying parties may make only one such request. Likewise, at any time following the initiation of proceedings, the periods set by the first subparagraph may be extended by the Commission with the agreement of the notifying parties. The total duration of any extension or extensions effected pursuant to this subparagraph shall not exceed 20 working days.

4. The periods set by paragraphs 1 and 3 shall exceptionally be suspended where, owing to circumstances for which one of the undertakings involved in the concentration is responsible, the Commission has had to request information by decision pursuant to Article 11 or to order an inspection by decision pursuant to Article 13.

   The first subparagraph shall also apply to the period referred to in Article 9(4)(b).

5. Where the Court of Justice gives a judgment which annuls the whole or part of a Commission decision which is subject to a time limit set by this Article, the concentration shall be reexamined by the Commission with a view to adopting a decision pursuant to Article 6(1).

   The concentration shall be re-examined in the light of current market conditions.

   The notifying parties shall submit a new notification or supplement the original notification, without delay, where the original notification becomes incomplete by reason of intervening changes in market conditions or in the information provided.

   Where there are no such changes, the parties shall certify this fact without delay.

   The periods laid down in paragraph 1 shall start on the working day following that of the receipt of complete information in a new notification, a supplemented notification, or a certification within the meaning of the third subparagraph.

   The second and third subparagraphs shall also apply in the cases referred to in Article 6(4) and Article 8(7).

6. Where the Commission has not taken a decision in accordance with Article 6(1)(b), (c), 8(1), (2) or (3) within the time limits set in paragraphs 1 and 3 respectively, the concentration shall be deemed to have been declared compatible with the common market, without prejudice to Article 9.

Article 11 Requests for information

1. In order to carry out the duties assigned to it by this Regulation, the Commission may, by simple request or by decision, require the persons referred to in Article 3(1)(b), as well as undertakings and associations of undertakings, to provide all necessary information.

2. When sending a simple request for information to a person, an undertaking or an association of undertakings, the Commission shall state the legal basis and the purpose of the request, specify what information is required and fix the time limit within which the information is to be provided, as well as the penalties provided for in Article 14 for supplying incorrect or misleading information.

3. Where the Commission requires a person, an undertaking or an association of undertakings to supply information by decision, it shall state the legal basis and the purpose of the request, specify what information is required and fix the time limit within which it is to be provided. It shall also indicate the penalties provided for in Article 14 and indicate or impose the penalties provided for in Article 15. It shall further indicate the right to have the decision reviewed by the Court of Justice.

4. The owners of the undertakings or their representatives and, in the case of legal persons, companies or firms, or associations having no legal personality, the persons authorised to represent them by law or by their constitution, shall supply the information requested on behalf of the undertaking concerned. Persons duly authorised to act may supply the information on behalf of their clients. The latter shall remain fully responsible if the information supplied is incomplete, incorrect or misleading.

5. The Commission shall without delay forward a copy of any decision taken pursuant to paragraph 3 to the competent authorities of the Member State in whose territory the residence of the person or the seat of the undertaking or association of undertakings is situated, and to the competent authority of the Member State whose territory is affected. At the specific request of the competent authority of a Member State, the Commission shall also forward to that authority copies of simple requests for information relating to a notified concentration.

6. At the request of the Commission, the governments and competent authorities of the Member States shall provide the Commission with all necessary information to carry out the duties assigned to it by this Regulation.

7. In order to carry out the duties assigned to it by this Regulation, the Commission may interview any natural or legal person who consents to be interviewed for the purpose of collecting information relating to the subject matter of an investigation. At the beginning of the interview, which may be conducted by telephone or other electronic means, the Commission shall state the legal basis and the purpose of the interview.
Where an interview is not conducted on the premises of the Commission or by telephone or other electronic means, the Commission shall inform in advance the competent authority of the Member State in whose territory the interview takes place. If the competent authority of that Member State so requests, officials of that authority may assist the officials and other persons authorised by the Commission to conduct the interview.

Article 12 Inspections by the authorities of the Member States

1. At the request of the Commission, the competent authorities of the Member States shall undertake the inspections which the Commission considers to be necessary under Article 13(1), or which it has ordered by decision pursuant to Article 13(4). The officials of the competent authorities of the Member States who are responsible for conducting these inspections as well as those authorised or appointed by them shall exercise their powers in accordance with their national law.

2. If so requested by the Commission or by the competent authority of the Member State within whose territory the inspection is to be conducted, officials and other accompanying persons authorised by the Commission may assist the officials of the authority concerned.

Article 13 The Commission's powers of inspection

1. In order to carry out the duties assigned to it by this Regulation, the Commission may conduct all necessary inspections of undertakings and associations of undertakings.
2. The officials and other accompanying persons authorised by the Commission to conduct an inspection shall have the power:
    (a) to enter any premises, land and means of transport of undertakings and associations of undertakings;
    (b) to examine the books and other records related to the business, irrespective of the medium on which they are stored;
    (c) to take or obtain in any form copies of or extracts from such books or records;
    (d) to seal any business premises and books or records for the period and to the extent necessary for the inspection;
    (e) to ask any representative or member of staff of the undertaking or association of undertakings for explanations on facts or documents relating to the subject matter and purpose of the inspection and to record the answers.
3. Officials and other accompanying persons authorised by the Commission to conduct an inspection shall exercise their powers upon production of a written authorisation specifying the subject matter and purpose of the inspection and the penalties provided for in Article 14, in the production of the required books or other records related to the business which is incomplete or where answers to questions asked under paragraph 2 of this Article are incorrect or misleading. In good time before the inspection, the Commission shall give notice of the inspection to the competent authority of the Member State in whose territory the inspection is to be conducted.
4. Undertakings and associations of undertakings are required to submit to inspections ordered by decision of the Commission. The decision shall specify the subject matter and purpose of the inspection, appoint the date on which it is to begin and indicate the penalties provided for in Articles 14 and 15 and the right to have the decision reviewed by the Court of Justice. The Commission shall take such decisions after consulting the competent authority of the Member State in whose territory the inspection is to be conducted.
5. Officials of, and those authorised or appointed by, the competent authority of the Member State in whose territory the inspection is to be conducted shall, at the request of that authority or of the Commission, actively assist the officials and other accompanying persons authorised by the Commission. To this end, they shall enjoy the powers specified in paragraph 2.
6. Where the officials and other accompanying persons authorised by the Commission find that an undertaking opposes an inspection, including the sealing of business premises, books or records, ordered pursuant to this Article, the Member State concerned shall afford them the necessary assistance, requesting where appropriate the assistance of the police or of an equivalent enforcement authority, so as to enable them to conduct their inspection.
7. If the assistance provided for in paragraph 6 requires authorisation from a judicial authority according to national rules, such authorisation shall be applied for. Such authorisation may also be applied for as a precautionary measure.
8. Where authorisation as referred to in paragraph 7 is applied for, the national judicial authority shall ensure that the Commission decision is authentic and that the coercive measures envisaged are neither arbitrary nor excessive having regard to the subject matter of the inspection. In its control of proportionality of the coercive measures, the national judicial authority may ask the Commission, directly or through the competent authority of that Member State, for detailed explanations relating to the subject matter of the inspection. However, the national judicial authority may not call into question the necessity for the inspection nor demand that it be provided with the information in the Commission's file. The lawfulness of the Commission's decision shall be subject to review only by the Court of Justice.

Article 14 Fines

1. The Commission may by decision impose on the persons referred to in Article 3(1)b, undertakings or associations of undertakings, fines not exceeding 1% of the aggregate turnover of the undertaking or association of undertakings concerned within the meaning of Article 5 where, intentionally or negligently:

    (a) they supply incorrect or misleading information in a submission, certification, notification or supplement thereto, pursuant to Article 4, Article 10(5) or Article 22(3);

    (b) they supply incorrect or misleading information in response to a request made pursuant to Article 11(2);

    (c) in response to a request made by decision adopted pursuant to Article 11(3), they supply incorrect, incomplete or misleading information or do not supply information within the required time limit;

    (d) they produce the required books or other records related to the business in incomplete form during inspections under Article 13, or refuse to submit to an inspection ordered by decision taken pursuant to Article 13(4);

    (e) in response to a question asked in accordance with Article 13(2)(e),
    — they give an incorrect or misleading answer,
    — they fail to rectify within a time limit set by the Commission an incorrect, incomplete or misleading answer given by a member of staff, or
    — they fail or refuse to provide a complete answer on facts relating to the subject matter and purpose of an inspection ordered by a decision adopted pursuant to Article 13(4);

    (f) seals affixed by officials or other accompanying persons authorised by the Commission in accordance with Article 13(2)(d) have been broken.

2. The Commission may by decision impose fines not exceeding 10% of the aggregate turnover of the undertaking concerned within the meaning of Article 5 on the persons referred to in Article 3(1)b or the undertakings concerned where, either intentionally or negligently, they:

    (a) fail to notify a concentration in accordance with Articles 4 or 22(3) prior to its implementation, unless they are expressly authorised to do so by Article 7(2) or by a decision taken pursuant to Article 7(3);

    (b) implement a concentration in breach of Article 7;

    (c) implement a concentration declared incompatible with the common market by decision pursuant to Article 8(3) or do not comply with any measure ordered by decision pursuant to Article 8(4) or (5);

    (d) fail to comply with a condition or an obligation imposed by decision pursuant to Articles 6(1)(b), Article 7(3) or Article 8(2), second subparagraph.

3. In fixing the amount of the fine, regard shall be had to the nature, gravity and duration of the infringement.

4. Decisions taken pursuant to paragraphs 1, 2 and 3 shall not be of a criminal law nature.

Article 15 Periodic penalty payments

1. The Commission may by decision impose on the persons referred to in Article 3(1)b, undertakings or associations of undertakings, periodic penalty payments not exceeding 5% of the average daily aggregate turnover of the undertaking or association of undertakings concerned within the meaning of Article 5 for each working day of delay, calculated from the date set in the decision, in order to compel them:

    (a) to supply complete and correct information which it has requested by decision taken pursuant to Article 11(3);

    (b) to submit to an inspection which it has ordered by decision taken pursuant to Article 13(4); (c) to comply with an obligation imposed by decision pursuant to Article 6(1)(b), Article 7(3) or Article 8(2), second subparagraph; or;

    (d) to comply with any measures ordered by decision pursuant to Article 8(4) or (5).

2. Where the persons referred to in Article 3(1)(b), undertakings or associations of undertakings have satisfied the obligation which the periodic penalty payment was intended to enforce, the

Commission may fix the definitive amount of the periodic penalty payments at a figure lower than that which would arise under the original decision.

Article 16 Review by the Court of Justice

The Court of Justice shall have unlimited jurisdiction within the meaning of Article 229 of the Treaty to review decisions whereby the Commission has fixed a fine or periodic penalty payments; it may cancel, reduce or increase the fine or periodic penalty payment imposed.

Article 17 Professional secrecy

1. Information acquired as a result of the application of this Regulation shall be used only for the purposes of the relevant request, investigation or hearing.
2. Without prejudice to Article 4(3), Articles 18 and 20, the Commission and the competent authorities of the Member States, their officials and other servants and other persons working under the supervision of these authorities as well as officials and civil servants of other authorities of the Member States shall not disclose information they have acquired through the application of this Regulation of the kind covered by the obligation of professional secrecy.
3. Paragraphs 1 and 2 shall not prevent publication of general information or of surveys which do not contain information relating to particular undertakings or associations of undertakings.

Article 18 Hearing of the parties and of third persons

1. Before taking any decision provided for in Article 6(3), Article 7(3), Article 8(2) to (6), and Articles 14 and 15, the Commission shall give the persons, undertakings and associations of undertakings concerned the opportunity, at every stage of the procedure up to the consultation of the Advisory Committee, of making known their views on the objections against them.
2. By way of derogation from paragraph 1, a decision pursuant to Articles 7(3) and 8(5) may be taken provisionally, without the persons, undertakings or associations of undertakings concerned being given the opportunity to make known their views beforehand, provided that the Commission gives them that opportunity as soon as possible after having taken its decision.
3. The Commission shall base its decision only on objections on which the parties have been able to submit their observations. The rights of the defence shall be fully respected in the proceedings. Access to the file shall be open at least to the parties directly involved, subject to the legitimate interest of undertakings in the protection of their business secrets.
4. In so far as the Commission or the competent authorities of the Member States deem it necessary, they may also hear other natural or legal persons. Natural or legal persons showing a sufficient interest and especially members of the administrative or management bodies of the undertakings concerned or the recognised representatives of their employees shall be entitled, upon application, to be heard.

Article 19 Liaison with the authorities of the Member States

1. The Commission shall transmit to the competent authorities of the Member States copies of notifications within three working days and, as soon as possible, copies of the most important documents lodged with or issued by the Commission pursuant to this Regulation. Such documents shall include commitments offered by the undertakings concerned vis-à-vis the Commission with a view to rendering the concentration compatible with the common market pursuant to Article 6(2) or Article 8(2), second subparagraph.
2. The Commission shall carry out the procedures set out in this Regulation in close and constant liaison with the competent authorities of the Member States, which may express their views upon those procedures. For the purposes of Article 9 it shall obtain information from the competent authority of the Member State as referred to in paragraph 2 of that Article and give it the opportunity to make known its views at every stage of the procedure up to the adoption of a decision pursuant to paragraph 3 of that Article; to that end it shall give it access to the file.
3. An Advisory Committee on concentrations shall be consulted before any decision is taken pursuant to Article 8(1) to (6), Articles 14 or 15 with the exception of provisional decisions taken in accordance with Article 18(2).

4.   The Advisory Committee shall consist of representatives of the competent authorities of the Member States. Each Member State shall appoint one or two representatives; if unable to attend, they may be replaced by other representatives.

At least one of the representatives of a Member State shall be competent in matters of restrictive practices and dominant positions.

5.   Consultation shall take place at a joint meeting convened at the invitation of and chaired by the Commission. A summary of the case, together with an indication of the most important documents and a preliminary draft of the decision to be taken for each case considered, shall be sent with the invitation. The meeting shall take place not less than 10 working days after the invitation has been sent. The Commission may in exceptional cases shorten that period as appropriate in order to avoid serious harm to one or more of the undertakings concerned by a concentration.

6.   The Advisory Committee shall deliver an opinion on the Commission's draft decision, if necessary by taking a vote. The Advisory Committee may deliver an opinion even if some members are absent and unrepresented. The opinion shall be delivered in writing and appended to the draft decision. The Commission shall take the utmost account of the opinion delivered by the Committee. It shall inform the Committee of the manner in which its opinion has been taken into account.

7.   The Commission shall communicate the opinion of the Advisory Committee, together with the decision, to the addressees of the decision. It shall make the opinion public together with the decision, having regard to the legitimate interest of undertakings in the protection of their business secrets.

Article 20 Publication of decisions

1.   The Commission shall publish the decisions which it takes pursuant to Article 8(1) to (6), Articles 14 and 15 with the exception of provisional decisions taken in accordance with Article 18(2) together with the opinion of the Advisory Committee in the *Official Journal of the European Union*.

2.   The publication shall state the names of the parties and the main content of the decision; it shall have regard to the legitimate interest of undertakings in the protection of their business secrets.

Article 21 Application of the Regulation and jurisdiction

1.   This Regulation alone shall apply to concentrations as defined in Article 3, and Council Regulations (EC) No 1/2003, (EEC) No 1017/68, (EEC) No 4056/86 and (EEC) No 3975/87 shall not apply, except in relation to joint ventures that do not have a Community dimension and which have as their object or effect the coordination of the competitive behaviour of undertakings that remain independent.

2.   Subject to review by the Court of Justice, the Commission shall have sole jurisdiction to take the decisions provided for in this Regulation.

3.   No Member State shall apply its national legislation on competition to any concentration that has a Community dimension.

The first subparagraph shall be without prejudice to any Member State's power to carry out any enquiries necessary for the application of Articles 4(4), 9(2) or after referral, pursuant to Article 9(3), first subparagraph, indent (b), or Article 9(5), to take the measures strictly necessary for the application of Article 9(8).

4.   Notwithstanding paragraphs 2 and 3, Member States may take appropriate measures to protect legitimate interests other than those taken into consideration by this Regulation and compatible with the general principles and other provisions of Community law.

Public security, plurality of the media and prudential rules shall be regarded as legitimate interests within the meaning of the first subparagraph.

Any other public interest must be communicated to the Commission by the Member State concerned and shall be recognised by the Commission after an assessment of its compatibility with the general principles and other provisions of Community law before the measures referred to above may be taken. The Commission shall inform the Member State concerned of its decision within 25 working days of that communication.

Article 22 Referral to the Commission

1. One or more Member States may request the Commission to examine any concentration as defined in Article 3 that does not have a Community dimension within the meaning of Article 1 but affects trade between Member States and threatens to significantly affect competition within the territory of the Member State or States making the request.

    Such a request shall be made at most within 15 working days of the date on which the concentration was notified, or if no notification is required, otherwise made known to the Member State concerned.

2. The Commission shall inform the competent authorities of the Member States and the undertakings concerned of any request received pursuant to paragraph 1 without delay.

    Any other Member State shall have the right to join the initial request within a period of 15 working days of being informed by the Commission of the initial request.

    All national time limits relating to the concentration shall be suspended until, in accordance with the procedure set out in this Article, it has been decided where the concentration shall be examined. As soon as a Member State has informed the Commission and the undertakings concerned that it does not wish to join the request, the suspension of its national time limits shall end.

3. The Commission may, at the latest 10 working days after the expiry of the period set in paragraph 2, decide to examine, the concentration where it considers that it affects trade between Member States and threatens to significantly affect competition within the territory of the Member State or States making the request. If the Commission does not take a decision within this period, it shall be deemed to have adopted a decision to examine the concentration in accordance with the request.

    The Commission shall inform all Member States and the undertakings concerned of its decision. It may request the submission of a notification pursuant to Article 4.

    The Member State or States having made the request shall no longer apply their national legislation on competition to the concentration.

4. Article 2, Article 4(2) to (3), Articles 5, 6, and 8 to 21 shall apply where the Commission examines a concentration pursuant to paragraph 3. Article 7 shall apply to the extent that the concentration has not been implemented on the date on which the Commission informs the undertakings concerned that a request has been made.

    Where a notification pursuant to Article 4 is not required, the period set in Article 10(1) within which proceedings may be initiated shall begin on the working day following that on which the Commission informs the undertakings concerned that it has decided to examine the concentration pursuant to paragraph 3.

5. The Commission may inform one or several Member States that it considers a concentration fulfils the criteria in paragraph 1. In such cases, the Commission may invite that Member State or those Member States to make a request pursuant to paragraph 1.

Article 23 Implementing provisions

1. The Commission shall have the power to lay down in accordance with the procedure referred to in paragraph 2:

    (a) implementing provisions concerning the form, content and other details of notifications and submissions pursuant to Article 4;

    (b) implementing provisions concerning time limits pursuant to Article 4(4), (5) Articles 7, 9, 10 and 22;

    (c) the procedure and time limits for the submission and implementation of commitments pursuant to Article 6(2) and Article 8(2);

    (d) implementing provisions concerning hearings pursuant to Article 18.

2. The Commission shall be assisted by an Advisory Committee, composed of representatives of the Member States.

    (a) Before publishing draft implementing provisions and before adopting such provisions, the Commission shall consult the Advisory Committee.

    (b) Consultation shall take place at a meeting convened at the invitation of and chaired by the Commission. A draft of the implementing provisions to be taken shall be sent with the invitation. The meeting shall take place not less than 10 working days after the invitation has been sent.

(c)   The Advisory Committee shall deliver an opinion on the draft implementing provisions, if necessary by taking a vote. The Commission shall take the utmost account of the opinion delivered by the Committee.

Article 24   Relations with third countries

1. The Member States shall inform the Commission of any general difficulties encountered by their undertakings with concentrations as defined in Article 3 in a third country.

2. Initially not more than one year after the entry into force of this Regulation and, thereafter periodically, the Commission shall draw up a report examining the treatment accorded to undertakings having their seat or their principal fields of activity in the Community, in the terms referred to in paragraphs 3 and 4, as regards concentrations in third countries.

   The Commission shall submit those reports to the Council, together with any recommendations.

3. Whenever it appears to the Commission, either on the basis of the reports referred to in paragraph 2 or on the basis of other information, that a third country does not grant undertakings having their seat or their principal fields of activity in the Community, treatment comparable to that granted by the Community to undertakings from that country, the Commission may submit proposals to the Council for an appropriate mandate for negotiation with a view to obtaining comparable treatment for undertakings having their seat or their principal fields of activity in the Community.

4. Measures taken under this Article shall comply with the obligations of the Community or of the Member States, without prejudice to Article 307 of the Treaty, under international agreements, whether bilateral or multilateral.

Article 25   Repeal

1. Without prejudice to Article 26(2), Regulations (EEC) No 4064/89 and (EC) No 1310/97 shall be repealed with effect from 1 May 2004.

2. References to the repealed Regulations shall be construed as references to this Regulation and shall be read in accordance with the correlation table in the Annex.

Article 26   Entry into force and transitional provisions

1. This Regulation shall enter into force on the 20th day following that of its publication in the Official Journal of the European Union.

   It shall apply from 1 May 2004.

2. Regulation (EEC) No 4064/89 shall continue to apply to any concentration which was the subject of an agreement or announcement or where control was acquired within the meaning of Article 4(1) of that Regulation before the date of application of this Regulation, subject, in particular, to the provisions governing applicability set out in Article 25(2) and (3) of Regulation (EEC) No 4064/89 and Article 2 of Regulation (EEC) No 1310/97.

3. As regards concentrations to which this Regulation applies by virtue of accession, the date of accession shall be substituted for the date of application of this Regulation.

COMMISSION NOTICE ON AGREEMENTS OF MINOR IMPORTANCE WHICH DO NOT APPRECIABLY RESTRICT COMPETITION UNDER ARTICLE 81(1) OF THE TREATY ESTABLISHING THE EUROPEAN COMMUNITY (*DE MINIMIS*)
[2001] OJ C368/07

I

1. Article 81(1) prohibits agreements between undertakings which may affect trade between Member States and which have as their object or effect the prevention, restriction or distortion of competition within the common market. The Court of Justice of the European Communities

has clarified that this provision is not applicable where the impact of the agreement on intra-Community trade or on competition is not appreciable.

2. In this notice the Commission quantifies, with the help of market share thresholds, what is not an appreciable restriction of competition under Article 81 of the EC Treaty. This negative definition of appreciability does not imply that agreements between undertakings which exceed the thresholds set out in this notice appreciably restrict competition. Such agreements may still have only a negligible effect on competition and may therefore not be prohibited by Article 81(1).

3. Agreements may in addition not fall under Article 81(1) because they are not capable of appreciably affecting trade between Member States. This notice does not deal with this issue. It does not quantify what does not constitute an appreciable effect on trade. It is however acknowledged that agreements between small and medium-sized under-takings, as defined in the Annex to Commission Recommendation 96/280/EC, are rarely capable of appreciably affecting trade between Member States. Small and medium-sized undertakings are currently defined in that recommendation as undertakings which have fewer than 250 employees and have either an annual turnover not exceeding EUR 40 million or an annual balance-sheet total not exceeding EUR 27 million.

4. In cases covered by this notice the Commission will not institute proceedings either upon application or on its own initiative. Where undertakings assume in good faith that an agreement is covered by this notice, the Commission will not impose fines. Although not binding on them, this notice also intends to give guidance to the courts and authorities of the Member States in their application of Article 81.

5. This notice also applies to decisions by associations of undertakings and to concerted practices.

6. This notice is without prejudice to any interpretation of Article 81 which may be given by the Court of Justice or the Court of First Instance of the European Communities.

II

7. The Commission holds the view that agreements between undertakings which affect trade between Member States do not appreciably restrict competition within the meaning of Article 81(1):

    (a)   if the aggregate market share held by the parties to the agreement does not exceed 10% on any of the relevant markets affected by the agreement, where the agreement is made between undertakings which are actual or potential competitors on any of these markets (agreements between competitors); or

    (b)   if the market share held by each of the parties to the agreement does not exceed 15% on any of the relevant markets affected by the agreement, where the agreement is made between undertakings which are not actual or potential competitors on any of these markets (agreements between non-competitors).

    In cases where it is difficult to classify the agreement as either an agreement between competitors or an agreement between non-competitors the 10% threshold is applicable.

8. Where in a relevant market competition is restricted by the cumulative effect of agreements for the sale of goods or services entered into by different suppliers or distributors (cumulative foreclosure effect of parallel networks of agreements having similar effects on the market), the market share thresholds under point 7 are reduced to 5%, both for agreements between competitors and for agreements between non-competitors. Individual suppliers or distributors with a market share not exceeding 5% are in general not considered to contribute significantly to a cumulative foreclosure effect. A cumulative foreclosure effect is unlikely to exist if less than 30% of the relevant market is covered by parallel (networks of) agreements having similar effects.

9. The Commission also holds the view that agreements are not restrictive of competition if the market shares do not exceed the thresholds of respectively 10%, 15% and 5% set out in point 7 and 8 during two successive calendar years by more than 2 percentage points.

10. In order to calculate the market share, it is necessary to determine the relevant market. This consists of the relevant product market and the relevant geographic market. When defining the relevant market, reference should be had to the notice on the definition of the relevant market for the purposes of Community competition law. The market shares are to be calculated on the basis of sales value data or, where appropriate, purchase value data. If value data are not available, estimates based on other reliable market information, including volume data, may be used.

11. Points 7, 8 and 9 do not apply to agreements containing any of the following hardcore restrictions:

    (1)   as regards agreements between competitors as defined in point 7, restrictions which, directly or indirectly, in isolation or in combination with other factors under the control of the parties, have as their object (3):

        (a)   the fixing of prices when selling the products to third parties;

        (b)   the limitation of output or sales;

        (c)   the allocation of markets or customers;

    (2)   as regards agreements between non-competitors as defined in point 7, restrictions which, directly or indirectly, in isolation or in combination with other factors under the control of the parties, have as their object:

        (a)   the restriction of the buyer's ability to determine its sale price, without prejudice to the possibility of the supplier imposing a maximum sale price or recommending a sale price, provided that they do not amount to a fixed or minimum sale price as a result of pressure from, or incentives offered by, any of the parties;

        (b)   the restriction of the territory into which, or of the customers to whom, the buyer may sell the contract goods or services, except the following restrictions which are not hardcore:

          — the restriction of active sales into the exclusive territory or to an exclusive customer group reserved to the supplier or allocated by the supplier to another buyer, where such a restriction does not limit sales by the customers of the buyer,

          — the restriction of sales to end users by a buyer operating at the wholesale level of trade,

          — the restriction of sales to unauthorised distributors by the members of a selective distribution system, and

          — the restriction of the buyer's ability to sell components, supplied for the purposes of incorporation, to customers who would use them to manufacture the same type of goods as those produced by the supplier;

        (c)   the restriction of active or passive sales to end users by members of a selective distribution system operating at the retail level of trade, without prejudice to the possibility of prohibiting a member of the system from operating out of an unauthorised place of establishment;

        (d)   the restriction of cross-supplies between distributors within a selective distribution system, including between distributors operating at different levels of trade;

        (e)   the restriction agreed between a supplier of components and a buyer who incorporates those components, which limits the supplier's ability to sell the components as spare parts to end users or to repairers or other service providers not entrusted by the buyer with the repair or servicing of its goods;

    (3)   as regards agreements between competitors as defined in point 7, where the competitors operate, for the purposes of the agreement, at a different level of the production or distribution chain, any of the hardcore restrictions listed in paragraph (1) and (2) above.

12. (1)   For the purposes of this notice, the terms 'under-taking', 'party to the agreement', 'distributor', 'supplier' and 'buyer' shall include their respective connected undertakings.

(2)   'Connected undertakings' are:
- (a)   undertakings in which a party to the agreement, directly or indirectly:
  - — has the power to exercise more than half the voting rights, or
  - — has the power to appoint more than half the members of the supervisory board, board of management or bodies legally representing the undertaking, or
  - — has the right to manage the undertaking's affairs;
- (b)   undertakings which directly or indirectly have, over a party to the agreement, the rights or powers listed in (a);
- (c)   undertakings in which an undertaking referred to in (b) has, directly or indirectly, the rights or powers listed in (a);
- (d)   undertakings in which   a party to the agreement together with one or more of the undertakings referred to in (a), (b) or (c), or in which two or more of the latter undertakings, jointly have the rights or powers listed in (a);
- (e)   undertakings in which the rights or the powers listed in (a) are jointly held by:
  - — parties to the agreement or their respective connected undertakings referred to in (a) to (d), or
  - — one or more of the parties to the agreement or one or more of their connected undertakings referred to in (a) to (d) and one or more third parties.

(3)   For the purposes of paragraph 2(e), the market share held by these jointly held undertakings shall be apportioned equally to each undertaking having the rights or the powers listed in paragraph 2(a).

COMMISSION NOTICE ON THE DEFINITION OF RELEVANT MARKET FOR THE PURPOSES OF COMMUNITY COMPETITION LAW [1997] OJ C372/03

I INTRODUCTION

1.   The purpose of this notice is to provide guidance as to how the Commission applies the concept of relevant product and geographic market in its ongoing enforcement of Community competition law, in particular the application of Council Regulation No 17 and (EEC) No 4064/89, their equivalents in other sectoral applications such as transport, coal and steel, and agriculture, and the relevant provisions of the EEA Agreement. Throughout this notice, references to Articles 85 and 86 of the Treaty and to merger control are to be understood as referring to the equivalent provisions in the EEA Agreement and the ECSC Treaty.

2.   Market definition is a tool to identify and define the boundaries of competition between firms. It serves to establish the framework within which competition policy is applied by the Commission. The main purpose of market definition is to identify in a systematic way the competitive constraints that the undertakings involved face. The objective of defining a market in both its product and geographic dimension is to identify those actual competitors of the undertakings involved that are capable of constraining those undertakings' behaviour and of preventing them from behaving independently of effective competitive pressure. It is from this perspective that the market definition makes it possible inter alia to calculate market shares that would convey meaningful information regarding market power for the purposes of assessing dominance or for the purposes of applying Article 85.

3.   It follows from point 2 that the concept of 'relevant market' is different from other definitions of market often used in other contexts. For instance, companies often use the term 'market' to refer to the area where it sells its products or to refer broadly to the industry or sector where it belongs.

4.   The definition of the relevant market in both its product and its geographic dimensions often has a decisive influence on the assessment of a competition case. By rendering public the procedures which the Commission follows when considering market definition and by indicating the criteria and evidence on which it relies to reach a decision, the Commission

expects to increase the transparency of its policy and decision-making in the area of competition policy.

5.   Increased transparency will also result in companies and their advisers being able to better anticipate the possibility that the Commission may raise competition concerns in an individual case. Companies could, therefore, take such a possibility into account in their own internal decision-making when contemplating, for instance, acquisitions, the creation of joint ventures, or the establishment of certain agreements. It is also intended that companies should be in a better position to understand what sort of information the Commission considers relevant for the purposes of market definition.

6.   The Commission's interpretation of 'relevant market' is without prejudice to the interpretation which may be given by the Court of Justice or the Court of First Instance of the European Communities.

II DEFINITION OF RELEVANT MARKET

Definition of relevant product market and relevant geographic market

7.   The Regulations based on Article 85 and 86 of the Treaty, in particular in section 6 of Form A/B with respect to Regulation No 17, as well as in section 6 of Form CO with respect to Regulation (EEC) No 4064/89 on the control of concentrations having a Community dimension have laid down the following definitions, 'Relevant product markets' are defined as follows:

'A relevant product market comprises all those products and/or services which are regarded as interchangeable or substitutable by the consumer, by reason of the products' characteristics, their prices and their intended use'.

8.   'Relevant geographic markets' are defined as follows:

'The relevant geographic market comprises the area in which the undertakings concerned are involved in the supply and demand of products or services, in which the conditions of competition are sufficiently homogeneous and which can be distinguished from neighbouring areas because the conditions of competition are appreciably different in those area'.

9.   The relevant market within which to assess a given competition issue is therefore established by the combination of the product and geographic markets. The Commission interprets the definitions in paragraphs 7 an 8 (which reflect the case-law of the Court of Justice and the Court of First Instance as well as its own decision-making practice) according to the orientations defined in this notice.

Concept of relevant market and objectives of Community competition policy

10.   The concept of relevant market is closely related to the objectives pursued under Community competition policy. For example, under the Community's merger control, the objective in controlling structural changes in the supply of a product/service is to prevent the creation or reinforcement of a dominant position as a result of which effective competition would be significantly impeded in a substantial part of the common market. Under the Community's competition rules, a dominant position is such that a firm or group of firms would be in a position to behave to an appreciable extent independently of its competitors, customers and ultimately of its consumers. Such a position would usually arise when a firm or group of firms accounted for a large share of the supply in any given market, provided that other factors analysed in the assessment (such as entry barriers, customers' capacity to react, etc.) point in the same direction.

11.   The same approach is followed by the Commission in its application of Article 86 of the Treaty to firms that enjoy a single or collective dominant position. Within the meaning of Regulation No 17, the Commission has the power to investigate and bring to an end abuses of such a dominant position, which must also be defined by reference to the relevant market. Markets may also need to be defined in the application of Article 85 of the Treaty, in particular, in determining whether an appreciable restriction of competition exists or in establishing if the condition pursuant to Article 85(3)(b) for an exemption from the application of Article 85(1) is met.

12. The criteria for defining the relevant market are applied generally for the analysis of certain types of behaviour in the market and for the analysis of structural changes in the supply of products. This methodology, though, might lead to different results depending on the nature of the competition issue being examined. For instance, the scope of the geographic market might be different when analysing a concentration, where the analysis is essentially prospective, from an analysis of past behaviour. The different time horizon considered in each case might lead to the result that different geographic markets are defined for the same products depending on whether the Commission is examining a change in the structure of supply, such as a concentration or a cooperative joint venture, or examining issues relating to certain past behaviour.

Basic principles for market definition

Competitive constraints

13. Firms are subject to three main sources or competitive constraints: demand substitutability, supply substitutability and potential competition. From an economic point of view, for the definition of the relevant market, demand substitution constitutes the most immediate and effective disciplinary force on the suppliers of a given product, in particular in relation to their pricing decisions. A firm or a group of firms cannot have a significant impact on the prevailing conditions of sale, such as prices, if its customers are in a position to switch easily to available substitute products or to suppliers located elsewhere. Basically, the exercise of market definition consists in identifying the effective alternative sources of supply for the customers of the undertakings involved, in terms both of products/services and of geographic location of suppliers.

14. The competitive constraints arising from supply side substitutability other then those described in paragraphs 20 to 23 and from potential competition are in general less immediate and in any case require an analysis of additional factors. As a result such constraints are taken into account at the assessment stage of competition analysis.

Demand substitution

15. The assessment of demand substitution entails a determination of the range of products which are viewed as substitutes by the consumer. One way of making this determination can be viewed as a speculative experiment, postulating a hypothetical small, lasting change in relative prices and evaluating the likely reactions of customers to that increase. The exercise of market definition focuses on prices for operational and practical purposes, and more precisely on demand substitution arising from small, permanent changes in relative prices. This concept can provide clear indications as to the evidence that is relevant in defining markets.

16. Conceptually, this approach means that, starting from the type of products that the undertakings involved sell and the area in which they sell them, additional products and areas will be included in, or excluded from, the market definition depending on whether competition from these other products and areas affect or restrain sufficiently the pricing of the parties' products in the short term.

17. The question to be answered is whether the parties' customers would switch to readily available substitutes or to suppliers located elsewhere in response to a hypothetical small (in the range 5% to 10%) but permanent relative price increase in the products and areas being considered. If substitution were enough to make the price increase unprofitable because of the resulting loss of sales, additional substitutes and areas are included in the relevant market. This would be done until the set of products and geographical areas is such that small, permanent increases in relative prices would be profitable. The equivalent analysis is applicable in cases concerning the concentration of buying power, where the starting point would then be the supplier and the price test serves to identify the alternative distribution channels or outlets for the supplier's products. In the application of these principles, careful account should be taken of certain particular situations as described within paragraphs 56 and 58.

18. A practical example of this test can be provided by its application to a merger of, for instance, soft-drink bottlers. An issue to examine in such a case would be to decide whether different

flavours of soft drinks belong to the same market. In practice, the question to address would be whether consumers of flavour A would switch to other flavours when confronted with a permanent price increase of 5% to 10% for flavour A. If a sufficient number of consumers would switch to, say, flavour B, to such an extent that the price increase for flavour A would not be profitable owing to the resulting loss of sales, then the market would comprise at least flavours A and B. The process would have to be extended in addition to other available flavours until a set of products is identified for which a price rise would not induce a sufficient substitution in demand.

19. Generally, and in particular for the analysis of merger cases, the price to take into account will be the prevailing market price. This may not be the case where the prevailing price has been determined in the absence of sufficient competition. In particular for the investigation of abuses of dominant positions, the fact that the prevailing price might already have been substantially increased will be taken into account.

Supply substitution

20. Supply-side substitutability may also be taken into account when defining markets in those situations in which its effects are equivalent to those of demand substitution in terms of effectiveness and immediacy. This means that suppliers are able to switch production to the relevant products and market them in the short term without incurring significant additional costs or risks in response to small and permanent changes in relative prices. When these conditions are met, the additional production that is put on the market will have a disciplinary effect on the competitive behaviour of the companies involved. Such an impact in terms of effectiveness and immediacy is equivalent to the demand substitution effect.

21. These situations typically arise when companies market a wide range of qualities or grades of one product; even if, for a given final customer or group of consumers, the different qualities are not substitutable, the different qualities will be grouped into one product market, provided that most of the suppliers are able to offer and sell the various qualities immediately and without the significant increases in costs described above. In such cases, the relevant product market will encompass all products that are substitutable in demand and supply, and the current sales of those products will be aggregated so as to give the total value or volume of the market. The same reasoning may lead to group different geographic areas.

22. A practical example of the approach to supply-side substitutability when defining product markets is to be found in the case of paper. Paper is usually supplied in a range of different qualities, from standard writing paper to high quality papers to be used, for instance, to publish art books. From a demand point of view, different qualities of paper cannot be used for any given use, i.e. an art book or a high quality publication cannot be based on lower quality papers. However, paper plants are prepared to manufacture the different qualities, and production can be adjusted with negligible costs and in a short time-frame. In the absence of particular difficulties in distribution, paper manufacturers are able therefore, to compete for orders of the various qualities, in particular if orders are placed with sufficient lead time to allow for modification of production plans. Under such circumstances, the Commission would not define a separate market for each quality of paper and its respective use. The various qualities of paper are included in the relevant market, and their sales added up to estimate total market value and volume.

23. When supply-side substitutability would entail the need to adjust significantly existing tangible and intangible assets, additional investments, strategic decisions or time delays, it will not be considered at the stage of market definition. Examples where supply-side substitution did not induce the Commission to enlarge the market are offered in the area of consumer products, in particular for branded beverages. Although bottling plants may in principle bottle different beverages, there are costs and lead times involved (in terms of advertising, product testing and distribution) before the products can actually be sold. In these cases, the effects of supply-side substitutability and other forms of potential competition would then be examined at a later stage.

Potential competition

24. The third source of competitive constraint, potential competition, is not taken into account when defining markets, since the conditions under which potential competition will actually represent an effective competitive constraint depend on the analysis of specific factors and circumstances related to the conditions of entry. If required, this analysis is only carried out at a subsequent stage, in general once the position of the companies involved in the relevant market has already been ascertained, and when such position gives rise to concerns from a competition point of view.

III EVIDENCE RELIED ON TO DEFINE RELEVANT MARKETS

The process of defining the relevant market in practice

Product dimension

25. There is a range of evidence permitting an assessment of the extent to which substitution would take place. In individual cases, certain types of evidence will be determinant, depending very much on the characteristics and specificity of the industry and products or services that are being examined. The same type of evidence may be of no importance in other cases. In most cases, a decision will have to be based on the consideration of a number of criteria and different items of evidence. The Commission follows an open approach to empirical evidence, aimed at making an effective use of all available information which may be relevant in individual cases. The Commission does not follow a rigid hierarchy of different sources of information or types of evidence.

26. The process of defining relevant markets may be summarised as follows: on the basis of the preliminary information available or information submitted by the undertakings involved, the Commission will usually be in a position to broadly establish the possible relevant markets within which, for instance, a concentration or a restriction of competition has to be assessed. In general, and for all practical purposes when handling individual cases, the question will usually be to decide on a few alternative possible relevant markets. For instance, with respect to the product market, the issue will often be to establish whether product A and product B belong or do not belong to the same product market. It is often the case that the inclusion of product B would be enough to remove any competition concerns.

27. In such situations it is not necessary to consider whether the market includes additional products, or to reach a definitive conclusion on the precise product market. If under the conceivable alternative market definitions the operation in question does not raise competition concerns, the question of market definition will be left open, reducing thereby the burden on companies to supply information.

Geographic dimension

28. The Commission's approach to geographic market definition might be summarised as follows: it will take a preliminary view of the scope of the geographic market on the basis of broad indications as to the distribution of market shares between the parties and their competitors, as well as a preliminary analysis of pricing and price differences at national and Community or EEA level. This initial view is used basically as a working hypothesis to focus the Commission's enquiries for the purposes of arriving at a precise geographic market definition.

29. The reasons behind any particular configuration of prices and market shares need to be explored. Companies might enjoy high market shares in their domestic markets just because of the weight of the past, and conversely, a homogeneous presence of companies throughout the EEA might be consistent with national or regional geographic markets. The initial working hypothesis will therefore be checked against an analysis of demand characteristics (importance of national or local preferences, current patterns of purchases of customers, product differentiation/brands, other) in order to establish whether companies in different areas do indeed constitute a real alternative source of supply for consumers. The theoretical experiment is again based on substitution arising from changes in relative prices, and the question to answer is again whether the customers of the parties would switch their orders to companies located elsewhere in the short term and at a negligible cost.

30. If necessary, a further check on supply factors will be carried out to ensure that those companies located in differing areas do not face impediments in developing their sales on competitive terms throughout the whole geographic market. This analysis will include an examination of requirements for a local presence in order to sell in that area the conditions of access to distribution channels, costs associated with setting up a distribution network, and the presence or absence of regulatory barriers arising from public procurement, price regulations, quotas and tariffs limiting trade or production, technical standards, monopolies, freedom of establishment, requirements for administrative authorisations, packaging regulations, etc. In short, the Commission will identify possible obstacles and barriers isolating companies located in a given area from the competitive pressure of companies located outside that area, so as to determine the precise degree of market interpenetration at national, European or global level.

31. The actual pattern and evolution of trade flows offers useful supplementary indications as to the economic importance of each demand or supply factor mentioned above, and the extent to which they may or may not constitute actual barriers creating different geographic markets. The analysis of trade flows will generally address the question of transport costs and the extent to which these may hinder trade between different areas, having regard to plant location, costs of production and relative price levels.

Market integration in the Community

32. Finally, the Commission also takes into account the continuing process of market integration, in particular in the Community, when defining geographic markets, especially in the area of concentrations and structural joint ventures. The measures adopted and implemented in the internal market programme to remove barriers to trade and further integrate the Community markets cannot be ignored when assessing the effects on competition of a concentration or a structural joint venture. A situation where national markets have been artifically isolated from each other because of the existence of legislative barriers that have now been removed will generally lead to a cautious assessment of past evidence regarding prices, market shares or trade patterns. A process of market integration that would, in the short term, lead to wider geographic markets may therefore be taken into consideration when defining the geographic market for the purposes of assessing concentrations and joint ventures.

The process of gathering evidence

33. When a precise market definition is deemed necessary, the Commission will often contact the main customers and the main companies in the industry to enquire into their views about the boundaries of product and geographic markets and to obtain the necessary factual evidence to reach a conclusion. The Commission might also contact the relevant professional associations, and companies active in upstream markets, so as to be able to define, in so far as necessary, separate product and geographic markets, for different levels of production or distribution of the products/services in question. It might also request additional information to the undertakings involved.

34. Where appropriate, the Commission will address written requests for information to the market players mentioned above. These requests will usually include questions relating to the perceptions of companies about reactions to hypothetical price increases and their views of the boundaries of the relevant market. They will also ask for provision of the factual information the Commission deems necessary to reach a conclusion on the extent of the relevant market. The Commission might also discuss with marketing directors or other officers of those companies to gain a better understanding on how negotiations between suppliers and customers take place and better understand issues relating to the definition of the relevant market. Where appropriate, they might also carry out visits or inspections to the premises of the parties, their customers and/or their competitors, in order to better understand how products are manufactured and sold.

35. The type of evidence relevant to reach a conclusion as to the product market can be categorised as follows:

Evidence to define markets — product dimension

36. An analysis of the product characteristics and its intended use allows the Commission, as a first step, to limit the field of investigation of possible substitutes. However, product characteristics and intended use are insufficient to show whether two products are demand substitutes. Functional interchangeability or similarity in characteristics may not, in themselves, provide sufficient criteria, because the responsiveness of customers to relative price changes may be determinded by other considerations as well. For example, there may be different competitive contraints in the original equipment market for car components and in spare parts, thereby leading to a separate delineation of two relevant markets. Conversely, differences in product characteristics are not in themselves sufficient to exclude demand substitutability, since this will depend to a large extent on how customers value different characteristics.

37. The type of evidence the Commission considers relevant to assess whether two products are demand substitutes can be categorised as follows:

38. Evidence of substitution in the recent past. In certain cases, it is possible to analyse evidence relating to recent past events or shocks in the market that offer actual examples of substitution between two products. When available, this sort of information will normally be fundamental for market definition. If there have been changes in relative prices in the past (all else being equal), the reactions in terms of quantities demanded will be determinant in establishing substitutability. Launches of new products in the past can also offer useful information, when it is possible to precisely analyse which products have lost sales to the new product.

39. There are a number of quantitative tests that have specifically been designed for the purpose of delineating markets. These tests consist of various econometric and statistical approaches estimates of elasticities and cross-price elasticities for the demand of a product, tests based on similarity of price movements over time, the analysis of causality between price series and similarity of price levels and/or their convergence. The Commission takes into account the available quantitative evidence capable of withstanding rigorous scrutiny for the purposes of establishing patterns of substitution in the past.

40. Views of customers and competitors. The Commission often contacts the main customers and competitors of the companies involved in its enquiries, to gather their views on the boundaries of the product market as well as most of the factual information it requires to reach a conclusion on the scope of the market. Reasoned answers of customers and competitors as to what would happen if relative prices for the candidate products were to increase in the candidate geographic area by a small amount (for instance of 5% to 10%) are taken into account when they are sufficiently backed by factual evidence.

41. Consumer preferences. In the case of consumer goods, it may be difficult for the Commission to gather the direct views of end consumers about substitute products. Marketing studies that companies have commissioned in the past and that are used by companies in their own decision-making as to pricing of their products and/or marketing actions may provide useful information for the Commission's delineation of the relevant market. Consumer surveys on usage patterns and attitudes, data from consumer's purchasing patterns, the views expressed by retailers and more generally, market research studies submitted by the parties and their competitors are taken into account to establish whether an economically significant proportion of consumers consider two products as substitutable, also taking into account the importance of brands for the products in question. The methodology followed in consumer surveys carried out ad hoc by the undertakings involved or their competitors for the purposes of a merger procedure or a procedure pursuant to Regulation No 17 will usually be scrutinised with utmost care. Unlike preexisting studies, they have not been prepared in the normal course of business for the adoption of business decisions.

42. Barriers and costs associated with switching demand to potential substitutes. There are a number of barriers and costs that might prevent the Commission from considering two prima facie demand substitutes as belonging to one single product market. It is not possible to provide an exhaustive list of all the possible barriers to substitution and of switching costs. These barriers or obstacles might have a wide range of origins, and in its decisions, the

Commission has been confronted with regulatory barriers or other forms of State intervention, constraints arising in downstream markets, need to incur specific capital investment or loss in current output in order to switch to alternative inputs, the location of customers, specific investment in production process, learning and human capital investment, retooling costs or other investments, uncertainty about quality and reputation of unknown suppliers, and others.

43. Different categories of customers and price discrimination. The extent of the product market might be narrowed in the presence of distinct groups of customers. A distinct group of customers for the relevant product may constitute a narrower, distinct market when such ha group could be subject to price discrimination. This will usually be the case when two conditions are met: (a) it is possible to identify clearly which group an individual customer belongs to at the moment of selling the relevant products to him, and (b) trade among customers or arbitrage by third parties should not be feasible.

Evidence for defining markets — geographic dimension

44. The type of evidence the Commission considers relevant to reach a conclusion as to the geographic market can be categorised as follows:

45. Past evidence of diversion of orders to other areas. In certain cases, evidence on changes in prices between different areas and consequent reactions by customers might be available. Generally, the same quantitative tests used for product market definition might as well be used in geographic market definition, bearing in mind that international comparisons of prices might be more complex due to a number of factors such as exchange rate movements, taxation and product differentiation.

46. Basic demand characteristics. The nature of demand for the relevant product may in itself determine the scope of the geographical market. Factors such as national preferences or preferences for national brands, language, culture and life style, and the need for a local presence have a strong potential to limit the geographic scope of competition.

47. Views of customers and competitors. Where appropriate, the Commission will contact the main customers and competitors of the parties in its enquiries, to gather their views on the boundaries of the geographic market as well as most of the factual information it requires to reach a conclusion on the scope of the market when they are sufficiently backed by factual evidence.

48. Current geographic pattern of purchases. An examination of the customers' current geographic pattern of purchases provides useful evidence as to the possible scope of the geographic market. When customers purchase from companies located anywhere in the Community or the EEA on similar terms, or they procure their supplies through effective tendering procedures in which companies from anywhere in the Community or the EEA submit bids, usually the geographic market will be considered to be Community-wide.

49. Trade flows/pattern of shipments. When the number of customers is so large that it is not possible to obtain through them a clear picture of geographic purchasing patterns, information on trade flows might be used alternatively, provided that the trade statistics are available with a sufficient degree of detail for the relevant products. Trade flows, and above all, the rationale behind trade flows provide useful insights and information for the purpose of establishing the scope of the geographic market but are not in themselves conclusive.

50. Barriers and switching costs associated to divert orders to companies located in other areas. The absence of trans-border purchases or trade flows, for instance, does not necessarily mean that the market is at most national in scope. Still, barriers isolating the national market have to identified before it is concluded that the relevant geographic market in such a case is national. Perhaps the clearest obstacle for a customer to divert its orders to other areas is the impact of transport costs and transport restrictions arising from legislation or from the nature of the relevant products. The impact of transport costs will usually limit the scope of the geographic market for bulky, low-value products, bearing in mind that a transport disadvantage might also be compensated by a comparative advantage in other costs (labour costs or raw materials). Access to distribution in a given area, regulatory barriers still existing in certain sectors, quotas and custom tariffs might also constitute barriers isolating a geographic area from the competitive pressure of companies located outside that area. Significant switching costs in

procuring supplies from companies located in other countries constitute additional sources of such barriers.

51. On the basis of the evidence gathered, the Commission will then define a geographic market that could range from a local dimension to a global one, and there are examples of both local and global markets in past decisions of the Commission.

52. The paragraphs above describe the different factors which might be relevant to define markets. This does not imply that in each individual case it will be necessary to obtain evidence and assess each of these factors. Often in practice the evidence provided by a susbset of these factors will be sufficient to reach a conclusion, as shown in the past decisional practice of the Commission.

IV CALCULATION OF MARKET SHARE

53. The definition of the relevant market in both its product and geographic dimensions allows the identification the suppliers and the customers/consumers active on that market. On that basis, a total market size and market shares for each supplier can be calculated on the basis of their sales of the relevant products in the relevant area. In practice, the total market size and market shares are often available from market sources, i.e. companies' estimates, studies commissioned from industry consultants and/or trade associations. When this is not the case, or when available estimates are not reliable, the Commission will usually ask each supplier in the relevant market to provide its own sales in order to calculate total market size and market shares.

54. If sales are usually the reference to calculate market shares, there are nevertheless other indications that, depending on the specific products or industry in question, can offer useful information such as, in particular, capacity, the number of players in bidding markets, units of fleet as in aerospace, or the reserves held in the case of sectors such as mining.

55. As a rule of thumb, both volume sales and value sales provide useful information. In cases of differentiated products, sales in value and their associated market share will usually be considered to better reflect the relative position and strength of each supplier.

V ADDITIONAL CONSIDERATIONS

56. There are certain areas where the application of the principles above has to be undertaken with care. This is the case when considering primary and secondary markets, in particular, when the behaviour of undertakings at a point in time has to be analysed pursuant to Article 86. The method of defining markets in these cases is the same, i.e. assessing the responses of customers based on their purchasing decisions to relative price changes, but taking into account as well, constraints on substitution imposed by conditions in the connected markets. A narrow definition of market for secondary products, for instance, spare parts, may result when compatibility with the primary product is important. Problems of finding compatible secondary products together with the existence of high prices and a long lifetime of the primary products may render relative price increases of secondary products profitable. A different market definition may result if significant substitution between secondary products is possible or if the characteristics of the primary products make quick and direct consumer responses to relative price increases of the secondary products feasible.

57. In certain cases, the existence of chains of substitution might lead to the definition of a relevant market where products or areas at the extreme of the market are not directly substitutable. An example might be provided by the geographic dimension of a product with significant transport costs. In such cases, deliveries from a given plant are limited to a certain area around each plant by the impact of transport costs. In principle, such an area could constitute the relevant geographic market. However, if the distribution of plants is such that there are considerable overlaps between the areas around different plants, it is possible that the pricing of those products will be constrained by a chain substitution effect, and lead to the definition of a broader geographic market. The same reasoning may apply if product B is a demand substitute for products A and C. Even if products A and C are not direct demand substitutes, they might be found to be in the same relevant product market since their respective pricing might be constrained by substitution to B.

58. From a practical perspective, the concept of chains of substitution has to be corroborated by actual evidence, for instance related to price interdependence at the extremes of the chains of substitution, in order to lead to an extension of the relevant market in an individual case. Price levels at the extremes of the chains would have to be of the same magnitude as well.

FREE MOVEMENT OF GOODS

COMMISSION DIRECTIVE (EEC) No 70/50 of 22 DECEMBER 1969
based on the provisions of Article 33(7), on the abolition of measures which have an effect equivalent to quantitative restrictions on imports and are not covered by other provisions adopted in pursuance of the EEC Treaty
[1970] OJ L13/29, 17

Article 1

The purpose of this Directive is to abolish the measures referred to in Articles 2 and 3, which were operative at the date of entry into force of the EEC Treaty.

Article 2

1. This Directive covers measures, other than those applicable equally to domestic or imported products, which hinder imports which could otherwise take place, including measures which make importation more difficult or costly than the disposal of domestic production.

2. In particular, it covers measures which make imports or the disposal, at any marketing stage, of imported products subject to a condition — other than a formality — which is required in respect of imported products only, or a condition differing from that required for domestic products and more difficult to satisfy. Equally, it covers, in particular, measures which favour domestic products or grant them a preference, other than an aid, to which conditions may or may not be attached.

3. The measures referred to must be taken to include those measures which:

    (a) lay down, for imported products only, minimum or maximum prices below or above which imports are prohibited, reduced or made subject to conditions liable to hinder importation;

    (b) lay down less favourable prices for imported products than for domestic products;

    (c) fix profit margins or any other price components for imported products only or fix these differently for domestic products and for imported products, to the detriment of the latter;

    (d) preclude any increase in the price of the imported product corresponding to the supplementary costs and charges inherent in importation;

    (e) fix the prices of products solely on the basis of the cost price or the quality of domestic products at such a level as to create a hindrance to importation;

    (f) lower the value of an imported product, in particular by causing a reduction in its intrinsic value, or increase its costs;

    (g) make access of imported products to the domestic market conditional upon having an agent or representative in the territory of the importing Member State;

    (h) lay down conditions of payment in respect of imported products only, or subject imported products to conditions which are different from those laid down for domestic products and more difficult to satisfy;

    (i) require, for imports only, the giving of guarantees or making of payments on account;

    (j) subject imported products only to conditions, in respect, in particular of shape, size, weight, composition, presentation, identification or putting up, or subject imported products to conditions which are different from those for domestic products and more difficult to satisfy;

    (k) hinder the purchase by private individuals of imported products only, or encourage, require or give preference to the purchase of domestic products only;

    (l) totally or partially preclude the use of national facilities or equipment in respect of imported products only, or totally or partially confine the use of such facilities or equipment to domestic products only;

    (m) prohibit or limit publicity in respect of imported products only, or totally or partially confine publicity to domestic products only;

    (n) prohibit, limit or require stocking in respect of imported products only; totally or partially confine the use of stocking facilities to domestic products only, or make the stocking of imported products subject to conditions which are different from those required for domestic products and more difficult to satisfy;

(o)   make importation subject to the granting of reciprocity by one or more Member States;

(p)   prescribe that imported products are to conform, totally or partially, to rules other than those of the importing country;

(q)   specify time limits for imported products which are insufficient or excessive in relation to the normal course of the various transactions to which these time limits apply;

(r)   subject imported products to controls or, other than those inherent in the customs clearance procedure, to which domestic products are not subject or which are stricter in respect of imported products than they are in respect of domestic products, without this being necessary in order to ensure equivalent protection;

(s)   confine names which are not indicative of origin or source to domestic products only.

Article 3

This Directive also covers measures governing the marketing of products which deal, in particular, with shape, size, weight, composition, presentation, identification or putting up and which are equally applicable to domestic and imported products, where the restrictive effect of such measures on the free movement of goods exceeds the effects intrinsic to trade rules.

This is the case, in particular, where:

— the restrictive effects on the free movement of goods are out of proportion to their purpose;

— the same objective can be attained by other means which are less of a hindrance to trade.

COMMISSION PRACTICE NOTE ON IMPORT PROHIBITIONS

Communication from the Commission concerning the consequences of the judgment given by the Court of Justice on 20 February 1979 in Case 120/78 ('Cassis De Dijon') [1980] OJ C256/2

The following is the text of a letter which has been sent to the Member States; the European Parliament and the Council have also been notified of it.

In the Commission's Communication of 6 November 1978 on 'Safeguarding free trade within the Community', it was emphasised that the free movement of goods is being affected by a growing number of restrictive measures.

The judgment delivered by the Court of Justice on 20 February 1979 in Case 120/78 (the 'Cassis de Dijon' case), and recently reaffirmed in the judgment of 26 June 1980 in Case 788/79, has given the Commission some interpretative guidance enabling it to monitor more strictly the application of the Treaty rules on the free movement of goods, particularly Articles 30 to 36 of the EEC Treaty.

The Court gives a very general definition of the barriers to free trade which are prohibited by the provisions of Article 30 et seq. of the EEC Treaty. These are taken to include 'any national measure capable of hindering, directly or indirectly, actually or potentially, intra-Community trade'.

In its judgment of 20 February 1979 the Court indicates the scope of this definition as it applies to technical and commercial rules.

Any product lawfully produced and marketed in one Member State must, in principle, be admitted to the market of any other Member State.

Technical and commercial rules, even those equally applicable to national and imported products, may create barriers to trade only where those rules are necessary to satisfy mandatory requirements and to serve a purpose which is in the general interest and for which they are an essential guarantee. This purpose must be such as to take precedence over the requirements of the free movement of goods, which constitutes one of the fundamental rules of the Community.

The conclusions in terms of policy which the Commission draws from this new guidance are set out below.

— Whereas Member States may, with respect to domestic products and in the absence of relevant Community provisions, regulate the terms on which such products are marketed, the case is different for products imported from other Member States.

Any product imported from another Member State must in principle be admitted to the territory of the importing Member State if it has been lawfully produced, that is, conforms to the rules and processes of manufacture that are customarily and traditionally accepted in the exporting country, and is marketed in the territory of the latter.

This principle implies that Member States, when drawing up commercial or technical rules liable to affect the free movement of goods, may not take an exclusively national viewpoint and take account only of requirements confined to domestic products. The proper functioning of the common market demands that each Member State also give consideration to the legitimate requirements of the other Member States.

- — Only under very strict conditions does the Court accept exceptions to this principle; barriers to trade resulting from differences between commercial and technical rules are only admissible:
- — if the rules are necessary, that is appropriate and not excessive, in order to satisfy mandatory requirements (public health, protection of consumers or the environment, the fairness of commercial transactions, etc.);
- — if the rules serve a purpose in the general interest which is compelling enough to justify an exception to a fundamental rule of the Treaty such as the free movement of goods;
- — if the rules are essential for such a purpose to be attained, i.e., are the means which are the most appropriate and at the same time least hinder trade. The Court's interpretation has induced the Commission to set out a number of guidelines.
- — The principles deduced by the Court imply that a Member State may not in principle prohibit the sale in its territory of a product lawfully produced and marketed in another Member State even if the product is produced according to technical or quality requirements which differ from those imposed on its domestic products. Where a product 'suitably and satisfactorily' fulfils the legitimate objective of a Member State's own rules (public safety, protection of the consumer or the environment, etc.), the importing country cannot justify prohibiting its sale in its territory by claiming that the way it fulfils the objective is different from that imposed on domestic products.

In such a case, an absolute prohibition of sale could not be considered 'necessary' to satisfy a 'mandatory requirement' because it would not be an 'essential guarantee' in the sense defined in the Court's judgment.

The Commission will therefore have to tackle a whole body of commercial rules which lay down that products manufactured and marketed in one Member State must fulfil technical or qualitative conditions in order to be admitted to the market of another and specifically in all cases where the trade barriers occasioned by such rules are inadmissible according to the very strict criteria set out by the Court.

The Commission is referring in particular to rules covering the composition, designation, presentation and packaging of products as well as rules requiring compliance with certain technical standards.

- — The Commission's work of harmonisation will henceforth have to be directed mainly at national laws having an impact on the functioning of the common market where barriers to trade to be removed arise from national provisions which are admissible under the criteria set by the Court.

The Commission will be concentrating on sectors deserving priority because of their economic relevance to the creation of a single internal market.

To forestall later difficulties, the Commission will be informing Member States of potential objections, under the terms of Community law, to provisions they may be considering introducing which come to the attention of the Commission.

It will be producing suggestions soon on the procedures to be followed in such cases.

The Commission is confident that this approach will secure greater freedom of trade for the Community's manufacturers, so strengthening the industrial base of the Community, while meeting the expectations of consumers.

COUNCIL REGULATION (EC) No 2679/98 of 7 DECEMBER 1998
on the functioning of the internal market in relation to the free movement of
goods among the Member States
[1998] OJ L337/8

Article 1

For the purpose of this Regulation:

1. the term 'obstacle' shall mean an obstacle to the free movement of goods among Member States which is attributable to a Member State, whether it involves action or inaction on its part, which may constitute a breach of Articles 30 to 36 of the Treaty and which:

    (a) leads to serious disruption of the free movement of goods by physically or otherwise preventing, delaying or diverting their import into, export from or transport across a Member State,

    (b) causes serious loss to the individuals affected, and

    (c) requires immediate action in order to prevent any continuation, increase or intensification of the disruption or loss in question;

2. the term 'inaction' shall cover the case when the competent authorities of a Member State, in the presence of an obstacle caused by actions taken by private individuals, fail to take all necessary and proportionate measures within their powers with a view to removing the obstacle and ensuring the free movement of goods in their territory.

Article 2

This Regulation may not be interpreted as affecting in any way the exercise of fundamental rights as recognised in Member States, including the right or freedom to strike. These rights may also include the right or freedom to take other actions covered by the specific industrial relations systems in Member States.

Article 3

1. When an obstacle occurs or when there is a threat thereof

    (a) any Member State (whether or not it is the Member State concerned) which has relevant information shall immediately transmit it to the Commission, and

    (b) the Commission shall immediately transmit to the Member States that information and any information from any other source which it may consider relevant.

2. The Member State concerned shall respond as soon as possible to requests for information from the Commission and from other Member States concerning the nature of the obstacle or threat and the action which it has taken or proposes to take. Information exchange between Member States shall also be transmitted to the Commission.

Article 4

1. When an obstacle occurs, and subject to Article 2, the Member State concerned shall

    (a) take all necessary and proportionate measures so that the free movement of goods is assured in the territory of the Member State in accordance with the Treaty, and

    (b) inform the Commission of the actions which its authorities have taken or intend to take.

2. The Commission shall immediately transmit the information received under paragraph 1(b) to the other Member States.

Article 5

1. Where the Commission considers that an obstacle is occurring in a Member State, it shall notify the Member State concerned of the reasons that have led the Commission to such a conclusion and shall request the Member State to take all necessary and proportionate measures to remove the said obstacle within a period which it shall determine with reference to the urgency of the case.

2. In reaching its conclusion, the Commission shall have regard to Article 2.

3. The Commission may publish in the Official Journal of the European Communities the text of the notification which it has sent to the Member State concerned and shall immediately transmit the text to any party which requests it.

4. The Member State shall, within five working days of receipt of the text, either:
   — inform the Commission of the steps which it has taken or intends to take to implement paragraph 1, or
   — communicate a reasoned submission as to why there is no obstacle constituting a breach of Articles 30 to 36 of the Treaty.
5. In exceptional cases, the Commission may allow an extension of the deadline mentioned in paragraph 4 if the Member State submits a duly substantiated request and the grounds cited are deemed acceptable.

FREE MOVEMENT OF PERSONS

COUNCIL REGULATION (EEC) No 1612/68 of 15 OCTOBER 1968
on freedom of movement for workers within the Community as amended by
Regulation 312/76
[1968] OJ L257/2, 475

PART I   EMPLOYMENT AND WORKERS' FAMILIES
TITLE I   ELIGIBILITY FOR EMPLOYMENT

Article 1

1.   Any national of a Member State, shall, irrespective of his place of residence, have the right to take up an activity as an employed person, and to pursue such activity, within the territory of another Member State in accordance with the provisions laid down by law, regulation or administrative action governing the employment of nationals of that State.

2.   He shall, in particular, have the right to take up available employment in the territory of another Member State with the same priority as nationals of the State.

Article 2

Any national of a Member State and any employer pursuing an activity in the territory of a Member State may exchange their applications for and offers of employment, and may conclude and perform contracts of employment in accordance with the provisions in force laid down by law, regulation or administrative action, without any discrimination resulting therefrom.

Article 3

1.   Under this Regulation, provisions laid down by law, regulation or administrative action or administrative practices of a Member State shall not apply:
   — where they limit application for and offers of employment, or the right of foreign nationals to take up and pursue employment or subject these to conditions not applicable in respect of their own nationals; or
   — where, though applicable irrespective of nationality, their exclusive or principal aim or effect is to keep nationals of other Member States away from the employment offered.
   This provision shall not apply to conditions relating to linguistic knowledge required by reason of the nature of the post to be filled.

2.   There shall be included in particular among the provisions or practices of a Member State referred to in the first subparagraph of paragraph 1 those which:
   (a)   prescribe a special recruitment procedure for foreign nationals;
   (b)   limit or restrict the advertising or vacancies in the press or through any other medium or subject it to conditions other than those applicable in respect of employers pursuing their activities in the territory of that Member State;
   (c)   subject eligibility for employment to conditions of registration with employment offices or impede recruitment of individual workers, where persons who do not reside in the territory of that State are concerned.

Article 4

1.   Provisions laid down by law, regulation or administrative action of the Member States which restrict by number of percentage the employment of foreign nationals in any undertaking, branch of activity or region, or at a national level, shall not apply to nationals of the other Member States.

2.   When in a Member State the granting of any benefit to undertakings is subject to a minimum percentage of national workers being employed, nationals of the other Member States shall be counted as national workers, subject to the provisions of the Council Directive of 15 October 1963.

Article 5

A national of a Member State who seeks employment in the territory of another Member State shall receive the same assistance there as that afforded by the employment offices in that State to their own nationals seeking employment.

Article 6

1. The engagement and recruitment of a national of one Member State for a post in another Member State shall not depend on medical, vocational or other criteria which are discriminatory on grounds of nationality by comparison with those applied to nationals of the other Member State who wish to pursue the same activity.

2. Nevertheless, a national who holds an offer in his name from an employer in a Member State other than that of which he is a national may have to undergo a vocational test, if the employer expressly requests this when making his offer of employment.

TITLE II   EMPLOYMENT AND EQUALITY OF TREATMENT

Article 7

1. A worker who is a national of a Member State may not, in the territory of another Member State, be treated differently from national workers by reason of his nationality in respect of any conditions of employment and work, in particular as regards remuneration, dismissal, and should he become unemployed, reinstatement or reemployment.

2. He shall enjoy the same social and tax advantages as national workers.

3. He shall also, by virtue of the same right and under the same conditions as national workers, have access to training in vocational schools and retraining centres.

4. Any clause of a collective or individual agreement or of any other collective regulation concerning eligibility for employment, employment, remuneration and other conditions of work or dismissal shall be null and void in so far as it lays down or authorises discriminatory conditions in respect of workers who are nationals of the other Member States.

Article 8

1. A worker who is a national of a Member State and who is employed in the territory of another Member State shall enjoy equality of treatment as regards membership of trade unions and the exercise of rights attaching thereto, including the right to vote and to be eligible for the administration or management posts of a trade union; he may be excluded from taking part in the management of bodies governed by public law and from holding an office governed by public law. Furthermore, he shall have the right of eligibility for workers' representative bodies in the undertaking. The provisions of this Article shall not affect laws or regulations in certain Member States which grant more extensive rights to workers coming from the other Member States.

2. ...

Article 9

1. A worker who is a national of a Member State and who is employed in the territory of another Member State shall enjoy all the rights and benefits accorded to national workers in matters of housing, including ownership of the housing he needs.

2. Such worker may, with the same right as nationals, put his name down on the housing lists in the region in which he is employed, where such lists exist; he shall enjoy the resultant benefits and priorities.

   If his family has remained in the country whence he came, they shall be considered for this purpose as residing in the said region, where national workers benefit from a similar presumption.

TITLE III   WORKERS' FAMILIES

Article 12

The children of a national of a Member State who is or has been employed in the territory of another Member State shall be admitted to that State's general educational, apprenticeship and vocational training courses under the same conditions as the nationals of that State, if such children are residing in its territory.

Member States shall encourage all efforts to enable such children to attend these courses under the best possible conditions.

COUNCIL DIRECTIVE (EEC) No 77/249 of 22 MARCH 1977
to facilitate the effective exercise by lawyers of freedom to provide services
[1977] OJ L78/17

Article 1

1. This Directive shall apply, within the limits and under the conditions laid down herein, to the activities of lawyers pursued by way of provision of services.

    Notwithstanding anything contained in this Directive, Member States may reserve to prescribed categories of lawyers the preparation of formal documents for obtaining title to administer estates of deceased persons, and the drafting of formal documents creating or transferring interests in land.

2. 'Lawyers' means any person entitled to pursue his professional activities under one of the following designations:

Austria:	Rechtsanwalt
Belgium:	Avocat/Advocaat
Denmark:	Advokat
Germany:	Rechtsanwalt
Greece:	Δικηγόρος
Finland:	AsianajajaAdvokat
France:	Avocat
Ireland:	Barrister
	Solicitor
Italy:	Avvocato
Luxembourg:	Avocat-avoué
Netherlands:	Advocaat
Portugal:	Advogado
Spain:	Abogado
Sweden:	Advokat
United Kingdom:	Advocate
	Barrister
	Solicitor
Czech Republic:	Advokát
Estonia:	Vandeadvokaat
Cyprus:	Δικηγόρος
Latvia:	Zvērināts advokāts
Lithuania:	Advokatas
Hungary:	Ügyvéd
Malta:	Avukat/Prokuratur Legali
Poland:	Adwokat/Radca prawny
Slovenia:	Odvetnik/Odvetnica
Slovakia:	Advokát/Komerčný právnik.
Bulgaria:	Aпвокат
Romania:	Avocat

Article 2

Each Member State shall recognise as a lawyer for the purpose of pursuing the activities specified in Article 1(1) any person listed in paragraph 2 of that Article.

Article 3

A person referred to in Article 1 shall adopt the professional title used in the Member State from which he comes, expressed in the language or one of the languages, of that State, with an indication of the professional organisation by which he is authorised to practise or the court of law before which he is entitled to practise pursuant to the laws of that State.

Article 4

1. Activities relating to the representation of a client in legal proceedings or before public authorities shall be pursued in each host Member State under the conditions laid down for lawyers established in that State, with the exception of any conditions requiring residence, or registration with a professional organisation, in that State.

2. A lawyer pursuing these activities shall observe the rules of professional conduct of the host Member State, without prejudice to his obligations in the Member State from which he comes.

3. When these activities are pursued in the United Kingdom, 'rules of professional conduct of the host Member State' means the rules of professional conduct applicable to solicitors, where such activities are not reserved for barristers and advocates. Otherwise the rules of professional conduct applicable to the latter shall apply. However, barristers from Ireland shall always be subject to the rules of professional conduct applicable in the United Kingdom to barristers and advocates.

   When these activities are pursued in Ireland 'rules of professional conduct of the host Member State' means, in so far as they govern the oral presentation of a case in court, the rules of professional conduct applicable to barristers. In all other cases the rules of professional conduct applicable to solicitors shall apply. However, barristers and advocates from the United Kingdom shall always be subject to the rules of professional conduct applicable in Ireland to barristers.

4. A lawyer pursuing activities other than those referred to in paragraph 1 shall remain subject to the conditions and rules of professional conduct of the Member State from which he comes without prejudice to respect for the rules, whatever their source, which govern the profession in the host Member State, especially those concerning the incompatibility of the exercise of the activities of a lawyer with the exercise of other activities in that State, professional secrecy, relation with other lawyers, the prohibition on the same lawyer acting for parties with mutually conflicting interests, and publicity. The latter rules are applicable only if they are capable of being observed by a lawyer who is not established in the host Member State and to the extent to which their observance is objectively justified to ensure, in that State, the proper exercise of a lawyer's activities, the standing of the profession and respect for the rules concerning incompatibility.

Article 5

For the pursuit of activities relating to the representation of a client in legal proceedings, a Member State may require lawyers to whom Article 1 applies:

— to be introduced, in accordance with local rules or customs, to the presiding judge and, where appropriate, to the President of the relevant Bar in the host Member State;

— to work in conjunction with a lawyer who practises before the judicial authority in question and who would, where necessary, be answerable to that authority, or with an 'avoué' or 'procuratore' practising before it.

Article 6

Any Member State may exclude lawyers who are in the salaried employment of a public or private undertaking from pursuing activities relating to the representation of that undertaking in legal proceedings in so far as lawyers established in that State are not permitted to pursue those activities.

Article 7

1. The competent authority of the host Member State may request the person providing the services to establish his qualifications as a lawyer.

2. In the event of non-compliance with the obligations referred to in Article 4 and in force in the host Member State, the competent authority of the latter shall determine in accordance with its own rules and procedures the consequences of such noncompliance, and to this end may obtain an appropriate professional information concerning the person providing services. It shall notify the competent authority of the Member State from which the person comes of any decision taken. Such exchanges shall not affect the confidential nature of the information supplied.

DIRECTIVE 98/5/EC OF THE EUROPEAN PARLIAMENT AND OF THE COUNCIL of 16 FEBRUARY 1998
to facilitate practice of the profession of lawyer on a permanent basis in a Member State other than that in which the qualification was obtained
[1998] OJ L77/36

THE EUROPEAN PARLIAMENT AND THE COUNCIL OF THE EUROPEAN UNION,

Having regard to the Treaty establishing the European Community, and in particular Article 49, Article 57(1) and the first and third sentences of Article 57(2) thereof,

Having regard to the proposal from the Commission,

Having regard to the Opinion of the Economic and Social Committee,

Acting in accordance with the procedure laid down in Article 189b of the Treaty,

(1)   Whereas, pursuant to Article 7a of the Treaty, the internal market is to comprise an area without internal frontiers; whereas, pursuant to Article 3(c) of the Treaty, the abolition, as between Member States, of obstacles to freedom of movement for persons and services constitutes one of the objectives of the Community; whereas, for nationals of the Member States, this means among other things the possibility of practising a profession, whether in a self-employed or a salaried capacity, in a Member State other than that in which they obtained their professional qualifications;

(2)   Whereas, pursuant to Council Directive 89/48/EEC of 21 December 1988 on a general system for the recognition of higher-education diplomas awarded on completion of professional education and training of at least three years' duration, a lawyer who is fully qualified in one Member State may already ask to have his diploma recognised with a view to establishing himself in another Member State in order to practise the profession of lawyer there under the professional title used in that State; whereas the objective of Directive 89/48/EEC is to ensure that a lawyer is integrated into the profession in the host Member State, and the Directive seeks neither to modify the rules regulating the profession in that State nor to remove such a lawyer from the ambit of those rules;

(3)   Whereas while some lawyers may become quickly integrated into the profession in the host Member State, *inter alia* by passing an aptitude test as provided for in Directive 89/48/EEC, other fully qualified lawyers should be able to achieve such integration after a certain period of professional practice in the host Member State under their home-country professional titles or else continue to practise under their home-country professional titles;

(4)   Whereas at the end of that period the lawyer should be able to integrate into the profession in the host Member States after verification that the possesses professional experience in that Member State;

(5)   Whereas action along these lines is justified at Community level not only because, compared with the general system for the recognition of diplomas, it provides lawyers with an easier means whereby they can integrate into the profession in a host Member State, but also because, by enabling lawyers to practise under their home-country professional titles on a permanent basis in a host Member State, it meets the needs of consumers of legal services who, owing to the increasing trade flows resulting, in particular, from the internal market, seek advice when carrying out cross-border transactions in which international law, Community law and domestic laws often overlap;

(6)   Whereas action is also justified at Community level because only a few Member States already permit in their territory the pursuit of activities of lawyers, otherwise than by way of provision of services, by lawyers from other Member States practising under their home-country professional titles; whereas, however, in the Member States where this possibility exists, the practical details concerning, for example, the area of activity and the obligation to register with the competent authorities differ considerably; whereas such a diversity of situations leads to inequalities and distortions in competition between lawyers from the Member States and constitutes an obstacle to freedom of movement; whereas only a directive laying down the conditions governing practice of the profession, otherwise than by way of provision of services, by lawyers practising under their home-country professional titles is

capable of resolving these difficulties and of affording the same opportunities to lawyers and consumers of legal services in all Member States;

(7) Whereas, in keeping with its objective, this Directive does not lay down any rules concerning purely domestic situations, and where it does affect national rules regulating the legal profession it does so no more than is necessary to achieve its purpose effectively; whereas it is without prejudice in particular to national legislation governing access to and practice of the profession of lawyer under the professional title used in the host Member State;

(8) Whereas lawyers covered by the Directive should be required to register with the competent authority in the host Member State in order that that authority may ensure that they comply with the rules of professional conduct in force in that State; whereas the effect of such registration as regards the jurisdictions in which, and the levels and types of court before which, lawyers may practise is determined by the law applicable to lawyers in the host Member State;

(9) Whereas lawyers who are not integrated into the profession in the host Member State should practise in that State under their home-country professional titles so as to ensure that consumers are properly informed and to distinguish between such lawyers and lawyers from the host Member State practising under the professional title used there;

(10) Whereas lawyers covered by this Directive should be permitted to give legal advice in particular on the law of their home Member States, on Community law, on international law and on the law of the host Member State; whereas this is already allowed as regards the provision of services under Council Directive 77/249/EEC of 22 March 1977 to facilitate the effective exercise by lawyers of freedom to provide services; whereas, however, provision should be made, as in Directive 77/249/EEC, for the option of excluding from the activities of lawyers practising under their home-country professional titles in the United Kingdom and Ireland the preparation of certain formal documents in the conveyancing and probate spheres; whereas this Directive in no way affects the provisions under which, in every Member State, certain activities are reserved for professions other than the legal profession; whereas the provision in Directive 77/249/EEC concerning the possibility of the host Member State to require a lawyer practising under his home-country professional title to work in conjunction with a local lawyer when representing or defending a client in legal proceedings should also be incorporated in this Directive; whereas that requirement must be interpreted in the light of the case law of the Court of Justice of the European Communities, in particular its judgment of 25 February 1988 in Case 427/85, Commission v. Germany;

(11) Whereas to ensure the smooth operation of the justice system Member States should be allowed, by means of specific rules, to reserve access to their highest courts to specialist lawyers, without hindering the integration of Member States' lawyers fulfilling the necessary requirements;

(12) Whereas a lawyer registered under his home-country professional title in the host Member State must remain registered with the competent authority in his home Member State if he is to retain his status of lawyer and be covered by this Directive; whereas for that reason close collaboration between the competent authorities is indispensable, in particular in connection with any disciplinary proceedings;

(13) Whereas lawyers covered by this Directive, whether salaried or self-employed in their home Member States, may practise as salaried lawyers in the host Member State, where that Member State offers that possibility to its own lawyers;

(14) Whereas the purpose pursued by this Directive in enabling lawyers to practise in another Member State under their home-country professional titles is also to make it easier for them to obtain the professional title of that host Member State; whereas under Articles 48 and 52 of the Treaty as interpreted by the Court of Justice the host Member State must take into consideration any professional experience gained in its territory; whereas after effectively and regularly pursuing in the host Member State an activity in the law of that State including Community law for a period of three years, a lawyer may reasonably be assumed to have gained the aptitude necessary to become fully integrated into the legal profession there; whereas at the end of that period the lawyer who can, subject to verification, furnish evidence of his professional competence in the host Member State should be able to obtain the professional title of that Member State; whereas if the period

of effective and regular professional activity of at least three years includes a shorter period of practice in the law of the host Member State, the authority shall also take into consideration any other knowledge of that State's law, which it may verify during an interview; whereas if evidence of fulfilment of these conditions is not provided, the decision taken by the competent authority of the host State not to grant the State's professional title under the facilitation arrangements linked to those conditions must be substantiated and subject to appeal under national law;

(15) Whereas, for economic and professional reasons, the growing tendency for lawyers in the Community to practise jointly, including in the form of associations, has become a reality; whereas the fact that lawyers belong to a grouping in their home Member State should not be used as a pretext to prevent or deter them from establishing themselves in the host Member State; whereas Member States should be allowed, however, to take appropriate measures with the legitimate aim of safeguarding the profession's independence; whereas certain guarantees should be provided in those Member States which permit joint practice,

HAVE ADOPTED THIS DIRECTIVE:

Article 1   Object, scope and definitions

1. The purpose of this Directive is to facilitate practice of the profession of lawyer on a permanent basis in a self-employed or salaried capacity in a Member State other than that in which the professional qualification was obtained.

2. For the purposes of this Directive:

   (a) '*lawyer*' means any person who is a national of a Member State and who is authorised to pursue his professional activities under one of the following professional titles:

Belgium	Avocat/Advocaat/Rechtsanwalt
Bulgaria	Адвокат
Czech Republic	Advokát
Denmark	Advokat
Germany	Rechtsanwalt
Estonia	Vandeadvokaat
Greece	Δικηγόρος
Spain	Abogado/Advocat/Avogado/Abokatu
France	Avocat
Ireland	Barrister/Solicitor
Italy	Avvocato
Cyprus	Δικηγόρος
Latvia	Zvērināts advokāts
Lithuania	Advokatas
Luxembourg	Avocat
Hungary	Ügyvéd
Malta	Avukat/Prokuratur Legali
Netherlands	Advocaat
Austria	Rechtsanwalt
Poland	Adwokat/Radca prawny
Portugal	Advogado
Romania	Avocat
Slovenia	Odvetnik/Odvetnica
Slovakia	Advokát/Komercny právnik
Finland	Asianajaja/Advokat
Sweden	Advokat
United Kingdom	Advocate/Barrister/Solicitor

   (b) '*home Member State*' means the Member State in which a lawyer acquired the right to use one of the professional titles referred to in (a) before practising the profession of lawyer in another Member State;

(c)   '*host Member State*' means the Member State in which a lawyer practises pursuant to this Directive;

(d)   '*home-country professional title*' means the professional title used in the Member State in which a lawyer acquired the right to use that title before practising the profession of lawyer in the host Member State;

(e)   '*grouping*' means any entity, with or without legal personality, formed under the law of a Member State, within which lawyers pursue their professional activities jointly under a joint name;

(f)   '*relevant professional title*' or '*relevant profession*' means the professional title or profession governed by the competent authority with whom a lawyer has registered under Article 3, and 'competent authority' means that authority.

3.   This Directive shall apply both to lawyers practising in a self-employed capacity and to lawyers practising in a salarial capacity in the home Member State and, subject to Article 8, in the host Member State.

4.   Practice of the profession of lawyer within the meaning of this Directive shall not include the provision of services, which is covered by Directive 77/249/EEC.

Article 2   Right to practise under the home-country professional title

Any lawyer shall be entitled to pursue on a permanent basis, in any other Member State under his home-country professional title, the activities specified in Article 5.

Integration into the profession of lawyer in the host Member State shall be subject to Article 10.

Article 3   Registration with the competent authority

1.   A lawyer who wishes to practise in a Member State other than that in which he obtained his professional qualification shall register with the competent authority in that State.

2.   The competent authority in the host Member State shall register the lawyer upon presentation of a certificate attesting to his registration with the competent authority in the home Member State. It may require that, when presented by the competent authority of the home Member State, the certificate be not more than three months old. It shall inform the competent authority in the home Member State of the registration.

3.   For the purpose of applying paragraph 1:

— in the United Kingdom and Ireland, lawyers practising under a professional title other than those used in the United Kingdom or Ireland shall register either with the authority responsible for the profession of barrister or advocate or with the authority responsible for the profession of solicitor,

— in the United Kingdom, the authority responsible for a barrister from Ireland shall be that responsible for the profession of barrister or advocate, and the authority responsible for a solicitor from Ireland shall be that responsible for the profession of solicitor,

— in Ireland, the authority responsible for a barrister or an advocate from the United Kingdom shall be that responsible for the profession of barrister, and the authority responsible for a solicitor from the United Kingdom shall be that responsible for the profession of solicitor.

4.   Where the relevant competent authority in a host Member State publishes the names of lawyers registered with it, it shall also publish the names of lawyers registered pursuant to this Directive.

Article 4   Practice under the home-country professional title

1.   A lawyer practising in a host Member State under his home-country professional title shall do so under that title, which must be expressed in the official language or one of the official languages of his home Member State, in an intelligible manner and in such a way as to avoid confusion with the professional title of the host Member State.

2.   For the purpose of applying paragraph 1, a host Member State may require a lawyer practising under his home-country professional title to indicate the professional body of which he is a member in his home Member State or the judicial authority before which he is entitled to practise pursuant to the laws of his home Member State. A host Member State may also require a lawyer practising under his home-country professional title to include a reference to his registration with the competent authority in that State.

Article 5   Area of activity

1. Subject to paragraphs 2 and 3, a lawyer practising under his home-country professional title carries on the same professional activities as a lawyer practising under the relevant professional title used in the host Member State and may, *inter alia*, give advice on the law of his home Member State, on Community law, on international law and on the law of the host Member State. He shall in any event comply with the rules of procedure applicable in the national courts.

2. Member States which authorise in their territory a prescribed category of lawyers to prepare deeds for obtaining title to administer estates of deceased persons and for creating or transferring interests in land which, in other Member States, are reserved for professions other than that of lawyer may exclude from such activities lawyers practising under a home-country professional title conferred in one of the latter Member States.

3. For the pursuit of activities relating to the representation or defence of a client in legal proceedings and insofar as the law of the host Member State reserves such activities to lawyers practising under the professional title of that State, the latter may require lawyers practising under their home-country professional titles to work in conjunction with a lawyer who practises before the judicial authority in question and who would, where necessary, be answerable to that authority or with an 'avoué' practising before it.

   Nevertheless, in order to ensure the smooth operation of the justice system, Member States may lay down specific rules for access to supreme courts, such as the use of specialist lawyers.

Article 6   Rules of professional conduct applicable

1. Irrespective of the rules of professional conduct to which he is subject in his home Member State, a lawyer practising under his home-country professional title shall be subject to the same rules of professional conduct as lawyers practising under the relevant professional title of the host Member State in respect of all the activities he pursues in its territory.

2. Lawyers practising under their home-country professional titles shall be granted appropriate representation in the professional associations of the host Member State.

   Such representation shall involve at least the right to vote in elections to those associations' governing bodies.

3. The host Member State may require a lawyer practising under his home-country professional title either to take out professional indemnity insurance or to become a member of a professional guarantee fund in accordance with the rules which that State lays down for professional activities pursued in its territory. Nevertheless, a lawyer practising under his home-country professional title shall be exempted from that requirement if he can prove that he is covered by insurance taken out or a guarantee provided in accordance with the rules of his home Member State, insofar as such insurance or guarantee is equivalent in terms of the conditions and extent of cover.

   Where the equivalence is only partial, the competent authority in the host Member State may require that additional insurance or an additional guarantee be contracted to cover the elements which are not already covered by the insurance or guarantee contracted in accordance with the rules of the home Member State.

Article 7   Disciplinary proceedings

1. In the event of failure by a lawyer practising under his home-country professional title to fulfil the obligations in force in the host Member State, the rules of procedure, penalties and remedies provided for in the host Member State shall apply.

2. Before initiating disciplinary proceedings against a lawyer practising under his home-country professional title, the competent authority in the host Member State shall inform the competent authority in the home Member State as soon as possible, furnishing it with all the relevant details.

   The first subparagraph shall apply *mutatis mutandis* where disciplinary proceedings are initiated by the competent authority of the home Member State, which shall inform the competent authority of the host Member State(s) accordingly.

3.   Without prejudice to the decision-making power of the competent authority in the host Member State, that authority shall cooperate throughout the disciplinary proceedings with the competent authority in the home Member State. In particular, the host Member State shall take the measures necessary to ensure that the competent authority in the home Member State can make submissions to the bodies responsible for hearing any appeal.

4.   The competent authority in the home Member State shall decide what action to take, under its own procedural and substantive rules, in the light of a decision of the competent authority in the host Member State concerning a lawyer practising under his home-country professional title.

5.   Although it is not a prerequisite for the decision of the competent authority in the host Member State, the temporary or permanent withdrawal by the competent authority in the home Member State of the authorisation to practise the profession shall automatically lead to the lawyer concerned being temporarily or permanently prohibited from practising under his home-country professional title in the host Member State.

Article 8   Salaried practice

A lawyer registered in a host Member State under his home-country professional title may practise as a salaried lawyer in the employ of another lawyer, an association or firm of lawyers, or a public or private enterprise to the extent that the host Member State so permits for lawyers registered under the professional title used in that State.

Article 9   Statement of reasons and remedies

Decisions not to effect the registration referred to in Article 3 or to cancel such registration and decisions imposing disciplinary measures shall state the reasons on which they are based.

A remedy shall be available against such decisions before a court or tribunal in accordance with the provisions of domestic law.

Article 10   Like treatment as a lawyer of the host Member State

1.   A lawyer practising under his home-country professional title who has effectively and regularly pursued for a period of at least three years an activity in the host Member State in the law of that State including Community law shall, with a view to gaining admission to the profession of lawyer in the host Member State, be exempted from the conditions set out in Article 4(1)(b) of Directive 89/48/EEC, *'Effective and regular pursuit'* means actual exercise of the activity without any interruption other than that resulting from the events of everyday life.

It shall be for the lawyer concerned to furnish the competent authority in the host Member State with proof of such effective regular pursuit for a period of at least three years of an activity in the law of the host Member State. To that end:

(a)   the lawyer shall provide the competent authority in the host Member State with any relevant information and documentation, notably on the number of matters he has dealt with and their nature;

(b)   the competent authority of the host Member State may verify the effective and regular nature of the activity pursued and may, if need be, request the lawyer to provide, orally or in writing, clarification of or further details on the information and documentation mentioned in point (a).

Reasons shall be given for a decision by the competent authority in the host Member State not to grant an exemption where proof is not provided that the requirements laid down in the first subparagraph have been fulfilled, and the decision shall be subject to appeal under domestic law.

2.   A lawyer practising under his home-country professional title in a host Member State may, at any time, apply to have his diploma recognised in accordance with Directive 89/48/EEC with a view to gaining admission to the profession of lawyer in the host Member State and practising it under the professional title corresponding to the profession in that Member State.

3.   A lawyer practising under his home-country professional title who has effectively and regularly pursued a professional activity in the host Member State for a period of at least three years but for a lesser period in the law of that Member State may obtain from the competent

authority of that State admission to the profession of lawyer in the host Member State and the right to practise it under the professional title corresponding to the profession in that Member State, without having to meet the conditions referred to in Article 4(1)(b) of Directive 89/ 48/EEC, under the conditions and in accordance with the procedures set out below:

(a) The competent authority of the host Member State shall take into account the effective and regular professional activity pursued during the abovementioned period and any knowledge and professional experience of the law of the host Member State, and any attendance at lectures or seminars on the law of the host Member State, including the rules regulating professional practice and conduct.

(b) The lawyer shall provide the competent authority of the host Member State with any relevant information and documentation, in particular on the matters he has dealt with. Assessment of the lawyer's effective and regular activity in the host Member State and assessment of his capacity to continue the activity he has pursued there shall be carried out by means of an interview with the competent authority of the host Member State in order to verify the regular and effective nature of the activity pursued.

Reasons shall be given for a decision by the competent authority in the host Member State not to grant authorisation where proof is not provided that the requirements laid down in the first subparagraph have been fulfilled, and the decision shall be subject to appeal under domestic law.

4. The competent authority of the host Member State may, by reasoned decision subject to appeal under domestic law, refuse to allow the lawyer the benefit of the provisions of this Article if it considers that this would be against public policy, in a particular because of disciplinary proceedings, complaints or incidents of any kind.

5. The representatives of the competent authority entrusted with consideration of the application shall preserve the confidentiality of any information received.

6. A lawyer who gains admission to the profession of lawyer in the host Member State in accordance with paragraphs 1, 2 and 3 shall be entitled to use his home-country professional title, expressed in the official language or one of the official languages of his home Member State, alongside the professional title corresponding to the profession of lawyer in the host Member State.

Article 11 Joint practice

Where joint practise is authorised in respect of lawyers carrying on their activities under the relevant professional title in the host Member State, the following provisions shall apply in respect of lawyers wishing to carry on activities under that title or registering with the competent authority:

(1) One or more lawyers who belong to the same grouping in their home Member State and who practise under their home-country professional title in a host Member State may pursue their professional activities in a branch or agency of their grouping in the host Member State. However, where the fundamental rules governing that grouping in the home Member State are incompatible with the fundamental rules laid down by law, regulation or administrative action in the host Member State, the latter rules shall prevail insofar as compliance therewith is justified by the public interest in protecting clients and third parties.

(2) Each Member State shall afford two or more lawyers from the same grouping or the same home Member State who practise in its territory under their home-country professional titles access to a form of joint practice. If the host Member State gives its lawyers a choice between several forms of joint practice, those same forms shall also be made available to the aforementioned lawyers. The manner in which such lawyers practise jointly in the host Member State shall be governed by the laws, regulations and administrative provisions of that State.

(3) The host Member State shall take the measures necessary to permit joint practice also between:

(a) several lawyers from different Member States practising under their home-country professional titles;

(b)   one or more lawyers covered by point (a) and one or more lawyers from the host Member State.

The manner in which such lawyers practice jointly in the host Member State shall be governed by the laws, regulations and administrative provisions of that State.

(4)   A lawyer who wishes to practise under his home-country professional title shall inform the competent authority in the host Member State of the fact that he is a member of a grouping in his home Member State and furnish any relevant information on that grouping.

(5)   Notwithstanding points 1 to 4, a host Member State, insofar as it prohibits lawyers practising under its own relevant professional title from practising the profession of lawyer within a grouping in which some persons are not members of the profession, may refuse to allow a lawyer registered under his home-country professional title to practice in its territory in his capacity as a member of his grouping. The grouping is deemed to include persons who are not members of the profession if

— the capital of the grouping is held entirely or partly, or

— the name under which it practises is used, or

— the decision-making power in that grouping is exercised, *de facto or de jure*,

by persons who do not have the status of lawyer within the meaning of Article 1(2).

Where the fundamental rules governing a grouping of lawyers in the home Member State are incompatible with the rules in force in the host Member State or with the provisions of the first subparagraph, the host Member State may oppose the opening of a branch or agency within its territory without the restrictions laid down in point (1).

Article 12   Name of the grouping

Whatever the manner in which lawyers practise under their home-country professional titles in the host Member State, they may employ the name of any grouping to which they belong in their home Member State.

The host Member State may require that, in addition to the name referred to in the first subparagraph, mention be made of the legal form of the grouping in the home Member State and/or of the names of any members of the grouping practising in the host Member State.

Article 13   Cooperation between the competent authorities in the home and host Member States and confidentiality

In order to facilitate the application of this Directive and to prevent its provisions from being misapplied for the sole purpose of circumventing the rules applicable in the host Member State, the competent authority in the host Member State and the competent authority in the home Member State shall collaborate closely and afford each other mutual assistance.

They shall preserve the confidentiality of the information they exchange.

Article 14   Designation of the competent authorities

Member States shall designate the competent authorities empowered to receive the applications and to take the decisions referred to in this Directive by 14 March 2000.

They shall communicate this information to the other Member States and to the Commission.

Article 15   Report by the Commission

Ten years at the latest from the entry into force of this Directive, the Commsision shall report to the European Parliament and to the Council on progress in the implementation of the Directive.

After having held all the necessary consultations, it shall on that occasion present its conclusions and any amendments which could be made to the existing system.

Article 16   Implementation

1.   Member States shall bring into force the laws, regulations and administrative provisions necessary to comply with this Directive by 14 March 2000. They shall forthwith inform the Commission thereof.

When Member States adopt these measures, they shall contain a reference to this Directive or shall be accompanied by such reference on the occasion of their official publication. The methods of making such reference shall be adopted by Member States.

2.   Member States shall communicate to the Commission the texts of the main provisions of domestic law which they adopt in the field covered by this Directive.

Article 17

This Directive shall enter into force on the date of its publication in the Official Journal of the European Communities.

Article 18

This Directive is addressed to the Member States.

COUNCIL AND PARLIAMENT DIRECTIVE (EC) No 2004/38
of 29 APRIL 2004
on the right of citizens of the Union and their family members to move and reside freely within the territory of the Member States amending Regulation (EEC) No 1612/68 and repealing Directives 64/221/EEC, 68/360/EEC, 72/194/EEC, 73/148/EEC, 75/34/EEC, 75/35/EEC, 90/364/EEC, 90/365/EEC and 93/96/EEC
[2004] OJ L158/77

THE EUROPEAN PARLIAMENT AND THE COUNCIL OF THE EUROPEAN UNION,

Having regard to the Treaty establishing the European Community, and in particular Articles 12, 18, 40, 44 and 52 thereof,

Having regard to the proposal from the Commission,

Having regard to the Opinion of the European Economic and Social Committee,

Having regard to the Opinion of the Committee of the Regions,

Acting in accordance with the procedure laid down in Article 251 of the Treaty,

Whereas:

(1)   Citizenship of the Union confers on every citizen of the Union a primary and individual right to move and reside freely within the territory of the Member States, subject to the limitations and conditions laid down in the Treaty and to the measures adopted to give it effect.

(2)   The free movement of persons constitutes one of the fundamental freedoms of the internal market, which comprises an area without internal frontiers, in which freedom is ensured in accordance with the provisions of the Treaty.

(3)   Union citizenship should be the fundamental status of nationals of the Member States when they exercise their right of free movement and residence. It is therefore necessary to codify and review the existing Community instruments dealing separately with workers, self-employed persons, as well as students and other inactive persons in order to simplify and strengthen the right of free movement and residence of all Union citizens.

(4)   With a view to remedying this sector-by-sector, piecemeal approach to the right of free movement and residence and facilitating the exercise of this right, there needs to be a single legislative act to amend Council Regulation (EEC) No 1612/68 of 15 October 1968 on freedom of movement for workers within the Community, and to repeal the following acts: Council Directive 68/360/EEC of 15 October 1968 on the abolition of restrictions on movement and residence within the Community for workers of Member States and their families, Council Directive 73/148/EEC of 21 May 1973 on the abolition of restrictions on movement and residence within the Community for nationals of Member States with regard to establishment and the provision of services, Council Directive 90/364/EEC of 28 June 1990 on the right of residence, Council Directive 90/365/EEC of 28 June 1990 on the right of residence for employees and self-employed persons who have ceased their occupational activity and Council Directive 93/96/EEC of 29 October 1993 on the right of residence for students.

(5)   The right of all Union citizens to move and reside freely within the territory of the Member States should, if it is to be exercised under objective conditions of freedom and dignity, be also granted to their family members, irrespective of nationality. For the purposes of this Directive, the definition of "family member" should also include the registered partner if the legislation of the host Member State treats registered partnership as equivalent to marriage.

(6) In order to maintain the unity of the family in a broader sense and without prejudice to the prohibition of discrimination on grounds of nationality, the situation of those persons who are not included in the definition of family members under this Directive, and who therefore do not enjoy an automatic right of entry and residence in the host Member State, should be examined by the host Member State on the basis of its own national legislation, in order to decide whether entry and residence could be granted to such persons, taking into consideration their relationship with the Union citizen or any other circumstances, such as their financial or physical dependence on the Union citizen.

(7) The formalities connected with the free movement of Union citizens within the territory of Member States should be clearly defined, without prejudice to the provisions applicable to national border controls.

(8) With a view to facilitating the free movement of family members who are not nationals of a Member State, those who have already obtained a residence card should be exempted from the requirement to obtain an entry visa within the meaning of Council Regulation (EC) No 539/2001 of 15 March 2001 listing the third countries whose nationals must be in possession of visas when crossing the external borders and those whose nationals are exempt from that requirement or, where appropriate, of the applicable national legislation.

(9) Union citizens should have the right of residence in the host Member State for a period not exceeding three months without being subject to any conditions or any formalities other than the requirement to hold a valid identity card or passport, without prejudice to a more favourable treatment applicable to job-seekers as recognised by the case-law of the Court of Justice.

(10) Persons exercising their right of residence should not, however, become an unreasonable burden on the social assistance system of the host Member State during an initial period of residence. Therefore, the right of residence for Union citizens and their family members for periods in excess of three months should be subject to conditions.

(11) The fundamental and personal right of residence in another Member State is conferred directly on Union citizens by the Treaty and is not dependent upon their having fulfilled administrative procedures.

(12) For periods of residence of longer than three months, Member States should have the possibility to require Union citizens to register with the competent authorities in the place of residence, attested by a registration certificate issued to that effect.

(13) The residence card requirement should be restricted to family members of Union citizens who are not nationals of a Member State for periods of residence of longer than three months.

(14) The supporting documents required by the competent authorities for the issuing of a registration certificate or of a residence card should be comprehensively specified in order to avoid divergent administrative practices or interpretations constituting an undue obstacle to the exercise of the right of residence by Union citizens and their family members.

(15) Family members should be legally safeguarded in the event of the death of the Union citizen, divorce, annulment of marriage or termination of a registered partnership. With due regard for family life and human dignity, and in certain conditions to guard against abuse, measures should therefore be taken to ensure that in such circumstances family members already residing within the territory of the host Member State retain their right of residence exclusively on a personal basis.

(16) As long as the beneficiaries of the right of residence do not become an unreasonable burden on the social assistance system of the host Member State they should not be expelled. Therefore, an expulsion measure should not be the automatic consequence of recourse to the social assistance system. The host Member State should examine whether it is a case of temporary difficulties and take into account the duration of residence, the personal circumstances and the amount of aid granted in order to consider whether the beneficiary has become an unreasonable burden on its social assistance system and to proceed to his expulsion. In no case should an expulsion measure be adopted against workers, self-employed persons or job-seekers as defined by the Court of Justice save on grounds of public policy or public security.

(17) Enjoyment of permanent residence by Union citizens who have chosen to settle long term in the host Member State would strengthen the feeling of Union citizenship and is a key element in promoting social cohesion, which is one of the fundamental objectives of the Union. A right of permanent residence should therefore be laid down for all Union citizens and their family members who have resided in the host Member State in compliance with the conditions laid down in this Directive during a continuous period of five years without becoming subject to an expulsion measure.

(18) In order to be a genuine vehicle for integration into the society of the host Member State in which the Union citizen resides, the right of permanent residence, once obtained, should not be subject to any conditions.

(19) Certain advantages specific to Union citizens who are workers or self-employed persons and to their family members, which may allow these persons to acquire a right of permanent residence before they have resided five years in the host Member State, should be maintained, as these constitute acquired rights, conferred by Commission Regulation (EEC) No 1251/70 of 29 June 1970 on the right of workers to remain in the territory of a Member State after having been employed in that State and Council Directive 75/34/EEC of 17 December 1974 concerning the right of nationals of a Member State to remain in the territory of another Member State after having pursued therein an activity in a self-employed capacity.

(20) In accordance with the prohibition of discrimination on grounds of nationality, all Union citizens and their family members residing in a Member State on the basis of this Directive should enjoy, in that Member State, equal treatment with nationals in areas covered by the Treaty, subject to such specific provisions as are expressly provided for in the Treaty and secondary law.

(21) However, it should be left to the host Member State to decide whether it will grant social assistance during the first three months of residence, or for a longer period in the case of job-seekers, to Union citizens other than those who are workers or self-employed persons or who retain that status or their family members, or maintenance assistance for studies, including vocational training, prior to acquisition of the right of permanent residence, to these same persons.

(22) The Treaty allows restrictions to be placed on the right of free movement and residence on grounds of public policy, public security or public health. In order to ensure a tighter definition of the circumstances and procedural safeguards subject to which Union citizens and their family members may be denied leave to enter or may be expelled, this Directive should replace Council Directive 64/221/EEC of 25 February 1964 on the coordination of special measures concerning the movement and residence of foreign nationals, which are justified on grounds of public policy, public security or public health.

(23) Expulsion of Union citizens and their family members on grounds of public policy or public security is a measure that can seriously harm persons who, having availed themselves of the rights and freedoms conferred on them by the Treaty, have become genuinely integrated into the host Member State. The scope for such measures should therefore be limited in accordance with the principle of proportionality to take account of the degree of integration of the persons concerned, the length of their residence in the host Member State, their age, state of health, family and economic situation and the links with their country of origin.

(24) Accordingly, the greater the degree of integration of Union citizens and their family members in the host Member State, the greater the degree of protection against expulsion should be. Only in exceptional circumstances, where there are imperative grounds of public security, should an expulsion measure be taken against Union citizens who have resided for many years in the territory of the host Member State, in particular when they were born and have resided there throughout their life. In addition, such exceptional circumstances should also apply to an expulsion measure taken against minors, in order to protect their links with their family, in accordance with the United Nations Convention on the Rights of the Child, of 20 November 1989.

(25) Procedural safeguards should also be specified in detail in order to ensure a high level of protection of the rights of Union citizens and their family members in the event of their being

denied leave to enter or reside in another Member State, as well as to uphold the principle that any action taken by the authorities must be properly justified.

(26) In all events, judicial redress procedures should be available to Union citizens and their family members who have been refused leave to enter or reside in another Member State.

(27) In line with the case-law of the Court of Justice prohibiting Member States from issuing orders excluding for life persons covered by this Directive from their territory, the right of Union citizens and their family members who have been excluded from the territory of a Member State to submit a fresh application after a reasonable period, and in any event after a three year period from enforcement of .the final exclusion order, should be confirmed.

(28) To guard against abuse of rights or fraud, notably marriages of convenience or any other form of relationships contracted for the sole purpose of enjoying the right of free movement and residence, Member States should have the possibility to adopt the necessary measures.

(29) This Directive should not affect more favourable national provisions.

(30) With a view to examining how further to facilitate the exercise of the right of free movement and residence, a report should be prepared by the Commission in order to evaluate the opportunity to present any necessary proposals to this effect, notably on the extension of the period of residence with no conditions.

(31) This Directive respects the fundamental rights and freedoms and observes the principles recognised in particular by the Charter of Fundamental Rights of the European Union. In accordance with the prohibition of discrimination contained in the Charter, Member States should implement this Directive without discrimination between the beneficiaries of this Directive on grounds such as sex, race, colour, ethnic or social origin, genetic characteristics, language, religion or beliefs, political or other opinion, membership of an ethnic minority, property, birth, disability, age or sexual orientation,

HAVE ADOPTED THIS DIRECTIVE:

CHAPTER I
GENERAL PROVISIONS

Article 1   Subject

This Directive lays down:

(a) the conditions governing the exercise of the right of free movement and residence within the territory of the Member States by Union citizens and their family members;

(b) the right of permanent residence in the territory of the Member States for Union citizens and their family members;

(c) the limits placed on the rights set out in (a) and (b) on grounds of public policy, public security or public health.

Article 2   Definitions

For the purposes of this Directive:

(1) "Union citizen" means any person having the nationality of a Member State;

(2) "Family member" means:

(a) the spouse;

(b) the partner with whom the Union citizen has contracted a registered partnership, on the basis of the legislation of a Member State, if the legislation of the host Member State treats registered partnerships as equivalent to marriage and in accordance with the conditions laid down in the relevant legislation of the host Member State;

(c) the direct descendants who are under the age of 21 or are dependants and those of the spouse or partner as defined in point (b);

(d) the dependent direct relatives in the ascending line and those of the spouse or partner as defined in point (b);

(3) "Host Member State" means the Member State to which a Union citizen moves in order to exercise his/her right of free movement and residence.

Article 3   Beneficiaries

.1.   This Directive shall apply to all Union citizens who move to or reside in a Member State other than that of which they are a national, and to their family members as defined in point 2 of Article 2 who accompany or join them.

·2.   Without prejudice to any right to free movement and residence the persons concerned may have in their own right, the host Member State shall, in accordance with its national legislation, facilitate entry and residence for the following persons:

(a)   any other family members, irrespective of their nationality, not falling under the definition in point 2 of Article 2 who, in the country from which they have come, are dependants or members of the household of the Union citizen having the primary right of residence, or where serious health grounds strictly require the personal care of the family member by the Union citizen;

(b)   the partner with whom the Union citizen has a durable relationship, duly attested.

The host Member State shall undertake an extensive examination of the personal circumstances and shall justify any denial of entry or residence to these people.

CHAPTER II
RIGHT OF EXIT AND ENTRY

Article 4   Right of exit

1.   Without prejudice to the provisions on travel documents applicable to national border controls, all Union citizens with a valid identity card or passport and their family members who are not nationals of a Member State and who hold a valid passport shall have the right to leave the territory of a Member State to travel to another Member State.

2.   No exit visa or equivalent formality may be imposed on the persons to whom paragraph 1 applies.

3.   Member States shall, acting in accordance with their laws, issue to their own nationals, and renew, an identity card or passport stating their nationality.

4.   The passport shall be valid at least for all Member States and for countries through which the holder must pass when travelling between Member States. Where the law of a Member State does not provide for identity cards to be issued, the period of validity of any passport on being issued or renewed shall be not less than five years.

Article 5   Right of entry

1.   Without prejudice to the provisions on travel documents applicable to national border controls, Member States shall grant Union citizens leave to enter their territory with a valid identity card or passport and shall grant family members who are not nationals of a Member State leave to enter their territory with a valid passport.

No entry visa or equivalent formality may be imposed on Union citizens.

2.   Family members who are not nationals of a Member State shall only be required to have an entry visa in accordance with Regulation (EC) No 539/2001 or, where appropriate, with national law. For the purposes of this Directive, possession of the valid residence card referred to in Article 10 shall exempt such family members from the visa requirement.

Member States shall grant such persons every facility to obtain the necessary visas. Such visas shall be issued free of charge as soon as possible and on the basis of an accelerated procedure.

3.   The host Member State shall not place an entry or exit stamp in the passport of family members who are not nationals of a Member State provided that they present the residence card provided for in Article 10.

4.   Where a Union citizen, or a family member who is not a national of a Member State, does not have the necessary travel documents or, if required, the necessary visas, the Member State concerned shall, before turning them back, give such persons every reasonable opportunity to obtain the necessary documents or have them brought to them within a reasonable period of time or to corroborate or prove by other means that they are covered by the right of free movement and residence.

5.   The Member State may require the person concerned to report his/her presence within its territory within a reasonable and non-discriminatory period of time. Failure to comply with

this requirement may make the person concerned liable to proportionate and non-discriminatory sanctions.

CHAPTER III
RIGHT OF RESIDENCE

Article 6   Right of residence for up to three months

1.   Union citizens shall have the right of residence on the territory of another Member State for a period of up to three months without any conditions or any formalities other than the requirement to hold a valid identity card or passport.

2.   The provisions of paragraph 1 shall also apply to family members in possession of a valid passport who are not nationals of a Member State, accompanying or joining the Union citizen.

Article 7   Right of residence for more than three months

1.   All Union citizens shall have the right of residence on the territory of another Member State for a period of longer than three months if they:

(a)   are workers or self-employed persons in the host Member State; or

(b)   have sufficient resources for themselves and their family members not to become a burden on the social assistance system of the host Member State during their period of residence and have comprehensive sickness insurance cover in the host Member State; or

(c)   — are enrolled at a private or public establishment, accredited or financed by the host Member State on the basis of its legislation or administrative practice, for the principal purpose of following a course of study, including vocational training; and

— have comprehensive sickness insurance cover in the host Member State and assure the relevant national authority, by means of a declaration or by such equivalent means as they may choose, that they have sufficient resources for themselves and their family members not to become a burden on the social assistance system of the host Member State during their period of residence; or

(d)   are family members accompanying or joining a Union citizen who satisfies the conditions referred to in points (a), (b) or (c).

2.   The right of residence provided for in paragraph 1 shall extend to family members who are not nationals of a Member State, accompanying or joining the Union citizen in the host Member State, provided that such Union citizen satisfies the conditions referred to in paragraph 1(a), (b) or (c).

3.   For the purposes of paragraph 1(a), a Union citizen who is no longer a worker or self-employed person shall retain the status of worker or self-employed person in the following circumstances:

(a)   he/she is temporarily unable to work as the result of an illness or accident;

(b)   he/she is in duly recorded involuntary unemployment after having been employed for more than one year and has registered as a job-seeker with the relevant employment office;

(c)   he/she is in duly recorded involuntary unemployment after completing a fixed-term employment contract of less than a year or after having become involuntarily unemployed during the first twelve months and has registered as a job-seeker with the relevant employment office. In this case, the status of worker shall be retained for no less than six months;

(d)   he/she embarks on vocational training. Unless he/she is involuntarily unemployed, the retention of the status of worker shall require the training to be related to the previous employment.

4.   By way of derogation from paragraphs 1(d) and 2 above, only the spouse, the registered partner provided for in Article 2(2)(b) and dependent children shall have the right of residence as family members of a Union citizen meeting the conditions under 1(c) above. Article 3(2) shall apply to his/her dependent direct relatives in the ascending lines and those of his/her spouse or registered partner.

Article 8   Administrative formalities for Union citizens

1.   Without prejudice to Article 5(5), for periods of residence longer than three months, the host Member State may require Union citizens to register with the relevant authorities.

2.   The deadline for registration may not be less than three months from the date of arrival. A registration certificate shall be issued immediately, stating the name and address of the person registering and the date of the registration. Failure to comply with the registration requirement may render the person concerned liable to proportionate and non-discriminatory sanctions.

3.   For the registration certificate to be issued, Member States may only require that
— Union citizens to whom point (a) of Article 7(1) applies present a valid identity card or passport, a confirmation of engagement from the employer or a certificate of employment, or proof that they are self-employed persons;
— Union citizens to whom point (b) of Article 7(1) applies present a valid identity card or passport and provide proof that they satisfy the conditions laid down therein;
— Union citizens to whom point (c) of Article 7(1) applies present a valid identity card or passport, provide proof of enrolment at an accredited establishment and of comprehensive sickness insurance cover and the declaration or equivalent means referred to in point (c) of Article 7(1). Member States may not require this declaration to refer to any specific amount of resources.

4.   Member States may not lay down a fixed amount which they regard as "sufficient resources", but they must take into account the personal situation of the person concerned. In all cases this amount shall not be higher than the threshold below which nationals of the host Member State become eligible for social assistance, or, where this criterion is not applicable, higher than the minimum social security pension paid by the host Member State.

5.   For the registration certificate to be issued to family members of Union citizens, who are themselves Union citizens, Member States may require the following documents to be presented:
(a)   a valid identity card or passport;
(b)   a document attesting to the existence of a family relationship or of a registered partnership;
(c)   where appropriate, the registration certificate of the Union citizen whom they are accompanying or joining;
(d)   in cases falling under points (c) and (d) of Article 2(2), documentary evidence that the conditions laid down therein are met;
(e)   in cases falling under Article 3(2)(a), a document issued by the relevant authority in the country of origin or country from which they are arriving certifying that they are dependants or members of the household of the Union citizen, or proof of the existence of serious health grounds which strictly require the personal care of the family member by the Union citizen;
(f)   in cases falling under Article 3(2)(b), proof of the existence of a durable relationship with the Union citizen.

Article 9   Administrative formalities for family members who are not nationals of a Member State

1.   Member States shall issue a residence card to family members of a Union citizen who are not nationals of a Member State, where the planned period of residence is for more than three months.

2.   The deadline for submitting the residence card application may not be less than three months from the date of arrival.

3.   Failure to comply with the requirement to apply for a residence card may make the person concerned liable to proportionate and non-discriminatory sanctions.

Article 10   Issue of residence cards

1.   The right of residence of family members of a Union citizen who are not nationals of a Member State shall be evidenced by the issuing of a document called "Residence card of a family member of a Union citizen" no later than six months from the date on which they submit the application. A certificate of application for the residence card shall be issued immediately.

2. For the residence card to be issued, Member States shall require presentation of the following documents:

    (a) a valid passport;

    (b) a document attesting to the existence of a family relationship or of a registered partnership;

    (c) the registration certificate or, in the absence of a registration system, any other proof of residence in the host Member State of the Union citizen whom they are accompanying or joining;

    (d) in cases falling under points (c) and (d) of Article 2(2), documentary evidence that the conditions laid down therein are met;

    (e) in cases falling under Article 3(2)(a), a document issued by the relevant authority in the country of origin or country from which they are arriving certifying that they are dependants or members of the household of the Union citizen, or proof of the existence of serious health grounds which strictly require the personal care of the family member by the Union citizen;

    (f) in cases falling under Article 3(2)(b), proof of the existence of a durable relationship with the Union citizen.

Article 11 Validity of the residence card

1. The residence card provided for by Article 10(1) shall be valid for five years from the date of issue or for the envisaged period of residence of the Union citizen, if this period is less than five years.

2. The validity of the residence card shall not be affected by temporary absences not exceeding six months a year, or by absences of a longer duration for compulsory military service or by one absence of a maximum of twelve consecutive months for important reasons such as pregnancy and childbirth, serious illness, study or vocational training, or a posting in another Member State or a third country.

Article 12 Retention of the right of residence by family members in the event of death or departure of the Union citizen

1. Without prejudice to the second subparagraph, the Union citizen's death or departure from the host Member State shall not affect the right of residence of his/her family members who are nationals of a Member State.

    Before acquiring the right of permanent residence, the persons concerned must meet the conditions laid down in points (a), (b), (c) or (d) of Article 7(1).

2. Without prejudice to the second subparagraph, the Union citizen's death shall not entail loss of the right of residence of his/her family members who are not nationals of a Member State and who have been residing in the host Member State as family members for at least one year before the Union citizen's death.

    Before acquiring the right of permanent residence, the right of residence of the persons concerned shall remain subject to the requirement that they are able to show that they are workers or self-employed persons or that they have sufficient resources for themselves and their family members not to become a burden on the social assistance system of the host Member State during their period of residence and have comprehensive sickness insurance cover in the host Member State, or that they are members of the family, already constituted in the host Member State, of a person satisfying these requirements. "Sufficient resources" shall be as defined in Article 8(4).

    Such family members shall retain their right of residence exclusively on a personal basis.

3. The Union citizen's departure from the host Member State or his/her death shall not entail loss of the right of residence of his/her children or of the parent who has actual custody of the children, irrespective of nationality, if the children reside in the host Member State and are enrolled at an educational establishment, for the purpose of studying there, until the completion of their studies.

Article 13 Retention of the right of residence by family members in the event of divorce, annulment of marriage or termination of registered partnership

    1.   Without prejudice to the second subparagraph, divorce, annulment of the Union citizen's marriage or termination of his/her registered partnership, as referred to in point 2(b) of Article 2 shall not affect the right of residence of his/her family members who are nationals of a Member State.

    . 2.   Without prejudice to the second subparagraph, divorce, annulment of marriage or termination of the registered partnership referred to in point 2(b) of Article 2 shall not entail loss of the right of residence of a Union citizen's family members who are not nationals of a Member State where:

Before acquiring the right of permanent residence, the persons concerned must meet the conditions laid down in points (a), (b), (c) or (d) of Article 7(1).

    (a)   prior to initiation of the divorce or annulment proceedings or termination of the registered partnership referred to in point 2(b) of Article 2, the marriage or registered partnership has lasted at least three years, including one year in the host Member State; or

    (b)   by agreement between the spouses or the partners referred to in point 2(b) of Article 2 or by court order, the spouse or partner who is not a national of a Member State has custody of the Union citizen's children; or

    (c)   this is warranted by particularly difficult circumstances, such as having been a victim of domestic violence while the marriage or registered partnership was subsisting; or

    (d)   by agreement between the spouses or partners referred to in point 2(b) of Article 2 or by court order, the spouse or partner who is not a national of a Member State has the right of access to a minor child, provided that the court has ruled that such access must be in the host Member State, and for as long as is required.

Before acquiring the right of permanent residence, the right of residence of the persons concerned shall remain subject to the requirement that they are able to show that they are workers or self-employed persons or that they have sufficient resources for themselves and their family members not to become a burden on the social assistance system of the host Member State during their period of residence and have comprehensive sickness insurance cover in the host Member State, or that they are members of the family, already constituted in the host Member State, of a person satisfying these requirements. "Sufficient resources" shall be as defined in Article 8(4).

Such family members shall retain their right of residence exclusively on personal basis.

Article 14 Retention of the right of residence

    1.   Union citizens and their family members shall have the right of residence provided for in Article 6, as long as they do not become an unreasonable burden on the social assistance system of the host Member State.

    2.   Union citizens and their family members shall have the right of residence provided for in Articles 7, 12 and 13 as long as they meet the conditions set out therein.

In specific cases where there is a reasonable doubt as to whether a Union citizen or his/her family members satisfies the conditions set out in Articles 7, 12 and 13, Member States may verify if these conditions are fulfilled. This verification shall not be carried out systematically.

    3.   An expulsion measure shall not be the automatic consequence of a Union citizen's or his or her family member's recourse to the social assistance system of the host Member State.

    4.   By way of derogation from paragraphs 1 and 2 and without prejudice to the provisions of Chapter VI, an expulsion measure may in no case be adopted against Union citizens or their family members if:

    (a)   the Union citizens are workers or self-employed persons, or

    (b)   the Union citizens entered the territory of the host Member State in order to seek employment. In this case, the Union citizens and their family members may not be expelled for as long as the Union citizens can provide evidence that they are continuing to seek employment and that they have a genuine chance of being engaged.

Article 15   Procedural safeguards

1. The procedures provided for by Articles 30 and 31 shall apply by analogy to all decisions restricting free movement of Union citizens and their family members on grounds other than public policy, public security or public health.

2. Expiry of the identity card or passport on the basis of which the person concerned entered the host Member State and was issued with a registration certificate or residence card shall not constitute a ground for expulsion from the host Member State.

3. The host Member State may not impose a ban on entry in the context of an expulsion decision to which paragraph 1 applies.

CHAPTER IV
RIGHT OF PERMANENT RESIDENCE

SECTION I
ELIGIBILITY

Article 16   General rule for Union citizens and their family members

1. Union citizens who have resided legally for a continuous period of five years in the host Member State shall have the right of permanent residence there. This right shall not be subject to the conditions provided for in Chapter III.

2. Paragraph 1 shall apply also to family members who are not nationals of a Member State and have legally resided with the Union citizen in the host Member State for a continuous period of five years.

3. Continuity of residence shall not be affected by temporary absences not exceeding a total of six months a year, or by absences of a longer duration for compulsory military service, or by one absence of a maximum of twelve consecutive months for important reasons such as pregnancy and childbirth, serious illness, study or vocational training, or a posting in another Member State or a third country.

4. Once acquired, the right of permanent residence shall be lost only through absence from the host Member State for a period exceeding two consecutive years.

Article 17   Exemptions for persons no longer working in the host Member State and their family members

1. By way of derogation from Article 16, the right of permanent residence in the host Member State shall be enjoyed before completion of a continuous period of five years of residence by:

    (a)   workers or self-employed persons who, at the time they stop working, have reached the age laid down by the law of that Member State for entitlement to an old age pension or workers who cease paid employment to take early retirement, provided that they have been working in that Member State for at least the preceding twelve months and have resided there continuously for more than three years.

    If the law of the host Member State does not grant the right to an old age pension to certain categories of self-employed persons, the age condition shall be deemed to have been met once the person concerned has reached the age of 60;

    (b)   workers or self-employed persons who have resided continuously in the host Member State for more than two years and stop working there as a result of permanent incapacity to work.

    If such incapacity is the result of an accident at work or an occupational disease entitling the person concerned to a benefit payable in full or in part by an institution in the host Member State, no condition shall be imposed as to length of residence;

    (c)   workers or self-employed persons who, after three years of continuous employment and residence in the host Member State, work in an employed or self-employed capacity in another Member State, while retaining their place of residence in the host Member State, to which they return, as a rule, each day or at least once a week.

    For the purposes of entitlement to the rights referred to in points (a) and (b), periods of employment spent in the Member State in which the person concerned is working shall be regarded as having been spent in the host Member State.

Periods of involuntary unemployment duly recorded by the relevant employment office, periods not worked for reasons not of the person's own making and absences from work or cessation of work due to illness or accident shall be regarded as periods of employment.

2.	The conditions as to length of residence and employment laid down in point (a) of paragraph 1 and the condition as to length of residence laid down in point (b) of paragraph 1 shall not apply if the worker's or the self-employed person's spouse or partner as referred to in point 2(b) of Article 2 is a national of the host Member State or has lost the nationality of that Member State by marriage to that worker or self-employed person.

3.	Irrespective of nationality, the family members of a worker or a self-employed person who are residing with him in the territory of the host Member State shall have the right of permanent residence in that Member State, if the worker or self-employed person has acquired himself the right of permanent residence in that Member State on the basis of paragraph 1.

4.	If, however, the worker or self-employed person dies while still working but before acquiring permanent residence status in the host Member State on the basis of paragraph 1, his family members who are residing with him in the host Member State shall acquire the right of permanent residence there, on condition that:

(a)	the worker or self-employed person had, at the time of death, resided continuously on the territory of that Member State for two years; or

(b)	the death resulted from an accident at work or an occupational disease; or

(c)	the surviving spouse lost the nationality of that Member State following marriage to the worker or self-employed person.

## Article 18	Acquisition of the right of permanent residence by certain family members who are not nationals of a Member State

Without prejudice to Article 17, the family members of a Union citizen to whom Articles 12(2) and 13(2) apply, who satisfy the conditions laid down therein, shall acquire the right of permanent residence after residing legally for a period of five consecutive years in the host Member State.

SECTION II
ADMINISTRATIVE FORMALITIES

## Article 19	Document certifying permanent residence for Union citizens

1.	Upon application Member States shall issue Union citizens entitled to permanent residence, after having verified duration of residence, with a document certifying permanent residence.

2.	The document certifying permanent residence shall be issued as soon as possible.

## Article 20	Permanent residence card for family members who are not nationals of a Member State

1.	Member States shall issue family members who are not nationals of a Member State entitled to permanent residence with a permanent residence card within six months of the submission of the application. The permanent residence card shall be renewable automatically every ten years.

2.	The application for a permanent residence card shall be submitted before the residence card expires. Failure to comply with the requirement to apply for a permanent residence card may render the person concerned liable to proportionate and non-discriminatory sanctions.

3.	Interruption in residence not exceeding two consecutive years shall not affect the validity of the permanent residence card.

## Article 21	Continuity of residence

For the purposes of this Directive, continuity of residence may be attested by any means of proof in use in the host Member State. Continuity of residence is broken by any expulsion decision duly enforced against the person concerned.

CHAPTER V
PROVISIONS COMMON TO THE RIGHT OF RESIDENCE AND THE RIGHT OF PERMANENT RESIDENCE

Article 22 Territorial scope

The right of residence and the right of permanent residence shall cover the whole territory of the host Member State. Member States may impose territorial restrictions on the right of residence and the right of permanent residence only where the same restrictions apply to their own nationals.

· Article 23 Related rights

Irrespective of nationality, the family members of a Union citizen who have the right of residence or the right of permanent residence in a Member State shall be entitled to take up employment or self-employment there.

Article 24 Equal treatment

1. Subject to such specific provisions as are expressly provided for in the Treaty and secondary law, all Union citizens residing on the basis of this Directive in the territory of the host Member State shall enjoy equal treatment with the nationals of that Member State within the scope of the Treaty. The benefit of this right shall be extended to family members who are not nationals of a Member State and who have the right of residence or permanent residence.

2. By way of derogation from paragraph 1, the host Member State shall not be obliged to confer entitlement to social assistance during the first three months of residence or, where appropriate, the longer period provided for in Article 14(4)(b), nor shall it be obliged, prior to acquisition of the right of permanent residence, to grant maintenance aid for studies, including vocational training, consisting in student grants or student loans to persons other than workers, self-employed persons, persons who retain such status and members of their families.

Article 25 General provisions concerning residence documents

1. Possession of a registration certificate as referred to in Article 8, of a document certifying permanent residence, of a certificate attesting submission of an application for a family member residence card, of a residence card or of a permanent residence card, may under no circumstances be made a precondition for the exercise of a right or the completion of an administrative formality, as entitlement to rights may be attested by any other means of proof.

2. All documents mentioned in paragraph 1 shall be issued free of charge or for a charge not exceeding that imposed on nationals for the issuing of similar documents.

Article 26 Checks

Member States may carry out checks on compliance with any requirement deriving from their national legislation for non-nationals always to carry their registration certificate or residence card, provided that the same requirement applies to their own nationals as regards their identity card. In the event of failure to comply with this requirement, Member States may impose the same sanctions as those imposed on their own nationals for failure to carry their identity card.

CHAPTER VI
RESTRICTIONS ON THE RIGHT OF ENTRY AND THE RIGHT OF RESIDENCE ON GROUNDS OF PUBLIC POLICY, PUBLIC SECURITY OR PUBLIC HEALTH

Article 27 General principles

1. Subject to the provisions of this Chapter, Member States may restrict the freedom of movement and residence of Union citizens and their family members, irrespective of nationality, on grounds of public policy, public security or public health. These grounds shall not be invoked to serve economic ends.

2.   Measures taken on grounds of public policy or public security shall comply with the principle of proportionality and shall be based exclusively on the personal conduct of the individual concerned. Previous criminal convictions shall not in themselves constitute grounds for taking such measures.

The personal conduct of the individual concerned must represent a genuine, present and sufficiently serious threat affecting one of the fundamental interests of society. Justifications that are isolated from the particulars of the case or that rely on considerations of general prevention shall not be accepted.

3.   In order to ascertain whether the person concerned represents a danger for public policy or public security, when issuing the registration certificate or, in the absence of a registration system, not later than three months from the date of arrival of the person concerned on its territory or from the date of reporting his/her presence within the territory, as provided for in Article 5(5), or when issuing the residence card, the host Member State may, should it consider this essential, request the Member State of origin and, if need be, other Member States to provide information concerning any previous police record the person concerned may have. Such enquiries shall not be made as a matter of routine. The Member State consulted shall give its reply within two months.

4.   The Member State which issued the passport or identity card shall allow the holder of the document who has been expelled on grounds of public policy, public security, or public health from another Member State to re-enter its territory without any formality even if the document is no longer valid or the nationality of the holder is in dispute.

Article 28 Protection against expulsion

1.   Before taking an expulsion decision on grounds of public policy or public security, the host Member State shall take account of considerations such as how long the individual concerned has resided on its territory, his/her age, state of health, family and economic situation, social and cultural integration into the host Member State and the extent of his/her links with the country of origin.

2.   The host Member State may not take an expulsion decision against Union citizens or their family members, irrespective of nationality, who have the right of permanent residence on its territory, except on serious grounds of public policy or public security.

3.   An expulsion decision may not be taken against Union citizens, except if the decision is based on imperative grounds of public security, as defined by Member States, if they:

(a)   have resided in the host Member State for the previous ten years; or

(b)   are a minor, except if the expulsion is necessary for the best interests of the child, as provided for in the United Nations Convention on the Rights of the Child of 20 November 1989.

Article 29 Public health

1.   The only diseases justifying measures restricting freedom of movement shall be the diseases with epidemic potential as defined by the relevant instruments of the World Health Organisation and other infectious diseases or contagious parasitic diseases if they are the subject of protection provisions applying to nationals of the host Member State.

2.   Diseases occurring after a three-month period from the date of arrival shall not constitute grounds for expulsion from the territory.

3.   Where there are serious indications that it is necessary, Member States may, within three months of the date of arrival, require persons entitled to the right of residence to undergo, free of charge, a medical examination to certify that they are not suffering from any of the conditions referred to in paragraph 1. Such medical examinations may not be required as a matter of routine.

Article 30 Notification of decisions

1.   The persons concerned shall be notified in writing of any decision taken under Article 27(1), in such a way that they are able to comprehend its content and the implications for them.

2. The persons concerned shall be informed, precisely and in full, of the public policy, public security or public health grounds on which the decision taken in their case is based, unless this is contrary to the interests of State security.

3. The notification shall specify the court or administrative authority with which the person concerned may lodge an appeal, the time limit for the appeal and, where applicable, the time allowed for the person to leave the territory of the Member State. Save in duly substantiated cases of urgency, the time allowed to leave the territory shall be not less than one month from the date of notification.

Article 31 Procedural safeguards

1. The persons concerned shall have access to judicial and, where appropriate, administrative redress procedures in the host Member State to appeal against or seek review of any decision taken against them on the grounds of public policy, public security or public health.

2. Where the application for appeal against or judicial review of the expulsion decision is accompanied by an application for an interim order to suspend enforcement of that decision, actual removal from the territory may not take place until such time as the decision on the interim order has been taken, except:
   — where the expulsion decision is based on a previous judicial decision; or
   — where the persons concerned have had previous access to judicial review; or
   — where the expulsion decision is based on imperative grounds of public security under Article 28(3).

3. The redress procedures shall allow for an examination of the legality of the decision, as well as of the facts and circumstances on which the proposed measure is based. They shall ensure that the decision is not disproportionate, particularly in view of the requirements laid down in Article 28.

4. Member States may exclude the individual concerned from their territory pending the redress procedure, but they may not prevent the individual from submitting his/her defence in person, except when his/her appearance may cause serious troubles to public policy or public security or when the appeal or judicial review concerns a denial of entry to the territory.

Article 32 Duration of exclusion orders

1. Persons excluded on grounds of public policy or public security may submit an application for lifting of the exclusion order after a reasonable period, depending on the circumstances, and in any event after three years from enforcement of the final exclusion order which has been validly adopted in accordance with Community law, by putting forward arguments to establish that there has been a material change in the circumstances which justified the decision ordering their exclusion.

   The Member State concerned shall reach a decision on this application within six months of its submission.

2. The persons referred to in paragraph 1 shall have no right of entry to the territory of the Member State concerned while their application is being considered.

Article 33 Expulsion as a penalty or legal consequence

1. Expulsion orders may not be issued by the host Member State as a penalty or legal consequence of a custodial penalty, unless they conform to the requirements of Articles 27, 28 and 29.

2. If an expulsion order, as provided for in paragraph 1, is enforced more than two years after it was issued, the Member State shall check that the individual concerned is currently and genuinely a threat to public policy or public security and shall assess whether there has been any material change in the circumstances since the expulsion order was issued.

CHAPTER VII
FINAL PROVISIONS

Article 34 Publicity

Member States shall disseminate information concerning the rights and obligations of Union citizens and their family members on the subjects covered by this Directive, particularly by means of awareness-raising campaigns conducted through national and local media and other means of communication.

Article 35 Abuse of rights

Member States may adopt the necessary measures to refuse, terminate or withdraw any right conferred by this Directive in the case of abuse of rights or fraud, such as marriages of convenience. Any such measure shall be proportionate and subject to the procedural safeguards provided for in Articles 30 and 31.

Article 36 Sanctions

Member States shall lay down provisions on the sanctions applicable to breaches of national rules adopted for the implementation of this Directive and shall take the measures required for their application. The sanctions laid down shall be effective and proportionate. Member States shall notify the Commission of these provisions not later than [30 April 2006] and as promptly as possible in the case of any subsequent changes.

Article 37 More favourable national provisions

The provisions of this Directive shall not affect any laws, regulations or administrative provisions laid down by a Member State which would be more favourable to the persons covered by this Directive.

Article 38 Repeals

1. Articles 10 and 11 of Regulation (EEC) No 1612/68 shall be repealed with effect from [30 April 2006].
2. Directives 64/221/EEC, 68/360/EEC, 72/194/EEC, 73/148/EEC, 75/34/EEC, 75/35/EEC, 90/364/EEC, 90/365/EEC and 93/96/EEC shall be repealed with effect from [30 April 2006].
3. References made to the repealed provisions and Directives shall be construed as being made to this Directive.

Article 39 Report

No later than [30 April 2008] the Commission shall submit a report on the application of this Directive to the European Parliament and the Council, together with any necessary proposals, notably on the opportunity to extend the period of time during which Union citizens and their family members may reside in the territory of the host Member State without any conditions. The Member States shall provide the Commission with the information needed to produce the report.

Article 40 Transposition

1. Member States shall bring into force the laws, regulations and administrative provisions necessary to comply with this Directive by [30 April 2006].
   When Member States adopt those measures, they shall contain a reference to this Directive or shall be accompanied by such a reference on the occasion of their official publication. The methods of making such reference shall be laid down by the Member States.
2. Member States shall communicate to the Commission the text of the provisions of national law which they adopt in the field covered by this Directive together with a table showing how the provisions of this Directive correspond to the national provisions adopted.

Article 41   Entry into force

This Directive shall enter into force on the day of its publication in the Official Journal of the European Union.

Article 42   Addressees

This Directive is addressed to the Member States.

DIRECTIVE 2005/36/EC OF THE EUROPEAN PARLIAMENT AND OF THE COUNCIL of 7 SEPTEMBER 2005
on the recognition of professional qualifications
[2005] OJ L255/22

THE EUROPEAN PARLIAMENT AND THE COUNCIL OF THE EUROPEAN UNION,
Having regard to the Treaty establishing the European Community, and in particular Article 40, Article 47(1), the first and third sentences of Article 47(2), and Article 55 thereof,
Having regard to the proposal from the Commission,
Having regard to the opinion of the European Economic and Social Committee,
Acting in accordance with the procedure laid down in Article 251 of the Treaty,

Whereas:

(1) Pursuant to Article 3(1)(c) of the Treaty, the abolition, as between Member States, of obstacles to the free movement of persons and services is one of the objectives of the Community. For nationals of the Member States, this includes, in particular, the right to pursue a profession, in a self-employed or employed capacity, in a Member State other than the one in which they have obtained their professional qualifications. In addition, Article 47(1) of the Treaty lays down that directives shall be issued for the mutual recognition of diplomas, certificates and other evidence of formal qualifications.

(2) Following the European Council of Lisbon on 23 and 24 March 2000, the Commission adopted a Communication on 'An Internal Market Strategy for Services', aimed in particular at making the free provision of services within the Community as simple as within an individual Member State. Further to the Communication from the Commission entitled 'New European Labour Markets, Open to All, with Access to All', the European Council of Stockholm on 23 and 24 March 2001 entrusted the Commission with presenting for the 2002 Spring European Council specific proposals for a more uniform, transparent and flexible regime of recognition of qualifications.

(3) The guarantee conferred by this Directive on persons having acquired their professional qualifications in a Member State to have access to the same profession and pursue it in another Member State with the same rights as nationals is without prejudice to compliance by the migrant professional with any non-discriminatory conditions of pursuit which might be laid down by the latter Member State, provided that these are objectively justified and proportionate.

(4) In order to facilitate the free provision of services, there should be specific rules aimed at extending the possibility of pursuing professional activities under the original professional title. In the case of information society services provided at a distance, the provisions of Directive 2000/31/EC of the European Parliament and of the Council of 8 June 2000 on certain legal aspects of information society services, in particular electronic commerce, in the Internal Market, should also apply.

(5) In view of the different systems established for the cross-border provision of services on a temporary and occasional basis on the one hand, and for establishment on the other, the criteria for distinguishing between these two concepts in the event of the movement of the service provider to the territory of the host Member State should be clarified.

(6) The facilitation of service provision has to be ensured in the context of strict respect for public health and safety and consumer protection. Therefore, specific provisions should be envisaged for regulated professions having public health or safety implications, which provide cross-frontier services on a temporary or occasional basis.

(7) Host Member States may, where necessary and in accordance with Community law, provide for declaration requirements. These requirements should not lead to a disproportionate burden on service providers nor hinder or render less attractive the exercise of the freedom to provide services. The need for such requirements should be reviewed periodically in the light of the progress made in establishing a Community framework for administrative cooperation between Member States.

(8) The service provider should be subject to the application of disciplinary rules of the host Member State having a direct and specific link with the professional qualifications, such as the definition of the profession, the scope of activities covered by a profession or reserved to it, the use of titles and serious professional malpractice which is directly and specifically linked to consumer protection and safety.

(9) While maintaining, for the freedom of establishment, the principles and safeguards underlying the different systems for recognition in force, the rules of such systems should be improved in the light of experience. Moreover, the relevant directives have been amended on several occasions, and their provisions should be reorganised and rationalised by standardising the principles applicable. It is therefore necessary to replace Council Directives 89/48/EEC and 92/51/EEC, as well as Directive 1999/42/EC of the European Parliament and of the Council on the general system for the recognition of professional qualifications, and Council Directives 77/452/EEC, 77/453/EEC, 78/686/EEC, 78/687/EEC, 78/1026/EEC, 78/1027/EEC, 80/154/EEC, 80/155/EEC, 85/384/EEC, 85/432/EEC, 85/433/EEC and 93/16/EEC concerning the professions of nurse responsible for general care, dental practitioner, veterinary surgeon, midwife, architect, pharmacist and doctor, by combining them in a single text.

(10) This Directive does not create an obstacle to the possibility of Member States recognising, in accordance with their rules, the professional qualifications acquired outside the territory of the European Union by third country nationals. All recognition should respect in any case minimum training conditions for certain professions.

(11) In the case of the professions covered by the general system for the recognition of qualifications, hereinafter referred to as 'the general system', Member States should retain the right to lay down the minimum level of qualification required to ensure the quality of the services provided on their territory. However, pursuant to Articles 10, 39 and 43 of the Treaty, they should not require a national of a Member State to obtain qualifications, which they generally lay down only in terms of the diplomas awarded under their national educational system, where the person concerned has already obtained all or part of those qualifications in another Member State. As a result, it should be laid down that any host Member State in which a profession is regulated must take account of the qualifications obtained in another Member State and assess whether they correspond to those which it requires. The general system for recognition, however, does not prevent a Member State from making any person pursuing a profession on its territory subject to specific requirements due to the application of professional rules justified by the general public interest. Rules of this kind relate, for example, to organisation of the profession, professional standards, including those concerning ethics, and supervision and liability. Lastly, this Directive is not intended to interfere with Member States' legitimate interest in preventing any of their citizens from evading enforcement of the national law relating to professions.

(12) This Directive concerns the recognition by Member States of professional qualifications acquired in other Member States. It does not, however, concern the recognition by Member States of recognition decisions adopted by other Member States pursuant to this Directive. Consequently, individuals holding professional qualifications which have been recognised pursuant to this Directive may not use such recognition to obtain in their Member State of origin rights different from those conferred by the professional qualification obtained in that Member State, unless they provide evidence that they have obtained additional professional qualifications in the host Member State.

(13) In order to define the mechanism of recognition under the general system, it is necessary to group the various national education and training schemes into different levels. These levels, which are established only for the purpose of the operation of the general system, have no effect upon the national education and training structures nor upon the competence of Member States in this field.

(14) The mechanism of recognition established by Directives 89/48/EEC and 92/51/EEC remains unchanged. As a consequence, the holder of a diploma certifying successful completion of training at post-secondary level of a duration of at least one year should be permitted access to

a regulated profession in a Member State where access is contingent upon possession of a diploma certifying successful completion of higher or university education of four years' duration, regardless of the level to which the diploma required in the host Member State belongs. Conversely, where access to a regulated profession is contingent upon successful completion of higher or university education of more than four years, such access should be permitted only to holders of a diploma certifying successful completion of higher or university education of at least three years' duration.

(15) In the absence of harmonisation of the minimum training conditions for access to the professions governed by the general system, it should be possible for the host Member State to impose a compensation measure. This measure should be proportionate and, in particular, take account of the applicant's professional experience. Experience shows that requiring the migrant to choose between an aptitude test or an adaptation period offers adequate safeguards as regards the latter's level of qualification, so that any derogation from that choice should in each case be justified by an imperative requirement in the general interest.

(16) In order to promote the free movement of professionals, while ensuring an adequate level of qualification, various professional associations and organisations or Member States should be able to propose common platforms at European level. This Directive should take account, under certain conditions, in compliance with the competence of Member States to decide the qualifications required for the pursuit of professions in their territory as well as the contents and the organisation of their systems of education and professional training and in compliance with Community law, and in particular Community law on competition, of those initiatives, while promoting, in this context, a more automatic character of recognition under the general system. Professional associations which are in a position to submit common platforms should be representative at national and European level. A common platform is a set of criteria which make it possible to compensate for the widest range of substantial differences which have been identified between the training requirements in at least two thirds of the Member States including all the Member States which regulate that profession. These criteria could, for example, include requirements such as additional training, an adaptation period under supervised practice, an aptitude test, or a prescribed minimum level of professional practice, or combinations thereof.

(17) In order to take into account all situations for which there is still no provision relating to the recognition of professional qualifications, the general system should be extended to those cases which are not covered by a specific system, either where the profession is not covered by one of those systems or where, although the profession is covered by such a specific system, the applicant does not for some particular and exceptional reason meet the conditions to benefit from it.

(18) There is a need to simplify the rules allowing access to a number of industrial, commercial and craft activities, in Member States where those professions are regulated, in so far as those activities have been pursued for a reasonable and sufficiently recent period of time in another Member State, while maintaining for those activities a system of automatic recognition based on professional experience.

(19) Freedom of movement and the mutual recognition of the evidence of formal qualifications of doctors, nurses responsible for general care, dental practitioners, veterinary surgeons, midwives, pharmacists and architects should be based on the fundamental principle of automatic recognition of the evidence of formal qualifications on the basis of coordinated minimum conditions for training. In addition, access in the Member States to the professions of doctor, nurse responsible for general care, dental practitioner, veterinary surgeon, midwife and pharmacist should be made conditional upon the possession of a given qualification ensuring that the person concerned has undergone training which meets the minimum conditions laid down. This system should be supplemented by a number of acquired rights from which qualified professionals benefit under certain conditions.

(20) To allow for the characteristics of the qualification system for doctors and dentists and the related acquis communautaire in the area of mutual recognition, the principle of automatic recognition of medical and dental specialities common to at least two Member States should

continue to apply to all specialities recognised on the date of adoption of this Directive. To simplify the system, however, automatic recognition should apply after the date of entry into force of this Directive only to those new medical specialities common to at least two fifths of Member States. Moreover, this Directive does not prevent Member States from agreeing amongst themselves on automatic recognition for certain medical and dental specialities common to them but not automatically recognised within the meaning of this Directive, according to their own rules.

(21) Automatic recognition of formal qualifications of doctor with basic training should be without prejudice to the competence of Member States to associate this qualification with professional activities or not.

(22) All Member States should recognise the profession of dental practitioner as a specific profession distinct from that of medical practitioner, whether or not specialised in odontostomatology. Member States should ensure that the training given to dental practitioners equips them with the skills needed for prevention, diagnosis and treatment relating to anomalies and illnesses of the teeth, mouth, jaws and associated tissues. The professional activity of the dental practitioner should be carried out by holders of a qualification as dental practitioner set out in this Directive.

(23) It did not appear desirable to lay down standardised training for midwives for all the Member States. Rather, the latter should have the greatest possible freedom to organise their training.

(24) With a view to simplifying this Directive, reference should be made to the concept of 'pharmacist' in order to delimit the scope of the provisions relating to the automatic recognition of the qualifications, without prejudice to the special features of the national regulations governing those activities.

(25) Holders of qualifications as a pharmacist are specialists in the field of medicines and should, in principle, have access in all Member States to a minimum range of activities in this field. In defining this minimum range, this Directive should neither have the effect of limiting the activities accessible to pharmacists in the Member States, in particular as regards medical biology analyses, nor create a monopoly for those professionals, as this remains a matter solely for the Member States. The provisions of this Directive are without prejudice to the possibility for the Member States to impose supplementary training conditions for access to activities not included in the coordinated minimum range of activities. This means that the host Member State should be able to impose these conditions on the nationals who hold qualifications which are covered by automatic recognition within the meaning of this Directive.

(26) This Directive does not coordinate all the conditions for access to activities in the field of pharmacy and the pursuit of these activities. In particular, the geographical distribution of pharmacies and the monopoly for dispensing medicines should remain a matter for the Member States. This Directive leaves unchanged the legislative, regulatory and administrative provisions of the Member States forbidding companies from pursuing certain pharmacists' activities or subjecting the pursuit of such activities to certain conditions.

(27) Architectural design, the quality of buildings, their harmonious incorporation into their surroundings, respect for natural and urban landscapes and for the public and private heritage are a matter of public interest. Mutual recognition of qualifications should therefore be based on qualitative and quantitative criteria which ensure that the holders of recognised qualifications are in a position to understand and translate the needs of individuals, social groups and authorities as regards spatial planning, the design, organisation and realisation of structures, conservation and the exploitation of the architectural heritage, and protection of natural balances.

(28) National regulations in the field of architecture and on access to and the pursuit of the professional activities of an architect vary widely in scope. In most Member States, activities in the field of architecture are pursued, de jure or de facto, by persons bearing the title of architect alone or accompanied by another title, without those persons having a monopoly on the pursuit of such activities, unless there are legislative provisions to the contrary. These activities, or some of them, may also be pursued by other professionals, in particular by

engineers who have undergone special training in the field of construction or the art of building. With a view to simplifying this Directive, reference should be made to the concept of 'architect' in order to delimit the scope of the provisions relating to the automatic recognition of the qualifications in the field of architecture, without prejudice to the special features of the national regulations governing those activities.

(29) Where a national and European-level professional organisation or association for a regulated profession makes a reasoned request for specific provisions for the recognition of qualifications on the basis of coordination of minimum training conditions, the Commission shall assess the appropriateness of adopting a proposal for the amendment of this Directive.

(30) In order to ensure the effectiveness of the system for the recognition of professional qualifications, uniform formalities and rules of procedure should be defined for its implementation, as well as certain details of the pursuit of the profession.

(31) Since collaboration among the Member States and between them and the Commission is likely to facilitate the implementation of this Directive and compliance with the obligations deriving from it, the means of collaboration should be organised.

(32) The introduction, at European level, of professional cards by professional associations or organisations could facilitate the mobility of professionals, in particular by speeding up the exchange of information between the host Member State and the Member State of origin. This professional card should make it possible to monitor the career of professionals who establish themselves in various Member States. Such cards could contain information, in full respect of data protection provisions, on the professional's professional qualifications (university or institution attended, qualifications obtained, professional experience), his legal establishment, penalties received relating to his profession and the details of the relevant competent authority.

(33) The establishment of a network of contact points with the task of providing the citizens of the Member States with information and assistance will make it possible to ensure that the system of recognition is transparent. These contact points will provide any citizen who so requests and the Commission with all the information and addresses relevant to the recognition procedure. The designation of a single contact point by each Member State within this network does not affect the organisation of competencies at national level. In particular, it does not prevent the designation at national level of several offices, the contact point designated within the aforementioned network being in charge of coordinating with the other offices and informing the citizen, where necessary, of the details of the relevant competent office.

(34) Administering the various systems of recognition set up by the sectoral directives and the general system has proved cumbersome and complex. There is therefore a need to simplify the administration and updating of this Directive to take account of scientific and technical progress, in particular where the minimum conditions of training are coordinated with a view to automatic recognition of qualifications. A single committee for the recognition of professional qualifications should be set up for this purpose, and suitable involvement of representatives of the professional organisations, also at European level, should be ensured.

(35) The measures necessary for the implementation of this Directive should be adopted in accordance with Council Decision 1999/468/EC of 28 June 1999 laying down the procedures for the exercise of implementing powers conferred on the Commission.

(36) The preparation by the Member States of a periodic report on the implementation of this Directive, containing statistical data, will make it possible to determine the impact of the system for the recognition of professional qualifications.

(37) There should be a suitable procedure for adopting temporary measures if the application of any provision of this Directive were to encounter major difficulties in a Member State.

(38) The provisions of this Directive do not affect the powers of the Member States as regards the organisation of their national social security system and determining the activities which must be pursued under that system.

(39) In view of the speed of technological change and scientific progress, life-long learning is of particular importance for a large number of professions. In this context, it is for the Member States to adopt the detailed arrangements under which, through suitable ongoing training, professionals will keep abreast of technical and scientific progress.

(40) Since the objectives of this Directive, namely the rationalisation, simplification and improvement of the rules for the recognition of professional qualifications, cannot be sufficiently achieved by the Member States and can therefore be better achieved at Community level, the Community may adopt measures, in accordance with the principle of subsidiarity as set out in Article 5 of the Treaty. In accordance with the principle of proportionality, as set out in that Article, this Directive does not go beyond what is necessary in order to achieve those objectives.

(41) This Directive is without prejudice to the application of Articles 39(4) and 45 of the Treaty concerning notably notaries.

(42) This Directive applies, concerning the right of establishment and the provision of services, without prejudice to other specific legal provisions regarding the recognition of professional qualifications, such as those existing in the field of transport, insurance intermediaries and statutory auditors. This Directive does not affect the operation of Council Directive 77/249/EEC of 22 March 1977 to facilitate the effective exercise by lawyers of freedom to provide services, or of Directive 98/5/EC of the European Parliament and of the Council of 16 February 1998 to facilitate practice of the profession of lawyer on a permanent basis in a Member State other than that in which the qualification was obtained. The recognition of professional qualifications for lawyers for the purpose of immediate establishment under the professional title of the host Member State should be covered by this Directive.

(43) To the extent that they are regulated, this Directive includes also liberal professions, which are, according to this Directive, those practised on the basis of relevant professional qualifications in a personal, responsible and professionally independent capacity by those providing intellectual and conceptual services in the interest of the client and the public. The exercise of the profession might be subject in the Member States, in conformity with the Treaty, to specific legal constraints based on national legislation and on the statutory provisions laid down autonomously, within that framework, by the respective professional representative bodies, safeguarding and developing their professionalism and quality of service and the confidentiality of relations with the client.

(44) This Directive is without prejudice to measures necessary to ensure a high level of health and consumer protection,

HAVE ADOPTED THIS DIRECTIVE:

TITLE I
GENERAL PROVISIONS

Article 1   Purpose

This Directive establishes rules according to which a Member State which makes access to or pursuit of a regulated profession in its territory contingent upon possession of specific professional qualifications (referred to hereinafter as the host Member State) shall recognise professional qualifications obtained in one or more other Member States (referred to hereinafter as the home Member State) and which allow the holder of the said qualifications to pursue the same profession there, for access to and pursuit of that profession.

Article 2   Scope

1. This Directive shall apply to all nationals of a Member State wishing to pursue a regulated profession in a Member State, including those belonging to the liberal professions, other than that in which they obtained their professional qualifications, on either a self-employed or employed basis.

2. Each Member State may permit Member State nationals in possession of evidence of professional qualifications not obtained in a Member State to pursue a regulated profession within the meaning of Article 3(1)(a) on its territory in accordance with its rules. In the case of professions covered by Title III, Chapter III, this initial recognition shall respect the minimum training conditions laid down in that Chapter.

3. Where, for a given regulated profession, other specific arrangements directly related to the recognition of professional qualifications are established in a separate instrument of Community law, the corresponding provisions of this Directive shall not apply.

Article 3 Definitions

1. For the purposes of this Directive, the following definitions apply:

(a) 'regulated profession': a professional activity or group of professional activities, access to which, the pursuit of which, or one of the modes of pursuit of which is subject, directly or indirectly, by virtue of legislative, regulatory or administrative provisions to the possession of specific professional qualifications; in particular, the use of a professional title limited by legislative, regulatory or administrative provisions to holders of a given professional qualification shall constitute a mode of pursuit. Where the first sentence of this definition does not apply, a profession referred to in paragraph 2 shall be treated as a regulated profession;

(b) 'professional qualifications': qualifications attested by evidence of formal qualifications, an attestation of competence referred to in Article 11, point (a)(i) and/or professional experience;

(c) 'evidence of formal qualifications': diplomas, certificates and other evidence issued by an authority in a Member State designated pursuant to legislative, regulatory or administrative provisions of that Member State and certifying successful completion of professional training obtained mainly in the Community. Where the first sentence of this definition does not apply, evidence of formal qualifications referred to in paragraph 3 shall be treated as evidence of formal qualifications;

(d) 'competent authority': any authority or body empowered by a Member State specifically to issue or receive training diplomas and other documents or information and to receive the applications, and take the decisions, referred to in this Directive;

(e) 'regulated education and training': any training which is specifically geared to the pursuit of a given profession and which comprises a course or courses complemented, where appropriate, by professional training, or probationary or professional practice.

The structure and level of the professional training, probationary or professional practice shall be determined by the laws, regulations or administrative provisions of the Member State concerned or monitored or approved by the authority designated for that purpose;

(f) 'professional experience': the actual and lawful pursuit of the profession concerned in a Member State;

(g) 'adaptation period': the pursuit of a regulated profession in the host Member State under the responsibility of a qualified member of that profession, such period of supervised practice possibly being accompanied by further training. This period of supervised practice shall be the subject of an assessment. The detailed rules governing the adaptation period and its assessment as well as the status of a migrant under supervision shall be laid down by the competent authority in the host Member State.

The status enjoyed in the host Member State by the person undergoing the period of supervised practice, in particular in the matter of right of residence as well as obligations, social rights and benefits, allowances and remuneration, shall be established by the competent authorities in that Member State in accordance with applicable Community law;

(h) 'aptitude test': a test limited to the professional knowledge of the applicant, made by the competent authorities of the host Member State with the aim of assessing the ability of the applicant to pursue a regulated profession in that Member State. In order to permit this test to be carried out, the competent authorities shall draw up a list of subjects which, on the basis of a comparison of the education and training required in the Member State and that received by the applicant, are not covered by the diploma or other evidence of formal qualifications possessed by the applicant.

The aptitude test must take account of the fact that the applicant is a qualified professional in the home Member State or the Member State from which he comes. It shall cover subjects to be selected from those on the list, knowledge of which is essential in order to be able to pursue the profession in the host Member State. The test may also include knowledge of the professional rules applicable to the activities in question in the host Member State.

The detailed application of the aptitude test and the status, in the host Member State, of the applicant who wishes to prepare himself for the aptitude test in that State shall be determined by the competent authorities in that Member State;

(i) 'manager of an undertaking': any person who in an undertaking in the occupational field in question has pursued an activity:

    (i) as a manager of an undertaking or a manager of a branch of an undertaking; or

    (ii) as a deputy to the proprietor or the manager of an undertaking where that post involves responsibility equivalent to that of the proprietor or manager represented; or

    (iii) in a managerial post with duties of a commercial and/or technical nature and with responsibility for one or more departments of the undertaking.

2. A profession practised by the members of an association or organisation listed in Annex I shall be treated as a regulated profession.

The purpose of the associations or organisations referred to in the first subparagraph is, in particular, to promote and maintain a high standard in the professional field concerned. To that end they are recognised in a special form by a Member State and award evidence of formal qualifications to their members, ensure that their members respect the rules of professional conduct which they prescribe, and confer on them the right to use a title or designatory letters or to benefit from a status corresponding to those formal qualifications.

On each occasion that a Member State grants recognition to an association or organisation referred to in the first subparagraph, it shall inform the Commission, which shall publish an appropriate notification in the Official Journal of the European Union.

3. Evidence of formal qualifications issued by a third country shall be regarded as evidence of formal qualifications if the holder has three years' professional experience in the profession concerned on the territory of the Member State which recognised that evidence of formal qualifications in accordance with Article 2(2), certified by that Member State.

Article 4   Effects of recognition

1. The recognition of professional qualifications by the host Member State allows the beneficiary to gain access in that Member State to the same profession as that for which he is qualified in the home Member State and to pursue it in the host Member State under the same conditions as its nationals.

2. For the purposes of this Directive, the profession which the applicant wishes to pursue in the host Member State is the same as that for which he is qualified in his home Member State if the activities covered are comparable.

TITLE II

FREE PROVISION OF SERVICES

Article 5   Principle of the free provision of services

1. Without prejudice to specific provisions of Community law, as well as to Articles 6 and 7 of this Directive, Member States shall not restrict, for any reason relating to professional qualifications, the free provision of services in another Member State:

(a) if the service provider is legally established in a Member State for the purpose of pursuing the same profession there (hereinafter referred to as the Member State of establishment), and

(b) where the service provider moves, if he has pursued that profession in the Member State of establishment for at least two years during the 10 years preceding the provision of services when the profession is not regulated in that Member State. The condition requiring two years' pursuit shall not apply when either the profession or the education and training leading to the profession is regulated.

2. The provisions of this title shall only apply where the service provider moves to the territory of the host Member State to pursue, on a temporary and occasional basis, the profession referred to in paragraph 1.

    The temporary and occasional nature of the provision of services shall be assessed case by case, in particular in relation to its duration, its frequency, its regularity and its continuity.

3. Where a service provider moves, he shall be subject to professional rules of a professional, statutory or administrative nature which are directly linked to professional qualifications, such as the definition of the profession, the use of titles and serious professional malpractice which is directly and specifically linked to consumer protection and safety, as well as disciplinary provisions which are applicable in the host Member State to professionals who pursue the same profession in that Member State.

Article 6   Exemptions

Pursuant to Article 5(1), the host Member State shall exempt service providers established in another Member State from the requirements which it places on professionals established in its territory relating to:

(a) authorisation by, registration with or membership of a professional organisation or body. In order to facilitate the application of disciplinary provisions in force on their territory according to Article 5(3), Member States may provide either for automatic temporary registration with or for pro forma membership of such a professional organisation or body, provided that such registration or membership does not delay or complicate in any way the provision of services and does not entail any additional costs for the service provider. A copy of the declaration and, where applicable, of the renewal referred to in Article 7(1), accompanied, for professions which have implications for public health and safety referred to in Article 7(4) or which benefit from automatic recognition under Title III Chapter III, by a copy of the documents referred to in

Article 7(2) shall be sent by the competent authority to the relevant professional organisation or body, and this shall constitute automatic temporary registration or pro forma membership for this purpose;

(b) registration with a public social security body for the purpose of settling accounts with an insurer relating to activities pursued for the benefit of insured persons.

     The service provider shall, however, inform in advance or, in an urgent case, afterwards, the body referred to in point (b) of the services which he has provided.

Article 7   Declaration to be made in advance, if the service provider moves

1. Member States may require that, where the service provider first moves from one Member State to another in order to provide services, he shall inform the competent authority in the host Member State in a written declaration to be made in advance including the details of any insurance cover or other means of personal or collective protection with regard to professional liability. Such declaration shall be renewed once a year if the service provider intends to provide temporary or occasional services in that Member State during that year. The service provider may supply the declaration by any means.

2. Moreover, for the first provision of services or if there is a material change in the situation substantiated by the documents, Member States may require that the declaration be accompanied by the following documents:

    (a) proof of the nationality of the service provider;

    (b) an attestation certifying that the holder is legally established in a Member State for the purpose of pursuing the activities concerned and that he is not prohibited from practising, even temporarily, at the moment of delivering the attestation;

    (c) evidence of professional qualifications;

    (d) for cases referred to in Article 5(1)(b), any means of proof that the service provider has pursued the activity concerned for at least two years during the previous ten years;

    (e) for professions in the security sector, where the Member State so requires for its own nationals, evidence of no criminal convictions.

3. The service shall be provided under the professional title of the Member State of establishment, in so far as such a title exists in that Member State for the professional activity in question. That title shall be indicated in the official language or one of the official languages of the Member State of establishment in such a way as to avoid any confusion with the professional title of the host Member State. Where no such professional title exists in the Member State of establishment, the service provider shall indicate his formal qualification in the official language or one of the official languages of that Member State. By way of exception, the service shall be provided under the professional title of the host Member State for cases referred to in Title III Chapter III.

4. For the first provision of services, in the case of regulated professions having public health or safety implications, which do not benefit from automatic recognition under Title III Chapter III, the competent authority of the host Member State may check the professional qualifications of the service provider prior to the first provision of services. Such a prior check shall be possible only where the purpose of the check is to avoid serious damage to the health or safety of the service recipient due to a lack of professional qualification of the service provider and where this does not go beyond what is necessary for that purpose.

    Within a maximum of one month of receipt of the declaration and accompanying documents, the competent authority shall endeavour to inform the service provider either of its decision not to check his qualifications or of the outcome of such check. Where there is a difficulty which would result in delay, the competent authority shall notify the service provider within the first month of the reason for the delay and the timescale for a decision, which must be finalised within the second month of receipt of completed documentation.

    Where there is a substantial difference between the professional qualifications of the service provider and the training required in the host Member State, to the extent that that difference is such as to be harmful to public health or safety, the host Member State shall give the service provider the opportunity to show, in particular by means of an aptitude test, that he has acquired the knowledge or competence lacking. In any case, it must be possible to provide the service within one month of a decision being taken in accordance with the previous subparagraph.

    In the absence of a reaction of the competent authority within the deadlines set in the previous subparagraphs, the service may be provided.

    In cases where qualifications have been verified under this paragraph, the service shall be provided under the professional title of the host Member State.

Article 8   Administrative cooperation

1. The competent authorities of the host Member State may ask the competent authorities of the Member State of establishment, for each provision of services, to provide any information relevant to the legality of the service provider's establishment and his good conduct, as well as the absence of any disciplinary or criminal sanctions of a professional nature. The competent authorities of the Member State of establishment shall provide this information in accordance with the provisions of Article 56.

2. The competent authorities shall ensure the exchange of all information necessary for complaints by a recipient of a service against a service provider to be correctly pursued. Recipients shall be informed of the outcome of the complaint.

Article 9   Information to be given to the recipients of the service

In cases where the service is provided under the professional title of the Member State of establishment or under the formal qualification of the service provider, in addition to the other requirements relating to information contained in Community law, the competent authorities of the host Member State may require the service provider to furnish the recipient of the service with any or all of the following information:

(a) if the service provider is registered in a commercial register or similar public register, the register in which he is registered, his registration number, or equivalent means of identification contained in that register;

(b) if the activity is subject to authorisation in the Member State of establishment, the name and address of the competent supervisory authority;

(c)   any professional association or similar body with which the service provider is registered;

(d)   the professional title or, where no such title exists, the formal qualification of the service provider and the Member State in which it was awarded;

(e)   if the service provider performs an activity which is subject to VAT, the VAT identification number referred to in Article 22(1) of the sixth Council Directive 77/388/EEC of 17 May 1977 on the harmonisation of the laws of the Member States relating to turnover taxes – Common system of value added tax: uniform basis of assessment;

(f)   details of any insurance cover or other means of personal or collective protection with regard to professional liability.

TITLE III

FREEDOM OF ESTABLISHMENT

CHAPTER I

GENERAL SYSTEM FOR THE RECOGNITION OF EVIDENCE OF TRAINING

Article 10   Scope

This Chapter applies to all professions which are not covered by Chapters II and III of this Title and in the following cases in which the applicant, for specific and exceptional reasons, does not satisfy the conditions laid down in those Chapters:

(a)   for activities listed in Annex IV, when the migrant does not meet the requirements set out in Articles 17, 18 and 19;

(b)   for doctors with basic training, specialised doctors, nurses responsible for general care, dental practitioners, specialised dental practitioners, veterinary surgeons, midwives, pharmacists and architects, when the migrant does not meet the requirements of effective and lawful professional practice referred to in Articles 23, 27, 33, 37, 39, 43 and 49;

(c)   for architects, when the migrant holds evidence of formal qualification not listed in Annex V, point 5.7;

(d)   without prejudice to Articles 21(1), 23 and 27, for doctors, nurses, dental practitioners, veterinary surgeons, midwives, pharmacists and architects holding evidence of formal qualifications as a specialist, which must follow the training leading to the possession of a title listed in Annex V, points 5.1.1, 5.2.2, 5.3.2, 5.4.2, 5.5.2, 5.6.2 and 5.7.1, and solely for the purpose of the recognition of the relevant specialty;

(e)   for nurses responsible for general care and specialised nurses holding evidence of formal qualifications as a specialist which follows the training leading to the possession of a title listed in Annex V, point 5.2.2, when the migrant seeks recognition in another Member State where the relevant professional activities are pursued by specialised nurses without training as general care nurse;

(f)   for specialised nurses without training as general care nurse, when the migrant seeks recognition in another Member State where the relevant professional activities are pursued by nurses responsible for general care, specialised nurses without training as general care nurse or specialised nurses holding evidence of formal qualifications as a specialist which follows the training leading to the possession of the titles listed in Annex V, point 5.2.2;

(g)   for migrants meeting the requirements set out in Article 3(3).

Article 11   Levels of qualification

For the purpose of applying Article 13, the professional qualifications are grouped under the following levels as described below:

(a)   an attestation of competence issued by a competent authority in the home Member State designated pursuant to legislative, regulatory or administrative provisions of that Member State, on the basis of:

(i)   either a training course not forming part of a certificate or diploma within the meaning of points (b), (c), (d) or (e), or a specific examination without prior training, or full-time pursuit of the profession in a Member State for three consecutive years or for an equivalent duration on a part-time basis during the previous 10 years,

(ii)   or general primary or secondary education, attesting that the holder has acquired general knowledge;

(b)   a certificate attesting to a successful completion of a secondary course,

(i)   either general in character, supplemented by a course of study or professional training other than those referred to in point (c) and/or by the probationary or professional practice required in addition to that course,

(ii)   or technical or professional in character, supplemented where appropriate by a course of study or professional training as referred to in point (i), and/or by the probationary or professional practice required in addition to that course;

(c)   a diploma certifying successful completion of

(i)   either training at post-secondary level other than that referred to in points (d) and (e) of a duration of at least one year or of an equivalent duration on a part-time basis, one of the conditions of entry of which is, as a general rule, the successful completion of the secondary course required to obtain entry to university or higher education or the completion of equivalent school education of the second secondary level, as well as the professional training which may be required in addition to that post-secondary course; or

(ii)   in the case of a regulated profession, training with a special structure, included in Annex II, equivalent to the level of training provided for under (i), which provides a comparable professional standard and which prepares the trainee for a comparable level of responsibilities and functions. The list in Annex II may be amended in accordance with the procedure referred to in Article 58(2) in order to take account of training which meets the requirements provided for in the previous sentence;

(d)   a diploma certifying successful completion of training at post-secondary level of at least three and not more than four years' duration, or of an equivalent duration on a part-time basis, at a university or establishment of higher education or another establishment providing the same level of training, as well as the professional training which may be required in addition to that post-secondary course;

(e)   a diploma certifying that the holder has successfully completed a post-secondary course of at least four years' duration, or of an equivalent duration on a part-time basis, at a university or establishment of higher education or another establishment of equivalent level and, where appropriate, that he has successfully completed the professional training required in addition to the post-secondary course.

Article 12 Equal treatment of qualifications

Any evidence of formal qualifications or set of evidence of formal qualifications issued by a competent authority in a Member State, certifying successful completion of training in the Community which is recognised by that Member State as being of an equivalent level and which confers on the holder the same rights of access to or pursuit of a profession or prepares for the pursuit of that profession, shall be treated as evidence of formal qualifications of the type covered by Article 11, including the level in question.

Any professional qualification which, although not satisfying the requirements contained in the legislative, regulatory or administrative provisions in force in the home Member State for access to or the pursuit of a profession, confers on the holder acquired rights by virtue of these provisions, shall also be treated as such evidence of formal qualifications under the same conditions as set out in the first subparagraph. This applies in particular if the home Member State raises the level of training required for admission to a profession and for its exercise, and if an individual who has undergone former training, which does not meet the requirements of the new qualification, benefits from acquired rights by virtue of national legislative, regulatory or administrative provisions; in such case this former training is considered by the host Member State, for the purposes of the application of Article 13, as corresponding to the level of the new training.

## Article 13	Conditions for recognition

1. If access to or pursuit of a regulated profession in a host Member State is contingent upon possession of specific professional qualifications, the competent authority of that Member State shall permit access to and pursuit of that profession, under the same conditions as apply to its nationals, to applicants possessing the attestation of competence or evidence of formal qualifications required by another Member State in order to gain access to and pursue that profession on its territory.

   Attestations of competence or evidence of formal qualifications shall satisfy the following conditions:

   (a)	they shall have been issued by a competent authority in a Member State, designated in accordance with the legislative, regulatory or administrative provisions of that Member State;

   (b)	they shall attest a level of professional qualification at least equivalent to the level immediately prior to that which is required in the host Member State, as described in Article 11.

2. Access to and pursuit of the profession, as described in paragraph 1, shall also be granted to applicants who have pursued the profession referred to in that paragraph on a full-time basis for two years during the previous 10 years in another Member State which does not regulate that profession, providing they possess one or more attestations of competence or documents providing evidence of formal qualifications.

   Attestations of competence and evidence of formal qualifications shall satisfy the following conditions:

   (a)	they shall have been issued by a competent authority in a Member State, designated in accordance with the legislative, regulatory or administrative provisions of that Member State;

   (b)	they shall attest a level of professional qualification at least equivalent to the level immediately prior to that required in the host Member State, as described in Article 11;

   (c)	they shall attest that the holder has been prepared for the pursuit of the profession in question.

   The two years' professional experience referred to in the first subparagraph may not, however, be required if the evidence of formal qualifications which the applicant possesses certifies regulated education and training within the meaning of Article 3(1)(e) at the levels of qualifications described in Article 11, points (b), (c), (d) or (e). The regulated education and training listed in Annex III shall be considered as such regulated education and training at the level described in Article 11, point (c). The list in Annex III may be amended in accordance with the procedure referred to in Article 58(2) in order to take account of regulated education and training which provides a comparable professional standard and which prepares the trainee for a comparable level of responsibilities and functions.

3. By way of derogation from paragraph 1, point (b) and to paragraph 2, point (b), the host Member State shall permit access and pursuit of a regulated profession where access to this profession is contingent in its territory upon possession of a qualification certifying successful completion of higher or university education of four years' duration, and where the applicant possesses a qualification referred to in Article 11, point (c).

## Article 14	Compensation measures

1. Article 13 does not preclude the host Member State from requiring the applicant to complete an adaptation period of up to three years or to take an aptitude test if:

   (a)	the duration of the training of which he provides evidence under the terms of Article 13, paragraph 1 or 2, is at least one year shorter than that required by the host Member State;

   (b)	the training he has received covers substantially different matters than those covered by the evidence of formal qualifications required in the host Member State;

(c)   the regulated profession in the host Member State comprises one or more regulated professional activities which do not exist in the corresponding profession in the applicant's home Member State within the meaning of Article 4(2), and that difference consists in specific training which is required in the host Member State and which covers substantially different matters from those covered by the applicant's attestation of competence or evidence of formal qualifications.

2.   If the host Member State makes use of the option provided for in paragraph 1, it must offer the applicant the choice between an adaptation period and an aptitude test.

Where a Member State considers, with respect to a given profession, that it is necessary to derogate from the requirement, set out in the previous subparagraph, that it give the applicant a choice between an adaptation period and an aptitude test, it shall inform the other Member States and the Commission in advance and provide sufficient justification for the derogation.

If, after receiving all necessary information, the Commission considers that the derogation referred to in the second subparagraph is inappropriate or that it is not in accordance with Community law, it shall, within three months, ask the Member State in question to refrain from taking the envisaged measure. In the absence of a response from the Commission within the abovementioned deadline, the derogation may be applied.

3.   By way of derogation from the principle of the right of the applicant to choose, as laid down in paragraph 2, for professions whose pursuit requires precise knowledge of national law and in respect of which the provision of advice and/or assistance concerning national law is an essential and constant aspect of the professional activity, the host Member State may stipulate either an adaptation period or an aptitude test.

This applies also to the cases provided for in Article 10 points (b) and (c), in Article 10 point (d) concerning doctors and dental practitioners, in Article 10 point (f) when the migrant seeks recognition in another Member State where the relevant professional activities are pursued by nurses responsible for general care or specialised nurses holding evidence of formal qualifications as a specialist which follows the training leading to the possession of the titles listed in Annex V, point 5.2.2 and in Article 10 point (g).

In the cases covered by Article 10 point (a), the host Member State may require an adaptation period or an aptitude test if the migrant envisages pursuing professional activities in a self-employed capacity or as a manager of an undertaking which require the knowledge and the application of the specific national rules in force, provided that knowledge and application of those rules are required by the competent authorities of the host Member State for access to such activities by its own nationals.

4.   For the purpose of applying paragraph 1 points (b) and (c), 'substantially different matters' means matters of which knowledge is essential for pursuing the profession and with regard to which the training received by the migrant shows important differences in terms of duration or content from the training required by the host Member State.

5.   Paragraph 1 shall be applied with due regard to the principle of proportionality. In particular, if the host Member State intends to require the applicant to complete an adaptation period or take an aptitude test, it must first ascertain whether the knowledge acquired by the applicant in the course of his professional experience in a Member State or in a third country, is of a nature to cover, in full or in part, the substantial difference referred to in paragraph 4.

Article 15   Waiving of compensation measures on the basis of common platforms

1.   For the purpose of this Article, 'common platforms' is defined as a set of criteria of professional qualifications which are suitable for compensating for substantial differences which have been identified between the training requirements existing in the various Member States for a given profession. These substantial differences shall be identified by comparison between the duration and contents of the training in at least two thirds of the Member States, including all Member States which regulate this profession. The differences in the contents of the training may result from substantial differences in the scope of the professional activities.

2.   Common platforms as defined in paragraph 1 may be submitted to the Commission by Member States or by professional associations or organisations which are representative at national and European level. If the Commission, after consulting the Member States, is of the

opinion that a draft common platform facilitates the mutual recognition of professional qualifications, it may present draft measures with a view to their adoption in accordance with the procedure referred to in Article 58(2).

3.   Where the applicant's professional qualifications satisfy the criteria established in the measure adopted in accordance with paragraph 2, the host Member State shall waive the application of compensation measures under Article 14.

4.   Paragraphs 1 to 3 shall not affect the competence of Member States to decide the professional qualifications required for the pursuit of professions in their territory as well as the contents and the organisation of their systems of education and professional training.

5.   If a Member State considers that the criteria established in a measure adopted in accordance with paragraph 2 no longer offer adequate guarantees with regard to professional qualifications, it shall inform the Commission accordingly, which shall, if appropriate, present a draft measure in accordance with the procedure referred to in Article 58(2).

6.   The Commission shall, by 20 October 2010, submit to the European Parliament and the Council a report on the operation of this Article and, if necessary, appropriate proposals for amending this Article.

CHAPTER II
RECOGNITION OF PROFESSIONAL EXPERIENCE

Article 16 Requirements regarding professional experience

If, in a Member State, access to or pursuit of one of the activities listed in Annex IV is contingent upon possession of general, commercial or professional knowledge and aptitudes, that Member State shall recognise previous pursuit of the activity in another Member State as sufficient proof of such knowledge and aptitudes. The activity must have been pursued in accordance with Articles 17, 18 and 19.

Article 17 Activities referred to in list I of Annex IV

1.   For the activities in list I of Annex IV, the activity in question must have been previously pursued:

   (a)   for six consecutive years on a self-employed basis or as a manager of an undertaking; or

   (b)   for three consecutive years on a self-employed basis or as a manager of an undertaking, where the beneficiary proves that he has received previous training of at least three years for the activity in question, evidenced by a certificate recognised by the Member State or judged by a competent professional body to be fully valid; or

   (c)   for four consecutive years on a self-employed basis or as a manager of an undertaking, where the beneficiary can prove that he has received, for the activity in question, previous training of at least two years' duration, attested by a certificate recognised by the Member State or judged by a competent professional body to be fully valid; or

   (d)   for three consecutive years on a self-employed basis, if the beneficiary can prove that he has pursued the activity in question on an employed basis for at least five years; or

   (e)   for five consecutive years in an executive position, of which at least three years involved technical duties and responsibility for at least one department of the company, if the beneficiary can prove that he has received, for the activity in question, previous training of at least three years' duration, as attested by a certificate recognised by the Member State or judged by a competent professional body to be fully valid.

2.   In cases (a) and (d), the activity must not have finished more than 10 years before the date on which the complete application was submitted by the person concerned to the competent authority referred to in Article 56.

3.   Paragraph 1(e) shall not apply to activities in Group ex 855, hairdressing establishments, of the ISIC Nomenclature.

Article 18 Activities referred to in list II of Annex IV

1.   For the activities in list II of Annex IV, the activity in question must have been previously pursued:

(a) for five consecutive years on a self-employed basis or as a manager of an undertaking, or

(b) for three consecutive years on a self-employed basis or as a manager of an undertaking, where the beneficiary proves that he has received previous training of at least three years for the activity in question, evidenced by a certificate recognised by the Member State or judged by a competent professional body to be fully valid, or

(c) for four consecutive years on a self-employed basis or as a manager of an undertaking, where the beneficiary can prove that he has received, for the activity in question, previous training of at least two years' duration, attested by a certificate recognised by the Member State or judged by a competent professional body to be fully valid, or

(d) for three consecutive years on a self-employed basis or as a manager of an undertaking, if the beneficiary can prove that he has pursued the activity in question on an employed basis for at least five years, or

(e) for five consecutive years on an employed basis, if the beneficiary can prove that he has received, for the activity in question, previous training of at least three years' duration, as attested by a certificate recognised by the Member State or judged by a competent professional body to be fully valid, or

(f) for six consecutive years on an employed basis, if the beneficiary can prove that he has received previous training in the activity in question of at least two years' duration, as attested by a certificate recognised by the Member State or judged by a competent professional body to be fully valid.

2. In cases (a) and (d), the activity must not have finished more than 10 years before the date on which the complete application was submitted by the person concerned to the competent authority referred to in Article 56.

Article 19 Activities referred to in list III of Annex IV

1. For the activities in list III of Annex IV, the activity in question must have been previously pursued:

(a) for three consecutive years, either on a self-employed basis or as a manager of an undertaking, or

(b) for two consecutive years, either on a self-employed basis or as a manager of an undertaking, if the beneficiary can prove that he has received previous training for the activity in question, as attested by a certificate recognised by the Member State or judged by a competent professional body to be fully valid, or

(c) for two consecutive years, either on a self-employed basis or as a manager of an undertaking, if the beneficiary can prove that he has pursued the activity in question on an employed basis for at least three years, or

(d) for three consecutive years, on an employed basis, if the beneficiary can prove that he has received previous training for the activity in question, as attested by a certificate recognised by the Member State or judged by a competent professional body to be fully valid.

2. In cases (a) and (c), the activity must not have finished more than 10 years before the date on which the complete application was submitted by the person concerned to the competent authority referred to in Article 56.

Article 20 Amendment of the lists of activities in Annex IV

The lists of activities in Annex IV which are the subject of recognition of professional experience pursuant to Article 16 may be amended in accordance with the procedure referred to in Article 58(2) with a view to updating or clarifying the nomenclature, provided that this does not involve any change in the activities related to the individual categories.

CHAPTER III
RECOGNITION ON THE BASIS OF COORDINATION OF MINIMUM TRAINING CONDITIONS
SECTION 1
GENERAL PROVISIONS

Article 21 Principle of automatic recognition

1. Each Member State shall recognise evidence of formal qualifications as doctor giving access to the professional activities of doctor with basic training and specialised doctor, as nurse responsible for general care, as dental practitioner, as specialised dental practitioner, as veterinary surgeon, as pharmacist and as architect, listed in Annex V, points 5.1.1, 5.1.2, 5.2.2, 5.3.2, 5.3.3, 5.4.2, 5.6.2 and 5.7.1 respectively, which satisfy the minimum training conditions referred to in Articles 24, 25, 31, 34, 35, 38, 44 and 46 respectively, and shall, for the purposes of access to and pursuit of the professional activities, give such evidence the same effect on its territory as the evidence of formal qualifications which it itself issues.

    Such evidence of formal qualifications must be issued by the competent bodies in the Member States and accompanied, where appropriate, by the certificates listed in Annex V, points 5.1.1, 5.1.2, 5.2.2, 5.3.2, 5.3.3, 5.4.2, 5.6.2 and 5.7.1 respectively.

    The provisions of the first and second subparagraphs do not affect the acquired rights referred to in Articles 23, 27, 33, 37, 39 and 49.

2. Each Member State shall recognise, for the purpose of pursuing general medical practice in the framework of its national social security system, evidence of formal qualifications listed in Annex V, point 5.1.4 and issued to nationals of the Member States by the other Member States in accordance with the minimum training conditions laid down in Article 28.

    The provisions of the previous subparagraph do not affect the acquired rights referred to in Article 30.

3. Each Member State shall recognise evidence of formal qualifications as a midwife, awarded to nationals of Member States by the other Member States, listed in Annex V, point 5.5.2, which complies with the minimum training conditions referred to in Article 40 and satisfies the criteria set out in Article 41, and shall, for the purposes of access to and pursuit of the professional activities, give such evidence the same effect on its territory as the evidence of formal qualifications which it itself issues. This provision does not affect the acquired rights referred to in Articles 23 and 43.

4. Member States shall not be obliged to give effect to evidence of formal qualifications referred to in Annex V, point 5.6.2, for the setting up of new pharmacies open to the public. For the purposes of this paragraph, pharmacies which have been open for less than three years shall also be considered as new pharmacies.

5. Evidence of formal qualifications as an architect referred to in Annex V, point 5.7.1, which is subject to automatic recognition pursuant to paragraph 1, proves completion of a course of training which began not earlier than during the academic reference year referred to in that Annex.

6. Each Member State shall make access to and pursuit of the professional activities of doctors, nurses responsible for general care, dental practitioners, veterinary surgeons, midwives and pharmacists subject to possession of evidence of formal qualifications referred to in Annex V, points 5.1.1, 5.1.2, 5.1.4, 5.2.2, 5.3.2, 5.3.3, 5.4.2, 5.5.2 and 5.6.2 respectively, attesting that the person concerned has acquired, over the duration of his training, and where appropriate, the knowledge and skills referred to in Articles 24(3), 31(6), 34(3), 38(3), 40(3) and 44(3).

    The knowledge and skills referred to in Articles 24(3), 31(6), 34(3), 38(3), 40(3) and 44(3) may be amended in accordance with the procedure referred to in Article 58(2) with a view to adapting them to scientific and technical progress.

    Such updates shall not entail, for any Member State, an amendment of its existing legislative principles regarding the structure of professions as regards training and conditions of access by natural persons.

7. Each Member State shall notify the Commission of the legislative, regulatory and administrative provisions which it adopts with regard to the issuing of evidence of formal qualifications in the area covered by this Chapter. In addition, for evidence of formal qualifications in the area referred to in Section 8, this notification shall be addressed to the other Member States.

The Commission shall publish an appropriate communication in the Official Journal of the European Union, indicating the titles adopted by the Member States for evidence of formal qualifications and, where appropriate, the body which issues the evidence of formal qualifications, the certificate which accompanies it and the corresponding professional title referred to in Annex V, points 5.1.1, 5.1.2, 5.1.4, 5.2.2, 5.3.2, 5.3.3, 5.4.2, 5.5.2, 5.6.2 and 5.7.1 respectively.

Article 22 Common provisions on training

With regard to the training referred to in Articles 24, 25, 28, 31, 34, 35, 38, 40, 44 and 46:

(a) Member States may authorise part-time training under conditions laid down by the competent authorities; those authorities shall ensure that the overall duration, level and quality of such training is not lower than that of continuous full-time training;

(b) in accordance with the procedures specific to each Member State, continuing education and training shall ensure that persons who have completed their studies are able to keep abreast of professional developments to the extent necessary to maintain safe and effective practice.

Article 23 Acquired rights

1. Without prejudice to the acquired rights specific to the professions concerned, in cases where the evidence of formal qualifications as doctor giving access to the professional activities of doctor with basic training and specialised doctor, as nurse responsible for general care, as dental practitioner, as specialised dental practitioner, as veterinary surgeon, as midwife and as pharmacist held by Member States nationals does not satisfy all the training requirements referred to in Articles 24, 25, 31, 34, 35, 38, 40 and 44, each Member State shall recognise as sufficient proof evidence of formal qualifications issued by those Member States insofar as such evidence attests successful completion of training which began before the reference dates laid down in Annex V, points 5.1.1, 5.1.2, 5.2.2, 5.3.2, 5.3.3, 5.4.2, 5.5.2 and 5.6.2 and is accompanied by a certificate stating that the holders have been effectively and lawfully engaged in the activities in question for at least three consecutive years during the five years preceding the award of the certificate.

2. The same provisions shall apply to evidence of formal qualifications as doctor giving access to the professional activities of doctor with basic training and specialised doctor, as nurse responsible for general care, as dental practitioner, as specialised dental practitioner, as veterinary surgeon, as midwife and as pharmacist, obtained in the territory of the former German Democratic Republic, which does not satisfy all the minimum training requirements laid down in Articles 24, 25, 31, 34, 35, 38, 40 and 44 if such evidence certifies successful completion of training which began before:

(a) 3 October 1990 for doctors with basic training, nurses responsible for general care, dental practitioners with basic training, specialised dental practitioners, veterinary surgeons, midwives and pharmacists, and

(b) 3 April 1992 for specialised doctors.

The evidence of formal qualifications referred to in the first subparagraph confers on the holder the right to pursue professional activities throughout German territory under the same conditions as evidence of formal qualifications issued by the competent German authorities referred to in Annex V, points 5.1.1, 5.1.2, 5.2.2, 5.3.2, 5.3.3, 5.4.2, 5.5.2 and 5.6.2.

3. Without prejudice to the provisions of Article 37(1), each Member State shall recognise evidence of formal qualifications as doctor giving access to the professional activities of doctor with basic training and specialised doctor, as nurse responsible for general care, as veterinary surgeon, as midwife, as pharmacist and as architect held by Member States nationals and issued by the former Czechoslovakia, or whose training commenced, for the Czech Republic and Slovakia, before 1 January 1993, where the authorities of either of the two

aforementioned Member States attest that such evidence of formal qualifications has the same legal validity within their territory as the evidence of formal qualifications which they issue and, with respect to architects, as the evidence of formal qualifications specified for those Member States in Annex VI, point 6, as regards access to the professional activities of doctor with basic training, specialised doctor, nurse responsible for general care, veterinary surgeon, midwife, pharmacist with respect to the activities referred to in Article 45(2), and architect with respect to the activities referred to in Article 48, and the pursuit of such activities.

Such an attestation must be accompanied by a certificate issued by those same authorities stating that such persons have effectively and lawfully been engaged in the activities in question within their territory for at least three consecutive years during the five years prior to the date of issue of the certificate.

4.   Each Member State shall recognise evidence of formal qualifications as doctor giving access to the professional activities of doctor with basic training and specialised doctor, as nurse responsible for general care, as dental practitioner, as specialised dental practitioner, as veterinary surgeon, as midwife, as pharmacist and as architect held by nationals of the Member States and issued by the former Soviet Union, or whose training commenced

(a)   for Estonia, before 20 August 1991,

(b)   for Latvia, before 21 August 1991,

(c)   for Lithuania, before 11 March 1990,

where the authorities of any of the three aforementioned Member States attest that such evidence has the same legal validity within their territory as the evidence which they issue and, with respect to architects, as the evidence of formal qualifications specified for those Member States in Annex VI, point 6, as regards access to the professional activities of doctor with basic training, specialised doctor, nurse responsible for general care, dental practitioner, specialised dental practitioner, veterinary surgeon, midwife, pharmacist with respect to the activities referred to in Article 45(2), and architect with respect to the activities referred to in Article 48, and the pursuit of such activities.

Such an attestation must be accompanied by a certificate issued by those same authorities stating that such persons have effectively and lawfully been engaged in the activities in question within their territory for at least three consecutive years during the five years prior to the date of issue of the certificate.

With regard to evidence of formal qualifications as veterinary surgeons issued by the former Soviet Union or in respect of which training commenced, for Estonia, before 20 August 1991, the attestation referred to in the preceding subparagraph must be accompanied by a certificate issued by the Estonian authorities stating that such persons have effectively and lawfully been engaged in the activities in question within their territory for at least five consecutive years during the seven years prior to the date of issue of the certificate.

5.   Each Member State shall recognise evidence of formal qualifications as doctor giving access to the professional activities of doctor with basic training and specialised doctor, as nurse responsible for general care, as dental practitioner, as specialised dental practitioner, as veterinary surgeon, as midwife, as pharmacist and as architect held by nationals of the Member States and issued by the former Yugoslavia, or whose training commenced, for Slovenia, before 25 June 1991, where the authorities of the aforementioned Member State attest that such evidence has the same legal validity within their territory as the evidence which they issue and, with respect to architects, as the evidence of formal qualifications specified for those Member States in Annex VI, point 6, as regards access to the professional activities of doctor with basic training, specialised doctor, nurse responsible for general care, dental practitioner, specialised dental practitioner, veterinary surgeon, midwife, pharmacist with respect to the activities referred to in Article 45(2), and architect with respect to the activities referred to in Article 48, and the pursuit of such activities.

Such an attestation must be accompanied by a certificate issued by those same authorities stating that such persons have effectively and lawfully been engaged in the activities in question within their territory for at least three consecutive years during the five years prior to the date of issue of the certificate.

6. Each Member State shall recognise as sufficient proof for Member State nationals whose evidence of formal qualifications as a doctor, nurse responsible for general care, dental practitioner, veterinary surgeon, midwife and pharmacist does not correspond to the titles given for that Member State in Annex V, points 5.1.1, 5.1.2, 5.1.3, 5.1.4, 5.2.2, 5.3.2, 5.3.3, 5.4.2, 5.5.2 and 5.6.2, evidence of formal qualifications issued by those Member States accompanied by a certificate issued by the competent authorities or bodies.

    The certificate referred to in the first subparagraph shall state that the evidence of formal qualifications certifies successful completion of training in accordance with Articles 24, 25, 28, 31, 34, 35, 38, 40 and 44 respectively and is treated by the Member State which issued it in the same way as the qualifications whose titles are listed in Annex V, points 5.1.1, 5.1.2, 5.1.3, 5.1.4, 5.2.2, 5.3.2, 5.3.3, 5.4.2, 5.5.2 and 5.6.2.

SECTION 2
DOCTORS OF MEDICINE

Article 24 Basic medical training

1. Admission to basic medical training shall be contingent upon possession of a diploma or certificate providing access, for the studies in question, to universities.

2. Basic medical training shall comprise a total of at least six years of study or 5 500 hours of theoretical and practical training provided by, or under the supervision of, a university.

    For persons who began their studies before 1 January 1972, the course of training referred to in the first subparagraph may comprise six months of full-time practical training at university level under the supervision of the competent authorities.

3. Basic medical training shall provide an assurance that the person in question has acquired the following knowledge and skills:

    (a) adequate knowledge of the sciences on which medicine is based and a good understanding of the scientific methods including the principles of measuring biological functions, the evaluation of scientifically established facts and the analysis of data;

    (b) sufficient understanding of the structure, functions and behaviour of healthy and sick persons, as well as relations between the state of health and physical and social surroundings of the human being;

    (c) adequate knowledge of clinical disciplines and practices, providing him with a coherent picture of mental and physical diseases, of medicine from the points of view of prophylaxis, diagnosis and therapy and of human reproduction;

    (d) suitable clinical experience in hospitals under appropriate supervision.

Article 25 Specialist medical training

1. Admission to specialist medical training shall be contingent upon completion and validation of six years of study as part of a training programme referred to in Article 24 in the course of which the trainee has acquired the relevant knowledge of basic medicine.

2. Specialist medical training shall comprise theoretical and practical training at a university or medical teaching hospital or, where appropriate, a medical care establishment approved for that purpose by the competent authorities or bodies.

    The Member States shall ensure that the minimum duration of specialist medical training courses referred to in Annex V, point 5.1.3 is not less than the duration provided for in that point. Training shall be given under the supervision of the competent authorities or bodies. It shall include personal participation of the trainee specialised doctor in the activity and responsibilities entailed by the services in question.

3. Training shall be given on a full-time basis at specific establishments which are recognised by the competent authorities. It shall entail participation in the full range of medical activities of the department where the training is given, including duty on call, in such a way that the trainee specialist devotes all his professional activity to his practical and theoretical training throughout the entire working week and throughout the year, in accordance with the procedures laid down by the competent authorities. Accordingly, these posts shall be the subject of appropriate remuneration.

4.   The Member States shall make the issuance of evidence of specialist medical training contingent upon possession of evidence of basic medical training referred to in Annex V, point 5.1.1.

5.   The minimum periods of training referred to in Annex V, point 5.1.3 may be amended in accordance with the procedure referred to in Article 58(2) with a view to adapting them to scientific and technical progress.

Article 26   Types of specialist medical training

Evidence of formal qualifications as a specialised doctor referred to in Article 21 is such evidence awarded by the competent authorities or bodies referred to in Annex V, point 5.1.2 as corresponds, for the specialised training in question, to the titles in use in the various Member States and referred to in Annex V, point 5.1.3.

The inclusion in Annex V, point 5.1.3 of new medical specialties common to at least two fifths of the Member States may be decided on in accordance with the procedure referred to in Article 58(2) with a view to updating this Directive in the light of changes in national legislation.

Article 27   Acquired rights specific to specialised doctors

1.   A host Member State may require of specialised doctors whose part-time specialist medical training was governed by legislative, regulatory and administrative provisions in force as of 20 June 1975 and who began their specialist training no later than 31 December 1983 that their evidence of formal qualifications be accompanied by a certificate stating that they have been effectively and lawfully engaged in the relevant activities for at least three consecutive years during the five years preceding the award of that certificate.

2.   Every Member State shall recognise the qualification of specialised doctors awarded in Spain to doctors who completed their specialist training before 1 January 1995, even if that training does not satisfy the minimum training requirements provided for in Article 25, in so far as that qualification is accompanied by a certificate issued by the competent Spanish authorities and attesting that the person concerned has passed the examination in specific professional competence held in the context of exceptional measures concerning recognition laid down in Royal Decree 1497/99, with a view to ascertaining that the person concerned possesses a level of knowledge and skill comparable to that of doctors who possess a qualification as a specialised doctor defined for Spain in Annex V, points 5.1.2 and 5.1.3.

3.   Every Member State which has repealed its legislative, regulatory or administrative provisions relating to the award of evidence of formal qualifications as a specialised doctor referred to in Annex V, points 5.1.2 and 5.1.3 and which has adopted measures relating to acquired rights benefiting its nationals, shall grant nationals of other Member States the right to benefit from those measures, in so far as such evidence of formal qualifications was issued before the date on which the host Member State ceased to issue such evidence for the specialty in question. The dates on which these provisions were repealed are set out in Annex V, point 5.1.3.

Article 28   Specific training in general medical practice

1.   Admission to specific training in general medical practice shall be contingent on the completion and validation of six years of study as part of a training programme referred to in Article 24.

2.   The specific training in general medical practice leading to the award of evidence of formal qualifications issued before 1 January 2006 shall be of a duration of at least two years on a full-time basis. In the case of evidence of formal qualifications issued after that date, the training shall be of a duration of at least three years on a full-time basis.

Where the training programme referred to in Article 24 comprises practical training given by an approved hospital possessing appropriate general medical equipment and services or as part of an approved general medical practice or an approved centre in which doctors provide primary medical care, the duration of that practical training may, up to a maximum of one year, be included in the duration provided for in the first subparagraph for certificates of training issued on or after 1 January 2006.

The option provided for in the second subparagraph shall be available only for Member States in which the specific training in general medical practice lasted two years as of 1 January 2001.

3. The specific training in general medical practice shall be carried out on a full-time basis, under the supervision of the competent authorities or bodies. It shall be more practical than theoretical.

The practical training shall be given, on the one hand, for at least six months in an approved hospital possessing appropriate equipment and services and, on the other hand, for at least six months as part of an approved general medical practice or an approved centre at which doctors provide primary health care.

The practical training shall take place in conjunction with other health establishments or structures concerned with general medicine. Without prejudice to the minimum periods laid down in the second subparagraph, however, the practical training may be given during a period of not more than six months in other approved establishments or health structures concerned with general medicine.

The training shall require the personal participation of the trainee in the professional activity and responsibilities of the persons with whom he is working.

4. Member States shall make the issuance of evidence of formal qualifications in general medical practice subject to possession of evidence of formal qualifications in basic medical training referred to in Annex V, point 5.1.1.

5. Member States may issue evidence of formal qualifications referred to in Annex V, point 5.1.4 to a doctor who has not completed the training provided for in this Article but who has completed a different, supplementary training, as attested by evidence of formal qualifications issued by the competent authorities in a Member State. They may not, however, award evidence of formal qualifications unless it attests knowledge of a level qualitatively equivalent to the knowledge acquired from the training provided for in this Article.

Member States shall determine, inter alia, the extent to which the complementary training and professional experience already acquired by the applicant may replace the training provided for in this Article.

The Member States may only issue the evidence of formal qualifications referred to in Annex V, point 5.1.4 if the applicant has acquired at least six months' experience of general medicine in a general medical practice or a centre in which doctors provide primary health care of the types referred to in paragraph 3.

Article 29 Pursuit of the professional activities of general practitioners

Each Member State shall, subject to the provisions relating to acquired rights, make the pursuit of the activities of a general practitioner in the framework of its national social security system contingent upon possession of evidence of formal qualifications referred to in Annex V, point 5.1.4. Member States may exempt persons who are currently undergoing specific training in general medicine from this condition.

Article 30 Acquired rights specific to general practitioners

1. Each Member State shall determine the acquired rights. It shall, however, confer as an acquired right the right to pursue the activities of a general practitioner in the framework of its national social security system, without the evidence of formal qualifications referred to in Annex V, point 5.1.4, on all doctors who enjoy this right as of the reference date stated in that point by virtue of provisions applicable to the medical profession giving access to the professional activities of doctor with basic training and who are established as of that date on its territory, having benefited from the provisions of Articles 21 or 23.

The competent authorities of each Member State shall, on demand, issue a certificate stating the holder's right to pursue the activities of general practitioner in the framework of their national social security systems, without the evidence of formal qualifications referred to in Annex V, point 5.1.4, to doctors who enjoy acquired rights pursuant to the first subparagraph.

2. Every Member State shall recognise the certificates referred to in paragraph 1, second subparagraph, awarded to nationals of Member States by the other Member States, and shall

give such certificates the same effect on its territory as evidence of formal qualifications which it awards and which permit the pursuit of the activities of a general practitioner in the framework of its national social security system.

SECTION 3
NURSES RESPONSIBLE FOR GENERAL CARE

Article 31 Training of nurses responsible for general care

1. Admission to training for nurses responsible for general care shall be contingent upon completion of general education of 10 years, as attested by a diploma, certificate or other evidence issued by the competent authorities or bodies in a Member State or by a certificate attesting success in an examination, of an equivalent level, for admission to a school of nursing.

2. Training of nurses responsible for general care shall be given on a full-time basis and shall include at least the programme described in Annex V, point 5.2.1.

   The content listed in Annex V, point 5.2.1 may be amended in accordance with the procedure referred to in Article 58(2) with a view to adapting it to scientific and technical progress.

   Such updates may not entail, for any Member State, any amendment of its existing legislative principles relating to the structure of professions as regards training and the conditions of access by natural persons.

3. The training of nurses responsible for general care shall comprise at least three years of study or 4 600 hours of theoretical and clinical training, the duration of the theoretical training representing at least one-third and the duration of the clinical training at least one half of the minimum duration of the training. Member States may grant partial exemptions to persons who have received part of their training on courses which are of at least an equivalent level.

   The Member States shall ensure that institutions providing nursing training are responsible for the coordination of theoretical and clinical training throughout the entire study programme.

4. Theoretical training is that part of nurse training from which trainee nurses acquire the professional knowledge, insights and skills necessary for organising, dispensing and evaluating overall health care. The training shall be given by teachers of nursing care and by other competent persons, in nursing schools and other training establishments selected by the training institution.

5. Clinical training is that part of nurse training in which trainee nurses learn, as part of a team and in direct contact with a healthy or sick individual and/or community, to organise, dispense and evaluate the required comprehensive nursing care, on the basis of the knowledge and skills which they have acquired. The trainee nurse shall learn not only how to work in a team, but also how to lead a team and organise overall nursing care, including health education for individuals and small groups, within the health institute or in the community.

   This training shall take place in hospitals and other health institutions and in the community, under the responsibility of nursing teachers, in cooperation with and assisted by other qualified nurses. Other qualified personnel may also take part in the teaching process.

   Trainee nurses shall participate in the activities of the department in question insofar as those activities are appropriate to their training, enabling them to learn to assume the responsibilities involved in nursing care.

6. Training for nurses responsible for general care shall provide an assurance that the person in question has acquired the following knowledge and skills:

   (a) adequate knowledge of the sciences on which general nursing is based, including sufficient understanding of the structure, physiological functions and behaviour of healthy and sick persons, and of the relationship between the state of health and the physical and social environment of the human being;

   (b) sufficient knowledge of the nature and ethics of the profession and of the general principles of health and nursing;

(c)   adequate clinical experience; such experience, which should be selected for its training value, should be gained under the supervision of qualified nursing staff and in places where the number of qualified staff and equipment are appropriate for the nursing care of the patient;

(d)   the ability to participate in the practical training of health personnel and experience of working with such personnel;

(e)   experience of working with members of other professions in the health sector.

Article 32 Pursuit of the professional activities of nurses responsible for general care

For the purposes of this Directive, the professional activities of nurses responsible for general care are the activities pursued on a professional basis and referred to in Annex V, point 5.2.2.

Article 33 Acquired rights specific to nurses responsible for general care

1.   Where the general rules of acquired rights apply to nurses responsible for general care, the activities referred to in Article 23 must have included full responsibility for the planning, organisation and administration of nursing care delivered to the patient.

2.   As regards the Polish qualification of nurse responsible for general care, only the following acquired rights provisions shall apply. In the case of nationals of the Member States whose evidence of formal qualifications as nurse responsible for general care was awarded by, or whose training started in, Poland before 1 May 2004 and who do not satisfy the minimum training requirements laid down in Article 31, Member States shall recognise the following evidence of formal qualifications as nurse responsible for general care as being sufficient proof if accompanied by a certificate stating that those Member State nationals have effectively and lawfully been engaged in the activities of a nurse responsible for general care in Poland for the period specified below:

(a)   evidence of formal qualifications as a nurse at degree level (dyplom licencjata pielegniarstwa) — at least three consecutive years during the five years prior to the date of issue of the certificate,

(b)   evidence of formal qualifications as a nurse certifying completion of post-secondary education obtained from a medical vocational school (dyplom pielegniarki albo pielegniarki dyplomowanej) — at least five consecutive years during the seven years prior to the date of issue of the certificate.

The said activities must have included taking full responsibility for the planning, organisation and administration of nursing care delivered to the patient.

3.   Member States shall recognise evidence of formal qualifications in nursing awarded in Poland, to nurses who completed training before 1 May 2004, which did not comply with the minimum training requirements laid down in Article 31, attested by the diploma 'bachelor' which has been obtained on the basis of a special upgrading programme contained in Article 11 of the Act of 20 April 2004 on the amendment of the Act on professions of nurse and midwife and on some other legal acts (Official Journal of the Republic of Poland of 30 April 2004 No 92, pos. 885), and the Regulation of the Minister of Health of 11 May 2004 on the detailed conditions of delivering studies for nurses and midwives, who hold a certificate of secondary school (final examination — matura) and are graduates of medical lyceum and medical vocational schools teaching in a profession of a nurse and a midwife (Official Journal of the Republic of Poland of 13 May 2004 No 110, pos. 1170), with the aim of verifying that the person concerned has a level of knowledge and competence comparable to that of nurses holding the qualifications which, in the case of Poland, are defined in Annex V, point 5.2.2.

SECTION 4
DENTAL PRACTITIONERS

Article 34 Basic dental training

1.   Admission to basic dental training presupposes possession of a diploma or certificate giving access, for the studies in question, to universities or higher institutes of a level recognised as equivalent, in a Member State.

2.   Basic dental training shall comprise a total of at least five years of full-time theoretical and practical study, comprising at least the programme described in Annex V, point 5.3.1 and given in a university, in a higher institute providing training recognised as being of an equivalent level or under the supervision of a university.

The content listed in Annex V, point 5.3.1 may be amended in accordance with the procedure referred to in Article 58(2) with a view to adapting it to scientific and technical progress.

Such updates may not entail, for any Member State, any amendment of its existing legislative principles relating to the system of professions as regards training and the conditions of access by natural persons.

3.   Basic dental training shall provide an assurance that the person in question has acquired the following knowledge and skills:

(a)   adequate knowledge of the sciences on which dentistry is based and a good understanding of scientific methods, including the principles of measuring biological functions, the evaluation of scientifically established facts and the analysis of data;

(b)   adequate knowledge of the constitution, physiology and behaviour of healthy and sick persons as well as the influence of the natural and social environment on the state of health of the human being, in so far as these factors affect dentistry;

(c)   adequate knowledge of the structure and function of the teeth, mouth, jaws and associated tissues, both healthy and diseased, and their relationship to the general state of health and to the physical and social well-being of the patient;

(d)   adequate knowledge of clinical disciplines and methods, providing the dentist with a coherent picture of anomalies, lesions and diseases of the teeth, mouth, jaws and associated tissues and of preventive, diagnostic and therapeutic dentistry;

(e)   suitable clinical experience under appropriate supervision.

This training shall provide him with the skills necessary for carrying out all activities involving the prevention, diagnosis and treatment of anomalies and diseases of the teeth, mouth, jaws and associated tissues.

Article 35   Specialist dental training

1.   Admission to specialist dental training shall entail the completion and validation of five years of theoretical and practical instruction within the framework of the training referred to in Article 34, or possession of the documents referred to in Articles 23 and 37.

2.   Specialist dental training shall comprise theoretical and practical instruction in a university centre, in a treatment teaching and research centre or, where appropriate, in a health establishment approved for that purpose by the competent authorities or bodies.

Full-time specialist dental courses shall be of a minimum of three years' duration supervised by the competent authorities or bodies. It shall involve the personal participation of the dental practitioner training to be a specialist in the activity and in the responsibilities of the establishment concerned.

The minimum period of training referred to in the second sub-paragraph may be amended in accordance with the procedure referred to in Article 58(2) with a view to adapting it to scientific and technical progress.

3.   The Member States shall make the issuance of evidence of specialist dental training contingent upon possession of evidence of basic dental training referred to in Annex V, point 5.3.2.

Article 36   Pursuit of the professional activities of dental practitioners

1.   For the purposes of this Directive, the professional activities of dental practitioners are the activities defined in paragraph 3 and pursued under the professional qualifications listed in Annex V, point 5.3.2.

2.   The profession of dental practitioner shall be based on dental training referred to in Article 34 and shall constitute a specific profession which is distinct from other general or specialised medical professions. Pursuit of the activities of a dental practitioner requires the possession of evidence of formal qualifications referred to in Annex V, point 5.3.2. Holders of such

evidence of formal qualifications shall be treated in the same way as those to whom Articles 23 or 37 apply.

3. The Member States shall ensure that dental practitioners are generally able to gain access to and pursue the activities of prevention, diagnosis and treatment of anomalies and diseases affecting the teeth, mouth, jaws and adjoining tissue, having due regard to the regulatory provisions and rules of professional ethics on the reference dates referred to in Annex V, point 5.3.2.

Article 37 Acquired rights specific to dental practitioners

1. Every Member State shall, for the purposes of the pursuit of the professional activities of dental practitioners under the qualifications listed in Annex V, point 5.3.2, recognise evidence of formal qualifications as a doctor issued in Italy, Spain, Austria, the Czech Republic and Slovakia to persons who began their medical training on or before the reference date stated in that Annex for the Member State concerned, accompanied by a certificate issued by the competent authorities of that Member State.

    The certificate must show that the two following conditions are met:

    (a) that the persons in question have been effectively, lawfully and principally engaged in that Member State in the activities referred to in Article 36 for at least three consecutive years during the five years preceding the award of the certificate;

    (b) that those persons are authorised to pursue the said activities under the same conditions as holders of evidence of formal qualifications listed for that Member State in Annex V, point 5.3.2.

    Persons who have successfully completed at least three years of study, certified by the competent authorities in the Member State concerned as being equivalent to the training referred to in Article 34, shall be exempt from the three-year practical work experience referred to in the second subparagraph, point (a).

    With regard to the Czech Republic and Slovakia, evidence of formal qualifications obtained in the former Czechoslovakia shall be accorded the same level of recognition as Czech and Slovak evidence of formal qualifications and under the same conditions as set out in the preceding subparagraphs.

2. Each Member State shall recognise evidence of formal qualifications as a doctor issued in Italy to persons who began their university medical training after 28 January 1980 and no later than 31 December 1984, accompanied by a certificate issued by the competent Italian authorities.

    The certificate must show that the three following conditions are met:

    (a) that the persons in question passed the relevant aptitude test held by the competent Italian authorities with a view to establishing that those persons possess a level of knowledge and skills comparable to that of persons possessing evidence of formal qualifications listed for Italy in Annex V, point 5.3.2;

    (b) that they have been effectively, lawfully and principally engaged in the activities referred to in Article 36 in Italy for at least three consecutive years during the five years preceding the award of the certificate;

    (c) that they are authorised to engage in or are effectively, lawfully and principally engaged in the activities referred to in Article 36, under the same conditions as the holders of evidence of formal qualifications listed for Italy in Annex V, point 5.3.2.

    Persons who have successfully completed at least three years of study certified by the competent authorities as being equivalent to the training referred to in Article 34 shall be exempt from the aptitude test referred to in the second subparagraph, point (a).

    Persons who began their university medical training after 31 December 1984 shall be treated in the same way as those referred to above, provided that the abovementioned three years of study began before 31 December 1994.

SECTION 5
VETERINARY SURGEONS

Article 38 The training of veterinary surgeons

1. The training of veterinary surgeons shall comprise a total of at least five years of full-time theoretical and practical study at a university or at a higher institute providing training recognised as being of an equivalent level, or under the supervision of a university, covering at least the study programme referred to in Annex V, point 5.4.1.

    The content listed in Annex V, point 5.4.1 may be amended in accordance with the procedure referred to in Article 58(2) with a view to adapting it to scientific and technical progress.

    Such updates may not entail, for any Member State, any amendment of its existing legislative principles relating to the structure of professions as regards training and conditions of access by natural persons.

2. Admission to veterinary training shall be contingent upon possession of a diploma or certificate entitling the holder to enter, for the studies in question, university establishments or institutes of higher education recognised by a Member State to be of an equivalent level for the purpose of the relevant study.

3. Training as a veterinary surgeon shall provide an assurance that the person in question has acquired the following knowledge and skills:

    (a) adequate knowledge of the sciences on which the activities of the veterinary surgeon are based;

    (b) adequate knowledge of the structure and functions of healthy animals, of their husbandry, reproduction and hygiene in general, as well as their feeding, including the technology involved in the manufacture and preservation of foods corresponding to their needs;

    (c) adequate knowledge of the behaviour and protection of animals;

    (d) adequate knowledge of the causes, nature, course, effects, diagnosis and treatment of the diseases of animals, whether considered individually or in groups, including a special knowledge of the diseases which may be transmitted to humans;

    (e) adequate knowledge of preventive medicine;

    (f) adequate knowledge of the hygiene and technology involved in the production, manufacture and putting into circulation of animal foodstuffs or foodstuffs of animal origin intended for human consumption;

    (g) adequate knowledge of the laws, regulations and administrative provisions relating to the subjects listed above;

    (h) adequate clinical and other practical experience under appropriate supervision.

Article 39 Acquired rights specific to veterinary surgeons

Without prejudice to Article 23(4), with regard to nationals of Member States whose evidence of formal qualifications as a veterinary surgeon was issued by, or whose training commenced in, Estonia before 1 May 2004, Member States shall recognise such evidence of formal qualifications as a veterinary surgeon if it is accompanied by a certificate stating that such persons have effectively and lawfully been engaged in the activities in question in Estonia for at least five consecutive years during the seven years prior to the date of issue of the certificate.

SECTION 6
MIDWIVES

Article 40 The training of midwives

1. The training of midwives shall comprise a total of at least:

    (a) specific full-time training as a midwife comprising at least three years of theoretical and practical study (route I) comprising at least the programme described in Annex V, point 5.5.1, or

    (b) specific full-time training as a midwife of 18 months' duration (route II), comprising at least the study programme described in Annex V, point 5.5.1, which was not the subject of equivalent training of nurses responsible for general care.

The Member States shall ensure that institutions providing midwife training are responsible for coordinating theory and practice throughout the programme of study.

The content listed in Annex V, point 5.5.1 may be amended in accordance with the procedure referred to in Article 58(2) with a view to adapting it to scientific and technical progress.

Such updates must not entail, for any Member State, any amendment of existing legislative principles relating to the structure of professions as regards training and the conditions of access by natural persons.

2.   Access to training as a midwife shall be contingent upon one of the following conditions:
   (a)   completion of at least the first 10 years of general school education for route I, or
   (b)   possession of evidence of formal qualifications as a nurse responsible for general care referred to in Annex V, point 5.2.2 for route II.

3.   Training as a midwife shall provide an assurance that the person in question has acquired the following knowledge and skills:
   (a)   adequate knowledge of the sciences on which the activities of midwives are based, particularly obstetrics and gynaecology;
   (b)   adequate knowledge of the ethics of the profession and the professional legislation;
   (c)   detailed knowledge of biological functions, anatomy and physiology in the field of obstetrics and of the newly born, and also a knowledge of the relationship between the state of health and the physical and social environment of the human being, and of his behaviour;
   (d)   adequate clinical experience gained in approved institutions under the supervision of staff qualified in midwifery and obstetrics;
   (e)   adequate understanding of the training of health personnel and experience of working with such.

Article 41   Procedures for the recognition of evidence of formal qualifications as a midwife

1.   The evidence of formal qualifications as a midwife referred to in Annex V, point 5.5.2 shall be subject to automatic recognition pursuant to Article 21 in so far as they satisfy one of the following criteria:
   (a)   full-time training of at least three years as a midwife:
      (i)   either made contingent upon possession of a diploma, certificate or other evidence of qualification giving access to universities or higher education institutes, or otherwise guaranteeing an equivalent level of knowledge; or
      (ii)   followed by two years of professional practice for which a certificate has been issued in accordance with paragraph 2;
   (b)   full-time training as a midwife of at least two years or 3 600 hours, contingent upon possession of evidence of formal qualifications as a nurse responsible for general care referred to in Annex V, point 5.2.2;
   (c)   full-time training as a midwife of at least 18 months or 3 000 hours, contingent upon possession of evidence of formal qualifications as a nurse responsible for general care referred to in Annex V, point 5.2.2 and followed by one year's professional practice for which a certificate has been issued in accordance with paragraph 2.

2.   The certificate referred to in paragraph 1 shall be issued by the competent authorities in the home Member State. It shall certify that the holder, after obtaining evidence of formal qualifications as a midwife, has satisfactorily pursued all the activities of a midwife for a corresponding period in a hospital or a health care establishment approved for that purpose.

Article 42   Pursuit of the professional activities of a midwife

1.   The provisions of this section shall apply to the activities of midwives as defined by each Member State, without prejudice to paragraph 2, and pursued under the professional titles set out in Annex V, point 5.5.2.

2.   The Member States shall ensure that midwives are able to gain access to and pursue at least the following activities:
   (a)   provision of sound family planning information and advice;

(b)   diagnosis of pregnancies and monitoring normal pregnancies; carrying out the examinations necessary for the monitoring of the development of normal pregnancies;

(c)   prescribing or advising on the examinations necessary for the earliest possible diagnosis of pregnancies at risk;

(d)   provision of programmes of parenthood preparation and complete preparation for childbirth including advice on hygiene and nutrition;

(e)   caring for and assisting the mother during labour and monitoring the condition of the foetus in utero by the appropriate clinical and technical means;

(f)   conducting spontaneous deliveries including where required episiotomies and in urgent cases breech deliveries;

(g)   recognising the warning signs of abnormality in the mother or infant which necessitate referral to a doctor and assisting the latter where appropriate; taking the necessary emergency measures in the doctor's absence, in particular the manual removal of the placenta, possibly followed by manual examination of the uterus;

(h)   examining and caring for the new-born infant; taking all initiatives which are necessary in case of need and carrying out where necessary immediate resuscitation;

(i)   caring for and monitoring the progress of the mother in the post-natal period and giving all necessary advice to the mother on infant care to enable her to ensure the optimum progress of the new-born infant;

(j)   carrying out treatment prescribed by doctors;

(k)   drawing up the necessary written reports.

Article 43 Acquired rights specific to midwives

1.   Every Member State shall, in the case of Member State nationals whose evidence of formal qualifications as a midwife satisfies all the minimum training requirements laid down in Article 40 but, by virtue of Article 41, is not recognised unless it is accompanied by a certificate of professional practice referred to in Article 41(2), recognise as sufficient proof evidence of formal qualifications issued by those Member States before the reference date referred to in Annex V, point 5.5.2, accompanied by a certificate stating that those nationals have been effectively and lawfully engaged in the activities in question for at least two consecutive years during the five years preceding the award of the certificate.

2.   The conditions laid down in paragraph 1 shall apply to the nationals of Member States whose evidence of formal qualifications as a midwife certifies completion of training received in the territory of the former German Democratic Republic and satisfying all the minimum training requirements laid down in Article 40 but where the evidence of formal qualifications, by virtue of Article 41, is not recognised unless it is accompanied by the certificate of professional experience referred to in Article 41(2), where it attests a course of training which began before 3 October 1990.

3.   As regards the Polish evidence of formal qualifications as a midwife, only the following acquired rights provisions shall apply.

In the case of Member States nationals whose evidence of formal qualifications as a midwife was awarded by, or whose training commenced in, Poland before 1 May 2004, and who do not satisfy the minimum training requirements as set out in Article 40, Member States shall recognise the following evidence of formal qualifications as a midwife if accompanied by a certificate stating that such persons have effectively and lawfully been engaged in the activities of a midwife for the period specified below:

(a)   evidence of formal qualifications as a midwife at degree level (dyplom licencjata poloznictwa): at least three consecutive years during the five years prior to the date of issue of the certificate,

(b)   evidence of formal qualifications as a midwife certifying completion of post-secondary education obtained from a medical vocational school (dyplom poloznej): at least five consecutive years during the seven years prior to the date of issue of the certificate.

4.   Member States shall recognise evidence of formal qualifications in midwifery awarded in Poland, to midwives who completed training before 1 May 2004, which did not comply with

the minimum training requirements laid down in Article 40, attested by the diploma 'bachelor' which has been obtained on the basis of a special upgrading programme contained in Article 11 of the Act of 20 April 2004 on the amendment of the Act on professions of nurse and midwife and on some other legal acts (Official Journal of the Republic of Poland of 30 April 2004 No 92, pos. 885), and the Regulation of the Minister of Health of 11 May 2004 on the detailed conditions of delivering studies for nurses and midwives, who hold a certificate of secondary school (final examination — matura) and are graduates of medical lyceum and medical vocational schools teaching in a profession of a nurse and a midwife (Official Journal of the Republic of Poland of 13 May 2004 No 110, pos 1170), with the aim of verifying that the person concerned has a level of knowledge and competence comparable to that of midwives holding the qualifications which, in the case of Poland, are defined in Annex V, point 5.5.2.

SECTION 7
PHARMACIST

Article 44   Training as a pharmacist

1.   Admission to a course of training as a pharmacist shall be contingent upon possession of a diploma or certificate giving access, in a Member State, to the studies in question, at universities or higher institutes of a level recognised as equivalent.

2.   Evidence of formal qualifications as a pharmacist shall attest to training of at least five years' duration, including at least:
   (a)   four years of full-time theoretical and practical training at a university or at a higher institute of a level recognised as equivalent, or under the supervision of a university;
   (b)   six-month traineeship in a pharmacy which is open to the public or in a hospital, under the supervision of that hospital's pharmaceutical department.

   That training cycle shall include at least the programme described in Annex V, point 5.6.1. The contents listed in Annex V, point 5.6.1 may be amended in accordance with the procedure referred to in Article 58(2) with a view to adapting them to scientific and technical progress.

   Such updates must not entail, for any Member State, any amendment of existing legislative principles relating to the structure of professions as regards training and the conditions of access by natural persons.

3.   Training for pharmacists shall provide an assurance that the person concerned has acquired the following knowledge and skills:
   (a)   adequate knowledge of medicines and the substances used in the manufacture of medicines;
   (b)   adequate knowledge of pharmaceutical technology and the physical, chemical, biological and microbiological testing of medicinal products;
   (c)   adequate knowledge of the metabolism and the effects of medicinal products and of the action of toxic substances, and of the use of medicinal products;
   (d)   adequate knowledge to evaluate scientific data concerning medicines in order to be able to supply appropriate information on the basis of this knowledge;
   (e)   adequate knowledge of the legal and other requirements associated with the pursuit of pharmacy.

Article 45   Pursuit of the professional activities of a pharmacist

1.   For the purposes of this Directive, the activities of a pharmacist are those, access to which and pursuit of which are contingent, in one or more Member States, upon professional qualifications and which are open to holders of evidence of formal qualifications of the types listed in Annex V, point 5.6.2.

2.   The Member States shall ensure that the holders of evidence of formal qualifications in pharmacy at university level or a level deemed to be equivalent, which satisfies the provisions of Article 44, are able to gain access to and pursue at least the following activities, subject to the requirement, where appropriate, of supplementary professional experience:
   (a)   preparation of the pharmaceutical form of medicinal products;
   (b)   manufacture and testing of medicinal products;

      (c)   testing of medicinal products in a laboratory for the testing of medicinal products;

      (d)   storage, preservation and distribution of medicinal products at the wholesale stage;

      (e)   preparation, testing, storage and supply of medicinal products in pharmacies open to the public;

      (f)   preparation, testing, storage and dispensing of medicinal products in hospitals;

      (g)   provision of information and advice on medicinal products.

3.   If a Member State makes access to or pursuit of one of the activities of a pharmacist contingent upon supplementary professional experience, in addition to possession of evidence of formal qualifications referred to in Annex V, point 5.6.2, that Member State shall recognise as sufficient proof in this regard a certificate issued by the competent authorities in the home Member State stating that the person concerned has been engaged in those activities in the home Member State for a similar period.

4.   The recognition referred to in paragraph 3 shall not apply with regard to the two-year period of professional experience required by the Grand Duchy of Luxembourg for the grant of a State public pharmacy concession.

5.   If, on 16 September 1985, a Member State had a competitive examination in place designed to select from among the holders referred to in paragraph 2, those who are to be authorised to become owners of new pharmacies whose creation has been decided on as part of a national system of geographical division, that Member State may, by way of derogation from paragraph 1, proceed with that examination and require nationals of Member States who possess evidence of formal qualifications as a pharmacist referred to in Annex V, point 5.6.2 or who benefit from the provisions of Article 23 to take part in it.

SECTION 8

ARCHITECT

Article 46 Training of architects

1.   Training as an architect shall comprise a total of at least four years of full-time study or six years of study, at least three years of which on a full-time basis, at a university or comparable teaching institution. The training must lead to successful completion of a university-level examination.

That training, which must be of university level, and of which architecture is the principal component, must maintain a balance between theoretical and practical aspects of architectural training and guarantee the acquisition of the following knowledge and skills:

      (a)   ability to create architectural designs that satisfy both aesthetic and technical requirements;

      (b)   adequate knowledge of the history and theories of architecture and the related arts, technologies and human sciences;

      (c)   knowledge of the fine arts as an influence on the quality of architectural design;

      (d)   adequate knowledge of urban design, planning and the skills involved in the planning process;

      (e)   understanding of the relationship between people and buildings, and between buildings and their environment, and of the need to relate buildings and the spaces between them to human needs and scale;

      (f)   understanding of the profession of architecture and the role of the architect in society, in particular in preparing briefs that take account of social factors;

      (g)   understanding of the methods of investigation and preparation of the brief for a design project;

      (h)   understanding of the structural design, constructional and engineering problems associated with building design;

      (i)   adequate knowledge of physical problems and technologies and of the function of buildings so as to provide them with internal conditions of comfort and protection against the climate;

      (j)   the necessary design skills to meet building users' requirements within the constraints imposed by cost factors and building regulations;

(k)   adequate knowledge of the industries, organisations, regulations and procedures involved in translating design concepts into buildings and integrating plans into overall planning.

2.   The knowledge and skills listed in paragraph 1 may be amended in accordance with the procedure referred to in Article 58(2) with a view to adapting them to scientific and technical progress.

Such updates must not entail, for any Member State, any amendment of existing legislative principles relating to the structure of professions as regards training and the conditions of access by natural persons.

Article 47   Derogations from the conditions for the training of architects

1.   By way of derogation from Article 46, the following shall also be recognised as satisfying Article 21: training existing as of 5 August 1985, provided by 'Fachhochschulen' in the Federal Republic of Germany over a period of three years, satisfying the requirements referred to in Article 46 and giving access to the activities referred to in Article 48 in that Member State under the professional title of 'architect', in so far as the training was followed by a four-year period of professional experience in the Federal Republic of Germany, as attested by a certificate issued by the professional association in whose roll the name of the architect wishing to benefit from the provisions of this Directive appears.

The professional association must first ascertain that the work performed by the architect concerned in the field of architecture represents convincing application of the full range of knowledge and skills listed in Article 46(1). That certificate shall be awarded in line with the same procedure as that applying to registration in the professional association's roll.

2.   By way of derogation from Article 46, the following shall also be recognised as satisfying Article 21: training as part of social betterment schemes or part-time university studies which satisfies the requirements referred to in Article 46, as attested by an examination in architecture passed by a person who has been working for seven years or more in the field of architecture under the supervision of an architect or architectural bureau. The examination must be of university level and be equivalent to the final examination referred to in Article 46(1), first subparagraph.

Article 48   Pursuit of the professional activities of architects

1.   For the purposes of this Directive, the professional activities of an architect are the activities regularly carried out under the professional title of 'architect'.

2.   Nationals of a Member State who are authorised to use that title pursuant to a law which gives the competent authority of a Member State the power to award that title to Member States nationals who are especially distinguished by the quality of their work in the field of architecture shall be deemed to satisfy the conditions required for the pursuit of the activities of an architect, under the professional title of 'architect'. The architectural nature of the activities of the persons concerned shall be attested by a certificate awarded by their home Member State.

Article 49   Acquired rights specific to architects

1.   Each Member State shall accept evidence of formal qualifications as an architect listed in Annex VI, point 6, awarded by the other Member States, and attesting a course of training which began no later than the reference academic year referred to in that Annex, even if they do not satisfy the minimum requirements laid down in Article 46, and shall, for the purposes of access to and pursuit of the professional activities of an architect, give such evidence the same effect on its territory as evidence of formal qualifications as an architect which it itself issues.

Under these circumstances, certificates issued by the competent authorities of the Federal Republic of Germany attesting that evidence of formal qualifications issued on or after 8 May 1945 by the competent authorities of the German Democratic Republic is equivalent to such evidence listed in that Annex, shall be recognised.

2.   Without prejudice to paragraph 1, every Member State shall recognise the following evidence of formal qualifications and shall, for the purposes of access to and pursuit of the professional

activities of an architect performed, give them the same effect on its territory as evidence of formal qualifications which it itself issues: certificates issued to nationals of Member States by the Member States which have enacted rules governing the access to and pursuit of the activities of an architect as of the following dates:

(a)   1 January 1995 for Austria, Finland and Sweden;

(b)   1 May 2004 for the Czech Republic, Estonia, Cyprus, Latvia, Lithuania, Hungary, Malta, Poland, Slovenia and Slovakia;

(c)   5 August 1987 for the other Member States.

The certificates referred to in paragraph 1 shall certify that the holder was authorised, no later than the respective date, to use the professional title of architect, and that he has been effectively engaged, in the context of those rules, in the activities in question for at least three consecutive years during the five years preceding the award of the certificate.

CHAPTER IV
COMMON PROVISIONS ON ESTABLISHMENT

Article 50 Documentation and formalities

1.   Where the competent authorities of the host Member State decide on an application for authorisation to pursue the regulated profession in question by virtue of this Title, those authorities may demand the documents and certificates listed in Annex VII.

The documents referred to in Annex VII, point 1(d), (e) and (f), shall not be more than three months old by the date on which they are submitted.

The Member States, bodies and other legal persons shall guarantee the confidentiality of the information which they receive.

2.   In the event of justified doubts, the host Member State may require from the competent authorities of a Member State confirmation of the authenticity of the attestations and evidence of formal qualifications awarded in that other Member State, as well as, where applicable, confirmation of the fact that the beneficiary fulfils, for the professions referred to in Chapter III of this Title, the minimum training conditions set out respectively in Articles 24, 25, 28, 31, 34, 35, 38, 40, 44 and 46.

3.   In cases of justified doubt, where evidence of formal qualifications, as defined in Article 3(1)(c), has been issued by a competent authority in a Member State and includes training received in whole or in part in an establishment legally established in the territory of another Member State, the host Member State shall be entitled to verify with the competent body in the Member State of origin of the award:

(a)   whether the training course at the establishment which gave the training has been formally certified by the educational establishment based in the Member State of origin of the award;

(b)   whether the evidence of formal qualifications issued is the same as that which would have been awarded if the course had been followed entirely in the Member State of origin of the award; and

(c)   whether the evidence of formal qualifications confers the same professional rights in the territory of the Member State of origin of the award.

4.   Where a host Member State requires its nationals to swear a solemn oath or make a sworn statement in order to gain access to a regulated profession, and where the wording of that oath or statement cannot be used by nationals of the other Member States, the host Member State shall ensure that the persons concerned can use an appropriate equivalent wording.

Article 51 Procedure for the mutual recognition of professional qualifications

1.   The competent authority of the host Member State shall acknowledge receipt of the application within one month of receipt and inform the applicant of any missing document.

2.   The procedure for examining an application for authorisation to practise a regulated profession must be completed as quickly as possible and lead to a duly substantiated decision by the competent authority in the host Member State in any case within three months after the date on which the applicant's complete file was submitted. However, this deadline may be extended by one month in cases falling under Chapters I and II of this Title.

3.   The decision, or failure to reach a decision within the deadline, shall be subject to appeal under national law.

Article 52   Use of professional titles

1.   If, in a host Member State, the use of a professional title relating to one of the activities of the profession in question is regulated, nationals of the other Member States who are authorised to practise a regulated profession on the basis of Title III shall use the professional title of the host Member State, which corresponds to that profession in that Member State, and make use of any associated initials.

2.   Where a profession is regulated in the host Member State by an association or organisation within the meaning of Article 3(2), nationals of Member States shall not be authorised to use the professional title issued by that organisation or association, or its abbreviated form, unless they furnish proof that they are members of that association or organisation.

      If the association or organisation makes membership contingent upon certain qualifications, it may do so, only under the conditions laid down in this Directive, in respect of nationals of other Member States who possess professional qualifications.

TITLE IV
DETAILED RULES FOR PURSUING THE PROFESSION

Article 53   Knowledge of languages

Persons benefiting from the recognition of professional qualifications shall have a knowledge of languages necessary for practising the profession in the host Member State.

Article 54   Use of academic titles

Without prejudice to Articles 7 and 52, the host Member State shall ensure that the right shall be conferred on the persons concerned to use academic titles conferred on them in the home Member State, and possibly an abbreviated form thereof, in the language of the home Member State. The host Member State may require that title to be followed by the name and address of the establishment or examining board which awarded it. Where an academic title of the home Member State is liable to be confused in the host Member State with a title which, in the latter Member State, requires supplementary training not acquired by the beneficiary, the host Member State may require the beneficiary to use the academic title of the home Member State in an appropriate form, to be laid down by the host Member State.

Article 55   Approval by health insurance funds

Without prejudice to Article 5(1) and Article 6, first subparagraph, point (b), Member States which require persons who acquired their professional qualifications in their territory to complete a preparatory period of in-service training and/or a period of professional experience in order to be approved by a health insurance fund, shall waive this obligation for the holders of evidence of professional qualifications of doctor and dental practitioner acquired in other Member States.

TITLE V
ADMINISTRATIVE COOPERATION AND RESPONSIBILITY FOR IMPLEMENTATION

Article 56   Competent authorities

1.   The competent authorities of the host Member State and of the home Member State shall work in close collaboration and shall provide mutual assistance in order to facilitate application of this Directive. They shall ensure the confidentiality of the information which they exchange.

2.   The competent authorities of the host and home Member States shall exchange information regarding disciplinary action or criminal sanctions taken or any other serious, specific circumstances which are likely to have consequences for the pursuit of activities under this Directive, respecting personal data protection legislation provided for in Directives 95/46/EC of the European Parliament and of the Council of 24 October 1995 on the protection of individuals with regard to the processing of personal data and on the free movement of such data and 2002/58/EC of the European Parliament and of the Council of 12 July 2002 concerning the processing of personal data and the protection of privacy in the electronic communications sector (Directive on privacy and electronic communications).

The home Member State shall examine the veracity of the circumstances and its authorities shall decide on the nature and scope of the investigations which need to be carried out and shall inform the host Member State of the conclusions which it draws from the information available to it.

3.   Each Member State shall, no later than 20 October 2007, designate the authorities and bodies competent to award or receive evidence of formal qualifications and other documents or information, and those competent to receive applications and take the decisions referred to in this Directive, and shall forthwith inform the other Member States and the Commission thereof.

4.   Each Member State shall designate a coordinator for the activities of the authorities referred to in paragraph 1 and shall inform the other Member States and the Commission thereof.
The coordinators' remit shall be:
(a)   to promote uniform application of this Directive;
(b)   to collect all the information which is relevant for application of this Directive, such as on the conditions for access to regulated professions in the Member States.
For the purpose of fulfilling the remit described in point (b), the coordinators may solicit the help of the contact points referred to in Article 57.

Article 57   Contact points

Each Member State shall designate, no later than 20 October 2007, a contact point whose remit shall be:
(a)   to provide the citizens and contact points of the other Member States with such information as is necessary concerning the recognition of professional qualifications provided for in this Directive, such as information on the national legislation governing the professions and the pursuit of those professions, including social legislation, and, where appropriate, the rules of ethics;
(b)   to assist citizens in realising the rights conferred on them by this Directive, in cooperation, where appropriate, with the other contact points and the competent authorities in the host Member State.
At the Commission's request, the contact points shall inform the Commission of the result of enquiries with which they are dealing pursuant to the provisions of point (b) within two months of receiving them.

Article 58   Committee on the recognition of professional qualifications

1.   The Commission shall be assisted by a Committee on the recognition of professional qualifications, hereinafter referred to as 'the Committee', made up of representatives of the Member States and chaired by a representative of the Commission.

2.   Where reference is made to this paragraph, Articles 5 and 7 of Decision 1999/468/EC shall apply, having due regard to the provisions of Article 8 thereof.
The period laid down in Article 5(6) of Decision 1999/468/EC shall be set at two months.

3.   The Committee shall adopt its rules of procedure.

Article 59   Consultation

The Commission shall ensure the consultation of experts from the professional groups concerned in an appropriate manner in particular in the context of the work of the committee referred to in Article 58 and shall provide a reasoned report on these consultations to that committee.

TITLE VI
OTHER PROVISIONS

Article 60   Reports

1.   As from 20 October 2007, Member States shall, every two years, send a report to the Commission on the application of the system. In addition to general observations, the report shall contain a statistical summary of decisions taken and a description of the main problems arising from the application of this Directive.

2.   As from 20 October 2007, the Commission shall draw up every five years a report on the implementation of this Directive.

Article 61 Derogation clause

If, for the application of one of the provisions of this Directive, a Member State encounters major difficulties in a particular area, the Commission shall examine those difficulties in collaboration with the Member State concerned.

Where appropriate, the Commission shall decide, in accordance with the procedure referred to in Article 58(2), to permit the Member State in question to derogate from the provision in question for a limited period.

Article 62 Repeal

Directives 77/452/EEC, 77/453/EEC, 78/686/EEC, 78/687/EEC, 78/1026/EEC, 78/1027/EEC, 80/154/EEC, 80/155/EEC, 85/384/EEC, 85/432/EEC, 85/433/EEC, 89/48/EEC, 92/51/EEC, 93/16/EEC and 1999/42/EC are repealed with effect from 20 October 2007. References to the repealed Directives shall be understood as references to this Directive and the acts adopted on the basis of those Directives shall not be affected by the repeal.

Article 63 Transposition

Member States shall bring into force the laws, regulations and administrative provisions necessary to comply with this Directive by 20 October 2007 at the latest. They shall forthwith inform the Commission thereof.

When Member States adopt these measures, they shall contain a reference to this Directive or be accompanied by such a reference on the occasion of their official publication. Member States shall determine how such reference is to be made.

Article 64 Entry into force

This Directive shall enter into force on the 20th day following its publication in the Official Journal of the European Union.

Article 65 Addressees

This Directive is addressed to the Member States.

ANNEX I
LIST OF PROFESSIONAL ASSOCIATIONS OR ORGANISATIONS FULFILLING THE CONDITIONS OF ARTICLE 3(2)

IRELAND
1.   The Institute of Chartered Accountants in Ireland
2.   The Institute of Certified Public Accountants in Ireland
3.   The Association of Certified Accountants
4.   Institution of Engineers of Ireland
5.   Irish Planning Institute

UNITED KINGDOM
1.   Institute of Chartered Accountants in England and Wales
2.   Institute of Chartered Accountants of Scotland
3.   Institute of Chartered Accountants in Ireland
4.   Chartered Association of Certified Accountants
5.   Chartered Institute of Loss Adjusters
6.   Chartered Institute of Management Accountants
7.   Institute of Chartered Secretaries and Administrators
8.   Chartered Insurance Institute
9.   Institute of Actuaries
10. Faculty of Actuaries
11. Chartered Institute of Bankers
12. Institute of Bankers in Scotland
13. Royal Institution of Chartered Surveyors
14. Royal Town Planning Institute
15. Chartered Society of Physiotherapy
16. Royal Society of Chemistry

17. British Psychological Society
18. Library Association
19. Institute of Chartered Foresters
20. Chartered Institute of Building
21. Engineering Council
22. Institute of Energy
23. Institution of Structural Engineers
24. Institution of Civil Engineers
25. Institution of Mining Engineers
26. Institution of Mining and Metallurgy
27. Institution of Electrical Engineers
28. Institution of Gas Engineers
29. Institution of Mechanical Engineers
30. Institution of Chemical Engineers
31. Institution of Production Engineers
32. Institution of Marine Engineers
33. Royal Institution of Naval Architects
34. Royal Aeronautical Society
35. Institute of Metals
36. Chartered Institution of Building Services Engineers
37. Institute of Measurement and Control
38. British Computer Society

FREE MOVEMENT OF SERVICES

DIRECTIVE 2006/123/EC OF THE EUROPEAN PARLIAMENT AND OF THE COUNCIL of 12 DECEMBER 2006
on services in the internal market
[2006] OJ L376/36

CHAPTER I
GENERAL PROVISIONS

Article 1   Subject matter

1.   This Directive establishes general provisions facilitating the exercise of the freedom of establishment for service providers and the free movement of services, while maintaining a high quality of services.

2.   This Directive does not deal with the liberalisation of services of general economic interest, reserved to public or private entities, nor with the privatisation of public entities providing services.

3.   This Directive does not deal with the abolition of monopolies providing services nor with aids granted by Member States which are covered by Community rules on competition.

This Directive does not affect the freedom of Member States to define, in conformity with Community law, what they consider to be services of general economic interest, how those services should be organised and financed, in compliance with the State aid rules, and what specific obligations they should be subject to.

4.   This Directive does not affect measures taken at Community level or at national level, in conformity with Community law, to protect or promote cultural or linguistic diversity or media pluralism.

5.   This Directive does not affect Member States' rules of criminal law. However, Member States may not restrict the freedom to provide services by applying criminal law provisions which specifically regulate or affect access to or exercise of a service activity in circumvention of the rules laid down in this Directive.

6.   This Directive does not affect labour law, that is any legal or contractual provision concerning employment conditions, working conditions, including health and safety at work and the relationship between employers and workers, which Member States apply in accordance with national law which respects Community law. Equally, this Directive does not affect the social security legislation of the Member States.

7.   This Directive does not affect the exercise of fundamental rights as recognised in the Member States and by Community law. Nor does it affect the right to negotiate, conclude and enforce collective agreements and to take industrial action in accordance with national law and practices which respect Community law.

Article 2   Scope

1.   This Directive shall apply to services supplied by providers established in a Member State.

2.   This Directive shall not apply to the following activities:

(a)   non-economic services of general interest;

(b)   financial services, such as banking, credit, insurance and re-insurance, occupational or personal pensions, securities, investment funds, payment and investment advice, including the services listed in Annex I to Directive 2006/48/EC;

(c)   electronic communications services and networks, and associated facilities and services, with respect to matters covered by Directives 2002/19/EC, 2002/20/EC, 2002/21/EC, 2002/22/EC and 2002/58/EC;

(d)   services in the field of transport, including port services, falling within the scope of Title V of the Treaty;

(e)   services of temporary work agencies;

(f)   healthcare services whether or not they are provided via healthcare facilities, and regardless of the ways in which they are organised and financed at national level or whether they are public or private;

(g) audiovisual services, including cinematographic services, whatever their mode of production, distribution and transmission, and radio broadcasting;

(h) gambling activities which involve wagering a stake with pecuniary value in games of chance, including lotteries, gambling in casinos and betting transactions;

(i) activities which are connected with the exercise of official authority as set out in Article 45 of the Treaty;

(j) social services relating to social housing, childcare and support of families and persons permanently or temporarily in need which are provided by the State, by providers mandated by the State or by charities recognised as such by the State;

(k) private security services;

(l) services provided by notaries and bailiffs, who are appointed by an official act of government.

3. This Directive shall not apply to the field of taxation.

Article 3 Relationship with other provisions of Community law

1. If the provisions of this Directive conflict with a provision of another Community act governing specific aspects of access to or exercise of a service activity in specific sectors or for specific professions, the provision of the other Community act shall prevail and shall apply to those specific sectors or professions. These include:

(a) Directive 96/71/EC;

(b) Regulation (EEC) No 1408/71;

(c) Council Directive 89/552/EEC of 3 October 1989 on the coordination of certain provisions laid down by law, regulation or administrative action in Member States concerning the pursuit of television broadcasting activities;

(d) Directive 2005/36/EC.

2. This Directive does not concern rules of private international law, in particular rules governing the law applicable to contractual and non contractual obligations, including those which guarantee that consumers benefit from the protection granted to them by the consumer protection rules laid down in the consumer legislation in force in their Member State.

3. Member States shall apply the provisions of this Directive in compliance with the rules of the Treaty on the right of establishment and the free movement of services.

Article 4 Definitions

For the purposes of this Directive, the following definitions shall apply:

(1) 'service' means any self-employed economic activity, normally provided for remuneration, as referred to in Article 50 of the Treaty;

(2) 'provider' means any natural person who is a national of a Member State, or any legal person as referred to in Article 48 of the Treaty and established in a Member State, who offers or provides a service;

(3) 'recipient' means any natural person who is a national of a Member State or who benefits from rights conferred upon him by Community acts, or any legal person as referred to in Article 48 of the Treaty and established in a Member State, who, for professional or non-professional purposes, uses, or wishes to use, a service;

(4) 'Member State of establishment' means the Member State in whose territory the provider of the service concerned is established;

(5) 'establishment' means the actual pursuit of an economic activity, as referred to in Article 43 of the Treaty, by the provider for an indefinite period and through a stable infrastructure from where the business of providing services is actually carried out;

(6) 'authorisation scheme' means any procedure under which a provider or recipient is in effect required to take steps in order to obtain from a competent authority a formal decision, or an implied decision, concerning access to a service activity or the exercise thereof;

(7) 'requirement' means any obligation, prohibition, condition or limit provided for in the laws, regulations or administrative provisions of the Member States or in consequence of case-law, administrative practice, the rules of professional bodies, or the collective rules of professional associations or other professional organisations, adopted in the exercise of their legal

autonomy; rules laid down in collective agreements negotiated by the social partners shall not as such be seen as requirements within the meaning of this Directive;

(8) 'overriding reasons relating to the public interest' means reasons recognised as such in the case law of the Court of Justice, including the following grounds: public policy; public security; public safety; public health; preserving the financial equilibrium of the social security system; the protection of consumers, recipients of services and workers; fairness of trade transactions; combating fraud; the protection of the environment and the urban environment; the health of animals; intellectual property; the conservation of the national historic and artistic heritage; social policy objectives and cultural policy objectives;

(9) 'competent authority' means any body or authority which has a supervisory or regulatory role in a Member State in relation to service activities, including, in particular, administrative authorities, including courts acting as such, professional bodies, and those professional associations or other professional organisations which, in the exercise of their legal autonomy, regulate in a collective manner access to service activities or the exercise thereof;

(10) 'Member State where the service is provided' means the Member State where the service is supplied by a provider established in another Member State;

(11) 'regulated profession' means a professional activity or a group of professional activities as referred to in Article 3(1)(a) of Directive 2005/36/EC;

(12) 'commercial communication' means any form of communication designed to promote, directly or indirectly, the goods, services or image of an undertaking, organisation or person engaged in commercial, industrial or craft activity or practising a regulated profession. The following do not in themselves constitute commercial communications:

   (a) information enabling direct access to the activity of the undertaking, organisation or person, including in particular a domain name or an electronic-mailing address;

   (b) communications relating to the goods, services or image of the undertaking, organisation or person, compiled in an independent manner, particularly when provided for no financial consideration.

CHAPTER II
ADMINISTRATIVE SIMPLIFICATION

Article 5   Simplification of procedures

1. Member States shall examine the procedures and formalities applicable to access to a service activity and to the exercise thereof. Where procedures and formalities examined under this paragraph are not sufficiently simple, Member States shall simplify them.

2. The Commission may introduce harmonised forms at Community level, in accordance with the procedure referred to in Article 40(2). These forms shall be equivalent to certificates, attestations and any other documents required of a provider.

3. Where Member States require a provider or recipient to supply a certificate, attestation or any other document proving that a requirement has been satisfied, they shall accept any document from another Member State which serves an equivalent purpose or from which it is clear that the requirement in question has been satisfied. They may not require a document from another Member State to be produced in its original form, or as a certified copy or as a certified translation, save in the cases provided for in other Community instruments or where such a requirement is justified by an overriding reason relating to the public interest, including public order and security.

   The first subparagraph shall not affect the right of Member States to require non-certified translations of documents in one of their official languages.

4. Paragraph 3 shall not apply to the documents referred to in Article 7(2) and 50 of Directive 2005/36/EC, in Articles 45(3), 46, 49 and 50 of Directive 2004/18/EC of the European Parliament and of the Council of 31 March 2004 on the coordination of procedures for the award of public works contracts, public supply contracts and public service contracts, in Article 3(2) of Directive 98/5/EC of the European Parliament and of the Council of 16 February 1998 to facilitate practice of the profession of lawyer on a permanent basis in a Member State other than that in which the qualification was obtained, in the First Council Directive 68/151/EEC of 9 March 1968 on coordination of safeguards which, for the protection of the interests of

members and others, are required by Member States of companies within the meaning of the second paragraph of Article 58 of the Treaty, with a view to making such safeguards equivalent throughout the Community and in the Eleventh Council Directive 89/666/EEC of 21 December 1989 concerning disclosure requirements in respect of branches opened in a Member State by certain types of company governed by the law of another State.

Article 6 Points of single contact

1. Member States shall ensure that it is possible for providers to complete the following procedures and formalities through points of single contact:

   (a) all procedures and formalities needed for access to his service activities, in particular, all declarations, notifications or applications necessary for authorisation from the competent authorities, including applications for inclusion in a register, a roll or a database, or for registration with a professional body or association;

   (b) any applications for authorisation needed to exercise his service activities.

2. The establishment of points of single contact shall be without prejudice to the allocation of functions and powers among the authorities within national systems.

Article 7 Right to information

1. Member States shall ensure that the following information is easily accessible to providers and recipients through the points of single contact:

   (a) requirements applicable to providers established in their territory, in particular those requirements concerning the procedures and formalities to be completed in order to access and to exercise service activities;

   (b) the contact details of the competent authorities enabling the latter to be contacted directly, including the details of those authorities responsible for matters concerning the exercise of service activities;

   (c) the means of, and conditions for, accessing public registers and databases on providers and services;

   (d) the means of redress which are generally available in the event of dispute between the competent authorities and the provider or the recipient, or between a provider and a recipient or between providers;

   (e) the contact details of the associations or organisations, other than the competent authorities, from which providers or recipients may obtain practical assistance.

2. Member States shall ensure that it is possible for providers and recipients to receive, at their request, assistance from the competent authorities, consisting in information on the way in which the requirements referred to in point (a) of paragraph 1 are generally interpreted and applied. Where appropriate, such advice shall include a simple step-by-step guide. The information shall be provided in plain and intelligible language.

3. Member States shall ensure that the information and assistance referred to in paragraphs 1 and 2 are provided in a clear and unambiguous manner, that they are easily accessible at a distance and by electronic means and that they are kept up to date.

4. Member States shall ensure that the points of single contact and the competent authorities respond as quickly as possible to any request for information or assistance as referred to in paragraphs 1 and 2 and, in cases where the request is faulty or unfounded, inform the applicant accordingly without delay.

5. Member States and the Commission shall take accompanying measures in order to encourage points of single contact to make the information provided for in this Article available in other Community languages. This does not interfere with Member States' legislation on the use of languages.

6. The obligation for competent authorities to assist providers and recipients does not require those authorities to provide legal advice in individual cases but concerns only general information on the way in which requirements are usually interpreted or applied.

Article 8 Procedures by electronic means

1. Member States shall ensure that all procedures and formalities relating to access to a service activity and to the exercise thereof may be easily completed, at a distance and by electronic

means, through the relevant point of single contact and with the relevant competent authorities.

2.   Paragraph 1 shall not apply to the inspection of premises on which the service is provided or of equipment used by the provider or to physical examination of the capability or of the personal integrity of the provider or of his responsible staff.

3.   The Commission shall, in accordance with the procedure referred to in Article 40(2), adopt detailed rules for the implementation of paragraph 1 of this Article with a view to facilitating the interoperability of information systems and use of procedures by electronic means between Member States, taking into account common standards developed at Community level.

CHAPTER III
FREEDOM OF ESTABLISHMENT FOR PROVIDERS

SECTION 1
AUTHORISATIONS

Article 9   **Authorisation schemes**

1.   Member States shall not make access to a service activity or the exercise thereof subject to an authorisation scheme unless the following conditions are satisfied:

    (a)   the authorisation scheme does not discriminate against the provider in question;

    (b)   the need for an authorisation scheme is justified by an overriding reason relating to the public interest;

    (c)   the objective pursued cannot be attained by means of a less restrictive measure, in particular because an a posteriori inspection would take place too late to be genuinely effective.

2.   In the report referred to in Article 39(1), Member States shall identify their authorisation schemes and give reasons showing their compatibility with paragraph 1 of this Article.

3.   This section shall not apply to those aspects of authorisation schemes which are governed directly or indirectly by other Community instruments.

Article 10   **Conditions for the granting of authorisation**

1.   Authorisation schemes shall be based on criteria which preclude the competent authorities from exercising their power of assessment in an arbitrary manner.

2.   The criteria referred to in paragraph 1 shall be:

    (a)   non-discriminatory;

    (b)   justified by an overriding reason relating to the public interest;

    (c)   proportionate to that public interest objective;

    (d)   clear and unambiguous;

    (e)   objective;

    (f)   made public in advance;

    (g)   transparent and accessible.

3.   The conditions for granting authorisation for a new establishment shall not duplicate requirements and controls which are equivalent or essentially comparable as regards their purpose to which the provider is already subject in another Member State or in the same Member State. The liaison points referred to in Article 28(2) and the provider shall assist the competent authority by providing any necessary information regarding those requirements.

4.   The authorisation shall enable the provider to have access to the service activity, or to exercise that activity, throughout the national territory, including by means of setting up agencies, subsidiaries, branches or offices, except where an authorisation for each individual establishment or a limitation of the authorisation to a certain part of the territory is justified by an overriding reason relating to the public interest.

5.   The authorisation shall be granted as soon as it is established, in the light of an appropriate examination, that the conditions for authorisation have been met.

6.   Except in the case of the granting of an authorisation, any decision from the competent authorities, including refusal or withdrawal of an authorisation, shall be fully reasoned and shall be open to challenge before the courts or other instances of appeal.

7.   This Article shall not call into question the allocation of the competences, at local or regional level, of the Member States' authorities granting authorisations.

Article 11   Duration of authorisation

1.   An authorisation granted to a provider shall not be for a limited period, except where:
  (a)   the authorisation is being automatically renewed or is subject only to the continued fulfilment of requirements;
  (b)   the number of available authorisations is limited by an overriding reason relating to the public interest; or
  (c)   a limited authorisation period can be justified by an overriding reason relating to the public interest.

2.   Paragraph 1 shall not concern the maximum period before the end of which the provider must actually commence his activity after receiving authorisation.

3.   Member States shall require a provider to inform the relevant point of single contact provided for in Article 6 of the following changes:
  (a)   the creation of subsidiaries whose activities fall within the scope of the authorisation scheme;
  (b)   changes in his situation which result in the conditions for authorisation no longer being met.

4.   This Article shall be without prejudice to the Member States' ability to revoke authorisations, when the conditions for authorisation are no longer met.

Article 12   Selection from among several candidates

1.   Where the number of authorisations available for a given activity is limited because of the scarcity of available natural resources or technical capacity, Member States shall apply a selection procedure to potential candidates which provides full guarantees of impartiality and transparency, including, in particular, adequate publicity about the launch, conduct and completion of the procedure.

2.   In the cases referred to in paragraph 1, authorisation shall be granted for an appropriate limited period and may not be open to automatic renewal nor confer any other advantage on the provider whose authorisation has just expired or on any person having any particular links with that provider.

3.   Subject to paragraph 1 and to Articles 9 and 10, Member States may take into account, in establishing the rules for the selection procedure, considerations of public health, social policy objectives, the health and safety of employees or self-employed persons, the protection of the environment, the preservation of cultural heritage and other overriding reasons relating to the public interest, in conformity with Community law.

Article 13   Authorisation procedures

1.   Authorisation procedures and formalities shall be clear, made public in advance and be such as to provide the applicants with a guarantee that their application will be dealt with objectively and impartially.

2.   Authorisation procedures and formalities shall not be dissuasive and shall not unduly complicate or delay the provision of the service. They shall be easily accessible and any charges which the applicants may incur from their application shall be reasonable and proportionate to the cost of the authorisation procedures in question and shall not exceed the cost of the procedures.

3.   Authorisation procedures and formalities shall provide applicants with a guarantee that their application will be processed as quickly as possible and, in any event, within a reasonable period which is fixed and made public in advance. The period shall run only from the time when all documentation has been submitted. When justified by the complexity of the issue, the time period may be extended once, by the competent authority, for a limited time. The extension and its duration shall be duly motivated and shall be notified to the applicant before the original period has expired.

4.   Failing a response within the time period set or extended in accordance with paragraph 3, authorisation shall be deemed to have been granted. Different arrangements may nevertheless

be put in place, where justified by overriding reasons relating to the public interest, including a legitimate interest of third parties.

5.   All applications for authorisation shall be acknowledged as quickly as possible. The acknowledgement must specify the following:

    (a)   the period referred to in paragraph 3;

    (b)   the available means of redress;

    (c)   where applicable, a statement that in the absence of a response within the period specified, the authorisation shall be deemed to have been granted.

6.   In the case of an incomplete application, the applicant shall be informed as quickly as possible of the need to supply any additional documentation, as well as of any possible effects on the period referred to in paragraph 3.

7.   When a request is rejected because it fails to comply with the required procedures or formalities, the applicant shall be informed of the rejection as quickly as possible.

SECTION 2
REQUIREMENTS PROHIBITED OR SUBJECT TO EVALUATION

Article 14   Prohibited requirements

Member States shall not make access to, or the exercise of, a service activity in their territory subject to compliance with any of the following:

(1)   discriminatory requirements based directly or indirectly on nationality or, in the case of companies, the location of the registered office, including in particular:

    (a)   nationality requirements for the provider, his staff, persons holding the share capital or members of the provider's management or supervisory bodies;

    (b)   a requirement that the provider, his staff, persons holding the share capital or members of the provider's management or supervisory bodies be resident within the territory;

(2)   a prohibition on having an establishment in more than one Member State or on being entered in the registers or enrolled with professional bodies or associations of more than one Member State;

(3)   restrictions on the freedom of a provider to choose between a principal or a secondary establishment, in particular an obligation on the provider to have its principal establishment in their territory, or restrictions on the freedom to choose between establishment in the form of an agency, branch or subsidiary;

(4)   conditions of reciprocity with the Member State in which the provider already has an establishment, save in the case of conditions of reciprocity provided for in Community instruments concerning energy;

(5)   the case-by-case application of an economic test making the granting of authorisation subject to proof of the existence of an economic need or market demand, an assessment of the potential or current economic effects of the activity or an assessment of the appropriateness of the activity in relation to the economic planning objectives set by the competent authority; this prohibition shall not concern planning requirements which do not pursue economic aims but serve overriding reasons relating to the public interest;

(6)   the direct or indirect involvement of competing operators, including within consultative bodies, in the granting of authorisations or in the adoption of other decisions of the competent authorities, with the exception of professional bodies and associations or other organisations acting as the competent authority; this prohibition shall not concern the consultation of organisations, such as chambers of commerce or social partners, on matters other than individual applications for authorisation, or a consultation of the public at large;

(7)   an obligation to provide or participate in a financial guarantee or to take out insurance from a provider or body established in their territory. This shall not affect the possibility for Member States to require insurance or financial guarantees as such, nor shall it affect requirements relating to the participation in a collective compensation fund, for instance for members of professional bodies or organisations;

(8)   an obligation to have been pre-registered, for a given period, in the registers held in their territory or to have previously exercised the activity for a given period in their territory.

Article 15 Requirements to be evaluated

1. Member States shall examine whether, under their legal system, any of the requirements listed in paragraph 2 are imposed and shall ensure that any such requirements are compatible with the conditions laid down in paragraph 3. Member States shall adapt their laws, regulations or administrative provisions so as to make them compatible with those conditions.

2. Member States shall examine whether their legal system makes access to a service activity or the exercise of it subject to compliance with any of the following non-discriminatory requirements:
    (a) quantitative or territorial restrictions, in particular in the form of limits fixed according to population or of a minimum geographical distance between providers;
    (b) an obligation on a provider to take a specific legal form;
    (c) requirements which relate to the shareholding of a company;
    (d) requirements, other than those concerning matters covered by Directive 2005/36/EC or provided for in other Community instruments, which reserve access to the service activity in question to particular providers by virtue of the specific nature of the activity;
    (e) a ban on having more than one establishment in the territory of the same State;
    (f) requirements fixing a minimum number of employees;
    (g) fixed minimum and/or maximum tariffs with which the provider must comply;
    (h) an obligation on the provider to supply other specific services jointly with his service.

3. Member States shall verify that the requirements referred to in paragraph 2 satisfy the following conditions:
    (a) non-discrimination: requirements must be neither directly nor indirectly discriminatory according to nationality nor, with regard to companies, according to the location of the registered office;
    (b) necessity: requirements must be justified by an overriding reason relating to the public interest;
    (c) proportionality: requirements must be suitable for securing the attainment of the objective pursued; they must not go beyond what is necessary to attain that objective and it must not be possible to replace those requirements with other, less restrictive measures which attain the same result.

4. Paragraphs 1, 2 and 3 shall apply to legislation in the field of services of general economic interest only insofar as the application of these paragraphs does not obstruct the performance, in law or in fact, of the particular task assigned to them.

5. In the mutual evaluation report provided for in Article 39(1), Member States shall specify the following:
    (a) the requirements that they intend to maintain and the reasons why they consider that those requirements comply with the conditions set out in paragraph 3;
    (b) the requirements which have been abolished or made less stringent.

6. From 28 December 2006 Member States shall not introduce any new requirement of a kind listed in paragraph 2, unless that requirement satisfies the conditions laid down in paragraph 3.

7. Member States shall notify the Commission of any new laws, regulations or administrative provisions which set requirements as referred to in paragraph 6, together with the reasons for those requirements. The Commission shall communicate the provisions concerned to the other Member States. Such notification shall not prevent Member States from adopting the provisions in question.

    Within a period of 3 months from the date of receipt of the notification, the Commission shall examine the compatibility of any new requirements with Community law and, where appropriate, shall adopt a decision requesting the Member State in question to refrain from adopting them or to abolish them.

    The notification of a draft national law in accordance with Directive 98/34/EC shall fulfil the obligation of notification provided for in this Directive.

CHAPTER IV
FREE MOVEMENT OF SERVICES

SECTION 1
FREEDOM TO PROVIDE SERVICES AND RELATED DEROGATIONS

Article 16 Freedom to provide services

1. Member States shall respect the right of providers to provide services in a Member State other than that in which they are established.

    The Member State in which the service is provided shall ensure free access to and free exercise of a service activity within its territory.

    Member States shall not make access to or exercise of a service activity in their territory subject to compliance with any requirements which do not respect the following principles:

    (a) non-discrimination: the requirement may be neither directly nor indirectly discriminatory with regard to nationality or, in the case of legal persons, with regard to the Member State in which they are established;

    (b) necessity: the requirement must be justified for reasons of public policy, public security, public health or the protection of the environment;

    (c) proportionality: the requirement must be suitable for attaining the objective pursued, and must not go beyond what is necessary to attain that objective.

2. Member States may not restrict the freedom to provide services in the case of a provider established in another Member State by imposing any of the following requirements:

    (a) an obligation on the provider to have an establishment in their territory;

    (b) an obligation on the provider to obtain an authorisation from their competent authorities including entry in a register or registration with a professional body or association in their territory, except where provided for in this Directive or other instruments of Community law;

    (c) a ban on the provider setting up a certain form or type of infrastructure in their territory, including an office or chambers, which the provider needs in order to supply the services in question;

    (d) the application of specific contractual arrangements between the provider and the recipient which prevent or restrict service provision by the self-employed;

    (e) an obligation on the provider to possess an identity document issued by its competent authorities specific to the exercise of a service activity;

    (f) requirements, except for those necessary for health and safety at work, which affect the use of equipment and material which are an integral part of the service provided;

    (g) restrictions on the freedom to provide the services referred to in Article 19.

3. The Member State to which the provider moves shall not be prevented from imposing requirements with regard to the provision of a service activity, where they are justified for reasons of public policy, public security, public health or the protection of the environment and in accordance with paragraph 1. Nor shall that Member State be prevented from applying, in accordance with Community law, its rules on employment conditions, including those laid down in collective agreements.

4. By 28 December 2011 the Commission shall, after consultation of the Member States and the social partners at Community level, submit to the European Parliament and the Council a report on the application of this Article, in which it shall consider the need to propose harmonisation measures regarding service activities covered by this Directive.

Article 17 Additional derogations from the freedom to provide services

Article 16 shall not apply to:

(1) services of general economic interest which are provided in another Member State, inter alia:

    (a) in the postal sector, services covered by Directive 97/67/EC of the European Parliament and of the Council of 15 December 1997 on common rules for the development of the internal market of Community postal services and the improvement of quality of service;

(b)   in the electricity sector, services covered by Directive 2003/54/EC of the European Parliament and of the Council of 26 June 2003 concerning common rules for the internal market in electricity;

(c)   in the gas sector, services covered by Directive 2003/55/EC of the European Parliament and of the Council of 26 June 2003 concerning common rules for the internal market in natural gas;

(d)   water distribution and supply services and waste water services;

(e)   treatment of waste;

(2)   matters covered by Directive 96/71/EC;

(3)   matters covered by Directive 95/46/EC of the European Parliament and of the Council of 24 October 1995 on the protection of individuals with regard to the processing of personal data and on the free movement of such data;

(4)   matters covered by Council Directive 77/249/EEC of 22 March 1977to facilitate the effective exercise by lawyers of freedom to provide services;

(5)   the activity of judicial recovery of debts;

(6)   matters covered by Title II of Directive 2005/36/EC, as well as requirements in the Member State where the service is provided which reserve an activity to a particular profession;

(7)   matters covered by Regulation (EEC) No 1408/71;

(8)   as regards administrative formalities concerning the free movement of persons and their residence, matters covered by the provisions of Directive 2004/38/EC that lay down administrative formalities of the competent authorities of the Member State where the service is provided with which beneficiaries must comply;

(9)   as regards third country nationals who move to another Member State in the context of the provision of a service, the possibility for Member States to require visa or residence permits for third country nationals who are not covered by the mutual recognition regime provided for in Article 21 of the Convention implementing the Schengen Agreement of 14 June 1985 on the gradual abolition of checks at the common borders or the possibility to oblige third country nationals to report to the competent authorities of the Member State in which the service is provided on or after their entry;

(10) as regards the shipment of waste, matters covered by Council Regulation (EEC) No 259/93 of 1 February 1993 on the supervision and control of shipments of waste within, into and out of the European Community;

(11) copyright, neighbouring rights and rights covered by Council Directive 87/54/EEC of 16 December 1986 on the legal protection of topographies of semiconductor products and by Directive 96/9/EC of the European Parliament and of the Council of 11 March 1996 on the legal protection of databases, as well as industrial property rights;

(12) acts requiring by law the involvement of a notary;

(13) matters covered by Directive 2006/43/EC of the European Parliament and of the Council of 17 May 2006 on statutory audit of annual accounts and consolidated accounts;

(14) the registration of vehicles leased in another Member State;

(15) provisions regarding contractual and non-contractual obligations, including the form of contracts, determined pursuant to the rules of private international law.

Article 18   Case-by-case derogations

1.   By way of derogation from Article 16, and in exceptional circumstances only, a Member State may, in respect of a provider established in another Member State, take measures relating to the safety of services.

2.   The measures provided for in paragraph 1 may be taken only if the mutual assistance procedure laid down in Article 35 is complied with and the following conditions are fulfilled:

(a)   the national provisions in accordance with which the measure is taken have not been subject to Community harmonisation in the field of the safety of services;

(b)   the measures provide for a higher level of protection of the recipient than would be the case in a measure taken by the Member State of establishment in accordance with its national provisions;

(c)   the Member State of establishment has not taken any measures or has taken measures which are insufficient as compared with those referred to in Article 35(2);

(d)   the measures are proportionate.

3.   Paragraphs 1 and 2 shall be without prejudice to provisions, laid down in Community instruments, which guarantee the freedom to provide services or which allow derogations therefrom.

SECTION 2
RIGHTS OF RECIPIENTS OF SERVICES

Article 19 Prohibited restrictions

Member States may not impose on a recipient requirements which restrict the use of a service supplied by a provider established in another Member State, in particular the following requirements:

(a)   an obligation to obtain authorisation from or to make a declaration to their competent authorities;

(b)   discriminatory limits on the grant of financial assistance by reason of the fact that the provider is established in another Member State or by reason of the location of the place at which the service is provided.

Article 20 Non-discrimination

1.   Member States shall ensure that the recipient is not made subject to discriminatory requirements based on his nationality or place of residence.

2.   Member States shall ensure that the general conditions of access to a service, which are made available to the public at large by the provider, do not contain discriminatory provisions relating to the nationality or place of residence of the recipient, but without precluding the possibility of providing for differences in the conditions of access where those differences are directly justified by objective criteria.

Article 21 Assistance for recipients

1.   Member States shall ensure that recipients can obtain, in their Member State of residence, the following information:

(a)   general information on the requirements applicable in other Member States relating to access to, and exercise of, service activities, in particular those relating to consumer protection;

(b)   general information on the means of redress available in the case of a dispute between a provider and a recipient;

(c)   the contact details of associations or organisations, including the centres of the European Consumer Centres Network, from which providers or recipients may obtain practical assistance.

Where appropriate, advice from the competent authorities shall include a simple step-by-step guide. Information and assistance shall be provided in a clear and unambiguous manner, shall be easily accessible at a distance, including by electronic means, and shall be kept up to date.

2.   Member States may confer responsibility for the task referred to in paragraph 1 on points of single contact or on any other body, such as the centres of the European Consumer Centres Network, consumer associations or Euro Info Centres.

Member States shall communicate to the Commission the names and contact details of the designated bodies. The Commission shall transmit them to all Member States.

3.   In fulfilment of the requirements set out in paragraphs 1 and 2, the body approached by the recipient shall, if necessary, contact the relevant body for the Member State concerned. The latter shall send the information requested as soon as possible to the requesting body which shall forward the information to the recipient. Member States shall ensure that those bodies give each other mutual assistance and shall put in place all possible measures for effective cooperation. Together with the Commission, Member States shall put in place practical arrangements necessary for the implementation of paragraph 1.

4.   The Commission shall, in accordance with the procedure referred to in Article 40(2), adopt measures for the implementation of paragraphs 1, 2 and 3 of this Article, specifying the technical mechanisms for the exchange of information between the bodies of the various Member States and, in particular, the interoperability of information systems, taking into account common standards.

CHAPTER V
QUALITY OF SERVICES

Article 22 Information on providers and their services

1.   Member States shall ensure that providers make the following information available to the recipient:

(a)   the name of the provider, his legal status and form, the geographic address at which he is established and details enabling him to be contacted rapidly and communicated with directly and, as the case may be, by electronic means;

(b)   where the provider is registered in a trade or other similar public register, the name of that register and the provider's registration number, or equivalent means of identification in that register;

(c)   where the activity is subject to an authorisation scheme, the particulars of the relevant competent authority or the single point of contact;

(d)   where the provider exercises an activity which is subject to VAT, the identification number referred to in Article 22(1) of Sixth Council Directive 77/388/EEC of 17 May 1977 on the harmonisation of the laws of the Member States relating to turnover taxes – Common system of value added tax: uniform basis of assessment;

(e)   in the case of the regulated professions, any professional body or similar institution with which the provider is registered, the professional title and the Member State in which that title has been granted;

(f)   the general conditions and clauses, if any, used by the provider;

(g)   the existence of contractual clauses, if any, used by the provider concerning the law applicable to the contract and/or the competent courts;

(h)   the existence of an after-sales guarantee, if any, not imposed by law;

(i)   the price of the service, where a price is pre-determined by the provider for a given type of service;

(j)   the main features of the service, if not already apparent from the context;

(k)   the insurance or guarantees referred to in Article 23(1), and in particular the contact details of the insurer or guarantor and the territorial coverage.

2.   Member States shall ensure that the information referred to in paragraph 1, according to the provider's preference:

(a)   is supplied by the provider on his own initiative;

(b)   is easily accessible to the recipient at the place where the service is provided or the contract concluded;

(c)   can be easily accessed by the recipient electronically by means of an address supplied by the provider;

(d)   appears in any information documents supplied to the recipient by the provider which set out a detailed description of the service he provides.

3.   Member States shall ensure that, at the recipient's request, providers supply the following additional information:

(a)   where the price is not pre-determined by the provider for a given type of service, the price of the service or, if an exact price cannot be given, the method for calculating the price so that it can be checked by the recipient, or a sufficiently detailed estimate;

(b)   as regards the regulated professions, a reference to the professional rules applicable in the Member State of establishment and how to access them;

(c)   information on their multidisciplinary activities and partnerships which are directly linked to the service in question and on the measures taken to avoid conflicts of interest. That information shall be included in any information document in which providers give a detailed description of their services;

(d) any codes of conduct to which the provider is subject and the address at which these codes may be consulted by electronic means, specifying the language version available;

(e) where a provider is subject to a code of conduct, or member of a trade association or professional body which provides for recourse to a non-judicial means of dispute settlement, information in this respect. The provider shall specify how to access detailed information on the characteristics of, and conditions for, the use of non-judicial means of dispute settlement.

4. Member States shall ensure that the information which a provider must supply in accordance with this Chapter is made available or communicated in a clear and unambiguous manner, and in good time before conclusion of the contract or, where there is no written contract, before the service is provided.

5. The information requirements laid down in this Chapter are in addition to requirements already provided for in Community law and do not prevent Member States from imposing additional information requirements applicable to providers established in their territory.

6. The Commission may, in accordance with the procedure referred to in Article 40(2), specify the content of the information provided for in paragraphs 1 and 3 of this Article according to the specific nature of certain activities and may specify the practical means of implementing paragraph 2 of this Article.

Article 23 Professional liability insurance and guarantees

1. Member States may ensure that providers whose services present a direct and particular risk to the health or safety of the recipient or a third person, or to the financial security of the recipient, subscribe to professional liability insurance appropriate to the nature and extent of the risk, or provide a guarantee or similar arrangement which is equivalent or essentially comparable as regards its purpose.

2. When a provider establishes himself in their territory, Member States may not require professional liability insurance or a guarantee from the provider where he is already covered by a guarantee which is equivalent, or essentially comparable as regards its purpose and the cover it provides in terms of the insured risk, the insured sum or a ceiling for the guarantee and possible exclusions from the cover, in another Member State in which the provider is already established. Where equivalence is only partial, Member States may require a supplementary guarantee to cover those aspects not already covered.

   When a Member State requires a provider established in its territory to subscribe to professional liability insurance or to provide another guarantee, that Member State shall accept as sufficient evidence attestations of such insurance cover issued by credit institutions and insurers established in other Member States.

3. Paragraphs 1 and 2 shall not affect professional insurance or guarantee arrangements provided for in other Community instruments.

4. For the implementation of paragraph 1, the Commission may, in accordance with the regulatory procedure referred to in Article 40(2), establish a list of services which exhibit the characteristics referred to in paragraph 1 of this Article. The Commission may also, in accordance with the procedure referred to in Article 40(3), adopt measures designed to amend non-essential elements of this Directive by supplementing it by establishing common criteria for defining, for the purposes of the insurance or guarantees referred to in paragraph 1 of this Article, what is appropriate to the nature and extent of the risk.

5. For the purpose of this Article
   — 'direct and particular risk' means a risk arising directly from the provision of the service,
   — 'health and safety' means, in relation to a recipient or a third person, the prevention of death or serious personal injury,
   — 'financial security' means, in relation to a recipient, the prevention of substantial losses of money or of value of property,
   — 'professional liability insurance' means insurance taken out by a provider in respect of potential liabilities to recipients and, where applicable, third parties arising out of the provision of the service.

Article 24 Commercial communications by the regulated professions

1. Member States shall remove all total prohibitions on commercial communications by the regulated professions.

2. Member States shall ensure that commercial communications by the regulated professions comply with professional rules, in conformity with Community law, which relate, in particular, to the independence, dignity and integrity of the profession, as well as to professional secrecy, in a manner consistent with the specific nature of each profession. Professional rules on commercial communications shall be non-discriminatory, justified by an overriding reason relating to the public interest and proportionate.

Article 25 Multidisciplinary activities

1. Member States shall ensure that providers are not made subject to requirements which oblige them to exercise a given specific activity exclusively or which restrict the exercise jointly or in partnership of different activities.

   However, the following providers may be made subject to such requirements:

   (a) the regulated professions, in so far as is justified in order to guarantee compliance with the rules governing professional ethics and conduct, which vary according to the specific nature of each profession, and is necessary in order to ensure their independence and impartiality;

   (b) providers of certification, accreditation, technical monitoring, test or trial services, in so far as is justified in order to ensure their independence and impartiality.

2. Where multidisciplinary activities between providers referred to in points (a) and (b) of paragraph 1 are authorised, Member States shall ensure the following:

   (a) that conflicts of interest and incompatibilities between certain activities are prevented;

   (b) that the independence and impartiality required for certain activities is secured;

   (c) that the rules governing professional ethics and conduct for different activities are compatible with one another, especially as regards matters of professional secrecy.

3. In the report referred to in Article 39(1), Member States shall indicate which providers are subject to the requirements laid down in paragraph 1 of this Article, the content of those requirements and the reasons for which they consider them to be justified.

Article 26 Policy on quality of services

1. Member States shall, in cooperation with the Commission, take accompanying measures to encourage providers to take action on a voluntary basis in order to ensure the quality of service provision, in particular through use of one of the following methods:

   (a) certification or assessment of their activities by independent or accredited bodies;

   (b) drawing up their own quality charter or participation in quality charters or labels drawn up by professional bodies at Community level.

2. Member States shall ensure that information on the significance of certain labels and the criteria for applying labels and other quality marks relating to services can be easily accessed by providers and recipients.

3. Member States shall, in cooperation with the Commission, take accompanying measures to encourage professional bodies, as well as chambers of commerce and craft associations and consumer associations, in their territory to cooperate at Community level in order to promote the quality of service provision, especially by making it easier to assess the competence of a provider.

4. Member States shall, in cooperation with the Commission, take accompanying measures to encourage the development of independent assessments, notably by consumer associations, in relation to the quality and defects of service provision, and, in particular, the development at Community level of comparative trials or testing and the communication of the results.

5. Member States, in cooperation with the Commission, shall encourage the development of voluntary European standards with the aim of facilitating compatibility between services supplied by providers in different Member States, information to the recipient and the quality of service provision.

Article 27 Settlement of disputes

1. Member States shall take the general measures necessary to ensure that providers supply contact details, in particular a postal address, fax number or e-mail address and telephone number to which all recipients, including those resident in another Member State, can send a complaint or a request for information about the service provided. Providers shall supply their legal address if this is not their usual address for correspondence. Member States shall take the general measures necessary to ensure that providers respond to the complaints referred to in the first subparagraph in the shortest possible time and make their best efforts to find a satisfactory solution.

2. Member States shall take the general measures necessary to ensure that providers are obliged to demonstrate compliance with the obligations laid down in this Directive as to the provision of information and to demonstrate that the information is accurate.

3. Where a financial guarantee is required for compliance with a judicial decision, Member States shall recognise equivalent guarantees lodged with a credit institution or insurer established in another Member State. Such credit institutions must be authorised in a Member State in accordance with Directive 2006/48/EC and such insurers in accordance, as appropriate, with First Council Directive 73/239/EEC of 24 July 1973 on the coordination of laws, regulations and administrative provisions relating to the taking-up and pursuit of the business of direct insurance other than life assurance and Directive 2002/83/EC of the European Parliament and of the Council of 5 November 2002 concerning life assurance.

4. Member States shall take the general measures necessary to ensure that providers who are subject to a code of conduct, or are members of a trade association or professional body, which provides for recourse to a non-judicial means of dispute settlement inform the recipient thereof and mention that fact in any document which presents their services in detail, specifying how to access detailed information on the characteristics of, and conditions for, the use of such a mechanism.

CHAPTER VI

ADMINISTRATIVE COOPERATION

Article 28 Mutual assistance – general obligations

1. Member States shall give each other mutual assistance, and shall put in place measures for effective cooperation with one another, in order to ensure the supervision of providers and the services they provide.

2. For the purposes of this Chapter, Member States shall designate one or more liaison points, the contact details of which shall be communicated to the other Member States and the Commission. The Commission shall publish and regularly update the list of liaison points.

3. Information requests and requests to carry out any checks, inspections and investigations under this Chapter shall be duly motivated, in particular by specifying the reason for the request. Information exchanged shall be used only in respect of the matter for which it was requested.

4. In the event of receiving a request for assistance from competent authorities in another Member State, Member States shall ensure that providers established in their territory supply their competent authorities with all the information necessary for supervising their activities in compliance with their national laws.

5. In the event of difficulty in meeting a request for information or in carrying out checks, inspections or investigations, the Member State in question shall rapidly inform the requesting Member State with a view to finding a solution.

6. Member States shall supply the information requested by other Member States or the Commission by electronic means and within the shortest possible period of time.

7. Member States shall ensure that registers in which providers have been entered, and which may be consulted by the competent authorities in their territory, may also be consulted, in accordance with the same conditions, by the equivalent competent authorities of the other Member States.

8. Member States shall communicate to the Commission information on cases where other Member States do not fulfil their obligation of mutual assistance. Where necessary, the Commission shall take appropriate steps, including proceedings provided for in Article 226 of the Treaty, in order to ensure that the Member States concerned comply with their obligation of mutual assistance. The Commission shall periodically inform Member States about the functioning of the mutual assistance provisions.

Article 29 Mutual assistance – general obligations for the Member State of establishment

1. With respect to providers providing services in another Member State, the Member State of establishment shall supply information on providers established in its territory when requested to do so by another Member State and, in particular, confirmation that a provider is established in its territory and, to its knowledge, is not exercising his activities in an unlawful manner.

2. The Member State of establishment shall undertake the checks, inspections and investigations requested by another Member State and shall inform the latter of the results and, as the case may be, of the measures taken. In so doing, the competent authorities shall act to the extent permitted by the powers vested in them in their Member State. The competent authorities can decide on the most appropriate measures to be taken in each individual case in order to meet the request by another Member State.

3. Upon gaining actual knowledge of any conduct or specific acts by a provider established in its territory which provides services in other Member States, that, to its knowledge, could cause serious damage to the health or safety of persons or to the environment, the Member State of establishment shall inform all other Member States and the Commission within the shortest possible period of time.

Article 30 Supervision by the Member State of establishment in the event of the temporary movement of a provider to another Member State

1. With respect to cases not covered by Article 31(1), the Member State of establishment shall ensure that compliance with its requirements is supervised in conformity with the powers of supervision provided for in its national law, in particular through supervisory measures at the place of establishment of the provider.

2. The Member State of establishment shall not refrain from taking supervisory or enforcement measures in its territory on the grounds that the service has been provided or caused damage in another Member State.

3. The obligation laid down in paragraph 1 shall not entail a duty on the part of the Member State of establishment to carry out factual checks and controls in the territory of the Member State where the service is provided. Such checks and controls shall be carried out by the authorities of the Member State where the provider is temporarily operating at the request of the authorities of the Member State of establishment, in accordance with Article 31.

Article 31 Supervision by the Member State where the service is provided in the event of the temporary movement of the provider

1. With respect to national requirements which may be imposed pursuant to Articles 16 or 17, the Member State where the service is provided is responsible for the supervision of the activity of the provider in its territory. In conformity with Community law, the Member State where the service is provided:
    (a) shall take all measures necessary to ensure the provider complies with those requirements as regards the access to and the exercise of the activity;
    (b) shall carry out the checks, inspections and investigations necessary to supervise the service provided.

2. With respect to requirements other than those referred to in paragraph 1, where a provider moves temporarily to another Member State in order to provide a service without being established there, the competent authorities of that Member State shall participate in the supervision of the provider in accordance with paragraphs 3 and 4.

3. At the request of the Member State of establishment, the competent authorities of the Member State where the service is provided shall carry out any checks, inspections and investigations

necessary for ensuring the effective supervision by the Member State of establishment. In so doing, the competent authorities shall act to the extent permitted by the powers vested in them in their Member State. The competent authorities may decide on the most appropriate measures to be taken in each individual case in order to meet the request by the Member State of establishment.

4. On their own initiative, the competent authorities of the Member State where the service is provided may conduct checks, inspections and investigations on the spot, provided that those checks, inspections or investigations are not discriminatory, are not motivated by the fact that the provider is established in another Member State and are proportionate.

Article 32 Alert mechanism

1. Where a Member State becomes aware of serious specific acts or circumstances relating to a service activity that could cause serious damage to the health or safety of persons or to the environment in its territory or in the territory of other Member States, that Member State shall inform the Member State of establishment, the other Member States concerned and the Commission within the shortest possible period of time.

2. The Commission shall promote and take part in the operation of a European network of Member States' authorities in order to implement paragraph 1.

3. The Commission shall adopt and regularly update, in accordance with the procedure referred to in Article 40(2), detailed rules concerning the management of the network referred to in paragraph 2 of this Article.

Article 33 Information on the good repute of providers

1. Member States shall, at the request of a competent authority in another Member State, supply information, in conformity with their national law, on disciplinary or administrative actions or criminal sanctions and decisions concerning insolvency or bankruptcy involving fraud taken by their competent authorities in respect of the provider which are directly relevant to the provider's competence or professional reliability. The Member State which supplies the information shall inform the provider thereof. A request made pursuant to the first subparagraph must be duly substantiated, in particular as regards the reasons for the request for information.

2. Sanctions and actions referred to in paragraph 1 shall only be communicated if a final decision has been taken. With regard to other enforceable decisions referred to in paragraph 1, the Member State which supplies the information shall specify whether a particular decision is final or whether an appeal has been lodged in respect of it, in which case the Member State in question should provide an indication of the date when the decision on appeal is expected.
    Moreover, that Member State shall specify the provisions of national law pursuant to which the provider was found guilty or penalised.

3. Implementation of paragraphs 1 and 2 must comply with rules on the provision of personal data and with rights guaranteed to persons found guilty or penalised in the Member States concerned, including by professional bodies. Any information in question which is public shall be accessible to consumers.

Article 34 Accompanying measures

1. The Commission, in cooperation with Member States, shall establish an electronic system for the exchange of information between Member States, taking into account existing information systems.

2. Member States shall, with the assistance of the Commission, take accompanying measures to facilitate the exchange of officials in charge of the implementation of mutual assistance and training of such officials, including language and computer training.

3. The Commission shall assess the need to establish a multiannual programme in order to organise relevant exchanges of officials and training.

Article 35 Mutual assistance in the event of case-by-case derogations

1. Where a Member State intends to take a measure pursuant to Article 18, the procedure laid down in paragraphs 2 to 6 of this Article shall apply without prejudice to court proceedings,

including preliminary proceedings and acts carried out in the framework of a criminal investigation.

2. The Member State referred to in paragraph 1 shall ask the Member State of establishment to take measures with regard to the provider, supplying all relevant information on the service in question and the circumstances of the case.

The Member State of establishment shall check, within the shortest possible period of time, whether the provider is operating lawfully and verify the facts underlying the request. It shall inform the requesting Member State within the shortest possible period of time of the measures taken or envisaged or, as the case may be, the reasons why it has not taken any measures.

3. Following communication by the Member State of establishment as provided for in the second subparagraph of paragraph 2, the requesting Member State shall notify the Commission and the Member State of establishment of its intention to take measures, stating the following:

   (a) the reasons why it believes the measures taken or envisaged by the Member State of establishment are inadequate;

   (b) the reasons why it believes the measures it intends to take fulfil the conditions laid down in Article 18.

4. The measures may not be taken until fifteen working days after the date of notification provided for in paragraph 3.

5. Without prejudice to the possibility for the requesting Member State to take the measures in question upon expiry of the period specified in paragraph 4, the Commission shall, within the shortest possible period of time, examine the compatibility with Community law of the measures notified.

Where the Commission concludes that the measure is incompatible with Community law, it shall adopt a decision asking the Member State concerned to refrain from taking the proposed measures or to put an end to the measures in question as a matter of urgency.

6. In the case of urgency, a Member State which intends to take a measure may derogate from paragraphs 2, 3 and 4. In such cases, the measures shall be notified within the shortest possible period of time to the Commission and the Member State of establishment, stating the reasons for which the Member State considers that there is urgency.

Article 36 Implementing measures

In accordance with the procedure referred to in Article 40(3), the Commission shall adopt the implementing measures designed to amend non-essential elements of this Chapter by supplementing it by specifying the time-limits provided for in Articles 28 and 35. The Commission shall also adopt, in accordance with the procedure referred to in Article 40(2), the practical arrangements for the exchange of information by electronic means between Member States, and in particular the interoperability provisions for information systems.

CHAPTER VII
CONVERGENCE PROGRAMME

Article 37 Codes of conduct at Community level

1. Member States shall, in cooperation with the Commission, take accompanying measures to encourage the drawing up at Community level, particularly by professional bodies,organisations and associations, of codes of conduct aimed at facilitating the provision of services or the establishment of a provider in another Member State, in conformity with Community law.

2. Member States shall ensure that the codes of conduct referred to in paragraph 1 are accessible at a distance, by electronic means.

Article 38 Additional harmonisation

The Commission shall assess, by 28 December 2010 the possibility of presenting proposals for harmonisation instruments on the following subjects:

   (a) access to the activity of judicial recovery of debts;

   (b) private security services and transport of cash and valuables.

Article 39 Mutual evaluation

1. By 28 December 2009 at the latest, Member States shall present a report to the Commission, containing the information specified in the following provisions:
    (a) Article 9(2), on authorisation schemes;
    (b) Article 15(5), on requirements to be evaluated;
    (c) Article 25(3), on multidisciplinary activities.
2. The Commission shall forward the reports provided for in paragraph 1 to the Member States, which shall submit their observations on each of the reports within six months of receipt. Within the same period, the Commission shall consult interested parties on those reports.
3. The Commission shall present the reports and the Member States' observations to the Committee referred to in Article 40(1), which may make observations.
4. In the light of the observations provided for in paragraphs 2 and 3, the Commission shall, by 28 December 2010 at the latest, present a summary report to the European Parliament and to the Council, accompanied where appropriate by proposals for additional initiatives.
5. By 28 December 2009 at the latest, Member States shall present a report to the Commission on the national requirements whose application could fall under the third subparagraph of Article 16(1) and the first sentence of Article 16(3), providing reasons why they consider that the application of those requirements fulfil the criteria referred to in the third subparagraph of Article 16(1) and the first sentence of Article 16(3).

    Thereafter, Member States shall transmit to the Commission any changes in their requirements, including new requirements, as referred to above, together with the reasons for them.

    The Commission shall communicate the transmitted requirements to other Member States. Such transmission shall not prevent the adoption by Member States of the provisions in question. The Commission shall on an annual basis thereafter provide analyses and orientations on the application of these provisions in the context of this Directive.

Article 40 Committee procedure

1. The Commission shall be assisted by a Committee.
2. Where reference is made to this paragraph, Articles 5 and 7 of Decision 1999/468/EC shall apply, having regard to the provisions of Article 8 thereof. The period laid down in Article 5(6) of Decision 1999/468/EC shall be set at three months.
3. Where reference is made to this paragraph, Article 5a(1) to (4), and Article 7 of Decision 1999/468/EC shall apply, having regard to the provisions of Article 8 thereof.

Article 41 Review clause

The Commission, by 28 December 2011 and every three years thereafter, shall present to the European Parliament and to the Council a comprehensive report on the application of this Directive. This report shall, in accordance with Article 16(4), address in particular the application of Article 16. It shall also consider the need for additional measures for matters excluded from the scope of application of this Directive. It shall be accompanied, where appropriate, by proposals for amendment of this Directive with a view to completing the Internal Market for services.

Article 42 Amendment of Directive 98/27/EC

In the Annex to Directive 98/27/EC of the European Parliament and of the Council of 19 May 1998 on injunctions for the protection of consumers' interests, the following point shall be added:

> '13. Directive 2006/123/EC of the European Parliament and of the Council of 12 December 2006 on services in the internal market (OJ L 376, 27.12.2006, p. 36)'.

Article 43 Protection of personal data

The implementation and application of this Directive and, in particular, the provisions on supervision shall respect the rules on the protection of personal data as provided for in Directives 95/46/EC and 2002/58/EC.

CHAPTER VIII
FINAL PROVISIONS

Article 44 Transposition

1. Member States shall bring into force the laws, regulations and administrative provisions necessary to comply with this Directive before 28 December 2009.

    They shall forthwith communicate to the Commission the text of those measures.

    When Member States adopt these measures, they shall contain a reference to this Directive or shall be accompanied by such a reference on the occasion of their official publication. The methods of making such reference shall be laid down by Member States.

2. Member States shall communicate to the Commission the text of the main provisions of national law which they adopt in the field covered by this Directive.

Article 45 Entry into force

This Directive shall enter into force on the day following that of its publication in the *Official Journal of the European Union*.

Article 46 Addressees

This Directive is addressed to the Member States.

SOCIAL SECURITY

COUNCIL REGULATION (EC) No 1408/71 of 14 JUNE 1971
on the application of social security schemes to employed persons, to self-employed persons and to members of their families moving within the Community
[1971] OJ L149/2

Editor's Note: At the time of writing, an implementation date for Regulation 883/2004 is awaited. This Regulation has been adopted to simplify and clarify the Community rules on the coordination of Member States' social security schemes. It will repeal Regulation 1408/71 from the date the new implementing Regulation comes into force (expected to be 2009).

TITLE I
GENERAL PROVISIONS

Article 1   Definitions

For the purpose of this Regulation:

(a)   *employed person* and *self-employed person* mean respectively:

(i)   any person who is insured, compulsorily or on an optional continued basis, for one or more of the contingencies covered by the branches of a social security scheme for employed or self-employed persons or by a special scheme for civil servants;

(ii)   any person who is compulsorily insured for one or more of the contingencies covered by the branches of social security dealt with in this Regulation, under a social security dealt with in this Regulation, under a social security scheme for all residents or for the whole working population, if such person:

— can be identified as an employed or self-employed person by virtue of the manner in which such scheme is administered or financed, or,

— failing such criteria, is insured for some other contingency specified in Annex I under a scheme for employed or self-employed persons, or under a scheme referred to in (iii), either compulsorily or on an optional continued basis, or, where no such scheme exists in the Member State concerned, complies with the definition given in Annex I;

(iii)   any person who is compulsorily insured for several of the contingencies covered by the branches dealt with in this Regulation, under a standard social security scheme for the whole rural population in accordance with the criteria laid down in Annex I;

(iv)   any person who is voluntarily insured for one or more of the contingencies covered by the branches dealt with in this Regulation, under a social security scheme of a Member State for employed or self-employed persons or for all residents or for certain categories of residents:

— if such person carries out an activity as an employed or self-employed person, or

— if such person has previously been compulsorily insured for the same contingency under a scheme for employed or self-employed persons for the same Member State;

(b)   *frontier worker* means any employed or self-employed person who pursues his occupation in the territory of a Member State and resides in the territory of another Member State to which he returns as a rule daily or at least once a week; however, a frontier worker who is posted elsewhere in the territory of the same or another Member State by the undertaking to which he is normally attached, or who engages in the provision of services elsewhere in the territory of the same or another Member State, shall retain the status of frontier worker for a period not exceeding four month, even if he is prevented, during that period, from returning daily or at least once a week to the place where he resides;

(c)   *seasonal worker* means any employed person who goes to the territory of a Member State other than the one in which he is resident to do work there of a seasonal nature for an undertaking or an employer of that State for a period which may on no account exceed eight month, and who stays in the territory of the said State for the duration of this work; work of a seasonal nature shall be taken to mean work which, being dependent on the succession of the seasons, automatically recurs each year;

(ca)   *student* means any person other than an employed or self-employed person or a member of his family or survivor within the meaning of this Regulation who studies or receives vocational training leading to a qualification officially recognised by the authorities of a Member State, and is insured under a general social security scheme or a special social security scheme applicable to students;

(d)   *refugee* shall have the meaning assigned to it in Article 1 of the Convention of the Status of Refugees, signed at Geneva on 28 July 1951;

(e)   *stateless person* shall have the meaning assigned to it in Article 1 of the Convention on the Status of Stateless Persons, signed in New York on 28 September 1954;

(f)   (i)   *member of the family* means any person defined or recognised as a member of the family or designated as a member of the household by the legislation under which benefits are provided or, in the cases referred to in Articles 22(1)(a) and 31, by the legislation of the Member State in whose territory such person resides; where, however, the said legislations regard as a member of the family or a member of the household only a person living under the same roof as the employed or self-employed person or student, this condition shall be considered satisfied if the person in question is mainly dependent on that person. Where the legislation of a Member State does not enable members of the family to be distinguished from the other persons to whom it applies, the term 'member of the family' shall have the meaning given to it in Annex I;

    (ii)   where, however, the benefits concerned are benefits for disabled persons granted under the legislation of a Member State to all nationals of that State who fulfil the prescribed conditions, the term 'member of the family' means at least the spouse of an employed or self-employed person or student and the children of such person who are either minors or dependent upon such person;

(g)   *survivor* means any person defined or recognised as such by the legislation under which the benefits are granted; where, however, the said legislation regards as a survivor only a person who was living under the same roof as the deceased, this condition shall be considered satisfied if such person was mainly dependent on the deceased;

(h)   *residence* means habitual residence;

(i)   *stay* means temporary residence;

(j)   *legislation* means in respect of each Member State statutes, regulations and other provisions and all other implementing measures, present or future, relating to the branches and schemes of social security covered by Article 4(1) and (2) or those special non-contributory benefits covered by Article 4(2a).

The term excludes provisions of existing or future industrial agreements, whether or not they have been the subject of a decision by the authorities rendering them compulsory or extending their scope. However, in so far as such provisions:

    (i)   serve to put into effect compulsory insurance imposed by the laws and regulations referred to in the preceding subparagraph; or

    (ii)   set up a scheme administered by the same institution as that which administers the schemes set up by the laws and regulations referred to in the preceding subparagraph,

the limitation on the term may at any time be lifted by a declaration of the Member State concerned specifying the schemes of such a kind to which this Regulation applies. Such a declaration shall be notified and published in accordance with the provisions of Article 97.

The provisions of the preceding subparagraph shall not have the effect of exempting from the application of this Regulation the schemes to which Regulation No 3 applied.

The term 'legislation' also excludes provisions governing special schemes for self-employed persons the creation of which is left to the initiatives of those concerned or which apply only to a part of the territory of the Member State concerned, irrespective of whether or not the authorities decided to make them compulsory or extend their scope. The special schemes in question are specified in Annex II;

(ja)   'special scheme for civil servants' means any social security scheme which is different from the general social security scheme applicable to employed persons in the Member States concerned and to which all, or certain categories of, civil servants or persons treated as such are directly subject;

(k)   *social security convention* means any bilateral or multilateral instrument which binds or will bind two or more Member States exclusively, and any other multilateral instrument which binds or will bind at least two Member States and one or more other States in the field of social security, for all or part of the branches and schemes set out in Article 4(1) and (2), together with agreements, of whatever kind, concluded pursuant to the said instruments;

(l)   *competent authority* means, in respect of each Member State, the Minister, Ministers or other equivalent authority responsible for social security schemes throughout or in any part of the territory of the State in question;

(m)   *Administrative Commission* means the commission referred to in Article 80;

(n)   *institution* means, in respect of each Member State, the body or authority responsible for administering all or part of the legislation;

(o)   *competent institution* means:

(i)   the institution with which the person concerned is insured at the time of the application for benefit;
or

(ii)   the institution from which the person concerned is entitled or would be entitled to benefits if he or a member or members of his family were resident in the territory of the Member State in which the institution is situated; or

(iii)   the institution designated by the competent authority of the member State concerned; or

(iv)   in the case of a scheme relating to an employer's liability in respect of the benefits set out in Article 4(1), either the employer or the insurer involved or, in default thereof, a body or authority designated by the competent authority of the Member State concerned;

(p)   *institution of the place of residence* and *institution of the place of stay* means respectively the institution which is competent to provide benefits in the place where the person concerned resides and the institution which is competent to provide benefits in the place where the person concerned is staying, under the legislation administered by that institution or, where no such institution exists, the institution designated by the competent authority of the Member State in question;

(q)   *competent State* means the Member State in whose territory the competent institution is situated;

(r)   *periods of insurance* means periods of contribution or period of employment or self-employment as defined or recognised as periods of insurance by the legislation under which they were completed or considered as completed, and all periods treated as such, where they are regarded by the said legislation as equivalent to periods of insurance; periods completed under a special scheme for civil servants are also considered as periods of insurance;

(s)   *periods of employment* and *periods of self-employment* means periods so defined or recognised by the legislation under which they were completed, and all periods treated as such, where they are regarded by the said legislation as equivalent to periods of employment or of self-employment; periods completed under a special scheme for civil servants are also considered as periods of employment;

(sa)   *periods of residence* means periods as defined or recognised as such by the legislation under which they were completed or considered as completed;

(t)   *benefits* and *pensions* mean all benefits and pensions, including all elements thereof payable out of public funds, revalorisation increases and supplementary allowances, subject to the provisions of Title III, as also lump-sum benefits which may be paid in lieu of pensions, and payments made by way of reimbursement of contributions;

(u)   (i)   the term *family benefits* means all benefits in kind or in cash intended to meet family expenses under the legislation provided for in Article 4(1)(h), excluding the special childbirth or adoption allowances referred to in Annex II;

     (ii)   *family allowances* means periodical cash benefits granted exclusively by reference to the number and, where appropriate, the age of members of the family;

(v)   *death grants* means any once-for-all payment in the event of death exclusive of the lump-sum benefits referred to in subparagraph (t).

Article 2   Persons covered

1.   This Regulation shall apply to employed or self-employed persons and to students who are or have been subject to the legislation of one or more Member States and who are nationals of one of the Member States or who are stateless persons or refugees residing within the territory of one of the Member States, as well as to the members of their families and their survivors.

2.   This Regulation shall apply to the survivors of employed or self-employed persons and of students who have been subject to the legislation of one or more Member States, irrespective of the nationality of such persons, where their survivors are nationals of one of the Member States, or stateless persons or refugees residing within the territory of one of the Member States.

Article 3   Equality of treatment

1.   Subject to the special provisions of this Regulation, persons to whom this Regulation applies shall be subject to the same obligations and enjoy the same benefits under the legislation of any Member State as the nationals of the State.

2.   The provisions of paragraph 1 shall apply to the right to elect members of the organs of social security institutions or to participate in their nomination, but shall not affect the legislative provisions of any Member State relating to eligibility or methods of nomination of persons concerned to those organs.

3.   Save as provided in Annex III, the provisions of social security conventions which remain in force pursuant to Article 7 2. (c) shall apply to all persons to whom this Regulation applies.

Article 4   Matters covered

1.   This Regulation shall apply to all legislation concerning the following branches of social security:

(a)   sickness and maternity benefits;

(b)   invalidity benefits, including those intended for the maintenance or improvement of earning capacity;

(c)   old-age benefits;

(d)   survivors' benefits;

(e)   benefits in respect of accidents at work and occupational diseases;

(f)   death grants;

(g)   unemployment benefits;

(h)   family benefits.

2.   This Regulation shall apply to all general and special social security schemes, whether contributory or non-contributory, and to schemes concerning the liability of an employer or shipowner in respect of the benefits referred to in paragraph 1.

2a.   This Article shall apply to special non-contributory cash benefits which are provided under legislation which, because of its personal scope, objectives and/or conditions for entitlement has characteristics both of the social security legislation referred to in paragraph 1 and of social assistance.

'Special non-contributory cash benefits' means those:

(a)   which are intended to provide either:
       (i)   supplementary, substitute or ancillary cover against the risks covered by the branches of social security referred to in paragraph 1, and which guarantee the persons concerned a minimum subsistence income having regard to the economic and social situation in the Member State concerned;
              or
       (ii)   solely specific protection for the disabled, closely linked to the said person's social environment in the Member State concerned,
              and
(b)   where the financing exclusively derives from compulsory taxation intended to cover general public expenditure and the conditions for providing and for calculating the benefits are not dependent on any contribution in respect of the beneficiary. However, benefits provided to supplement a contributory benefit shall not be considered to be contributory benefits for this reason alone;
       and
(c)   which are listed in Annex IIa.

2b.   This Regulation shall not apply to the provisions in the legislation of a Member State concerning special non-contributory benefits, referred to in Annex II, Section III, the validity of which is confined to part of its territory.

3.   The provisions of Title III of this Regulation shall not, however, affect the legislative provisions of any Member State concerning a shipowner's liability.

4.   This Regulation shall not apply to social and medical assistance, to benefit schemes for victims of war or its consequences.

Article 9   Admission to voluntary or optional continued insurance

1.   The provisions of the legislation of any Member State which make admission to voluntary or optional continued insurance conditional upon residence in the territory of that State shall not apply to persons resident in the territory of another Member State, provided that at some time in their past working life they were subject to the legislation of the first State as employed or as self-employed persons.

2.   Where under the legislation of a Member State, admission to voluntary or optional continued insurance is conditional upon completion of periods of insurance, the periods of insurance or residence completed under the legislation of another Member State shall be taken into account, to the extent required, as if they were completed under the legislation of the first State.

Article 9a   Prolongation of the reference period

If the legislation of a Member State subordinates recognition of entitlement to a benefit to the completion of a minimum period of insurance during a determined period preceding the contingency insured against (reference period) and lays down that periods during which benefits were paid under the legislation of that Member State or periods devoted to child-rearing in the territory of that Member State shall extend this reference period, the periods during which invalidity or old age pensions or sickness, unemployment, industrial accidents at work or occupational disease benefits were paid under the legislation of another Member State and periods devoted to child-rearing in the territory of another Member State shall also extend this reference period.

Article 10   Waiving of residence clauses – Effect of compulsory insurance on reimbursement of contributions

1.   Save as otherwise provided in this Regulation invalidity, old-age or survivors' cash benefits, pension for accidents at work or occupational diseases and death grants acquired under the legislation of one or more Member States shall not be subject to any reduction, modification, suspension, withdrawal or confiscation by reason of the fact that the recipient resides in the territory of a Member State other than that in which the institution responsible for payment is situated.

The first subparagraph shall also apply to lump-sum benefits granted in cases of remarriage of a surviving spouse who was entitled to a survivors' pension.

2. Where under the legislation of a Member State reimbursement of contributions is conditional upon the person concerned having ceased to be subject to compulsory insurance, this condition shall not be considered satisfied as long as the person concerned is subject to compulsory insurance under the legislation of another Member State.

Article 10a Special non-contributory benefits

1. The provisions of Article 10 and of Title III shall not apply to the special non-contributory cash benefits referred to in Article 4(2a). The persons to whom this Regulation applies shall receive these benefits exclusively in the territory of the Member State in which they reside and under the legislation of that State, in so far as these benefits are mentioned in Annex IIa. Benefits shall be paid by, and at the expense of, the institution of the place of residence.

2. The institution of a Member State under whose legislation entitlement to benefits covered by paragraph 1 is subject to the completion of periods of employment, self-employment or residence shall regard, to the extent necessary, periods of employment, self-employment or residence completed in the territory of any other Member State as periods completed in the territory of the first Member State.

3. Where entitlement to a benefit covered by paragraph 1 but granted in the form of a supplement is subject, under the legislation of a Member State, to receipt of a benefit covered by Article 4(1)(a) to (h), and no such benefit is due under that legislation, any corresponding benefit granted under the legislation of any other Member State shall be treated as a benefit granted under the legislation of the first Member State for the purposes of entitlement to the supplement.

4. Where the granting of a disability or invalidity benefit covered by paragraph 1 is subject, under the legislation of a Member State, to the condition that the disability or invalidity should be diagnosed for the first time in the territory of that Member State, this condition shall be deemed to be fulfilled where such diagnosis is made for the first time in the territory of another Member State.

Article 11 Revalorisation of benefits

Rules for revalorisation provided by the legislation of a Member State shall apply to benefits due under that legislation taking into account the provisions of this Regulation.

Article 12 Prevention of overlapping of benefits

1. This Regulation can neither confer nor maintain the right to several benefits of the same kind for one and the same period of compulsory insurance. However, this provision shall not apply to benefits in respect of invalidity, old age, death (pensions) or occupational disease which are awarded by the institutions of two or more Member States, in accordance with the provisions of Articles 41, 43(2) and (3), 46, 50 and 51 or Article 60(1)(b).

2. Save as otherwise provided in this Regulation, the provisions of the legislations of a Member State governing the reduction, suspension or withdrawal of benefits in cases of overlapping with other social security benefits or any other form of income may be invoked even where such benefits were acquired under the legislation of another Member State or where such income was acquired in the territory of another Member State.

3. The provisions of the legislation of a Member State for reduction, suspension or withdrawal of benefit in the case of a person in receipt of invalidity benefits or anticipatory old-age benefits pursuing a professional or trade activity may be invoked against such person even though he is pursuing his activity in the territory of another Member State.

4. An invalidity pension payable under Netherlands legislation shall, in case where the Netherlands institution is bound under the provisions of Article 57(5) or 60(29)(b) to contribute also to the cost of benefits for occupational disease granted under the legislation of another Member State, be reduced by the amount payable to the institution of the other Member State which is responsible for granting the benefits for occupational disease.

TITLE II
DETERMINATION OF THE LEGISLATION APPLICABLE

Article 13   General rules

1. Subject to Articles 14c and 14f, persons to whom this Regulation applies shall be subject to the legislation of a single Member State only. That legislation shall be determined in accordance with the provisions of this Title.

2. Subject to Articles 14 to 17:

    (a) a person employed in the territory of one Member State shall be subject to the legislation of that State even if he resides in the territory of another Member State or if the registered office or place of business of the undertaking or individual employing him is situated in the territory of another Member State;

    (b) a person who is self-employed in the territory of one Member State shall be subjected to the legislation of that State even if he resides in the territory of another Member State;

    (c) a person employed on board a vessel flying the flag of a Member State shall be subject to the legislation of the State;

    (d) civil servants and persons treated as such shall be subject to the legislation of the Member State to which the administration employing them is subject;

    (e) a person called up or recalled for service in the armed forces, or for civilian service, of a Member State shall be subject to the legislation of that State. If entitlement under that legislation is subject to the completion of periods of insurance before entry into or after release from such military or civilian service, periods of insurance completed under the legislation of any other Member State shall betaken into account, to the extent necessary, as if they were periods of insurance completed under the legislation of the first State. The employed or self-employed person called up or recalled for service in the armed forces or for civilian service shall retain the status of employed or self-employed person;

    (f) a person to whom the legislation of a Member State ceases to be applicable, without the legislation of another Member State becoming applicable to him in accordance with one of the rules laid down in the aforegoing subparagraphs or in accordance with one of the exceptions or special provisions laid down in Articles 14 to 17 shall be subject to the legislation of the Member State in whose territory he resides in accordance with the provisions of that legislation alone.

Article 14   Special rules applicable to persons, other than mariners, engaged in paid employment Article 13(2)(a) shall apply subject to the following exceptions and circumstances:

1. (a) A person employed in the territory of a Member State by a undertaking to which he is normally attached who is posted by that undertaking to the territory of another Member State to perform work there for that undertaking shall continue to be subject to the legislation of the first Member State, provided that the anticipated duration of that work does not exceed 12 months and that he is not sent to replace another person who has completed his term of posting.

    (b) If the duration of the work to be done extends beyond the duration originally anticipated, owing to unforeseeable circumstances, and exceeds 12 months, the legislation of the first Member State shall continue to apply until the completion of such work, provided that the competent authority of the Member State in whose territory the person concerned is posted or the body designated by that authority gives its consent; such consent must be requested before the end of the initial 12 month period. Such consent cannot, however, be given for a period exceeding 12 months.

2. A person normally employed in the territory of two or more Member States shall be subject to the legislation determined as follows:

    (a) A person who is a member of the travelling or flying personnel of an undertaking which, for hire or reward or on its own account, operates international transport services for passengers or goods by rail, road, air or inland waterway and has its registered office or place of business in the territory of a Member State shall be subject to the legislation of the latter State, with the following restrictions:

(i) where the said undertaking has a branch or permanent representation in the territory of a Member State other than that in which it has its registered office or place of business, a person employed by such branch or permanent representation shall be subject to the legislation of the Member State in whose territory such branch or permanent representation is situated;

(ii) where a person is employed principally in the territory of the Member State in which he resides, he shall be subject to the legislation of that State, even if the undertaking which employs him has no registered office or place of business or branch or permanent representation in that territory.

(b) A person other than that referred to in (a) shall be subject:

(i) to the legislation of the Member State in whose territory he resides, if he pursues his activity partly in that territory or if he is attached to several undertakings or several employers who have their registered offices or places of business in the territory of different Member States;

(ii) to the legislation of the Member State in whose territory is situated the registered office or place of business of the undertaking or individual employing him, if he does not reside in the territory of any of the Member States where he is pursuing his activity.

3. A person who is employed in the territory of one Member State by an undertaking which has its registered office or place of business in the territory of another Member State and which straddles the common frontier of these States shall be subject to the legislation of the Member State in whose territory the undertaking has its registered office or place of business.

Article 14a Special rules applicable to persons, other than mariners, who are self-employed

Article 13(2)(b) shall apply subject to the following exceptions and circumstances:

1. (a) A person normally self-employed in the territory of a Member State and who performs work in the territory of another Member State shall continue to be subject to the legislation of the first Member State, provided that the anticipated duration of the work does not exceed 12 months.

(b) If the duration of the work to be done extends beyond the duration originally anticipated, owing to unforeseeable circumstances, and exceeds 12 months, the legislation of the first Member State shall continue to apply until the completion of such work, provided that the competent authority of the Member State in whose territory the person concerned has entered to perform the work in question or the body appointed by that authority gives its consent; such consent must be .

2. A person normally self-employed in the territory of two or more Member States shall be subject to the legislation of the Member State in whose territory he resides if he pursues any part of his activity in the territory of that Member State. If he does not pursue any activity in the territory of the Member State in which he resides, he shall be subject to the legislation of the Member State in whose territory he pursue his main activity. The criteria used to determine the principal activity are laid down in the Regulation referred to in Article 98.

3. A person who is self-employed in an undertaking which has its registered office or place of business in the territory of one Member State and which straddles the common frontier of two Member States shall be subject to the legislation of the Member State in whose territory the undertaking has its registered office or place of business.

4. If the legislation to which a person should be subject in accordance with paragraph 2 or 3 does not enable that person, even on a voluntary basis, to join a pension scheme, the person concerned shall be subject to the legislation of the other Member State which would apply apart from these particular provisions, or should the legislations of two or more Member States apply in this way, he shall be subject to the legislation decided on by common agreement amongst the Member States concerned or their competent authorities.

Article 15 Rules concerning voluntary insurance or optional continued insurance

1. Articles 13 to 14d shall not apply to voluntary insurance or to optional continued insurance unless, in respect of one of the branches referred to in Article 4, there exists in any Member State only a voluntary scheme of insurance.

2. Where application of the legislations of two or more Member States entails overlapping of insurance:
   — under a compulsory insurance scheme and one or more voluntary or optional continued insurance schemes, the person concerned shall be subject exclusively to the compulsory insurance scheme;
   — under two or more voluntary or optional continued insurance schemes, the person concerned may join only the voluntary or optional continued insurance scheme for which he has opted.

3. However, in respect of invalidity, old age and death (pensions), the person concerned may join the voluntary or optional continued insurance scheme of a Member State, even if he is compulsorily subject to the legislation of another Member State, to the extent that such overlapping is explicitly or implicitly admitted in the first Member State.

TITLE III

SPECIAL PROVISIONS RELATING TO THE VARIOUS CATEGORIES OF BENEFITS

CHAPTER I

SICKNESS AND MATERNITY

SECTION 1

COMMON PROVISIONS

Article 18 Aggregation of periods of insurance, employment or residence

1. The competent institution of a Member State whose legislation makes the acquisition, retention or recovery of the right to benefits conditional upon the completion of periods of insurance, employment or residence shall, to the extent necessary, take account of periods of insurance, employment or residence completed under the legislation of any other Member State as if they were periods completed under the legislation which it administers.

2. The provisions of paragraph 1 shall apply to seasonal workers, even in respect of periods prior to any break in insurance exceeding the period allowed by the legislation of the competent State, provided, however, that the person concerned has not ceased to be insured for a period exceeding four months.

SECTION 2

EMPLOYED OR SELF-EMPLOYED PERSONS AND MEMBERS OF THEIR FAMILIES

Article 19 Residence in a Member State other than the competent State – General rules

1. An employed or self-employed person residing in the territory of a Member State other than the competent State, who satisfies the conditions of the legislation of the competent State for entitlement to benefits, taking account where appropriate of the provisions of Article 18, shall receive in the State in which he is resident:
   (a) benefits in kind provided on behalf of the competent institution by the institution of the place of residence in accordance with the provisions of the legislation administered by that institution as though he were insured with it;
   (b) cash benefits provided by the competent institution in accordance with the legislation which it administers. However, by agreement between the competent institution and the institution of the place of residence, such benefits may be provided by the latter institution on behalf of the former, in accordance with the legislation of the competent State.

2. The provisions of paragraph 1 shall apply by analogy to members of the family who reside in the territory of a Member State other than the competent State in so far as they are not entitled to such benefits under the legislation of the State in whose territory they reside.
   Where the members of the family reside in the territory of a Member State under whose legislation the right to receive benefits in kind is not subject to condition of insurance or

employment, benefits in kind which they receive shall be considered as being on behalf of the institution with which the employed or self-employed person is insured, unless the spouse or the person looking after the children pursues a professional or trade activity in the territory of the said Member State.

Article 20   Frontier workers and members of their families – Special rules

A frontier worker may also obtain benefits in the territory of the competent State. Such benefits shall be provided by the competent institution in accordance with the provisions of the legislation of that State, as though the person concerned where resident in that State. Members of his family may receive benefits under the same conditions; however, receipt of such benefits shall, except in urgent cases, be conditional upon an agreement between the States concerned or between the competent authorities of those States or, in its absence, on prior authorisation by the competent institution.

Article 21   Stay in or transfer of residence to the competent State

1.   The employed or self-employed person referred to in Article 19(1) who is staying in the territory of the competent State shall receive benefits in accordance with the provisions of the legislation of that State as though he were resident there, even if he has already received benefits for the same case of sickness or maternity before his stay.

2.   Paragraph 1 shall apply by analogy to the members of the family referred to in Article 19(2). However, where the latter reside in the territory of a Member State other than the one in whose territory the employed or self-employed person resides, benefits in kind shall be provided by the institution of the place of stay on behalf of the institution of the place of residence of the persons concerned.

3.   Paragraphs 1 and 2 shall not apply to frontier workers and the members of their families.

4.   An employed or self-employed person and members of his family referred to in Article 19 who transfer their residence to the territory of the competent State shall receive benefits in accordance with the provisions of the legislation of that State even if they have already received benefits for the same case of sickness or maternity before transferring their residence.

Article 22   Stay outside the competent State – Return to or transfer of residence to another Member State during sickness or maternity – Need to go to another Member State in order to receive appropriate treatment

1.   An employed or self-employed person who satisfies the conditions of the legislation of the competent State for entitlement to benefits, taking account where appropriate of the provisions of Article 18, and:

   (a)   whose condition requires benefits in kind which become necessary on medical grounds during a stay in the territory of another Member State, taking into account the nature of the benefits and the expected length of the stay;

   (b)   who, having become entitled to benefits chargeable to the competent institution, is authorised by that institution to return to the territory of the Member State where he resides, or to transfer his residence to the territory of another Member State;
   or

   (c)   who is authorised by the competent institution to go to the territory of another Member State to receive there the treatment appropriate to his condition,

   shall be entitled:

      (i)   to benefits in kind provided on behalf of the competent institution by the institution of the place of stay or residence in accordance with the provisions of the legislation which it administers, as though he were insured with it; the length of the period during which benefits are provided shall be governed, however, by the legislation of the competent State;

      (ii)   to cash benefits provided by the competent institution in accordance with the provisions of the legislation which it administers. However, by agreement between the competent institution and the institution of the place of stay or residence, such benefits may be provided by the latter institution on behalf of the former, in accordance with the provisions of the legislation of the competent State.

1a The Administrative Commission shall establish a list of benefits in kind which, in order to be provided during a stay in another Member State, require, for practical reasons, a prior agreement between the person concerned and the institution providing the care;

2. The authorisation required under paragraph 1(b) may be refused only if it is established that movement of the person concerned would be prejudicial to his state of health or the receipt of medical treatment.

The authorisation required under paragraph 1(c) may not be refused where the treatment in question is among the benefits provided for by the legislation of the Member State on whose territory the person concerned resided and where he cannot be given such treatment within the time normally necessary for obtaining the treatment in question in the Member State of residence taking account of his current state of health and the probable course of the disease.

3. Paragraphs 1, 1a and 2 shall apply by analogy to members of the family of an employed or self-employed person.

However, for the purpose of applying paragraph 1(a) and (c)(i) to the members of the family referred to in Article 19(2) who reside in the territory of a Member State other than the one in whose territory the employed or self-employed person resides:

(a) benefits in kind shall be provided on behalf of the institution of the Member State in whose territory the members of the family are residing by the institution of the place of stay in accordance with the provisions of the legislation which it administers as if the employed or self-employed person were insured there. The period during which benefits are provided shall, however, be that laid down under the legislation of the Member State in whose territory the members of the family are residing;

(b) the authorisation required under paragraph 1(c) shall be issued by the institution of the Member State in whose territory the members of the family are residing.

4. The fact that the provisions of paragraph 1 apply to an employed or self-employed person shall not affect the right to benefit of members of his family.

Article 22a Special rules for certain categories of persons

Notwithstanding Article 2, Article 22(1)(a) and (c) and (1a) shall also apply to persons who are nationals of one of the Member States and who are insured under the legislation of a Member State and to the members of their families residing with them.

Article 23 Calculation of cash benefits

1. The competent institution of a Member State whose legislation provides that the calculation of cash benefits shall be based on average earnings or on average contributions, shall determine such average earnings or contributions exclusively by reference to earnings or contributions completed under the said legislation.

2a The provisions of paragraphs 1 and 2 shall also apply where the legislation applied by the competent institution provides for a specific reference period and this period coincides, where appropriate, with the whole or part of the periods completed by the person concerned under the legislation of one or more other Member States.

3. The competent institution of a Member State under whose legislation the amount of cash benefits varies with the number of members of the family, shall also take into account the members of the family of the person concerned who are resident in the territory of another Member State as if they were resident in the territory of the competent State.

Article 24 Substantial benefits in kind

1. Where the right of an employed or self-employed person or a member of his family to a prosthesis, a major appliance or other substantial benefits in kind has been recognised by the institution of a Member State before he becomes insured with the institution of another Member State, the said employed or self-employed person shall receive such benefits at the expense of the first institution, even if they are granted after he becomes insured with the second institution.

2.   The Administrative Commission shall draw up the list of benefits to which the provisions of paragraph 1 apply.

SECTION 3
UNEMPLOYED PERSONS AND MEMBERS OF THEIR FAMILIES

Article 25

1.   An unemployed person who was formerly employed or self-employed and to whom the provisions of Article 69(1) or Article 71(1)(b)(ii), second sentence apply and who satisfies the conditions laid down in the legislation of the competent State for entitlement to benefits in kind and cash benefits, taking account where necessary of the provisions of Article 18, shall receive for the period of time referred to in Article 69(1)(c):

   (a)   benefits in kind which become necessary on medical grounds for this person during his stay in the territory of the Member State where he is seeking employment, taking account of the nature of the benefits and the expected length of the stay. These benefits in kind shall be provided on behalf of the competent institution by the institution of the Member State in which the person is seeking employment, in accordance with the provisions of the legislation which the latter institution administers, as if he were insured with it;

   (b)   cash benefits provided by the competent institution in accordance with the provisions of the legislation which it administers. However, by agreement between the competent institution and the institution of the Member State in which the unemployed person seeks employment, benefits may be provided by the latter institution on behalf of the former institution in accordance with the provisions of the legislation of the competent State. Unemployment benefits under Article 69(1) shall not be granted for the period during which cash benefits are received.

1a. Article 22(1a) shall apply by analogy.

2.   A totally unemployed person who was formerly employed and to whom the provisions of Article 71(1)(a)(ii) or the first sentence of Article 71(1)(b)(ii) apply, shall receive benefits in kind and in cash in accordance with the provisions of the legislation of the Member State in whose territory he resides, as though he had been subject to that legislation during his last employment, taking account where appropriate of the provisions of Article 18; the cost of such benefits shall be met by the institution of the country of residence.

3.   Where an unemployed person satisfies the conditions of the legislation of the Member State which is responsible for the cost of unemployment benefits for entitlement to sickness and maternity benefits, taking account where appropriate of the provisions of Article 18, the members of his family shall receive these benefits, irrespective of the Member State in whose territory they reside or are staying. Such benefits shall be provided:

   (i)   with regard to the benefits in kind, by the institution of the place of residence or stay in accordance with the provisions of the legislation which it administers, on behalf of the competent institution of the Member State which is responsible for the cost of unemployment benefits;

   (ii) with regard to cash benefits, by the competent institution of the Member State which is responsible for the cost of unemployment benefits, in accordance with the legislation which it administers.

4.   Without prejudice to any provisions of the legislation of a Member State which permit an extension of the period during which sickness benefits may be granted, the period provided for in paragraph 1 may, in cases of force majeure, be extended by the competent institution within the limit fixed by the legislation administered by that institution.

Article 25a   Contributions payable by wholly unemployed persons

The institution which is responsible for granting benefits in kind and cash benefits to the unemployed persons referred to in Article 25(2) and which belongs to a Member State whose legislation provides for deduction of contributions payable by unemployed persons to cover sickness and maternity benefits shall be authorised to make such deductions in accordance with the provisions of its legislation.

CHAPTER 3
OLD AGE AND DEATH (PENSIONS)

Article 44 **General provisions for the award of benefits where an employed or self-employed person has been subject to the legislation of two or more Member States**

1. The rights to benefits of an employed or self-employed person who has been subject to the legislation of two or more Member States, or of his survivors, shall be determined in accordance with the provisions of this Chapter.

2. Save as otherwise provided in Article 49, the processing of a claim for an award submitted by the person concerned shall have regard to all the legislations to which the employed or self-employed person has been subject. Exception shall be made to this rule if the person concerned expressly asks for postponement of the award of old-age benefits to which he would be entitled under the legislation of one or more Member States.

3. This chapter shall not apply to increases in or supplements to pensions in respect of children or to orphans' pensions to be granted in accordance with the provisions of Chapter 8.

Article 45 **Consideration of periods of insurance or of residence completed under the legislations to which an employed person or self-employed person was subject, for the acquisition, retention or recovery of the right to benefits**

1. Where the legislation of a Member State makes the acquisition, retention or recovery of the right to benefits, under a scheme which is not a special scheme within the meaning of paragraph 2 or 3, subject to the completion of periods of insurance or of residence, the competent institution of that Member State shall take account, where necessary, of the periods of insurance or of residence completed under the legislation of any other Member State, be it under a general scheme or under a special scheme and either as an employed person or a self-employed person. For that purpose, it shall take account of these periods as if they had completed under its own legislation.

2. Where the legislation of a Member State makes the granting of certain benefits conditional upon the periods of insurance having been completed only in an occupation which is subject to a special scheme for employed persons or, where appropriate, in a specific employment, periods completed under the legislation of other Member States shall be taken into account for the granting of these benefits only if completed under a corresponding scheme or, failing that, in the same occupation or, where appropriate, in the same employment. If, account having been taken of the periods thus completed, the person concerned does not satisfy the conditions for receipt of these benefits, these periods shall be taken into account for the granting of the benefits under the general scheme or, failing that, under the scheme applicable to manual or clerical workers, as the case may be, subject to the condition that the person has been affiliated to one or other of these schemes.

3. Where the legislation of a Member State makes the granting of certain benefits conditional upon the periods of insurance having been completed only in an occupation subject to a special scheme for selfemployed persons, periods completed under the legislations of other Member States shall be taken into account for the granting of these benefits only if completed under a corresponding scheme or, failing that, in the same occupation. The special schemes for self-employed persons referred to in this paragraph are listed in Annex IV, part B, for each Member State concerned. If, account having been taken of the periods referred to in this paragraph, the person concerned does not satisfy the conditions for receipt of these benefits, these periods shall be taken into account for the granting of the benefits under the general scheme or, failing this, under the scheme applicable to manual or clerical workers, as the case may be, subject to the condition that the person concerned has been affiliated to one or other of these schemes.

4. The periods of insurance completed under a special scheme of a Member State shall be taken into account under the general scheme or, failing that, under the scheme applicable to manual or clerical workers, as the case may be, of another Member State for the acquisition, retention or recovery of the right to benefits, subject to the condition that the person concerned has been

affiliated to one or other of these schemes, even if these periods have already been taken into account in the latter State under a scheme referred to in paragraph 2 or in the first sentence of paragraph 3.

5. Where the legislation of a Member State makes the acquisition, retention or recovery of the right to benefits conditional upon the person concerned being insured at the time of the materialisation of the risk, this condition shall be regarded as having been satisfied in the case of insurance under the legislation of another Member State, in accordance with the procedures provided in Annex VI for each Member State concerned.

6. A period of full employment of a worker to whom Article 81(1)(a)(ii) or (b)(ii), first sentence, applies shall be taken into account by the competent institution of the Member State in whose territory the worker concerned resides in accordance with the legislation administered by that institution, as if that legislation applied to him during his last employment.

Where that institution applies legislation providing for deduction of contributions payable by unemployed persons to cover old age pensions and death, it shall be authorised to make such deductions in accordance with the provisions of its legislation.

If the period of full unemployment in the country of residence of the person concerned can be taken into account only if contribution periods have been completed in that country, this condition shall be deemed to be fulfilled if the contribution periods have been completed in another Member State.

Article 46   Award of benefits

1. Where the conditions required by the legislation of a Member State for entitlement to benefits have been satisfied without having to apply Article 45 or Article 40(3), the following rules shall apply:

(a) the competent institution shall calculate the amount of the benefit that would be due:

(i) on the one hand, only under the provisions of the legislation which it administers;

(ii) on the other hand, pursuant to paragraph 2;

(b) the competent institution may, however, waive the calculation to be carried out in accordance with (a)(ii) if the result of this calculation, apart from differences arising from the use of round figures, is equal to or lower than the result of the calculation carried out in accordance with (a)(i), in so far as that institution does not apply any legislation containing rules against overlapping as referred to in Articles 46b and 46c or if the aforementioned institution applies a legislation containing rules against overlapping in the case referred to in Article 46c, provided that the said legislation lays down that benefits of a different kind shall be taken into consideration only on the basis of the relation of the periods of insurance or of residence completed under that legislation alone to the periods of insurance or of residence required by that legislation in order to qualify for full benefit entitlement.

Annex IV, part C, lists for each Member State concerned the cases where the two calculations would lead to a result of this kind.

2. Where the conditions required by the legislation of a Member State for entitlement to benefits are satisfied only after application of Article 45 and or Article 40(3), the following rules shall apply:

(a) the competent institution shall calculate the theoretical amount of the benefit to which the person concerned could lay claim provided all periods of insurance and/or of residence, which have been completed under the legislation of the Member States to which the employed person or self-employed person was subject, have been completed in the State in question under the legislation which it administers on the date of the award of the benefit. If, under this legislation, the amount of the benefit is independent of the duration of the periods completed, the amount shall be regarded as being the theoretical amount referred to in this paragraph;

(b) the competent institution shall subsequently determine the actual amount of the benefit on the basis of the theoretical amount referred to in the preceding paragraph in accordance with the ratio of the duration of the periods of insurance or of residence completed before the materialisation of the risk under the legislation which it administers to the total duration of the periods of insurance and of residence completed before the materialisation of the risk under the legislations of all the Member States concerned.

3. The person concerned shall be entitled to the highest amount calculated in accordance with paragraphs 1 and 2 from the competent institution of each Member State without prejudice to any application of the provisions concerning reduction, suspension or withdrawal provided for by the legislation under which this benefit is due.

Where that is the case, the comparison to be carried out shall relate to the amounts determined after the application of the said provisions.

4. When, in the case of invalidity, old-age or survivor's pensions, the total of the benefits due from the competent institutions of two or more Member States under the provisions of a multilateral social security convention referred to in Article 6(b) does not exceed the total which would be due from such Member States under paragraphs 1 to 3, the person concerned shall benefit from the provisions of this Chapter.

Article 46a General provisions relating to reduction, suspension or withdrawal applicable to benefits in respect of invalidity, old age or survivors under the legislations of the Member States

1. For the purposes of the Chapter, overlapping of benefits of the same kind shall have the following meaning: all overlapping of benefits in respect of invalidity, old age and survivors calculated or provided on the basis of periods of insurance and/or residence completed by one and the same person.

2. For the purposes of this Chapter, overlapping of benefits of different kinds means all overlapping of benefits that cannot be regarded as being of the same kind within the meaning of paragraph 1.

3. The following rules shall be applicable for the application of provisions on reduction, suspension or withdrawal laid down by the legislation of a Member State in the case of overlapping of a benefit in respect of invalidity, old age or survivors with a benefit of the same kind or a benefit of a different kind or with other income:

   (a) account shall be taken of the benefits acquired under the legislation of another Member State or of other income acquired in another Member State only where the legislation of the first Member State provides for the taking into account of benefits or income acquired abroad;

   (b) account shall be taken of the amount of benefits to be granted by another Member State before deductions of taxes, social security contributions and other individual levies or deductions;

   (c) no account shall be taken of the amount of benefits acquired under the legislation of another Member State which are awarded on the basis of voluntary insurance or continued optional insurance;

   (d) where provisions on reduction, suspension or withdrawal are applicable under the legislation of only one Member State on account of the fact that the person concerned receives benefits of a similar or different kind payable under the legislation of other Member States or other income acquired within the territory of other Member States, the benefit payable under the legislation of the first Member State may be reduced only within the limit of the amount of the benefits payable under the legislation or the income acquired within the territory of other Member States.

Article 46b Special provisions applicable in the case of overlapping of benefits of the same kind under the legislation of two or more Member States

1. The provisions on reduction, suspension or withdrawal laid down by the legislation of a Member State shall not be applicable to a benefit calculated in accordance with Article 46(2).

2. The provisions on reduction, suspension or withdrawal laid down by the legislation of a Member State shall apply to a benefit calculated in accordance with Article 46(1)(a)(i) only if the benefit concerned is:

(a)   a benefit, the amount of which is determined on the basis of a credited period deemed to have been completed between the date on which the risk materialised and a later date. In the latter case, the said provisions shall apply in the case of overlapping of such a benefit:

or

(b)   a benefit, the amount of which is determined on the basis of a credited period deemed to have been completed between the date on which the risk materialised and a later date. In the latter case, the said provisions shall apply in the case of overlapping of such a benefit:

    (i)   either with a benefit of the same kind, except where an agreement has been concluded between two or more Member States providing that one and the same credited period may not be taken into account two or more times;

    (ii)   or with a benefit of the type referred to in (a).

The benefits referred to in (a) and (b) and agreements are mentioned in Annex IV, part D.

Article 46c Special provisions applicable in the case of overlapping of one or more benefits referred to in Article 46a(1) with one or more benefits of a different kind or with other income, where two or more Member States are concerned

1.   If the receipt of benefits of a different kind or other income entails the reduction, suspension or withdrawal of two or more benefits referred to in Article 46(1)(a)(i), the amounts which would not be paid in strict application of the provisions concerning reduction, suspension or withdrawal provided for by the legislation of the Member States concerned shall be divided by the number of benefits subject to reduction, suspension or withdrawal.

2.   Where the benefit in question is calculated in accordance with Article 46(2), the benefit or benefits of a different kind from other Member States or other income and all other elements provided for by the legislation of the Member State for the application of the provisions in the respect of reduction, suspension or withdrawal shall be taken into account in proportion to the periods of insurance and/or residence referred to in Article 46(2)(b), and shall be used for the calculation of the said benefit.

3.   If the receipt of benefits of a different kind or of other income entails the reduction, suspension or withdrawal of one or more benefits referred to in Article 46(1)(a)(i), and of one or more benefits referred to in Article 46(2), the following rules shall apply:

(a)   where in a case of a benefit or benefits referred to in Article 46(1)(a)(i), the amounts which would not be paid in strict application of the provisions concerning reduction, suspension or withdrawal provided for by the legislation of the Member States concerned shall be divided by the number of benefits subject to reduction, suspension or withdrawal;

(b)   where in a case of a benefit or benefits calculated in accordance with Article 46(2), the reduction suspension or withdrawal shall be carried out in accordance with paragraph 2.

4.   Where, in the case referred to in paragraphs 1 and 3(a), the legislation of a Member State provides that, for the application of provisions concerning reduction, suspension or withdrawal, account shall be taken of benefits of a different kind and/or other income and all other elements in proportion to the periods of insurance referred to in Article 46(2)(b), the division provided for in the said paragraphs shall not apply in respect of that Member State.

5.   All the above mentioned provisions shall apply mutatis mutandis where the legislation of one or more Member States provides that the right to a benefit cannot be acquired in the case where the person concerned is in receipt of a benefit of a different kind, payable under the legislation of another Member State, or of other income.

Article 50 Award of a supplement where the total of benefits payable under the legislations of the various Member States does not amount to the minimum laid down by the legislation of the State in whose territory the recipient resides

A recipient of benefits to whom this Chapter applies may not, in the State in whose territory he resides and under whose legislation a benefit is payable to him, be awarded a benefit which is less than the minimum benefit fixed by that legislation for a period of insurance or residence equal to all the periods of insurance or residence equal to all the periods of insurance taken into account for the payment in accordance with the preceding Articles. The competent institution of that State shall, if necessary, pay him throughout the period of his residence in its territory a supplement equal to the difference between the total of the benefits payable under this Chapter and the amount of the minimum benefit.

Article 51 Revalorization and recalculation of benefits

1.   If, by reason of an increase in the cost of living or changes in the level of wages or salaries or other reasons for adjustment, the benefits of the States concerned are altered by a fixed percentage or amount, such percentage or amount must be applied directly to the benefits determined under Article 46, without the need for a recalculation in accordance with that Article.

2.   On the other hand, if the method of determining benefits or the rules for calculating benefits should be altered, a recalculation shall be carried out in accordance with Article 46.

CHAPTER 4
ACCIDENTS AT WORK AND OCCUPATIONAL DISEASES

SECTION 1
RIGHTS TO BENEFITS

Article 52   Residence in a Member State other than the competent State – General rules

An employed or self-employed person who sustains an accident at work or contracts an occupational disease, and who is residing in the territory of a Member State other than the competent State, shall receive in the State in which he is residing:

(a)   benefits in kind, provided on behalf of the competent institution by the institutions of his place of residence in accordance with the provisions of the legislation which it administers as if he were insured with it;

(b)   cash benefits provided by the competent institution in accordance with the provisions of the legislation which it administers. However, by agreement between the competent institution and the institution of the place of residence, these benefits may be provided by the latter institution on behalf of the former in accordance with the legislation of the competent State.

CHAPTER 6
UNEMPLOYMENT BENEFITS

SECTION 1
COMMON PROVISIONS

Article 67 Aggregation of periods of insurance or employment

1.   The competent institution of a Member State whose legislation makes the acquisition, retention or recovery of the right to benefits subject to the completion of periods of insurance shall take into account, to the extent necessary, periods of insurance or employment completed as an employed person under the legislation of any other Member State, as though they were periods of insurance completed under the legislation which it administers, provided, however, that the periods of employment would have been counted as periods of insurance had they been completed under that legislation.

2.   The competent institution of a Member State whose legislation makes the acquisition, retention or recovery of the right to benefits subject to the completion of periods of employment shall take into account, to the extent necessary, periods of insurance or employment completed as an employed person under the legislation of any other Member State, as though they were periods of employment completed under the legislation which it administers.

3.   Except in the cases referred to in Article 71(1)(a)(ii) and (b)(ii), application of the provisions of paragraphs 1 and 2 shall be subject to the condition that the person concerned should have completed lastly:
— in the case of paragraph 1, periods of insurance,
— in the case of paragraph 2, periods of employment,
in accordance with the provisions of the legislation under which the benefits are claimed.

4.   Where the length of the period during which benefits may be granted depends on the length of periods of insurance or employment, the provisions of paragraph 1 or 2 shall apply, as appropriate.

Article 68   Calculation of benefits

1.   The competent institution of a Member State whose legislation provides that the calculation of benefits should be based on the amount of the previous wage or salary shall take into account exclusively the wage or salary received by the person concerned in respect of his last employment in the territory of that State. However, if the person concerned had been in his last employment in that territory for less than four weeks, the benefits shall be calculated on the basis of the normal wage or salary corresponding, in the place where the unemployed person is residing or staying, to an equivalent or similar employment to his last employment in the territory of another Member State.

2.   The competent institution of a Member State whose legislation provides that the amount of benefits varies with the number of members of the family, shall take into account also members of the family of the person concerned who are residing in the territory of another Member State, as though they were residing in the territory of the competent State. This provision shall not apply if, in the country of residence of the members of the family, another person is entitled to unemployment benefits for the calculation of which the members of the family are taken into consideration.

SECTION 2
UNEMPLOYED PERSONS GOING TO A MEMBER STATE OTHER THAN THE
COMPETENT STATE

Article 69   Conditions and limits for the retention of the right to benefits

1.   An employed or self-employed person who is wholly unemployed and who satisfies the conditions of the legislation of a Member State for entitlement to benefits and who goes to one or more other Member States in order to seek employment there shall retain his entitlement to such benefits under the following conditions and within the following limits:

(a)   Before his departure, he must have been registered as a person seeking work and have remained available to the employment services of the competent State for at least four weeks after becoming unemployed, However, the competent services or institutions may authorise his departure before such time has expired.

(b)   He must register as a person seeking work with the employment services of each of the Member States to which he goes and be subject to the control procedure organised therein. This condition shall be considered satisfied for the period before registration if the person concerned registered within seven days of the date when he ceased to be available to the employment services of the State he left. In exceptional cases, this period may be extended by the competent services or institutions.

(c)   Entitlement to benefits shall continue for a maximum period of three months from the date when the person concerned ceased to be available to the employment services of the State which he left, provided that the total duration of the benefits does not exceed the duration of the period of benefits he was entitled to under the legislation of that State. In the case of a seasonal worker such duration shall, moreover, be limited to the period remaining until the end of the season for which he was engaged.

2.   If the person concerned returns to the competent State before the expiry of the period during which he is entitled to benefits under the provisions of paragraph 1(c), he shall continue to be entitled to benefits under the legislation of that State; he shall lose all entitlement to benefits under the legislation of the competent State if he does not return there before the expiry of that

period. In exceptional cases, this time limit may be extended by the competent services or institutions.

3. The provisions of paragraph 1 may be invoked only once between two periods of employment.

Article 70 Provision of benefits and reimbursements

1. In the cases referred to in Article 69(1), benefits shall be provided by the institution of each of the States to which an unemployed person goes to seek employment.

    The competent institution of the Member State to whose legislation an employed or self-employed person was subject at the time of his last employment shall be obliged to reimburse the amount of such benefits.

2. The reimbursements referred to in paragraph 1 shall be determined and made in accordance with the procedure laid down by the implementing Regulation referred to in Article 98, on proof of actual expenditure, or by lump sum payments.

3. Two or more Member States, or the competent authorities of those States, may provide for other methods of reimbursement or payment, or may waive all reimbursement between the institutions coming under their jurisdiction.

SECTION 3
UNEMPLOYED PERSONS WHO, DURING THEIR LAST EMPLOYMENT, WERE RESIDING IN A MEMBER STATE OTHER THAN THE COMPETENT STATE

Article 71

1. An unemployed person who was formerly employed and who, during his last employment, was residing in the territory of a Member State other than the competent State shall receive benefits in accordance with the following provisions:

    (a) (i)   A frontier worker who is partially or intermittently unemployed in the undertaking which employs him, shall receive benefits in accordance with the provisions of the legislation of the competent State as if he were residing in the territory of that State; these benefits shall be provided by the competent institution.

    (ii)   A frontier worker who is wholly unemployed shall receive benefits in accordance with the provisions of the legislation of the Member State in whose territory he resides as though he had been subject to that legislation while last employed; these benefits shall be provided by the institution of the place of residence at its own expense.

    (b) (i)   An employed person, other than a frontier worker, who is partially, intermittently or wholly unemployed and who remains available to his employer or to the employment services in the territory of the competent State shall receive benefits in accordance with the provisions of the legislation of that State as though he were residing in its territory; these benefits shall be provided by the competent institution.

    (ii)   An employed person, other than a frontier worker, who is wholly unemployed and who makes himself available for work to the employment services in the territory of the Member State in which he resides, or who returns to that territory, shall receive benefits in accordance with the legislation of that State as if he had last been employed there; the institution of the place of residence shall provide such benefits at its own expense. However, if such an employed person has become entitled to benefits at the expense of the competent institution of the Member State to whose legislation he was last subject, he shall receive benefits under the provisions of Article 69. Receipt of benefits under the legislation of the State in which he resides shall be suspended for any period during which the unemployed person may, under the provisions of Article 69, make a claim for benefits under the legislation to which he was last subject.

2. An unemployed person may not claim benefits under the legislation of the Member State in whose territory he resides while he is entitled to benefits under the provisions of paragraph 1(a)(i) or (b)(i).

SECTION 4
PERSONS COVERED BY A SPECIAL SCHEME FOR CIVIL SERVANTS

Article 71a

1. The provisions of Sections 1 and 2 shall apply by analogy to persons covered by a special unemployment scheme for civil servants.

2. The provisions of Section 3 shall not apply to persons covered by a special unemployment scheme for civil servants. An unemployed person who is covered by a special unemployment scheme for civil servants, who is partially or wholly unemployed, and who, during his last employment, was residing in the territory of a Member State other than the competent State, shall receive benefits in accordance with the provisions of the legislation of the competent State as if he were residing in the territory of that State; these benefits shall be provided by the competent institution, at its expense.

CHAPTER 7
FAMILY BENEFITS

Article 72 Aggregation of periods of insurance, employment or self-employment

Where the legislation of a Member State makes acquisition of the right to benefits conditional upon completion of periods of insurance, employment or self-employment, the competent institution of that State shall take into account for this purpose, to the extent necessary, periods of insurance, employment or self-employment completed in any other Member State, as if they were periods completed under the legislation which it administers.

Article 72a Employed persons who have become fully unemployed

An employed person who has become fully unemployed and to whom Article 71(1)(a)(ii) or (b)(ii), first sentence, apply shall, for the members of his family residing in the territory of the same Member State as he, receive family benefits in accordance with the legislation of the State, as if he had been subject to that legislation during his last employment, taking account, where appropriate, of the provisions of Article 72. These benefits shall be provided by, and at the expense of, the institution of the place of residence.

Where that institution applies legislation providing for deduction of contributions payable by unemployed persons to cover family benefits, it shall be authorised to make such deductions in accordance with the provisions of its legislation.

Article 73 Employed or self-employed persons the members of whose families reside in a Member State other than the competent State

An employed or self-employed person subject to the legislation of a Member State shall be entitled, in respect of the members of his family who are residing in another Member State, to the family benefits provided for by the legislation of the former State, as if they were residing in that State, subject to the provisions of Annex VI.

Article 74 Unemployed persons the members of whose families reside in a Member State other than the competent State

An unemployed person who was formerly employed or self-employed and who draws unemployment benefits under the legislation of a Member State shall be entitled, in respect of the members of his family residing in another Member State, to the family benefits provided for by the legislation of the former State, as if they were residing in that State,
subject to the provisions of Annex VI.

Article 93 Rights of institutions responsible for benefits against liable third parties

1. If a person receives benefits under the legislation of one Member State in respect of an injury resulting from an occurrence in the territory of another State, any rights of the institution responsible for benefits against a third party bound to compensate for the injury shall be governed by the following rules:

   (a) Where the institution responsible for benefits is, by virtue of the legislation which it administers, subrogated to the rights which the recipient has against the third party, such subrogation shall be recognised by each Member State.

(b) Where the said institution has direct rights against the third party, such rights shall be recognised by each Member State.

2. If a person receives benefits under the legislation of one Member State in respect of an injury resulting from an occurrence in the territory of another Member State, the provisions of the said legislation which determine in which cases the civil liability of employers or of the persons employed by them is to be excluded shall apply with regard to the said person or to the competent institution.

The provisions of paragraph 1 shall also apply to any rights of the institution responsible for benefit against an employer or the persons employed by him in cases where their liability is not excluded.

3. Where, in accordance with the provisions of Article 36(3) and/or Article 63(3), two or more Member States or the competent authorities of those States have concluded an agreement to waive reimbursement between institutions under their jurisdiction, any rights arising against a liable third party shall be governed by the following rules:

(a) Where the institution of the Member State of stay or residence awards benefits to a person in respect of an injury which was sustained within its territory, that institution, in accordance with the legislation which it administers, shall exercise the right to subrogation or direct action against the third party liable to provide compensation for the injury.

(b) For the purpose of implementing (a):

(i) the person receiving benefits shall be deemed to be insured with the institution of the place of stay or residence, and

(ii) that institution shall be deemed to be the debtor institution.

(c) The provisions of paragraphs 1 and 2 shall remain applicable in respect of any benefits not covered by the waiver agreement referred to in this paragraph.

EMPLOYMENT: EQUALITY

COUNCIL DIRECTIVE (EEC) No 75/117 of 10 FEBRUARY 1975
on the approximation of the laws of the Member States relating to the application of the principle of equal pay for men and women
[1975] OJ L45/19

Article 1

The principle of equal pay for men and women outlined in Article 119 of the Treaty, hereinafter called 'principle of equal pay', means, for the same work or for work to which equal value is attributed, the elimination of all discrimination on grounds of sex with regard to all aspects and conditions of remuneration.

In particular, where a job classification system is used for determining pay, it must be based on the same criteria for both men and women and so drawn up as to exclude any discrimination on grounds of sex.

Article 2

Member States shall introduce into their national legal systems such measures as are necessary to enable all employees who consider themselves wronged by failure to apply the principle of equal pay to pursue their claims by judicial process after possible recourse to other competent authorities.

Article 3

Member States shall abolish all discrimination between men and women arising from laws, regulations or administrative provisions which is contrary to the principle of equal pay.

Article 4

Member States shall take the necessary measures to ensure that provisions appearing in collective agreements, wage scales, wage agreements or individual contracts of employment which are contrary to the principle of equal pay shall be, or may be declared, null and void or may be amended.

Article 5

Member States shall take the necessary measures to protect employees against dismissal by the employer as a reaction to a complaint within the undertaking or to any legal proceedings aimed at enforcing compliance with the principle of equal pay.

Article 6

Member States shall, in accordance with their national circumstances and legal systems, take the measures necessary to ensure that the principle of equal pay is applied. They shall see that effective means are available to take care that this principle is observed.

Article 7

Member States shall take care that the provisions adopted pursuant to this Directive, together with the relevant provisions already in force, are brought to the attention of employees by all appropriate means, for example at their place of employment.

COUNCIL DIRECTIVE (EEC) No 76/207 of 9 FEBRUARY 1976
on the implementation of the principle of equal treatment for men and women as regards access to employment, vocational training and promotion, and working conditions
[1976] OJ L39/40 as amended by Directive 2002/73 ([2002] OJ L269/15)

Article 1

1. The purpose of this Directive is to put into effect in the Member States the principle of equal treatment for men and women as regards access to employment, including promotion, and to vocational training and as regards working conditions and, on the conditions referred to in paragraph 2, social security. This principle is herinafter referred to as 'the principle of equal treatment.'

1a.   Member States shall actively take into account the objective of equality between men and women when formulating and implementing laws, regulations, administrative provisions, policies and activities in the areas referred to in paragraph 1.

2.   With a view to ensuring the progressive implementation of the principle of equal treatment in matters of social security, the Council, acting on a proposal from the Commission, will adopt provisions defining its substance, its scope and the arrangements for its application.

Article 2

1.   For the purposes of the following provisions, the principle of equal treatment shall mean that there shall be no discrimination whatsoever on grounds of sex either directly or indirectly by reference in particular to marital or family status.

2.   For the purposes of this Directive, the following definitions shall apply:
      — direct discrimination: where one person is treated less favourably on grounds of sex than another is, has been or would be treated in a comparable situation,
      — indirect discrimination: where an apparently neutral provision, criterion or practice would put persons of one sex at a particular disadvantage compared with persons of the other sex, unless that provision, criterion or practice is objectively justified by a legitimate aim, and the means of achieving that aim are appropriate and necessary,
      — harassment: where an unwanted conduct related to the sex of a person occurs with the purpose or effect of violating the dignity of a person, and of creating an intimidating, hostile, degrading, humiliating or offensive environment,
      — sexual harassment: where any form of unwanted verbal, non-verbal or physical conduct of a sexual nature occurs, with the purpose or effect of violating the dignity of a person, in particular when creating an intimidating, hostile, degrading, humiliating or offensive environment.

3.   Harassment and sexual harassment within the meaning of this Directive shall be deemed to be discrimination on the grounds of sex and therefore prohibited.
      A person's rejection of, or submission to, such conduct may not be used as a basis for a decision affecting that person.

4.   An instruction to discriminate against persons on grounds of sex shall be deemed to be discrimination within the meaning of this Directive.

5.   Member States shall encourage, in accordance with national law, collective agreements or practice, employers and those responsible for access to vocational training to take measures to prevent all forms of discrimination on grounds of sex, in particular harassment and sexual harassment at the workplace.

6.   Member States may provide, as regards access to employment including the training leading thereto, that a difference of treatment which is based on a characteristic related to sex shall not constitute discrimination where, by reason of the nature of the particular occupational activities concerned or of the context in which they are carried out, such a characteristic constitutes a genuine and determining occupational requirement, provided that the objective is legitimate and the requirement is proportionate.

7.   This Directive shall be without prejudice to provisions concerning the protection of women, particularly as regards pregnancy and maternity.
      A woman on maternity leave shall be entitled, after the end of her period of maternity leave, to return to her job or to an equivalent post on terms and conditions which are no less favourable to her and to benefit from any improvement in working conditions to which she would be entitled during her absence.
      Less favourable treatment of a woman related to pregnancy or maternity leave within the meaning of Directive 92/85/EEC shall constitute discrimination within the meaning of this Directive.
      This Directive shall also be without prejudice to the provisions of Council Directive 96/34/EC of 3 June 1996 on the framework agreement on parental leave concluded by UNICE, CEEP and the ETUC and of Council Directive 92/85/EEC of 19 October 1992 on the introduction of measures to encourage improvements in the safety and health at work of pregnant workers and workers who have recently given birth or are breastfeeding (tenth individual Directive within

the meaning of Article 16(1) of Directive 89/391/EEC). It is also without prejudice to the right of Member States to recognise distinct rights to paternity and/or adoption leave. Those Member States which recognise such rights shall take the necessary measures to protect working men and women against dismissal due to exercising those rights and ensure that, at the end of such leave, they shall be entitled to return to their jobs or to equivalent posts on terms and conditions which are no less favourable to them, and to benefit from any improvement in working conditions to which they would have been entitled during their absence.

8. Member States may maintain or adopt measures within the meaning of Article 141(4) of the Treaty with a view to ensuring full equality in practice between men and women.

Article 3

1. Application of the principle of equal treatment means that there shall be no direct or indirect discrimination on the grounds of sex in the public or private sectors, including public bodies, in relation to:
    (a) conditions for access to employment, to self-employment or to occupation, including selection criteria and recruitment conditions, whatever the branch of activity and at all levels of the professional hierarchy, including promotion;
    (b) access to all types and to all levels of vocational guidance, vocational training, advanced vocational training and retraining, including practical work experience;
    (c) employment and working conditions, including dismissals, as well as pay as provided for in Directive 75/117/EEC;
    (d) membership of, and involvement in, an organisation of workers or employers, or any organisation whose members carry on a particular profession, including the benefits provided for by such organisations.

2. To that end, Member States shall take the necessary measures to ensure that:
    (a) any laws, regulations and administrative provisions contrary to the principle of equal treatment are abolished;
    (b) any provisions contrary to the principle of equal treatment which are included in contracts or collective agreements, internal rules of undertakings or rules governing the independent occupations and professions and workers' and employers' organisations shall be, or may be declared, null and void or are amended.

Article 6

1. Member States shall ensure that judicial and/or administrative procedures, including where they deem it appropriate conciliation procedures, for the enforcement of obligations under this Directive are available to all persons who consider themselves wronged by failure to apply the principle of equal treatment to them, even after the relationship in which the discrimination is alleged to have occurred has ended.

2. Member States shall introduce into their national legal systems such measures as are necessary to ensure real and effective compensation or reparation as the Member States so determine for the loss and damage sustained by a person injured as a result of discrimination contrary to Article 3, in a way which is dissuasive and proportionate to the damage suffered; such compensation or reparation may not be restricted by the fixing of a prior upper limit, except in cases where the employer can prove that the only damage suffered by an applicant as a result of discrimination within the meaning of this Directive is the refusal to take his/her job application into consideration.

3. Member States shall ensure that associations, organisations or other legal entities which have, in accordance with the criteria laid down by their national law, a legitimate interest in ensuring that the provisions of this Directive are complied with, may engage, either on behalf or in support of the complainants, with his or her approval, in any judicial and/or administrative procedure provided for the enforcement of obligations under this Directive.

4. Paragraphs 1 and 3 are without prejudice to national rules relating to time limits for bringing actions as regards the principle of equal treatment.

Article 7

Member States shall introduce into their national legal systems such measures as are necessary to protect employees, including those who are employees' representatives provided for by national laws and/or practices, against dismissal or other adverse treatment by the employer as a reaction to a complaint within the undertaking or to any legal proceedings aimed at enforcing compliance with the principle of equal treatment.

Article 8

Member States shall take care that the provisions adopted pursuant to this Directive, together with the relevant provisions already in force, are brought to the attention of employees by all appropriate means, for example at their place of employment.

Article 8a

1. Member States shall designate and make the necessary arrangements for a body or bodies for the promotion, analysis, monitoring and support of equal treatment of all persons without discrimination on the grounds of sex. These bodies may form part of agencies charged at national level with the defence of human rights or the safeguard of individuals' rights.
2. Member States shall ensure that the competences of these bodies include:
   (a) without prejudice to the right of victims and of associations, organisations or other legal entities referred to in Article 6(3), providing independent assistance to victims of discrimination in pursuing their complaints about discrimination;
   (b) conducting independent surveys concerning discrimination;
   (c) publishing independent reports and making recommendations on any issue relating to such discrimination.

Article 8b

1. Member States shall, in accordance with national traditions and practice, take adequate measures to promote social dialogue between the social partners with a view to fostering equal treatment, including through the monitoring of workplace practices, collective agreements, codes of conduct, research or exchange of experiences and good practices.
2. Where consistent with national traditions and practice, Member States shall encourage the social partners, without prejudice to their autonomy, to promote equality between women and men and to conclude, at the appropriate level, agreements laying down anti-discrimination rules in the fields referred to in Article 1 which fall within the scope of collective bargaining. These agreements shall respect the minimum requirements laid down by this Directive and the relevant national implementing measures.
3. Member States shall, in accordance with national law, collective agreements or practice, encourage employers to promote equal treatment for men and women in the workplace in a planned and systematic way.
4. To this end, employers should be encouraged to provide at appropriate regular intervals employees and/or their representatives with appropriate information on equal treatment for men and women in the undertaking.
   Such information may include statistics on proportions of men and women at different levels of the organisation and possible measures to improve the situation in cooperation with employees' representatives.

Article 8c

Member States shall encourage dialogue with appropriate non-governmental organisations which have, in accordance with their national law and practice, a legitimate interest in contributing to the fight against discrimination on grounds of sex with a view to promoting the principle of equal treatment.

Article 8d

Member States shall lay down the rules on sanctions applicable to infringements of the national provisions adopted pursuant to this Directive, and shall take all measures necessary to ensure that they are applied.

The sanctions, which may comprise the payment of compensation to the victim, must be effective, proportionate and dissuasive. The Member States shall notify those provisions to the Commission by 5 October 2005 at the latest and shall notify it without delay of any subsequent amendment affecting them.

Article 8e

1. Member States may introduce or maintain provisions which are more favourable to the protection of the principle of equal treatment than those laid down in this Directive.
2. The implementation of this Directive shall under no circumstances constitute grounds for a reduction in the level of protection against discrimination already afforded by Member States in the fields covered by this Directive.

Article 9

1. Member States shall put into force the laws, regulations and administrative provisions necessary in order to comply with this Directive within 30 months of its notification and shall immediately inform the Commission thereof.
   However, as regards the first part of Article 3(2)(c) and the first part of Article 5(2)(c), Member States shall carry out a first examination and if necessary a first revision of the laws, regulations and administrative provisions referred to therein within four years of notification of this Directive.
2. Member States shall periodically assess the occupational activities referred to in Article 2 (2) in order to decide, in the light of social developments, whether there is justification for maintaining the exclusions concerned. They shall notify the Commission of the results of this assessment.
3. Member States shall also communicate to the Commission the texts of laws, regulations and administrative provisions which they adopt in the field covered by this Directive.

Article 10

Within two years following expiry of the 30-month period laid down in the first subparagraph of Article 9(1), Member States shall forward all necessary information to the Commission to enable it to draw up a report on the application of this Directive for submission to the Council.

Article 11

This Directive is addressed to the Member States.

COUNCIL AND PARLIAMENT DIRECTIVE (EC) No 2002/73 of 23 SEPTEMBER 2002
amending Council Directive 76/207/EEC on the implementation of the principle of equal treatment for men and women as regards access to employment, vocational training and promotion, and working conditions
[2002] OJ L296/15

THE EUROPEAN PARLIAMENT AND THE COUNCIL OF THE EUROPEAN UNION,
Having regard to the Treaty establishing the European Community and, in particular, Article 141(3) thereof,
Having regard to the proposal from the Commission,
Having regard to the Opinion of the Economic and Social Committee,
Acting in accordance with the procedure laid down in Article 251 of the Treaty, in the light of the joint text approved by the Conciliation Committee on 19 April 2002,
Whereas:
(1) In accordance with Article 6 of the Treaty on European Union, the European Union is founded on the principles of liberty, democracy, respect for human rights and fundamental freedoms, and the rule of law, principles which are common to the Member States, and shall respect fundamental rights as guaranteed by the European Convention for the Protection of Human Rights and Fundamental Freedoms and as they result from the constitutional traditions common to the Member States, as general principles of Community law.

(2) The right to equality before the law and protection against discrimination for all persons constitutes a universal right recognised by the Universal Declaration of Human Rights, the United Nations Convention on the Elimination of all forms of Discrimination Against Women, the International Convention on the Elimination of all Forms of Racial Discrimination and the United Nations Covenants on Civil and Political Rights and on Economic, Social and Cultural Rights and by the Convention for the Protection of Human Rights and Fundamental Freedoms, to which all Member States are signatories.

(3) This Directive respects the fundamental rights and observes the principles recognised in particular by the Charter of Fundamental Rights of the European Union.

(4) Equality between women and men is a fundamental principle, under Article 2 and Article 3(2) of the EC Treaty and the case-law of the Court of Justice. These Treaty provisions proclaim equality between women and men as a 'task' and an 'aim' of the Community and impose a positive obligation to 'promote' it in all its activities.

(5) Article 141 of the Treaty, and in particular paragraph 3, addresses specifically equal opportunities and equal treatment of men and women in matters of employment and occupation.

(6) Council Directive 76/207/EEC does not define the concepts of direct or indirect discrimination. On the basis of Article 13 of the Treaty, the Council has adopted Directive 2000/43/EC of 29 June 2000 implementing the principle of equal treatment between persons irrespective of racial or ethnic origin and Directive 2000/78/EC of 27 November 2000 establishing a general framework for equal treatment in employment and occupation which define direct and indirect discrimination. Thus it is appropriate to insert definitions consistent with these Directives in respect of sex.

(7) This Directive does not prejudice freedom of association, including the right to establish unions with others and to join unions to defend one's interests. Measures within the meaning of Article 141(4) of the Treaty may include membership or the continuation of the activity of organisations or unions whose main objective is the promotion, in practice, of the principle of equal treatment between women and men.

(8) Harassment related to the sex of a person and sexual harassment are contrary to the principle of equal treatment between women and men; it is therefore appropriate to define such concepts and to prohibit such forms of discrimination. To this end it must be emphasised that these forms of discrimination occur not only in the workplace, but also in the context of access to employment and vocational training, during employment and occupation.

(9) In this context, employers and those responsible for vocational training should be encouraged to take measures to combat all forms of sexual discrimination and, in particular, to take preventive measures against harassment and sexual harassment in the workplace, in accordance with national legislation and practice.

(10) The appreciation of the facts from which it may be inferred that there has been direct or indirect discrimination is a matter for national judicial or other competent bodies, in accordance with rules of national law or practice. Such rules may provide in particular for indirect discrimination to be established by any means including on the basis of statistical evidence. According to the case-law of the Court of Justice, discrimination involves the application of different rules to a comparable situation or the application of the same rule to different situations.

(11) The occupational activities that Member States may exclude from the scope of Directive 76/207/EEC should be restricted to those which necessitate the employment of a person of one sex by reason of the nature of the particular occupational activities concerned, provided that the objective sought is legitimate, and subject to the principle of proportionality as laid down by the case-law of the Court of Justice.

(12) The Court of Justice has consistently recognised the legitimacy, in terms of the principle of equal treatment, of protecting a woman's biological condition during and after pregnancy. It has moreover consistently ruled that any unfavourable treatment of women related to pregnancy or maternity constitutes direct sex discrimination. This Directive is therefore without prejudice to Council Directive 92/85/EEC of 19 October 1992 on the introduction of measures to encourage improvements in the safety and health at work of pregnant

workers and workers who have recently given birth or are breast-feeding (tenth individual Directive within the meaning of Article 16(1) of Directive 89/391/EEC), which aims to ensure the protection of the physical and mental state of women who are pregnant, women who have recently given birth or women who are breastfeeding. The preamble to Directive 92/85/EEC provides that the protection of the safety and health of pregnant workers, workers who have recently given birth or workers who are breastfeeding should not involve treating women who are on the labour market unfavourably nor work to the detriment of Directives concerning equal treatment for men and women. The Court of Justice has recognised the protection of employment rights of women, in particular their right to return to the same or an equivalent job, with no less favourable working conditions, as well as to benefit from any improvement in working conditions to which they would be entitled during their absence.

(13) In the Resolution of the Council and of the Ministers for Employment and Social Policy meeting within the Council of 29 June 2000 on the balanced participation of women and men in family and working life, Member States were encouraged to consider examining the scope for their respective legal systems to grant working men an individual and untransferable right to paternity leave, while maintaining their rights relating to employment. In this context, it is important to stress that it is for the Member States to determine whether or not to grant such a right and also to determine any conditions, other than dismissal and return to work, which are outside the scope of this Directive.

(14) Member States may, under Article 141(4) of the Treaty, maintain or adopt measures providing for specific advantages, in order to make it easier for the underrepresented sex to pursue a vocational activity or to prevent or compensate for disadvantages in professional careers. Given the current situation, and bearing in mind Declaration No 28 to the Amsterdam Treaty, Members States should, in the first instance, aim at improving the situation of women in working life.

(15) The prohibition of discrimination should be without prejudice to the maintenance or adoption of measures intended to prevent or compensate for disadvantages suffered by a group of persons of one sex. Such measures permit organisations of persons of one sex where their main object is the promotion of the special needs of those persons and the promotion of equality between women and men.

(16) The principle of equal pay for men and women is already firmly established by Article 141 of the Treaty and Council Directive 75/117/EEC of 10 February 1975 on the approximation of the laws of the Member States relating to the application of the principle of equal pay for men and women and is consistently upheld by the case-law of the Court of Justice; the principle constitutes an essential and indispensable part of the *acquis communautaire* concerning sex discrimination.

(17) The Court of Justice has ruled that, having regard to the fundamental nature of the right to effective judicial protection, employees enjoy such protection even after the employment relationship has ended. An employee defending or giving evidence on behalf of a person protected under this Directive should be entitled to the same protection.

(18) The Court of Justice has ruled that, in order to be effective, the principle of equal treatment implies that, whenever it is breached, the compensation awarded to the employee discriminated against must be adequate in relation to the damage sustained. It has furthermore specified that fixing a prior upper limit may preclude effective compensation and that excluding an award of interest to compensate for the loss sustained is not allowed.

(19) According to the case-law of the Court of Justice, national rules relating to time limits for bringing actions are admissible provided that they are not less favourable than time limits for similar actions of a domestic nature and that they do not render the exercise of rights conferred by the Community law impossible in practice.

(20) Persons who have been subject to discrimination based on sex should have adequate means of legal protection. To provide a more effective level of protection, associations, organisations and other legal entities should also be empowered to engage in proceedings, as the Member

States so determine, either on behalf or in support of any victim, without prejudice to national rules of procedure concerning representation and defence before the courts.

(21) Member States should promote dialogue between the social partners and, within the framework of national practice, with non-governmental organisations to address different forms of discrimination based on sex in the workplace and to combat them.

(22) Member States should provide for effective, proportionate and dissuasive sanctions in case of breaches of the obligations under Directive 76/207/EEC.

(23) In accordance with the principle of subsidiarity as set out in Article 5 of the Treaty, the objectives of the proposed action cannot be sufficiently achieved by the Member States and can therefore be better achieved by the Community. In accordance with the principle of proportionality, as set out in that Article, this Directive does not go beyond what is necessary for that purpose.

(24) Directive 76/207/EEC should therefore be amended accordingly,

HAVE ADOPTED THIS DIRECTIVE:

Editor's Note: Article 1 contains amendments to Directive 76/207 and is not reproduced here.

Article 2

1. Member States shall bring into force the laws, regulations and administrative provisions necessary to comply with this Directive by 5 October 2005 at the latest or shall ensure, by that date at the latest, that management and labour introduce the requisite provisions by way of agreement. Member States shall take all necessary steps to enable them at all times to guarantee the results imposed by this Directive. They shall immediately inform the Commission thereof. When Member States adopt those measures, they shall contain a reference to this Directive or be accompanied by such reference on the occasion of their official publication. Member States shall determine how such reference is to be made.

2. The Member States shall communicate to the Commission, within three years of the entry into force of this Directive, all the information necessary for the Commission to draw up a report to the European Parliament and the Council on the application of this Directive,

3. Without prejudice to paragraph 2, Member States shall communicate to the Commission, every four years, the texts of laws, regulations and administrative provisions of any measures adopted pursuant to Article 141(4) of the Treaty, as well as reports on these measures and their implementation. On the basis of that information, the Commission will adopt and publish every four years a report establishing a comparative assessment of any measures in the light of Declaration No 28 annexed to the Final Act of the Treaty of Amsterdam.

Article 3

This Directive shall enter into force on the day of its publication in the Official Journal of the European Communities.

Article 4

This Directive is addressed to the Member States.

DIRECTIVE 2006/54/EC OF THE EUROPEAN PARLIAMENT AND OF THE COUNCIL of 5 JULY 2006
on the implementation of the principle of equal opportunities and equal treatment of men and women in matters of employment and occupation (recast)
[2006] OJ L204/23

THE EUROPEAN PARLIAMENT AND THE COUNCIL OF THE EUROPEAN UNION,

Having regard to the Treaty establishing the European Community, and in particular Article 141(3) thereof,

Having regard to the proposal from the Commission,

Having regard to the opinion of the European Economic and Social Committee,

Acting in accordance with the procedure laid down in Article 251 of the Treaty,

Whereas:

(1) Council Directive 76/207/EEC of 9 February 1976 on the implementation of the principle of equal treatment for men and women as regards access to employment, vocational training and promotion, and working conditions and Council Directive 86/378/EEC of 24 July 1986 on the implementation of the principle of equal treatment for men and women in occupational social security schemes have been significantly amended. Council Directive 75/117/EEC of 10 February 1975 on the approximation of the laws of the Member States relating to the application of the principle of equal pay for men and women and Council Directive 97/80/EC of 15 December 1997 on the burden of proof in cases of discrimination based on sex also contain provisions which have as their purpose the implementation of the principle of equal treatment between men and women. Now that new amendments are being made to the said Directives, it is desirable, for reasons of clarity, that the provisions in question should be recast by bringing together in a single text the main provisions existing in this field as well as certain developments arising out of the case-law of the Court of Justice of the European Communities (hereinafter referred to as the Court of Justice).

(2) Equality between men and women is a fundamental principle of Community law under Article 2 and Article 3(2) of the Treaty and the case-law of the Court of Justice. Those Treaty provisions proclaim equality between men and women as a 'task' and an 'aim' of the Community and impose a positive obligation to promote it in all its activities.

(3) The Court of Justice has held that the scope of the principle of equal treatment for men and women cannot be confined to the prohibition of discrimination based on the fact that a person is of one or other sex. In view of its purpose and the nature of the rights which it seeks to safeguard, it also applies to discrimination arising from the gender reassignment of a person.

(4) Article 141(3) of the Treaty now provides a specific legal basis for the adoption of Community measures to ensure the application of the principle of equal opportunities and equal treatment in matters of employment and occupation, including the principle of equal pay for equal work or work of equal value.

(5) Articles 21 and 23 of the Charter of Fundamental Rights of the European Union also prohibit any discrimination on grounds of sex and enshrine the right to equal treatment between men and women in all areas, including employment, work and pay.

(6) Harassment and sexual harassment are contrary to the principle of equal treatment between men and women and constitute discrimination on grounds of sex for the purposes of this Directive. These forms of discrimination occur not only in the workplace, but also in the context of access to employment, vocational training and promotion. They should therefore be prohibited and should be subject to effective, proportionate and dissuasive penalties.

(7) In this context, employers and those responsible for vocational training should be encouraged to take measures to combat all forms of discrimination on grounds of sex and, in particular, to take preventive measures against harassment and sexual harassment in the workplace and in access to employment, vocational training and promotion, in accordance with national law and practice.

(8) The principle of equal pay for equal work or work of equal value as laid down by Article 141 of the Treaty and consistently upheld in the case-law of the Court of Justice constitutes an important aspect of the principle of equal treatment between men and women and an essential and indispensable part of the acquis communautaire, including the case-law of the Court concerning sex discrimination. It is therefore appropriate to make further provision for its implementation.

(9) In accordance with settled case-law of the Court of Justice, in order to assess whether workers are performing the same work or work of equal value, it should be determined whether, having regard to a range of factors including the nature of the work and training and working conditions, those workers may be considered to be in a comparable situation.

(10) The Court of Justice has established that, in certain circumstances, the principle of equal pay is not limited to situations in which men and women work for the same employer.

(11) The Member States, in collaboration with the social partners, should continue to address the problem of the continuing gender-based wage differentials and marked gender segregation on

the labour market by means such as flexible working time arrangements which enable both men and women to combine family and work commitments more successfully. This could also include appropriate parental leave arrangements which could be taken up by either parent as well as the provision of accessible and affordable child-care facilities and care for dependent persons.

(12) Specific measures should be adopted to ensure the implementation of the principle of equal treatment in occupational social security schemes and to define its scope more clearly.

(13) In its judgment of 17 May 1990 in Case C-262/88, the Court of Justice determined that all forms of occupational pension constitute an element of pay within the meaning of Article 141 of the Treaty.

(14) Although the concept of pay within the meaning of Article 141 of the Treaty does not encompass social security benefits, it is now clearly established that a pension scheme for public servants falls within the scope of the principle of equal pay if the benefits payable under the scheme are paid to the worker by reason of his/her employment relationship with the public employer, notwithstanding the fact that such scheme forms part of a general statutory scheme. According to the judgments of the Court of Justice in Cases C-7/93 and C-351/00, that condition will be satisfied if the pension scheme concerns a particular category of workers and its benefits are directly related to the period of service and calculated by reference to the public servant's final salary. For reasons of clarity, it is therefore appropriate to make specific provision to that effect.

(15) The Court of Justice has confirmed that whilst the contributions of male and female workers to a defined-benefit pension scheme are covered by Article 141 of the Treaty, any inequality in employers' contributions paid under funded defined-benefit schemes which is due to the use of actuarial factors differing according to sex is not to be assessed in the light of that same provision.

(16) By way of example, in the case of funded defined-benefit schemes, certain elements, such as conversion into a capital sum of part of a periodic pension, transfer of pension rights, a reversionary pension payable to a dependant in return for the surrender of part of a pension or a reduced pension where the worker opts to take earlier retirement, may be unequal where the inequality of the amounts results from the effects of the use of actuarial factors differing according to sex at the time when the scheme's funding is implemented.

(17) It is well established that benefits payable under occupational social security schemes are not to be considered as remuneration insofar as they are attributable to periods of employment prior to 17 May 1990, except in the case of workers or those claiming under them who initiated legal proceedings or brought an equivalent claim under the applicable national law before that date. It is therefore necessary to limit the implementation of the principle of equal treatment accordingly.

(18) The Court of Justice has consistently held that the Barber Protocol does not affect the right to join an occupational pension scheme and that the limitation of the effects in time of the judgment in Case C-262/88 does not apply to the right to join an occupational pension scheme. The Court of Justice also ruled that the national rules relating to time limits for bringing actions under national law may be relied on against workers who assert their right to join an occupational pension scheme, provided that they are not less favourable for that type of action than for similar actions of a domestic nature and that they do not render the exercise of rights conferred by Community law impossible in practice. The Court of Justice has also pointed out that the fact that a worker can claim retroactively to join an occupational pension scheme does not allow the worker to avoid paying the contributions relating to the period of membership concerned.

(19) Ensuring equal access to employment and the vocational training leading thereto is fundamental to the application of the principle of equal treatment of men and women in matters of employment and occupation. Any exception to this principle should therefore be limited to those occupational activities which necessitate the employment of a person of a particular sex by reason of their nature or the context in which they are carried out, provided that the objective sought is legitimate and complies with the principle of proportionality.

(20) This Directive does not prejudice freedom of association, including the right to establish unions with others and to join unions to defend one's interests. Measures within the meaning of Article 141(4) of the Treaty may include membership or the continuation of the activity of organisations or unions whose main objective is the promotion, in practice, of the principle of equal treatment between men and women.

(21) The prohibition of discrimination should be without prejudice to the maintenance or adoption of measures intended to prevent or compensate for disadvantages suffered by a group of persons of one sex. Such measures permit organisations of persons of one sex where their main object is the promotion of the special needs of those persons and the promotion of equality between men and women.

(22) In accordance with Article 141(4) of the Treaty, with a view to ensuring full equality in practice between men and women in working life, the principle of equal treatment does not prevent Member States from maintaining or adopting measures providing for specific advantages in order to make it easier for the under-represented sex to pursue a vocational activity or to prevent or compensate for disadvantages in professional careers. Given the current situation and bearing in mind Declaration No 28 to the Amsterdam Treaty, Member States should, in the first instance, aim at improving the situation of women in working life.

(23) It is clear from the case-law of the Court of Justice that unfavourable treatment of a woman related to pregnancy or maternity constitutes direct discrimination on grounds of sex. Such treatment should therefore be expressly covered by this Directive.

(24) The Court of Justice has consistently recognised the legitimacy, as regards the principle of equal treatment, of protecting a woman's biological condition during pregnancy and maternity and of introducing maternity protection measures as a means to achieve substantive equality. This Directive should therefore be without prejudice to Council Directive 92/85/EEC of 19 October 1992 on the introduction of measures to encourage improvements in the safety and health at work of pregnant workers and workers who have recently given birth or are breastfeeding. This Directive should further be without prejudice to Council Directive 96/34/EC of 3 June 1996 on the framework agreement on parental leave concluded by UNICE, CEEP and the ETUC.

(25) For reasons of clarity, it is also appropriate to make express provision for the protection of the employment rights of women on maternity leave and in particular their right to return to the same or an equivalent post, to suffer no detriment in their terms and conditions as a result of taking such leave and to benefit from any improvement in working conditions to which they would have been entitled during their absence.

(26) In the Resolution of the Council and of the Ministers for Employment and Social Policy, meeting within the Council, of 29 June 2000 on the balanced participation of women and men in family and working life, Member States were encouraged to consider examining the scope for their respective legal systems to grant working men an individual and non-transferable right to paternity leave, while maintaining their rights relating to employment.

(27) Similar considerations apply to the granting by Member States to men and women of an individual and nontransferable right to leave subsequent to the adoption of a child. It is for the Member States to determine whether or not to grant such a right to paternity and/or adoption leave and also to determine any conditions, other than dismissal and return to work, which are outside the scope of this Directive.

(28) The effective implementation of the principle of equal treatment requires appropriate procedures to be put in place by the Member States.

(29) The provision of adequate judicial or administrative procedures for the enforcement of the obligations imposed by this Directive is essential to the effective implementation of the principle of equal treatment.

(30) The adoption of rules on the burden of proof plays a significant role in ensuring that the principle of equal treatment can be effectively enforced. As the Court of Justice has held, provision should therefore be made to ensure that the burden of proof shifts to the respondent when there is a prima facie case of discrimination, except in relation to proceedings in which it is for the court or other competent national body to investigate the facts. It is however

necessary to clarify that the appreciation of the facts from which it may be presumed that there has been direct or indirect discrimination remains a matter for the relevant national body in accordance with national law or practice. Further, it is for the Member States to introduce, at any appropriate stage of the proceedings, rules of evidence which are more favourable to plaintiffs.

(31) With a view to further improving the level of protection offered by this Directive, associations, organisations and other legal entities should also be empowered to engage in proceedings, as the Member States so determine, either on behalf or in support of a complainant, without prejudice to national rules of procedure concerning representation and defence.

(32) Having regard to the fundamental nature of the right to effective legal protection, it is appropriate to ensure that workers continue to enjoy such protection even after the relationship giving rise to an alleged breach of the principle of equal treatment has ended. An employee defending or giving evidence on behalf of a person protected under this Directive should be entitled to the same protection.

(33) It has been clearly established by the Court of Justice that in order to be effective, the principle of equal treatment implies that the compensation awarded for any breach must be adequate in relation to the damage sustained. It is therefore appropriate to exclude the fixing of any prior upper limit for such compensation, except where the employer can prove that the only damage suffered by an applicant as a result of discrimination within the meaning of this Directive was the refusal to take his/her job application into consideration.

(34) In order to enhance the effective implementation of the principle of equal treatment, Member States should promote dialogue between the social partners and, within the framework of national practice, with non-governmental organisations.

(35) Member States should provide for effective, proportionate and dissuasive penalties for breaches of the obligations under this Directive.

(36) Since the objectives of this Directive cannot be sufficiently achieved by the Member States and can therefore be better achieved at Community level, the Community may adopt measures in accordance with the principle of subsidiarity as set out in Article 5 of the Treaty. In accordance with the principle of proportionality, as set out in that Article, this Directive does not go beyond what is necessary in order to achieve those objectives.

(37) For the sake of a better understanding of the different treatment of men and women in matters of employment and occupation, comparable statistics disaggregated by sex should continue to be developed, analysed and made available at the appropriate levels.

(38) Equal treatment of men and women in matters of employment and occupation cannot be restricted to legislative measures. Instead, the European Union and the Member States should continue to promote the raising of public awareness of wage discrimination and the changing of public attitudes, involving all parties concerned at public and private level to the greatest possible extent. The dialogue between the social partners could play an important role in this process.

(39) The obligation to transpose this Directive into national law should be confined to those provisions which represent a substantive change as compared with the earlier Directives. The obligation to transpose the provisions which are substantially unchanged arises under the earlier Directives.

(40) This Directive should be without prejudice to the obligations of the Member States relating to the time limits for transposition into national law and application of the Directives set out in Annex I, Part B.

(41) In accordance with paragraph 34 of the Interinstitutional agreement on better law-making, Member States are encouraged to draw up, for themselves and in the interest of the Community, their own tables, which will, as far as possible, illustrate the correlation between this Directive and the transposition measures and to make them public,

HAVE ADOPTED THIS DIRECTIVE:

TITLE I
GENERAL PROVISIONS

Article 1   Purpose

The purpose of this Directive is to ensure the implementation of the principle of equal opportunities and equal treatment of men and women in matters of employment and occupation.

To that end, it contains provisions to implement the principle of equal treatment in relation to:

(a)   access to employment, including promotion, and to vocational training;

(b)   working conditions, including pay;

(c)   occupational social security schemes.

It also contains provisions to ensure that such implementation is made more effective by the establishment of appropriate procedures.

Article 2   Definitions

1.   For the purposes of this Directive, the following definitions shall apply:

(a)   'direct discrimination': where one person is treated less favourably on grounds of sex than another is, has been or would be treated in a comparable situation;

(b)   'indirect discrimination': where an apparently neutral provision, criterion or practice would put persons of one sex at a particular disadvantage compared with persons of the other sex, unless that provision, criterion or practice is objectively justified by a legitimate aim, and the means of achieving that aim are appropriate and necessary;

(c)   'harassment': where unwanted conduct related to the sex of a person occurs with the purpose or effect of violating the dignity of a person, and of creating an intimidating, hostile, degrading, humiliating or offensive environment;

(d)   'sexual harassment': where any form of unwanted verbal, non-verbal or physical conduct of a sexual nature occurs, with the purpose or effect of violating the dignity of a person, in particular when creating an intimidating, hostile, degrading, humiliating or offensive environment;

(e)   'pay': the ordinary basic or minimum wage or salary and any other consideration, whether in cash or in kind, which the worker receives directly or indirectly, in respect of his/ her employment from his/her employer;

(f)   'occupational social security schemes': schemes not governed by Council Directive 79/7/EEC of 19 December 1978 on the progressive implementation of the principle of equal treatment for men and women in matters of social security whose purpose is to provide workers, whether employees or self-employed, in an undertaking or group of undertakings, area of economic activity, occupational sector or group of sectors with benefits intended to supplement the benefits provided by statutory social security schemes or to replace them, whether membership of such schemes is compulsory or optional.

2.   For the purposes of this Directive, discrimination includes:

(a)   harassment and sexual harassment, as well as any less favourable treatment based on a person's rejection of or submission to such conduct;

(b)   instruction to discriminate against persons on grounds of sex;

(c)   any less favourable treatment of a woman related to pregnancy or maternity leave within the meaning of Directive 92/85/EEC.

Article 3   Positive action

Member States may maintain or adopt measures within the meaning of Article 141(4) of the Treaty with a view to ensuring full equality in practice between men and women in working life.

TITLE II
SPECIFIC PROVISIONS

CHAPTER 1
EQUAL PAY

Article 4   Prohibition of discrimination

For the same work or for work to which equal value is attributed, direct and indirect discrimination on grounds of sex with regard to all aspects and conditions of remuneration shall be eliminated.

In particular, where a job classification system is used for determining pay, it shall be based on the same criteria for both men and women and so drawn up as to exclude any discrimination on grounds of sex.

CHAPTER 2
EQUAL TREATMENT IN OCCUPATIONAL SOCIAL SECURITY SCHEMES

Article 5   Prohibition of discrimination

Without prejudice to Article 4, there shall be no direct or indirect discrimination on grounds of sex in occupational social security schemes, in particular as regards:

  (a)   the scope of such schemes and the conditions of access to them;
  (b)   the obligation to contribute and the calculation of contributions;
  (c)   the calculation of benefits, including supplementary benefits due in respect of a spouse or dependants, and the conditions governing the duration and retention of entitlement to benefits.

Article 6   Personal scope

This Chapter shall apply to members of the working population, including self-employed persons, persons whose activity is interrupted by illness, maternity, accident or involuntary unemployment and persons seeking employment and to retired and disabled workers, and to those claiming under them, in accordance with national law and/or practice.

Article 7   Material scope

  1.   This Chapter applies to:

   (a)   occupational social security schemes which provide protection against the following risks:
      (i)   sickness,
      (ii)   invalidity,
      (iii)   old age, including early retirement,
      (iv)   industrial accidents and occupational diseases,
      (v)   unemployment;

   (b)   occupational social security schemes which provide for other social benefits, in cash or in kind, and in particular survivors' benefits and family allowances, if such benefits constitute a consideration paid by the employer to the worker by reason of the latter's employment.

  2.   This Chapter also applies to pension schemes for a particular category of worker such as that of public servants if the benefits payable under the scheme are paid by reason of the employment relationship with the public employer. The fact that such a scheme forms part of a general statutory scheme shall be without prejudice in that respect.

Article 8   Exclusions from the material scope

  1.   This Chapter does not apply to:

   (a)   individual contracts for self-employed persons;
   (b)   single-member schemes for self-employed persons;
   (c)   insurance contracts to which the employer is not a party, in the case of workers;
   (d)   optional provisions of occupational social security schemes offered to participants individually to guarantee them:
      (i)   either additional benefits,
      (ii)   or a choice of date on which the normal benefits for self-employed persons will start, or a choice between several benefits;
   (e)   occupational social security schemes in so far as benefits are financed by contributions paid by workers on a voluntary basis.

  2.   This Chapter does not preclude an employer granting to persons who have already reached the retirement age for the purposes of granting a pension by virtue of an occupational social security scheme, but who have not yet reached the retirement age for the purposes of granting a statutory retirement pension, a pension supplement, the aim of which is to make equal or more nearly equal the overall amount of benefit paid to these persons in relation to the amount

paid to persons of the other sex in the same situation who have already reached the statutory retirement age, until the persons benefiting from the supplement reach the statutory retirement age.

Article 9   Examples of discrimination

1. Provisions contrary to the principle of equal treatment shall include those based on sex, either directly or indirectly, for:

    (a) determining the persons who may participate in an occupational social security scheme;

    (b) fixing the compulsory or optional nature of participation in an occupational social security scheme;

    (c) laying down different rules as regards the age of entry into the scheme or the minimum period of employment or membership of the scheme required to obtain the benefits thereof;

    (d) laying down different rules, except as provided for in points (h) and (j), for the reimbursement of contributions when a worker leaves a scheme without having fulfilled the conditions guaranteeing a deferred right to long-term benefits;

    (e) setting different conditions for the granting of benefits or restricting such benefits to workers of one or other of the sexes;

    (f) fixing different retirement ages;

    (g) suspending the retention or acquisition of rights during periods of maternity leave or leave for family reasons which are granted by law or agreement and are paid by the employer;

    (h) setting different levels of benefit, except in so far as may be necessary to take account of actuarial calculation factors which differ according to sex in the case of defined contribution schemes; in the case of funded defined-benefit schemes, certain elements may be unequal where the inequality of the amounts results from the effects of the use of actuarial factors differing according to sex at the time when the scheme's funding is implemented;

    (i) setting different levels for workers' contributions;

    (j) setting different levels for employers' contributions, except:

        (i)   in the case of defined-contribution schemes if the aim is to equalise the amount of the final benefits or to make them more nearly equal for both sexes,

        (ii) in the case of funded defined-benefit schemes where the employer's contributions are intended to ensure the adequacy of the funds necessary to cover the cost of the benefits defined;

    (k) laying down different standards or standards applicable only to workers of a specified sex, except as provided for in points (h) and (j), as regards the guarantee or retention of entitlement to deferred benefits when a worker leaves a scheme.

2. Where the granting of benefits within the scope of this Chapter is left to the discretion of the scheme's management bodies, the latter shall comply with the principle of equal treatment.

Article 10   Implementation as regards self-employed persons

1. Member States shall take the necessary steps to ensure that the provisions of occupational social security schemes for self-employed persons contrary to the principle of equal treatment are revised with effect from 1 January 1993 at the latest or for Member States whose accession took place after that date, at the date that Directive 86/378/EEC became applicable in their territory.

2. This Chapter shall not preclude rights and obligations relating to a period of membership of an occupational social security scheme for self-employed persons prior to revision of that scheme from remaining subject to the provisions of the scheme in force during that period.

Article 11   Possibility of deferral as regards self-employed persons

As regards occupational social security schemes for self-employed persons, Member States may defer compulsory application of the principle of equal treatment with regard to:

    (a) determination of pensionable age for the granting of old age or retirement pensions, and the possible implications for other benefits:

        (i)   either until the date on which such equality is achieved in statutory schemes,

        (ii)   or, at the latest, until such equality is prescribed by a directive;

   (b)   survivors' pensions until Community law establishes the principle of equal treatment in statutory social security schemes in that regard;

   (c)   the application of Article 9(1)(i) in relation to the use of actuarial calculation factors, until 1 January 1999 or for Member States whose accession took place after that date until the date that Directive 86/378/EEC became applicable in their territory.

Article 12   Retroactive effect

1.   Any measure implementing this Chapter, as regards workers, shall cover all benefits under occupational social security schemes derived from periods of employment subsequent to 17 May 1990 and shall apply retroactively to that date, without prejudice to workers or those claiming under them who have, before that date, initiated legal proceedings or raised an equivalent claim under national law. In that event, the implementation measures shall apply retroactively to 8 April 1976 and shall cover all the benefits derived from periods of employment after that date. For Member States which acceded to the Community after 8 April 1976, and before 17 May 1990, that date shall be replaced by the date on which Article 141 of the Treaty became applicable in their territory.

2.   The second sentence of paragraph 1 shall not prevent national rules relating to time limits for bringing actions under national law from being relied on against workers or those claiming under them who initiated legal proceedings or raised an equivalent claim under national law before 17 May 1990, provided that they are not less favourable for that type of action than for similar actions of a domestic nature and that they do not render the exercise of rights conferred by Community law impossible in practice.

3.   For Member States whose accession took place after 17 May 1990 and which were on 1 January 1994 Contracting Parties to the Agreement on the European Economic Area, the date of 17 May 1990 in the first sentence of paragraph 1 shall be replaced by 1 January 1994.

4.   For other Member States whose accession took place after 17 May 1990, the date of 17 May 1990 in paragraphs 1 and 2 shall be replaced by the date on which Article 141 of the Treaty became applicable in their territory.

Article 13   Flexible pensionable age

Where men and women may claim a flexible pensionable age under the same conditions, this shall not be deemed to be incompatible with this Chapter.

CHAPTER 3
EQUAL TREATMENT AS REGARDS ACCESS TO EMPLOYMENT, VOCATIONAL TRAINING AND PROMOTION AND WORKING CONDITIONS

Article 14   Prohibition of discrimination

1.   There shall be no direct or indirect discrimination on grounds of sex in the public or private sectors, including public bodies, in relation to:

   (a)   conditions for access to employment, to self-employment or to occupation, including selection criteria and recruitment conditions, whatever the branch of activity and at all levels of the professional hierarchy, including promotion;

   (b)   access to all types and to all levels of vocational guidance, vocational training, advanced vocational training and retraining, including practical work experience;

   (c)   employment and working conditions, including dismissals, as well as pay as provided for in Article 141 of the Treaty;

   (d)   membership of, and involvement in, an organisation of workers or employers, or any organisation whose members carry on a particular profession, including the benefits provided for by such organisations.

2.   Member States may provide, as regards access to employment including the training leading thereto, that a difference of treatment which is based on a characteristic related to sex shall not constitute discrimination where, by reason of the nature of the particular occupational activities concerned or of the context in which they are carried out, such a characteristic

constitutes a genuine and determining occupational requirement, provided that its objective is legitimate and the requirement is proportionate.

Article 15 Return from maternity leave

A woman on maternity leave shall be entitled, after the end of her period of maternity leave, to return to her job or to an equivalent post on terms and conditions which are no less favourable to her and to benefit from any improvement in working conditions to which she would have been entitled during her absence.

Article 16 Paternity and adoption leave

This Directive is without prejudice to the right of Member States to recognise distinct rights to paternity and/or adoption leave. Those Member States which recognise such rights shall take the necessary measures to protect working men and women against dismissal due to exercising those rights and ensure that, at the end of such leave, they are entitled to return to their jobs or to equivalent posts on terms and conditions which are no less favourable to them, and to benefit from any improvement in working conditions to which they would have been entitled during their absence.

TITLE III

HORIZONTAL PROVISIONS

CHAPTER 1

REMEDIES AND ENFORCEMENT

SECTION 1

REMEDIES

Article 17 Defence of rights

1. Member States shall ensure that, after possible recourse to other competent authorities including where they deem it appropriate conciliation procedures, judicial procedures for the enforcement of obligations under this Directive are available to all persons who consider themselves wronged by failure to apply the principle of equal treatment to them, even after the relationship in which the discrimination is alleged to have occurred has ended.

2. Member States shall ensure that associations, organisations or other legal entities which have, in accordance with the criteria laid down by their national law, a legitimate interest in ensuring that the provisions of this Directive are complied with, may engage, either on behalf or in support of the complainant, with his/her approval, in any judicial and/or administrative procedure provided for the enforcement of obligations under this Directive.

3. Paragraphs 1 and 2 are without prejudice to national rules relating to time limits for bringing actions as regards the principle of equal treatment.

Article 18 Compensation or reparation

Member States shall introduce into their national legal systems such measures as are necessary to ensure real and effective compensation or reparation as the Member States so determine for the loss and damage sustained by a person injured as a result of discrimination on grounds of sex, in a way which is dissuasive and proportionate to the damage suffered. Such compensation or reparation may not be restricted by the fixing of a prior upper limit, except in cases where the employer can prove that the only damage suffered by an applicant as a result of discrimination within the meaning of this Directive is the refusal to take his/her job application into consideration.

SECTION 2

BURDEN OF PROOF

Article 19 Burden of proof

1. Member States shall take such measures as are necessary, in accordance with their national judicial systems, to ensure that, when persons who consider themselves wronged because the principle of equal treatment has not been applied to them establish, before a court or other competent authority, facts from which it may be presumed that there has been direct or indirect

discrimination, it shall be for the respondent to prove that there has been no breach of the principle of equal treatment.

2. Paragraph 1 shall not prevent Member States from introducing rules of evidence which are more favourable to plaintiffs.

3. Member States need not apply paragraph 1 to proceedings in which it is for the court or competent body to investigate the facts of the case.

4. Paragraphs 1, 2 and 3 shall also apply to:

 (a) the situations covered by Article 141 of the Treaty and, insofar as discrimination based on sex is concerned, by Directives 92/85/EEC and 96/34/EC;

 (b) any civil or administrative procedure concerning the public or private sector which provides for means of redress under national law pursuant to the measures referred to in (a) with the exception of out-of-court procedures of a voluntary nature or provided for in national law.

5. This Article shall not apply to criminal procedures, unless otherwise provided by the Member States.

CHAPTER 2
PROMOTION OF EQUAL TREATMENT — DIALOGUE

Article 20 Equality bodies

1. Member States shall designate and make the necessary arrangements for a body or bodies for the promotion, analysis, monitoring and support of equal treatment of all persons without discrimination on grounds of sex. These bodies may form part of agencies with responsibility at national level for the defence of human rights or the safeguard of individuals' rights.

2. Member States shall ensure that the competences of these bodies include:

 (a) without prejudice to the right of victims and of associations, organisations or other legal entities referred to in Article 17(2), providing independent assistance to victims of discrimination in pursuing their complaints about discrimination;

 (b) conducting independent surveys concerning discrimination;

 (c) publishing independent reports and making recommendations on any issue relating to such discrimination;

 (d) at the appropriate level exchanging available information with corresponding European bodies such as any future European Institute for Gender Equality.

Article 21 Social dialogue

1. Member States shall, in accordance with national traditions and practice, take adequate measures to promote social dialogue between the social partners with a view to fostering equal treatment, including, for example, through the monitoring of practices in the workplace, in access to employment, vocational training and promotion, as well as through the monitoring of collective agreements, codes of conduct, research or exchange of experience and good practice.

2. Where consistent with national traditions and practice, Member States shall encourage the social partners, without prejudice to their autonomy, to promote equality between men and women, and flexible working arrangements, with the aim of facilitating the reconciliation of work and private life, and to conclude, at the appropriate level, agreements laying down antidiscrimination rules in the fields referred to in Article 1 which fall within the scope of collective bargaining. These agreements shall respect the provisions of this Directive and the relevant national implementing measures.

3. Member States shall, in accordance with national law, collective agreements or practice, encourage employers to promote equal treatment for men and women in a planned and systematic way in the workplace, in access to employment, vocational training and promotion.

4. To this end, employers shall be encouraged to provide at appropriate regular intervals employees and/or their representatives with appropriate information on equal treatment for men and women in the undertaking.

Such information may include an overview of the proportions of men and women at different levels of the organisation; their pay and pay differentials; and possible measures to improve the situation in cooperation with employees' representatives.

Article 22 Dialogue with non-governmental organisations

Member States shall encourage dialogue with appropriate non-governmental organisations which have, in accordance with their national law and practice, a legitimate interest in contributing to the fight against discrimination on grounds of sex with a view to promoting the principle of equal treatment.

CHAPTER 3

GENERAL HORIZONTAL PROVISIONS

Article 23 Compliance

Member States shall take all necessary measures to ensure that:

(a)   any laws, regulations and administrative provisions contrary to the principle of equal treatment are abolished;

(b)   provisions contrary to the principle of equal treatment in individual or collective contracts or agreements, internal rules of undertakings or rules governing the independent occupations and professions and workers' and employers' organisations or any other arrangements shall be, or may be, declared null and void or are amended;

(c)   occupational social security schemes containing such provisions may not be approved or extended by administrative measures.

Article 24 Victimisation

Member States shall introduce into their national legal systems such measures as are necessary to protect employees, including those who are employees' representatives provided for by national laws and/or practices, against dismissal or other adverse treatment by the employer as a reaction to a complaint within the undertaking or to any legal proceedings aimed at enforcing compliance with the principle of equal treatment.

Article 25 Penalties

Member States shall lay down the rules on penalties applicable to infringements of the national provisions adopted pursuant to this Directive, and shall take all measures necessary to ensure that they are applied. The penalties, which may comprise the payment of compensation to the victim, must be effective, proportionate and dissuasive. The Member States shall notify those provisions to the Commission by 5 October 2005 at the latest and shall notify it without delay of any subsequent amendment affecting them.

Article 26 Prevention of discrimination

Member States shall encourage, in accordance with national law, collective agreements or practice, employers and those responsible for access to vocational training to take effective measures to prevent all forms of discrimination on grounds of sex, in particular harassment and sexual harassment in the workplace, in access to employment, vocational training and promotion.

Article 27 Minimum requirements

1.   Member States may introduce or maintain provisions which are more favourable to the protection of the principle of equal treatment than those laid down in this Directive.

2.   Implementation of this Directive shall under no circumstances be sufficient grounds for a reduction in the level of protection of workers in the areas to which it applies, without prejudice to the Member States' right to respond to changes in the situation by introducing laws, regulations and administrative provisions which differ from those in force on the notification of this Directive, provided that the provisions of this Directive are complied with.

Article 28 Relationship to Community and national provisions

1.   This Directive shall be without prejudice to provisions concerning the protection of women, particularly as regards pregnancy and maternity.

2.   This Directive shall be without prejudice to the provisions of Directive 96/34/EC and Directive 92/85/EEC.

Article 29 Gender mainstreaming

Member States shall actively take into account the objective of equality between men and women when formulating and implementing laws, regulations, administrative provisions, policies and activities in the areas referred to in this Directive.

Article 30 Dissemination of information

Member States shall ensure that measures taken pursuant to this Directive, together with the provisions already in force, are brought to the attention of all the persons concerned by all suitable means and, where appropriate, at the workplace.

TITLE IV

FINAL PROVISIONS

Article 31 Reports

1. By 15 February 2011, the Member States shall communicate to the Commission all the information necessary for the Commission to draw up a report to the European Parliament and the Council on the application of this Directive.

2. Without prejudice to paragraph 1, Member States shall communicate to the Commission, every four years, the texts of any measures adopted pursuant to Article 141(4) of the Treaty, as well as reports on these measures and their implementation. On the basis of that information, the Commission will adopt and publish every four years a report establishing a comparative assessment of any measures in the light of Declaration No 28 annexed to the Final Act of the Treaty of Amsterdam.

3. Member States shall assess the occupational activities referred to in Article 14(2), in order to decide, in the light of social developments, whether there is justification for maintaining the exclusions concerned. They shall notify the Commission of the results of this assessment periodically, but at least every 8 years.

Article 32 Review

By 15 February 2011 at the latest, the Commission shall review the operation of this Directive and if appropriate, propose any amendments it deems necessary.

Article 33 Implementation

Member States shall bring into force the laws, regulations and administrative provisions necessary to comply with this Directive by 15 August 2008 at the latest or shall ensure, by that date, that management and labour introduce the requisite provisions by way of agreement. Member States may, if necessary to take account of particular difficulties, have up to one additional year to comply with this Directive. Member States shall take all necessary steps to be able to guarantee the results imposed by this Directive. They shall forthwith communicate to the Commission the texts of those measures.

When Member States adopt these measures, they shall contain a reference to this Directive or be accompanied by such reference on the occasion of their official publication. They shall also include a statement that references in existing laws, regulations and administrative provisions to the Directives repealed by this Directive shall be construed as references to this Directive. Member States shall determine how such reference is to be made and how that statement is to be formulated.

The obligation to transpose this Directive into national law shall be confined to those provisions which represent a substantive change as compared with the earlier Directives. The obligation to transpose the provisions which are substantially unchanged arises under the earlier Directives.

Member States shall communicate to the Commission the text of the main provisions of national law which they adopt in the field covered by this Directive.

Article 34 Repeal

1. With effect from 15 August 2009 Directives 75/117/EEC, 76/207/EEC, 86/378/EEC and 97/80/EC shall be repealed without prejudice to the obligations of the Member States relating to the time-limits for transposition into national law and application of the Directives set out in Annex I, Part B.

2.   References made to the repealed Directives shall be construed as being made to this Directive and should be read in accordance with the correlation table in Annex II.

Article 35 Entry into force

This Directive shall enter into force on the 20th day following its publication in the *Official Journal of the European Union*.

Article 36 Addressees

This Directive is addressed to the Member States.

COUNCIL DIRECTIVE (EEC) No 79/7 of 19 DECEMBER 1978
on the progressive implementation of the principle of equal treatment for men and women in matters of social security
[1979] OJ L6/24

Article 1

The purpose of this Directive is the progressive implementation, in the field of social security and other elements of social protection provided for in Article 3, of the principle of equal treatment for men and women in matters of social security, hereinafter referred to as 'the principle of equal treatment'.

Article 2

This Directive shall apply to the working population—including self-employed persons, workers and self-employed persons whose activity is interrupted by illness, accident or involuntary unemployment and persons seeking employment—and to retired or invalided workers and self-employed persons.

Article 3

1.   This Directive shall apply to:
   (a)   statutory schemes which provide protection against the following risks:
      — sickness,
      — invalidity,
      — old age,
      — accidents at work and occupational diseases,
      — unemployment;
   (b)   social assistance, in so far as it is intended to supplement or replace the schemes referred to in (a).
2.   This Directive shall not apply to the provisions concerning survivors' benefits nor to those concerning family benefits, except in the case of family benefits granted by way of increases of benefits due in respect of the risks referred to in paragraph 1(a).
3.   With a view to ensuring implementation of the principle of equal treatment in occupational schemes, the Council, acting on a proposal from the Commission, will adopt provisions defining its substance, its scope and the arrangements for its application.

Article 4

1.   The principle of equal treatment means that there shall be no discrimination whatsoever on ground of sex either directly, or indirectly by reference in particular to marital or family status, in particular as concerns:
      — the scope of the schemes and the conditions of access thereto,
      — the obligation to contribute and the calculation of contributions,
      — the calculation of benefits including increases due in respect of a spouse and for dependants and the conditions governing the duration and retention of entitlement to benefits.
2.   The principle of equal treatment shall be without prejudice to the provisions relating to the protection of women on the grounds of maternity.

Article 5

Member States shall take the measures necessary to ensure that any laws, regulations and administrative provisions contrary to the principle of equal treatment are abolished.

Article 6

Member States shall introduce into their national legal systems such measures as are necessary to enable all persons who consider themselves wronged by failure to apply the principle of equal treatment to pursue their claims by judicial process, possibly after recourse to other competent authorities.

Article 7

1. This Directive shall be without prejudice to the right of Member States to exclude from its scope:
    (a) the determination of pensionable age for the purposes of granting old-age and retirement pensions and the possible consequences thereof for other benefits;
    (b) advantages in respect of old-age pension schemes granted to persons who have brought up children; the acquisition of benefit entitlements following periods of interruption of employment due to the bringing up of children;
    (c) the granting of old-age or invalidity benefit entitlements by virtue of the derived entitlements of a wife;
    (d) the granting of increases of long-term invalidity, old-age, accidents at work and occupational disease benefits for a dependent wife;
    (e) the consequences of the exercise, before the adoption of this Directive, of a right of option not to acquire rights or incur obligations under a statutory scheme.
2. Member States shall periodically examine matters excluded under paragraph 1 in order to ascertain, in the light of social developments in the matter concerned, whether there is justification for maintaining the exclusions concerned.

Article 8

1. Member States shall bring into force the laws, regulations and administrative provisions necessary to comply with this Directive within six years of its notification. They shall immediately inform the Commission thereof.
2. Member States shall communicate to the Commission the text of laws, regulations and administrative provisions which they adopt in the field covered by this Directive, including measures adopted pursuant to Article 7(2).
    They shall inform the Commission of their reasons for maintaining any existing provisions on the matters referred to in Article 7(1) and of the possibilities for reviewing them at a later date.

Article 9

Within seven years of notification of this Directive, Member States shall forward all information necessary to the Commission to enable it to draw up a report on the application of this Directive for submission to the Council and to propose such further measures as may be required for the implementation of the principle of equal treatment.

Article 10

This Directive is addressed to the Member States.

COUNCIL DIRECTIVE (EEC) No 86/378 of 24 JULY 1986
on the implementation of the principle of equal treatment for men and women in occupational social security schemes
[1986] OJ L225/40

Article 1

The object of this Directive is to implement, in occupational social security schemes, the principle of equal treatment for men and women, hereinafter referred to as 'the principle of equal treatment'.

Article 2

1. 'Occupational social security schemes' means schemes not governed by Directive 79/7/EEC whose purpose is to provide workers, whether employees or self-employed, in an undertaking or group of undertakings, area of economic activity or occupational sector or group of such sectors with benefits intended to supplement the benefits provided by statutory social security schemes or to replace them, whether membership of such schemes is compulsory or optional.

2. This Directive does not apply to:
    (a) individual contracts for self-employed workers;
    (b) schemes for self-employed workers having only one member;
    (c) insurance contracts to which the employer is not a party, in the case of salaried workers;
    (d) optional provisions of occupational schemes offered to participants individually to guarantee them:
        — either additional benefits, or
        — a choice of date on which the normal benefits for self-employed workers will start, or a choice between several benefits;
    (e) occupational schemes in so far as benefits are financed by contributions paid by workers on a voluntary basis.

3. This Directive does not preclude an employer granting to persons who have already reached the retirement age for the purposes of granting a pension by virtue of an occupational scheme, but who have not yet reached the retirement age for the purposes of granting a statutory retirement pension, a pension supplement, the aim of which is to make equal or more nearly equal the overall amount of benefit paid to these persons in relation to the amount paid to persons of the other sex in the same situation who have already reached the statutory retirement age, until the persons benefiting from the supplement reach the statutory retirement age.

Article 3

This Directive shall apply to members of the working population including self-employed persons, persons whose activity is interrupted by illness, maternity, accident or involuntary unemployment and persons seeking employment, to retired and disabled workers and to those claiming under them, in accordance with national law and/or practice.

Article 4

This Directive shall apply to:

(a) occupational schemes which provide protection against the following risks:
    — sickness,
    — invalidity,
    — old age, including early retirement,
    — industrial accidents and occupational diseases,
    — unemployment;

(b) occupational schemes which provide for other social benefits, in cash or in kind, and in particular survivors' benefits and family allowances, if such benefits are accorded to employed persons and thus constitute a consideration paid by the employer to the worker by reason of the latter's employment.

Article 5

1. Under the conditions laid down in the following provisions, the principle of equal treatment implies that there shall be no discrimination on the basis of sex, either directly or indirectly, by reference in particular to marital or family status, especially as regards:
    — the scope of the schemes and the conditions of access to them;
    — the obligation to contribute and the calculation of contributions;
    — the calculation of benefits, including supplementary benefits due in respect of a spouse or dependants, and the conditions governing the duration and retention of entitlement to benefits.

2. The principle of equal treatment shall not prejudice the provisions relating to the protection of women by reason of maternity.

Article 6

1. Provisions contrary to the principle of equal treatment shall include those based on sex, either directly or indirectly, in particular by reference to marital or family for:

    (a)   determining the persons who may participate in an occupational scheme;

    (b)   fixing the compulsory or optional nature of participation in an occupational scheme;

    (c)   laying down different rules as regards the age of entry into the scheme or the minimum period of employment or membership of the scheme required to obtain the benefits thereof;

    (d)   laying down different rules, except as provided for in points (h) and (i), for the reimbursement of contributions where a worker leaves a scheme without having fulfilled the conditions guaranteeing him a deferred right to long-term benefits;

    (e)   setting different conditions for the granting of benefits of restricting such benefits to workers of one or other of the sexes;

    (f)   fixing different retirement ages;

    (g)   suspending the retention or acquisition of rights during periods of maternity leave or leave for family reasons which are granted by law or agreement and are paid by the employer;

    (h)   setting different levels of benefit, except insofar as may be necessary to take account of actuarial calculation factors which differ according to sex in the case of defined contribution schemes. In the case of funded defined-benefit schemes, certain elements (examples of which are annexed) may be unequal where the inequality of the amounts results from the effects of the use of actuarial factors differing according to sex at the time when the scheme's funding is implemented;

    (i)   setting different levels of worker contribution;

    — in the case of defined-contribution schemes if the aim is to equalise the amount of the final benefits or to make them more nearly equal for both sexes,

    — in the case of funded defined-benefit schemes where the employer's contributions are intended to ensure the adequacy of the funds necessary to cover the cost of the benefits defined,

    (j)   laying down different standards or standards applicable only to workers of a specified sex, except as provided for in subparagraphs (h) and (i), as regards the guarantee or retention of entitlement to deferred benefits when a worker leaves a scheme.

2. Where the granting of benefits within the scope of this Directive is left to the discretion of the scheme's management bodies, the latter must comply with the principle of equal treatment.

Article 7

Member States shall take all necessary steps to ensure that:

(a)   provisions contrary to the principle of equal treatment in legally compulsory collective agreements, staff rules of undertakings or any other arrangements relating to occupational schemes are null and void, or may be declared null and void or amended;

(b)   schemes containing such provisions may not be approved or extended by administrative measures.

Article 8

1. Member States shall take all necessary steps to ensure that the provisions of occupational schemes contrary to the principle of equal treatment are revised by 1 January 1993 at the latest.

2. This Directive shall not preclude rights and obligations relating to a period of membership of an occupational scheme prior to revision of that scheme from remaining subject to the provisions of the scheme in force during that period.

Article 9

As regards schemes for self-employed workers, Member States may defer compulsory application of the principle of equal treatment with regard to:

(a)   determination of pensionable age for the granting of old-age or retirement pensions, and the possible implications for other benefits:

— either until the date on which such equality is achieved in statutory schemes,

— or, at the latest, until such equality is required by a directive;

(b)   survivors' pensions until Community law establishes the principle of equal treatment in statutory social security schemes in that regard;

(c)   the application of the first subparagraph of point (i) of Article 6(1) to take account of the different actuarial calculation factors, at the latest until 1 January 1999.

Article 9a

Where men and women may claim a flexible pensionable age under the same conditions, this shall not be deemed to be incompatible with this Directive.

Article 10

Member States shall introduce into their national legal systems such measures as are necessary to enable all persons who consider themselves injured by failure to apply the principle of equal treatment to pursue their claims before the courts, possibly after bringing the matters before other competent authorities.

Article 11

Member States shall take all the necessary steps to protect worker against dismissal where this constitutes a response on the part of the employer to a complaint made at undertaking level or to the institution of legal proceedings aimed at enforcing compliance with the principle of equal treatment.

Article 12

1.   Member States shall bring into force such laws, regulations and administrative provisions as are necessary in order to comply with this Directive at the latest three years after notification thereof. They shall immediately inform the Commission thereof.

2.   Member States shall communicate to the Commission at the latest five years after notification of this Directive all information necessary to enable the Commission to draw up a report on the application of this Directive for submission to the Council.

Article 13

This Directive is addressed to the Member States.

COUNCIL DIRECTIVE (EC) No 96/97 of 20 DECEMBER 1996 amending Directive 86/378/EEC on the implementation of the principle of equal treatment for men and women in occupational social security schemes [1996] OJ L46/20

The Council of the European Union,

Having regard to the Treaty establishing the European Community, and in particular Article 100 thereof,

Having regard to the proposal from the Commission,

Having regard to the opinion of the European Parliament,

Having regard to the opinion of the Economic and Social Committee,

Whereas Article 119 of the Treaty provides that each Member State shall ensure the application of the principle that men and women should receive equal pay for equal work; whereas 'pay' should be taken to mean the ordinary basic or minimum wage or salary and any other consideration, whether in cash or in kind, which the worker receives, directly or indirectly, from his employer in respect of his employment;

Whereas, in its judgment of 17 May 1990, in Case 262/88: *Barber v Guardian Royal Exchange Assurance Group*, the Court of Justice of the European Communities acknowledges that all forms of occupational pension constitute an element of pay within the meaning of Article 119 of the Treaty;

Whereas, in the abovementioned judgment, as clarified by the judgment of 14 December 1993 (Case C-110/91: *Moroni v Collo GmbH*), the Court interprets Article 119 of the Treaty in such a way that discrimination between men and women in occupational social security schemes is prohibited in general and not only in respect of establishing the age of entitlement to a pension or when an occupational pension is offered by way of compensation for compulsory retirement on economic grounds;

Whereas, in accordance with Protocol 2 concerning Article 119 of the Treaty annexed to the Treaty establishing the European Community, benefits under occupational social security schemes shall not be considered as remuneration if and in so far as they are attributable to periods of employment prior to 17 May 1990, except in the case of workers or those claiming under them who have, before that date, initiated legal proceedings or raised an equivalent claim under the applicable national law;

Whereas, in its judgments of 28 September 1994 (Case C-57/93: *Vroege v NCIV Instituut voor Volkshuisvesting BV* and Case C-128/93: *Fisscher v Voorhuis Hengelo BV*), the Court ruled that the abovementioned Protocol did not affect the right to join an occupational pension scheme, which continues to be governed by the judgment of 13 May 1986 in Case 170/84: *Bilka-Kaufhaus GmbH v Hartz*, and that the limitation of the effects in time of the judgment of 17 May 1990 in Case C-262/88: *Barber v Guardian Royal Exchange Assurance Group* does not apply to the right to join an occupational pension scheme; whereas the Court also ruled that the national rules relating to time limits for bringing actions under national law may be relied on against workers who assert their right to join an occupational pension scheme, provided that they are not less favourable for that type of action than for similar actions of a domestic nature and that they do not render the exercise of rights conferred by Community law impossible in practice; whereas the Court has also pointed out that the fact that a worker can claim retroactively to join an occupational pension scheme does not allow the worker to avoid paying the contributions relating to the period of membership concerned;

Whereas the exclusion of workers on the grounds of the nature of their work contracts from access to a company or sectoral social security scheme may constitute indirect discrimination against women;

Whereas, in its judgment of 9 November 1993 (Case C-132/92: *Birds Eye Walls Ltd v Friedel M. Roberts*), the Court has also specified that it is not contrary to Article 119 of the Treaty, when calculating the amount of a bridging pension which is paid by an employer to male and female employees who have taken early retirement on grounds of ill health and which is intended to compensate, in particular, for loss of income resulting from the fact that they have not yet reached the age required for payment of the State pension which they will subsequently receive and to reduce the amount of the bridging pension accordingly, even though, in the case of men and women aged between 60 and 65, the result is that a female ex-employee receives a smaller bridging pension than that paid to her male counterpart, the difference being equal to the amount of the State pension to which she is entitled as from the age of 60 in respect of the periods of service completed with that employer;

Whereas, in its judgment of 6 October 1993 (Case C-109/91: *Ten Oever v Stichting Bedrijfpensioenfonds voor het Glazenwassers-en Schoonmaakbedrijf*) and in its judgments of 14 December 1993 (Case C-110/91: *Moroni v Collo GmbH*), 22 December 1993 (Case C-152/91: *Neath v Hugh Steeper Ltd*) and 28 September 1994 (Case C-200/91: *Coloroll Pension Trustees Limited v Russell and Others*), the Court confirms that, by virtue of the judgment of 17 May 1990 (Case C-262/88: *Barber v Guardian Royal Exchange Assurance Group*), the direct effect of Article 119 of the Treaty may be relied on, for the purpose of claiming equal treatment in the matter of occupational pensions, only in relation to benefits payable in respect of periods of service subsequent to 17 May 1990, except in the case of workers or those claiming under them who have, before that date, initiated legal proceedings or raised an equivalent claim under the applicable national law;

Whereas, in its abovementioned judgments (Case C-109/91: *Ten Oever v Stichting Bedrijfpensioenfonds voor het Glazenwassers-en Schoonmaakbedrijf* and Case C-200/91: *Coloroll Pension Trustees Limited v Russell and Others*), the Court confirms that the limitation of the effects in time of the Barber judgment applies to survivors' pensions and, consequently, equal treatment in this matter may be claimed only in relation to periods of service subsequent to 17 May 1990, except in the case of those who have, before that date, initiated legal proceedings or raised an equivalent claim under the applicable national law;

Whereas, moreover, in its judgments in Case C-152/91 and Case C-200/91, the Court specifies that the contributions of male and female workers to a defined-benefit pension scheme must be the same, since they are covered by Article 119 of the Treaty, whereas inequality of employers' contributions paid under funded defined-benefit schemes, which is due to the use of actuarial factors differing according to sex, is not to be assessed in the light of that same provision;

Whereas, in its judgments of 28 September 1994 (Case C-408/92: *Smith v Advel Systems* and Case C-28/93: *Van den Akker v Stichting Shell Pensioenfonds*), the Court points out that Article 119 of the Treaty precludes an employer who adopts measures necessary to comply with the *Barber* judgment of 17 May 1990 (C-262/88) from raising the retirement age for women to that which exists for men in relation to periods of service completed between 17 May 1990 and the date on which those measures come into force; on the other hand, as regards periods of service completed after the latter date, Article 119 does not prevent an employer from taking that step; as regards periods of service prior to 17 May 1990, Community law imposed no obligation which would justify retroactive reduction of the advantages which women enjoyed;

Whereas, in its abovementioned judgment in Case C-200/91: *Coloroll Pension Trustees Limited v Russell and Others*), the Court ruled that additional benefits stemming from contributions paid by employees on a purely voluntary basis are not covered by Article 119 of the Treaty;

Whereas, among the measures included in its third medium-term action programme on equal opportunities for women and men (1991 to 1995), the Commission emphasises once more the adoption of suitable measures to take account of the consequences of the judgment of 17 May 1990 in Case 262/88 (*Barber v Guardian Royal Exchange Assurance Group*);

Whereas that judgment automatically invalidates certain provisions of Council Directive 86/378/EEC of 24 July 1986 on the implementation of the principle of equal treatment for men and women in occupational social security schemes in respect of paid workers;

Whereas Article 119 of the Treaty is directly applicable and can be invoked before the national courts against any employer, whether a private person or a legal person, and whereas it is for these courts to safeguard the rights which that provision confers on individuals;

Whereas, on grounds of legal certainty, it is necessary to amend Directive 86/378/EEC in order to adapt the provisions which are affected by the Barber case-law,

Has adopted this directive:

Article 2

1. Any measure implementing this Directive, as regards paid workers, must cover all benefits derived from periods of employment subsequent to 17 May 1990 and shall apply retroactively to that date, without prejudice to workers or those claiming under them who have, before that date, initiated legal proceedings or raised an equivalent claim under national law. In that event, the implementation measures must apply retroactively to 8 April 1976 and must cover all the benefits derived from periods of employment after that date. For Member States which acceded to the Community after 8 April 1976 and before 17 May 1990, that date shall be replaced by the date on which Article 119 of the Treaty became applicable on their territory.

2. The second sentence of paragraph 1 shall not prevent national rules relating to time limits for bringing actions under national law from being relied on against workers or those claiming under them who initiated legal proceedings or raise an equivalent claim under national law before 17 May 1990, provided that they are not less favourable for that type of action than for similar actions of a domestic nature and that they do not render the exercise of Community law impossible in practice.

3. For Member States whose accession took place after 17 May 1990 and who were on 1 January 1994 Contracting Parties to the Agreement on the European Economic Area, the date of 17 May 1990 in the first sentence of paragraph 1 of this Article is replaced by 1 January 1994.

Article 3

1. Member States shall bring into force the laws, regulations and administrative provisions necessary to comply with this Directive by 1 July 1997. They shall forthwith inform the Commission thereof.

When Member States adopt these provisions, they shall contain a reference to this Directive or be accompanied by such reference on the occasion of their official publication. The methods of making such a reference shall be laid down by the Member States.

2. Member States shall communicate to the Commission, at the latest two years after the entry into force of this Directive, all information necessary to enable the Commission to draw up a report on the application of this Directive.

Article 4

This Directive shall enter into force on the 20th day following that of its publication in the *Official Journal of the European Communities*.

Article 5

This Directive is addressed to the Member States.

COUNCIL DIRECTIVE (EEC) No 86/613 of 11 DECEMBER 1986
on the application of the principle of equal treatment between men and women engaged in an activity, including agriculture, in a self-employed capacity, and on the protection of self-employed women during pregnancy and motherhood
[1986] OJ L359/56

SECTION I
AIMS AND SCOPE

Article 1

The purpose of this Directive is to ensure, in accordance with the following provisions, application in the Member States of the principle of equal treatment as between men and women engaged in an activity in a self-employed capacity, or contributing to the pursuit of such an activity, as regards those aspects not covered by Directives 76/207/EEC and 79/7/EEC.

Article 2

This Directive covers:

(a) self-employed workers, i.e., all persons pursuing a gainful activity for their own account, under the conditions laid down by national law, including farmers and members of the liberal professions;

(b) their spouses, not being employees or partners, where they habitually, under the conditions laid down by national law, participate in the activities of the self-employed worker and perform the same tasks or ancillary tasks.

Article 3

For the purposes of this Directive the principle of equal treatment implies the absence of all discrimination on grounds of sex, either directly or indirectly, by reference in particular to marital or family status.

SECTION II
EQUAL TREATMENT BETWEEN SELF-EMPLOYED MALE AND FEMALE WORKERS — POSITION OF THE SPOUSES WITHOUT PROFESSIONAL STATUS OF SELF-EMPLOYED WORKERS — PROTECTION OF SELF-EMPLOYED WORKERS OR WIVES OF SELF-EMPLOYED WORKERS DURING PREGNANCY AND MOTHERHOOD

Article 4

As regards self-employed persons, Member States shall take the measures necessary to ensure the elimination of all provisions which are contrary to the principle of equal treatment as defined in Directive 76/207/EEC, especially in respect of the establishment, equipment or extension of a business or the launching or extension of any other form of self-employed activity including financial facilities.

Article 5

Without prejudice to the specific conditions for access to certain activities which apply equally to both sexes, Member States shall take the measures necessary to ensure that the conditions for the formation of a company between spouses are not more restrictive than the conditions for the formation of a company between unmarried persons.

Article 6

Where a contributory social security system for self-employed workers exists in a Member State, that Member State shall take the necessary measures to enable the spouses referred to in Article 2(b) who are not protected under the self-employed worker's social security scheme to join a contributory social security scheme voluntarily.

Article 7

Member States shall undertake to examine under what conditions recognition of the work of the spouses referred to in Article 2(b) may be encouraged and, in the light of such examination, consider any appropriate steps for encouraging such recognition.

Article 8

Member States shall undertake to examine whether, and under what conditions, female self-employed workers and the wives of self-employed workers may, during interruptions in their occupational activity owing to pregnancy or motherhood,
— have access to services supplying temporary replacements or existing national social services, or
— be entitled to cash benefits under a social security scheme or under any other public social protection system.

SECTION III
GENERAL AND FINAL PROVISIONS

Article 9

Member States shall introduce into their national legal systems such measures as are necessary to enable all persons who consider themselves wronged by failure to apply the principle of equal treatment in self-employed activities to pursue their claims by judicial process, possibly after recourse to other competent authorities.

Article 10

Member States shall ensure that the measures adopted pursuant to this Directive, together with the relevant provisions already in force, are brought to the attention of bodies representing self-employed workers and vocational training centres.

Article 11

The Council shall review this Directive, on a proposal from the Commission, before 1 July 1993.

Article 12

1. Member States shall bring into force the laws, regulations and administrative provisions necessary to comply with this Directive not later than 30 June 1989. However, if a Member State which, in order to comply with Article 5 of this Directive, has to amend its legislation on matrimonial rights and obligations, the date on which such Member State must comply with Article 5 shall be 30 June 1991.
2. Member States shall immediately inform the Commission of the measures taken to comply with this Directive.

Article 13

Member States shall forward to the Commission, not later than 30 June 1991, all the information necessary to enable it to draw up a report on the application of this directive for submission to the Council.

Article 14

This Directive is addressed to the Member States.

COUNCIL DIRECTIVE (EC) No 96/34 of 3 JUNE 1996
on the framework agreement on parental leave concluded by UNICE, CEEP and the ETUC
[1996] OJ L145/9

THE COUNCIL OF THE EUROPEAN UNION,

Having regard to the Agreement on social policy, annexed to the Protocol (No. 14) on social policy, annexed to the Treaty establishing the European Community, and in particular Article 4(2) thereof,

Having regard to the proposal from the Commission,

(1)   Whereas on the basis of the Protocol on social policy, the Member States, with the exception of the United Kingdom of Great Britain and Northern Ireland, (hereinafter referred to as 'the Member States'), wishing to pursue the course mapped out by the 1989 Social Charter have concluded an Agreement on social policy amongst themselves;

(2)   Whereas management and labour may, in accordance with Article 4(2) of the Agreement on social policy, request jointly that agreements at Community level be implemented by a Council decision on a proposal from the Commission;

(3)   Whereas paragraph 16 of the Community Charter of the Fundamental Social Rights of Workers on equal treatment for men and women provides, inter alia, that 'measures should also be developed enabling men and women to reconcile their occupational and family obligations;

(4)   Whereas the Council, despite the existence of a broad consensus, has not been able to act on the proposal for a Directive on parental leave for family reasons (1), as amended (2) on 15 November 1984;

(5)   Whereas the Commission, in accordance with Article 3(2) of the Agreement on social policy, consulted management and labour on the possible direction of Community action with regard to reconciling working and family life;

(6)   Whereas the Commission, considering after such consultation that Community action was desirable, once again consulted management and labour on the substance of the envisaged proposal in accordance with Article 3(3) of the said Agreement;

(7)   Whereas the general cross-industry organisations (UNICE, CEEP and the ETUC) informed the Commission in their joint letter of 5 July 1995 of their desire to initiate the procedure provided for by Article 4 of the said Agreement;

(8)   Whereas the said cross-industry organisations concluded, on 14 December 1995, a framework agreement on parental leave; whereas they have forwarded to the Commission their joint request to implement this framework agreement by a Council Decision on a proposal from the Commission in accordance with Article 4(2) of the said Agreement;

(9)   Whereas the Council, in its Resolution of 6 December 1994 on certain aspects for a European Union social policy; a contribution to economic and social convergence in the Union (3), asked the two sides of industry to make use of the possibilities for concluding agreements, since they are as a rule closer to social reality and to social problems; whereas in Madrid, the members of the European Council from those States which have signed the Agreement on social policy welcomed the conclusion of this framework agreement;

(10)   Whereas the signatory parties wanted to conclude a framework agreement setting out minimum requirements on parental leave and time off from work on grounds of force majeure and referring back to the Member States and/or management and labour for the definition of the conditions under which parental leave would be implemented, in order to take account of the situation, including the situation with regard to family policy, existing in each Member State, particularly as regards the conditions for granting parental leave and exercise of the right to parental leave;

(11)   Whereas the proper instrument for implementing this framework agreement is a Directive within the meaning of Article 189 of the Treaty; whereas it is therefore binding on the Member States as to the result to be achieved, but leaves them the choice of form and methods;

(12)   Whereas, in keeping with the principle of subsidiarity and the principle of proportionality as set out in Article 3b of the Treaty, the objectives of this Directive cannot be sufficiently

achieved by the Member States and can therefore be better achieved by the Community; whereas this Directive is confined to the minimum required to achieve these objectives and does not go beyond what is necessary to achieve that purpose;

(13) Whereas the Commission has drafted its proposal for a Directive, taking into account the representative status of the signatory parties, their mandate and the legality of the clauses of the framework agreement and compliance with the relevant provisions concerning small and medium-sized undertakings;

(14) Whereas the Commission, in accordance with its Communication of 14 December 1993 concerning the implementation of the Protocol on social policy, informed the European Parliament by sending it the text of the framework agreement, accompanied by its proposal for a Directive and the explanatory memorandum;

(15) Whereas the Commission also informed the Economic and Social Committee by sending it the text of the framework agreement, accompanied by its proposal for a Directive and the explanatory memorandum;

(16) Whereas clause 4 point 2 of the framework agreement states that the implementation of the provisions of this agreement does not constitute valid grounds for reducing the general level of protection afforded to workers in the field of this agreement. This does not prejudice the right of Member States and/or management and labour to develop different legislative, regulatory or contractual provisions, in the light of changing circumstances (including the introduction of non-transferability), as long as the minimum requirements provided for in the present agreement are complied with;

(17) Whereas the Community Charter of the Fundamental Social Rights of Workers recognises the importance of the fight against all forms of discrimination, especially based on sex, colour, race, opinions and creeds;

(18) Whereas Article F(2) of the Treaty on European Union provides that 'the Union shall respect fundamental rights, as guaranteed by the European Convention for the Protection of Human Rights and Fundamental Freedoms signed in Rome on 4 November 1950 and as they result from the constitutional traditions common to the Member States, as general principles of Community law;

(19) Whereas the Member States can entrust management and labour, at their joint request, with the implementation of this Directive, as long as they take all the necessary steps to ensure that they can at all times guarantee the results imposed by this Directive;

(20) Whereas the implementation of the framework agreement contributes to achieving the objectives under Article 1 of the Agreement on social policy,

HAS ADOPTED THIS DIRECTIVE:

Article 1   Implementation of the framework agreement

The purpose of this Directive is to put into effect the annexed framework agreement on parental leave concluded on 14 December 1995 between the general cross-industry organisations (UNICE, CEEP and the ETUC).

Article 2   Final provisions

1.   The Member States shall bring into force the laws, regulations and administrative provisions necessary to comply with this Directive by 3 June 1998 at the latest or shall ensure by that date at the latest that management and labour have introduced the necessary measures by agreement, the Member States being required to take any necessary measure enabling them at any time to be in a position to guarantee the results imposed by this Directive. They shall forthwith inform the Commission thereof.

1a.   As regards the United Kingdom of Great Britain and Northern Ireland, the date of 3 June 1998 in paragraph 1 shall be replaced by 15 December 1999.

2.   The Member States may have a maximum additional period of one year, if this is necessary to take account of special difficulties or implementation by a collective agreement.

      They must forthwith inform the Commission of such circumstances.

3.   When Member States adopt the measures referred to in paragraph 1, they shall contain a reference to this Directive or be accompanied by such reference on the occasion of their

official publication. The methods of making such reference shall be laid down by Member States.

Article 3

This Directive is addressed to the Member States.

ANNEX
FRAMEWORK AGREEMENT ON PARENTAL LEAVE
PREAMBLE

The enclosed framework agreement represents an undertaking by UNICE, CEEP and the ETUC to set out minimum requirements on parental leave and time off from work on grounds of force majeure, as an important means of reconciling work and family life and promoting equal opportunities and treatment between men and women.

ETUC, UNICE and CEEP request the Commission to submit this framework agreement to the Council for a Council Decision making these minimum requirements binding in the Member States of the European Community, with the exception of the United Kingdom of Great Britain and Northern Ireland.

I GENERAL
CONSIDERATIONS

1. Having regard to the Agreement on social policy annexed to the Protocol on social policy, annexed to the Treaty establishing the European Community, and in particular Articles 3(4) and 4(2) thereof;

2. Whereas Article 4(2) of the Agreement on social policy provides that agreements concluded at Community level shall be implemented, at the joint request of the signatory parties, by a Council Decision on a proposal from the Commission;

3. Whereas the Commission has announced its intention to propose a Community measure on the reconciliation of work and family life;

4. Whereas the Community Charter of Fundamental Social Rights stipulates at point 16 dealing with equal treatment that measures should be developed to enable men and women to reconcile their occupational and family obligations;

5. Whereas the Council Resolution of 6 December 1994 recognises that an effective policy of equal opportunities presupposes an integrated overall strategy allowing for better organisation of working hours and greater flexibility, and for an easier return to working life, and notes the important role of the two sides of industry in this area and in offering both men and women an opportunity to reconcile their work responsibilities with family obligations;

6. Whereas measures to reconcile work and family life should encourage the introduction of new flexible ways of organising work and time which are better suited to the changing needs of society and which should take the needs of both undertakings and workers into account;

7. Whereas family policy should be looked at in the context of demographic changes, the effects of the ageing population, closing the generation gap and promoting women's participation in the labour force;

8. Whereas men should be encouraged to assume an equal share of family responsibilities, for example they should be encouraged to take parental leave by means such as awareness programmes;

9. Whereas the present agreement is a framework agreement setting out minimum requirements and provisions for parental leave, distinct from maternity leave, and for time off from work on grounds of force majeure, and refers back to Member States and social partners for the establishment of the conditions of access and detailed rules of application in order to take account of the situation in each Member State;

10. Whereas Member States should provide for the maintenance of entitlements to benefits in kind under sickness insurance during the minimum period of parental leave;

11. Whereas Member States should also, where appropriate under national conditions and taking into account the budgetary situation, consider the maintenance of entitlements to relevant social security benefits as they stand during the minimum period of parental leave;

12. Whereas this agreement takes into consideration the need to improve social policy requirements, to enhance the competitiveness of the Community economy and to avoid imposing administrative, financial and legal constraints in a way which would impede the creation and development of small and medium-sized undertakings;

13. Whereas management and labour are best placed to find solutions that correspond to the needs of both employers and workers and must therefore have conferred on them a special role in the implementation and application of the present agreement,

THE SIGNATORY PARTIES HAVE AGREED THE FOLLOWING:

II CONTENT

Clause 1: Purpose and scope

1. This agreement lays down minimum requirements designed to facilitate the reconciliation of parental and professional responsibilities for working parents.

2. This agreement applies to all workers, men and women, who have an employment contract or employment relationship as defined by the law, collective agreements or practices in force in each Member State.

Clause 2: Parental leave

1. This agreement grants, subject to clause 2.2, men and women workers an individual right to parental leave on the grounds of the birth or adoption of a child to enable them to take care of that child, for at least three months, until a given age up to 8 years to be defined by Member States and/or management and labour.

2. To promote equal opportunities and equal treatment between men and women, the parties to this agreement consider that the right to parental leave provided for under clause 2.1 should, in principle, be granted on a non-transferable basis.

3. The conditions of access and detailed rules for applying parental leave shall be defined by law and/or collective agreement in the Member States, as long as the minimum requirements of this agreement are respected. Member States and/or management and labour may, in particular:

    (a) decide whether parental leave is granted on a full-time or part-time basis, in a piecemeal way or in the form of a time-credit system;

    (b) make entitlement to parental leave subject to a period of work qualification and/or a length of service qualification which shall not exceed one year;

    (c) adjust conditions of access and detailed rules for applying parental leave to the special circumstances of adoption;

    (d) establish notice periods to be given by the worker to the employer when exercising the right to parental leave, specifying the beginning and the end of the period of leave;

    (e) define the circumstances in which an employer, following consultation in accordance with national law, collective agreements and practices, is allowed to postpone the granting of parental leave for justifiable reasons related to the operation of the undertaking (e.g. where work is of a seasonal nature, where a replacement cannot be found within the notice period, where a significant proportion of the workforce applies for parental leave at the same time, where a specific function is of strategic importance). Any problem arising from the application of this provision should be dealt with in accordance with national law, collective agreements and practices;

    (f) in addition to (e), authorise special arrangements to meet the operational and organisational requirements of small undertakings.

4. In order to ensure that workers can exercise their right to parental leave, Member States and/or management and labour shall take the necessary measures to protect workers against dismissal on the grounds of an application for, or the taking of, parental leave in accordance with national law, collective agreements or practices.

5. At the end of parental leave, workers shall have the right to return to the same job or, if that is not possible, to an equivalent or similar job consistent with their employment contract or employment relationship.

6. Rights acquired or in the process of being acquired by the worker on the date on which parental leave starts shall be maintained as they stand until the end of parental leave. At the end of parental leave, these rights, including any changes arising from national law, collective agreements or practice, shall apply.

7. Member States and/or management and labour shall define the status of the employment contract or employment relationship for the period of parental leave.

8. All matters relating to social security in relation to this agreement are for consideration and determination by Member States according to national law, taking into account the importance of the continuity of the entitlements to social security cover under the different schemes, in particular health care.

Clause 3: Time off from work on grounds of force majeure

1. Member States and/or management and labour shall take the necessary measures to entitle workers to time off from work, in accordance with national legislation, collective agreements and/or practice, on grounds of force majeure for urgent family reasons in cases of sickness or accident making the immediate presence of the worker indispensable.

2. Member States and/or management and labour may specify the conditions of access and detailed rules for applying clause 3.1 and limit this entitlement to a certain amount of time per year and/or per case.

Clause 4: Final provisions

1. Member States may apply or introduce more favourable provisions that those set out in this agreement.

2. Implementation of the provisions of this agreement shall not constitute valid grounds for reducing the general level of protection afforded to workers in the field covered by this agreement. This shall not prejudice the right of Member States and/or management and labour to develop different legislative, regulatory or contractual provisions, in the light of changing circumstances (including the introduction of non-transferability), as long as the minimum requirements provided for in the present agreement are complied with.

3. The present agreement shall not prejudice the right of management and labour to conclude, at the appropriate level including European level, agreements adapting and/or complementing the provisions of this agreement in order to take into account particular circumstances.

4. Member States shall adopt the laws, regulations and administrative provisions necessary to comply with the Council decision within a period of two years from its adoption or shall ensure that management and labour (1) introduce the necessary measures by way of agreement by the end of this period. Member States may, if necessary to take account of particular difficulties or implementation by collective agreement, have up to a maximum of one additional year to comply with this decision.

5. The prevention and settlement of disputes and grievances arising from the application of this agreement shall be dealt with in accordance with national law, collective agreements and practices.

6. Without prejudice to the respective role of the Commission, national courts and the Court of Justice, any matter relating to the interpretation of this agreement at European level should, in the first instance, be referred by the Commission to the signatory parties who will give an opinion.

7. The signatory parties shall review the application of this agreement five years after the date of the Council decision if requested by one of the parties to this agreement.

COUNCIL DIRECTIVE (EC) No 97/80 of 15 DECEMBER 1997
on the burden of proof in cases of discrimination based on sex
[1998] OJ L14/6

THE COUNCIL OF THE EUROPEAN UNION,

Having regard to the Agreement on social policy annexed to the Protocol (No. 14) on social policy annexed to the Treaty establishing the European Community, and in particular Article 2(2) thereof,

Having regard to the proposal from the Commission, Having regard to the opinion of the Economic and Social Committee, Acting, in accordance with the procedure laid down in Article 189c of the Treaty, in cooperation with the European Parliament,

(1) Whereas, on the basis of the Protocol on social policy annexed to the Treaty, the Member States, with the exception of the United Kingdom of Great Britain and Northern Ireland (hereinafter called 'the Member States'), wishing to implement the 1989 Social Charter, have concluded an Agreement on social policy;

(2) Whereas the Community Charter of the Fundamental Social Rights of Workers recognises the importance of combating every form of discrimination, including discrimination on grounds of sex, colour, race, opinions and beliefs;

(3) Whereas paragraph 16 of the Community Charter of the Fundamental Social Rights of Workers on equal treatment for men and women, provides, inter alia, that 'action should be intensified to ensure the implementation of the principle of equality for men and women as regards, in particular, access to employment, remuneration, working conditions, social protection, education, vocational training and career development;

(4) Whereas, in accordance with Article 3(2) of the Agreement on social policy, the Commission has consulted management and labour at Community level on the possible direction of Community action on the burden of proof in cases of discrimination based on sex;

(5) Whereas the Commission, considering Community action advisable after such consultation, once again consulted management and labour on the content of the proposal contemplated in accordance with Article 3(3) of the same Agreement; whereas the latter have sent their opinions to the Commission;

(6) Whereas, after the second round of consultation, neither management nor labour have informed the Commission of their wish to initiate the process — possibly leading to an agreement — provided for in Article 4 of the same Agreement;

(7) Whereas, in accordance with Article 1 of the Agreement, the Community and the Member States have set themselves the objective, inter alia, of improving living and working conditions; whereas effective implementation of the principle of equal treatment for men and women would contribute to the achievement of that aim;

(8) Whereas the principle of equal treatment was stated in Article 119 of the Treaty, in Council Directive 75/117/EEC of 10 February 1975 on the approximation of the laws of the Member States relating to the application of the principle of equal pay for men and women and in Council Directive 76/207/EEC of 9 February 1976 on the implementation of the principle of equal treatment for men and women as regards access to employment, vocational training and promotion and working conditions;

(9) Whereas Council Directive 92/85/EEC of 19 October 1992 on the introduction of measures to encourage improvements in the safety and health at work of pregnant workers and workers who have recently given birth or are breastfeeding also contributes to the effective implementation of the principle of equal treatment for men and women; whereas that Directive should not work to the detriment of the aforementioned Directives on equal treatment; whereas, therefore, female workers covered by that Directive should likewise benefit from the adaptation of the rules on the burden of proof;

(10) Whereas Council Directive 96/34/EC of 3 June 1996 on the framework agreement on parental leave concluded by UNICE, CEEP and the ETUC, is also based on the principle of equal treatment for men and women;

(11) Whereas the references to 'judicial process' and 'court' cover mechanisms by means of which disputes may be submitted for examination and decision to independent bodies which may hand down decisions that are binding on the parties to those disputes;

(12) Whereas the expression 'out-of-court procedures' means in particular procedures such as conciliation and mediation;

(13) Whereas the appreciation of the facts from which it may be presumed that there has been direct or indirect discrimination is a matter for national judicial or other competent bodies, in accordance with national law or practice;

(14) Whereas it is for the Member States to introduce, at any appropriate stage of the proceedings, rules of evidence which are more favourable to plaintiffs;

(15) Whereas it is necessary to take account of the specific features of certain Member States' legal systems, inter alia where an inference of discrimination is drawn if the respondent fails to produce evidence that satisfies the court or other competent authority that there has been no breach of the principle of equal treatment;

(16) Whereas Member States need not apply the rules on the burden of proof to proceedings in which it is for the court or other competent body to investigate the facts of the case; whereas the procedures thus referred to are those in which the plaintiff is not required to prove the facts, which it is for the court or competent body to investigate;

(17) Whereas plaintiffs could be deprived of any effective means of enforcing the principle of equal treatment before the national courts if the effect of introducing evidence of an apparent discrimination were not to impose upon the respondent the burden of proving that his practice is not in fact discriminatory;

(18) Whereas the Court of Justice of the European Communities has therefore held that the rules on the burden of proof must be adapted when there is a prima facie case of discrimination and that, for the principle of equal treatment to be applied effectively, the burden of proof must shift back to the respondent when evidence of such discrimination is brought;

(19) Whereas it is all the more difficult to prove discrimination when it is indirect; whereas it is therefore important to define indirect discrimination;

(20) Whereas the aim of adequately adapting the rules on the burden of proof has not been achieved satisfactorily in all Member States and, in accordance with the principle of subsidiarity stated in Article 3b of the Treaty and with that of proportionality, that aim must be attained at Community level; whereas this Directive confines itself to the minimum action required and does not go beyond what is necessary for that purpose,

HAS ADOPTED THIS DIRECTIVE:

Article 1   Aim

The aim of this Directive shall be to ensure that the measures taken by the Member States to implement the principle of equal treatment are made more effective, in order to enable all persons who consider themselves wronged because the principle of equal treatment has not been applied to them to have their rights asserted by judicial process after possible recourse to other competent bodies.

Article 2   Definitions

1. For the purposes of this Directive, the principle of equal treatment shall mean that there shall be no discrimination whatsoever based on sex, either directly or indirectly.

2. For purposes of the principle of equal treatment referred to in paragraph 1, indirect discrimination shall exist where an apparently neutral provision, criterion or practice disadvantages a substantially higher proportion of the members of one sex unless that provision, criterion or practice is appropriate and necessary and can be justified by objective factors unrelated to sex.

Article 3   Scope

1. This Directive shall apply to:
    (a) the situations covered by Article 119 of the Treaty and by Directives 75/117/EEC, 76/207/EEC and, insofar as discrimination based on sex is concerned, 92/85/EEC and 96/34/EC;
    (b) any civil or administrative procedure concerning the public or private sector which provides for means of redress under national law pursuant to the measures referred to in (a) with the exception of out-of-court procedures of a voluntary nature or provided for in national law.

2. This Directive shall not apply to criminal procedures, unless otherwise provided by the Member States.

Article 4   Burden of proof

1. Member States shall take such measures as are necessary, in accordance with their national judicial systems, to ensure that, when persons who consider themselves wronged because the principle of equal treatment has not been applied to them establish, before a court or other competent authority, facts from which it may be presumed that there has been direct or indirect discrimination, it shall be for the respondent to prove that there has been no breach of the principle of equal treatment.

2. This Directive shall not prevent Member States from introducing rules of evidence which are more favourable to plaintiffs.

3. Member States need not apply paragraph 1 to proceedings in which it is for the court or competent body to investigate the facts of the case.

Article 5   Information

Member States shall ensure that measures taken pursuant to this Directive, together with the provisions already in force, are brought to the attention of all the persons concerned by all appropriate means.

Article 6   Non-regression

Implementation of this Directive shall under no circumstances be sufficient grounds for a reduction in the general level of protection of workers in the areas to which it applies, without prejudice to the Member States' right to respond to changes in the situation by introducing laws, regulations and administrative provisions which differ from those in force on the notification of this Directive, provided that the minimum requirements of this Directive are complied with.

Article 7   Implementation

The Member States shall bring into force the laws, regulations and administrative provisions necessary for them to comply with this Directive by 1 January 2001. They shall immediately inform the Commission thereof.

As regards the United Kingdom of Great Britain and Northern Ireland, the date of 1 January 2001 in paragraph 1 shall be replaced by 22 July 2001.

When the Member States adopt those measures they shall contain a reference to this Directive or shall be accompanied by such a reference on the occasion of their official publication. The methods of making such references shall be laid down by the Member States.

The Member States shall communicate to the Commission, within two years of the entry into force of this Directive, all the information necessary for the Commission to draw up a report to the European Parliament and the Council on the application of this Directive.

Article 8

This Directive is addressed to the Member States.

COUNCIL DIRECTIVE (EC) No 2000/43 of 29 JUNE 2000
implementing the principle of equal treatment between persons irrespective of racial or ethnic origin
[2000] OJ L180/22

THE COUNCIL OF THE EUROPEAN UNION,

Having regard to the Treaty establishing the European Community and in particular Article 13 thereof,

Having regard to the proposal from the Commission,

Having regard to the opinion of the European Parliament,

Having regard to the opinion of the Economic and Social Committee,

Having regard to the opinion of the Committee of the Regions,

Whereas:

(1) The Treaty on European Union marks a new stage in the process of creating an ever closer union among the peoples of Europe.

(2) In accordance with Article 6 of the Treaty on European Union, the European Union is founded on the principles of liberty, democracy, respect for human rights and fundamental freedoms, and the rule of law, principles which are common to the Member States, and should respect fundamental rights as guaranteed by the European Convention for the protection of Human Rights and Fundamental Freedoms and as they result from the constitutional traditions common to the Member States, as general principles of Community Law.

(3) The right to equality before the law and protection against discrimination for all persons constitutes a universal right recognised by the Universal Declaration of Human Rights, the United Nations Convention on the Elimination of all forms of Discrimination Against Women, the International Convention on the Elimination of all forms of Racial Discrimination and the United Nations Covenants on Civil and Political Rights and on Economic, Social and Cultural Rights and by the European Convention for the Protection of Human Rights and Fundamental Freedoms, to which all Member States are signatories.

(4) It is important to respect such fundamental rights and freedoms, including the right to freedom of association. It is also important, in the context of the access to and provision of goods and services, to respect the protection of private and family life and transactions carried out in this context.

(5) The European Parliament has adopted a number of Resolutions on the fight against racism in the European Union.

(6) The European Union rejects theories which attempt to determine the existence of separate human races. The use of the term 'racial origin' in this Directive does not imply an acceptance of such theories.

(7) The European Council in Tampere, on 15 and 16 October 1999, invited the Commission to come forward as soon as possible with proposals implementing Article 13 of the EC Treaty as regards the fight against racism and xenophobia.

(8) The Employment Guidelines 2000 agreed by the European Council in Helsinki, on 10 and 11 December 1999, stress the need to foster conditions for a socially inclusive labour market by formulating a coherent set of policies aimed at combating discrimination against groups such as ethnic minorities.

(9) Discrimination based on racial or ethnic origin may undermine the achievement of the objectives of the EC Treaty, in particular the attainment of a high level of employment and of social protection, the raising of the standard of living and quality of life, economic and social cohesion and solidarity. It may also undermine the objective of developing the European Union as an area of freedom, security and justice.

(10) The Commission presented a communication on racism, xenophobia and anti-Semitism in December 1995.

(11) The Council adopted on 15 July 1996 Joint Action (96/443/JHA) concerning action to combat racism and xenophobia under which the Member States undertake to ensure effective judicial cooperation in respect of offences based on racist or xenophobic behaviour.

(12) To ensure the development of democratic and tolerant societies which allow the participation of all persons irrespective of racial or ethnic origin, specific action in the field of discrimination based on racial or ethnic origin should go beyond access to employed and self-employed activities and cover areas such as education, social protection including social security and health-care, social advantages and access to and supply of goods and services.

(13) To this end, any direct or indirect discrimination based on racial or ethnic origin as regards the areas covered by this Directive should be prohibited throughout the Community. This prohibition of discrimination should also apply to nationals of third countries, but does not cover differences of treatment based on nationality and is without prejudice to provisions governing the entry and residence of third-country nationals and their access to employment and to occupation.

(14) In implementing the principle of equal treatment irrespective of racial or ethnic origin, the Community should, in accordance with Article 3(2) of the EC Treaty, aim to eliminate inequalities, and to promote equality between men and women, especially since women are often the victims of multiple discrimination.

(15) The appreciation of the facts from which it may be inferred that there has been direct or indirect discrimination is a matter for national judicial or other competent bodies, in accordance with rules of national law or practice. Such rules may provide in particular for indirect discrimination to be established by any means including on the basis of statistical evidence.

(16) It is important to protect all natural persons against discrimination on grounds of racial or ethnic origin. Member States should also provide, where appropriate and in accordance with their national traditions and practice, protection for legal persons where they suffer discrimination on grounds of the racial or ethnic origin of their members.

(17) The prohibition of discrimination should be without prejudice to the maintenance or adoption of measures intended to prevent or compensate for disadvantages suffered by a group of persons of a particular racial or ethnic origin, and such measures may permit organisations of persons of a particular racial or ethnic origin where their main object is the promotion of the special needs of those persons.

(18) In very limited circumstances, a difference of treatment may be justified where a characteristic related to racial or ethnic origin constitutes a genuine and determining occupational requirement, when the objective is legitimate and the requirement is proportionate. Such circumstances should be included in the information provided by the Member States to the Commission.

(19) Persons who have been subject to discrimination based on racial and ethnic origin should have adequate means of legal protection. To provide a more effective level of protection, associations or legal entities should also be empowered to engage, as the Member States so determine, either on behalf or in support of any victim, in proceedings, without prejudice to national rules of procedure concerning representation and defence before the courts.

(20) The effective implementation of the principle of equality requires adequate judicial protection against victimisation.

(21) The rules on the burden of proof must be adapted when there is a prima facie case of discrimination and, for the principle of equal treatment to be applied effectively, the burden of proof must shift back to the respondent when evidence of such discrimination is brought.

(22) Member States need not apply the rules on the burden of proof to proceedings in which it is for the court or other competent body to investigate the facts of the case. The procedures thus referred to are those in which the plaintiff is not required to prove the facts, which it is for the court or competent body to investigate.

(23) Member States should promote dialogue between the social partners and with non-governmental organisations to address different forms of discrimination and to combat them.

(24) Protection against discrimination based on racial or ethnic origin would itself be strengthened by the existence of a body or bodies in each Member State, with competence to analyse the problems involved, to study possible solutions and to provide concrete assistance for the victims.

(25) This Directive lays down minimum requirements, thus giving the Member States the option of introducing or maintaining more favourable provisions. The implementation of this Directive should not serve to justify any regression in relation to the situation which already prevails in each Member State.

(26) Member States should provide for effective, proportionate and dissuasive sanctions in case of breaches of the obligations under this Directive.

(27) The Member States may entrust management and labour, at their joint request, with the implementation of this Directive as regards provisions falling within the scope of collective agreements, provided that the Member States take all the necessary steps to ensure that they can at all times guarantee the results imposed by this Directive.

(28) In accordance with the principles of subsidiarity and proportionality as set out in Article 5 of the EC Treaty, the objective of this Directive, namely ensuring a common high level of protection against discrimination in all the Member States, cannot be sufficiently achieved by the Member States and can therefore, by reason of the scale and impact of the proposed action,

be better achieved by the Community. This Directive does not go beyond what is necessary in order to achieve those objectives,

HAS ADOPTED THIS DIRECTIVE:

CHAPTER I
GENERAL PROVISIONS

Article 1   Purpose

The purpose of this Directive is to lay down a framework for combating discrimination on the grounds of racial or ethnic origin, with a view to putting into effect in the Member States the principle of equal treatment.

Article 2   Concept of discrimination

1. For the purposes of this Directive, the principle of equal treatment shall mean that there shall be no direct or indirect discrimination based on racial or ethnic origin.
2. For the purposes of paragraph 1:
    (a) direct discrimination shall be taken to occur where one person is treated less favourably than another is, has been or would be treated in a comparable situation on grounds of racial or ethnic origin;
    (b) indirect discrimination shall be taken to occur where an apparently neutral provision, criterion or practice would put persons of a racial or ethnic origin at a particular disadvantage compared with other persons, unless that provision, criterion or practice is objectively justified by a legitimate aim and the means of achieving that aim are appropriate and necessary.
3. Harassment shall be deemed to be discrimination within the meaning of paragraph 1, when an unwanted conduct related to racial or ethnic origin takes place with the purpose or effect of violating the dignity of a person and of creating an intimidating, hostile, degrading, humiliating or offensive environment. In this context, the concept of harassment may be defined in accordance with the national laws and practice of the Member States.
4. An instruction to discriminate against persons on grounds of racial or ethnic origin shall be deemed to be discrimination within the meaning of paragraph 1.

Article 3   Scope

1. Within the limits of the powers conferred upon the Community, this Directive shall apply to all persons, as regards both the public and private sectors, including public bodies, in relation to:
    (a) conditions for access to employment, to self-employment and to occupation, including selection criteria and recruitment conditions, whatever the branch of activity and at all levels of the professional hierarchy, including promotion;
    (b) access to all types and to all levels of vocational guidance, vocational training, advanced vocational training and retraining, including practical work experience;
    (c) employment and working conditions, including dismissals and pay;
    (d) membership of and involvement in an organisation of workers or employers, or any organisation whose members carry on a particular profession, including the benefits provided for by such organisations;
    (e) social protection, including social security and healthcare;
    (f) social advantages;
    (g) education;
    (h) access to and supply of goods and services which are available to the public, including housing.
2. This Directive does not cover difference of treatment based on nationality and is without prejudice to provisions and conditions relating to the entry into and residence of third-country nationals and stateless persons on the territory of Member States, and to any treatment which arises from the legal status of the third-country nationals and stateless persons concerned.

Article 4   Genuine and determining occupational requirements

Notwithstanding Article 2(1) and (2), Member States may provide that a difference of treatment which is based on a characteristic related to racial or ethnic origin shall not constitute discrimination where, by reason of the nature of the particular occupational activities concerned or of the context in which they are carried out, such a characteristic constitutes a genuine and determining occupational requirement, provided that the objective is legitimate and the requirement is proportionate.

Article 5   Positive action

With a view to ensuring full equality in practice, the principle of equal treatment shall not prevent any Member State from maintaining or adopting specific measures to prevent or compensate for disadvantages linked to racial or ethnic origin.

Article 6   Minimum requirements

1.   Member States may introduce or maintain provisions which are more favourable to the protection of the principle of equal treatment than those laid down in this Directive.
2.   The implementation of this Directive shall under no circumstances constitute grounds for a reduction in the level of protection against discrimination already afforded by Member States in the fields covered by this Directive.

CHAPTER II

REMEDIES AND ENFORCEMENT

Article 7   Defence of rights

1.   Member States shall ensure that judicial and/or administrative procedures, including where they deem it appropriate conciliation procedures, for the enforcement of obligations under this Directive are available to all persons who consider themselves wronged by failure to apply the principle of equal treatment to them, even after the relationship in which the discrimination is alleged to have occurred has ended.
2.   Member States shall ensure that associations, organisations or other legal entities, which have, in accordance with the criteria laid down by their national law, a legitimate interest in ensuring that the provisions of this Directive are complied with, may engage, either on behalf or in support of the complainant, with his or her approval, in any judicial and/or administrative procedure provided for the enforcement of obligations under this Directive.
3.   Paragraphs 1 and 2 are without prejudice to national rules relating to time limits for bringing actions as regards the principle of equality of treatment.

Article 8   Burden of proof

1.   Member States shall take such measures as are necessary, in accordance with their national judicial systems, to ensure that, when persons who consider themselves wronged because the principle of equal treatment has not been applied to them establish, before a court or other competent authority, facts from which it may be presumed that there has been direct or indirect discrimination, it shall be for the respondent to prove that there has been no breach of the principle of equal treatment.
2.   Paragraph 1 shall not prevent Member States from introducing rules of evidence which are more favourable to plaintiffs.
3.   Paragraph 1 shall not apply to criminal procedures.
4.   Paragraphs 1, 2 and 3 shall also apply to any proceedings brought in accordance with Article 7(2).
5.   Member States need not apply paragraph 1 to proceedings in which it is for the court or competent body to investigate the facts of the case.

Article 9   Victimisation

Member States shall introduce into their national legal systems such measures as are necessary to protect individuals from any adverse treatment or adverse consequence as a reaction to a complaint or to proceedings aimed at enforcing compliance with the principle of equal treatment.

Article 10 Dissemination of information

Member States shall take care that the provisions adopted pursuant to this Directive, together with the relevant provisions already in force, are brought to the attention of the persons concerned by all appropriate means throughout their territory.

Article 11 Social dialogue

1.   Member States shall, in accordance with national traditions and practice, take adequate measures to promote the social dialogue between the two sides of industry with a view to fostering equal treatment, including through the monitoring of workplace practices, collective agreements, codes of conduct, research or exchange of experiences and good practices.

2.   Where consistent with national traditions and practice, Member States shall encourage the two sides of the industry without prejudice to their autonomy to conclude, at the appropriate level, agreements laying down anti-discrimination rules in the fields referred to in Article 3 which fall within the scope of collective bargaining. These agreements shall respect the minimum requirements laid down by this Directive and the relevant national implementing measures.

Article 12 Dialogue with non-governmental organisations

Member States shall encourage dialogue with appropriate non-governmental organisations which have, in accordance with their national law and practice, a legitimate interest in contributing to the fight against discrimination on grounds of racial and ethnic origin with a view to promoting the principle of equal treatment.

CHAPTER III

BODIES FOR THE PROMOTION OF EQUAL TREATMENT

Article 13

1.   Member States shall designate a body or bodies for the promotion of equal treatment of all persons without discrimination on the grounds of racial or ethnic origin. These bodies may form part of agencies charged at national level with the defence of human rights or the safeguard of individuals' rights.

2.   Member States shall ensure that the competences of these bodies include:

— without prejudice to the right of victims and of associations, organisations or other legal entities referred to in Article 7(2), providing independent assistance to victims of discrimination in pursuing their complaints about discrimination,

— conducting independent surveys concerning discrimination,

— publishing independent reports and making recommendations on any issue relating to such discrimination.

CHAPTER IV

FINAL PROVISIONS

Article 14 Compliance

Member States shall take the necessary measures to ensure that:

(a)   any laws, regulations and administrative provisions contrary to the principle of equal treatment are abolished;

(b)   any provisions contrary to the principle of equal treatment which are included in individual or collective contracts or agreements, internal rules of undertakings, rules governing profit-making or non-profit-making associations, and rules governing the independent professions and workers' and employers' organisations, are or may be declared, null and void or are amended.

Article 15 Sanctions

Member States shall lay down the rules on sanctions applicable to infringements of the national provisions adopted pursuant to this Directive and shall take all measures necessary to ensure that they are applied. The sanctions, which may comprise the payment of compensation to the victim, must be effective, proportionate and dissuasive. The Member States shall notify those provisions to the Commission by 19 July 2003 at the latest and shall notify it without delay of any subsequent amendment affecting them.

Article 16 Implementation

Member States shall adopt the laws, regulations and administrative provisions necessary to comply with this Directive by 19 July 2003 or may entrust management and labour, at their joint request, with the implementation of this Directive as regards provisions falling within the scope of collective agreements. In such cases, Member States shall ensure that by 19 July 2003, management and labour introduce the necessary measures by agreement, Member States being required to take any necessary measures to enable them at any time to be in a position to guarantee the results imposed by this Directive. They shall forthwith inform the Commission thereof.

When Member States adopt these measures, they shall contain a reference to this Directive or be accompanied by such a reference on the occasion of their official publication. The methods of making such a reference shall be laid down by the Member States.

Article 17 Report

1. Member States shall communicate to the Commission by 19 July 2005, and every five years thereafter, all the information necessary for the Commission to draw up a report to the European Parliament and the Council on the application of this Directive.

2. The Commission's report shall take into account, as appropriate, the views of the European Monitoring Centre on Racism and Xenophobia, as well as the viewpoints of the social partners and relevant non-governmental organisations. In accordance with the principle of gender mainstreaming, this report shall, inter alia, provide an assessment of the impact of the measures taken on women and men. In the light of the information received, this report shall include, if necessary, proposals to revise and update this Directive.

Article 18 Entry into force

This Directive shall enter into force on the day of its publication in the Official Journal of the European Communities.

Article 19 Addressees

This Directive is addressed to the Member States.

COUNCIL DIRECTIVE (EC) No 2000/78 of 27 NOVEMBER 2000 establishing a general framework for equal treatment in employment and occupation
[2000] OJ L303/16

THE COUNCIL OF THE EUROPEAN UNION,

Having regard to the Treaty establishing the European Community, and in particular Article 13 thereof,

Having regard to the proposal from the Commission,

Having regard to the Opinion of the European Parliament,

Having regard to the Opinion of the Economic and Social Committee,

Having regard to the Opinion of the Committee of the Regions,

Whereas:

(1) In accordance with Article 6 of the Treaty on European Union, the European Union is founded on the principles of liberty, democracy, respect for human rights and fundamental freedoms, and the rule of law, principles which are common to all Member States and it respects fundamental rights, as guaranteed by the European Convention for the Protection of Human Rights and Fundamental Freedoms and as they result from the constitutional traditions common to the Member States, as general principles of Community law.

(2) The principle of equal treatment between women and men is well established by an important body of Community law, in particular in Council Directive 76/207/EEC of 9 February 1976 on the implementation of the principle of equal treatment for men and women as regards access to employment, vocational training and promotion, and working conditions.

(3)   In implementing the principle of equal treatment, the Community should, in accordance with Article 3(2) of the EC Treaty, aim to eliminate inequalities, and to promote equality between men and women, especially since women are often the victims of multiple discrimination.

(4)   The right of all persons to equality before the law and protection against discrimination constitutes a universal right recognised by the Universal Declaration of Human Rights, the United Nations Convention on the Elimination of All Forms of Discrimination against Women, United Nations Covenants on Civil and Political Rights and on Economic, Social and Cultural Rights and by the European Convention for the Protection of Human Rights and Fundamental Freedoms, to which all Member States are signatories. Convention No 111 of the International Labour Organisation (ILO) prohibits discrimination in the field of employment and occupation.

(5)   It is important to respect such fundamental rights and freedoms. This Directive does not prejudice freedom of association, including the right to establish unions with others and to join unions to defend one's interests.

(6)   The Community Charter of the Fundamental Social Rights of Workers recognises the importance of combating every form of discrimination, including the need to take appropriate action for the social and economic integration of elderly and disabled people.

(7)   The EC Treaty includes among its objectives the promotion of coordination between employment policies of the Member States. To this end, a new employment chapter was incorporated in the EC Treaty as a means of developing a coordinated European strategy for employment to promote a skilled, trained and adaptable workforce.

(8)   The Employment Guidelines for 2000 agreed by the European Council at Helsinki on 10 and 11 December 1999 stress the need to foster a labour market favourable to social integration by formulating a coherent set of policies aimed at combating discrimination against groups such as persons with disability. They also emphasise the need to pay particular attention to supporting older workers, in order to increase their participation in the labour force.

(9)   Employment and occupation are key elements in guaranteeing equal opportunities for all and contribute strongly to the full participation of citizens in economic, cultural and social life and to realising their potential.

(10) On 29 June 2000 the Council adopted Directive 2000/43/EC implementing the principle of equal treatment between persons irrespective of racial or ethnic origin. That Directive already provides protection against such discrimination in the field of employment and occupation.

(11) Discrimination based on religion or belief, disability, age or sexual orientation may undermine the achievement of the objectives of the EC Treaty, in particular the attainment of a high level of employment and social protection, raising the standard of living and the quality of life, economic and social cohesion and solidarity, and the free movement of persons.

(12) To this end, any direct or indirect discrimination based on religion or belief, disability, age or sexual orientation as regards the areas covered by this Directive should be prohibited throughout the Community. This prohibition of discrimination should also apply to nationals of third countries but does not cover differences of treatment based on nationality and is without prejudice to provisions governing the entry and residence of third-country nationals and their access to employment and occupation.

(13) This Directive does not apply to social security and social protection schemes whose benefits are not treated as income within the meaning given to that term for the purpose of applying Article 141 of the EC Treaty, nor to any kind of payment by the State aimed at providing access to employment or maintaining employment.

(14) This Directive shall be without prejudice to national provisions laying down retirement ages. indirect discrimination is a matter for national judicial or other competent bodies, in accordance with rules of national law or practice. Such rules may provide, in particular, for indirect discrimination to be established by any means including on the basis of statistical evidence.

(15) The appreciation of the facts from which it may be inferred that there has been direct or (28) This Directive lays down minimum requirements, thus giving the Member States the option of introducing or maintaining more favourable provisions. The implementation of this Directive

should not serve to justify any regression in relation to the situation which already prevails in each Member State.

(16) The provision of measures to accommodate the needs of disabled people at the workplace plays an important role in combating discrimination on grounds of disability.

(17) This Directive does not require the recruitment, promotion, maintenance in employment or training of an individual who is not competent, capable and available to perform the essential functions of the post concerned or to undergo the relevant training, without prejudice to the obligation to provide reasonable accommodation for people with disabilities.

(18) This Directive does not require, in particular, the armed forces and the police, prison or emergency services to recruit or maintain in employment persons who do not have the required capacity to carry out the range of functions that they may be called upon to perform with regard to the legitimate objective of preserving the operational capacity of those services.

(19) Moreover, in order that the Member States may continue to safeguard the combat effectiveness of their armed forces, they may choose not to apply the provisions of this Directive concerning disability and age to all or part of their armed forces. The Member States which make that choice must define the scope of that derogation.

(20) Appropriate measures should be provided, i.e. effective and practical measures to adapt the workplace to the disability, for example adapting premises and equipment, patterns of working time, the distribution of tasks or the provision of training or integration resources.

(21) To determine whether the measures in question give rise to a disproportionate burden, account should be taken in particular of the financial and other costs entailed, the scale and financial resources of the organisation or undertaking and the possibility of obtaining public funding or any other assistance.

(22) This Directive is without prejudice to national laws on marital status and the benefits dependent thereon.

(23) In very limited circumstances, a difference of treatment may be justified where a characteristic related to religion or belief, disability, age or sexual orientation constitutes a genuine and determining occupational requirement, when the objective is legitimate and the requirement is proportionate. Such circumstances should be included in the information provided by the Member States to the Commission.

(24) The European Union in its Declaration No 11 on the status of churches and non-confessional organisations, annexed to the Final Act of the Amsterdam Treaty, has explicitly recognised that it respects and does not prejudice the status under national law of churches and religious associations or communities in the Member States and that it equally respects the status of philosophical and non-confessional organisations. With this in view, Member States may maintain or lay down specific provisions on genuine, legitimate and justified occupational requirements which might be required for carrying out an occupational activity.

(25) The prohibition of age discrimination is an essential part of meeting the aims set out in the Employment Guidelines and encouraging diversity in the workforce. However, differences in treatment in connection with age may be justified under certain circumstances and therefore require specific provisions which may vary in accordance with the situation in Member States. It is therefore essential to distinguish between differences in treatment which are justified, in particular by legitimate employment policy, labour market and vocational training objectives, and discrimination which must be prohibited.

(26) The prohibition of discrimination should be without prejudice to the maintenance or adoption of measures intended to prevent or compensate for disadvantages suffered by a group of persons of a particular religion or belief, disability, age or sexual orientation, and such measures may permit organisations of persons of a particular religion or belief, disability, age or sexual orientation where their main object is the promotion of the special needs of those persons.

(27) In its Recommendation 86/379/EEC of 24 July 1986 on the employment of disabled people in the Community, the Council established a guideline framework setting out examples of

positive action to promote the employment and training of disabled people, and in its Resolution of 17 June 1999 on equal employment opportunities for people with disabilities, affirmed the importance of giving specific attention inter alia to recruitment, retention, training and lifelong learning with regard to disabled persons.

(29) Persons who have been subject to discrimination based on religion or belief, disability, age or sexual orientation should have adequate means of legal protection. To provide a more effective level of protection, associations or legal entities should also be empowered to engage in proceedings, as the Member States so determine, either on behalf or in support of any victim, without prejudice to national rules of procedure concerning representation and defence before the courts.

(30) The effective implementation of the principle of equality requires adequate judicial protection against victimisation.

(31) The rules on the burden of proof must be adapted when there is a prima facie case of discrimination and, for the principle of equal treatment to be applied effectively, the burden of proof must shift back to the respondent when evidence of such discrimination is brought. However, it is not for the respondent to prove that the plaintiff adheres to a particular religion or belief, has a particular disability, is of a particular age or has a particular sexual orientation.

(32) Member States need not apply the rules on the burden of proof to proceedings in which it is for the court or other competent body to investigate the facts of the case. The procedures thus referred to are those in which the plaintiff is not required to prove the facts, which it is for the court or competent body to investigate.

(33) Member States should promote dialogue between the social partners and, within the framework of national practice, with non-governmental organisations to address different forms of discrimination at the workplace and to combat them.

(34) The need to promote peace and reconciliation between the major communities in Northern Ireland necessitates the incorporation of particular provisions into this Directive.

(35) Member States should provide for effective, proportionate and dissuasive sanctions in case of breaches of the obligations under this Directive.

(36) Member States may entrust the social partners, at their joint request, with the implementation of this Directive, as regards the provisions concerning collective agreements, provided they take any necessary steps to ensure that they are at all times able to guarantee the results required by this Directive.

(37) In accordance with the principle of subsidiarity set out in Article 5 of the EC Treaty, the objective of this Directive, namely the creation within the Community of a level playing-field as regards equality in employment and occupation, cannot be sufficiently achieved by the Member States and can therefore, by reason of the scale and impact of the action, be better achieved at Community level. In accordance with the principle of proportionality, as set out in that Article, this Directive does not go beyond what is necessary in order to achieve that objective,

HAS ADOPTED THIS DIRECTIVE:

CHAPTER I

GENERAL PROVISIONS

Article 1   Purpose

The purpose of this Directive is to lay down a general framework for combating discrimination on the grounds of religion or belief, disability, age or sexual orientation as regards employment and occupation, with a view to putting into effect in the Member States the principle of equal treatment.

Article 2   Concept of discrimination

1. For the purposes of this Directive, the 'principle of equal treatment' shall mean that there shall be no direct or indirect discrimination whatsoever on any of the grounds referred to in Article 1.

2. For the purposes of paragraph 1:

(a)   direct discrimination shall be taken to occur where one person is treated less favourably than another is, has been or would be treated in a comparable situation, on any of the grounds referred to in Article 1;

(b)   indirect discrimination shall be taken to occur where an apparently neutral provision, criterion or practice would put persons having a particular religion or belief, a particular disability, a particular age, or a particular sexual orientation at a particular disadvantage compared with other persons unless:

    (i)   that provision, criterion or practice is objectively justified by a legitimate aim and the means of achieving that aim are appropriate and necessary, or

    (ii)   as regards persons with a particular disability, the employer or any person or organisation to whom this Directive applies, is obliged, under national legislation, to take appropriate measures in line with the principles contained in Article 5 in order to eliminate disadvantages entailed by such provision, criterion or practice.

3.   Harassment shall be deemed to be a form of discrimination within the meaning of paragraph 1, when unwanted conduct related to any of the grounds referred to in Article 1 takes place with the purpose or effect of violating the dignity of a person and of creating an intimidating, hostile, degrading, humiliating or offensive environment. In this context, the concept of harassment may be defined in accordance with the national laws and practice of the Member States.

4.   An instruction to discriminate against persons on any of the grounds referred to in Article 1 shall be deemed to be discrimination within the meaning of paragraph 1.

5.   This Directive shall be without prejudice to measures laid down by national law which, in a democratic society, are necessary for public security, for the maintenance of public order and the prevention of criminal offences, for the protection of health and for the protection of the rights and freedoms of others.

Article 3   Scope

1.   Within the limits of the areas of competence conferred on the Community, this Directive shall apply to all persons, as regards both the public and private sectors, including public bodies, in relation to:

(a)   conditions for access to employment, to self-employment or to occupation, including selection criteria and recruitment conditions, whatever the branch of activity and at all levels of the professional hierarchy, including promotion;

(b)   access to all types and to all levels of vocational guidance, vocational training, advanced vocational training and retraining, including practical work experience;

(c)   employment and working conditions, including dismissals and pay;

(d)   membership of, and involvement in, an organisation of workers or employers, or any organisation whose members carry on a particular profession, including the benefits provided for by such organisations.

2.   This Directive does not cover differences of treatment based on nationality and is without prejudice to provisions and conditions relating to the entry into and residence of third-country nationals and stateless persons in the territory of Member States, and to any treatment which arises from the legal status of the third-country nationals and stateless persons concerned.

3.   This Directive does not apply to payments of any kind made by state schemes or similar, including state social security or social protection schemes.

4.   Member States may provide that this Directive, in so far as it relates to discrimination on the grounds of disability and age, shall not apply to the armed forces.

Article 4   Occupational requirements

1.   Notwithstanding Article 2(1) and (2), Member States may provide that a difference of treatment which is based on a characteristic related to any of the grounds referred to in Article 1 shall not constitute discrimination where, by reason of the nature of the particular occupational activities concerned or of the context in which they are carried out, such a

characteristic constitutes a genuine and determining occupational requirement, provided that the objective is legitimate and the requirement is proportionate.

2.   Member States may maintain national legislation in force at the date of adoption of this Directive or provide for future legislation incorporating national practices existing at the date of adoption of this Directive pursuant to which, in the case of occupational activities within churches and other public or private organisations the ethos of which is based on religion or belief, a difference of treatment based on a person's religion or belief shall not constitute discrimination where, by reason of the nature of these activities or of the context in which they are carried out, a person's religion or belief constitute a genuine, legitimate and justified occupational requirement, having regard to the organisation's ethos. This difference of treatment shall be implemented taking account of Member States' constitutional provisions and principles, as well as the general principles of Community law, and should not justify discrimination on another ground.

Provided that its provisions are otherwise complied with, this Directive shall thus not prejudice the right of churches and other public or private organisations, the ethos of which is based on religion or belief, acting in conformity with national constitutions and laws, to require individuals working for them to act in good faith and with loyalty to the organisation's ethos.

Article 5   Reasonable accommodation for disabled persons

In order to guarantee compliance with the principle of equal treatment in relation to persons with disabilities, reasonable accommodation shall be provided. This means that employers shall take appropriate measures, where needed in a particular case, to enable a person with a disability to have access to, participate in, or advance in employment, or to undergo training, unless such measures would impose a disproportionate burden on the employer. This burden shall not be disproportionate when it is sufficiently remedied by measures existing within the framework of the disability policy of the Member State concerned.

Article 6   Justification of differences of treatment on grounds of age

1.   Notwithstanding Article 2(2), Member States may provide that differences of treatment on grounds of age shall not constitute discrimination, if, within the context of national law, they are objectively and reasonably justified by a legitimate aim, including legitimate employment policy, labour market and vocational training objectives, and if the means of achieving that aim are appropriate and necessary. Such differences of treatment may include, among others:

   (a)   the setting of special conditions on access to employment and vocational training, employment and occupation, including dismissal and remuneration conditions, for young people, older workers and persons with caring responsibilities in order to promote their vocational integration or ensure their protection;

   (b)   the fixing of minimum conditions of age, professional experience or seniority in service for access to employment or to certain advantages linked to employment;

   (c)   the fixing of a maximum age for recruitment which is based on the training requirements of the post in question or the need for a reasonable period of employment before retirement.

2.   Notwithstanding Article 2(2), Member States may provide that the fixing for occupational social security schemes of ages for admission or entitlement to retirement or invalidity benefits, including the fixing under those schemes of different ages for employees or groups or categories of employees, and the use, in the context of such schemes, of age criteria in actuarial calculations, does not constitute discrimination on the grounds of age, provided this does not result in discrimination on the grounds of sex.

Article 7   Positive action

1.   With a view to ensuring full equality in practice, the principle of equal treatment shall not prevent any Member State from maintaining or adopting specific measures to prevent or compensate for disadvantages linked to any of the grounds referred to in Article 1.

2.   With regard to disabled persons, the principle of equal treatment shall be without prejudice to the right of Member States to maintain or adopt provisions on the protection of health and safety at work or to measures aimed at creating or maintaining provisions or facilities for safeguarding or promoting their integration into the working environment.

Article 8   Minimum requirements

1.   Member States may introduce or maintain provisions which are more favourable to the protection of the principle of equal treatment than those laid down in this Directive.
2.   The implementation of this Directive shall under no circumstances constitute grounds for a reduction in the level of protection against discrimination already afforded by Member States in the fields covered by this Directive.

CHAPTER II
REMEDIES AND ENFORCEMENT

Article 9   Defence of rights

1.   Member States shall ensure that judicial and/or administrative procedures, including where they deem it appropriate conciliation procedures, for the enforcement of obligations under this Directive are available to all persons who consider themselves wronged by failure to apply the principle of equal treatment to them, even after the relationship in which the discrimination is alleged to have occurred has ended.
2.   Member States shall ensure that associations, organisations or other legal entities which have, in accordance with the criteria laid down by their national law, a legitimate interest in ensuring that the provisions of this Directive are complied with, may engage, either on behalf or in support of the complainant, with his or her approval, in any judicial and/or administrative procedure provided for the enforcement of obligations under this Directive.
3.   Paragraphs 1 and 2 are without prejudice to national rules relating to time limits for bringing actions as regards the principle of equality of treatment.

Article 10   Burden of proof

1.   Member States shall take such measures as are necessary, in accordance with their national judicial systems, to ensure that, when persons who consider themselves wronged because the principle of equal treatment has not been applied to them establish, before a court or other competent authority, facts from which it may be presumed that there has been direct or indirect discrimination, it shall be for the respondent to prove that there has been no breach of the principle of equal treatment.
2.   Paragraph 1 shall not prevent Member States from introducing rules of evidence which are more favourable to plaintiffs.
3.   Paragraph 1 shall not apply to criminal procedures.
4.   Paragraphs 1, 2 and 3 shall also apply to any legal proceedings commenced in accordance with Article 9(2).
5.   Member States need not apply paragraph 1 to proceedings in which it is for the court or competent body to investigate the facts of the case.

Article 11   Victimisation

Member States shall introduce into their national legal systems such measures as are necessary to protect employees against dismissal or other adverse treatment by the employer as a reaction to a complaint within the undertaking or to any legal proceedings aimed at enforcing compliance with the principle of equal treatment.

Article 12   Dissemination of information

Member States shall take care that the provisions adopted pursuant to this Directive, together with the relevant provisions already in force in this field, are brought to the attention of the persons concerned by all appropriate means, for example at the workplace, throughout their territory.

Article 13 Social dialogue

1. Member States shall, in accordance with their national traditions and practice, take adequate measures to promote dialogue between the social partners with a view to fostering equal treatment, including through the monitoring of workplace practices, collective agreements, codes of conduct and through research or exchange of experiences and good practices.

2. Where consistent with their national traditions and practice, Member States shall encourage the social partners, without prejudice to their autonomy, to conclude at the appropriate level agreements laying down anti-discrimination rules in the fields referred to in Article 3 which fall within the scope of collective bargaining. These agreements shall respect the minimum requirements laid down by this Directive and by the relevant national implementing measures.

Article 14 Dialogue with non-governmental organisations

Member States shall encourage dialogue with appropriate non-governmental organisations which have, in accordance with their national law and practice, a legitimate interest in contributing to the fight against discrimination on any of the grounds referred to in Article 1 with a view to promoting the principle of equal treatment.

CHAPTER III
PARTICULAR PROVISIONS

Article 15 Northern Ireland

1. In order to tackle the under-representation of one of the major religious communities in the police service of Northern Ireland, differences in treatment regarding recruitment into that service, including its support staff, shall not constitute discrimination insofar as those differences in treatment are expressly authorised by national legislation.

2. In order to maintain a balance of opportunity in employment for teachers in Northern Ireland while furthering the reconciliation of historical divisions between the major religious communities there, the provisions on religion or belief in this Directive shall not apply to the recruitment of teachers in schools in Northern Ireland in so far as this is expressly authorised by national legislation.

CHAPTER IV
FINAL PROVISIONS

Article 16 Compliance

Member States shall take the necessary measures to ensure that:

(a) any laws, regulations and administrative provisions contrary to the principle of equal treatment are abolished;

(b) any provisions contrary to the principle of equal treatment which are included in contracts or collective agreements, internal rules of undertakings or rules governing the independent occupations and professions and workers' and employers' organisations are, or may be, declared null and void or are amended.

Article 17 Sanctions

Member States shall lay down the rules on sanctions applicable to infringements of the national provisions adopted pursuant to this Directive and shall take all measures necessary to ensure that they are applied. The sanctions, which may comprise the payment of compensation to the victim, must be effective, proportionate and dissuasive. Member States shall notify those provisions to the Commission by 2 December 2003 at the latest and shall notify it without delay of any subsequent amendment affecting them.

Article 18 Implementation

Member States shall adopt the laws, regulations and administrative provisions necessary to comply with this Directive by 2 December 2003 at the latest or may entrust the social partners, at their joint request, with the implementation of this Directive as regards provisions concerning collective agreements. In such cases, Member States shall ensure that, no later than 2 December 2003, the social partners introduce the necessary measures by agreement, the Member States concerned being required to take any necessary measures to enable them at any time to be in a position to guarantee the results imposed by this Directive. They shall forthwith inform the Commission thereof.

In order to take account of particular conditions, Member States may, if necessary, have an additional period of 3 years from 2 December 2003, that is to say a total of 6 years, to implement the provisions of this Directive on age and disability discrimination. In that event they shall inform the Commission forthwith. Any Member State which chooses to use this additional period shall report annually to the Commission on the steps it is taking to tackle age and disability discrimination and on the progress it is making towards implementation. The Commission shall report annually to the Council.

When Member States adopt these measures, they shall contain a reference to this Directive or be accompanied by such reference on the occasion of their official publication. The methods of making such reference shall be laid down by Member States.

Article 19 Report

1. Member States shall communicate to the Commission, by 2 December 2005 at the latest and every five years thereafter, all the information necessary for the Commission to draw up a report to the European Parliament and the Council on the application of this Directive.

2. The Commission's report shall take into account, as appropriate, the viewpoints of the social partners and relevant non-governmental organisations. In accordance with the principle of gender mainstreaming, this report shall, inter alia, provide an assessment of the impact of the measures taken on women and men. In the light of the information received, this report shall include, if necessary, proposals to revise and update this Directive.

Article 20 Entry into force

This Directive shall enter into force on the day of its publication in the Official Journal of the European Communities.

Article 21 Addressees

This Directive is addressed to the Member States.

EMPLOYMENT: WORKER PROTECTION

COUNCIL DIRECTIVE (EC) No 2001/23 of 12 MARCH 2001
on the approximation of the laws of the Member States relating to the safeguarding of employees' rights in the event of transfers of undertakings, businesses or parts of undertakings or businesses
[2001] OJ L82/16

THE COUNCIL OF THE EUROPEAN UNION,

Having regard to the Treaty establishing the European Community, and in particular Article 94 thereof,

Having regard to the proposal from the Commission,

Having regard to the opinion of the European Parliament,

Having regard to the opinion of the Economic and Social Committee,

Whereas:

(1) Council Directive 77/187/EEC of 14 February 1977 on the approximation of the laws of the Member States relating to the safeguarding of employees' rights in the event of transfers of undertakings, businesses or parts of undertakings or businesses has been substantially amended. In the interests of clarity and rationality, it should therefore be codified.

(2) Economic trends are bringing in their wake, at both national and Community level, changes in the structure of undertakings, through transfers of undertakings, businesses or parts of undertakings or businesses to other employers as a result of legal transfers or mergers.

(3) It is necessary to provide for the protection of employees in the event of a change of employer, in particular, to ensure that their rights are safeguarded.

(4) Differences still remain in the Member States as regards the extent of the protection of employees in this respect and these differences should be reduced.

(5) The Community Charter of the Fundamental Social Rights of Workers adopted on 9 December 1989 ('Social Charter') states, in points 7, 17 and 18 in particular that: 'The completion of the internal market must lead to an improvement in the living and working conditions of workers in the European Community. The improvement must cover, where necessary, the development of certain aspects of employment regulations such as procedures for collective redundancies and those regarding bankruptcies. Information, consultation and participation for workers must be developed along appropriate lines, taking account of the practice in force in the various Member States. Such information, consultation and participation must be implemented in due time, particularly in connection with restructuring operations in undertakings or in cases of mergers having an impact on the employment of workers'.

(6) In 1977 the Council adopted Directive 77/187/EEC to promote the harmonisation of the relevant national laws ensuring the safeguarding of the rights of employees and requiring transferors and transferees to inform and consult employees' representatives in good time.

(7) That Directive was subsequently amended in the light of the impact of the internal market, the legislative tendencies of the Member States with regard to the rescue of undertakings in economic difficulties, the case-law of the Court of Justice of the European Communities, Council Directive 75/129/EEC of 17 February 1975 on the approximation of the laws of the Member States relating to collective redundancies and the legislation already in force in most Member States.

(8) Considerations of legal security and transparency required that the legal concept of transfer be clarified in the light of the case-law of the Court of Justice. Such clarification has not altered the scope of Directive 77/187/EEC as interpreted by the Court of Justice.

(9) The Social Charter recognises the importance of the fight against all forms of discrimination, especially based on sex, colour, race, opinion and creed.

(10) This Directive should be without prejudice to the time limits set out in Annex I Part B within which the Member States are to comply with Directive 77/187/EEC, and the act amending it,

HAS ADOPTED THIS DIRECTIVE:

CHAPTER I
SCOPE AND DEFINITIONS

Article 1

1. (a) This Directive shall apply to any transfer of an undertaking, business, or part of an undertaking or business to another employer as a result of a legal transfer or merger.

    (b) Subject to subparagraph (a) and the following provisions of this Article, there is a transfer within the meaning of this Directive where there is a transfer of an economic entity which retains its identity, meaning an organised grouping of resources which has the objective of pursuing an economic activity, whether or not that activity is central or ancillary.

    (c) This Directive shall apply to public and private undertakings engaged in economic activities whether or not they are operating for gain. An administrative reorganisation of public administrative authorities, or the transfer of administrative functions between public administrative authorities, is not a transfer within the meaning of this Directive.

2. This Directive shall apply where and in so far as the undertaking, business or part of the undertaking or business to be transferred is situated within the territorial scope of the Treaty.

3. This Directive shall not apply to seagoing vessels.

Article 2

1. For the purposes of this Directive:

    (a) 'transferor' shall mean any natural or legal person who, by reason of a transfer within the meaning of Article 1(1), ceases to be the employer in respect of the undertaking, business or part of the undertaking or business;

    (b) 'transferee' shall mean any natural or legal person who, by reason of a transfer within the meaning of Article 1(1), becomes the employer in respect of the undertaking, business or part of the undertaking or business;

    (c) 'representatives of employees' and related expressions shall mean the representatives of the employees provided for by the laws or practices of the Member States;

    (d) 'employee' shall mean any person who, in the Member State concerned, is protected as an employee under national employment law.

2. This Directive shall be without prejudice to national law as regards the definition of contract of employment or employment relationship. However, Member States shall not exclude from the scope of this Directive contracts of employment or employment relationships solely because:

    (a) of the number of working hours performed or to be performed,

    (b) they are employment relationships governed by a fixed-duration contract of employment within the meaning of Article 1(1) of Council Directive 91/383/EEC of 25 June 1991 supplementing the measures to encourage improvements in the safety and health at work of workers with a fixed-duration employment relationship or a temporary employment relationship, or

    (c) they are temporary employment relationships within the meaning of Article 1(2) of Directive 91/383/EEC, and the undertaking, business or part of the undertaking or business transferred is, or is part of, the temporary employment business which is the employer.

CHAPTER II
SAFEGUARDING OF EMPLOYEES' RIGHTS

Article 3

1. The transferor's rights and obligations arising from a contract of employment or from an employment relationship existing on the date of a transfer shall, by reason of such transfer, be transferred to the transferee.

    Member States may provide that, after the date of transfer, the transferor and the transferee shall be jointly and severally liable in respect of obligations which arose before the date of transfer from a contract of employment or an employment relationship existing on the date of the transfer.

2. Member States may adopt appropriate measures to ensure that the transferor notifies the transferee of all the rights and obligations which will be transferred to the transferee under this Article, so far as those rights and obligations are or ought to have been known to the transferor at the time of the transfer. A failure by the transferor to notify the transferee of any such right or obligation shall not affect the transfer of that right or obligation and the rights of any employees against the transferee and/or transferor in respect of that right or obligation.

3. Following the transfer, the transferee shall continue to observe the terms and conditions agreed in any collective agreement on the same terms applicable to the transferor under that agreement, until the date of termination or expiry of the collective agreement or the entry into force or application of another collective agreement. Member States may limit the period for observing such terms and conditions with the proviso that it shall not be less than one year.

4. (a) Unless Member States provide otherwise, paragraphs 1 and 3 shall not apply in relation to employees' rights to old-age, invalidity or survivors' benefits under supplementary company or intercompany pension schemes outside the statutory social security schemes in Member States.

(b) Even where they do not provide in accordance with subparagraph (a) that paragraphs 1 and 3 apply in relation to such rights, Member States shall adopt the measures necessary to protect the interests of employees and of persons no longer employed in the transferor's business at the time of the transfer in respect of rights conferring on them immediate or prospective entitlement to old age benefits, including survivors' benefits, under supplementary schemes referred to in subparagraph (a).

Article 4

1. The transfer of the undertaking, business or part of the undertaking or business shall not in itself constitute grounds for dismissal by the transferor or the transferee. This provision shall not stand in the way of dismissals that may take place for economic, technical or organisational reasons entailing changes in the workforce. Member States may provide that the first subparagraph shall not apply to certain specific categories of employees who are not covered by the laws or practice of the Member States in respect of protection against dismissal.

2. If the contract of employment or the employment relationship is terminated because the transfer involves a substantial change in working conditions to the detriment of the employee, the employer shall be regarded as having been responsible for termination of the contract of employment or of the employment relationship.

Article 5

1. Unless Member States provide otherwise, Articles 3 and 4 shall not apply to any transfer of an undertaking, business or part of an undertaking or business where the transferor is the subject of bankruptcy proceedings or any analogous insolvency proceedings which have been instituted with a view to the liquidation of the assets of the transferor and are under the supervision of a competent public authority (which may be an insolvency practitioner authorised by a competent public authority).

2. Where Articles 3 and 4 apply to a transfer during insolvency proceedings which have been opened in relation to a transferor (whether or not those proceedings have been instituted with a view to the liquidation of the assets of the transferor) and provided that such proceedings are under the supervision of a competent public authority (which may be an insolvency practitioner determined by national law) a Member State may provide that:

(a) notwithstanding Article 3(1), the transferor's debts arising from any contracts of employment or employment relationships and payable before the transfer or before the opening of the insolvency proceedings shall not be transferred to the transferee, provided that such proceedings give rise, under the law of that Member State, to protection at least equivalent to that provided for in situations covered by Council Directive 80/987/EEC of 20 October 1980 on the approximation of the laws of the Member States relating to the protection of employees in the event of the insolvency of their employer, and, or alternatively, that,

(b)   the transferee, transferor or person or persons exercising the transferor's functions, on the one hand, and the representatives of the employees on the other hand may agree alterations, in so far as current law or practice permits, to the employees' terms and conditions of employment designed to safeguard employment opportunities by ensuring the survival of the undertaking, business or part of the undertaking or business.

3.   A Member State may apply paragraph 20(b) to any transfers where the transferor is in a situation of serious economic crisis, as defined by national law, provided that the situation is declared by a competent public authority and open to judicial supervision, on condition that such provisions already existed in national law on 17 July 1998.

The Commission shall present a report on the effects of this provision before 17 July 2003 and shall submit any appropriate proposals to the Council.

4.   Member States shall take appropriate measures with a view to preventing misuse of insolvency proceedings in such a way as to deprive employees of the rights provided for in this Directive.

Article 6

1.   If the undertaking, business or part of an undertaking or business preserves its autonomy, the status and function of the representatives or of the representation of the employees affected by the transfer shall be preserved on the same terms and subject to the same conditions as existed before the date of the transfer by virtue of law, regulation, administrative provision or agreement, provided that the conditions necessary for the constitution of the employee's representation are fulfilled.

The first subparagraph shall not apply if, under the laws, regulations, administrative provisions or practice in the Member States, or by agreement with the representatives of the employees, the conditions necessary for the reappointment of the representatives of the employees or for the reconstitution of the representation of the employees are fulfilled.

Where the transferor is the subject of bankruptcy proceedings or any analogous insolvency proceedings which have been instituted with a view to the liquidation of the assets of the transferor and are under the supervision of a competent public authority (which may be an insolvency practitioner authorised by a competent public authority), Member States may take the necessary measures to ensure that the transferred employees are properly represented until the new election or designation of representatives of the employees.

If the undertaking, business or part of an undertaking or business does not preserve its autonomy, the Member States shall take the necessary measures to ensure that the employees transferred who were represented before the transfer continue to be properly represented during the period necessary for the reconstitution or reappointment of the representation of employees in accordance with national law or practice.

2.   If the term of office of the representatives of the employees affected by the transfer expires as a result of the transfer, the representatives shall continue to enjoy the protection provided by the laws, regulations, administrative provisions or practice of the Member States.

CHAPTER III
INFORMATION AND CONSULTATION

Article 7

1.   The transferor and transferee shall be required to inform the representatives of their respective employees affected by the transfer of the following:
— the date or proposed date of the transfer,
— the reasons for the transfer,
— the legal, economic and social implications of the transfer for the employees,
— any measures envisaged in relation to the employees. The transferor must give such information to the representatives of his employees in good time, before the transfer is carried out.

The transferee must give such information to the representatives of his employees in good time, and in any event before his employees are directly affected by the transfer as regards their conditions of work and employment.

2.   Where the transferor or the transferee envisages measures in relation to his employees, he shall consult the representatives of his employees in good time on such measures with a view to reaching an agreement.

3.   Member States whose laws, regulations or administrative provisions provide that representatives of the employees may have recourse to an arbitration board to obtain a decision on the measures to be taken in relation to employees may limit the obligations laid down in paragraphs 1 and 2 to cases where the transfer carried out gives rise to a change in the business likely to entail serious disadvantages for a considerable number of the employees. The information and consultations shall cover at least the measures envisaged in relation to the employees.

The information must be provided and consultations take place in good time before the change in the business as referred to in the first subparagraph is effected.

4.   The obligations laid down in this Article shall apply irrespective of whether the decision resulting in the transfer is taken by the employer or an undertaking controlling the employer. In considering alleged breaches of the information and consultation requirements laid down by this Directive, the argument that such a breach occurred because the information was not provided by an undertaking controlling the employer shall not be accepted as an excuse.

5.   Member States may limit the obligations laid down in paragraphs 1, 2 and 3 to undertakings or businesses which, in terms of the number of employees, meet the conditions for the election or nomination of a collegiate body representing the employees.

6.   Member States shall provide that, where there are no representatives of the employees in an undertaking or business through no fault of their own, the employees concerned must be informed in advance of:
— the date or proposed date of the transfer,
— the reason for the transfer,
— the legal, economic and social implications of the transfer for the employees,
— any measures envisaged in relation to the employees.

CHAPTER IV
FINAL PROVISIONS

Article 8

This Directive shall not affect the right of Member States to apply or introduce laws, regulations or administrative provisions which are more favourable to employees or to promote or permit collective agreements or agreements between social partners more favourable to employees.

Article 9

Member States shall introduce into their national legal systems such measures as are necessary to enable all employees and representatives of employees who consider themselves wronged by failure to comply with the obligations arising from this Directive to pursue their claims by judicial process after possible recourse to other competent authorities.

Article 10

The Commission shall submit to the Council an analysis of the effect of the provisions of this Directive before 17 July 2006. It shall propose any amendment which may seem necessary.

Article 11

Member States shall communicate to the Commission the texts of the laws, regulations and administrative provisions which they adopt in the field covered by this Directive.

Article 12

Directive 77/187/EEC, as amended by the Directive referred to in Annex I, Part A, is repealed, without prejudice to the obligations of the Member States concerning the time limits for implementation set out in Annex I, Part B.

References to the repealed Directive shall be construed as references to this Directive and shall be read in accordance with the correlation table in Annex II.

Article 13

This Directive shall enter into force on the 20th day following its publication in the Official Journal of the European Communities.

Article 14

This Directive is addressed to the Member States.

ANNEX I

PART A

Repealed Directive and its amending Directive (referred to in Article 12)
Council Directive 77/187/EEC (OJ L61, 5.3.1977, p. 26)
Council Directive 98/50/EC (OJ L201, 17.7.1998, p. 88)

PART B

Deadlines for transposition into national law (referred to in Article 12)

Directive	Deadline for transposition
77/187/EEC	16 February 1979
98/50/EC 17	July 2001

ANNEX II

CORRELATION TABLE

Directive 77/187/EEC Article 1 This Directive	Article 1
Directive 77/187/EEC Article 2 This Directive	Article 2
Directive 77/187/EEC Article 3 This Directive	Article 3
Directive 77/187/EEC Article 4 This Directive	Article 4
Directive 77/187/EEC Article 4a This Directive	Article 5
Directive 77/187/EEC Article 5 This Directive	Article 6
Directive 77/187/EEC Article 6 This Directive	Article 7
Directive 77/187/EEC Article 7 This Directive	Article 8
Directive 77/187/EEC Article 7a This Directive	Article 9
Directive 77/187/EEC Article 7b This Directive	Article 10
Directive 77/187/EEC Article 7 This Directive	Article 9
Directive 77/187/EEC Article 7 This Directive	Article 10
Directive 77/187/EEC Article 8 This Directive	Article 11

Directive 77/187/EEC — This Directive	Article 12
Directive 77/187/EEC — This Directive	Article 13
Directive 77/187/EEC — This Directive	Article 14
Directive 77/187/EEC — This Directive	ANNEX I
Directive 77/187/EEC — This Directive	ANNEX II

COUNCIL DIRECTIVE (EEC) No 80/987 of 20 OCTOBER 1980
on the protection of employees in the event of the insolvency of their employer
[1980] OJ L283/23

SECTION I

SCOPE AND DEFINITIONS

Article 1

1. This Directive shall apply to employees' claims arising from contracts of employment or employment relationships and existing against employers who are in a state of insolvency within the meaning of Article 2(1).

2. Member States may, by way of exception, exclude claims by certain categories of employee from the scope of this Directive, by virtue of the existence of other forms of guarantee if it is established that these offer the persons concerned a degree of protection equivalent to that resulting from this Directive.

3. Where such provision already applies in their national legislation, Member States may continue to exclude from the scope of this Directive:
   (a)   domestic servants employed by a natural person;
   (b)   share-fishermen.

Article 2

1. For the purposes of this Directive, an employer shall be deemed to be in a state of insolvency where a request has been made for the opening of collective proceedings based on insolvency of the employer, as provided for under the laws, regulations and administrative provisions of a Member State, and involving the partial or total divestment of the employer's assets and the appointment of a liquidator or a person performing a similar task, and the authority which is competent pursuant to the said provisions has:
   (a)   either decided to open the proceedings, or
   (b)   established that the employer's undertaking or business has been definitively closed down and that the available assets are insufficient to warrant the opening of the proceedings.

2. This Directive is without prejudice to national law as regards the definition of the terms 'employee', 'employer', 'pay', 'right conferring immediate entitlement' and 'right conferring prospective entitlement'.
   However, the Member States may not exclude from the scope of this Directive:
   (a)   part-time employees within the meaning of Directive 97/81/EC;
   (b)   workers with a fixed-term contract within the meaning of Directive 1999/70/EC;
   (c)   workers with a temporary employment relationship within the meaning of Article 1(2) of Directive 91/383/EEC.

3. Member States may not set a minimum duration for the contract of employment or the employment relationship in order for workers to qualify for claims under this Directive.

4. This Directive does not prevent Member States from extending workers' protection to other situations of insolvency, for example where payments have been de facto stopped on a permanent basis, established by proceedings different from those mentioned in paragraph 1 as provided for under national law.

Such procedures shall not however create a guarantee obligation for the institutions of the other Member States in the cases referred to in Section IIIa.

SECTION II
PROVISIONS CONCERNING GUARANTEE INSTITUTIONS

Article 3

Member States shall take the measures necessary to ensure that guarantee institutions guarantee, subject to Article 4, payment of employees' outstanding claims resulting from contracts of employment or employment relationships, including, where provided for by national law, severance pay on termination of employment relationships.

The claims taken over by the guarantee institution shall be the outstanding pay claims relating to a period prior to and/or, as applicable, after a given date determined by the Member States.

Article 4

1. Member States shall have the option to limit the liability of the guarantee institutions referred to in Article 3.

2. When Member States exercise the option referred to in paragraph 1, they shall specify the length of the period for which outstanding claims are to be met by the guarantee institution. However, this may not be shorter than a period covering the remuneration of the last three months of the employment relationship prior to and/or after the date referred to in Article 3. Member States may include this minimum period of three months in a reference period with a duration of not less than six months.

   Member States having a reference period of not less than 18 months may limit the period for which outstanding claims are met by the guarantee institution to eight weeks. In this case, those periods which are most favourable to the employee are used for the calculation of the minimum period.

3. Furthermore, Member States may set ceilings on the payments made by the guarantee institution. These ceilings must not fall below a level which is socially compatible with the social objective of this Directive.

   When Member States exercise this option, they shall inform the Commission of the methods used to set the ceiling.

Article 5

Member States shall lay down detailed rules for the organisation, financing and operation of the guarantee institutions, complying with the following principles in particular:

   (a) the assets of the institutions shall be independent of the employers' operating capital and be inaccessible to proceedings for insolvency;

   (b) employers shall contribute to financing, unless it is fully covered by the public authorities;

   (c) the institutions' liabilities shall not depend on whether or not obligations to contribute to financing have been fulfilled.

SECTION III
PROVISIONS CONCERNING SOCIAL SECURITY

Article 6

Member States may stipulate that Articles 3, 4 and 5 shall not apply to contributions due under national statutory social security schemes or under supplementary company or inter-company pension schemes outside the national statutory social security schemes.

Article 7

Member States shall take the measures necessary to ensure that non-payment of compulsory contributions due from the employer, before the onset of his insolvency, to their insurance institutions under national statutory social security schemes does not adversely affect employees' benefit entitlement in respect of these insurance institutions inasmuch as the employees' contributions were deducted at source from the remuneration paid.

Article 8

Member States shall ensure that the necessary measures are taken to protect the interests of employees and of persons having already left the employer's undertaking or business at the date of the onset of the employer's insolvency in respect of rights conferring on them immediate or prospective entitlement to old-age benefits, including survivors' benefits, under supplementary company or inter-company pension schemes outside the national statutory social security schemes.

SECTION IIIa
PROVISIONS CONCERNING TRANSNATIONAL SITUATIONS

Article 8a

1.   When an undertaking with activities in the territories of at least two Member States is in a state of insolvency within the meaning of Article 2(l), the institution responsible for meeting employees' outstanding claims shall be that in the Member State in whose territory they work or habitually work.
2.   The extent of employees' rights shall be determined by the law governing the competent guarantee institution.
3.   Member States shall take the measures necessary to ensure that, in the cases referred to in paragraph 1, decisions taken in the context of insolvency proceedings referred to in Article 2(1), which have been requested in another Member State, are taken into account when determining the employer's state of insolvency within the meaning of this Directive.

Article 8b

1.   For the purposes of implementing Article 8a, Member States shall make provision for the sharing of relevant information between their competent administrative authorities and/or the guarantee institutions mentioned in Article 3, making it possible in particular to inform the guarantee institution responsible for meeting the employees' outstanding claims.
2.   Member States shall notify the Commission and the other Member States of the contact details of their competent administrative authorities and/or guarantee institutions. The Commission shall make these communications publicly accessible.

SECTION IV
GENERAL AND FINAL PROVISIONS

Article 9

This Directive shall not affect the option of Member States to apply or introduce laws, regulations or administrative provisions which are more favourable to employees.

Implementation of this Directive shall not under any circumstances be sufficient grounds for a regression in relation to the current situation in the Member States and in relation to the general level of protection of workers in the area covered by it.

Article 10

This Directive shall not affect the option of Member States:

    (a)   to take the measures necessary to avoid abuses;

    (b)   to refuse or reduce the liability referred to in Article 3 or the guarantee obligation referred to in Article 7 if it appears that fulfilment of the obligation is unjustifiable because of the existence of special links between the employee and the employer and of common interests resulting in collusion between them;

    (c)   to refuse or reduce the liability referred to in Article 3 or the guarantee obligation referred to in Article 7 in cases where the employee, on his or her own or together with his or her close relatives, was the owner of an essential part of the employer's undertaking or business and had a considerable influence on its activities.

Article 10a

Member States shall notify the Commission and the other Member States of the types of national insolvency proceedings falling within the scope of this Directive, and of any amendments relating thereto. The Commission shall publish these communications in the Official Journal of the European Communities.

Article 11

1. Member States shall bring into force the laws, regulations and administrative provisions necessary to comply with this Directive within 36 months of its notification. They shall forthwith inform the Commission thereof.

2. Member States shall communicate to the Commission the texts of the laws, regulations and administrative provisions which they adopt in the field governed by this Directive.

Article 12

Within 18 months of the expiry of the period of 36 months laid down in Article 11 (1), Member States shall forward all relevant information to the Commission in order to enable it to draw up a report on the application of this Directive for submission to the Council.

Article 13

This Directive is addressed to the Member States.

COUNCIL AND PARLIAMENT DIRECTIVE (EC) No 2002/74 of 23 SEPTEMBER 2002 AMENDING COUNCIL DIRECTIVE 80/987/EEC on the approximation of the laws of the Member States relating to the protection of employees in the event of the insolvency of their employer
[2002] OJ L270/10

THE EUROPEAN PARLIAMENT AND THE COUNCIL OF THE EUROPEAN UNION,

Having regard to the Treaty establishing the European Community, and in particular Article 137(2) thereof,

Having regard to the proposal from the Commission,

Having regard to the opinion of the Economic and Social Committee,

Having consulted the Committee of the Regions,

Acting in accordance with the procedure laid down in Article 251 of the Treaty,

Whereas:

(1) The Community Charter of Fundamental Social Rights for Workers adopted on 9 December 1989 states, in point 7, that the completion of the internal market must lead to an improvement in the living and working conditions of workers in the European Community and that this improvement must cover, where necessary, the development of certain aspects of employment regulations such as procedures for collective redundancies and those regarding bankruptcies.

(2) Directive 80/987/EEC aims to provide a minimum degree of protection for employees in the event of the insolvency of their employer. To this end, it obliges the Member States to establish a body which guarantees payment of the outstanding claims of the employees concerned.

(3) Changes in insolvency law in the Member States and the development of the internal market mean that certain provisions of that Directive must be adapted.

(4) Legal certainty and transparency also require clarification with regard to the scope and certain definitions of Directive 80/987/EEC. In particular the possible exclusions granted to the Member States should be indicated in the enacting provisions of the Directive and consequently the Annex thereto should be deleted.

(5) In order to ensure equitable protection for the employees concerned, the definition of the state of insolvency should be adapted to new legislative trends in the Member States and should also include within this concept insolvency proceedings other than liquidation. In this context, Member States should, in order to determine the liability of the guarantee institution, be able to lay down that where an insolvency situation results in several insolvency proceedings, the situation be treated as a single insolvency procedure.

(6) It should be ensured that the employees referred to in Directive 97/81/EC of 15 December 1997 concerning the Framework Agreement on part-time work concluded by UNICE, CEEP and the ETUC, Council Directive 1999/70/EC of 28 June 1999 concerning the framework agreement on fixed-term work concluded by the ETUC, UNICE and CEEP and Council Directive 91/383/EEC of 25 June 1991 supplementing the measures to encourage improvements in the safety and health at work of workers with a fixed-duration employment

relationship or a temporary employment relationship are not excluded from the scope of this Directive.

(7) In order to ensure legal certainty for employees in the event of insolvency of undertakings pursuing their activities in a number of Member States, and to strengthen workers' rights in line with the established case law of the Court of Justice, provisions should be introduced which expressly state which institution is responsible for meeting pay claims in these cases and establishes as the aim of cooperation between the competent administrative authorities of the Member States the early settlement of employees' outstanding claims. Furthermore it is necessary to ensure that the relevant arrangements are properly implemented by making provision for collaboration between the competent administrative authorities in the Member States.

(8) Member States may set limitations on the responsibility of the guarantee institutions which should be compatible with the social objective of the Directive and may take into account the different levels of claims.

(9) In order to make it easier to identify insolvency proceedings in particular in situations with a cross-border dimension, provision should be made for the Member States to notify the Commission and the other Member States about the types of insolvency proceedings which give rise to intervention by the guarantee institution.

(10) Directive 80/987/EEC should be amended accordingly.

(11) Since the objectives of the proposed action, namely the amendment of certain provisions of Directive 80/987/EEC to take account of changes in the activities of undertakings in the Community, cannot be sufficiently achieved by the Member States and can therefore be better achieved at Community level, the Community may adopt measures, in accordance with the principle of subsidiarity as set out in Article 5 of the Treaty. In accordance with the principle of proportionality, as set out in that Article, this Directive does not go beyond what is necessary in order to achieve that objective.

(12) The Commission should submit to the European Parliament and the Council a report on the implementation and application of this Directive in particular as regards the new forms of employment emerging in the Member States,

HAVE ADOPTED THIS DIRECTIVE:

Editor's Note: Article 1 contains amendments to Directive 80/987 and is not reproduced here.

Article 2

1. Member States shall bring into force the laws, regulations and administrative provisions necessary to comply with this Directive before 8 October 2005. They shall forthwith inform the Commission thereof.

   They shall apply the provisions referred to in the first subparagraph to any state of insolvency of an employer occurring after the date of entry into force of those provisions.

   When Member States adopt these measures, they shall contain a reference to this Directive or be accompanied by such reference on the occasion of their official publication. The methods of making such a reference shall be laid down by the Member States.

2. Member States shall communicate to the Commission the text of the provisions of national law which they adopt in the field covered by this Directive.

Article 3

This Directive shall enter into force on the day of its publication in the Official Journal of the European Communities.

Article 4

By 8 October 2010 at the latest, the Commission shall submit to the European Parliament and the Council a report on the implementation and application of this Directive in the Member States.

Article 5

This Directive is addressed to the Member States.

COUNCIL DIRECTIVE (EEC) No 89/391 of 12 JUNE 1989
on the introduction of measures to encourage improvements in the safety and health of workers at work
[1989] OJ L183/1

SECTION I
GENERAL PROVISIONS

Article 1 Object

1. The object of this Directive is to introduce measures to encourage improvements in the safety and health of workers at work.
2. To that end it contains general principles concerning the prevention of occupational risks, the protection of safety and health, the elimination of risk and accident factors, the informing, consultation, balanced participation in accordance with national laws and/or practices and training of workers and their representatives, as well as general guidelines for the implementation of the said principles.
3. This Directive shall be without prejudice to existing or future national and Community provisions which are more favourable to protection of the safety and health of workers at work.

Article 2 Scope

1. This Directive shall apply to all sectors of activity, both public and private (industrial, agricultural, commercial, administrative, service, educational, cultural, leisure, etc.).
2. This Directive shall not be applicable where characteristics peculiar to certain specific public service activities, such as the armed forces or the police, or to certain specific activities in the civil protection services inevitably conflict with it.
   In that event, the safety and health of workers must be ensured as far as possible in the light of the objectives of this Directive.

Article 3 Definitions

For the purposes of this Directive, the following terms shall have the following meanings:
   (a) worker: any person employed by an employer, including trainees and apprentices but excluding domestic servants;
   (b) employer: any natural or legal person who has an employment relationship with the worker and has responsibility for the undertaking and/or establishment;
   (c) workers' representative with specific responsibility for the safety and health of workers: any person elected, chosen or designated in accordance with national laws and/or practices to represent workers where problems arise relating to the safety and health protection of workers at work;
   (d) prevention: all the steps or measures taken or planned at all stages of work in the undertaking to prevent or reduce occupational risks.

Article 4

1. Member States shall take the necessary steps to ensure that employers, workers and workers' representatives are subject to the legal provisions necessary for the implementation of this Directive.
2. In particular, Member States shall ensure adequate controls and supervision.

SECTION II
EMPLOYERS' OBLIGATIONS

Article 5 General provision

1. The employer shall have a duty to ensure the safety and health of workers in every aspect related to the work.
2. Where, pursuant to Article 7(3), an employer enlists competent external services or persons, this shall not discharge him from his responsibilities in this area.
3. The workers' obligations in the field of safety and health at work shall not affect the principle of the responsibility of the employer.

4. This Directive shall not restrict the option of Member States to provide for the exclusion or the limitation of employers' responsibility where occurrences are due to unusual and unforeseeable circumstances, beyond the employers' control, or to exceptional events, the consequences of which could not have been avoided despite the exercise of all due care.

Member States need not exercise the option referred to in the first subparagraph.

Article 6   General obligations on employers

1. Within the context of his responsibilities, the employer shall take the measures necessary for the safety and health protection of workers, including prevention of occupational risks and provision of information and training, as well as provision of the necessary organisation and means. The employer shall be alert to the need to adjust these measures to take account of changing circumstances and aim to improve existing situations.

2. The employer shall implement the measures referred to in the first subparagraph of paragraph 1 on the basis of the following general principles of prevention:
   (a)   avoiding risks;
   (b)   evaluating the risks which cannot be avoided:
   (c)   combating the risks at source;
   (d)   adapting the work to the individual, especially as regards the design of work places, the choice of work equipment and the choice of working and production methods, with a view, in particular, to alleviating monotonous work and work at a predetermined work-rate and to reducing their effect on health.
   (e)   adapting to technical progress;
   (f)   replacing the dangerous by the non-dangerous or the less dangerous;
   (g)   developing a coherent overall prevention policy which covers technology, organisation of work, working conditions, social relationships and the influence of factors related to the working environment;
   (h)   giving collective protective measures priority over individual protective measures;
   (i)   giving appropriate instructions to the workers.

3. Without prejudice to the other provisions of this Directive, the employer shall, taking into account the nature of the activities of the enterprise and/or establishment:
   (a)   evaluate the risks to the safety and health of workers, inter alia in the choice of work equipment, the chemical substances or preparations used, and the fitting-out of work places.

   Subsequent to this evaluation and as necessary, the preventive measures and the working and production methods implemented by the employer must:
   — assure an improvement in the level of protection afforded to workers with regard to safety and health,
   — be integrated into all the activities of the undertaking and/or establishment and at all hierarchical levels;
   (b)   where he entrusts tasks to a worker, take into consideration the worker's capabilities as regards health and safety;
   (c)   ensure that the planning and introduction of new technologies are the subject of consultation with the workers and/or their representatives, as regards the consequences of the choice of equipment, the working conditions and the working environment for the safety and health of workers;
   (d)   take appropriate steps to ensure that only workers who have received adequate instructions may have access to areas where there is serious and specific danger.

4. Without prejudice to the other provisions of this Directive, where several undertakings share a work place, the employers shall cooperate in implementing the safety, health and occupational hygiene provisions and, taking into account the nature of the activities, shall coordinate their actions in matters of the protection and prevention of occupational risks, and shall inform one another and their respective workers and/or workers' representatives of these risks.

5. Measures related to safety, hygiene and health at work may in no circumstances involve the workers in financial cost.

Article 7   Protective and preventive services

1. Without prejudice to the obligations referred to in Articles 5 and 6, the employer shall designate one or more workers to carry out activities related to the protection and prevention of occupational risks for the undertaking and/or establishment.

2. Designated workers may not be placed at any disadvantage because of their activities related to the protection and prevention of occupational risks. Designated workers shall be allowed adequate time to enable them to fulfil their obligations arising from this Directive.

3. If such protective and preventive measures cannot be organised for lack of competent personnel in the undertaking and/or establishment, the employer shall enlist competent external services or persons.

4. Where the employer enlists such services or persons, he shall inform them of the factors known to affect, or suspected of affecting, the safety and health of the workers and they must have access to the information referred to in Article 10(2).

5. In all cases:
   — the workers designated must have the necessary capabilities and the necessary means,
   — the external services or persons consulted must have the necessary aptitudes and the necessary personal and professional means, and
   — the workers designated and the external services or persons consulted must be sufficient in number

   to deal with the organisation of protective and preventive measures, taking into account the size of the undertaking and/or establishment and/or the hazards to which the workers are exposed and their distribution throughout the entire undertaking and/or establishment.

6. The protection from, and prevention of, the health and safety risks which form the subject of this Article shall be the responsibility of one or more workers, of one service or of separate services whether from inside or outside the undertaking and/or establishment. The worker(s) and/or agency(ies) must work together whenever necessary.

7. Member States may define, in the light of the nature of the activities and size of the undertakings, the categories of undertakings in which the employer, provided he is competent, may himself take responsibility for the measures referred to in paragraph 1.

8. Member States shall define the necessary capabilities and aptitudes referred to in paragraph 5. They may determine the sufficient number referred to in paragraph 5.

Article 8   First aid, fire-fighting and evacuation of workers, serious and imminent danger

1. The employer shall:
   — take the necessary measures for first aid, fire-fighting and evacuation of workers, adapted to the nature of the activities and the size of the undertaking and/or establishment and taking into account other persons present,
   — arrange any necessary contacts with external services, particularly as regards first aid, emergency medical care, rescue work and fire-fighting.

2. Pursuant to paragraph 1, the employer shall, *inter alia*, for first aid, fire-fighting and the evacuation of workers, designate the workers required to implement such measures. The number of such workers, their training and the equipment available to them shall be adequate, taking account of the size and/or specific hazards of the undertaking and/or establishment.

3. The employer shall:
   (a) as soon as possible, inform all workers who are, or may be, exposed to serious and imminent danger of the risk involved and of the steps taken or to be taken as regards protection;
   (b) take action and give instructions to enable workers in the event of serious, imminent and unavoidable danger to stop work and/or immediately to leave the work place and proceed to a place of safety;
   (c) save in exceptional cases for reasons duly substantiated, refrain from asking workers to resume work in a working situation where there is still a serious and imminent danger.

4. Workers who, in the event of serious, imminent and unavoidable danger, leave their workstation and/or a dangerous area may not be placed at any disadvantage because of their

action and must be protected against any harmful and unjustified consequences, in accordance with national laws and/or practices.

5. The employer shall ensure that all workers are able, in the event of serious and imminent danger to their own safety and/or that of other persons, and where the immediate superior responsible cannot be contacted, to take the appropriate steps in the light of their knowledge and the technical means at their disposal, to avoid the consequences of such danger.

Their actions shall not place them at any disadvantage, unless they acted carelessly or there was negligence on their part.

Article 9 Various obligations on employers

1. The employer shall:
   (a) be in possession of an assessment of the risks to safety and health at work, including those facing groups of workers exposed to particular risks;
   (b) decide on the protective measures to be taken and, if necessary, the protective equipment to be used;
   (c) keep a list of occupational accidents resulting in a worker being unfit for work for more than three working days;
   (d) draw up, for the responsible authorities and in accordance with national laws and/or practices, reports on occupational accidents suffered by his workers.

2. Member States shall define, in the light of the nature of the activities and size of the undertakings, the obligations to be met by the different categories of undertakings in respect of the drawing-up of the documents provided for in paragraph 1(a) and (b) and when preparing the documents provided for in paragraph 1(c) and (d).

Article 10 Worker information

1. The employer shall take appropriate measures so that workers and/or their representatives in the undertaking and/or establishment receive, in accordance with national laws and/or practices which may take account, *inter alia*, of the size of the undertaking and/or establishment, all the necessary information concerning:
   (a) the safety and health risks and protective and preventive measures and activities in respect of both the undertaking and/or establishment in general and each type of workstation and/or job;
   (b) the measures taken pursuant to Article 8(2).

2. The employer shall take appropriate measures so that employers of workers from any outside undertakings and/or establishments engaged in work in his undertaking and/or establishment receive, in accordance with national laws and/or practices, adequate information concerning the points referred to in paragraph 1(a) and (b) which is to be provided to the workers in question.

3. The employer shall take appropriate measures so that workers with specific functions in protecting the safety and health of workers, or workers' representatives with specific responsibility for the safety and health of workers shall have access, to carry out their functions and in accordance with national laws and/or practices, to:
   (a) the risk assessment and protective measures referred to in Article 9(1)(a) and (b);
   (b) the list and reports referred to in Article 9(1)(c) and (d);
   (c) the information yielded by protective and preventive measures, inspection agencies and bodies responsible for safety and health.

Article 11 Consultation and participation of workers

1. Employers shall consult workers and/or their representatives and allow them to take part in discussions on all questions relating to safety and health at work.

This presupposes:
— the consultation of workers,
— the right of workers and/or their representatives to make proposals,
— balanced participation in accordance with national laws and/or practices.

2.   Workers or workers' representatives with specific responsibility for the safety and health of workers shall take part in a balanced way, in accordance with national laws and/or practices, or shall be consulted in advance and in good time by the employer with regard to:
     (a)   any measure which may substantially affect safety and health;
     (b)   the designation of workers referred to in Articles 7(1) and 8(2) and the activities referred to in Article 7(1);
     (c)   the information referred to in Articles 9(1) and 10;
     (d)   the enlistment, where appropriate, of the competent services or persons outside the undertaking and/or establishment, as referred to in Article 7(3);
     (e)   the planning and organisation of the training referred to in Article 12.
3.   Workers' representatives with specific responsibility for the safety and health of workers shall have the right to ask the employer to take appropriate measures and to submit proposals to him to that end to mitigate hazards for workers and/or to remove sources of danger.
4.   The workers referred to in paragraph 2 and the workers' representatives referred to in paragraphs 2 and 3 may not be placed at a disadvantage because of their respective activities referred to in paragraphs 2 and 3.
5.   Employers must allow workers' representatives with specific responsibility for the safety and health of workers adequate time off work, without loss of pay, and provide them with the necessary means to enable such representatives to exercise their rights and functions deriving from this Directive.
6.   Workers and/or their representatives are entitled to appeal, in accordance with national law and/or practice, to the authority responsible for safety and health protection at work if they consider that the measures taken and the means employed by the employer are inadequate for the purposes of ensuring safety and health at work.
     Workers' representatives must be given the opportunity to submit their observations during inspection visits by the competent authority.

Article 12 Training of workers

1.   The employer shall ensure that each worker receives adequate safety and health training, in particular in the form of information and instructions specific to his workstation or job:
     — on recruitment,
     — in the event of a transfer or a change of job,
     — in the event of the introduction of new work equipment or a change in equipment, — in the event of the introduction of any new technology.
     The training shall be:
     — adapted to take account of new or changed risks, and
     — repeated periodically if necessary.
2.   The employer shall ensure that workers from outside undertakings and/or establishments engaged in work in his undertaking and/or establishment have in fact received appropriate instructions regarding health and safety risks during their activities in his undertaking and/or establishment.
3.   Workers' representatives with a specific role in protecting the safety and health of workers shall be entitled to appropriate training.
4.   The training referred to in paragraphs 1 and 3 may not be at the workers' expense or at that of the workers' representatives.
     The training referred to in paragraph 1 must take place during working hours.
     The training referred to in paragraph 3 must take place during working hours or in accordance with national practice either within or outside the undertaking and/or the establishment.

SECTION III
WORKERS' OBLIGATIONS

Article 13

1.   It shall be the responsibility of each worker to take care as far as possible of his own safety and health and that of other persons affected by his acts or omissions at work in accordance with his training and the instructions given by his employer.

2. To this end, workers must in particular, in accordance with their training and the instructions given by their employer:

    (a) make correct use of machinery, apparatus, tools, dangerous substances, transport equipment and other means of production;

    (b) make correct use of the personal protective equipment supplied to them and, after use, return it to its proper place;

    (c) refrain from disconnecting, changing or removing arbitrarily safety devices fitted, e.g. to machinery, apparatus, tools, plant and buildings, and use such safety devices correctly;

    (d) immediately inform the employer and/or the workers with specific responsibility for the safety and health of workers of any work situation they have reasonable grounds for considering represents a serious and immediate danger to safety and health and of any shortcomings in the protection arrangements;

    (e) cooperate, in accordance with national practice, with the employer and/or workers with specific responsibility for the safety and health of workers, for as long as may be necessary to enable any tasks or requirements imposed by the competent authority to protect the safety and health of workers at work to be carried out;

    (f) cooperate, in accordance with national practice, with the employer and/or workers with specific responsibility for the safety and health of workers, for as long as may be necessary to enable the employer to ensure that the working environment and working conditions are safe and pose no risk to safety and health within their field of activity.

SECTION IV

MISCELLANEOUS PROVISIONS

Article 14 Health surveillance

1. To ensure that workers receive health surveillance appropriate to the health and safety risks they incur at work, measures shall be introduced in accordance with national law and/or practices.

2. The measures referred to in paragraph 1 shall be such that each worker, if he so wishes, may receive health surveillance at regular intervals.

3. Health surveillance may be provided as part of a national health system.

Article 15 Risk groups

Particularly sensitive risk groups must be protected against the dangers which specifically affect them.

Article 16 Individual Directives — Amendments — General scope of this Directive

1. The Council, acting on a proposal from the Commission based on Article 118a of the Treaty, shall adopt individual Directives, *inter alia*, in the areas listed in the Annex.

2. This Directive and, without prejudice to the procedure referred to in Article 17 concerning technical adjustments, the individual Directives may be amended in accordance with the procedure provided for in Article 118a of the Treaty.

3. The provisions of this Directive shall apply in full to all the areas covered by the individual Directives, without prejudice to more stringent and/or specific provisions contained in these individual Directives.

Article 17

1. For the purely technical adjustments to the individual Directives provided for in Article 16(1) to take account of:

    — the adoption of Directives in the field of technical harmonisation and standardisation, and/or

    — technical progress, changes in international regulations or specifications, and new findings,

the Commission shall be assisted by a committee.

2. Articles 5 and 7 of Decision 1999/468/EC shall apply, having regard to the provisions of Article 8 thereof. The period laid down in Article 5(6) of Decision 1999/468/EC shall be set at three months.

3. The Committee shall adopt its rules of procedure.

Article 17a Implementation reports

1. Every five years, the Member States shall submit a single report to the Commission on the practical implementation of this Directive and individual Directives within the meaning of Article 16(1), indicating the points of view of the social partners. The report shall assess the various points related to the practical implementation of the different Directives and, where appropriate and available, provide data disaggregated by gender.

2. The structure of the report, together with a questionnaire specifying its content, shall be defined by the Commission, in cooperation with the Advisory Committee on Safety and Health at Work.

    The report shall include a general part on the provisions of this Directive relating to the common principles and points applicable to all of the Directives referred to in paragraph 1.

    To complement the general part, specific chapters shall deal with implementation of the particular aspects of each Directive, including specific indicators, where available.

3. The Commission shall submit the structure of the report, together with the above-mentioned questionnaire specifying its content, to the Member States at least six months before the end of the period covered by the report. The report shall be transmitted to the Commission within 12 months of the end of the five-year period that it covers.

4. Using these reports as a basis, the Commission shall evaluate the implementation of the Directives concerned in terms of their relevance, of research and of new scientific knowledge in the various fields in question. It shall, within 36 months of the end of the five-year period, inform the European Parliament, the Council, the European Economic and Social Committee and the Advisory Committee on Safety and Health at Work of the results of this evaluation and, if necessary, of any initiatives to improve the operation of the regulatory framework.

5. The first report shall cover the period 2007 to 2012.

Article 18 Final provisions

1. Member States shall bring into force the laws, regulations and administrative provisions necessary to comply with this Directive by 31 December 1992.

    They shall forthwith inform the Commission thereof.

2. Member States shall communicate to the Commission the texts of the provisions of national law which they have already adopted or adopt in the field covered by this Directive.

Article 19

This Directive is addressed to the Member States.

ANNEX

List of areas referred to in Article 16 (1)

— Work places
— Work equipment
— Personal protective equipment
— Work with visual display units
— Handling of heavy loads involving risk of back injury
— Temporary or mobile work sites
— Fisheries and agriculture

COUNCIL DIRECTIVE (EEC) No 92/85 of 19 OCTOBER 1992
on the introduction of measures to encourage improvements in the safety and health at work of pregnant workers and workers who have recently given birth or are breastfeeding (tenth individual Directive within the meaning of Article 16(1) of Directive 89/391/EEC)
[1992] OJ L348/1

SECTION I
PURPOSE AND DEFINITIONS

Article 1   Purpose

    1.   The purpose of this Directive, which is the tenth individual Directive within the meaning of Article 16(1) of Directive 89/391/EEC, is to implement measures to encourage improvements in the safety and health at work of pregnant workers and workers who have recently given birth or who are breastfeeding.

    2.   The provisions of Directive 89/391/EEC, except for Article 2(2) thereof, shall apply in full to the whole area covered by paragraph 1, without prejudice to any more stringent and/or specific provisions contained in this Directive.

    3.   This Directive may not have the effect of reducing the level of protection afforded to pregnant workers, workers who have recently given birth or who are breastfeeding as compared with the situation which exists in each Member State on the date on which this Directive is adopted.

Article 2   Definitions

For the purposes of this Directive:

    (a)   pregnant worker shall mean a pregnant worker who informs her employer of her condition, in accordance with national legislation and/or national practice;

    (b)   worker who has recently given birth shall mean a worker who has recently given birth within the meaning of national legislation and/or national practice and who informs her employer of her condition, in accordance with that legislation and/or practice;

    (c)   worker who is breastfeeding shall mean a worker who is breastfeeding within the meaning of national legislation and/or national practice and who informs her employer of her condition, in accordance with that legislation and/or practice.

SECTION II
GENERAL PROVISIONS

Article 3   Guidelines

    1.   In consultation with the Member States and assisted by the Advisory Committee on Safety, Hygiene and Health Protection at Work, the Commission shall draw up guidelines on the assessment of the chemical, physical and biological agents and industrial processes considered hazardous for the safety or health of workers within the meaning of Article 2.

        The guidelines referred to in the first subparagraph shall also cover movements and postures, mental and physical fatigue and other types of physical and mental stress connected with the work done by workers within the meaning of Article 2.

    2.   The purpose of the guidelines referred to in paragraph 1 is to serve as a basis for the assessment referred to in Article 4(1).

        To this end, Member States shall bring these guidelines to the attention of all employers and all female workers and/or their representatives in the respective Member State.

Article 4   Assessment and information

    1.   For all activities liable to involve a specific risk of exposure to the agents, processes or working conditions of which a non-exhaustive list is given in Annex I, the employer shall assess the nature, degree and duration of exposure, in the undertaking and/or establishment concerned, of workers within the meaning of Article 2, either directly or by way of the protective and preventive services referred to in Article 7 of Directive 89/391/EEC, in order to:

        — assess any risks to the safety or health and any possible effect on the pregnancys or breastfeeding of workers within the meaning of Article 2,

— decide what measures should be taken.

2. Without prejudice to Article 10 of Directive 89/391/EEC, workers within the meaning of Article 2 and workers likely to be in one of the situations referred to in Article 2 in the undertaking and/or establishment concerned and/or their representatives shall be informed of the results of the assessment referred to in paragraph 1 and of all measures to be taken concerning health and safety at work.

Article 5   Action further to the results of the assessment

1. Without prejudice to Article 6 of Directive 89/391/EEC, if the results of the assessment referred to in Article 4(1) reveal a risk to the safety or health or an effect on the pregnancy or breastfeeding of a worker within the meaning of Article 2, the employer shall take the necessary measures to ensure that, by temporarily adjusting the working conditions and/or the working hours of the worker concerned, the exposure of that worker to such risks is avoided.

2. If the adjustment of her working conditions and/or working hours is not technically and/or objectively feasible, or cannot reasonably be required on duly substantiated grounds, the employer shall take the necessary measures to move the worker concerned to another job.

3. If moving her to another job is not technically and/or objectively feasible or cannot reasonably be required on duly substantiated grounds, the worker concerned shall be granted leave in accordance with national legislation and/or national practice for the whole of the period necessary to protect her safety or health.

4. The provisions of this Article shall apply mutatis mutandis to the case where a worker pursuing an activity which is forbidden pursuant to Article 6 becomes pregnant or starts breastfeeding and informs her employer thereof.

Article 6   Cases in which exposure is prohibited

In addition to the general provisions concerning the protection of workers, in particular those relating to the limit values for occupational exposure:

1. pregnant workers within the meaning of Article 2(a) may under no circumstances be obliged to perform duties for which the assessment has revealed a risk of exposure, which would jeopardise safety or health, to the agents and working conditions listed in Annex II, Section A;

2. workers who are breastfeeding, within the meaning of Article 2(c), may under no circumstances be obliged to perform duties for which the assessment has revealed a risk of exposure, which would jeopardise safety or health, to the agents and working conditions listed in Annex II, Section B.

Article 7   Night work

1. Member States shall take the necessary measures to ensure that workers referred to in Article 2 are not obliged to perform night work during their pregnancy and for a period following childbirth which shall be determined by the national authority competent for safety and health, subject to submission, in accordance with the procedures laid down by the Member States, of a medical certificate stating that this is necessary for the safety or health of the worker concerned.

2. The measures referred to in paragraph 1 must entail the possibility, in accordance with national legislation and/or national practice, of:
   (a) transfer to daytime work; or
   (b) leave from work or extension of maternity leave where such a transfer is not technically and/or objectively feasible or cannot reasonably by required on duly substantiated grounds.

Article 8   Maternity leave

1. Member States shall take the necessary measures to ensure that workers within the meaning of Article 2 are entitled to a continuous period of maternity leave of a least 14 weeks allocated before and/or after confinement in accordance with national legislation and/or practice.

2. The maternity leave stipulated in paragraph 1 must include compulsory maternity leave of at least two weeks allocated before and/or after confinement in accordance with national legislation and/or practice.

Article 9   Time off for ante-natal examinations

Member States shall take the necessary measures to ensure that pregnant workers within the meaning of Article 2(a) are entitled to, in accordance with national legislation and/or practice, time off, without loss of pay, in order to attend ante-natal examinations, if such examinations have to take place during working hours.

Article 10   Prohibition of dismissal

In order to guarantee workers, within the meaning of Article 2, the exercise of their health and safety protection rights as recognised under this Article, it shall be provided that:

1. Member States shall take the necessary measures to prohibit the dismissal of workers, within the meaning of Article 2, during the period from the beginning of their pregnancy to the end of the maternity leave referred to in Article 8(1), save in exceptional cases not connected with their condition which are permitted under national legislation and/or practice and, where applicable, provided that the competent authority has given its consent;

2. if a worker, within the meaning of Article 2, is dismissed during the period referred to in point 1, the employer must cite duly substantiated grounds for her dismissal in writing;

3. Member States shall take the necessary measures to protect workers, within the meaning of Article 2, from consequences of dismissal which is unlawful by virtue of point 1.

Article 11   Employment rights

In order to guarantee workers within the meaning of Article 2 the exercise of their health and safety protection rights as recognised in this Article, it shall be provided that:

1. in the cases referred to in Articles 5, 6 and 7, the employment rights relating to the employment contract, including the maintenance of a payment to, and/or entitlement to an adequate allowance for, workers within the meaning of Article 2, must be ensured in accordance with national legislation and/or national practice;

2. in the case referred to in Article 8, the following must be ensured:
    (a) the rights connected with the employment contract of workers within the meaning of Article 2, other than those referred to in point (b) below;
    (b) maintenance of a payment to, and/or entitlement to an adequate allowance for, workers within the meaning of Article 2;

3. the allowance referred to in point 2(b) shall be deemed adequate if it guarantees income at least equivalent to that which the worker concerned would receive in the event of a break in her activities on grounds connected with her state of health, subject to any ceiling laid down under national legislation;

4. Member States may make entitlement to pay or the allowance referred to in points 1 and 2(b) conditional upon the worker concerned fulfilling the conditions of eligibilty for such benefits laid down under national legislation.

    These conditions may under no circumstances provide for periods of previous employment in excess of 12 months immediately prior to the presumed date of confinement.

Article 12   Defence of rights

Member States shall introduce into their national legal systems such measures as are necessary to enable all workers who should themselves wronged by failure to comply with the obligations arising from this Directive to pursue their claims by judicial process (and/or, in accordance with national laws and/or practices) by recourse to other competent authorities.

Article 13   Amendments to the Annexes

1. Strictly technical adjustments to Annex I as a result of technical progress, changes in international regulations or specifications and new findings in the area covered by this Directive shall be adopted in accordance with the procedure laid down in Article 17 of Directive 89/391/EEC.

2. Annex II may be amended only in accordance with the procedure laid down in Article 118a of the Treaty.

Article 14 Final provisions

1. Member States shall bring into force the laws, regulations and administrative provisions necessary to comply with this Directive not later than two years after the adoption thereof or ensure, at the latest two years after adoption of this Directive, that the two sides of industry introduce the requisite provisions by means of collective agreements, with Member States being required to make all the necessary provisions to enable them at all times to guarantee the results laid down by this Directive. They shall forthwith inform the Commission thereof.

2. When Member States adopt the measures referred to in paragraph 1, they shall contain a reference of this Directive or shall be accompanied by such reference on the occasion of their official publication. The methods of making such a reference shall be laid down by the Member States.

3. Member States shall communicate to the Commission the texts of the essential provisions of national law which they have already adopted or adopt in the field governed by this Directive.

4. Member States shall report to the Commission every five years on the practical implementation of the provisions of this Directive, indicating the points of view of the two sides of industry.

   However, Member States shall report for the first time to the Commission on the practical implementation of the provisions of this Directive, indicating the points of view of the two sides of industry, four years after its adoption.

   The Commission shall inform the European Parliament, the Council, the Economic and Social Committee and the Advisory Committee on Safety, Hygiene and Health Protection at Work.

5. The Commission shall periodically submit to the European Parliament, the Council and the Economic and Social Committee a report on the implementation of this Directive, taking into account paragraphs 1, 2 and 3.

6. The Council will re-examine this Directive, on the basis of an assessment carried out on the basis of the reports referred to in the second subparagraph of paragraph 4 and, should the need arise, of a proposal, to be submitted by the Commission at the latest five years after adoption of the Directive.

Article 15

This Directive is addressed to the Member States.

ANNEX I

NON-EXHAUSTIVE LIST OF AGENTS, PROCESSES AND WORKING CONDITIONS

referred to in Article 4(1)

A. Agents

1. Physical agents where these are regarded as agents causing foetal lesions and/or likely to disrupt placental attachment, and in particular:

   (a) shocks, vibration or movement;

   (b) handling of loads entailing risks, particularly of a dorsolumbar nature;

   (c) noise;

   (d) ionizing radiation;*

   (e) non-ionizing radiation;

   (f) extremes of cold or heat;

   (g) movements and postures, travelling - either inside or outside the establishment — mental and physical fatigue and other physical burdens connected with the activity of the worker within the meaning of Article 2 of the Directive.

2. Biological agents

   Biological agents of risk groups 2, 3 and 3 within the meaning of Article 2(d) numbers 2, 3 and 4 of Directive 90/679/EEC, in so far as it is known that these agents or the therapeutic measures necessitated by such agents endanger the health of pregnant women and the unborn child and in so far as they do not yet appear in Annex II.

3. Chemical agents
    The following chemical agents in so far as it is known that they endanger the health of
    pregnant women and the unborn child and in so far as they do not yet appear in Annex II:
    (a) substances labelled R 40, R 45, R 46, and R 47 under Directive 67/548/EEC in so far as
         they do not yet appear in Annex II;
    (b) chemical agents in Annex I to Directive 90/394/EEC;
    (c) mercury and mercury derivatives;
    (d) antimitotic drugs;
    (e) carbon monoxide;
    (f) chemical agents of known and dangerous percutaneous absorption.

B.   Processes
Industrial processes listed in Annex I to Directive 90/394/EEC.

C.   Working conditions
Underground mining work.

*See Directive 80/836/Euratom

ANNEX II

NON-EXHAUSTIVE LIST OF AGENTS AND WORKING CONDITIONS

referred to in Article 6

A.   Pregnant workers within the meaning of Article 2(a)
1. Agents
    (a) Physical agents
         Work in hyperbaric atmosphere, e.g. pressurised enclosures and underwater diving.
    (b) Biological agents
         The following biological agents:
         — toxoplasma,
         — rubella virus, unless the pregnant workers are proved to be adequately protected
           against such agents by immunisation.
    (c) Chemical agents
         Lead and lead derivatives in so far as these agents are capable of being absorbed by the
         human organism.
2. Working conditions
    Underground mining work.

B.   Workers who are breastfeeding within the meaning of Article 2(c)
1. Agents
    (a) Chemical agents
         Lead and lead derivatives in so far as these agents are capable of being absorbed by the
         human organism.
2. Working conditions
    Underground mining work.

Statement of the Council and the Commission concerning Article 11(3) of Directive
92/85/EEC, entered in the minutes of the 1608th meeting of the Council (Luxembourg,
19 October 1992)

THE COUNCIL AND THE COMMISSION stated that:
'In determining the level of the allowances referred to in Article 11(2)(b) and (3), reference shall
be made, for purely technical reasons, to the allowance which a worker would receive in the
event of a break in her activities on grounds connected with her state of health. Such a reference
is not intended in any way to imply that pregnancy and childbirth be equated with sickness. The
national social security legislation of all Member States provides for an allowance to be paid
during an absence from work due to sickness. The link with such allowance in the chosen
formulation is simply intended to serve as a concrete, fixed reference amount in all Member

States for the determination of the minimum amount of maternity allowance payable. In so far as allowances are paid in individual Member States which exceed those provided for in the Directive, such allowances are, of course, retained. This is clear from Article 1(3) of the Directive.'

COUNCIL DIRECTIVE (EC) No 94/33 of 22 JUNE 1994
on the protection of young people at work
[1994] OJ L216/12

SECTION I

Article 1   Purpose

1. Member States shall take the necessary measures to prohibit work by children.
    They shall ensure, under the conditions laid down by this Directive, that the minimum working or employment age is not lower than the minimum age at which compulsory full-time schooling as imposed by national law ends or 15 years in any event.
2. Member States ensure that work by adolescents is strictly regulated and protected under the conditions laid down in this Directive.
3. Member States shall ensure in general that employers guarantee that young people have working conditions which suit their age.
    They shall ensure that young people are protected against economic exploitation and against any work likely to harm their safety, health or physical, mental, moral or social development or to jeopardise their education.

Article 2   Scope

1. This Directive shall apply to any person under 18 years of age having an employment contract or an employment relationship defined by the law in force in a Member State and/or governed by the law in force in a Member State.
2. Member States may make legislative or regulatory provision for this Directive not to apply, within the limits and under the conditions which they set by legislative or regulatory provision, to occasional work or short-term work involving:
    (a)   domestic service in a private household, or
    (b)   work regarded as not being harmful, damaging or dangerous to young people in a family undertaking.

Article 3   Definitions

For the purposes of this Directive:
(a)   'young person' shall mean any person under 18 years of age referred to in Article 2(1);
(b)   'child' shall mean any young person of less than 15 years of age or who is still subject to compulsory full-time schooling under national law;
(c)   'adolescent' shall mean any young person of at least 15 years of age but less than 18 years of age who is no longer subject to compulsory full-time schooling under national law;
(d)   'light work' shall mean all work which, on account of the inherent nature of the tasks which it involves and the particular conditions under which they are performed:
      (i)   is not likely to be harmful to the safety, health or development of children, and
      (ii)   is not such as to be harmful to their attendance at school, their participation in vocational guidance or training programmes approved by the competent authority or their capacity to benefit from the instruction received;
(e)   'working time' shall mean any period during which the young person is at work, at the employer's disposal and carrying out his activity or duties in accordance with national legislation and/or practice;
(f)   'rest period' shall mean any period which is not working time.

Article 4   Prohibition of work by children

1. Member States shall adopt the measures necessary to prohibit work by children.
2. Taking into account the objectives set out in Article 1, Member States may make legislative or regulatory provision for the prohibition of work by children not to apply to:

(a)   children pursuing the activities set out in Article 5;

(b)   children of at least 14 years of age working under a combined work/training scheme or an in-plant work-experience scheme, provided that such work is done in accordance with the conditions laid down by the competent authority;

(c)   children of at least 14 years of age performing light work other than that covered by Article 5; light work other than that covered by Article 5 may, however, be performed by children of 13 years of age for a limited number of hours per week in the case of categories of work determined by national legislation.

3.   Member States that make use of the opinion referred to in paragraph 2(c) shall determine, subject to the provisions of this Directive, the working conditions relating to the light work in question.

Article 5   Cultural or similar activities

1.   The employment of children for the purposes of performance in cultural, artistic, sports or advertising activities shall be subject to prior authorisation to be given by the competent authority in individual cases.

2.   Member States shall by legislative or regulatory provision lay down the working conditions for children in the cases referred to in paragraph 1 and the details of the prior authorisation procedure, on condition that the activities:

(i)   are not likely to be harmful to the safety, health or development of children, and

(ii)   are not such as to be harmful to their attendance at school, their participation in vocational guidance or training programmes approved by the competent authority or their capacity to benefit from the instruction received.

3.   By way of derogation from the procedure laid down in paragraph 1, in the case of children of at least 13 years of age, Member States may authorise, by legislative or regulatory provision, in accordance with conditions which they shall determine, the employment of children for the purposes of performance in cultural, artistic, sports or advertising activities.

4.   The Member States which have a specific authorisation system for modelling agencies with regard to the activities of children may retain that system.

SECTION II

Article 6   General obligations on employers

1.   Without prejudice to Article 4(1), the employer shall adopt the measures necessary to protect the safety and health of young people, taking particular account of the specific risks referred to in Article 7(1).

2.   The employer shall implement the measures provided for in paragraph 1 on the basis of an assessment of the hazards to young people in connection with their work. The assessment must be made before young people begin work and when there is any major change in working conditions and must pay particular attention to the following points:

(a)   the fitting-out and layout of the workplace and the workstation;

(b)   the nature, degree and duration of exposure to physical, biological and chemical agents;

(c)   the form, range and use of work equipment, in particular agents, machines, apparatus and devices, and the way in which they are handled;

(d)   the arrangement of work processes and operations and the way in which these are combined (organisation of work);

(e)   the level of training and instruction given to young people.

Where this assessment shows that there is a risk to the safety, the physical or mental health or development of young people, an appropriate free assessment and monitoring of their health shall be provided at regular intervals without prejudice to Directive 89/391/EEC. The free health assessment and monitoring may form part of a national health system.

3.   The employer shall inform young people of possible risks and of all measures adopted concerning their safety and health.

Furthermore, he shall inform the legal representatives of children of possible risks and of all measures adopted concerning children's safety and health.

4.   The employer shall involve the protective and preventive services referred to in Article 7 of Directive 89/391/EEC in the planning, implementation and monitoring of the safety and health conditions applicable to young people.

Article 7   Vulnerability of young people — Prohibition of work

1.   Member States shall ensure that young people are protected from any specific risks to their safety, health and development which are a consequence of their lack of experience, of absence of awareness of existing or potential risks or of the fact that young people have not yet fully matured.

2.   Without prejudice to Article 4(1), Member States shall to this end prohibit the employment of young people for:
   (a)   work which is objectively beyond their physical or psychological capacity;
   (b)   work involving harmful exposure to agents which are toxic, carcinogenic, cause heritable genetic damage, or harm to the unborn child or which in any other way chronically affect human health;
   (c)   work involving harmful exposure to radiation;
   (d)   work involving the risk of accidents which it may be assumed cannot be recognised or avoided by young persons owing to their insufficient attention to safety or lack of experience or training; or
   (e)   work in which there is a risk to health from extreme cold or heat, or from noise or vibration. Work which is likely to entail specific risks for young people within the meaning of paragraph 1 includes:
       — work involving harmful exposure to the physical, biological and chemical agents referred to in point I of the Annex, and
       — processes and work referred to in point II of the Annex.

3.   Member States may, by legislative or regulatory provision, authorise derogations from paragraph 2 in the case of adolescents where such derogations are indispensable for their vocational training, provided that protection of their safety and health is ensured by the fact that the work is performed under the supervision of a competent person within the meaning of Article 7 of Directive 89/391/EEC and provided that the protection afforded by that Directive is guaranteed.

SECTION III

Article 8   Working time

1.   Member States which make use of the option in Article 4(2)(b) or (c) shall adopt the measures necessary to limit the working time of children to:
   (a)   eight hours a day and 40 hours a week for work performed under a combined work/training scheme or an in-plant work-experience scheme;
   (b)   two hours on a school day and 12 hours a week for work performed in term-time outside the hours fixed for school attendance, provided that this is not prohibited by national legislation and/or practice; in no circumstances may the daily working time exceed seven hours; this limit may be raised to eight hours in the case of children who have reached the age of 15;
   (c)   seven hours a day and 35 hours a week for work performed during a period of at least a week when school is not operating; these limits may be raised to eight hours a day and 40 hours a week in the case of children who have reached the age of 15;
   (d)   seven hours a day and 35 hours a week for light work performed by children no longer subject to compulsory full-time schooling under national law.

2.   Member States shall adopt the measures necessary to limit the working time of adolescents to eight hours a day and 40 hours a week.

3.   The time spent on training by a young person working under a theoretical and/or practical combined work/training scheme or an in-plant work-experience scheme shall be counted as working time.

4.   Where a young person is employed by more than one employer, working days and working time shall be cumulative.

5. Member States may, by legislative or regulatory provision, authorise derogations from paragraph 1(a) and paragraph 2 either by way of exception or where there are objective grounds for so doing. Member States shall, by legislative or regulatory provision, determine the conditions, limits and procedure for implementing such derogations.

Article 9 Night work

1. (a) Member States which make use of the option in Article 4(2)(b) or (c) shall adopt the measures necessary to prohibit work by children between 8 p.m. and 6 a.m.
   (b) Member States shall adopt the measures necessary to prohibit work by adolescents either between 10 p.m. and 6 a.m. or between 11 p.m. and 7 a.m.

2. (a) Member States may, by legislative or regulatory provision, authorise work by adolescents in specific areas of activity during the period in which night work is prohibited as referred to in paragraph 1(b). In that event, Member States shall take appropriate measures to ensure that the adolescent is supervised by an adult where such supervision is necessary for the adolescent's protection.
   (b) If point (a) is applied, work shall continue to be prohibited between midnight and 4 a.m. However, Member States may, by legislative or regulatory provision, authorise work by adolescents during the period in which night work is prohibited in the following cases, where there are objective grounds for so doing and provided that adolescents are allowed suitable compensatory rest time and that the objectives set out in Article 1 are not called into question:
   — work performed in the shipping or fisheries sectors;
   — work performed in the context of the armed forces or the police;
   — work performed in hospitals or similar establishments;
   — cultural, artistic, sports or advertising activities.

3. Prior to any assignment to night work and at regular intervals thereafter, adolescents shall be entitled to a free assessment of their health and capacities, unless the work they do during the period during which work is prohibited is of an exceptional nature.

Article 10 Rest period

1. (a) Member States which make use of the option in Article 4(2)(b) or (c) shall adopt the measures necessary to ensure that, for each 24-hour period, children are entitled to a minimum rest period of 14 consecutive hours.
   (b) Member States shall adopt the measures necessary to ensure that, for each 24-hour period, adolescents are entitled to a minimum rest period of 12 consecutive hours.

2. Member States shall adopt the measures necessary to ensure that, for each seven-day period:
   — children in respect of whom they have made use of the option in Article 4(2)(b) or (c), and
   — adolescents
   are entitled to a minimum rest period of two days, which shall be consecutive if possible. Where justified by technical or organisation reasons, the minimum rest period may be reduced, but may in no circumstances be less than 36 consecutive hours. The minimum rest period referred to in the first and second subparagraphs shall in principle include Sunday.

3. Member States may, by legislative or regulatory provision, provide for the minimum rest periods referred to in paragraphs 1 and 2 to be interrupted in the case of activities involving periods of work that are split up over the day or are of short duration.

4. Member States may make legislative or regulatory provision for derogations from paragraph 1(b) and paragraph 2 in respect of adolescents in the following cases, where there are objective grounds for so doing and provided that they are granted appropriate compensatory rest time and that the objectives set out in Article 1 are not called into question:
   (a) work performed in the shipping or fisheries sectors;
   (b) work performed in the context of the armed forces or the police;
   (c) work performed in hospitals or similar establishments;
   (d) work performed in agriculture;
   (e) work performed in the tourism industry or in the hotel, restaurant and café sector;
   (f) activities involving periods of work split up over the day.

Article 11   Annual rest

Member States which make use of the option referred to in Article 4(2)(b) or (c) shall see to it that a period free of any work is included, as far as possible, in the school holidays of children subject to compulsory full-time schooling under national law.

Article 12   Breaks

Member States shall adopt the measures necessary to ensure that, where daily working time is more than four and a half hours, young people are entitled to a break of at least 30 minutes, which shall be consecutive if possible.

Article 13   Work by adolescents in the event of force majeure

Member States may, by legislative or regulatory provision, authorise derogations from Article 8(2), Article 9(1)(b), Article 10(1)(b) and, in the case of adolescents, Article 12, for work in the circumstances referred to in Article 5(4) of Directive 89/391/EEC, provided that such work is of a temporary nature and must be performed immediately, that adult workers are not available and that the adolescents are allowed equivalent compensatory rest time within the following three weeks.

SECTION IV

Article 14   Measures

Each Member State shall lay down any necessary measures to be applied in the event of failure to comply with the provisions adopted in order to implement this Directive; such measures must be effective and proportionate.

Article 15   Adaptation of the Annex

Adaptations of a strictly technical nature to the Annex in the light of technical progress, changes in international rules or specifications and advances in knowledge in the field covered by this Directive shall be adopted in accordance with the procedure provided for in Article 17 of Directive 89/391/EEC.

Article 16   Non-reducing clause

Without prejudice to the right of Member States to develop, in the light of changing circumstances, different provisions on the protection of young people, as long as the minimum requirements provided for by this Directive are complied with, the implementation of this Directive shall not constitute valid grounds for reducing the general level of protection afforded to young people.

Article 17   Final provisions

1.   (a)   Member States shall bring into force the laws, regulations and administrative provisions necessary to comply with this Directive not later than 22 June 1996 or ensure, by that date at the latest, that the two sides of industry introduce the requisite provisions by means of collective agreements, with Member States being required to make all the necessary provisions to enable them at all times to guarantee the results laid down by this Directive.

     (b)   The United Kingdom may refrain from implementing the first subparagraph of Article 8(1)(b) with regard to the provision relating to the maximum weekly working time, and also Article 8(2) and Article 9(1)(b) and (2) for a period of four years from the date specified in subparagraph (a).
     The Commission shall submit a report on the effects of this provision.
     The Council, acting in accordance with the conditions laid down by the Treaty, shall decide whether this period should be extended.

     (c)   Member States shall forthwith inform the Commission thereof.

2.   When Member States adopt the measures referred to in paragraph 1, such measures shall contain a reference to this Directive or shall be accompanied by such reference on the occasion of their official publication. The methods of making such reference shall be laid down by Member States.

3.   Member States shall communicate to the Commission the texts of the main provisions of national law which they have already adopted or adopt in the field governed by this Directive.

Article 17a   Implementation report

Every five years, the Member States shall submit to the Commission a report on the practical implementation of this Directive in the form of a specific chapter of the single report referred to in Article 17a(1), (2) and (3) of Directive 89/391/EEC, which serves as a basis for the Commission's evaluation, in accordance with Article 17a(4) of that Directive.

Article 18

This Directive is addressed to the Member States.

ANNEX

Non-exhaustive list of agents, processes and work (Article 7(2), second subparagraph)

I   Agents

1.   Physical agents:
     (a)   Ionizing radiation;
     (b)   Work in a high-pressure atmosphere, e.g., in pressurised containers, diving.
2.   Biological agents
     (a)   Biological agents belonging to groups 3 and 4 within the meaning of Article 2(d) of Council Directive 90/679/EEC of 26 November 1990 on the protection of workers from risks related to exposure to biological agents at work (Seventh individual Directive within the meaning of Article 16(1) of Directive 89/391/EEC).
3.   Chemical agents
     (a)   Substances and preparations classified according to Council Directive 67/548/EEC of 27 June 1967 on the approximation of laws, regulations and administrative provisions relating to the classification, packaging and labelling of dangerous substances with amendments and Council Directive 88/379/EEC of 7 June 1988 on the approximation of the laws, regulations and administrative provisions of the Member States relating to the classification, packaging and labelling of dangerous preparations as toxic (T), very toxic (Tx), corrosive (C) or explosive (E);
     (b)   Substances and preparations classified according to Directives 67/548/EEC and 88/379/EEC as harmful (Xn) and with one or more of the following risk phrases:
           — danger of very serious irreversible effects (R39),
           — possible risk of irreversible effects (R40),
           — may cause sensitisation by inhalation (R42),
           — may cause sensitisation by skin contact (R43),
           — may cause cancer (R45),
           — may cause heritable genetic damage (R46),
           — danger of serious damage to health by prolonged exposure (R48),
           — may impair fertility (R60),
           — may cause harm to the unborn child (R61);
     (c)   Substances and preparations classified according to Directives 67/548/EEC and 88/379/EEC as irritant (Xi) and with one or more of the following risk phrases:
           — highly flammable (R12),
           — may cause sensitisation by inhalation (R42),
           — may cause sensitisation by skin contact (R43),
     (d)   Substances and preparations referred to Article 2(c) of Council Directive 90/394/EEC of 28 June 1990 on the protection of workers from the risks related to exposure to carcinogens at work (Sixth individual Directive within the meaning of Article 16(1) of Directive 89/391/EEC;
     (e)   Lead and compounds thereof, inasmuch as the agents in question are absorbable by the human organism;
     (f)   Asbestos.

II   Processes and work

1.   Processes at work referred to in Annex I to Directive 90/394/EEC.
2.   Manufacture and handling of devices, fireworks or other objects containing explosives.

3.   Work with fierce or poisonous animals.
4.   Animal slaughtering on an industrial scale.
5.   Work involving the handling of equipment for the production, storage or application of compressed, liquified or dissolved gases.
6.   Work with vats, tanks, reservoirs or carboys containing chemical agents referred to in 1.3.
7.   Work involving a risk of structural collapse.
8.   Work involving high-voltage electrical hazards.
9.   Work the pace of which is determined by machinery and involving payment by results.

COUNCIL DIRECTIVE (EC) No 94/45 of 22 SEPTEMBER 1994
on the establishment of a European Works Council or a procedure in Community-scale undertakings and Community-scale groups of undertakings for the purposes of informing and consulting employees
[1994] OJ L254/64

THE COUNCIL OF THE EUROPEAN UNION,

Having regard to the Agreement on social policy annexed to Protocol 14 on social policy annexed to the Treaty establishing the European Community, and in particular Article 2(2) thereof,

Having regard to the proposal from the Commission,

Having regard to the opinion of the Economic and Social Committee,

Acting in accordance with the procedure referred to in Article 189c of the Treaty,

Whereas, on the basis of the Protocol on Social Policy annexed to the Treaty establishing the European Community, the Kingdom of Belgium, the Kingdom of Denmark, the Federal Republic of Germany, the Hellenic Republic, the Kingdom of Spain, the French Republic, Ireland, the Italian Republic, the Grand Duchy of Luxembourg, the Kingdom of the Netherlands and the Portuguese Republic (hereinafter referred to as 'the Member States'), desirous of implementing the Social Charter of 1989, have adopted an Agreement on Social Policy;

Whereas Article 2(2) of the said Agreement authorises the Council to adopt minimum requirements by means of directives;

Whereas, pursuant to Article 1 of the Agreement, one particular objective of the Community and the Member States is to promote dialogue between management and labour;

Whereas point 17 of the Community Charter of Fundamental Social Rights of Workers provides, inter alia, that information, consultation and participation for workers must be developed along appropriate lines, taking account of the practices in force in different Member States; whereas the Charter states that 'this shall apply especially in companies or groups of companies having establishments or companies in two or more Member States';

Whereas the Council, despite the existence of a broad consensus among the majority of Member States, was unable to act on the proposal for a Council Directive on the establishment of a European Works Council in Community-scale undertakings or groups of undertakings for the purposes of informing and consulting employees, as amended on 3 December 1991;

Whereas the Commission, pursuant to Article 3(2) of the Agreement on Social Policy, has consulted management and labour at Community level on the possible direction of Community action on the information and consultation of workers in Community-scale undertakings and Community-scale groups of undertakings;

Whereas the Commission, considering after this consultation that Community action was advisable, has again consulted management and labour on the content of the planned proposal, pursuant to Article 3(3) of the said Agreement, and management and labour have presented their opinions to the Commission;

Whereas, following this second phase of consultation, management and labour have not informed the Commission of their wish to initiate the process which might lead to the conclusion of an agreement, as provided for in Article 4 of the Agreement;

Whereas the functioning of the internal market involves a process of concentrations of undertakings, cross-border mergers, take-overs, joint ventures and, consequently, a transnationalisation of undertakings and groups of undertakings;

Whereas, if economic activities are to develop in a harmonious fashion, undertakings and groups of undertakings operating in two or more Member States must inform and consult the representatives of those of their employees that are affected by their decisions;

Whereas procedures for informing and consulting employees as embodied in legislation or practice in the Member States are often not geared to the transnational structure of the entity which takes the decisions affecting those employees;

Whereas this may lead to the unequal treatment of employees affected by decisions within one and the same undertaking or group of undertakings;

Whereas appropriate provisions must be adopted to ensure that the employees of Community-scale undertakings are properly informed and consulted when decisions which affect them are taken in a Member State other than that in which they are employed;

Whereas, in order to guarantee that the employees of undertakings or groups of undertakings operating in two or more Member States are properly informed and consulted, it is necessary to set up European Works Councils or to create other suitable procedures for the transnational information and consultation of employees;

Whereas it is accordingly necessary to have a definition of the concept of controlling undertaking relating solely to this Directive and not prejudging definitions of the concepts of group or control which might be adopted in texts to be drafted in the future;

Whereas the mechanisms for informing and consulting employees in such undertakings or groups must encompass all of the establishments or, as the case may be, the group's undertakings located within the Member States, regardless of whether the undertaking or the group's controlling undertaking has its central management inside or outside the territory of the Member States;

Whereas, in accordance with the principle of autonomy of the parties, it is for the representatives of employees and the management of the undertaking or the group's controlling undertaking to determine by agreement the nature, composition, the function, mode of operation, procedures and financial resources of European Works Councils or other information and consultation procedures so as to suit their own particular circumstances;

Whereas, in accordance with the principle of subsidiarity, it is for the Member States to determine who the employees' representatives are and in particular to provide, if they consider appropriate, for a balanced representation of different categories of employees;

Whereas, however, provision should be made for certain subsidiary requirements to apply should the parties so decide or in the event of the central management refusing to initiate negotiations or in the absence of agreement subsequent to such negotiations;

Whereas, moreover, employees' representatives may decide not to seek the setting-up of a European Works Council or the parties concerned may decide on other procedures for the transnational information and consultation of employees;

Whereas, without prejudice to the possibility of the parties deciding otherwise, the European Works Council set up in the absence of agreement between the parties must, in order to fulfil the objective of this Directive, be kept informed and consulted on the activities of the undertaking or group of undertakings so that it may assess the possible impact on employees' interests in at least two different Member States;

Whereas, to that end, the undertaking or controlling undertaking must be required to communicate to the employees' appointed representatives general information concerning the interests of employees and information relating more specifically to those aspects of the activities of the undertaking or group of undertakings which affect employees' interests; whereas the European Works Council must be able to deliver an opinion at the end of that meeting;

Whereas certain decisions having a significant effect on the interests of employees must be the subject of information and consultation of the employees' appointed representatives as soon as possible;

Whereas provision should be made for the employees' representatives acting within the framework of the Directive to enjoy, when exercising their functions, the same protection and guarantees similar to those provided to employees' representatives by the legislation and/or practice of the country of employment;

Whereas they must not be subject to any discrimination as a result of the lawful exercise of their activities and must enjoy adequate protection as regards dismissal and other sanctions;

Whereas the information and consultation provisions laid down in this Directive must be implemented in the case of an undertaking or a group's controlling undertaking which has its central management outside the territory of the Member States by its representative agent, to be designated if necessary, in one of the Member States or, in the absence of such an agent, by the establishment or controlled undertaking employing the greatest number of employees in the Member States;

Whereas special treatment should be accorded to Community-scale undertakings and groups of undertakings in which there exists, at the time when this Directive is brought into effect, an agreement, covering the entire workforce, providing for the transnational information and consultation of employees;

Whereas the Member States must take appropriate measures in the event of failure to comply with the obligations laid down in this Directive,

HAS ADOPTED THIS DIRECTIVE:

SECTION I

GENERAL

Article 1   Objective

1. The purpose of this Directive is to improve the right to information and to consultation of employees in Community-scale undertakings and Community-scale groups of undertakings.

2. To that end, a European Works Council or a procedure for informing and consulting employees shall be established in every Community-scale undertaking and every Community-scale group of undertakings, where requested in the manner laid down in Article 5(1), with the purpose of informing and consulting employees under the terms, in the manner and with the effects laid down in this Directive.

3. Notwithstanding paragraph 2, where a Community-scale group of undertakings within the meaning of Article 2(1)(c) comprises one or more undertakings or groups of undertakings which are Community-scale undertakings or Community-scale groups of undertakings within the meaning of Article 2(1)(a) or (c), a European Works Council shall be established at the level of the group unless the agreements referred to in Article 6 provide otherwise.

4. Unless a wider scope is provided for in the agreements referred to in Article 6, the powers and competence of European Works Councils and the scope of information and consultation procedures established to achieve the purpose specified in paragraph 1 shall, in the case of a Community-scale undertaking, cover all the establishments located within the Member States and, in the case of a Community-scale group of undertakings, all group undertakings located within the Member States.

5. Member States may provide that this Directive shall not apply to merchant navy crews.

Article 2   Definitions

1. For the purposes of this Directive:

   (a) 'Community-scale undertaking' means any undertaking with at least 1,000 employees within the Member States and at least 150 employees in each of at least two Member States;

   (b) 'group of undertakings' means a controlling undertaking and its controlled undertakings;

   (c) 'Community-scale group of undertakings' means a group of undertakings with the following characteristics:
   — at least 1,000 employees within the Member States,
   — at least two group undertakings in different Member States, and
   — at least one group undertaking with at least 150 employees in one Member State, and
   — at least one other group undertaking with at least 150 employees in another Member State;

(d)   'employees' representatives' means the employees' representatives provided for by national law and/or practice;

(e)   'central management' means the central management of the Community-scale undertaking or, in the case of a Community-scale group of undertakings, of the controlling undertaking;

(f)   'consultation' means the exchange of views and establishment of dialogue between employees' representatives and central management or any more appropriate level of management;

(g)   'European Works Council' means the council established in accordance with Article 1(2) or the provisions of the Annex, with the purpose of informing and consulting employees;

(h)   'special negotiating body' means the body established in accordance with Article 5(2) to negotiate with the central management regarding the establishment of a European Works Council or a procedure for informing and consulting employees in accordance with Article 1(2).

2.   For the purposes of this Directive, the prescribed thresholds for the size of the workforce shall be based on the average number of employees, including part-time employees, employed during the previous two years calculated according to national legislation and/or practice.

Article 3   Definition of 'controlling undertaking'

1.   For the purposes of this Directive, 'controlling undertaking' means an undertaking which can exercise a dominant influence over another undertaking ('the controlled undertaking') by virtue, for example, of ownership, financial participation or the rules which govern it.

2.   The ability to exercise a dominant influence shall be presumed, without prejudice to proof to the contrary, when, in relation to another undertaking directly or indirectly:

(a)   holds a majority of that undertaking's subscribed capital; or

(b)   controls a majority of the votes attached to that undertaking's issued share capital; or

(c)   can appoint more than half of the members of that undertaking's administrative, management or supervisory body.

3.   For the purposes of paragraph 2, a controlling undertaking's rights as regards voting and appointment shall include the rights of any other controlled undertaking and those of any person or body acting in his or its own name but on behalf of the controlling undertaking or of any other controlled undertaking.

4.   Notwithstanding paragraphs 1 and 2, an undertaking shall not be deemed to be a 'controlling undertaking' with respect to another undertaking in which it has holdings where the former undertaking is a company referred to in Article 3(5)(a) or (c) of Council Regulation (EEC) No. 4064/89 of 21 December 1989 on the control of concentrations between undertakings.

5.   A dominant influence shall not be presumed to be exercised solely by virtue of the fact that an office holder is exercising his functions, according to the law of a Member State relating to liquidation, winding up, insolvency, cessation of payments, compositions or analogous proceedings.

6.   The law applicable in order to determine whether an undertaking is a 'controlling undertaking' shall be the law of the Member State which governs that undertaking. Where the law governing that undertaking is not that of a Member State, the law applicable shall be the law of the Member State within whose territory the representative of the undertaking or, in the absence of such a representative, the central management of the group undertaking which employs the greatest number of employees is situated.

7.   Where, in the case of a conflict of laws in the application of paragraph 2, two or more undertakings from a group satisfy one or more of the criteria laid down in that paragraph, the undertaking which satisfies the criterion laid down in point (c) thereof shall be regarded as the controlling undertaking, without prejudice to proof that another undertaking is able to exercise a dominant influence.

SECTION II
ESTABLISHMENT OF A EUROPEAN WORKS COUNCIL OR AN EMPLOYEE INFORMATION
AND CONSULTATION PROCEDURE

Article 4   Responsibility for the establishment of a European Works Council or an employee information and consultation procedure

1.   The central management shall be responsible for creating the conditions and means necessary for the setting up of a European Works Council or an information and consultation procedure, as provided for in Article 1(2), in a Community-scale undertaking and a Community-scale group of undertakings.

2.   Where the central management is not situated in a Member State, the central management's representative agent in a Member State, to be designated if necessary, shall take on the responsibility referred to in paragraph 1. In the absence of such a representative, the management of the establishment or group undertaking employing the greatest number of employees in any one Member State shall take on the responsibility referred to in paragraph 1.

3.   For the purposes of this Directive, the representative or representatives or, in the absence of any such representatives, the management referred to in the second subparagraph of paragraph 2, shall be regarded as the central management.

Article 5   Special negotiating body

1.   In order to achieve the objective in Article 1(1), the central management shall initiate negotiations for the establishment of a European Works Council or an information and consultation procedure on its own initiative or at the written request of at least 100 employees or their representatives in at least two undertakings or establishments in at least two different Member States.

2.   For this purpose, a special negotiating body shall be established in accordance with the following guidelines:

(a)   The Member States shall determine the method to be used for the election or appointment of the members of the special negotiating body who are to be elected or appointed in their territories.

Member States shall provide that employees in undertakings and/or establishments in which there are no employees' representatives through no fault of their own, have the right to elect or appoint members of the special negotiating body.

The second subparagraph shall be without prejudice to national legislation and/or practice laying down thresholds for the establishment of employee representation bodies.

(b)   The special negotiating body shall have a minimum of three members and a maximum of members equal to the members of Member States.

(c)   In these elections or appointments, it must be ensured:

— firstly, that each Member State in which the Community-scale undertaking has one or more establishments or in which the Community-scale group of undertakings has the controlling undertaking or one or more controlled undertakings is represented by one member,

— secondly, that there are supplementary members in proportion to the number of employees working in the establishments, the controlling undertaking or the controlled undertakings as laid down by the legislation of the Member State within the territory of which the central management is situated.

(d)   The central management and local management shall be informed of the composition of the special negotiating body.

3.   The special negotiating body shall have the task of determining, with the central management, by written agreement, the scope, composition, functions, and term of office of the European Works Council(s) or the arrangements for implementing a procedure for the information and consultation of employees.

4.   With a view to the conclusion of an agreement in accordance with Article 6, the central management shall convene a meeting with the special negotiating body. It shall inform the local managements accordingly.

For the purpose of the negotiations, the special negotiating body may be assisted by experts of its choice.

5.   The special negotiating body may decide, by at least two-thirds of the votes, not to open negotiations in accordance with paragraph 4, or to terminate the negotiations already opened. Such a decision shall stop the procedure to conclude the agreement referred to in Article 6. Where such a decision has been taken, the provisions in the Annex shall not apply.

A new request to convene the special negotiating body may be made at the earliest two years after the abovementioned decision unless the parties concerned lay down a shorter period.

6.   Any expenses relating to the negotiations referred to in paragraphs 3 and 4 shall be borne by the central management so as to enable the special negotiating body to carry out its task in an appropriate manner.

In compliance with this principle, Member States may lay down budgetary rules regarding the operation of the special negotiating body. They may in particular limit the funding to cover one expert only.

Article 6   Content of the agreement

1.   The central management and the special negotiating body must negotiate in a spirit of cooperation with a view to reaching an agreement on the detailed arrangements for implementing the information and consultation of employees provided for in Article 1(1).

2.   Without prejudice to the autonomy of the parties, the agreement referred to in paragraph 1 between the central management and the special negotiating body shall determine:

(a)   the undertakings of the Community-scale group of undertakings or the establishments of the Community-scale undertaking which are covered by the agreement;

(b)   the composition of the European Works Council, the number of members, the allocation of seats and the term of office;

(c)   the functions and the procedure for information and consultation of the European Works Council;

(d)   the venue, frequency and duration of meetings of the European Works Council;

(e)   the financial and material resources to be allocated to the European Works Council;

(f)   the duration of the agreement and the procedure for its renegotiation.

3.   The central management and the special negotiating body may decide, in writing, to establish one or more information and consultation procedures instead of a European Works Council.

The agreement must stipulate by what method the employees' representatives shall have the right to meet to discuss the information conveyed to them. This information shall relate in particular to transnational questions which significantly affect workers' interests.

4.   The agreements referred to in paragraphs 2 and 3 shall not, unless provision is made otherwise therein, be subject to the subsidiary requirements of the Annex.

5.   For the purposes of concluding the agreements referred to in paragraphs 2 and 3, the special negotiating body shall act by a majority of its members.

Article 7   Subsidiary requirements

1.   In order to achieve the objective in Article 1(1), the subsidiary requirements laid down by the legislation of the Member State in which the central management is situated shall apply:

— where the central management and the special negotiating body so decide, or

— where the central management refuses to commence negotiations within six months of the request referred to in Article 5(1), or

— where, after three years from the date of this request, they are unable to conclude an agreement as laid down in Article 6 and the special negotiating body has not taken the decision provided for in Article 5(5).

2.   The subsidiary requirements referred to in paragraph 1 as adopted in the legislation of the Member States must satisfy the provisions set out in the Annex.

SECTION III
MISCELLANEOUS PROVISIONS

Article 8   Confidential information

1. Member States shall provide that members of special negotiating bodies or of European Works Councils and any experts who assist them are not authorised to reveal any information which has expressly been provided to them in confidence.

    The same shall apply to employees' representatives in the framework of an information and consultation procedure. This obligation shall continue to apply, wherever the persons referred to in the first and second subparagraphs are, even after the expiry of their terms of office.

2. Each Member State shall provide, in specific cases and under the conditions and limits laid down by national legislation, that the central management situated in its territory is not obliged to transmit information when its nature is such that, according to objective criteria, it would seriously harm the functioning of the undertakings concerned or would be prejudicial to them.

    A Member State may make such dispensation subject to prior administrative or judicial authorisation.

3. Each Member State may lay down particular provisions for the central management of undertakings in its territory which pursue directly and essentially the aim of ideological guidance with respect to information and the expression of opinions, on condition that, at the date of adoption of this Directive such particular provisions already exist in the national legislation.

Article 9   Operation of European Works Council and information and consultation procedure for workers

The central management and the European Works Council shall work in a spirit of cooperation with due regard to their reciprocal rights and obligations.

The same shall apply to cooperation between the central management and employees' representatives in the framework of an information and consultation procedure for workers.

Article 10   Protection of employees' representatives

Members of special negotiating bodies, members of European Works Councils and employees' representatives exercising their functions under the procedure referred to in Article 6(3) shall, in the exercise of their functions, enjoy the same protection and guarantees provided for employees' representatives by the national legislation and/or practice in force in their country of employment. This shall apply in particular to attendance at meetings of special negotiating bodies or European Works Councils or any other meetings within the framework of the agreement referred to in Article 6(3), and the payment of wages for members who are on the staff of the Community-scale undertaking or the Community-scale group of undertakings for the period of absence necessary for the performance of their duties.

Article 11   Compliance with this Directive

1. Each Member State shall ensure that the management of establishments of a Community-scale undertaking and the management of undertakings which form part of a Community-scale group of undertakings which are situated within its territory and their employees' representatives or, as the case may be, employees abide by the obligations laid down by this Directive, regardless of whether or not the central management is situated within its territory.

2. Member States shall ensure that the information on the number of employees referred to in Article 2(1)(a) and (c) is made available by undertakings at the request of the parties concerned by the application of this Directive.

3. Member States shall provide for appropriate measures in the event of failure to comply with this Directive; in particular, they shall ensure that adequate administrative or judicial procedures are available to enable the obligations deriving from this Directive to be enforced.

4. Where Member States apply Article 8, they shall make provision for administrative or judicial appeal procedures which the employees' representatives may initiate when the central management requires confidentiality or does not give information in accordance with that Article.

Such procedures may include procedures designed to protect the confidentiality of the information in question.

Article 12 Link between this Directive and other provisions

1. This Directive shall apply without prejudice to measures taken pursuant to Council Directive 75/129/EEC of 17 February 1975 on the approximation of the laws of the Member States relating to collective redundancies, and to Council Directive 77/187/EEC of 14 February 1977 on the approximation of the laws of the Member States relating to the safeguarding of employees' rights in the event of transfers of undertakings, businesses or parts of businesses.

2. This Directive shall be without prejudice to employees' existing rights to information and consultation under national law.

Article 13 Agreements in force

1. Without prejudice to paragraph 2, the obligations arising from this Directive shall not apply to Community-scale undertakings or Community-scale groups of undertakings in which, on the date laid down in Article 14(1) for the implementation of this Directive or the date of its transposition in the Member State in question, where this is earlier than the abovementioned date, there is already an agreement, covering the entire workforce, providing for the transnational information and consultation of employees.

2. When the agreements referred to in paragraph 1 expire, the parties to those agreements may decide jointly to renew them. Where this is not the case, the provisions of this Directive shall apply.

Article 14 Final provisions

1. Member States shall bring into force the laws, regulations and administrative provisions necessary to comply with this Directive no later than 22 September 1996 or shall ensure by that date at the latest that management and labour introduce the required provisions by way of agreement, the Member States being obliged to take all necessary steps enabling them at all times to guarantee the results imposed by this Directive. They shall forthwith inform the Commission thereof.

2. When Member States adopt these measures, they shall contain a reference to this Directive or shall be accompanied by such reference on the occasion of their official publication. The methods of making such reference shall be laid down by Member States.

Article 15 Review by the Commission

Not later than 22 September 1999, the Commission shall, in consultation with the Member States and with management and labour at European level, review its operation and, in particular examine whether the workforce size thresholds are appropriate with a view to proposing suitable amendments to the Council, where necessary.

Article 16

This Directive is addressed to the Member States.

ANNEX
SUBSIDIARY REQUIREMENTS REFERRED TO IN ARTICLE 7 OF THE DIRECTIVE

1. In order to achieve the objective in Article 1(1) of the Directive and in the cases provided for in Article 7(1) of the Directive, the establishment, composition and competence of a European Works Council shall be governed by the following rules:

    (a) The competence of the European Works Council shall be limited to information and consultation on the matters which concern the Community-scale undertaking or Community-scale group of undertakings as a whole or at least two of its establishments or group undertakings situated in different Member States. In the case of undertakings or groups of undertakings referred to in Article 4(2), the competence of the European Works Council shall be limited to those matters concerning all their establishments or group undertakings situated within the Member States or concerning at least two of their establishments or group undertakings situated in different Member States.

(b)   The European Works Council shall be composed of employees of the Community-scale undertaking or Community-scale group of undertakings elected or appointed from their number by the employees' representatives or, in the absence thereof, by the entire body of employees.

The election or appointment of members of the European Works Council shall be carried out in accordance with national legislation and/or practice.

(c)   The European Works Council shall have a minimum of three members and a maximum of 30. Where its size so warrants, it shall elect a select committee from among its members, comprising at most three members. It shall adopt its own rules of procedure.

(d)   In the election or appointment of members of the European Works Council, it must be ensured:

— firstly, that each Member State in which the Community-scale undertaking has one or more establishments or in which the Community-scale group of undertakings has the controlling undertaking or one or more controlled undertakings is represented by one member,

— secondly, that there are supplementary members in proportion to the number of employees working in the establishments, the controlling undertaking or the controlled undertakings as laid down by the legislation of the Member State within the territory of which the central management is situated.

(e)   The central management and any other more appropriate level of management shall be informed of the composition of the European Works Council.

(f)   Four years after the European Works Council is established it shall examine whether to open negotiations for the conclusion of the agreement referred to in Article 6 of the Directive or to continue to apply the subsidiary requirements adopted in accordance with this Annex.

Articles 6 and 7 of the Directive shall apply, mutatis mutandis, if a decision has been taken to negotiate an agreement according to Article 6 of the Directive, in which case 'special negotiating body' shall be replaced by 'European Works Council'.

2.   The European Works Council shall have the right to meet with the central management once a year, to be informed and consulted, on the basis of a report drawn up by the central management, on the progress of the business of the Community-scale undertaking or Community-scale group of undertakings and its prospects. The local managements shall be informed accordingly.

The meeting shall relate in particular to the structure, economic and financial situation, the probable development of the business and of production and sales, the situation and probable trend of employment, investments, and substantial changes concerning organisation, introduction of new working methods or production processes, transfers of production, mergers, cut-backs or closures of undertakings, establishments or important parts thereof, and collective redundancies.

3.   Where there are exceptional circumstances affecting the employees' interests to a considerable extent, particularly in the event of relocations, the closure of establishments or undertakings or collective redundancies, the select committee or, where no such committee exists, the European Works Council shall have the right to be informed. It shall have the right to meet, at its request, the central management, or any other more appropriate level of management within the Community-scale undertaking or group of undertakings having its own powers of decision, so as to be informed and consulted on measures significantly affecting employees' interests. Those members of the European Works Council who have been elected or appointed by the establishments and/or undertakings which are directly concerned by the measures in question shall also have the right to participate in the meeting organised with the select committee.

This information and consultation meeting shall take place as soon as possible on the basis of a report drawn up by the central management or any other appropriate level of management of the Community-scale undertaking or group of undertakings, on which an opinion may be delivered at the end of the meeting or within a reasonable time. This meeting shall not affect the prerogatives of the central management.

4.   The Member States may lay down rules on the chairing of information and consultation meetings.

Before any meeting with the central management, the European Works Council or the select committee, where necessary enlarged in accordance with the second paragraph of point 3, shall be entitled to meet without the management concerned being present.

5.   Without prejudice to Article 8 of the Directive, the members of the European Works Council shall inform the representatives of the employees of the establishments or of the undertakings of a Community-scale group of undertakings or, in the absence of representatives, the workforce as a whole, of the content and outcome of the information and consultation procedure carried out in accordance with this Annex.

6.   The European Works Council or the select committee may be assisted by experts of its choice, in so far as this is necessary for it to carry out its tasks.

7.   The operating expenses of the European Works Council shall be borne by the central management.

The central management concerned shall provide the members of the European Works Council with such financial and material resources as enable them to perform their duties in an appropriate manner.

In particular, the cost of organising meetings and arranging for interpretation facilities and the accommodation and travelling expenses of members of the European Works Council and its select committee shall be met by the central management unless otherwise agreed.

In compliance with these principles, the Member States may lay down budgetary rules regarding the operation of the European Works Council. They may in particular limit funding to cover one expert only.

COUNCIL DIRECTIVE (EC) No 97/81 of 15 DECEMBER 1997
concerning the framework agreement on part-time work concluded by UNICE, CEEP and the ETUC
[1998] OJ L14/9

THE COUNCIL OF THE EUROPEAN UNION,

Having regard to the Agreement on social policy annexed to the Protocol (No. 14) on social policy, annexed to the Treaty establishing the European Community, and in particular Article 4(2) thereof,

Having regard to the proposal from the Commission,

(1)   Whereas on the basis of the Protocol on social policy annexed to the Treaty establishing the European Community, the Member States, with the exception of the United Kingdom of Great Britain and Northern Ireland (hereinafter referred to as 'the Member States'), wishing to continue along the path laid down in the 1989 Social Charter, have concluded an agreement on social policy;

(2)   Whereas management and labour (the social partners) may, in accordance with Article 4(2) of the Agreement on social policy, request jointly that agreements at Community level be implemented by a Council decision on a proposal from the Commission;

(3)   Whereas point 7 of the Community Charter of the Fundamental Social Rights of Workers provides, inter alia, that 'the completion of the internal market must lead to an improvement in the living and working conditions of workers in the European Community. This process must result from an approximation of these conditions while the improvement is being maintained, as regards in particular … forms of employment other than open-ended contracts, such as fixed-term contracts, part-time working, temporary work and seasonal work';

(4)   Whereas the Council has not reached a decision on the proposal for a Directive on certain employment relationships with regard to distortions of competition, as amended, nor on the proposal for a Directive on certain employment relationships with regard to working conditions;

(5)   Whereas the conclusions of the Essen European Council stressed the need to take measures to promote employment and equal opportunities for women and men, and called for measures with a view to increasing the employment-intensiveness of growth, in particular by a more flexible organisation of work in a way which fulfils both the wishes of employees and the requirements of competition;

(6)   Whereas the Commission, in accordance with Article 3(2) of the Agreement on social policy, has consulted management and labour on the possible direction of Community action with regard to flexible working time and job security;

(7)   Whereas the Commission, considering after such consultation that Community action was desirable, once again consulted management and labour at Community level on the substance of the envisaged proposal in accordance with Article 3(3) of the said Agreement;

(8)   Whereas the general cross-industry organisations, the Union of Industrial and Employer's Confederations of Europe (UNICE), the European Centre of Enterprises with Public Participation (CEEP) and the European Trade Union Confederation (ETUC) informed the Commission in their joint letter of 19 June 1996 of their desire to initiate the procedure provided for in Article 4 of the Agreement on social policy; whereas they asked the Commission, in a joint letter dated 12 March 1997, for a further three months; whereas the Commission complied with this request;

(9)   Whereas the said cross-industry organisations concluded, on 6 June 1997, a Framework Agreement on part-time work; whereas they forwarded to the Commission their joint request to implement this Framework Agreement by a Council decision on a proposal from the Commission, in accordance with Article 4(2) of the said Agreement;

(10) Whereas the Council, in its Resolution of 6 December 1994 on prospects for a European Union social policy: contribution to economic and social convergence in the Union, asked management and labour to make use of the opportunities for concluding agreements, since they are as a rule closer to social reality and to social problems;

(11) Whereas the signatory parties wished to conclude a framework agreement on part-time work setting out the general principles and minimum requirements for part-time working; whereas they have demonstrated their desire to establish a general framework for eliminating discrimination against part-time workers and to contribute to developing the potential for part-time work on a basis which is acceptable for employers and workers alike;

(12) Whereas the social partners wished to give particular attention to part-time work, while at the same time indicating that it was their intention to consider the need for similar agreements for other flexible forms of work;

(13) Whereas, in the conclusions of the Amsterdam European Council, the Heads of State and Government of the European Union strongly welcomed the agreement concluded by the social partners on part-time work;

(14) Whereas the proper instrument for implementing the Framework Agreement is a Directive within the meaning of Article 189 of the Treaty; whereas it therefore binds the Member States as to the result to be achieved, whilst leaving national authorities the choice of form and methods;

(15) Whereas, in accordance with the principles of subsidiarity and proportionality as set out in Article 3(b) of the Treaty, the objectives of this Directive cannot be sufficiently achieved by the Member States and can therefore be better achieved by the Community; whereas this Directive does not go beyond what is necessary for the attainment of those objectives;

(16) Whereas, with regard to terms used in the Framework Agreement which are not specifically defined therein, this Directive leaves Member States free to define those terms in accordance with national law and practice, as is the case for other social policy Directives using similar terms, providing that the said definitions respect the content of the Framework Agreement;

(17) Whereas the Commission has drafted its proposal for a Directive, in accordance with its Communication of 14 December 1993 concerning the application of the Protocol (No. 14) on social policy and its Communication of 18 September 1996 concerning the development of the social dialogue at Community level, taking into account the representative status of the signatory parties and the legality of each clause of the Framework Agreement;

(18) Whereas the Commission has drafted its proposal for a Directive in compliance with Article 2(2) of the Agreement on social policy which provides that Directives in the social policy domain'shall avoid imposing administrative, financial and legal constraints in a way which would hold back the creation and development of small and medium-sized undertakings';

(19) Whereas the Commission, in accordance with its Communication of 14 December 1993 concerning the application of the Protocol (No. 14) on social policy, informed the European Parliament by sending it the text of its proposal for a Directive containing the Framework Agreement;

(20) Whereas the Commission also informed the Economic and Social Committee;

(21) Whereas Clause 6.1 of the Framework Agreement provides that Member States and/or the social partners may maintain or introduce more favourable provisions;

(22) Whereas Clause 6.2 of the Framework Agreement provides that implementation of this Directive may not serve to justify any regression in relation to the situation which already exists in each Member State;

(23) Whereas the Community Charter of the Fundamental Social Rights of Workers recognises the importance of the fight against all forms of discrimination, especially based on sex, colour, race, opinion and creed;

(24) Whereas Article F(2) of the Treaty on European Union states that the Union shall respect fundamental rights, as guaranteed by the European Convention for the Protection of Human Rights and Fundamental Freedoms and as they result from the constitutional traditions common to the Member States, as general principles of Community law;

(25) Whereas the Member States may entrust the social partners, at their joint request, with the implementation of this Directive, provided that the Member States take all the necessary steps to ensure that they can at all times guarantee the results imposed by this Directive;

(26) Whereas the implementation of the Framework Agreement contributes to achieving the objectives under Article 1 of the Agreement on social policy,

HAS ADOPTED THIS DIRECTIVE:

Article 1

The purpose of this Directive is to implement the Framework Agreement on part-time work concluded on 6 June 1997 between the general cross-industry organisations (UNICE, CEEP and the ETUC) annexed hereto.

Article 2

1.   Member States shall bring into force the laws, regulations and administrative provisions necessary to comply with this Directive not later than 20 January 2000, or shall ensure that, by that date at the latest, the social partners have introduced the necessary measures by agreement, the Member States being required to take any necessary measures to enable them at any time to be in a position to guarantee the results imposed by this Directive. They shall forthwith inform the Commission thereof.

   Member States may have a maximum of one more year, if necessary, to take account of special difficulties or implementation by a collective agreement.

   They shall inform the Commission forthwith in such circumstances.

   When Member States adopt the measures referred to in the first subparagraph, they shall contain a reference to this Directive or shall be accompanied by such reference on the occasion of their official publication. The methods of making such a reference shall be laid down by the Member States.

1a.   As regards the United Kingdom of Great Britain and Northern Ireland, the date of 20 January 2000 in paragraph 1 shall be replaced by the date of 7 April 2000.

2.   Member States shall communicate to the Commission the text of the main provisions of domestic law which they have adopted or which they adopt in the field governed by this Directive.

Article 3

This Directive shall enter into force on the day of its publication in the Official Journal of the European Communities.

Article 4

This Directive is addressed to the Member States.

ANNEX
UNION OF INDUSTRIAL AND EMPLOYERS' CONFEDERATIONS OF EUROPE, EUROPEAN TRADE UNION CONFEDERATION, EUROPEAN CENTRE OF ENTERPRISES WITH PUBLIC PARTICIPATION FRAMEWORK AGREEMENT ON PART-TIME WORK

This Framework Agreement is a contribution to the overall European strategy on employment. Part-time work has had an important impact on employment in recent years. For this reason, the parties to this agreement have given priority attention to this form of work. It is the intention of the parties to consider the need for similar agreements relating to other forms of flexible work.

Recognising the diversity of situations in Member States and acknowledging that part-time work is a feature of employment in certain sectors and activities, this Agreement sets out the general principles and minimum requirements relating to part-time work. It illustrates the willingness of the social partners to establish a general framework for the elimination of discrimination against part-time workers and to assist the development of opportunities for part-time working on a basis acceptable to employers and workers.

This Agreement relates to employment conditions of part-time workers recognising that matters concerning statutory social security are for decision by the Member States. In the context of the principle of non-discrimination, the parties to this Agreement have noted the Employment Declaration of the Dublin European Council of December 1996, wherein the Council inter alia emphasised the need to make social security systems more employment-friendly by 'developing social protection systems capable of adapting to new patterns of work and of providing appropriate protection to people engaged in such work'. The parties to this Agreement consider that effect should be given to this Declaration.

ETUC, UNICE and CEEP request the Commission to submit this Framework Agreement to the Council for a decision making these requirements binding in the Member States which are party to the Agreement on social policy annexed to the Protocol (No. 14) on social policy annexed to the Treaty establishing the European Community.

The parties to this Agreement ask the Commission, in its proposal to implement this Agreement, to request that Member States adopt the laws, regulations and administrative provisions necessary to comply with the Council decision within a period of two years from its adoption or ensure that the social partners establish the necessary measures by way of agreement by the end of this period. Member States may, if necessary to take account of particular difficulties or implementation by collective agreement, have up to a maximum of one additional year to comply with this provision. Without prejudice to the role of national courts and the Court of Justice, the parties to this agreement request that any matter relating to the interpretation of this agreement at European level should, in the first instance, be referred by the Commission to them for an opinion.

General considerations

1. Having regard to the Agreement on social policy annexed to the Protocol (No. 14) on social policy annexed to the Treaty establishing the European Community, and in particular Articles 3(4) and 4(2) thereof;

2. Whereas Article 4(2) of the Agreement on social policy provides that agreements concluded at Community level may be implemented, at the joint request of the signatory parties, by a Council decision on a proposal from the Commission.

3. Whereas, in its second consultation document on flexibility of working time and security for workers, the Commission announced its intention to propose a legally binding Community measure;

4.   Whereas the conclusions of the European Council meeting in Essen emphasised the need for measures to promote both employment and equal opportunities for women and men, and called for measures aimed at 'increasing the employment intensiveness of growth, in particular by more flexible organisation of work in a way which fulfils both the wishes of employees and the requirements of competition';

5.   Whereas the parties to this agreement attach importance to measures which would facilitate access to part-time work for men and women in order to prepare for retirement, reconcile professional and family life, and take up education and training opportunities to improve their skills and career opportunities for the mutual benefit of employers and workers and in a manner which would assist the development of enterprises;

6.   Whereas this Agreement refers back to Member States and social partners for the arrangements for the application of these general principles, minimum requirements and provisions, in order to take account of the situation in each Member State;

7.   Whereas this Agreement takes into consideration the need to improve social policy requirements, to enhance the competitiveness of the Community economy and to avoid imposing administrative, financial and legal constraints in a way which would hold back the creation and development of small and medium-sized undertakings;

8.   Whereas the social partners are best placed to find solutions that correspond to the needs of both employers and workers and must therefore be given a special role in the implementation and application of this Agreement.

THE SIGNATORY PARTIES HAVE AGREED THE FOLLOWING:

Clause 1: Purpose

The purpose of this Framework Agreement is:

(a)   to provide for the removal of discrimination against part-time workers and to improve the quality of part-time work;

(b)   to facilitate the development of part-time work on a voluntary basis and to contribute to the flexible organisation of working time in a manner which takes into account the needs of employers and workers.

Clause 2: Scope

1.   This Agreement applies to part-time workers who have an employment contract or employment relationship as defined by the law, collective agreement or practice in force in each Member State.

2.   Member States, after consultation with the social partners in accordance with national law, collective agreements or practice, and/or the social partners at the appropriate level in conformity with national industrial relations practice may, for objective reasons, exclude wholly or partly from the terms of this Agreement part-time workers who work on a casual basis. Such exclusions should be reviewed periodically to establish if the objective reasons for making them remain valid.

Clause 3: Definitions

For the purpose of this agreement:

1.   The term 'part-time worker' refers to an employee whose normal hours of work, calculated on a weekly basis or on average over a period of employment of up to one year, are less than the normal hours of work of a comparable full-time worker.

2.   The term 'comparable full-time worker' means a full-time worker in the same establishment having the same type of employment contract or relationship, who is engaged in the same or a similar work/occupation, due regard being given to other considerations which may include seniority and qualification/skills.

Where there is no comparable full-time worker in the same establishment, the comparison shall be made by reference to the applicable collective agreement or, where there is no applicable collective agreement, in accordance with national law, collective agreements or practice.

Clause 4: Principle of non-discrimination

1. In respect of employment conditions, part-time workers shall not be treated in a less favourable manner than comparable full-time workers solely because they work part time unless different treatment is justified on objective grounds.

2. Where appropriate, the principle of pro rata temporis shall apply.

3. The arrangements for the application of this clause shall be defined by the Member States and/or social partners, having regard to European legislation, national law, collective agreements and practice.

4. Where justified by objective reasons, Member States after consultation of the social partners in accordance with national law, collective agreements or practice and/or social partners may, where appropriate, make access to particular conditions of employment subject to a period of service, time worked or earnings qualification.

   Qualifications relating to access by part-time workers to particular conditions of employment should be reviewed periodically having regard to the principle of non-discrimination as expressed in Clause 4.1.

Clause 5: Opportunities for part-time work

1. In the context of Clause 1 of this Agreement and of the principle of nondiscrimination between part-time and full-time workers:

   (a) Member States, following consultations with the social partners in accordance with national law or practice, should identify and review obstacles of a legal or administrative nature which may limit the opportunities for part-time work and, where appropriate, eliminate them;

   (b) the social partners, acting within their sphere of competence and through the procedures set out in collective agreements, should identify and review obstacles which may limit opportunities for part-time work and, where appropriate, eliminate them.

2. A worker's refusal to transfer from full-time to part-time work or vice-versa should not in itself constitute a valid reason for termination of employment, without prejudice to termination in accordance with national law, collective agreements and practice, for other reasons such as may arise from the operational requirements of the establishment concerned.

3. As far as possible, employers should give consideration to:

   (a) requests by workers to transfer from full-time to part-time work that becomes available in the establishment;

   (b) requests by workers to transfer from part-time to full-time work or to increase their working time should the opportunity arise;

   (c) the provision of timely information on the availability of part-time and full-time positions in the establishment in order to facilitate transfers from full-time to part-time or vice versa;

   (d) measures to facilitate access to part-time work at all levels of the enterprise, including skilled and managerial positions, and where appropriate, to facilitate access by part-time workers to vocational training to enhance career opportunities and occupational mobility;

   (e) the provision of appropriate information to existing bodies representing workers about part-time working in the enterprise.

Clause 6: Provisions on implementation

1. Member States and/or social partners may maintain or introduce more favourable provisions than set out in this agreement.

2. Implementation of the provisions of this Agreement shall not constitute valid grounds for reducing the general level of protection afforded to workers in the field of this agreement. This does not prejudice the right of Member States and/or social partners to develop different legislative, regulatory or contractual provisions, in the light of changing circumstances, and does not prejudice the application of Clause 5.1 as long as the principle of non-discrimination as expressed in Clause 4.1 is complied with.

3. This Agreement does not prejudice the right of the social partners to conclude, at the appropriate level, including European level, agreements adapting and/or complementing the

provisions of this Agreement in a manner which will take account of the specific needs of the social partners concerned.

4. This Agreement shall be without prejudice to any more specific Community provisions, and in particular Community provisions concerning equal treatment or opportunities for men and women.

5. The prevention and settlement of disputes and grievances arising from the application of this Agreement shall be dealt with in accordance with national law, collective agreements and practice.

6. The signatory parties shall review this Agreement, five years after the date of the Council decision, if requested by one of the parties to this Agreement.

COUNCIL DIRECTIVE (EC) No 98/59 of 20 JULY 1998
on the approximation of the laws of the Member States relating to collective redundancies
[1998] OJ L225/16

THE COUNCIL OF THE EUROPEAN UNION,

Having regard to the Treaty establishing the European Community, and in particular Article 100 thereof,

Having regard to the proposal from the Commission,

Having regard to the opinion of the European Parliament,

Having regard to the opinion of the Economic and Social Committee,

(1) Whereas for reasons of clarity and rationality Council Directive 75/129/EEC of 17 February 1975 on the approximation of the laws of the Member States relating to collective redundancies should be consolidated;

(2) Whereas it is important that greater protection should be afforded to workers in the event of collective redundancies while taking into account the need for balanced economic and social development within the Community;

(3) Whereas, despite increasing convergence, differences still remain between the provisions in force in the Member States concerning the practical arrangements and procedures for such redundancies and the measures designed to alleviate the consequences of redundancy for workers;

(4) Whereas these differences can have a direct effect on the functioning of the internal market;

(5) Whereas the Council resolution of 21 January 1974 concerning a social action programme made provision for a directive on the approximation of Member States' legislation on collective redundancies;

(6) Whereas the Community Charter of the fundamental social rights of workers, adopted at the European Council meeting held in Strasbourg on 9 December 1989 by the Heads of State or Government of 11 Member States, states, inter alia, in point 7, first paragraph, first sentence, and second paragraph; in point 17, first paragraph; and in point 18, third indent:

'7.   The completion of the internal market must lead to an improvement in the living and working conditions of workers in the European Community.

The improvement must cover, where necessary, the development of certain aspects of employment regulations such as procedures for collective redundancies and those regarding bankruptcies.

17. Information, consultation and participation for workers must be developed along appropriate lines, taking account of the practices in force in the various Member States.

18. Such information, consultation and participation must be implemented in due time, particularly in the following cases:

— in cases of collective redundancy procedures'

(7) Whereas this approximation must therefore be promoted while the improvement is being maintained within the meaning of Article 117 of the Treaty;

(8) Whereas, in order to calculate the number of redundancies provided for in the definition of collective redundancies within the meaning of this Directive, other forms of termination of

employment contracts on the initiative of the employer should be equated to redundancies, provided that there are at least five redundancies;

(9) Whereas it should be stipulated that this Directive applies in principle also to collective redundancies resulting where the establishment's activities are terminated as a result of a judicial decision;

(10) Whereas the Member States should be given the option of stipulating that workers' representatives may call on experts on grounds of the technical complexity of the matters which are likely to be the subject of the informing and consulting;

(11) Whereas it is necessary to ensure that employers' obligations as regards information, consultation and notification apply independently of whether the decision on collective redundancies emanates from the employer or from an undertaking which controls that employer;

(12) Whereas Member States should ensure that workers' representatives and/or workers have at their disposal administrative and/or judicial procedures in order to ensure that the obligations laid down in this Directive are fulfilled;

(13) Whereas this Directive must not affect the obligations of the Member States concerning the deadlines for transposition of the Directives set out in Annex I, Part B,

HAS ADOPTED THIS DIRECTIVE:

SECTION I
DEFINITIONS AND SCOPE

Article 1

1. For the purposes of this Directive:

    (a) 'collective redundancies' means dismissals effected by an employer for one or more reasons not related to the individual workers concerned where, according to the choice of the Member States, the number of redundancies is:

        (i) either, over a period of 30 days:
            — at least 10 in establishments normally employing more than 20 and less than 100 workers,
            — at least 10 % of the number of workers in establishments normally employing at least 100 but less than 300 workers,
            — at least 30 in establishments normally employing 300 workers or more,

        (ii) or, over a period of 90 days, at least 20, whatever the number of workers normally employed in the establishments in question;

    (b) 'workers' representatives' means the workers' representatives provided for by the laws or practices of the Member States.

    For the purpose of calculating the number of redundancies provided for in the first subparagraph of point (a), terminations of an employment contract which occur on the employer's initiative for one or more reasons not related to the individual workers concerned shall be assimilated to redundancies, provided that there are at least five redundancies.

2. This Directive shall not apply to:

    (a) collective redundancies effected under contracts of employment concluded for limited periods of time or for specific tasks except where such redundancies take place prior to the date of expiry or the completion of such contracts;

    (b) workers employed by public administrative bodies or by establishments governed by public law (or, in Member States where this concept is unknown, by equivalent bodies);

    (c) the crews of seagoing vessels.

SECTION II
INFORMATION AND CONSULTATION

Article 2

1. Where an employer is contemplating collective redundancies, he shall begin consultations with the workers' representatives in good time with a view to reaching an agreement.

2. These consultations shall, at least, cover ways and means of avoiding collective redundancies or reducing the number of workers affected, and of mitigating the consequences by recourse

to accompanying social measures aimed, inter alia, at aid for redeploying or retraining workers made redundant.

Member States may provide that the workers' representatives may call on the services of experts in accordance with national legislation and/or practice.

3. To enable workers' representatives to make constructive proposals, the employers shall in good time during the course of the consultations:

    (a) supply them with all relevant information and

    (b) in any event notify them in writing of:

        (i) the reasons for the projected redundancies;

        (ii) the number of categories of workers to be made redundant;

        (iii) the number and categories of workers normally employed;

        (iv) the period over which the projected redundancies are to be effected;

        (v) the criteria proposed for the selection of the workers to be made redundant in so far as national legislation and/or practice confers the power therefore upon the employer;

        (vi) the method for calculating any redundancy payments other than those arising out of national legislation and/or practice.

The employer shall forward to the competent public authority a copy of, at least, the elements of the written communication which are provided for in the first subparagraph, point (b), subpoints (i) to (v).

4. The obligations laid down in paragraphs 1, 2 and 3 shall apply irrespective of whether the decision regarding collective redundancies is being taken by the employer or by an undertaking controlling the employer.

In considering alleged breaches of the information, consultation and notification requirements laid down by this Directive, account shall not be taken of any defence on the part of the employer on the ground that the necessary information has not been provided to the employer by the undertaking which took the decision leading to collective redundancies.

SECTION III
PROCEDURE FOR COLLECTIVE REDUNDANCIES

Article 3

1. Employers shall notify the competent public authority in writing of any projected collective redundancies.

However, Member States may provide that in the case of planned collective redundancies arising from termination of the establishment's activities as a result of a judicial decision, the employer shall be obliged to notify the competent public authority in writing only if the latter so requests.

This notification shall contain all relevant information concerning the projected collective redundancies and the consultations with workers' representatives provided for in Article 2, and particularly the reasons for the redundancies, the number of workers to be made redundant, the number of workers normally employed and the period over which the redundancies are to be effected.

2. Employers shall forward to the workers' representatives a copy of the notification provided for in paragraph 1.

The workers' representatives may send any comments they may have to the competent public authority.

Article 4

1. Projected collective redundancies notified to the competent public authority shall take effect not earlier than 30 days after the notification referred to in Article 3(1) without prejudice to any provisions governing individual rights with regard to notice of dismissal.

Member States may grant the competent public authority the power to reduce the period provided for in the preceding subparagraph.

2. The period provided for in paragraph 1 shall be used by the competent public authority to seek solutions to the problems raised by the projected collective redundancies.

3. Where the initial period provided for in paragraph 1 is shorter than 60 days, Member States may grant the competent public authority the power to extend the initial period to 60 days following notification where the problems raised by the projected collective redundancies are not likely to be solved within the initial period.

    Member States may grant the competent public authority wider powers of extension. The employer must be informed of the extension and the grounds for it before expiry of the initial period provided for in paragraph 1.

4. Member States need not apply this Article to collective redundancies arising from termination of the establishment's activities where this is the result of a judicial decision.

SECTION IV
FINAL PROVISIONS

Article 5

This Directive shall not affect the right of Member States to apply or to introduce laws, regulations or administrative provisions which are more favourable to workers or to promote or to allow the application of collective agreements more favourable to workers.

Article 6

Member States shall ensure that judicial and/or administrative procedures for the enforcement of obligations under this Directive are available to the workers' representatives and/or workers.

Article 7

Member States shall forward to the Commission the text of any fundamental provisions of national law already adopted or being adopted in the area governed by this Directive.

Article 8

1. The Directives listed in Annex I, Part A, are hereby repealed without prejudice to the obligations of the Member States concerning the deadlines for transposition of the said Directive set out in Annex I, Part B.

2. References to the repealed Directives shall be construed as references to this Directive and shall be read in accordance with the correlation table in Annex II.

Article 9

This Directive shall enter into force on the 20th day following its publication in the Official Journal of the European Communities.

Article 10

This Directive is addressed to the Member States.

ANNEX I

PART A

Repealed Directives (referred to by Article 8)

Council Directive 75/129/EEC and its following amendment: Council Directive 92/56/EEC.

PART B

DEADLINES FOR TRANSPOSITION INTO NATIONAL LAW

(referred to by Article 8)

Directive	Deadline for transposition
75/129/EEC (OJ L48, 22.2.1975, p. 29)	19 February 1977
92/56/EEC (OJ L245, 26.8.1992, p. 3)	24 June 1994

ANNEX II

CORRELATION TABLE

Directive 75/129/EEC	This Directive
Article 1(1), first subparagraph, point (a), first indent, point 1	Article 1(1),first subparagraph, point (a)(i), first indent
Article 1(1), first subparagraph, point (a), first indent, point 2	Article 1(1),first subparagraph, point (a)(i), second indent
Article 1(1), first subparagraph, point (a), first indent, point 3	Article 1(1),first subparagraph, point (a)(i), third indent
Article 1(1), first subparagraph, point (a), second indent	Article 1(1),first subparagraph, point (a)(ii)
Article 1(1), first subparagraph, point (b)	Article 1(1), first subparagraph, point (b)
Article 1(1), second subparagraph	Article 1(1), second subparagraph
Article 1(2)	Article 1(2)
Article 2	Article 2
Article 3	Article 3
Article 4	Article 4
Article 5	Article 5
Article 5a	Article 6
Article 6(1)	—
Article 6(2)	Article 7
Article 7	—
—	Article 8
—	Article 9
—	Article 10
—	Annex I
—	Annex II

COUNCIL DIRECTIVE (EC) No 1999/70 of 28 JUNE 1999
concerning the framework agreement on fixed-term work concluded by ETUC, UNICE and CEEP
[1999] OJ L175/43

THE COUNCIL OF THE EUROPEAN UNION,

Having regard to the Treaty establishing the European Community, and in particular Article 139(2) thereof,

Having regard to the proposal from the Commission,

Whereas:

(1) Following the entry into force of the Treaty of Amsterdam the provisions of the Agreement on social policy annexed to the Protocol on social policy, annexed to the Treaty establishing the European Community have been incorporated into Articles 136 to 139 of the Treaty establishing the European Community;

(2) Management and labour (the social partners) may, in accordance with Article 139(2) of the Treaty, request jointly that agreements at Community level be implemented by a Council decision on a proposal from the Commission;

(3) Point 7 of the Community Charter of the Fundamental Social Rights of Workers provides, *inter alia*, that 'the completion of the internal market must lead to an improvement in the living and working conditions of workers in the European Community. This process must result from an approximation of these conditions while the improvement is being maintained, as regards in particular forms of employment other than open-ended contracts, such as fixed-term contracts, part-time working, temporary work and seasonal work';

(4) The Council has been unable to reach a decision on the proposal for a Directive on certain employment relationships with regard to distortions of competition, nor on the proposal for a Directive on certain employment relationships with regard to working conditions;

(5) The conclusions of the Essen European Council stressed the need to take measures with a view to 'increasing the employment-intensiveness of growth, in particular by a more flexible organisation of work in a way which fulfils both the wishes of employees and the requirements of competition';

(6) The Council Resolution of 9 February 1999 on the 1999 Employment Guidelines invites the social partners at all appropriate levels to negotiate agreements to modernise the organisation of work, including flexible working arrangements, with the aim of making under-takings productive and competitive and achieving the required balance between flexibility and security;

(7) The Commission, in accordance with Article 3(2) of the Agreement on social policy, has consulted management and labour on the possible direction of Community action with regard to flexible working time and job security;

(8) The Commission, considering after such consultation that Community action was desirable, once again consulted management and labour on the substance of the envisaged proposal in accordance with Article 3(3) of the said Agreement;

(9) The general cross-industry organisations, namely the Union of Industrial and Employers' Confederations of Europe (UNICE), the European Centre of Enterprises with Public Participation (CEEP) and the European Trade Union Confederation (ETUC), informed the Commission in a joint letter dated 23 March 1998 of their desire to initiate the procedure provided for in Article 4 of the said Agreement; they asked the Commission, in a joint letter, for a further period of three months; the Commission complied with this request extending the negotiation period to 30 March 1999;

(10) The said cross-industry organisations on 18 March 1999 concluded a framework agreement on fixed-term work; they forwarded to the Commission their joint request to implement the framework agreement by a Council Decision on a proposal from the Commission, in accordance with Article 4(2) of the Agreement on social policy;

(11) The Council, in its Resolution of 6 December 1994 on 'certain aspects for a European Union social policy: a contribution to economic and social convergence in the Union', asked management and labour to make use of the opportunities for concluding agreements, since they are as a rule closer to social reality and to social problems;

(12) The signatory parties, in the preamble to the framework agreement on part-time work concluded on 6 June 1997, announced their intention to consider the need for similar agreements relating to other forms of flexible work;

(13) Management and labour wished to give particular attention to fixed-term work, while at the same time indicating that it was their intention to consider the need for a similar agreement relating to temporary agency work;

(14) The signatory parties wished to conclude a framework agreement on fixed-term work setting out the general principles and minimum requirements for fixed-term employment contracts and employment relationships; they have demonstrated their desire to improve the quality of fixed-term work by ensuring the application of the principle of non-discrimination, and to establish a framework to prevent abuse arising from the use of successive fixed-term employment contracts or relationships;

(15) The proper instrument for implementing the framework agreement is a directive within the meaning of Article 249 of the Treaty; it therefore binds the Member States as to the result to be achieved, whilst leaving them the choice of form and methods;

(16) In accordance with the principles of subsidiarity and proportionality as set out in Article 5 of the Treaty, the objectives of this Directive cannot be sufficiently achieved by the Member States and can therefore be better achieved by the Community; this Directive limits itself to the minimum required for the attainment of those objectives and does not go beyond what is necessary for that purpose;

(17) As regards terms used in the framework agreement but not specifically defined therein, this Directive allows Member States to define such terms in conformity with national law or practice as is the case for other Directives on social matters using similar terms, provided that the definitions in question respect the content of the framework agreement;

(18) The Commission has drafted its proposal for a Directive, in accordance with its Communication of 14 December 1993 concerning the application of the agreement on social policy and its Communication of 20 May 1998 on adapting and promoting the social dialogue at Community level, taking into account the representative status of the contracting parties, their mandate and the legality of each clause of the framework agreement; the contracting parties together have a sufficiently representative status;

(19) The Commission informed the European Parliament and the Economic and Social Committee by sending them the text of the agreement, accompanied by its proposal for a Directive and the explanatory memorandum, in accordance with its communication concerning the implementation of the Protocol on social policy;

(20) On 6 May 1999 the European Parliament adopted a Resolution on the framework agreement between the social partners;

(21) The implementation of the framework agreement contributes to achieving the objectives in Article 136 of the Treaty,

HAS ADOPTED THIS DIRECTIVE:

Article 1

The purpose of the Directive is to put into effect the frame-work agreement on fixed-term contracts concluded on 18 March 1999 between the general cross-industry organisations (ETUC, UNICE and CEEP) annexed hereto.

Article 2

Member States shall bring into force the laws, regulations and administrative provisions necessary to comply with this Directive by 10 July 2001*, or shall ensure that, by that date at the latest, management and labour have introduced the necessary measures by agreement, the Member States being required to take any necessary measures to enable them at any time to be in a position to guarantee the results imposed by this Directive. They shall forthwith inform the Commission thereof.

Member States may have a maximum of one more year, if necessary, and following consultation with management and labour, to take account of special difficulties or implementation by a collective agreement. They shall inform the Commission forthwith in such circumstances.

When Member States adopt the provisions referred to in the first paragraph, these shall contain a reference to this Directive or shall be accompanied by such reference at the time of their official publication. The procedure for such reference shall be adopted by the Member States.

Article 3

This Directive shall enter into force on the day of its publication in the Official Journal of the European Communities.

Article 4

This Directive is addressed to the Member States.

Note

*Corrected by Corrigendum OJ L 244, 16.9.1999, p. 64 (1999/70/EC).

ANNEX

ETUC-UNICE-CEEP

FRAMEWORK AGREEMENT ON FIXED-TERM WORK

Preamble

This framework agreement illustrates the role that the social partners can play in the European employment strategy agreed at the 1997 Luxembourg extraordinary summit and, following the framework agreement on part-time work, represents a further contribution towards achieving a better balance between 'flexibility in working time and security for workers'.

The parties to this agreement recognise that contracts of an indefinite duration are, and will continue to be, the general form of employment relationship between employers and workers. They also recognise that fixed-term employment contracts respond, in certain circumstances, to the needs of both employers and workers.

This agreement sets out the general principles and minimum requirements relating to fixed-term work, recognising that their detailed application needs to take account of the realities of specific national, sectoral and seasonal situations. It illustrates the willingness of the Social Partners to establish a general framework for ensuring equal treatment for fixed-term workers by protecting them against discrimination and for using fixed-term employment contracts on a basis acceptable to employers and workers.

This agreement applies to fixed-term workers with the exception of those placed by a temporary work agency at the disposition of a user enterprise. It is the intention of the parties to consider the need for a similar agreement relating to temporary agency work.

This agreement relates to the employment conditions of fixed-term workers, recognising that matters relating to statutory social security are for decision by the Member States. In this respect the Social Partners note the Employment Declaration of the Dublin European Council in 1996 which emphasised inter alia, the need to develop more employment-friendly social security systems by 'developing social protection systems capable of adapting to new patterns of work and providing appropriate protection to those engaged in such work'. The parties to this agreement reiterate the view expressed in the 1997 part-time agreement that Member States should give effect to this Declaration without delay.

In addition, it is also recognised that innovations in occupational social protection systems are necessary in order to adapt them to current conditions, and in particular to provide for the transferability of rights.

The ETUC, UNICE and CEEP request the Commission to submit this framework agreement to the Council for a decision making these requirements binding in the Member States which are party to the Agreement on social policy annexed to the Protocol (No 14) on social policy annexed to the Treaty establishing the European Community.

The parties to this agreement ask the Commission, in its proposal to implement the agreement, to request Member States to adopt the laws, regulations and administrative provisions necessary to comply with the Council Decision within two years from its adoption or ensure that the social partners establish the necessary measures by way of agreement by the end of this period. Member States may, if necessary and following consultation with the social partners, and in order to take account of particular difficulties or implementation by collective agreement have up to a maximum of one additional year to comply with this provision.

The parties to this agreement request that the social partners are consulted prior to any legislative, regulatory or administrative initiative taken by a Member State to conform to the present agreement.

Without prejudice to the role of national courts and the Court of Justice, the parties to this agreement request that any matter relating to the interpretation of this agreement at European level should in the first instance be referred by the Commission to them for an opinion.

General considerations

1. Having regard to the Agreement on social policy annexed to the Protocol (No 14) on social policy annexed to the Treaty establishing the European Community, and in particular Article 3.4 and 4.2 thereof;

2. Whereas Article 4.2 of the Agreement on social policy provides that agreements concluded at Community level may be implemented, at the joint request of the signatory parties, by a Council decision on a proposal from the Commission;

3. Whereas, in its second consultation document on flexibility in working time and security for workers, the Commission announced its intention to propose a legally-binding Community measure;

4. Whereas in its opinion on the proposal for a Directive on part-time work, the European Parliament invited the Commission to submit immediately proposals for directives on other forms of flexible work, such as fixed-term work and temporary agency work;

5. Whereas in the conclusions of the extraordinary summit on employment adopted in Luxembourg, the European Council invited the social partners to negotiate agreements to 'modernise the organisation of work, including flexible working arrangements, with the aim of making undertakings productive and competitive and achieving the required balance between flexibility and security';

6. Whereas employment contracts of an indefinite duration are the general form of employment relationships and contribute to the quality of life of the workers concerned and improve performance;

7. Whereas the use of fixed-term employment contracts based on objective reasons is a way to prevent abuse;

8. Whereas fixed-term employment contracts are a feature of employment in certain sectors, occupations and activities which can suit both employers and workers;

9. Whereas more than half of fixed-term workers in the European Union are women and this agreement can therefore contribute to improving equality of opportunities between women and men;

10. Whereas this agreement refers back to Member States and social partners for the arrangements for the application of its general principles, minimum requirements and provisions, in order to take account of the situation in each Member State and the circumstances of particular sectors and occupations, including the activities of a seasonal nature;

11. Whereas this agreement takes into consideration the need to improve social policy requirements, to enhance the competitiveness of the Community economy and to avoid imposing administrative, financial and legal constraints in a way which would hold back the creation and development of small and medium-sized undertakings;

12. Whereas the social partners are best placed to find solutions that correspond to the needs of both employers and workers and shall therefore be given a special role in the implementation and application of this agreement.

THE SIGNATORY PARTIES HAVE AGREED THE FOLLOWING

Purpose (clause 1)

The purpose of this framework agreement is to:

   (a) improve the quality of fixed-term work by ensuring the application of the principle of non-discrimination;

   (b) establish a framework to prevent abuse arising from the use of successive fixed-term employment contracts or relationships.

Scope (clause 2)

1. This agreement applies to fixed-term workers who have an employment contract or employment relationship as defined in law, collective agreements or practice in each Member State.

2. Member States after consultation with the social partners and/or the social partners may provide that this agreement does not apply to:

    (a) initial vocational training relationships and apprenticeship schemes;

    (b) employment contracts and relationships which have been concluded within the framework of a specific public or publicly-supported training, integration and vocational retraining programme.

Definitions (clause 3)

1. For the purpose of this agreement the term 'fixed-term worker' means a person having an employment contract or relationship entered into directly between an employer and a worker where the end of the employment contract or relationship is determined by objective conditions such as reaching a specific date, completing a specific task, or the occurrence of a specific event.

2. For the purpose of this agreement, the term 'comparable permanent worker' means a worker with an employment contract or relationship of indefinite duration, in the same establishment, engaged in the same or similar work/occupation, due regard being given to qualifications/skills.

    Where there is no comparable permanent worker in the same establishment, the comparison shall be made by reference to the applicable collective agreement, or where there is no applicable collective agreement, in accordance with national law, collective agreements or practice.

Principle of non-discrimination (clause 4)

1. In respect of employment conditions, fixed-term workers shall not be treated in a less favourable manner than comparable permanent workers solely because they have a fixed-term contract or relation unless different treatment is justified on objective grounds.

2. Where appropriate, the principle of pro rata temporis shall apply.

3. The arrangements for the application of this clause shall be defined by the Member States after consultation with the social partners and/or the social partners, having regard to Community law and national law, collective agreements and practice.

4. Period of service qualifications relating to particular conditions of employment shall be the same for fixed-term workers as for permanent workers except where different length-of service qualifications are justified on objective grounds.

Measures to prevent abuse (clause 5)

1. To prevent abuse arising from the use of successive fixed-term employment contracts or relationships, Member States, after consultation with social partners in accordance with national law, collective agreements or practice, and/or the social partners, shall, where there are no equivalent legal measures to prevent abuse, introduce in a manner which takes account of the needs of specific sectors and/or categories of workers, one or more of the following measures:

    (a) objective reasons justifying the renewal of such contracts or relationships;

    (b) the maximum total duration of successive fixed-term employment contracts or relationships;

    (c) the number of renewals of such contracts or relationships.

2. Member States after consultation with the social partners and/or the social partners shall, where appropriate, determine under what conditions fixed-term employment contracts or relationships:

    (a) shall be regarded as 'successive'

    (b) shall be deemed to be contracts or relationships of indefinite duration.

Information and employment opportunities (clause 6)

1. Employers shall inform fixed-term workers about vacancies which become available in the undertaking or establishment to ensure that they have the same opportunity to secure permanent positions as other workers. Such information may be provided by way of a general announcement at a suitable place in the undertaking or establishment.
2. As far as possible, employers should facilitate access by fixed-term workers to appropriate training opportunities to enhance their skills, career development and occupational mobility.

Information and consultation (clause 7)

1. Fixed-term workers shall be taken into consideration in calculating the threshold above which workers' representative bodies provided for in national and Community law may be constituted in the undertaking as required by national provisions.
2. The arrangements for the application of clause 7.1 shall be defined by Member States after consultation with the social partners and/or the social partners in accordance with national law, collective agreements or practice and having regard to clause 4.1.
3. As far as possible, employers should give consideration to the provision of appropriate information to existing workers' representative bodies about fixed-term work in the undertaking.

Provisions on implementation (clause 8)

1. Member States and/or the social partners can maintain or introduce more favourable provisions for workers than set out in this agreement.
2. This agreement shall be without prejudice to any more specific Community provisions, and in particular Community provisions concerning equal treatment or opportunities for men and women.
3. Implementation of this agreement shall not constitute valid grounds for reducing the general level of protection afforded to workers in the field of the agreement.
4. The present agreement does not prejudice the right of the social partners to conclude at the appropriate level, including European level, agreements adapting and/or complementing the provisions of this agreement in a manner which will take note of the specific needs of the social partners concerned.
5. The prevention and settlement of disputes and grievances arising from the application of this agreement shall be dealt with in accordance with national law, collective agreements and practice.
6. The signatory parties shall review the application of this agreement five years after the date of the Council decision if requested by one of the parties to this agreement.

COUNCIL AND PARLIAMENT DIRECTIVE (EC) No 2002/14
of 11 MARCH 2002
establishing a general framework for informing and consulting employees in the European Community
[2000] OJ L80/29

THE EUROPEAN PARLIAMENT AND THE COUNCIL OF THE EUROPEAN UNION,

Having regard to the Treaty establishing the European Community, and in particular Article 137(2) thereof,

Having regard to the proposal from the Commission,

Having regard to the opinion of the Economic and Social Committee ,

Having regard to the opinion of the Committee of the Regions,

Acting in accordance with the procedure referred to in Article 251, and in the light of the joint text approved by the Conciliation Committee on 23 January 2002,

Whereas:

(1) Pursuant to Article 136 of the Treaty, a particular objective of the Community and the Member States is to promote social dialogue between management and labour.

(2) Point 17 of the Community Charter of Fundamental Social Rights of Workers provides, inter alia, that information, consultation and participation for workers must be developed along appropriate lines, taking account of the practices in force in different Member States.

(3) The Commission consulted management and labour at Community level on the possible direction of Community action on the information and consultation of employees in undertakings within the Community.

(4) Following this consultation, the Commission considered that Community action was advisable and again consulted management and labour on the contents of the planned proposal; management and labour have presented their opinions to the Commission.

(5) Having completed this second stage of consultation, management and labour have not informed the Commission of their wish to initiate the process potentially leading to the conclusion of an agreement.

(6) The existence of legal frameworks at national and Community level intended to ensure that employees are involved in the affairs of the undertaking employing them and in decisions which affect them has not always prevented serious decisions affecting employees from being taken and made public without adequate procedures having been implemented beforehand to inform and consult them.

(7) There is a need to strengthen dialogue and promote mutual trust within undertakings in order to improve risk anticipation, make work organisation more flexible and facilitate employee access to training within the undertaking while maintaining security, make employees aware of adaptation needs, increase employees' availability to undertake measures and activities to increase their employability, promote employee involvement in the operation and future of the undertaking and increase its competitiveness.

(9) There is a need, in particular, to promote and enhance information and consultation on the situation and likely development of employment within the undertaking and, where the employer's evaluation suggests that employment within the undertaking may be under threat, the possible anticipatory measures envisaged, in particular in terms of employee training and skill development, with a view to offsetting the negative developments or their consequences and increasing the employability and adaptability of the employees likely to be affected.

(9) Timely information and consultation is a prerequisite for the success of the restructuring and adaptation of undertakings to the new conditions created by globalisation of the economy, particularly through the development of new forms of organisation of work.

(10) The Community has drawn up and implemented an employment strategy based on the concepts of 'anticipation', 'prevention' and 'employability', which are to be incorporated as key elements into all public policies likely to benefit employment, including the policies of individual undertakings, by strengthening the social dialogue with a view to promoting change compatible with preserving the priority objective of employment.

(11) Further development of the internal market must be properly balanced, maintaining the essential values on which our societies are based and ensuring that all citizens benefit from economic development.

(12) Entry into the third stage of economic and monetary union has extended and accelerated the competitive pressures at European level. This means that more supportive measures are needed at national level.

(13) The existing legal frameworks for employee information and consultation at Community and national level tend to adopt an excessively a posteriors approach to the process of change, neglect the economic aspects of decisions taken and do not contribute either to genuine anticipation of employment developments within the undertaking or to risk prevention.

(14) All of these political, economic, social and legal developments call for changes to the existing legal framework providing for the legal and practical instruments enabling the right to be informed and consulted to be exercised.

(15) This Directive is without prejudice to national systems regarding the exercise of this right in practice where those entitled to exercise it are required to indicate their wishes collectively.

(16) This Directive is without prejudice to those systems which provide for the direct involvement of employees, as long as they are always free to exercise the right to be informed and consulted through their representatives.

(17) Since the objectives of the proposed action, as outlined above, cannot be adequately achieved by the Member States, in that the object is to establish a framework for employee information

and consultation appropriate for the new European context described above, and can therefore, in view of the scale and impact of the proposed action, be better achieved at Community level, the Community may adopt measures in accordance with the principle of subsidiarity as set out in Article 5 of the Treaty. In accordance with the principle of proportionality, as set out in that Article, this Directive does not go beyond what is necessary in order to achieve these objectives.

(18) The purpose of this general framework is to establish minimum requirements applicable throughout the Community while not preventing Member States from laying down provisions more favourable to employees.

(19) The purpose of this general framework is also to avoid any administrative, financial or legal constraints which would hinder the creation and development of small and medium-sized undertakings. To this end, the scope of this Directive should be restricted, according to the choice made by Member States, to undertakings with at least 50 employees or establishments employing at least 20 employees.

(20) This takes into account and is without prejudice to other national measures and practices aimed at fostering social dialogue within companies not covered by this Directive and within public administrations.

(21) However, on a transitional basis, Member States in which there is no established statutory system of information and consultation of employees or employee representation should have the possibility of further restricting the scope of the Directive as regards the numbers of employees.

(22) A Community framework for informing and consulting employees should keep to a minimum the burden on undertakings or establishments while ensuring the effective exercise of the rights granted.

(23) The objective of this Directive is to be achieved through the establishment of a general framework comprising the principles, definitions and arrangements for information and consultation, which it will be for the Member States to comply with and adapt to their own national situation, ensuring, where appropriate, that management and labour have a leading role by allowing them to define freely, by agreement, the arrangements for informing and consulting employees which they consider to be best suited to their needs and wishes.

(24) Care should be taken to avoid affecting some specific rules in the field of employee information and consultation existing in some national laws, addressed to undertakings or establishments which pursue political, professional, organisational, religious, charitable, educational, scientific or artistic aims, as well as aims involving information and the expression of opinions.

(25) Undertakings and establishments should be protected against disclosure of certain particularly sensitive information.

(26) The employer should be allowed not to inform and consult where this would seriously damage the undertaking or the establishment or where he has to comply immediately with an order issued to him by a regulatory or supervisory body.

(27) Information and consultation imply both rights and obligations for management and labour at undertaking or establishment level.

(28) Administrative or judicial procedures, as well as sanctions that are effective, dissuasive and proportionate in relation to the seriousness of the offence, should be applicable in cases of infringement of the obligations based on this Directive.

(29) This Directive should not affect the provisions, where these are more specific, of Council Directive 98159/EC of 20 July 1998 on the approximation of the laws of the Member States relating to collective redundancies and of Council Directive 2001123/EC of 12 March 2001 on the approximation of the laws of the Member States relating to the safeguarding of employees' rights in the event of transfers of undertakings, businesses or parts of undertakings or businesses.

(30) Other rights of information and consultation, including those arising from Council Directive 94/45/EEC of 22 September 1994 on the establishment of a European Works Council or a procedure in Community-scale undertakings and Community-scale groups of undertakings for the purposes of informing and consulting employees, should not be affected by this Directive.

(31) Implementation of this Directive should not be sufficient grounds for a reduction in the general level of protection of workers in the areas to which it applies,

HAVE ADOPTED THIS DIRECTIVE:

Article 1 Object and principles

1. The purpose of this Directive is to establish a general framework setting out minimum requirements for the right to information and consultation of employees in undertakings or establishments within the Community.

2. The practical arrangements for information and consultation shall be defined and implemented in accordance with national law and industrial relations practices in individual Member States in such a way as to ensure their effectiveness.

3. When defining or implementing practical arrangements for information and consultation, the employer and the employees' representatives shall work in a spirit of cooperation and with due regard for their reciprocal rights and obligations, taking into account the interests both of the undertaking or establishment and of the employees.

Article 2 Definitions

For the purposes of this Directive:

(a) 'undertaking' means a public or private undertaking carrying out an economic activity, whether or not operating for gain, which is located within the territory of the Member States;

(b) 'establishment' means a unit of business defined in accordance with national law and practice, and located within the territory of a Member State, where an economic activity is carried out on an ongoing basis with human and material resources;

(c) 'employer' means the natural or legal person party to employment contracts or employment relationships with employees, in accordance with national law and practice;

(d) 'employee' means any person who, in the Member State concerned, is protected as an employee under national employment law and in accordance with national practice;

(e) 'employees' representatives' means the employees' representatives provided for by national laws and/or practices;

(f) 'information' means transmission by the employer to the employees' representatives of data in order to enable them to acquaint themselves with the subject matter and to examine it;

(g) 'consultation' means the exchange of views and establishment of dialogue between the employees' representatives and the employer.

Article 3 Scope

1. This Directive shall apply, according to the choice made by Member States, to:

(a) undertakings employing at least 50 employees in any one Member State, or

(b) establishments employing at least 20 employees in any one Member State.

Member States shall determine the method for calculating the thresholds of employees employed.

2. In conformity with the principles and objectives of this Directive, Member States may lay down particular provisions applicable to undertakings or establishments which pursue directly and essentially political, professional organisational, religious, charitable, educational, scientific or artistic aims, as well as aims involving information and the expression of opinions, on condition that, at the date of entry into force of this Directive, provisions of that nature already exist in national legislation.

3. Member States may derogate from this Directive through particular provisions applicable to the crews of vessels plying the high seas.

Article 4 Practical arrangements for information and consultation

1. In accordance with the principles set out in Article 1 and without prejudice to any provisions and/or practices in force more favourable to employees, the Member States shall determine the practical arrangements for exercising the right to information and consultation at the appropriate level in accordance with this Article.

2.   Information and consultation shall cover:
    (a)   information on the recent and probable development of the undertaking's or the establishment's activities and economic situation;
    (b)   information and consultation on the situation, structure and probable development of employment within the undertaking or establishment and on any anticipatory measures envisaged, in particular where there is a threat to employment;
    (c)   information and consultation on decisions likely to lead to substantial changes in work organisation or in contractual relations, including those covered by the Community provisions referred to in Article 9(1).

3.   Information shall be given at such time, in such fashion and with such content as are appropriate to enable, in particular, employees' representatives to conduct an adequate study and, where necessary, prepare for consultation.

4.   Consultation shall take place:
    (a)   while ensuring that the timing, method and content thereof are appropriate;
    (b)   at the relevant level of management and representation, depending on the subject under discussion;
    (c)   on the basis of information supplied by the employer in accordance with Article 2(f) and of the opinion which the employees' representatives are entitled to formulate;
    (d)   in such a way as to enable employees' representatives to meet the employer and obtain a response, and the reasons for that response, to any opinion they might formulated
    (e)   with a view to reaching an agreement on decisions within the scope of the employer's powers referred to in paragraph 2(c).

Article 5   Information and consultation deriving from an agreement

Member States may entrust management and labour at the appropriate level, including at undertaking or establishment level, with defining freely and at any time through negotiated agreement the practical arrangements for informing and consulting employees. These agreements, and agreements existing on the date laid down in Article 11, as well as any subsequent renewals of such agreements, may establish, while respecting the principles set out in Article 1 and subject to conditions and limitations laid down by the Member States, provisions which are different from those referred to in Article 4.

Article 6   Confidential information

1.   Member States shall provide that, within the conditions and limits laid down by national legislation, the employees' representatives, and any experts who assist them, are not authorised to reveal to employees or to third parties, any information which, in the legitimate interest of the undertaking or establishment, has expressly been provided to them in confidence. This obligation shall continue to apply, wherever the said representatives or experts are, even after expiry of their terms of office. However, a Member State may authorise the employees' representatives and anyone assisting them to pass on confidential information to employees and to third parties bound by an obligation of confidentiality.

2.   Member States shall provide, in specific cases and within the conditions and limits laid down by national legislation, that the employer is not obliged to communicate information or undertake consultation when the nature of that information or consultation is such that, according to objective criteria, it would seriously harm the functioning of the undertaking or establishment or would be prejudicial to it.

3.   Without prejudice to existing national procedures, Member States shall provide for administrative or judicial review procedures for the case where the employer requires confidentiality or does not provide the information in accordance with paragraphs 1 and 2. They may also provide for procedures intended to safeguard the confidentiality of the information in question.

Article 7   Protection of employees' representatives

Member States shall ensure that employees' representatives, when carrying out their functions, enjoy adequate protection and guarantees to enable them to perform properly the duties which have been assigned to them.

Article 8   Protection of rights

    1.   Member States shall provide for appropriate measures in the event of non-compliance with this Directive by the employer or the employees' representatives. In particular, they shall ensure that adequate administrative or judicial procedures are available to enable the obligations deriving from this Directive to be enforced.

    2.   Member States shall provide for adequate sanctions to be applicable in the event of infringement of this Directive by the employer or the employees' representatives. These sanctions must be effective, proportionate and dissuasive.

Article 9   Link between this Directive and other Community and national provisions

    1.   This Directive shall be without prejudice to the specific information and consultation procedures set out in Article 2 of Directive 98/59/EC and Article 7 of Directive 2001/23/EC.

    2.   This Directive shall be without prejudice to provisions adopted in accordance with Directives 94/45/EC and 97/74/EC.

    3.   This Directive shall be without prejudice to other rights to information, consultation and participation under national law,

    4.   Implementation of this Directive shall not be sufficient grounds for any regression in relation to the situation which already prevails in each Member State and in relation to the general level of protection of workers in the areas to which it applies.

Article 10   Transitional provisions

Notwithstanding Article 3, a Member State in which there is, at the date of entry into force of this Directive, no general, permanent and statutory system of information and consultation of employees, nor a general, permanent and statutory system of employee representation at the workplace allowing employees to be represented for that purpose, may limit the application of the national provisions implementing this Directive to:

    (a)   undertakings employing at least 150 employees or establishments employing at least 100 employees until 23 March 2007, and

    (b)   undertakings employing at least 100 employees or establishments employing at least 50 employees during the year following the date in point (a).

Article 11   Transposition

    1.   Member States shall adopt the laws, regulations and administrative provisions necessary to comply with this Directive not later than 23 March 2005 or shall ensure that management and labour introduce by that date the required provisions by way of agreement, the Member States being obliged to take all necessary steps enabling them to guarantee the results imposed by this Directive at all times. They shall forthwith inform the Commission thereof.

    2.   Where Member States adopt these measures, they shall contain a reference to this Directive or shall be accompanied by such reference on the occasion of their official publication. The methods of making such reference shall be laid down by the Member States.

Article 12   Review by the Commission

Not later than 23 March 2007, the Commission shall, in consultation with the Member States and the social partners at Community level, review the application of this Directive with a view to proposing any necessary amendments.

Article 13   Entry into force

This Directive shall enter into force on the day of its publication in the *Official Journal of the European Communities*.

Article 14   Addresses

This Directive is addressed to the Member States.

COUNCIL AND PARLIAMENT DIRECTIVE (EC) No 2003/88 of 4 NOVEMBER 2003
concerning certain aspects of the organisation of working time
[2003] OJ L299/9

THE EUROPEAN PARLIAMENT AND THE COUNCIL, OF THE EUROPEAN UNION,

Having regard to the Treaty establishing the European Community, and in particular Article 137(2) thereof,

Having regard to the proposal from the Commission,

Having regard to the opinion of the European Economic and Social Committee,

Having consulted the Committee of the Regions,

Acting in accordance with the procedure referred to in Article 251 of the Treaty,

Whereas:

(1) Council Directive 93/104/EC of 23 November 1993, concerning certain aspects of the organisation of working time, which lays down minimum safety and health requirements for the organisation of working time, in respect of periods of daily rest, breaks, weekly rest, maximum weekly working time, annual leave and aspects of night work, shift work and patterns of work, has been significantly amended. In order to clarify matters, a codification of the provisions in question should be drawn up.

(2) Article 137 of the Treaty provides that the Community is to support and complement the activities of the Member States with a view to improving the working environment to protect workers' health and safety. Directives adopted on the basis of that Article are to avoid imposing administrative, financial and legal constraints in a way which would hold back the creation and development of small and medium-sized undertakings.

(3) The provisions of Council Directive 89/391/EEC of 12 June 1989 on the introduction of measures to encourage improvements in the safety and health of workers at work remain fully applicable to the areas covered by this Directive without prejudice to more stringent and/or specific provisions contained herein.

(4) The improvement of workers' safety, hygiene and health at work is an objective which should not be suborditiated to purely economic considerations.

(5) All workers should have adequate rest periods. The concept of 'rest' must be expressed in units of time, i.e. in days, hours and/or fractions thereof. Community workers must be granted minimum daily, weekly and annual periods of rest and adequate breaks. It is also necessary in this context to place a maximum limit on weekly working hours.

(6) Account should be taken of the principles of the International Labour Organisation with regard to the organisation of working time, including those relating to night work.

(7) Research has shown that the human body is more sensitive at night to environmental disturbances and also to certain burdensome forms of work organisation and that long periods of night work can be detrimental to the health of workers and can endanger safety at the workplace.

(8) There is a need to limit the duration of periods of night work, including overtime, and to provide for employers who regularly use night workers to bring this information to the attention of the competent authorities if they so request.

(9) It is important that night workers should be entitled to a free health assessment prior to their assignment and thereafter at regular intervals and that whenever possible they should be transferred to day work for which they are suited if they suffer from health problems.

(10) The situation of night and shift workers requires that the level of safety and health protection should be adapted to the nature of their work and that the organisation and functioning of protection and prevention services and resources should be efficient.

(11) Specific working conditions may have detrimental effects on the safety and health of workers. The organisation of work according to a certain pattern must take account of the general principle of adapting work to the worker.

(12) A European Agreement in respect of the working time of seafarers has been put into effect by means of Council Directive 1999163/EC of 21 June 1999 concerning the Agreement on the organisation of working time of seafarers concluded by the European Community Shipowners' Association (ECSA) and the Federation of Transport Workers' Unions in the

European Union (FST) based on Article 139(2) of the Treaty. Accordingly, the provisions of this Directive should not apply to seafarers.

(13) In the case of those 'share-fishermen' who are employees, it is for the Member States to determine, pursuant to this Directive, the conditions for entitlement to, and granting of, annual leave, including the arrangements for payments.

(14) Specific standards laid down in other Community instruments relating, for example, to rest periods, working time, annual leave and night work for certain categories of workers should take precedence over the provisions of this Directive.

(15) In view of the question likely to be raised by the organisation of working time within an undertaking, it appears desirable to provide for flexibility in the application of certain provisions of this Directive, whilst ensuring compliance with the principles of protecting the safety and health of workers.

(16) It is necessary to provide that certain provisions may be subject to derogations implemented, according to the case, by the Member States or the two sides of industry. As a general rule, in the event of a derogation, the workers concerned must be given equivalent compensatory rest periods.

(17) This Directive should not affect the obligations of the Member States concerning the deadlines for transposition of the Directives set out in Annex 1, part B,

HAVE ADOPTED THIS DIRECTIVE:

CHAPTER 1
SCOPE AND DEFINITIONS

Article 1 Purpose and scope

1. This Directive lays down minimum safety and health requirements for the organisation of working time.

2. This Directive applies to:

    (a) minimum periods of daily rest, weekly rest and annual leave, to breaks and maximum weekly working time; and

    (b) certain aspects of night work, shift work and patterns of work.

3. This Directive shall apply to all sectors of activity, both public and private, within the meaning of Article 2 of Directive 89/391/EEC, without prejudice to Articles 14, 17, 18 and 19 of this Directive.

    This Directive shall not apply to seafarers, as defined in Directive 1999/63/EC without prejudice to Article 2(8) of this Directive.

4. The provisions of Directive 89/391/EEC are fully applicable to the matters referred to in paragraph 2, without prejudice to more stringent and/or specific provisions contained in this Directive.

Article 2 Definitions

For the purposes of this Directive, the following definitions shall apply:

1. 'working time' means any period during which the worker is working, at the employer's disposal and carrying out his activity or duties, in accordance with national laws and/or practice;

2. 'rest period' means any period which is not working time;

3. 'night time' means any period of not less than seven hours, as defined by national law, and which must include, in any case, the period between midnight and 5.00;

4. 'night worker' means:

    (a) on the one hand, any worker, who, during night time, works at least three hours of his daily working time as a normal course; and

    (b) on the other hand, any worker who is likely during night time to work a certain proportion of his annual working time, as defined at the choice of the Member State concerned:

        (i) by national legislation, following consultation with the two sides of industry; or

        (ii) by collective agreements or agreements concluded between the two sides of industry at national or regional level;

5. 'shift work' means any method of organising work in shifts whereby workers succeed each other at the same work stations according to a certain pattern, including a rotating pattern, and which may be continuous or discontinuous, entailing the need for workers to work at different times over a given period of days or weeks:

6. 'shift worker' means any worker whose work schedule is part of shift work;

7. 'mobile worker' means any worker employed as a member of travelling or flying personnel by an undertaking which operates transport services for passengers or goods by road, air or inland waterway:

8. 'offshore work' means work performed mainly on or from offshore installations (including drilling rigs), directly or indirectly in connection with the exploration, extraction or exploitation of mineral resources, including hydrocarbons, and diving in connection with such activities, whether performed from an offshore installation or a vessel;

9. 'adequate rest' means that workers have regular rest periods, the duration of which is expressed in units of time and which are sufficiently long and continuous to ensure that, as a result of fatigue or other irregular working patterns, they do not cause injury to themselves, to fellow workers or to others and that they do not damage their health, either in the short term or in the longer term.

CHAPTER 2
MINIMUM REST PERIODS — OTHER ASPECTS OF THE ORGANISATION
OF WORKING TIME

Article 3   Daily rest

Member States shall take the measures necessary to ensure that every worker is entitled to a minimum daily rest period of 11 consecutive hours per 24-hour period.

Article 4   Breaks

Member States shall take the measures necessary to ensure that, where the working day is longer than six hours, every worker is entitled to a rest break, the details of which, including duration and the terms on which it is granted, shall be laid down in collective agreements or agreements between the two sides of industry or, failing that, by national legislation.

Article 5   Weekly rest period

Member States shall take the measures necessary to ensure that, per each seven-day period, every worker is entitled to a minimum uninterrupted rest period of 24 hours plus the 11 hours' daily rest referred to in Article 3.

If objective, technical or work organisation conditions so justify, a minimum rest period of 24 hours may be applied.

Article 6   Maximum weekly working time

Member States shall take the measures necessary to ensure that, in keeping with the need to protect the safety and health of workers:

(a)   the period of weekly working time is limited by means of laws, regulations or administrative provisions or by collective agreements or agreements between the two sides of industry;

(b)   the average working time for each seven-day period, including overtime, does not exceed 48 hours.

Article 7   Annual leave

1.   Member States shall take the measures necessary to ensure that every worker is entitled to paid annual leave of at least four weeks in accordance with the conditions for entitlement to, and granting of, such leave laid down by national legislation and/or practice.

2.   The minimum period of paid annual leave may not be replaced by an allowance in lieu, except where the employment relationship is terminated.

CHAPTER 3
NIGHT WORK — SHIFT WORK — PATTERNS OF WORK

Article 8   Length of night work

Member States shall take the measures necessary to ensure that:

(a)   normal hours of work for night workers do not exceed an average of eight hours in any 24-hour period;

(b)   night workers whose work involves special hazards or heavy physical or mental strain do not work more than eight hours in any period of 24 hours during which they perform night work.

For the purposes of point (b), work involving special hazards or heavy physical or mental strain shall be defined by national legislation and/or practice or by collective agreements or agreements concluded between the two sides of industry, taking account of the specific effects and hazards of night work.

Article 9   Health assessment and transfer of night workers to day work

1.   Member States shall take the measures necessary to ensure that:

(a)   night workers are entitled to a free health assessment before their assignment and thereafter at regular intervals;

(b)   night workers suffering from health problems recognised as being connected with the fact that they perform night work are transferred whenever possible to day work to which they are suited.

2.   The free health assessment referred to in paragraph 1(a) must comply with medical confidentiality.

3.   The free health assessment referred to in paragraph 1(a) may be conducted within the national health system.

Article 10   Guarantees for night-time working

Member States may make the work of certain categories of night workers subject to certain guarantees, under conditions laid down by national legislation and/or practice, in the case of workers who incur risks to their safety or health linked to night-time working.

Article 11   Notification of regular use of night workers

Member States shall take the measures necessary to ensure that an employer who regularly uses night workers brings this information to the attention of the competent authorities if they so request.

Article 12   Safety and health protection

Member States shall take the measures necessary to ensure that:

(a)   night workers and shift workers have safety and health protection appropriate to the nature of their work;

(b)   appropriate protection and prevention services or facilities with regard to the safety and health of night workers and shift workers are equivalent to those applicable to other workers and are available at all times.

Article 13   Pattern of work

Member States shall take the measures necessary to ensure that an employer who intends to organise work according to a certain pattern takes account of the general principle of adapting work to the worker, with a view, in particular, to alleviating monotonous work and work at a predetermined workrate, depending on the type of activity, and of safety and health requirements, especially as regards breaks during working time.

CHAPTER 4
MISCELLANEOUS PROVISIONS

Article 14   More specific Community provisions

This Directive shall not apply where other Community instruments contain more specific requirements relating to the organisation of working time for certain occupations or occupational activities.

Article 15 More favourable provisions

This Directive shall not affect Member States' right to apply or introduce laws, regulations or administrative provisions more favourable to the protection of the safety and health of workers or to facilitate or permit the application of collective agreements or agreements concluded between the two sides of industry which are more favourable to the protection of the safety and health of workers.

Article 16 Reference periods

Member States may lay down:

(a)   for the application of Article 5 (weekly rest period), a reference period not exceeding 14 days;

(b)   for the application of Article 6 (maximum weekly working time), a reference period not exceeding four months,

The periods of paid annual leave, granted in accordance with Article 7, and the periods of sick leave shall not be included or shall be neutral in the calculation of the average;

(c)   for the application of Article 8 (length of night work), a reference period defined after consultation of the two sides of industry or by collective agreements or agreements concluded between the two sides of industry at national or regional level.

If the minimum weekly rest period of 24 hours required by Article 5 falls within that reference period, it shall not be included in the calculation of the average.

CHAPTER 5
DEROGATIONS AND EXCEPTIONS

Article 17 Derogations

1.   With due regard for the general principles of the protection of the safety and health of workers, Member States may derogate from Articles 3 to 6, 8 and 16 when, on account of the specific characteristics of the activity concerned, the duration of the working time is not measured and/or predetermined or can be determined by the workers themselves, and particularly in the case of.

(a)   managing executives or other persons with autonomous decision-taking powers;

(b)   family workers; or

(c)   workers officiating at religious ceremonies in churches and religious communities.

2.   Derogations provided for in paragraphs 3, 4 and 5 may be adopted by means of laws, regulations or administrative provisions or by means of collective agreements or agreements between the two sides of industry provided that the workers concerned are afforded equivalent periods of compensatory rest or that, in exceptional cases in which it is not possible, for objective reasons, to grant such equivalent periods of compensatory rest, the workers concerned are afforded appropriate protection.

3.   In accordance with paragraph 2 of this Article derogations may be made from Articles 3, 4, 5, 8 and 16:

(a)   in the case of activities where the worker's place of work and his place of residence are distant from one another, including offshore work, or where the worker's different places of work are distant from one another;

(b)   in the case of security and surveillance activities requiring a permanent presence in order to protect property and persons, particularly security guards and caretakers or security firms;

(c)   in the case of activities involving the need for continuity of service or production, particularly:

(i)   services relating to the reception, treatment and/or care provided by hospitals or similar establishments, including the activities of doctors in training, residential institutions and prisons;

(ii)   dock or airport workers;

(iii)   press, radio, television, cinematographic production, postal and tele-communications services, ambulance, fire and civil protection services;

          (iv)   gas, water and electricity production, transmission and distribution, household refuse collection and incineration plants;

          (v)   industries in which work cannot be interrupted on technical grounds;

          (vi)   research and development activities;

          (vii) agriculture;

          (viii) workers concerned with the carriage of passengers on regular urban transport services;

    (d)   where there is a foreseeable surge of activity, particularly in:

          (i)   agriculture;

          (ii)   tourism;

          (iii) postal services;

    (e)   in the case of persons working in railway transport:

          (i)   whose activities are intermittent;

          (ii)   who spend their working time on board trains; or

          (iii) whose activities are linked to transport timetables and to ensuring the continuity and regularity of traffic;

    (f)   in the circumstances described in Article 5(4) of Directive 891391/EEC;

    (g)   in cases of accident or imminent risk of accident.

4.   In accordance with paragraph 2 of this Article derogations may be made from Articles 3 and 5:

    (a)   in the case of shift work activities, each time the worker changes shift and cannot take daily and/or weekly rest periods between the end of one shift and the start of the next one;

    (b)   in the case of activities involving periods of work split up over the day, particularly those of cleaning staff.

5.   In accordance with paragraph 2 of this Article, derogations may be made from Article 6 and Article 16(b), in the case of doctors in training, in accordance with the provisions set out in the second to the seventh subparagraphs of this paragraph.

With respect to Article 6 derogations referred to in the first subparagraph shall be permitted for a transitional period of five years from 1 August 2004.

Member States may have up to two more years, if necessary, to take account of difficulties in meeting the working time provisions with respect to their responsibilities for the organisation and delivery of health services and medical care. At least six months before the end of the transitional period, the Member State concerned shall inform the Commission giving its reasons, so that the Commission can give an opinion, after appropriate consultations, within the three months following receipt of such information. If the Member State does not follow the opinion of the Commission, it will justify its decision. The notification and justification of the Member State and the opinion of the Commission shall be published in the *Official Journal of the European Union* and forwarded to the European Parliament.

Member States may have an additional period of up to one year, if necessary, to take account of special difficulties in meeting the responsibilities referred to in the third subparagraph. They shall follow the procedure set out in that subparagraph.

Member States shall ensure that in no case will the number of weekly working hours exceed an average of 58 during the first three years of the transitional period, an average of 56 for the following two years and an average of 52 for any remaining period.

The employer shall consult the representatives of the employees in good time with a view to reaching an agreement, wherever possible, on the arrangements applying to the transitional period. Within the limits set out in the fifth subparagraph, such an agreement may cover:

    (a)   the average number of weekly hours of work during the transitional period; and

    (b)   the measures to be adopted to reduce weekly working hours to an average of 48 by the end of the transitional period.

With respect to Article 16(b) derogations referred to in the first subparagraph shall be permitted provided that the reference period does not exceed 12 months, during the first part of the transitional period specified in the fifth subparagraph, and six months thereafter.

Article 18 Derogations by collective agreements

Derogations may be made from Articles 3, 4, 5, 8 and 16 by means of collective agreements or agreements concluded between the two sides of industry at national or regional level or, in conformity with the rules laid down by them, by means of collective agreements or agreements concluded between the two sides of industry at a lower level.

Member States in which there is no statutory system ensuring the conclusion of collective agreements or agreements concluded between the two sides of industry at national or regional level, on the matters covered by this Directive, or those Member States in which there is a specific legislative framework for this purpose and within the limits thereof, may, in accordance with national legislation and/or practice, allow derogations from Articles 3, 4, 5, 8 and 16 by way of collective agreements or agreements concluded between the two sides of industry at the appropriate collective level.

The derogations provided for in the first and second subparagraphs shall be allowed on condition that equivalent compensating rest periods are granted to the workers concerned or, in exceptional cases where it is not possible for objective reasons to grant such periods, the workers concerned are afforded appropriate protection.

Member States may lay down rules:

(a)   for the application of this Article by the two sides of industry; and

(b)   for the extension of the provisions of collective agreements or agreements concluded in conformity with this Article to other workers in accordance with national legislation and/or practice.

Article 19 Limitations to derogations from reference periods

The option to derogate from Article 16(b), provided for in Article 17(3) and in Article 18, may not result in the establishment of a reference period exceeding six months.

However, Member States shall have the option, subject to compliance with the general principles relating to the protection of the safety and health of workers, of allowing, for objective or technical reasons or reasons concerning the organisation of work, collective agreements or agreements concluded between the two sides of industry to set reference periods in no event exceeding 12 months. Before 23 November 2003, the Council shall, on the basis of a Commission proposal accompanied by an appraisal report, reexamine the provisions of this Article and decide what action to take.

Article 20 Mobile workers and offshore work

1.   Articles 3, 4, 5 and 8 shall not apply to mobile workers.

      Member States shall, however, take the necessary measures to ensure that such mobile workers are entitled to adequate rest, except in the circumstances laid down in Article 17(3)(f) and (g).

2.   Subject to compliance with the general principles relating to the protection of the safety and health of workers, and provided that there is consultation of representatives of the employer and employees concerned and efforts to encourage all relevant forms of social dialogue, including negotiation if the parties so wish, Member States may, for objective or technical reasons or reasons concerning the organisation of work, extend the reference period referred to in Article 16(b) to 12 months in respect of workers who mainly perform offshore work.

3.   Not later than 1 August 2005 the Commission shall, after consulting the Member States and management and labour at European level, review the operation of the provisions with regard to offshore workers from a health and safety perspective with a view to presenting, if need be, the appropriate modifications.

Article 21 Workers on board seagoing fishing vessels

1.   Articles 3 to 6 and 8 shall not apply to any worker on board a seagoing fishing vessel flying the flag of a Member State.

      Member States shall, however, take the necessary measures to ensure that any worker on board a seagoing fishing vessel flying the flag of a Member State is entitled to adequate rest and to limit the number of hours of work to 48 hours a week on average calculated over a reference period not exceeding 12 months.

2.   Within the limits set out in paragraph 1, second subparagraph, and paragraphs 3 and 4 Member States shall take the necessary measures to ensure that, in keeping with the need to protect the safety and health of such workers:

(a)   the working hours are limited to a maximum number of hours which shall not be exceeded in a given period of time; or

(b)   a minimum number of hours of rest are provided within a given period of time.

The maximum number of hours of work or minimum number of hours of rest shall be specified by law, regulations, administrative provisions or by collective agreements or agreements between the two sides of the industry.

3.   The limits on hours of work or rest shall be either:

(a)   maximum hours of work which shall not exceed:

(i)   14 hours in any 24-hour period; and

(ii)   72 hours in any seven-day period;

or

(b)   minimum hours of rest which shall not be less than:

(i)   10 hours in any 24-hour period; and

(ii)   77 hours in any seven-day period.

4.   Hours of rest may be divided into no more than two periods, one of which shall be at least six hours in length, and the interval between consecutive periods of rest shall not exceed 14 hours.

5.   In accordance with the general principles of the protection of the health and safety of workers, and for objective or technical reasons or reasons concerning the organisation of work, Member States may allow exceptions, including the establishment of reference periods, to the limits laid down in paragraph 1, second subparagraph, and paragraphs 3 and 4. Such exceptions shall, as far as possible, comply with the standards laid down but may take account of more frequent or longer leave periods or the granting of compensatory leave for the workers. These exceptions may be laid down by means of:

(a)   laws, regulations or administrative provisions provided there is consultation, where possible, of the representatives of the employers and workers concerned and efforts are made to encourage all relevant forms of social dialogue; or

(b)   collective agreements or agreements between the two sides of industry.

6.   The master of a seagoing fishing vessel shall have the right to require workers on board to perform any hours of work necessary for. the immediate safety of the vessel, persons on board or cargo, or for the purpose of giving assistance to other vessels or persons in distress at sea.

7.   Members States may provide that workers on board seagoing fishing vessels for which national legislation or practice determines that these vessels are not allowed to operate in a specific period of the calendar year exceeding one month, shall take annual leave in accordance with Article 7 within that period.

Article 22 Miscellaneous provisions

1.   A Member State shall have the option not to apply Article 6, while respecting the general principles of the protection of the safety and health of workers, and provided it takes the necessary measures to ensure that:

(a)   no employer requires a worker to work more than 48 hours over a seven-day period, calculated as an average for the reference period referred to in Article 16(b), unless he has first obtained the worker's agreement to perform such work:

(b)   no worker is subjected to any detriment by his employer because he is not willing to give his agreement to perform such work;

(c)   the employer keeps up-to-date records of all workers who carry out such work;

(d)   the records are placed at the disposal of the competent authorities, which may, for reasons connected with the safety and/or health of workers, prohibit or restrict the possibility of exceeding the maximum weekly working hours;

(e)   the employer provides the competent authorities at their request with information on cases in which agreement has been given by workers to perform work exceeding 48 hours over a period of seven days, calculated as an average for the reference period referred to in Article 16(b).

Before 23 November 2003, the Council shall, on the basis of a Commission proposal accompanied by an appraisal report, reexamine the provisions of this paragraph and decide on what action to take.

2.   Member States shall have the option, as regards the application of Article 7, of making use of a transitional period of not more than three years from 23 November 1996, provided that during that transitional period:

(a)   every worker receives three weeks' paid annual leave in accordance with the conditions for the entitlement to, and granting of, such leave laid down by national legislation and/or practice: and

(b)   the three-week period of paid annual leave may not be replaced by an allowance in lieu, except where the employment relationship is terminated.

3.   If Member States avail themselves of the options provided for in this Article, they shall forthwith inform the Commission thereof.

<h2 style="text-align:center">CHAPTER 6
FINAL PROVISIONS</h2>

Article 23   Level of protection

Without prejudice to the right of Member States to develop, in the light of changing circumstances, different legislative, regulatory or contractual provisions in the field of working time, as long as the minimum requirements provided for in this Directive are complied with, implementation of this Directive shall not constitute valid grounds for reducing the general level of protection afforded to workers.

Article 24   Reports

1.   Member States shall communicate to the Commission the texts of the provisions of national law already adopted or being adopted in the field governed by this Directive.

2.   Member States shall report to the Commission every five years on the practical implementation of the provisions of this Directive, indicating the viewpoints of the two sides of industry.

The Commission shall inform the European Parliament, the Council, the European Economic and Social Committee and the Advisory Committee on Safety, Hygiene and Health Protection at Work thereof.

3.   Every five years from 23 November 1996 the Commission shall submit to the European Parliament, the Council and the European Economic and Social Committee a report on the application of this Directive taking into account Articles 22 and 23 and paragraphs 1 and 2 of this Article.

Article 25   Review of the operation of the provisions with regard to workers on board seagoing fishing vessels

Not later than 1 August 2009 the Commission shall, after consulting the Member States and management and labour at European level, review the operation of the provisions with regard to workers on board seagoing fishing vessels, and, in particular examine whether these provisions remain appropriate, in particular, as far as health and safety are concerned with a view to proposing suitable amendments, if necessary.

Article 26   Review of the operation of the provisions with regard to workers concerned with the carriage of passengers

Not later than 1 August 2005 the Commission shall, after consulting the Member States and management and labour at European level, review the operation of the provisions with regard to workers concerned with the carriage of passengers on regular urban transport services, with a view to presenting, if need be, the appropriate modifications to ensure a coherent and suitable approach in the sector.

Article 27 Repeal

1. Directive 93/104/EC, as amended by the Directive referred to in Annex 1, part A, shall be repealed, without prejudice to the obligations of the Member States in respect of the deadlines for transposition laid down in Annex I, part B.

2. The references made to the said repealed Directive shall be construed as references to this Directive and shall be read in accordance with the correlation table set out in Annex II.

Article 28 Entry into force

This Directive shall enter into force on 2 August 2004.

Article 29 Addressees

This Directive is addressed to the Member States.

ANNEX I

PART A

REPEALED DIRECTIVE AND ITS AMENDMENT

(Article 27)

Council Directive 93/104/EC	(OJ L 307, 13.12.1993, p. 18)
Directive 2000/34/EC of the European Parliament and of the Council	(OJ L 195, 1.8.2000, p. 41)

PART B

DEADLINES FOR TRANSPOSITION INTO NATIONAL LAW

(Article 27)

Directive	Deadline for transposition
93/104/EC	23 November 1996
2000/34/EC	1 August 2000[1]

[1] 1 August 2004 in the case of doctors in training. See Article 2 of Directive 2000/34/EC.

ANNEX II

CORRELATION TABLE

Directive 93/104/EEC	This Directive
Article 1 to 5	Article 1 to 5
Article 6, introductory words	Article 6, introductory words
Article 6(1)	Article 6(a)
Article 6(2)	Article 6(b)
Article 7	Article 7
Article 8, introductory words	Article 8, introductory words
Article 8(1)	Article 8(a)
Article 8(2)	Article 8(b)
Article 9, 10 and 11	Article 9, 10 and 11
Article 12, introductory words	Article 12, introductory words
Article 12(1)	Article 12(a)
Article 12(2)	Article 12(b)
Article 13, 14 and 15	Article 13, 14 and 15
Article 16, introductory words	Article 16, introductory words
Article 16(1)	Article 16(a)

Directive 93/104/EEC	This Directive
Article 16(2)	Article 16(b)
Article 16(3)	Article 16(c)
Article 17(1)	Article 17(1)
Article 17(2), introductory words	Article 17(2)
Article 17(2)(1)	Article 17(3)(a) to (e)
Article 17(2)(2)	Article 17(3)(f) to (g)
Article 17(2)(3)	Article 17(4)
Article 17(2)(4)	Article 17(5)
Article 17(3)	Article 18
Article 17(4)	Article 19
Article 17a(1)	Article 20(1), first subparagraph
Article 17a(2)	Article 20(1), second subparagraph
Article 17a(3)	Article 20(2)
Article 17a(4)	Article 20(3)
Article 17b(1)	Article 21(1), first subparagraph
Article 17b(2)	Article 21(1), second subparagraph
Article 17b(3)	Article 21(2)
Article 17b(4)	Article 21(3)
Article 17b(5)	Article 21(4)
Article 17b(6)	Article 21(5)
Article 17b(7)	Article 21(6)
Article 17b(8)	Article 21(7)
Article 18(1)(a)	—
Article 18(1)(b)(i)	Article 22(1)
Article 18(1)(b)(ii)	Article 22(2)
Article 18(1)(c)	Article 22(3)
Article 18(2)	—
Article 18(3)	Article 23
Article 18(4)	Article 24(1)
Article 18(5)	Article 24(2)
Article 18(6)	Article 24(3)
—	Article 25[1]
—	Article 25[2]
—	Article 27
—	Article 28
Article 19	Article 29
—	Annex I
—	Annex II

[1] Directive 2000/34/EC, Article 3.
[2] Directive 2000/34/EC, Article 4.

CONSUMER PROTECTION

COUNCIL DIRECTIVE (EEC) No 85/374 of 25 JULY 1985
on the approximation of the laws, regulations and administrative provisions of the Member States concerning liability for defective products
[1985] OJ L210/29

Article 1

The producer shall be liable for damage caused by a defect in his product.

Article 2

For the purpose of this Directive 'product' means all movables even if incorporated into another movable or into an immovable. 'Product' includes electricity.

Article 3

1. 'Producer' means the manufacturer of a finished product, the producer of any raw material or the manufacturer of a component part and any person who, by putting his name, trade mark or other distinguishing feature on the product presents himself as its producer.
2. Without prejudice to the liability of the producer, any person who imports into the Community a product for sale, hire, leasing or any form of distribution in the course of his business shall be deemed to be a producer within the meaning of this Directive and shall be responsible as a producer.
3. Where the producer of the product cannot be identified, each supplier of the product shall be treated as its producer unless he informs the injured person, within a reasonable time, of the identity of the producer or of the person who supplied him with the product. The same shall apply, in the case of an imported product, if this product does not indicate the identity of the importer referred to in paragraph 2, even if the name of the producer is indicated.

Article 4

The injured person shall be required to prove the damage, the defect and the causal relationship between defect and damage.

Article 5

Where, as a result of the provisions of this Directive, two or more persons are liable for the same damage, they shall be liable jointly and severally, without prejudice to the provisions of national law concerning the rights of contribution or recourse.

Article 6

1. A product is defective when it does not provide the safety which a person is entitled to expect, taking all circumstances into account, including:
   (a) the presentation of the product;
   (b) the use to which it could reasonably be expected that the product would be put;
   (c) the time when the product was put into circulation.
2. A product shall not be considered defective for the sole reason that a better product is subsequently put into circulation.

Article 7

The producer shall not be liable as a result of this Directive if he proves:
   (a) that he did not put the product into circulation; or
   (b) that, having regard to the circumstances, it is probable that the defect which caused the damage did not exist at the time when the product was put into circulation by him or that this defect came into being afterwards; or
   (c) that the product was neither manufactured by him for sale or any form of distribution for economic purpose nor manufactured or distributed by him in the course of his business; or
   (d) that the defect is due to compliance of the product with mandatory regulations issued by the public authorities; or

(e)   that the state of scientific and technical knowledge at the time when he put the product into circulation was not such as to enable the existence of the defect to be discovered; or

(f)   in the case of a manufacturer of a component, that the defect is attributable to the design of the product in which the component has been fitted or to the instructions given by the manufacturer of the product.

Article 8

1.   Without prejudice to the provisions of national law concerning the right of contribution or recourse, the liability of the producer shall not be reduced when the damage is caused both by a defect in product and by the act or omission of a third party.

2.   The liability of the producer may be reduced or disallowed when, having regard to all the circumstances, the damage is caused both by a defect in the product and by the fault of the injured person or any person for whom the injured person is responsible.

Article 9

For the purpose of Article 1, 'damage' means:

(a)   damage caused by death or by personal injuries;

(b)   damage to, or destruction of, any item of property other than the defective product itself, with a lower threshold of 500 ECU, provided that the item of property:

(i)   is of a type ordinarily intended for private use or consumption, and

(ii)   was used by the injured person mainly for his own private use or consumption.

This Article shall be without prejudice to national provisions relating to non-material damage.

Article 10

1.   Member States shall provide in their legislation that a limitation period of three years shall apply to proceedings for the recovery of damages as provided for in this Directive. The limitation period shall begin to run from the day on which the plaintiff became aware, or should reasonably have become aware, of the damage, the defect and the identity of the producer.

2.   The laws of Member States regulating suspension or interruption of the limitation period shall not be affected by this Directive.

Article 11

Member States shall provide in their legislation that the rights conferred upon the injured person pursuant to this Directive shall be extinguished upon the expiry of a period of 10 years from the date on which the producer put into circulation the actual product which caused the damage, unless the injured person has in the meantime instituted proceedings against the producer.

Article 12

The liability of the producer arising from this Directive may not, in relation to the injured person, be limited or excluded by a provision limiting his liability or exempting him from liability.

Article 13

This Directive shall not affect any rights which an injured person may have according to the rules of the law of contractual or non-contractual liability or a special liability system existing at the moment when this Directive is notified.

Article 14

This Directive shall not apply to injury or damage arising from nuclear accidents and covered by international conventions ratified by the Member States.

Article 15

1.   Each Member State may:

(a)   ...

(b)   by way of derogation from Article 7(e), maintain or, subject to the procedure set out in paragraph 2 of this Article, provide in this legislation that the producer shall be liable even if he proves that the state of scientific and technical knowledge at the time when he put the product into circulation was not such as to enable the existence of a defect to be discovered.

2. A Member State wishing to introduce the measure specified in paragraph 1(b) shall communicate the text of the proposed measure to the Commission. The Commission shall inform the other Member States thereof.

    The Member State concerned shall hold the proposed measure in abeyance for nine months after the Commission is informed and provided that in the meantime the Commission has not submitted to the Council a proposal amending this Directive on the relevant matter. However, if within three months of receiving the said information, the Commission does not advise the Member State concerned that it intends submitting such a proposal to the Council, the Member State may take the proposed measure immediately.

    If the Commission does submit to the Council such a proposal amending this Directive within the aforementioned nine months, the Member State concerned shall hold the proposed measure in abeyance for a further period of 18 months from the date on which the proposal is submitted.

3. Ten years after the date of notification of this Directive, the Commission shall submit to the Council a report on the effect that rulings by the courts as to the application of Article 7(e) and of paragraph 1(b) of this Article have on consumer protection and the functioning of the common market. In the light of this report the Council, acting on a proposal from the Commission and pursuant to the terms of Article 100 of the Treaty, shall decide whether to repeal Article 7(e).

Article 16

1. Any Member State may provide that a producer's total liability for damage resulting from a death or personal injury and caused by identical items with the same defect shall be limited to an amount which may not be less than 70 million ECU.

2. Ten years after the date of notification of this Directive, the Commission shall submit to the Council a report on the effect on consumer protection and the functioning of the common market of the implementation of the financial limit on liability by those Member States which have used the option provided for in paragraph 1. In the light of this report the Council, acting on a proposal from the Commission and pursuant to the terms of Article 100 of the Treaty, shall decide whether to repeal paragraph 1.

Article 17

This Directive shall not apply to products put into circulation before the date on which the provisions referred to in Article 19 enter into force.

Article 18

1. For the purposes of this Directive, the ECU shall be that defined by Regulation (EEC) No 3180/78, as amended by Regulation (EEC) No 2626/84. The equivalent in national currency shall initially be calculated at the rate obtaining on the date of adoption of this Directive.

2. Every five years the Council, acting on a proposal from the Commission, shall examine and, if need be, revise the amounts in this Directive, in the light of economic and monetary trends in the Community.

Article 19

1. Member States shall bring into force, not later than three years from the date of notification of this Directive, the laws, regulations and administrative provisions necessary to comply with this Directive. They shall forthwith inform the Commission thereof.

2. The procedure set out in Article 15(2) shall apply from the date of notification of this Directive.

Article 20

Member States shall communicate to the Commission the texts of the main provisions of national law which they subsequently adopt in the field governed by this Directive.

Article 21

Every five years the Commission shall present a report to the Council on the application of this Directive and, if necessary, shall submit appropriate proposals to it.

Article 22

This Directive is addressed to the Member States.

COUNCIL DIRECTIVE 93/13/EEC of 5 April 1993
on unfair terms in consumer contracts
[1993] OJ L95/29

Article 1

1. The purpose of this Directive is to approximate the laws, regulations and administrative provisions of the Member States relating to unfair terms in contracts concluded between a seller or supplier and a consumer.

2. The contractual terms which reflect mandatory statutory or regulatory provisions and the provisions or principles of international conventions to which the Member States or the Community are party, particularly in the transport area, shall not be subject to the provisions of this Directive.

Article 2

For the purposes of this Directive:

(a)   'unfair terms' means the contractual terms defined in Article 3;

(b)   'consumer' means any natural person who, in contracts covered by this Directive, is acting for purposes which are outside his trade, business or profession;

(c)   'seller or supplier' means any natural or legal person who, in contracts covered by this Directive, is acting for purposes relating to his trade, business or profession, whether publicly owned or privately owned.

Article 3

1. A contractual term which has not been individually negotiated shall be regarded as unfair if, contrary to the requirement of good faith, it causes a significant imbalance in the parties' rights and obligations arising under the contract, to the detriment of the consumer.

2. A term shall always be regarded as not individually negotiated where it has been drafted in advance and the consumer has therefore not been able to influence the substance of the term, particularly in the context of a pre-formulated standard contract.

    The fact that certain aspects of a term or one specific term have been individually negotiated shall not exclude the application of this Article to the rest of a contract if an overall assessment of the contract indicates that it is nevertheless a pre-formulated standard contract.

    Where any seller or supplier claims that a standard term has been individually negotiated, the burden of proof in this respect shall be incumbent on him.

3. The Annex shall contain an indicative and non-exhaustive list of the terms which may be regarded as unfair.

Article 4

1. Without prejudice to Article 7, the unfairness of a contractual term shall be assessed, taking into account the nature of the goods or services for which the contract was concluded and by referring, at the time of conclusion of the contract, to all the circumstances attending the conclusion of the contract and to all the other terms of the contract or of another contract on which it is dependent.

2. Assessment of the unfair nature of the terms shall relate neither to the definition of the main subject matter of the contract nor to the adequacy of the price and remuneration, on the one hand, as against the services or goods supplies in exchange, on the other, in so far as these terms are in plain intelligible language.

Article 5

In the case of contracts where all or certain terms offered to the consumer are in writing, these terms must always be drafted in plain, intelligible language. Where there is doubt about the meaning of a term, the interpretation most favourable to the consumer shall prevail. This rule on interpretation shall not apply in the context of the procedures laid down in Article 7 (2).

Article 6

1. Member States shall lay down that unfair terms used in a contract concluded with a consumer by a seller or supplier shall, as provided for under their national law, not be binding on the consumer and that the contract shall continue to bind the parties upon those terms if it is capable of continuing in existence without the unfair terms.

2. Member States shall take the necessary measures to ensure that the consumer does not lose the protection granted by this Directive by virtue of the choice of the law of a non-Member country as the law applicable to the contract if the latter has a close connection with the territory of the Member States.

Article 7

1. Member States shall ensure that, in the interests of consumers and of competitors, adequate and effective means exist to prevent the continued use of unfair terms in contracts concluded with consumers by sellers or suppliers.

2. The means referred to in paragraph 1 shall include provisions whereby persons or organisations, having a legitimate interest under national law in protecting consumers, may take action according to the national law concerned before the courts or before competent administrative bodies for a decision as to whether contractual terms drawn up for general use are unfair, so that they can apply appropriate and effective means to prevent the continued use of such terms.

3. With due regard for national laws, the legal remedies referred to in paragraph 2 may be directed separately or jointly against a number of sellers or suppliers from the same economic sector or their associations which use or recommend the use of the same general contractual terms or similar terms.

Article 8

Member States may adopt or retain the most stringent provisions compatible with the Treaty in the area covered by this Directive, to ensure a maximum degree of protection for the consumer.

Article 9

The Commission shall present a report to the European Parliament and to the Council concerning the application of this Directive five years at the latest after the date in Article 10 (1).

Article 10

1. Member States shall bring into force the laws, regulations and administrative provisions necessary to comply with this Directive no later than 31 December 1994. They shall forthwith inform the Commission thereof.

   These provisions shall be applicable to all contracts concluded after 31 December 1994.

2. When Member States adopt these measures, they shall contain a reference to this Directive or shall be accompanied by such reference on the occasion of their official publication. The methods of making such a reference shall be laid down by the Member States.

3. Member States shall communicate the main provisions of national law which they adopt in the field covered by this Directive to the Commission.

Article 11

This Directive is addressed to the Member States.

ANNEX

TERMS REFERRED TO IN ARTICLE 3 (3)

1. Terms which have the object or effect of:
   (a) excluding or limiting the legal liability of a seller or supplier in the event of the death of a consumer or personal injury to the latter resulting from an act or omission of that seller or supplier;

(b)   inappropriately excluding or limiting the legal rights of the consumer vis-à-vis the seller or supplier or another party in the event of total or partial non-performance or inadequate performance by the seller or supplier of any of the contractual obligations, including the option of offsetting a debt owed to the seller or supplier against any claim which the consumer may have against him;

(c)   making an agreement binding on the consumer whereas provision of services by the seller or supplier is subject to a condition whose realisation depends on his own will alone;

(d)   permitting the seller or supplier to retain sums paid by the consumer where the latter decides not to conclude or perform the contract, without providing for the consumer to receive compensation of an equivalent amount from the seller or supplier where the latter is the party cancelling the contract;

(e)   requiring any consumer who fails to fulfil his obligation to pay a disproportionately high sum in compensation;

(f)   authorising the seller or supplier to dissolve the contract on a discretionary basis where the same facility is not granted to the consumer, or permitting the seller or supplier to retain the sums paid for services not yet supplied by him where it is the seller or supplier himself who dissolves the contract;

(g)   enabling the seller or supplier to terminate a contract of indeterminate duration without reasonable notice except where there are serious grounds for doing so;

(h)   automatically extending a contract of fixed duration where the consumer does not indicate otherwise, when the deadline fixed for the consumer to express this desire not to extend the contract is unreasonably early;

(i)   irrevocably binding the consumer to terms with which he had no real opportunity of becoming acquainted before the conclusion of the contract;

(j)   enabling the seller or supplier to alter the terms of the contract unilaterally without a valid reason which is specified in the contract;

(k)   enabling the seller or supplier to alter unilaterally without a valid reason any characteristics of the product or service to be provided;

(l)   providing for the price of goods to be determined at the time of delivery or allowing a seller of goods or supplier of services to increase their price without in both cases giving the consumer the corresponding right to cancel the contract if the final price is too high in relation to the price agreed when the contract was concluded;

(m)   giving the seller or supplier the right to determine whether the goods or services supplied are in conformity with the contract, or giving him the exclusive right to interpret any term of the contract;

(n)   limiting the seller's or supplier's obligation to respect commitments undertaken by his agents or making his commitments subject to compliance with a particular formality;

(o)   obliging the consumer to fulfil all his obligations where the seller or supplier does not perform his;

(p)   giving the seller or supplier the possibility of transferring his rights and obligations under the contract, where this may serve to reduce the guarantees for the consumer, without the latter's agreement;

(q)   excluding or hindering the consumer's right to take legal action or exercise any other legal remedy, particularly by requiring the consumer to take disputes exclusively to arbitration not covered by legal provisions, unduly restricting the evidence available to him or imposing on him a burden of proof which, according to the applicable law, should lie with another party to the contract.

2.   Scope of subparagraphs (g), (j) and (l)

(a)   Subparagraph (g) is without hindrance to terms by which a supplier of financial services reserves the right to terminate unilaterally a contract of indeterminate duration without notice where there is a valid reason, provided that the supplier is required to inform the other contracting party or parties thereof immediately.

(b)   Subparagraph (j) is without hindrance to terms under which a supplier of financial services reserves the right to alter the rate of interest payable by the consumer or due to the latter, or the amount of other charges for financial services without notice where there is a valid reason, provided that the supplier is required to inform the other contracting party or parties thereof at the earliest opportunity and that the latter are free to dissolve the contract immediately.

Subparagraph (j) is also without hindrance to terms under which a seller or supplier reserves the right to alter unilaterally the conditions of a contract of indeterminate duration, provided that he is required to inform the consumer with reasonable notice and that the consumer is free to dissolve the contract.

(c)   Subparagraphs (g), (j) and (l) do not apply to:

— transactions in transferable securities, financial instruments and other products or services where the price is linked to fluctuations in a stock exchange quotation or index or a financial market rate that the seller or supplier does not control;

— contracts for the purchase or sale of foreign currency, traveller's cheques or international money orders denominated in foreign currency;

(d)   Subparagraph (l) is without hindrance to price-indexation clauses, where lawful, provided that the method by which prices vary is explicitly described.

UK STATUTES

EUROPEAN COMMUNITIES ACT 1972
(1972, c. 68)

PART 1
GENERAL PROVISIONS

1   Short title and interpretation

(1)   This Act may be cited as the European Communities Act 1972.

(2)   In this Act …

"the Communities" means the European Economic Community, the European Coal and Steel Community and the European Atomic Energy Community;

"the Treaties" or "the Community Treaties" means, subject to subsection (3) below, the pre-accession treaties, that is to say, those described in Part 1 of Schedule 1 to this Act, taken with

(a)   the treaty relating to the accession of the United Kingdom to the European Economic Community and to the European Atomic Energy Community, signed at Brussels on the 22nd January 1972; and

(b)   the decision, of the same date, of the Council of the European Communities relating to the accession of the United Kingdom to the European Coal and Steel Community; and

   …

(j)   the following provisions of the Single European Act signed at Luxembourg and The Hague on 17th and 28th February 1986, namely Title II (amendment of the treaties establishing the Communities) and, so far as they relate to any of the Communities or any Community institution, the preamble and Titles I (common provisions) and IV (general and final provisions); and

(k)   Titles II, III and IV of the Treaty on European Union signed at Maastricht on 7th February 1992, together with the other provisions of the Treaty so far as they relate to those Titles, and the Protocols adopted at Maastricht on that date and annexed to the Treaty establishing the European Community with the exception of the Protocol on Social Policy on page 117 of Cm 1934; and

(l)   the decision, of 1st February 1993, of the Council amending the Act concerning the election of the representatives of the European Parliament by direct universal suffrage annexed to Council Decision 76/787/ECSC, EEC, Euratom of 20th September 1976; and

(m)   the Agreement on the European Economic Area signed at Oporto on 2nd May 1992 together with the Protocol adjusting that Agreement signed at Brussels on 17th March 1993; and

   …

(o)   the following provisions of the Treaty signed at Amsterdam on 2nd October 1997 amending the Treaty on European Union, the Treaties establishing the European Communities and certain related Acts

    (i)   Articles 2 to 9,

    (ii)   Article 12, and

    (iii)   the other provisions of the Treaty so far as they relate to those Articles,

and the Protocols adopted on that occasion other than the Protocol on Article J.7 of the Treaty on European Union; and

(p)   the following provisions of the Treaty signed at Nice on 26th February 2001 amending the Treaty on European Union, the Treaties establishing the European Communities and certain related Acts

    (i)   Articles 2 to 10, and

    (ii)   the other provisions of the Treaty so far as they relate to those Articles, and the Protocols adopted on that occasion;

and any other treaty entered into by any of the Communities, with or without any of the member States, or entered into, as a treaty ancillary to any of the Treaties, by the United Kingdom; and

...

and any expression defined in Schedule 1 to this Act has the meaning there given to it.

(3) If Her Majesty by Order in Council declares that a treaty specified in the Order is to be regarded as one of the Community Treaties as herein defined, the Order shall be conclusive that it is to be so regarded; but a treaty entered into by the United Kingdom after the 22nd January 1972, other than a pre-accession treaty to which the United Kingdom accedes on terms settled on or before that date, shall not be so regarded unless it is so specified, nor be so specified unless a draft of the Order in Council has been approved by resolution of each House of Parliament.

(4) For purposes of subsections (2) and (3) above, "treaty" includes any international agreement, and any protocol or annex to a treaty or international agreement.

2 General implementation of Treaties

(1) All such rights, powers, liabilities, obligations and restrictions from time to time created or arising by or under the Treaties, and all such remedies and procedures from time to time provided for by or under the Treaties, as in accordance with the Treaties are without further enactment to be given legal effect or used in the United Kingdom shall be recognised and available in law, and be enforced, allowed and followed accordingly; and the expression "enforceable Community right" and similar expressions shall be read as referring to one to which this subsection applies.

(2) Subject to Schedule 2 to this Act, at any time after its passing Her Majesty may by Order in Council, and any designated Minister or department may by order, rules, regulations or scheme, make provision—

    (a) for the purpose of implementing any Community obligation of the United Kingdom, or enabling any such obligation to be implemented, or of enabling any rights enjoyed or to be enjoyed by the United Kingdom under or by virtue of the Treaties to be exercised; or

    (b) for the purpose of dealing with matters arising out of or related to any such obligation or rights or the coming into force, or the operation from time to time, of subsection (1) above;

and in the exercise of any statutory power or duty, including any power to give directions or to legislate by means of orders, rules, regulations or other subordinate instrument, the person entrusted with the power or duty may have regard to the objects of the Communities and to any such obligation or rights as aforesaid.

In this subsection "designated Minister or department" means such Minister of the Crown or government department as may from time to time be designated by Order in Council in relation to any matter or for any purpose, but subject to such restrictions or conditions (if any) as may be specified by the Order in Council.

(3) There shall be charged on and issued out of the Consolidated Fund or, if so determined by the Treasury, the National Loans Fund the amounts required to meet any Community obligation to make payments to any of the Communities or member States, or any Community obligation in respect of contributions to the capital or reserves of the European Investment Bank or in respect of loans to the Bank, or to redeem any notes or obligations issued or created in respect of any such Community obligation; and, except as otherwise provided by or under any enactment,

    (a) any other expenses incurred under or by virtue of the Treaties or this Act by any Minister of the Crown or government department may be paid out of moneys provided by Parliament; and

    (b) any sums received under or by virtue of the Treaties or this Act by any Minister of the Crown or government department, save for such sums as may be required for disbursements permitted by any other enactment, shall be paid into the Consolidated Fund or, if so determined by the Treasury, the National Loans Fund.

(4) The provision that may be made under subsection (2) above includes, subject to Schedule 2 to this Act, any such provision (of any such extent) as might be made by Act of Parliament, and any enactment passed or to be passed, other than one contained in this Part of this Act, shall be construed and have effect subject to the foregoing provisions of this section; but, except as may be provided by any Act passed after this Act, Schedule 2 shall have effect in connection with the powers conferred by this and the following sections of this Act to make Orders in Council or orders, rules, regulations or schemes.

...

3   Decisions on, and proof of, Treaties and Community instruments, etc.

(1) For the purposes of all legal proceedings any question as to the meaning or effect of any of the Treaties, or as to the validity, meaning or effect of any Community instrument, shall be treated as a question of law (and, if not referred to the European Court, be for determination as such in accordance with the principles laid down by and any relevant decision of the European Court or any court attached thereto).

(2) Judicial notice shall be taken of the Treaties, of the Official Journal of the Communities and of any decision of, or expression of opinion by, the European Court or any court attached thereto on any such question as aforesaid; and the Official Journal shall be admissible as evidence of any instrument or other act thereby communicated of any of the Communities or of any Community institution.

...

EUROPEAN PARLIAMENTARY ELECTIONS ACT 2002
(2002, c. 24)

An Act to consolidate the European Parliamentary Elections Acts 1978, 1993 and 1999.

Introductory

1   Number of MEPs and electoral regions

(1) There shall be 78 members of the European Parliament ("MEPs") elected for the United Kingdom.

(2) For the purposes of electing those MEPs—

   (a)   the area of England and Gibraltar is divided into the nine electoral regions specified in Schedule 1; and

   (b)   Scotland, Wales and Northern Ireland are each single electoral regions.

(3) The number of MEPs to be elected for each electoral region is as follows—

East Midlands	6
Eastern	7
London	9
North East	3
North West	9
South East	10
South West	7
West Midlands	7
Yorkshire and the Humber	6
Scotland	7
Wales	7
Northern Ireland	3

General elections

2   Voting system in Great Britain and Gibraltar

(1) The system of election of MEPs in an electoral region other than Northern Ireland in Great Britain is to be a regional list system.

(2) The Secretary of State must by regulations—

   (a)   make provision for the nomination of registered parties in relation to an election in such a region, and

Sixth Edition

Law of the European Union

JOHN FAIRHURST
Anglia Ruskin University

PEARSON
Longman

Harlow, England • London • New York • Boston • San Francisco • Toronto • Sydney • Singapore • Hong Kong
Tokyo • Seoul • Taipei • New Delhi • Cape Town • Madrid • Mexico City • Amsterdam • Munich • Paris • Milan

Pearson Education Limited
Edinburgh Gate
Harlow
Essex CM20 2JE
England

and Associated Companies throughout the world

Visit us on the World Wide Web at:
www.pearsoned.co.uk

First published 1996
Second edition published under the Financial Times/Pitman Publishing imprint in 1999
Third edition 2002
Fourth edition 2003
Fifth edition 2006
Sixth edition published in Great Britain 2007

ISBN 978-1-4058-4688-2

British Library Cataloguing-in-Publication Data
A catalogue record for this book is available from the British Library

Library of Congress Cataloging-in-Publication Data
Fairhurst, John.
   Law of the European Union / John Fairhurst. - 6th ed.
      p. cm. - (The foundation studies in law series)
   Includes bibliographical references and index.
   ISBN 978-1-4058-4688-2
   1. Law-European Union countries. 2. Courts-European Union countries. 3.
   Treaties-European Union countries. 4. European Union. I. Title.

KJE947.F342 2007
341.242'2-dc22

                                                    2006053276

10 9 8 7 6 5 4 3 2
11 10 09 08

Typeset in 9pt Stone Serif by 3
Printed and bound in Malaysia (CTP - PJB)

The publisher's policy is to use paper manufactured from sustainable forests.

To my brother Philip
(1958–2005)
and to all the medical and support staff
at the Intensive Care Unit,
Hope Hospital, Salford

Supporting resources

Visit www.pearsoned.co.uk/fsls to find valuable online resources

- Interactive multiple choice questions to test your factual knowledge of the topics
- Tutorial style questions and answer guidance to test your ability to apply knowledge
- Links to relevant sites on the web
- An online glossary providing definitions of key legal terms
- Interactive online flashcards that allow you to check definitions against the key terms during revision
- Regular updates on major legal changes affecting the book

For instructors
- A testbank of questions allowing for class assessment

Also: The regularly maintained Companion Website provides the following features:
- Search tool to help locate specific items of content
- E-mail results and profile tools to send results of quizzes to instructors
- Online help and support to assist with website usage and troubleshooting

For more information please contact your local Pearson Education sales representative or visit www.mylawchamber/fairhurst

Brief contents

Contents

Part 1 Constitutional and administrative law of the European Communities and the European Union   1

1 An introduction to the European Communities and the European Union   3

Preface to the sixth edition

Since the fifth edition of this book was published, there have been two important events in the continuing evolvement of the European Communities and the European Union: (i) the failure to ratify the Constitutional Treaty; and (ii) enlargement of the European Union from 25 Member States to 27 on 1 January 2007, with the admission of Bulgaria and Romania.

The Constitutional Treaty would only have come into force if it had been ratified by each of the then 25 Member States. Many commentators forecast that the ratification process would be a tumultuous affair, particularly when Tony Blair (the UK Prime Minister) announced that the UK would only ratify the Treaty if the electorate voted in favour of such in a referendum. However, it never got that far, because France and The Netherlands held their referenda before the UK and the electorates in both of these countries rejected the Treaty. The UK (along with some of the other Member States) subsequently decided to suspend their referenda. The EU embarked on a period of reflection, and decisions on the future of the Constitutional Treaty will be taken during 2007. My own view is that the Constitutional Treaty, in its current format, will be abandoned. If the EU attempts to press on with the ratification process, a further setback would be politically damaging. If either France or The Netherlands rejected the Treaty in a second referendum this could set the reform process back indefinitely. There is a clear need for a new Treaty which either replaces the existing Treaties or amends them. In particular, a new Treaty is required so that the necessary changes can be made to the Community institutions' composition and procedures, to prepare for future EU enlargement. Chapter 1 has been revamped to reflect this current impasse, and to explore how this issue might develop. Throughout Chapter 1 and the remainder of the book I have decided to include a discussion of the changes which the Constitutional Treaty would have effected, because at this stage it is unclear if the Treaty is 'dead or alive' or whether a replacement Treaty will be adopted.

With regard to EU enlargement, Bulgaria and Romania joined on 1 January 2007. The constitutional and administrative impact of this latest expansion is explored throughout Part 1 of the book, in particular with regard to its impact on the Community institutions: their composition and procedures.

In addition to covering these two developments within this new edition, I have included recent EU legislation and legislative proposals, and recent judgments of the Court of Justice and Court of First Instance, where these seem relevant. The format of this edition follows the same format as the previous edition.

Part 1 (Constitutional and Administrative Law of the European Communities and the European Union) has been substantially revised to incorporate the two developments discussed above. Throughout Chapters 1 to 5 in particular, there is a thorough review of the impact which the Constitutional Treaty would have had on the EU's constitutional structure.

Chapter 1 consists of an introduction to the European Communities and the European Union. Chapter 2 is devoted to the sources of Community law, including a commentary on fundamental rights and the European Convention on Human Rights. The rationale for this approach is that I consider it preferable to have an understanding of such sources before embarking upon a consideration of the Community institutions (Chapter 3) and the decision-making process (Chapter 4). There is a separate chapter on the Court of Justice and Court of First Instance, together with their methods of interpretation (Chapter 5). Included within Chapter 5 is an exploration of the role of the new EU Civil Service Tribunal. Chapters 6–8 are devoted to the preliminary ruling jurisdiction of the Court of Justice (Art 234 EC Treaty), direct actions against Member States (Arts 226–228 EC Treaty), and judicial review of acts of the Community institutions, respectively. Chapter 8 has been substantially rewritten to provide a clearer structure. Chapter 9 examines the principles of supremacy, direct and indirect effect, and state liability and their application in UK courts. The extension of state liability to include national courts of last instance is fully discussed. The final chapter of Part 1 (Chapter 10) is devoted to the application of Community law in UK courts and the adapting of remedies to the requirements of Community law.

The final three parts of the book (Parts 2 to 4) relate to three areas of substantive law: free movement of persons and services, and rights of establishment (Part 2, Chapters 11–16); free movement of goods (Part 3, Chapters 17–18); and competition law (Part 4, Chapters 19–22). In each of these three parts, judgments of the Court of Justice and Court of First Instance have been extracted to provide a deeper exposure to the methodology adopted by the Courts in the development of the Community's substantive law. The impact of new EU legislation has had a most marked impact on Part 2 of the book (free movement of persons). Part 2 includes a detailed commentary on Directive 2004/38 which relates to the entry and residence rights of EU citizens and their family members. The UK's implementing legislation (the Immigration (European Economic Area) Regulations 2006) is fully reviewed in Chapter 15. A new section on the Schengen *acquis* has been included within Chapter 11. Previously, although the Schengen *acquis* was referred to, it had never been incorporated into the book as an important area of EU law in its own right. This has now been addressed. Directive 2005/36 which reforms the law on the recognition of professional qualifications is comprehensively discussed within Chapter 13. Within this chapter there is also a consideration of the proposed directive relating to services in the internal market.

The EU's institutional websites provide a vast array of resources, including free full-text copies of legislation and judgments of the Court of Justice and Court of First Instance. Almost without exception, the website addresses (URLs) have changed from those published in the last edition. This edition includes the updated URLs.

A Companion Website accompanies this edition of the book, which can be accessed at: (www.pearsoned.co.uk/fsls). A variety of resources will be available, including the following:

- Regular comprehensive updates to the book (it is planned to provide updates in September 2007, March 2008 and November 2008).

- Seminar/tutorial style Questions and Answers.

- Multiple choice questions (MCQs) for each of the 22 chapters. The MCQs can be completed online, providing the participant with instant feedback.

- Up-to-date listing of the URLs for relevant websites.

- An additional databank of MCQs which lecturers can use for in-class tests or during tutorials/seminars.

I hope these online resources prove useful, and I would welcome feedback from lecturers on their usefulness. I also welcome views about how the range of these resources can be expanded in the future.

Finally, I would like to thank the following staff at Pearson Education for their support and guidance throughout this latest rewrite: Zoë Botterill (acquisitions editor for law), Cheryl Cheasley (editorial assistant for law), Joe Vella (senior desk editor) and Melanie Beard (electronic project editor).

I have endeavoured to state the law as at 31 October 2006.

John Fairhurst
October 2006

Preface to the first edition

Over the last few years the number of books on European Community law has proliferated, and it might seem that there could not be any need for yet another. The breadth and depth of Community law has, however, meant that all those books, especially those primarily written for students, have had to be selective, emphasising either the institutional and administrative aspects of Community law, or selecting a limited range of substantive topics, such as social and employment policy, free movement of persons, competition or agriculture. The tendency, until recently, has been to treat the working of the Community and the application of Community law as essentially matters for the Community institutions. Community law tended to seem a somewhat exotic subject for common law students, located somewhere between international law, constititional law and jurisprudence. Decisions of the European Court of Justice on the need for effective judicial protection in the national courts, and the growing realisation in those courts that much of what appeared to be national legislation had, in fact, originated in Community measures, have brought the importance of Community law home to practising lawyers in the United Kingdom.

This has resulted in Community law becoming a 'core' subject for those hoping to qualify as a solicitor. The widening legislative competence of the Community, so that Community law now reaches into almost every aspect of law, both public and private, has meant that an understanding of the fundamentals of Community law is essential for every working lawyer. In making a selection of topics for this book I have, therefore, had three principal aims, The first is to provide an account of the institutions of the Community and the selected topics in a way which I hope is accessible to those who have not already studied other areas of law in depth. The second is to provide a selection of topics of substantive Community law in the areas of free movement of persons, goods and services, competition law and policy which, though far from exhaustive, provide illustrations of much wider principles of Community law, how these relate to the national legal systems, and how they can be applied in areas of Community law which have not been examined. The third, and most important, distinctive aim of the book is to illustrate the links between Community institutions and the government, legislature and judiciary of the United Kingdom, including the effect of Community law on the law within the United Kingdom.

I have endeavoured to look at how Community principles of the supremacy of Community law and the direct effects of directives have been applied by our courts. Specific sections, and in some cases, whole chapters, have been devoted to show how the United Kingdom has met, and in some cases failed to meet, its obligations under Community law in the areas of substantive law which have been examined. This will, I hope, help the reader to see how Community law is integrated into our own and how far it has developed so as to give effects to Community rights. Even though only a necessarily limited range of topics has been covered, it is hoped that these will provide the reader with a good grounding in those areas. There is, however, a further reading section at the end of each chapter providing titles of books and articles in which the issues covered can be explored in more depth. I have endeavoured to state the law as at 1 November 1995.

I acknowledge, with thanks, permission by the Incoporated Council of Law Reporting for England and Wales to publish extracts from the *Law Reports Appeal Cases* and the *Weekly Law Reports*, by Blackstone Press Ltd in relation to an extract from *Textbook on Constititional and Administrative Law* (2nd Edition) (1995) by Brian Thompson; by Butterworths for consent to publish an extract from *An Introduction to Intellectual Property Law* (1995) by Jeremy Phillips and Alison Firth, and extracts from the *All England Law Reports* and the *New Law Journal*; and for leave from Kluer Academic Publishers to publish an extract from an article by Judge Federico Mancini published in the *Common Market Law Review*. I am also grateful to Advocate-General Francis Jacobs and the *European Advocate* for permission to publish extracts from an article in the Winter 1994 edition of that journal, and to Professor Terence Daintith, Professor Noreen Burrows, Hilary Hiram and John Wiley & Sons for consent to publish extracts from *Implemeting EC Law in the United Kingdom: Structures for Indirect Rule* (1995). Extracts from judgments of the European Court of Justice and the Court of First Instance are taken with leave of the publishers either from the summaries of the judgments published by the Court or from the official reports.

I am also most grateful to my publishers and especially to Patrick Bond and Julianne Mulholland for all their help and advice. Finally, the greatest debt I owe is to my wife Ruth, without whose support and continuing encouragement this book would never have been completed.

Christopher Vincenzi
June 1996

Guided tour

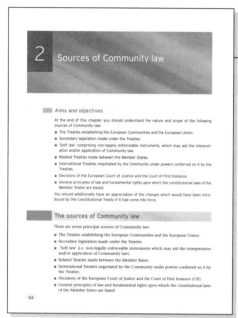

Aims and objectives – Located at the start of each chapter, a list of aims and objectives indicates the essential points you should look out for in your reading.

Chapter summaries – Located at the end of each chapter, chapter summaries draw together the key points that you should be aware of following your reading, and provide a useful checklist for revision.

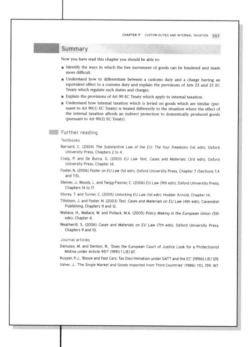

Further reading – At the end of each chapter, use the further reading section to delve deeper into the topic, and read those books and articles that will help you to gain higher marks in both exams and assessments.

Case summaries – Highlight the facts and key legal principles of essential cases that you need to be aware of in your study of EU Law.

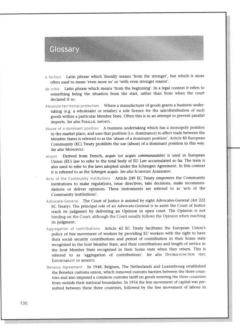

Glossary – *Have you forgotten the meaning of a word?* Turn to the glossary at the back of the book to remind yourself of its meaning.

Companion Website – *Want to test your knowledge of a topic, practice answering exam-style questions, visit useful EU Law sites on the web or just check if the law has changed?*
Visit **www.mylawchamber/fairhurst** to find extensive resources designed to aid you in your study, including multiple choice questions, tutorial questions and answer guidance, web links to further resources, flashcards to test your knowledge of key terms, an online glossary and regular web updates on major legal changes.

For Instructors – The Companion Website also includes a testbank of multiple choice questions that can be used to access students' progress.

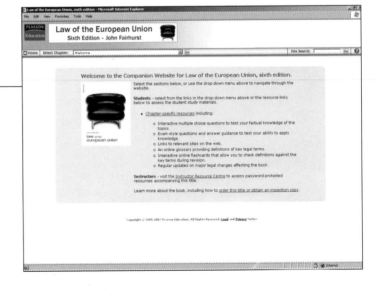

Table of cases before the European Court of Justice and the Court of First Instance (numerical)

Table of cases before the European Court of Justice and the Court of First Instance (alphabetical)

Table of cases before the European Court of Human Rights

Table of cases before national courts

Table of European Commission Decisions

Table of European Community Treaties

Table of equivalences referred to in Article 12 of the Treaty of Amsterdam (renumbered Articles of the EC Treaty)*

A. Treaty on European Union

	Previous numbering		New numbering
	Title I		Title I
Article A		Article 1	
Article B		Article 2	
Article C		Article 3	
Article D		Article 4	
Article E		Article 5	
Article F		Article 6	
Article F.1[1]		Article 7	
	Title II		Title II
Article G		Article 8	
	Title III		Title III
Article H		Article 9	
	Title IV		Title IV
Article I		Article 10	
	Title V[2]		Title V
Article J.1		Article 11	
Article J.2		Article 12	
Article J.3		Article 13	
Article J.4		Article 14	
Article J.5		Article 15	
Article J.6		Article 16	

*Excerpt from the Treaty of Amsterdam © European Communities, 1995–2007.
[1]New Article introduced by the Treaty of Amsterdam.
[2]Title restructured by the Treaty of Amsterdam.

Previous numbering		New numbering
Article J.7	Article 17	
Article J.8	Article 18	
Article J.9	Article 19	
Article J.10	Article 20	
Article J.11	Article 21	
Article J.12	Article 22	
Article J.13	Article 23	
Article J.14	Article 24	

	Title V[2]		Title V
Article J.15		Article 25	
Article J.16		Article 26	
Article J.17		Article 27	
Article J.18		Article 28	

	Title VI[2]		Title V
Article K.1		Article 29	
Article K.2		Article 30	
Article K.3		Article 31	
Article K.4		Article 32	
Article K.5		Article 33	
Article K.6		Article 34	
Article K.7		Article 35	
Article K.8		Article 36	
Article K.9		Article 37	
Article K.10		Article 38	
Article K.11		Article 39	
Article K.12		Article 40	
Article K.13		Article 41	
Article K.14		Article 42	

	Title VIa[1]		Title VII
Article K.15[2]		Article 43	
Article K.16[2]		Article 44	
Article K.17[2]		Article 45	

	Title VII		Title VIII
Article L		Article 46	
Article M		Article 47	
Article N		Article 48	
Article O		Article 49	
Article P		Article 50	
Article Q		Article 51	
Article R		Article 52	
Article S		Article 53	

[1]New Title introduced by the Treaty of Amsterdam.
[2]New Article introduced by the Treaty of Amsterdam.

B. Treaty establishing the European Community

Previous numbering		New numbering
Part One		Part One
Article 1	Article 1	
Article 2	Article 2	
Article 3	Article 3	
Article 3a	Article 4	
Article 3b	Article 5	
Article 3c[1]	Article 6	
Article 4	Article 7	
Article 4a	Article 8	
Article 4b	Article 9	
Article 5	Article 10	

Previous numbering		New numbering	
Article 5a[1]		Article 11	
Article 6		Article 12	
Article 6a[1]		Article 13	
Article 7 (repealed)		–	
Article 7a		Article 14	
Article 7b (repealed)		–	
Article 7c		Article 15	
Article 7d[1]		Article 16	
	Part Two		Part Two
Article 8		Article 17	
Article 8a		Article 18	
Article 8b		Article 19	
Article 8c		Article 20	
Article 8d		Article 21	
Article 8e		Article 22	
	Part Three		Part Three
	Title I		Title I
Article 9		Article 23	
Article 10		Article 24	
Article 11 (repealed)		–	
	Chapter 1		Chapter 1
	Section 1 (deleted)		–
Article 12		Article 25	
Article 13 (repealed)		–	
Article 14 (repealed)		–	
Article 15 (repealed)		–	
Article 16 (repealed)		–	
Article 17 (repealed)		–	
	Section 2 (deleted)	–	
Article 18 (repealed)		–	
Article 19 (repealed)		–	

[1]New Article introduced by the Treaty of Amsterdam.

Previous numbering		New numbering	
Article 20 (repealed)		–	
Article 21 (repealed)		–	
Article 22 (repealed)		–	
Article 23 (repealed)		–	
Article 24 (repealed)		–	
Article 26 (repealed)		–	
Article 27 (repealed)		–	
Article 28		Article 26	
Article 29		Article 27	
	Chapter 2		Chapter 2
Article 30		Article 28	
Article 31 (repealed)		–	
Article 32 (repealed)		–	
Article 33 (repealed)		–	

Article 34	Article 29
Article 35 (repealed)	–
Article 36	Article 30
Article 37	Article 31

Title II		Title II
Article 38	Article 32	
Article 39	Article 33	
Article 40	Article 34	
Article 41	Article 35	
Article 42	Article 36	
Article 43	Article 37	
Article 44 (repealed)	–	
Article 45 (repealed)	–	
Article 46	Article 38	
Article 47 (repealed)	–	

Title III		Title III
Chapter 1		Chapter 1
Article 48	Article 39	
Article 49	Article 40	
Article 50	Article 41	
Article 51	Article 42	

Chapter 2		Chapter 2
Article 52	Article 43	
Article 53 (repealed)	–	
Article 54	Article 44	
Article 55	Article 45	
Article 56	Article 46	
Article 57	Article 47	
Article 58	Article 48	

Chapter 3		Chapter 3
Article 59	Article 49	
Article 60	Article 50	
Article 61	Article 51	
Article 62 (repealed)	–	
Article 63	Article 52	
Article 64	Article 53	
Article 65	Article 54	
Article 66	Article 55	

Chapter 4		Chapter 4
Article 67 (repealed)	–	
Article 68 (repealed)	–	
Article 69 (repealed)	–	
Article 70 (repealed)	–	
Article 71 (repealed)	–	
Article 72 (repealed)	–	
Article 73 (repealed)	–	
Article 73a (repealed)	–	
Article 73b	Article 56	

Article 73c	Article 57	
Article 73d	Article 58	
Article 73e (repealed)	–	
Article 73f	Article 59	
Article 73g	Article 60	
Article 73h (repealed)	–	

Title IIIa[1]		Title IV
Article 73i[2]	Article 61	
Article 73j[2]	Article 62	
Article 73k[2]	Article 63	
Article 73l[2]	Article 64	
Article 73m[2]	Article 65	
Article 73n[2]	Article 66	
Article 73o[2]	Article 67	
Article 73p[2]	Article 68	
Article 73q[2]	Article 69	

Title IV		Title V
Article 74	Article 70	
Article 75	Article 71	
Article 76	Article 72	
Article 77	Article 73	
Article 78	Article 74	
Article 79	Article 75	
Article 80	Article 76	
Article 81	Article 77	

[1] New Title introduced by the Treaty of Amsterdam.
[2] New Article introduced by the Treaty of Amsterdam.

	Previous numbering		New numbering
	Title IV		Title V
Article 82		Article 78	
Article 83		Article 79	
Article 84		Article 80	
	Title V		Title VI
	Chapter 1		Chapter 1
	Section 1		Section 1
Article 85		Article 81	
Article 86		Article 82	
Article 87		Article 83	
Article 88		Article 84	
Article 89		Article 85	
Article 90		Article 86	
	Section 2 (deleted)	–	
Article 91 (repealed)		–	
	Section 3		Section 2
Article 92		Article 87	
Article 93		Article 88	
Article 94		Article 89	

	Chapter 2		Chapter 2
Article 95		Article 90	
Article 96		Article 91	
Article 97 (repealed)		–	
Article 98		Article 92	
Article 99		Article 93	
	Chapter 3		Chapter 3
Article 100		Article 94	
Article 100a		Article 95	
Article 100b (repealed)		–	
Article 100c (repealed)		–	
Article 100d (repealed)		–	
Article 101		Article 96	
Article 102		Article 97	

	Title VI		Title VII
	Chapter 1		Chapter 1
Article 102a		Article 98	
Article 103		Article 99	
Article 103a		Article 100	
Article 104		Article 101	
Article 104a		Article 102	
Article 104b		Article 103	
Article 104c		Article 104	

	Chapter 2		Chapter 2
Article 105		Article 105	
Article 105a		Article 106	
Article 106		Article 107	
Article 107		Article 108	
Article 108		Article 109	
Article 108a		Article 110	
Article 109		Article 111	

	Chapter 3		Chapter 3
Article 109a		Article 112	
Article 109b		Article 113	
Article 109c		Article 114	
Article 109d		Article 115	

	Chapter 4		Chapter 4
Article 109e		Article 116	
Article 109f		Article 117	
Article 109g		Article 118	
Article 109h		Article 119	
Article 109I		Article 120	
Article 109j		Article 121	
Article 109k		Article 122	
Article 109l		Article 123	
Article 109m		Article 124	

	Title Va[1]		Title VIII
Article 109n[2]		Article 125	

Previous numbering		New numbering
	Title VII	Title IX
Article 109o[2]	Article 126	
Article 109p[2]	Article 127	
Article 109q[2]	Article 128	
Article 109r[2]	Article 129	
Article 109s[2]	Article 130	
Article 110	Article 131	
Article 111 (repealed)	–	
Article 112	Article 132	
Article 113	Article 133	
Article 114 (repealed)	–	
Article 115	Article 134	
Article 115	Article 134	
	Title VIIa1	Title X
Article 116[2]	Article 135	

[1] New Title introduced by the Treaty of Amsterdam.
[2] New Article introduced by the Treaty of Amsterdam.

	Previous numbering	New numbering
	Title VIII	Title XI
Chapter 1[1]	Chapter 1	
Article 117	Article 136	
Article 118	Article 137	
Article 118a	Article 138	
Article 118b	Article 139	
Article 118c	Article 140	
Article 119	Article 141	
Article 119a	Article 142	
Article 120	Article 143	
Article 121	Article 144	
Article 122	Article 145	
	Chapter 2	Chapter 2
Article 123	Article 146	
Article 124	Article 147	
Article 125	Article 148	
	Chapter 3	Chapter 3
Article 126	Article 149	
Article 127	Article 150	
	Title IX	Title XII
Article 128	Article 151	
	Title X	Title XIII
Article 129	Article 152	
	Title XI	Title XIV
Article 129a	Article 153	
	Title XII	Title XV
Article 129b	Article 154	

Article 129c	Article 155	
Article 129d	Article 156	

Title XIII		Title XVI
Article 130	Article 157	

Title XIV		Title XVII
Article 130a	Article 158	
Article 130b	Article 159	
Article 130c	Article 160	
Article 130d	Article 161	
Article 130e	Article 162	

[1]Chapter 1 restructured by the Treaty of Amsterdam.

Previous numbering		**New numbering**
Title XV		Title XVIII
Article 130f	Article 163	
Article 130g	Article 164	
Article 130h	Article 165	
Article 130I	Article 166	
Article 130j	Article 167	
Article 130k	Article 168	
Article 130l	Article 169	
Article 130m	Article 170	
Article 130n	Article 171	
Article 130o	Article 172	
Article 130p	Article 173	
Article 130q (repealed)	–	

Title XVI		Title XIX
Article 130r	Article 174	
Article 130s	Article 175	
Article 130t	Article 176	

Title XVII		Title XX
Article 130u	Article 177	
Article 130v	Article 178	
Article 130w	Article 179	
Article 130x	Article 180	
Article 130y	Article 181	

Part Four		Part Four
Article 131	Article 182	
Article 132	Article 183	
Article 133	Article 184	
Article 134	Article 185	
Article 135	Article 186	
Article 136	Article 187	
Article 136a	Article 188	

Part Five		Part Five
Title I		Title I
Chapter 1		Chapter 1

	Title I Section 1		Title I Section 1
Article 137		Article 189	
Article 138		Article 190	
Article 138a		Article 191	
Article 138b		Article 192	
Article 138c		Article 193	
Article 138d		Article 194	
Article 138e		Article 195	
Article 139		Article 196	
Article 140		Article 197	
Article 141		Article 198	
Article 142		Article 199	
Article 143		Article 200	
Article 144		Article 201	
	Section 2		Section 2
Article 145		Article 202	
Article 146		Article 203	
Article 147		Article 204	
Article 148		Article 205	
Article 149 (repealed)		–	
Article 150		Article 206	
Article 151		Article 207	
Article 152		Article 208	
Article 153		Article 209	
Article 154		Article 210	
	Section 3		Section 3
Article 155		Article 211	
Article 156		Article 212	
Article 157		Article 213	
Article 158		Article 214	
Article 159		Article 215	
Article 160		Article 216	
Article 161		Article 217	
Article 162		Article 218	
Article 163		Article 219	
	Section 4		Section 4
Article 164		Article 220	
Article 165		Article 221	
Article 166		Article 222	
Article 167		Article 223	
Article 168		Article 224	
Article 168a		Article 225	
Article 169		Article 226	
Article 170		Article 227	
Article 171		Article 228	
Article 172		Article 229	
Article 173		Article 230	
Article 174		Article 231	

Article 175	Article 232	
Article 176	Article 233	
Article 177	Article 234	
Article 178	Article 235	
Article 179	Article 236	
Article 180	Article 237	
Article 181	Article 238	
Article 182	Article 239	
Article 183	Article 240	
Article 184	Article 241	
Article 185	Article 242	
Article 186	Article 243	
Article 187	Article 244	
Article 188	Article 245	
Section 5		Section 5
Article 188a	Article 246	
Article 188b	Article 247	
Article 188c	Article 248	
Chapter 2		Chapter 2
Article 189	Article 249	
Article 189a	Article 250	
Article 189b	Article 251	
Article 189c	Article 252	
Article 190	Article 253	
Article 191	Article 254	
Article 191a[1]	Article 255	
Article 192	Article 256	
Chapter 3		Chapter 3
Article 193	Article 257	
Article 194	Article 258	
Article 195	Article 259	
Article 196	Article 260	
Article 197	Article 261	
Article 198	Article 262	
Chapter 4		Chapter 4
Article 198a	Article 263	
Article 198b	Article 264	
Article 198c	Article 265	
Chapter 5		Chapter 5
Article 198d	Article 266	
Article 198e	Article 267	
Title II		Title II
Article 199	Article 268	
Article 200 (repealed)	–	
Article 201	Article 269	
Article 201a	Article 270	
Article 202	Article 271	
Article 203	Article 272	

Article 204	Article 273
Article 205	Article 274
Article 205a	Article 275
Article 206	Article 276

[1]New Title introduced by the Treaty of Amsterdam.

Previous numbering	New numbering
Article 206a (repealed)	–
Article 207	Article 277
Article 208	Article 278
Article 209	Article 279
Article 209a	Article 280

Part Six	Part Six
Article 210	Article 281
Article 211	Article 282
Article 212[1]	Article 283
Article 213	Article 284
Article 213a[1]	Article 285
Article 213b[1]	Article 286
Article 214	Article 287
Article 215	Article 288
Article 216	Article 289
Article 217	Article 290
Article 218[1]	Article 291
Article 219	Article 292
Article 220	Article 293
Article 221	Article 294
Article 222	Article 295
Article 223	Article 296
Article 224	Article 297
Article 225	Article 298
Article 226 (repealed)	–
Article 227	Article 299
Article 228	Article 300
Article 228a	Article 301
Article 229	Article 302
Article 230	Article 303
Article 231	Article 304
Article 232	Article 305
Article 233	Article 306
Article 234	Article 307
Article 235	Article 308
Article 236[1]	Article 309
Article 237 (repealed)	–
Article 238	Article 310
Article 239	Article 311
Article 240	Article 312
Article 241 (repealed)	–
Article 242 (repealed)	–
Article 243 (repealed)	–

Article 244 (repealed)   –
Article 245 (repealed)   –
Article 246 (repealed)   –

[1]New Article introduced by the Treaty of Amsterdam.

Previous numbering	New numbering
Final Provisions	Final Provisions
Article 247	Article 313
Article 248	Article 314

Table of other Treaties

Table of European Community Directives

Rules of Procedure of the European Court of Justice

Table of Statutes

Table of Statutory Instruments

List of abbreviations

AC	Appeal Cases
ACP	African Caribbean Pacific states
AJCL	American Journal of Comparative Law
AJIL	American Journal of International Law
All ER	All England Law Reports
Anglo-Am LRev	Anglo-American Law Review
BDMA	British Direct Mailing Association
Bull EC	Bulletin of the European Communities
BYIL	British Yearbook of International Law
CAP	Common Agricultural Policy
CE	Compulsory Expenditure
CEEs	Charges having an equivalent effect to a customs duty
CEN	European Committee for Standardisation
CENELEC	European Committee of Electrotechnical Standardisation
CFI	Court of First Instance
CFSP	Common Foreign and Security Policy
CJHA	Cooperation in Justice and Home Affairs
CLJ	Cambridge Law Journal
CLP	Current Legal Problems
CMLR	Common Market Law Reports
CML Rev	Common Market Law Review
COM	Common Organisation of the Market or Commission Document
COREPER	Committee of Permanent Representatives (*Comité des Représentants Permanents*)
DG	Directorate General
EAFFG	European Agricultural Guidance and Guarantee Fund (often referred to as FEOGA – *Fonds européen d'orientation et de garantie agricole*)
EC	European Community
ECB	European Central Bank
ECHR	European Convention of Human Rights
ECJ	European Court of Justice
ECLR	European Competition Law Review
ECOFIN	Council of Economic and Finance Ministers
ECOSOC	Economic and Social Committee
ECR	European Court Reports
ECSC	European Coal and Steel Community
ECU	European Currency Unit
EEA	European Economic Area
EEC	European Economic Community

EELR	European Environmental Law Review
EFTA	European Free Trade Association
EHRR	European Human Rights Reports Review
EIPL	European Intellectual Property Law
EL Rev	European Law Review
EP	European Parliament
EPC	European Political Cooperation
EPL	European Public Law
ESCB	European System of Central Banks
EU	European Union
Euratom	European Atomic Energy Community
FamLaw	Family Law
FAO	Food and Agriculture Organisation of the United Nations
FSR	Fleet Street Reports
GATT	General Agreement on Tariffs and Trade
GNP	Gross National Product
HarvLR or Harvard LR	Harvard Law Review
HRLJ	Human Rights Law Journal
IAT	Immigration Appeals Tribunal
IBL	International Business Lawyer
ICLQ	International and Comparative Law Quarterly
IGC	Intergovernmental Conference
IndLJ	Industrial Law Journal
Int Lawyer	International Lawyer
IRLR	Industrial Relations Law Reports
JBL	Journal of Business Law
JCMS	Journal of Common Market Studies
JESP	Journal of European Social Policy
JHA	Justice and Home Affairs
JLIS	Journal of Law and Information Science
JLS	Journal of Law and Society
JPL	Journal of Planning and Environmental Law
JSWL	Journal of Social Welfare Law (now JSWFL – Journal of Social Welfare and Family Law)
LIEI	Legal Issues of European Integration
LQR	Law Quarterly Review
MCA	Monetary Compensatory Amount
MEQR	Measure having Equivalent Effect to Quantitative Restrictions
MEP	Member of the European Parliament
MGQ	Maximum Guaranteed Quantities
MLR	Modern Law Review
NATO	North Atlantic Treaty Organization
NCE	Non-Compulsory Expenditure
NILQ	Northern Ireland Legal Quarterly
NLJ	New Law Journal
OECD	Organisation for Economic Cooperation and Development
OJ	Official Journal of the European Communities
OJLS	Oxford Journal of Legal Studies
PA	Public Administration

PL	Public Law
PPLR	Public Procurement Law Review
QMV	Qualified Majority Voting
SCA	Special Committee on Agriculture
SEA	Single European Act
SJ	Solicitors' Journal
SRWT	Société Régionale Walloon du Transport
TEU	Treaty on European Union
ToA	Treaty of Amsterdam
ToN	Treaty of Nice
WLR	Weekly Law Reports
Yale LJ	Yale Law Journal
YEL	Yearbook of European Law

PART 1

Constitutional and administrative law of the European Communities and the European Union

1 An introduction to the European Communities and the European Union

Aims and objectives

At the end of this chapter you should understand:

- How and why the European Communities were established and understand their aims and objectives.
- How the European Union has evolved from its initial six Member States to 27 Member States and beyond.
- How the Single European Act amended the founding Treaties.
- What effect the Treaty on European Union had on the founding Treaties and the nature of the European Union and its three pillars.
- How the Treaty of Amsterdam amended the founding Treaties and the Treaty on European Union.
- What effect the Treaty of Nice had on the founding Treaties and the Treaty on European Union.
- The status of the proposed Constitutional Treaty and the possible future development of EU constitutional reform.
- The role of the European Free Trade Association and the relevance of the European Economic Area.
- The legal status, within the context of Community law, of the European Convention on Human Rights and the European Court of Human Rights.

The post-war years

The European Communities came into existence in the aftermath of the Second World War, but the impetus for their creation, to a large extent, came from a desire not to repeat the mistakes made by the victorious powers in the inter-war years. The Treaty of Versailles of 1919 recognised the new nation-states of Central and Eastern Europe that had emerged following the collapse of the Austro-Hungarian and Ottoman empires. It also imposed heavy reparations on Germany, which the new Weimar Republic was unable to pay. The hyper-inflation that followed, and the crash of 1929, wiped out the savings of the large German middle class and pushed unemployment in Germany to more than 40 per cent of the labour force (Hobsbawm, 1994). The instability that this created led directly to the rise of the Nazi Party and the outbreak of the Second World War. It also gravely affected the economies of the other Western European powers. The UK, France and Italy, the victors who were the architects of Versailles, suffered almost as much as the vanquished from its consequences. Attempts at protecting national economies by tariff barriers were largely unsuccessful and did little more than maintain the economies of Western Europe in a state of stagnation until they were lifted by preparations for another world war. The experience of the inter-war years made clear beyond doubt that it was no longer possible for the states of Western Europe, including states like the UK and France which still had large colonial markets, to operate their national economies without regard to the effect on their immediate neighbours.

Another important lesson of the First World War and its aftermath was learned from the failure of linked defence treaties and the new League of Nations to avert war. The French, above all, grasped the importance of binding Germany's coal and steel industry, the sinews of its war machine, into a new political and economic alliance. At the same time, fear of the apparently expansionist Soviet Union that now occupied the whole of Eastern and Central Europe, including the former East Germany, impelled the democratic states of Western Europe and North America to come together in 1949 into the North Atlantic Treaty Organisation (NATO). The former West Germany did not join NATO until October 1954 (The Paris Agreements). The USA, instead of withdrawing from Europe as it had in 1919, was a founder member of NATO, the new defence organisation, and took a major part in European rehabilitation and reconstruction. Millions of dollars were poured into West Germany in grants and loans under the Marshall Plan, and it started on a rapid economic recovery. Other European states were also assisted under the Plan.

The recognition of the reality and, indeed, the need for mutual interdependence by Western European states, created a receptive atmosphere for resurgent ideas about European political unity. These were expressed with force and vision by Winston Churchill (the former UK Prime Minister) at Zurich in September 1946, when he proposed a 'sovereign remedy' to European tensions. He proposed the creation of 'a European family, or as much of it as we can, and provide it with a structure under which it can dwell in peace, in safety and in freedom. We must build a kind of United States of Europe'. Although he did not envisage the UK becoming a member of this 'European family', he stated that the first step in its creation should be based on a partnership between France and Germany. This would have required an imaginative leap by the French, who were only just beginning to recover from German occupation and who had been the victims of three wars of aggression by Germany. The idea of European federation, based on a Franco-German partnership, was, however, taken up with enthusiasm by two French politicians, Jean Monnet and Robert Schumann, the former with responsibility for French economic planning and the latter as Foreign Minister. The first step in the construction of a new European order was the creation of the European Coal and Steel Community.

The remainder of this chapter contains a sequential historical examination of the development of the European Union (EU) and the European Communities, from their humble beginnings through the establishment of the European Coal and Steel Community (with the participation of six Member States) to the establishment of the European Union (with the participation of 27 Member States ... and rising). The rationale for this approach is to facilitate an understanding of how the EU has evolved, in order to appreciate how it might evolve in the future. A table of key dates and events is included towards the end of this chapter. The European Coal and Steel Community is considered first.

23 July 1952: the European Coal and Steel Community

Less than four years after Churchill made his Zurich speech, Robert Schumann (the former French Foreign Minister) stated on 9 May 1950 that a united Europe was essential for the maintenance of world peace. He further stated that a European alliance was essential and that would require the century-old opposition between France and Germany to be eliminated. He proposed that the first stage on this road to European integration would require the whole of France and Germany's coal and steel production to be placed under one authority. His proposal provided that other countries within Europe could participate in the organisation which would be created.

France, Germany, Italy and the Benelux countries (i.e. Belgium, The Netherlands and Luxembourg) accepted the proposal in principle and negotiations started immediately. The UK was not a party to these negotiations, as it was not yet interested in joining the European family (at this time the UK still had strong connections with the Commonwealth). The negotiations progressed rapidly, and less than one year later, on 18 April 1951, the Treaty Establishing the European Coal and Steel Community (ECSC) was signed by these six countries in Paris. Because it was signed in Paris it is often referred to as the Treaty of Paris. However, its official title is 'The Treaty Establishing the ECSC'. Ratification of the Treaty by the six states was a mere formality.

Following ratification (i.e. approval), the Treaty entered into force on 23 July 1952, thus establishing the ECSC. This Treaty had a 50-year lifespan and therefore this Community came to an end on 23 July 2002. It was one of the three Communities which were collectively referred to as the European Communities; this is discussed further below.

Earlier in the discussion of the historical evolvement of the European Communities, it was stated that European integration was necessary to ensure world peace. So how did the ECSC further this aim? Coal and steel were, in the 1950s, essential components in the production of arms and munitions. Thus, by depriving France and Germany of their independence in the production of these commodities, it was widely believed that future conflicts between France and Germany would be avoided. However, the Preamble to the Treaty made it quite clear that the long-term aims of the participants went a great deal further than the control of the production of coal and steel. The Treaty recognised that 'Europe can be built only through practical achievements which will first of all create solidarity, and through the establishment of common bases for economic solidarity'. The participants were 'resolved to substitute for age-old rivalries the merging of their essential interests; to create, by establishing an economic community, the basis for a deeper and broader community among peoples long divided by bloody conflicts' (Preamble). There was little UK enthusiasm for involvement, and successive UK governments (including the then Conservative administration under the Premiership of Winston Churchill) were prepared to support only the loosest association with their Continental neighbours. These fell far short of the aspirations of the six founding states and, for two decades, the UK remained on the sidelines of Community developments.

The ECSC Treaty created five institutions:

- an executive, called the High Authority;
- a Consultative Committee attached to the High Authority;
- a Special Council of Ministers;

- an Assembly; and
- a Court of Justice.

The most striking thing about the new Community was the fact that it had legal personality. The High Authority was to be responsible for policy relating to the coal and steel industries in the Member States and had the power to make decisions directly affecting the economic agents in each country without regard to the wishes of the governments of those states. Investment in the coal and steel industries was to be influenced by the High Authority, though not subject to much control. Powers were reserved to regulate prices and production, but only if there were crises of shortage or over-production. There was also a social dimension to this Community: policies were to be framed for training, housing and redeployment. Competition was, at the same time, to be stimulated by rules on price transparency, as well as anti-trust laws which were modelled on those of the United States. These decisions could be enforced against the Member States in the new Court of Justice.

1 July 1958: the European Economic Community and the European Atomic Energy Community

Three of the founding states of the ECSC (Belgium, The Netherlands and Luxembourg) had already formed themselves into the Benelux customs union. From 1 January 1948, customs barriers were removed between Belgium, The Netherlands and Luxembourg and a common customs tariff was agreed between them in relation to the outside world. The effect of this was that goods could freely pass between the three countries, with minimal formalities. Customs duties levied on goods originating within the three countries were abolished and goods entering from outside had a uniform customs tariff applied to them. In 1954 they also authorised the free flow of capital, which meant a freedom of investment and unrestricted transfer of currency within the three countries, and in 1956 they accepted the free movement of labour. The internal trade of these countries between 1948 and 1956 increased by 50 per cent. This mini common market proved to be profitable to all three countries involved and its success whetted the appetites of neighbouring states and led to pressure to project this experiment on a European scale.

That pressure created the political climate for a much more ambitious project. On 25 March 1957 the EEC Treaty was signed in Rome by the six founding states of the ECSC, the aim being to establish a European Economic Community (EEC) in goods, labour, capital and services among these six states. The common market established by the EEC Treaty was, at the time, the biggest free trade area in the world. At the same time, the Treaty Establishing the European Atomic Energy Community (Euratom) for cooperation in the use of atomic energy was signed. The UK participated in the initial negotiations for both Treaties but withdrew because it feared a loss of national sovereignty and damage to its favourable trading links with the Commonwealth. The EEC and Euratom Treaties came into force on 1 July 1958, following their ratification (i.e. approval) by the six states. This resulted in the existence of three communities: EEC, ECSC and Euratom, which were collectively referred to as the European Communities. As stated above, the ECSC came to an end on 23 July 2002, and therefore it is the EEC (later to be renamed the EC) and Euratom which are now collectively referred to as the European Communities.

The Preamble to the EEC Treaty set out the objective of the contracting parties:

> to lay the foundations of an ever closer union among the peoples of Europe ... to ensure the economic and social progress of their countries by common action to eliminate the barriers which divide Europe ... [to secure] the constant improvement of the living and working conditions of their peoples ... [and] to strengthen the unity of their economies and to ensure their harmonious development by reducing differences existing between various regions ... [and] by means of a common commercial policy, to [secure] the progressive abolition of restrictions on international trade.

The common market, which was created by the EEC Treaty, covered the whole economic field except those areas falling within the scope of the ECSC or Euratom. It involved the creation of a customs union, which required the abolition of all customs duties and quantitative restrictions in trade between the Member States, a common external tariff, and provisions for the free movement of labour, business and capital. These objectives reflected what had already largely been achieved in the Benelux states, the aim being to create, on a Community scale, economic conditions similar to those in the market of a single state; similar to the position in the UK where there is free movement of goods, persons, business and capital between England, Scotland, Wales and Northern Ireland.

As initially formulated, Art 3 EEC Treaty vested the Community with power to pursue the following activities:

- the elimination, as between Member States, of customs duties and of quantitative restrictions on the import and export of goods, and of all other measures having equivalent effect;
- the establishment of a common customs tariff and a common commercial policy towards third countries (i.e. countries not within the Community);
- the abolition, as between Member States, of obstacles to the free movement of persons, services and capital;
- the adoption of a common agricultural policy;
- the adoption of a common transport policy;
- the creation of a Community competition policy;
- the approximation of the laws of the Member States to the extent required for the proper functioning of the common market; and
- the association of overseas countries and territories in order to increase trade and promote economic development.

Article 3 was vital to empower the Community (through its institutions) to pursue these *economic* activities and thus secure the four features of the common market discussed above, i.e. the free movement of goods, labour, business and capital.

The main institutions of the EEC – the Commission, the Council of Ministers, the Assembly and the Court of Justice – were modelled on those of the ECSC, and the Community had a similar legal structure.

In contrast, the object of Euratom was to develop nuclear energy, distribute it within the Community and sell the surplus to the outside world. For political reasons originally associated with France's nuclear weapons programme and, subsequently, as a result of widespread doubts about the safety and viability of nuclear power, Euratom never developed as originally envisaged. Euratom has, however, remained an important focus for research and the promotion of nuclear safety.

8 April 1965: the merger of the institutions

Immediately following the signing of the EEC and Euratom Treaties, agreement was reached so that there would be only one Parliamentary Assembly and one Court of Justice for the ECSC, EEC and Euratom. For some time after the new Treaties came into effect, however, there remained separate Councils of Ministers and separate executive bodies – a High Authority in the case of the ECSC and a Commission each for the EEC and Euratom.

On 8 April 1965, the simplification of the institutional structure of the Communities was completed by the signature of a Merger Treaty, the result of which was that there was thereafter one Council, one European Commission, one European Court of Justice and one Assembly (later to be renamed the European Parliament) for all three Communities.

1 July 1973: enlargement

The UK's response to the creation of the EEC in 1958 was to propose a much looser 'free trade area'. This proposal was not welcomed by the Community, but in 1959 it resulted in the creation of a rival organisation, the European Free Trade Association (EFTA), comprising Austria, Denmark, Norway, Portugal, Sweden, Switzerland and the UK. Although trade increased between these states, EFTA lacked the structure and coherence of the EEC, and its members' economies grew only modestly by comparison. By 1961, the UK government had realised that its failure to join the European Communities had been a mistake and, in that year, the Macmillan government applied for membership. After prolonged negotiations, the application, which needed the unanimous agreement of the Member States, was vetoed by the French President, General de Gaulle. The French were reluctant to accept the UK's membership because it was feared that the UK would attempt to retain preferences for Commonwealth trade and that the UK government was, politically, too close to the USA. They were afraid that the special relationship between the UK and the USA would obstruct French efforts to create a European defence community free from US dominance. A further attempt was made by the government of Harold Wilson in 1967, but this was again vetoed by the French. In 1970, a third application was made by the Heath government and on this occasion the application was successful. The Treaty of Accession was signed on 22 January 1972 and the UK, together with Denmark and Ireland, became members of the European Communities on 1 January 1973. Norway, which had participated in the accession negotiations, did not join, as a result of a hostile national referendum.

The Treaty of Accession bound the new Member States to accept the three Treaties and to accept the existing rules of the Communities. The UK Parliament, after a debate that split both the Conservative and Labour parties, enacted the European Communities Act 1972, which was intended to give effect to both present and future Community law in the UK. Divisions within the Labour Party about membership of the European Communities led the Labour government (which had been elected to office in 1974) to promise a referendum. This was held in 1975 and resulted in endorsement of continuing membership by a majority of almost 2:1.

1 January 1981: enlargement

Greece became a member of the European Communities on 1 January 1981, increasing the number of Member States to ten.

1 January 1986: enlargement

Portugal and Spain became members of the European Communities on 1 January 1986, increasing the number of Member States to twelve.

1 July 1987: the Single European Act

The Single European Act (SEA) was a response to both development and the lack of it in the three Communities and was the first major amendment to the founding Treaties. The SEA is *not* a UK Act of Parliament. It is a Treaty which was concluded between the Member States, the purpose of which was to amend the three founding Treaties: ECSC, EEC and Euratom. It was signed in February 1986 and came into force on 1 July 1987.

A European Union?

The Preamble to the SEA set out the Member States' commitment to transform relations as a whole between the Member States into a European Union; a Union which would have activities way beyond the solely economic sphere. Political cooperation between the Member States was considered to be of paramount importance in the creation of this European Union.

The SEA separated provisions relating to political cooperation from those relating to economic integration. Those provisions relating to economic integration were to be implemented by amending the founding EEC Treaty. However, in relation to political cooperation, those provisions were to be implemented outside the existing Treaty. It was provided for the representatives of the Member States (i.e. Prime Minister/President and Foreign Secretary) to meet regularly for the purpose of drawing up common political objectives (through a body to be referred to as the European Council).

Therefore, at one level (the economic level) policies were implemented through the structure of the EEC (having its own special methods of decision-making and enforcement), whereas political policies were achieved outside this structure, through cooperation between the Member States; an intergovernmental arrangement which would not bind the Member States unless *all* the Member States were in agreement.

The main amendments made to the EEC Treaty consisted of the following:

Completing the internal market and new policy objectives

Since the signing of the Treaties in the 1950s, concerns about war in Western Europe and mass unemployment tended, by the mid-1970s and early 1980s, to have given way to pressure for greater consumer protection and protection at work. There were also growing anxieties about the degradation of the natural environment. The response to these new concerns was initially tackled at a national level, rather than Community level, which resulted in a whole range of different national standards for both goods and industrial production that seriously threatened the growth in a genuinely common market in goods and services. The development of a multiplicity of national standards was accompanied by a slowing down of the economies of all the Member States, following the explosion of oil prices in 1973. Implementing the recommendations of the Commission's White Paper, *Completing the Internal Market* (1985), the SEA attempted to tackle this problem on two fronts. It extended the competence of the EEC to enable it to legislate for the whole area of the Community on: environmental matters; economic and social cohesion, including health and safety; consumer protection; academic, professional and vocational qualifications; public procurement (i.e. competition for public contracts); VAT (i.e. Value Added Tax, which is a tax levied internally on goods and services); excise duties and frontier controls; and research and technological development. It also aimed to give the completion of the common market a new boost by setting a target for creating a new internal market by removing all the remaining legal, technical and physical obstacles to the free movement of goods, persons, services and capital by 1 January 1993. This objective was set out in Art 8a of the EEC Treaty (added by the SEA), where the internal market was described as 'an area without internal frontiers in which the free movement of goods, persons, services and capital is ensured' (Art 8a was renumbered Art 7a by the Treaty on European Union and Art 14 by the Treaty of Amsterdam (see below)).

Increasing the European Parliament's legislative powers

Until 1979 members of the European Assembly were nominated by their national parliaments. The first direct elections to the newly named European Parliament took place in June 1979 (see Chapter 3), and their effect was that the Parliament became the only directly elected Community institution. It had, at the same time, only a consultative status in the legislative process (see Chapter 4). It was often said that the European Commission proposed legislation and the Council of Ministers disposed of it (i.e. adopted it). This situation generated pressure on the Member States to address the 'democratic deficit' in the Communities' decision-making process. The SEA added a new 'cooperation procedure' to the Treaties, giving the Parliament a much more important role in the legislative process in four areas:

- prohibition of discrimination on the grounds of nationality (Art 12 EC Treaty, previously Art 6);
- the achievement of the free movement of workers (Art 40 EC Treaty, previously Art 49);
- promotion of the right of establishment (Art 44 EC Treaty, previously Art 54); and
- measures for implementation of the internal market (Art 95 EC Treaty, previously Art 100a).

This new legislative procedure required the Council of Ministers to cooperate with the Parliament. The Parliament would for the first time have a real input into the legislative process (being able to propose amendments). In addition to Parliamentary input, legislative measures in these four areas could be adopted by the Council by 'qualified majority' rather than unanimity, thus overriding the objections of a Member State. The legislative process will be considered in detail in Chapter 4.

1 November 1993: the Treaty on European Union

The next step in the constitutional development of the Communities was the adoption of the Treaty on European Union (TEU), which was negotiated at Maastricht and signed on 7 February 1992. It came into force on 1 November 1993 once it had been ratified by the Member States. A summary of the main provisions is followed by a more substantive discussion of the key features of the TEU.

Summary

The TEU was intended to extend further the competencies of the Communities by creating two new 'pillars' outside the legally binding, formal decision-making processes of the European Communities (the EC, ECSC and Euratom), which continued to exist. The two new 'pillars' of the European Union were Common Foreign and Security Policy (CFSP) and Cooperation in the fields of Justice and Home Affairs (JHA). These two pillars of the Union were really only intergovernmental in character and, like the foreign policy provisions of the SEA, created a broad framework for cooperation between the Member States rather than a process for the making of binding rules. The whole structure, which included the European Communities and the two new pillars, was called 'the European Union' (EU).

Of more constitutional and legal significance were the amendments to the EEC Treaty. The EEC was renamed 'the European Community' (EC), giving legal recognition to the fact that the activities and competencies of the former economic Community ranged far beyond its original economic goals. The European Parliament's role in the legislative process was further strengthened by the introduction of the co-decision procedure which, for the first time, gave the Parliament the power to veto legislation in certain circumstances. The reunification of Germany in 1990 was reflected by an increased representation in the Parliament, so that Germany now had the largest group of MEPs. It did not, however, gain any more votes in the qualified majority voting procedure within the Council of Ministers (see Chapter 4). A further institution was also created, the Committee of the Regions, having a role analogous to the Economic and Social Committee (see Chapter 3).

The central economic feature of the TEU was the section designed to lead to economic and monetary union by three stages. The UK and Denmark opted out of compulsory participation in the third stage. Sweden negotiated a similar opt-out when it joined the EU on 1 January 1995. The UK also refused to participate in the social chapter which incorporated principles which had previously been agreed by the heads of government (excluding the UK) in Strasbourg in December 1989: the Community Charter of Fundamental Social Rights of Workers. Both of these opt-outs are considered in further detail below.

Some of the key features of the TEU are now considered.

The TEU provisions

The TEU consisted of seven *titles* as follows:

- Title I: Common provisions *(Arts A to F)*;
- Title II: Provisions amending the EEC Treaty *(Art G)*;

- Title III: Provisions amending the ECSC Treaty *(Art H)*;
- Title IV: Provisions amending the Euratom Treaty *(Art I)*;
- Title V: Provisions on a Common Foreign and Security Policy *(Arts J.1 to J.11)*;
- Title VI: Provisions on Cooperation in Justice and Home Affairs *(Arts K.1 to K.9)*;
- Title VII: Final Provisions *(Arts L to S)*.

Titles II, III and IV of the TEU simply amended the three founding treaties (as previously amended by the SEA).

The European Union

Title I contained common provisions which set out the basic objectives of the TEU. This title did not amend the founding treaties, but simply set out the basic aims and principles of the newly formed European Union.

The three pillars of the European Union

Article A TEU provided for the establishing of a European Union:

> The Union shall be founded on the European Communities, supplemented by the policies and forms of cooperation established by this Treaty.

It followed from this that the European Union (EU) was to be founded upon three pillars:

- the European Communities – EC, ECSC (now expired), Euratom;
- Common Foreign and Security Policy – Title V (Art J);
- Cooperation in Justice and Home Affairs – Title VI (Art K).

Figure 1.1 illustrates the structure of the European Union.

Objectives of the European Union

Article B set out the objectives of the Union, some of which mirrored those contained in the founding Treaties as amended.

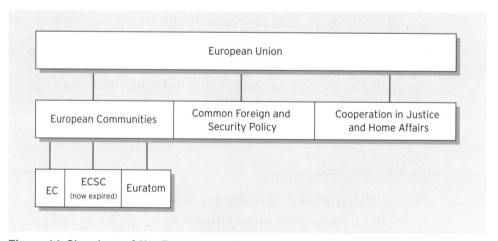

Figure 1.1 Structure of the European Union as at 1 November 1993

Protection of human rights

Article F(2) TEU provided that the Union would respect fundamental rights 'as guaranteed by the European Convention for the Protection of Human Rights and Fundamental Freedoms . . . as general principles of Community law'.

However, Art L TEU provided that all the common provisions (which included Art F(2) TEU) were not justiciable by the European Court of Justice, i.e. the Court did not have the power to rule on their application or validity. Despite this, it was possible that the Court of Justice would take the common provisions into account, including Art F(2), when interpreting the founding Treaties, as amended. This is considered further in Chapter 2.

The two intergovernmental pillars

The second and third pillars of the Union, not being inserted into the amended founding Treaties, remained outside the formal structures of the European Communities. These two pillars, as previously mentioned, related to (i) a Common Foreign and Security Policy; and (ii) Cooperation in the fields of Justice and Home Affairs.

Although being intergovernmental in nature, and thus falling outside the formal Community structure, they did have a connection in that some of the Community institutions (in particular the Council of Ministers) played a part in these policy areas.

It was argued that, over a period of time, these two pillars would be subsumed into the formal Community structure. This would be achieved by amending the founding Treaties. If this happened, all Community institutions could play a part in developing these policy areas, perhaps with a greater role for the European Parliament. Germany's former Chancellor Kohl favoured this approach which had already occurred in relation to the Single European Currency policy. This policy had initially been introduced on an intergovernmental basis by the SEA, but was subsequently incorporated into the formal EC structure (with its own special decision-making and enforcement powers) following amendments to the EC Treaty by the TEU. It is now governed by Arts 98–124 EC Treaty (previously Arts 102a–109m pre-Treaty of Amsterdam).

Under the TEU, prior to its amendment by the Treaty of Amsterdam, the Court of Justice was excluded from exercising its powers in matters dealt with under these two pillars (except in certain *very limited* situations) – Art L TEU.

As its name suggests, the second pillar (Common Foreign and Security Policy) provided for joint foreign action and security (i.e. defence) action by the Member States. This action would be adopted by a *unanimous* vote of the Council of Ministers. However, there was provision for the Council to provide that certain decisions could be taken by a qualified majority vote (Art J.3, para 2 TEU). There was minimal involvement of the Parliament and the Commission in the process. Article L TEU excluded the Court of Justice from ruling on these provisions.

The third pillar (Cooperation in Justice and Home Affairs) provided for cooperation in policy areas such as asylum, immigration, 'third country' (i.e. non-EU) nationals, international crime (e.g. drug trafficking) and various forms of judicial cooperation. Action would again be taken by the Council of Ministers acting unanimously, with very limited provision for qualified majority voting (Art K.4, para 3 TEU). There was very little involvement of the Parliament and the Commission. Once again, Art L TEU applied to exclude the Court of Justice from ruling on these provisions.

Amendments to the EEC Treaty

Following amendments made by the TEU, as discussed below, the EEC Treaty provisions increasingly covered tasks and activities which were not purely economic-based and therefore the TEU amended the title of the EEC Treaty to the European Community Treaty (EC Treaty). From here on the EEC Treaty will be referred to as the EC Treaty.

The EC Treaty is the most important of the three founding Treaties. Amendments made to the EC Treaty by Art G (i.e. Title II) TEU were as follows:

- creation of a citizenship of the European Union (formerly Art 8 EC Treaty, now Art 17 following renumbering by the Treaty of Amsterdam (see below));
- common economic and monetary policy, with a timetable for the implementation of a common currency (formerly Arts 102a–109m EC Treaty, now Arts 98–124);
- adoption of the principle of subsidiarity (formerly Art 3b EC Treaty, now Art 5);
- amendment of the decision-making process – extension of qualified majority voting for the adoption of Council acts into new policy areas, and further powers given to Parliament; and
- introduction of new areas of tasks and activities (Arts 2 and 3 EC Treaty were amended).

Articles 2 and 3 EC Treaty, as amended by the TEU, extended the tasks and activities of the European Community beyond the purely economic, and incorporated political and social goals. Article 2 (post-TEU, but pre-Treaty of Amsterdam) provided that:

> The Community shall have as its task, by establishing a common market and an economic and monetary union and by implementing the common policies or activities referred to in Articles 3 and 3a, to promote throughout the Community a harmonious and balanced development of economic activities, sustainable and non-inflationary growth respecting the environment, a high degree of convergence of economic performance, a high level of employment and of social protection, the raising of the standard of living and quality of life, and economic and social cohesion and solidarity among Member States.

Article 3 (post-TEU, but pre-Treaty of Amsterdam) provided that:

> For the purposes set out in Article 2, the activities of the Community shall include, as provided in this Treaty and in accordance with the timetable set out therein:
> (a) the elimination, as between Member States, of customs duties and quantitative restrictions on the import and export of goods, and of all measures having equivalent effect;
> (b) a common commercial policy;
> (c) an internal market characterised by the abolition, as between Member States, of obstacles to the free movement of goods, persons, services and capital;
> (d) measures concerning the entry and movement of persons in the internal market as provided for in Article 100c;
> (e) a common policy in the sphere of agriculture and fisheries;
> (f) a common policy in the sphere of transport;
> (g) a system ensuring that competition in the internal market is not distorted;
> (h) the approximation of the laws of the Member States to the extent required for the functioning of the common market;
> (i) a policy in the social sphere comprising a European Social Fund;
> (j) the strengthening of economic and social cohesion;
> (k) a policy in the sphere of the environment;

(l) the strengthening of the competitiveness of Community industry;

(m) the promotion of research and technological development;

(n) encouragement for the establishment and development of trans-European networks;

(o) a contribution to the attainment of a high level of health protection;

(p) a contribution to education and training of quality and to the flowering of the cultures of the Member States;

(q) a policy in the sphere of development cooperation;

(r) the association of the overseas countries and territories in order to increase trade and promote jointly economic and social development;

(s) a contribution to the strengthening of consumer protection;

(t) measures in the spheres of energy, civil protection and tourism.

Article 2 provided that the Community's tasks included the promotion of 'a high level of employment and of social protection, the raising of the standard of living and quality of life, and economic and social cohesion and solidarity'. This is indicative of the fact that the European Community now had tasks and activities which were not purely economic-based, hence its amendment from EEC to EC.

Protocols

Annexed to the EC Treaty, as amended by the TEU, were a number of protocols. Protocols form part of the Treaty by virtue of Art 311 EC Treaty (previously Art 239):

> The protocols annexed to this Treaty by common accord of the Member States shall form an integral part thereof.

Two highly controversial protocols provided for the UK to opt out of certain Community policies which the UK government of the day found unacceptable:

Protocol on social policy

All the Member States, except the UK's then Conservative government under the Premiership of Margaret Thatcher, supported an amendment to the EC Treaty for greater Community competence to legislate in the area of social policy (e.g. employee protection rights). The UK objected to this and would not compromise its position. Therefore, the UK agreed to a protocol providing for the remaining Member States to enter into an agreement which would permit them to have recourse to the Community institutions and Treaty procedures and mechanisms when adopting acts and decisions in the social policy area not otherwise covered by the Treaties. This agreement was annexed to the protocol (and was labelled: Agreement on Social Policy).

Following the election of a Labour government in the UK on 1 May 1997, it was announced that the UK would no longer retain its opt-out, and would take the necessary steps to be bound by the Agreement. This was put into effect by the Treaty of Amsterdam which incorporated an amended version of the Agreement on Social Policy into the EC Treaty (this is discussed further, below).

Protocol on certain provisions relating to the UK of Great Britain and Northern Ireland

Under the SEA, economic and monetary policy, including working towards a single European currency, was introduced outside the formal structures of the Communities, to be dealt with on an intergovernmental basis. Thus each Member State retained direct control of its destiny. However, the TEU amended the EC Treaty to provide for this policy area (including a timetable for the introduction of a single European currency) to be dealt with under the formal structure of the Communities, thus removing such control from the Member States. The UK was not ready to sign up to full economic and monetary union, being somewhat cautious about agreeing to the single currency timetable. This protocol provides that the UK will not be:

> ... obliged or committed to move to the third stage of Economic and Monetary Union without a separate decision to do so by its Government and Parliament.

It is often referred to as the UK's opt-out from the single currency, but it is more akin to an 'opt-in'. Denmark has a similar opt-out to the UK's (this is provided for by the 'Protocol on certain provisions relating to Denmark'). Denmark rejected entry to the single currency in a referendum held on 28 September 2000 by a 53 per cent to 46 per cent majority. Sweden negotiated a similar opt-out to the UK and Denmark when it became a member of the Community on 1 January 1995 (see below). Sweden rejected entry in a referendum held on 14 September 2003. The current UK government has indicated its desire to join the single currency, provided the economic circumstances are favourable. Once the government considers that the economic circumstances are favourable, it will put the question of joining the Euro to the UK electorate in a referendum.

The third stage was the final stage on the road to Monetary Union, when the Member States decided which of them had met the criteria laid down in the Treaty for the forming of a common currency. The third stage started on 1 January 1999 (see Art 121(4) EC Treaty (previously Art 109j(4))). All Member States satisfied the criteria, except Greece. However, Greece was subsequently adjudged to have satisfied the economic criteria and joined the original eleven qualifying states.

A European Central Bank has been established which sets a common European interest rate for these twelve Member States. The currencies of these twelve Member States have fixed conversion rates, quoted in euros. From 1 January 2002 foreign exchange operations were completed in euros, and euro banknotes and coins were placed in circulation. On 1 July 2002 national currencies in these twelve Member States were no longer legal tender and all transactions are now completed in euros.

1 January 1995: enlargement

Three of the remaining EFTA members – Finland, Austria and Sweden – joined the European Communities on 1 January 1995, increasing the number of Member States to fifteen. Norway, having once more successfully negotiated terms for entry, again failed to join after another adverse national referendum.

1 May 1999: the Treaty of Amsterdam

The Treaty of Amsterdam (ToA) was agreed by the Member States in June 1997 and was formally signed by the Member States in Amsterdam on 2 October 1997. This Treaty was concluded on behalf of the UK by the Labour government which had been elected to office on 1 May 1997, under the Premiership of Tony Blair. The Treaty came into force on 1 May 1999 once it had been ratified by the then 15 Member States. A summary of the main provisions is followed by a more substantive discussion of the key features of the Treaty.

Summary

It was anticipated that the ToA would take the first major steps towards restructuring the institutions of the European Union. This was widely seen as essential if the institutions, which were originally set up for a European Community of six states, were to continue functioning effectively in an enlarged European Union of 25-plus states. In the event, the Treaty achieved little in the way of institutional reform. A limit was set on the number of MEPs in the European Parliament, the powers of the President of the Commission were made more specific and the administrative support for the Council of Ministers was strengthened. The difficult decisions which further enlargement would inevitably bring were postponed. These decisions were partially addressed by the Treaty of Nice (see below).

The ToA did, however, broaden the objectives of the EU, moving it further away from the narrower economic base of its early years. There are specific commitments to a number of important non-economic goals, with much more emphasis placed on the rights and duties of EU citizenship, and the EU's commitment to human and civil rights. Decisions within the EU are to be taken 'as openly as possible', and as closely as possible to the citizen. The EU firmly proclaims, in the common provisions of the revised TEU, that it is founded on respect for human rights, democracy and the rule of law, and respect for these principles has been made an explicit condition of application for membership. Under a new Art 7 TEU, the rights of Member States can be suspended if the Council of Ministers finds that a Member State has been in 'serious and persistent breach' of its obligation to respect civil, political and human rights. Article 2 EC Treaty describes equality between men and women as one of the principal objectives of the Community. Article 13 EC Treaty confers power on the Community to legislate to combat discrimination based on sex, racial or ethnic origin, religion or belief, disability, age or sexual orientation. Environmental protection has become one of the principal aims of the Community.

The TEU had created a three-pillar structure for the Union, under which the European Communities (the EC, ECSC and Euratom) comprised the first pillar, Common Foreign and Security Policy (CFSP) the second, and Cooperation in the fields of Justice and Home Affairs (JHA) the third. Under the TEU, only the first pillar of the old Communities used the legally binding decision-making structures described in Chapter 4. Decisions made under the other two pillars were taken 'intergovernmentally' (i.e. politically) and they could not be enforced or challenged in the Court of Justice. The sharpness of this division between legally binding decisions and the political decision-making process has, unfortunately, been blurred by the ToA. A large part of JHA (the third pillar) has been brought within the framework of the Communities (the first pillar). Decisions in what remains of the third pillar (renamed: Police Cooperation in Criminal Matters) now have a limited input from the European Parliament and potential involvement by the Court of Justice. Decision-making in relation to the second pillar (CFSP) remains intergovernmental, outside the formal, legally binding Community decision-making structure. Important changes were also made to the decision-making structure of the Communities (the first pillar), giving the European Parliament even greater powers to amend and block legislative proposals. These changes are discussed in Chapter 4.

For anyone with any prior knowledge of Community law, the most obvious change brought about by the ToA is the renumbering of the EC Treaty. All the familiar landmarks have gone: the obligation of Member States to observe Community law is now Art 10 EC Treaty, and not Art 5; proceedings against Member States are to be brought under Art 226 EC Treaty, and not Art 169; references to the Court of Justice under what used to be Art

177 EC Treaty are now to be brought under Art 234. The wording of these provisions remains identical in most cases. A table of equivalent provisions is published at the beginning of this book. Care must be taken when referring to older cases of the Court of Justice, to ensure that the numbering of old provisions are distinguished from the new. The new numbering structure contained in Art 12 ToA came into effect on 1 May 1999. For some time, however, it will be necessary to be aware of both the old and new numbering. Subsequent chapters of this book are based on the new Treaty numbers but, where relevant, cross-references to the old Treaty numbers are made.

ToA provisions

The Treaty is divided into three parts:

- Part One (Arts 1–5) contains substantive amendments to, *inter alia*, the TEU and the EC Treaty.
- Part Two (Arts 6–11) contains provisions to simplify the TEU and Community Treaties, which includes the deleting of lapsed provisions.
- Part Three (Arts 12–15) contains general and final provisions, which includes provisions which renumber articles of the TEU and the EC Treaty. This renumbering will create some confusion because case law and legislation which predates the coming into force of the ToA will refer to the old numbering.

Amendments made to the TEU by the ToA will be considered first, followed by those made to the EC Treaty.

Amendments to the TEU

The TEU articles have been renumbered by the ToA. Amendments made will be considered under the relevant Titles of the TEU.

Title I – common provisions

The articles of Title I have been renumbered from Arts A–F TEU to 1–7 TEU. The provisions themselves have also been amended. In particular, Art 6(1) TEU now provides that:

> The Union is founded on the principles of liberty, democracy, respect for human rights and fundamental freedoms, and the rule of law, principles which are upheld by the Member States.

A new Art 6(3) TEU provides that:

> The Union shall respect the national identities of its Member States.

A new Art 7 TEU has been inserted which provides for the Council of Ministers to suspend certain rights under the Treaty (including voting rights) of any Member State if the Council determines that the Member State has committed a 'serious and persistent breach' of the Art 6 TEU principles.

As discussed above, the former Art F(2) TEU (now Art 6(2)) provides that:

> The Union shall respect fundamental rights as guaranteed by the European Convention of Human Rights and Fundamental Freedoms . . . as general principles of Community law.

The former Art L TEU provided that all the common provisions (which included the former Art F(2)) were not justiciable by the Court of Justice. Article L TEU has been renumbered Art 46 and has been amended by the ToA to provide that Art 6(2) TEU shall now be justiciable by the Court of Justice, meaning that the Court can explicitly take account of the Convention rights.

Titles II, III, IV – amendments to the founding Treaties

The articles of Titles II, III and IV have simply been renumbered from Arts G, H and I TEU to Arts 8, 9 and 10 TEU respectively.

The three pillars of the European Union

It was discussed above that the EU was founded upon three pillars:

- the European Communities – EC, ECSC (now expired), Euratom;
- Common Foreign and Security Policy (Title V);
- Cooperation in Justice and Home Affairs (Title VI).

The major substantive change made by the ToA is to amend this structure and incorporate part of the third pillar (Justice and Home Affairs) into the EC Treaty, thus forming part of the first pillar. This is discussed further below, when considering the amendments made to the EC Treaty by the ToA.

Title V – common foreign and security policy

The articles of Title V have been renumbered from J.1–J.11 TEU to Arts 11–28 TEU. This remains the second pillar of the EU. Although the ToA has made some amendments to the main provisions of Title V, the role of the European Parliament has not changed and the exclusion of the Court of Justice from adjudicating on the provisions remains. The Secretary General of the Council of Ministers will now act as the 'High Representative' (i.e. the spokesperson) for the Common Foreign and Security Policy.

Title VI – police and judicial cooperation in criminal matters

The articles of Title VI have been renumbered from K.1–K.9 TEU to Arts 29–42 TEU. This is the third pillar of the EU and, as discussed above, it should be noted that the title has changed from 'Cooperation in Justice and Home Affairs' to 'Police and Judicial Cooperation in Criminal Matters'. This is to reflect the fact that those provisions of the former third pillar relating to visas, asylum, immigration and other policies relating to the free movement of persons have been incorporated into the EC Treaty with the insertion of a new Title VI EC Treaty.

The new third pillar states the Union's objective as being able to 'provide citizens with a high level of safety within an area of freedom, security and justice' (Art 29 TEU), and to develop 'common action' among the Member States in the field of police and judicial cooperation and by preventing and combating racism and xenophobia.

Article 29 TEU stipulates that this will be achieved by:

Preventing and combating crime, organised or otherwise, in particular terrorism, trafficking in persons and offences against children, illicit drug trafficking and illicit arms trafficking, corruption and fraud . . .

The European Parliament is given an increased consultative role in the decision-making process and the Court of Justice will generally have jurisdiction over most of the provisions.

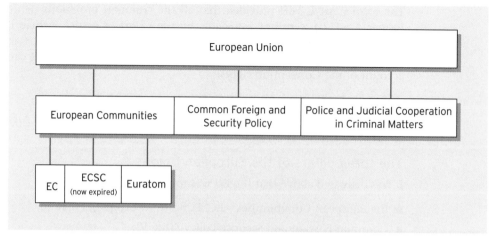

Figure 1.2 Structure of the European Union as at 1 May 1999, following the ToA

Figure 1.2 illustrates the structure of the EU, following the ToA's amendments to the third pillar.

Title VII – closer cooperation

This new title was inserted into the TEU by the ToA and contains three articles (Arts 43–45) which enable Member States to establish closer cooperation between themselves and to use the institutions, procedures and mechanisms of the TEU and EC Treaty. However, Art 43(c) TEU provides that these provisions can only be used as a 'last resort where the objectives of the ... Treaties could not be attained by applying the relevant procedures laid down therein'.

These provisions will therefore allow flexibility in the future development of the ECs and the EU, recognising the right of Member States to 'opt-out' from *new* policy initiatives not otherwise covered by the Treaties (this formalises the situation whereby the UK opted out of the Social Policy Agreement and single currency, for example).

A similar flexibility clause has been inserted into the EC Treaty (Art 11 (see below)).

Title VIII – final provisions

The Articles of Title VIII have been renumbered from L–S TEU to Arts 46–53 TEU. Article 49 TEU (previously Art O) has amended the procedure for the admission of new Member States. New Member States must have respect for the fundamental principles set out in Art 6 TEU (see above). The Council of Ministers will act unanimously after receiving the opinion of the Commission and the assent of the European Parliament.

Amendments to the EC Treaty

Article 2 EC Treaty has been amended to include new tasks:

- promotion of equality between men and women;
- a high level of protection and improvement of the quality of the environment;
- promotion of a high degree of competitiveness; and

■ economic development which must be 'sustainable' as well as 'balanced and harmonious'.

The new Art 2 EC Treaty provides that:

> The Community shall have as its task, by establishing a common market and an economic and monetary union and by implementing common policies or activities referred to in Articles 3 and 4, to promote throughout the Community a harmonious, balanced and sustainable development of economic activities, a high level of employment and of social protection, equality between men and women, sustainable and non inflationary growth, a high degree of competitiveness and convergence of economic performance, a high level of protection and improvement of the quality of the environment, the raising of the standard of living and quality of life, and economic and social cohesion and solidarity among Member States.

Article 3 EC Treaty lists the activities of the Community which can be undertaken in order to achieve the tasks set out in Art 2. Article 3 has been amended to include a new activity (the other activities already cover the new Art 2 tasks):

> The promotion of coordination between employment policies of the Member States with a view to enhancing their effectiveness by developing a coordinated strategy for employment.

A new Art 3(2) EC Treaty provides that:

> In all the activities referred to in this Article, the Community shall aim to eliminate inequalities, and to promote equality, between men and women.

The other main amendments to the EC Treaty by the ToA include:

■ Article 11 EC Treaty inserts a flexibility clause similar to that in Title VII TEU (discussed above) allowing Member States to establish closer cooperation between themselves and to make use of the institutions, procedures and mechanisms laid down in the EC Treaty, provided the cooperation proposed does not, *inter alia,* 'concern areas which fall within the exclusive competence of the Community'.

■ Article 13 EC Treaty (previously Art 6a) provides a new non-discriminatory provision which confers legislative competence on the Community to combat discrimination based on sex, racial or ethnic origin, religion or belief, disability, age, or sexual orientation.

■ Articles 61–69 (Title IV) EC Treaty incorporate part of the former third pillar of the European Union which covers visas, asylum, immigration and other policies relating to the free movement of persons.

■ Articles 125–130 (Title VIII) EC Treaty insert a new title on employment, reflecting the new activity set out in Art 3 EC Treaty.

■ Articles 136–143 EC Treaty incorporate an amended version of the Social Policy Agreement, which will apply to *all* Member States. At Amsterdam the then newly elected UK Labour government agreed to end its opt-out.

■ Titles XIII and XIV EC Treaty on public health and consumer protection, respectively, have been enhanced.

■ The decision-making process has been amended and the European Parliament has been given a greater role in more policy areas.

■ Minor amendments have been made to the composition and/or role of some of the Community institutions.

Conclusion

The TEU provided for the European Union to be founded upon three pillars; these pillars were amended by the ToA. The European Communities (the first pillar) now comprises two separate and distinct Communities, the most important of which is the European Community (previously referred to as the European Economic Community) which was established by the Treaty Establishing the European Community.

The ECs and the EU have evolved over a period of little more than 50 years. During this time the change that has been brought about has resulted in more, not less, integration. What started off as a predominantly economic market now has a political and social agenda. Each time the founding Treaties are amended the end result is that more areas of competence are transferred by the Member States to the Community.

1 February 2003: the Treaty of Nice

The Treaty of Nice (ToN) was agreed by the Member States in December 2000. It was formally signed by the Member States on 26 February 2001 but it could only come into force once they had ratified it. In a referendum during June 2001, the Irish, by a majority of 54 per cent to 46 per cent, refused to ratify the Treaty. The other fourteen Member States had already, or subsequently, ratified it. Ireland held a second referendum during October 2002, and this time there was a positive vote in favour of ratification (63 per cent to 37 per cent). Having now been ratified by the fifteen Member States, the Treaty came into force on 1 February 2003.

Below is a summary of the main amendments which the ToN made to the EC Treaty and TEU.

Institutional reform

The main reason for a new Treaty amending the EC Treaty and TEU was to reform the institutions in preparation for enlargement of membership of the Communities. The EC Treaty was amended to enable an enlarged membership of up to 27 Member States. The changes made will be discussed in Chapters 3 to 5.

Fundamental rights

Article 7 TEU provides for the suspension of a Member State's Treaty rights if there has been a 'serious and persistent' breach of the Art 6(1) TEU principles (i.e. the principles of liberty, democracy, respect for human rights and fundamental freedoms, and the rule of law). The ToN amends Art 7 to provide that the suspension can be imposed where the Council of Ministers votes by a four-fifths majority of its membership. Prior to the ToN it had required a unanimous vote by the Council. The role of the other institutions in this process has not been changed.

Security and defence

Article 25 TEU provides for the monitoring of the international situation within the areas covered by the second pillar (Common Foreign and Security Policy), and the development of associated policies. In a meeting of the European Council, immediately prior to the meeting at which the ToN was agreed, a policy for the establishment of a European rapid reaction force was adopted. This 60,000-strong force will be used primarily for peace-keeping and emergency missions within the region.

Eurojust

Articles 29 and 31 TEU have been amended to provide that in the application of the third pillar (Police and Judicial Cooperation in Criminal Matters) there shall be cooperation with, *inter alia,* the European Judicial Cooperation Unit (Eurojust). A declaration specifies that Eurojust shall comprise national prosecutors and magistrates (or police officers of equivalent competence) who are detached from each Member State.

Enhanced cooperation

Articles 43–45 (Title VII) TEU have been substantially amended to further the prospect of a minimum of eight Member States establishing closer cooperation between themselves and to use the institutions, procedures and mechanisms of the TEU and EC Treaty. Similar to the existing provisions, the amended provisions provide that closer cooperation can be undertaken only if it is 'aimed at furthering the objectives of the Union and the Community, at protecting and serving its interests'. The new provision also requires that 'enhanced cooperation may be engaged in only as a last resort, when it has been established within the Council that the objectives of such cooperation cannot be attained within a reasonable period by applying the relevant provisions of the Treaties'.

New policies

Only a few new policies have been introduced, although some polices have been refined. One new policy relates to economic, financial and technical cooperation with third states following the insertion of a new Title XXI EC Treaty. This new policy will 'contribute to the general objective of developing and consolidating democracy and the rule of law, and to that of respecting human rights and fundamental freedoms'.

Decision-making process

Some legal bases for the adoption of secondary Community instruments (see Chapter 2), which originally required a unanimous vote by the Council of Ministers in order to be adopted, have been amended to provide for their adoption by a qualified majority. In addition, the role of the Parliament has been enhanced within selected policy areas.

1 May 2004: enlargement

On 1 May 2004 membership of the European Union increased to 25, with the admission of ten new Member States:

- Cyprus (South)
- Czech Republic

- Estonia
- Hungary
- Latvia
- Lithuania
- Malta
- Poland
- Slovakia
- Slovenia.

Political differences within Cyprus resulted in Northern Cyprus being excluded from membership for the time being. Cyprus has been divided between its Greek and Turkish Cypriot peoples since 1974, when Turkey invaded the north of the island. The United Nations attempted to broker an agreement between the two sides to reunite the island, but no agreement was forthcoming. The United Nations therefore drafted its own agreement which was voted on by the citizens from the north and south (in simultaneous referenda) on 24 April 2004. The Greek Cypriots rejected the agreement, whereas the Turkish Cypriots accepted the agreement. Given the Greek Cypriots' rejection, the agreement was not concluded and the division between north and south remains. This being the case, it is only Southern Cyprus which is a member of the European Union. However, accession negotiations with Turkey opened on 3 October 2005 and Turkey has signalled an intent to recognise the Greek Cypriot southern part of the island. This intent may have a positive impact on future reunification negotiations.

Economic and Monetary Union

The ten new Member States did not join the Euro on 1 May 2004. They will only do so once they have achieved the high degree of sustainable economic convergence with the Euro area which is required for membership of the single currency. They will thus need to fulfil the same convergence criteria which were applied to the existing euro area members, namely a high degree of price stability, sustainable government finances (in terms of both public deficit and public debt levels), a stable exchange rate, and convergence in long-term interest rates.

There is no pre-defined timetable for adoption of the euro by the new Member States, but the levels of convergence required for membership will be assessed by the Council of Ministers on a proposal from the European Commission and on the basis of convergence reports by the Commission and the European Central Bank. These reports are produced at least every two years or at the request of a Member State seeking to adopt the euro.

On 11 July 2006, the Council adopted a decision allowing Slovenia to join the euro area on 1 January 2007. Slovenia will become the first of the ten new Member States to adopt the euro as its currency, joining the twelve current members. The UK, together with Denmark and Sweden, continue to exercise their opt-out from the single currency (see above).

1 January 2007: enlargement

On 25 April 2005, the then 25 Member States, together with Bulgaria and Romania, signed the Accession Treaty (OJ 2005 L 157/01), paving the way for Bulgaria and Romania's membership of the EU.

On 26 September 2006, the Commission approved the Monitoring Report on Bulgaria and Romania's state of preparedness for EU membership (COM (2006)). This enabled Bulgaria and Romania to become EU Member States on 1 January 2007, increasing the European Union from 25 to 27 Member States.

The Monitoring Report of 26 September 2006 highlighted a number of areas where both Bulgaria and Romania required further progress in the months leading up to accession on 1 January 2007, and beyond. Section 3 of the Monitoring Report set out a number of safeguards and other measures which the Commission will apply following Bulgaria and Romania's entry into the EU. Section 3 provides as follows:

3. SAFEGUARDS AND OTHER MEASURES

Upon accession, the Commission will, as for any other Member State, monitor the implementation of the *acquis*. Like for any other Member State, it will apply all the tools available within the EU legislation (*acquis*) where necessary. In addition, there are specific tools which only apply to Bulgaria and Romania. They are laid down in the Accession Treaty.

Section 3.1 provides an overview of the tools available under the *acquis*. Section 3.2 presents the tools based on the Accession Treaty. Section 3.3 indicates which specific accompanying measures are foreseen for the actual accession of Bulgaria and Romania.

3.1. Tools applicable to all Member States

These tools consist of the necessary preventive or remedial actions which the Commission is obliged to use to address any shortcoming which may impede the proper functioning of EU policies. These include safeguard measures, financial corrections of EU funds, competition policy measures and infringement procedures. They are based on the *acquis*.

Moreover, for some aspects related to human rights, the European Monitoring Centre on Racism and Xenophobia (EUMC) will continue its monitoring after accession of both countries with respect to the fight against racism and related discrimination and to support of positive integration of minority communities. The scope of the EUMC, which covers all Member States, has already been extended to Bulgaria and Romania.

Safeguard measures based on the *acquis* can be invoked upon accession, as for any Member State, in many policy areas (transport, food safety, aviation safety etc). Such measures are applied as long as the underlying problems exist. The decision-making procedures depend on the relevant EU legislation and may therefore vary across different policy areas. For example, the *acquis* contains several measures to ensure the food safety within the EU. For each of the animal or plant diseases, different Directives specify measures to be taken in case such a disease occurs in a current or new Member State. Such measures often consist of prohibitions to export certain animals or products from a Member State to the internal market until the disease is under control or eradicated. The Commission can decide on food safety measures after having received the favourable opinion of the EU Standing Committee on the Food Chain and Animal Health by qualified majority voting.

The Commission may apply safeguard measures in relation to the EU funds, including financial corrections. Any shortcomings on the proper use of EU funds may delay the disbursement of funds or allow the Commission to claim financial corrections (i.e. reduction on future payments) or to recover payments.

For **agricultural funds**, the *acquis* provides different types of controls. Firstly, Member States are obliged to have accredited and efficient paying agencies to ensure the sound management and control of agricultural expenditure. Secondly, Member States are also required to operate functioning control systems, in particular a functioning integrated administrative and control system (IACS), for the direct payments to farmers and parts of rural development expenditures, notably in order to avoid fraudulent practices and irregular payments. Thirdly, if Member States fail to operate such control systems properly, the Commission, based on the *acquis*, decides ex-post on financial corrections through clearance of accounts procedures. In that case, the Commission refuses to finance parts of the agricultural expenditure. Finally, if the Commission concludes that there is a non-respect of Community rules or an abusive use of EU funds, it may suspend or temporarily reduce the payment of advances on a case-by-case basis.

For **structural funds**, the *acquis* provides four types of control that may lead to financial corrections. Firstly, every Member State needs to submit operational programmes indicating how the funds will be spent within each sector. These programmes have to be approved by the Commission before any payments can be made. No advance payments can be made until the Commission formally adopts the programmes. Secondly, any Member State needs to prove that it has established adequate management, certification and audit authorities. If the Commission does not consider these authorities to function efficiently, no interim payments will be made. Thirdly, the corresponding disbursement of funds for these programme or programmes can be interrupted, suspended or cancelled if, on the basis of Commission findings, the Commission suspects or detects cases of irregularities or fraud including corrupt practices. Finally, further to this range of safeguard measures to the EU funds, financial corrections can take place in case of individual or systemic irregularities are found during the regular ex-post controls.

3.2. Tools based on the Accession Treaty

Under the Accession Treaty, there are three types of safeguard measures: the economic, internal market, and justice and home affairs (JHA) safeguards, which can be taken up to three years after accession. The latter two can be invoked prior to accession. Once in place, such measures will be applied until the Commission decides to lift the measures upon the resolution of the underlying problems.

In addition, there are two types of transitional arrangements, which are also outlined below.

The **economic** safeguard can be invoked to address serious economic difficulties in the current or new Member States after accession.

The **internal market** safeguard can be invoked when a new Member State causes, or risks causing, a serious breach of the functioning of the internal market. The Commission can take appropriate measures such as excluding this state from the benefits of certain internal market legislation. This safeguard encompasses the internal market in the broad sense, i.e. not only the four freedoms, but also the sectoral policies (e.g. competition, agriculture, transport, telecommunications, energy, consumer and health protection, environment etc.) insofar as they have cross-border effects.

The **justice and home affairs (JHA)** safeguard allows the unilateral suspension of the current Member States' obligations in the field of judicial cooperation with the country concerned, both in civil and criminal law as far as legal instruments falling under the principle of mutual recognition are concerned. It can be invoked in case there are serious shortcomings or the risk thereof in these two areas.

In addition, there are **transitional arrangements** in the Accession Treaty. The first category exists of arrangements which have been agreed during the negotiations for several areas to avoid possible regional or sectoral disturbances in either the new or old Member

States. For example, the free movement of workers from new Member States may be restricted by the Member States for up to seven years after accession. Access to the national road transport markets (cabotage) has been temporarily restricted.

Finally, the Accession Treaty foresees a second category of transitional arrangements which the Commission can take during a period of three years after accession on veterinary, phytosanitary and food safety rules. These measures aim to prevent, for example, non-compliant food establishments from selling their products on the internal market during the transitional period of maximum three years. During this period, such establishments are allowed only to produce goods bearing a specific label and only for the national market. After the transition period, they have to comply with the EU rules or close down.

3.3. Accompanying measures foreseen for the accession of Bulgaria and Romania

Based on the findings of this report, the Commission will take remedial measures, where necessary, to ensure the functioning of EU policies. This concerns cases in the areas of food safety, air safety, EU agricultural funds and the judiciary and fight against corruption, as described below. In case other shortcomings are identified before or after accession, appropriate measures will equally be taken to ensure the proper functioning of EU policies.

3.3.1. Judiciary and the fight against corruption

The report shows that further progress is still necessary in the area of judicial reform and the fight against organised crime and corruption. The Commission will establish a mechanism to cooperate and verify progress in these areas after accession. This will be based on Articles 37 and 38 of the Act of Accession.

Both Bulgaria and Romania shall report regularly on progress in addressing specific benchmarks. The first report should be submitted by 31 March 2007. The Commission will provide internal and external expertise to cooperate and provide guidance in the reform process and to verify progress. The Commission will then report to the European Parliament and the Council by June on the progress made in addressing the benchmarks.

The Commission's reports will assess whether the benchmarks have been met, need to be adjusted and may request further reports on progress if necessary. The mechanism will continue until the benchmarks have been met.

Should either country fail to address the benchmarks adequately, the Commission will apply the safeguard measures of the Accession Treaty. They lead to the suspension of the current Member States' obligation to recognise those judgments and execute warrants issued by either country's courts or prosecutors falling under the principle of mutual recognition.

Based on the findings of this report, the benchmarks to be addressed are as follows:

Bulgaria

– Adopt constitutional amendments removing any ambiguity regarding the independence and accountability of the judicial system.

– Ensure a more transparent and efficient judicial process by adopting and implementing a new judicial system act and the new civil procedure code. Report on the impact of these new laws and of the penal and administrative procedure codes, notably on the pre-trial phase.

– Continue the reform of the judiciary in order to enhance professionalism, accountability and efficiency. Evaluate the impact of this reform and publish the results annually.

– Conduct and report on professional, non-partisan investigations into allegations of high-level corruption. Report on internal inspections of public institutions and on the publication of assets of high-level officials.

– Take further measures to prevent and fight corruption, in particular at the borders and within local government.

– Implement a strategy to fight organised crime, focussing on serious crime, money laundering as well as on the systematic confiscation of assets of criminals. Report on new and ongoing investigations, indictments and convictions in these areas.

Romania

– Ensure a more transparent, and efficient judicial process notably by enhancing the capacity and accountability of the Superior Council of Magistracy. Report and monitor the impact of the new civil and penal procedures codes.

– Establish, as foreseen, an integrity agency with responsibilities for verifying assets, incompatibilities and potential conflicts of interest, and for issuing mandatory decisions on the basis of which dissuasive sanctions can be taken.

– Building on progress already made, continue to conduct professional, non-partisan investigations into allegations of high-level corruption.

– Take further measures to prevent and fight against corruption, in particular within the local government.

The Commission will adopt a Decision implementing and defining the modalities of this mechanism after consulting the Member States. It will enter into force on 1 January 2007. This list of benchmarks will be amended in case either country complies with one or more of the benchmarks before accession.

3.3.2. Agricultural funds

In Bulgaria and Romania there is a real risk that the IACS will not be functioning properly by the time of accession. In both countries, the timetable for completing such a properly functioning IACS is very tight due to the late start of preparations. As a result, the necessary quality of the work to be carried out risks not to be achieved.

The agricultural funds covered by the IACS constitute by far the largest part (around 80%) of the agricultural expenditure of Bulgaria and Romania and, therefore, a proper functioning IACS is of the utmost importance.

To address these risks, a mechanism is needed which provides for the possibility of a future decision on measures relating to the proper use of agricultural funding covered by IACS. Such measures are necessary to avoid undue payments during the first years after accession and to address the imminent risk of a serious breach of the functioning of the internal market in agricultural products. This risk is due to the specific nature of agricultural expenditure, which is under a strict timeframe. In addition, the funds covered by the IACS are characterised by a high volume of transactions early after accession.

They have to be managed, controlled and paid soon after accession. Moreover, efficient controls can only be carried out during a limited period in the year concerned.

The mechanism, based on the Accession Treaty, is laid down in a regulation adopted simultaneously with this communication. In practice the mechanism gives the two countries time to complete the necessary work on a properly functioning IACS. The measures will not be introduced if they succeed in doing so within that timeframe. To achieve the timely completion of the work, continued increased efforts are needed.

3.3.3. Food safety

Bulgaria and Romania are currently prohibited to export live pigs, pig meat, and certain pig meat products to the EU due to the existence of *classical swine fever* in both countries. The situation as regards classical swine fever requires the adoption of certain decisions by the Commission by the date of accession.

Bulgaria has submitted for formal approval a plan finalising the eradication of classical swine fever in feral pigs. Approval of this plan would lead to the integration of Bulgaria in the community regime already set up for those Member States which are affected by classical swine fever. Romania has submitted for formal approval a plan for the eradication of classical swine fever in feral and domestic pigs. However, the current situation in both countries still require the prohibition to trade live pigs, pig meat, and certain pig meat products to the EU after accession. The corresponding measures enter into force upon accession.

Both countries do not fully comply with the *acquis* on *TSE*. If Bulgaria and Romania will be not in position before accession to set up an adequate collection system and treatment of dead animals and animal by-products throughout their countries and to complete the upgrading of the rendering establishments, restrictions on the use of certain animal by-products (for example for feeding to animals) will be decided. These measures will be based on the Act of Accession or the *acquis*. They enter into force upon accession.

The list of Bulgarian and Romanian agri-food establishments which were not allowed to sell their products in the other Member States during a period of three years as they do not comply yet with EU rules will be updated by the date of accession. The updated lists will include, if needed, other non-compliant establishments. This procedure is based on transitional measures provided for in the Act of Accession.

In addition, specific transitional measures based on Article 42 of the Act of Accession may need to be adopted in the milk sector due to the discrepancy between the capacity of treatment of compliant establishment and the availability of compliant raw milk. These measures will prevent the selling of some products made from this non-compliant raw milk in the other Member States.

3.3.4. Aviation safety

In view of the serious deficiencies identified by the European Aviation Safety Agency (EASA) and the Joint Aviation Authorities (JAA) in the area of aviation safety, the JAA refused Bulgaria's mutual recognition within the JAA system in the relevant safety areas, namely airworthiness, maintenance, operations and flight crew licensing. In order to comply with EU law, Bulgaria needs to submit a corrective action plan to rectify all deficiencies and implement it within a strict timetable, in close cooperation with, and under guidance from EASA. An inspection by EASA will then be carried out as soon as possible before accession to verify the implementation of this plan.

Unless Bulgaria takes the necessary corrective actions, it risks that the Commission, at its own initiative or at the request of a Member State, may restrict access to the internal aviation market. Also, Bulgarian registered aircraft which do not comply with EU civil aviation safety rules may be subject to appropriate safeguard measures, based on the *acquis*.

Furthermore, non-complying Bulgarian air carriers may be added to the EU list of banned air carriers which may not fly into, over or out of air space of the EU. These measures are all based on the *acquis*.

Economic and Monetary Union

Bulgaria and Romania did not join the euro on 1 January 2007. Similar to the ten states joining the EU on 1 May 2004, Bulgaria and Romania will only join once they have achieved the high degree of sustainable economic convergence with the euro area which is required for membership of the single currency. They will thus need to fulfil the same convergence criteria which were applied to the existing euro area members, namely a high degree of price stability, sustainable government finances (in terms of both public deficit and public debt levels), a stable exchange rate, and convergence in long-term interest rates.

There is no pre-defined timetable for adoption of the euro by Bulgaria and Romania, but the levels of convergence required for membership will be assessed by the Council of Ministers on a proposal from the European Commission and on the basis of convergence reports by the Commission and the European Central Bank. These reports are produced at least every two years or at the request of a Member State seeking to adopt the euro.

The euro is currently in circulation in thirteen Member States:

- Austria
- Belgium
- Finland
- France
- Germany
- Greece
- Ireland
- Italy
- Luxembourg
- Netherlands
- Portugal
- Slovenia (from 1 January 2007)
- Spain.

Future enlargement

Three countries have applied for membership of the European Union: Croatia, Turkey and the Former Yugoslav Republic of Macedonia. In order to join the Union, each prospective Member State is required to fulfil the economic and political conditions known as the 'Copenhagen criteria' (which was adopted in 1993), according to which they must:

- be a stable democracy, respecting human rights, the rule of law, and the protection of minorities;
- have a functioning market economy;
- adopt the common rules, standards and policies that make up the body of European Community and Union law.

Croatia applied for EU membership on 21 February 2003. Formal accession negotiations opened on 17 March 2005, but it is likely to be a few years before Croatia is considered ready for entry.

The Former Yugoslav Republic of Macedonia applied for EU membership during December 2005, but formal accession negotiations have not yet been opened.

Turkey applied for EU membership as long ago as 14 April 1987, but its passage to entry has not been smooth. At its December 2004 meeting, the Council invited the Commission to present to the Council a proposal for a framework for negotiations with Turkey, on the basis set out below. It requested the Council to agree on that framework with a view to opening negotiations on 3 October 2005. The framework for negotiations (which will also apply to future candidate countries) is as follows:

The European Council agreed that accession negotiations with individual candidate states will be based on a framework for negotiations. Each framework, which will be established by the Council on a proposal by the Commission, taking account of the experience of the fifth enlargement process and of the evolving *acquis*, will address the following elements, according to own merits and specific situations and characteristics of each candidate state:

1. As in previous negotiations, the substance of the negotiations, which will be conducted in an Intergovernmental Conference (IGC) with the participation of all Member States on the one hand and the candidate State concerned on the other, where decisions require unanimity, will be broken down into a number of chapters, each covering a specific policy area. The Council, acting by unanimity on a proposal by the Commission, will lay down benchmarks for the provisional closure and, where appropriate, for the opening of each chapter; depending on the chapter concerned, these benchmarks will refer to legislative alignment and a satisfactory track record of implementation of the *acquis* as well as obligations deriving from contractual relations with the European Union.

2. Long transition periods, derogations, specific arrangements or permanent safeguard clauses, i.e. clauses which are permanently available as a basis for safeguard measures, may be considered. The Commission will include these, as appropriate, in its proposals for each framework, for areas such as freedom of movement of persons, structural policies or agriculture. Furthermore, the decision-taking process regarding the eventual establishment of freedom of movement of persons should allow for a maximum role of individual Member States. Transitional arrangements or safeguards should be reviewed regarding their impact on competition or the functioning of the internal market.

3. The financial aspects of accession of a candidate state must be allowed for in the applicable Financial Framework. Hence, accession negotiations yet to be opened with candidates whose accession could have substantial financial consequences can only be concluded after the establishment of the Financial Framework for the period from 2014 together with possible consequential financial reforms.

4. The shared objective of the negotiations is accession. These negotiations are an open-ended process, the outcome of which cannot be guaranteed beforehand. While taking account of all Copenhagen criteria, if the Candidate State is not in a position to assume in full all the obligations of membership it must be ensured that the Candidate State concerned is fully anchored in the European structures through the strongest possible bond.

5. In the case of a serious and persistent breach in a candidate state of the principles of liberty, democracy, respect for human rights and fundamental freedoms and the rule of law on which the Union is founded, the Commission will, on its own initiative or on the request of one third of the Member States, recommend the suspension of negotiations and propose the conditions for eventual resumption. The Council will decide by qualified majority on such a recommendation, after having heard the Candidate State, whether to suspend the negotiations and on the conditions for their resumption. The Member States will act in the IGC in accordance with the Council decision, without prejudice to the general requirement for unanimity in the IGC. The European Parliament will be informed.

6. Parallel to accession negotiations, the Union will engage with every candidate state in an intensive political and cultural dialogue. With the aim of enhancing mutual understanding by bringing people together, this inclusive dialogue also will involve civil society.

Accession negotiations have subsequently been opened with Turkey, although Turkey's entry to the EU is not envisaged for a number of years.

The Commission's website on enlargement is available at:

http://europa.eu/pol/enlarg/index_en.htm

Key dates and events

23 July 1952	The European Coal and Steel Community (ECSC) comes into force.
1 July 1958	The European Economic Community (EEC) and the European Atomic Energy Community (Euratom) come into force.
8 April 1965	Merger of the Community institutions.
1 January 1973	EU enlargement from six Member States to nine. The new Member States are Denmark, Ireland and the UK.
1 January 1981	EU enlargement from nine Member States to ten. The new Member State is Greece.
1 January 1986	EU enlargement from ten Member States to twelve. The new Member States are Portugal and Spain.
1 July 1987	The Single European Act (SEA) comes into force.
1 January 1993	The target date for completion of the internal market: 'an area without frontiers where the free movement of goods, persons, services and capital is ensured'.
1 November 1993	The Treaty on European Union (TEU) comes into force.
1 January 1995	EU enlargement from twelve Member States to fifteen. The new Member States are Austria, Finland and Sweden.
1 May 1999	The Treaty of Amsterdam (ToA) comes into force.
1 January 2002	The euro becomes legal tender in twelve Member States.
23 July 2002	The European Coal and Steel Community (ECSC) comes to an end.
1 February 2003	The Treaty of Nice (ToN) comes into force.
1 May 2004	EU enlargement from 15 Member States to 25. The new Member States are Cyprus (South), Czech Republic, Estonia, Hungary, Latvia, Lithuania, Malta, Poland, Slovakia and Slovenia.
1 January 2007	EU enlargement from 25 Member States to 27. The new Member States are Bulgaria and Romania.
1 January 2007	Slovenia joins the euro.

The Charter of Fundamental Rights of the European Union

The Charter of Fundamental Rights of the European Union was signed by the then fifteen Member States during December 2000 at the meeting of the European Council held in Nice, France. The Charter combines in a single text the civil, political, economic, social and societal rights which have previously been laid down in a variety of international, European and national sources. It includes rights of dignity (e.g. the right to life; respect for private and family life); freedoms (e.g. freedom of assembly and of association); equality (e.g. respect for cultural, religious and linguistic diversity); solidarity (e.g. right of collective bargaining and action); citizens' rights (e.g. freedom of movement and residence); and justice (e.g. presumption of innocence and right of defence).

The Charter is not legally binding, but despite the protestations of the UK government, it is highly probable that the Court of Justice will draw on its provisions when interpreting and applying Community law (see Chapters 2 and 5). A Declaration annexed to the ToN provided that an Intergovernmental Conference would be held in 2004 to consider, *inter alia,* the status of the Charter. This resulted in the adoption of the proposed Constitutional Treaty. The Charter was incorporated into the proposed Treaty (Arts II-61 to II-114). Article I-9 Constitutional Treaty provided that the EU shall 'recognise the rights, freedoms and principles set out in the Charter'. Clearly therefore, if the Treaty had been ratified and had come into force, the Charter would have been given explicit legal recognition; however, the Constitutional Treaty did not come into force because it was not ratified by all the Member States (see below).

The Constitutional Treaty

At the European Council meeting in Laeken on 14 and 15 December 2001, a declaration on the 'Future of the Union' was adopted (SN 300/1/01). This declaration provided for the establishment of a Convention on the Future of Europe, to work towards the adoption of a Constitution for the European Union.

The Convention formed the basis of an Intergovernmental Conference (IGC) during 2004 when the 'Future of the Union' was the subject of detailed discussion. This resulted in the text of a Constitutional Treaty being agreed at the meeting of the European Council on 18 June 2004, and the 'Treaty establishing a Constitution for Europe' was formally signed in Rome on 29 October 2004 (OJ 2004 C 310/1).

The Constitutional Treaty could only come into force once it had been ratified (i.e. approved) by *all* the then 25 Member States. The ratification process varies from Member State to Member State. The ratification process in an individual Member State depends upon the constitutional requirements of the respective Member State. Some Member States were constitutionally required to hold a referendum before being able to ratify the Treaty. Although the UK's constitution did not require a referendum to be held before the Treaty could be ratified, Tony Blair (the UK Prime Minister) stated that he would hold a referendum. The UK's referendum was not scheduled to be held before 2006, because in the first half of 2005 the government was preoccupied with the May 2005 general election, and in the second half the UK held the presidency of the European Union's Council of Ministers.

It had been anticipated that ratification would prove to be a tumultuous affair; if all the then 25 Member States did not ratify it, then it would not come into force. If it was ratified by all the then 25 Member States then Art IV-447(2) provided that 'This Treaty shall enter into force on 1 November 2006, provided that all the instruments of ratification have been deposited [with the Italian government], or, failing that, on the first day of the second month following the deposit of the instrument of ratification by the last signatory State to take this step'.

The ratification process

On 29 May 2005, France held a referendum; 54.68 per cent rejected the Treaty. A few days later, on 1 June 2005, The Netherlands held a referendum; 61.7 per cent rejected the Treaty.

Despite the Treaty having been rejected by two Member States, the European Union did not officially declare the Constitutional Treaty 'dead'.

Following the no votes in France and The Netherlands, the UK stated that it was suspending the ratification process (i.e. no referendum would be held).

Other Member States postponed their scheduled referenda: Czech Republic, Denmark, Ireland and Portugal. Two other Member States put the ratification process on hold: Poland and Sweden. Finland is in the process of ratifying the Treaty. To date, 15 Member States have ratified the Treaty.

Developments with regard to the ratification process are available at:
http://europa.eu.int/constitution/index_en.htm

The Constitutional Treaty – 'dead or alive'?

At the meeting of the European Council on 16–17 June 2005, the Heads of State and government agreed to come back to the issue of ratification of the Constitutional Treaty in the first half of 2006 in order to make an overall assessment of the national debates launched as part of a 'period of reflection' and to agree on how to proceed.

Following this meeting a further five Member States ratified the Treaty (bringing the total to 15, as stated above).

At its meeting on 15–16 June 2006, the European Council stated that the 'period of reflection' had been useful in enabling the EU to assess the concerns and worries expressed in the course of the ratification process. The Council stated that ratification should continue with regard to the ten Member States that had not yet ratified the Treaty. However, it also stated that further work was needed before decisions on the future of the Constitutional Treaty could be taken.

This is an implicit admission that the Constitutional Treaty will *not* come into force in its current format.

The Council stated that the Presidency would present a report to the European Council during the first half of 2007, based on extensive consultations with the Member States. This report will contain an assessment of the state of discussion with regard to the Constitutional Treaty and explore possible future developments.

The Council stated that the European Council would subsequently examine this report. The outcome of this examination will serve as the basis for further decisions on how to continue the reform process, it being understood that the necessary steps to that effect will have been taken during the second half of 2008 at the latest.

Therefore, assuming that the Constitutional Treaty does not come into force because all Member States have not ratified it, the following timetable will apply:

Early 2007 – The President of the European Council will present a report to the Council which will advise on (i) whether or not the Constitutional Treaty should be abandoned (is it 'dead or alive'?); and (ii) if it should be abandoned, what future developments could be pursued (e.g. a replacement Constitutional Treaty).

2007 to early 2008 – The European Council will examine the report and further decisions will be taken with regard to a replacement Constitutional Treaty (if the report recommends abandoning the current Treaty). It is quite possible that any new proposed Treaty will not be referred to as a Constitutional Treaty.

Once the Council has adopted a new Treaty, it will require ratification (i.e. approval) by *all* 27 Member States before it can come into force.

Although the changes which the Constitutional Treaty would have made will not come into effect as initially scheduled, it is now clear that there will be another attempt to adopt and ratify an alternative to the Constitutional Treaty. For that reason, included below is a summary of the main provisions of the Constitutional Treaty; this will provide a foundation of what *could* be included within a replacement Constitutional Treaty.

The Constitutional Treaty: Parts I–IV

The Constitutional Treaty is divided into four parts:

- Part I (Arts I-1 to I-60) is concerned with the main constitutional provisions.

- Part II (Arts II-61 to II-114) contains the entire Charter of Fundamental Rights.

- Part III (Arts III-115 to III-436) relates to the policies of the Union and detailed provisions on how the institutions function.

- Part IV (Arts IV-437 to IV-438) sets out the general and final provisions.

The European Union

The construction of the European Union (and its three pillars), as discussed above, is complicated, and therefore the Constitutional Treaty would have established a single European Union which would have replaced the current European Community and European Union (Art I-1 Constitutional Treaty). The three pillars would have been merged even though special procedures would have been maintained in the fields of foreign policy, security and defence (see below). Art I-1(2) would have provided that 'The Union shall be open to all European States which respect its values and are committed to promoting them together'.

The Union's values

Article I-2 would have provided that the Union was founded on 'the values of respect for human dignity, freedom, democracy, equality, the rule of law and respect for human rights, including the right of persons belonging to minorities', to a large extent mirroring the provisions of Art 6(1) TEU (as amended by the ToA).

The Union's objectives

The Union's objectives, set out in Art I-3, were much more succinct than the combined objectives in Art 3 EC Treaty (in respect of the European Community) and Art 2 TEU (in respect of the EU). Art I-3 would have provided that:

1. The Union's aim is to promote peace, its values and the well-being of its peoples.
2. The Union shall offer its citizens an area of freedom, security and justice without internal frontiers, and an internal market where competition is free and undistorted.
3. The Union shall work for the sustainable development of Europe based on balanced economic growth and price stability, a highly competitive social market economy, aiming at full employment and social progress, and a high level of protection and improvement of the quality of the environment. It shall promote scientific and technological advance.

    It shall combat social exclusion and discrimination, and shall promote social justice and protection, equality between women and men, solidarity between generations and protection of the rights of the child.

    It shall promote economic, social and territorial cohesion, and solidarity among Member States.

    It shall respect its rich cultural and linguistic diversity, and shall ensure that Europe's cultural heritage is safeguarded and enhanced.
4. In its relations with the wider world, the Union shall uphold and promote its values and interests. It shall contribute to peace, security, the sustainable development of the Earth,

solidarity and mutual respect among peoples, free and fair trade, eradication of poverty and the protection of human rights, in particular the rights of the child, as well as to the strict observance and the development of international law, including respect for the principles of the United Nations Charter.

5. The Union shall pursue its objectives by appropriate means commensurate with the competences which are conferred upon it in the Constitution.

Fundamental freedoms and non-discrimination

Article I-4(2) would have replaced the non-discrimination provision in Art 12 EC Treaty, providing that 'Within the scope of the Constitution, and without prejudice to any of its specific provisions, any discrimination on grounds of nationality shall be prohibited'.

The Treaty would have established the free movement of persons, services, goods and capital, and the freedom of establishment, as fundamental rights, stating that 'they shall be guaranteed within and by the Union, in accordance with the Constitution' (Art I-4(1)).

Relations between the Union and the Member States

Article I-5(1) would have provided that the Union shall respect the 'equality of Member States before the Constitution' and shall also respect national identities. The Union would have also respected the essential State functions of each Member State, which included 'ensuring the territorial integrity of the State, maintaining law and order and safeguarding national security'.

Similar to Art 10 EC Treaty, Art I-5(2) would have provided that:

> Pursuant to the principle of sincere cooperation, the Union and the Member States shall, in full mutual respect, assist each other in carrying out tasks which flow from the Constitution.
>
> The Member States shall take any appropriate measure, general or particular, to ensure fulfilment of the obligations arising out of the Constitution or resulting from the acts of the institutions of the Union.
>
> The Member States shall facilitate the achievement of the Union's tasks and refrain from any measure which could jeopardise the attainment of the Union's objectives.

Supremacy of EU Law

Although supremacy of Community law was established in the 1960s by the Court of Justice (see Chapter 9), this principle has never been explicitly set out within a Treaty. However, Art I-6 would have provided that 'The Constitution and law adopted by the institutions of the Union in exercising competences conferred on it shall have primacy over the law of the Member States'.

Legal personality

Article I-7 would have provided that the Union shall have legal personality.

Symbols of the Union

Article I-8 would have provided for a flag, anthem, motto and currency. The anthem would have been based on the 'Ode to Joy' from Beethoven's Ninth Symphony. An annual 'Europe Day' would have been celebrated throughout the Union on 9 May.

Fundamental rights and citizenship of the Union

Article I-9(1) would have provided that the Union would recognise the rights, freedoms and principles which were set out in the Charter of Fundamental Rights (which formed Part II of the Constitutional Treaty). Article I-9(1) would have provided that the Union would accede to the European Convention on Human Rights, although it stated that 'such accession shall not affect the Union's competences as defined in the Constitution'. It would also have provided that the fundamental rights guaranteed by the Convention and which also resulted from the constitutional traditions common to the Member States 'shall constitute general principles of the Union's law'.

Article I-10 would have provided for European Citizenship, stating that EU citizens would enjoy the rights and be subject to the duties provided for in the Constitution. This provision would have been similar to Arts 17 and 18 EC Treaty, and would likewise have provided that 'These rights shall be exercised in accordance with the conditions and limits defined by the Constitution and by the measures adopted thereunder'.

European Union competences

Article I-11 would have provided that the limits of Union competences were governed by 'the principle of conferral', which meant that the Union would act 'within the limits of the competences conferred upon it ... in the Constitution'. The corollary of this, was that 'Competences not conferred upon the Union in the Constitution remain with the Member States'. The use of Union competences was also stated to be governed by 'the principles of subsidiarity and proportionality' (Art 1-11(1)). This provision would have been complemented by a Protocol on the application of these two principles, which would have provided for an 'early-warning system' involving national parliaments in monitoring how subsidiarity was applied. National parliaments would have been informed of all new legislative initiatives and if at least one-third of them considered that a proposal infringed the principle of subsidiarity, the Commission would have had to reconsider its proposal.

The Constitutional Treaty would have distinguished between three categories of Union powers:

- areas of exclusive competence (where the Constitution conferred on the Union exclusive competence in a specific area) – Arts I-12(1) and I-13;
- areas of shared competence (where the Constitution conferred on the Union a competence which was shared with the Member States in a specific area) – Arts I-12(2) and I-14; and
- areas where the Union could take supporting action (provided this conformed with the provisions of Part III relative to the area in which action was to be taken) – Arts I-12(5) and I-17.

Particular cases which did not fit into this threefold general classification would have been dealt with separately: for example, the coordination of economic and employment policies (Art I-15) and common foreign and security policy (Art I-16).

The flexibility which the system required was guaranteed by a 'flexibility clause' which would have allowed the adoption of measures necessary to attain any of the objectives laid down by the Constitution where there was no provision for powers of action to that effect in the Constitution (Art I-18). Its scope would therefore have been wider than that of the current Art 308 EC Treaty, which is confined to the internal market, but the conditions for its implementation would have been stricter in that, as well as requiring unanimity in the Council, Parliament's approval would also have been needed.

The Union's institutions and bodies

The institutional framework

Article I-19 would have provided that the Union shall have an 'institutional framework' comprising:

- the European Parliament
- the European Council
- the Council of Ministers (to be referred to as the 'Council')
- the European Commission (to be referred to as the 'Commission')
- the Court of Justice of the European Union.

It should be noted that for the first time the European Council would have been treated as a full institution in its own right.

Articles I-20 to I-29 would have clarified the role of these five institutions. Part III, Title VI Constitutional Treaty would have concerned the functioning of the Union. Chapter 1 (of Part III, Title VI) would have contained the detailed provisions governing the institutions:

> **Part III The Policies and Functioning of the Union (Arts III-115 to III-436)**
> **Title VI The Functioning of the Union (Arts III-330 to III-436)**
> *Chapter 1   Provisions Governing the Institutions (Arts III-330 to III-401)*
> Section 1   The Institutions (Arts III-330 to III-385)
> Section 2   The Union's Advisory Bodies (Arts III-386 to III-392)
> Section 3   The European Investment Bank (Arts III-393 to III-394)
> Section 4   Common Provisions (Arts III-395 to III-401)

Changes which would have affected the institutions are discussed briefly below. These changes are also considered in Chapters 3 to 5.

The European Parliament

The European Parliament would have had the power, jointly with the Council of Ministers, to enact legislation and exercise the budgetary function, as well as exercise functions of political control and consultation (Art I-20(1)). It would have elected the President of the European Commission on a proposal from the European Council (adopted by qualified majority), which would have had to take into account the results of the elections (Art I-27(1)). The Parliament would also have approved the Commission as a whole (Art I-27(2)). The number of MEPs would have been limited to 750 (Art I-20(2)). The Constitution did not make provision for the allocation of seats by Member State as is currently the case, but Art I-20(2) would have contained a legal base giving the European Council, on a proposal from Parliament and with its consent, the responsibility to have determined the allocation of seats before the elections scheduled for 2009, on the basis of the principle of 'degressively proportional' representation of citizens, with a minimum threshold of six seats and a maximum of 96 per Member State (the Convention had proposed a minimum threshold of four with no upper limit).

The European Council

The European Council would have become a full institution (Art I-19). The revolving presidency would have been abolished and replaced by a permanent presidency with limited powers, elected by a qualified majority of its members for a renewable term of two and a half years (Art I-22(1)). The general rule regarding the adoption of decisions would have been consensus (Art I-22(4)). The European Council would have provided impetus and defined political priorities but would not have exercised a legislative function (Art I-21(1)). Respect for this principle was ensured during the negotiations in the IGC, despite an extremely difficult debate on the role of the European Council in the field of judicial cooperation in criminal matters (compare this with the description of the compromise found on the definition of the 'emergency brake' mechanism, see below).

The Council of Ministers

Article I-24(3) would have provided for the creation of a Foreign Affairs Council chaired by the EU Minister for Foreign Affairs (see below), separate from the General Affairs Council. The latter would have continued to ensure the coherence of the Council's deliberations with the aid of COREPER. The meetings of special formations of the Council would have been split into two parts, one devoted to legislative deliberations, the other to non-legislative deliberations. In order to meet the requirement of transparency, Art I-24(6) would have provided that legislative deliberations would be held in public.

The organisation of the Council's work was fiercely debated in the IGC until an advanced stage, with a majority of the Member States in favour of maintaining the rotation of the Council presidency (except for the Foreign Affairs Council). Finally, the Constitution stated the principle of equal rotation in the context of a system of 'team' presidency which would have been defined by a European Council decision (Art I-24(7)).

Qualified majority

Qualified majority was one of the key issues which resurfaced throughout the debates in the Convention and the IGC, with regard to both its definition and its sphere of application.

With regard to its definition, the formula finally adopted by the IGC was based on the double majority principle devised by the Convention (based upon the number of Member States and the population). Article I-25 would have provided that this double majority principle would have required two thresholds to be achieved before a measure could be adopted: the first would have required the support of at least 55 per cent of the Member States (the Convention had proposed a majority of the Member States) comprising at least fifteen of them; the second would have required the support of Member States which comprised at least 65 per cent of the population (the Convention had proposed 60 per cent). The IGC added an extra clause specifying that a blocking minority (*a priori* 35 per cent of the population) would have to include at least four Member States, failing which a decision would in any case be considered to have been adopted (Art I-25(1)). This could have had the effect of lowering the population threshold and have allowed, for example, the adoption of a law by 22 Member States representing only around 55.5 per cent. This system would have applied from 1 November 2009. In order to overcome the remaining reluctance of certain Member States, the Conference also adopted a decision containing a revised 'Ioannina' compromise (see Chapter 4). If Council members representing at least three-quarters of the Member States or the percentage of the population required to block a decision indicated their opposition to the

Council's adoption of an act by qualified majority, the Council would have continued to debate the proposed act in order to achieve broader agreement within a reasonable period of time.

When a Commission proposal is not required or when a decision is not adopted on the initiative of the Minister for Foreign Affairs, Art I-25(2) would have provided that the qualified majority required would be enhanced: 72 per cent of the Member States (two-thirds was proposed by the Convention) representing at least 65 per cent of the population (60 per cent was proposed by the Convention).

Qualified majority would have become the general rule for the adoption of decisions within the Council of Ministers (Art I-23(3)). Unanimity would have remained the rule for taxation and partly in the fields of foreign and common security policy and social policy. Furthermore, it would also have applied to the system of own resources and the multiannual financial framework. Finally, for cases in which the Convention failed to achieve consensus on changing over to qualified majority voting, Art IV-444 would have introduced a general measure (known in French as a 'passerelle'), whereby the European Council would have had the opportunity to decide unanimously that the Council would in future act by qualified majority and, if necessary, according to the ordinary legislative procedure, without the need to amend the Constitution, which would in turn have required ratification by each Member State. The formal opposition of a single national parliament would have been enough to block the application of the 'passerelle' (Art IV-444(3)).

The Union Minister for Foreign Affairs

An institutional innovation proposed by the Convention, Art I-28, would have provided that the Union Minister for Foreign Affairs, appointed by the European Council by qualified majority with the agreement of the President of the Commission, would conduct the Union's common foreign and security policy, chair the Foreign Affairs Council and serve as Vice-President of the Commission (as such he would have been subject to a collective vote of approval by the European Parliament and, possibly, a vote of censure). In this 'two-hatted' role (Commission-Council), he would have been responsible for carrying out the Union's external policy as a whole (Art III-296). He would have had the power of proposal (Art III-299(1)), to represent the Union alone or with the Commission, and would have been aided by a European External Action Service (Art III-296(3)). The Service would consist of officials from the relevant departments of the Council's Secretariat and the Commission, as well as staff seconded from national diplomatic services. Its organisation and operation would be determined by a Council decision after obtaining the opinion of the Parliament and the approval of the Commission (Art III-296).

The European Commission

The Commission's power of legislative initiative would have been clearly restated (Art I-26(2)). However, the IGC did not take up the Convention's proposal regarding its composition. The final agreement reached meant that the Commission would have been made up of one Commissioner per Member State until 2014 (Art I-26(5)). From then on it would have consisted of a number of Members corresponding to two-thirds the number of Member States, chosen on the basis of equal rotation between the Member States (Art I-26(6)).

The political role of the President of the Commission, elected by the European Parliament (Art I-27(1)), would have been reinforced, and would have included the appointment of Commissioners (Art I-27(2)), the allocation of portfolios (Art III-350) and the right to request the resignation of a Commissioner (Art I-27(3)).

The Court of Justice

The Court of Justice's competence would have been broadened, particularly in the area of freedom, security and justice and certain aspects of foreign policy (see below). There would also have been provision for a degree of individual access to the Court (Art III-365).

The other institutions and advisory bodies

Articles I-30 to I-32 would have set out the Union's other institutions (the European Central Bank and the Court of Auditors) and advisory bodies (the Committee of the Regions and the Economic and Social Committee). These articles would also have clarified the role of these two institutions and two advisory bodies.

Exercise of Union competence

The Union's competences were dealt with above. Articles I-33 to I-44 would have clarified how these competences would be exercised.

Legal acts of the Union

Article I-33 would have replaced Art 249 EC Treaty (see Chapter 2). Article I-33 would have provided that:

1. To exercise the Union's competences the institutions shall use as legal instruments, in accordance with Part III, European laws, European framework laws, European regulations, European decisions, recommendations and opinions.

   A **European law** shall be a legislative act of general application. It shall be binding in its entirety and directly applicable in all Member States.

   A **European framework law** shall be a legislative act binding, as to the result to be achieved, upon each Member State to which it is addressed, but shall leave to the national authorities the choice of form and methods.

   A **European regulation** shall be a non-legislative act of general application for the implementation of legislative acts and of certain provisions of the Constitution. It may either be binding in its entirety and directly applicable in all Member States, or be binding, as to the result to be achieved, upon each Member State to which it is addressed, but shall leave to the national authorities the choice of form and methods.

   A **European decision** shall be a non-legislative act, binding in its entirety. A decision which specifies those to whom it is addressed shall be binding only on them.

   Recommendations and **opinions** shall have no binding force.
2. When considering draft legislative acts, the European Parliament and the Council shall refrain from adopting acts not provided for by the relevant legislative procedure in the area in question. [emphasis added]

This Article would have provided that the following instruments would have been used by the European Union:

- European law – equivalent to the current regulation;
- European framework law – equivalent to the current directive;
- European decision – equivalent to the current decision;

- European regulation – a non-legislative act of general application for the implementation of legislative acts; a completely new act;
- Recommendations and opinions – equivalent to the current recommendations and opinions.

The Constitution would work on the basis of a hierarchy of acts, clarifying the legal acts used by the institutions to put the Union's powers into practice and how they were adopted. It made two successive distinctions:

- between legally binding acts (laws, framework laws, regulations and decisions) and non-binding acts (opinions and recommendations);
- in terms of legally binding acts, it would have distinguished between legislative acts (laws and framework laws) and non-legislative acts (regulations and decisions).

Legislative acts

The power of legislative initiative would have rested with the Commission (Art I-26(2)), although this would have been shared with at least a quarter of Member States as regards certain aspects of the area of freedom, security and justice (Art III-264).

The Constitution stated that, as a general rule, laws and framework laws would have been adopted by co-decision of the Parliament and the Council, the latter with a qualified majority, through a procedure which would have been known as the 'ordinary legislative procedure', which was practically a carbon copy of the current co-decision procedure (Art I-34(1)); see Chapter 4.

Non-legislative acts

As far as implementing acts in the strict sense of the term are concerned, the Constitution would have stated from the outset that it was the responsibility of Member States to implement legally binding acts of the European institutions (Art I-37(1)). Where uniform conditions for implementing acts were required, Art I-37(2) would have given the Commission the power to take the necessary implementing measures, or, exceptionally, have given this power to the Council (in cases involving implementing acts based directly on the Constitution, apart from the common foreign and security policy). As regards 'commitology', a European law would have laid down in advance the rules and general principles for the mechanisms for control by Member States of these implementing acts (Art I-37(3)). The Parliament would therefore have had a decisive role in this area in future.

Article I-36 would also have created *delegated regulations*, delegated to the Commission by the legislative authority; that is, the Parliament and the Council. These delegated regulations, which could have amended or supplemented certain aspects of laws or framework laws without changing their essential elements, would therefore have required specific authorisation in the text on which they were based and would have been subject to a specific system of control exercised by the co-legislators. Each of the two branches could have revoked the delegation, and the delegated regulation could only have entered into force if neither branch of the legislative authority had raised an objection within a period set by the law or framework law. There would have been no provision for delegated Council regulations.

Specific provisions relating to the common foreign and security policy

Article I-40 would have provided that:

1. The European Union shall conduct a common foreign and security policy, based on the development of mutual political solidarity among Member States, the identification of questions of general interest and the achievement of an ever-increasing degree of convergence of Member States' actions.
2. The European Council shall identify the Union's strategic interests and determine the objectives of its common foreign and security policy. The Council shall frame this policy within the framework of the strategic guidelines established by the European Council and in accordance with Part III.
3. The European Council and the Council shall adopt the necessary European decisions.
4. The common foreign and security policy shall be put into effect by the Union Minister for Foreign Affairs and by the Member States, using national and Union resources.
5. Member States shall consult one another within the European Council and the Council on any foreign and security policy issue which is of general interest in order to determine a common approach. Before undertaking any action on the international scene or any commitment which could affect the Union's interests, each Member State shall consult the others within the European Council or the Council. Member States shall ensure, through the convergence of their actions, that the Union is able to assert its interests and values on the international scene. Member States shall show mutual solidarity.
6. European decisions relating to the common foreign and security policy shall be adopted by the European Council and the Council unanimously, except in the cases referred to in Part III. The European Council and the Council shall act on an initiative from a Member State, on a proposal from the Union Minister for Foreign Affairs or on a proposal from that Minister with the Commission's support. European laws and framework laws shall be excluded.
7. The European Council may, unanimously, adopt a European decision authorising the Council to act by a qualified majority in cases other than those referred to in Part III.
8. The European Parliament shall be regularly consulted on the main aspects and basic choices of the common foreign and security policy. It shall be kept informed of how it evolves.

Specific provisions relating to the common security and defence policy

Article I-41 would have provided that:

1. The common security and defence policy shall be an integral part of the common foreign and security policy. It shall provide the Union with an operational capacity drawing on civil and military assets. The Union may use them on missions outside the Union for peace-keeping, conflict prevention and strengthening international security in accordance with the principles of the United Nations Charter. The performance of these tasks shall be undertaken using capabilities provided by the Member States.
2. The common security and defence policy shall include the progressive framing of a common Union defence policy. This will lead to a common defence, when the European Council, acting unanimously, so decides. It shall in that case recommend to the Member States the adoption of such a decision in accordance with their respective constitutional requirements.

   The policy of the Union in accordance with this Article shall not prejudice the specific character of the security and defence policy of certain Member States, it shall respect the obligations of certain Member States, which see their common defence realised in the

North Atlantic Treaty Organisation, under the North Atlantic Treaty, and be compatible with the common security and defence policy established within that framework.

3. Member States shall make civilian and military capabilities available to the Union for the implementation of the common security and defence policy, to contribute to the objectives defined by the Council. Those Member States which together establish multinational forces may also make them available to the common security and defence policy.

   Member States shall undertake progressively to improve their military capabilities. An Agency in the field of defence capabilities development, research, acquisition and armaments (European Defence Agency) shall be established to identify operational requirements, to promote measures to satisfy those requirements, to contribute to identifying and, where appropriate, implementing any measure needed to strengthen the industrial and technological base of the defence sector, to participate in defining a European capabilities and armaments policy, and to assist the Council in evaluating the improvement of military capabilities.

4. European decisions relating to the common security and defence policy, including those initiating a mission as referred to in this Article, shall be adopted by the Council acting unanimously on a proposal from the Union Minister for Foreign Affairs or an initiative from a Member State. The Union Minister for Foreign Affairs may propose the use of both national resources and Union instruments, together with the Commission where appropriate.

5. The Council may entrust the execution of a task, within the Union framework, to a group of Member States in order to protect the Union's values and serve its interests. The execution of such a task shall be governed by Article III-310.

6. Those Member States whose military capabilities fulfil higher criteria and which have made more binding commitments to one another in this area with a view to the most demanding missions shall establish permanent structured cooperation within the Union framework. Such cooperation shall be governed by Article III-312. It shall not affect the provisions of Article III-309.

7. If a Member State is the victim of armed aggression on its territory, the other Member States shall have towards it an obligation of aid and assistance by all the means in their power, in accordance with Article 51 of the United Nations Charter. This shall not prejudice the specific character of the security and defence policy of certain Member States. Commitments and cooperation in this area shall be consistent with commitments under the North Atlantic Treaty Organisation, which, for those States which are members of it, remains the foundation of their collective defence and the forum for its implementation.

8. The European Parliament shall be regularly consulted on the main aspects and basic choices of the common security and defence policy. It shall be kept informed of how it evolves.

Specific provisions relating to the area of freedom, security and justice

Article I-42 would have provided that:

1. The Union shall constitute an area of freedom, security and justice:
   (a) by adopting European laws and framework laws intended, where necessary, to approximate laws and regulations of the Member States in the areas referred to in Part III;
   (b) by promoting mutual confidence between the competent authorities of the Member States, in particular on the basis of mutual recognition of judicial and extrajudicial decisions;
   (c) including the police, customs and other services specialising in the prevention and detection of criminal offences.

2. National Parliaments may, within the framework of the area of freedom, security and justice, participate in the evaluation mechanisms provided for in Article III-260. They shall be involved in the political monitoring of Europol and the evaluation of Eurojust's activities in accordance with Articles III-276 and III-273.

3. Member States shall have a right of initiative in the field of police and judicial cooperation in criminal matters, in accordance with Article III-264.

Solidarity clause

Article I-43 would have provided that:

1. The Union and its Member States shall act jointly in a spirit of solidarity if a Member State is the object of a terrorist attack or the victim of a natural or man-made disaster. The Union shall mobilise all the instruments at its disposal, including the military resources made available by the Member States, to:

   (a) – prevent the terrorist threat in the territory of the Member States;

   – protect democratic institutions and the civilian population from any terrorist attack;

   – assist a Member State in its territory, at the request of its political authorities, in the event of a terrorist attack;

   (b) assist a Member State in its territory, at the request of its political authorities, in the event of a natural or man-made disaster.

2. The detailed arrangements for implementing this Article are set out in Article III-329.

Enhanced cooperation

Article I-44 would have provided for a system of 'enhanced cooperation'. This would have replaced Art 11 EC Treaty (see below). The detailed provisions for enhanced cooperation would have been set out within Arts III-416 to III-423.

Enhanced cooperation would have required the involvement of a third of the Member States. It would have only applied to the Union's non-exclusive competences (but could also have covered defence policy). Authorisation to proceed with enhanced cooperation would have been granted by the Council by a qualified majority, after obtaining the consent of the European Parliament, on a proposal from the Commission (except with regard to the common foreign and security policy, where it would have required the opinion of the Union Minister for Foreign Affairs and of the Commission, in which case the European Parliament would simply have been informed). Member States not participating in enhanced cooperation would have taken part in Council meetings even though they would not have been involved in the decision-making.

As a result of efforts made by a number of delegations and the European Parliament representatives in particular, the Conference also adopted a 'passerelle' provision, which was proposed by the Convention but was called into question during the negotiations. This provision would have enabled the Member States taking part in enhanced cooperation to change over to qualified-majority voting or the ordinary legislative procedure by virtue of a decision adopted unanimously by these Member States. However, this passerelle clause could not have been used in the field of defence.

The democratic life of the Union

Articles I-45 to I-52 would have set out a number of provisions relating to the democratic life of the European Union, which would have included:

- the principle of democratic equality (Art I-45);
- the principle of representative democracy (Art I-46);
- the principle of participatory democracy (Art I-47);
- the social partners and autonomous social dialogue (Art I-48);
- the European Ombudsman (Art I-49);
- transparency of proceedings of Union institutions, bodies, offices and agencies (Art I-50);
- protection of personal data (Art I-51);
- status of churches and non-confessional organisations (Art I-52).

The Union's finances

The finances of the European Union would have been dealt with by Arts I-53 to I-56.

The Union and its neighbours

Article I-57 would have provided that the Union would have developed a 'special relationship with neighbouring countries', the aim of which would have been to establish 'an area of prosperity and good friendliness, founded on the values of the Union and characterised by close and peaceful relations based on cooperation'. The Union would have been empowered to conclude specific agreements with the countries concerned, in order to have achieved this special relationship.

Union membership

Article I-58 would have set out the conditions of eligibility and the procedure for accession to the Union. The Council would have acted unanimously after consulting the Commission and after having obtained the consent of the European Parliament, which would act by a majority of its component members.

Article I-59 would have provided for the suspension of certain rights resulting from Union membership, along similar grounds to those contained in Art 7 TEU, although the provision in the Constitutional Treaty would have been more comprehensive.

Article I-60 would have provided, for the first time, the procedure for a Member State's voluntary withdrawal from the Union.

Policies

Part III of the Constitutional Treaty would have opened with a number of articles of general application, devoted to the Union's policies on: general consistency of policy (Art III-115); the promotion of equality between men and women (Art III-116); social protection (Art III-117); the fight against discrimination (Art III-118); the requirements of environmental protection (Art III-119); consumer protection (Art III-120); and animal welfare (Art III-121). The final article of Part III would have acknowledged the existence of 'services of general economic interest' whose 'principles and conditions' of operation must be defined by law (Art III-122).

External policies: external action

It is in the area of external action that the Constitutional Treaty would have made the most radical changes, more by means of institutional modifications, notably in the creation of the post of Union Minister for Foreign Affairs (see above), than by improvement of procedures, which would have remained practically unchanged. The role of the European Parliament in foreign policy would not have changed fundamentally, although it would have played a more prominent role in common commercial policy and the conclusion of international agreements.

Common foreign and security policy

The implementation of the common foreign and security policy – by unanimous European Council or Council decision, except in certain cases provided for by the Constitution or where the European Council decided otherwise – would not have been subject to the 'ordinary legislative procedure' (see above). The Parliament would have been consulted as a matter of course.

Some new legal bases would have been created (see above): a solidarity clause between Member States in the event of a terrorist attack or natural disaster (Art I-43), and international agreements with neighbouring countries (Arts III-323 to III-326). Security policy (Arts III-294 to III-312) would have been modernised in a number of areas (since the IGC approved some important advances not envisaged by the Convention), in particular in the area of defence:

- updating the Petersburg tasks (addition of a reference to tasks involving disarmament, military advice, post-conflict stabilisation and the fight against terrorism, including actions carried out on the territory of third countries);

- creation of new forms of flexibility and cooperation in defence matters;

- the possibility for the Council to entrust a group of Member States with a mission to uphold the Union's values;

- the possibility of creating, by a Council decision adopted by a qualified majority, a permanent structure for cooperation between the countries that meet the criteria and subscribe to the commitments with regard to military capability contained in a Protocol annexed to the Constitution;

- the introduction of closer cooperation in the sphere of reciprocal defence, envisaging in particular the obligation to aid and assist a Member State subjected to armed aggression on its own territory (without prejudice to the specific nature of the security and defence policy of certain Member States);

- the creation of a start-up fund for military defence independent of the Union budget;

- the creation of a European Armaments, Research and Military Capabilities Agency;

- defining a procedure to allow rapid access to appropriations in the Union budget.

Humanitarian aid

Article III-321 would have created a specific legal base for humanitarian aid, which would have included the creation of a Voluntary Humanitarian Aid Corps (using the ordinary legislative procedure).

Internal policies

Area of freedom, security and justice

Of all the policies referred to as internal policies, it was in the area of freedom, security and justice that the Constitution would have made most changes to the status quo, not least as a result of the removal of the distinction between measures covered by the EC Treaty and those covered by the 'third pillar', and the general application of co-decision (ordinary legislative procedure) and qualified majority voting (see above).

The Union's political objectives would have been clarified: the Union's actions would have been explicitly subordinate to fundamental rights (Art III-257(1)); access to justice would have been a general objective (Art III-257(4)); the challenges posed by mutual recognition of different systems and approximation of legislation would have been brought together (Art III-257(3) and (4)).

Policy-making would have been deepened: asylum and immigration policy would have been made common Union policy governed by the principles of solidarity and fair sharing of responsibility between Member States (Art III-257(2)).

But it is with regard to the measures relating to judicial cooperation in criminal matters that the most innovative changes were to be found, above all because they would have broadly been subject to qualified majority voting. The Constitution would have called for thorough approximation of criminal legislation (descriptions of criminal offences and punishments), partly in order to fight against crimes 'of European interest', of which a list was given, and partly to have ensured the implementation of Union legislation (Art III-270).

This legislation would have had to take into account the differences between legal traditions and the (judicial) systems of the Member States. Furthermore, in order to allay the fears of certain Member States, Art III-270(3) and (4) and Art III-271(3) and (4) would have provided a special 'emergency brake' procedure. If a Member State considered that a legislative proposal in this area may jeopardise fundamental aspects of its criminal justice system, it could have requested that the matter be referred back to the European Council and the procedure would have been suspended. The European Council would then have had to, within a period of four months, refer the matter back to the Council, so that the procedure could have continued, or requested that a new legislative proposal be submitted by the Commission or the group of Member States that had taken the initiative. If the European Council had not taken the aforementioned decision within four months, or if the new legislative procedure initiated at its request had not produced a result within a twelve-month deadline, enhanced cooperation would automatically have been initiated, provided at least one-third of the Member States had so wished.

The Court of Justice would have had a general role in monitoring the Union's activities in this area. However, Art III-377 would have provided that:

> In exercising its powers regarding the provisions of Sections 4 [judicial cooperation in criminal matters] and 5 [police cooperation] of Chapter IV of Title III relating to the area of freedom, security and justice, the Court of Justice of the European Union shall have no jurisdiction to review the validity or proportionality of operations carried out by the police or other law-enforcement services of a Member State or the exercise of the responsibilities incumbent upon Member States with regard to the maintenance of law and order and the safeguarding of internal security.

Some specific institutional characteristics would have remained, however, including: the definition by the European Council (and therefore by consensus) of strategic guidelines for legislative and operational planning, without European Parliament involvement (Art III-258); sharing of the legislative initiative between the Commission and a quarter of the Member States (one Member State would no longer have been able to submit a proposal on its own) in the area of judicial cooperation in criminal matters and police cooperation (Art III-264); unanimity would have been retained in certain areas, particularly as regards cross-border aspects of family law (Art III-269(3)) and all forms of police cooperation (Art III-275(3)); definition of a more prominent role for national parliaments, with particular regard to monitoring whether the principle of subsidiarity was being respected (Art III-259). However, the possibility of subsequent developments would have been left open by transitional ('passerelle') measures regarding family law (Art III-269(3)) and the list of serious crimes for which a European framework law could have laid down minimum rules (Art III-271(1)). The Council, acting unanimously following consent by the Parliament, could have expanded the list of crimes (Art III-271(1)).

Finally, and despite keen opposition from a number of delegations, the Constitution envisaged the creation, by means of a European law adopted unanimously by the Council, of a European Public Prosecutor's Office, which would have been competent to combat offences against the Union's financial interests and could have prosecuted those responsible for such infringements (Art III-274). Article III-274(4) would have incorporated a 'passerelle' clause to provide for the possibility of extending the remit of the European Public Prosecutor's Office to combating serious crime with a cross-border dimension, by means of a European decision adopted unanimously by the Council, following consent by the European Parliament (and after having consulted the Commission).

A two-speed Europe?

The idea of a 'two-speed Europe' was much canvassed before the Amsterdam Intergovernmental Conference. This would mean that those states who were keen to embrace closer political and economic cooperation would be free to do so, while the other more reluctant states could follow at their own pace. To some extent, this had already happened in relation to Economic and Monetary Union, with the UK, Denmark and Sweden negotiating opt-outs (see above).

The ToA went some way to giving formal recognition to this kind of 'variable geometry'. Under the new Art 11 EC Treaty, the Council of Ministers could authorise 'closer cooperation' between Member States. The Council would act on a proposal from the Commission. The use of Art 11 is, however, strictly limited and closer cooperation between Member States cannot be undertaken if the area in question is already part of the Community's exclusive competence – i.e. if it affects Community policies, actions or programmes; if it would lead to discrimination between nationals of Member States; or if it would restrict trade between Member States. It has proven to be the case, given these limitations, that no use has been made of this new provision. It was always thought unlikely that the Commission would want to initiate a process of separate development. This will arguably remain the case following the amendments made by the ToN (see above).

There are two main reasons for this. First, a European Union in which there are different rules between the 'outer' and 'inner' areas will be extremely difficult to operate in practice. The Commission would not be in favour of having a body of rules operating in different parts of the Union. Second, any further development of an inner 'core' of

Member States moving towards greater integration will tend to accentuate what is already a tendency in the Union: the already serious drift of commerce and industry towards the geographical centre of Western Europe. If Germany, with its usually strong economy and having the largest market of all the Member States, is in the 'inner circle', businesses may tend to re-establish themselves nearer to the heart of Europe. Businesses from outside the Union seeking to jump over the Community's external tariff wall may tend to look to the centre rather than to states on the periphery for new locations. For both these reasons, the Commission is likely to resist any further measures which may make the integration of European markets more difficult rather than less difficult, which is likely to be the case if any body of rules is adopted which applies only in part of the Union.

The European Economic Area

The remaining European Free Trade Association (EFTA) states continued to work together as a free-trade area after the departure of Ireland, Denmark and the UK in 1973 (see above). On 2 May 1992 the then seven EFTA states, and the EC and its Member States, signed an agreement to establish the European Economic Area (EEA). The EEA, which some initially saw as an alternative to full membership of the European Communities, was intended to integrate the EFTA states *economically* into the Community without giving them a role in its institutions. The EEA gave the EFTA states access for their goods, services, workers and capital to the markets of the Community. Equally, the same facilities were granted by EFTA states in their territories to Member States of the Community. Only Switzerland refused to participate in the EEA, after a hostile national referendum. In this new trading area, all the rules of the EC apply, although the Member States of EFTA are not represented in any of the EC institutions and do not participate in the EC's decision-making process. There are, however, four new bodies to coordinate the functioning of this new trading area:

- the EEA Council;
- Joint Committee;
- Joint Parliamentary Committee; and
- Consultative Committee.

The EEA came into effect on 1 January 1994. On 1 January 1995, three of the remaining EFTA members became full members of the EU, so that the EEA states now comprise the existing 27 EU Member States together with Iceland, Liechtenstein and Norway.

The Council of Europe, The European Convention on Human Rights and the European Court of Human Rights: a structure outside the Communities and the Union

It is important to distinguish the international structure created by the European Convention on Human Rights (ECHR) from the quite separate supranational institutions of the EC. Newspapers talk loosely about taking a case 'to Europe', without identifying whether or not the case is a human rights matter involving the ECHR and to be dealt with by the European Court of Human Rights in Strasbourg, or a matter of Community law to be referred to the Court of Justice in Luxembourg. Decisions made by the European Court of Human Rights are not legally binding on national courts, although they will be taken into account by these courts. Decisions by the Court of Justice are legally binding on all national courts.

The ECHR was drafted in 1950 under the auspices of the Council of Europe, an international organisation composed of 21 Western European states. It is intended to uphold common political traditions of individual civil liberties and the rule of law. All the Member States of the EU are members. Although the ECHR became part of English law on 2 October 2000 under the Human Rights Act 1998, it does *not* automatically prevail where there is a clear conflict, whereas, as discussed in Chapter 9, under some circumstances Community obligations *are* part of national law *and* prevail over it in the event of conflict.

Decisions of the European Court of Human Rights may result in compensation being paid by the UK government to victims of human rights abuses, but such decisions are not binding on the government, and could (in legal theory) be ignored. The Court of Justice, like national courts, takes account of the ECHR when interpreting Community law. Unlike national courts, however, the Court of Justice treats the ECHR as a source of basic Community law principles (see Chapter 5). The ECHR has been formally accepted in the TEU as part of the Community's fundamental principles, but it has no application under Community law to matters outside the Community's legal competence. Although the ECHR is recognised by the ToA as an important source of Community law, it remains the case that it is only important when interpreting and applying *Community* law. This would have remained the case if the Constitutional Treaty had come into force (see above). However, although the ECHR has only a limited application to Community law, the decision by the UK to incorporate it into UK law by the Human Rights Act 1998 means that it will be unlawful for courts or tribunals and any person whose functions are of a public nature in the UK, to act in a way which is incompatible with it. Unlike the position of Community law which has immediate primacy, if there is a clear conflict between a UK statute and one of the articles of the ECHR, the UK courts will only be able to make a 'declaration of incompatibility'. Ministers will then have to ensure that the offending legislation is amended to give full effect to the ECHR.

Summary

Now you have read this chapter you should be able to:

- Outline the aims and objectives of the European Communities.
- Explain how and why the European Communities came into existence.
- Understand how membership of the European Communities and Union has evolved to accommodate 27 Member States.
- Evaluate the impact the following Treaties have had on the founding Treaties and the composition, role and function of the European Communities and Union:
  – Single European Act;
  – Treaty of European Union;

– Treaty of Amsterdam; and

– Treaty of Nice.

- Assess the impact which the proposed Constitutional Treaty would have had on the European Communities and Union if it had been ratified, and evaluate the current status of this Treaty.

- Identify possible future developments in EU Constitutional Reform.

- Understand the nature of the European Free Trade Association and the European Economic Area in terms of their membership, reason for existence, role and relevance.

- Explain the legal status of the European Convention on Human Rights and the European Court of Human Rights, in the context of Community law.

References

Hobsbawm, E. (1994) *Age of Extremes: The Short Twentieth Century*, Michael Joseph, Chapters 2, 3 and 8.

Further reading

Text books

Craig, P. and De Burca, G. (2003) *EU Law Text, Cases and Materials* (3rd edn), Oxford University Press, Chapter 1.

Foster, N. (2006) *Foster on EU Law* (1st edn), Oxford University Press, Chapters 1 and 4 (Sections 4.3 and 4.5).

Hobsbawm, E. (1994) *Age of Extremes: The Short Twentieth Century*, Michael Joseph, Chapters 2, 3 and 8.

Inglis, K. and Ott, A. (2005) *The Constitution for Europe and an Enlarging Union: Unity in Diversity* (1st edn), Europa Law Publishing.

Piris, J. (2006) *The Constitution for Europe: A Legal Analysis* (1st edn), Cambridge University Press.

Steiner, J., Woods, L. and Twigg-Flesner, C. (2006) *EU Law* (9th edn), Oxford University Press, Chapter 1.

Storey, T. and Turner C. (2005) *Unlocking EU Law* (1st edn), Hodder Arnold, Chapters 1 and 2.

Tillotson, J. and Foster N. (2003) *Text, Cases and Materials on EU Law* (4th edn), Cavendish Publishing, Chapters 1 and 2.

Wallace, H., Wallace, W. and Pollack, M.A. (2005) *Policy Making in the European Union* (5th edn), Chapters 1, 2, 16, 17 and 18.

Weatherill, S. (2006) *Cases and Materials on EU Law* (7th edn), Oxford University Press, Chapter 1.

Weigall, D. and Stirk, A. (eds) (1992) *The Origins and Development of the European Community*, Leicester University Press.

Journal articles

Bradley, K., 'Institutional Design in the Treaty of Nice' (2001) 38 CML Rev 1095.

Cremona, M., 'EU enlargement: Solidarity and conditionality' (2005) 30 EL Rev 3.

Davies, G., 'Subsidiarity: The wrong idea, in the wrong place at the wrong time' (2006) 43 CML Rev 63.

Dehousse, R., 'European Institutional Architecture after Amsterdam' (1998) 35 CML Rev 595.

Dyèvre, A., 'The constitutionalisation of the European Union: Discourse, present, future and facts' (2005) 30 EL Rev 165.

Georgopoulos, T., 'What kind of treaty-making power for the EU?' (2005) 30 EL Rev 190.

Halberstam, D., 'The bride of Messina: Constitutionalism and democracy in Europe' (2005) 30 EL Rev 775.

Joerges, C., 'What is left of the European Economic Constitution? A melancholic eulogy' (2005) 30 EL Rev 461.

Meyring, B., 'Intergovernmentalism and Supranationality: Two Stereotypes for a Complex Reality' (1997) 22 EL Rev 221.

Peers, S., 'Taking Supremacy Seriously' (1998) 23 EL Rev 146.

Szyszczak, E., 'Making Europe more Relevant to its Citizens' (1996) 21 EL Rev 351.

Usher, J.A., 'Variable Geometry or Concentric Circles: Patterns for the European Union' (1996) 46 ICLQ 243.

van Bogdandy, A., 'The prospect of a European republic: What European citizens are voting on' (2005) 42 CML Rev 913.

Verhoeven, A., 'How Democratic Need European Union Members Be?' (1998) 23 EL Rev 217.

Wouters, J., 'Institutional and Constitutional Challenges for the European Union: Some Reflections in the Light of the Treaty of Nice' (2001) 26 EL Rev 342.

Yataganas, X., 'The Treaty of Nice: The Sharing of Power and the Institutional Balance in the European Union - A Continental Perspective' (2001) ELJ 242.

2 Sources of Community law

Aims and objectives

At the end of this chapter you should understand the nature and scope of the following sources of Community law:

- The Treaties establishing the European Communities and the European Union.
- Secondary legislation made under the Treaties.
- 'Soft law' comprising non-legally enforceable instruments, which may aid the interpretation and/or application of Community law.
- Related Treaties made between the Member States.
- International Treaties negotiated by the Community under powers conferred on it by the Treaties.
- Decisions of the European Court of Justice and the Court of First Instance.
- General principles of law and fundamental rights upon which the constitutional laws of the Member States are based.

You should additionally have an appreciation of the changes which would have been introduced by the Constitutional Treaty if it had come into force.

The sources of Community law

There are seven principal sources of Community law:

- The Treaties establishing the European Communities and the European Union.
- Secondary legislation made under the Treaties.
- 'Soft law' (i.e. non-legally enforceable instruments which may aid the interpretation and/or application of Community law).
- Related Treaties made between the Member States.
- International Treaties negotiated by the Community under powers conferred on it by the Treaties.
- Decisions of the European Court of Justice and the Court of First Instance (CFI).
- General principles of law and fundamental rights upon which the constitutional laws of the Member States are based.

The Treaties establishing the European Communities and the European Union

The three founding Treaties (EC, ECSC and Euratom), as amended principally by the SEA, TEU, ToA and ToN, together with the TEU which established the European Union, form the 'constitution' of the European Communities and the Union and are therefore an important source of Community law. The ECSC (one of the three founding Treaties) has now expired. The EC Treaty is the most extensive of the three founding Treaties and will be considered further. Although the EC Treaty does not purport to create the constitution of a federal state, it does, in some respects, have that effect, and has been interpreted in that way by the Court of Justice:

Opinion 1/91 on the Draft Agreement between the EEC [renamed EC by the TEU] and EFTA [the European Free Trade Association (see Chapter 1)] [1991] ECR 6079

The Court of Justice stated that:

> The EEC Treaty [renamed the EC Treaty by the TEU], albeit concluded in the form of an international agreement, nonetheless constitutes the constitutional charter of a Community based on the rule of law. As the Court of Justice has consistently held, the Community Treaties established a new legal order for the benefit of which the States had limited their sovereign rights, in ever wider fields, and the subjects of which comprised not only the Member States but also their nationals.
>
> The essential characteristics of the Community legal order which had thus been established were, in particular, its primacy over the law of Member States and the direct effect of a whole series of provisions which were applicable to their nationals and to the Member States themselves.

Although fulfilling many of the functions of a constitution for the Community, the EC Treaty still falls far short of creating a federal state, and even though Community law prevails in Member States, the Community depends on the courts and the enforcement agencies of the Member States to implement it. There is no Community police or military force, and defence and foreign policy remains in the hands of national governments; although important steps were taken in the TEU, ToA and ToN to coordinate action in those areas, as well as in the area of drugs enforcement, illegal immigration and justice and home affairs. These areas are, ultimately, still a matter of national policy over which Member States retain final control in their territories. In a federal state, defence and foreign policy would be the sole prerogative of the central, federal government. The Community is, therefore, at the most, only an embryonic federal state.

The Treaty most nearly resembles a constitution in the way in which it defines the competence of the Community itself, and each of its constituent parts and, to a lesser extent, the rights of its citizens. Although the Treaty does not contain a complete catalogue of citizens' rights, it does confer a number of rights which can be enforced directly in the national courts. Ultimately, the Court of Justice acts as guarantor of those rights and has, in fact, quite consciously used the doctrine of direct enforcement to empower citizens in their own courts and, if need be, against their own governments. A whole range of Treaty provisions have been held to create directly enforceable rights, among them the right not to be discriminated against on grounds of nationality (Art 12 EC Treaty); the right to equal pay for work of equal value, regardless of gender (Art 141); the right to seek work and remain as a worker in another Member State (Art 39); the right to receive and provide services (Art 49); the right not to be subjected to import taxes (Art 25); and the right to take action against another undertaking for breach of the competition rules (Art 82; see **Garden Cottage Foods** *v* **Milk Marketing Board** [1984] AC 130). This principle of direct enforcement is considered in detail in Chapter 9.

The Constitutional Treaty

As discussed in Chapter 1, the Constitutional Treaty has not come into force because all the Member States did not ratify it. Although the changes which the Constitutional Treaty would have made will not come into effect as initially scheduled, it is now clear that there will be another attempt to adopt and ratify an alternative to the Constitutional Treaty. For that reason, included throughout this chapter is a summary of the relevant provisions of the Constitutional Treaty; this will provide a foundation of what *could* be included within a replacement Constitutional Treaty.

Documents and information relevant to the Constitutional Treaty (and its replacement) are available at: http://europa.eu.int/constitution/index_en.htm

The EC Treaty

The EC Treaty, being the most substantive of the three founding Treaties, requires further consideration. As the Court of Justice stated in **Opinion 1/91** (see above): '... the Community Treaties established a new legal order for the benefit of which the States had limited their sovereign rights, in ever wider fields'. The reference to 'ever wider fields' in part refers to the limited nature of the Community's competence, in that the Community can act only in those policy areas where the Member States have given it the power to act through the EC Treaty, but also recognises the fact that each time the Treaty has been amended the result has been that the powers of the Community have been enhanced, through, for example, the inclusion of more policy areas. In order to understand the extent of the EC's legal competence it is essential to be familiar with the contents of the Treaty itself. A useful starting point is to consider the index to the EC Treaty as amended by subsequent Treaties (the SEA, TEU, ToA and ToN).

Index to the EC Treaty

The index to the EC Treaty, following amendments made to it by the SEA, TEU, ToA and ToN, is as follows:

Preamble
Part One　　Principles (Arts 1–16)
Part Two　　Citizenship of the Union (Arts 17–22)
Part Three　Community Policies (Arts 23–181a)
　　　　　　　Title I　　　*Free Movement of Goods (Arts 23–31)*
　　　　　　　Chapter 1　*The Customs Union (Arts 25–27)*
　　　　　　　Chapter 2　*Prohibition of Quantitative Restrictions (Arts 28–31)*
　　　　　　　Title II　　*Agriculture (Arts 32–38)*
　　　　　　　Title III　*Free Movement of Persons, Services and Capital (Arts 39–60)*
　　　　　　　Chapter 1　*Workers (Arts 39–42)*
　　　　　　　Chapter 2　*Right of Establishment (Arts 43–48)*
　　　　　　　Chapter 3　*Services (Arts 49–55)*
　　　　　　　Chapter 4　*Capital and Payments (Arts 56–60)*

The full text of the EC Treaty, as amended, is available at:

http://eur-lex.europa.eu/en/treaties/index.htm

The Treaty is followed by a number of protocols, declarations and agreements. Protocols are given legal effect within the Community legal system by Art 311 EC Treaty, which provides that:

The Protocols annexed to this Treaty by common accord of the Member States shall form an integral part thereof.

Declarations and agreements may be legally effective within the Community legal system, if they are adopted by the Council of Ministers (as most are). The agreement taken at the Edinburgh Summit, for example, following Denmark's rejection of the TEU in a referendum, is an example of a non-legally enforceable agreement. At this summit a decision and declaration on Denmark was taken, not by the Council, but by the heads of state and governments meeting within the European Council. This is more akin to an international agreement and does not form part of the Community legal system.

In Chapter 1 there was a brief discussion of Part One of the Treaty (Principles), considering in particular Art 2 (the tasks of the Community) and Art 3 (the activities of the Community to achieve the Art 2 tasks). Articles 2 and 3 set out the broad aims and objectives of the Community; aims and objectives which include not only economic policies but also social and political policies. But how does the Community operate; is it run by the Member States?

Article 7 EC Treaty – institutions of the Community

Article 7 EC Treaty (previously Art 4) provides that:

1. The tasks entrusted to the Community shall be carried out by the following institutions:
   – a European Parliament,
   – a Council,
   – a Commission,
   – a Court of Justice,
   – a Court of Auditors.
   Each institution shall act within the limits of the powers conferred upon it by this Treaty.
2. The Council and the Commission shall be assisted by an Economic and Social Committee and a Committee of the Regions acting in an advisory capacity.

Article 7 EC Treaty creates five institutions which are responsible for carrying out the aims and objectives of the Community as set out in Arts 2 and 3 of the Treaty and the other provisions within it. It is provided that each of these institutions must act within the powers granted to them under the Treaty. There is a more in-depth discussion of this in subsequent chapters: suffice to say at this point that the founding Treaty (as amended) created institutions to run the Community and defined the powers of each Community institution (see, for example, Part Five, EC Treaty). If any institution exceeds its powers as defined, any resultant act can be struck down as being *ultra vires*, i.e. in excess of its powers.

In the next three chapters it will be noted that in addition to these five institutions, the Treaty provides for other named bodies to be created, and defines their role. Two such bodies are specifically referred to in Art 7(2) EC Treaty: the Economic and Social Committee, and the Committee of the Regions.

Constitutional Treaty

If the Constitutional Treaty had come into force, Art I-19 would have provided that the Union would have an 'institutional framework' comprising:

■ the European Parliament;

■ the European Council;

- the Council of Ministers (to be referred to as the 'Council');
- the European Commission (to be referred to as the 'Commission');
- the Court of Justice of the European Union.

For the first time the European Council would have been treated as a full institution in its own right.

Articles I-20 to I-29 would have clarified the role of these five institutions. This clarification, together with some related issues (which are covered within these articles), are considered in more detail in Chapters 3 to 5.

Articles I-30 to I-32 would have set out the Union's other institutions (the European Central Bank and the Court of Auditors) and advisory bodies (the Committee of the Regions, and the Economic and Social Committee). These articles would also have clarified the role of these two institutions and two advisory bodies.

Community policies

Part Three of the EC Treaty amplifies the broad Arts 2 and 3 aims and objectives of the Community by setting out, in more detail, the substantive Community policies. For example, in Title II 'Free Movement of Workers', four articles are concerned specifically with this policy area:

- Article 2: 'The Community shall have as its task, by establishing a common market ...'
- Article 3: 'For the purposes set out in Article 2, the activities of the Community shall include ...

  (c) an internal market characterised by the abolition, as between Member States, of obstacles to the free movement of ... persons ...'
- Articles 39–42 (previously Arts 48–51): Free Movement of Workers. These articles set out the detailed provisions relating to this policy area.

Article 39 EC Treaty (previously Art 48) defines the policy area in more detail than Arts 2 and 3, but it is still stated in quite broad terms. The first thing to note about Art 39 is that it is limited to the free movement of *workers*, not persons generally. Article 39 (previously Art 48) provides:

1. Freedom of movement for workers shall be secured within the Community.
2. Such freedom of movement shall entail the abolition of any discrimination based on nationality between workers of the Member States as regards employment, remuneration and other conditions of work and employment.
3. It shall entail the right, subject to limitations justified on grounds of public policy, public security or public health:
   (a) to accept offers of employment actually made;
   (b) to move freely within the territory of Member States for this purpose;
   (c) to stay in a Member State for the purpose of employment in accordance with the provisions governing the employment of nationals of that State laid down by law, regulation or administrative action;
   (d) to remain in the territory of a Member State after having been employed in that State, subject to conditions which shall be embodied in implementing regulations to be drawn up by the Commission.
4. The provisions of this Article shall not apply to employment in the public service.

Article 40 (previously Art 49) provides for the Council to issue directives or to make regulations setting out the measures required to bring about the free movement of workers as defined in Art 39 (previously Art 48). Article 40 (previously Art 49) provides:

> The Council shall . . . issue directives or make regulations setting out the measures required to bring about freedom of movement for workers, as defined in Article 39 . . .

In many instances, the EC Treaty provides a framework of broad policies, which are to be supplemented by further *measures* to be adopted by certain Community institutions. In the case of Art 40, these further measures are in the form of directives and regulations, and the institution which will adopt the directive or regulation is the Council. The institutions and the legislative process will be considered further in the next three chapters. The measures which may be adopted are the next source of Community law.

Secondary legislation made under the Treaties

Article 249 EC Treaty (previously Art 189) sets out the different types of Community legislative act:

> In order to carry out their task and in accordance with the provisions of this Treaty, the European Parliament acting jointly with the Council, the Council and the Commission, shall make regulations, issue directives, take decisions, make recommendations or deliver opinions.

The consequences of the legislative act depends upon its specific nature:

- A *regulation* shall have general application. It shall be binding in its entirety and directly applicable in all Member States (Art 249, para 2).
- A *directive* shall be binding, as to the result to be achieved, upon each Member State to which it is addressed, but shall leave to the national authorities the choice of form and methods (Art 249, para 3).
- A *decision* shall be binding in its entirety upon those to whom it is addressed (Art 249, para 4).
- *Recommendations and opinions* shall have no binding force (Art 249, para 5).

Article 249 EC Treaty provides that regulations, directives and decisions are 'binding' and they are therefore legally enforceable. In contrast, Art 249 provides that recommendations have 'no binding force' and they are therefore not legally enforceable. The former three legally enforceable measures will be considered below, whereas the latter two will be considered in the section entitled 'Soft law'.

Regulations

Article 249 EC Treaty (previously Art 189) provides that a regulation shall be binding upon all Member States and is *directly applicable* within all such states. Article 254 (previously Art 191) provides that all regulations must be published in the *Official Journal*. The *Official Journal* is an official Community publication. It consists of two related series and a supplement:

- **The L series (legislation)** contains all the legislative acts whose publication is obligatory under the Treaties, as well as other acts.

- **The C series (information and notices)** covers the complete range of information other than legislation.

- **The S series** is a supplement containing invitations to tender for public works and supply contracts.

The L and C series are published daily (except Sunday) and the supplement is published every day from Tuesday to Saturday. Being a legislative act, a regulation will be published in the L series. The regulation will be cited alongside a reference such as OJ 1990 L 257/13 (this is a reference for an EC Regulation on the control of concentrations between businesses). The reference is decoded as: the L series of the *Official Journal*, Year 1990, issue number 257, page 13. The regulation enters into force on the date specified in the regulation, or if there is no such date specified, on the twentieth day following its publication in the *Official Journal* (Art 254 (previously Art 191)).

Issues of the *Official Journal* which have been published since 1998 can be accessed at:

http://eur-lex.europa.eu/JOIndex.do?ihmlang=en

Directly applicable

As stated above, Art 249 provides that a regulation shall be *directly applicable*. Normally if a state enters into an agreement with another state, although that agreement may be binding in international law, it will only be effective in the legal system of that state if it is implemented in accordance with the state's constitutional requirements.

For example, if the UK entered into an agreement with France, in order for the agreement to be enforceable in UK courts an Act of Parliament would normally have to be enacted. The Act may transpose the agreement into the relevant Act, or it may simply refer to the agreement and provide for it to be effective in the UK.

An EC regulation is an agreement, made by an international body, the European Community. For the regulation to be incorporated into the national legal system, implementing legislation would have to be enacted by the national legislature. This would be very burdensome, because the Community adopts a vast number of regulations each year. The whole Community system would very quickly grind to a halt if a regulation had to be incorporated into the national law of each of the 27 Member States before it was effective. Regulations, especially in the agricultural policy area, quite often require speedy implementation in order to have the desired effect. Such regulations would lose their effect if the Community had to await incorporation by each Member State into their respective national legal systems.

It is for this reason that Art 249 EC Treaty provides that a regulation shall be *directly applicable*. This means regulations shall be taken to have been incorporated into the national legal system of each of the Member States automatically, and come into force in accordance with Art 254 (see above). They are binding on anyone falling within their terms in all Member States. They require no further action by Member States, and can be applied by the courts of the Member States as soon as they become operative.

In the UK, the European Communities Act 1972 (as amended) provides for the direct applicability of EC regulations.

Directives

A directive differs to a regulation in that it applies only to those Member States to whom it is addressed, although normally a directive will be addressed to all 27 Member States. A directive sets out the result to be achieved, but leaves some choice to each Member State as to the form and method of achieving the end result. A directive will quite often provide a Member State with a range of options it can choose from when implementing the measure.

A directive is not directly applicable. It requires each Member State to incorporate the directive in order for it to be given effect in the national legal system. In the UK, this requires the enactment of an Act of Parliament or delegated legislation.

Article 254 EC Treaty provides that directives which are addressed to all Member States (of which the vast majority are), and those which are adopted in accordance with the legislative procedure prescribed by Art 251 (the co-decision procedure (see Chapter 4)), must (like all regulations) be published in the *Official Journal*. Such directives will come into force on the date specified in the directive or, if no date is specified, 20 days after publication in the *Official Journal* (Art 254).

All other directives (i.e. those which do not need to be published in the *Official Journal* (this will be rare)) must be communicated to the Member States to whom they are addressed. Such directives will take effect on the date of communication (Art 254(3)).

Regulation or directive?

Enabling the Community to legislate by means of either a regulation or a directive gives the Community some flexibility. Very few Treaty articles provide that a specific instrument must be used; therefore, there is a choice available.

This flexibility is necessary given the difference between the instruments. As discussed above, regulations are directly applicable in that they become part of the Member States' national legal systems just as they are. It is therefore necessary for a regulation to be precise and clear. Compare this to a directive which is a much more flexible instrument. A directive sets out the result to be achieved, while leaving some degree of discretion to the Member State as to the choice of form and method for achieving that end result. However, despite this apparent flexibility, a directive may nevertheless contain very specific provisions, leaving very little discretion to the Member State.

Usually the Community institution empowered to adopt an instrument is given flexibility as to the mode of instrument chosen, be it a regulation, a directive or some other instrument. However, some Treaty articles will actually specify the mode of instrument. For example, Art 89 EC Treaty (previously Art 94) provides that:

> The Council acting by a qualified majority on a proposal from the Commission and after consulting the European Parliament, may make any appropriate **regulations** for the application of Articles 87 and 88 ... [emphasis added]

Also, Art 94 EC Treaty (previously Art 100) provides that:

> The Council shall, acting unanimously on a proposal from the Commission and after consulting the European Parliament and the Economic and Social Committee, issue **directives** for the approximation of such laws, regulations or administrative provisions of the Member States as directly affect the establishment or functioning of the common market. [emphasis added]

Decisions

Article 249 EC Treaty provides that a decision is binding in its entirety on those to whom it is addressed. Article 254(3) (previously Art 191(3)) provides that a decision must be notified to the person or Member State to whom it is addressed and that it will take effect upon such notification. However, if a decision is adopted using the legislative procedure prescribed by Art 251 (previously Art 189(b) (the co-decision procedure)), then the decision must be published in the *Official Journal*, and it will take effect either on the date specified in the decision or, if there is no such date specified, on the twentieth day following its publication in the *Official Journal*.

The same can be said of decisions as can be said of regulations and directives, in that the Treaty articles are generally left open to allow the relevant institution to decide the actual mode of the instrument. However, some articles actually specify that the mode of the instrument shall be a decision. For example, Art 85(2) EC Treaty (previously Art 89(2)) provides that:

> If the infringement is not brought to an end, the Commission shall record such infringement of the principles in a reasoned **decision** . . . [emphasis added]

Article 85(2) concerns infringement of Community competition rules.

Legal base

The relevant institution, so empowered by the Treaty, may choose the relevant mode for an instrument, unless the Treaty specifies that a particular mode must be used. Articles 39 and 40 EC Treaty (previously Arts 48 and 49) relating to the free movement of workers were discussed above. Article 40 provides that:

> The Council shall issue **directives or** make **regulations** setting out the measures required to bring about freedom of movement for workers, as defined in Article 39 . . . [emphasis added]

The Council has adopted a number of directives and regulations pursuant to the former Art 49 (now 40). For example:

- Regulation 1612/68 of the Council of 15 October 1968 on Freedom of Movement for Workers within the Community [OJ Sp. Ed. 1968, No. L257/2, p. 475].
- Directive 2004/38 of the European Parliament and the Council of 29 April 2004 on the right of citizens of the Union and their family members to move and reside freely within the territory of the Member States [OJ 2004 L229/35].

Article 40 EC Treaty is said to be the *legal base* for the Community institutions, empowering them to adopt secondary legislation in relation to the policy of free movement of workers. Whenever the institutions seek to adopt secondary legislation, the institution which makes the proposal (more often than not the European Commission) must find a relevant legal base within the Treaty. Without a legal base the institutions are prevented from acting.

Constitutional Treaty

If the Constitutional Treaty had come into force, Art I-33 would have replaced Art 249 EC Treaty. Article I-33 would have provided that:

1. To exercise the Union's competences the institutions shall use as legal instruments, in accordance with Part III, European laws, European framework laws, European regulations, European decisions, recommendations and opinions.

   A **European law** shall be a legislative act of general application. It shall be binding in its entirety and directly applicable in all Member States.

   A **European framework law** shall be a legislative act binding, as to the result to be achieved, upon each Member State to which it is addressed, but shall leave to the national authorities the choice of form and methods.

   A **European regulation** shall be a non-legislative act of general application for the implementation of legislative acts and of certain provisions of the Constitution. It may either be binding in its entirety and directly applicable in all Member States, or be binding, as to the result to be achieved, upon each Member State to which it is addressed, but shall leave to the national authorities the choice of form and methods.

   A **European decision** shall be a non-legislative act, binding in its entirety. A decision which specifies those to whom it is addressed shall be binding only on them.

   Recommendations and **opinions** shall have no binding force.

2. When considering draft legislative acts, the European Parliament and the Council shall refrain from adopting acts not provided for by the relevant legislative procedure in the area in question. [emphasis added]

This article provides that the following instruments would have been used by the European Union:

- European law – equivalent to the current regulation;
- European framework law – equivalent to the current directive;
- European decision – equivalent to the current decision;
- European regulation – a non-legislative act of general application for the implementation of legislative acts; a completely new act;
- recommendations and opinions – equivalent to the current recommendations and opinions.

The Constitutional Treaty would have worked on the basis of a hierarchy of acts, clarifying the legal acts used by the institutions to put the Union's powers into practice and stipulating how the acts would have been adopted.

The Constitutional Treaty would have made two successive distinctions:

- between legally binding acts (laws, framework laws, regulations and decisions) and non-binding acts (opinions and recommendations);
- in terms of legally binding acts, it would have distinguished between legislative acts (laws and framework laws) and non-legislative acts (regulations and decisions).

The legally binding acts would have constituted a source of Union law: i.e. secondary legislation made under the Constitutional Treaty. The non-binding acts would have constituted 'soft law'.

Soft law

Non-legally enforceable instruments which may aid the interpretation and/or application of Community law are referred to as 'soft law' (Snyder, 1993). Such instruments may be referred to by the Court of Justice and Court of First Instance (CFI) when interpreting and/or applying Community law. Two particular forms of 'soft law' will be considered further: (i) recommendations and opinions; and (ii) The Charter of Fundamental Rights of the European Union.

Recommendations and opinions

Article 249 EC Treaty explicitly states that recommendations and opinions shall not have any binding force. However, the use of these two instruments may be useful to clarify matters in a formal way. Article 211 EC Treaty (previously Art 155) empowers the Commission to formulate recommendations or deliver opinions on matters dealt with in the Treaty, not only where expressly provided for, but also whenever it considers it necessary.

Although recommendations and opinions have no immediate legal force, they may achieve some legal effect as persuasive authority if they are subsequently referred to, and taken notice of, in a decision of the Court of Justice or CFI. National courts are bound to take them into account when interpreting Community measures, where they throw light on the purpose of the legislation: **Grimaldi *v* Fonds des Maladies Professionelles** (Case C-322/88).

The Charter of Fundamental Rights of the European Union

The Charter of Fundamental Rights of the European Union was signed by the then 15 Member States during December 2000 at the meeting of the European Council held in Nice, France. The Charter combines in a single text the civil, political, economic, social and societal rights which have previously been laid down in a variety of international, European and national sources. It includes rights of dignity (e.g. the right to life; respect for private and family life); freedoms (e.g. freedom of assembly and of association); equality (e.g. respect for cultural, religious and linguistic diversity); solidarity (e.g. right of collective bargaining and action); citizens' rights (e.g. freedom of movement and residence); and justice (e.g. presumption of innocence and right of defence).

The Charter is not legally binding but, despite the protestations of the UK government, it is highly probable that the Court of Justice will draw on its provisions when interpreting and applying Community law. It would therefore achieve the status of 'soft law'. A declaration annexed to the ToN provided that an Intergovernmental Conference would be held in 2004 to consider, *inter alia*, the status of the Charter. This resulted in the adoption of the proposed Constitutional Treaty. The Charter was incorporated into the proposed Treaty (Arts II-61 to II-114). However, as stated above, the Constitutional Treaty will not come into force because it has not been ratified by all the Member States.

Constitutional Treaty

If the Constitutional Treaty had come into force, it would have continued to provide that recommendations and opinions were not legally binding (Art I-33). These would therefore have retained their 'soft law' status under the Constitutional Treaty.

In contrast, the Charter of Fundamental Rights would have been incorporated into the Constitutional Treaty (Part II) and would therefore have become legally enforceable principles which the Court of Justice and CFI would have been bound to uphold. Article I-9(1) would have provided that the Union would 'recognise the rights, freedoms and principles set out in the Charter of Fundamental Rights which constitutes Part II'.

Related treaties made between Member States

These are treaties related to the original Treaties, either amending or enlarging them. Within this category, as a source of law, are the Merger Treaties, the Single European Act, the Treaty on European Union, the Treaty of Amsterdam, the Treaty of Nice, and the Treaties of Accession. A Treaty of Accession is necessary when the Community is enlarged (thus there were separate Accession Treaties for enlargement in 1973, 1981, 1986, 1995, 2004 and 2007).

Like the original Treaties themselves, the Treaties of Accession have been held to confer directly enforceable rights on individuals (**Rush Portuguesa *v* Office National d'Immigration** (Case C-113/89)).

International treaties negotiated by the Community under powers conferred by the Treaty

This category includes not only multilateral treaties to which the Community is a party, such as the General Agreement on Tariffs and Trade (GATT), but Association Agreements concluded by the Community with individual states. The GATT agreement was held in **International Fruit** (Case 21–24/72) to be binding on the Community, and the Court of Justice has also held that undertakings which complain to the Commission of illicit commercial practices which breach the Community's commercial policy instrument may rely upon the GATT as forming part of the rules of international law to which the instrument applies (**Fediol** (Case 70/87)).

In **Kupferberg** (Case 104/81), the Court of Justice held that Art 21 of the EEC–Portugal Association Agreement was directly enforceable in the national courts. The principle of the direct enforcement of such agreements has enabled the nationals of the states which are parties to such agreements to enforce their provisions against Member States of the Community (the principle of direct enforcement is considered further in Chapter 9). In **Kziber** (Case C-18/90), the Court of Justice held that parts of the EEC–Morocco Cooperation Agreement are directly enforceable (see also, **Yousfi *v* Belgium** (Case C-58/93)).

Decisions of the European Court of Justice and Court of First Instance

The jurisprudence (i.e. case law) of the Court of Justice and CFI is a major source of law. It comprises not only all the formal decisions of the Court of Justice and CFI, but also the principles enunciated by them in their judgments and through opinions sought from them. The Treaties and the implementing legislation do not, between them, contain an exhaustive statement of the relevant law, and much of the work of the Court of Justice and CFI has been to put flesh on the legislative bones. The creative jurisprudence of the Court of Justice in particular, and its willingness to interpret measures in such a way as to make them effective, to achieve the *effet utile*, has done much to assist in the attainment of the general objectives of the Treaties.

The role of the Court of Justice and CFI in developing the law of the Community is discussed below and in Chapter 5.

General principles of law and fundamental rights upon which the constitutional laws of the Member States are based

Article 6(1) TEU (as amended by the ToA) now states, unequivocally, that 'The Union is founded on the principles of liberty, democracy, respect for human rights and fundamental freedoms, and the rule of law, principles which are common to the Member States'. The importance of these principles is emphasised by the powers conferred on the Council of Ministers by Art 7(2) TEU to suspend the voting rights of states found to be in breach.

In interpreting primary and secondary Community legislation, the Court has developed a number of general principles of law, some based on the fundamental laws of the constitutions of the Member States, some based on principles of international law and some derived directly from the European Convention on Human Rights (ECHR). Although the jurisdiction of the Court of Justice is, as is discussed in Chapter 5, limited by Art 220 EC Treaty to the interpretation of the Treaties and the subordinate legislation made under them, this is to be done in such a way as to ensure that 'the law is observed'. This has been widely interpreted to mean not only the law established by the Treaties but 'any rule of law relating to the Treaty's application' (Pescatore, 1970). The principles of the ECHR are to be applied insofar as they relate to matters within the competence of the Community. The Union shall 'respect fundamental rights, as guaranteed by the European Convention for the Protection of Fundamental Freedoms signed in Rome on 4 November 1950 and as they result from the constitutional traditions common to Member States, as general principles of Community law' (Art 6(2) TEU).

The development and application of these principles of Community law are considered further below, but prior to this, there is a brief discussion on the changes which would have been brought about if the Constitutional Treaty had come into force.

Constitutional Treaty

Article I-2 of the Constitutional Treaty would have provided that the Union was founded on 'the values of respect for human dignity, freedom, democracy, equality, the rule of law and respect for human rights, including the right of persons belonging to minorities', to a large extent mirroring the provisions of Art 6(1) TEU (as amended by the ToA). Article I-59 would have provided for the suspension of certain rights resulting from Union membership, along similar grounds to those contained in Art 7 TEU, although the provision in the Constitutional Treaty would have been more comprehensive.

As stated above, Art I-9(1) would have provided that the Union would recognise the rights, freedoms and principles which are set out in the Charter of Fundamental Rights (which would have formed Part II of the Constitutional Treaty). Article I-9(1) would have provided that the Union would have acceded to the ECHR, although it stated that 'such accession shall not affect the Union's competences as defined in the Constitution'. It would also have provided that the fundamental rights guaranteed by the ECHR and which also resulted from the constitutional traditions common to the Member States 'shall constitute general principles of the Union's law'.

There now follows a discussion of the development and application of the principles, as discussed above.

Human rights

Article 6 TEU (as amended by the ToA) declares that:

(1) The Union is founded on the principles of liberty, democracy, respect for human rights and fundamental freedoms, and the rule of law, principles which are common to the Member States.

(2) The Union shall respect fundamental rights, as guaranteed by the European Convention for the Protection of Human Rights and Fundamental Freedoms signed in Rome on 4 November 1950 and as they result from the constitutional traditions common to the Member States, as general principles of Community Law.

The effect of Art 6 is to give formal recognition in the Treaty to what has been part of the jurisprudence of the Court since **Stauder** (Case 29/69). In that case the Court of Justice declared that 'fundamental human rights are enshrined in the general principles of Community law and protected by the Court'. In **A v Commission** (Case T-10/93) the CFI noted the commitment in Art F.2 TEU (now Art 6) to respect the fundamental rights guaranteed by the ECHR and said, repeating the words of the Court of Justice in **ERT** (Case C-260/89), 'the Court draws inspiration from the constitutional traditions common to Member States and from the guidelines supplied by international treaties for the protection of human rights on which Member States have collaborated or of which they are signatories' (see, in particular, the judgment in **Nold v Commission** (Case 4/73)). The ECHR has special significance in that respect (see, in particular, **Johnston v Chief Constable of the Royal Ulster Constabulary** (Case 222/84)). It follows that, as the Court of Justice held in its judgment in **Wachauf v Germany** (Case 5/88), the Community cannot accept measures which are incompatible with observance of the human rights thus recognised and guaranteed.

What this means is that when there is a conflict between a national law which is, for example, intended to implement Community law, but does so in such a way as to breach the Convention, the Court will rule that the national measure is contrary to Community law. In the **Johnston** case, national measures intended to prohibit sexual discrimination in Northern Ireland and to provide a remedy for those alleging discriminatory behaviour, were held contrary to Community law because the Court of Justice held that they did not give complainants an effective remedy as required by Art 13, ECHR. It must, however, be emphasised that the Court of Justice can only rule on compatibility between the ECHR and Community law in those areas of national law affected by Community law. It could not, for example, rule on the compatibility of a criminal trial in a Member State with the ECHR's provisions on fair process, if the trial was unrelated to any rules of Community law, even though the individual involved was an EU citizen (**Kremzow v Austria** (Case C-299/95)). The Court of Justice defined the limits of its powers in the following case:

Demirel v *Stadt Schwabisch Gmund* (Case 12/86)

The Court of Justice held that it has:

> ... no power to examine the compatibility with the European Convention on Human Rights of national legislation lying outside the scope of Community law.

The application of the ECHR and the development of the jurisprudence of fundamental rights has been a somewhat erratic process, depending very much on the kind of cases which have come before the Court. Some provisions of the ECHR, particularly those relating to due process under Art 6 ECHR, have been discussed frequently by the Court, while others, such as that relating to the right to life, hardly at all. Fundamental rights have been drawn both from the ECHR and from the constitutions of the Member States; rights and freedoms recognised by national constitutions as being 'fundamental' both in the sense that they protect and promote the most essential human values, such as the dignity, the personality, the intellectual and physical integrity, or the economic and social well-being of the individual, and in the sense that they are inseparably attached to the person. The Court of Justice has emphasised its commitment to human rights in general on several occasions, over a period of 30 years, starting with **Stauder** (Case 29/69). However, until the Treaty on European Union came into effect in 1993, there were no specific provisions for the protection of human rights as such in the Treaties. It is arguable that the Court has been reluctant to take on the protection of fundamental rights, and did so largely to protect the supremacy of its jurisdiction:

> Reading an unwritten bill of rights into Community law is indeed the most striking contribution the Court made to the development of a new constitution for Europe. This statement should be qualified in two respects. First ... that contribution was forced on the court from outside, by the German and, later, the Italian Constitutional Courts. Second, the court's effort to safeguard the fundamental rights of the Community citizens stopped at the threshold of national legislations. (Mancini, 1989)

Even where a right is recognised by the Court as a 'fundamental' Community right, that recognition is not conclusive. The designation by the Court of a right as fundamental does not always mean that all other rules must give way before it. In some circumstances, one fundamental right may have to give way to another which the Court regards as even more important. Much will depend on the context in which the fundamental right is called upon, and the nature of the right itself.

Some of the specific rights are now considered.

The right to property and the freedom to choose a trade or profession

This right is contained in Art 1 of the First Protocol ECHR (1952 Cmd 9221) (and see **Nold v Commission** (Case 4/73)). The Court of Justice has declared 'The right to property is guaranteed in the Community legal order' (**Hauer v Land Rheinland-Pfalz** (Case

44/79)). In the following case, the Court of Justice applied the principle of the right to property:

Wachauf (Case 5/88)

A German tenant farmer was deprived of his right to compensation under Regulation 857/84 for loss of a milk quota when his lease expired, as a result of the way in which the German government had interpreted the regulation. He argued that this amounted to expropriation without compensation. The case was referred to the Court of Justice which held:

> It must be observed that Community rules which, upon the expiry of the lease, had the effect of depriving the lessee, without compensation, of the fruits of his labour and of his investments in the tenanted holding would be incompatible with the requirements of the protection of fundamental rights in the Community legal order. Since those requirements are also binding on Member States when they implement Community rules, the Member States must, as far as possible, apply those rules in accordance with those requirements.

However, the Court of Justice held in **R v Ministry of Agriculture, ex parte Bostock** (Case C2/92), that where a lessor 'inherited' the benefit of a milk quota, neither the milk quota scheme itself nor the Community principles of fundamental rights required a Member State to introduce a scheme for compensation for the outgoing lessee, nor did they confer directly on the lessee a right to such compensation.

In the following case, the Court affirmed that both the right to property and the freedom to pursue a trade or business formed part of the general principles of Community law:

Commission v Germany (Case C-280/93)

The Court of Justice stated that the two principles (i.e. the right to property and the freedom to pursue a trade or business) were not absolute, and:

> ... had to be viewed in relation to their social function. Consequently, the exercise of the right to property and the freedom to pursue a trade or profession could be restricted, particularly in the context of a common organisation of a market, provided that those restrictions in fact corresponded to objectives of general interest pursued by the Community and did not constitute a disproportionate and intolerable interference, impairing the very substance of the rights guaranteed.

In relation to access to a trade or profession, the principle of equality should ensure equal access to available employment and the professions between EU citizens and nationals of the host state (see **Thieffry** (Case 71/76)). In **UNECTEF v Heylens** (Case 222/86), the Court of Justice stated that 'free access to employment is a fundamental right which the Treaty confers individually on each worker of the Community'.

The right to carry on an economic activity

The right to carry on an economic activity is closely connected with the right to property. The Court has held that the right to property is guaranteed in the Community legal order. However, it has also decided that a Community-imposed restriction on the planting of vines constitutes a legitimate exception to the principle, which is recognised in the constitutions of Member States (see **Hauer** (Case 44/79), **Eridania** (Case 230/78) and **S M Winsersett v Land Rheinland-Pfalz** (Case C-306/93)).

Freedom of trade

Procureur de la République v *ADBHU* (Case 240/83)

The Court of Justice stated that:

> It should be borne in mind that the principles of free movement of goods and freedom of competition, together with freedom of trade as a fundamental right, are general principles of Community law of which the Court ensures observance.

The Court has held on several occasions that the right of goods to be allowed access to markets in other Member States under Art 28 EC Treaty is, subject to the exceptions in Art 30, a directly enforceable right. This decision elevates that right to a fundamental principle, in the face of which inconsistent Community and national legislation must generally give way (see Chapter 9). But, the freedom to trade is not absolute, and may have to give way to the imperatives of the Single Market (see **Commission** *v* **Germany** (above)).

The right to an effective judicial remedy before national courts (Articles 6, 13 ECHR)

The right to an effective judicial remedy before national courts has become one of the most developed fundamental principles in the jurisprudence of the Court of Justice:

Johnston v *Chief Constable of the RUC* (Case 222/84)

The RUC maintained a general policy of refraining from issuing firearms to female members of the force. The policy was defended on the ground, *inter alia*, that Art 53, Sex Discrimination (Northern Ireland) Order 1976 (SI 1976/1042 (NI 15)) permitted sex discrimination for the purpose of 'safeguarding national security or of protecting public safety or public order'. A certificate issued by the Secretary of State was to be 'conclusive evidence' that the action was necessary on security grounds. The complainant argued that the rule effectively barred her promotion, and that Directive 76/207 (which prohibited discrimination on grounds of sex in relation to conditions of employment) should take priority over national law. Article 6 of the directive provided that complainants should be able to 'pursue their claims by judicial process'. On a reference to the Court of Justice, the Court held that the national tribunal had to be given enough information to determine whether or not the policy of the Chief Constable was objectively justified. This was necessary in the interests of effective judicial control:

> The requirements of judicial control stipulated by that Article [Art 6 Dir 76/207] reflect a general principle of law which underlines the constitutional traditions common to the Member States. That principle is also laid down in Articles 6 and 13 of the European Convention of Human Rights and Fundamental Freedoms ... As the European Parliament, Council and Commission recognised in their joint declaration of 5 April 1977 (OJ 1977 C 103 p. 1) and as the Court has recognised in its own decisions, the principles on which the Convention is based must be taken into consideration in Community law.

The Court of Justice's approach in the above case was endorsed by the European Court of Human Rights in the following case:

Tinnelly & Sons Ltd and McElduff v UK (1999) 27 EHRR 249

With regard to similar Northern Ireland legislation permitting discrimination on religious grounds, the European Court of Human Rights declared that:

> The right of a court guaranteed by Article 6.1 . . . cannot be replaced by the *ipse dixit* of the executive even if national security considerations constitute a highly material aspect of the case.

The principles of effective judicial control and effective remedies underlies several decisions relating to difficulties encountered by individuals in seeking to establish themselves in businesses and professions in other Member States. These principles require that sufficient reasons must be given for official decisions, to enable them to be challenged in court, should the need arise:

UNECTEF v Heylens (Case 222/86)

The Court of Justice stated that:

> Effective judicial review, which must be able to cover the legality of the reasons for the contested decision, presupposes in general that the court to which the matter is referred may require the competent authority to notify its reasons. But where, as in this case, it is more particularly a question of securing the effective protection of a fundamental right conferred by the Treaty on Community workers, the latter must also be able to defend that right under the best possible conditions and have the possibility of deciding, with a full knowledge of the relevant facts, whether there is any point in their applying to the courts. Consequently, in such circumstances the competent national authority is under a duty to inform them of the reasons on which its refusal is based, either in the decision itself or in a subsequent communication made at their request.

The right to due judicial process also involves a fair investigative process in accordance with the ECHR when the European Commission is investigating alleged breaches of competition law. In interpreting its investigative powers under Regulation 17/62 (which has now been replaced by Regulation 1/2003 (OJ 2003 L 1/1); see Chapter 22), the Commission has to have regard to the ECHR and, particularly, the rights of the defence to be informed of the matters under investigation (see **Hoechst** *v* **Commission** (Case 46/87)). This principle has come to be known as 'equality of arms' (**Solvay SA** *v* **Commission** (Case T-30/91)). The same principle entitles protection to be given to certain communications between the person under investigation and his lawyer (see **Australia Mining & Smelting Ltd** *v* **Commission** (Case 155/79)).

The protection of family life, home and family correspondence (Article 8 ECHR)

In **National Panasonic** (Case 136/79), the Court of Justice held that the principles of Art 8 ECHR were applicable to an investigation by the Commission of an alleged anticompetitive practice, but held that the exception in Art 8(2) justified the action taken by the Commission under Regulation 17/62 (which, as stated above, has now been replaced by Regulation 1/2003).

In the following case, the applicant had applied for an appointment as a temporary member of the Commission's staff. He had agreed to undergo the normal medical examination but refused to be subjected to a test which might disclose whether or not he carried the AIDS virus:

X v *Commission* (Case C-404/92)

The Court of Justice held that he was entitled to refuse the test:

> The right to respect for private life, embodied in Art 8 ECHR and deriving from the common consti-
> tutional traditions of the Member States, is one of the fundamental rights protected by the legal order
> of the Community. It includes in particular a person's right to keep his state of health secret.

The right of EU citizens in other Member States to have only those restrictions imposed on them as are necessary in the interests of national security or public safety in a democratic society (Article 2 Fourth Protocol ECHR)

This right has a wide application. The position of EU citizens in other Member States, in relation to their human rights, has been described in the most comprehensive terms by Advocate-General Jacobs in the following case:

Christos Konstantinidis v *Stadt Altensteig-Standesamt* (Case C-168/91)

Advocate-General Jacobs stated that:

> In my opinion, a Community national who goes to another Member State as a worker or a self-
> employed person under Articles 48, 52 or 59 [now Articles 39, 43 or 49] of the Treaty is entitled . . .
> to assume that, wherever he goes to earn his living in the European Community, he will be treated in
> accordance with a common code of fundamental values, in particular those laid down in the European
> Convention on Human Rights. In other words, he is entitled to say 'civis Europeus sum' and to invoke
> that status in order to oppose any violation of his fundamental rights.

The principle applies, *a fortiori*, since the creation of EU citizenship by Art 17 EC Treaty, because such citizenship carries with it, under Art 18, a general right of residence any-where in the Community, subject only to the limitations contained in the Treaty and in the implementing legislation (see Chapters 11–15).

Prohibition of discrimination on the grounds of sex in relation to pay and working conditions (Article 14 ECHR)

The prohibition of discrimination on the grounds of sex in relation to pay and working conditions is now one of the principal objectives of the Community (Art 3(2) EC Treaty which is more specifically spelt out in Art 141 EC Treaty). In **P/S and Cornwall County Council** (C-13/94), a case involving the dismissal of a transsexual, the Court of Justice held that the right not to be discriminated against on grounds of sex is 'simply the expression, in the relevant field, of the principle of equality, which is one of the funda-mental principles of Community law'. However, since the Court was not prepared to regard cohabitees of the same sex as being in an 'equal' situation, the principle of equality did not apply to them (**Grant *v* South-Western Trains** (Case C-249/96)). Despite this decision, the creation by the ToA of a power for the Council of Ministers in Art 13 EC Treaty to 'combat' discrimination on grounds of sexual orientation, could well per-suade the Court of Justice that the situation of same-sex couples is now an 'equal' situation.

Pursuant to Art 13 EC Treaty, the Council adopted Directive 2000/78 (OJ 2000 L 303/16) which establishes a general framework for equal treatment in employment and occupation. The directive had to be implemented by 3 December 2003. The directive prohibits direct and indirect discrimination as regards access to employment and occupation on grounds of religion or belief, disability, age or sexual orientation. It applies to both the public and private sectors. Although the directive applies to EU and non-EU citizens, the prohibition does not cover national provisions relating to the entry into and residence of third-country (i.e. non-EU) nationals (Art 3(2)). The directive does not, therefore, extend the free movement provisions, *per se*, to non-EU citizens (see Chapter 11).

Freedom of expression (Article 10 ECHR)

The right to freedom of expression has been considered on several occasions by the Court in the context of freedom to provide and receive services, and in relation to the establishment of businesses in other Member States. In the following case, the Court of Justice had to consider a challenge by an independent broadcasting company to the monopoly of the state broadcasting company:

Elleneki Radiophonia Tileorasi (ERT) (Case C-260/89)

Greek law forbade any party other than the state television company from broadcasting television programmes within Greek territory. The defendant company defied the ban and, when prosecuted, pleaded in their defence that the television monopoly was contrary both to Community law (in relation to, *inter alia*, the free movement of goods and services) and to Art 10 ECHR. The Greek government defended the television monopoly as a public policy derogation from the free movement of goods and services under Arts 56 and 66 EC Treaty (now Arts 46 and 55). The Court of Justice accepted that these derogations were subject to the ECHR and said:

> When a Member State invokes Articles 56 and 66 of the Treaty [now Articles 46 and 55] in order to justify rules which hinder the free movement of services, this justification, which is provided for in Community law, must be interpreted in the light of general principles of law, notably fundamental rights ... The limitations imposed on the power of Member States to apply the provisions of Articles 66 and 56 [now Articles 55 and 46] of the Treaty, for reasons of public order, public security and public health must be understood in the light of the general principles of freedom of expression, enshrined in Article 10 of the Convention. (para 45)

Access to information is an important corollary to the effective exercise both of freedom of expression (Art 10 ECHR) and of the right to know the basis of a decision under the general rules requiring a fair decision-making process. Article 253 EC Treaty (formerly Art 190) has long required that reasons for all decisions by Community institutions be given. The ToA has gone further, conferring a right of information on consumers (Art 153 EC Treaty), and a right of access for all EU citizens and those resident in the Community to documents produced by the institutions (Art 255(3) EC Treaty). This right of access is, however, subject to the rules made by each body. The CFI has recognised that the policy decision of the Commission to make its documents available could be subject to its power to withhold documents on grounds of public security, international relations, monetary stability, court proceedings and investigations, but these limitations must be specifically justified in the case of each document, and interpreted strictly (**Van der Wal v Commission** (Case T-83/96)). The Treaty of Amsterdam amended the EC Treaty to include a new Art 255 which provides for access to European Parliament, Council of Ministers and Commission documents. Pursuant to Art 255, Regulation 1049/2001 was adopted by the Council of Ministers and this Regulation replaced Decision 94/90 with effect from 3 December 2001. Refusal to grant access must now be based on one of the exceptions provided for in the Regulation and must be justified on the grounds that disclosure of the document would be harmful (see Chapter 3).

Freedom of religion (Article 9 ECHR)

The question of religious discrimination came before the Court of Justice in the following case:

Prais v *The Council* (Case 130/75)

A woman of Jewish faith applied for a post as a Community official. She did not mention her faith in her application form, but when she was informed that she would have to sit a competitive examination on a particular day, she explained that she could not do so because it was an important Jewish festival. She asked to be able to take the examination on another day. She was refused, because the Council decided that it was essential for all candidates to sit the examination on the same day. The Court upheld the decision of the Council, because it had not been told, in advance, about the difficulty. The Court of Justice accepted, as did the Council, that freedom of religion was a general principle of Community law, but decided that it had not been breached in this case (see also Directive 2000/78 above).

Freedom of trade union activity including the right to join and form staff associations

Union Syndicale *v* **Council** (Case 175/73) recognised the right to trade union membership. It is doubtful if this right extends to a right to engage in industrial action, although Art 13 of the Community Charter of the Fundamental Social Rights of Workers of 1989 provides that the worker shall have the right:

> . . . to resort to collective action in the event of a conflict of interests and shall have the right to strike, subject to the obligations arising under national regulations and collective agreements.

These rights are now, by implication, recognised by all Member States (Art 136 EC Treaty, added by the ToA). Individuals benefiting from the protection of Community law are entitled to participate equally in trade unions and staff associations, and should not be penalised for taking part in legitimate trade union activity (see **Rutili** (Case 36/75) and **Association de Soutien aux Travailleurs Immigrés** (Case C-213/90)). This includes the right to vote and stand for office in such bodies (**Commission** *v* **Luxembourg** (Case C-118/92)). The European Court of Human Rights, in **Schmidt and Dahlstom**, held that the ECHR safeguards the freedom to protect the occupational interests of trade union members by trade union action, but leaves each state a free choice of the means to be used to this end. Article 8, Regulation 1612/68, which gives migrant workers equal rights with national workers as far as membership of trade unions and the election to office in them is concerned, refers only to 'the rights attaching' to such membership, without further elaboration.

Constitutional Treaty

As previously discussed, if the Constitutional Treaty had come into force it would have incorporated the Charter of Fundamental Rights of the European Union. Article II-12 Constitutional Treaty would have provided that:

1. Everyone has the right to freedom of peaceful assembly and to freedom of association at all levels, in particular in political, trade union and civic matters, which implies the right of everyone to form and to join trade unions for the protection of his or her interests ...

It should be noted that this provision does not explicitly include a right to strike.

Fundamental rights and the UK's Human Rights Act 1998

Applying the rule of supremacy of Community law (see Chapter 9), the principles referred to in this chapter must be recognised and implemented by the courts of the UK as part of its national law. In addition, since the incorporation of the ECHR into the law of England, Wales, Scotland and Northern Ireland by the Human Rights Act 1998, all public bodies, including courts and tribunals, and even private bodies implementing public law, will have to abide by the principles of the ECHR. Therefore ECHR rights may be applied either as a matter of Community law, where they concern a measure within the competence of the Community, or under national law, following the procedures set out in the Act, where Community law is not involved.

The following are additional general principles which have been embraced by the Court of Justice and CFI when interpreting and applying Community law.

Proportionality

Proportionality is a general principle imported from German law, and is often invoked to determine whether a piece of subordinate legislation or an action purported to be taken under the Treaties goes beyond what is necessary to achieve the declared, lawful objects. It holds that 'the individual should not have his freedom of action limited beyond the degree necessary for the public interest' (**Internationale Handelsgesellschaft** (Case 11/70)). The principle applies in relation to action by the Community in the sphere of legislation, to determine whether a regulation has, for example, gone beyond what was necessary to achieve the aim contained in the enabling Treaty provision, or whether a Community institution has exceeded the necessary action to be taken in relation to an infraction (i.e. breach) of Community law. It may thus be invoked to challenge fines imposed by undertakings found by the Commission to have breached the competition rules in Arts 81 and 82 EC Treaty (see Chapter 22).

It is also applicable to action by Member States in relation to permitted derogations from Community law. While, for example, restrictions on imports from other Member States, and also other measures having an equivalent effect, are prohibited by Art 28 EC Treaty, an exception is permitted under Art 30 in relation to action taken on the grounds of, *inter alia*, public health (see Chapter 18). A total ban on a product will in almost every case be disproportionate, while some sampling and testing, in proportion to the degree of the perceived risk, may be legitimate. Excessive action may constitute a disguised restriction on trade (**Commission v Germany (Re Crayfish Imports)** (Case C-131/93)).

The principle of equality

The EC Treaty includes three specific types of prohibition against discrimination:

- prohibition against discrimination on grounds of nationality under Art 12 EC Treaty;
- prohibition of discrimination between producers and consumers in relation to the operation of the Common Agricultural Policy under Art 34(2) EC Treaty; and

■ entitlement to equal pay for work of equal value for both men and women under Art 141 EC Treaty.

Article 2 EC Treaty was amended by the ToA to set a new general goal of 'equality between men and women'. Hitherto, this objective was confined to the workplace. Article 13 EC Treaty (post-ToA) created a new power for the Council of Ministers: 'within the limits of the powers conferred upon it by the Community ... [to] take appropriate action to combat discrimination based on sex, racial or ethnic origin, religion or belief, disability, age or sexual orientation'. Two directives have been adopted pursuant to Art 13 EC Treaty:

Directive 2000/43 (OJ 2000 L 180/22) implements the principle of equal treatment between persons irrespective of racial or ethnic origin. The directive had to be implemented by 19 July 2003. The principle of equal treatment prohibits direct or indirect discrimination based on racial or ethnic origin (Art 1). It applies to EU and non-EU citizens and covers both public and private sectors in relation to employment, self-employment, education, social protection including social security and healthcare, social advantages, and access to and supply of goods and services (Art 3(1)). The prohibition of racial or ethnic discrimination does not, however, cover national provisions relating to the entry into and residence of third-country (i.e. non-EU) nationals (Art 13(2)). The directive does not, therefore, extend the free movement provisions *per se* to non-EU citizens (see Chapter 11).

Directive 2000/78 (OJ 2000 L 303/16) establishes a general framework for equal treatment in employment and occupation, prohibiting direct and indirect discrimination as regards access to employment and occupation on grounds of religion or belief, disability, age or sexual orientation (see above).

The principle of equality has been recognised by the Court of Justice as one of general application and requires that comparable situations should not be treated differently, and different situations should not be treated in the same way, unless such differentiation is objectively justified (**Graff** *v* **Hauptzollamt Köln-Rheinau** (Case C-351/92)). Besides the specific Treaty provisions, the Court of Justice has held that the fixing and collection of financial charges which make up the Community's own resources are governed by the general principle of equality (**Grosoli** (Case 131/73)), as is the allocation of Community tariff quotas by the Member States (**Krohn** (Case 165/84)).

The principle is also evident in the Court's requirement of equality of arms under which undertakings which are subject to investigation by the Commission for breach of competition law should have full knowledge of the allegations and evidence in the Commission's file (**Solvay SA** *v* **Commission** (Case T-30/91)).

Constitutional Treaty

If the Constitutional Treaty had come into force Art I-3 would have set out the Union's objectives, stating that the Union would 'combat social exclusion and discrimination, and shall promote social justice and protection, equality between women and men, solidarity between generations and protection of the rights of the child'. Article I-4(2) would have provided that 'within the scope of the Constitution, and without prejudice to any of its specific provisions, any discrimination on grounds of nationality shall be prohibited'.

Part II of the Constitutional Treaty would have incorporated the Charter of Fundamental Rights of the European Union (see above). Article II-81 would have provided that:

1. Any discrimination based on any ground such as sex, race, colour, ethnic or social origin, genetic features, language, religion or belief, political or any other opinion, membership of a national minority, property, birth, disability, age or sexual orientation shall be prohibited.
2. Within the scope of application of the Constitution and without prejudice to any of its specific provisions, any discrimination on grounds of nationality shall be prohibited.

Part III of the Treaty would have set out the Union's policies. Article III-118 would have provided that in defining and implementing the policies and activities referred to in Part III, the Union would have aimed to combat discrimination based on sex, racial or ethnic origin, religion or belief, disability, age or sexual orientation. Article III-223 would have provided that European laws (i.e. regulations under the EC Treaty) or framework laws (i.e. directives under the EC Treaty) could have been adopted to 'lay down rules to prohibit discrimination on grounds of nationality as referred to in Article I-4(2)'. Article III-124 would have further provided that:

1. Without prejudice to the other provisions of the Constitution and within the limits of the powers assigned by it to the Union, a European law or framework law of the Council may establish the measures needed to combat discrimination based on sex, racial or ethnic origin, religion or belief, disability, age or sexual orientation. The Council shall act unanimously after obtaining the consent of the European Parliament.
2. By way of derogation from paragraph 1, European laws or framework laws may establish basic principles for Union incentive measures and define such measures, to support action taken by Member States in order to contribute to the achievement of the objectives referred to in paragraph 1, excluding any harmonisation of their laws and regulations.

Similar to the provisions under the EC Treaty, Art III-214 would have specifically provided the right to equal pay for work of equal value for both men and women, and Art III-228(2) would have specifically prohibited discrimination between producers and consumers in relation to the operation of the Common Agricultural Policy.

Legal certainty and non-retroactivity

Legal certainty and non-retroactivity is a general principle of law familiar to all the legal systems of the Member States. In its broadest sense, it means that 'Community legislation must be unequivocal and its application must be predictable for those who are subject to it' (**Kloppenburg** (Case 70/81)). It means, for example, that the principle of the indirect effect of directives does not apply in relation to national provisions with criminal sanctions, because the need for legal certainty requires that the effect of national criminal law should be absolutely clear to those subject to it. In **Kolpinghuis Nijmegen** (Case 80/86), the Court of Justice stated that the national court's obligation to interpret domestic law to comply with Community law was 'limited by the general principles of law which form part of Community law, and in particular, the principles of legal certainty and non-retroactivity' (see Chapter 9).

The following case raised the question of the imposition by national courts of penalties for breach of Community law. This case concerned an EU Regulation, whereas previous cases had been concerned with EU Directives:

X (Case C-60/02)

During November 2000, Rolex, a company which holds various trade marks for watches, applied in Austria for a judicial investigation to be opened against 'persons unknown', following the discovery of a consignment of counterfeit watches which persons unknown had attempted to transport from Italy to Poland, thus infringing its trade mark rights. Rolex asked for the goods to be seized and destroyed following that investigation. In July 2001 Tommy Hilfiger, Gucci and Gap likewise requested the opening of judicial investigations concerning imitation goods from China intended to be transported to Slovakia.

The Austrian court was faced with the following problem: the opening of a judicial investigation under the Austrian Code of Criminal Procedure requires that the conduct complained of is a criminal offence. However, the court said, under the national law on the protection of trade marks only the import and export of counterfeit goods constituted a criminal offence; the mere transit across the national territory did not constitute a criminal offence. This interpretation of national law was disputed; the Austrian government, for example, was of the opinion that mere transit was a criminal offence under Austrian law.

The Austrian court referred a question to the Court of Justice on the compatibility of the Austrian law with Regulation 3295/94, which in the national court's view covers mere transit.

The Court of Justice first confirmed that view: the regulation applies also to goods in transit from one non-member country to another, where the goods are temporarily detained in a Member State by the customs authorities of that state.

The Court further stated that the interpretation of the scope of the regulation does not depend on the type of national proceedings (civil, criminal or administrative) in which that interpretation is relied on.

The Court then noted that there was no unanimity as to the interpretation to be given to the Austrian law on trade marks. The Austrian government and the claimant companies contested the view taken by the national court; in their opinion, mere transit was a criminal offence under Austrian law. That, said the Court, concerned the interpretation of national law, which was a matter for the national court, not the Court of Justice.

The Court of Justice stated that if the national court were to find that the relevant provisions of national law did **not** in fact penalise mere transit contrary to the regulation, it would have to interpret its national law within the limits set by Community law, in order to achieve the result intended by the Community rule (see Chapter 9: principles of direct effect and indirect effect). In relation to the transit of counterfeit goods across the national territory, the Austrian court would have to apply the civil law remedies applicable under national law to the other offences, provided that they were effective and proportionate and constituted an effective deterrent.

The Court noted, however, that a particular problem arose where the principle of compatible interpretation was applied to **criminal matters. Since Regulation 3295/94 empowers Member States to adopt penalties for the conduct it prohibits** (i.e. requiring the Member States to make an election as to the penalties it will impose), **the Court's case law on directives must be extended to it, according to which directives cannot, of themselves and independently of a national law adopted by a Member State for their implementation, have the effect of determining or aggravating the liability in criminal law of persons who act in contravention of their provisions.**

The Court reached the conclusion that, if the national court considered that Austrian law did not prohibit the mere transit of counterfeit goods, the principle of non-retroactivity of penalties, which is a general principle of Community law, would prohibit the imposition of criminal penalties for such conduct, despite the fact that national law was contrary to Community law.

Legitimate expectation

Legitimate expectation is based on the concept that 'trust in the Community's legal order must be respected' (**Deuka** (Case 5/75) (A–G Trabucchi)). Under this principle, 'assurances relied on in good faith should be honoured' (**Compagnie Continentale _v_ Council** (Case 169/73) (A–G Trabucchi)). It is closely linked to the principle of legal certainty. The relationship between the two principles is illustrated in the following case:

Mulder (Case 120/86)

In order to stabilise milk production, Community rules required dairy farmers to enter into a five-year non-marketing agreement, in exchange for which they would receive a premium. In 1984, the Community introduced a system of milk quotas, under which milk producers would have to pay a levy on milk produced in excess of their quota in any one year. Those who had entered into the non-marketing agreement for 1983 were not allowed any quota, because there was no provision in the regulations for them to do so. Having suspended production for the non-marketing period, they were effectively excluded from subsequent milk production. A farmer excluded in this way challenged the validity of the regulations. The Court of Justice held that:

> ... where such a producer, as in the present case, has been encouraged by a Community measure to suspend marketing for a limited period in the general interest and against payment of a premium, he may legitimately expect not to be subject, upon the expiry of his undertaking, to restrictions which specifically affect him because he has availed himself of the possibilities offered by the Community provisions.

The principle of legitimate expectation seeks to ensure a fair process, although it cannot fetter the Community's freedom of action. The balance is not always easily struck, but the issues involved in doing so were applied in an English court by Sedley J in the following case:

R v Ministry of Agriculture and Fisheries, ex parte Hamble Fisheries [1995] 2 All ER 714

Sedley J stated that:

> The principle of legal certainty and the protection of legitimate expectation are fundamental to European Community law. Yet these principles are merely general maxims derived from the notion that the Community is based on the rule of law and can be applied to individual cases only if expressed in enforceable rules. Moreover, in most instances there are other principles which run counter to legal certainty and the protection of legitimate expectations; here the right balance will need to be struck. For instance, in the field of Community legislation the need for changes in the law can conflict with the expectation of those affected by such a change that the previous legal situation will remain in force ...

In the above case, the court decided that the legitimate expectation of the holders of fishing licences had not been infringed when the Ministry introduced a more restrictive fishing licensing policy to protect the remaining fish stocks allocated to the UK under the Community's quota system. The CFI has held that operators in the Community's agricultural markets cannot have a legitimate expectation that an existing situation will prevail since the Community's intervention in these markets involves constant adjustments to meet changes in the economic situation (**O'Dwyer and Others *v* Council** (Cases T-466, 469, 473 and 477/93)).

Natural justice

Natural justice is a concept derived from English administrative law, but closely linked to the United States' 'due process'. It is sometimes used by the Court of Justice to mean no more than 'fairness', and is not always distinguishable from 'equity'. In the English administrative law sense, it implies, however, two basic principles: (i) the right to an unbiased hearing; and (ii) the right to be heard before the making of a potentially adverse decision affecting the person concerned (see, for example, **Ridge *v* Baldwin** [1964] AC 40). In the following case, the Court of Justice referred to a general principle of good administration:

Kuhner (Case 33/79)

The Court of Justice stated the principle as:

> ... a general principle of good administration to the effect that an administration which has to take decisions, even legally, which cause serious detriment to the person concerned, must allow the latter to make known their point of view, unless there is a serious reason for not doing so.

The principle is explicit in relation to decisions affecting an individual's free movement rights on the grounds of public policy, public security and public health (Arts 27-32, Directive 2004/38), and implicit in other decisions affecting the exercise of those rights. It involves the right to be given full reasons for the decision in order that they may be challenged. The right to natural justice is thus closely linked to the right to an effective remedy, as stated by the Court of Justice in the following case:

UNECTEF v Heylens and Others (Case 222/86)

The Court of Justice stated that:

> 15. Where, as in this case, it is more particularly a question of securing the effective protection of a fundamental right conferred by the Treaty on Community workers, the latter must ... be able to defend that right under the best possible conditions and have the possibility of deciding, with a full knowledge of the relevant facts, whether there is any point in their applying to the courts.

Summary

Now you have read this chapter you should be able to:

- Explain the nature and scope of the different sources of Community law, including:
  - Treaties; and
  - secondary legislation.
- Understand the nature of following different forms of secondary Community legislation which may be adopted pursuant to Article 249 EC Treaty:
  - Regulations;
  - Directives;
  - Decisions; and
  - Recommendations.
- Assess the impact which the proposed Constitutional Treaty would have had on the form of secondary Community legislation if it had been ratified.
- Explain how soft law may be used as an aid to the interpretation and application of Community law.
- Understand the role which the European Court of Justice and the Court of First Instance play in the creation and development of Community law.
- Evaluate how the decisions of these Courts have been influenced by general principles of law and fundamental rights.

References

Mancini, G.F., 'The Making of a Constitution for Europe' (1989) 26 CML Rev 595.

Pescatore, P., 'Fundamental Rights and Freedoms in the System of the European Communities', (1970) AJIL, 343.

Snyder, F., 'The Effectiveness of European Community Law: Institutions, Processes, Tools and Techniques' (1993) 56 MLR 19, 32.

Further reading

Textbooks

Craig, P. and De Burca, G. (2003) *EU Law Text, Cases and Materials* (3rd edn), Oxford University Press, Chapters 3, 8 and 9.

Foster, N. (2006) *Foster on EU Law* (1st edn), Oxford University Press, Chapter 3 (Sections 3.1 to 3.3).

Prechal, S. (2005) *Directives in EC Law* (1st edn), Oxford University Press, Chapters 1 to 5.

Steiner, J., Woods, L. and Twigg-Flesner, C. (2006) *EU Law* (9th edn), Oxford University Press, Chapters 3 and 6.

Storey, T. and Turner C. (2005) *Unlocking EU Law* (1st edn), Hodder Arnold, Chapter 4.

Tillotson, J. and Foster, N. (2003) *Text, Cases and Materials on EU Law* (4th edn), Cavendish Publishing, Chapters 4 and 10.

Weatherill, S. (2006) *Cases and Materials on EU Law* (7th edn), Oxford University Press, Chapter 2.

Journal articles

Besselink, L., 'Entrapped by the Maximum Standard: On Fundamental Rights, Pluralism and Subsidiarity in the European Union' (1998) 35 CML Rev 629.

Coppel, J. and O'Neill, A., 'The European Court of Justice: Taking Rights Seriously?' (1992) Legal Studies 227.

Goldsmith, T., 'A Charter of Rights, Freedoms and Principles' (2001) 38 CML Rev 1201.

Jacobs, F., 'Human Rights in the EU: The Role of the Court of Justice' (2001) 26 EL Rev 331.

Jowell, J., 'Is Proportionality an Alien Concept?' (1996) 2 EPL 401.

Lenaerts, K., 'Fundamental Rights to be included in a Community Catalogue' (1991) 16 EL Rev 367.

Lenaerts, K. and De Smijter, E., 'A Bill of Rights for the EU' (2001) 38 CML Rev 273.

Liisberg, J. 'Does the EU Charter of Fundamental Rights Threaten the Supremacy of Community Law?' (2001) 38 CML Rev 1171.

Mancini, G.F., 'The Making of a Constitution for Europe' (1989) 26 CML Rev 595.

Pescatore, P., 'Fundamental Rights and Freedoms in the System of the European Communities' (1970) AJIL 343.

Schilling, T., 'The Autonomy of the Community Legal Order: An Analysis of Possible Foundations' (1996) 37 Harv Int LJ 389.

Sharpston, E., 'Legitimate Expectation and Economic Reality' (1990) 15 EL Rev 103.

Snyder, F., 'The Effectiveness of European Community Law: Institutions, Processes, Tools and Techniques' (1993) 56 MLR 19, 32.

Toth, A.G., 'The European Union and Human Rights: The Way Forward' (1997) 34 CML Rev 491.

Weiler, J. and Lockhart, N., 'Taking Rights Seriously: The European Court of Justice and its Fundamental Rights Jurisprudence' (1995) 32 CML Rev 579.

3 Community institutions and related bodies

At the end of this chapter you should understand the composition and role of:

- The European Commission and the President of the Commission.
- The Council of Ministers, COREPER and the European Council.
- The European Parliament.
- The Court of Auditors.
- The advisory committees: the Economic and Social Committee, and the Committee of the Regions.

You should additionally have an appreciation of the changes which would have been introduced by the Constitutional Treaty if it had come into force.

Article 7 EC Treaty

The EC Treaty initially created four institutions to enable 'the tasks entrusted to the Community ... [to be] ... carried out' (Art 7(1) EC Treaty). Those institutions were:

- the European Commission;
- the Council of Ministers;
- the European Parliament; and
- the Court of Justice.

A fifth institution, the Court of Auditors, was added by the TEU in 1993.

Article 7(1) EC Treaty further provides that each institution is obliged to act within the limits of the powers conferred on it by the Treaty. It can, in other words, only do those things which it has been expressly authorised by the Treaty to do. The Court of Justice has, by and large, been strict in limiting the activities of the other institutions to their specified functions, although it has been more liberal when interpreting the powers of the European Parliament (**Les Verts** (Case 294/83); **Parliament v Council** (Case C-388/92)).

There are two other bodies which are expressly mentioned in Art 7(2) EC Treaty, but which have only an advisory function in the decision-making process: the Economic and Social Committee and the Committee of the Regions.

The role of each of the above institutions will be considered in turn in this chapter, except for the Court of Justice and Court of First Instance (which will be considered in Chapter 5). The institutions that are to be examined are considered in the context of their role in the European Community (which, until the TEU, was called the European *Economic* Community (Art G TEU (now Art 8)), unless otherwise stated. In this chapter, and throughout the book, the focus will be on the European *Community* and not the European *Union*. This is because the European Union created by the TEU includes not only the European Community, but also Euratom (the European Coal and Steel Community was also included, but this community expired on 23 July 2002), and the non-legally binding cooperative decision-making processes of the Member States on foreign and security policy, and police and judicial cooperation in criminal matters (i.e. the second and third pillars of the EU (see Chapter 1)), which are generally outside the competence of the institutions. The focus of this book is on the institutions as the constituent parts of those Community acts which have *legal* effect. Each institution has a defined role (i) in the decision-making and law-making processes, (ii) in relation to adjudication, and/or (iii) in the audit of the Community's accounts.

The institutions do not fit easily into categories such as legislature, executive and judiciary. Although the Community performs legislative, executive and judicial functions, there is no formal 'separation of powers' doctrine in-built into the Community's constitution. The competence of each institution has not remained static. Amendments to the founding Treaty have generally resulted in changes to the balance of power between these institutions: e.g. the Parliament started off as a mere debating chamber with limited supervisory powers, but following the introduction of direct elections in 1979, subsequent amendments to the EC Treaty (by the SEA, TEU, ToA and ToN) have resulted in its powers being enhanced, at the cost of some of the other institutions. This shifting of the balance of powers will be explored throughout this and the following chapter.

The detailed Treaty provisions which apply to the Community institutions are contained in Part Five of the EC Treaty. Part Five is structured as follows:

Part Five   **Institutions of the Community (Arts 189–280)**
Title I   *Provisions Governing the Institutions (Arts 189–267)*
Chapter 1   *The Institutions (Arts 189–248)*
  Section 1   *The European Parliament (Arts 189–201)*
  Section 2   *The Council (Arts 202–210)*
  Section 3   *The Commission (Arts 211–219)*
  Section 4   *The Court of Justice (Arts 220–245)*
  Section 5   *The Court of Auditors (Arts 246–248)*
Chapter 2   *Provisions Common to Several Institutions (Arts 249–256)*
Chapter 3   *The Economic and Social Committee (Arts 257–262)*
Chapter 4   *The Committee of the Regions (Arts 263–265)*
Chapter 5   *The European Investment Bank (Arts 266–267)*

Constitutional Treaty

As discussed in Chapter 1, the proposed Constitutional Treaty did not come into force because it was not ratified by all of the then 25 Member States. If the Constitutional Treaty had come into force, it would have replaced all the existing treaties (with the exception of Euratom). It would have established a single European Union which would have replaced the current European Communities and the European Union (Art I-1 Constitutional Treaty). The three pillars would have been merged, although special procedures would have been maintained in the fields of foreign policy, security and defence (see Chapter 1).

Article I-19 Constitutional Treaty would have provided that the Union would have an 'institutional framework' comprising:

- the European Parliament;
- the European Council;
- the Council of Ministers (to be referred to as the 'Council');
- the European Commission (to be referred to as the 'Commission');
- the Court of Justice of the European Union.

For the first time the European Council would have been treated as a full institution in its own right.

Articles I-20 to I-29 would have clarified the role of these five institutions. Part Three, Title VI Constitutional Treaty would have concerned the functioning of the Union. Chapter 1 (of Part Three, Title VI) would have contained the provisions governing the institutions:

Part Three   **The Policies and Functioning of the Union (Arts III-115 to III-436)**
Title VI   ***The Functioning of the Union (Arts III-330 to III-436)***
Chapter 1   *Provisions Governing the Institutions (Arts III-330 to III-401)*
               Section 1   *The Institutions (Arts III-330 to III-385)*
               Section 2   *The Union's Advisory Bodies (Arts III-386 to III-392)*
               Section 3   *The European Investment Bank (Arts III-393 to III-394)*
               Section 4   *Common Provisions (Arts III-395 to III-401)*

The changes to the structure and role of the institutions which would have been made by the Constitutional Treaty are discussed further below. Each of the institutions is now considered.

The European Council

The European Council did not exist when the Community came into being on 1 January 1958. The European Council was created following a meeting of heads of government in Paris in 1974 and received formal recognition in the Single European Act (see Chapter 1).

The role of the European Council (not to be confused with the Council of Ministers, see below) is described, in Art 4 TEU, as being to 'provide the Union with the necessary impetus for its development ... [and to] ... define the general political guidelines'. It is, essentially, a political forum in which the heads of government, meeting at least twice a year, accompanied by their foreign ministers, thrash out the political agenda for the Community in the ensuing months and years. These meetings are often referred to as European Summits. General programmes worked at in outline at these meetings are taken up and fleshed out by the European Commission and may, in some cases, form the background to a whole raft of legislation or more detailed policy-making in such areas as monetary policy and the measures necessary to complete the single market. It is here also that discussions will take place on matters which fall within the second and third pillars of the European Union (i.e. Common Foreign and Security Policy; and Police and Judicial Cooperation in Criminal Matters (see Chapter 1)).

The subject matter of European Council meetings depends on a number of different factors but the following factors are relevant in determining what is discussed. The work of the European Council will depend, to some extent, on the political issues which currently preoccupy a majority of the heads of government. These might involve, for example, a foreign policy crisis, a run on the national currencies in the financial markets, or a major environmental disaster. To illustrate this point, the Copenhagen meeting of the European Council on 12 and 13 December 2002 considered the crises in Iraq and the Middle East; two declarations were adopted. Other items will appear regularly on the Council's agenda, such as the general economic situation, the level of unemployment, and a review of the development of the single market. The Commission will quite often be involved in bringing forward new policy initiatives, usually with some support from the head of government of the state which holds the presidency of the Council of Ministers (see below). Major initiatives have started in this way, such as those leading to the adoption of the Social Charter at the Strasbourg Summit in 1989, and the programmes that led up to the signing of the TEU in 1992, the ToA in 1997 and the ToN in 2000.

It is the task of the European Commission to carry forward the Community towards its goals as set out in the Treaty (see below), but the European Council has proved valuable for ensuring that measures proposed by the Commission are actually approved. Once they have been accepted by the European Council they are much more likely to be accepted by the Council of Ministers because they will, in principle at least, have been accepted by the heads of the governments of which the Ministers are part.

Constitutional Treaty

As stated above, if the Constitutional Treaty had come into force, Art I-19 would, for the first time, have treated the European Council as a full institution in its own right.

Articles I-21, I-22 and III-341 would have set out the provisions which would have applied to the European Council.

Similar to Art 4 TEU, Art I-21(1) Constitutional Treaty would have provided that the role of the European Council was to 'provide the Union with the necessary impetus for its development ... [and to] ... define the general political directions and priorities thereof'. Article I-21(1) would have stated that the European Council would not exercise legislative functions.

Article I-22(1) would have established the position of President of the European Council. The President would have been elected by the members of the European Council, by a qualified majority, for a term of two-and-a-half years, renewable once. The President would not have been allowed to hold a national office (Art I-22(3)), therefore current elected politicians would have been excluded. The President would have:

- chaired the meetings of the European Council and driven forward its work;
- ensured the preparation and continuity of the work of the European Council in cooperation with the President of the Commission, and on the basis of the work of the General Affairs Council;
- endeavoured to facilitate cohesion and consensus with the European Council;
- presented a report to the European Parliament after each meeting; and
- ensured the external representation of the Union (at his or her level, and in that capacity) on issues concerning its common foreign and security policy, without prejudice to the powers of the Union Minister for Foreign Affairs (Art I-22(2)).

Article I-22(2) would have provided that the European Council would consist of the 'Heads of State or Government of the Member States, together with its President and the President of the European Commission'. A Union Minister for Foreign Affairs would have been established by the Constitutional Treaty (see Chapter 1), and this minister would have taken part in the European Council's work (Art I-22(2)). The heads of state or government could have been assisted by a minister, and the President of the European Commission by a member of the Commission (Art I-22(3)).

Rather than meeting every six months, Art I-22(3) would have provided that the European Council would meet quarterly (i.e. every three months). There would also have been provision for special meetings to be convened by the President.

Article I-22(4) would have provided that decisions would be taken by consensus, except where the Treaty provided otherwise (e.g. Art III-341(3) would have provided that the European Council would act by a simple majority with regard to procedural questions and for the adoption of its Rules of Procedure). When a vote was taken, any member of the European Council could also have acted on behalf of one other member (Art III-341(1)). Abstentions by members present at the meeting, or who were represented by another member, would not have prevented the European Council from adopting an act which required unanimity (Art III-341(1)).

The European Council could have invited the President of the European Parliament to speak at one of its meetings (Art III-341(2)).

The European Commission

The provisions of the EC Treaty which govern the Commission are Arts 211–219 EC Treaty (previously Arts 155–163). The Commission's website can be accessed at:

http://ec.europa.eu/index_en.htm

The role of the Commission is set out in Art 211 EC Treaty. It has four primary duties:

- to ensure that the provisions of the Treaty and the measures taken by the institutions under the Treaty are applied;

- to formulate recommendations or deliver opinions on matters dealt with in the Treaty if the Treaty either expressly requires it or if the Commission considers it necessary;

- to take part in the decision-making and legislative processes of the Community with the Council of Ministers and the European Parliament; and

- to exercise the powers conferred on it by the Council of Ministers for the implementation of rules laid down by the latter.

Essentially, the Commission's function is, generally, to act as the executive of the Community and to see that Community policy is carried out, to formulate new policy and to draft legislation to give it effect, to police observance of Community rules (whether primary, in the form of Treaty provisions; or secondary, in the form of regulations, directives and decisions) and, to a lesser extent, to act as a legislative body in its own right. This fourth function is largely related to the making (and enforcement) of detailed rules for the implementation of the Common Agricultural Policy.

Constitutional Treaty

If the Constitutional Treaty had come into force, Arts I-26, I-27 and III-347 to III-352 would have set out the provisions which would have applied to the European Commission. Article I-26(1) would have set out the role of the Commission:

> The Commission shall promote the general interest of the Union and take appropriate initiatives to that end. It shall ensure the application of the Constitution, and measures adopted by the institutions pursuant to the Constitution. It shall oversee the application of Union law under the control of the Court of Justice of the European Union. It shall execute the budget and manage programmes. It shall exercise coordinating, executive and management functions, as laid down in the Constitution. With the exception of the common foreign and security policy, and other cases provided for in the Constitution, it shall ensure the Union's external representation. It shall initiate the Union's annual and multiannual programming with a view to achieving interinstitutional agreements.

Composition

15 Member States (pre 1 May 2004)

Following entry to the European Union of Austria, Finland and Sweden on 1 January 1995, the Commission consisted of 20 Commissioners (Art 156(1) Act of Accession, Art 30 Decision 95/1/EC OJ 1995 L 1/1; this was set out in Art 213 EC Treaty). Article 213 EC Treaty further provided that only nationals of the Member States were eligible as Commission members, and that the Commission must include at least one national of each of the Member States, with no more than two. Although Art 213 did not stipulate this, in practice the five largest Member States (France, Germany, Italy, Spain and the UK) each had two Commissioners appointed, with one each from the remaining ten Member States. Under Art 213 EC Treaty, the numbers could be increased by a unanimous vote of the Council of Ministers.

25 Member States (pre 1 January 2007)

Following the accession of the ten new Member States on 1 May 2004, the number of Commissioners increased. For a transitional period, ten new Commissioners were appointed, one from each of the ten new Member States. This increased the total number of Commissioners from 20 to 30 (there being two Commissioners from France, Germany, Italy, Spain and the UK).

In February 2004 the European Commission set out the measures it was going to put in place to ensure the smooth integration of the ten new Commissioners from 1 May 2004. The Commissioners from the new Member States were full members of the Commission and would play a full and active role in the decision-making process. While they did not have specific portfolios, they were associated with the work of an existing Commissioner in order to ease their integration into the Commission's work. The new Commissioners each had a cabinet (see below).

Due to the transitional and short-term nature of their mandate, the new Commissioners did not hold a specific portfolio. Instead they were twinned with current members of the Commission in their work. Cabinets of the new Commissioners worked closely with the cabinet of the Commissioner with whom they were associated during this transitional period (which had been planned to be 1 May to 31 October 2004). These cabinets comprised three A-grade officials, including either a Head of Cabinet (A2) or Deputy Head of Cabinet (A3). At least one A-grade was an existing Commission official and at least one a national of a different Member State from that of the Commissioner.

Article 4 of the Protocol on EU Enlargement, which was attached to the ToN, provided that from 1 January 2005, Art 213(1) EC Treaty would be amended to provide that the Commission would include one national from each of the Member States. This amendment would reduce the five larger Member States' representation from two to one.

Although the term of office of the transitional Commission had been due to expire on 31 December 2004, the Accession Treaty that was signed in Athens in April 2003 provided that the new Commission would take office on 1 November 2004, two months early (see below). However, the end of the transitional Commission was brought forward so that the operational difficulties of a 30-member Commission did not continue any longer than necessary. As it happened, political problems were encountered during the appointment process of the new Commission, which resulted in the transitional arrangement being continued until the new Commission took office on 22 November 2004 (see below).

27 Member States (from 1 January 2007)

Article 4 of the Protocol on EU Enlargement further provided that when the Union consisted of 27 Member States, Art 213(1) would be further amended to provide that the number of members of the Commission would be less than the number of Member States. The number would be set by the Council of Ministers acting unanimously. The members would be chosen according to a rotation system based on the principle of equality, the implementing arrangements for which would be adopted by the Council, again acting unanimously.

However, the Accession Treaty which provided for Bulgaria and Romania's entry into the EU included an Act which set out amendments to the founding treaties. Article 45 of this Act provides that:

> A national of each new Member State [i.e. Bulgaria and Romania] shall be appointed to the Commission as from the date of accession. The new Members of the Commission shall be appointed by the Council, acting by qualified majority and by common accord with the President of the Commission, after consulting the European Parliament.
>
> The terms of office of the Members thus appointed shall expire at the same time as those of the Members in office at the time of accession.

Article 45 therefore provided for the number of Commissioners, following enlargement on 1 January 2007, to be increased from 25 to 27.

Constitutional Treaty

The Intergovernmental Conference which met during December 2004 to agree the text for the proposed Constitutional Treaty did not accept the Convention's proposal regarding the Commission's composition (see Chapter 1); the Convention had proposed a reduction in their number. However, the final text of the proposed Constitutional Treaty provided that the first Commission to have been appointed under the Constitutional Treaty would have consisted of one national of each Member State, including the President of the Commission and the Union Minister for Foreign Affairs (who would have been one of the Commission's Vice-Presidents); Art I-26(5). At the end of the first Commission's term of office (which, if the Constitutional Treaty had been adopted, would have been scheduled to be 31 December 2014), the Commission would have consisted of a number of Members corresponding to two-thirds of the number of Member States, chosen on the basis of equal rotation between the Member States, unless the European Council, acting unanimously, decided to alter this number (Art I-26(6)).

Independence and integrity of the Commission

Article 213(2) EC Treaty (previously Art 157(2)) provides that:

> The Members of the Commission shall, in the general interest of the Community, be completely independent in the performance of their duties.
>
> In the performance of these duties, they shall neither seek nor take instructions from any government or from any other body. They shall refrain from any action incompatible with their duties. Each Member State undertakes to respect this principle and not to seek to influence the Members of the Commission in the performance of their tasks.
>
> The Members of the Commission may not, during their term of office, engage in any other occupation, whether gainful or not. When entering upon their duties they shall give a solemn undertaking that, both during and after their term of office, they will respect the obligations arising therefrom and in particular their duty to behave with integrity and discretion as regards the acceptance, after they have ceased to hold office, of certain appointments or benefits. In the event of any breach of these obligations, the Court of Justice may, on application by the Council or the Commission, rule that the Member concerned be, according to the circumstances, either compulsorily retired in accordance with Article 216 or deprived of his right to a pension or other benefits in its stead.

It is thereby provided that the Commission shall act in the general interests of the Community. The Commission members are not representatives of the Member States of their nationality.

The following case, decided by the Court of Justice in 2006, concerns the issue of whether or not a former Commissioner had breached Art 213(2) EC Treaty, in failing to respect the obligations arising from her office as Commissioner:

Commission v Edith Cresson (Case C-432/04)

Mrs Cresson was a member of the European Commission from 24 January 1995 to 8 September 1999, when the Commission left office, having resigned collectively on 16 March 1999. During her term of office at the Commission, Mrs Cresson's portfolio comprised: science, research and development, human resources, education, training and youth, together with the Joint Research Centre (JRC).

When Mrs Cresson took up her functions, she sought to appoint one of her close acquaintances, Mr Berthelot, a dental surgeon, as a 'personal adviser'. Because he was 66 years old, Mr Berthelot could not be appointed as a member of a Commissioner's Cabinet, and Mrs Cresson was advised accordingly. Moreover, when Mrs Cresson took up office, her Cabinet was already fully staffed, as far as personal advisers were concerned. Mrs Cresson asked the administration to consider how it might be possible to appoint him. Mr Berthelot was then engaged as a visiting scientist from September 1995 until the end of February 1997. Although appointment as a visiting scientist implies that the person concerned is mainly to work either in the JRC or the services dealing with research, Mr Berthelot worked exclusively as a personal adviser to Mrs Cresson.

On the expiry of his contract on 1 March 1997, Mr Berthelot was offered another visiting scientist's contract, for a period of one year expiring at the end of February 1998. His appointment as a visiting scientist thus lasted for a total period of two and a half years, whereas the rules specify a maximum duration of 24 months. On 31 December 1997, Mr Berthelot requested the termination of his contract from that date on medical grounds. His application was accepted.

Following a complaint by a Member of the European Parliament, a criminal investigation concerning Mr Berthelot's file was opened in Belgium in 1999. In June 2004, the Chambre du conseil of the Tribunal de première instance de Bruxelles (Court of First Instance, Brussels) decided that no further action should be taken in the case, taking the view that there was no ground for continuing the criminal procedure.

At the same time, in January 2003, the Commission sent Mrs Cresson a statement of the complaints against her as regards the breach of her obligations as a Commissioner in relation to Mr Berthelot's appointment. After hearing Mrs Cresson, the Commission brought an action before the Court of Justice based on Art 213 EC Treaty.

The Court noted, first, that Art 213 EC Treaty requires Members of the Commission to respect the 'obligations arising from [their office]'. As there is nothing which restricted that concept, it was to be understood as extending not only to the duties of integrity and discretion expressly mentioned in that article, but also to all of the duties which arise from the office of Member of the Commission, which include the obligation to be completely independent, to act in the general interest of the Community, and to observe the highest standards of conduct. It is therefore the duty of Members of the Commission to ensure that the general interest of the Community takes precedence at all times not only over national interests but also over personal ones.

However, while Members of the Commission are under an obligation to conduct themselves in a manner which is beyond reproach, the Court of Justice stated that **a breach of a certain gravity is required if a breach of Art 213(2) EC Treaty is to be committed.**

The Court went on to hold that Mrs Cresson acted in breach of the obligations arising from her office as a Member of the Commission in relation to the appointment of Mr Berthelot and the terms under which he worked. It essentially held that Mr Berthelot's appointment constituted a circumvention of the rules relating to the appointment of Members of a Cabinet and of visiting scientists.

Having regard to her personal involvement in that appointment, since it took place at her express request, after she had been informed that she could not recruit Mr Berthelot to her Cabinet, Mrs Cresson was held responsible for that appointment and the circumvention of the rules which it involved.

Thus, in appointing a close acquaintance, Mr Berthelot, as a visiting scientist, when he was not going to be engaged in the activities associated with that position, in order to allow him to undertake the role of personal adviser within her Cabinet, even though the latter was fully staffed and, additionally, Mr Berthelot had passed the permitted age limit for performing that role, Mrs Cresson became liable for a breach of her obligations of a certain degree of gravity.

While the breach of the obligations arising from the office of Member of the Commission calls, in principle, for the imposition of a penalty, the Court held that the finding of breach constitutes, of itself, an appropriate penalty. The Court therefore decided not to impose on Mrs Cresson a penalty in the form of a deprivation of her right to a pension or other benefits in its stead.

Constitutional Treaty

Similar to Art 113(2) EC Treaty, if the Constitutional Treaty had come into force, Art III-347 would have provided that '... Member States shall respect ... [the] independence [of

the members of the Commission] and shall not seek to influence them in the performance of their tasks'.

Appointment

Article 214 EC Treaty (previously Art 158), as amended by the ToN, provides for the
appointment of the President and the other members. The governments of the Member
States nominate by qualified majority the person they wish to appoint as President (prior
to the ToN the governments acted by *common accord* (i.e. they all had to agree)). That
nomination is subject to a vote of approval by the European Parliament (this requirement was inserted by the ToA). The last two Presidents were: Jacques Santer (who
resigned on 15 March 1999) and Romano Prodi (whose period of office ended on 21
November 2004). The current Commission President is José Manuel Barroso, the former
Portuguese Prime Minister.

The governments, by a qualified majority, and in *common accord* with the nominee for
President, nominate the persons they wish to appoint as Commissioners. The body *as a
whole* is subject to a vote of approval by the European Parliament. Once approved by the
Parliament the body is appointed by qualified majority of the Member States. The
members are appointed for a renewable period of five years.

It should be noted that the power of the Parliament to veto the appointment of the
Commission is only a power to block the appointment of the Commission as a body; it
cannot block the appointment of an individual member (other than blocking the
President's appointment). However, the Parliament may be able to negotiate a redistrib-
ution of portfolios to ensure that a member of which it disapproves does not have
responsibility for a high-profile portfolio. The Parliament may threaten to veto the
appointment of the whole Commission if its request is not met.

The current Commission's five-year period of office started on 22 November 2004. This
was three weeks later than planned, due to political problems which surfaced during the
appointments process. During the European Parliamentary approval process, the
Parliament opposed the appointment of Rocco Buttiglione (from Italy) because of his
views on homosexuality and marriage. As stated above, the Parliament cannot block the
appointment of an individual member; it can only vote to block the appointment of the
Commission as a whole. The Parliament felt so strongly about Buttiglione's appointment
that it became clear they would vote against the appointment of the proposed
Commissioners *en bloc*. At this stage, the Commission-elect was withdrawn. Franco
Frattini (from Italy) took the place of Rocco Buttiglione. The President-elect also
requested the replacement of Latvia's Ingridia Udre because of her views on EU taxation.
He also reshuffled two portfolios. Following these changes, on 18 November 2004 the
European Parliament approved the new Commission by 449 votes to 149, with 82
abstentions.

Constitutional Treaty

If the Constitutional Treaty had come into force, Art I-27(1) would have provided that
the European Council, acting by a qualified majority, would propose a candidate for
President of the Commission to the European Parliament. The Parliament would elect
the candidate by a majority of its component members. If this majority was not obtained,
then the European Council, again acting by a qualified majority, would propose a new
candidate within one month, who would again have been subject to election by the
Parliament by the same majority (Art I-27(1)).

Article I-27(2) would have further provided that the Council, by common accord with the President-elect, would adopt a list of the proposed Commissioners. The President and the other members of the Commission would have been subject to 'a vote of consent' by the European Parliament, following which the European Council would appoint the Commission by a qualified majority (Art I-27(2)).

Termination of office

Termination may occur by:

- expiry of their five-year period of office (Art 214(1) (previously Art 158(1)));
- death (Art 215 (previously Art 159));
- voluntary resignation (Art 215 (previously Art 159));
- compulsory resignation pursuant to Art 216 (previously Art 160): 'If any member of the Commission no longer fulfils the conditions required for the performance of his duties or if he is guilty of serious misconduct, the Court of Justice may, on application by the Council or the Commission, compulsorily retire him'; or
- compulsory collective resignation where the Parliament passes a vote of no confidence pursuant to Art 201 (previously Art 144). Such a vote requires a two-thirds majority of the votes cast which must represent a majority of the total membership of the Parliament (i.e. 393 votes because, following enlargement of the EU to 27 Member States, there are currently 785 MEPs for the transitional period 1 January 2007 to the beginning of the 2009–2014 European Parliamentary term (see below)). On 15 March 1999 the dominant socialist bloc of Members of the European Parliament withdrew support for the President (Jacques Santer) and his 19 Commissioners following a damning report by an external fraud inquiry that charged them with losing political control over the Brussels executive. Their immediate resignation was demanded, and this was forthcoming. If they had not resigned a vote of no confidence would have been carried and the President and Commissioners would have been legally required to resign.

The ToN amended Art 217 EC Treaty to provide that a member of the Commission must resign if the President requests such resignation, having first of all obtained the collective approval of the Commission. This amendment was a response to the forced collective resignation of Jacques Santer's administration during 1999. The external fraud inquiry, which precipitated the mass resignation, had pointed the finger at two members who refused to resign individually. This amendment empowers the President to require an individual member's resignation.

Constitutional Treaty

If the Constitutional Treaty had come into force, Art III-340 would have substantially re-enacted the European Parliament's power to vote on a motion of censure to force the collective resignation of the European Commission.

Compulsory resignation of an individual Commissioner, upon an application to the Court of Justice, would have been provided for by Art III-349. This is similar to Art 216 EC Treaty.

Art III-348 Constitutional Treaty would have set out the procedures which would have applied when a Commissioner's term of office came to an end early (through death, resignation or compulsory resignation).

Role of the President

The ToA inserted a new paragraph into Art 219 EC Treaty (previously Art 163) which provides that the 'Commission shall work under the political guidance of its President'. The President therefore has authority to lead the Commission and it will depend upon the President as to how influential and powerful he is. The former President Jacques Delors was a very influential and powerful leader, and contributed greatly to the future shaping of the Community. During the 1980s under Jacques Delors, it was said that 'the office became a key focus of power, not just in the Commission, but in Europe as a whole. He gave the Commission a purpose and taught it to respond to his will' (Grant, 1994). Under a weak President, it becomes a fragmented bureaucracy, as demonstrated during Jacques Santer's period of office, which culminated in his resignation on 15 March 1999. Although the President has few special powers, the office is designed to deliver a powerful figure who represents the Community; this can be contrasted to that of other countries which are represented by their head of state.

Article 217 EC Treaty was amended by the ToN. The amended Art 217 provides that the Commission shall work under the political guidance of its President (this was previously the first para of Art 219), but it additionally provides that the President shall decide on the Commission's internal organisation in order to ensure that it acts consistently, efficiently and on the basis of collective responsibility. It is explicitly provided that the President shall allocate responsibilities to individual members and that he can reshuffle those responsibilities during the Commission's term of office. This amendment strengthens the hand of the President and was a response to the events leading up to the Commission's mass resignation during 1999.

Constitutional Treaty

In addition to the re-enactment of the President's powers set out in Art 217 EC Treaty (as amended by the ToN), if the Constitutional Treaty had come into force a new provision would have empowered the President to request the resignation of the Union Minister for Foreign Affairs, in which case the Minister's term of office would have been ended by the European Council acting by a qualified majority (Art I-27(3)).

Structure

Each member of the Commission will be responsible for one or more policy areas (portfolios), to be allocated by the President. Each member will be assisted by a small Cabinet of officials (similar to UK civil servants) whom he personally appoints. The Cabinet is headed by a Chef de Cabinet, who will liase closely with the member.

The Commission itself is divided into a number of departments labelled Directorates-General (DGs), and each DG is headed by a Director General who is individually responsible to the relevant member of the Commission. Each Directorate-General is further divided into a number of Directorates (usually between four and six), each headed by a Director. The Director is individually responsible to the relevant Director General. Each Directorate is further sub-divided into a number of Divisions each headed by a Head of Division who is individually responsible to the relevant Director (see Table 3.1).

Each Directorate-General used to be referred to by a number (e.g. DGI External Economic Affairs; DGV Employment, Industrial Relations and Social Affairs). However, in 1999 it was decided to label each DG with a clear name, in what was largely a symbolic change designed to facilitate understanding by outsiders. It was also announced that the

Table 3.1 Structure of the Commission following the ToN

Commission	Commissioner
Directorate-General	Director General
Directorate	Director
Division	Head of Division

number of DGs would be reduced from 42 to 36 (although this has since increased to 40). The website for the Directorates-General can be accessed at:

http://ec.europa.eu/dgs_en.htm

There are approximately 20,000 staff employed by the Commission; the administration of a medium-sized European city will often employ more people.

The Commission acts as a collegiate body and decisions are made by a simple majority. Once taken, they bind the Commissioners (see Chapter 4). Although, as discussed above, the Commissioners are bound to act as a collegiate body on behalf of the Community rather than for the states from which they originate, it would be unrealistic to expect them to divest themselves of all political contacts with their national governments. Indeed, it would not be helpful to the Community for them to do so. They frequently use such contacts within the governments and civil services of Member States to promote Community policies, and to sound out the extent of support which new legislation might secure in the Parliament and the Council of Ministers. Tensions do arise, however, when they appear to be too assiduous in promoting the policies of their own states. Equally, they may also experience difficulties if their approach is seen by their home government as too *Communautaire*. After a period of five years, Commissioners need to be reappointed and will be nominated (or not, as the case may be) by their national state. The UK Commissioner largely responsible for creating and promoting the development of the Single Market in 1986, Lord Cockfield, is widely believed to have failed to achieve reappointment because he was seen by the then UK Prime Minister, Margaret Thatcher, as having 'gone native' in Brussels and lost sight of UK interests.

Despite this, most Commissioners see themselves as having a much freer hand in devising and promoting new policies. Unlike national politicians, they have no political platform to which they must adhere. They simply need to follow the very broad objectives established by the Treaties and, increasingly, by the European Council (see above). They need to promote a good working relationship with the European Parliament, although there will be few issues which will unite the Parliament sufficiently to secure the Commission's removal *en bloc*.

The Commission as initiator of changes in policy and legislation

In recent years the Commission has annually adopted a *Work Programme*. The Work Programme for 2006 was published during October 2005 (COM (2005) 531 final) and it gives a useful indication of the Commission's current priorities. The current Work Programme and related documents are available at:

http://ec.europa.eu/atwork/programmes/index_en.htm

Although the Commission is often described as the Community's executive, that description does less than justice to its major policy-making role. Although the Treaty does not expressly stipulate, in general terms, that law and policy changes must be initiated by the Commission, it contains a large number of references such as 'The Council . . . acting on a proposal from the Commission' may draw up a programme, adopt appropriate regulations and/or directives, and so forth. The Work Programme referred to above is part of that process. The references in the Treaty to the role of the Commission have been interpreted as providing a more or less exclusive role for the Commission in policy initiation, so much so that the position has often been summarised by the maxim that 'the Commission proposes and the Council disposes'. However, when considering the decision-making process this no longer accurately reflects the position, partly because of the increasingly important role of the European Council and partly because of the much enhanced role of the European Parliament (see Chapter 4). Directorates-General, assisted by a large number of specialist advisory committees drawn from the appropriate industrial, commercial and other sectors in the Member States, take an active part in drafting new provisions. This process has been particularly visible in the measures proposed to harmonise product standards, consumer safety measures, and health and safety at work measures in the Single Market under Art 95 EC Treaty.

Policy initiation takes place at many levels within the Commission. Senior Commission officials who have moved from civil service posts within their Member States are often surprised by the extent to which they are enabled to bring forward their own policy initiatives. Since there is no equivalent of a Cabinet with a political programme, either at Council of Ministers or Commission level, there is much greater scope for even middle-ranking officials to bring forward proposals to implement the Work Programme.

The Commission also has an important external role, representing the Community in negotiations with other groups of states and trading organisations. This is specifically recognised by Art 133(3) EC Treaty which provides that:

> Where agreements with one or more States or international organisations need to be negotiated, the Commission shall make recommendations to the Council, which shall authorise the Commission to open the necessary negotiations.
>
> The Commission shall conduct these negotiations in consultation with a special committee appointed by the Council to assist the Commission in its task and within the framework of such directives as the Council may issue to it.

Under Art 133, the Commission is empowered, subject to the necessary Council approval, to negotiate world trade agreements.

The Commission represents the EU at a number of important international organisations, three of which are specifically mentioned in the EC Treaty:

■ Article 302 – United Nations;

■ Article 303 – Council of Europe;

■ Article 304 – Organisation for Economic Cooperation and Development (OECD).

It is also the holder of Community funds and administers four special funds:

■ the European Social Fund;

■ the Cohesion Fund;

■ the European Agricultural Guidance and Guarantee Fund; and

■ the European Regional Development Fund.

The European Social Fund seeks mainly to expand vocational training for workers in order to promote employment and occupational mobility (Arts 146, 147 EC Treaty).

The Cohesion Fund was established in 1993 to provide financial support for projects in the environment and in relation to trans-European networks in the area of transport infrastructure (Art 161 EC Treaty). It was created as part of a process of transferring resources from some of the Community's wealthier states to those with less-developed economies. The four countries which initially benefited from the Cohesion Fund – those with Gross National Products (GNP) per capita at 90 per cent or less of the Community average – were Spain, Portugal, Greece and Ireland.

The European Agricultural Guidance and Guarantee Fund was set up to assist in the restructuring of national agricultural economies (Art 37 EC Treaty).

The European Regional Development Fund is intended to help to redress the main regional imbalances in the Community through participation in the development of regions which are lagging behind economically (Art 160 EC Treaty).

Constitutional Treaty

If the Constitutional Treaty had come into force, Art I-26(2) would have explicitly provided that 'Union legislative acts may be adopted only on the basis of a Commission proposal, except where the Constitution provides otherwise. Other acts shall be adopted on the basis of a Commission proposal where the Constitution so provides'.

Article 133(3) EC Treaty would have been substantially re-enacted by Art III-217(3). Articles 302–304 EC Treaty would have been substantially re-enacted by Art III-229 which would have provided that the Union Minister for Foreign Affairs and the Commission would implement the Union's policy to 'establish all appropriate forms of cooperation with the organs of the United Nations and its specialised agencies, the Council of Europe, the Organisation for Security and Cooperation in Europe and the Organisation for Economic Cooperation and Development', and to 'maintain such relations as are appropriate with other international organisations'.

The Commission as 'Guardian of the Treaties'

The expression 'Guardian of the Treaties' is used to describe the Commission's role both as the keeper of the 'soul' of the Community, maintaining its course towards its declared aims of political and economic unity, and the more mundane, but equally important, role of ensuring that the Member States honour their obligation to give effect to the Treaty and the implementing legislation (Art 10 EC Treaty). This role is discharged both through political contact and, if need be, by the initiation of proceedings against Member States under Art 226 EC Treaty (previously Art 169). The Commission is empowered by Art 226 to bring an action against a Member State which is acting in breach of Community law. This is a very important provision and is considered in greater detail in Chapter 7. The Commission will first of all ask the defaulting Member State for its own observations on the default. The Commission will then, if the matter cannot be settled, deliver a reasoned opinion. This will set out why the Commission considers the Member State to be in breach of Community law and what the Member State must do to remedy the situation. If the Member State still fails to act, the Commission may take proceedings against the Member State, such proceedings being brought before the Court of Justice. The action will be listed as **Commission *v* Member State**.

The Commission has another important policing and regulating function in relation to Arts 81 and 82 EC Treaty. The preservation of a genuine common market within the Community of goods, services and capital is dependent not just on the collaboration of governments in removing both visible and invisible barriers, but also on the exercise, by the Community, of substantial powers to prevent large private and state undertakings using restrictive agreements, and other abuses of their dominant market position, to exclude Community-produced goods and services from domestic markets (see Chapters 20 and 21).

Access to Commission documents

The attitude towards openness and transparency has changed rapidly over the last few years within all the European institutions, including the Commission. A number of measures have been taken to open up the work of the Commission to public scrutiny, as a means of enabling citizens to take part in an informed way in the debate on the future of Europe. The Commission makes frequent use of Green Papers and White Papers. Green Papers are communications published by the Commission on a specific policy area. Primarily they are documents addressed to interested parties, organisations and individuals, who are invited to participate in a process of consultation and debate. In some cases they provide an impetus for subsequent legislation. White Papers are documents containing proposals for Community action in a specific area, which often follow a Green Paper. While Green Papers set out a range of ideas presented for public discussion and debate, White Papers contain an official set of proposals in specific policy areas and are used as vehicles for their development. These documents can be accessed on the Commission's website:

> http://europa.eu/documents/comm/index_en.htm
The vast catalogue of documents available on the Europa website
> http://europa.eu/index_en.htm

has added to this openness and transparency.

In accordance with the wish expressed at several European Council meetings, the Commission adopted a decision on public access to Commission documents in February 1994. This implemented a joint code of conduct between the Commission and the Council. The general principle expressed in it was that the public should have the widest possible access to documents held by these two institutions, subject to public or private interests being protected (Commission Decision 94/90 of 8 February 1994 on public access to Commission documents).

The Treaty of Amsterdam amended the EC Treaty to include a new Art 255 which provides for access to documents of the European Parliament, Council of Ministers and Commission. Pursuant to Art 255, Regulation 1049/2001 was adopted by the Council of Ministers and this Regulation replaced Decision 94/90 with effect from 3 December 2001. Refusal to grant access must be based on one of the exceptions provided for in the Regulation and must be justified on the ground that disclosure of the document would be harmful. Article 4 of the Regulation sets out the exceptions, for example:

1. The institutions shall refuse access to a document where disclosure would undermine the protection of:
   (a) the public interest, as regards:
   – public security
   – defence and military matters
   – international relations
   – the financial, monetary or economic policy of the Community or a Member State
   (b) privacy and the integrity of the individual, in particular in accordance with Community legislation regarding the protection of personal data.

2. The institutions shall refuse access to a document where disclosure would undermine the protection of:
- commercial interests of a natural or legal person, including intellectual property
- court proceedings and legal advice
- the purpose of inspections, investigations and audits unless there is an overriding public interest in disclosure.

Article 4(4) provides that an institution which is requested to disclose a document originating from a third party has to consult the third party with a view to assessing whether one of the exceptions provided for by the Regulation is applicable, unless it is clear that the document is or is not to be disclosed. Article 4(5) provides that a Member State may request the institution not to disclose a document originating from that Member State without its prior agreement.

In a case brought by an individual against the Commission, the CFI examined whether the Commission could lawfully refuse access to documents which were in its possession but which had been drawn up by the Italian authorities. The CFI pointed out in this regard that the institutions may be required, in appropriate cases, to communicate documents originating from third parties, including, in particular, the Member States. The CFI noted, however, that the Member States are subject to special treatment inasmuch as Art 4(5), Regulation 1049/2001 confers on a Member State the power to request an institution not to disclose documents originating from that State without its prior agreement. In this case the Italian authorities had opposed communication to the applicant of the documents emanating from them, and therefore the Commission had been entitled to reject the application for access (**Messina v Commission** (Case T-76/02)).

The same issue arose in the following case:

IFAW Internationaler Tierschutz-Fonds v Commission (Case T-168/02)

Germany had refused to agree to the disclosure to the applicant of certain documents originating from the German authorities, and therefore the Commission refused to disclose them to that applicant. On an application for annulment of the decision refusing access, the CFI upheld that decision. Pointing out that the Member States are in a different position from that of other third parties, the CFI observed that a Member State has the power to request an institution not to disclose a document originating from it and the institution is obliged not to disclose it without its 'prior agreement'. That obligation imposed on the institution to obtain the Member State's prior agreement, which is clearly laid down in Art 4(5), Regulation 1049/2001, would risk becoming a dead letter if the Commission was able to decide to disclose that document despite an explicit request not to do so from the Member State concerned. Thus, where a request is made by a Member State under that provision, the institution is obliged not to disclose the document in question.

In the following case, the CFI clarified the conditions governing the treatment by the institutions of a request for access to a large number of documents:

VKI v Commission (Case T-2/03)

The Verein für Konsumenteninformation (VKI), an association of Austrian consumers, had made a request to the Commission for access to its administrative file in a competition procedure that had resulted in a decision censuring eight Austrian banks for their participation in a cartel (known as the 'Lombard Club'). The Commission refused that request in its entirety and the VKI brought an action for annulment of that refusal before the CFI.

The CFI held that since the purpose of the concrete, individual examination which the institution must in principle undertake in response to a request for access is to enable the institution in question to assess, on the one hand, the extent to which an exception to the right of access is applicable and, on the other, the possibility of partial access, such an examination may not be necessary where, due to the particular circumstances of the individual case, it is obvious that access must be refused or, on the contrary, granted.

In this case, the CFI found that the exceptions relied on by the Commission did not necessarily apply to the whole of the Lombard Club file and that, even in the case of the documents to which they may apply, they may concern only certain passages in those documents. Consequently, **the Commission was bound, in principle, to carry out a concrete, individual examination of each of the documents referred to in the request, in order to determine whether any exceptions applied or whether partial access was possible.**

However, the CFI added that **a derogation from that obligation to examine the documents may be permissible in exceptional cases where the administrative burden entailed by a concrete, individual examination of the documents proves to be particularly heavy, thereby exceeding the limits of what may reasonably be required. In such a situation, the institution is obliged to try to consult with the applicant in order, on the one hand, to ascertain or to ask him to specify his interest in obtaining the documents in question and, on the other, to consider specifically whether and how it may adopt a measure less onerous than a concrete, individual examination of the documents. The institution nevertheless remains obliged, against that background, to prefer the option which, whilst not itself constituting a task which exceeds the limits of what may reasonably be required, remains the most favourable to the applicant's right of access.**

In this case, it was not apparent from the contested decision that the Commission considered specifically and exhaustively the various options available to it in order to take steps which would not impose an unreasonable amount of work on it but would, on the other hand, increase the chances that the applicant might receive, at least in respect of part of its request, access to the documents concerned. As a result, the CFI annulled the Commission's decision.

Documents on this transparency policy are available at:
    http://ec.europa.eu/transparency/access_documents/index_en.htm

Constitutional Treaty

If the Constitutional Treaty had come into force, Art I-50(3) would have provided that 'Any citizen of the Union, and any natural or legal person residing or having its registered office in a Member State shall have, under the conditions laid down in Part III, a right of access to documents of the Union institutions . . .' Article III-399 would have provided that:

1. The institutions . . . of the Union shall ensure transparency in their work and shall, pursuant to Article I-50, determine in their rules of procedure specific provisions for public access to their documents . . .

Reforming the Commission

Following the removal from office of Jacques Santer's Commission, there was considered to be a need for reform to take place. The former Vice-President, Neil Kinnock, was given responsibility for the Administrative Reform of the Commission. A White Paper 'Reforming the Commission' was adopted by the Commission on 1 March 2000 (COM (2000) 200 final). The White Paper, and other documents associated with the reform agenda, are available at:

http://ec.europa.eu/reform/index_en.htm

The White Paper set out a strategy with three related themes:

- *Reform of the way political priorities are set and resources allocated.* New policy-driven decision-taking mechanisms will ensure that activities undertaken by the Commission are carried out with the necessary human, administrative, IT and financial resources. The evaluation of results will become a routine part of management activities.

- *Important changes to human resources policy*, placing a premium on performance, continuous training and quality of management, as well as improving recruitment and career development. These changes will also place an emphasis on improving the working environment and equal opportunities, as well as the evaluation of management and staff, and will enable disciplinary matters or cases of under-performance to be dealt with properly and fairly.

- *An overhaul of financial management*, empowering each department to establish an effective internal control system appropriate to its own needs. In doing so, departments will be able to draw on the advice of the Commission's specialist services. Reform is predicated upon a precise definition of the responsibilities of each actor, and upon regular checks by the Internal Audit Service on the quality and reliability of each internal control system.

Progress was relatively slow, but two notable achievements are as follows:

- New Staff Regulations entered into force on 1 May 2004, setting out the terms and conditions of employment for EU civil servants (Regulation 723/2004 (OJ 2004 L 124/1)).

- A new Code of Conduct for Commissioners entered into force in November 2004.

Both of the above measures are available at:

http://ec.europa.eu/reform/index_en.htm

The Council of Ministers

The provisions of the EC Treaty which govern the Council of Ministers are Arts 202–210 (previously Arts 145–154). The Council's website can be accessed at:

http://www.consilium.europa.eu/cms3_fo/showPage.ASP?lang=en

The EC Treaty refers to the Council; many commentators refer to the Council of Ministers. However, in November 1993, the Council chose to rename itself the Council of the European Union. This reflects the fact that it is the only institution which is truly an institution of all three pillars of the European Union. As discussed in Chapter 1, the other institutions have their principal role in the European Communities pillar.

Constitutional Treaty

If the Constitutional Treaty had come into force, Arts I-23 to I-25 and III-342 to III-346 would have set out the provisions which would have applied to the Council of Ministers.

As discussed in Chapter 1, the Constitutional Treaty would have established a single European Union which would have replaced the current European Communities and the European Union (Art I-1 Constitutional Treaty). The three pillars would have been merged although special procedures would have been maintained in the fields of foreign policy, security and defence. For this reason, the Council of Ministers would no longer have been referred to as the Council of the European Union. It would simply have been referred to as 'the Council'.

Composition

The Council consists of members of the governments of the Member States 'authorised to commit the government of that Member State' (Art 203 EC Treaty). The Council is therefore made up of politicians from the Member States who are authorised to bind the Member State they represent. The membership will vary according to the matter under discussion within the specialised Council meetings (referred to as 'configurations'). During the 1990s there were 22 configurations; this was reduced to 16 in June 2000, and further reduced to nine in June 2002. The nine configurations are as follows:

- General Affairs and External Relations
- Economic and Financial Affairs
- Competitiveness
- Cooperation in the fields of Justice and Home Affairs (JHA)
- Employment, Social Policy, Health and Consumer Affairs
- Transport, Telecommunications and Energy
- Agriculture and Fisheries
- Environment
- Education, Youth and Culture.

The President of the European Commission, although not a member of the Council and not entitled to vote, will in practice attend these meetings, or another Commissioner may attend on his behalf.

Although Member States are normally represented by the senior minister in each department, this may not always be possible and there are occasions when Council meetings comprise ministers of different levels of seniority.

Constitutional Treaty

Article 203 EC Treaty, relating to composition of the Council, would have been substantially re-enacted by Art I-23 Constitutional Treaty, if the Treaty had come into force.

Article I-24(1) would have provided that the Council would meet in different configurations. The General Affairs Council would have ensured consistency in the work of the different Council configurations, and it would have prepared and ensured the follow-up to meetings of the European Council, in liaison with the President of the European Council and the Commission (Art I-24(2)). Article I-24(3) would have established the Foreign Affairs Council which 'shall elaborate the Union's external action on the basis of strategic guidelines laid down by the European Council and ensure that the Union's action is consistent'. A list of additional Council configurations would have been adopted by the European Council acting by a qualified majority (Art I-24(4)).

President of the Council

Article 203 EC Treaty provides for the office of President to be held in turn by each Member State for a period of six months in the order decided by the Council acting unanimously. Pursuant to Art 203, the Council decided that for the first six months of 2005 the presidency would be held by Luxembourg, followed by the UK (last six months 2005), Austria (first six months 2006), Finland (last six months 2006) and Germany (first six months of 2007).

The President is responsible for preparing the agenda for Council meetings, so that holding the presidency provides an opportunity for Member States to ensure that issues that are of importance to them are placed at the top of the agenda. There is also an element of competition between Member States, so that success or failure of a presidency will, to some extent, be judged by the volume of legislation adopted during that six-month period.

Council of Ministers' meetings are normally convened by the country holding the presidency. In some cases, however, the Commission, or another Member State, may take the initiative in convening a meeting.

The government of the Member State holding the presidency is primarily responsible for arranging and chairing ministerial meetings of the Council and of its sub-committees. It also has to attempt to gain support among the other Member States for new initiatives, for maintaining their momentum once they are launched and for representing the Council's views to the other institutions. The presidency's control of the agenda allows it considerable scope to change and affect the pace of policy changes in the Community. Achievement of the policy goals set by the presidency will depend to a large extent on its ability to persuade the other Member States to go along with new initiatives, often by a process of trade-offs and mutual concessions in other, sometimes quite unrelated, policy areas. Continuity between successive presidencies is maintained by a close process of cooperation between the outgoing and incoming Member States.

Constitutional Treaty

If the Constitutional Treaty had come into force it would have provided for the presidency of the Council configurations, other than that of Foreign Affairs, to be held by Member State representatives in the Council on the basis of 'equal rotation'. This basis would have been set out in a European decision of the European Council which would have been adopted by a qualified majority (Art I-25).

Function

The function of the Council is set out in Art 202 EC Treaty in very broad terms:

> To ensure that the objectives set out in this Treaty are attained the Council shall, in accordance with the provisions of the Treaty:
> - ensure coordination of the general economic policies of the Member States;
> - have power to take decisions ...

Decision-making remains the central role of the Council and the different methods of decision-making are considered in detail in Chapter 4. Despite the increasingly important role of the Parliament, in the overwhelming majority of cases the Council is the place where final decisions will be made. Hitherto, discussions in the Council of Ministers have been held in secret. However, Art 255 EC Treaty now confers a right of access to all Council documents for all citizens of the Union or anyone living in a Member State. As discussed above, this has been implemented by Regulation 1049/2001 which came into effect on 3 December 2001. Refusal to grant access must be based on one of the exceptions provided for in the Regulation and must be justified on the grounds that disclosure of the document would be harmful.

The CFI considered the application of Regulation 1049/2001, in relation to access to Council documents, in the following case:

Turco v Council (Case T-84/03)

The Council refused to disclose to the applicant an opinion of the Council's legal service on a proposal for a Council Directive. The Council had relied on Art 4(2), Regulation 1049/2001 which provides that the institutions are to refuse access to a document where disclosure would undermine the protection of, *inter alia*, court proceedings and legal advice unless there is an overriding public interest in disclosure.

The CFI held in favour of the Council. It held that the words 'legal advice' must be understood as meaning that the protection of the public interest may preclude the disclosure of the contents of documents drawn up by the Council's legal service in the context of court proceedings but also for any other purpose. It pointed out that legal advice drawn up in the context of court proceedings was already covered by the exception relating to the protection of such proceedings.

The CFI stated that exceptions to the right of access to the institutions' documents under the Regulation must be interpreted and applied strictly, and therefore the fact that the document in question is a legal opinion cannot, of itself, justify application of the exception relied upon. However, since (i) the Council made no error of assessment in considering that the disclosure of such advice could give rise to lingering doubts as to the lawfulness of the legislative act in question and there was, therefore, an interest in the protection of that opinion; and (ii) the applicant had not cited any matter of public interest liable to justify the disclosure of such a document, the CFI dismissed the action in its entirety.

Constitutional Treaty

If the Constitutional Treaty had come into force, Art I-23(1) would have provided that 'The Council shall, jointly with the European Parliament, exercise legislative and budgetary functions. It shall carry out policy-making and coordinating functions as laid down in the Constitution'.

Art I-24(6) would have provided that the Council would meet in public when it deliberated and voted on a draft legislative act.

COREPER

COREPER, which is the French acronym for the Committee of Permanent Representatives, plays an important role in providing continuity during the inevitable absences of relevant ministers from the Council. The Committee consists of senior national officials who are permanently located in Brussels. The Committee was originally established by Art 4 of the Merger Treaty in 1965, but it has now been formally integrated into the Community's decision-making structure by Art 207 EC Treaty. The Committee 'shall be responsible for preparing the work of the Council and for carrying out the tasks assigned to it by the Council' (Art 207(1) EC Treaty).

The Committee operates on two levels: COREPER I, which consists of the ambassadors from the Member States who are seconded to the Community in Brussels, and COREPER II, which is staffed by the ambassadors' deputies. The primary task of COREPER is to prepare items for discussion at Council meetings and it will be assisted in this by a whole range of specialist advisory committees. If the text of a policy statement or legislation can be agreed before the meeting, it will be tabled in Part A of the Council agenda, where it will normally be adopted without further discussion. More difficult, controversial items, on which agreement has not been possible, will appear in Part B of the agenda. In these cases the issue may, subject to the appropriate legal base, have to be decided by a qualified majority vote (see Chapter 4).

Constitutional Treaty

If the Constitutional Treaty had come into force, Art I-24(5) would have provided that 'A Committee of Permanent Representatives of the Governments of the Member States shall be responsible for preparing the work of the Council'. Article III-344(1) would have further provided that 'A committee consisting of the Permanent Representatives of the Governments of the Member States shall be responsible for preparing the work of the Council and for carrying out the tasks assigned to it by the latter. The Committee may adopt procedural decisions in cases provided for in the Council's Rules of Procedure'.

The European Parliament

The provisions of the EC Treaty governing the European Parliament are Arts 189–201 (previously Arts 137–144). The European Parliament's website can be accessed at:

http://www.europarl.europa.eu/news/public/default_en.htm

The EC Treaty, as it was originally drawn in 1957, included provision for 'an Assembly' whose task was to 'exercise the advisory and supervisory powers' conferred upon it (Art 189 EC Treaty). The Assembly is now called 'The European Parliament' and the words 'advisory and supervisory' have disappeared. The Parliament, which in 1979 became a directly elected body, now simply exercises the powers conferred on it by the Treaty (Art 189 EC Treaty (as amended by the TEU)). Prior to that date, its members were drawn from nominees from the national parliaments. It is currently the only directly elected institution in the Community, but the name 'Parliament' is misleading. It shares a number of important features with national parliaments and has considerable influence but it falls far short of being a real, sovereign parliament as would be understood in the UK. The principal difference is that it lacks the power both to initiate legislation and to impose taxes. Its powers have increased, however, and are likely to continue to do so following the changes to decision-making made by the SEA, TEU, ToA and ToN. The rationale for the increase in Parliament's powers was to counter the argument that the Community was democratically deficient because its only directly elected body had no real powers.

Constitutional Treaty

If the Constitutional Treaty had come into force, Arts I-20 and III-330 to III-340 would have set out the provisions which would have applied to the European Parliament.

Article I-20(1) would have provided that 'The European Parliament shall, jointly with the Council, exercise legislative and budgetary functions. It shall exercise functions of political control and consultation as laid down in the Constitution ...'

Composition

25 Member States (pre 1 January 2007)

Following enlargement of the European Union from 15 Member States to 25 on 1 May 2004, and the subsequent elections to the European Parliament during June 2004, the Parliament consisted of 732 Members of the European Parliament (MEPs). This was an increase from 626 pre-enlargement. MEPs are elected on different variants of proportional representation. The last elections to the European Parliament took place in June 2004. Prior to the June 1999 election, UK MEPs were elected by the first-past-the-post system as used for general elections (except in Northern Ireland where MEPs had previously been elected by a system of proportional representation). The UK Labour Party, which was elected to government following a landslide general election victory on 1 May 1997, had stated in its manifesto that: 'We have long supported a proportional voting system for election to the European Parliament'. The European Parliamentary Elections Act 1999 was duly enacted and was in force in time for the June 1999 MEP elections. The Act divides the UK into electoral regions:

- England (9 regions) – 71 MEPs
- Scotland (1 region) – 8 MEPs
- Wales (1 region) – 5 MEPs
- Northern Ireland (1 region) – 3 MEPs.

The electoral system (which was used within the UK for the first time on 10 June 1999) provides that in each region within England, Scotland and Wales, MEPs are elected by a regional list system. The electorate votes either for a registered party (e.g. Labour, Conservatives, etc. – i.e. a closed party list system) or an individual candidate who stands

Table 3.2 UK results in European Parliamentary elections 1994, 1999 and 2004

Parties	1994			1999			2004		
	% vote	% seats	Seats	% vote	% seats	Seats	% vote	% seats	Seats
Conservatives	27.8	21.4	18	35.8	42.9	36	27.4	34.6	27
Labour	44.2	73.8	62	28.0	34.5	29	22.3	24.4	19
UK Independence Party				7.0	3.6	3	16.8	15.4	12
Liberal Democrats	16.7	2.4	2	12.7	12.0	10	15.1	15.4	12
Greens	3.2	0	0	6.3	2.4	2	6.2	2.6	2
Scottish Nationalists	3.2	2.4	2	2.7	2.4	2	3.0	2.6	2
Plaid Cymru	1.1	0	0	1.9	2.4	2	1.1	1.3	1
Ulster Unionists							1.0	1.3	1
Democratic Unionists							1.0	1.3	1
Sinn Fein							1.0	1.3	1
Pro-Euro Conservatives				7.0	3.6	3			
Others	3.7	0	0	3.7	0	0			

as an independent. The first seat is allocated to the party or individual candidate with the greatest number of votes. The second and subsequent seats are allocated in the same way, but the number of votes given to a party to which one or more seats have already been allocated is divided by the number of seats allocated **plus 1**.

Northern Ireland uses a different system, which is the same as that used for elections to the Northern Ireland Assembly.

Table 3.2 sets out the UK's results in the European Parliamentary elections in 1994 (which used the first-past-the-post system), and 1999 and 2004 (which used the new proportional system).

Article 11 of the Accession Treaty 2003 (which paved the way for enlargement of the European Union on 1 May 2004) amended Art 190(2) EC Treaty to provide that from the start of the 2004–09 Parliamentary term the number of representatives to be elected by each Member State would be as follows, alphabetically:

Table 3.3 Member State MEP allocation, 2004-09 term (alphabetical)

Member State	Representatives	Member State	Representatives
Austria	18	Latvia	9
Belgium	24	Lithuania	13
Cyprus	6	Luxembourg	6
Czech Republic	24	Malta	5
Denmark	14	Netherlands	27
Estonia	6	Poland	54
Finland	14	Portugal	24
France	78	Slovakia	14
Germany	99	Slovenia	7
Greece	24	Spain	54
Hungary	24	Sweden	19
Ireland	13	UK	78
Italy	78	**Total**	**732**

... and as follows, numerically:

Table 3.4 Member State MEP allocation, 2004-09 term (numerical)

Member State	Representatives	Member State	Representatives
Germany	99	Austria	18
France	78	Denmark	14
Italy	78	Finland	14
UK	78	Slovakia	14
Poland	54	Ireland	13
Spain	54	Lithuania	13
Netherlands	27	Latvia	9
Belgium	24	Estonia	7
Czech Republic	24	Slovenia	7
Greece	24	Cyprus	6
Hungary	24	Luxembourg	6
Portugal	24	Malta	5
Sweden	19	**Total**	**732**

The number of MEPs allocated to each Member State is not in proportion to its population. However, Art 190(2) EC Treaty provided that in the event of an amendment being made to the number of MEPs, 'the number of representatives elected in each Member State must ensure appropriate representation of the peoples of the States brought together in the Community'. Article 189 provided that the number of MEPs shall not exceed the current 732.

27 Member States (from 1 January 2007)

Transitional period: 1 January 2007 to the beginning of the 2009-2014 European Parliamentary term

The Accession Treaty which provided for Bulgaria and Romania's entry into the EU included an Act which set out transitional arrangements and amendments to the founding treaties. Article 9(1) of the Act amended Art 189(2) EC Treaty to provide that 'the number of Members of the European Parliament shall not exceed 736'. This is an increase from the previous maximum of 732.

Article 24(1) of the Act provides that the number of MEPs shall be increased to take account of the accession of Bulgaria and Romania, notwithstanding the 736 maximum stipulated in Art 189(2) EC Treaty. From the date of accession (i.e. 1 January 2007), until the beginning of the 2009–2014 term, Bulgaria will have 18 MEPs and Romania will have 35. Therefore, the numbers of MEPs from 1 January 2007 until the beginning of the 2009–2014 term will be as follows, alphabetically:

Table 3.5 Member State MEP allocation from 1 January 2007 to the start of the 2009-2014 European Parliamentary term (alphabetical)

Member State	Representatives	Member State	Representatives
Austria	18	Latvia	9
Belgium	24	Lithuania	13
Bulgaria	18	Luxembourg	6
Cyprus	6	Malta	5
Czech Republic	24	Netherlands	27
Denmark	14	Poland	54
Estonia	6	Portugal	24
Finland	14	Romania	35
France	78	Slovakia	14
Germany	99	Slovenia	7
Greece	24	Spain	54
Hungary	24	Sweden	19
Ireland	13	UK	78
Italy	78	**Total**	**785**

. . . and as follows, numerically:

Table 3.6 Member State MEP allocation from 1 January 2007 to the start of the 2009–2014 European Parliamentary term (numerical)

Member State	Representatives	Member State	Representatives
Germany	99	Austria	18
France	78	Bulgaria	18
Italy	78	Denmark	14
UK	78	Finland	14
Poland	54	Slovakia	14
Spain	54	Ireland	13
Romania	35	Lithuania	13
Netherlands	27	Latvia	9
Belgium	24	Estonia	7
Czech Republic	24	Slovenia	7
Greece	24	Cyprus	6
Hungary	24	Luxembourg	6
Portugal	24	Malta	5
Sweden	19	**Total**	**785**

Article 24(2) of the Act provides that before 31 December 2007, Bulgaria and Romania will hold elections for the appointment of their MEPs. Article 24(3) provides that in the interim period (i.e. from 1 January 2007 until elections are held, which must be no later than 31 December 2007), the Bulgarian and Romanian MEPs will be appointed by their respective national parliaments.

2009–2014 European Parliamentary term

Article 20 of the Declaration adopted by the Nice Intergovernmental Conference, which is attached to the ToN, provided that in an enlarged Union of 27 Member States the number of MEPs would be as follows:

Table 3.7 Member State MEP allocation (27 Member States)

Member State	Representatives	Member State	Representatives
Germany	99	Austria	17
France	72	Bulgaria	17
Italy	72	Denmark	13
UK	72	Finland	13
Poland	50	Slovakia	13
Spain	50	Ireland	12
Romania	33	Lithuania	12
Netherlands	25	Latvia	8
Belgium	22	Slovenia	7
Greece	22	Cyprus	6
Portugal	22	Estonia	6
Czech Republic	20	Luxembourg	6
Hungary	20	Malta	5
Sweden	18	**Total**	**732**

However, the Act attached to the Accession Treaty which provided for Bulgaria and Romania's entry into the EU has amended the EC Treaty to alter these allocations. As stated above, Art 9(1) of the Act has amended Art 189(2) EC Treaty to provide that 'the number of Members of the European Parliament shall not exceed 736'. This is an increase from the previous maximum of 732. Article 190(2) EC Treaty previously provided that in the event of an amendment being made to the number of MEPs, 'the number of representatives elected in each Member State must ensure appropriate representation of the peoples of the States brought together in the Community'.

Article 9(2) of the Act has amended Art 190(2) EC Treaty to remove the above provision, and also to provide that from the start of the 2009-2014 European Parliamentary term, the number of MEPs will be as follows, alphabetically:

Table 3.8 Member State MEP allocation from the start of the 2009-2014 European Parliamentary term (alphabetical)

Member State	Representatives	Member State	Representatives
Austria	17	Latvia	8
Belgium	22	Lithuania	12
Bulgaria	17	Luxembourg	6
Cyprus	6	Malta	5
Czech Republic	22	Netherlands	25
Denmark	13	Poland	50
Estonia	6	Portugal	22
Finland	13	Romania	33
France	72	Slovakia	13
Germany	99	Slovenia	7
Greece	22	Spain	50
Hungary	22	Sweden	18
Ireland	12	UK	72
Italy	72	**Total**	**736**

... and as follows, numerically:

Table 3.9 Member State MEP allocation from the start of the 2009-2014 European Parliamentary term (numerical)

Member State	Representatives	Member State	Representatives
Germany	99	Austria	17
France	72	Bulgaria	17
Italy	72	Denmark	13
UK	72	Finland	13
Poland	50	Slovakia	13
Spain	50	Ireland	12
Romania	33	Lithuania	12
Netherlands	25	Latvia	8
Belgium	22	Slovenia	7
Greece	22	Cyprus	6
Portugal	22	Estonia	6
Czech Republic	22	Luxembourg	6
Hungary	22	Malta	5
Sweden	18	**Total**	**736**

Only Estonia, Germany, Luxembourg, Malta and Slovenia have retained the same number of MEPs as before, with all other Member States having had their representation reduced. The two new Member States, Bulgaria and Romania, have been allocated 17 and 33 MEPs respectively.

Constitutional Treaty

The Constitutional Treaty, if it had come into force, would have made alternative arrangements for membership of the European Parliament. Article I-20(2) would have provided that the number of MEPs would not exceed 750 (compare this to Art 189 EC Treaty which sets an upper limit of 736). It would also have provided that:

> Representation of citizens shall be degressively proportional, with a minimum threshold of six members per Member State. No Member State shall be allocated more than ninety-six seats.
>
> The European Council shall adopt by unanimity, on the initiative of the European Parliament and with its consent, a European decision establishing the composition of the European Parliament, respecting the principles referred to in the first paragraph.

Political groups

MEPs are elected for a term of five years. They stand as members of national political parties, but sit within broad political rather than national groupings in the Parliament. As at 15 October 2006, excluding the Bulgarian and Romanian MEPs, the political groups were represented within the European Parliament as follows:

Table 3.10 European Parliament political groups (not including Bulgaria and Romania MEPs) as at 15 October 2006

Political Party	Number of seats
European People's Party and European Democrats (includes UK Conservative Party MEPs)	264
Socialist Group (includes UK Labour Party MEPs)	201
Alliance of Liberals and Democrats for Europe (includes UK Liberal Democrat MEPs)	89
Greens/European Free Alliance	42
European United Left/Nordic Green Left	41
Union for Europe of the Nations	30
Independence/Democracy Group	28
Others (unattached) (includes the Reverend Ian Paisley, the Northern Ireland MEP)	37
Total	**732**

From 1 January 2007, for a transitional period (see above), the number of MEPs will increase to 785 (Bulgaria being allocated 18 MEPs and Romania 35).

Under the EC Treaty (as amended by the TEU), political parties at European level are now recognised as 'a factor for integration within the Union' and 'contribute to forming a European awareness and to expressing the political will of the citizens of the Union' (Art 191 EC Treaty).

Political activity in the European Parliament largely takes place through the groups. Under the previous Rules of Procedure (2002) a political group had to comprise MEPs from more than one Member State (rule 29(2)). The minimum number of MEPs required to form a political group was 23 if they came from two Member States, 18 if they came from three Member States, and 14 if they came from four or more Member States. The 16th edition of the European Parliament's Rules of Procedure (July 2004, updated version July 20( )) amended the rules relating to the formation of political parties within the Parliament. Rule 29(2) now provides that:

> A political group shall comprise Members elected in at least one-fifth of the Member States. The minimum number of Members required to form a political group shall be nineteen.

The effect of this amendment is that a political group can only be formed if it includes at least 19 MEPs from at least 6 Member States (it had previously been 5 Member States prior to 1 January 2007 when the EU comprised 25 Member States).

There are a number of reasons why groups have developed. Primarily they are formed to provide mutual ideological support and identification. In addition, there are organisational benefits, including funds for administrative and research purposes which are better deployed in support of groups than for individuals. There are also advantages in the conduct of Parliamentary business that stem from group status, since the Parliament arranges much of its business around the groups. Although non-attached members are not formally excluded, and indeed are guaranteed many rights under the Rules of Procedure, they can, in practice, be disadvantaged in the distribution of committee chairmanships or in the preparation of the agendas for plenary sessions (i.e. meetings of the full Parliament).

A section of the Parliament's website is set aside for the political groups, each of which publishes a plethora of information. The website for the political groups can be accessed at:

http://www.europarl.europa.eu/groups/default_en.htm

The following case, which came before the CFI, concerned 29 formerly unattached MEPs who sought to form a group (and therefore receive the financial and organisational benefits bestowed upon groups).

Jean Claude Martinez, Charles de Gaulle, Front National, Emma Bonino, Marco Pannella, Marco Cappato, Gianfranco Dell'Alba, Benedetto Della Vedova, Olivier Dupuis, Maurizio Turco, Lista Emma Bobino v *European Parliament* (Joined Cases T-222/99, T-327/99 and T-329/99)

Twenty-nine MEPs informed the President of the European Parliament (as they were required to under Rule 29(4) of the Rules of Procedure) of the formation of their group: Technical Group of Independent Members – Mixed Group. The 'rules of constitution' for this new group declared that:

> ... the individual signatory members affirm their total independence of one another. And hence: freedom to vote independently both in committee and plenary session; each member shall refrain from speaking on behalf of the Members of the group as a whole; the purpose of meetings of the group shall be to allocate speaking time and to settle any administrative and financial matters concerning the group; and the Bureau of the group shall be made up of the representatives of the individual members.

Rule 29(1) provides that 'members may form themselves into groups according to their political affinities'. Having been through various Parliamentary procedures, on 13 September 1999 the Parliament determined that Rule 29(1) should be interpreted such that 'the formation of a group which openly rejects any political character and all political affiliation between its Members is not acceptable within the meaning of this Rule'. Given the new group's constitution which guaranteed its members total independence, the Parliament resolved to dissolve the group. Members of the group issued proceedings before the CFI contesting these decisions. The Court dismissed the applications.

The above case provides that political groups within Parliament must share some common ideological platform and must work together within Parliament. If that is not the case then Parliament can refuse to recognise the group and thus prevent it from being provided with the financial and organisational benefits which are bestowed upon groups. In the above case it did seem quite clear that the group members shared very little in common, were not prepared to work together within the Parliament, and were simply forming the group so that they could take advantage of the benefits. Rule 29(1) now further provides as follows:

> Parliament need not normally evaluate the political affinity of members of a group. In forming a group together under this Rule, Members concerned accept by definition that they have political affinity. Only when this is denied by the Members concerned is it necessary for Parliament to evaluate whether the group has been constituted in conformity with the Rules.

The ToN amended Art 191 EC Treaty to require the Council of Ministers to adopt regulations governing political parties and in particular regarding their funding.

Constitutional Treaty

If the Constitutional Treaty had come into force, Art I-46(4) would have provided that 'European parties at European level contribute to forming European political awareness and to expressing the will of citizens of the Union'. Art III-331 would have provided that European laws would lay down the regulations governing political parties at European level and in particular the rules regarding their funding.

Parliamentary meetings

The Parliament holds plenary sessions (i.e. all 785 MEPs (decreasing to 736 MEPs from the start of the 2009–2014 European Parliamentary term) congregating together in one chamber) in Strasbourg, committee meetings in Brussels and is serviced by staff located in Luxembourg. A new building has been erected in Brussels for full Parliamentary sessions but the European Council meeting in Edinburgh in December 1992 confirmed that the Parliament would remain in Strasbourg. A new Parliament building was opened in Strasbourg in December 1999 to ensure that the chamber could accommodate all the MEPs. Enlargement of Community membership, and the resultant increase in the number of MEPs, meant that the previous chamber was too small. A decision by the Parliament to increase the number of plenary sessions held in Brussels was struck down by the Court of Justice in October 1997 (**France v European Parliament** (Case C-345/95)). MEPs and officials will continue to live a highly peripatetic existence, largely because the Parliament is a major employer and the Member States cannot agree on a single, permanent site for it.

Except in August, the Parliament sits for one week in each month, usually in Strasbourg. It occasionally sits for additional periods to discuss special items, such as the budget. Between the monthly part-sessions, two weeks are set aside for meetings of the Parliamentary committees, and one week for meetings of the political groups.

Full details of the Parliamentary agenda and post-session report are available on the Parliament's website at:

http://www.europarl.europa.eu/activities.do?language=EN

Committee meetings

The Parliament has a large range of specialist committees. Some are permanent, while others are *ad hoc* (i.e. set up to consider a particular matter). The committees cover such matters as Internal Market and Consumer Protection; Economic and Monetary Affairs; Employment and Social Affairs; Transport and Tourism; Budgets; Foreign Affairs.

Much of Parliament's legislative groundwork will be conducted in committee. When Parliament receives a request from the Council or Commission for an opinion, approval or assent, the request will be sent to the relevant committee for a report to be prepared for full debate and vote in the chamber. The committee will appoint a member to be responsible for preparing the report. This person is called the 'Rapporteur'. The Rapporteur will lead the debate when the report of the committee comes before the full Parliament (i.e. when the Parliament sits in plenary session in Strasbourg).

The committees follow legislative and policy matters in detail and, as they usually meet *in camera* (i.e. the public are excluded from their meetings unless invited to attend by the Chairperson), they are given confidential information, both by Commission officials and by the independent experts and representatives of pressure groups who appear before them.

Powers of the Parliament

There are three main powers exercised by the Parliament:

- participation in the legislative processes of the Community;
- acting as the budgetary authority; and
- supervision of the Commission.

In addition to these formal powers, the Parliament takes an active part in the political life of Europe, commissioning reports and passing resolutions on social and political issues, human rights, defence and foreign policy, and on many other matters. It can, however, do little more than express a view on the issues about which the majority of MEPs are concerned.

The TEU strengthened the position of the Parliament by the addition of Art 192 to the EC Treaty, which provides that it may:

> ... request the Commission to submit any appropriate proposal on matters on which it considers that a Community act is required for the purposes of implementing this Treaty.

The Parliament also gained the important power under the SEA (now Art 49 TEU) of approval of new Member States. This is, potentially, an important bargaining counter in relation to the acquisition by the Parliament of more powers, although the opportunity was not taken at the time of enlargement in 1995, 2004 and 2007. The TEU also gave Parliament the power to set up *Committees of Inquiry* to 'investigate alleged contraventions or maladministration in the implementation of Community law' (Art 193 EC Treaty), and to appoint a *Parliamentary Ombudsman* to investigate complaints about any of the other institutions, except the Court of Justice and the CFI acting judicially (Art 195 EC Treaty). Jacob Söderman was elected the first European Ombudsman by the European

Parliament in 1995 and he remained in office until 2003. P. Nikiforos Diamandouros is the current European Ombudsman. The Ombudsman can investigate complaints against the Community institutions of maladministration, which includes such matters as unfairness, discrimination, abuse of power, lack or refusal of information or unnecessary delay. The Ombudsman's website can be accessed at:

http://www.euro-ombudsman.eu.int/home/en/default.htm

The role of Parliament in the decision-making process is discussed in Chapter 4.

The budget

In relation to the budget, the Parliament has an important function, which it shares with the Council of Ministers. The Community's budget is drafted by the Commission and placed before the Council of Ministers and Parliament before 1 September each year. This is necessary because the Community's financial year runs from 1 January to 31 December. The budget is divided into two parts: compulsory expenditure (CE) and non-compulsory expenditure (NCE). Compulsory expenditure relates to those items where the expenditure is required by the Treaty, primarily the Common Agricultural Policy which usually absorbs almost 50 per cent of the total budget, whereas NCE covers such items as social and regional policy, research and aid to non-EU countries in Central and Eastern Europe.

The Treaty gives Parliament wide powers to amend NCE items, but its powers to modify CE items are more limited under Art 272 EC Treaty. Parliament may, however, acting by a majority of its members (i.e. at least 393, because there are 785 MEPs (from the start of the 2009–2014 European Parliamentary term, this will reduce to 369 because the number of MEPs will be decreased to 736)), which must also represent a two-thirds majority of the votes actually cast, reject the whole of the draft budget and ask for a new draft to be submitted to it (Art 272(8) EC Treaty). If that occurs, the Community institutions have to continue on a month-by-month basis, spending no more than one-twelfth per month of the previous year's budget until a new budget is approved (Art 273 EC Treaty).

Supervision of the Commission

There is close and continuous contact between the Commissioners and Parliament. Although Commissioners are not members of Parliament, they frequently take part in debates where legislation is under discussion, and they will often attend the specialist committees of the Parliament to deal with detailed points arising from Commission proposals. Under the Treaty, they have the right to attend and to be heard (Art 197 EC Treaty).

Commissioners have a duty to respond, orally or in writing, to questions put to them by MEPs (Art 197 EC Treaty). Since 1974, this has become formalised into a Westminster-type Question Time during every week when Parliament is in full session (Rule 109, Rules of Procedure). Outside plenary sessions, there are regular exchanges between the Commission, the various Parliamentary Committees and individual MEPs.

The Parliament has the right to dismiss the Commission *en bloc* under Art 201 EC Treaty. Although it has never done so, as discussed above, it effectively forced Jacques Santer's Commission from office when Parliament threatened to use its censuring powers. The Commission accepted defeat and resigned, rather than face the humiliation of a certain defeat.

Since the TEU, the powers of the Parliament have been reinforced by the requirement that the new Commission, before it starts its term of office, is subject to a vote of approval by the Parliament (Art 214(2) EC Treaty). Prior to taking up office in 1995, individual Commissioners in the Santer administration were subjected to intensive questioning in American-style appointment committees. As a result of this questioning, Padraig Flynn, the Commissioner for Social Affairs, gave up the chair of the Commission's women's rights committee to the President of the Commission, Jacques Santer. As discussed above, the current Commission's five-year period of office started on 22 November 2004. This was three weeks later than planned, due to political problems which surfaced during the appointments process. During the European Parliamentary approval process, the Parliament opposed the appointment of Rocco Buttiglione (from Italy). Franco Frattini (from Italy) took the place of Rocco Buttiglione. The President-elect also requested the replacement of Latvia's Ingridia Udre, and he also reshuffled two portfolios. Following these changes, on 18 November 2004 the European Parliament approved the new Commission by 449 votes to 149, with 82 abstentions.

As previously discussed, the Commission's Work Programme is put together and implemented in close conjunction with Parliament, and there is a considerable coincidence of interest to both the Commission and Parliament in developing Community-wide policies. Where these fail to materialise, it is often as a result of the more nationally orientated policies of the Member States, reflected in the Council of Ministers. One of the most striking examples of this is the failure of the Community to develop a common transport policy, as required by Art 70 EC Treaty. The failure of the Council to make progress on the policy led to the initiation of proceedings in the Court of Justice by the Parliament (under Art 232 EC Treaty) with the support of the Commission. However, the Court of Justice declared that the provisions of Art 70 were not sufficiently precise to create a legally enforceable obligation (**European Parliament v Council** (Case 13/83)).

Enlargement of the powers of the European Parliament

The most obvious difference between the European Parliament and national parliaments is its inability to initiate legislation. As discussed in Chapter 4, although Parliament has, in most cases, the right to be consulted, such consultation may mean no more than the right to comment on a draft prepared by the Commission. Under some Treaty provisions there is no right of consultation at all, although Commission and Council practice is, nonetheless, to seek Parliament's views. In other cases, especially in relation to decisions in the field of economic and monetary policy, Parliament has no more than the right to be informed of the decision reached by the Council of Ministers (Arts 99(2) and 104(11) EC Treaty). Even where Parliament's opinion must be sought, there remains considerable scope for rejection of its views by the Council of Ministers, provided that Parliament's opinion is properly considered by the Council. It was widely felt that these limitations were inappropriate for the only democratically elected institution in the Union, and that the Treaty of Amsterdam should have conferred on Parliament the right to draft and initiate legislation, and to be involved at every level as a co-decision-maker; but most Member States, including the UK, were opposed to extending Parliament's powers in this way. Nevertheless, the role of Parliament in the legislative process has been strengthened following amendments to the EC Treaty by the SEA, TEU, ToA and ToN (see Chapter 4).

There is, arguably, a 'democratic deficit' in relation to Parliament's inability to dismiss individual Commissioners and to make Ministers accountable to Parliament for their decisions in the Council of Ministers. Although Council documents are now available after meetings and Council deliberations on legislative acts to be adopted by the co-decision procedure (see Chapter 4) are now generally open to the public (i.e. open sessions), the meetings of the Council generally take place in more or less complete secrecy. There is considerable support, largely among MEPs, for a Minister from the Council to be required to attend the Parliamentary debate and to report back to the Parliament at the conclusion of the ministerial meeting. Although there is some support for these proposals in Germany and The Netherlands, the UK government has remained firmly opposed to them, on the grounds that they would further undermine the powers of the UK Parliament to which national ministers are, in the last resort, solely accountable.

Court of Auditors

The Court was established by an amendment to the Treaties in 1975 (second Budgetary Treaty 1975). It is not, strictly speaking, a court, but more an audit commission. It is responsible for the external audit of the general budget of the European Communities. The internal audit is the responsibility of the Financial Controller of each institution.

The Court came into being partly as a result of the desire of some of the newer Member States to establish more effective audit arrangements and partly as a result of the desire of the Parliament to have greater power in the financial affairs of the Communities. An independent audit body is seen by Parliament as an important part in establishing greater financial control. It had, initially, the status of a separate body but, since the TEU came into effect in 1993, it has been classed by Art 7 EC Treaty as one of the institutions of the Community.

The Court consists of 27 full-time members (one from each Member State). Article 47 of the Act attached to the Accession Treaty which provided for Bulgaria and Romania's entry into the EU, increased the number of members from 25 to 27. The members who are chosen by the Council of Ministers (after consulting the European Parliament) from among persons who have had relevant auditing experience and whose independence is beyond doubt (Art 247(2) EC Treaty).

The Court of Auditors' website is available at: http://www.eca.eu.int/index_en.htm

The Economic and Social Committee (ECOSOC)

This Committee was established by Art 257 EC Treaty to assist the Council and the Commission in an advisory capacity. The Committee originally consisted of 'representatives of the various categories of economic and social activity, in particular, representatives of producers, farmers, carriers, workers, dealers, craftsmen, professional occupations and representatives of the general public'. The ToN amended Art 257 EC Treaty to provide that the Committee shall now consist of representatives 'of the various economic and social components of organised civil society, and in particular representatives of producers, farmers, carriers, workers, dealers, craftsmen, professional occupations, consumers and the general public'. Consumers are explicitly included for the first time. The Committee's website can be accessed at:

http://eesc.europa.eu/index_en.asp

The members of the Committee are appointed by the Council of Ministers, acting unanimously, for a period of four years (Art 259 EC Treaty) and they may be reappointed. Membership is allocated according to the size of the Member State. Following the accession of the ten new Member States on 1 May 2004, the number of ECOSOC members was increased from 222 to 317 (Art 258 EC Treaty), as follows:

Table 3.11 Member State ECOSOC membership prior to 1 January 2007
(25 Member States)

Member State	ECOSOC Members	Member State	ECOSOC Members
Austria	12	Latvia	7
Belgium	12	Lithuania	9
Cyprus	6	Luxembourg	6
Czech Republic	12	Malta	5
Denmark	9	Netherlands	12
Estonia	7	Poland	21
Finland	9	Portugal	12
France	24	Slovakia	9
Germany	24	Slovenia	7
Greece	12	Spain	21
Hungary	12	Sweden	12
Ireland	9	UK	24
Italy	24	**Total**	**317**

Article 20 of the Declaration adopted by the Nice Intergovernmental Conference, which is attached to the ToN, provided that in an enlarged Union of 27 Member States (Bulgaria and Romania joined the European Union on 1 January 2007), the number of ECOSOC members would be as follows:

Table 3.12 Member State ECOSOC membership from 1 January 2007 (27 Member States)

Member State	ECOSOC Members	Member State	ECOSOC Members
France	24	Portugal	12
Germany	24	Sweden	12
Italy	24	Denmark	9
UK	24	Finland	9
Poland	21	Ireland	9
Spain	21	Lithuania	9
Romania	15	Slovakia	9
Austria	12	Estonia	7
Belgium	12	Latvia	7
Bulgaria	12	Slovenia	7
Czech Republic	12	Cyprus	6
Greece	12	Luxembourg	6
Hungary	12	Malta	5
Netherlands	12	**Total**	**344**

These new membership figures have been confirmed by Art 12 of the Act attached to the Accession Treaty which provided for Bulgaria and Romania's entry into the EU. Article 12 of the Act amended Art 258 EC Treaty accordingly. Article 48 of the Act sets out the transitional arrangements which will apply from Bulgaria and Romania's date of accession (i.e. 1 January 2007):

The Economic and Social Committee shall be enlarged by the appointment of 27 members [i.e. 15 allocated to Romania and 12 to Bulgaria] representing the various economic and social components of organised civil society in Bulgaria and Romania. The terms of office of the members thus appointed shall expire at the same time as those of the members in office at the time of accession.

Members of the Committee must be completely independent and act 'in the general interests of the Community'. The members serve on three interest groups of Employers, Workers and General Interest, although they are prohibited from being bound by any mandate from that group in their own state or any other (Art 259 EC Treaty). The appointment of members is from a list of candidates provided by each Member State, and is to take account of the need to ensure adequate representation of the various categories of economic and social activity. The Court of Justice has held that adequate representation must be ensured at Community level but that, because of the limited number of seats available, it is not possible to guarantee that all the elements from every category of economic and social activity are represented by nationals from each Member State (**CIDA v Council** (Case 297/86)).

Constitutional Treaty

If the Constitutional Treaty had come into force, Arts I-32 and III-389 to III-392 would have set out the provisions which would have applied to ECOSOC. Article I-32(3) would have provided that 'The Economic and Social Committee shall consist of representatives of organisations of employers, of the employed, and of other parties representative of civil society, notably in socio-economic, civic, professional and cultural areas' (compare this with the amended Art 257 EC Treaty).

The members of the Committee would not have been bound by mandatory instructions, and they would have been completely independent in the performance of their duties 'in the Union's general interest' (Art I-32(4)).

Article III-389 would have provided that the number of ECOSOC members would not exceed 350. The Council, acting unanimously on a proposal from the Commission, would have adopted a European decision determining the Committee's composition.

Function of the Committee

The Economic and Social Committee (ECOSOC) is not recognised by Art 7 EC Treaty as being one of the institutions of the Community, although it receives a mention in Art 7(2). A requirement in Art 24 of the Merger Treaty that the Council consult 'other institutions' when adopting or amending staff regulations was held not to apply to ECOSOC (**Adam v Commission** (Case 828/79)). It must be consulted by the Council or the Commission where the Treaty provides for it, and in other cases consultation is at the discretion of those institutions. When the Committee is consulted, it responds by the submission of an opinion to the Commission and Council. These institutions can, if they wish, impose a deadline for the submission of an opinion, but this must not be less than one month (Art 262 EC Treaty). Failure to deliver an opinion cannot prevent further action by the institutions. The Committee also has the right to submit opinions on its own initiative where it considers such action appropriate (Art 262). Opinions of ECOSOC are prepared by a Section designated by the Chairperson and then discussed and adopted at plenary sessions of the full Committee which are held during the last seven days of the month (Title II, ECOSOC's Rules of Procedure). Although the Committee's opinions are not legally binding, the expertise of the Committee's membership does mean that they carry considerable weight with the institutions. Where the Treaty requires consultation of ECOSOC, failure to do so could lead to the annulment of a measure by the Court of Justice, on the basis of failure to meet an essential procedural requirement (see Chapter 8). The ToA amended the EC Treaty to create a new right for the European Parliament to consult ECOSOC (Art 262).

Constitutional Treaty

If the Constitutional Treaty had come into force, the Committee would have continued in its advisory capacity; it would not have been a formal institution (Art I-32(1)). Article II-392 would have provided as follows:

> The Economic and Social Committee shall be consulted by the European Parliament, by the Council or by the Commission where the Constitution so provides. It may be consulted by these institutions in all cases in which they consider it appropriate. It may also issue an opinion on its own initiative.
>
> The European Parliament, the Council or the Commission shall, if it considers it necessary, set the Committee, for the submission of its opinion, a time-limit which shall not be less than one month from the date on which the chairman receives notification to this effect. Upon expiry of the time-limit, the absence of an opinion shall not prevent further action.
>
> The opinion of the Committee, together with a record of its proceedings, shall be forwarded to the European Parliament, to the Council and to the Commission.

The Committee of the Regions

The Committee of the Regions was set up as an advisory body by the TEU (Art 263 EC Treaty) and, like ECOSOC, it is not recognised by Art 7 EC Treaty as one of the Community institutions, although it is mentioned in Art 7(2). It was intended to represent a move towards more region-orientated decision-making, and to bring the Community and the EU closer to the peoples of Europe, as required by Art 1 TEU. The Committee's website can be accessed at:

http://www.cor.europa.eu/en/index.htm

Following the accession of the ten new Member States on 1 May 2004, the number of members was increased from 222 to 317 (Art 263 EC Treaty), with the same allocation of members to each state as ECOSOC.

The Declaration adopted by the Nice Intergovernmental Conference, which is attached to the ToN, provided that in an enlarged Union of 27 Member States (Bulgaria and Romania became members of the EU on 1 January 2007), the number of members would be changed. This new allocation was the same as that for ECOSOC (see above). These new membership figures have been confirmed by Art 13 of the Act attached to the Accession Treaty which provided for Bulgaria and Romania's entry into the EU. Article 13 of the Act amended Art 263 EC Treaty accordingly. Article 49 of the Act sets out the transitional arrangements which will apply from Bulgaria and Romania's date of accession (i.e. 1 January 2007):

> The Committee of the Regions shall be enlarged by the appointment of 27 members [i.e. 15 allocated to Romania and 12 to Bulgaria] representing regional and local bodies in Bulgaria and Romania, who either hold a regional or local authority electoral mandate or are politically accountable to an elected assembly. The terms of office of the members thus

appointed shall expire at the same time as those of the members in office at the time of accession.

The members were previously representatives of regional and representative bodies in the Member States. Article 263 EC Treaty was amended by the ToN to provide that the Committee shall consist of representatives 'of regional and local bodies *who either hold a regional or local authority electoral mandate or are politically accountable to an elected assembly*' (emphasis added). Members therefore need to have an electoral mandate to represent citizens at a local level. Where a member's mandate comes to an end, their membership of the Committee shall automatically terminate.

Its basic role is comparable to ECOSOC: the members of the Committee, whose principal role is to deliver opinions on legislation when consulted by the Council of Ministers and to issue own-initiative opinions in appropriate cases, are completely independent in the performance of their duties and act in the general interests of the Community.

The Committee must be consulted in relation to proposed legislation on culture (Art 151(5) EC Treaty), public health (Art 152(4) EC Treaty), economic and social cohesion (Arts 158–162 EC Treaty) and environmental policy (Arts 174 and 175 EC Treaty).

Constitutional Treaty

If the Constitutional Treaty had come into force, Arts I-32 and III-386 to III-388 would have set out the provisions which would have applied to the Committee of the Regions. Article I-32(2) would have provided that 'The Committee of the Regions shall consist of representatives of regional and local bodies who either hold a regional or local authority electoral mandate or are politically accountable to an elected assembly' (this is identical to the amended Art 263 EC Treaty).

The members of the Committee would not have been bound by mandatory instructions, and they would have been completely independent in the performance of their duties 'in the Union's general interest' (Art I-32(4)).

Article III-386 would have provided that the number of Committee members would not exceed 350. The Council, acting unanimously on a proposal from the Commission, would have adopted a European decision determining the Committee's composition.

The Committee would have continued in its advisory capacity; it would not have been a formal institution (Art I-32(1)). Article II-388 would have provided as follows:

> The Committee of the Regions shall be consulted by the European Parliament, by the Council or by the Commission where the Constitution so provides and in all other cases in which one of these institutions considers it appropriate, in particular those which concern cross-border cooperation.
>
> The European Parliament, the Council or the Commission shall, if it considers it necessary, set the Committee, for the submission of its opinion, a time-limit which shall not be less than one month from the date on which the chairman receives notification to this effect. Upon expiry of the time-limit, the absence of an opinion shall not prevent further action.
>
> Where the Economic and Social Committee is consulted, the Committee of the Regions shall be informed by the European Parliament, the Council or the Commission of the request for an opinion. Where it considers that specific regional interests are involved, the Committee of the Regions may issue an opinion on the matter. It may also issue an opinion on its own initiative.
>
> The opinion of the Committee, together with a record of its proceedings, shall be forwarded to the European Parliament, to the Council and to the Commission.

The European Central Bank and the European Investment Bank

Article 8 EC Treaty established the European Central Bank (ECB). It is an innovation of the TEU and is linked to the establishment of a European System of Central Banks. The ECB was set up as part of the progression towards Economic and Monetary Union. It is not a Community institution within the definition of Art 7 EC Treaty. It can, however, enact legislation, impose fines, submit opinions and be consulted within its field of operation (Title VII EC Treaty: Arts 105, 106, 107 and 110). The European Central Bank's website can be accessed at:

> http://www.ecb.int/home/html/index.en.html

The European Investment Bank (EIB) was established by Art 9 EC Treaty and is the long-term lending bank and the regional development bank for the EU. It makes grants and loans to projects affecting more than one Member State, where they cannot be funded sufficiently from within those Member States themselves. The European Investment Bank's website can be accessed at:

> http://eib.eu.int

Summary

Now you have read this chapter you should be able to:

- Name the institutions of the European Communities which were established by Art 7(1) EC Treaty.
- Outline the composition, role and powers of each Community institution.
- Explain the difference between the Council of Ministers and the European Council.
- Understand the changes which would have been made to the composition, role and powers of each Community institution by the proposed Constitutional Treaty if it had been ratified.

References

Grant, C., 'The House that Jacques Built', *Independent*, 29 June 1994.

Further reading

Textbooks

Craig, P. and De Burca, G. (2003) *EU Law Text, Cases and Materials* (3rd edn), Oxford University Press, Chapter 2.

Duff, A., Pinder, J. and Pryce, R. (1994) *Maastricht and Beyond*, Federal Trust.

Dunnett, D.R.R. (1994) 'Legal and Institutional Issues Affecting Economic and Monetary Union', in O'Keefe, D. and Twomey, P. (eds) *Legal Issues of the Maastricht Treaty*, Chancery Publications.

Edwards, G. and Spence, D. (1997) *The European Commission*, Cartermill International Ltd.

Foster, N. (2006) *Foster on EU Law* (1st edn), Oxford University Press, Chapter 2 (Sections 2.1 to 2.5, and 2.7).

Steiner, J., Woods, L. and Twigg-Flesner, C. (2006) *EU Law* (9th edn), Oxford University Press, Chapter 2.

Storey, T. and Turner C. (2005) *Unlocking EU Law* (1st edn), Hodder Arnold, Chapter 3 (Sections 3.1 to 3.4, and 3.6).

Tillotson, J. and Foster, N. (2003) *Text, Cases and Materials on EU Law* (4th edn), Cavendish Publishing, Chapter 5.

Wallace, H., Wallace, W. and Pollack, M.A. (2005) *Policy Making in the European Union* (5th edn), Chapter 3.

Journal articles

Dehousse, R., 'European Institutional Architecture after Amsterdam: Parliamentary System or Regulatory Structure?' (1998) 35 CML Rev 595.

Driessen, B., 'The Council of the European Union and access to documents' (2005) 30 EL Rev 675.

Grant, C., 'The House that Jacques Built', *Independent*, 29 June 1994.

Heliskoski, J. and Leino, P., 'Darkness at the break of noon: The case law on Regulation No. 1049/2001 on access to documents' (2006) 43 CML Rev 735.

Söderman, J., 'A Thousand and One Complaints: The European Ombudsman en Route' (1997) 3 EPL 351.

4 The decision-making process

Aims and objectives

At the end of this chapter you should understand:

- The decision-making process and the interaction between the Community institutions and the national parliaments within this process.

- The changes which the Constitutional Treaty would have made to the decision-making process if the Treaty had come into force.

Decision-making within the Community

Decision-making is central to the effective functioning of the Community. Decisions made by Community institutions may relate to the implementation of a policy, such as enlargement of the Community, or the adoption of a trade agreement with other states, or they may be part of a number of different legislative programmes. The type of process will be determined by the subject matter of the decision, as interpreted by the European Commission, which will then choose the appropriate legal base in the Treaties (see below). That choice will determine which institutions and other bodies will be involved in the process, the voting system used in the Council of Ministers and the extent to which the Parliament will be able to influence the content of the measure and, in some cases, whether it is approved at all. Although, as discussed in Chapter 3, the European Council plays an increasingly important role in setting policy goals, the task of translating those goals into specific policy decisions and legislation still belongs almost exclusively to the Commission. The European Parliament does now have the power under Art 192 EC Treaty to suggest new areas for legislation, but the decision on whether or not to bring forward such legislation and in what form is for the Commission alone. Apart from a few exceptional situations where the Council may act on its own initiative (i.e. Arts 113 and 210 EC Treaty), in most cases the EC Treaty provides that it shall act on a proposal from the Commission.

Constitutional Treaty

The Constitutional Treaty has not come into force because it was not ratified (i.e. approved) by all of the then 25 Member States.

If it had come into force, the Constitutional Treaty, as discussed in Chapter 1, would have replaced all the existing treaties (except Euratom). It would have established a single European Union which would have replaced the current European Communities and the European Union (Art I-1 Constitutional Treaty). The three pillars would have been merged, although special procedures would have been maintained in the fields of foreign policy, security and defence (see Chapter 1).

Changes which would have been made to the decision-making process by the Constitutional Treaty will be considered throughout this chapter.

The respective roles of the Commission, Council and European Parliament with regard to the initiation of a legislative proposal would have been explicitly set out in Art I-26(2):

> Union legislative acts may be adopted only on the basis of a Commission proposal, except where the Constitution provides otherwise. Other acts shall be adopted on the basis of a Commission proposal where the Constitution so provides.

Article III-332 (which would have replaced Art 192 EC Treaty) would have set out the circumstances in which the European Parliament could request the Commission to submit a proposal:

> The European Parliament may, by a majority of its component Members, request the Commission to submit any appropriate proposal on matters on which it considers that a Union act is required for the purpose of implementing the Constitution. If the Commission does not submit a proposal, it shall inform the European Parliament of the reasons.

Article 249 EC Treaty would have set out the measures which could be adopted (i.e. regulations, directives, decisions, recommendations and opinions), and the characteristics of each measure (see Chapter 2). Article I-33 Constitutional Treaty would have replaced Art 249 EC Treaty, providing that:

1. To exercise the Union's competences the institutions shall use as legal instruments, in accordance with Part III, European laws, European framework laws, European regulations, European decisions, recommendations and opinions.

   A **European law** shall be a legislative act of general application. It shall be binding in its entirety and directly applicable in all Member States.

   A **European framework law** shall be a legislative act binding, as to the result to be achieved, upon each Member State to which it is addressed, but shall leave to the national authorities the choice of form and methods.

   A **European regulation** shall be a non-legislative act of general application for the implementation of legislative acts and of certain provisions of the Constitution. It may either be binding in its entirety and directly applicable in all Member States, or be binding, as to the result to be achieved, upon each Member State to which it is addressed, but shall leave to the national authorities the choice of form and methods.

   A **European decision** shall be a non-legislative act, binding in its entirety. A decision which specifies those to whom it is addressed shall be binding only on them.

   Recommendations and **opinions** shall have no binding force.
2. When considering draft legislative acts, the European Parliament and the Council shall refrain from adopting acts not provided for by the relevant legislative procedure in the area in question. [emphasis added]

This article would have provided that the following instruments would be used by the European Union:

- European law – equivalent to the current regulation;
- European framework law – equivalent to the current directive;
- European decision – equivalent to the current decision;
- European regulation – a non-legislative act of general application for the implementation of legislative acts; a completely new act;
- Recommendations and opinions – equivalent to the current recommendations and opinions.

The Constitution would have worked on the basis of a hierarchy of acts, clarifying the legal acts used by the institutions to put the Union's powers into practice and how they were adopted.

It made two successive distinctions:

- between legally binding acts (laws, framework laws, regulations and decisions) and non-binding acts (opinions and recommendations);
- in terms of legally binding acts, it would have distinguished between legislative acts (laws and framework laws) and non-legislative acts (regulations and decisions).

Dialogue between Commission, Council and Parliament

The virtual monopoly which the Commission enjoys over the legislative process could cause serious problems. If it submits no proposals, the Council is paralysed and the progress of the Community comes to a halt, whether in the field of agriculture, transport, commercial policy or the environment. However, except for a period of relative stagnation during the economic crisis of the 1970s, the Commission has always been active in promoting the development of the Community through a series of legislative programmes. As discussed in Chapter 3, the Commission outlines its annual Work Programme each year. The programme provides a framework of policy and legislative objectives. The Commission then brings forward a series of proposals within that programme. Once a proposal is lodged, a dialogue begins between Commission officials and the representatives of the Council in COREPER. This will continue until the legislation has passed through all its stages and the Council has finally approved it. Where the legislative process requires Parliamentary involvement the Commission will similarly open a dialogue with the Parliament.

Legislative proposals

Legislative proposals may result from the implementation of a wide programme of action, such as that laid down in the plans for the Single European Market, or the Social Chapter (which was incorporated into the EC Treaty by the ToA), or in response to particular circumstances calling for specific legislation. The appropriate Directorate-General, assisted by one of the Commission's advisory committees, will prepare the first draft, which will initially be approved by the appropriate Commissioner holding the relevant portfolio. The views of these advisory committees, which will contain representatives of industrial, commercial and social interests in Member States, are not in any sense binding on the Commission. The Commission, voting as a collegiate body on a simple majority basis, will then consider the proposal.

Legal base

Before the Commission considers drafting a proposal, it must ensure that it has the necessary power, i.e. it must find a legal base within the relevant Treaty. Articles 39 and 40 EC Treaty (previously 48 and 49) were discussed in Chapter 2, and it was noted that the Commission is empowered to propose legislation in relation to the free movement of workers. The extent of this power is set out in Art 40 and must not be exceeded, i.e. 'The Council shall issue directives or make regulations setting out the measures required to bring about freedom of movement for workers, as defined in Article 39 ...'. If it is exceeded, the resulting instrument may be struck down by the Court of Justice, as being *ultra vires*; i.e. in excess of power (see below).

Article 308 EC Treaty (previously 235) provides a *general* legislative power, if the Treaty has not provided the necessary *specific* power. However, the general legislative power will only be available if the proposal is necessary to attain one of the objectives of the Community, in the course of the operation of the common market:

> If action by the Community should prove necessary to attain, in the course of the operation of the common market, one of the objectives of the Community and this Treaty has not provided the necessary powers, the Council shall, acting unanimously on a proposal from the Commission and after consulting the European Parliament, take the appropriate measures.

It should be noted that a Commission proposal under Art 308 EC Treaty must be approved by *all* the Member States (excluding any abstentions) because the Council must act *unanimously*.

Constitutional Treaty

Similar to Art 308 EC Treaty, Art I-18 Constitutional Treaty would have established a 'flexibility clause'. This flexibility clause would have provided a general legislative power for the adoption of measures which were necessary to attain any of the objectives laid down by the Constitution, if the Constitution had not provided a specific power. Its scope would have been wider than that of the current Art 308 EC Treaty, which is confined to the internal market, but the conditions for its implementation would have been stricter in that, as well as requiring unanimity in the Council, Parliament's approval would also have been needed.

Voting procedures

The Commission

Decisions by the Commission on whether or not to adopt a proposal are taken by a simple majority of the Commissioners. Although the initiative for specific measures will be taken up by the appropriate Directorate-General, other Commissioners have no power to delegate approval of the details of that measure to that Commissioner. The Court of Justice made the position clear in the following case:

Commission v BASF and Others (Case C-137/92)

The Court of Justice stated that:

> The functioning of the Commission is governed by the principle of collegiate responsibility. The principle of collegiate responsibility is based on the equal participation of the Commissioners in the adoption of decisions, from which it follows in particular that decisions should be the subject of collective deliberation and that all the members of the college of Commissioners should bear collective responsibility at political level for all decisions adopted.

Constitutional Treaty

Article III-351 would have provided that 'The Commission shall act by a majority of its members. Its Rules of Procedure shall determine the quorum'.

The European Parliament

Except as otherwise provided in the Treaties, the European Parliament acts by an *absolute majority of the votes cast* (Art 198 EC Treaty, Art 111 Euratom Treaty). This is sometimes referred to as a simple majority, so that abstentions by MEPs within the chamber, and MEPs not present, are not taken into account. However, some Treaty articles provide for something more than an absolute majority of the votes cast; e.g. Art 252(c) EC Treaty provides that 'The European Parliament may ... [vote] by *an absolute majority of its component members*' (emphasis added). There are currently 785 MEPs; therefore a minimum of 393 votes will be required. From the start of the 2009–2014 European Parliamentary term, the number of MEPs will decrease to 736 and therefore a minimum of 369 votes will be required to satisfy the *absolute majority* requirement. Article 201 (a censure motion against the Commission) requires a 'two-thirds majority of the votes cast, representing a majority of the Members of the European Parliament'. The second limb of this is similar to that under Art 252, in that there must be at least 393 votes in favour. However, the first limb provides an additional hurdle which needs to be overcome: of the votes cast, there must be a two-thirds majority in favour. To illustrate this, on a vote under Art 201, if 690 MEPs voted, with 450 in favour and 240 against, although the second limb would have been satisfied, the first limb would not have been (because the majority in favour is less than two-thirds of the votes cast). If 360 MEPs vote, with 250 in favour and 110 against, although this time the first limb has been satisfied, the second limb has not (because it requires a minimum of 393 votes in favour in any event).

A quorum exists when one-third of the current MEPs are present in the Chamber (Rule 149(2), Rules of Procedure 2006); because there are currently 785 MEPs, at least 262 MEPs must be present in the Chamber to satisfy this requirement. However, all votes are valid whatever the number of voters unless the President of the Parliament, acting on a request made by at least 37 MEPs, ascertains that, at the moment of voting, the quorum is not present. In that case, the vote is placed on the agenda of the next sitting (Rule 149(3), Rules of Procedure 2006). The right to vote is a personal right and MEPs are required to cast their votes individually and in person (Rule 158). Although members of the European Council and Commissioners have the right to attend debates of the European Parliament and to participate in the discussion, they have no right to vote (Art 197 EC Treaty).

Constitutional Treaty

Similar to Art 198 EC Treaty, Art III-338 Constitutional Treaty would have provided that 'Save as otherwise provided in the Constitution, the European Parliament shall act by a majority of the votes cast. Its Rules of Procedure shall determine the quorum'.

The Council of Ministers

The Treaties set up three voting methods in the Council:

- simple majority;
- qualified majority; and
- unanimity.

All three methods have been in existence since the earliest days of the Community.

Simple majority

Although Art 205(1) EC Treaty provides that simple majority voting is the system to be used unless otherwise provided in the Treaty, the Treaty almost invariably provides for some other system. Under the 'simple majority' voting system, one vote is allocated to each Member State, and the decision is simply made in favour of the largest number of votes cast. It is largely used for the establishment of sub-committees of the Council and for procedural matters.

Constitutional Treaty

The Constitutional Treaty would have departed from Art 205(1) EC Treaty. Article I-23(3) Constitutional Treaty would have provided that the Council would act by a qualified majority except where the Constitution provided otherwise.

Qualified majority

Qualified majority voting (QMV) is a system of voting, weighted according to the population size of the Member State (Art 205(2)).

25 Member States (pre 1 January 2007)

Article 11 of the Accession Treaty 2003 (which paved the way for enlargement of the European Union on 1 May 2004) amended Art 205(2) EC Treaty to provide for the allocation of votes as follows, alphabetically:

Table 4.1 QMV Member State vote allocation (alphabetical)

Member State	QMV allocation	Member State	QMV allocation
Austria	10	Latvia	4
Belgium	12	Lithuania	7
Cyprus	4	Luxembourg	4
Czech Republic	12	Malta	3
Denmark	7	Netherlands	13
Estonia	4	Poland	27
Finland	7	Portugal	12
France	29	Slovakia	7
Germany	29	Slovenia	4
Greece	12	Spain	27
Hungary	12	Sweden	10
Ireland	7	UK	29
Italy	29	**Total**	**321**

... and as follows, numerically:

Table 4.2 QMV Member State vote allocation (numerical)

Member State	QMV allocation	Member State	QMV allocation
France	29	Sweden	10
Germany	29	Denmark	7
Italy	29	Finland	7
UK	29	Ireland	7
Poland	27	Lithuania	7
Spain	27	Slovakia	7
Netherlands	13	Cyprus	4
Belgium	12	Estonia	4
Czech Republic	12	Latvia	4
Greece	12	Luxembourg	4
Hungary	12	Slovenia	4
Portugal	12	Malta	3
Austria	10	**Total**	**321**

To secure approval by a qualified majority, a measure proposed by the Commission needed to be supported by at least 232 votes, cast by a majority of the members. In other cases the 232 votes in favour had to be cast by at least two-thirds of the members (Art 205(2) EC Treaty). Conversely, to block a proposal, opponents needed to secure at least 90 votes. Since the six largest Member States could only muster 170 votes between them, they were not in a position to force through legislation which tended to favour them, without the support of some of the smaller States. A new requirement, which was inserted by the ToN, further provided that when a decision was to be adopted by the Council by a qualified majority, a member of the Council could request verification that the Member States constituting the qualified majority represented at least 62 per cent of the total population of the Union. If that condition was not shown to have been met, the decision in question would not be adopted (Art 205(4) EC Treaty). This was additional to the numerical requirements set out in Art 205(2).

The majority of decisions were made by qualified majority vote even before the SEA. There was, however, a substantial increase in qualified majority voting following the inclusion of Art 95 EC Treaty, which was intended to secure more rapid decision-making in the run up to the Single Market (see below).

27 Member States (from 1 January 2007)

Article 20 of the Declaration adopted by the Nice Intergovernmental Conference, which is attached to the ToN, provided that in an enlarged Union of 27 Member States (Bulgaria and Romania joined the EU on 1 January 2007), the allocation of votes will be as follows, alphabetically:

Table 4.3 QMV Member State vote allocation from 1 January 2007 (alphabetical)

Member State	QMV allocation	Member State	QMV allocation
Austria	10	Latvia	4
Belgium	12	Lithuania	7
Bulgaria	10	Luxembourg	4
Cyprus	4	Malta	3
Czech Republic	12	Netherlands	13
Denmark	7	Poland	27
Estonia	4	Portugal	12
Finland	7	Romania	14
France	29	Slovakia	7
Germany	29	Slovenia	4
Greece	12	Spain	27
Hungary	12	Sweden	10
Ireland	7	UK	29
Italy	29	**Total**	**345**

... and as follows numerically:

Table 4.4 QMV Member State vote allocation from 1 January 2007 (numerical)

Member State	QMV allocation	Member State	QMV allocation
France	29	Bulgaria	10
Germany	29	Sweden	10
Italy	29	Denmark	7
UK	29	Finland	7
Poland	27	Ireland	7
Spain	27	Lithuania	7
Romania	14	Slovakia	7
Netherlands	13	Cyprus	4
Belgium	12	Estonia	4
Czech Republic	12	Latvia	4
Greece	12	Luxembourg	4
Hungary	12	Slovenia	4
Portugal	12	Malta	3
Austria	10	**Total**	**345**

The Act attached to the Accession Treaty which provided for Bulgaria and Romania's entry into the EU confirmed these new vote allocations. Article 10(1) of the Act has amended Art 205(2) EC Treaty to this effect. Article 205(2) EC Treaty also provides that:

> Acts of the Council shall require for their adoption at least 255 votes in favour cast by a majority of the members where this Treaty requires them to be adopted on a proposal from the Commission.
>
> In other cases, for their adoption acts of the Council shall require at least 255 votes in favour, cast by at least two-thirds of the members.

Now that the EU comprises of 27 Member States, the number of votes required to adopt a measure has increased to 255. The requirement for a majority of Member States to vote in favour in respect of a Commission proposal and two-thirds otherwise, is unaffected. Art 10(2) of the Act, has amended Arts 28(2) and 34(3) TEU to provide that:

> ... When a decision is to be adopted by the Council by a qualified majority, a member of the Council may request verification that the Member States constitute 62% of the total population of the Union. If that condition is shown not to have been met, the decision in question shall not be adopted.

Therefore, the 62 per cent population verification measure is likewise unaffected.

Constitutional Treaty

Article I-25 would have set out new provisions with regard to qualified majority voting which would have applied from 1 November 2009. The definition of 'qualified majority' for decision-making in the Council would have continued on the basis of 'double majority'. Article I-25 would have provided that this double majority principle required two thresholds to be achieved before a measure could be adopted: (i) the support of at least 55 per cent of the Member States comprising at least 15 of them; and (ii) the support of Member States which comprised at least 65 per cent of the population of the Union. In order to avoid the situation where, in an extreme case, only three (large) Member States would be able to block a Council decision due to an increase in the population threshold, a blocking minority would have needed to comprise of at least four Member States (Art I-25(1)). This may have had the effect of lowering the population threshold and have allowed, for example, the adoption of a law by 22 Member States representing only around 55.5 per cent.

If the Council was not acting on a proposal from the Commission or the Union Minister for Foreign Affairs, then the qualified majority would have required the support of 72 per cent of the members of the Council (rather than 55 per cent), representing Member States comprising at least 65 per cent of the population of the Union.

In order to overcome the remaining reluctance of certain Member States, the Council adopted a decision containing a revised 'Ioannina' compromise (see below). If Council members representing at least three-quarters of the Member States or the percentage of the population required to block a decision indicated their opposition to the Council's adoption of an act by qualified majority, the Council would have continued to debate the subject in order to achieve broader agreement within a reasonable period of time.

Article 2(3), Protocol 34 to the Constitutional Treaty would have provided that when the Union was enlarged further, the threshold referred to in Art 2(2) 'shall be calculated to ensure that the qualified majority threshold expressed in votes does not exceed that resulting from the table in the Declaration on the enlargement of the European Union in the Final Act of the Conference which adopted the Treaty of Nice'.

Qualified majority would have become the general rule for the adoption of decisions within the Council of Ministers (Art I-23(3)). For cases in which the Constitutional Treaty did not provide for qualified majority voting, Art IV-444 would have introduced a general measure (known in French as a 'passerelle'), whereby the European Council would have had the opportunity to decide unanimously that the Council would in future act by qualified majority and, if necessary, according to the 'ordinary legislative procedure' (see below), without the need to amend the Constitution, which would in turn have required ratification by each Member State. However, the formal opposition of a single national parliament would have been enough to block the application of the 'passerelle' (Art IV-444(3)).

Unanimity

Unanimity is reserved for the most important decisions, or those for which Member States are least prepared to pool their national sovereignty. Although this effectively gives Member States a veto, that veto must be exercised for a measure to be blocked. Abstention by Members present or represented does not prevent the adoption of an act which requires unanimity (Art 205(3)). Unanimity is, for example, required for the admission of new States (Art 49 TEU), and for approval of any other matter within the competence of the Community for which the Treaty does not provide a legal base (Art 308 EC Treaty, see above).

Constitutional Treaty

As stated above, qualified majority would have become the general rule for the adoption of decisions within the Council of Ministers (Art I-23(3)). Unanimity would have remained the rule for taxation and partly in the fields of foreign and common security policy and social policy. Furthermore, it would also have applied to the system of own resources and the multiannual financial framework.

The Luxembourg Accords

The Luxembourg Accords (which are also referred to as the Luxembourg Compromise) were the result of an impasse between France and the other Member States in relation to farm prices in 1965. The decision had to be determined, under the Treaty, by the Council acting by a qualified majority. The French insisted on the right to secure a unanimous decision in cases such as this, where a vital national interest was at stake. The other Member States could not agree. France then remained absent from all but technical meetings of the Council for seven months, and important decision-making in the Community virtually drew to a halt. The Accords were negotiated in a reconvened meeting of the Council in January 1966. The three points that emerged from this meeting, as far as voting procedures are concerned, were as follows:

1. Where, in the case of decisions which may be taken by majority vote on a proposal of the Commission, very important interests of one or more partners are at stake, the members of Council will endeavour, within a reasonable time, to reach solutions which can be adopted by all the members of the Council while respecting their mutual interests and those of the Community, in accordance with Art 2 of the Treaty.

2. With regard to the preceding paragraph, the French delegation considers that where very important interests are at stake the discussion must be continued until unanimous agreement is reached.

3. The six delegates note that there is a divergence of views on what should be done in the event of a failure to reach complete agreement.

The six delegations concluded by observing that the divergence noted in point 3 did not prevent the Community's work from being resumed in accordance with the normal procedure. There are a number of things to be said about the Accords. In the first place, the title 'Accord' is inappropriate. There was, in fact, no agreement, only an agreement to disagree. Secondly, the Accords have no standing in law. Insofar as they purport to amend the voting procedure laid down by the Treaty in certain circumstances, they cannot be effective. Changes to the text and substance of the EC Treaty have to be carried out in the appropriate form, after consultation with the Parliament and the Commission. This was not done in the case of the Accords. The Commission has never accepted that the Accords had any validity, and has disassociated itself from them (Bull EC 5 1982, p. 8).

Pierre Pescatore, a former judge of the Court of Justice has described the Accords as 'a mere press release', without the least force of law (Pescatore, 1987 at p. 13). The Court of Justice has stated (but not in the context of the Accords) that 'the rules regarding the manner in which the Community institutions arrive at their decisions [i.e. by a qualified majority vote or by unanimity] are laid down in the Treaty and are not at the disposal of the Member States or of the institutions themselves' (**United Kingdom** *v* **Council** (Case 68/86)). There is no *general* right to veto proposed legislation. What there has been is a willingness, in some cases where Member States appear to be in difficulties in relation to a domestic political situation, to refrain from pressing to a qualified majority vote where the Treaty authorises it.

The Accords have undoubtedly encouraged Member States to reach a compromise wherever possible. The formal invocation of the Accords has been rare, and has not always achieved the desired result. In 1982, for example, when the UK sought to block the adoption of an agricultural price package in order to put pressure on the other Member States to agree to a reduction of the UK's contributions, its purported 'veto' was ignored and a vote was taken. However, in 1985, Germany invoked the Accords to forestall an increase in cereal prices, and was successful. It is significant that no Member State which has been overridden, following an appeal to the Accords, has ever taken the decision to the Court of Justice. The trend in voting procedures in recent Treaty changes has been to more qualified majority voting and less unanimous decision taking, and it is likely that appeals to vital national interests under the Accords will become even rarer than at present.

The Ioannina Declaration

Some recognition of the continuing need to take into account the genuine difficulties of some Member States when a qualified majority vote is to be taken was shown early in 1994. Under a declaration made in March 1994 at the Ioannina Summit, if members of the Council representing a total of between 23 and 26 votes indicated their intention to oppose the adoption by the Council of a decision by a qualified majority vote, the Council was committed to do all in its power to reach, within a reasonable time, and without infringing the obligatory time limits in Arts 251 and 252 EC Treaty procedures (see below), a satisfactory solution that could be adopted by at least 65 votes (Bull EU 3 1994 p. 65: OJ 1994 C 105/1 as amended by Council Decision of 1 January 1995).

This did no more than provide an opportunity to delay a qualified majority vote, but could not prevent one from being held, because the new Treaty time limits had still to be respected. However, unlike the Luxembourg Accords, the Declaration had the force of law. It was intended to continue to apply until the amendments to the Treaties following the Intergovernmental Conference of 1996 came into effect, but it was continued by the Treaty of Amsterdam until the 2004 enlargement of the Community (Declaration 50, ToA). Although the Declaration was given legal effect by a Decision of the Council of Ministers, its vagueness must have meant that it was most unlikely to have been the subject of litigation before the Court of Justice.

Constitutional Treaty

The Council adopted a decision containing a revised 'Ioannina' compromise. If Council members representing at least three-quarters of the Member States or the percentage of the population required to block a decision indicated their opposition to the Council's adoption of an act by qualified majority, the Council would have continued to debate the subject in order to achieve broader agreement within a reasonable period of time.

The legislative process

Due to allegations that the Community was democratically deficient, the powers of the Parliament were broadened by the SEA, broadened further by the TEU, and still further by the ToA and ToN.

There are six separate and distinct methods of enacting Community legislation, each of which will be considered. In addition, the Council has power to delegate its legislative powers to the Commission. Under Art 211 EC Treaty the Commission shall 'exercise the powers conferred on it by the Council for the implementation of the rules laid down by the latter'.

Commission acting alone

The Commission is, in very limited policy areas, empowered by the EC Treaty to enact legislation. One example is Art 86(3) EC Treaty (previously Art 90(3)), which provides that:

> The Commission shall ensure the application of the provisions of this Article and shall, where necessary, address appropriate directives or decisions to Member States.

This article is concerned with the role of the state in relation to public bodies or other bodies, to which the state has granted special or exclusive rights (e.g. privatised utility companies: water, gas, electricity, etc.). The Commission has adopted the following directive pursuant to the former Art 90(3) (now Art 86(3)):

- Directive 80/723 on the transparency of financial relations between Member States and public undertakings (OJ 1980 L 195/35).

Constitutional Treaty

The above situation would have been similar under the Constitutional Treaty in that the Commission would only have been empowered to enact legislation in very limited situations. For example, Art III-165(3) (which would have replaced Art 86(3) EC Treaty) would have provided that:

> The Commission shall ensure the application of the provisions of this Article and shall, where necessary, adopt appropriate European regulations or decisions to Member States.

As discussed above, under the Constitutional Treaty, a European regulation would have been a non-legislative act of general application for the implementation of legislative acts (such a measure is not currently in use). A European decision would have been equivalent to the current decision and would have been a legislative act.

Council and Commission acting alone

There are a number of policy areas where the EC Treaty provides for the Council to adopt a Commission proposal without the involvement of any other institution (most notably the Parliament). Although there is no formal duty to consult with the Parliament, consultation may (and usually will) occur.

However, if there is no consultation there is nothing the Parliament can do; the legislative measure will be effective. The relevant Treaty article (i.e. the legal base) will specify the voting mode to be used by the Council (i.e. qualified majority or unanimity; otherwise simple majority). Some of the policy areas where this method for adopting an act is prescribed are of major importance. The areas (post-ToN) are:

- Article 26 EC Treaty (previously 28) relating to the fixing of Common Customs Tariff duties – the Council acts by a qualified majority.

- Article 45 EC Treaty (previously 55) relating to derogations from the right of establishment – the Council acts by a qualified majority.

- Article 49 EC Treaty (previously 59) relating to the extension of provisions on the freedom to provide services to nationals of third countries who provide services within the Community – the Council acts by a qualified majority.

- Articles 57 and 60 EC Treaty (previously 73c and 73g) relating to the free movement of capital – the Council acts by a qualified majority.

- Article 96 EC Treaty (previously 101) relating to harmonisation of laws necessary to eliminate a distortion in competition – the Council acts by a qualified majority.

- Articles 99 and 104 EC Treaty (previously 103 and 104c) relating to economic and monetary policy – the Council acts by a qualified majority.

- Article 133 (previously 113) relating to implementation of the Common Commercial Policy – the Council acts by a qualified majority.

- Article 301 (previously 228a) relating to economic sanctions against a third country – the Council acts by a qualified majority.

For example, Article 301 EC Treaty provides that:

... the Council shall act by a qualified majority on a proposal from the Commission.

Constitutional Treaty

As discussed above, unlike Art 205(1) EC Treaty which provides that the Council shall act by a simply majority except where the Treaty provides otherwise, Art I-23(3) Constitutional Treaty would have provided that the Council would act by a qualified majority except where the Constitution provided otherwise.

The Constitutional Treaty would have empowered the Council to adopt a Commission proposal without the involvement of any other institution in a very limited number of policy areas, for example:

- Article III-151(5) relating to the fixing of Common Customs Tariff duties – the Council would have acted by a qualified majority.

Council, Commission and consultation with Parliament

From the earliest days of the Community, this was the commonest legislative procedure in the Treaty, and the only one which gave the Parliament a significant role in the process. New procedures were introduced by both the SEA and the TEU to give the Parliament a greater involvement. Article 249 EC Treaty refers to the making of regulations and directives, the taking of decisions, the making of recommendations or the delivery of opinions, as a joint function of the Parliament and the Council, and the Council and the Commission. However, the Parliament is still far from being a joint legislator in the sense known to national legislatures. Under this procedure, measures are proposed by the Commission, the Parliament is consulted and delivers an opinion, and the Council of Ministers makes the final decision. The opinion is prepared by the Rapporteur of one of the Parliament's specialist committees (see Chapter 3). Its preparation follows the hearing of evidence by the Committee from specialist advisers, interested individuals and organisations, and members of the officials of the Directorate-General originally responsible for drafting the proposal. Although the Council of Ministers is not required to follow the opinion of Parliament, the consultation must be genuine. Parliament must have a proper opportunity to respond to the proposal. This was recognised as an essential procedural requirement by the Court of Justice in the following case:

Roquette Frères v *Council* (Case 138/79)

The Court of Justice stated that:

> The consultation provided for in ... the Treaty is the means which allows the Parliament to play an actual part in the legislative process of the Community. Such power represents an essential factor in the institutional balance intended by the Treaty. Although limited, it reflects at Community level the fundamental principle that the peoples should take part in the exercise of power through the intermediary of a representative assembly. Due consultation of the Parliament in the cases provided for by the Treaty therefore constitutes an essential formality disregard of which means that the measure concerned is void. (at p. 3360)

This principle was further developed to require re-consultation when a measure on which Parliament had already given an opinion was subsequently changed. In **European Parliament** v **Council** (Case C-65/90) the Court of Justice said that further consultation was required unless the amendments essentially corresponded to the wishes already expressed by the Parliament. In **European Parliament** v **Council** (Case C-388/92) the Court of Justice held that the obligation arose to re-consult 'on each occasion when the text finally adopted, viewed as a whole, departs substantially from the text on which Parliament has already been consulted'. On that basis the Court found that the Council had disregarded the prerogatives of Parliament and annulled Regulation 2454/92 on the operation by non-resident carriers of transport services in Member States. However, consultation is a two-way process. Where Parliament wilfully fails to respond it cannot subsequently complain that its views have not been taken into account, as illustrated in the following case:

European Parliament v *Council* (Case C-65/93)

The Council had informed the Parliament of the urgent need for approval of draft regulations on tariff preference relating to agricultural products to be made under Art 43 EC Treaty (now Art 37(2)). Having agreed to deal with the draft regulations as a matter of urgency, Parliament then decided to adjourn discussion of them for reasons wholly unconnected with their content. The draft regulations were subsequently adopted by the Council without having received Parliament's opinion. The Parliament sought to annul the regulations on the ground of failure of consultation. The Court of Justice rejected the application:

> ... Inter-institutional dialogue, on which the consultation procedure in particular is based, is subject to the same mutual duties of sincere cooperation as those which govern relations between Member States and the Community institutions. By adopting that course of action [adjournment of consideration of the draft regulation] the Parliament failed to discharge its obligation to cooperate sincerely with the Council ... In those circumstances the Parliament is not entitled to complain of the Council's failure to await its opinion before adopting the contested regulation ...

Although the Council should not come to a final decision without giving the Parliament an opportunity to respond, it does not have to suspend all discussion until it receives that opinion (**European Parliament _v_ Council** (Case C-417/93)).

This mode of legislating has been retained in certain policy areas (post-ToN):

- Article 19 (previously 8b) concerns the right of EU citizens to vote and stand in local elections, and European Parliament elections – the Council acts unanimously.

- Article 22 (previously 8e) relates to provisions increasing the rights of an EU citizen – the Council acts unanimously.

- Article 67(1) concerns visas, etc. – the Council acts unanimously.

- Article 89 (previously 94) relates to the grant of state aids – the Council acts by a qualified majority.

- Article 93 (previously 99) concerns the harmonisation of indirect taxes – the Council acts unanimously.

- Article 94 (previously 100) provides for the approximation of national laws which directly affect the operation of the common market – the Council acts unanimously.

- Article 107(6) (previously 106(6)) relates to the adoption of certain provisions contained in the Statute of the European System of Central Banks (ESCB) – the Council acts by a qualified majority.

- Article 128 concerns employment – the Council acts by a qualified majority.

- Article 175(2) (previously 130s(2)) provides for fiscal planning and energy measures affecting the environment – the Council acts unanimously (although in some circumstances it acts by a qualified majority).

The Treaty article (i.e. the legal base) will specify the voting mechanism to be used in Council for the adoption of the measure (as stated above, unanimously or by a qualified majority). There may be a duty to consult other bodies e.g. the Economic and Social Committee. For example, Art 128(2) provides:

> ... the Council, acting by a qualified majority on a proposal from the Commission and after consulting the European Parliament, the Economic and Social Committee, the Committee of the Regions and the Employment Committee referred to in Article 130 ...

If consultation was the full extent of Parliament's involvement in the legislative process, it could quite genuinely be questioned whether or not the Community was democratically deficient; the only directly elected institution, comprising 'representatives of the Peoples of the States brought together in the Community' (Art 189 EC Treaty (previously 137)), has no real say in the legislative process. It was for this reason that the SEA, TEU, ToA and ToN increased the involvement of the European Parliament in the legislative process.

Constitutional Treaty

This mode of legislating would have been included within the Constitutional Treaty in certain limited policy areas, for example:

- Article III-169 related to state aid – the Council would have acted by a qualified majority.

Council, Commission and European Parliament – Article 252 (previously 189c) cooperation procedure

The election of the European Parliament by direct franchise for the first time in 1979 produced pressure to address the Community's 'democratic deficit'. The Community institutions were seen as essentially undemocratic, in that the only body that was directly accountable to an electorate played only a peripheral part in the legislative process. Parliament attacked the issue by commissioning a report on wholesale constitutional reform of the Community. That report, the Spinelli Report, appeared in 1984 and although many of the recommendations were not taken up by the Commission, an attempt was made in the SEA to address the issue of lack of significant Parliamentary input. This was referred to as the cooperation procedure, but since the TEU it is called 'the procedure referred to in Art 252'. It is still widely referred to as 'the cooperation procedure'.

This procedure starts off similar to the consultation procedure, whereby the Commission makes a proposal which is submitted to the Council and the Parliament. The Parliament gives its opinion to the Council which, acting by a qualified majority, adopts a common position. However, if the Council's common position amends the Commission's proposal, the Council must act unanimously (Art 250(1) EC Treaty (previously 189a(1))). This common position is then forwarded to the Parliament together with the Council's reasons as to why it has adopted that position. The Commission also informs the Parliament as to its opinion on the Council's common position. This will be the second occasion that Parliament considers the matter and it is therefore said that the procedure provides Parliament with a Second Reading.

The Parliament has three months from receipt of the above to take action, with the following results:

- if the Parliament approves the common position or does nothing, then the Council, within three months, shall adopt the proposal, in accordance with the common position. If the Council fails to act within this three months, the proposal shall be deemed not to have been adopted;

- if the Parliament rejects the common position by *an absolute majority of its membership* (i.e. 393, because there are 785 MEPs; at the start of the 2009–2014 European Parliamentary term this will decrease to 369, because the number of MEPs will be reduced to 736) then the Council can, within three months, only adopt the act by unanimity; or

- if the Parliament proposes amendments to the common position by *an absolute majority of its membership*, then the Commission has one month within which to re-examine its proposal and the Parliament's amendments to the common position. The Commission shall forward its re-examined proposal to the Council together with any of the Parliament's amendments which it has not accepted, and the reasons why it has not accepted them. Following this the Council may:

- adopt the re-examined proposal acting by a qualified majority;
- amend the re-examined proposal acting unanimously; or
- adopt any of Parliament's amendments not accepted by the Commission, acting unanimously.

The Council must act within three months, otherwise the proposal will be deemed not to have been adopted.

Under this procedure there is a duty on the Council, after Parliament's First Reading, to inform the Parliament why it has adopted its common position. This will include reasons why, if applicable, it has rejected Parliament's opinion. The Commission is under a duty to inform the Parliament, after Second Reading, why it rejects any of its proposed amendments to the common position, if applicable.

In the final analysis, the Commission can reject the Parliament's proposals (except that it does not have a say if Parliament rejects the common position), and the Council can override Parliament and the Commission provided it acts unanimously. It may be appreciated therefore, that although under this procedure Parliament's involvement in the legislative process is more significant, real legislative power still lies with the Council. It is for this reason that Parliament pushed for enhanced legislative powers in the build-up to the TEU, ToA and ToN.

The policy areas in which the Art 252 (previously 189c) procedure applies are now very limited because the ToA and ToN transferred the majority of provisions into the Art 251 (previously 189b) procedure, discussed below, which gives the European Parliament an enhanced role in the legislative process. The following provisions continue to be governed by Art 252 (post-ToN):

■ Articles 102, 103 and 106 EC Treaty (previously 104a, 104b and 105a) which concern aspects of economic and monetary policy.

For example, Art 106(2) EC Treaty (previously 105a(2)) provides that:

The Council, acting in accordance with the procedure referred to in Article 252 . . .

Constitutional Treaty

The Constitutional Treaty would not have incorporated the Art 252 cooperation procedure. The vast majority of measures would have been adopted under the co-decision procedure which would have been renamed 'the ordinary legislative procedure' (Art III-396).

Council, Commission and Parliament – Article 251 (previously 189b) co-decision procedure

The TEU introduced a new decision-making procedure, 'co-decision making', which gave substantial new powers of amendment and, ultimately, a veto to the European Parliament. This system has been simplified, and much extended by the ToA (and to a more limited extent by the ToN), so that it now applies to the vast majority of legislative decisions made by the Community. This procedure was amended by the ToA and renumbered Art 251 from 189b. It must be applied wherever the legal base provides that an act shall be adopted 'in accordance with the procedure referred to in Article 251'.

This procedure starts off very similar to the Art 252 procedure, in that the Commission proposal is submitted to both the Council and the Parliament. The Parliament gives its opinion on the proposal to the Council. The Council may adopt the proposal by a qualified majority if:

- it approves *all* the amendments contained in the European Parliament's opinion; or
- if the European Parliament does not propose any amendments.

Otherwise, the Council, by a qualified majority, adopts a common position. Article 250(1) provides that if the Council amends the Commission's proposal, then the Council must act unanimously.

The common position is communicated to the Parliament, together with the Council's reasons as to why it has adopted the common position. This will obviously include reasons as to why the Council rejects the Parliament's opinion, in whole or in part (if applicable). The Commission informs the Parliament as to its view on the Council's common position. Within three months of the common position being communicated to Parliament, if Parliament either fails to take a decision, or approves the common position, the Council will be deemed to adopt the act in accordance with the common position. Alternatively, within this three-month period, Parliament may:

- by *an absolute majority of its membership* (i.e. 393 because there are 785 MEPs; at the start of the 2009–2014 European Parliamentary term this will decrease to 369, because the number of MEPs will be reduced to 736) reject the common position, in which case the act is deemed *not* to have been adopted (i.e. a veto); or
- by *an absolute majority of its membership*, propose amendments to the common position.

Where amendments have been proposed by Parliament, the amended text is forwarded to both the Council and the Commission. The Commission then delivers an opinion on the amendments. It will adopt one of three positions; it may:

- accept them all;
- reject them all; or
- accept some and reject others.

Within three months of receiving the Parliament's amended text, the Council may:

- approve all the amendments of the Parliament and adopt the act. It will do so by qualified majority if the Commission has also accepted all the amendments, by unanimity if the Commission has rejected all the amendments, and by a mixture of the two if the Commission has accepted some (qualified majority) and rejected others (unanimity). In this case the act is adopted; or
- fail to adopt the act, in which case a Conciliation Committee may be convened.

The Conciliation Committee consists of an equal number of representatives from the Council and the Parliament. Their task is to agree a joint text. This will be reached by the Council representatives acting by a qualified majority and the Parliament representatives acting by a majority. The Commission will act as mediator to encourage the parties to reach an agreement. There are two possible outcomes. If within six weeks of it being convened the Committee:

- approves a joint text, then the act will be adopted in accordance with the joint text, by the Parliament acting by an absolute majority of the votes cast (i.e. simple majority), and the Council acting by a qualified majority. The act will be deemed not adopted if approval is not obtained from either institution; or

■ does not approve a joint text, then the act is deemed not to have been adopted unless positive action is taken.

There are provisions in Art 251 for the above periods of three months and six weeks to be extended by one month and two weeks respectively.

It should be appreciated that this is a very complicated and cumbersome procedure. It is necessary to understand that this is a reflection of the competing interests between the three institutions involved in the legislative process. The Parliament demands more powers, but the Council resists such demands. However, Art 251 has shifted some power from the Council to the Parliament because now the Parliament can actually veto a proposal, although Parliament cannot demand that its amendments be accepted. The Parliament ultimately either has to accept the proposal in totality or reject it in totality. It is therefore a negative power rather than a true (positive) legislative power.

The Art 251 procedure can be seen to be a balancing act of competing interests. The Commission will resist any inroad into its role as policy initiator and developer. Article 251 has made an inroad into the Commission's territory because if a Conciliation Committee is set up, the Council and Parliament can agree a joint text by qualified majority and simple majority respectively. This joint text may amend the Commission's proposal. The joint text (if agreed) can then be adopted by the whole Council acting by a qualified majority and the Parliament acting by a majority of the votes cast.

While the Art 251 procedure is an important development in the evolution of Parliament's legislative powers it should be remembered that:

■ it only involves an ultimate power to veto;

■ the Parliament must cooperate with the Council in order to seek its agreement to amendments (or at least seek a qualified majority if the matter proceeds to a Conciliation Committee); and

■ it is limited to certain policy areas, although the policy areas have been substantially extended by amendments made by the ToA, and to a more limited extent by the ToN.

The post-ToN policy areas governed by Art 251 include:

■ Article 40 (previously 49) – free movement of workers.

■ Article 44 (previously 54) – freedom of establishment.

■ Article 47 (previously 57) – mutual recognition of qualifications.

■ Article 71 (previously 75) – transport.

■ Article 95 (previously 100a) – completion of the internal market.

■ Article 148 (previously 125) – provisions relating to the European Social Fund.

■ Article 151(5) (previously 128(5)) – incentive measures relating to culture.

■ Article 152(4) (previously 129(4)) – incentive measures relating to public health.

■ Article 162 (previously 130e) – provisions relating to the European Regional Development Fund.

For example, Art 40 EC Treaty provides that:

The Council shall, acting in accordance with the procedure referred to in Article 251 . . .

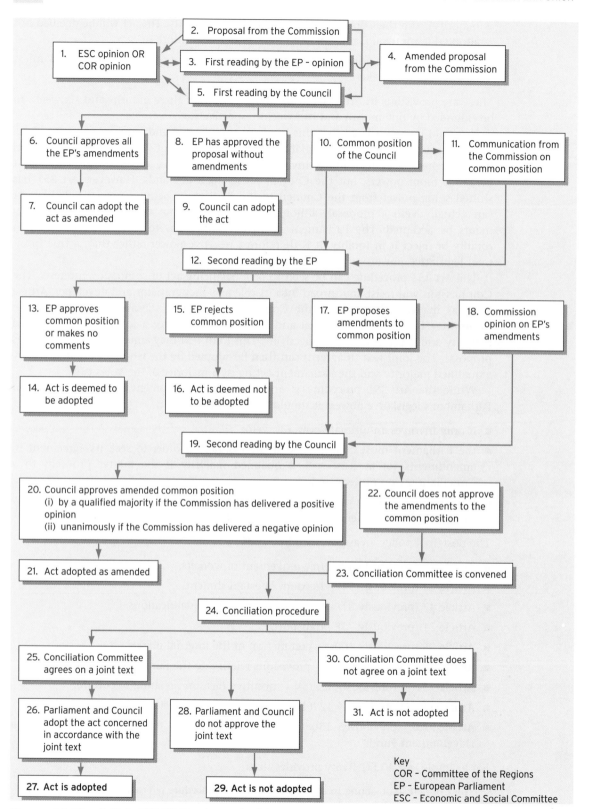

Figure 4.1 The Article 251 EC Treaty co-decision procedure
Source: http://ec.europa.eu/codecision/stepbystep/diagram_en.htm. © European Communities, 1995–2007.

Figure 4.1 consists of a flowchart setting out the application of the Art 251 EC Treaty co-decision procedure.

Constitutional Treaty

Article III-396 would have substantially re-enacted Art 251 EC Treaty. Under the Constitutional Treaty the procedure would have been referred to as 'the ordinary legislative procedure'. Article III-396(1) would have provided that:

> Where, pursuant to the Constitution, European laws or framework laws are adopted under **the ordinary legislative procedure**, the following provisions shall apply. [emphasis added]

The vast majority of European laws and framework laws would have been adopted pursuant to the ordinary legislative procedure, thus enhancing Parliament's legislative role.

Article I-34 would have provided 'special legislative procedures' in specific cases provided for in the Constitution. For example, Art I-40(6), which related to the common foreign and security policy, would have provided that 'European decisions relating to the common foreign and security policy shall be adopted by the European Council and the Council unanimously, except in the cases referred to in Part III . . .'. However, Art I-40(7) would have provided that the European Council, acting unanimously, may adopt a European decision authorising the Council to act by a qualified majority in cases other than those referred to in Part III. Article I-40(8) would have provided that the Parliament would be regularly consulted on the main aspects and basic choices of the policy and it would be kept informed of how the policy evolved.

Council, Commission and assent of Parliament

This quite simply provides for an act to be adopted by the Council (by a qualified majority or unanimously) upon a proposal by the Commission and 'after obtaining the assent of the Parliament'. The Parliament will only need to act by a *majority of the votes cast* and this procedure is a true co-decision of the two institutions: the Council and Parliament. There is no special majority required in the Parliament.

The assent procedure was introduced by the SEA and following amendments made to the EC Treaty by the ToA and ToN, this procedure currently applies to the following:

- Article 105(6) EC Treaty – certain functions of the European Central Bank (ECB).
- Article 107(5) EC Treaty – amendments to the Statute of the European System of Central Banks.
- Article 161 EC Treaty – application of structure and cohesion funds.
- Article 190(4) EC Treaty – uniform election procedures for MEPs.
- Article 300(3) EC Treaty – making of association agreements with foreign states.
- Article 49 TEU (previously Article O) – enlarging membership of the Communities.

For example, Art 105(6) provides that:

> The Council may, acting unanimously . . . and after receiving the assent of the European Parliament . . .

Constitutional Treaty

The Constitutional Treaty would have retained this procedure, but it would only have applied in a limited number of situations. The Constitutional Treaty would have referred to Parliament's 'consent' rather than 'assent'. For example, Art III-223(2) would have provided that '... The Council shall act unanimously after obtaining the consent of the European Parliament'. There would have been no requirement for a 'special' Parliamentary majority.

The involvement of the UK Parliament

National parliaments become involved in the decision-making process at two or sometimes three points in the process. In the first place, draft directives and regulations are sent for scrutiny by national parliaments at the same time as they are sent to the European Parliament. They are examined by the UK Parliament through a Select Committee on European legislation which reports to the House of Commons on their political and legal consequences. In addition, more general discussion takes place about Community legislative proposals before the biennial meetings of the European Council.

If the Select Committee recommends that further consideration should be given to any particular proposal, it will be referred to a Standing Committee. The UK government has given an undertaking to Parliament that they will not approve proposals for legislation in the Council of Ministers if they are awaiting consideration by the House or are still subject to scrutiny. However, ministers may agree to proposals which:

- are subject to scrutiny if they are confidential, routine, trivial or substantially the same as an item which has already been scrutinised;
- are awaiting consideration but the Select Committee has indicated that agreement could be given; or
- are either awaiting consideration or are still subject to scrutiny, and the minister has special reasons why agreement should be given, provided that these reasons are given at the first opportunity (HC Debates Vol 178 Col 399 (24 October 1990)).

By a Declaration annexed to the TEU, Member States committed themselves to ensuring that 'national parliaments receive Commission proposals for legislation in good time for information or possible examination' (Declaration 13 TEU).

A Protocol attached to the EC Treaty by the ToA requires all Community Green and White Papers to be 'promptly forwarded' to national parliaments and legislative proposals to be forwarded 'in good time'. Not less than six weeks should elapse after a proposal is made available in all the languages of the Community and its adoption by the Council of Ministers (CM 3780, p. 89).

Constitutional Treaty

The Constitutional Treaty would have made a number of references to the interaction between the Community institutions and national parliaments particularly with regard to the application of the principle of subsidiarity (see below). A Protocol (Number 1) which was annexed to the Constitutional Treaty would have specifically related to the role of national parliaments.

The appropriate legal base

In almost every case, as the initiator of the legislative process, the choice of legal base is made by the Commission. It is not always clear, especially in relation to proposals which touch on a number of different activities, which Treaty provision, and hence which decision-making process, is appropriate. Article 5 EC Treaty provides that the Community shall act within the limits of the powers conferred on it by the Treaty and the objectives of the Treaty. When legislating, the Commission is bound to give reasons for its proposal, the legal basis on which it is made, and the process through which it passed, including the institutions and other bodies which participated in the decision (Art 253 EC Treaty). This information is normally contained in the preamble to the measure. Prior to the SEA, the choice of legal base rarely gave rise to controversy. However, disputes have subsequently arisen, largely either because Member States contested the competence of the Community to legislate at all or because a legal base was chosen allowing for a qualified majority vote within the Council of Ministers, when some Member States demanded a basis requiring unanimity and the opportunity to block the measure by a national veto (see above).

Defects in the legal base may be one of three kinds:

- lack of competence of the Community;
- lack of competence of an institution;
- inappropriate Treaty provision for the subject matter of the legislation.

The Court of Justice has not yet found that a proposed action is without a Community base, but some challenges have been successful. In **Germany v Commission** (Case 281/85) Germany, France, The Netherlands and the UK sought to annul a decision made by the Commission in relation to migration policy from non-Member States. Although free movement of persons is central to the working of the Community, the law is largely directed at the facilitation of free movement by EU citizens and their families (but see now the enlarged powers of the Community under Arts 62 and 65 EC Treaty in relation to immigration from outside the Community (see Chapters 11 and 12)). It was argued by the applicant Member States that neither the former Art 118 EC Treaty (which then related to social policy) nor any other Treaty provision empowered the Commission to adopt a binding decision. The Court of Justice held that the Commission did have the power to consult with Member States on the impact of third-country (i.e. non-EU) immigration on the employment market, and how this was affecting Community workers, but that it did not have the power to make a binding measure restricting the way in which Member States could regulate immigration into their territories from outside the Community. The Commission will generally choose the legal base offering the best chance of approval for a measure, if there is at least an arguable alternative:

Commission v Council (Generalised Tariff Preferences) (Case 45/86)

The Court of Justice stated that:

> The choice of a legal base for a measure may not depend simply on an institution's conviction as to the objective pursued but must be based on objective factors which are amenable to judicial review.

In the following case, a conflict arose between the Council, on the one hand, and the Parliament and the Commission, on the other, as to the choice of the appropriate legal base:

Commission v Council (Case C-300/89)

The Commission (supported by the Parliament) applied to the Court of Justice for the annulment of Directive 89/428 on procedures for harmonising the programmes for the reduction and elimination of pollution caused by waste from the titanium dioxide industry. The Commission had proposed that the directive should be based on the former Art 100a EC Treaty (now Art 95), which provided for the Council to act by a qualified majority in cooperation with the Parliament. However, despite the Parliament's objections, the Council adopted the directive on the basis of environmental policy, pursuant to the former Art 130s EC Treaty. This article provided at the time (but see, now, Art 175 EC Treaty) that decisions in Council should be taken unanimously, and only after consultation with the Parliament. The Court decided that Art 100a, which provided that decisions should be taken by qualified majority in Council, in cooperation with the European Parliament, was the appropriate legal base. Although the directive had the dual objectives of environmental protection and the removal of distortions of competition by establishing harmonised production conditions, it was not possible to have recourse to two legal bases, and the unanimity rule in Art 130s was incompatible with the cooperation procedure in Art 130a. The decision of the Court of Justice has a strong political flavour:

> [20] The very purpose of the cooperation procedure, which is to increase the involvement of the European Parliament in the legislative process of the Community would thus be jeopardised. As the Court stated in its judgment in **Roquette Frères v Council** (Case 138/79) and **Maizena v Council** (Case C-139/79), para. 34, that participation reflects a fundamental democratic principle that the peoples should take part in the exercise of power through the intermediary of a representative assembly.

The Commission has continued to show a disinclination to use Treaty provisions, on which decisions in the Council are to be taken unanimously, and a preference for articles for which qualified majority voting is the appropriate procedure in the Council of Ministers. The following case is an example in the field of higher education:

European Parliament v Council (Case C-295/90)

The Court of Justice had decided in **Gravier v City of Liège** (Case 293/83) that the former Art 128 EC Treaty, which contained some fairly general provisions on the promotion of a common vocational training policy, created a directly enforceable right of access to vocational training in other Member States. As a Treaty right, it was to be delivered in accordance with the principles of equality contained in the former Art 7 EC Treaty (now Art 12).

The former Arts 7 and 128 EC Treaty were, therefore, taken as the basis for a new directive on student mobility (Directive 90/366). Article 7 provided for measures to eliminate discrimination on grounds of nationality to be decided by a qualified majority vote, and it was on this basis that the measure was proposed. The Council of Ministers substituted the former Art 235 EC Treaty (now Art 308) as the legal base, on the grounds that since Art 128 contained no voting procedure, the residual voting system in Art 235 (a unanimous vote) was more appropriate. Although the directive was unanimously approved by the Council of

Ministers, its legal base was challenged by the Parliament, since it did not want to see a precedent established of unanimous decision-making in relation to future educational measures. The Court of Justice upheld the challenge on the basis that the measure was, fundamentally, about equal access to vocational training, and that Art 7, which required only a qualified majority vote, was the proper legal basis. The Court ordered that the directive be annulled and a new measure be proposed with Art 7 as the legal base.

Under the Constitutional Treaty, such conflict would have become less pronounced because the majority of legislative acts would have been adopted under the 'ordinary legislative procedure' set out in Art III-396. However, Art I-18 Constitutional Treaty would have included what is termed a 'flexibility clause'. This would have allowed the adoption of measures necessary to attain any of the objectives laid down by the Constitution where there was no provision for powers of action to that effect in the Constitution. Its scope would therefore have been wider than that of the current Art 308 EC Treaty, which is confined to the internal market (see above), but the conditions for its implementation would have been stricter in that, as well as requiring unanimity in the Council, Parliament's approval would also have been needed.

Competence under Title VI TEU

The following case concerned the adoption of a Framework Decision under Title VI TEU (Police and Judicial Cooperation in Criminal Matters; see Chapter 1). The issue before the Court of Justice was whether or not the Framework Decision should be annulled because it encroached upon the powers conferred on the Community by the EC Treaty:

Commission v *Council* (Case C-176/03)

Framework Decision 2003/80/JHA was adopted on the basis of Title VI TEU. The aim of the Framework Decision was to respond with concerted action to the disturbing increase in offences posing a threat to the environment. Articles 2 and 3 of the Framework Decision provided that the Member States were to prescribe criminal penalties for seven types of environmental offences committed either intentionally or negligently. Article 4 provided for the classification as offences of forms of participating in, and of instigating, offending conduct. Under Art 5, the criminal penalties laid down had to be 'effective, proportionate and dissuasive'. Article 5(1) provided that serious offences were to be punished with penalties involving deprivation of liberty which could give rise to extradition. Article 6 governed the liability, for an act or omission, of legal persons in respect of the offences set out in Arts 2 to 4, while Art 7 made them subject to 'effective, proportionate and dissuasive' penalties. Article 7 set out five specific criminal penalties where legal persons were found liable for those offences.

Before the contested Framework Decision was adopted, the Commission had presented a proposal for a directive of the European Parliament and of the Council, on the basis of Art 175(1) EC Treaty on the protection of the environment through criminal law. The European Parliament had expressed its view on both pieces of legislation and had called on the Council:

(1) to use the Framework Decision as a measure complementing the proposed directive that would take effect in relation to the protection of the environment through criminal law solely in respect of judicial cooperation; and

(2) to refrain from adopting the Framework Decision before adoption of the proposed directive.

The Council did not adopt the proposed directive but instead adopted the Framework Decision, mentioning the proposal for a directive in the fifth and seventh recitals and stating that a majority of its members had taken the view that the proposal went beyond the powers attributed to the Community, since its objective was to require the Member States to provide for criminal sanctions. The Commission had expressed its disagreement on this point.

Before the Court of Justice, in support of its application for annulment of the Framework Decision, the Commission challenged the choice of the provisions of the TEU as the legal basis for Arts 1 to 7 of the Framework Decision. It pointed out that, under Art 2 EC Treaty, the Community is competent to require the Member States to impose penalties at national level, including criminal penalties if appropriate, where that proves necessary in order to attain a Community objective.

The Council replied that the division of powers in criminal matters as between the Member States and the European Community is clearly established and that the Court has never obliged the Member States to adopt criminal penalties.

The Court began by observing that it is its task to ensure that acts which, according to the Council, fall within the scope of Title VI TEU do not encroach upon the powers conferred by the EC Treaty on the Community.

In relation to the specific problem before it, the Court noted that protection of the environment constitutes one of the objectives of the Community, fundamental in nature and extending across Community policies and activities. The Court also noted that Arts 174 to 176 EC Treaty provide the appropriate instruments for achieving that objective, pointing out that the measures referred to in the three indents of the first subparagraph of Art 175(2) EC Treaty all imply the involvement of the Community institutions in areas such as fiscal policy, energy policy or town and country planning policy, in which, apart from Community policy on the environment, either the Community has no legislative powers or unanimity within the Council is required.

The Court then applied its settled case law, according to which the choice of the legal base for a Community measure must rest on objective factors which are amenable to judicial review, including in particular the aim and the content of the measure. The Court noted that the objective of the Framework Decision was the protection of the environment and that Arts 2 to 7 entailed partial harmonisation of the criminal laws of the Member States, a sphere in which, as a general rule, the Community does not have competence. The Court held that the last-mentioned finding does not, however, prevent the Community legislature, when the application of effective, proportionate and dissuasive criminal penalties by the competent national authorities is an essential measure for combating serious environmental offences, from taking measures which relate to the criminal law of the Member States which it considers necessary in order to ensure that the rules it lays down on environmental protection are fully effective. Since those conditions were specifically met in the present case, Arts 1 to 7 of the Framework Decision could have been properly adopted on the basis of Art 175 EC Treaty and therefore the entire Framework Decision, being indivisible, infringed Art 47 TEU because it encroached on the powers which Art 175 EC Treaty confers on the Community. The Framework Decision was therefore annulled by the Court of Justice.

Subsidiary

Following an amendment made to the EC Treaty by the TEU, there is the recognition of a national dimension to the decision-making process. Article 5 EC Treaty (post-TEU) provides that:

> The Community shall act within the limits of the powers conferred upon it by this Treaty and of the objectives assigned to it therein. In areas which do not fall within its exclusive competence, the Community shall take action, in accordance with the principle of subsidiarity, only if and in so far as the objectives of the proposed action cannot be sufficiently achieved by the Member States and can, therefore, by reason of the scale or effects of the proposed action, be better achieved by the Community. Any action by the Community shall not go beyond what is necessary to achieve the objectives of this Treaty.

Although subsidiarity was not a new concept for the Community, the TEU made it a central criterion to be applied by the Commission when it proposes new legislation. Hitherto, subsidiarity had been implicit in Art 249 EC Treaty in relation to the implementation of directives, where the Community set the objectives, and the Member States chose the 'manner and form of implementation'. It was first made specific by the former Art 130(4) in relation to the environment, where legislation was only to be introduced if the environmental objectives could 'be attained better at Community level than at the level of individual Member States'. Article 5 EC Treaty makes the principle applicable to all new legislation where the issue of competing competencies arises.

At the Edinburgh European Council Meeting of October 1993, it was decided that the Commission should consult more widely before proposing legislation and should include in the recitals to any new measure its justification for initiating the measure, under the subsidiarity principle. If legislation had to be made at Community level, directives were to be preferred to regulations, and 'framework directives' (allowing Member States considerable leeway in the manner of implementation) to be preferred to specific and detailed directives.

As part of the process of implementing the new subsidiarity principle, the Commission embarked on a so-called 'bonfire of measures' and the abandonment of some legislative programmes, with a view to the policies which they were intended to implement being carried out at national level. It announced the withdrawal of proposals for more than 15 directives, including proposals on the liability of suppliers of services, minimum standards for the keeping of animals in zoos, speed limits for motor vehicles and maximum alcohol levels for vehicle drivers (Bull EU 6 1994, p. 26).

There are, however, both legal and practical limits to the implementation of policies at national level, as envisaged in Art 5. Article 5 refers to matters which are not within the exclusive competence of the Community, implying that there are matters of shared competence.

It is at the national level that practical difficulties arise. Experience has shown that there are major divergences in the extent of implementation of Community law by Member States. The briefest examination of the European Court Reports and the Annual General Report of the Commission indicates the extent of the problem.

If more legislation and enforcement take place at state level, there will be even greater local variations in the degree of regulation in each Member State. The 'level playing field' for business may then become even less attainable. The Court of Justice may be called upon to decide, according to the effects or scale of a measure, whether its objectives could be 'sufficiently' achieved by legislation in the Member States. It may have to apply conflicting criteria.

Ironically, subsidiarity was championed by those Member States, among them the UK, that were concerned about the centralising of decision making in Brussels, and the apparent movement of the Community towards a federal structure. If the Court of Justice has to determine which decisions can and should be taken at the centre, and which at national level by national parliaments, then Art 5 could become the cornerstone in the constitution of a new federal Europe. Subsidiarity was again discussed at the Amsterdam Conference in 1997 and some attempt was made to build the principle into the decision-making process. A Protocol added to the ToA provides that:

> Subsidiarity is a dynamic concept and should be applied in the light of the objectives set out in the Treaty. It allows Community action within the limits of its powers to be expanded where circumstances so require, and conversely, to be restricted or discontinued where it is no longer justified.

The Protocol requires every proposed piece of Community legislation to state how it complies with the principle of subsidiarity and proportionality (see Chapter 2) and why 'a Community objective can be better achieved by the Community'. Essentially, Member States retain powers only in those areas where the Treaties confer no powers on the Community, or where the Community has general powers in a given area but has not yet chosen to act. Once it does act, its measures prevail over national rules, and it has exclusive competence.

Constitutional Treaty

Article I-11 would have provided that the limits of Union competences were governed by 'the principle of conferral', which meant that the Union would act 'within the limits of the competences conferred upon it . . . in the Constitution'. The corollary of this, would be that 'Competences not conferred upon the Union in the Constitution remain with the Member States'. The use of Union competences was also stated to be governed by 'the principles of subsidiarity and proportionality' (Art I-11(1)). This provision would have been complemented by a Protocol (Number 2) on the application of these two principles, which provided for an 'early-warning system' involving national parliaments in monitoring how subsidiarity was applied. National parliaments would have been informed of all new legislative initiatives and if at least one-third of them considered that a proposal infringed the principle of subsidiarity, the Commission would have had to reconsider its proposal.

The Constitutional Treaty would have distinguished between three categories of Union powers:

- areas of exclusive competence (where the Constitution conferred on the Union exclusive competence in a specific area) – Arts I-12(1) and I-13;

- areas of shared competence (where the Constitution conferred on the Union a competence which was shared with the Member States in a specific area) – Arts I-12(2) and I-14; and

- areas where the Union may take supporting action (provided this conformed with the provisions of Part III relative to the area in which action was to be taken) – Arts I-12(5) and I-17.

Particular cases which did not fit into this threefold general classification would have been dealt with separately: for example, the coordination of economic and employment policies (Art I-15) and common foreign and security policy (Art I-16).

Summary

Now you have read this chapter you should be able to:

- Compare and contrast the respective roles of the Community institutions and national parliaments within the Community's legislative process.

- Understand the importance of choosing the appropriate legal base when adopting secondary Community legislation, and discuss how this choice of legal base impacts upon the voting systems used in the Council of Ministers.

- Understand and evaluate the relevance of the principle of subsidiarity to the Community's decision-making process.

- Assess the impact which the proposed Constitutional Treaty would have had on the Community's decision-making process if it had been ratified.

References

Pescatore, P., 'Some Critical Remarks on the Single European Act' (1987) CML Rev 9.

Further reading

Textbooks

Craig, P. and De Burca, G. (2003) *EU Law Text, Cases and Materials* (3rd edn), Oxford University Press, Chapter 4.

Foster, N. (2006) *Foster on EU Law* (1st edn), Oxford University Press, Chapter 3 (Sections 3.4 to 3.6).

Tillotson, J. and Foster, N. (2003) *Text, Cases and Materials on EU Law* (4th edn), Cavendish Publishing, Chapter 5.

Steiner, J., Woods, L. and Twigg-Flesner, C. (2006) *EU Law* (9th edn), Oxford University Press, Chapter 3.

Storey, T. and Turner, C. (2005) *Unlocking EU Law* (1st edn), Hodder Arnold, Chapter 5.

Toth, A.G. (1994) 'A Legal Analysis of Subsidiarity', in O'Keefe, D. and Twomey, P. (eds) *Legal Issues of the Maastricht Treaty*, Chancery Publications.

Weatherill, S. (2006) *Cases and Materials on EU Law* (7th edn), Oxford University Press, Chapter 2.

Journal articles

Hosli, M., 'Coalitions and Power: Effects of Qualified Majority Voting on the Council of the European Union' (1996) 34 JCMS 255.

Langrish, S., 'The Treaty of Amsterdam: Selected Highlights' (1998) 23 EL Rev 3.

Nicholl, W., 'The Code of Conduct of the Commission towards the European Parliament' (1996) 34 JCMS 275.

Obradovic, D. and Alonso Vizcaino, J.M., 'Good governance requirements concerning the participation of interest groups in EU consultations' (2006) 43 CML Rev 1049.

Pescatore, P., 'Some Critical Remarks on the Single European Act' (1987) CML Rev 9.

Timmermans, C., 'How Can One Improve the Quality of Community Legislation?' (1997) 34 CML Rev 1229.

5 The European Court of Justice and the Court of First Instance

Aims and objectives

At the end of this chapter you should understand:

■ The composition and role of the European Court of Justice, with a particular reference to judges and Advocates-General.

■ The structure of the Court of Justice and how it reaches a judgment.

■ The various methods of interpretation used by the Court of Justice, and how these methods differ to those used by the UK judiciary.

■ How the Court of Justice's jurisdiction is defined and the various heads of jurisdiction.

■ The composition, role and powers of the Court of First Instance.

■ The role of the EU Civil Service Tribunal.

■ Changes which the Constitutional Treaty would have made to the constitutional structure of the Court of Justice and the Court of First Instance, if it had come into force.

Statute of the Court of Justice and the Rules of Procedure

Article 7(1) EC Treaty (previously Art 4(1)) establishes the Community institutions. In addition to the European Parliament, Council, Commission and Court of Auditors (which were considered in Chapter 3), Art 7(1) also established as a Community institution the Court of Justice (it may also be referred to as the European Court, or European Court of Justice). It should not be confused with the European Court of Human Rights, which is not a Community institution and does not have jurisdiction to adjudicate on Community law. The European Court of Human Rights has jurisdiction to adjudicate on breaches of the European Convention on Human Rights, of which the UK is a signatory (see Chapter 1). The Court of Justice is permanently in session in Luxembourg and vacations are fixed according to the workload. The European Court of Human Rights sits in Strasbourg.

The Court of Justice plays a pivotal role in the Community. Some of the legal principles which govern the way the Community functions are not found in the Treaty or the legislative acts made under it, but they are to be found in the case law of the Court. This has been considered in Chapter 2 and is considered further in Chapter 9.

Statute of the Court of Justice

The Court of Justice is itself governed by the founding Treaties as amended, and the Statute of the Court of Justice which is appended to the Treaties as a protocol. The statute annexed to the EC Treaty has the title: 'Protocol on the Statute of the Court of Justice of the European Community', as amended by Council Decision 94/993 (OJ 1994 L 397/1). A new version of the Statute of the Court of Justice (OJ 2002 C 325/167) came into effect when the Treaty of Nice came into force on 1 February 2003. This Statute has been amended on a number of occasions:

- 15 July 2003 by Council Decision (OJ 2003 L 188/1);

- 19 April 2004 by Council Decision (OJ 2004 L 132/1, with corrigendum in OJ 2004 L 194/3);

- 1 May 2004 by Art 13(2) of the Act concerning the conditions of accession of 16 April 2003 (OJ 2003 L 236/37);

- 2 November 2004 by Council Decision (OJ 2004 L 333/7);

- 1 January 2007 by Art 13(2) of the Act concerning the conditions of accession of 25 April 2005 (OJ 2005 L 157/203).

The full text of the consolidated Statute is available at:
> http://curia.europa.eu/en/instit/txtdocfr/index.htm

Rules of Procedure of the Court of Justice

Detailed effect is given to the statute by the Court's Rules of Procedure. The third paragraph of Art 245 EC Treaty provides that 'the Court of Justice shall adopt its rules of procedure. These shall require the unanimous approval of the Council'. The rules were adopted on 19 June 1991 (OJ 1991 L 176/1, with corrigendum in OJ 1992 L 383/117). They have been amended on a number of occasions:

- 21 February 1995 (OJ 1995 L 44/61);

- 11 March 1997 (OJ 1997 L 103/1, with corrigendum in OJ 1997 L 351/72);

- 16 May 2000 (OJ 2000 L 122/43);

- 28 November 2000 (OJ 2000 L 122/1);

- 3 April 2001 (OJ 2001 L 119/1);

- 17 September 2002 (OJ 2002 L 272/1, with corrigendum in OJ 2002 L 281/24);

- 8 April 2003 (OJ 2003 L 147/17);

- 10 June 2003 (OJ 2003 L 172/12);

- 19 April 2004 (OJ 2004 L 132/2);

- 20 April 2004 (OJ 2004 L 127/107);

- 15 May 2005 (OJ 2005 L 203/19);

- 18 October 2005 (OJ 2005 L 288/51).

A consolidated version of the Rules is available at:
> http://curia.europa.eu/en/instit/txtdocfr/index.htm

The amendments made in 2000 were designed to improve the conduct of procedures, to expedite (i.e. accelerate) the treatment of certain references for a preliminary ruling which are of exceptional urgency, and to adapt the Rules to the amendments introduced by the ToA. In its submission to the Nice 2000 Intergovernmental Conference (IGC) the Court of Justice and the Court of First Instance (CFI, see below) requested the power to amend their Rules of Procedure themselves:

> In an enlarged Union, the requirement that amendments to the Rules of Procedure of the Court of Justice and the Court of First Instance be unanimously approved by the Council may give rise to a lack of flexibility which is incompatible with the need for the courts to adapt to their new work. Such inflexibility is unnecessary, particularly since most of the procedural provisions having any special importance in terms of institutional considerations or matters of policy are contained in the Statute. It will also be noted that other courts, such as the International Court of Justice and the European Court of Human Rights, have the power to adopt their own rules of procedure.
>
> The Court of Justice and the Court of First Instance therefore propose the removal of the words 'Those rules shall require the unanimous approval of the Council' from the end of the third paragraph of Article 245 and the end of Article 225(4).
>
> (*Contribution by the Court of Justice and the Court of First Instance to the Intergovernmental Conference*, Luxembourg, 2000)

Although the ToN (which came into force on 1 February 2003) did not accommodate the Court's request, the ToN amended Art 223 to provide that the Council's approval of the Court's rules of procedure shall be by a qualified majority vote rather than by unanimity. The ToN made other amendments affecting the composition, rules and procedures of both the Court of Justice and the CFI, which will be discussed throughout this chapter. In addition, amendments made by the new Statute and amended Rules of Procedure will be referred to. The changes which would have been brought about by the Constitutional Treaty (if it had come into force) will be considered separately.

The provisions of the EC Treaty applicable to the Court of Justice are Arts 220–245 (previously Arts 164–188). The Court of Justice's website can be accessed at:

http://curia.europa.eu/en/instit/presentationfr/index_cje.htm

Constitutional Treaty

The Constitutional Treaty has not come into force because it was not ratified by all of the then 25 Member States. Articles I-29 and III-353 to III-381 would have set out the provisions which would have applied to the Court of Justice. Art I-29(1) would have provided that:

> The Court of Justice of the European Union shall include the Court of Justice, the General Court [the new name for the CFI] and specialised courts . . .

A new Statute of the Court of Justice would have come into force at the same time as the Constitutional Treaty. The new Statute was attached to the Constitutional Treaty as a protocol (Number 4): 'Protocol on the Statute of the Court of Justice of the European Union'.

Article III-355 would have provided that the Court of Justice would adopt its Rules of Procedure which would require the consent of the Council (i.e. by qualified majority, because Art I-23(3) Constitutional Treaty provided that the Council would act by a qualified majority except where the Constitution provided otherwise).

Organisation of the Court of Justice

Members

Prior to the ToN, the Court consisted of 15 judges (Art 221 EC Treaty (previously Art 165)) assisted by 8 Advocates-General (Art 222 EC Treaty (previously Art 166)). The ToN amended Art 221 EC Treaty to provide that the Court of Justice will consist of one judge from each Member State. Therefore, on 1 May 2004 (when the European Union was enlarged to 25 Member States), the number of judges increased from 15 to 25, and on 1 January 2007 (when the European Union was enlarged to 27 Member States), the number of judges increased from 25 to 27. The ToN also amended Art 222 EC Treaty, and although it still provides for 8 Advocates-General to assist the Court, it now provides that if the Court requests the number to be increased, the Council may do so acting unanimously.

Article 223 (previously Art 167) provides that both judges and Advocates-General:

> ... shall be chosen from persons whose independence is beyond doubt and who possess the qualifications required for appointment to the highest judicial offices in their respective countries or who are jurisconsults of recognised competence.

The requirements for these appointments are therefore not intended to be confined to those who have made a career in the courts and are destined for, or already sit, on the bench in their Member State. Appointments may also be made from the ranks of distinguished academic lawyers or 'jurisconsults of recognised competence'.

Although the Treaty (pre-ToN) did not contain any provisions regarding the nomination and nationality of judges and Advocates-General, it was the practice that each Member State would nominate one judge who was a national, and each of the four larger states (France, Germany, Italy and the UK) did the same in relation to four of the Advocates-General. However, on the accession of Austria, Finland and Sweden on 1 January 1995, a Declaration was made by the Member States in relation to the allocation of the posts of Advocates-General. Under the Declaration, France, Germany, Italy, Spain and the UK would be allocated a 'permanent' Advocate-General each. Spanish, Irish and Italian Advocates-General were appointed from 1 January 1995, and replacements for the non-permanent posts were then filled by the Member States taking part in rotation, in alphabetical order (Joint Declaration 1 January 1995, OJ 1995 L 1/21).

A new judge is required to take an oath to perform his duties impartially and conscientiously and to preserve the secrecy of the deliberations of the Court. He also signs a solemn declaration to behave with integrity and discretion in relation to the acceptance of benefits after he has left office (Arts 2 and 4 Statute of the Court of Justice). Judges may not hold any political or administrative office and may not follow any other occupation, paid or unpaid, during their period of office (Art 4 Statute).

Article 223 EC Treaty (previously Art 167) provides for the appointments to be for a renewable six-year term. Appointment and reappointment of the judges and Advocates-General is staggered, taking place every three years. It has been argued that this necessity to seek reappointment could threaten the impartiality of the judiciary, because if a particular judge acts against the interests of the Member State of his nationality it is likely he would not be nominated for reselection. Accordingly, there may be pressure on the judge to be sympathetic to national issues. This argument may be rejected because the Court delivers one judgment, and therefore it is impossible for a Member

State to ascertain the actual views of their nominee (see below). The same, however, could not be said of Advocates-General, the role of whom is considered below.

The UK judge, from 8 January 2004, is Konrad Schiemann (a QC and Lord Justice of Appeal (1995–2003)). His term of office has been renewed for the period from 7 October 2006 to 6 October 2012. He replaced the UK judge, David Edward.

The UK's Advocate-General is Ms Eleanor Sharpston (QC). Her period of office runs from 10 January 2006 until 6 October 2009.

Constitutional Treaty

Membership of the Court has been increased as a matter of course as membership of the EU has increased. The Court expressed anxiety about the indefinite application of this policy in its submission to the 1996 IGC. In relation to membership, two factors must be balanced:

> On the one hand, any significant increase in the number of judges might mean that the plenary session of the Court would cross the invisible boundary between a collegiate body and a deliberative assembly. Moreover, as the great majority of cases would be heard by Chambers, this increase would pose a threat to the consistency of the case law.
>
> On the other hand, the presence of members from all the national legal systems on the Court is undoubtedly conducive to harmonious development of Community case law, taking into account concepts regarded as fundamental in the various Member States and thus enhancing the acceptability of the solutions arrived at. It may also be considered that the presence of a judge from each of the Member States enhances the legitimacy of the Court.

Despite these recurring discussions, the Constitutional Treaty failed to address the issue. If the Constitutional Treaty had come into force, Art III-353 would not have stipulated the number of judges, Art III-354 simply stating that: 'Every three years there shall be a partial replacement of the Judges . . . in accordance with the conditions laid down in the Statute of the Court of Justice'. Article 9 of the new Statute would have provided that 'When, every three years, the Judges are partially replaced, fourteen and thirteen judges shall be replaced alternately', thus retaining the current structure of 27 judges. Article III-354 would have been similar to Art 222 EC Treaty, providing for eight Advocates-General but providing for that number to have been increased by the Council acting unanimously, at the request of the Court of Justice.

While Art III-355 would have followed the principle of independence set out in Art 223 EC Treaty, Art III-355 would also have provided that judges and Advocates-General would be appointed by common accord of the governments of the Member States 'after consultation of the panel provided for in Article III-357'. This panel would have comprised seven persons chosen from among former members of the Court of Justice and the General Court (this would have been the new name given to the CFI, see below), members of national supreme courts and lawyers of recognised competence, one of whom would have been proposed by the European Parliament (Art III-357). The purpose of the panel would have been to give an opinion on the candidates' suitability to perform the duties.

President of the Court

Article 223 EC Treaty (previously Art 167) provides for the election by the judges of a President for a term of three years, which may be renewed. The current President of the

Court is Mr Vassilios Skouris, who was elected for the period from 7 October 2003 to 8 October 2006; he has subsequently been re-elected for the period 9 October 2006 to 6 October 2009. He replaced Mr Gill Carlos Rodriguez Iglesias who had been President of the Court since 7 October 1994.

The President directs the judicial business and administration of the Court: thus he presides at hearings of the full court, fixes and extends time limits for lodging pleadings, documents, etc., and usually deals with interlocutory applications (i.e. applications within the course of the proceedings, prior to the full hearing).

Article 9(2) of the Rules provides for the President to appoint a Judge-Rapporteur to each case before the Court. The function of the Judge-Rapporteur is to manage the case throughout its progression through the Court's system. The Judge-Rapporteur will be responsible for drafting the final judgment.

From 1 February 2003 (the date the ToN came into force), Article 13 of the Statute of the Court of Justice provides that the Council (acting unanimously) may provide for the appointment of Assistant Rapporteurs to assist the Judge-Rapporteur. These assistants will be legally qualified persons and shall be appointed by the Council.

Constitutional Treaty

Identical to Art 223 EC Treaty, Art III-355 Constitutional Treaty would have provided for the election of the President of the Court for a renewable period of three years. All provisions relating to the President would have remained the same, with the exception that the appointments panel (see above) would have acted 'on the initiative of the President' (Art III-357).

Article 13 of the new Statute would have provided for the appointment of Assistant Rapporteurs:

> A European law may provide for the appointment of Assistant Rapporteurs and lay down the rules governing their service. It shall be adopted at the request of the Court of Justice. The Assistant Rapporteurs may be required, under conditions laid down in the Rules of Procedure, to participate in preparatory inquiries in cases pending before the Court of Justice and to cooperate with the Judge who acts as Rapporteur.
>
> The Assistant Rapporteurs shall be chosen from persons whose independence is beyond doubt and who possess the necessary legal qualifications; they shall be appointed by a European decision of the Council, acting by a simple majority. They shall take an oath before the Court of Justice to perform their duties impartially and conscientiously and to preserve the secrecy of the deliberations of the Court of Justice.

Advocate-General

The title 'Advocate' is something of a misnomer, because the Advocate-General represents no one and does not present a case on anyone's behalf. Although not a judge, the Advocate-General enjoys equal status with the judges. For that reason, the Report by the Court of Justice to the 1996 IGC suggested that Advocates-General should be able to take part in the election of the President of the Court, but the recommendation was not acted upon (and has not been acted upon at subsequent IGCs). Article 10(1) of the Rules provides for the office of First Advocate-General to rotate annually among the Advocates-General. Once the President has assigned a Judge-Rapporteur to a case, the First Advocate-General assigns an Advocate-General to the case. Thus each case will have one Judge-Rapporteur and one Advocate-General.

Article 222 (previously Art 166) prescribes the role of the Advocate-General as being:

... to make, in open court, reasoned submissions on cases which, in accordance with the Statute of the Court of Justice, require his involvement.

The various Court stages are considered below. Once all the formal stages have been completed, but before the judges deliberate upon their judgment, the Advocate-General will prepare his personal opinion as to the decision the Court should reach, which he will deliver in open court. He is an independent adviser to the Court.

From 1 February 2003 (the date the ToN came into force), Art 20 of the Statute of the Court of Justice provides that, after hearing the Advocate-General assigned to a particular case, if the Court considers that the case raises no new point of law, it may decide to determine the case without a submission (i.e. Opinion) from the Advocate-General. In 2004, 30 per cent of judgments delivered by the Court of Justice were determined without an Advocate-General's Opinion; this increased to 35 per cent in 2005.

The recommendation in the Opinion is not binding on the Court, or on the parties, and the Court is free to follow it or not, as it chooses. However, in spite of their non-binding nature, the Opinions of Advocates-General carry considerable weight on account of the very high standard of legal analysis which they contain and they are frequently cited in the Court as well as in legal writing as persuasive sources of authority.

The Opinion is fully reasoned. It normally deals with every aspect of the case, and will generally be much longer and more wide-ranging than the judgment of the Court. It will usually attempt to set the case in a broader context than the issues which divide the parties. It will set out the relevant facts and any applicable legislation (e.g. Treaty articles, regulations, directives, etc.), the issues that have been raised will be discussed, there will be a full review of any relevant past case law of the Court, and it will conclude with a recommendation for a solution which the Court may adopt.

An Opinion that is particularly persuasive may strongly influence the Court, especially if it suggests creating a new principle, or departing from a previous decision of the Court. In the vast majority of cases, judgments of the Court will follow the Opinion. However, for example, in **Paola Faccini Dori** *v* **Recreb SRL** (Case C-91/92) the Court did not follow the Advocate-General's Opinion. In this case the Advocate-General recommended a departure from existing case law of the Court, which the Court was not minded to depart from.

The reasoning of the Court's judgment may not be as clear and fully argued as the Advocate-General's Opinion, due to the fact that the Court must reach a single judgment. The Opinion therefore may be persuasive in future cases on broadly the same theme. The Opinion will be published together with the judgment in the European Court Reports (the official Community law reports, abbreviated to ECR) and both are also available at:

http://curia.europa.eu/en/content/juris/index.htm

Constitutional Treaty

The Constitutional Treaty would have made no changes to the role of the Advocate-General (Art III-354).

Similar to the current Art 20 of the Statute, Art 20 of the new Statute would have provided that 'When it considers the case raises no new point of law, the Court of Justice may decide, after hearing the Advocate-General, that the case shall be determined without a submission from the Advocate-General'.

Registrar

Article 223 EC Treaty provides that:

> The Court of Justice shall appoint its Registrar and lay down the rules governing his service.

The Rules provide for him to be appointed for a six-year renewable term (Art 12(4), Rules). The current Registrar is Roger Grass from France. He has been in post since 10 February 1994.

The Registrar heads the Registry, which is responsible for the filing of documents, distribution of documents to relevant parties, etc. The Registrar is also responsible for the administration of the Court of Justice, and is directly responsible to the President of the Court.

Constitutional Treaty

The Constitutional Treaty made no reference to the Registrar, although the new Statute would have made similar references to the Registrar as are contained in the current Statute.

Chambers

Prior to the ToN, Art 221 EC Treaty (previously Art 165) provided that:

> The Court of Justice shall sit in plenary session [i.e. all 15 judges sitting together, subject to the rules on quorum]. It may, however, form chambers, each consisting of three, five or seven Judges, either to undertake certain preparatory inquiries or to adjudicate on particular categories of cases in accordance with rules laid down for these purposes. The Court of Justice shall sit in plenary session when a Member State or Community institution that is a party to the proceedings so requests.

Also prior to the ToN, Art 15 of the Statute provided that decisions were valid only if there was an uneven number of judges sitting in the deliberations. Decisions of the full Court (i.e. in plenary session) were valid if nine judges were sitting, and decisions of chambers consisting of three or five judges were valid if three judges were sitting, while chambers of seven were valid if five were sitting.

Article 95(1) of the Rules provided that any type of case could be assigned to a chamber:

> ... in so far as the difficulty or the importance of the case or particular circumstances are not such as to require that the Court decide it in plenary session.

However, prior to the ToN, a Member State or Community institution which was a party to a case could demand that the case be heard by the full Court (Art 221 EC Treaty (previously Art 165)), i.e. sitting in plenary session.

The ToN amended Art 221 EC Treaty to provide for the sitting of the Court in chambers, in a new Grand Chamber, and in plenary session (i.e. the full Court).

Article 16 of the Statute now provides that the Court shall form chambers of three or five judges (thus dispensing with the seven-judge chamber). The Grand Chamber shall consist of thirteen judges and will be presided over by the President of the Court. The Grand Chamber shall sit whenever a Member State or Community institution that is a party to the proceedings so requests. Where it is considered that a case before it is of exceptional importance, the Court may decide, after hearing the Advocate-General, to refer the case to the full Court.

Article 16 provides that the Court shall sit as a full Court where cases are brought to it pursuant to:

- Art 195(2) EC Treaty – dismissal of the Ombudsman.

- Art 213(2) EC Treaty – compulsory retirement of a Commission member, or removing his right to a pension or other benefits, on the ground of his breach of his Art 213 obligations.

- Art 216 EC Treaty – compulsory retirement of a Commission member on the ground that he no longer fulfils the conditions required for the performance of his duties or he is guilty of serious misconduct.

- Art 247(7) EC Treaty – compulsory retirement of a member of the Court of Auditors, or removing his right to a pension or other benefits, on the ground that he no longer fulfils the requisite conditions or meets the obligations arising from his office.

Article 17 of the Statute provides that decisions of the court shall be valid only when an uneven number of its members is sitting in the deliberations. It further provides that chambers consisting of three or five judges shall be valid only if they are taken by at least three judges, those of the Grand Chamber valid only if at least nine judges are sitting, and those of the full Court valid only if at least fifteen judges are sitting.

As regards the distribution of cases between the formations of the Court of Justice, of the cases brought to a close in 2004 and 2005:

- The full Court (full Court, Grand Chamber, former plenary formations) dealt with nearly 12 per cent of the cases brought to a close in 2004 and 13 per cent in 2005.

- Chambers of five judges dealt with 54 per cent of the cases brought to a close in both 2004 and 2005.

- Chambers of three judges dealt with 34 per cent of the cases brought to a close in 2004 and 33 per cent in 2005.

Five-judge Chambers are becoming the usual formation for hearing cases brought before the Court.

Constitutional Treaty

The Constitutional Treaty would have made no changes to the above provisions (Art III-353). Articles 16 and 17 of the new Statute would have been identical to Arts 16 and 17 of the current Statute.

Language

The case may be conducted in any one of the Community's official languages, and it may also be conducted in Irish (Art 29(1), Rules). It is for the applicant to choose the language (Art 29(2), Rules). This is overridden by Art 29(2)(a) of the Rules, which provides that where the defendant is a Member State or a natural or legal person with the nationality of a Member State, then the case shall be conducted in the official language of that state. References for a preliminary ruling pursuant to Art 234 EC Treaty (previously Art 177) (see Chapter 6) shall be conducted in the language of the referring national court (Art 29(2), Rules).

The Court itself will use French as its working language. This is despite a majority of citizens of the Member States now speaking English rather than French. French was chosen as the working language of the Court, because when the first Community (the ECSC, which expired on 23 July 2002) was created by the six founding Member States, French was the official language of three of them (France, Belgium and Luxembourg).

Procedure of the Court

The rules concerning the procedure of the Court are laid down in the Statute of the Court and the Rules of Procedure (see above). The process is essentially inquisitorial. Unlike an English adversarial process, the procedure of the Court, after the initiation of the case by one or more of the parties, is Court-led. The Court can request the parties to provide documents and statements; witnesses are heard at the instigation of the Court. Their evidence is part of the investigation by the Judge-Rapporteur and not, as in an English case, part of the oral hearing. The procedure in a direct action (as opposed to a reference under Art 234 EC Treaty, which is considered in Chapter 6) generally has four stages:

- written proceedings
- preparatory inquiry
- oral hearing
- judgment.

These four stages are now considered in further detail.

Written proceedings

Article 20 of the Statute provides that:

> The written procedure shall consist of the communication to the parties and to the institutions of the Communities whose decisions are in dispute, of applications, statements of case, defences and observations, and of replies, if any, as well as of all papers and documents in support or of certified copies of them.

Direct actions are initiated by the applicant filing an application (this is known as a 'pleading') at the Court's registry in accordance with Art 21 of the Statute. At this stage, following the ToN, the case may be assigned to a chamber or Grand Chamber, and a Judge-Rapporteur and Advocate-General will be appointed. Articles 39 and 40 of the Rules require the Registrar to serve the application on the defendant and any Community institution affected, following which the defendant has one month within which to lodge his defence, if any (this is also known as a 'pleading').

After the close of pleadings, the defendant can argue separately that the application is not admissible, e.g. he may argue that the proceedings were not issued within any relevant time limit. The Court may hear this application at this stage and, if successful, the action will be struck out. Alternatively, the Court may decide to hear the argument as to admissibility at the substantive hearing (i.e. the hearing of the main application).

Preparatory inquiry

It is at this stage that the Court takes over the future direction of the case. Unlike the English legal system, the Court will decide what evidence is required. Article 45(1) of the Rules provides that:

> The Court, after hearing the Advocate-General, shall prescribe the measures of inquiry that it considers appropriate by means of an order setting out the facts to be proved . . .

At the close of pleadings, the Judge-Rapporteur prepares a report which considers the issues of fact. The Court will decide at an administrative meeting what evidence is required to prove the facts which have not otherwise been agreed by the applicant and the defendant. Article 45(2) of the Rules provides that the following measures of inquiry may be adopted:

■ the personal appearance of the parties

■ a request for information and production of documents

■ oral testimony

■ the commissioning of an expert's report

■ an inspection of the place or thing in question.

Oral hearing

Articles 55 to 62 of the Rules govern the procedural aspects associated with the oral procedure. Once the preparatory inquiry has been concluded, the President of the Court fixes the date for the public hearing. A few days before the hearing the Judge-Rapporteur issues his report for the hearing. This sets out the facts of the case and summarises the arguments of the parties. Copies of the report are given to all the judges in the chamber and the parties, and are made available to members of the public before the hearing.

The oral proceedings are brief compared to those in an English court in a contested action. They consist of the addresses by counsel for the parties and the Opinion of the Advocate-General. There is usually a gap of some months between the conclusion of the addresses and the delivery of the Opinion to the reconvened Court. Addresses by counsel tend to be quite brief. They are expected to have lodged a copy of their submission before the hearing, and will normally use their address to emphasise their strongest arguments and to attack the weakest points in those of their opponents. The judges will quite frequently challenge points made, but the cut and thrust of forensic debate is somewhat blunted by the need for instant translation by interpreters as the argument proceeds.

Following the addresses the Advocate-General prepares his Opinion, which will be delivered in open court at some future date. Although he takes no part in the discussions between the judges which precede the judgment, his Opinion will have a significant influence on their decision. The Court has held that it is not open to the parties to submit written observations in response to the Advocate-General's Opinion (**Emesa Sugar (Free Zone) NV** *v* **Aruba** (Case C-17/98)). Immediately after delivery of the Opinion the Court goes into deliberation.

Article 44a of the Rules, which provides for the oral procedure, was amended on 1 July 2000 (OJ 2000 L 122/43). The new Art 44a provides that:

> Without prejudice to any special provisions laid down in these Rules, the procedure before the Court shall also include an oral part. However, after the pleadings referred to in Article 40(1) [i.e. service of a defence] and, as the case may be, in Article 41(1) have been lodged, the Court, acting on a report from the Judge-Rapporteur and after hearing the Advocate-General, and if none of the parties has submitted an application setting out the reasons for which he wishes to be heard, may decide otherwise . . .

The effect of this provision is that the Court can decide to dispense with the oral procedure, having received a report from the Judge-Rapporteur, and having listened to the Advocate-General and the parties to the case. This was incorporated into the Statute of the Court of Justice (by Art 20) which came into force at the same time as the ToN (i.e. 1 February 2003). However, Art 20 of the Statute limits the dispensing of the oral procedure to cases which raise no new point of law.

Judgment

Articles 63 to 68 of the Rules govern the procedural aspects associated with the delivering of a judgment. Judgment is always reserved by the Court, i.e. it goes into secret deliberation and will deliver its judgment in open court at some future date. This is necessary because a single judgment is delivered. The deliberation may be lengthy, taking many weeks (or months) to conclude.

A draft judgment will be prepared by the Judge-Rapporteur. This draft will form the basis of the deliberations. It may be necessary to go through the judgment sentence by sentence, voting on individual sentences. The votes of the judges are taken in ascending order of seniority; this is to ensure that the younger judges do not merely follow their seniors. The judgment may be short on reasons, or it may include differing (maybe conflicting) reasons, in order to obtain the necessary majority. It will be recalled (from above) that Art 17 of the Statute provides that a judgment will be valid only if an uneven number of judges sit in on the deliberations.

The deliberations will be conducted in French, and the judgment will be drafted in French, being translated into the language of the hearing (the authentic version of the judgment) once agreed.

Publication of judgments

The formal ruling of the judgment (the 'operative part') is published in the *Official Journal*. Prior to May 2004, the whole of the judgment together with the Advocate-General's Opinion would be published in the official European Court Reports (ECR). The reports are published in each of the official languages. They are not published in Irish, Irish not being one of the official languages. The series of reports are distinguished by colour, the UK version being purple.

The correct mode of citation is for the case number to precede the title, followed by the year of publication of the judgment in square brackets, the abbreviation ECR, and ending with the page number of the report – e.g. Case 20/59 **Italy** *v* **High Authority** [1960] ECR 423.

Since the CFI was established (see below), cases before that court are prefixed with a capital letter 'T' (from the French version of 'Tribunal') and those of the Court of Justice by 'C'. From 1990, the volumes of law reports are divided into two sections, so that the page number is now preceded by the numeral 'I' for cases before the Court of Justice and the numeral 'II' for cases before the CFI: e.g. Case C-79/89 **Brown Boveri** *v* **Hauptzollamt Mannheim** [1991] ECR I-1853. The two sections may be bound in two separate volumes depending upon the number of cases reported.

Due to the fact that judgments are always drafted in French, the bound French volume will usually be available six months following the end of the month to which it relates. There are eleven monthly paperback volumes: no judgments are delivered in August. They will subsequently be bound into one yearly volume. Following certain changes at the Court of Justice (for example, it decided not to publish the Report for the Hearing in all the official languages) the printed volumes are usually available in all languages quite soon after publication of the French version. It had previously been two years later.

Judgments are available from the Court's Registry (at a charge) on the day of the judgment, or very shortly thereafter. Judgments (and Opinions of Advocates-General) are now available (free of charge) at:

http://curia.europa.eu/en/content/juris/index.htm

An alternative means of accessing the Court's case law is through electronic and online databases such as LexisNexis. There are several independent unofficial law reports, e.g. the Common Market Law Reports (CMLR). The advantage of these reports is that, because they employ their own translators, a case may appear in them before it appears in the official ECR. The cases published are selective. The judgments may omit the Advocate-General's Opinion and will rarely include the Report for the Hearing. The downside is that their translations may differ from the version of the official report (ECR). When conducting research or litigation, it is always advisable to refer to the ECRs; alternatives should be used only if the official report is not available.

Some important cases may be reported in the domestic law reports, e.g. All ER, Weekly Law Reports, etc.

Publication of judgments from May 2004

During early 2004 the Court of Justice reviewed its methods of work, in order to make them more efficient and to counteract the expanding average length of proceedings. The result was the adoption of a series of measures which were put into practice progressively from May 2004.

The Reports for the Hearing drawn up by the Judge-Rapporteur are now drafted in a shorter and more summary form and contain only the essential elements of the case. Where the procedure in a case, in accordance with the Rules of Procedure, does not require an oral hearing, a report of the Judge-Rapporteur is no longer produced.

In accordance with Art 20 of the Statute of the Court, such a report is compulsory only if a hearing takes place.

The Court also re-examined its practice of publishing judgments in the European Court Reports. Two factors were identified at the centre of the problem:

(i)   it was found that the volume of the Reports, which exceeded 12,000 pages in 2002 and 13,000 pages in 2003, is liable to compromise the accessibility of the case law; and

(ii)   all judgments published in the Reports necessarily have to be translated into all the official languages of the Union, which represents a substantial workload for the Court's translation department.

Given that not all the judgments it delivers are equally significant from the point of view of the development of Community law, the Court decided to adopt a policy of *selective publication* of its decisions in the European Court Reports.

In an initial stage, as regards direct actions and appeals, judgments will no longer be published in the Reports if they come from a chamber of three judges or five judges if, pursuant to the last paragraph of Art 20 of the Statute of the Court, the case is decided without an Opinion of the Advocate General. It will, however, be open to the formation giving judgment to decide to publish such a decision in whole or in part in exceptional circumstances. Texts of the decisions not published in the Reports will still be accessible in electronic form in the language or languages available. The Reports are available electronically at:

http://www.curia.europa.eu/en/content/juris/index_form.htm

The Court decided not to extend this new practice to references for a preliminary ruling, in view of their importance for the interpretation and uniform application of Community law in all the Member States.

This reduction in the workload of the Court's translation department following the adoption of the selective publication policy was already noticeable in 2004. The total saving as a result of selective publication amounted in 2004 to approximately 20,000 pages.

ToA renumbering of Treaties – future citation

As a consequence of the renumbering of the Treaties provided for by the Treaty of Amsterdam, the Court of Justice has opted for a uniform system for citing provisions of the Treaty (see *Proceedings of the Court of Justice and the Court of First Instance of the European Communities* 7–11 December 1998 No. 31/98):

> In their pre-ToA versions, the Community Treaties (ECSC, Euratom, EC) and the TEU numbered their respective provisions differently to each other.
>
> They used Roman and Arabic numerals (ECSC and Euratom Treaties) or a combination of Roman and Arabic numerals and letters of the alphabet (EC and TEU).
>
> Article 12 of the ToA provides that, as from 1 May 1999 (the date it came into force), the provisions (articles, chapters and sections) of the EC Treaty and TEU are to be renumbered in Arabic numerals.
>
> The amendment of those Treaties involved not only an amendment of their content and the insertion of new provisions, but also the renumbering of most of the already existing provisions.
>
> This could obviously cause confusion in the mind of the user between the version of an article before the entry into force of the ToA and that subsequent to that date, as well as confusion between the provisions of the EC Treaty and the TEU, which are ever more frequently bound to be cited in the same document.
>
> The Court of Justice has therefore decided, in the interests of clarity and consistency, to implement a uniform system of citation of the provisions of the four Treaties in the judgments of the Court and the Opinions of the Advocates-General.
>
> Thus, from 1 May 1999, references to the provisions of the Treaties are to consist of an Arabic numeral designating the article plus two letters designating the Treaty, for example 'Article 2 EC' refers to Article 2 of the EC Treaty.
>
> In English, each of the four Treaties will be designated by two letters:
> - ECSC CS
> - Euratom Treaty EA
> - EC Treaty EC
> - Treaty on European Union EU.
>
> These rules are to be applied in all cases brought *after* 1 May 1999 which concern the renumbered provisions.
>
> However, the Court of Justice has provided for a transitional period. The Court has adopted different rules of citation for documents relating to cases brought *before* 1 May 1999 and for cases brought *after* 1 May 1999 but concerning the Treaties as they applied before this date. These transitional rules are as follows:
> - Where an article has simply been renumbered with no change to its wording, the example to be followed is '*Article 81 EC (ex Article 85)*'

- Where the article has been both renumbered and amended but the version concerned is that prior to the amendment, the formula used is *'Article 51 of the EC Treaty (now, after amendment, Article 41 EC)'*
- Where the article has been repealed by the ToA, it should be referred to as, for example, *'Article 53 of the EC Treaty (repealed by the Treaty of Amsterdam)'*.

Precedent

The doctrine of precedent (*stare decisis*) does not apply to the Court of Justice. However, the Court generally follows its own previous decisions; this is necessary for the sake of legal certainty. Nonetheless, faced with a very persuasive Advocate-General's Opinion, the Court may be persuaded to deviate from its past case law (e.g. to develop a new Community legal principle). The Court may, of its own volition, depart from its own previous case law: e.g. on policy grounds.

An example of a departure from its past case law is illustrated in the following case:

Criminal Proceedings against Keck and Mithouard (Cases C-267 and 268/91)

The Court of Justice held that:

14 . . . the Court considers it necessary to re-examine and clarify its case law on this matter . . .
16. . . . contrary to what has previously been decided . . .

It is usual for lawyers to cite previous case law when arguing a point of law before the Court. Indeed, the Advocate-General in his Opinion, and the Court in its judgment, will generally refer to previous cases. It may be difficult, if not impossible, to extract a *ratio decidendi* (i.e. principle of law applied to the facts) from the judgment because of the style of the Court's single judgment.

Methods of interpretation

The task of the Court of Justice is stated as being to '. . . ensure that in the interpretation and application of [the] Treaty the law is observed' (Art 220 EC Treaty). The sources of law to which the Court has to give effect are diverse (and are considered in detail in Chapter 2). Many of the Treaty provisions, and some of the implementing legislation, are expressed in the broadest terms, and the Court of Justice plays a crucial role in developing the law and constitution of the Community. It emphasised the importance and the breadth of that role in its submission to the 1996 IGC:

The Court . . . carries out tasks which, in the legal systems of the Member States, are those of the constitutional courts, the courts of general jurisdiction or the administrative courts or tribunals, as the case may be.

In its constitutional role, the Court rules on the respective powers of the Communities and of the Member States, and on those of the Communities in relation to other forms of cooperation within the framework of the Union and, generally, determines the scope of the provisions of the Treaties whose observance it is its duty to ensure. It ensures that the delimitation of powers between the institutions is safeguarded, thereby helping to maintain the institutional balance. It examines whether fundamental rights and general principles of law have been observed by the institutions, and by the Member States when their actions fall within the scope of Community law. It rules on the relationship between Community law and national law and on the reciprocal obligations between the Member States and the Community institutions. Finally, it may be called upon to judge whether international commitments envisaged by the Communities are compatible with the Treaties.

(*Report of the Court of Justice on Certain Aspects of the Application of the Treaty on European Union for the Purposes of the 1996 Inter-Governmental Conference* (May 1995))

The methods of interpretation which the Court of Justice employs when interpreting Community law, whether it is a provision of the Treaty, a regulation, a directive, etc., are considered further below. This 'European way' of interpretation is totally different to that employed by the English judiciary. This was recognised by Lord Denning, sitting in the English Court of Appeal, in the following case:

Bulmer v *Bollinger* [1974] 3 WLR 202

Lord Denning stated that:

> The [EC] Treaty is quite unlike any of the enactments to which we have become accustomed ... It lays down general principles. It expresses its aims and purposes. All in sentences of moderate length and commendable style. But it lacks precision. It uses words and phrases without defining what they mean. An English lawyer would look for an interpretation clause, but he would look in vain. There is none. All the way through the Treaty there are gaps and lacunae. These have to be filled by the judges, or by regulations or directives.
>
> It is the European way ... Seeing these differences, what are the English courts to do when they are faced with a problem of interpretation? They must follow the European pattern. No longer must they argue about the precise grammatical sense. They must look to the purpose and intent ... They must divine the spirit of the Treaty and gain inspiration from it. If they find a gap, they must fill it as best they can ... These are the principles, as I understand it, on which the European Court acts.

The approach of Lord Denning in the above case has its source in s 3(1), European Communities Act 1972, which provides:

> For the purposes of all legal proceedings any question as to the meaning or effect of any of the Treaties, or as to the validity, meaning or effect of any Community instrument, shall be treated as a question of law (and, if not referred to the European Court, be for determination as such in accordance with the principles laid down by and any relevant decision of the European Court or any court attached thereto).

The 'principles laid down by ... the European Court' is certainly wide enough to include the Court of Justice's method of interpretation. The European Communities Act 1972 was enacted by the UK Parliament to enable the UK to become a Member State of the Communities with effect from 1 January 1973.

The Court employs four separate methods of interpretation, each of which is considered further:

- literal
- historical
- contextual
- teleological.

It has emerged that the last two (and the last one in particular) are most often employed by the Court of Justice, these two being novel to the English legal system. The four methods of interpretation are now considered.

Literal interpretation

This rule is commonly used by the English judiciary when interpreting national legislation. You begin with the words of the text and give them their natural, plain meaning. The Court of Justice may refuse to employ this method, even where the words of the measure in question appear to be perfectly clear (see, e.g., **Commission v Council** (Case 22/70)).

Literal interpretation may be more difficult for the Court of Justice to apply because of the lack of interpretation sections in the relevant legislative measure. It will therefore be left to judicial interpretation to develop the meanings of certain words and phrases. Examples of words and phrases from the EC Treaty which have required interpretation include:

- 'Charges having equivalent effect' (Arts 23 and 25 (previously Arts 9 and 12)).
- 'Worker' (Art 39 (previously Art 48)).
- 'Public policy' (Art 39 (previously Art 48)).
- 'Abuse of a dominant position' (Art 82 (previously Art 86)).

Secondary legislation may be drafted more specifically (especially regulations which are to be directly applicable as they stand (see Chapter 2)). Nevertheless, the Court of Justice may apply one of the other methods rather than the literal method.

Historical interpretation

Historical interpretation requires a consideration of the subjective intention of the author of the text. This will involve an examination of the preliminary debates. This may be equated with the English mischief rule, where the judge seeks to establish the legislative intent, i.e. ascertain why the legislation was enacted; what its purpose was conceived to be at the time of enactment.

Historical interpretation is occasionally used by the Court of Justice. Generally the Court is not prepared to examine records of debates, and it should be remembered that meetings of the Council and Commission are usually conducted in secret, although there is now a greater tendency to openness and transparency (see Chapter 3). With regard to regulations, directives and decisions, Art 253 EC Treaty (previously Art 190) provides that reasons on which they are based must be given, i.e. the reasons as to why they have been enacted. These reasons will be contained in the preamble. The Court of Justice may be guided by these historical reasons in ascertaining the legislative intention of the relevant Community institutions. They are often referred to in judgments of the Court of Justice, as illustrated in the following case:

Markus v Hauptzollamt Hamburg-Jonas (Case 14/69)

The Court of Justice held that:

> ... according to the seventh recital of the preamble to the regulation in question ... the eight recital of the same preamble states ... It must therefore be assumed that the authors of the first paragraph

of Article 16 intended ... The solution is confirmed by the penultimate recital of the preamble to the said regulation according to which ...

Contextual interpretation

This method is extensively used by the Court of Justice when interpreting the Treaties and secondary legislation. It involves placing the provision within its context and interpreting it in relation to the other provisions. A particular paragraph of a directive or regulation, etc., must be considered not in isolation, but within the context of the whole instrument. When interpreting an article of the Treaty the Court of Justice may have regard to 'the general scheme of the Treaty as a whole', as illustrated in the following case:

Commission v Luxembourg and Belgium (Cases 2 and 3/62)

The Court of Justice was considering the former Art 12 (now Art 25), which provides that:

> Customs duties on imports and exports and charges having equivalent effect shall be prohibited between Member States. This prohibition shall also apply to customs duties of a fiscal nature.

The Court of Justice held that:

> The position of those Articles [former Arts 9 and 12 (now Arts 23 and 25)] towards the beginning of that Part of the Treaty dealing with the 'Foundations of the Community' – [former] Article 9 [now Art 23] being placed at the beginning of the Title relating to 'Free Movement of Goods' and [former] Article 12 [now Art 25] at the beginning of the section dealing with the 'Elimination of Customs Duties' – is sufficient to emphasise the essential nature of the prohibitions which they impose.

The Court, relying upon the 'general scheme' of these provisions and of the Treaty as a whole, went on to state that there was:

> ... a general intention to prohibit not only measures which obviously take the form of the classic customs duty but also all those which, presented under other names or introduced by the indirect means of other procedures, would lead to the same discriminatory or protective results as customs duties.

In the above case, the Court of Justice gave a wide interpretation to the general words 'charges having equivalent effect', whereas an English court may have applied the *ejusdem generis* rule to limit its scope: i.e. where specific categories are followed by general words, then the general words are limited to the context of the specific categories. The Court of Justice used the general expression as a catch-all provision, looking at the specific provision in context and in relation to the Treaty as a whole, the aim of which is to abolish all restrictions on the free movement of goods.

Teleological interpretation

When applying this method of interpretation, the Court will interpret the provision in question in furtherance of the aims and objectives of the Community and Union as a whole. As discussed in Chapter 1, the EC Treaty sets out a broad programme rather than a detailed plan. The preamble to the Treaty and some of the introductory articles (especially Arts 2 and 3) set out the broad aims and objectives of the Community in very general terms. When interpreting the Treaties or other Community legislation, the Court of Justice may be guided by these overarching aims and objectives (the grand scheme), thus adopting a teleological approach.

Therefore, the contextual approach considers a specific section of a provision in the context of all the sections of that provision, whereas the teleological approach goes outside the actual provision and considers the whole purpose, the aims and objectives, of the Community and the Union.

The Court has become accustomed to interpreting Community law teleologically, by reference to the broad policy objectives of the Treaty, rather than, as would an English court, by the meaning of the words before it and their immediate context. It was, for example, accepted that the European Parliament had the right to bring an action for annulment against the Council or Commission, although only Member States, the Council and affected individuals had specifically been given such a right in Art 230(1) EC Treaty. The Court of Justice held that not to imply such a right for the Parliament would deprive it of the legal means with which to protect its privileges against incursions by the other institutions (**Parliament** v **Council** (Case C-70/88)). Article 230 EC Treaty (as amended by the TEU), now gives the Parliament the right to take such action to protect its prerogatives. The Court has also extended the right of free movement of workers to those looking for work, even though Art 39 EC Treaty appears to confer the right only on those to whom an offer of work has actually been made. The Court of Justice considered that the object of the Treaty to secure the free movement of labour would not be achieved if only those with an offer of employment from another Member State were enabled to move (**Procureur du Roi** v **Royer** (Case 48/75)). In these, and in many other matters, the Court has used its interpretative powers to put flesh on the bones of Treaty provisions, and to do so in such a way as to facilitate the effective development of the Community.

Underlying these decisions is what can only be described as the *policy* of the Court. All national courts have unstated policy objectives, such as the maintenance of the rule of law or the discouragement of what is seen as anti-social behaviour. The law will be interpreted as far as possible to achieve those ends. The Court's objectives are more clearly discernible. Broadly, the Court's policies could be said to consist of strengthening the Union's structure, increasing the scope and effectiveness of Community law and enhancing the powers of the Community institutions. The series of cases in which Parliament's ability to bring proceedings to protect its prerogatives has effectively been extended beyond those powers conferred by the EC Treaty, and the decisions under which its consultative role has been enhanced, all reflect the concern of the Court to ensure that the Community's only democratically elected institution is given proper weight in the decision-making process.

The Court's policy of securing greater effectiveness for Community law is achieved partly by interpreting the law in such a way that it achieves the broader objectives of the Treaty, even if this has to be done, in some cases, by ignoring the express words of Community legislation. It can also be seen in the doctrine of the direct effect of directives under which the measures originally intended to bind only the Member States have become the means by which individuals can secure their rights in national courts (see Chapter 9). In pursuit of the same policy objective, remedies in national courts, which were originally seen as being of purely national concern and beyond the competence of the Court, are now judged by the Court in terms of their effectiveness to secure the implementation of Community law. If they are not effective, they must be set aside and an effective remedy provided: **R** v **Secretary of State for Transport, ex parte Factortame** (Case C-213/89, see Chapter 10).

The Court of First Instance

To cope with the great increase in the work of the Court of Justice, the SEA provided for the creation of a Court of First Instance (CFI) to be attached to the Court of Justice (Art 225 EC Treaty).

The CFI has its own Rules of Procedure, which are available at:

http://curia.europa.eu/en/instit/txtdocfr/index.htm

The number of cases disposed of by the CFI during 2005 increased by 69 per cent to 610, although this included 117 cases which were transferred to the Civil Service Tribunal (see below). Excluding these 117 cases, the number of cases determined by the CFI increased by 37 per cent.

From 1 February 2003, Art 50 of the Statute provides that the CFI may sit in chambers of three or five judges. The Rules of Procedure can determine when the CFI may sit in plenary session or even be constituted by a single judge. As with the Court of Justice, a Grand Chamber can be established. In 2005, 83 per cent of the cases determined were decided by a chamber of three judges, 10 per cent were decided by a chamber of five judges, and 1 per cent by the Court sitting as a single judge. In 2005 the CFI delivered its first judgments by a Grand Chamber (composed of 11 judges) in six cases concerning actions for damages against the Community.

Jurisdiction

Article 225 EC Treaty (pre-ToN) provided for the determination of the categories of case which could be heard by the CFI. Article 225(1) expressly provided that the CFI 'shall not be competent to hear and determine questions referred for a preliminary ruling under Article 234 [EC Treaty]'. However, the ToN amended Art 225, providing for a sharing of the Art 234 jurisdiction between the Court of Justice and the CFI. Article 225(3) EC Treaty now provides that:

> The Court of First Instance shall have jurisdiction to hear and determine questions referred for a preliminary ruling under Article 234, in specific areas laid down by the Statute.
>
> Where the Court of First Instance considers that the case requires a decision of principle likely to affect the unity or consistency of Community law, it may refer the case to the Court of Justice for a ruling.
>
> Decisions given by the Court of First Instance on questions referred for a preliminary ruling may exceptionally be subject to review by the Court of Justice, under the conditions and within the limits laid down by the Statute, where there is a serious risk of the unity or consistency of Community law being affected.

Therefore, the CFI will have jurisdiction to hear and determine questions referred for a preliminary ruling under Art 234 EC Treaty, in the areas specified in the Court's Statute. In such a situation, if the CFI considers that the case requires a decision of principle likely to affect the unity or consistency of Community law, it may refer the case to the Court of Justice for a ruling. In addition, CFI decisions may exceptionally be subject to review by the Court of Justice, under the conditions and within the limits laid down by the Court's Statute, where there is a serious risk of the unity or consistency of Community law being affected.

A Declaration annexed to the ToN called on the Court of Justice and the Commission to give overall consideration as soon as possible to the division of competence between the Court of Justice and the CFI. The Court's Statute has subsequently been amended but these amendments have not made provision for the division of competence between the Court of Justice and the CFI, with regard to the application of Art 234. However, the Statute does set out the conditions for review by the Court of Justice, where the CFI has jurisdiction to hear and determine an application for a preliminary ruling referred by a national court or tribunal pursuant to Art 234 EC Treaty.

The Decision establishing the CFI (Council Decision 88/591, OJ 1988 L 319/1) laid down four categories of cases which could be heard by the CFI:

1. Staff cases (these have now been transferred to the EU Civil Service Tribunal, see below).

2. Actions by undertakings (but not by Community institutions or Member States) against the Commission concerning individual acts relating to the ECSC Treaty provisions on levies, production controls, price regulation or competition. The ECSC Treaty expired on 23 July 2002.

3. Actions by natural or legal persons against a Community institution relating to the implementation of EC competition rules applicable to undertakings.

4. Damages claims by natural or legal persons where the damage is alleged to arise from an act or failure to act which is the subject of an action under 1, 2, or 3 above or from a breach of contract.

In addition, Art 4, Decision 88/591 provided for the CFI to have unlimited jurisdiction in relation to penalties, and gave it jurisdiction to suspend measures and to grant interim relief during the course of proceedings.

Following amendments made to the EC Treaty by the TEU, the CFI was empowered to determine claims brought by natural and legal persons under Arts 230 and 232 EC Treaty (including anti-dumping cases). The CFI initially had no competence to hear applications by institutions or Member States. However, on 26 April 2004 the Council adopted Decision 2004/407 amending Arts 51 and 54 of the Court's Statute (OJ 2004 L 132, p. 5; corrigendum at OJ 2004 L 194, p. 3).

As a result of these amendments, a new division of direct actions between the Court of Justice and the CFI came into effect on 1 June 2004. Actions for annulment and for failure to act brought by a Member State against an act of, or failure to act by, the Commission fall within the jurisdiction of the CFI. The same is true of actions brought by the Member States against:

■ decisions of the Council concerning state aid;

■ acts of the Council adopted pursuant to a Council regulation concerning measures to protect trade;

■ acts of the Council by which it exercises implementing powers;

■ acts of the European Central Bank.

On account of this new division of jurisdiction for direct actions, during 2004, cases which had initially brought before the Court of Justice but in which the written procedure had not yet been brought to a close were transferred to the CFI. These cases related mostly to state aid and to the European Agriculture Guidance and Guarantee Fund.

Article 62 of the Court's Statute provides that in the cases provided for in the amended Art 225(2) and (3) EC Treaty, if the Court of Justice's First Advocate-General considers that there is a serious risk of the unity or consistency of Community law being affected, he may propose that the Court of Justice review the decision of the CFI. The proposal by the First Advocate-General must be made within one month of delivery of the CFI's decision. Within one month of receiving the proposal, the Court of Justice has to decide whether or not to review the decision.

Judicial panels

The ToN came into force on 1 February 2003, introducing substantial changes to the structure, functions, rules and procedures of the CFI. This was considered to be essential given the fact that it was taking about two years to finally determine a case; and with an enlarged membership of 25 Member States on 1 May 2004, increasing to 27 Member States on 1 January 2007, reform was all the more necessary.

Article 220 EC Treaty now provides for judicial panels to be attached to the CFI. By Art 225a, the Council, acting unanimously, may set up these panels to hear and determine at first instance certain classes of action or proceeding brought in specific areas. A judicial panel has been established to deal with Community patents. Decisions of the panel may be subject to a right of appeal on points of law (and in certain circumstances matters of fact) to the CFI. Article 225(2) EC Treaty provides that the Court of Justice may exceptionally review a decision of the CFI (where the CFI has acted as a court of appeal from a judicial panel) if there is a serious risk to the unity or consistency of Community law. The members of the judicial panels are appointed by the Council, acting unanimously. A Declaration attached to the ToN provides that the Court and the Commission should prepare as swiftly as possible a draft decision establishing a judicial panel which is competent to deliver judgments at first instance on disputes between the Community and its servants (i.e. actions pursuant to Art 236 EC Treaty). Such a judicial panel (the EU Civil Service Tribunal) has been established (see below).

Membership of the Court of First Instance

Although it is attached to the Court of Justice, the CFI is staffed by judges who are separately appointed according to slightly different criteria. This partly relates to the type of work allocated to the CFI, and partly to the role of the CFI in hearing evidence and determining questions of fact.

Article 225(3) EC Treaty (pre-ToN) provided that the then 15 Members of the CFI should be chosen from persons whose independence was beyond doubt and who 'possess the ability required for appointment to judicial office' (Art 21, Act of Accession; Art 12, Decision 95/1/EC). Like the members of the Court of Justice, members of the CFI were appointed by common accord of the governments of the Member States for terms of six years, with partial renewal of membership every three years.

Following the ToN coming into force on 1 February 2003, Art 224 EC Treaty provides that the CFI shall consist of *at least* one judge from each Member State (there are currently 27 judges) and they shall be chosen from persons whose independence is beyond doubt and who 'possess the ability required for appointment to judicial office'. The number of judges will be determined by the Court's Statute. This therefore provides the possibility of increasing the CFI's membership in the light of the shifting of jurisdiction from the Court of Justice to the CFI. Given the increasing competence of the CFI, it would not be sensible to increase the workload of the CFI while at the same time standing still in terms of number of judges. As discussed above, there is a safeguard in that cases before the CFI can be referred to, or reviewed by, the Court of Justice in certain circumstances.

Constitutional Treaty

If the Constitutional Treaty had come into force, the CFI would have undergone a name change, being referred to as the General Court (the draft Treaty had suggested High Court). The judicial panels, which had been established by Arts 220 and 225a EC Treaty, would have been referred to as specialised courts (Art III-359).

Article III-358 would have set out the jurisdiction of the General Court. This article substantially re-enacted Art 225 EC Treaty.

Article III-356 would have provided for the number of judges of the General Court to be determined by the Statute of the Court (there would have been no reference within the Constitutional Treaty to the Court consisting of at least one judge from each Member State). Another change would have been to require members of the General Court to possess the ability required for appointment to '*high* judicial office'. This would have been the same requirement as that for membership of the Court of Justice, and would have deviated from the position in Art 224 EC Treaty which provides that members of the General Court (i.e. the CFI) must possess the ability required for appointment to 'judicial office'.

Art III-356 would also have provided that judges of the General Court would be appointed by common accord of the governments of the Member States 'after consultation of the panel provided for in Article III-357'. This would have been identical to appointment of judges and Advocates-General of the Court of Justice under Art III-355. The panel under Art III-357 would have comprised seven persons chosen from among former members of the Court of Justice and the General Court, members of national supreme courts and lawyers of recognised competence, one of whom would have been proposed by the European Parliament. The purpose of the panel would have been to give an opinion on the candidates' suitability to perform the duties.

EU Civil Service Tribunal

As discussed above, Art 220 EC Treaty provides for judicial panels to be attached to the CFI. Article 225a EC Treaty further provides that such judicial panels may be set up by the Council, acting unanimously.

On 2 November 2004 the Council adopted Decision 2004/752 establishing the European Union Civil Service Tribunal (OJ 2004 L 333/7).

The CFI was in favour of this reform because of the special nature of this field of litigation and the workload which was anticipated as a result of application of the provisions of new Staff Regulations. This new specialised tribunal, consisting of seven judges, can be called on to hear disputes involving the EU civil service (i.e. staff cases), in respect of which jurisdiction was previously exercised by the CFI.

Its decisions are subject to appeal, limited to points of law, before the CFI and, exceptionally, subject to review by the Court of Justice in the circumstances prescribed by the Court's Statute.

The seven new judges of the Tribunal took their oath on 5 October 2005. On 2 December 2005 the President of the Court of Justice recorded that the tribunal had been constituted in accordance with the law (the decision is published at OJ 2005 L 325/1). As a result, on 15 December 2005, 117 cases which had originally been brought before the

CFI, in which the written procedure had not been completed by that date, were transferred (by order) to the Civil Service Tribunal.

The provisions relating to the Tribunal's composition, jurisdiction etc. are contained in an Annex to the Court's Statute.

The jurisdiction of the European Court of Justice and the Court of First Instance

Besides the general function of ensuring that Community law is observed, the Court of Justice and the CFI (the Courts) have a number of other tasks. Since the Courts, like the other Community institutions, can act only within the limits of their powers, they have jurisdiction only if jurisdiction has been expressly conferred upon them (Art 7 EC Treaty). This means that the Courts have, unlike English courts, no 'residual' or 'inherent' powers and, consequently, cannot hear cases not expressly falling within their jurisdiction. It has, for example, been held that judicial protection cannot be afforded to private individuals who might otherwise be deprived of all legal redress at both national and Community level, since there is no express provision authorising them to do so (**Schlieker *v* HA** (Case 12/63)). The Courts were specifically excluded by the ToA from ruling on any measure or decision relating to the maintenance of law and order and the safeguarding of internal security in a Member State (Art 68(2) EC Treaty). The Court of Justice has also ruled that, in hearing appeals from the CFI, it has no jurisdiction to review the facts established by the CFI (**John Deere Ltd *v* Commission** (Case C-7/95)). However, the Court of Justice has shown some flexibility in ruling on cases which it might, hitherto, have refused to adjudicate (**Imm Zwartveld** (Case 2/88); **Dzodzi *v* Belgium** (Case C297/88)).

The main heads of jurisdiction for the Court of Justice are as follows:

- To establish whether or not a Member State has failed to fulfil an obligation under the Treaty. Actions for this purpose can be brought by the Commission under Art 226 EC Treaty, or a Member State under Art 227 EC Treaty; see Chapter 7.

- To exercise unlimited jurisdiction with regard to penalties in actions brought by the Commission under Arts 228(1) and 229 EC Treaty; see Chapter 7.

- To review the legality of an act, or of a failure to act, of, *inter alia*, the Council, the Commission, or the Parliament, at the request of Member States, the Council or the Commission. Applications by the Parliament and the European Central Bank are limited to the protection of their prerogatives (Arts 230 and 231 EC Treaty (as amended by TEU) and Art 9 of the Protocol on the Statute of the European System of Central Banks and of the European Central Bank); see Chapter 8.

- To give preliminary rulings under Art 234 EC Treaty at the request of a national court or tribunal; see Chapter 6.

- To grant compensation for damage caused by the institutions in actions brought by Member States, and natural and legal persons under Arts 235 and 288 EC Treaty; see Chapter 8.

- To act as a Court of Appeal from the CFI under Art 225(1) EC Treaty.

Summary

Now you have read this chapter you should be able to:

- Explain the respective roles of the European Court of Justice and the European Court of Human Rights in the interpretation and application of Community law.
- Outline the membership composition of the European Court of Justice.
- Assess the European Court of Justice's role in the development of Community law.
- Explain how the European Court of Justice interprets Community law through the use of the following methods of interpretation:
  - literal;
  - historical;
  - contextual; and
  - teleological.
- Understand how a UK national court's approach to interpretation differs to that of the European Court of Justice.
- Explain the role of the Court of First Instance with a particular reference to its membership composition, jurisdiction and powers.
- Identify the main heads of jurisdiction of the European Court of Justice.
- Evaluate the impact which the proposed Constitutional Treaty would have had on the constitutional structure of the European Court of Justice and the Court of First Instance if it had been ratified.

Further reading

Textbooks

Brown, N. and Jacobs, F. (2000) *The Court of Justice of the European Communities* (5th edn), Sweet & Maxwell.

Craig, P. and De Burca, G. (2003) *EU Law Text, Cases and Materials* (3rd edn), Oxford University Press, Chapter 2.

Foster, N. (2006) *Foster on EU Law* (1st edn), Oxford University Press, Chapter 2 (Section 2.6).

Steiner, J., Woods, L. and Twigg-Flesner, C. (2006) *EU Law* (9th edn), Oxford University Press, Chapters 2 and 10.

Storey, T. and Turner, C. (2005) *Unlocking EU Law* (1st edn), Hodder Arnold, Chapter 3 (Section 3.5).

Tillotson, J. and Foster, N. (2003) *Text, Cases and Materials on EU Law* (4th edn), Cavendish Publishing, Chapter 7.

Wallace, H., Wallace, W. and Pollack, M.A. (2005) *Policy Making in the European Union* (5th edn), Chapter 3.

Journal articles

Arnull, A., 'Owning up to Fallibility: Precedent and the Court of Justice' (1993) 30 CML Rev 247.

Arnull, A., 'Judicial Architecture or Judicial Folly? The Challenge facing the European Union' (1999) 24 EL Rev 516.

Barbier de la Serre, F., 'Accelerated and expedited procedures before the EC courts: A review of the practice' (2006) 43 CML Rev 783.

Coppel, J. and O'Neill, A., 'The European Court of Justice: Taking Rights Seriously?' (1992) Legal Studies 227.

Jacobs, F., 'Human Rights in the EU: The Role of the Court of Justice' (2001) 26 EL Rev 331.

Johnston, A., 'Judicial Reform and the Treaty of Nice' (2001) 21 EL Rev 499.

Liisberg, J., 'Does the EU Charter of Fundamental Rights Threaten the Supremacy of Community Law?' (2001) 38 CML Rev 1171.

Pescatore, P., 'Fundamental Rights and Freedoms in the System of the European Communities' (1970) AJIL 343.

Tridimas, T., 'The Court of Justice and Judicial Activism' (1996) 21 EL Rev 199.

6

Preliminary ruling jurisdiction of the Court of Justice (Article 234 EC Treaty)

Aims and objectives

At the end of this chapter you should understand:

- The purpose of the Art 234 EC Treaty preliminary ruling procedure.

- The scope of 'national courts and tribunals' within Art 234.

- The types of question which a national court is empowered to refer to the Court of Justice under Art 234.

- How to distinguish between the national courts and tribunals which have a *discretion* to refer a question to the Court of Justice under Art 234 from those which are under an *obligation* to make a referral.

- Why a national court or tribunal may not consider it *necessary* to make a reference to the Court of Justice under Art 234, with a particular reference to the doctrines of precedent and *acte clair*.

- The role of the national court once a referral to the Court of Justice under Art 234 has been made.

Introduction to the Court of Justice's premlinary ruling jurisdiction

National courts perform a crucial role in administering and applying Community law. The Court of Justice has developed an important body of case law on the application of directly enforceable Community provisions in the courts of Member States (see Chapter 9), but it depends on the national courts to cooperate with it to make those provisions effective, as the Court intimated in the following case:

Simmenthal (Case 106/77)

The Court of Justice stated that:

> A national court which is called upon, within the limits of its jurisdiction, to apply provisions of Community law is under a duty to give full effect to those provisions, if necessary refusing of its own motion to apply any conflicting provisions of national legislation, even if adopted subsequently, and

it is not necessary for the court to request or await the prior setting aside of such provisions by legislative or other constitutional means.

There is a clear danger that, given the disparate national legal traditions of the Member
States, Community law will develop differently in the national courts. If this were to
happen, individuals and businesses would be operating under different rules and many
of the benefits of an open Community and a genuine common market would be lost.
The Community has, therefore, a fundamental interest in ensuring that its law has the
same meaning and effect in all the Member States. The only effective way of doing this
is to provide that ultimate authority for deciding the meaning of Community law
should reside in one court. That court is, of course, the Court of Justice. The best way
to ensure the harmonious development of Community law would have been to have
established the Court of Justice as a final Court of Appeal on matters of Community law.
That course seemed to constitute too direct a challenge to the supremacy of national
legal systems, and was rejected by the founders of the Community. They opted, instead,
for a system of references by national courts. Article 234 EC Treaty (previously Art 177),
which establishes the preliminary reference procedure, is the only provision of the
Treaty which expressly acknowledges the enforcement role of the courts of the Member
States.

Jursidiction

The Court of Justice has recognised that there is some concern about the effectiveness of
the system because of the time which such references take. However, in its Report to the
1996 Intergovernmental Conference (*Report of the Court of Justice on Certain Aspects of the
Application of the Treaty on European Union for the Purposes of the 1996 Inter-Governmental
Conference* (May 1995)) it unequivocally rejected suggestions that the scope for references
be limited:

> To limit access to the Court would have the effect of jeopardising the uniform application
> and interpretation of Community law. But that is not all. The preliminary ruling system is
> the veritable cornerstone of the operation of the internal market, since it plays a funda-
> mental role in ensuring that the law established by the Treaties retains its Community
> character with a view to guaranteeing that the law has the same effect in all circumstances
> in all the Member States of the European Union. Any weakening, even if only potential, of
> the uniform application and interpretation of Community law throughout the Union
> would be liable to give rise to distortions of competition and discrimination between econ-
> omic operators, thus jeopardising equality of opportunity between those operators and
> consequently the proper functioning of the internal market.

However, the Court's position changed in the light of its increasing caseload and
resulting delays. With the May 2004 enlargement of the Community and Union on the
horizon, the ToN (which came into force on 1 February 2003) sought to address the issue
of reform of the Court of Justice and Court of First Instance (CFI). The ToN, as discussed
in Chapter 5, opted for a sharing of the Art 234 jurisdiction between the Court of Justice
and the CFI. The ToN amended the EC Treaty, Art 225(3) now providing that:

> The Court of First Instance shall have jurisdiction to hear and determine questions referred
> for a preliminary ruling under Article 234, in specific areas laid down by the Statute.
> Where the Court of First Instance considers that the case requires a decision of principle

likely to affect the unity or consistency of Community law, it may refer the case to the Court of Justice for a ruling.

Decisions given by the Court of First Instance on questions referred for a preliminary ruling may exceptionally be subject to review by the Court of Justice, under the conditions and within the limits laid down by the Statute, where there is a serious risk of the unity or consistency of Community law being affected.

A Declaration annexed to the ToN called on the Court of Justice and the Commission to give overall consideration as soon as possible to the division of competence between the Court of Justice and the CFI. The Court's Statute has subsequently been amended, but these amendments have not made provision for the division of competence between the Court of Justice and the CFI, with regard to the application of Art 234. However, the Statute sets out the conditions for review by the Court of Justice, where the CFI has juris-diction to hear and determine an application for a preliminary ruling referred by a national court or tribunal pursuant to Art 234 EC Treaty.

Article 62, Statute of the Court of Justice provides that:

> In the cases provided for in Article 225 . . . (3) of the EC Treaty . . . where the First Advocate General considers that there is a serious risk of the unity or consistency of Community law being affected, he may propose that the Court of Justice review the decision of the Court of First Instance.
>
> The proposal must be made within one month of delivery of the decision by the Court of First Instance. Within one month of receiving the proposal made by the First Advocate General, the Court of Justice shall decide whether or not the decision should be reviewed.

Article 62b, Statute of the Court of Justice provides that:

> . . . In the cases provided for in Article 225(3) of the EC Treaty . . . in the absence of proposals for review or decisions to open the review procedure, the answer(s) given by the Court of First Instance to the questions submitted to it shall take effect upon expiry of the periods prescribed for that purpose in the second paragraph of Article 62. Should a review pro-cedure be opened, the answer(s) subject to review shall take effect following that procedure, unless the Court of Justice decides otherwise. If the Court of Justice finds that the decision of the Court of First Instance affects the unity or consistency of Community law, the answer given by the Court of Justice to the questions subject to review shall be substituted for that given by the Court of First Instance.

The need for jurisdictional reform has primarily been due to the fact that the majority of cases which come before the Court of Justice are cases which have been referred by national courts pursuant to Art 234 EC Treaty. This has impacted upon the effective oper-ation of the Court, although during 2004 and 2005 there was a reduction in the length of time taken before a judgment was delivered by the Court of Justice in cases referred to it pursuant to Art 234.

The number of cases referred to the Court of Justice under Art 234 EC Treaty and which were completed, together with the *total* number of cases completed by the Court, during the period 1999–2005, were as follows:

1999　192 Art 234 EC Treaty cases were completed during 1999, out of a total of 395 cases which were completed by the Court during that year.

2000　268 Art 234 EC Treaty cases were completed during 2000, out of a total of 526 cases which were completed by the Court during that year.

2001　182 Art 234 EC Treaty cases were completed during 2001, out of a total of 434 cases which were completed by the Court during that year.

2002   241 Art 234 EC Treaty cases were completed during 2002, out of a total of 513 cases which were completed by the Court during that year.

2003   233 Art 234 EC Treaty cases were completed during 2003, out of a total of 494 cases which were completed by the Court during that year.

2004   262 Art 234 EC Treaty cases were completed during 2004, out of a total of 665 cases which were completed by the Court during that year.

2005   254 Art 234 EC Treaty cases were completed during 2005, out of a total of 574 cases which were completed by the Court during that year.

The length of time taken for a judgment to be delivered in cases referred to the Court of Justice under Art 234 EC Treaty has steadily increased, although, as stated above, this decreased in 2004, and decreased further in 2005:

1999   21.2 months

2000   21.6 months

2001   22.7 months

2002   24.1 months

2003   25.5 months

2004   23.5 months

2005   20.4 months.

Simplified procedure and expedited hearing

The amendments to the Rules of Procedure of the Court of Justice which came into effect from 1 July 2000 introduced a simplified procedure for certain types of case referred to it under Art 234, and in other situations to provide for an accelerated procedure (OJ 2000 L 122/43).

The simplified procedure will be applied to those questions referred to the Court which are identical to questions that have been answered previously, where the answer to the question can be clearly deduced from existing case law and where the answer admits of no reasonable doubt. The amended Art 104(3) of the Rules provides that:

> Where a question referred to the Court for a preliminary ruling is identical to a question on which the Court has already ruled, or where the answer to such a question may be clearly deduced from existing case-law, the Court may, after hearing the Advocate General, at any time give its decision by reasoned order in which reference is made to its previous judgment or to the relevant case-law.
>
> The Court may also give its decision by reasoned order, after informing the court or tribunal which referred the question to it, hearing any observations submitted by the persons referred to in Article 23 of the Statute and after hearing the Advocate General, where the answer to the question referred to the Court for a preliminary ruling admits of no reasonable doubt.

The accelerated procedure was introduced by Art 104a of the Rules, which provides that:

> At the request of the national court, the President may exceptionally decide, on a proposal from the Judge-Rapporteur and after hearing the Advocate General, to apply an accelerated procedure derogating from the provisions of these Rules to a reference for a preliminary ruling, where the circumstances referred to establish that a ruling on the question put to the Court is a matter of exceptional urgency.

> In that event, the President may immediately fix the date for the hearing, which shall be notified to the parties in the main proceedings and to the other persons referred to in Article 23 of the Statute when the decision making the reference is served.
>
> The parties and other interested persons referred to in the preceding paragraph may lodge statements of case or written observations within a period prescribed by the President, which shall not be less than 15 days. The President may request the parties and other interested persons to restrict the matters addressed in their statement of case or written observations to the essential points of law raised by the question referred.
>
> The statements of case or written observations, if any, shall be notified to the parties and to the other persons referred to above prior to the hearing.
>
> The Court shall rule after hearing the Advocate General.

During 2004, the Court of Justice used the simplified procedure provided for in Art 104(3) of the Rules and made 22 orders on the basis of that provision; during 2005, the Court of Justice made 12 orders on the basis of that provision, bringing 29 cases to a close. This has undoubtedly had an effect on reducing the average time taken to deliver a judgment in Art 234 proceedings (see above). Although use of the accelerated procedure was requested during both 2004 and 2005 in relation to Art 234 EC Treaty proceedings, the requirement of exceptional urgency was not satisfied.

References from national courts under Article 234 EC Treaty

Article 234 EC Treaty envisages a partnership role between the Court of Justice and the national court, with jurisdiction divided between the Court of Justice which interprets the law, and the national courts which apply it. It must be emphasised that Art 234 references have a different function to an appeal. In an appeal, the initiative lies with the parties, and if the appeal is successful the appellate court can substitute its own decision for that of the lower court. In a reference, however, it is the lower (national) court itself which takes the decision to refer the case. The Court of Justice rules on the issues which have been raised, but it is then for the lower (national) court to apply the ruling of the Court of Justice to the facts of the case before it. At the end of the day, the decision in that case will be that of the national court. The objective of the reference procedure is to retain the independence of the national courts, while at the same time preventing 'a body of national case law not in accord with the rules of Community law from coming into existence in any Member State' (**Hoffmann La Roche** *v* **Centrafarm** (Case 107/76)). It must, however, be emphasised that in many instances the national court will be able to give judgment *without* making a reference to the Court of Justice. National courts do so throughout the Community, quite properly, in many hundreds of cases each day.

Article 234 provides:

> The Court of Justice shall have jurisdiction to give preliminary rulings concerning:
> (a) the interpretation of this Treaty;
> (b) the validity and interpretation of acts of the institutions of the Community and of the ECB [i.e. the European Central Bank];
> (c) the interpretation of the statutes of bodies established by an act of the Council, where those statutes so provide.
>
> Where such a question is raised before any court or tribunal of a Member State, that

court or tribunal may, if it considers that a decision on the question is necessary to enable it to give judgment, request the Court of Justice to give a ruling thereon.

Where any such question is raised in a case pending before a court or tribunal of a Member State against whose decisions there is no judicial remedy under national law, that court or tribunal shall bring the matter before the Court of Justice.

Constitutional Treaty

As discussed in Chapter 1, the proposed Constitutional Treaty did not come into force because it was not ratified by all the Member States. If it had come into force, Art 234 EC Treaty would have been replaced with Art III-369, Constitutional Treaty:

> The Court of Justice of the European Union shall have jurisdiction to give preliminary rulings concerning:
> (a) the interpretation of the Constitution;
> (b) the validity and interpretation of acts of the institutions, bodies, offices and agencies of the Union.
>
> Where such a question is raised before any court or tribunal of a Member State, that court or tribunal may, if it considers that a decision on the question is necessary to enable it to give judgment, request the Court of Justice to give a ruling thereon.
>
> If such a question is raised in a case pending before a court or tribunal of a Member State with regard to a person in custody, the Court shall act with the minimum of delay.

This wording is very similar to that in the current Art 234 EC Treaty, with the exception of the acts upon which the Court of Justice could provide preliminary rulings. An additional provision would have been added which would have required the Court to act 'with the minimum of delay' if the case related to a person who is in custody. This is understandable given the length of time it normally takes for the Court to provide its judgment.

What matters can be the subject of a reference under Article 234?

Article 234 refers to three types of provision which can be the subject of a reference to the Court of Justice for a preliminary ruling:

(a) the interpretation of the Treaty;

(b) the validity and interpretation of acts of the institutions of the Community and of the ECB;

(c) the interpretation of the statutes of bodies established by an act of the Council, where those statutes so provide.

The most common of these are now considered.

Interpretation of the Treaty

'Interpretation of the Treaty' covers any part of the EC Treaty, the amending Treaties and the Treaties of Accession, the last normally being made expressly subject to Art 234. In the case of the UK's entry to the Community, this was achieved by Art 1(3) of the Treaty of Accession of 1972 (**Department of Health and Social Security v Barr and Montrose Holdings Ltd** (Case C-355/89)).

Parts of the TEU relating to Common Foreign and Security Policy, and Police and Judicial Cooperation in Criminal Matters (i.e. the second and third pillars of the European Union (see Chapter 1)) are excluded from the referral procedure (Art 46 TEU): **Grau Gomis** (Case C-167/94R).

Constitutional Treaty

Title V, Chapter II, Section 1–3, Arts III-294 to III-313 of the proposed Constitutional Treaty would have related to the Common Foreign and Security Policy. Title III, Chapter IV, Section 4, Arts III-270 to III-274 would have related to Judicial Cooperation in Criminal Matters. Title III, Chapter IV, Section 5, Arts III-275 to III-277 would have related to Police Cooperation. As discussed in Chapter 1, if the Constitutional Treaty had come into force, these provisions would have been incorporated into the Constitutional Treaty itself, and there would no longer have been any separate pillars. Article III-376 would have provided that 'The Court of Justice of the European Union shall not have jurisdiction with respect to ... the provisions of Chapter II of Title V concerning the common foreign and security policy and Article III-293 insofar as it concerns the common foreign and security policy'. Similarly, Art III-377 would have provided that 'In exercising its powers regarding the provisions of Sections 4 and 5 of Chapter IV of Title III relating to the area of freedom, security and justice, the Court of Justice of the European Union shall have no jurisdiction to review the validity or proportionality of operations carried out by the police or other law enforcement services of a Member State or the exercise of the responsibilities incumbent on Member States with regard to the maintenance of law and order and the safeguarding of internal security'.

Therefore, if the Constitutional Treaty had come into force there would have been a similar restriction to the Court's jurisdiction as there is currently under the existing Treaties.

Validity and interpretation of acts of the institutions of the Community

'Community acts' includes not only legally binding acts, such as regulations, directives and decisions, but also opinions and recommendations where these are relevant to the interpretation of Community law by the courts of Member States: **Frecassetti** (Case 113/75); **Grimaldi v Fonds des Maladies Professionnelles** (Case C-322/88). In **Deutsche Shell AG v Hauptzollamt Hamburg** (Case C-188/91), the Court of Justice held that 'arrangements' made by a joint committee responsible for implementing a convention on a common transit policy between the EEC and EFTA formed 'part of the Community legal order'. The Court noted that the fact that a Community legal measure lacked compulsory effect did not exclude the Court from giving a legal ruling on it, because national courts were obliged to take it into account when interpreting the convention.

In the **Deutsche Shell** case the Court of Justice emphasised that it did not have jurisdiction under Art 234 to give a ruling on the compatibility of a national measure with Community law. However, it does in fact come very close to doing so. Characteristically, it will describe the national measure in hypothetical terms and state that, if there was such a measure, it would not be compatible with Community law! Although the Court can only give a ruling on the interpretation (and validity – see below) of *Community* law, it has been prepared to rule on the meaning of *national* provisions which are not intended to implement Community law but which are based on the wording of a Community provision: **Gmurzynska-Bscher** (Case C-231/89).

With regard to 'Community acts', the Court has power to give preliminary rulings concerning their *validity* in addition to their interpretation. However, it should be noted that the Court does not have the power to question the validity of the Treaties. 'Validity' relates to the question of whether or not the act is void (i.e. of no effect). It may, for example, have been made *ultra vires* (where, for example, the opinion of the European Parliament has not been obtained despite the relevant Treaty article requiring this).

Consider the following scenario: a levy is imposed by a regulation; the regulation may provide for the levy to be collected by a national agency. An individual may be sued when he refuses to pay the levy. In his defence he may argue that the regulation is not valid because a procedural step in the legislative process has not been followed. The national court may refer the matter to the Court of Justice pursuant to Art 234 to ascertain if the regulation (i.e. a Community act) is valid. The Court of Justice will make the ruling and pass the case back to the national court. The national court will then apply the law as determined by the Court of Justice. If the Court of Justice rules that the regulation is invalid, the national court will be obliged to rule in favour of the defendant. As will be discussed in Chapter 8, this indirect way of challenging the validity of a Community act may be a much more effective mechanism than the restricted power to challenge such an act directly under Art 230 EC Treaty (previously Art 173).

Which courts or tribunals are able to refer?

Depending on the status of the court or tribunal, some *may*, while others *must*, refer questions of interpretation of the Treaty or interpretation/validity of Community acts to the Court of Justice. Before discussing the issue of which courts and tribunals have a discretion to refer, and which are under an obligation to make a referral, it is necessary to ascertain which courts or tribunals should consider the possibility of a reference under Art 234. Article 234 refers to 'any court or tribunal of a Member State' so that, at first glance, it would appear that references can only be made by courts and tribunals within the state's judicial structure. However, the essential elements to determine the status of the body in relation to Art 234 are its power to make legally binding decisions, its independence from the parties and the recognition of its decision-making function by the state. To be able to make references under Art 234 it will have to satisfy all these criteria. An arbitrator, although conferred with a power by contract to make legally binding decisions on the parties, and also being independent of the parties, lacks the official state recognition to make his decisions 'judicial' in character, and he cannot, therefore, make a reference under Art 234 (**Nordsee** v **Reederei Mond** (Case 102/81)). However, an arbitration board or a disciplinary body which is recognised by the state as having a function in making legally binding decisions in relation to an industry or a professional body may well be a 'court or tribunal' for the purpose of Art 234.

Broekmeulen v *Huisarts Registratie Commissie* (Case 246/80)

A Dutch body called the Appeals Committee for General Medicine heard appeals from the Dutch body responsible for registering persons seeking to practise medicine in The Netherlands. Without registration, it was practically impossible to practise. Both of these bodies were established by the Royal Netherlands Society for the Promotion of Medicine, a private association, but were recognised indirectly in some Dutch legal provisions. The Appeals Committee was not a court or tribunal under Dutch law. It followed an adversarial procedure and allowed legal representation.

The applicant was a Dutch national and had qualified in Belgium. He wanted to practise in The Netherlands and applied for registration. This was refused and he appealed. The case was referred to the Court of Justice pursuant to the former Art 177 (now Art 234) and the question arose whether the Appeals Committee was a 'court or tribunal of a Member State'. If it was not, then the Court of Justice would not have jurisdiction to give a preliminary ruling. The Court of Justice stated that:

17. In order to deal with the question of applicability in the present case of Article 177 of the Treaty [now Article 234], it should be noted that it is incumbent upon Member States to take the necessary steps to ensure within their own territory the provisions adopted by the Community institutions are implemented in their entirety. **If, under the legal system of a Member State, the task of implementing such provisions is assigned to a professional body acting under a degree of governmental supervision, and if that body, in conjunction with the public authorities concerned, creates appeal procedures which may affect the exercise of rights granted by Community law, it is imperative, in order to ensure the proper functioning of Community law, that the Court should have an opportunity of ruling on issues of interpretation and validity arising out of such proceedings.**

18. As a result of all the foregoing considerations and in the absence, in practice, of any right of appeal to the ordinary courts, the Appeals Committee, which operates with the consent of the public authorities and with their cooperation, and which, after an adversarial procedure, delivers decisions which are recognised as final, must, in a matter involving the application of Community law, be considered as a court or tribunal of a Member State within the meaning of Article 177 of the Treaty [now Art 234]. Therefore, the Court has jurisdiction to reply to the question asked. [emphasis added]

In **Walter Schmid** (Case C-516/99), the Court of Justice held that the Fifth Appeal Chamber of the regional finance authority for Vienna (Austria) was not a 'court or tribunal' within the scope of Art 234, because it was not independent. The Chamber was established to enable taxpayers to resolve any dispute with the tax authority. However, the tax authority personnel would sit as adjudicators (together with others not employed by the tax authority). The adjudicators who were not employed by the tax authority were nevertheless selected by the authority, and they did not have a sufficient period of tenure to detach themselves closely enough from the tax authority.

The concept of 'court or tribunal' was the issue in the following case:

De Coster v Collège des Bourgmestres et Échevins de Watermael-Boitsfort (Case C-17/00)

A dispute arose between De Coster and the Collège, when the Collège levied a municipal charge on De Coster in respect of his satellite dish. He contended, *inter alia*, that this tax breached Art 49 EC Treaty because it was a restriction on the free movement of services (i.e. the freedom to receive television programmes coming from other Member States). The Collège decided to refer the case to the Court of Justice pursuant to Art 234 for a preliminary ruling. The first question before the Court was whether or not the Collège was a 'court or tribunal'. The Court stated that:

9. First of all, the question of whether the Collège juridictionnel de la Région de Bruxelles-Capitale should be considered to be a national court or tribunal for the purposes of Article 234 EC must be examined.

10. It is settled case-law that in order to determine whether a body making a reference is a court or tribunal for the purposes of Article 234 EC, which is a question governed by Community law alone, the Court takes account of a number of factors, such as whether the body is established by law, whether it is permanent, whether its jurisdiction is compulsory, whether its procedure is *inter partes*, whether it applies rules of law and whether it is independent (see, in particular, Case C-54/96 Dorsch Consult [1997] ECR I-4961, paragraph 23 and the case law cited therein, and Joined Cases C-110/98 to C-147/98 Gabalfrisa and Others [2000] ECR I-1577, paragraph 33).

11. In the case of the Collège juridictionnel de la Région de Bruxelles-Capitale, Article 83d(2) of the Law of 12 January 1989 concerning the Brussels institutions (*Moniteur belge* of 14 January 1989, p. 667), states:

> 'The judicial functions which in the provinces are exercised by the permanent deputation are exercised in respect of the territory referred to in Article 2(1) by a board of 9 members appointed by the Council of the Brussels-Capital Region on the proposal of its government. At least three members must come from the smallest linguistic group.
>
> The members of this board are subject to the same rules on ineligibility as those which apply to the members of the permanent deputations in the provinces.
>
> In proceedings before the board, the same rules must be respected as those which apply when the permanent deputation exercises a judicial function in the provinces'.

12. It is thus established that the Collège juridictionnel de la Région de Bruxelles-Capitale is a permanent body, established by law, that it gives legal rulings and that the jurisdiction thereby invested in it concerning local tax proceedings is compulsory.

13. However, the Commission maintains that no assurance can be gained from examination of Article 83d of the Law of 12 January 1989 that the procedure followed before the Collège juridictionnel is inter partes, or that the latter exercises its functions completely independently and impartially in applications by taxpayers challenging taxes charged them by the municipal councils. In particular, the Commission raises the question of whether the Collège juridictionnel is independent of the executive.

14. Regarding the requirement that the procedure be inter partes, it must first be noted that that is not an absolute criterion (**Dorsch Consult**, paragraph 31, and **Gabalfrisa**, paragraph 37, both cited above).

15. Secondly, it must be noted that in the present case Article 104a of the Provincial Law of 30 April 1836, a provision inserted by the Law of 6 July 1987 (*Moniteur belge* of 18 August 1987, p. 12309), and the Royal Decree of 17 September 1987 concerning the procedure before the permanent deputation when it exercises a judicial function (*Moniteur belge* of 29 September 1987, p. 14073), both of which are applicable to the Collège juridictionnel de la Région de Bruxelles-Capitale by virtue of Article 83d(2) of the Law of 12 January 1989, indicate that the procedure followed before the latter is indeed inter partes.

16. Article 104a of the abovementioned Provincial Law and Article 5 of the Royal Decree of 17 September 1987 indicate that a copy of the application is sent to the defendant, who has 30 days in which to submit a reply (which is then sent to the applicant), that the preparatory inquiries are adversarial, that the file may be consulted by the parties and that they may present their oral observations at a public hearing.

17. As to the criteria of independence and impartiality, it must be noted that there is no reason to consider that the Collège juridictionnel does not satisfy such requirements.

18. First, as is clear from Article 83d(2) of the Law of 12 January 1989, it is the Conseil de la Région de Bruxelles-Capitale that appoints the members of the Collège juridictionnel and not the municipal authorities whose tax decisions the Collège juridictionnel is, as in the main proceedings, required to examine.

19. Secondly, it is apparent *inter alia* from the Belgian Government's answers to the questions put to it by the Court that members of the Collège juridictionnel may not be members of a municipal council or of the staff of a municipal authority.

20. Thirdly, Articles 22 to 25 of the Royal Decree of 17 September 1987 establish procedure for challenging appointment which is applicable to the members of the Collège juridictionnel by virtue of Article 83d(2) of the Law of 12 January 1989, and which is to be based on reasons essentially identical to those which apply in the case of members of the judiciary.

21. Finally, it appears from the explanations provided by the Belgian Government at the request of the Court that appointments of members of the Collège juridictionnel are for an unlimited period of time and cannot be revoked.

22. It is clear from the above that the Collège juridictionnel de la Région de Bruxelles-Capitale must

be considered to be a court or tribunal for the purposes of Article 234 EC; accordingly, the reference for a preliminary ruling is admissible.

In the above case, the Court of Justice held that the Collège was a 'court or tribunal' for the purpose of Art 234 EC Treaty, such that the Court could provide the Collège with a preliminary ruling. Paragraph 10 of the Court's judgment sets out the legal test to be applied when determining this question.

A national court determining an appeal against an arbitration award, not according to law but according to what is 'fair and reasonable', may be regarded as a 'court or tribunal' for the purpose of Art 234 (**Municipality of Almelo and Others** *v* **Energiebedvijf NV** (Case C-394/92)). A court delivering an advisory 'opinion' may likewise be a 'court or tribunal' for the purpose of Art 234. In **Garofalo and Others** *v* **Ministero della Sanità and Others** (Joined Cases C-69–79/96) an opinion delivered by the Italian Consiglio del Stato to the Italian President, although not binding on him, was held to be a proper subject for a reference under Art 234. In the UK, besides references from magistrates' courts, Crown Courts and county courts, there have also been references from VAT tribunals, employment tribunals and the Social Security Commissioners.

Admissibility

In the following case, the Court of Justice had an opportunity to clarify its case law on the admissibility of a reference for a preliminary ruling where the circumstances of the dispute in the main proceedings are confined to a single Member State:

Salzmann (Case C-300/01)

The Court of Justice noted that the referring court was seeking an interpretation of Community law for the purpose of determining the scope of rules of national law which refer to it. The Court cited its own case law in that connection, according to which (i) it is for the national courts alone to determine, having regard to the particular features of each case, both the need to refer a question for a preliminary ruling and the relevance of such a question (**Guimont** (Case C-448/98), para 22, and **Reisch** (Joined Cases C-515/99, C-519/99 to C-524/99 and C-526/99 to C-540/99), para 25); and (ii) it is only in the exceptional case, where it is quite obvious that the interpretation of Community law sought bears no relation to the facts or the purpose of the main action, that the Court refrains from giving a ruling (**Konle** (Case C-302/97), para 33, and **Angonese** (Case C-281/98), para 18). However, the Court pointed out that a situation where national law requires that a national be allowed to enjoy the same rights as those which nationals of other Member States would derive from Community law in the same situation does not correspond to such an exceptional case. Moreover, the Court held that 'where, in relation to purely internal situations, domestic legislation adopts solutions which are consistent with those adopted in Community law in order, in particular, to avoid discrimination against foreign nationals, it is clearly in the Community interest that, in order to forestall future differences of interpretation, provisions or concepts taken from Community law should be interpreted uniformly, irrespective of the circumstances in which they are to apply' (para 34).

What is the appropriate stage in the proceedings for a reference to be made?

A reference to the Court of Justice may be made at any stage in the proceedings, even before a full hearing, either during the interim stage (i.e. a hearing on a preliminary matter before the full hearing) or where the case is being dealt with in the absence of one of the parties (**Simmenthal *v* Amministrazione delle Finanze dello Stato** (Case 70/77); **Balocchi *v* Ministero delle Finanze dello Stato** (Case C-10/92)). The Court does, however, think it desirable that an *inter partes* hearing (i.e. a hearing where all the parties are invited to take part) takes place before the reference, if that is possible (**Eurico Italia Srl *v* Ente Nazionale Risi** (Case C-332/92)).

The Court of Justice will not hear arguments that the national court or tribunal should not, under national law, have made the reference (**Reina *v* Landeskreditbank Baden-Württemberg** (Case 65/81)). However, the Court does expect the case to have reached a stage at which the relevant facts have been established and the issues identified on which the assistance of the Court is required:

Irish Creamery Milk Suppliers Association v *Ireland* (Case 36/80)

The Court of Justice stated that:

> It might be convenient, in certain circumstances, for the facts in the case to be established and for questions of purely national law to be settled at the time the reference is made to the Court of Justice so as to enable the latter to take cognisance of all the features of fact and of law which may be relevant.

In **Telemarsicabruzzo SpA** (Joined Cases C-320–322/90), the Court refused to give a ruling, stating that the need to give a practical interpretation of Community law requires the national court to define the factual and legal framework in which the questions arise, or that at least it explains the factual assumptions on which those questions are based. Neither had been done in this case. In **Venntveld** (Case C-316/93), however, although all the relevant facts were not included, the Court held that there was sufficient information in the case file and in the pleadings to give a preliminary ruling.

More recently, in the following case, the Court of Justice held inadmissible a question referred to it to enable the referring court to decide whether the legislation of another Member State is in accordance with Community law:

Bacardi-Martini and Cellier des Dauphins (Case C-318/00)

The Court observed that, when such a question is before it, the Court must display special vigilance and 'must be informed in some detail of [the referring court's] reasons for considering that an answer to the question is necessary to enable it to give judgment' (para 46). The Court pointed out, *inter alia*, that where the national court has confined itself to repeating the argument of one of the parties, without indicating whether and to what extent it considers that a reply to the question is necessary to enable it to give judgment, and, as a result, the Court does not have the material before it to show that it is necessary to rule on the question referred, that question is inadmissible.

A *discretion* to refer

The second paragraph of Art 234 EC Treaty provides that:

> Where such a question is raised before any court or tribunal of a Member State, that court or tribunal **may**, if it considers that a decision on the question is necessary to enable it to give judgment, request the Court of Justice to give a ruling thereon. [emphasis added]

It contemplates a situation in which the national court or tribunal considers that it is 'necessary' to refer a question to the Court of Justice to enable it to give judgment in the case. In such a case, it *may* refer the question to the Court. The question to be referred must relate to one of the matters considered above (e.g. (i) interpretation of the Treaty; or (ii) the validity or interpretation of a regulation, directive or decision). Therefore, before the discretion to refer arises, the national court must be of the view that 'a decision on the question is *necessary* in order to enable it to give judgment' (emphasis added (see below)). The decision on whether or not to make a reference is essentially a matter for the national court, as explained by the Court of Justice in the following case:

Dzodzi v *Belgium* (Joined Cases C-297/88 and C-197/89)

The Court of Justice stated that:

> In the context of the division of judicial functions between national courts and the Court of Justice, provided for by Article 177 [now Art 234], the Court of Justice gives preliminary rulings without, in principle, needing to enquire as to the circumstances which led to the national court submitting questions to it ... The only exception to that principle would be in cases in which it appeared that the procedure provided for in Article 177 had been abused and where the question submitted sought, in reality, to lead the Court of Justice to make a ruling on the basis of an artificial dispute, or where it is obvious that the provision of Community law submitted to the Court of Justice could not be applied.

In the above case, the Court of Justice allowed a reference where the national court needed a ruling to determine a question of national law in an area of law that was outside the competence of the Community but which had been based on Community law.

Although the national court has the discretion to assess the need for a reference, it should explain how it has come to the conclusion that a reference is necessary, so that the Court of Justice can be satisfied that it has the jurisdiction to deal with the matter (**Foglia** *v* **Novello (No. 2)** (Case 244/80)). Once it is satisfied that it has the jurisdiction to deal with a reference, the Court is, in principle, bound to give a ruling. It cannot refuse to do so on the basis that, if its ruling were to have the effect of annulling a Community or national provision, this would create a 'legal vacuum' in a Member State. It then would be for the national court to interpret national law in such a way as to fill any gap (**Gmurzynska** (Case C-231/89); **Helmig and Others** (Joined Cases C-399, 409 and 425/92 and C-34, 50 & 78/93)). However, the national court does have 'the widest discretion' (**Rheinmuhlen** (Case 166/73), paras 3 and 4); the power to make a reference arises 'as soon as the judge perceives either of his own motion or at the request of the parties that the litigation depends on a point referred to in the first paragraph of Art 177 [now Art 234]'. Even if the national judge decided that it was 'necessary' to make a referral, he has a total discretion whether or not to do so (see below).

If one of the parties to the national proceedings withdraws from them, the Court of Justice cannot continue to deliver a judgment on the reference, because such a judgment would then no longer be 'necessary' for the outcome of the case (**Teres Zabala Erasun and Others** *v* **Instituto Nacional de Empleo** (Joined Cases C-422–424/93)). Even if a superior national court has decided the issue, the lower court is not precluded from making a reference by national rules. Although the national court has a discretion to refer if it is a lower court and where its decisions are subject to appeal (see below), it has little real discretion in cases where its decision depends on the disputed *validity* of a Community measure. It has itself no power to declare the Community measure invalid, so it has no choice but to refer the matter to the Court of Justice for a ruling on its validity (**Foto-Frost** (Case 314/85)).

An *obligation* to refer

The third paragraph of Art 234 EC Treaty provides that:

> Where any such question is raised in a case pending before a court or tribunal of a Member State against whose decisions there is no judicial remedy under national law, that court or tribunal **shall** bring the matter before the Court of Justice. [emphasis added]

Therefore, a court or tribunal which satisfies the above criteria has no discretion; it is *required* to refer the case to the Court of Justice for a preliminary ruling. The criteria are as follows.

'No judicial remedy under national law'

The concept of 'no judicial remedy under national law' clearly includes situations where there is no further appeal. That situation may arise where the national court is, like the English House of Lords, the highest in the hierarchy of courts. It may also arise in specific cases where no appeal is possible from a court which is very low in the hierarchy. In some jurisdictions, for example, there may be no appeal where the amount claimed or the value of the goods concerned is below a certain figure. In the landmark case of **Costa** *v* **ENEL** (Case 6/64), the amount claimed was less than £2. There was no appeal from the magistrate's decision because of the smallness of the sum. The magistrate was, therefore, under Art 177 (now Art 234) obliged to refer the question before him to the Court of Justice. In **Parfums Christian Dior BV** *v* **Evora BV** (Case C-337/95), the Dutch Court of Appeal (the *Hoge Raad*) had the power to refer a question on trade mark law to the Benelux Court, the highest court for points of law affecting the Benelux Agreement. The Court of Justice held that, if the *Hoge Raad* decided *not* to refer the case to the Benelux Court, it was *obliged* to refer the case to the Court of Justice. If it did refer the case to the Benelux Court, the Benelux Court was itself, as the ultimate court *in that case*, obliged to refer the matter to the Court of Justice.

In the following case, the Court of Justice was directly required to consider the application of the third paragraph of Art 234 to the Swedish District Court:

Kenny Roland Lyckeskog (Case C-99/00)

The Swedish District Court had referred the case to the Court of Justice, asking the court whether it came within the third paragraph of Art 234, because an appeal from its decision to the Swedish Supreme Court would only apply if the supreme court declared that the appeal was admissible. The Court of Justice stated that decisions of a national court which can be challenged before a supreme court are not decisions of a 'court or tribunal of a Member State against whose decisions there is no judicial remedy under national law' within the meaning of Art 234. The fact that examination of the merits of such appeals is subject to a declaration of admissibility by the Swedish Supreme Court does not have the effect of depriving the parties of a judicial remedy. Therefore, because there was an appeal to the Supreme Court, the District Court did not come within the scope of the third paragraph of Art 234, even though the Supreme Court could refuse to hear the appeal (if it held the appeal to be inadmissible).

The question arises as to the impact the above case has on the English legal system. In the English legal system a litigant whose case comes before the Court of Appeal can request leave to appeal to the House of Lords if he loses the case. If the Court of Appeal refuses leave to appeal, the litigant can then request it from the House of Lords, but the House of Lords could also refuse leave. According to the judgment of the Court of Justice in the above case, in these circumstances the Court of Appeal would not be considered to be a court 'against whose decisions there is no judicial remedy'.

Within the English legal system, the term 'judicial remedy' is wide enough to include applications for judicial review. Even when, therefore, there is no appeal from, say, the Immigration Appeal Tribunal, its decisions are subject to judicial review and may subsequently be referred to the Court of Justice in the course of those judicial review proceedings (see, for example, **R v Immigration Appeal Tribunal, ex parte Antonissen** (Case C-292/89)). In such a case, it would appear that there is no obligation on the tribunal to refer and an English tribunal has, in fact, refused to refer a case because it has held that it was not obliged to do so because of the availability of judicial review of its decisions (**Re a Holiday in Italy** [1975] 1 CMLR 184 (National Insurance Commissioner)). This would seem to be compatible with the Court of Justice's decision in **Lyckeskog** (Case C-99/00).

Having considered the concept of 'no judicial remedy' the other two criteria are as follows:

'Where any such question is raised'

This was considered above, and includes a question relating to (i) the interpretation of the Treaty; or (ii) the validity or interpretation of a Community act (i.e. a regulation, directive or decision).

'A decision on the question is necessary to enable it to give judgment'

There is no express reference to this criterion in the third paragraph of Art 234, although there is such a reference in the second paragraph. However, in the following case the Court of Justice stated that it is also applicable to the third paragraph:

CILFIT (Case 283/81)

The Court of Justice stated that:

> 10. . . . it follows from the relationship between the second and third paragraphs of Article 177 [now Art 234] that the courts or tribunals referred to in paragraph 3 have the same discretion as any other national court or tribunal to ascertain whether a decision on a question of Community law is necessary to enable them to give judgment.

To conclude this section, a court or tribunal which satisfies the above three criteria has no discretion; it must refer the question to the Court of Justice for a preliminary ruling.

Is it necessary to make the referral?

As discussed above, a court or tribunal will have a discretion (pursuant to the second paragraph of Art 234) or be under an obligation (pursuant to the third paragraph) to refer a case to the Court of Justice for a preliminary ruling only if it 'considers a decision on the question to be *necessary* to enable it to give judgment' (emphasis added). There may be a number of reasons why the court or tribunal does not consider it *necessary* to have the question answered by the Court of Justice. Two of these reasons are now considered further: (i) the development of precedent; and (ii) the doctrine of *acte clair*.

The development of precedent

Not every question concerning the interpretation of Community law which is relevant to the outcome of a case requires a reference under Art 234. In Chapter 5 it was stated that the doctrine of precedent does not apply to the Court of Justice, but the Court generally follows its own previous decisions for the sake of legal certainty. This has been acknowledged by the Court of Justice in the following case:

CILFIT (Case 283/81)

The Court of Justice stated that:

> the authority of an interpretation under Article 177 [now Art 234] already given by the Court may deprive the obligation of its purpose and thus empty it of its substance. Such is the case when the question raised is materially identical with a question which has already been the subject of a preliminary ruling in a similar case.

In the above case, the Court of Justice held that it may not be *necessary* to make a referral to it because the question may already have been answered in a previous case (e.g. the Court of Justice may already have interpreted the relevant Treaty article). However, a national court can refer any question on interpretation or validity, whether or not the Court of Justice has ruled on the point. The case before the national court may raise some new fact or argument. However, if it does not raise any new fact or argument, the Court may, in its ruling, simply restate the substance of the earlier case, as it did in the following case:

Da Costa (Cases 28-30/62)

The Court of Justice held that:

> The questions of interpretation posed in this case are identical with those settled [in the case of **Van Gend en Loos**] and no new factor has been presented to the Court. In these circumstances the Tariefcommissie must be referred to the previous judgment.

In the above case, it would appear that the Court of Justice is actively encouraging national courts to apply the Court's previous decisions: thus a system of precedent is emerging by default. This is apparent in the following case:

International Chemical Corporation (Case 66/80)

The Court of Justice had previously ruled in a former Art 177 EC Treaty (now Art 234) referral that Regulation 563/76 was invalid. This case concerned the regulation's validity. The Italian court hearing the case referred the matter to the Court of Justice asking whether the previous decision that the regulation was invalid applied only to that particular case, or whether it was effective in any subsequent litigation. The Court of Justice held that the purpose of the former Art 177 (now Art 234) was to ensure that Community law was applied uniformly by national courts. Uniform application did not only concern the interpretation of Community law, it also concerned the validity of a Community act. The Court said that in the previous case, the ruling that the regulation in question was void was addressed to the national court making the reference. **However, since it was declared to be void, any other national court could likewise regard the act as void for the purpose of a judgment which it had to give.**

In the following case the Court of Justice applied this principle when it was called upon to interpret a measure (rather than decide on its validity):

Kühne & Heitz (Case C-453/00)

The Court of Justice stated that in view of the obligation on all the authorities of the Member States to ensure observance of Community law, and also of the retroactive effect inherent in interpretative judgments, **a rule of Community law which has been interpreted on the occasion of a reference for a preliminary ruling must be applied by all State bodies within the sphere of their competence, even to legal relationships which arose or were formed before the Court gave its ruling on the request for interpretation.**

With regard to compliance with that obligation, the Court stated that account must be taken of the demands of the principle of legal certainty, which is one of the general principles of Community law.

An interesting situation arose in the following case, which was decided by the English Court of Appeal:

R v Secretary of State for the Home Department, ex parte A ([2002] EWCA Civ 1008, unreported)

In judicial review proceedings, the English High Court thought that it was necessary to make a referral to the Court of Justice pursuant to Art 234, because it concerned interpretation of Community law. The claimant challenged this decision to refer the case to the Court of Justice, and the Court of Appeal held that a judgment of the Court of Justice in 2000 had made it perfectly clear the interpretation which should be placed on the Community law provisions; it therefore followed that it was not necessary to make the referral.

It should be noted, however, that the Court of Justice is the sole arbitrator upon the *validity* of an act of the Community institutions. To decide otherwise would put the objective of uniform application of Community law at risk. It is not open to a national court to declare an act of the Community (e.g. a regulation or directive) to be void, unless the Court of Justice has decided this in an earlier judgment (see **Firma Foto-Frost** (Case 314/85)).

The doctrine of *acte clair*

In **CILFIT** (Case 283/81), the Court of Justice held that a court which is bound by the mandatory reference provisions in the third paragraph of Art 234 is not obliged to refer a case where the answer to a question of interpretation of Community law is 'so obvious as to leave no scope for any reasonable doubt' (para 16). This situation of an apparently transparent interpretative point is normally referred to in Community law as *acte clair*. In the following case, the Court described the circumstances in which a reference should be made:

CILFIT (Case 283/81)

The Court of Justice stated that:

16. Finally, the correct application of Community law may be so obvious as to leave no scope for reasonable doubt as to the manner in which the question raised is to be resolved. Before it comes to the conclusion that such is the case, the national court or tribunal must be convinced that the matter is equally obvious to the Courts of the other Member States and to the Court of Justice. Only if those conditions are satisfied, may the national court or tribunal refrain from submitting the question to the Court of Justice and take upon itself the responsibility for resolving it.
17. However, the existence of such a possibility must be assessed on the basis of the characteristic feature of Community law and the particular difficulties to which its interpretation gives rise.
18. To begin with, it must be borne in mind that Community legislation is drafted in several languages and that the different language versions are equally authentic. An interpretation of a provision of Community law thus involves a comparison of the different language versions.
19. It must also be borne in mind, even where the different language versions are entirely in accord with one another, that **Community law uses terminology which is peculiar to it.** Furthermore, it must be emphasised that **legal concepts do not necessarily have the same meaning in Community law and in the law of the various Member States.**
20. Finally, every provision of Community law must be placed in its context and interpreted in the light of the provisions of Community law as a whole, regard being had to the objectives thereof and to its state of evolution at the date on which the provision in question is to be applied. [emphasis added]

The approach adopted by the Court of Justice when interpreting Community law has been considered in Chapter 5; suffice to say at this point, the Court of Justice does not interpret such law literally, but generally favours a contextual or teleological approach. Quite often the interpretation of the Court could not have been predicted. Hence, although the Court has given permission to national courts to apply the doctrine of *acte clair*, the national court must do so with the utmost caution.

The responsibility imposed on a court in declining to refer a question which, by virtue of the lack of possibility for further appeal or review of its decisions, it, *prima facie*, ought to refer, is thus an onerous one. In the following case, an English judge recognised the advantages enjoyed by the Court of Justice in this context:

Customs and Excise Commissioners v *Samex* [1983] 3 CMLR 194

Bingham J stated that:

... [the Court of Justice] has a panoramic view of the Community and its institutions, a detailed knowledge of the treaties and of much subordinate legislation made under them, and an intimate familiarity with the functioning of the Community market which no national judge denied the collective experience of the Court of Justice could hope to achieve.

Other English courts have not been so mindful of their limitations. **R v London Boroughs Transport Committee, ex parte Freight Transport Association** [1991] 3 All ER 915 involved the interpretation of directives on vehicle brake construction and the powers of national authorities to impose further restrictions on vehicles. The House of Lords refused to make a reference although the issues were complex. Lord Templeman noted that 'no plausible grounds had been advanced for a reference to the European Court'. The refusal to refer was criticised, and one of the parties made a complaint to the Commission about the refusal. The case is not, however, indicative of a general unwillingness to refer cases by the House of Lords, as the **Factortame** and the equal treatment cases demonstrate (**R v Secretary of State for Transport, ex parte Factortame (No. 1)** (Case C-221/89); **R v Secretary of State for Transport, ex parte Factortame (No. 2)** (Case C-213/89); **Webb v EMO Cargo** [1993] 1 WLR 49; **R v Secretary of State for Employment, ex parte EOC** [1995] 1 CMLR 345). There is, however, continuing evidence of a reluctance to refer by English courts and tribunals, not least because of the time which such references take (see, for example: **Johnson v Chief Adjudication Officer** [1994] 1 CMLR 829; **Gould and Cullen v Commissioners of Customs and Excise (VAT Tribunal)** [1994] 1 CMLR 347; **R v Ministry of Agriculture, Fisheries and Food, ex parte Portman Agrochemicals Ltd** [1994] 1 CMLR 18). As discussed above, there is one situation in which *any* national court *must* refer a question to the Court of Justice. If 'a national court (even one whose decision is still subject to appeal) intends to question the validity of a Community act, it *must* refer the question to the Court of Justice' (emphasis added) (**Foto-Frost v Hauptzollamt Lubeck-Ost** (Case 314/85)).

Interim measures

It may be as long as two years before a decision on a reference under Art 234 is available from the Court of Justice. The Court of Justice has jurisdiction under Art 243 EC Treaty to 'prescribe any interim measures' and will sometimes do so where the legality of a Community measure is being challenged under Art 230 EC Treaty (see Chapter 8). Under Art 234, the validity of any act of the institutions may be raised in a reference. The following questions need to be addressed: Can the allegedly invalid Community measure be suspended by the national court pending the outcome of the reference? Will the Court of Justice suspend it? Should national courts suspend national legislation which is alleged to conflict with Community law or which implements a Community measure whose validity is disputed?

The Court of Justice may use its power under Art 243 EC Treaty to order a Member State to cease pursuing a course of conduct which *prima facie* breaches Community law, and which is requested by a party to the proceedings (**Commission v UK (Re Nationality of Fishermen)** (Case 246/89R); **Commission v Germany** (Case C-195/90)). This will normally be an interim measure in the course of Art 226 proceedings against a Member State (see Chapter 7). Alternatively, national courts may be required to suspend a provision of national law which, arguably, conflicts with Community law (see **Factortame**, above). Although the criteria for granting interim relief are national, presumptions about the validity of primary national law should not act as a bar to its interim suspension.

The position with regard to the suspension of national measures implementing a provision of Community law, the validity of which is challenged, was discussed by the Court of Justice in the following case:

Zuckerfabrik Suderdithmarschen v *HZA Itzehoe* (Case C-143/88)

The Court of Justice declared that, to enable Art 234 references to work effectively, national courts must have the power to grant interim relief in the situation where a national measure is disputed on the grounds of the validity of the Community measure on which it is based, on the same grounds as when the compatibility of a national measure with Community law is contested. However, the national court has to be careful before doing so:

> Where a national court or tribunal has serious doubts about the validity of a Community act on which a national measure is based, it may, in exceptional circumstances, temporarily suspend application of the latter measure or grant other interim relief with respect to it. It must then refer the question of validity to the Court of Justice, stating the reasons for which it considers that the Community act is not valid.

National courts can apply national criteria when deciding, in the particular circumstances, whether or not to grant suspensory relief, but the national measures must be effective in providing the necessary remedies to protect rights conferred by Community law (**Factortame (No. 2)** (Case C-213/89)) and to prevent 'irreparable damage' to the person seeking relief, pending the outcome of the reference (**Atlanta Fruchthandelsgesellschaft GmbH** *v* **Bundesamt für Ernährung und Forstwirtschaft** (Case C-465/93)).

Interpretation or application

Article 234 EC Treaty empowers the Court of Justice to interpret Community law, but not to apply it to the facts of a case. The application of the law to the facts is the role of the national court. The national court, if it considers a decision of the Court of Justice is necessary in order for it to give a judgment, will refer the matter to the Court of Justice requesting an answer to a given question (or series of questions) which concerns the interpretation or validity of Community law. The Court of Justice answers the question(s) and sends the case back to the national court for the national court to apply the law to the facts of the case. However, this distinction may become blurred in practice, as illustrated in the following case:

Cristini (Case 32/75)

Article 7(2), Regulation 1612/68, provides that a Community worker who is working in another Member State should be entitled to the same 'social advantages' as workers of that Member State (see Chapter 12). Large *French* families were allowed reduced fares on the French railways. The question referred to the Court of Justice by the French court was whether this was a 'social advantage' within the meaning of the regulation and thus should be available to large families of all Member State nationals working in France. The Court of Justice stated that it was not empowered to decide the actual case, it being its duty simply to interpret the provision of the regulation in question. The Court, however, went on to hold that the concept of 'social advantage' included this type of fare reduction offered by the French Railways.

In the above case, the Court of Justice not only interpreted Community law, but also applied it to the particular facts. However, to be fair to the Court, in answering the

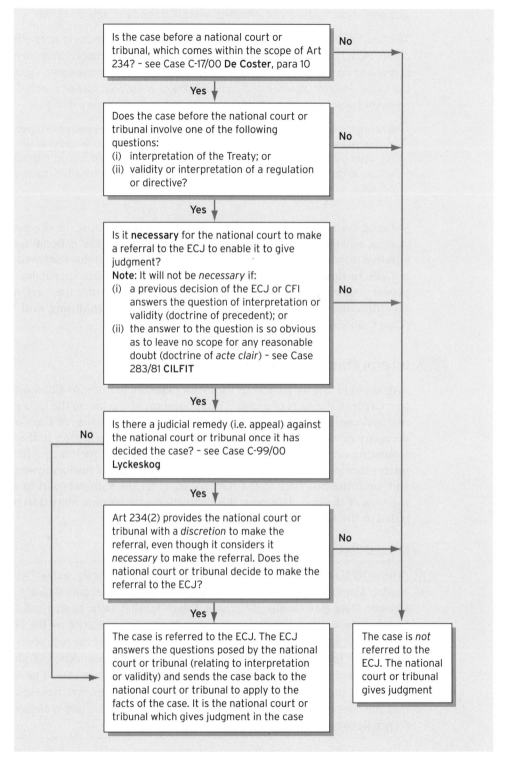

Figure 6.1 The Art 234 EC Treaty preliminary ruling jurisdiction of the Court of Justice

national court's question it would have been difficult for the Court of Justice to have done anything else.

Figure 6.1 consists of a flowchart setting out the application of the Art 234 EC Treaty preliminary ruling jurisdiction of the Court of Justice.

Summary

Now you have read this chapter you should be able to:

- Explain how the Art 234 EC Treaty preliminary ruling procedure seeks to ensure the harmonious development of Community law.

- Distinguish between the Art 234 EC Treaty procedure and an appeal.

- Understand the scope of 'national courts and tribunals' within the context of Art 234 EC Treaty.

- Outline the different types of question which may be the subject of a reference from a national court or tribunal to the European Court of Justice pursuant to Art 234 EC Treaty.

- Identify when a national court or tribunal has an obligation to refer a question to the European Court of Justice (pursuant to the third paragraph of Art 234 EC Treaty).

- Identify when a national court or tribunal has discretion to refer a question to the European Court of Justice (pursuant to the second paragraph of Art 234 EC Treaty).

- Assess how the doctrines of precedent and acte clair impact upon the decision of a national court or tribunal to make a reference to the European Court of Justice pursuant to Art 234 EC Treaty.

- Assess the extent to which the European Court of Justice not only interprets Community law but applies it to the facts of an individual case, and discuss whether this is a role which, under Art 234 EC Treaty, falls within the sole jurisdiction of the national court or tribunal which referred the case.

Further reading

Textbooks

Brown, L.N. and Jacobs, F. (2000) *The Court of Justice of the European Communities* (5th edn), Sweet & Maxwell, Chapter 10.

Craig, P. and De Burca, G. (2003) *EU Law Text, Cases and Materials* (3rd edn), Oxford University Press, Chapter 11.

Foster, N. (2006) *Foster on EU Law* (1st edn), Oxford University Press, Chapter 5 (Sections 5.1, 5.2 and 5.5).

Steiner, J., Woods, L. and Twigg-Flesner, C. (2006) *EU Law* (9th edn), Oxford University Press, Chapter 9.

Storey, T. and Turner, C. (2005) *Unlocking EU Law* (1st edn), Hodder Arnold, Chapter 7.

Tillotson, J. and Foster, N. (2003) *Text, Cases and Materials on EU Law* (4th edn), Cavendish Publishing, Chapter 9.

Vincenzi, C. (1995) 'Private Initiative and Public Control in the Regulatory Process', in Daintith, T. (ed.) *Implementing EC Law in the UK: Structures for Indirect Rule*, John Wiley & Sons.

Weatherill, S. (2006) *Cases and Materials on EU Law* (7th edn), Oxford University Press, Chapter 7.

Journal articles

Barnard, C. and Sharpston, E., 'The Changing Face of Article 177 References' (1997) 34 CML Rev 1113.

Mancini, F. and Keeling, D., 'From CILFIT to ERT: The Constitutional Challenge Facing the European Court' (1991) 11 YEL 1.

O'Neill, M., 'Article 177 and Limits to the Right to Refer: An End to Confusion' (1996) 2 EPL 375.

Rasmussen, H., 'The European Court's Acte Clair Strategy in CILFIT' (1984) 9 CML Rev 242.

Weatherill, S., 'Regulating the Internal Market: Result Orientation in the House of Lords' (1992) 17 EL Rev 299, 318.

7 Direct actions against Member States (Articles 226-228 EC Treaty)

Aims and objectives

At the end of this chapter you should understand:

■ The Art 226 EC Treaty (previously Art 169) procedure.

■ The interaction between the Commission's power under Art 226 with that of a Member State under Art 227 EC Treaty (previously Art 170).

■ The nature of the Commission's discretion on whether to initiate action against a defaulting Member State.

■ The purpose of a reasoned opinion and the powers available to a Member State to challenge a defective opinion.

■ The different forms of breach of Community law and whether or not the Commission can continue to pursue an action under Art 226 if a defaulting Member State remedies the breach.

■ Any defences which a Member State can rely upon to justify a breach of Community law.

■ The Court of Justice's power to impose a lump sum or penalty payment on a defaulting Member State, pursuant to Art 228 EC Treaty.

The obligation of Member States under the EC Treaty

Member States have a general duty, under Art 10 EC Treaty (previously Art 5), to 'take all appropriate measures, whether general or particular, to ensure fulfilment of the obligations arising out of this Treaty or resulting from action taken by the institutions of the Community. They shall facilitate the achievement of the Community's tasks'. The obligation to observe Community law extends beyond the Treaties and secondary legislation to agreements made by the Community with other states under Art 300(1) EC Treaty (**SZ Service** (Case 192/89), para 13; First EEA Case Opinion 1/94). This positive duty to do what is required of them both under the Treaty and under legislation enacted by the institutions is underpinned by a negative obligation in the second limb of Art 10 to 'abstain from any measure which could jeopardise the attainment of the objectives of this Treaty'. The Commission, in order 'to ensure the proper functioning and development of the common market' shall ensure 'that the provisions of this Treaty and the measures taken by the institutions pursuant thereto are applied' (Art 211 EC Treaty (previously Art 155)).

The obligation to observe Community law binds, as shall be seen in the discussion on the direct enforcement of directives (referred to as the principle of 'direct effect'), not only the state, but organs and emanations of the state (see Chapter 9). Those organs include government departments, state-funded and regulated agencies providing public services, state governments in federal systems (the *Länder*, for example, in Germany), local authorities (**Costanzo** (Case 103/88), **Johnston** *v* **RUC** (Case 222/84)), and the courts. All are, potentially, the subject of enforcement proceedings, although the actual defendant in each case will be the state itself.

In some cases where action is required, lack of Commission resources may limit or delay its response to unlawful action or inaction by Member States. A more appropriate response than a Commission initiative may be reliance by individuals on the direct enforcement of Treaty and other Community provisions in the courts of the offending Member State (see Chapter 9). Despite the liberal interpretation of the Treaties and the secondary legislation by the Court of Justice, not every Community provision is sufficiently precise and unconditional to be directly enforceable. In addition, individuals may not have the means to start proceedings or to obtain the evidence to prove a breach. Action by individuals in the courts of the state alleged to have breached Community law does not preclude action by the Commission in the Court of Justice. For example, in 1977 the UK government banned the importation of main crop potatoes. A Dutch potato exporter challenged this by applying for a declaration in the English High Court that the ban breached Art 28 EC Treaty. A reference was made to the Court of Justice under Art 234 EC Treaty which confirmed that the ban was indeed unlawful. A parallel case was also brought by the Commission in the Court of Justice under Art 226 EC Treaty (**Meijer** *v* **Department of Trade** (Case 118/78); **Commission** *v* **UK** (Case 231/78)).

Action by the Commission: Article 226 EC Treaty

If an individual is unable or unwilling to commence proceedings in relation to the alleged breach, there may be no practical alternative to action by the Commission. The Commission has the power to commence proceedings. Where Member States fail to implement Community law, or fail to eliminate obstacles to its implementation, it can take the necessary action under Art 226 EC Treaty (previously Art 169):

> If the Commission considers that a Member State has failed to fulfil an obligation under this Treaty, it shall deliver a reasoned opinion on the matter after giving the State concerned the opportunity to submit its observations.
>
> If the State concerned does not comply with the opinion within the period laid down by the Commission the latter may bring the matter before the Court of Justice.

Constitutional Treaty

As discussed in Chapter 1, the proposed Constitutional Treaty has not come into force because it was not ratified by all the Member States. If it had come into force, Art III-360 would have replaced Art 226 EC Treaty. Article III-360 would have been worded similarly to Art 226 EC Treaty, although the reference in Art III-360 would have been to a breach of the Constitutional Treaty rather than the EC Treaty.

Action by another Member State: Article 227 EC Treaty

As an alternative to Art 226, action can be commenced by other Member States under Art 227 EC Treaty (previously Art 170):

> A Member State which considers that another Member State has failed to fulfil an obligation under this Treaty may bring the matter before the Court of Justice.
>
> Before a Member State brings an action against another Member State for an alleged infringement of an obligation under this Treaty, it shall bring the matter before the Commission.
>
> The Commission shall deliver a reasoned opinion after each of the States concerned has been given the opportunity to submit its own case and its observations on that of the other party both orally and in writing.
>
> If the Commission has not delivered an opinion within three months of the date on which the matter was brought before it, the absence of such opinion shall not prevent the matter from being brought before the Court of Justice.

Member States have shown a marked reluctance to use Art 227, and although states have quite frequently brought breaches of Community law to the attention of the Commission, it could be politically damaging for a Member State to take action all the way to the Court of Justice. The increased use of qualified majority voting has made the governments of Member States more aware of the need to retain the goodwill of fellow states. A very public confrontation in the Court of Justice is not likely to be regarded as helpful. In fact, only one case has come to judgment in the life of the Community: **France** *v* **UK** (Case 141/78). For that reason, any action in the Court of Justice that results from a complaint to the Commission about the failure of a Member State to meet its obligations is likely to be brought by the Commission under Art 226.

Nevertheless, Art 227 can be usefully employed by a Member State to focus the Commission's mind to take action under Art 226. During 1999, when the Community lifted the worldwide ban on UK beef (which had originally been imposed for health reasons), France (and Germany) refused to allow UK beef to enter their markets. The UK informed the Commission that it intended to take action against France under Art 227. The Commission, which had been involved in negotiations with France in an attempt to resolve the dispute, eventually decided to take action against France under Art 226, and thus prevent the UK from taking its own independent action under Art 227. The case eventually came before the Court of Justice and France was held to be in breach of the Treaty (**Commission** *v* **France** (Case C-1/00)). France eventually lifted its ban.

Constitutional Treaty

If the proposed Constitutional Treaty had come into force, Art III-361 would have replaced Art 227 EC Treaty. Article III-361 would have been worded similarly to Art 227 EC Treaty, although the reference in Art III-361 would have been to a breach of the Constitutional Treaty rather than the EC Treaty.

The stages of Article 226 proceedings

The administrative stage

Suspected breaches of Community law generally come to the notice of the Commission as a result of the complaints of individuals or businesses affected by the breach. The first stage is usually an informal inquiry by letter to the government of the Member State concerned to ascertain the relevant facts. Member States have a legal duty to cooperate with Commission investigations into alleged breaches by them (**Commission v Spain** (Case C-375/92)).

In **Greece v Commission** (Case 240/86), the Commission was investigating the possible breach by Greece of certain Treaty articles relating to the free movement of goods. The Commission requested certain information which Greece refused to give. Accordingly the Commission could not ascertain whether Greece was in breach of the Treaty. The Commission initiated Art 226 proceedings against Greece, alleging that Greece was in breach of its duty under the former Art 5 EC Treaty (now Art 10) because of its failure to cooperate with the Commission. The Court of Justice held that Greece was in breach of the former Art 5 (now Art 10).

Therefore, if the Commission requires information from a Member State to enable it to ascertain if that Member State is in breach of its Community law obligations, it will have to pursue Art 226 proceedings for breach of Art 10 EC Treaty if the Member State refuses to cooperate. If successful, the Member State will have to 'take the necessary measures to comply with the judgment' (Art 228(1) EC Treaty) and thus hand the information over. If this information discloses a breach, the Commission will have to start fresh Art 226 proceedings with regard to this breach.

Commission's discretion or obligation?

Article 226 EC Treaty provides that:

> ... If the Commission **considers** ... it **shall** deliver a reasoned opinion ... [the Commission] **may** bring the matter before the Court of Justice. [emphasis added]

The Commission does not have to carry out a formal investigation, but it does at least have to 'consider' whether or not there may have been a breach. Where the Commission does consider there has been a breach, it must, after giving the Member State an opportunity to submit observations on the suspected breach, deliver a reasoned opinion to the government of the state concerned. The reasoned opinion will often follow prolonged correspondence between the Member State and the Commission. The Commission will have to decide, at some stage in its discussions with (or, in some cases, non-cooperation by) Member States, whether or not to proceed to the delivery of a formal opinion which will stipulate a date by which time the necessary remedial action should have taken place. The Commission may decide to take no further action if it considers the breach is not serious and that its resources would be better applied to other infractions.

It would seem that the Commission does have a discretion, but it also has a duty under Art 226. It must consider the possibility of whether or not there has been a breach and it must take the most appropriate action. This may be to decide not to commence proceedings. Advocate-General Roemer gave some indication of the appropriate considerations which the Commission should have in mind in the following case:

Commission v *France* (Case 7/71)

Advocate-General Roemer said that it might be justifiable not to start formal proceedings where (i) there is a possibility that an amicable settlement may be achieved if formal proceedings are delayed; (ii) the effects of the violation are only minor; (iii) there is a major political crisis which could be aggravated if proceedings are commenced in relation to relatively minor matters; and (iv) there is a possibility that the Community provision in issue might be altered in the near future. The Advocate-General commented that Member States resent proceedings being brought against them and the Commission is not always anxious, on this account alone, to take action.

Many breaches go for years without being remedied. For example, the UK government failed to implement Directive 64/221 for more than 20 years after it had been held to have been in default in **Van Duyn** (see now, the Immigration (European Economic Area) Regulations 2006, SI 2006/1003; Chapter 16). In 1996 the French government was again before the Court of Justice for failing to amend its Code du Travail Maritime, 22 years after the Court in **Commission** *v* **France (Re French Merchant Seamen)** (Case 167/73) had held that the Code breached Arts 12 and 39 EC Treaty (**Commission** *v* **France** (Case C-334/94), and see **Commission** *v* **Belgium** (Case C-37/93), which concerned similar restrictions on Belgian ships). Some of the cases in which action has not been taken involve immigration and social issues which tend to be more politically sensitive.

Despite the embarrassment which Art 226 proceedings may occasionally cause to Member States, the Commission has shown an increasing willingness to use them. In its *23rd Annual Report on Monitoring the Application of Community Law* (2005) (COM (2006) 416 final), the Commission reported that pursuant to Art 226 EC Treaty, during 2005 it initiated 2653 infringement proceedings. Although this was less than the 2993 initiated by the Commission during 2004, it was a marked increase on the number initiated during the previous four years (1552 in 2003; 996 in 2002; 1050 in 2001; and 1317 in 2000).

The reasoned opinion

If the Commission decides that a violation of Community law has occurred it must record the infringement in a reasoned opinion or decision served on the offending Member State. In arriving at that opinion the Commission must take into account the replies to its inquiries from the state and any defences which may have been advanced. The Court of Justice has said that an opportunity to submit such observations before a reasoned opinion is served is an essential procedural requirement. A failure to observe it may invalidate the whole process (**Commission** *v* **Italy** (Case 31/69), para 13).

Types of infringement

A large number of infringements concern either the failure to implement directives or a failure to implement them properly, or to observe their terms when implemented. Other infringements may involve direct breaches of Treaty provisions. Whether or not there is an infringement will often depend on the nature and effect of national legal provisions and of the administrative steps taken to give effect to the Community provision, and it is on these legal and factual issues that many disputes with the Commission over implementation occur. A few examples will serve to indicate the diversity of the actions brought by the Commission under Art 226 and the issues involved.

In **Commission** *v* **UK** (Case C-337/89) proceedings were brought by the Commission against the UK for failing to legislate to implement Directive 80/778 to ensure that water used for food production met the maximum nitrate levels in the directive. The UK government argued that most food production was carried out with water from the domestic supply and that legislation was not necessary. The Court of Justice upheld the Commission's view that, in the absence of a specific derogation in the directive, all water used for food production should be made to comply. However, in **Commission** *v* **Belgium** (Case C-376/90), the Court rejected the Commission's interpretation of Directive 80/836/Euratom which required the adoption of national laws protecting the general public and workers against specified levels of ionising radiation. The Commission considered that Member States were not allowed to fix different dose limits to those laid down in the directive, even if they were stricter than those specified. The Court disagreed, holding that the directive only laid down maximum exposure levels and Belgium was not, therefore, in breach for enacting lower permitted exposure levels.

It will also be a breach by the Member State if, while implementing the directive, it does not provide an effective remedy or uses means which cannot be relied upon by individuals in the national courts. Directive 77/187 protects employees who are employed by an undertaking which is transferred to a new owner. The Directive had been implemented in the UK by the Transfer of Undertakings (Protection of Employment) Regulations 1981 (SI 1981/1794) and, *inter alia*, provided for consultation with employees' representatives. The UK's implementing regulations, however, provided no means for recognising such employee representatives. Effectively, in the UK the duty to consult could be negated by the employer's refusal to recognise employee representatives, and there was no effective remedy for this failure to consult. The Court of Justice held that where a Community directive does not specifically provide any penalty for an infringement, Art 10 EC Treaty requires the Member States to guarantee the application and effectiveness of Community law. For that purpose, while the choice of penalties remains within the discretion of the Member State, it must ensure in particular that infringements of Community law are penalised under conditions, both procedural and substantive, which are analogous to those applicable to infringements of national law of a similar nature and importance and which, in any event, make the penalty effective, proportionate and dissuasive (**Commission** *v* **UK** (Case C-382/92), para 55).

Contents of the opinion

The opinion must set out the Community provision and specific details of the breach, together with a response to the Member State's arguments that there has been compliance or attempting to justify delay in compliance, and it must detail the steps to be taken by the Member State to correct its infringement. The opinion has to be more fully reasoned than a legislative act under Art 253 EC Treaty (**Commission** *v* **Germany (Re Brennwein)** (Case 24/62) and **Commission** *v* **Italy** (Case C-439/99)).

Time limit

The Commission must set a time limit within which the Member State must end its violation. The Court of Justice has held that a Member State must be given a 'reasonable period of time' within which to comply with the opinion and thus negate the Commission's power to institute proceedings before the Court of Justice (**Commission** *v* **Ireland** (Case 74/82)).

It is normal practice for a Member State to be given at least two months to respond to a reasoned opinion, but a shorter period might be permissible in certain cases. In the case of the French ban on British beef, the Commission issued a letter of formal notice to France on 16 November 1999. The Commission gave France only two weeks to explain its continued ban. Following the expiry of this two-week period a reasoned opinion was served on France, giving an equally short period within which to lift the ban, after which proceedings were issued in the Court of Justice (**Commission v France** (Case C-1/00)).

Effect of complying with the reasoned opinion

If a Member State complies with the reasoned opinion within the time limit laid down, the Commission does not have the power to bring the matter before the Court of Justice. This in effect gives the Member State a period of grace within which it is protected from the threat of legal proceedings. If the Commission does subsequently bring proceedings, it has the obligation of proving that the violation was not ended before the expiry of the time limit (**Commission v Belgium** (Case 298/86)). In the following case, the Court of Justice articulated the effect of complying with, and not complying with, the reasoned opinion:

Commission v *Italy* (Case 7/61)

The Court of Justice stated:

> It is true that the second paragraph of Article 169 [now Art 226] gives the Commission the right to bring the matter before the Court only if the State concerned does not comply with the Commission's opinion within the period laid down by the Commission, the period being such as to allow the State in question to regularise its position in accordance with the provisions of the Treaty.
>
> However, if the Member State does not comply with the opinion within the prescribed period, there is no question that the Commission has the right to obtain the Court's judgment on that Member State's failure to fulfil the obligations flowing from the Treaty.

This was reaffirmed by the Court of Justice in **Commission v Italy** (Case C-439/99), where part of the proceedings were ruled inadmissible by the Court because Italy had complied, in part, with the reasoned opinion, within the time period laid down in the opinion.

The effect of this can be appreciated by considering the situation where a Member State fails to implement a directive within the time limit stipulated in the directive. Once this time limit has expired the Commission may move swiftly against the defaulting Member State. If it has still failed to implement it by the date specified in the reasoned opinion, the Commission may take enforcement action in the Court of Justice irrespective of whether the Member State subsequently implements the directive. However, if the directive has been implemented within the time period laid down within the reasoned opinion, no further action can be taken pursuant to Art 226.

Take as an example the case of the Working Time Directive 93/104 (OJ 1993 L 307/18) which should have been implemented by all Member States by 23 November 1996. The UK failed to implement it on time. The Directive provides rights for individual workers (e.g. four weeks' paid annual leave, minimum daily and weekly rest periods and a 48-hour maximum working week; all of which are subject to certain exceptions and derogations). A relatively short breach by the UK would have an enormous impact on an indeterminate number of workers. The UK eventually implemented the Directive by the Working Time Regulations 1998 (SI 1998/1833) which came into force on 1 October 1998 (almost two years after the date stipulated in the Directive). The Commission had taken no action against the UK under Art 226. Even if it had taken action, provided the UK had implemented the directive before expiry of the time limit laid down in the reasoned opinion, the UK could not have been brought before the Court of Justice. A sceptic could therefore argue that a Member State may view the period from the date of implementation specified in the directive, to expiry of the reasoned opinion, as an extra period of time within which to implement the directive (although see Chapter 9 for the development of principles by the Court of Justice, which in certain situations empower citizens to enforce their Community law rights in national courts, and ultimately to claim damages from the state if loss has been suffered due to the Member State's breach of Community law). The following case further illustrates this point:

Commission v UK (Cases C-382 and 383/92)

The Acquired Rights Directive 77/187 (OJ 1977 L 61/27) had been implemented in the UK by delegated legislation: the Transfer of Undertakings (Protection of Employment) Regulations 1981 (SI 1981/1974). The aim of the directive was, *inter alia*, to ensure that when a business or part of a business was transferred to another party (e.g. sold), the employees would continue in the employment of the new employer on the same conditions as before (i.e. same hours of work, pay, etc.). Any dismissal connected with the transfer would be unlawful.

Article 1, Directive 77/187 provided it would apply to an 'undertaking, business or part of a business'. This was transposed into Reg 2(1) of the UK regulations as applying to an undertaking, which would include any trade or business 'but not including any undertaking ... which is not in the nature of a commercial venture'.

The English courts held that a local authority was not 'in the nature of a commercial venture', because it was not a profit-making organisation, and therefore the regulations did not apply. Accordingly, where part of a local authority's activities was transferred to a private contractor, because the regulations did not apply, the employees could be dismissed lawfully, or those re-employed could have their pay reduced, etc. Therefore, where, following a competitive tender, responsibility for refuse collection was transferred to a private contractor, the employees affected were the former local authority refuse collectors.

Following subsequent rulings of the Court of Justice on the interpretation of the directive, it became clear that the directive applied in these circumstances and therefore the UK had incorrectly implemented the directive by providing that it would not apply to undertakings 'not in the nature of a commercial venture' (see, for example, **Dr Sophie Redmond Stichting Foundation** v **Bartol and Others** (Case C-29/91)).

The Commission initiated Art 226 proceedings against the UK once the time limit specified in the reasoned opinion had expired. Although the UK had remedied the breach by the time the matter reached the Court of Justice, the Court nevertheless held that the UK was in breach of its obligations under the Treaty, i.e. to implement the directive correctly by the date of implementation specified in the directive.

Altering the subject matter

When the case comes before the Court of Justice, the Commission cannot rely on matters which have not been included in the reasoned opinion (**Commission** v **Belgium** (Case 186/85), para 13).

In the following case, the Court of Justice held that this applies even if both parties consent:

Commission v *Italy* (Case 7/69)

After the date for complying with a reasoned opinion which had been served on Italy had expired, the Commission started enforcement proceedings in the Court of Justice. After starting these proceedings, Italy amended its law in an attempt to comply with the reasoned opinion, but the Commission still considered Italy to be in breach of Community law. Both parties agreed that the Court of Justice should decide whether the new Italian law complied with Community obligations, rather than adjudicate on Italy's initial breach.

The Court of Justice refused to consider this question. The nature of the proceedings could not be altered, even by consent. The subject matter of the Commission's complaint had changed significantly since it had issued the reasoned opinion, the issuing of which is a compulsory part of the Art 226 procedure. The proceedings (as set out in the reasoned opinion) only concerned a default existing at the time the proceedings were initiated. What transpired afterwards was irrelevant for the current proceedings. If the Commission wished to have the new law tested, the full Art 226 proceedings must be started afresh, i.e. formal letter, reasoned opinion and enforcement proceedings.

Disclosure of draft reasoned opinion

In the following case, the Court of First Instance (CFI) held that the European Commission was not obliged to disclose a draft reasoned opinion which it subsequently decided not to serve on a Member State because it was satisfied with the action taken by that Member State to remedy the alleged breach of Community law:

Bavarian Lager Company Ltd v *Commission* (Case T-309/97)

The CFI stated that:

> The Joint Code of Conduct concerning access to Council and Commission documents (OJ 1993 L 340/4) laid down the general principle that the public was to have the widest access to documents held by the Commission and the Council, and on the basis of that and Case T-105/95 **UK** v **Commission** [1997] ECR II-313, the applicant [Bavarian Lager Company Ltd] asserted that it had a right to access to the document in issue [i.e. the draft reasoned opinion].
>
> The grounds which could be relied on by a Community institution to reject an application for access were listed in the Code of Conduct which provided, *inter alia*:
>
> 'The institutions will refuse access to any documents where disclosure could undermine the protection of the public interest (public security, ... inspections and investigations) ...'
>
> It was on that exception that the Commission grounded its refusal.
>
> The applicant classified the document to which it sought access as a reasoned opinion, but that was wrong in fact and in law.
>
> The document was in fact a draft reasoned opinion drawn up by Commission staff after the members of the Commission had decided to deliver a reasoned opinion.
>
> In view of the decision to suspend the procedure, that document was in the end never signed by the Commissioner responsible or communicated to the Member State.
>
> The procedure initiated under article 169 [now 226] thus only got as far as the stage of inspection and investigation and never reached the stage where the Commission delivered a reasoned opinion, and the 'opinion' remained a purely preparatory document.
>
> The Member States were entitled to expect confidentiality from the Commission during investigations which could lead to an infringement procedure, and the disclosure of documents relating thereto, during the negotiations between the Commission and the Member State concerned, could jeopardise the purpose of the infringement procedures: to enable the Member State to comply of its own accord with the requirements of the Treaty or, if appropriate, to justify its position.

The safeguarding of that objective warranted, under the heading of the protection of the public interest, the refusal of access to a preparatory document relating to the investigation stage of the article 169 [now 226] procedure.

On the grounds set out above, the CFI dismissed the application.

The judicial stage

The Commission does not have to commence proceedings immediately on the expiry of the period specified in its opinion. In one case it waited six years before commencing proceedings (**Commission** v **Germany** (Case C-422/92)). It is envisaged that the Commission may wish to give the offending state more time to take the necessary remedial action (**Commission** v **France** (Case 7/71), para 5).

Member States have attempted to rely upon a number of defences to breaches of Community law, but the Court has not, generally, been receptive. In relation to non-transposition of directives, it is frequently argued either that there has been a shortage of parliamentary time or, alternatively, that transposition is not necessary because the terms of the directive are, in fact, observed and conflicting national legislative provisions are not adhered to. The first defence was resolutely disposed of by the Court of Justice in the following case:

Commission v Belgium (Case 77/69)

Belgium had imposed a discriminatory tax on wood which violated Art 95 EC Treaty (now Art 90) (see Chapter 17). A draft law to amend the tax scheme had been laid before the Belgian Parliament, but had fallen when the Parliament was dissolved. The Belgian government argued that these were matters out of its control and it had been prevented from legislating by *force majeure*. The Court of Justice was curt in its dismissal of the argument:

> The obligations arising from Article 95 [now Art 90] of the Treaty devolve upon States as such and the liability of a Member State under Article 169 [now Art 226] arises whatever the agency of the State whose action or inaction is the cause of the failure to fulfil its obligations, even in the case of a constitutionally independent institution. The objection raised by the defendant cannot therefore be sustained. [paras 15 and 16] [see also **Commission** v **Belgium** (Case 1/86)]

Nor is the fact that the requirements imposed by a directive are difficult to meet accepted as a defence, as illustrated in the following case:

Commission v UK (Case C-56/90)

The UK attempted to justify its failure to take all necessary measures to ensure that bathing beaches in Blackpool and Southport met the environmental and health standards set by Directive 76/160 by arguing that implementation was made more difficult by local circumstances. The Court of Justice stated that, even assuming that absolute physical impossibility to carry out the obligations imposed by the Directive might justify failure to fulfil them, the UK had not established such impossibility in this case.

Nor can Member States qualify their obligations imposed by directives in response to the demands of 'special' local circumstances or particular economic or social interest groups.

In **Commission** *v* **Hellenic Republic** (Case C-45/91), the Greek government attempted to justify its failure to implement a directive on the safe disposal of toxic waste because of 'opposition by the local population'. The Court commented that it had consistently held that a Member State cannot rely on an internal situation to justify disregard of its obligations. Similar defences relating to local conditions have been advanced, and rejected, in two Art 226 proceedings following the failure of Member States to implement

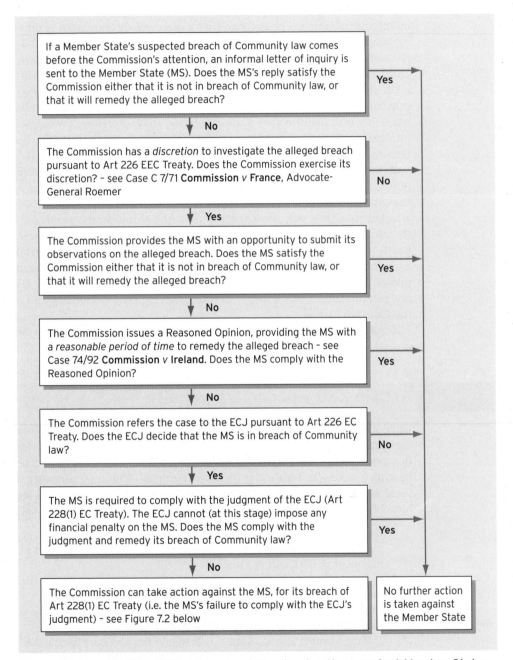

Figure 7.1 The Art 226 EC Treaty procedure: direct actions against Member States

Directive 79/409 on the protection of wild birds (**Commission** *v* **Netherlands (Re Protection of Wild Birds)** (Case 339/87); **Commission** *v* **Spain** (Case C-355/90)).

In **Commission** *v* **Greece** (Case C-105/91), the Greek government defended its admittedly unlawful and discriminatory tax on foreign vehicles by arguing that the Greek vehicles concerned constituted no more than 10 per cent of the internal demand and that there was no manifest discrimination. The Court of Justice rejected the defence on the ground that it had consistently held that a Member State was guilty of a failure to fulfil its obligations under the Treaty regardless of the frequency or the scale of the infringement. The defence that a directive or regulation is observed in practice or 'administratively' where there are conflicting national provisions has also been rejected by the Court of Justice on a number of occasions (**Commission** *v* **Italy** (Case 166/82); **Commission** *v* **Germany (Re Nursing Directives)** (Case 29/84); **Commission** *v* **UK (Re Tachographs)** (Case 128/78)). However, the use of existing, legally binding provisions of national law may be acceptable if they provide an effective means of implementing the directive. Such legislation may, therefore, provide a defence to non-implementation (**Commission** *v* **Netherlands** (Case C-190/90)). Individuals must, nonetheless, be able to rely on a text of national law that accurately reflects their rights and on which they can rely in the event of a judicial challenge (**Commission** *v* **France** (Case 167/73)). For this reason, a Community obligation cannot be implemented by the government of a Member State simply by accepting assurances from the bodies affected that they will meet the terms of the Community provision. It is suggested, therefore, that **R** *v* **Secretary of State for the Environment, ex parte Friends of the Earth** [1994] 2 CMLR 760, in which Schiemann J held that an undertaking from water authorities given to the Secretary of State that they would meet Community requirements on water quality was an acceptable way of meeting the UK's Community obligations, is probably wrongly decided; this case was decided by an English court, not the Court of Justice.

Figure 7.1 consists of a flowchart setting out the application of the Art 226 EC Treaty procedure: direct actions against Member States.

Article 228 - pecuniary penalty

Once judgment has been given against a Member State, failure to observe the terms of that judgment will constitute a breach of Art 228(1) EC Treaty (previously Art 171). A number of judgments have not been implemented for as long as five years after the hearing (Audretsch, 1986). The Treaty on European Union significantly strengthened the hand of the Court of Justice in those cases in which Member States are found to have breached Community law. Article 228 (as amended by the TEU) provides:

1. If the Court of Justice finds that a Member State has failed to fulfil an obligation under this Treaty, the State shall be required to take the necessary measures to comply with the judgment of the Court of Justice.
2. If the Commission considers that the Member State concerned has not taken such measures it shall, after giving that State the opportunity to submit its observations, issue a reasoned opinion specifying the points on which the Member State concerned has not complied with the judgment of the Court of Justice.

   If the Member State concerned fails to take the necessary measures to comply with the Court's judgment within the time limit laid down by the Commission, the latter may bring the case before the Court of Justice. In so doing it shall specify the amount of the lump sum or penalty to be paid by the Member State concerned which it considers appropriate in the circumstances.

If the Court of Justice finds that the Member State concerned has not complied with its judgment it may impose a lump sum or penalty payment on it.

This procedure shall be without prejudice to Article 227.

Following a judgment of the Court of Justice pursuant to Art 226, the Member State is obliged to take the necessary measures to give effect to the judgment (Art 228(1)). This may require national legislation being implemented, amended or repealed to remedy the breach of Community law. If the Member State fails to comply with the judgment it will be in breach of its Art 228(1) duty. The Commission is then empowered by Art 228(2) to initiate fresh enforcement proceedings for breach of Art 228(1). The three Art 226 stages will apply (Art 228(2)). If the Commission decides to implement stage three (i.e. referral to the Court of Justice), the Commission will recommend a lump sum or penalty payment which should be imposed against the defaulting Member State. However, this is only a recommendation; the Court of Justice can levy any amount it wishes. There is no upper limit.

Prior to the TEU, Art 228(2) carried no sanction. All the Court of Justice was empowered to do was to make a declaration that a Member State was acting in breach of its Community law obligations. The incorporation of financial sanctions into the Art 228 procedure strengthens the Commission's hand in ensuring that Member States comply with their Community obligations. However, the Commission will still seek to resolve the conflict informally; it will explore every possible avenue before initiating Court proceedings.

On 8 January 1997 the Commission agreed a procedure with regard to recommending to the Court the use of penalties (OJ 1997 C 63/2). It started with a basic penalty of 55 euros per day, which would be multiplied by factors to account for the gravity of the breach, the length of time it had lasted and the relative wealth of the state. The UK would face a minimum daily penalty of 90,000 euros and a maximum of 537,500 euros. France and Germany have larger economies and therefore would face increased penalties, while Italy would be liable to a slightly lower penalty.

In the following case, the Court of Justice imposed a financial penalty on Greece in Art 228(2) proceedings and commented upon the Commission's pecuniary penalty guidelines:

Commission v *Hellenic Republic* (Case C-387/97)

Greece had failed to fulfil its obligations under Art 4, Directive 75/442 on waste (OJ 1975 L 194/39) and Art 5, Directive 78/319 on toxic and dangerous waste (OJ 1978 L 84/43), whereby Member States had to take measures to ensure that, respectively, waste and toxic and dangerous waste were disposed of without endangering human health and harming the environment. In addition, Greece had failed to comply with Art 6, Directive 74/442 and Art 12, Directive 78/319, whereby the competent authorities were required to draw up plans in relation to waste disposal.

The Commission received a complaint in September 1987 about the uncontrolled tipping in the mouth of the River Kouroupitos in Chania, Crete, of waste including household refuse, refuse from military bases, hospitals and clinics, and residues from salt factories, poultry farms, slaughterhouses and industrial sites. The Commission brought the matter to the attention of the Greek government which in reply referred, *inter alia*, to the opposition of the Chania population to the creation of new landfill sites in the area.

The Commission in due course brought proceedings under the former Art 169 EC Treaty (now Art 226) which culminated in the judgment in Case C-45/91, given on 7 April 1992. In finding against Greece, the Court of Justice pointed out, *inter alia*, that a Member State could not plead internal circumstances such as difficulties of implementation to justify a failure to comply with obligations laid down by Community law (see above).

After further communications between the Commission and the Greek government between 1993 and 1996, the Commission issued a reasoned opinion to the effect that, by continuing not to draw up or implement requisite waste disposal plans, Greece had failed to comply with the 1992 judgment. The Commission therefore brought an action under Art 171(2) EC Treaty (now Art 228(2)).

In its judgment, the Court of Justice concluded that waste was still being tipped into the Kouroupitos in an uncontrolled and unlawful manner and, although the Greek government had stated that it was going to end the operation of the Chania tip after August 1988 and create new disposal sites, that had still not been done.

It had not been proved that Greece had failed to comply with the judgment in Case C-45/91 in relation to Art 5, Directive 78/319, but in other respects that judgment had not been complied with.

The Court of Justice stated that Art 171(2) EC Treaty (now Art 228(2)) did not specify the period within which a judgment had to be complied with, but the importance of immediate and uniform application of Community law meant that the process of compliance had to be initiated at once and completed as soon as possible.

In the absence of provisions in the Treaty, the Court stated that the Commission could adopt guidelines for determining how the lump sums or penalty payments which it intended to propose to the Court were calculated, so as in particular to ensure equal treatment between the Member States. The Court of Justice then referred to the Commission's guidelines and continued:

> The Commission's suggestion that account should be taken both of the gross domestic product of the Member State concerned, and of the number of votes in the Council, appeared appropriate in that it enabled that State's ability to pay to be reflected while keeping the variation between Member States within a reasonable range.
>
> Those suggestions could not bind the court but were a useful point of reference.
>
> First, since the principal aim of penalty payments was that the Member State should remedy the breach of obligations as soon as possible, a penalty payment had to be set that was appropriate to the circumstances and proportionate both to the breach which had been found and to the State's ability to pay.
>
> Second, the degree of urgency that the Member State should fulfil its obligations could vary in accordance with the breach.
>
> In that light, and as the Commission had suggested, the basic criteria which were to be taken into account in order to ensure that penalty payments had coercive force and Community law was applied uniformly and effectively were, in principle, the duration of the infringement, its degree of seriousness and the ability of the Member State to pay.
>
> In applying those criteria, regard should be had in particular to the effects of the failure to comply on private and public interests, and to the urgency of getting the Member State to fulfil its obligations.
>
> In the present case, having regard to the nature of the breaches of obligations, which continued to the present day, a penalty payment was the means best suited to the circumstances.
>
> The duration of the infringement was considerable, as was its degree of seriousness and in particular the effect on private and public interests, given, *inter alia*, that the failure to comply with the obligation in article 4 of Directive 75/442 could, by the very nature of that obligation, directly endanger human health and harm the environment.

In the above case, the Court of Justice ordered Greece to pay to the Commission, into the account of 'EC own resources', a penalty payment of 20,000 euros for each day of delay in implementing the measures necessary to comply with the judgment in Case C-45/91 from delivery of the present judgment (4 July 2000) until the judgment in Case C-45/91 had been complied with. The interesting point here is that the Court only applied the daily penalty from the date of the current judgment and not 'a reasonable period' after its initial judgment when it had been held that Greece was in breach of its Community law obligations (7 April 1992). Nevertheless, the potency of the amended Art 228 is clearly amplified in the above case.

In the following case, an action was brought before the Court of Justice for France's failure to fulfil its obligations under Art 228(2) EC Treaty:

Commission v France (Case C-304/02)

It was alleged that France had failed to comply with the judgment of 11 June 1991 in **Commission v France** (Case C-64/88), in which it had been found that France had failed to fulfil its obligations under regulations concerning fishing and the control of fishing activities. The Commission concluded, following large numbers of inspections in various French ports that: (i) there continued to be inadequate controls; and (ii) it was widely known that the action taken in respect of infringements was inadequate. Consequently, in its submission, France's failure to fulfil its obligations persisted after the judgment had been delivered, in breach of the Common Fisheries Policy, even though the French government had made efforts to implement the Community provisions.

The Court of Justice began by recalling the importance of complying with Community rules in the area of the Common Fisheries Policy, since compliance with such obligations is to 'ensure the protection of fishing grounds, the conservation of the biological resources of the sea and their exploitation on a sustainable basis in appropriate economic and social conditions'. The Court found, following an examination of the facts submitted to it in the Commission's inspection reports, that France had not carried out controls of fishing activities in accordance with the Community rules and had not taken all the necessary measures to comply with the judgment in **Commission v France** (Case C-64/88).

As regards the second complaint raised by the Commission, maintaining that France was taking insufficient action in respect of infringements of the Common Fisheries Policy, the Court pointed out that if 'the competent authorities of a Member State were systematically to refrain from taking action against the persons responsible for such infringements, both the conservation and management of fishery resources and the uniform application of the common fisheries policy would be jeopardised'. Since France had not done what was necessary to take action systematically against offenders, the Court concluded that there was a failure to fulfil obligations on the part of France, which had not taken all the necessary measures to comply with the judgment in **Commission v France** (Case C-64/88).

In relation to the financial penalties which could be imposed on France and in the light of the Advocate-General's Opinion of 29 April 2004, the Court raised the issue (i) of its ability to impose a lump sum penalty, although the Commission had requested a penalty payment; and (ii) of its right to impose both a lump sum penalty *and* a penalty payment. The Court of Justice reopened the oral procedure because there had been no argument in the proceedings on these two issues.

In relation to the possibility of imposing both a penalty payment and a lump sum, the Court observed that Art 228(2) EC Treaty has the objective 'of inducing a defaulting

Member State to comply with a judgment establishing a breach of obligations and thereby of ensuring that Community law is in fact applied'. The Court considered the measures provided for by that provision (the lump sum and the penalty payment) to pursue the same objective. **The purpose of a penalty payment is to induce a Member State to put an end as soon as possible to a breach of obligations which, in the absence of the measure, would tend to persist (persuasive effect), while the lump sum 'is based more on assessment of the effects on public and private interests of the failure of the Member State concerned to comply with its obligations, in particular where the breach has persisted for a long period since the judgment which initially established it' (deterrent effect).** The Court concluded that where the breach of obligations both has continued for a long period and is inclined to persist, it is possible to have recourse to both types of penalty. **Therefore, the conjunction 'or' in Art 228(2) EC Treaty, 'may ... have an alternative or a cumulative sense and must therefore be read in the context in which it is used'. The fact that both measures were not imposed in previous cases cannot constitute an obstacle, if imposing both measures appears appropriate, regard being had to the circumstances of the case. Thus, 'it is for the Court, in each case, to assess in light of its circumstances the financial penalties to be imposed', since the Court is not bound by the Commission's suggestions.**

Finally, the Court considered its discretion as to the financial penalties that can be imposed. When a penalty payment is to be imposed on a Member State in order to penalise non-compliance with a judgment establishing a breach of obligations, it is for the Court to set the penalty payment so that it is appropriate to the circumstances and proportionate both to the breach that has been established and to the ability to pay of the Member State concerned. For that purpose, the basic criteria which must be taken into account in order to ensure that penalty payments have coercive force and Community law is applied uniformly and effectively are, in principle, the duration of the infringement, its degree of seriousness and the ability of the Member State concerned to pay. In applying those criteria, regard should be had in particular to the effects of failure to comply on private and public interests and to the urgency of getting the Member State concerned to fulfil its obligations.

The Court found that France's breach of obligations had persisted over a long period and imposed a dual financial penalty:

(i)   EUR 57,761,250, by way of a **penalty payment** for each period of six months from delivery of the current judgment at the end of which the judgment in **Commission v France** (Case C-64/88) had not yet been fully complied with; and

(ii) EUR 20,000,000 as a **lump sum penalty.**

The above case clearly establishes the principle that the Court of Justice can impose both a penalty payment and a lump sum penalty; a penalty payment is imposed to persuade the defaulting Member State to comply with the judgment, whereas a lump sum penalty is imposed to deter all Member States from breaching their Community law obligations.

In the following case, despite Italy's breach of Art 228(2) EC Treaty, the Court of Justice decided **not** to impose a penalty payment which had been suggested by the Commission:

Commission v *Italy* (Case C-119/04)

In 1995 Italy adopted a law to reform foreign language teaching. The post of 'foreign-language assistant' was abolished and replaced by that of 'linguistic associate'. Following that law's entry into force, the Commission received several complaints from former foreign-language assistants that, in the conversion to linguistic associate, their length of service as assistants had not been taken into account for the purposes of pay and social security. The Commission therefore instigated legal proceedings against Italy.

On 26 June 2001, in **Commission** *v* **Italy** (Case C-212/99), the Court of Justice found that Italy had failed to fulfil its obligations under the provisions of the EC Treaty guaranteeing freedom of movement for workers, by not guaranteeing recognition of the acquired rights of former foreign-language assistants in six Italian universities, even though such recognition was guaranteed to Italian nationals.

Believing that Italy had still not complied with that judgment, on 4 March 2004, the Commission commenced the present action (C-119/04) against Italy requesting that the Court find Italy in breach of the judgment of June 2001 and impose a penalty payment of EUR 309,750 per day from the date of judgment in the present case until Italy had complied.

The case was decided by the Court in July 2006. The Court held that, by not ensuring, at the date of expiry of the period prescribed in the reasoned opinion, recognition of the rights acquired by former assistants who had become associates and linguistic experts, even though such recognition was guaranteed to all national workers, Italy had failed to take all the measures necessary to comply with the judgment of 26 June 2001 in **Commission** *v* **Italy** (Case C-212/99) and had therefore failed to fulfil its obligations under the EC Treaty.

However, **in view of the fact that the breach of obligations no longer persisted on the date of the Court's examination of the facts, the Court rejected the Commission's application for the imposition of a penalty payment.**

Figure 7.2 consists of a flowchart setting out the application of the Art 228(2) EC Treaty procedure: imposition of a financial penalty on a Member State which fails to comply with Art 228(1) EC Treaty.

Constitutional Treaty

If the proposed Constitutional Treaty had come into force, Art III-362 would have replaced Art 228 EC Treaty. Article III-362 would have been worded similarly to Art 228, although under Art III-362 there would have been no explicit requirement to issue a reasoned opinion before bringing proceedings before the Court of Justice.

Interim measures

Breaches of Community law may occur inadvertently or intentionally. In the former case, Member States will normally take remedial action when the breach is brought to their attention by the Commission. In the latter case, Member States may risk action by the Commission when they are confronted by internal political pressures which they cannot, or will not, resist. They will often do so in the hope that, by the time the Commission commences proceedings, a solution can be found and the illegal action can be terminated. Such considerations appear to have motivated the French government in the ban

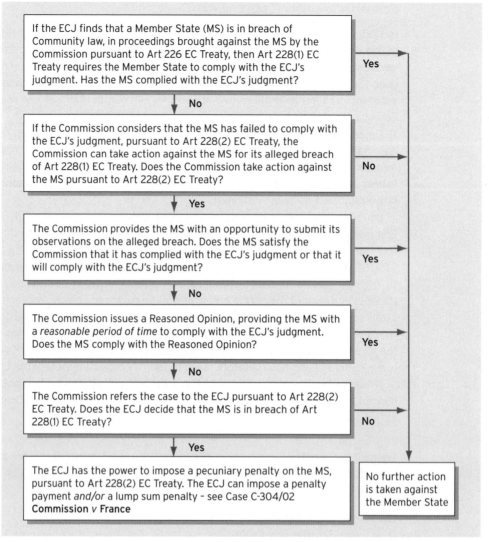

Figure 7.2 The Art 228(2) EC Treaty procedure: imposition of a financial penalty on a Member State which fails to comply with Art 228(1) EC Treaty

it imposed on the import of lamb and mutton from other Member States, principally the UK (**Commission v France (Re Sheepmeat)** (Case 232/78)). Similar considerations seem, at least, to have been in the mind of the French government during 1999 when it refused to lift the ban on the sale of UK beef. A worldwide ban had earlier been imposed by the Community in response to concerns about UK beef being affected by Bovine Spongiform Encephalitis (BSE) or 'mad cow disease'. When the ban was lifted during 1999 the French refused to comply, and the Commission issued proceedings against France pursuant to Art 226 (**Commission v France** (Case C-1/00).

Given that several years may elapse between the initial complaint to the Commission and the hearing before the Court of Justice, the Commission, in circumstances where continuing damage is being caused while the case is processed, may apply to the Court for interim relief. Interim relief may be granted by the Court under Art 243 EC Treaty (previously Art 186), which simply states:

> The Court of Justice may in any cases before it prescribe any necessary interim measures.

The speed of the relief available is demonstrated by **Commission v Ireland** (Case 61/77R). In this case, Ireland had introduced fisheries conservation measures which the Commission regarded as contrary to the Treaty. The Commission commenced Art 226 proceedings and, at the same time, made an application for an interim order requiring Ireland to suspend the operation of the legislation. Only nine days later the Court gave judgment. It doubted the validity of the Irish legislation on grounds of discrimination and, after several adjournments to promote a settlement, ordered the Irish Government to suspend the measures within five days. The following case also concerned the issue of conservation of diminishing fishing stocks:

Commission v UK (Case C-246/89R)

The UK government, concerned about fishing vessels from other Member States operating in UK waters under UK 'flags of convenience' to gain access to UK fishing quotas, enacted the Merchant Shipping Act 1988. The Act confined the issue of fishing licences to companies registered in the UK and whose owners or shareholders were UK nationals or were ordinarily resident in the UK. The Act was clearly discriminatory under Art 7 EC Treaty (now Art 12), and it was an obstacle to establishment under Art 43 EC Treaty. The UK government argued that the measures were necessary to protect the UK fishing quota. Pending the hearing of the case, could the Spanish shipowners who had challenged the licensing system continue to fish? The Court of Justice noted that the owners of the vessels were suffering heavy losses while their ships remained idle, and would soon have to sell them under very adverse conditions. *Prima facie*, the companies had a right to continue in business and, given the urgency of the situation, the Court ordered the UK to suspend the relevant provisions of the Merchant Shipping Act 1988. The Court of Justice subsequently found that there was unlawful discrimination (**Factortame** (Case C-221/89)).

The following case concerned Germany's imposition of a new tax on heavy goods vehicles with a view to encouraging greater use of water transport on the country's inland waterways:

Commission v Germany (Case C-195/90R)

The German tax, which was to be imposed largely for environmental reasons, was to take effect on 1 July 1990. The Commission applied for what was, in effect, an *ex parte* interim order from the President of the Court of Justice, which was ordered on 28 June, pending the full hearing of the interim application. Under the Court's Rules of Procedure, applicants need to state grounds indicating (i) a *prima facie* case establishing the breach of the law alleged; and (ii) urgency and the need for the interim measures.

On the law allegedly infringed, the Commission argued that the new German tax breached the 'stand-still' provisions of Art 72 EC Treaty, which were intended to protect the present position until a common Community transport policy was adopted under Art 70. It also breached Art 90 EC Treaty (the prohibition against discriminatory taxation, see Chapter 17), since the charge, although payable by all vehicles of the appropriate weight, was offset in relation to German vehicles by a reduction in German vehicle tax. The Court of Justice accepted that these arguments constituted a sufficiently strong case to meet the first requirement of the rules of procedure, but were the circumstances sufficiently urgent for interim relief? The Court has laid down that the urgency of an application for an interim measure is to be assessed in the light of the extent to which an interim order is necessary to avoid serious and irreparable damage (**Commission** v **Greece** (Case C-170/94R)). The Commission argued that the new German tax would disrupt its attempts to create a common transport policy and would drive a number of carriers out of business before the full proceedings could be heard. The German government insisted that if the tax was suspended it would suffer irreparable damage in the loss of tax, which could not be recovered subsequently if the tax was found to be lawful in the main proceedings. The Court accepted the Commission's argument of the need to protect the *status quo* and the need to avoid irreparable damage to transport undertakings. The German government could hardly be said to be suffering a loss to its exchequer, since the tax had never existed before. The interim order to suspend the operation of the new tax was, therefore, confirmed.

Subsequently, an application for interim relief arose out of the award of contracts to replace old buses in Belgium and the alleged breach of the procedures laid down in Directive 90/531 by the Société Régionale Walloon du Transport (SRWT). The contract had been awarded (wrongly, the Commission maintained) and the delivery of the first buses was due to take place before the full hearing could take place. The Commission argued that there was a risk of serious and irreparable damage, in that the award of the contract and the first deliveries would confront the Commission with a *fait accompli*, and would create the conditions for a serious and immediate threat to the Community legal order. The Court agreed that the failure to comply with a directive applicable to a public contract constituted a serious threat to the Community legal order, and that a declaration at the conclusion of Art 226 proceedings could not cancel the damage suffered. However, the Court felt that an application for interim relief should be pursued with due diligence. The Commission had taken more than two months to apply for relief after one of the unsuccessful tenderers had informed it of the situation. The formal contract was, in the meantime, concluded. The Commission's application for interim relief was refused (**Commission** v **Belgium** (Case C-87/94)).

Constitutional Treaty

If the Constitutional Treaty had come into force, Art III-379(2) would have replaced Art 243 EC Treaty. Article III-379(2) would have been worded similarly to Art 243.

Other actions against Member States

The power of the Commission to take cases directly to the Court of Justice where a Member State has granted aid to an undertaking in breach of Art 87 EC Treaty will be considered in Chapter 19. Failure to abolish the offending aid within the time specified will entitle the Commission to proceed without giving a reasoned opinion as required under Arts 226 and 227.

There are also special powers given to the Commission under Art 95(9) EC Treaty to enable it to bring Member States before the Court of Justice without going through the

Art 226 procedure in cases where a Member State has used its power to derogate from a harmonising directive on grounds of major needs or protection of the environment or the working environment. This could apply if the Commission believes that the Member State is using its power of derogation improperly.

Summary

Now you have read this chapter you should be able to:

- Explain the function of the Art 226 EC Treaty procedure, and understand the circumstances in which the Commission may commence proceedings against a Member State.

- Explain the purpose of Art 227 EC Treaty and identify why a Member State may be reluctant to initiate action pursuant to it.

- Outline the following key events which occur during the course of Art 226 EC Treaty proceedings:

  - investigation of the alleged breach by the Commission;

  - submission of a Member State's observations on the alleged breach to the Commission;

  - the Commission's issue of a reasoned opinion setting out details of the alleged breach;

  - the Member State's compliance (or otherwise) with such reasoned opinion within a reasonable period of time;

  - the Commission's referral of the case to the European Court of Justice if the Member State fails to comply with such reasoned opinion;

  - a Member State's obligation to comply with a judgment of the European Court of Justice (pursuant to Art 228(1) EC Treaty); and

  - the Commission's power to take action pursuant to Art 228(2) EC Treaty if a Member State fails to comply with the judgment of the European Court of Justice.

- Understand the purpose of Art 228(2) EC Treaty and the circumstances in which the European Court of Justice may impose a lump sum and/or penalty payment on a Member State which has failed to comply with a judgment of the European Court of Justice pursuant to Art 228(1) EC Treaty.

References

Audretsch, H.A.H. (1986) *Supervision in European Community Law* (2nd edn), North-Holland.

Further reading

Textbooks

Audretsch, H.A.H. (1986) *Supervision in European Community Law* (2nd edn), North-Holland.

Craig, P. and De Burca, G. (2003) *EU Law Text, Cases and Materials* (3rd edn), Oxford University Press, Chapter 10.

Foster, N. (2006) *Foster on EU Law* (1st edn), Oxford University Press, Chapter 6 (Sections 6.1 to 6.3).

Steiner, J., Woods, L. and Twigg-Flesner, C. (2006) *EU Law* (9th edn), Oxford University Press, Chapter 10.

Storey, T. and Turner, C. (2005) *Unlocking EU Law* (1st edn), Hodder Arnold, Chapter 6 (Sections 6.1 and 6.2).

Tillotson, J. and Foster, N. (2003) *Text, Cases and Materials on EU Law* (4th edn), Cavendish Publishing, Chapter 20.

Weatherill, S. (2006) *Cases and Materials on EU Law* (7th edn), Oxford University Press, Chapter 4.

Journal articles

Dashwood, A. and White, R., 'Enforcement Actions and Articles 169 & 170' (1989) 14 EL Rev 388.

Harding, C., 'Member State Enforcement of European Community Measures: The Chimera of "Effective Enforcement"' (1997) 4 MJ 5.

Harlow, C. and Rawlings, R., 'Accountability and law enforcement: The centralised EU infringement procedure' (2006) 31 EL Rev 447.

Rawlings, R., 'Engaged Elites, Citizen Action and Institutional Attitudes in Commission Enforcement' (2000) 6 ELJ 4.

Van den Bossche, P., 'In Search of Remedies for Non-compliance: The Experience of the European Community' (1996) 3 MJ 371.

Wennerås, P., 'A new dawn for Commission enforcement under Articles 226 and 228 EC: General and persistent (gap) infringements, lump sums and penalty payments' (2006) 43 CML Rev 31.

Judicial review of acts of Community institutions

Aims and objectives

At the end of this chapter you should understand:

- The range of Community acts which can be reviewed by the CFI and the Court of Justice pursuant to Art 230 EC Treaty and be able to compare and contrast the conditions which apply to a 'privileged applicant' and a 'non-privileged applicant'.

- The four grounds for review under Art 230.

- How an indirect challenge to a Community act could be pursued under Arts 241 and 234 EC Treaty.

- The power under Art 232 EC Treaty to challenge a Community institution's failure to act.

- How the Court of Justice applies the rules relating to a claim for damages against a Community institution for unlawful acts, pursuant to Art 288 EC Treaty.

Legality of Community acts: Article 230 EC Treaty

Although the Community does not have a formal constitution, the EC Treaty confers specific powers and duties on each of the institutions and establishes what the Court of Justice has, on a number of occasions, referred to as 'a new legal order' (**Opinion 1/91** [1991] ECR I-6079). Each of the institutions has a limited competence and must carry out its functions in the way specified in the Treaty and according to general principles of Community law (Art 7(1) EC Treaty).

If an institution exceeds its powers or uses them unlawfully, its acts may be subject to review by the Court of Justice under Art 230 (as amended by the ToA):

The Court of Justice shall review the legality of acts adopted jointly by the European Parliament and the Council, of acts of the Council, of the Commission and of the European Central Bank, other than recommendations and opinions, and of acts of the European Parliament intended to produce legal effects vis-à-vis third parties.

It shall for this purpose have jurisdiction in actions brought by a Member State, the Council or the Commission on grounds of lack of competence, infringement of an essential procedural requirement, infringement of this Treaty or of any rule of law relating to its application, or misuse of powers.

The Court shall have jurisdiction under the same conditions in actions brought by the

European Parliament, by the Court of Auditors and by the ECB for the purpose of protecting their prerogatives.

Any natural or legal person may, under the same conditions, institute proceedings against a decision addressed to that person or against a decision which, although in the form of a regulation or a decision addressed to another person, is of direct and individual concern to the former.

The proceedings provided for in this Article shall be instituted within two months of the publication of the measure, or of its notification to the plaintiff, or, in the absence thereof, of the day on which it came to the knowledge of the latter, as the case may be.

The constituent parts of Art 230 EC Treaty raise *five* issues:

1. When is an action barred by lapse of time?
2. What type of act may be reviewed?
3. Who may challenge such an act, i.e. who has, in the language of English administrative law, the *locus standi* to mount a challenge?
4. What are the grounds for challenge?
5. What are the consequences of an annulment?

These five issues are now considered further.

Time limits

Article 230 EC Treaty provides that proceedings should be instituted within two months of:

- the date of publication of the measure; or
- notification of the measure to the applicant; or, in the absence thereof
- the day on which the measure came to the knowledge of the applicant, as the case may be.

The third criterion, i.e. the day on which the measure came to the knowledge of the applicant, is subsidiary to the first and second criteria of publication or notification of the measure. Moreover, if the third criterion applies, the period for bringing an action can begin to run only from the moment when the applicant acquires precise knowledge of the content of the decision in question and of the reasons on which it is based in such a way as to enable him to exercise his right of action. It is for the party who has knowledge of a decision to request the whole text thereof within a reasonable period. Accordingly, the Court of First Instance (CFI) held in **COBB v Commission** (Case T-485/04) that where an applicant requests communication of a decision excluding eligible expenditure under a programme implemented under the European Regional Development Fund (ERDF) more than four months after becoming aware of it, a reasonable time within the meaning of the case law cited is exceeded.

In the following case, the CFI had an opportunity to add an important rider to the application of those principles in a case concerning litigation on state aid:

Olsen v Commission (Case T-17/02) (under appeal, Case C-320/05P)

The applicant contested a Commission decision authorising state aid paid to a Spanish competitor. Its action was lodged just over six months after Spain, the only addressee of the

contested decision, was notified of it. As the applicant was not the addressee of the contested decision, the CFI held in its judgment that the criterion of notification of the decision was not applicable to it. As to whether, in this case, the criterion of publication or that of the day on which a measure came to the knowledge of an applicant was applicable, the CFI cited the case law according to which, with regard to measures which are published in the *Official Journal*, the criterion of the day on which a measure came to the knowledge of an applicant was not applicable; **in such circumstances it was the date of publication which marked the starting point of the period prescribed for instituting proceedings** (Case C-122/95 **Germany** *v* **Council** [1998] ECR I-973, at para 39).

In the area of state aid, decisions by means of which the Commission, after a preliminary examination, finds that no doubts are raised as to the compatibility with the common market of a notified measure and decides that the measure is compatible with the common market, are to be the subject of a summary notice published in the *Official Journal* (Regulation 659/1999). Moreover, in accordance with the recent but established practice of the Commission, the summary notice includes a reference to the website of the Secretariat General of the Commission and the statement that the full text of the decision in question, from which all confidential information has been removed, can be found there, in the authentic language version or versions. **The CFI held that the fact that the Commission gives third parties full access to the text of a decision placed on its website, combined with publication of a summary notice in the *Official Journal* enabling interested parties to identify the decision in question and notifying them of this possibility of access via the Internet, must be considered to be publication for the purposes of Art 230(5) EC Treaty.** In this case, the applicant could legitimately expect that the contested decision would be published in the *Official Journal*. As its application was lodged **even before such publication,** it was held admissible.

The two-month period expires at the end of the day in the last month which bears the same number as the day of the occurrence of the event which caused time to start running (**Misset** *v* **Council** (Case 152/85)). So, for example, if the measure had been published in the *Official Journal* on 2 February 2001, the two-month period would expire at midnight on 2 April 2001. The CFI has held that where an applicant lets the time limit for bringing an action against a decision unequivocally affecting his interests expire, he cannot start time running again by asking the institution to reconsider its decision and then start proceedings against the confirmation of the decision (**Cobrecaf SA** *v* **Commission** (Case T-514/93)). The expiry of the period of time allowed for bringing proceedings will not be fatal if the applicant can rely on Art 45 of the Statute of the Court, which provides:

> No right shall be prejudiced in consequence of the expiry of the time limit if the party concerned proves the existence of unforeseeable circumstances or of force majeure.

The Court of Justice has, however, shown reluctance in allowing applications outside the statutory time limits. Time limits do not apply where the issue of the legality of a Community measure is raised in Art 234 EC Treaty proceedings (see below). However, a national court cannot refer a case under Art 234 to the Court of Justice if the applicant could have challenged the Community measure within the time limit under Art 230, but failed to do so (**TWD Deggendorf** (Case C-188/92); see Chapter 6).

Reviewable acts

Not every act of an institution may be reviewed. *Prima facie*, it is only those acts which Art 249 EC Treaty defines as legally binding – i.e. regulations, directives and decisions – which are subject to review. Opinions and recommendations are not reviewable. However, other acts, not specified in Art 249, have been treated by the Court of Justice as subject to review. In **Commission v Council** (Case 22/70), the Court of Justice held that a resolution passed by the Council to participate in a European Transport Agreement was reviewable under Art 230. The Court refused to interpret Art 249 restrictively, and declared that 'an action for annulment must ... be available in the case of all measures adopted by the institutions, whatever their nature and form, which are intended to have legal effects'. In the following case, the Court of Justice emphasised that the determining factor is whether or not an act has legal consequences, no matter how it has been arrived at:

IBM v Commission (Case 60/81)

The Court of Justice stated that:

> In order to ascertain whether the measures in question are acts within the meaning of Article 173 [now Art 230] it is necessary ... to look to their substance. According to the consistent case law of the Court any measure the legal effects of which are binding on, and capable of affecting the interests of, the applicant by bringing about a distinct change in his legal position is an act or decision which may be the subject of an action under Article 173 [now Art 230] for a declaration that it is void. However, the form in which such acts or decisions are cast is, in principle, immaterial as regards the question whether they are open to challenge under that article.

It is, however, often difficult to distinguish between form and substance. An act may not have any legal consequence precisely because it has not been adopted in the form required. In **Air France v Commission** (Case T-3/93) the Commissioner responsible for competition policy, Sir Leon Brittan, had issued a press statement about the merger between Dan Air and British Airways, declaring that it would result in a sufficient concentration of air transport to have a Community dimension. Air France's attempt to challenge the statement failed at the first hurdle, because the statement had not been adopted by the whole Commission and did not have the *form* of a legal act. It could, therefore, have no legal consequences (see also **Nefarma v Commission** (Case T-113/89)).

As it was originally drawn, Art 230 made no mention of measures adopted by the European Parliament. Despite this, the Court of Justice held, in **Parti Ecologiste ('Les Verts') v European Parliament** (Case 294/83) that measures adopted by the Parliament intended to have legal effects *vis-à-vis* third parties were subject to annulment under Art 230 (see also **Luxembourg v European Parliament** (Case C-213/88)). The Court of Justice has also held that a declaration made by the President of the Parliament at the conclusion of the debate by Parliament on the Community's budget has the character of a legal act and is also subject to annulment (**Council v Parliament** (Case 34/86); **Council v European Parliament** (Case C-284/90)). That case should be contrasted with that of the following which likewise concerned whether a declaration of the President of the Parliament was a measure open to challenge:

Le Pen v *Parliament* (Case T-353/00)

The declaration of the President of the Parliament stated that, in accordance with Art 12(2) of the Act concerning the election of representatives to the Parliament by direct universal suffrage, annexed to the Council Decision of 20 September 1976, 'the ... Parliament takes note of the notification of the French government declaring the disqualification of Mr Le Pen from holding office'. The CFI held that the declaration was not open to challenge. In its judgment, the CFI stated that the intervention of the European Parliament under the first subparagraph of Art 12(2) of the abovementioned Act was restricted to taking note of the declaration, already made by the national authorities, that the applicant's seat was vacant. The CFI accordingly held that the declaration of the President of the Parliament was not intended to produce legal effects of its own, distinct from those of the decree dated 31 March 2000 of the French Prime Minister stating that the applicant's ineligibility brought to an end his term of office as a representative in the European Parliament.

Le Pen's appeal to the Court of Justice was dismissed (Case C-208/03P).

Measures taken by the Parliament affecting third parties are now specifically subject to review as a result of amendments made to Art 230 by the TEU. A measure adopted by the Court of Auditors has also been held to be reviewable under Art 230 (**Maurissen and Others** *v* **Court of Auditors** (Cases 193 & 194/87)). A decision by the Commission to close the file on a complaint alleging breach of Art 82 EC Treaty has also been held to be a 'decision' reviewable under Art 230 (**SFEI and Others** *v* **Commission** (Case C-39/93P)).

Although the acts of the Council are reviewable, the representatives of the Member States must be acting *as* the Council for Art 230 to apply. In **Parliament** *v* **Council** (Cases C-181/91 & C-248/91), the Parliament attempted to challenge a decision made at a Council meeting granting special aid to Bangladesh. The Court of Justice held that acts adopted by representatives of the Member States acting not as members of the Council but as representatives of their governments amounted to the collective exercise of the competencies of the Member States. They were not, therefore, acts of the Council and were not, consequently, subject to review by the Court of Justice.

Some acts are specifically excluded from review. For example, Art 35(5) TEU (as amended by the ToA) provides that the Court of Justice shall have no jurisdiction to review the validity or proportionality of operations carried out by the police or other law enforcement services of a Member State. The Court has, however, decided that it does have jurisdiction to determine the *scope* of such exclusions. In **Svenska Journalistforbundet** *v* **Council of European Union** (Case T-174/95) the CFI ruled that, although it could not rule on the substance of decisions contained in Council documents, it did have jurisdiction to review the refusal to journalists of access to the documents themselves. The CFI accordingly annulled a decision by the Council refusing access to certain documents concerning the European Police Office.

Continuing the theme of acts which are not subject to review, in the following case the CFI held that decisions by the Commission to commence legal proceedings against certain American cigarette manufacturers before a federal court in the USA did not constitute measures that were open to challenge:

Philip Morris International and Others v Commission (Joined Cases T-377/00, T-379/00, T 380/00, T-260/01 and T-272/01)

The CFI held that a decision to bring court proceedings does not in itself alter the legal position in question, but has the effect merely of opening a procedure whose purpose is to achieve a change in that position through a judgment. While noting that the commencement of legal proceedings may give rise to certain consequences by operation of law, the CFI held that their commencement does not in itself determine definitively the obligations of the parties to the case and that that determination results only from the judgment of the court. The CFI stated that this finding applies both to proceedings before the Community Courts and to proceedings before courts of the Member States and even of non-member countries, such as the United States.

Philip Morris International's appeal to the Court of Justice was dismissed (Case C-131/03P).

The CFI has held that where, in the context of an action for annulment, the contested measure is *negative*, it must be appraised in the light of the nature of the request to which it constitutes a reply.

In particular, the refusal by a Community institution to withdraw or amend a measure may constitute a decision whose legality may be reviewed under Art 230 EC Treaty only if the measure which the Community institution refuses to withdraw or amend could itself have been contested under that provision (**Institouto N. Avgerinopoulou and Others** *v* **Commission** (Case T-139/02), and **Comunidad Autónoma de Andalucía** *v* **Commission** (Case T-29/03)).

In **Comunidad Autónoma de Andalucía** *v* **Commission**, the European Anti-Fraud Office (OLAF) issued a final report following an external investigation. OLAF forwarded the report to the competent Spanish authorities in accordance with Art 9, Regulation 1073/1999. The CFI held that a letter from the Director-General of OLAF, informing the applicant that it was not possible to investigate its complaint directed against the final report, could not be regarded as a decision against which proceedings could be brought. This was due to the fact that the report did not constitute a measure producing binding legal effects such as to affect the applicant's interests; rather, it was a recommendation or an opinion which lacked binding legal effects.

Competition law cases

In the field of Community competition law, a number of cases have concerned the issue of whether or not the act is reviewable. In **Coe Clerici Logistics** *v* **Commission** (Case T-52/00), a letter from the Commission refusing to act on an undertaking's complaint based on Arts 82 and 86 EC Treaty was not, in principle, a measure against which an action for annulment could be brought. After recalling that the exercise of the Commission's power conferred by Art 86(3) EC Treaty to assess the compatibility of State measures with the Treaty rules was not coupled with an obligation on the part of the Commission to take action, the CFI held that legal or natural persons who request the Commission to take action under Art 86(3) do not, in principle, have the right to bring an action against a Commission decision not to use the powers which it has under that article. However, since the applicant relied at the hearing on the judgment in **max.mobil** *v* **Commission** (Case T-54/99), the CFI added that 'if the contested act, in so far as it concerns infringement of Art 82 EC in conjunction with Article 86 EC, must be classified as a decision rejecting a complaint' as referred to in **max.mobil** *v* **Commission**, the applicant should, as complainant and addressee of that decision, be regarded as entitled to bring his action. In the present case the question as to the admissibility of the action did not affect the outcome of the dispute because the CFI held on the merits that the action was unfounded.

However, since the CFI gave judgment in **Coe Clerici Logistics** *v* **Commission**, the Court of Justice reversed the decision of **max.mobil** *v* **Commission** (Case T-54/99) on appeal:

Commission v *T-Mobile Austria GmbH* (Case C-141/02P)

[Note: max.mobil had become T-Mobile Austria GmbH prior to the appeal.]
The Court of Justice held that the CFI had erred in declaring max.mobil's action was admissible and therefore held that the judgment had to be set aside.

The case gave the Court an opportunity to be more specific about the scope of its decision in **Bundesverband der Bilanzbuchhalter** *v* **Commission** (Case C-107/95P), according to which the Commission is empowered to determine, using the powers conferred on it by Art 90(3) EC Treaty (now Art 86(3) EC Treaty), that a given State measure is incompatible with the rules of the Treaty and to indicate what measures the state to which a decision is addressed must adopt in order to comply with its obligations under Community law. It observed that it followed from that judgment that individuals may, in certain circumstances, be entitled to bring an action for annulment against a decision which the Commission addresses to a Member State on the basis of Art 90(3) EC Treaty if the conditions laid down in the fourth paragraph of Art 173 EC Treaty (now, the fourth paragraph of Art 230 EC Treaty) are satisfied. The Court held, however, that it follows from the wording of Art 90(3) EC Treaty and from the scheme of that article as a whole that **the Commission is not obliged to bring proceedings within the terms of those provisions, as individuals cannot require the Commission to take a position in a specific sense.** It held that the fact that max.mobil had a direct and individual interest in annulment of the Commission's decision to refuse to act on its complaint was not such as to confer on it a right to challenge that decision; nor could the applicant claim a right to bring an action pursuant to Regulation No 17 (now Regulation 1/2003), which is not applicable to Art 90 EC Treaty (see Chapter 22). According to the Court, that finding was not at variance with the principle of sound administration or with any other general principle of Community law. **No general principle of Community law requires that an undertaking be recognised as having standing before the Community judicature to challenge a refusal by the Commission to bring proceedings against a Member State on the basis of Art 90(3) EC Treaty (now Art 86(3) EC Treaty).**

The orders of the CFI in **Commerzbank** *v* **Commission** (Case T-219/01), **Dresdner Bank** *v* **Commission** (Case T-250/01) and **Reisebank** *v* **Commission** (Case T-216/01) resulted from challenges to decisions of the hearing officer which had been made pursuant to Art 8, Commission Decision 2001/462. Article 8 relates to the terms of reference of hearing officers in certain competition proceedings. By those decisions, several banks which were subject to administrative investigation to establish their participation in an arrangement contrary to Art 81 EC Treaty had been refused access to information relating to the circumstances which had led to the hearing officer terminating some of the administrative procedures which had been initiated against other banks. In each of the three cases the CFI held that the decision of the hearing officer in itself produced only limited effects, characteristic of a preparatory measure in the course of an administrative procedure initiated by the Commission, and could not therefore justify the action being admissible before that procedure had been completed. It followed that any infringement of rights of defence by the refusal, capable of rendering the administrative procedure unlawful, could properly be pleaded only in an action brought against the final decision finding that Art 81 had been infringed.

Finally, in the field of state aid, the CFI had the opportunity to clarify the case law concerning the ability to challenge decisions to initiate the formal investigation procedure envisaged in Art 88(2) EC Treaty. The CFI distinguished between cases which concerned the provisional classification of *new* aid and that of *existing* aid. Decisions initiating the formal examination procedure with regard to measures that have been provisionally classified as *new* aid have previously been held to have independent legal effects *vis-à-vis* the final decision for which they are a preparatory step (see judgments in **Government of Gibraltar *v* Commission** (Joined Cases T-195/01 and T-207/01), **Territorio Histórico de Guipúzcoa and Others *v* Commission** (Joined Cases T-269/99, T-271/99 and T-272/99) and **Territorio Histórico de Álava and Others *v* Commission** (Joined Cases T-346/99, T-347/99 and T-348/99)). This can be contrasted with the decision initiating the formal examination procedure which gave rise to the order in **Forum 187 *v* Commission** (Case T-276/02), in which the Belgian scheme at issue – the coordination centres scheme – was classified as a scheme of *existing* aid. The CFI held that such a decision does not produce any independent legal effects and, as such, did not constitute a challengeable measure.

Who may apply for review?

There are two categories of applicant:

- specified Community institutions and Member States – referred to as a 'privileged applicant';
- any natural or legal person – referred to as a 'non-privileged applicant'.

Different rules apply depending upon whether the applicant is privileged or non-privileged. It is much more difficult to prove standing for a non-privileged applicant.

Privileged applicants

Article 230 confers specific and unlimited rights of challenge on Member States, the Council of Ministers and the Commission. The European Parliament, the Court of Auditors and the European Central Bank have more limited rights of challenge to enable them to protect their prerogatives. Their powers to do so reflect decisions of the Court of Justice made on the basis of Art 230 in relation to the Parliament as it was originally framed, before amendment by the TEU. Member States may apply for review, even though they have no direct or indirect interest in the subject matter of the case but, for example, are concerned that the appropriate procedure should be used (**Italy *v* Commission** (Case 41/83)).

Non-privileged applicant

Article 230 limits access to challenge by a non-privileged applicant. A non-privileged applicant can only challenge the legality of a specified act in three cases:

- a decision addressed to the applicant;

- a decision addressed to another person which is of direct and individual concern to the applicant; and

- a decision in the form of a regulation, which is of direct and individual concern to the applicant.

The first of these is relatively straightforward. An applicant to whom a decision is addressed has standing to challenge the legality of such a decision in the Court of Justice, within the time limits specified in Art 230 (see above). Many decisions which are subject to challenge are made by the Commission in relation to competition law, and are challenged by those against whom they are made.

In contrast to a decision addressed to the applicant, the latter two are not so straightforward, and have produced a catalogue of litigation. Each of these is considered further below. However, before considering these two issues, the question of whether or not the applicant has a legal interest in bringing the proceedings is discussed.

Legal interest in bringing proceedings

An action for annulment brought by a natural or legal person is admissible only in so far as the applicant has a legal interest in seeing the contested measure annulled. Although a legal interest in bringing proceedings is not expressly required by Art 230 EC Treaty, the applicant must prove that he has such an interest in bringing proceedings. The CFI stated that this is an essential and fundamental prerequisite for any legal proceedings (**Schmitz-Gotha Fahrzeugwerke v Commission** (Case T-167/01)) and that, in the absence of a legal interest in bringing proceedings, it is unnecessary to examine whether the contested decision is of direct and individual concern to the applicant (**Olivieri v Commission and European Agency for the Evaluation of Medicinal Products** (Case T-326/99)).

That interest must be a vested and present interest and is assessed as at the date when the action is brought. If the interest which an applicant claims concerns a future legal situation, he must demonstrate that the prejudice to that situation is already certain (**NBV v Commission** (Case T-138/89), at para 33). Such an interest is not established by an applicant who seeks the annulment of a decision addressed to a Member State ordering it to recover State aid from various companies where, contrary to the applicant's assertions, the decision does not impose any joint and several obligation on him to repay the contested aid (**Schmitz-Gotha Fahrzeugwerke**).

The following case concerned a future legal situation, but on its particular facts the CFI held that there was a vested and present interest in bringing proceedings:

MCI v Commission (Case T-310/00)

The applicant (MCI) had notified the Commission of an agreement it had entered into with Sprint, for the two companies to merge. During the Commission's investigations, MCI informed the Commission that it was abandoning the proposed merger. The Commission refused to regard this as amounting to a formal withdrawal of the notified agreement, and went on to adopt a decision prohibiting the proposed merger.

The CFI held that MCI had an interest in obtaining the annulment of this decision. The CFI added that, as long as the Commission decision continues to stand, MCI is prevented by law from merging with Sprint, at least in the configuration and under the conditions put forward in the notification, should it again have the intention to do so. The fact that the undertaking does not necessarily have that intention, or that it will perhaps not carry it out, is a purely subjective circumstance that cannot be taken into account when assessing its legal interest in bringing proceedings for the annulment of a measure which, unquestionably, produces binding legal effects such as to affect its interests by bringing about a distinct change in its legal position.

Although the applicant's interest in bringing proceedings must be assessed as at the time when the application is lodged, in the following case the CFI decided otherwise.

First Data v Commission (Case T-28/02)

The applicants contested a decision by which the Commission opposed, on the basis of Art 81 EC Treaty, certain rules governing membership of a bank card scheme. Those rules were withdrawn after the action was brought so that, in the view of the CFI, the applicants' interest in bringing proceedings, in so far as it had any, had ceased to exist.

The CFI held that, in the interest of the proper administration of justice, that consideration relating to the time when the admissibility of the action is assessed cannot prevent the Court from finding that there is no longer any need to adjudicate on the action in the event that an applicant who initially had a legal interest in bringing proceedings has lost all personal interest in having the contested decision annulled on account of an event occurring after that application was lodged.

The facts of the above case gave the CFI an opportunity to apply the established principle that an interest in bringing proceedings cannot be assessed on the basis of a future, hypothetical event. In particular, if it is claimed that the interest concerns a future legal situation, the applicant must demonstrate that the prejudice to that situation is already certain (**NBV v Commission**, at para 33).

The CFI applied those principles in the following cases:

Gruppo ormeggiatori del porto di Venezia and Others v Commission (Joined Cases T-228/00, T-229/00, T-242/00, T-243/00, T-245/00 to T-248/00, T-250/00, T-252/00, T-256/00 to T-259/00, T-267/00, T-268/00, T-271/00, T-275/00, T-276/00, T-281/00, T-287/00 and T-296/00), Sagar v Commission (Case T-269/00) and Gardena Hotels and Comitato Venezia Vuole Vivere v Commission (Case T-288/00)

The CFI declared the actions inadmissible because of a lack of a legal interest in bringing the proceedings. The actions were brought by Italian undertakings contesting a Commission decision declaring incompatible with the common market certain aid to firms in Venice and Chioggia. Raising an absolute bar to proceeding of its own motion, **the CFI found that the applicants had no legal interest in bringing proceedings on the basis essentially of the decision of Italy not to proceed to recover the aid from the applicants. To substantiate their interest in bringing proceedings the applicants confined themselves to citing future and uncertain circumstances, namely the possibility that the Commission would make a different assessment from that made by Italy and would require it to recover the alleged aid from the applicant undertakings.**

Accordingly, since it is only in the future and uncertain event of a Commission decision calling into question Italy's implementing decision that their legal position would be affected, **the applicant undertakings have not demonstrated that there was a vested, present interest in seeking the annulment of the contested decision.** Moreover, even in that event, the applicant undertakings would not thereby be deprived of any effective legal remedy, given the possibility they had of bringing actions in the national courts against any decisions of the competent national authority requiring them to return the alleged aid.

Again applying the case law on interest in bringing proceedings, the CFI declared the following action inadmissible:

Sniace v Commission (Case T-88/01) (under appeal, Case C-260/05P)

The CFI declared as inadmissible the action brought by Sniace contesting a decision of the Commission declaring aid it had received incompatible with the common market. Sniace disputed the classification of the aid as state aid in the decision, claiming that it affected it adversely, in particular because of the risk of legal action and certain effects on its relations with the credit institution which granted the aid. The Court dismissed the action on the basis that the applicant had no legal interest in bringing proceedings, citing the case law mentioned above according to which **if the interest upon which an applicant relies concerns a future legal situation, he must demonstrate that the prejudice to that situation is already certain** (NBV v Commission). The CFI held that the applicant had not shown at all that: (i) the alleged risk of legal proceedings was, in this case, vested and present, nor that the classification as state aid could entail the obligation to notify the Commission in future of any measure adopted by that credit institution in favour of the applicant; nor (ii) that the damage, which, according to the applicant, results from the conduct of the administrative procedure, could be linked to the classification as state aid in the contested decision.

The CFI has also held that an applicant does not have a legal interest in bringing proceedings where he seeks the annulment of a Commission decision granting marketing authorisation for a medicinal product and it is established that the scientific information forwarded by him to the European Agency for the Evaluation of Medicinal Products has, first, justified the reopening of the assessment procedure and, second, been examined and taken into account under that procedure (**Olivieri v Commission and European Agency for the Evaluation of Medicinal Products (Case T-326/99)**).

A decision addressed to another person which is of direct and individual concern to the applicant

Article 230 EC Treaty limits access to challenge by a non-privileged applicant. Other than a decision which is addressed to the applicant, a non-privileged applicant can only challenge the legality of a specified act in two cases:

(i)   a decision addressed to another person which is of *direct and individual concern* to the applicant; and

(ii) a decision in the form of a regulation which is of *direct and individual concern* to the applicant.

The Court considers the issue of *direct concern* and *individual concern* as two separate issues, both of which have to be satisfied.

Direct concern

With regard to 'direct concern', in the following case the CFI denied the *locus standi* of employees' representatives to challenge Commission decisions approving mergers which were likely to result in redundancies:

Comité Centrale d'Enterprise de la Société Générale des Grandes Sources and Others v *Commission* and *Comité Centrale d'Enterprise de la Société Anonyme Vittel and Others* v *Commission* (Case T-96/92)

The CFI held that the employee representatives had standing to challenge the decisions of the Commission only in so far as the mergers that would result following the Commission's approval affected rights of representation of the employee organisations concerned. The CFI was not satisfied that redundancies were an inevitable consequence of the mergers. Even if they were, the effect on the *representatives* of the redundancies would 'only be of an indirect nature' and they did not, therefore, have standing to challenge the decisions.

Even individuals who the Court acknowledged ought to have been consulted as a matter of good environmental practice before a decision was made were held not to have standing to challenge the decision when it was made because the regulation did not give them a *right* to challenge it: **Associazone Agricoltori di Rovigo** v **Commission** (Case C-142/95).

The following cases concerned Regulation 2004/2003, which governs political parties at European level and the rules regarding their funding:

Bonde and Others v *Parliament and Council* (Case T-13/04), *Bonino and Others* v *Parliament and Council* (Case T-40/04) and *Front national and Others* v *Parliament and Council* (Case T-17/04) (under appeal, Case C-338/05P)

The CFI held that Members of Parliament acting in their own name (and not on behalf of the party to which they belong) were not directly concerned by Regulation 2004/2003 because, *inter alia*, the economic consequences of that Regulation did not affect their legal position but only their factual situation. On the other hand, in the **Bonino** and **Front national** cases, the CFI held that the Regulation, which creates a status for political parties at European level, directly affects certain political groupings. First, the creation of an advantageous legal status from which some political groupings may benefit while others are excluded from it, is likely to affect equality of opportunity between political parties. Second, decisions on the financing of political parties taken in accordance with the criteria established by the contested Regulation fall within the limited discretion of the competent authority. Such decisions are thus purely automatic in nature deriving solely from the contested Regulation without the application of other intermediary rules.

So far as concerns the circumstances in which an applicant is regarded as directly concerned by the measure whose annulment he seeks, in the three cases considered below the CFI recalled that a Community measure is of direct concern to an individual if it directly produces effects on his legal position and its implementation leaves no discretion to the addressees of the measure, implementation being a purely automatic matter flowing solely from the Community legislation without the application of other intermediate rules.

In **Institouto N. Avgerinopoulou and Others** v **Commission** (T-139/02) and **Regione Siciliana** v **Commission** (Case T-341/02 – under appeal, Case C-417/04P), the CFI dismissed both applications for lack of direct interest because the national authorities had a *discretion* in implementing the contested measures.

In the following case, the CFI clarified certain details of the application of the criterion of direct concern where decisions are adopted relating to aid granted by the European Regional Development Fund (ERDF). This judgment marks a certain development in relation to previous decisions made in slightly different contexts (see **SLIM Sicilia *v* Commission** (Case T-105/01)):

Regione Siciliana v *Commission* (Case T-341/02) (under appeal Case C-417/04P)

The applicant disputed a decision relating to the cancellation of ERDF aid granted to Italy and then paid to the applicant for the construction of a dam. The Commission argued that the decision was not of direct concern to the applicant as the Member States formed a screen between the Commission and the final beneficiary of the assistance. However, **the CFI dismissed that plea of inadmissibility, citing case law to the effect that for a person to be directly concerned by a measure that is not addressed to him, the measure must directly affect the individual's legal situation and its implementation must be purely automatic, resulting from Community rules alone to the exclusion of other intermediate rules** (see **P Dreyfus** v **Commission** (Case C-386/96), at para 43).

With regard, first of all, to the alteration of the applicant's legal situation, the CFI held that **the contested decision had had the initial direct and immediate effect of changing the applicant's financial situation** by depriving it of the balance of the assistance remaining to be paid by the Commission and requiring it to repay the sums paid by way of advances. As regards, next, the criterion that the contested decision should be automatically applicable, the CFI observed that **it is automatically and of itself that the contested decision produces its legal effects on the applicant, that is to say, as a result of Community law alone, and the national authorities enjoy no discretion in their duty to implement the decision.** The CFI dismissed the argument that the national authorities may in theory decide to release the applicant from the financial consequences that the contested decision entails for it directly. A national decision providing funding of that magnitude would remain extraneous to the application in Community law of the contested decision and its effect would be to put the applicant back in the situation it occupied before the contested decision was adopted, by bringing about in its turn a second alteration of the applicant's legal situation which was changed in the first place, and automatically, by the contested decision.

Individual concern

In the following case, the Court of Justice established a test which would be applied in future cases to ascertain whether the applicant was 'individually concerned' with the measure:

Plaumann & Co v *Commission* (Case 25/62)

Following a request to it from some German importers of clementines, the German government requested the Commission to grant it permission to suspend the collection of taxes on imports of clementines into Germany from non-Member States. The Commission refused the request, informing the government in a letter addressed to the German government (i.e. a decision addressed to the government). The applicant was an importer of clementines who sought to challenge the legality of the decision. The Court of Justice had to consider whether the decision which was addressed to another person (i.e. the German government) was of direct and *individual* concern to the applicant. The Court of Justice adopted the following highly restrictive test to ascertain if the applicant was *individually* concerned by the decision addressed to the German government:

> **Persons other than those to whom a decision is addressed may only claim to be individually concerned if that decision affects them by reason of certain attributes which are peculiar to them or by reason of circumstances in which they are differentiated from all other persons and by virtue of these factors distinguishes them individually just as in the case of the person addressed.** In the present case the applicant is affected by the disputed Decision as an importer of clementines, that is to say, by reason of a commercial activity which may at any time be practised by any person and is not therefore such as to distinguish the applicant in relation to the contested Decision as in the case of the addressee. For these reasons the present action for annulment must be declared inadmissible. [emphasis added]

The **Plaumann** test has been cited in a number of later cases and should therefore be considered to be authoritative. The test can be stated as follows:

> The applicant must be differentiated from all other persons, and by reason of these distinguishing features singled out in the same way that the initial addressee was singled out.

In **Plaumann**, the applicant failed, because in applying the test to the facts of the case, the Court of Justice held that the applicant practised a commercial activity (i.e. importing of clementines) which could be carried on by any other person in the future. He did not belong to a *closed-class* of persons on the date of the decision.

The application of the test is open to severe criticism, the Court not being concerned with economic reality. First, the fact that the sector of the market (e.g. importing of clementines) may be dominated exclusively by one person or a few persons may realistically prevent other persons entering that particular sector of the market. This has, in the past, been ignored by the Court of Justice. Second, the application of the test may make it virtually impossible for an individual to succeed. The Court of Justice will nearly always be able to say that the applicant does not have distinguishing features because any other person *may*, in the future, take on such distinguishing features.

The **Plaumann** test was applied in the following case:

A E Piraiki-Patraiki v Commission (Case 11/82)

The applicants were Greek exporters of yarn to France. They sought to contest a Commission decision permitting France to impose a quota system on the amount of yarn that could be imported into France from Greece during the period November 1981 to January 1982. The Court of Justice quoted the **Plaumann** test and then continued:

> 12. The applicants argue that they fulfil the conditions set out above since they are the main Greek undertakings which produce and export cotton yarn to France. They argue that they therefore belong to a class of traders individually identifiable on the basis of criteria having to do with the product in question, the business activities carried on and the length of time during which they have been carried on. In that regard the applicants emphasise that the production and export to France of cotton yarn of Greek origin requires industrial and commercial organisation which cannot be established from one day to the next, and certainly not during the short period of application of the decision in question.
>
> 13. That proposition cannot be accepted. It must be pointed out that the applicants are affected by the decision at issue only in their capacity as exporters to France of cotton yarn of Greek origin.

> The decision is not intended to limit the production of those products in any way, nor does it have such a result.
>
> 14. As for the exportation of those products to France, **that is clearly a commercial activity which can be carried on at any time by any undertaking whatever.** It follows that the decision at issue concerns the applicants in the same way as any other trader actually or potentially finding himself in the same position. The mere fact that the applicants export goods to France is not therefore sufficient to establish that they are individually concerned by the contested decision. [emphasis added]

In the following case, the Court of Justice held that there was an exception to this general restrictive principle, provided the decision concerned a set of past events.

Alfred Toepfer and Getreide-Import Gesellschaft v *Commission* (Cases 106 and 107/63)

The applicants were importers of grain. They applied to the German authorities on 1 October 1963 for an import licence. On this date the duty on such imports was zero. However, Germany had requested the Commission to raise the duty with immediate effect. To comply with this request, the Commission, in a decision addressed to the German authorities, confirmed that all applications made on 1 October would be rejected and that duty would be imposed from 2 October. The applicants sought to have this decision annulled. The Court of Justice held the applicant had standing because:

> ... the only persons concerned by the said measures were importers who had applied for an import licence during the course of the day of 1 October 1963. The number and identity of these importers had already become fixed and ascertainable before 4 October, when the contested decision was made. The Commission was in a position to know that its decision affected the interests and the position of the said importers alone.
>
> The factual situation thus created differentiates the said importers, including the applicants, from all other persons and distinguishes them individually just as in the case of the person addressed.
>
> Therefore the objection of inadmissibility which has been raised is unfounded and the applications are admissible.

Similar to the **Piraiki-Patraiki** case above, some of the Greek exporters had already entered into contracts for the export of cotton yarn to France on the date the decision to impose quotas was made. Accordingly, the Court of Justice held that such exporters satisfied the test in so far as they could show that:

> 17. ... before the date of the contested decision they had entered into contracts with French customers for the delivery of cotton yarn from Greece during the period of application of that decision.

Some greater flexibility has, however, been shown by the CFI in allowing a journalist to apply for annulment of a decision refusing access to documents without requiring him to show a special interest above others affected by the refusal (**Svenska Journalistforbundet** v **Council of the European Union** (Case T-174/95)). Also, individuals who have complained that the conduct of an undertaking infringes Art 82 EC Treaty, where the Commission refuses to investigate the complaint, will have standing to challenge that refusal (**Demo-Studio Schmidt** v **Commission** (Case 210/81); compare, **Lord Bethell** v **Commission** (Case 246/81)).

In the following two cases, the CFI considered the issue of 'individual concern' where the applicant is an association of undertakings (e.g. a group of companies):

Bundesverband der Nahrungsmittel-und Speiseresteverwertung and Kloh v Parliament and Council (Case T-391/02) and Schmoldt and Others v Commission (Case T-264/03)

The CFI held that where a legal person bringing an action for annulment is an **association of undertakings** (e.g. a group of companies), it may, when it has taken part in the procedure leading to the adoption of the contested measure, be granted standing in at least three kinds of circumstances:

(i)   where a legal provision expressly grants it a series of procedural powers;
(ii) where the association itself is distinguished individually because its own interests as an association are affected, in particular because its negotiating position has been affected by the measure whose annulment is being sought; and
(iii) where it represents the interests of undertakings which would themselves be entitled to bring proceedings.

In these cases, the CFI refused to accept that the applicant associations had occupied a clearly circumscribed position as negotiator which was intimately linked to the subject-matter of the contested measure.

A more flexible application of the 'individual concern' test

More recently, the CFI and Court of Justice have reconsidered past case law, and addressed the issue of whether or not the strict application of the test, with regard to 'individual concern', should be relaxed. In the following case, the CFI decided that there should be a departure from application of the **Plaumann** test:

Jégo-Quéré et Cie SA v Commission of the European Communities (Case T-177/01)

The case concerned the legality of a regulation which was adopted with the aim of preserving stocks of junior hake in certain specified seas. The applicant fished whiting in Irish waters (which was covered by this regulation). The terms of the regulation were such that the applicant would have to stop fishing. The applicant sought the annulment of certain provisions of the regulation, pursuant to Art 230 EC Treaty. The Commission sought to have the application dismissed because the applicant, applying the Court of Justice's and the CFI's previous case law, did not have *locus standi* to bring an action for annulment because the regulation was not of *individual concern* to the applicant. There is little doubt that if the CFI had applied past case law then the applicant would not have had *locus standi*. However, the CFI deviated from past case law and relaxed its previous very restrictive application of *individual concern*.

In this case, the CFI first of all decided (at para 26) that the *direct concern* criterion was satisfied; this was decided in accordance with past case law.

With regard to *individual concern* the Court stated at para 47 that in this particular case it was only through Art 230 EC Treaty that the applicant could challenge the legality of the regulation. The regulation could not be challenged indirectly through proceedings before a national court, and a preliminary reference to the Court under Art 234 EC Treaty, because there was no national implementing law (a regulation does not require implementation). Therefore, the only way that the applicant could come before a national court (which could then make a reference to the Court) in order to challenge the regulation's legality would be by breaching the regulation. The CFI was concerned that the applicant would have to commit its own unlawful action before being able to challenge the legality of the regulation. Also, an application for non-contractual damages, pursuant to Art 288 EC Treaty, would not enable the Court to judicially review the legality of the regulation in the same way it is empowered to in Art 230 EC Treaty proceedings. However, the CFI stated at para 48 that the fact that the applicant had no judicial remedy did not enable the Court to change the system of remedies and procedures established by the Treaty. Its only option was to relax the previous restrictive application of *individual concern*.

Therefore, at para 50, the CFI stated that 'the strict interpretation, applied until now, of the notion of a person individually concerned according to the fourth paragraph of Article 230 EC [Treaty], must be reconsidered'. At para 51 the CFI relaxed its previous restrictive application of *individual concern* when it stated that 'a natural or legal person is to be regarded as individually concerned by a Community measure of general application that concerns him directly if the measure in question affects his legal position, in a manner which is both definite and immediate, by restricting his rights or imposing obligations on him. The number and position of other persons who are likewise affected by the measure, or who may be so, are of no relevance in that regard'. Since the applicant satisfied this test, the CFI held that it was individually concerned with the regulation and therefore had *locus standi* to challenge its legality. The Commission's objection was therefore dismissed.

However, the judgment of the CFI in the above case received a swift rebuff from the Court of Justice less than three months later:

Unión de Pequeños Agricultores v *Council of the European Union* (*supported by the Commission*) (Case C-50/00P)

The Unión had applied for the partial annulment of a regulation pursuant to Art 230. The CFI rejected the application and the Unión appealed to the Court of Justice. The Court of Justice held as follows:

40. By Article 173 [now Article 230] and Article 184 [now Article 241 EC], on the one hand, and by Article 177 [now Article 234], on the other, the Treaty has established a complete system of legal remedies and procedures designed to ensure judicial review of the legality of acts of the institutions, and has entrusted such review to the Community Courts (see, to that effect, **Les Verts** v **Parliament**, paragraph 23). Under that system, where natural or legal persons cannot, by reason of the conditions for admissibility laid down in the fourth paragraph of Article 173 of the Treaty, directly challenge Community measures of general application, they are able, depending on the case, either indirectly to plead the invalidity of such acts before the Community Courts under Article 184 of the Treaty or to do so before the national courts and ask them, since they have no jurisdiction themselves to declare those measures invalid (see Case 314/85 **Foto-Frost** [1987] ECR 4199, paragraph 20), to make a reference to the Court of Justice for a preliminary ruling on validity.

41. Thus it is for the Member States to establish a system of legal remedies and procedures which ensure respect for the right to effective judicial protection.

42. In that context, in accordance with the principle of sincere cooperation laid down in Article 5 of the Treaty [now Article 10], national courts are required, so far as possible, to interpret and apply national procedural rules governing the exercise of rights of action in a way that enables natural and legal persons to challenge before the courts the legality of any decision or other national measure relative to the application to them of a Community act of general application, by pleading the invalidity of such an act.

43. As the Advocate General has pointed out in paragraphs 50 to 53 of his Opinion, it is not accept-able to adopt an interpretation of the system of remedies, such as that favoured by the appellant, to the effect that a direct action for annulment before the Community Court will be available where it can be shown, following an examination by that Court of the particular national procedural rules, that those rules do not allow the individual to bring proceedings to contest the validity of the Community measure at issue. Such an interpretation would require the Community Court, in each individual case, to examine and interpret national procedural law. That would go beyond its jurisdiction when reviewing the legality of Community measures.

44. Finally, it should be added that, according to the system for judicial review of legality established by the Treaty, a natural or legal person can bring an action challenging a regulation only if it is concerned both directly and individually. Although this last condition must be interpreted in the light of the principle of effective judicial protection by taking account of the various circum-stances that may distinguish an applicant individually (see, for example, Joined Cases 67/85, 68/85 and 70/85 **Van der Kooy v Commission** [1988] ECR 219, paragraph 14; **Extramet Industrie v Council**, paragraph 13, and **Codorniu v Council**, paragraph 19), such an interpretation cannot have the effect of setting aside the condition in question, expressly laid down in the Treaty, without going beyond the jurisdiction conferred by the Treaty on the Community Courts.

45. While it is, admittedly, possible to envisage a system of judicial review of the legality of Community measures of general application different from that established by the founding Treaty and never amended as to its principles, it is for the Member States, if necessary, in accor-dance with Article 48 [T]EU, to reform the system currently in force.

46. In the light of the foregoing, the Court finds that the Court of First Instance did not err in law when it declared the appellant's application inadmissible without examining whether, in the par-ticular case, there was a remedy before a national court enabling the validity of the contested regulation to be examined.

In the above case, the Court of Justice held that the pre-**Jégo-Quéré** case law was correct, and that to depart from this case law would be to depart from the Treaty provisions. If the Member States sought to extend the rights of individuals to challenge Community measures, then that could only come about by an amendment to the Treaty. The CFI's judgment in **Jégo-Quéré** was overruled. The Court of Justice subsequently reversed the CFI's judgment when **Jégo-Quéré** came before it on appeal from the CFI (Case C-263/02P).

Constitutional Treaty

The Court of Justice disagreed with the CFI's judgment in **Jégo-Quéré et Cie SA v Commission of the European Communities** (Case T-177/01), in which the CFI sought to relax the rules relating to 'individual concern'. The Court of Justice stated that a relax-ation of the rules could only come about by an amendment to Art 230 EC Treaty. If the Constitutional Treaty had come into force, Article III-365 would have provided that:

4. Any natural or legal person may . . . institute proceedings against an act addressed to that person or which is of direct and individual concern to him or her, and against a regu-latory act which is of direct concern to him or her and does not entail implementing measures.

While this provision would have potentially opened up the range of acts which could have been reviewed, at the request of an individual, it is the latter part of this provision which is of interest. Provided the measure which the individual was seeking to have reviewed was 'a regulatory act which . . . does not entail implementing measures', then in order to have standing, an individual would only have needed to show 'direct concern' rather than direct *and individual* concern. This indicates that when the EC Treaty is amended in the future, the Member States may seek to relax the currently very strict rules relating to individual concern.

Competition cases

In the field of state aid, actions mainly seek the annulment either of (i) a decision taken without opening the formal investigation procedure referred to in Art 88(2) EC Treaty; or (ii) a decision taken at the end of that procedure (see Chapter 19). Since those decisions are addressed to the Member State concerned, it is for the undertaking, which is not the addressee, to show that that measure is of *direct and individual concern* to it.

Where the Commission, without opening the formal investigation procedure, finds in the course of a preliminary investigation that state aid is compatible with the common market, the parties concerned within the meaning of Art 88(2) EC Treaty, who are entitled to the guarantees of the formal investigation procedure when it is implemented, must be regarded as individually concerned by the decision making that finding.

In **Danske Busvognmaend v Commission** (Case T-157/01), a trade association representing the interests of the majority of Danish bus companies was recognised by the CFI as having the status of a 'party concerned', on the ground that it made a complaint to the Commission that its interventions influenced the course of the administrative procedure and that at least some of its members were in competition with the undertaking which benefited from the disputed aid.

In **Kronofrance v Commission** (Case T-27/02), the CFI held that the applicant, who had pleaded the failure to open the formal investigation procedure, was a 'party concerned' in light of its status as a competitor, a status established by having regard to the identity of the products manufactured by it with those of the undertaking benefiting from the aid and to the fact that their sales areas overlapped.

In **Thermenhotel Stoiser Franz and Others v Commission** (Case T-158/99), the CFI held that hotel operators in a tourist resort in the Province of Styria (Austria) were entitled to challenge the legality of a Commission decision declaring the public financing of the construction of a luxury hotel in the same resort to be compatible with the common market. The CFI observed that the applicants were direct competitors of the hotel receiving the aid in question and that they were recognised as having this status in the contested decision.

In the above three cases it was held that the applicant undertakings were, in their capacity as parties concerned within the meaning of Art 88(2) EC Treaty, individually concerned by the decisions declaring at the end of the preliminary investigation procedure that aid was compatible with the common market. It should be noted, with regard to the extent of the review of the pleas, that in one instance the CFI regarded the pleas for annulment in their entirety as seeking to establish that the Commission had unlawfully failed to open the formal investigation procedure (**Thermenhotel Stoiser Franz**), whereas in another instance it annulled the decision approving the grant of aid on its merits (**Danske Busvognmaend**).

Where the contested decision has been adopted at the end of the formal investigation procedure provided for by Art 88(2) EC Treaty, it is not sufficient, in order for an undertaking to be distinguished individually in the same way as the addressee of the decision, that it has the status of a 'party concerned'.

According to the case law, such a decision is of individual concern to the undertakings which were at the origin of the complaint which led to that procedure and whose views were heard and determined the conduct of the procedure, provided, however, that their position on the market is *substantially affected* by the aid which is the subject of that decision.

Applying those criteria, the CFI held that the Austrian company Lenzing was individually concerned by a Commission decision concerning the state aid granted by Spain to the company Sniace, since Lenzing, a competitor of the recipient company: (i) was at the origin of the complaint that led to the opening of the procedure and participated actively in the procedure; and (ii) provided information such as would show that its position on the market was substantially affected by the contested decision, for instance information concerning the characteristics of the market in question, namely a very limited number of producers, fierce competition and significant production surpluses (**Lenzing** *v* **Commission** (Case T-36/99) (under appeal, Case C-525/04P)).

On the other hand, in **Deutsche Post and DHL** *v* **Commission** (Case T-358/02) (under appeal, Case C-367/04P), the CFI found that Deutsche Post and DHL International, two companies operating on the Italian market in postal services open to competition, had not played an active role during the administrative procedure which preceded the adoption of the decision relating to state aid granted by Italy in favour of Poste Italiane. It therefore examined whether the measure authorised by that decision was nevertheless liable to affect significantly their position on the market in question and concluded, in the absence of sufficient proof of the magnitude of the prejudice to their position on the market, that that was not the case.

This was likewise the situation in the following case (which has been considered above):

Sniace v Commission (Case T-88/01) (under appeal, Case C-260/05P)

Sniace disputed a Commission decision finding measures adopted for the benefit of Lenzing Lyocell, an Austrian company, to be compatible with the common market. The CFI raised of its own motion the question of the applicant's standing to bring proceedings over that decision and, in particular, the question whether it was of individual concern to it in the light of the criteria defined for the first time by the Court of Justice in its judgment **COFAZ and Others** v **Commission** (Case 169/84), at para 25. According to those criteria, in the field of state aid, not only the undertaking in receipt of the aid but also the undertakings competing with it which have played an active role in the procedure initiated pursuant to Art 88(2) EC Treaty in respect of an individual grant of aid are recognised as being individually concerned by the Commission decision closing that procedure, provided that their position on the market is *substantially affected* by the aid which is the subject of the contested decision. That was not the position in this case. First, the applicant played only a minor role in the course of the administrative procedure, as it lodged no complaint nor any observations which had a significant impact on the conduct of the procedure. Second, analysis of the physical characteristics, the price and the manufacturing processes of the products sold by the applicant and Lenzing Lyocell did not lead the CFI to find that they were in direct competition, as the applicant did not establish that the contested decision was capable of significantly affecting its position on the market.

Decisions in the form of regulations

An individual may challenge the legality of a regulation provided it is in reality a decision which is of direct and individual concern to him. The test which the Court of Justice has applied in this situation is just as stringent as that applied in the **Plaumann** case (above), as illustrated in the following case:

Calpak SpA and Società Emiliana Lavorazione Frutta SpA v *Commission* (Cases 789 and 790/79)

Under the terms of a regulation, aid was to be granted to the producers of pears calculated on the basis of the average production over the previous three years. A later regulation provided that aid would now be assessed on the basis of one marketing year in which production was low. The applicants, pear producers, challenged the legality of the latter regulation, claiming it was in fact a decision, and argued that because they belonged to a closed class of persons (i.e. they were readily identifiable by the Commission on the date the regulation was passed), they therefore had the necessary standing. The Court of Justice held as follows:

6. The Commission's main contention is that as the disputed provisions were adopted in the form of regulations, their annulment may only be sought if their content shows them to be, in fact, decisions. But in the Commission's view the provisions in question, which lay down rules of general application, are truly in the nature of regulations within the meaning of Article 189 of the Treaty [now Art 249] . . .

7. The second paragraph of Article 173 [now 230] empowers individuals to contest, *inter alia*, any decision which, although in the form of a regulation, is of direct and individual concern to them. The objective of that provision is in particular to prevent the Community institutions from being in a position, merely by choosing the form of a regulation, to exclude an application by an individual against a decision which concerns him directly and individually; it therefore stipulates that the choice of form cannot change the nature of the measure.

8. By virtue of the second paragraph of Article 189 of the Treaty [now Art 249] **the criterion for distinguishing between a regulation and a decision is whether the measure is of general application or not . . .**

9. A provision which limits the granting of production aid for all producers in respect of a particular product to a uniform percentage of the quantity produced by them during a uniform period is by nature a measure of general application within the meaning of Article 189 of the Treaty [now Art 249]. In fact **the measure applies to objectively determined situations and produces legal effects with regard to categories of persons described in a generalised and abstract manner.** The nature of the measure as a regulation is not called in question by the mere fact that it is possible to determine the number or even the identity of the producers to be granted the aid which is limited thereby.

10. Nor is the fact that the choice of reference period is particularly important for the applicants, whose production is subject to considerable variation from one marketing year to another as a result of their own programme of production, sufficient to entitle them to an individual remedy. Moreover, the applicants have not established the existence of circumstances such as to justify describing that choice . . . as a decision adopted specifically in relation to them and, as such, entitling them to institute proceedings under the second paragraph of Article 173 [now 230].

11. It follows that the objection raised by the Commission must be accepted as regards the applications for the annulment of the provisions in the two regulations in question. [emphasis added]

Paragraph 9 of the above judgment is particularly important, as it demonstrates the very restrictive nature of the test. A regulation is the correct form of Community instrument (rather than a decision) provided it applies to 'objectively determined situations and produces legal effects with regard to persons described in a generalised and abstract manner'. It must be possible for the Commission to draft a regulation in such terms in almost every situation, thus ensuring the regulation could not be challenged by an aggrieved individual.

The Court of Justice has made an exception in relation to a regulation which applies to a completed set of past events. For example, in **International Fruit Company BV** *v*

Commission (Cases 41–44/70), the Court held that the regulation in question applied to a closed category of persons on the date the regulation was passed, i.e. those who had made import applications in the previous week. Accordingly, an action to challenge the regulation by a person falling within this class was admissible.

Also, in the case of anti-dumping regulations, the Court has accepted the standing of a company to challenge a regulation of a general character (**Codorniu** (Case C-309/89)). If the regulation is intended to affect a specific group of undertakings, it may be 'a conglomeration of individual decisions ... under the guise of a regulation', and those affected may have the status to challenge it (**International Fruit Co v Commission** (Case 41/70)).

The legal basis for a challenge

Article 230 provides four possible bases for a challenge. These are:

- lack of competence;
- infringement of an essential procedural requirement;
- infringement of the Treaty or any rule of law relating to its application; and
- misuse of powers.

These are not mutually exclusive and two or even three may be cited together in an application for judicial review.

Lack of competence

This corresponds in English law to *substantive ultra vires;* a body can only do that which it is authorised to do by law. A number of challenges have been mounted on the grounds that the Commission has chosen the wrong legal base for a legislative proposal (see **Commission v Council (Re Titanium Dioxide Waste)** (Case C-300/89)) or a decision. In **Germany, France, Netherlands, Denmark and the UK v Commission** (Cases 281, 283–285, 287/85) the Commission had adopted a decision under Art 137 EC Treaty (then Art 118) under which Member States were required to consult with the Commission on measures relating to the integration of workers from states outside the Community. The Court of Justice held that the social policy objects of Art 137 were confined to measures that affected migrants from other Member States, and did not extend, as this decision purported to do, to measures affecting only migrants from states outside the Community.

There are not a great many challenges which are successful on this basis, but the following two cases are examples of where such challenges were successful:

France v Commission (Case C-327/91)

The Commission had concluded an agreement with the USA to promote cooperation and coordination and to lessen the possibility of conflict between the parties in the application of their competition laws. The case concerned the competence of the Commission to conclude the agreement. In a challenge by the French government, the Court held that the Commission did not have the competence to do so. Under the former Art 228 EC Treaty (before amendment by the TEU) the Commission had the power to negotiate agreements with states outside the Community or with international organisations, but they had to be concluded by the Council.

Laboratoires Servier v *Commission* (Case T-147/00)

The CFI annulled a Commission decision withdrawing marketing authorisation for certain medicinal products, on the basis of a ground relating to a matter of public policy raised by it of its own motion. The CFI observed that the lack of competence of an institution which has adopted a contested measure constitutes a ground for annulment for reasons of public policy, which must be raised by the Community judicature of its own motion. The decision of the CFI was appealed to the Court of Justice; the appeal was dismissed (Case C-156/03 P).

The relationship between the power of the Community judicature to raise a ground of its own motion and the existence of a public policy interest underlying the ground was confirmed in **Strabag Benelux** *v* **Council** (Case T-183/00), para 37 and in **Henkel** *v* **OHIM – LHS (UK)** (Case T-308/01), para 34.

Infringement of an essential procedural requirement

This is probably the most oft-cited basis of challenge and is equivalent in English law to *procedural ultra vires*. It comprises breaches of both formal procedural requirements laid down in the EC Treaty and in secondary legislation and the more informal rules of fairness required by general principles of Community law (see Chapter 2). The most important general procedural requirement in the EC Treaty is that laid down in Art 253, under which secondary legislation must state the reasons on which it is based. The CFI emphasised the importance of this provision in the following case:

Eugénio Branco Ld v *Commission* (Case T-85/94)

The CFI stated that:

> According to a consistent line of case law, the purpose of the obligation to state the reasons on which an individual decision is based is to enable the Community judicature to review the legality of the decision and to provide the person concerned with sufficient information to make it possible to ascertain whether the decision is well founded or whether it is vitiated by a defect which may permit its legality to be contested. The extent of that obligation depends on the nature of the measure in question and on the context in which it was adopted.

In the above case, and two similar previous cases, the Court annulled Commission decisions withdrawing approval or partial support of projects financed by the European Social Fund. Besides the obligation imposed by Art 253 EC Treaty, there was also a breach of the requirement imposed by Art 6(1), Regulation 2950/83 under which the Commission, before deciding to suspend, reduce or withdraw fund aid, had to give the relevant Member State the opportunity to comment (**Consorgan Lda** *v* **Commission** (Case C-181/90); **Socurte Ld and Others** *v* **Commission** (Cases T-432, 434/93)).

Breach of a procedural requirement may be so fundamental that the decision or other measure may be void *ab initio*, i.e. the decision will be held to have never existed. This issue arose in the following case:

Commission v *BASF AG and Others* (Case C-137/92P)

The CFI had dismissed as inadmissible actions for annulment of a measure which purported to have been taken by the Commission under Art 81 EC Treaty on the ground that the measure was 'non-existent'. The Court of Justice allowed an appeal. The Court stated that acts of the Community institutions are presumed to be lawful and accordingly produce legal effects, even if they are tainted by irregularities, until such time as they are annulled or withdrawn. However, it held that there are some acts which are so tainted by irregularity, whose gravity is so obvious, that they cannot be tolerated by the Community legal order. They must be treated as having no legal effect, even provisional. The Court said that such a conclusion, with all its potentially serious consequences, should be reached only in 'quite extreme circumstances'. In this case, both the operative part of the decision and the reasons for it had been adopted by a single Commissioner and three of the texts of the decision in the relevant languages had never been seen by the full Commission, contrary to the Commission's Rules of Procedure. It amounted to breach of an essential procedural requirement and was consequently annulled by the Court under Art 230. The decision of the Commission had not, however, been 'non-existent'.

Infringement of the Treaty or any rule relating to its application

There is an obvious overlap between Art 253 EC Treaty, the need to give reasons, procedural requirements, and the general principles of fairness and natural justice which are fundamental principles of Community law. In addition there are also the rights set out in the European Convention on Human Rights (ECHR), together with the principles of non-discrimination, proportionality, legitimate expectation, respect for property rights and equal treatment (see Chapter 2). These latter rights and principles are not absolute and may, in appropriate circumstances, have to give way to restrictions imposed in the interest of the common organisation of the internal market, 'provided that those restrictions in fact correspond to objectives of general interest pursued by the Community, and do not constitute a disproportionate and intolerable interference, impairing the very substance of the rights guaranteed' (**Germany v Commission (Re Banana Market)** (Case C-280/93)).

Before and after the terrorist attacks of 11 September 2001, the Security Council of the United Nations adopted several resolutions concerning the Taliban, Osama bin Laden, the Al-Qaeda network and the persons and bodies associated with them. By those resolutions, all the Member States of the United Nations were required to freeze funds and other financial resources under the direct or indirect control of those persons and bodies. A sanctions committee was tasked with identifying the subjects concerned and the financial resources to be frozen and considering requests for derogations. Those resolutions were implemented in the Community by several common positions and Council regulations ordering the freezing of the funds of the persons and bodies concerned. Several of them sought the annulment of those regulations before the CFI:

Yusuf and Al Barakaat International Foundation v *Council and Commission* (Case T-306/01) (under appeal, Case C-415/05P), and *Kadi* v *Council and Commission* (Case T-315/01) (under appeal, Case C-402/05P)

The CFI held, first, that reliance on Arts 60, 301 and 308 EC Treaty in combination as a legal basis made it possible, in the field of economic and financial sanctions, to attain the objective pursued by the Union and its Member States under the Common Foreign and Security Policy (CFSP). Having held that the Council was competent to adopt the contested regulation, the CFI considered the applicants' plea alleging breach of their fundamental rights enshrined in Community law and the ECHR. Since the contested regulations applied decisions taken by the Security Council of the United Nations, consideration of that plea led the CFI to consider, as a preliminary issue, the relationship between the international legal order under the United Nations and the domestic or Community legal order. The CFI found, on that point, that **under international law, the obligations of the Member States of the United Nations under the Charter of that organisation clearly prevail over every other obligation including their obligations under the ECHR and under the EC Treaty and that primacy exends to decisions of the Security Council taken pursuant to Title VII of the Charter. Moreover, although it is not itself a Member of the United Nations, the Community must be considered to be bound by the obligations under the Charter of the United Nations in the same way as its Member States, by virtue of the Treaty establishing it.** Accordingly, first, the Community may not infringe the obligations imposed on its Member States by the Charter of the United Nations or impede their performance. Second, in the exercise of its powers it is bound, by the very Treaty by which it was established, to adopt all the measures necessary to enable its Member States to fulfil those obligations.

The CFI went on to analyse the implications of this principle for its judicial review of regulations which merely implement the decisions of the Security Council of the United Nations. The CFI observed in that regard that any review of the internal lawfulness of the contested regulation would therefore imply that the CFI is to consider, indirectly, the lawfulness of those decisions. **In view of their primacy, those decisions fall outside the ambit of the CFI's judicial review so that it has no authority to call in question, even indirectly, their lawfulness in the light of Community law or of the fundamental rights enshrined in the Community legal order.** On the contrary, the CFI is bound, so far as possible, to interpret and apply that law in a manner compatible with the obligations of the Member States under the Charter of the United Nations. **Nonetheless, the CFI considered itself empowered to check the lawfulness of the contested regulation and, indirectly, the lawfulness of the decisions of the Security Council which that regulation implements, with regard to superior rules of international law falling within the ambit of** *jus cogens* **(i.e. the fundamental rights of the human person), understood as a body of higher rules of public international law from which neither the Member States nor the bodies of the United Nations may derogate and which include,** *inter alia,* **mandatory provisions concerning the universal protection of fundamental human rights.**

The CFI then reviewed the regulation in the light of those principles and found that the freezing of funds provided for by the contested regulation does not infringe the applicants' fundamental rights, as protected by *jus cogens*. In particular, the regulation does not infringe the applicants' right to property provided that it is protected by *jus cogens*. As regards the right to a fair hearing, the CFI observed that no rule of *jus cogens* requires a prior hearing for the persons concerned by the Sanctions Committee, and, moreover, the resolutions at issue set up a mechanism for the re-examination of individual cases.

On the question of the right to an effective judicial remedy, the CFI stated that, in dealing with the action brought by the applicants it carries out a complete review of the lawfulness of the contested regulation with regard to observance by the Community institutions of the rules of jurisdiction and the rules of external lawfulness and the essential procedural requirements which bind their actions. It also reviews the lawfulness of the contested regulation having regard to the Security Council's decisions. Further, it reviews the lawfulness of the contested regulation and, indirectly, the lawfulness of the resolutions of the Security Council in the light of *jus cogens*. On the other hand, it is not for the CFI to review indirectly whether the Security Council's resolutions are themselves compatible with fundamental rights as protected by the Community legal order, nor to verify that there has been no error of assessment of the facts and evidence relied on by the Security Council in support of the measures it has taken or to check indirectly the appropriateness and proportionality of those measures. To that extent, and in the absence of an independent international court responsible for ruling in actions brought against decisions taken by the Sanctions Committee, there is no judicial remedy available to the applicant.

However, the CFI acknowledged that any such lacuna in the judicial protection available to the applicants is not in itself contrary to *jus cogens*, as the right of access to the courts is not absolute. The applicants' interest in having a court hear their case on its merits is not enough to outweigh the essential public interest in the maintenance of international peace and security in the face of a threat clearly identified by the Security Council. **Consequently, the CFI dismissed the actions as unfounded.**

Misuse of powers

This ground for challenge stems from the French *détournement de pouvoir*. This is the equivalent, in English administrative law, of using a power for an improper or illegitimate purpose. Since the power is itself lawful, a challenger must prove a subjective matter, the purpose for which it has been used (**Netherlands *v* High Authority** (Case 6/54)). Since outsiders are not privy to the reasons for institutional decisions unless they are made public, most of the few successful cases have relied on published documents, or the reasons given under Art 253 EC Treaty, which indicate that the institution has misunderstood the purpose for which a power has been conferred on it (**Giuffrida *v* Council** (Case 105/75)).

The UK's challenge to the Working Time Directive: a case study

In 1990, the Commission proposed a directive to regulate working time, under the health and safety provisions of the former Art 118a EC Treaty (now Art 137 (OJ 1990 C 254/4)). The legislative procedure which applied to Art 118a was the cooperation procedure (see Chapter 4). The Working Time Directive 93/104 was adopted by the Council, acting by a qualified majority, on 23 November 1993, with an implementation date of 23 November 1996 (OJ 1993 L 307/18). Eleven of the then twelve Member States voted in favour; the UK abstained and indicated that it would challenge the legality of the directive.

On 8 March 1994 the UK brought an action under Art 173 EC Treaty (now Art 230) for the annulment of the directive and, in the alternative, the annulment of specific parts of the directive including, *inter alia*, the second sentence of Art 5 of the directive. The second sentence of Art 5 provided that the minimum weekly rest period should 'in principle include Sunday'. In **UK *v* Council of the European Union** (Case C-84/94), in support of its action, the UK relied on four pleas:

1. that the legal base of the directive was defective;
2. breach of the principle of proportionality;
3. misuse of powers; and
4. infringement of essential procedural requirements.

Defective legal base

The main thrust of the UK's argument centred around the first plea that the directive was not concerned with the improvement of the health and safety of workers and therefore should not have been adopted under Art 118a (now Art 137). It was contended that the correct legal base was either Art 100 (now Art 94) or Art 235 (now Art 308), which both required unanimity within the Council of Ministers.

Article 100 (now Art 94) empowers the Council of Ministers to adopt directives which directly affect the establishment or functioning of the common market, by a *unanimous* vote. Article 100a (now Art 95) derogates from Art 100 (now Art 94) in that it empowers the Council of Ministers to adopt directives which directly affect the establishment or functioning of the internal market by a *qualified majority* while specifically excluding provisions 'relating to the rights and interests of employed persons'.

The UK first argued that provisions which related to the rights and interests of employed persons and which directly affected the internal or common market would as a general rule have to be enacted under Art 100 (now Art 94). The Court of Justice rejected this submission. It held that Art 118a (now Art 137) is a more specific legal base than Arts 100 (now Art 94) and 100a (now Art 95) and this is confirmed by the actual wording of Art 100a(1) (now Art 95(1)) which states that its provisions apply 'save where otherwise provided in this Treaty'. Therefore the more specific legal base of Art 118a (now Art 137) was to be preferred.

Second, the UK argued that a strict interpretation of Art 118a (now Art 137) only permitted the adoption of directives which had a genuine and objective link to the health and safety of workers and which therefore related to physical conditions and risks at the workplace. This did not apply to measures concerning, in particular, weekly working time (Art 6 of the Directive), paid annual leave (Art 7) and rest periods (Arts 4 and 5) whose connection with the health and safety of workers was tenuous. The UK's alternative plea was for the annulment of these specific provisions. This was also rejected by the Court of Justice, which held that a broad scope was to be given to health and safety. This was supported by reference to the Constitution of the World Health Organisation (to which all the Member States belong); health is there defined as 'a state of complete physical, mental and social well-being which does not consist only in the absence of illness or infirmity'. The UK additionally argued that the reference to the adoption of 'minimum requirements' in Art 118a(2) (now Art 137(2)) empowered the Council of Ministers only to adopt measures which were at a level acceptable to all Member States, and which constituted a minimum benchmark. This was similarly rejected by the Court. The reference to 'minimum requirements' enabled Member States to adopt more stringent measures than those contained in the directive, as confirmed by Art 118a(3) (now Art 137(5)).

Third, it was argued by the UK that Art 118a (now Art 137) did not empower the Council to adopt directives which deal with the question of health and safety in a 'generalised, unspecific and unscientific manner'. The UK supported this argument with reference to previous directives which had been adopted under Art 118a (now Art 137), which covered specific areas of activity. The Court likewise rejected this argument. Past practice of the Council cannot create a precedent binding on the Community institutions with regard to the correct legal basis. In any event, the Health and Safety Framework Directive 89/391 (OJ 1989 L 183/1), which had been adopted under Art 118a (now Art 137), had a general, unspecific scope.

The Court of Justice concluded that 'where the principal aim of the measure in question is the protection of the health and safety of workers, Art 118a (now Art 137) must be used, albeit such a measure may have ancillary effects on the establishment and functioning of the internal market'.

Having set out the legal basis for the adoption of a directive under Art 118a (now Art 137), the Court examined whether, in the particular circumstances of this case, the Working Time Directive had been properly adopted under this article. The Court noted that the approach taken by the directive, viewing the organisation of working time essentially in terms of the favourable impact it may have on the health and safety of workers, was apparent from its preamble. While it could not be denied that the directive might affect employment, its essential and overriding objective was one of health and safety. However, the Court did not accept that choosing Sunday as the weekly rest day (Art 5, second sentence) was more closely connected to the health and safety of workers than any other day of the week. The Court therefore upheld this part of the UK's alternative claim; the second sentence of Art 5, which could be severed from the other provisions of the directive, was annulled.

With regard to Art 235 EC Treaty (now Art 308), the Court of Justice simply noted that the article could be used as the legal basis for a measure only where no other Treaty provision conferred on the Community institutions the necessary power to adopt it; this was not the case here.

Breach of the principle of proportionality

First, the UK argued that not all measures which may 'improve' the level of the health and safety protection of workers constitute minimum requirements. This was rejected by the Court of Justice which reiterated the point made above that the concept of 'minimum requirements' does not limit Community action to the lowest level of protection provided by the various Member States, but means a Member State can adopt provisions more stringent than those of the directive.

Second, it was argued by the UK that the application of the principle of proportionality would require the directive's objective of safeguarding the health and safety of workers to be attained by measures which were less restrictive and involved fewer obstacles to the competitiveness of industry and the earning capacity of individuals. The Court held that the Council, acting as legislature, must be allowed a wide discretion where it was making social policy choices and was required to carry out complex assessments. The Court would only rule the measure to be disproportionate if the exercise of the Council's discretion had been vitiated by manifest error or misuse of powers, or if it had manifestly exceeded the limits of its power. This could not be proven and was therefore rejected by the Court.

Third, the UK argued that a measure will only be proportionate if it complies with the principle of subsidiarity. It is for the Community institutions to demonstrate that the aims of the directive could be better achieved at Community level rather than national level. The Court held that it had been demonstrated that Community action was necessary to adopt minimum requirements with the objective of raising the level of the health and safety protection of workers.

Misuse of powers

Misuse of powers is defined by the Court of Justice as the adoption of a measure with the exclusive or main purpose of achieving an end other than that stated, or evading a procedure specifically prescribed by the Treaty. The Court had already held that Art 118a (now Art 137) was the appropriate legal base and therefore this plea was also dismissed.

Infringement of essential procedural requirements

The UK argued that the directive was inadequately reasoned because there was a failure to demonstrate a connection between the health and safety of workers and the provisions of the directive. Many of the provisions were concerned with improving the living and working conditions of workers, or the internal market, rather than the health and safety of workers. This was rejected; the various recitals in the preamble to the directive clearly reasoned the connection between the provisions and the health and safety of workers. There was no necessity to include in the preamble specific references to scientific material justifying the adoption of the various provisions.

Consequences of annulment

Under Art 231 EC Treaty:

> If the action is well founded, the Court of Justice shall declare the act concerned to be void.
>
> In the case of a regulation, however, the Court of Justice shall, if it considers this necessary, state which of the effects of the regulation which it has declared void shall be considered as definitive.

Under Art 233 EC Treaty:

> The institution or institutions whose act has been declared void or whose failure to act has been declared contrary to the Treaty shall be required to take the necessary measures to comply with the judgment of the Court of Justice.
>
> The obligation shall not affect any obligation which may result from the application of the second paragraph of Article 288.

Since decisions and other acts having legal consequences will affect only single undertakings or individuals or groups of undertakings, the Court of Justice, if it finds the decision or other act to be void, will declare it to be void from the moment of delivery of the judgment. It can, of course, declare an act non-existent, but, as can be seen in the **BASF Case** (Case C-137/92), it is reluctant to do this because of the disruption which this may cause to actions which may have been based on the assumption that the act was valid. The second paragraph of Art 230 enables the Court to declare part of a decision void. In the case of Community legislation, it will frequently declare that, for example, the provisions of an annulled directive or regulation will remain effective until a new regulation is adopted (see, e.g., the Court of Justice's declaration on annulling Directive 90/366 on students' rights in **European Parliament** *v* **Council** (Case C-295/90), and on Council Regulation 2454/92 on transport undertakings operating in other Member States in **European Parliament** *v* **Council** (Case C-388/92)).

Article 233 requires the institution concerned to take the necessary remedial action to correct the failure which has been established by the judgment of the Court. There is no time limit for this, but the Court of Justice has held that such steps should be taken within a reasonable period from the date of the judgment (**European Parliament** *v* **Council** (Case 13/83)).

Indirect challenge to a Community act under Articles 241 and 234 EC Treaty

The legality of a Community act may become an issue in proceedings in which the object is not the Community act itself but some action of an institution which purports to be based upon it. The issue can be raised only if it is relevant to the proceedings (**Italy** *v* **Commission** (Case 32/65)). Attacks on the legality of Community acts in this way are normally called indirect challenges and they may result in the judicial review of the legality of Community acts long after the time has passed for an application for review under Art 230. The issue of legality may arise before both the Court of Justice and the CFI at Community level, or in national courts. Where it arises at Community level it is subject to the rules laid down in Art 241 EC Treaty which provides:

> Notwithstanding the expiry of the period laid down in the third paragraph of Article 230, any party may, in proceedings in which a regulation of the Council or of the Commission is in issue, plead the grounds specified in the first paragraph of Article 230 in order to invoke before the Court of Justice the inapplicability of that regulation.

The first point to note is that an indirect challenge in this way is only available in relation to regulations and cannot, therefore, be used in relation to other Community acts having legal effect. Second, the effect of Art 241 is limited to proceedings brought before the Court of Justice (**Wöhrmann** *v* **Commission** (Case 31/62)). Although Art 241 excludes an indirect challenge to other acts having legal effect, this rule may, in some cases, be circumvented where the issue arises in a national court. The question of the legality of the Community measure may then be raised, as we have already noted in connection with time limits under Art 230, in the national court and referred to the Court of Justice under Art 234 EC Treaty. The operation of Art 234 is examined in Chapter 6; the relevant part of that article enables national courts to ask for a preliminary ruling, *inter alia*, in relation to 'the validity . . . of acts of the institutions of the Community'.

If a national body purports to act on the basis of, for example, a decision or a directive which is invalid, a party to the proceedings may ask the national court to refer the question of the validity of that measure to the Court of Justice pursuant to Art 234 EC Treaty. Such a reference will be necessary if the issue arises, because national courts have no power themselves to rule on the validity of a Community measure (**Foto-Frost** *v* **HZA Lübeck-Ost** (Case 314/85)). An important restriction on that principle is, however, the rule laid down by the Court in **TWD Deggendorf** (Case C-188/92). In that case the Court of Justice held that no indirect challenge to a Commission decision could be made under Art 234 where the party had been informed of the Commission decision and could 'without doubt' have challenged it directly before the Court under Art 230, but had not done so.

Challenging a failure to act: Article 232 EC Treaty

Institutions may act unlawfully not only by exceeding or abusing their powers, but also by failing to carry out a duty imposed on them by the Treaty or some other provision having legal effect. This form of inaction may result in proceedings brought under Art 232 EC Treaty:

> Should the European Parliament, the Council or the Commission, in infringement of this Treaty, fail to act, the Member States and the other institutions of the Community may bring an action before the Court of Justice to have the infringement established.
>
> The action shall be admissible only if the institution concerned has first been called upon to act. If, within two months of being called upon, the institution concerned has not defined its position, the action may be brought within a further period of two months.
>
> Any natural or legal person may, under the conditions laid down in the preceding paragraphs, complain to the Court of Justice that an institution of the Community has failed to address to that person any act other than a recommendation or an opinion.
>
> The Court of Justice shall have jurisdiction, under the same conditions, in actions or proceedings brought by the European Central Bank in the areas falling within the latter's field of competence and in actions and proceedings brought against the latter.

Standing to challenge a failure to act

The position of 'privileged' applicants (i.e. Member States and institutions) that can bring proceedings under Art 232 EC Treaty irrespective of any particular interest, and 'non-privileged' applicants (i.e. legal and natural persons) that need to establish a special interest, is the same under Art 232 as in relation to challenges under Art 230. The Court has, in fact, stated that 'in the system of legal remedies provided for by the Treaty, there is a close relationship between the right of action given in Article 173 [now Art 230] . . . and that based on Article 175 [now Art 232]' (**European Parliament** *v* **Council (Re Transport Policy)** (Case 13/83)).

Scope for challenge

There have not been many successful actions brought on this basis. Many of the duties which are conferred on the institutions involve both a duty and a discretion of whether, and how, to exercise that duty. To satisfy Art 232 EC Treaty, the institution generally only needs to have addressed the issue and defined its position. In the case of natural or legal persons, if the only outcome of the institution's deliberations will be an opinion or a recommendation, a failure to produce either is not a failure which can be dealt with by Art 232. Where there is a clear duty to act, as was imposed on the Commission by Art 85(1) EC Treaty in relation to breaches of Arts 81 and 82, a statement by the Commission that was not going to respond to a complaint might give grounds for an action under Art 232, after the appropriate warning has been given. For example, in **Ladbroke Racing (Deutschland) GmbH** *v* **Commission** (Case T-74/92), Ladbroke had complained to the Commission about a denial of access for the televising of horse racing, alleging a breach of Arts 81 and 82 EC Treaty by German and French companies in the horse racing and communications businesses. After deciding to investigate the complaint in December 1990, the Commission had still not defined its position on the alleged breach of Art 82 by June 1992, when it was formally requested to do so. The CFI found that there was a breach following the instigation of Art 232 proceedings. The Commission could have either initiated the procedure for establishing a breach of Art 82, dismissed the complaint in a formal letter to the complainant, or made a reasoned decision not to pursue the complaint on the ground of a lack of Community interest. It had, however, done none of these things. If there is a refusal to pursue an investigation, it may in itself constitute a decision which is best attacked under Art 230 (**SFEI and Others** *v* **Commission** (Case C-39/93P)). It should be noted that the enforcement procedures, in relation to Community Competition law, have changed following the coming into force of Regulation 1/2003 (see Chapter 22).

The difficulty of launching a successful action under Art 232 is illustrated by the **Transport Policy** case ((Case 13/83), see above) concerning Arts 70 and 71 EC Treaty that require the Council to adopt a common transport policy for the Community. More than 20 years after the Treaty had come into force no such policy had been adopted, and the Parliament brought proceedings against the Council for failure to act under Art 232, after a number of requests had been made to the Council for progress in this area. The Court of Justice agreed that the Council had been 'called upon to act, by the Parliament, as required by Article 175(2) EC Treaty [now Art 232], and had produced equivocal replies as to what, if any, action it proposed to take'. The requirement in Arts 70 and 71 EC Treaty was not sufficiently precise, however, to amount to an enforceable obligation. Other cases have failed because the Court decided that all that was required was an opinion (**Chevally *v* Commission** (Case 15/70)), or because the decision which the applicant required was not to be addressed to him (**Lord Bethell *v* Commission** (Case 246/81)).

Claims for damages against Community institutions for unlawful acts: Article 288 EC Treaty

Article 233 EC Treaty specifically preserves the question of non-contractual liability as a separate issue from the legality or otherwise of institutional acts. As in English law, the fact that a public body has acted unlawfully does not, *per se*, mean that the body concerned is under a duty to compensate those adversely affected by its action, although a court does have the power to order the payment of compensation at the conclusion of an application for judicial review. Whether or not damages are payable under Community law depends on the way in which the Court has interpreted the provisions of Art 288 EC Treaty. The liability of Community institutions in contract will generally be governed by the law of the Member State where the institution is situated. Liability in non-contractual matters (tort, in English law) is governed by Art 288, second indent, which provides that:

> In the case of non-contractual liability, the Community shall, in accordance with the general principles common to the laws of the Member States, make good any damage caused by its institutions or by its servants in the performance of their duties.

The Court of Justice laid down some basic rules for liability in the following case:

Lütticke v *Commission* (Case 4/69)

The Court of Justice stated that there must be actual damage to the claimant and a causal link between the damage and the alleged unlawful conduct of the institution. Fault is not an essential element in liability, in the sense that the institution does not have to be conscious of any wrongdoing. The only type of fault that need be established is an unlawful act by the relevant institution. Where there is a positive duty to do something, there must be an omission to do it and where there is a discretion, it must have been exercised in an unlawful way. The wrongdoing is likely to have been the result of carelessness, failure to make appropriate inquiries or the giving of misleading information. The conduct giving rise to a claim under Art 288 will usually amount to no more than *faute de service* or poor administrative practice causing loss to the claimant. The scope for liability is much wider than under English law, however, and institutions can be liable for wrongful legislative acts.

This liability was, however, limited by the so-called **Schöppenstedt formula** (**Zückerfabrik Schöppenstedt *v* Council** (Case 5/71)). Under the formula the Court held that 'the Community does not incur liability on account of a legislative measure which involves choices of economic policy unless a sufficiently serious breach of a superior rule of law for the protection of the individual has occurred' (see **HNL *v* Council and Commission** (Case 83/77), para 4; **Unifruit Hellas *v* Commission** (Case T-489/93)).

The Court of Justice has subsequently extended the requirement of a 'sufficiently serious breach' to all cases for damages under Art 288 EC Treaty, unless there is a particular justification for a departure from this requirement:

Bergaderm and Goupil v Commission (Case C-352/98P)

The Court of Justice stated as follows:

39. The second paragraph of Article 215 of the Treaty [now Art 288] provides that, in the case of non-contractual liability, the Community is, in accordance with the general principles common to the laws of the Member States, to make good any damage caused by its institutions or by its servants in the performance of their duties.

40. The system of rules which the Court has worked out with regard to that provision takes into account, *inter alia*, the complexity of the situations to be regulated, difficulties in the application or interpretation of the texts and, more particularly, the margin of discretion available to the author of the act in question (Joined Cases C-46/93 and C-48/93 **Brasserie du Pêcheur** and **Factortame** [1996] ECR I-1029, paragraph 43).

41. **The Court has stated that the conditions under which the State may incur liability for damage caused to individuals by a breach of Community law cannot, in the absence of particular justification, differ from those governing the liability of the Community in like circumstances.** The protection of the rights which individuals derive from Community law cannot vary depending on whether a national authority or a Community authority is responsible for the damage (**Brasserie du Pêcheur** and **Factortame**, paragraph 42).

42. As regards Member State liability for damage caused to individuals, the Court has held that Community law confers a right to reparation where three conditions are met: the rule of law infringed must be intended to confer rights on individuals; the breach must be sufficiently serious; and there must be a direct causal link between the breach of the obligation resting on the State and the damage sustained by the injured parties (**Brasserie du Pêcheur** and **Factortame**, paragraph 51).

43. As to the second condition, as regards both Community liability under Article 215 of the Treaty [now Art 288] and Member State liability for breaches of Community law, **the decisive test for finding that a breach of Community law is sufficiently serious is whether the Member State or the Community institution concerned manifestly and gravely disregarded the limits on its discretion** (**Brasserie du Pêcheur** and **Factortame**, paragraph 55; and Joined Cases C-178/94, C-179/94, C-188/94, C-189/94, C-190/94 **Dillenkofer and Others** *v* Germany [1996] ECR I-4845, paragraph 25).

44. Where the Member State or the institution in question has only considerably reduced, or even no, discretion, the mere infringement of Community law may be sufficient to establish the existence of a sufficiently serious breach (see, to that effect, Case C-5/94 **Hedley Lomas** [1996] ECR I-2553, paragraph 28). [emphasis added]

In the above case, the Court of Justice reviewed its case law establishing Member States' liability for damage caused to individuals by a breach of Community law (referred to as state liability or **Francovich** damages, see Chapter 9). At para 41 the Court stated that 'the conditions under which the state may incur liability for damage caused to individuals by a breach of Community law cannot, in the absence of particular justification, differ from those governing the liability of the Community in like circumstances'. For the Community to incur non-contractual liability for an unlawful act, three conditions therefore have to be satisfied:

(i) the rule of law infringed must be intended to confer rights on individuals;

(ii) the breach of that rule of law must be sufficiently serious; and

(iii) there must be a direct causal link between the breach of the obligation resting on the Community institution and the damage sustained by the injured party.

The issue of 'sufficiently serious breach' has subsequently been considered by the CFI in the following case:

Afrikanische Frucht-Compagnie and Internationale Fruchtimport Gesellschaft Weichert & Co. v *Commission* (Joined Cases T-64/01 and T-65/01), and *Cantina sociale di Dolianova and Others* v *Commission* (Case T-166/98)

The CFI stated that as regards the requirement that the breach must be sufficiently serious, the decisive test for finding that there has been such a breach is whether the Member State or the Community institution concerned **manifestly and gravely disregarded the limits on its discretion.** Where the Member State or the institution in question has only considerably reduced discretion, or even no discretion at all, the mere infringement of Community law may be sufficient to establish the existence of a sufficiently serious breach.

The expression 'rule of law intended to confer rights on individuals' has been analysed on several occasions by the CFI. For instance, it has been held that the aim of the rules applicable to the system of the division of powers between the various Community institutions is to ensure that the balance between the institutions provided for in the Treaty is maintained and not to confer rights on individuals. Accordingly, any unlawful delegation of the Council's powers to the Commission is not such as to incur liability (**Afrikanische Frucht-Compagnie and Internationale Fruchtimport Gesellschaft Weichert & Co.** *v* **Commission**).

It has also been held, by reference to the case law of the Court of Justice, that infringement of the obligation to state reasons is not such as to give rise to the liability of the Community (**Afrikanische Frucht-Compagnie and Internationale Fruchtimport Gesellschaft Weichert & Co.** *v* **Commission**).

On the other hand, in its judgment in **Cantina sociale di Dolianova and Others** *v* **Commission**, the CFI held that the prohibition on unjust enrichment and the principle of non-discrimination were intended to confer rights on individuals. The breach by the Commission of those principles was held to be sufficiently serious.

Liability for a lawful act

Under Art 288 EC Treaty, in the case of non-contractual liability, the Community has, in accordance with the general principles common to the laws of the Member States, to make good any damage caused by its institutions or by its servants in the performance of their duties. In a series of judgments delivered in December 2005, the CFI, sitting as a Grand Chamber, expressly recognised that the Community could incur liability even in the absence of unlawful conduct:

FIAMM and FIAMM Technologies v *Council and Commission* (Case T-69/00); *Laboratoire du Bain* v *Council and Commission* (Case T-151/00); *Groupe Fremaux and Palais Royal* v *Council and Commission* (Case T-301/00); *CD Cartondruck* v *Council and Commission* (Case T-320/00); *Beamglow* v *Parliament and Others*; and *Fedon & Figli and Others* v *Council and Commission* (Case T-383/00)

In 1993, the Council adopted Regulation 404/93 introducing for the Member States common rules for the import of bananas (the COM for bananas). This Regulation contained preferential provisions for bananas from certain African, Caribbean and Pacific States. Following complaints lodged by certain states, the Dispute Settlement Board (DSB) of the World Trade Organisation (WTO) held that the Community regime governing the import of bananas was incompatible with the WTO agreements. In 1998 the Council therefore adopted a regulation amending that regime. Since the United States took the view that the new regime was still not compatible with the WTO agreements, it requested, and obtained, authorisation from the DSB to impose increased customs duty on imports of Community products appearing on a list drawn up by the United States' authorities. Six companies established in the EU brought proceedings before the CFI claiming compensation from the Commission and the Council for the damage alleged to have been suffered by them because the United States' retaliatory measures applied to their exports to the United States.

In its judgment the CFI first held that the Community could not incur liability in this case for unlawful conduct. However, it held that **where it has not been established that conduct attributed to the Community institutions is unlawful, that does not mean that undertakings which, as a category of economic operators, are required to bear a disproportionate part of the burden resulting from a restriction of access to export markets, can in no circumstances obtain compensation by virtue of the Community's non-contractual liability.** National laws on non-contractual liability allow individuals, albeit to varying degrees, in specific fields and in accordance with differing rules, to obtain compensation in legal proceedings for certain kinds of damage, even in the absence of unlawful action by the perpetrator of the damage. Where the damage caused by the conduct of the Community institution is not shown to be unlawful, the Community can incur non-contractual liability if the conditions as to (i) sustaining actual damage; (ii) the causal link between that damage and the conduct of the Community institution; and (iii) the unusual and special nature of the damage in question, are all met.

This is the first time that the Court has held that the Community could incur non-contractual liability in the absence of unlawful conduct on the part of its bodies, other than in a purely hypothetical case. In the above case, the CFI held that the condition requiring the applicants to have sustained damage was satisfied. That was also true of the condition relating to the causal link between that damage and the conduct of the institutions. The withdrawal of concessions in relation to the Community which took the form of the increased customs duties on imports was to be regarded as a consequence resulting objectively, in accordance with the normal and foreseeable operation of the WTO dispute settlement system which was accepted by the Community, from the retention in force by the defendant institutions of a banana import regime incompatible with the WTO agreements. Thus, the conduct of the defendant institutions necessarily led to the adoption of the retaliatory measure, and 'must be regarded as the immediate cause of the damage suffered by the applicants following imposition of the United States' increased customs duty.' On the other hand, the applicants had not succeeded in proving that they sustained unusual damage, that is to say, damage which exceeded the limits of the economic risks inherent in operating in the sector concerned. The possibility of tariff concessions being suspended is among the vicissitudes inherent in the current system of international trade and, accordingly, has to be borne by every operator who decides to sell his products on the market of one of the WTO members. The CFI therefore dismissed the six actions.

Remedies

The Court has not developed a comprehensive set of principles concerning the type and extent of damages which may be recovered, but certain rules have emerged in the case law. Actual financial loss that results from the unlawful action by the Commission may be recovered, but it must be established that this results directly from the unlawful conduct (**Dumortier Frères v Council** (Case 64/76)). The Court has also awarded damages for shock, disturbance and uneasiness, in Community staff cases (**Algera v Common Assembly** (Case 7/56)).

Difficulties may arise where a national authority has acted on what subsequently transpires to have been an unlawful act by a Community institution. Who is liable? Should the injured party sue the institution which promulgated the unlawful act, or the national institution which implemented it, or both? Where the claimant's loss has occurred as a result of being obliged to pay money under an unlawful act, and he is claiming restitution, he will be expected to claim in the national courts against the national institution (**Vreugdenhil v Commission** (Case C-282/90)). Where there is no remedy in the national courts, claims can be brought against the relevant institution in the Court of Justice (**Krohn v Commission** (Case 175/84), paras 24–29).

In the following case, the CFI reiterated the principle of the autonomy of remedies:

Holcim (France) v *Commission* (Case T-86/03)

The CFI held that where an applicant could have brought an action for annulment or for failure to act against an act or abstention allegedly causing it loss, but failed to do so, the failure to exercise such remedies does not in itself make the action for damages time-barred. On the question of autonomous remedies this case also allowed the CFI to clarify the scope of the case law according to which an action for damages is inadmissible where it actually seeks the withdrawal of an individual decision which has become definitive. That case law concerns 'the exceptional case where an application for compensation is brought for the payment of an amount precisely equal to the duty which the applicant was required to pay under an individual decision, so that the application seeks in fact the withdrawal of that individual decision' (see, for example, **Krohn v Commission** (Case 175/84), at para 33). The CFI made clear that this case law was relevant only where the alleged damage results solely from an individual administrative measure which has become definitive and which the person concerned could have contested in an action for annulment. In this case the loss alleged by the applicant did not result from an individual administrative measure which the applicant could have contested, but from the wrongful failure of the Commission to take a measure necessary to comply with a judgment. The action was therefore held admissible.

Summary

Now you have read this chapter you should be able to:

- Explain the range of Community acts which may be judicially reviewed by the Court of First Instance or the European Court of Justice pursuant to Art 230 EC Treaty.

- Outline the conditions which are applied to determine whether a 'privileged' applicant has the standing to challenge the legality of a Community act, and compare and contrast such conditions with those which are applied to determine a 'non-privileged' applicant's standing.

- Explain the four grounds upon which a Community act may be challenged: 1) lack of competence; 2) infringement of an essential procedural requirement; 3) infringement of the Treaty or any rule of law relating to its application; and 4) misuse of powers.

- Understand how Arts 241 and 234 EC Treaty may be utilised to enable an indirect challenge to be made against a Community act.

- Discuss the extent of the power to challenge a Community institution's failure to act, pursuant to Art 232 EC Treaty.

- Explain how the European Court of Justice applies the rules relating to a claim for damages against a Community institution for unlawful acts, pursuant to Art 288 EC Treaty.

References

Hunnings, N.M., 'The Stanley Adams Affair or the Biter Bit' (1987) 24 CML Rev 65.

Further reading

Textbooks

Craig, P. and De Burca, G. (2003) *EU Law Text, Cases and Materials* (3rd edn), Oxford University Press, Chapters 12 and 13.

Foster, N. (2006) *Foster on EU Law* (1st edn), Oxford University Press, Chapter 6 (Sections 6.4 to 6.8).

Schermers, H.G., Mead, P. and Heukels, T. (eds) (1988) *Non-Contractual Liability of the European Communities*, Nijhoff Publications.

Steiner, J., Woods, L. and Twigg-Flesner, C. (2006) *EU Law* (9th edn), Oxford University Press, Chapters 11 to 13.

Storey, T. and Turner, C. (2005) *Unlocking EU Law* (1st edn), Hodder Arnold, Chapter 6 (Section 6.3).

Tillotson, J. and Foster, N. (2003) *Text, Cases and Materials on EU Law* (4th edn), Cavendish Publishing, Chapter 19.

Weatherill, S. (2006) *Cases and Materials on EU Law* (7th edn), Oxford University Press, Chapter 8.

Journal articles

Arnull, A., 'Private Applicants and the Action for Annulment under Art 173 of the EC Treaty' (1995) 32 CML Rev 7.

Arnull, A., 'Private Applicants and the Action for Annulment since **Codorniu**' (2001) 38 CML Rev 7.

Greaves, R.M., 'Locus Standi under Article 173 when Seeking Annulment of a Regulation' (1986) 11 EL Rev 119.

Harlow, C., 'Towards a Theory of Access for the European Court of Justice' (1992) 12 YEL 213.

Hunnings, N.M., 'The Stanley Adams Affair or the Biter Bit' (1987) 24 CML Rev 65.

Koch, C., '*Locus standi* of private applicants under the EU Constitution: Preserving gaps in the protection of individuals' right to an effective remedy' (2005) 30 EL Rev 511.

Lefevre, S., 'Rules of procedure do matter: The legal status of the institutions' power of self-organisation' (2005) 30 EL Rev 802.

Tridimas, T., 'Liability for breach of Community law: Growing up and mellowing down?' (2001) 38 CML Rev 301.

Vogt, M., 'Indirect judicial protection in EC law – the case of the plea of illegality' (2006) 31 EL Rev 364.

Wils, W., 'Concurrent liability of the Community and a Member State' (1992) 17 EL Rev 191.

Principles of supremacy, direct effect, indirect effect and state liability

Aims and objectives

At the end of this chapter you should understand:

- What is meant by 'the supremacy of Community law'.
- The principle of direct effect, how to apply the test for ascertaining whether a provision of Community law is capable of having direct effect, and the rule that 'generally' excludes directives from having horizontal direct effect.
- The **Marleasing** interpretative obligation and how UK courts and tribunals have applied this obligation.
- The principle of state liability established by the Court of Justice in **Francovich** and how this principle has developed.

The supremacy of Community law

Nowhere in the Treaty is there a reference to the supremacy of Community law. However, the Court of Justice has consistently held that this principle of supremacy is implied in the Treaty. The Court addressed this issue of supremacy in the following case:

Flaminio Costa v ENEL (Case 6/64)

In an oft-quoted statement, the Court of Justice stated that:

> By creating a Community of unlimited duration, having its own institutions, its own personality, its own legal capacity and capacity of representation on the international plane and, more particularly, real powers stemming from a limitation of sovereignty or a transfer of powers from the States of the Community, **the Member States have limited their sovereign rights**, albeit within limited fields, and have thus **created a body of law which binds both their nationals and themselves.** [emphasis added]

This principle of supremacy has never been explicitly set out within a Treaty. However, Art I–6 of the proposed Constitutional Treaty (which has not come into force because it has not been ratified by all the Member States) would have provided that 'The Constitution and law adopted by the institutions of the Union in exercising competences conferred on it shall have primacy over the law of the Member States'.

Article 226 EC Treaty – ineffective means of enforcement

As discussed in Chapter 7, Art 226 EC Treaty (previously Art 169) expressly provides a mechanism for infraction proceedings to be initiated by the Commission against a defaulting Member State to ensure the state complies with its Community law obligations. The weakness in the Art 226 EC Treaty procedure, as initially formulated, was that there was no provision for imposing a penalty on a defaulting Member State; it proved ineffective in dealing with a recalcitrant Member State. However, as discussed in Chapter 7, following amendments made to the EC Treaty by the TEU, if a Member State fails to comply with a declaration made by the Court of Justice that it is in breach of Community law, the Commission may take action against that state under Art 228(2) EC Treaty. In this instance the Court of Justice can impose a financial penalty (a penalty payment and/or a lump sum penalty) on the defaulting Member State.

An additional weakness is Art 226's failure to sufficiently safeguard the rights of individuals (e.g. a compensation order cannot be made against the defaulting Member State in favour of an aggrieved individual). The UK, for example, may have failed to implement a directive or may have implemented it incorrectly. With regard to employment-related directives, the purpose of such directives is to provide protection for employees. Breach of such a directive may have a significant impact upon an indeterminate number of workers. The fact that the UK may be brought before the Court of Justice will be of little comfort to this group of persons deprived of their rights under Community law. The fact that Community law is considered by the Court of Justice to be supreme is irrelevant. It does not repair the possible damage suffered by them, unless they are provided with rights which they can enforce in the courts of Member States.

The impact on individuals can be illustrated by considering the Working Time Directive 93/104 (OJ 1993 L 307/18) which should have been implemented by all Member States by 23 November 1996. The UK failed to implement it on time. The directive provides rights for individual workers (e.g. four weeks' paid annual leave, minimum daily and weekly rest periods and a 48-hour maximum working week; all of which are subject to certain exceptions and derogations). A relatively short breach by the UK could have an enormous impact on an indeterminate number of workers. The UK implemented the directive by the Working Time Regulations 1998 (SI 1998/1833) which came into force on 1 October 1998 (almost two years after the date stipulated in the directive). The Commission had taken no action against the UK under Art 226. Even if it had taken action, provided the UK implemented the directive before expiry of the time limit laid down in the reasoned opinion, the UK could not have been brought before the Court of Justice. In addition, if the Court had ruled against the UK, it would not have had the power to award compensation to those workers whose rights had been infringed by the UK's failure to implement the directive.

Development of Community law principles

In an attempt to address the problem of ineffective individual rights, the Court of Justice developed principles whereby an aggrieved national of a Member State would be afforded rights based upon Community law which could, in certain circumstances, be enforced in the courts of Member States. These rights are enshrined in the three principles of direct effect, indirect effect and state liability (also referred to as **Francovich** damages).

These principles have been established by the Court of Justice following referrals to it from national courts pursuant to Art 234 EC Treaty (previously Art 177) (see Chapter 6). These three principles will be considered further.

The principle of direct effect

The Court of Justice developed the principle of direct effect in the following case:

Van Gend en Loos v Nederlandse Administratie der Belastingen (Case 26/62)

Van Gend en Loos had imported ureaformaldehyde from Germany into The Netherlands. It had been charged a customs duty. This breached the rules on the free movement of goods between Member States, and in particular Art 12 EC Treaty (now Art 25). Van Gend en Loos issued proceedings in a Dutch court, claiming reimbursement of the customs duty from the Dutch government. The court referred the question of whether or not the claimant could rely on Art 12 in the national court to the Court of Justice. The Court of Justice first of all addressed the general question of whether Treaty provisions could confer directly effective rights on individuals, and held as follows:

> The Community constitutes a new legal order of international law for the benefit of which the States have limited their sovereign rights, albeit within limited fields, and the subjects of which comprise not only the Member States but also their nationals. **Independently of the legislation of Member States Community law therefore not only imposes obligations on individuals but is also intended to confer on them rights which become part of their legal heritage. These rights arise not only where they are expressly granted by the Treaty, but also by reason of obligations which the Treaty imposes in a clearly defined way upon individuals as well as upon Member States** and upon institutions of the Community. [emphasis added]

Effective supervision

Prior to **Van Gend en Loos** the accepted method of enforcement was, as stated above, for the Commission to issue infraction proceedings against the defaulting Member State under the former Art 169 EC Treaty (now Art 226). However, even if such proceedings proved successful, this would have been of no assistance to Van Gend en Loos. It would not have resulted in the repayment to it of the customs duty levied in breach of Community law. The Court of Justice accordingly dismissed the suggestion (by Belgium, The Netherlands and (West) Germany) that, because there existed machinery under the former Art 169 to bring offending states before the Court of Justice, this must preclude the possibility of the use of Treaty provisions before national courts:

Van Gend en Loos v Nederlandse Administratie der Belastingen (Case 26/62)

The Court of Justice stated that:

> the argument based on Articles 169 and 170 of the Treaty [now Articles 226 and 227] put forward by the three Governments ... is misconceived. The fact that these Articles of the Treaty enable the Commission and the Member States to bring before the Court a State which has not fulfilled its obligations does not mean that individuals cannot plead these obligations, should the occasion arise, before a national court, any more than the fact that the Treaty places at the disposal of the

Commission ways of ensuring that obligations imposed upon those subject to the Treaty are observed, precludes the possibility, in actions between individuals before a national court, of pleading infringement of these obligations ... The vigilance of individuals concerned to protect their rights amounts to an effective supervision in addition to the supervision entrusted by Articles 169 and 170 [now 226 and 227] to the diligence of the Commission and of the Member States. [emphasis added]

In this landmark judgment the Court of Justice created the principle of direct effect which was based upon the premise that the Treaty created rights for citizens of Member States which, if enforced by them in the courts of the Member States, would provide an additional supervisory function to that already contained in the former Arts 169 and 170 EC Treaty (now Arts 226 and 227).

The scope of direct effect

The Court of Justice, in establishing the general principle of direct effect, limited its scope only to those provisions which were *sufficiently precise and unconditional*. This has been applied quite flexibly by the Court and has resulted in articles of the Treaty and provisions of directives being held to be directly effective by the Court in circumstances where a national court could have been excused from coming to the opposite conclusion.

Before considering the three forms of Community legislation (EC Treaty, regulations and directives) separately, the following examples give an indication of the Court of Justice's approach in determining whether or not a provision is *sufficiently precise and unconditional*.

Sufficiently precise

In **Van Duyn** *v* **Home Office** (Case 41/74) the Court of Justice held that Art 3(1) of the Residence and Public Policy, Security and Health Directive 64/221 (OJ Sp. Ed. 1964 850/64 p. 117), which provides that 'measures taken on the grounds of *public policy* or of *public security* shall be based exclusively on the personal conduct of the individual concerned' (emphasis added), was sufficiently precise to be capable of having direct effect, despite the fact that the scope of 'public policy' and 'public security' would require determination by the Court. Directive 64/221 has since been replaced by Directive 2004/38.

Similarly, in **Defrenne** *v* **SABENA** (Case 43/75) the Court of Justice held that the former Art 119 EC Treaty (now Art 141), which set out a principle that men and women 'should receive equal pay for equal work', was sufficiently precise to be capable of having direct effect despite the fact that the scope of 'equal pay' and 'equal work' would likewise have to be determined by the Court.

The above two cases illustrate the Court of Justice's approach in determining whether or not a provision is 'sufficiently precise'.

Unconditional

A Community provision is 'unconditional' if it is not subject, in its implementation or effects, to any additional measure by either the Community institutions or Member States.

In **Van Gend en Loos** *v* **Administratie der Belastingen** (Case 26/62), the former Art 12 EC Treaty (now Art 25) was held by the Court of Justice to be unconditional because it imposed a negative obligation on Member States to 'refrain from introducing between themselves any new customs duties on imports and exports ... and from increasing those which they already apply in their trade with each other'. It was not qualified by any reservation on the part of the Member States which would make its implementation conditional upon a positive legislative measure being enacted under national law.

This case can be contrasted with **Costa v ENEL** (Case 6/64), where the Court of Justice held, *inter alia*, that the former Art 102 EC Treaty (now Art 97) was not unconditional. The former Art 102 provided that, where a Member State intended to adopt or amend its laws in such a way that there was a reason to fear this might cause distortion of the conditions of competition in the common market, there was an obligation of prior consultation between the Member State and the Commission. It was held that this was *not* unconditional because it was subject to additional measures in the form of 'prior consultation' and therefore was not capable of having direct effect.

Treaty articles

As a general principle, treaties and international agreements are not capable, in international law, of conferring rights on individuals in the courts of their own state. However, as discussed above, the Court of Justice has developed the principle of direct effect to provide otherwise with regard to Community law (**Van Gend en Loos v Nederlandse Administratie der Belastingen** (Case 26/62)).

The principle of direct effect was established in **Van Gend en Loos** but its application was still unclear. Certain Treaty provisions were to be enforceable against Member States, provided that the obligations imposed were 'sufficiently precise' and 'unconditional'. These were necessary preconditions, because many Treaty provisions are set out in the most general terms and do not appear to impose a commitment to do anything. Sometimes they express no more than a statement or an aspiration. Article 191 EC Treaty, for example, provides that 'Political parties at European level are important as a factor for integration within the Union'. Following **Van Gend en Loos**, and largely on the basis of the chance appearance of appropriate cases before it, the Court of Justice has developed its criteria for determining whether particular Treaty provisions have direct effect, and if so, against whom.

In **Van Gend en Loos** the Court had found that the former Art 12 EC Treaty (now Art 25) was directly effective against the state. It had reached this position to some extent, at least, on the basis that the state had entered into a commitment when it signed the Treaty. That commitment was owed not only to the other Member States as parties, but also to its own citizens as actual or potential beneficiaries of the Treaty. However, the decision did not resolve the status of Treaty provisions between private citizens. Could a private citizen rely on an article of the Treaty, provided that it was sufficiently precise and unconditional, against another private citizen or undertaking? The Court did not give an unequivocal reply to this question until 13 years later in the following case:

Defrenne v *SABENA* (Case 43/75)

An air stewardess made a claim against her employer for equal pay to that received by male stewards. Article 119 EC Treaty (now Art 141) provided that 'Each Member State shall during the first stage ensure and subsequently maintain the application of the principle that men and women should receive equal pay for equal work'. Belgium had not enacted legislation to bring this about. The issue was whether the claimant could rely on Art 119 in her national court. The case was referred to the Court of Justice on a reference under Art 177 (now Art 234) (see Chapter 6).

The Court of Justice dismissed the suggestion that the wording of the article confined the obligation to the Member State itself, and held as follows:

[35]   In its reference to 'Member States', Article 119 [now Art 141] is alluding to those States in the exercise of all those of their functions which may usefully contribute to the implementation of the principle of equal pay ... Thus ... this provision is far from merely referring the matter to the powers of the national legislative authorities. Therefore, the reference to 'Member States' in Article 119 cannot be interpreted as excluding the intervention of the courts in the direct application of the Treaty ... Since Article 119 is mandatory in nature, the prohibition on discrimination between men and women applies not only to the action of public authorities, but also extends to all agreements which are intended to regulate paid labour collectively, as well as to contracts between individuals. [emphasis added]

The effect of the above judgment was, therefore, that the former Art 119 (now Art 141) could be used between individuals in relation to a contract of employment. Some articles of the Treaty could thus be vertically effective (i.e. directly enforceable by private individuals/undertakings against the state, as in **Van Gend en Loos**) or both vertically and horizontally effective (i.e. directly enforceable by private individuals/undertakings against the state, *and* by private individuals/undertakings against other private individuals/undertakings) according to their wording and the context. In subsequent years the Court has found the former Art 7 EC Treaty (now Art 12), prohibiting discrimination on grounds of nationality, to be both vertically and horizontally effective. This was the situation in the following case:

Walrave and Koch v Association Union Cycliste Internationale (Case 36/74)

The Court of Justice held that:

... prohibition of such discrimination does not only apply to the acts of public authorities, but extends likewise to rules of any other nature aimed at regulating in a collective manner gainful employment and the provision of services.

Other Treaty provisions have also been held to be both horizontally and vertically effective, including:

- Articles 28 and 29 (prohibiting the imposition of restrictions on the export and import of goods: **Dansk Supermarked** (Case 58/80));
- Article 39 (free movement of workers: **Donà** v **Mantero** (Case 13/76));
- Articles 43 and 49 (the right of establishment of businesses and professions and the right to provide services: **Thieffry** v **Paris Bar Association** (Case 71/76)); and
- Articles 81 and 82 (the prohibition of restrictive agreements and the abuse of a monopoly position: **Brasseries de Haecht** (Case 48/72); **Marty** (Case 37/79)).

The accumulation of case law in relation to a number of these provisions has resulted in a subtle change in the terminology of the Court of Justice. In the jurisprudence of the Court, many of these Treaty provisions, especially those relating to freedom of movement, have come to be regarded not merely as directly effective Treaty provisions at the suit of individuals in national courts, but also as *fundamental rights* of EU citizens. The principle of direct effect is regarded as fundamentally important to the development of the Community. As a judge of the Court of Justice has declared: 'Without direct effect, we should have a very different Community today – a more obscure, more remote Community barely distinguishable from so many other international organisations whose existence passes unnoticed by ordinary citizens' (Mancini and Keeling, 1994).

Regulations

The EC Treaty provides in Art 249(2) that 'A regulation shall have general application. It shall be binding in its entirety and directly applicable'. The reference to 'directly applicable' means that domestic legislation is not required in order to incorporate a regulation into national law. Community regulations are thus part of UK law without any further need of implementation. Indeed, any attempt at express incorporation is illegal, unless it is explicitly or implicitly required by the regulation itself (**Fratelli Variola SpA v Amministrazione Italiana delle Finanze** (Case 34/73)). Whether or not a directly applicable measure is 'directly effective' (i.e. is capable of creating individual rights which a national court must recognise) will depend on the terms of the regulation; it must be 'sufficiently precise and unconditional' (see above). In practice, many are directly effective and are a fruitful source of individual rights (see e.g., Reg 1612/68 on employment rights of migrant workers, and Reg 1408/71 on social security benefits for those employed and self-employed in other Member States; see also Chapters 12 and 14). Regulations which are 'sufficiently precise and unconditional' will be both vertically and horizontally effective (i.e. directly enforceable by private individuals/undertakings against the state, *and* by private individuals/undertakings against other private individuals/undertakings).

Directives

Implementation of directives

Directives were not originally seen as being capable of creating directly effective rights. In contrast to regulations, they are not described as having direct applicability:

> A directive shall be binding, as to the result to be achieved, upon each Member State to which it is addressed, but shall leave to the national authorities the choice of form and method. (Art 249 EC Treaty (third indent))

Unlike regulations, directives are not directed at the world at large but at Member States. In the case of Treaty articles, this did not deter the Court from finding that individuals could also be bound by them (see **Defrenne**, above). However, unlike Treaty articles, directives are always conditional. They depend, under Art 249 EC Treaty, on the Member State giving effect to them. They have, since the inception of the Treaty, been a form of legislative subsidiarity, giving the Member State the option of the way in which it will legislate to meet the Community's objectives. The problem, as it became clear to both the Commission and the Court of Justice, was that Member States either simply did not implement directives by the date required, or implemented them in such a way as to fail, in whole or in part, to achieve their objectives.

Implementation does not mean that a directive must be directly transposed into national law. The Court described the Member States' obligations in the following case:

Commission v Germany (Re Nursing Directives) (Case 29/84)

The Court of Justice stated:

> The implementation of a directive does not necessarily require legislative action in each Member State. In particular, the existence of general principles of constitutional and administrative law may render the implementation by specific legislation superfluous, provided, however, that those principles guarantee that the national authorities will, in fact, apply the directive fully, and where the directive is intended to create rights for individuals, the legal position arising from those principles is sufficiently clear and precise, and the persons concerned are made fully aware of their rights, and, where appropriate, are afforded the possibility of relying upon them before national courts. (para 23)

Although legislation may not always be necessary in relation to directives which are not intended to confer rights on individuals, the vast majority have either that intention, or at least that effect if implemented. In such cases, the issue of circular letters, urging a change of policy or a change in administrative practice, will not constitute implementation. Such practices, which may alter from time to time at the whim of the authority, and be quite unknown to the ordinary citizen, completely lack the certainty and transparency which Community law demands (**Commission** v **Belgium** (Case 102/79)).

A failure to correctly implement a directive often results in a complaint by interested individuals and groups to the relevant Directorate-General in the Commission. This will usually be followed by protracted correspondence between the Commission and the offending state. If this is unsuccessful, formal Art 226 EC Treaty proceedings may be instituted by the Commission in the Court of Justice. Finally, if non-implementation persists, the case may come before the Court, and the Court may impose a financial penalty on the Member State if its judgment is not complied with (Arts 226 and 228 EC Treaty, see Chapter 7). The process, from first complaint to judgment, may take several years. Enforcement procedures, given the limited resources of the Commission, can only be a partial solution to the problem. Until all Member States have implemented a directive, however, those states which fail to do so may gain an unfair competitive advantage. Many directives, for example those aimed at enhancing workers' rights, can significantly increase business costs. In addition, individuals may be deprived of rights which Community law has sought to provide them with. It is this situation to which the Court of Justice responded in its approach to unimplemented (or incorrectly implemented) directives.

Direct effect of directives

It is clear from the wording of Art 249 EC Treaty that directives were not to be directly applicable in the same way as regulations. They required Member States to act to give the directives effect in their territories. However, in **Grad** (Case 9/70) the Court suggested, in a case turning on the effect of a regulation, that a directive might have some effect in a state where it had not been implemented by the due date. In the following case, the Court of Justice took its first important step towards recognising the direct effect of a directive:

❧ Van Duyn v Home Office (Case 41/74)

The claimant in the case, Ms Van Duyn, a Dutch national, was a member of the Church of Scientology. She wished to enter the UK to work at the headquarters of the organisation. She was refused leave to enter. The UK government had decided some years previously that the

Church of Scientology was an undesirable organisation, although no steps had been taken against it, except to publicise the government's view.

In this case, *prima facie*, Ms Van Duyn, as a worker, had a right of entry under Art 39 EC Treaty. That right was, and remains, subject to the right of the host state to exclude and expel on public policy and public security grounds. The limits of the powers of the host state to derogate from its Treaty obligation on these grounds, and the extent of the procedural rights of those affected by such a decision, were set out in the former Directive 64/221 (which has been repealed and replaced by Directive 2004/38). In particular, Art 3(1), Directive 64/221 provided that a decision should be based 'exclusively on the personal conduct of the individual concerned'. Ms Van Duyn argued that membership of an organisation could not be 'personal conduct' under Art 3(1). The UK government maintained that its power to refuse entry could not be limited in this way, because the UK had not yet implemented Directive 64/221 (it remained unimplemented for 20 years, see Chapter 16). The case was referred to the Court of Justice under the former Art 177 EC Treaty (now Art 234). The Court refused to accept the position taken by the UK government, and held as follows:

> The UK observes that, since Article 189 [now Art 249] of the Treaty distinguishes between the effects ascribed to regulations, directives and decisions, it must therefore be presumed that the Council, in issuing a directive rather than making a regulation, must have intended that the directive should have had an effect other than that of a regulation and accordingly that the former should not be directly applicable .. However ... it does not follow from this that other categories of acts mentioned in that article can never have similar effects. It would be incompatible with the binding effect attributed to a directive by Article 189 to exclude, in principle, the possibility that the obligation which it imposes may be invoked by those concerned. In particular, where the Community authorities have, by directive, imposed on Member States the obligation to pursue a particular course of conduct, the useful effect of such an act would be weakened if individuals were prevented from relying on it before their national courts and if the latter were prevented from taking it into consideration as an element of Community law.

The guiding principle adopted by the Court of Justice in the above case is that of ensuring the *effet utile* (the useful effect) of a measure in the territories and courts of Member States. In addition to this guiding principle is another (implied) principle, known to continental as well as to common law lawyers. This principle is referred to as the equitable doctrine of estoppel, or the continental doctrine of the impermissibility of reliance on one's own turpitude. Application of this principle prevents a Member State from defending itself against a claim by an individual by raising as a defence its own failure to implement a directive (Advocate-General Van Gerven in **Barber** (Case C–262/88)). Once the deadline for implementing a directive has passed, and not before (see **Ratti** (Case 148/78)), an individual may enforce the directive against the government of the state which has failed to implement it. The directive is therefore *vertically* effective.

Not every directive is, however, effective in this way. As the Court said in **Van Duyn**, 'it is necessary to examine in every case, whether the nature, general scheme and wording of the provision in question are capable of having direct effects'; i.e. are the provisions 'unconditional and sufficiently precise?' (**Becker** (Case 8/81)).

Directives – 'sufficiently precise and unconditional'

The fact that a directive requires Member States to perform a positive act to implement it does not in itself prevent it from being capable of being unconditional.

The Court of Justice held in **Francovich *v* Republic of Italy** (Cases C–6 & 9/90) that in the case of employment-related directives in general, in order to be sufficiently precise and unconditional, it is necessary to be able to:

- identify the persons who are entitled to the right;
- ascertain the content of that right; and
- identify the person/body liable to provide that right.

A similar approach was adopted by the Court of Justice in **Kampelmann *v* Landschaftsverband Westfalen-Lippe** (Cases C–253–258/96) in which it was held that Art 2(2)(c), Directive 91/583 (OJ 1991 L 288/32), which imposed an obligation on employers to inform their employees of the conditions applicable to their contract or employment relationship, was sufficiently clear and precise to be capable of having direct effect.

The **Francovich** case concerned Directive 80/987 (OJ 1980 L 283/23) which sought to protect employees on their employers' insolvency:

Francovich v *Republic of Italy* (Case C-6 &9/90)

The persons entitled to the rights under Directive 80/987 were employees (Art 2(2) of the directive refers to national law for the definition of the terms 'employee' and 'employer'). The Court of Justice held this was sufficiently precise to allow a national judge to ascertain whether an applicant had the status of employee under national law and whether the applicant was excluded from the scope of the directive under the specific exclusions set out therein.

The content of the right was more problematic. In implementing the directive, the Member State was given a number of choices, which included, *inter alia*:

- Choice of date from which the payment of wages would accrue. As a result Member States could limit the payment of wages to periods of three months or eight weeks.
- A discretion to set a liability ceiling so that payment of wages would not exceed a certain sum.

Given these legislative choices it would appear that the directive was not unconditional or sufficiently precise. However, the Court of Justice held that it was possible to calculate the minimum guarantee provided for by the directive which would impose the least burden on the body liable to provide the benefit (i.e. the 'guarantee institution'). With regard to the discretion to set a liability ceiling, the Court of Justice held that this discretion would not be available, however, unless the Member State had actually implemented the directive and taken advantage of the derogation in its implementing legislation.

The identity of the person/body liable to provide the benefit was subject to the Member State making a legislative choice as to whether the body should be public or private, or whether it would be publicly or privately funded. Under the directive, Member States enjoyed a wide discretion with regard to the functioning and financing of the 'guarantee institution'. The Member State had to identify the institution which would be liable to provide the benefit. The Court of Justice held this provision was not sufficiently precise or unconditional and therefore the directive was not capable of having direct effect.

The state . . .

As discussed above, the Court of Justice held that if a directive was 'sufficiently precise and unconditional' then it could be enforced against the state (i.e. vertical direct effect). It was not until 1986 in the following case that the Court explicitly stated that directives could *not* be enforced against private individuals and legal persons (although see below on this issue):

Marshall v Southampton Area Health Authority (Case 152/84)

The Court of Justice declared that a directive could only be directly enforced against the *state*. After considering the effect of the third paragraph of the former Art 189 (now Art 249), the Court stated (at paras 46 and 48) that:

> a Member State which has not adopted the implementing measures required by the directive within the prescribed period may not plead, as against individuals, its own failure to perform the obligations which the directive entails . . . According to Article 189 [now Art 249] . . . the binding nature of a directive . . . exists only in relation to 'each Member State to which it is addressed'. It follows that a directive may not of itself impose obligations on an individual and that a provision of a directive may not be relied upon as such against such a person.

In the above case, the Court of Justice's reasoning for distinguishing between vertical and horizontal effect was based upon the fact that the former Art 189 EC Treaty (now Art 249) does not provide for directives to bind individuals and therefore it would be unfair for the Court to give them such an effect. The Court of Justice, however, was anxious to prevent a Member State from defending an action on the basis of its own wrongdoing.

So, if the directive is sufficiently precise and unconditional, the individual can enforce the unimplemented directive against 'the state'. But what constitutes 'the state'? Under Art 10 EC Treaty, the obligation to implement Community law binds the Member States. The Court of Justice has been prepared to give that term a broad interpretation. Initially, it referred to the state exercising various functions and it was not necessary that it should be engaged in activities normally carried on by (or associated with) the state, such as operating immigration controls, collecting taxes, enforcing public health measures. In addition, directives were enforceable against the state when it was, for example, simply acting as an employer, as illustrated in the following case:

Marshall v Southampton Area Health Authority (Case 152/84)

The claimant was employed by the Health Authority. She wished to retire at 65, the same age as her male colleagues. The rules of the authority required her to retire at the age of 60. She was dismissed on the grounds of her age at 62, and brought proceedings against the Authority on grounds of sex discrimination. Discrimination on grounds of sex in relation to conditions of employment is prohibited by Directive 76/207. The UK's Sex Discrimination Act 1975, which had been enacted to implement the directive while it was still in draft form, contained an exception, allowing differential male and female retirement ages. There was no such exception in the directive. To that extent, therefore, the UK had failed to correctly implement the directive. The question to be determined was whether Marshall could enforce the directive against the Health Authority. The Court of Justice, on a referral under Art 177 EC Treaty (now Art 234), held that she could:

> Where a person involved in legal proceedings is able to rely on a directive as against the State, he

may do so regardless of the capacity in which the latter is acting, whether employer or public authority. In either case it is necessary to prevent the State from taking advantage of its own failure to comply with Community law.

In the above case, the Court of Justice added that it was for the national courts to determine the status of a body for the purposes of determining whether or not a directive could be directly enforced against it. It has, however, continued to give guidance. It decided in **Costanzo** *v* **Comune di Milano** (Case 103/88) that 'the state' included 'all organs of the administration, including decentralised authorities such as municipalities'. How 'decentralised' a body could be, and still be bound, was still to be determined by the Court of Justice.

... or emanation of the state

In the following case, the Court of Justice addressed the issue of how 'decentralised' a body could be, and still be bound by an unimplemented or incorrectly implemented directive:

Foster v *British Gas* (Case C-188/89)

The UK's House of Lords requested a preliminary ruling from the Court of Justice, pursuant to the former Art 177 EC Treaty (now Art 234), on the question of whether the British Gas Corporation (BGC) was, at the material time, a body of such a type that individuals could directly enforce a directive against it in the national courts and tribunals. At the material time, BGC had not been privatised (it was privatised on 24 August 1986 by the UK's Gas Act 1986). Foster was employed by BGC and was made to retire at the age of 60. This was in line with company policy which required women to retire at the age of 60 and men at the age of 65. As discussed above, under English law (the Sex Discrimination Act 1975, which was in force at the material time) although it was unlawful for any employer to discriminate against a woman employed in Great Britain 'by dismissing her or subjecting her to any other detriment', this did not apply to 'provisions in relation to death or retirement'. Foster therefore sought to rely upon the Equal Treatment Directive (Council Directive 76/207) which did not allow discriminatory retirement ages.

In the **Marshall** case, the Court of Justice interpreted the Equal Treatment Directive as meaning that such a general policy of discriminatory retirement ages constituted discrimination on grounds of sex, contrary to the directive, which could be relied upon against a state authority. Foster's application to an employment tribunal was dismissed on the ground the BGC was not a state authority within the meaning of **Marshall** and therefore the directive could not be relied upon against it. This decision was subsequently confirmed by both the Employment Appeal Tribunal and the Court of Appeal. The question of 'state authority' was critical to the outcome of the case, hence the House of Lords' referral of such question to the Court of Justice.

The Court of Justice (at para 20) developed a test to be applied to ascertain if the body against whom a directive was sought to be enforced was an *emanation of the state*:

> ... a body, whatever its legal form, which has been made responsible, pursuant to a measure adopted by the State, for providing a public service under the control of the State and has for that purpose special powers beyond those which result from the normal rules applicable in relations between individuals **is included** in any event among the bodies against which the provisions of a directive capable of having direct effect may be relied upon. [emphasis added]

The three **Foster** criteria, established by the Court of Justice in the above case, for determining whether a body is an 'emanation of the state' can be summarised as:

- provision of a public service;
- under state control; and
- having special powers.

The Court of Justice returned the case to the House of Lords for the test to be applied to the facts of the case:

Foster v British Gas (No. 2) [1991] 2 AC 306

Lord Templeman was of the view that there was no justification for a narrow or strained construction of the Court of Justice's ruling (at p. 315, paras E–F). He further stated (at p. 315, paras G–H):

> I decline to apply the ruling of the European Court of Justice, couched in terms of broad principle and purposive language characteristic of Community law, in a manner which is ... sometimes applied to an enactment of the UK ... I can find no warrant in the present circumstances for the limited and speculative approach of [British Gas plc] and have no means of judging whether the relevant provisions of the Directive are enforceable against the BGC save by applying the plain words of the ruling of the European Court of Justice.

Lord Templeman reviewed the regulatory provisions under the UK's Gas Act 1972 whereby the Secretary of State was authorised to make regulations and whereby the BGC was obliged to develop and maintain a gas supply for the UK (see s 2, Gas Act 1972) and he concluded (at p. 313, para F):

> Thus the BGC was a body which was made responsible pursuant to a measure adopted by the State [i.e. the Gas Act 1972] for providing a public service.

He further held (at p. 314, para B) that the BGC performed its public service under the control of the state:

> The BGC was not independent, its members were appointed by the State; the BGC was responsible to the minister acting on behalf of the State, and the BGC was subject to directions given by the Secretary of State.

Under s 29, Gas Act 1972 the BGC was afforded a monopoly for the supply of gas. This was sufficient for it to satisfy the Court's third criterion that the BGC had conferred upon it 'special powers beyond those which result from the normal rules applicable in relations between individuals' (at p. 314, para D).

The House of Lords held that the BGC satisfied the three criteria established by the Court of Justice and therefore the BGC was an 'emanation of the state' against which the directive could be enforced. The inconsistent provisions of the Sex Discrimination Act 1975 would be overridden.

Three important post-**Foster** cases in the UK have considered the concept of 'emanation of the state' and the application of the **Foster** test.

The first case was factually similar to the **Marshall** and **Foster** cases:

Doughty v Rolls-Royce plc [1992] CMLR 1045

Ms Doughty was compulsorily retired at age 60, in accordance with company policy that women retire at 60 whereas men retire only at 65. As considered above, such discrimination was, at the material time, expressly permitted under English law. Doughty sought to rely upon the Equal Treatment Directive. The question before the Court of Appeal was whether or not Rolls-Royce was an emanation of the state. Lord Justice Mustill gave the leading judgment with which Lord Justice Butler-Sloss and Sir John Megaw agreed.

Mustill LJ quoted extensively from the employment tribunal's findings of fact as to the nature of Rolls-Royce, which at the material time had not been privatised (see p. 1048, para 8). All of Rolls-Royce's shares were held on behalf of the Crown; the ultimate power in relation to the company and its business rested with the shareholder (i.e. the Crown) by virtue of its ability to pass resolutions in General Meeting. In December 1980 a 'Memorandum of Understanding with Rolls-Royce – Relationship with Government' was issued. This provided that the government had three separate roles in its relationship with Rolls-Royce:

- that of 100 per cent shareholder;
- that of principal customer for the development and production of military engines; and
- that of its overall sponsorship of the aerospace industry.

The employment tribunal held that Rolls-Royce was an emanation of the state because as 100 per cent shareholder the state had the power to require the directors to alter the contracts of employment of the company's employees so as to comply with the directive.

This decision was reversed by the Employment Appeal Tribunal ([1987] IRLR 447), which held that the crucial question was whether or not Rolls-Royce could be said to be an organ or agent of the state carrying out a state function (see paras 11–12).

The appeal to the Court of Appeal was heard after the decisions of the Court of Justice and the House of Lords in **Foster**. Mustill LJ stated that the **Foster** test was not intended to be an exhaustive statement for determining the status of the entity, but, nevertheless, it was Mustill LJ's opinion that in a case which was factually similar to **Foster**, the test:

> ... **must always be the starting point and will usually be the finishing point.** If all the factors identified by the Court are present it is likely to require something very unusual to produce the result that an entity is not to be identified with the State. Conversely, although the absence of a factor will not necessarily be fatal, it will need the addition of something else, not contemplated by the formula ... (para 24) [emphasis added]

Mustill LJ went on to examine whether or not the three **Foster** criteria were satisfied. He accepted that the second criterion, requiring the service to be provided under the control of the state, was satisfied. However, he stated that if this point had been crucial to the outcome it would have required detailed examination. He stated that with regard to this criterion, the relevant question was whether the public *service* (rather than the *body* providing the service) was under the state's control. He concluded that the other two criteria were not satisfied: Rolls-Royce could not be said to have been made responsible for providing a public service, pursuant to a measure adopted by the state, nor was there any evidence that Rolls-Royce possessed or exercised any 'special powers'.

Accordingly, Doughty could not enforce the directive against Rolls-Royce, because Rolls-Royce was deemed not to be an emanation of the state.

The second case centred around the question of whether the provisions of the Collective Redundancies Directive 92/129 could be enforced directly against the privatised company, South West Water:

Griffin and Others v *South West Water Services Ltd* [1995] IRLR 15

The English High Court first considered the question of whether South West Water (SWW) was an emanation of the state. It was common ground between the parties that the correct approach was to consider whether the three **Foster** criteria were fulfilled. Blackburne J relied upon Mustill LJ's dicta in **Doughty** that the **Foster** criteria must be the starting point and will usually be the finishing point. In deciding the question, Blackburne J conducted a detailed examination of the powers and duties conferred upon the newly privatised SWW and of the control to which it was subject.

It was common ground between the parties that the first criterion, the 'public service' condition, and the third criterion, the 'special powers' condition, were fulfilled. The crucial question was whether or not the second criterion, the 'state control' condition, was satisfied. Blackburne J, as did Mustill LJ in **Doughty**, made it clear (at para 94) that:

> The question is not whether the body in question is under the control of the State, but whether the public service in question is under the control of the State ... It is also irrelevant that the body does not carry out any of the traditional functions of the State and is not an agent of the State ... It is irrelevant too that the State does not possess day-to-day control over the activities of the body.

The question therefore was whether or not the public services of water and sewerage provision performed by SWW were under the control of the state. There were a whole number of powers available to the Secretary of State and the Director General of Water Services to conclude that the public service of water and sewerage provision performed by SWW were under the control of the state, thus fulfilling the 'control' condition (see paras 96–110).

The three **Foster** criteria being satisfied, SWW was an emanation of the state, a body against which the directive was capable of being enforced.

It should be noted that, as discussed above, the directive could therefore be directly enforced, provided the provisions of the directive were *sufficiently precise and unconditional*. In the above case, the High Court decided that the relevant provisions were *not* sufficiently precise and unconditional and therefore the directive could not be enforced against SWW.

The following is the third and final case:

National Union of Teachers and Others v *The Governing Body of St Mary's Church of England (Aided) Junior School and Others* [1997] IRLR 242

The individual applicants had been employed at a school which had been closed down, following which a new school was established under the control of a temporary governing body. The applicants were not re-employed. It was argued by the applicants that the Acquired Rights Directive 77/187 applied automatically to transfer their contracts of employment and therefore their dismissals were unlawful. It was common ground that, at the material time, English law would not assist the applicants.

To determine whether the governing body was an emanation of the state, the employment tribunal applied the **Foster** test and concluded that it did not satisfy the 'special powers' criterion. The directive could therefore not be directly enforced against the governing body because it was not an emanation of the state. The appeal to the Employment Appeal Tribunal ([1995] ICR 317) was dismissed. The Court of Appeal unanimously allowed the appeal. The leading judgment was delivered by Schiemann LJ.

Schiemann LJ quite correctly recognised that the Court of Justice had not established a test which should be applied to all situations. Although each party to the case had relied upon the **Foster** test, he stated that:

> It is clear from the wording of paragraph 20 [of the Court's judgment in **Foster**] and in particular the words 'is included among' that the formula there used was not intended to be an exclusive formula.

The governing body relied heavily upon the Court of Appeal's decision in **Doughty**, and in particular on Mustill LJ's observation that in a case of the same general type as **Foster**, the test formulated by the Court of Justice will always be the starting point and will usually be the finishing point. However, Schiemann LJ was of the view that this case was not of the same general type as that of **Foster**:

> That case and **Rolls-Royce** were both concerned with commercial undertakings in which the Government had a stake. The present case is not concerned with any commercial undertaking but rather with the provision of what would generally in the Community be regarded as the provision of a public service.

He said that the Employment Appeal Tribunal was wrong in applying the **Foster** test as if it was a statutory definition. Even though the parties had relied upon the test, Schiemann LJ did not think it was appropriate to apply it in a similar fashion to the Appeal Tribunal. Nevertheless, in view of the parties' submissions, he made his own observations on the application of the three **Foster** criteria to the particular facts.

The first two criteria, 'public service' provision and 'state control', were fulfilled. However, he was not satisfied that the governing body had 'special powers'. Despite this reservation, he held that the governing body was an emanation of the state. He was no doubt influenced by the financial benefit accruing to the local education authority if the appeal was dismissed:

> The financial position is that the failure to transpose the Directive will, if the present appeal is dismissed, have the effect of allowing the local education authority and the State to benefit from the failure to transpose the Directive. The Rolls-Royce case indicates that the mere fact that some incidental benefit may arise to the State from a failure to implement a directive does not necessarily bring the doctrine of vertical effect into play. In the present case the benefit is direct to the local education authority, as is conceded because of the provisions of s 46 of the Education Reform Act 1988, and the local education authority, as is further conceded, is an emanation of the State for the purposes of the doctrine of direct vertical effect.

Section 46 of the 1988 Act provided that local education authorities were responsible for redundancy payments. The nature of the service being provided and the fact that the body providing the service was financially dependent upon the local education authority were indicative to the outcome of the case. Schiemann LJ quite correctly departed from a strict application of the **Foster** test, preferring to address the question on the basis that the state should not benefit from its own failure to implement a directive.

The Court of Justice subsequently delivered a judgment which considered the **Foster** test further:

Kampelmann v *Landschaftsverband Westfalen-Lippe* (Cases C-253-258/96)

The Court of Justice held that, in accordance with its **Foster** *v* **British Gas plc** judgment:

46. ... a directive ... may ... be relied on against organisations or bodies which are subject to the authority or control of the State **or** have special powers beyond those which result from the normal rules applicable to relations between individuals, such as local or regional authorities **or** other bodies which, irrespective of their legal form, have been given responsibility by the public authorities and under their supervision, for providing a public service. [emphasis added]

Although in the above case the Court of Justice stated that this judgment was in line with its **Foster** judgment, in the operative part of **Foster** the three criteria were stated to be cumulative, whereas in the **Kampelmann** judgment the Court of Justice set out the criteria as alternatives. If this had been subsequently reaffirmed by the Court of Justice as a departure from **Foster** then the bodies and organisations against which a directive may be capable of having direct effect could have been extended. However, this would have required the Court to explicitly depart from its previous reasoning as to why a directive should only be enforceable vertically (i.e. to prevent a Member State from profiting from its own failure to implement (or correctly implement) a directive). The Court of Justice has subsequently considered the concept of 'emanation of the state' in the following case, and made no reference to its **Kampelmann** judgment:

Rieser Internationale Transporte GmbH v *Autobahnen-und Schnellstraßen-Finanzierungs-AG (Asfinag)* (Case C-157/02)

With regard to enforcement of a direction against an 'emanation of the state', the Court of Justice held as follows:

22. It ought to be borne in mind that the Court has consistently held (Case 8/81 *Becker* [1982] ECR 53, paragraphs 23 to 25, and Case C-188/89 **Foster and Others** [1990] ECR I-3313, paragraph 16) that where the Community authorities have, by means of a directive, placed Member States under an obligation to adopt a certain course of action, the effectiveness of such a measure would be diminished if persons were prevented from relying upon it in proceedings before a court and national courts were prevented from taking it into consideration as an element of Community law. Consequently, a Member State which has not adopted the implementing measures required by the directive within the prescribed period may not plead, as against individuals, its own failure to perform the obligations which the directive entails. Thus, wherever the provisions of a directive appear, as far as their subject-matter is concerned, to be unconditional and sufficiently precise, those provisions may, in the absence of implementing measures adopted within the prescribed period, be relied upon as against any national provision which is incompatible with the directive or in so far as the provisions define rights which individuals are able to assert against the State.

23. The Court has further held (Case 152/84 **Marshall** [1986] ECR 723, paragraph 49, and **Foster and Others**, cited above, paragraph 17) that where a person is able to rely on a directive as against the State he may do so regardless of the capacity in which the latter is acting, whether as employer or as public authority. In either case it is necessary to prevent the State from taking advantage of its own failure to comply with Community law.

24. A body, whatever its legal form, which has been made responsible, pursuant to a measure adopted by the State, for providing a public service under the control of the State and has for that purpose special powers beyond those which result from the normal rules applicable in relations between individuals is included in any event among the bodies against which the provisions of a directive capable of having direct effect may be relied upon (**Foster and**

Others, paragraph 20, and Case C-343/98 **Collino and Chiappero** [2000] ECR I-6659, paragraph 23).

25. It is clear from the information contained in the order for reference that the Austrian State is the sole shareholder in Asfinag. It has the right to check all measures taken by that company and its subsidiaries and at any time to demand information about their activities. It is entitled to impose objectives with regard to the organisation of traffic, safety and construction. Every year Asfinag is required to draw up a plan for the maintenance of the motorways and expressways and to submit to the State the calculation of the costs involved. Furthermore, every year within the periods necessary for the drawing-up of the State's budget, it must present to the State calculations with the estimated costs of planning, constructing, maintaining and managing motorways and national expressways.

26. In addition, the order for reference makes it clear that Asfinag is not entitled of its own authority to fix the amount of the tolls to be levied. That amount is fixed by law. Paragraphs 4 and 8 of the law known as the Asfinag Law (BGBl. 1982/591) provide that the amount of the payment must be fixed by the Bundesminister für Wirtschaftliche Angelegenheiten (Federal Minister for Economic Affairs) in concert with the Bundesminister für Finanzen (Federal Minister for Finance), according to certain criteria including, inter alia, the type of vehicle.

27. Those facts clearly show that Asfinag is a body to which, pursuant to an act adopted by the public authorities, the performance of a public-interest service (namely: the constructing, planning, operating, maintaining and financing of motorways and expressways in addition to the levying of tolls and user charges), has been entrusted, under the supervision of those public authorities, and which for that purpose possesses special powers beyond those resulting from the normal rules applicable in relations between individuals.

28. According to the decisions cited in paragraph 24 above, such a body, whatever its legal form, is included among those against which the provisions of a directive capable of having direct effect may be relied upon.

29. In consequence, the answer to be given to the first question must be that, when contracts are concluded with road users, the provisions of a directive capable of having direct effect may be relied upon against a legal person governed by private law where the State has entrusted to that legal person the task of levying tolls for the use of public road networks and where it has direct or indirect control of that legal person.

In the above case, the Court of Justice, at para 24, set out the **Foster** criteria as being cumulative; the Court did not refer to the **Kampelmann** judgment. The Court then applied the three criteria to the facts of the case, at paras 25–27. The Court concluded, at para 28, that in the case of a company which had been entrusted by Austria to levy toll charges for the use of public roads, and where Austria had direct or indirect control of the toll-levying company, the three **Foster** criteria were satisfied. Such a company was therefore an emanation of the state against which a directive (which was sufficiently precise and unconditional) could be enforced. The above case would suggest that the Court of Justice had not deliberately departed from the **Foster** case in **Kampelmann**, and it has probably confirmed that the **Foster** criteria will be applied cumulatively in the future.

Directives: horizontal effect?

The following case concerned the question of whether or not an EC directive could have horizontal direct effect:

Paola Faccini Dori v *Recreb SRL* (Case C-91/92)

The issue before the Court of Justice was whether Miss Faccini Dori could rely upon an unimplemented directive in the national (Italian) court against a private company (which was not an emanation of the state).

On 9 February 1994 the opinion of Advocate-General Lenz was delivered at a sitting of the full Court. The Advocate-General recognised that the Court of Justice had consistently held that directives could not have direct effect in relations between individuals, and that for reasons of legal certainty this should be maintained with regard to situations in the past. However, as regards the future, the Advocate-General was of the opinion that those provisions of a directive which are sufficiently precise and unconditional should have direct effect; for future cases the Community should recognise that directives may be directly effective both vertically and horizontally.

As discussed in Chapter 5, the Court of Justice is not bound by the doctrine of precedent and accordingly could have departed from its own previous decisions. However, for the sake of legal certainty the Court generally follows and builds upon its own previous case law. The Court of Justice rejected the Advocate-General's opinion. The Court stated that ever since the **Marshall** case it had been held that a directive could not of itself impose obligations on an individual. Accordingly, a directive could not be relied upon against such an individual.

Although the above judgment would appear to have settled the issue, certainly for the foreseeable future, on occasion the Court of Justice has implicitly allowed horizontal direct enforcement, provided no particular obligation was placed on the defendant. For example, in **CIA Security International** *v* **Signalson and Securitel** (Case C–194/94) a directive required the Commission to be notified of certain technical regulations. This was effectively not implemented by the relevant Member State. The claimant sought to rely on the directive to relieve him from an obligation, without it imposing an obligation on the defendant under the directive, and the Court of Justice allowed this. In effect the Court allowed the claimant to directly enforce the directive horizontally.

In **Criminal Proceedings against Rafael Ruiz Bernáldez** (Case C–129/94), Spain had a law requiring drivers of vehicles to have a valid motor insurance policy. However, Spanish law, contrary to a directive, provided that an insurance company was not liable to compensate a third party victim of a driver who was under the influence of alcohol at the time of the accident. The Court of Justice held that the unimplemented directive should apply, thus indirectly imposing an obligation on the insurance company. The practical effect, once again, was to allow the directive to be directly enforced horizontally, although the Court of Justice did not explicitly state this to be the case.

The principle of indirect effect

The obvious limitation of the application of the direct effect of directives is that, however generously the Court of Justice has interpreted 'emanation of the state' in favour of individual claimants, the term clearly cannot apply to the private commercial employer. In the following case, the Court of Justice adopted a novel approach to enable the claimant to indirectly enforce, horizontally, an incorrectly implemented directive:

Harz v *Deutsche Tradax* (Case 79/83)

Germany had incorrectly implemented Directive 76/207 on equal employment rights, because the German law provided only nominal compensation whereas the directive required proper compensation to be available (see **Marshall (No. 2)** (Case C-271/91)). Ms Harz was employed by a private company and therefore was unable to rely on the directive in the national court. The case was referred to the Court of Justice by the (West) German Labour Court.

The Court's starting point was Art 10 EC Treaty (previously Art 5): the obligation of Member States to take all appropriate measures to give effect to Community law. The Court of Justice stated that this obligation 'is binding on all the authorities of Member States including, for matters within their jurisdiction, the courts. It follows that, in applying the national law ... national courts are required to interpret their national law in the light of the wording and the purpose of the directive in order to achieve the result referred to in the third paragraph of Art 189 EC Treaty [now Art 249]' (para 26). The national court was therefore under an obligation to 'interpret' the national law on sexual discrimination in such a way that there was no limit on proper compensation to which injured parties were entitled. On this basis, the German court which had referred the case could award proper compensation to Ms Harz.

The above case concerned the interpretation of legislation which had been put into place to implement the directive in question. It was questionable whether this new interpretative obligation was confined to cases where the Member State had implemented the directive but had done so incorrectly. The Court of Justice answered this question in the negative in the following case:

Marleasing SA v *La Commercial SA* (Case C-106/89)

A Spanish court was confronted with a national law on the constitution of companies which conflicted with Directive 68/71. The directive had not been implemented in Spain. The Court of Justice, nevertheless, held that:

> ... in applying national law, whether the provisions concerned **pre-date** or post-date the directive, the national court asked to interpret national law is bound to do so in every way possible in the light of the text and the aims of the directive to achieve the results envisaged by it and thus comply with Article 189(3) of the Treaty. [emphasis added]

The above judgment provides that, for example, a national court could be required to 'interpret' a provision of national law that preceded a directive by many years, and which had been enacted with quite different considerations in mind, 'in the light of the text and the aims of the directive'. The extent of this interpretative obligation has caused particular problems for UK courts. These are considered below. The Court of Justice has made it clear that the courts of Member States should act on the presumption that relevant national legislation, whether passed before or after the relevant directive, was intended to implement it. However, whether this is in fact possible, in the light of the wording of the national provision, is essentially a matter of interpretation by those courts (**Wagner Miret** (Case 334/92)).

There is one exception to the obligation to interpret national law in conformity with an unimplemented directive. That is where the national measure, which ought to be interpreted in this way, imposes criminal liability. The Court of Justice held in **Arcaro** (Case C–168/95) that no obligation could be imposed on an individual by an unimplemented directive. Nor could there be any liability in criminal law of persons who act in contravention of that directive's provisions. The Court of Justice has, however, held that a person can be convicted of a driving offence in a national court, even where that conviction rests upon evidence obtained under national legislation made in breach of a Community directive (**Lemmens** (Case C–226/97)).

Framework decisions

The interpretative obligation, which forms the basis of the principle of indirect effect, was considered by the Court of Justice during 2005 in the following case, which concerned a framework decision rather than a directive:

Pupino (Case C-105/03)

Framework Decision 2001/220/JHA (OJ 2001 L 82/1) had been adopted under the Justice and Home Affairs provisions of the third pillar of the TEU (i.e. Title VI TEU, Police and Judicial Cooperation in Criminal Matters). The framework decision relates to the standing of victims in criminal proceedings.

An Italian court had made a reference for a preliminary ruling to the Court of Justice pursuant to Art 35(2) TEU. The referring court sought guidance on the scope of Arts 2, 3 and 8 of the framework decision. Article 2 provides for the recognition of the rights of victims; Art 3 provides for the possibility of victims being heard; and Art 8 provides for the protection of victims, in particular from the effects of giving evidence in public.

The Court of Justice held that the wording of Art 34(2)(b) TEU confers a binding character on framework decisions, which entails **an obligation for national authorities to interpret national law in conformity, as in the case of directives, under the third paragraph of Art 249 EC Treaty. Therefore, when applying national law, 'the national court that is called upon to interpret it must do so as far as possible in the light of the wording and purpose of the framework decision in order to attain the result which it pursues'.** The obligation on the national court to refer to the content of a framework decision when interpreting the relevant rules of its national law is, however, limited 'by general principles of law, particularly those of legal certainty and non-retroactivity'. Likewise, 'the principle of conforming interpretation cannot serve as the basis for an interpretation of national law *contra legem* ... That principle does, however, require that, where necessary, the national court consider the whole of national law in order to assess how far it can be applied in such a way as not to produce a result contrary to that envisaged by the framework decision'.

Therefore, although framework decisions are intergovernmental in character inasmuch as they are part of the third pillar and although they do not have direct effect, the national law incorporating them should be interpreted in the light of their wording and purpose. That is in keeping with the intention of the Member States to create an 'ever closer Union', which has recourse to legal instruments with effects similar to those provided for by the EC Treaty which are concerned with further integration (paragraph 36).

The principle of state liability

The possibility of taking action against the state for failing to implement a directive was first considered in the following case:

Francovich and Bonifaci v *Republic of Italy* (Cases C-6 & 9/90)

An Italian company went into liquidation, leaving Mr Francovich and other employees with unpaid arrears of salary. Directive 80/987 required Member States to set up a compensation scheme for employees in these circumstances, but Italy had not established one. Mr Francovich therefore sought compensation from the Italian government. The case was referred to the Court of Justice. The Court was asked (i) whether the directive had direct effect; (ii) whether the Member State was liable for the damage arising from its failure to implement the directive; and (iii) to what extent it was liable for damages for violation of its obligations under Community law.

The Court decided that the directive was insufficiently precise to have direct effect (see above). However, it emphasised that the EC Treaty creates a legal order which is binding upon Member States and citizens. The *effet utile* (i.e. the useful effect) of Community law would be diminished if individuals were not able to obtain damages after suffering loss incurred because of a violation of Community law by a Member State. There was an implied obligation under the former Art 5 EC Treaty (now Art 10) to compensate individuals affected by such a violation. The Court held that, in cases such as this, where there was a violation of the state's obligation to implement Community law under the former Art 189 EC Treaty (now Art 249), there was a right to compensation from the state, provided that three conditions were satisfied:

- The result which had to be attained by the directive involved rights conferred on individuals.
- The content of those rights could be identified from the provisions of the directive.
- There must exist a causal link between the failure by the Member State to fulfil its obligations and the damage suffered by the person affected.

The Court did not decide how the extent of liability was to be determined as this was to be a matter for national law. National procedures had, however, 'to ensure the full protection of rights which individuals might derive from Community law'. In this particular case, the failure of Italy to implement the directive in question had already been established by the Court.

Generally, there will not be a defence to simple non-implementation because, whatever practical difficulties there may be, the obligation to implement is strict (**Commission** *v* **Belgium** (Case 1/86)).

The Court has developed the concept of state liability and entitlement to damages in a number of subsequent judgments.

Legislative acts

The following (joined) cases concerned directly effective Treaty articles which had been breached:

Brasserie du Pêcheur v Germany; R v Secretary of State for Transport, ex parte Factortame Ltd and Others (Cases C-46 & 48/93)

The former case concerned a pre-existing German law which breached the former Art 30 EC Treaty (now Art 28), and the latter a UK Act of Parliament which was enacted in breach of, *inter alia*, the former Art 52 EC Treaty (now Art 43). The claimants sought damages against the respective states for the *legislature's* breach of Community law. The national courts referred a number of questions to the Court of Justice for a preliminary ruling pursuant to the former Art 177 EC Treaty (now Art 234).

The first question in both cases concerned whether or not the **Francovich** principle of state liability would oblige Member States to make good damage caused to individuals by a breach of Community law by the state legislature, no matter what form that breach took. In assessing this question, the Court of Justice initially stated that it was irrelevant that the breach concerned a directly effective Treaty article and that it was irrelevant which organ of state was responsible for the breach:

31. ... the Court held in **Francovich and Others**, at paragraph 35, that the principle of State liability for loss and damage caused to individuals as a result of breaches of Community law for which it can be held responsible is inherent in the system of the Treaty.

32. It follows that that principle holds good for any case in which a Member State breaches Community law, whatever be the organ of the State whose act or omission was responsible for the breach.

The Court of Justice then gave consideration to the conditions under which state liability may be incurred. Reiterating its **Francovich** judgment, the Court stated that:

38. Although Community law imposes State liability, the conditions under which that liability gives rise to a right to reparation depend on the nature of the breach of Community law giving rise to the loss and damage.

In examining the facts of the two cases, the Court of Justice stated that the national legislatures had a wide discretion in the relevant fields of activity. Where there was such a wide discretion, three conditions had to be met in order to incur state liability (at para 51):

- the rule of law infringed must be intended to *confer rights on individuals;*
- the breach must be *sufficiently serious;* and
- there must be a *direct causal link* between the breach of the obligation resting on the state and the damage sustained by the injured parties.

The former Arts 30 and 52 EC Treaty (now Arts 28 and 43) are directly effective and therefore the first condition was satisfied *per se*. It is the second condition which is the most interesting. The Court of Justice stated that the decisive test for finding that a breach of Community law is *sufficiently serious* is whether the Member State 'manifestly and gravely disregarded the limits on its discretion' (at para 55). The Court of Justice then set out a number of factors which may be taken into consideration by the national court when assessing whether or not there was such a manifest and grave disregard by the Member State of the limit on its discretion:

56. **The factors which the competent court may take into consideration include the clarity and precision of the rule breached, the measure of discretion left by that rule to the national or Community authorities, whether the infringement and the damage caused was intentional or involuntary, whether any error of law was excusable or inexcusable, the fact that the position**

taken by a Community institution may have contributed towards the omission, and the adoption or retention of national measures or practices contrary to Community law.

57. On any view, a breach of Community law will clearly be sufficiently serious if it has persisted despite a judgment finding the infringement in question to be established, or a preliminary ruling or settled case law of the Court on the matter from which it is clear that the conduct in question constituted an infringement. [emphasis added]

The **Factortame** case returned to the UK court for it to apply the three conditions of state liability. The case reached the House of Lords (**R v Secretary of State for Transport, ex parte Factortame Ltd and Others (No. 5)** [1999] 3 WLR 1062). The House of Lords held that the adoption of legislation which was discriminatory on the ground of nationality in respect of the registration of UK fishing vessels, in breach of clear and unambiguous rules of Community law, was *sufficiently serious* to give rise to liability in damages to individuals who suffered loss as a consequence. Factortame would then have to prove its losses (i.e. prove that there was a *direct causal link* between the breach and the damage they had sustained).

Legislative act – incorrect implementation of a directive

The following case concerned the incorrect implementation of a directive by the UK, a situation in which a Member State does not enjoy a wide discretion (the former Art 189(3) (now Art 249(3)) requires a Member State to implement a directive within the time period laid down):

R v HM Treasury, ex parte British Telecommunications plc (Case C-392/93)

The Court of Justice (at para 39) restated the three conditions in the previous joined cases. Where a Member State acts in a field in which it has a wide discretion in the taking of legislative decisions, for the defaulting Member State to incur liability:

the rule of law infringed must be intended to confer rights on individuals; the breach must be sufficiently serious; and there must be a direct causal link between the breach ... and the damage sustained.

The Court of Justice held (at para 40) that this restrictive approach was equally applicable to the facts of this case, where the UK had incorrectly transposed a directive. Once again the Court stated that it was for the national court to determine whether or not there was a *sufficiently serious* breach. However, because the Court of Justice had all the necessary facts before it, it went on to advise the national court as to the determination of the factual situation.

In the **Brasserie du Pêcheur** and **Factortame** joined cases the Court of Justice held (at para 56) that one of the relevant factors was the clarity and precision of the rule breached. In this case the directive was imprecisely worded and was reasonably capable of bearing the interpretation given to it by the UK. Moreover, the UK had acted in good faith (at para 43). The Court of Justice noted that this interpretation was shared by other Member States and 'was not manifestly contrary to the wording of the directive or to the objective pursued by it' (at para 43).

Additionally, there had been no case law from the Court of Justice to guide the UK. The Commission had not questioned the UK's implementing legislation. In those circumstances, the Court of Justice held that the breach could not be regarded as *sufficiently serious*.

Executive act - breach of the Treaty

The following case again involved the UK courts:

R v Ministry of Agriculture, Fisheries and Food, ex parte Hedley Lomas (Ireland) Ltd (Case C-5/94)

The Ministry refused licences for the exporting of livestock to Spain for slaughter because it was of the view that Spain was acting contrary to Directive 74/557 which concerns the stunning of animals before slaughter. Unlike the previous cases, this involved an act of the executive rather than an act of the legislature. The Court of Justice held that the refusal by the Ministry was a quantitative restriction contrary to the former Art 34 EC Treaty (now Art 29) which could not be justified under the former Art 36 (now Art 30). The UK was therefore in breach of Community law.

In reaching its judgment, the Court of Justice restated that part of its judgment in **Brasserie du Pêcheur** and **Factortame** where it held that in a field in which a Member State has a wide discretion to make legislative choices, a defaulting Member State will incur liability where three conditions are satisfied:

> 25. ... the rule of law infringed must be intended to confer rights on individuals; the breach must be sufficiently serious; and there must be a direct causal link between the breach of the obligation resting on the State and the damage sustained by the injured parties.

In an attempt to impose a common standard for state liability throughout the Community, the Court of Justice held that:

> 26. Those three conditions are also applicable in the circumstances of this case.

This was despite the fact that the breach did not involve a legislative act and despite the fact that the Member State did not enjoy a wide discretion. Although the Court of Justice introduced the three conditions in order to impose a uniform test for state liability throughout the Community, it acknowledged that the concept of 'sufficiently serious breach' will vary, depending upon the facts of the case. With regard to this particular case, the Court of Justice stated:

> 28. ... where, at the time when it committed the infringement, the Member State in question was not called upon to make any legislative choices and had only considerably reduced, or even no, discretion, **the mere infringement of Community law may be sufficient to establish the existence of a sufficiently serious breach.** [emphasis added]

Failure to implement a directive - *Francovich* revisited

The next case concerned Germany's failure to transpose Directive 90/314/EEC:

Dillenkofer and Others v Federal Republic of Germany (Joined Cases C-178, 179 & 188-190/94)

This case was factually similar to **Francovich**. In **Francovich** the Court of Justice did *not* make it a condition that the breach of Community law must be sufficiently serious in order for state liability to be incurred. However, in this case, the Court of Justice stated that this was a condition, but by the very nature of the breach (i.e. a complete disregard of the Member State's obligation under the former Art 189(3) EC Treaty (now Art 249(3))) the breach was sufficiently serious *per se* (i.e. automatically).

National courts – failure to apply Community law

Köbler (Case C-224/01)

A German national had worked as an ordinary professor in an Austrian university for 10 years. He applied for a special length-of-service increment which was normally paid to professors with 15 years' experience exclusively at Austrian universities, arguing that he had completed the requisite length of service if the duration of his service in universities of other Member States were taken into consideration. After it had referred a question on this point for a preliminary ruling, the Austrian court took account of the judgment in **Schöning-Kougebetopoulou** (Case C-15/96). In this case, the Court of Justice had held that the provisions of Community law on freedom of movement for workers within the Community precluded a clause in a collective agreement which applied to the public service of a Member State, which provided for promotion on grounds of seniority for employees of that service after eight years' employment in a salary group determined by that agreement, without taking any account of previous periods of comparable employment completed in the public service of another Member State. The Austrian court then withdrew the question it had referred for a preliminary ruling and, without referring a second question to the Court of Justice, confirmed that the refusal of the application of the person concerned was justified, on the ground that the special length-of-service increment was a loyalty bonus which objectively justified a derogation from the Community law provisions on freedom of movement for workers.

Köbler then brought an action for damages before the referring court for breach of Community law. In its preliminary ruling the Court of Justice confirmed that the principle, stated in particular in **Brasserie du Pêcheur** and **Factortame** (Cases C-46/93 and C-48/93), where **Member States are obliged to make good damage caused to individuals by infringements of Community law for which they are responsible applies in cases where the alleged infringement stems from a decision of a court adjudicating at last instance** where the rule of Community law infringed is intended to confer rights on individuals, the breach is sufficiently serious and there is a direct causal link between that breach and the loss or damage sustained by the injured parties. **The Court of Justice made clear that, as regards the second condition, in order to determine whether the infringement is sufficiently serious when the infringement at issue stems from a decision of a court, the competent national court, taking into account the specific nature of the judicial function, must determine whether that infringement is manifest.** Finally, it added that it is for the legal system of each Member State to designate the court competent to determine disputes relating to that reparation.

Although it is generally for the national courts to consider the abovementioned criteria, the Court of Justice took the view that it had available to it all the material facts enabling it to establish whether the conditions necessary for liability to be incurred by the Member State concerned were fulfilled. As regards the existence of a sufficiently serious breach, it held that an infringement of Community law does not have the requisite manifest character for liability under Community law to be incurred by a Member State for a decision of one of its courts adjudicating at last instance, where, first, Community law does not expressly cover the point of law at issue, no reply was to be found to that question in the Court's case law and that reply was not obvious, and, second, that infringement was not intentional but was the result of an incorrect reading of a judgment of the Court.

Although in the above case the applicant was unsuccessful, this is an important case in that it extends the principle of state liability to courts of last instance which infringe Community law obligations. The applicant did not succeed because the Court of Justice held that the Austrian court's infringement of Community law was not 'sufficiently serious'. The Court of Justice stated that in a case where the infringement concerns the decision of a court of last instance (i.e. a court from which there is no appeal (e.g. the House of Lords in the UK)), in order to establish that the infringement is 'sufficiently serious' it must be determined whether or not the infringement is *manifest*. This decision quite clearly affords national courts with a degree of protection; the necessity to show that the infringement is manifest could be an onerous task.

The following case, decided by the Court of Justice during 2006, builds upon the **Köbler** case:

Traghetti del Mediterraneo SpA v Italy (Case C-173/03)

In 1981, the maritime transport undertaking Traghetti del Mediterraneo (TDM) brought proceedings against a competing undertaking, Tirrenia di Navigazione, before the Tribunale di Napoli. TDM sought compensation for the damage that its competitor had allegedly caused it through its policy of low fares on the maritime cabotage market between mainland Italy and the islands of Sardinia and Sicily, which had been made possible by public subsidies.

TDM submitted in particular that the conduct in question constituted unfair competition and abuse of a dominant position which was prohibited by Art 82 EC Treaty.

The action for compensation was dismissed by all the Italian courts which had heard the case, namely, at first instance, the Tribunale di Napoli, then, on appeal, the Corte d'appello di Napoli and the Corte suprema di cassazione (the supreme court). Taking the view that the judgment of the latter court was founded on an incorrect interpretation of the Community rules, the administrator of TDM, which had in the meantime been put into liquidation, brought proceedings against Italy before the Tribunale di Genova. That action sought compensation for the damage suffered by TDM as a result of the errors of interpretation committed by the supreme court (the court of last instance in this case) and of the breach of its obligation to make a reference for a preliminary ruling to the Court of Justice.

In those circumstances, the Tribunale di Genova asked the Court of Justice whether Community law and, in particular, the principles laid down by the Court in the **Köbler** judgment preclude national legislation such as the Italian law which, on the one hand, excludes all liability of a Member State for damage caused to individuals by an infringement of Community law committed by a national court adjudicating at last instance, where that infringement is the result of an interpretation of provisions of law or of an assessment of the facts and evidence carried out by that court, and, on the other hand, also limits such liability solely to cases of intentional fault and serious misconduct on the part of the court.

The Court of Justice observed that the principle that a **Member State is obliged to make good damage caused to individuals as a result of breaches of Community law for which it is responsible applies to any case in which a Member State breaches Community law, whichever is the authority of the Member State whose act or omission was responsible for the breach.**

The Court then noted that the essential role played by the judiciary in the protection of individuals' rights under Community law would be weakened if individuals could not, under certain conditions, obtain compensation for damage caused by an infringement of Community law attributable to a court of a Member State adjudicating at last instance. In such a case, individuals must be able to rely on state liability in order to obtain legal protection of their rights.

The Court stated that the interpretation of provisions of law and the assessment of facts and evidence constitute an essential part of judicial activity and may lead, in certain cases, to a manifest infringement of the applicable law.

To exclude any possibility that state liability may be incurred where the infringement allegedly committed by the national court relates to its interpretation of provisions of law or its assessment of facts or evidence would amount to depriving the principle of state liability of all practical effect and lead to a situation where individuals would have no judicial protection if a national court adjudicating at last instance committed a manifest error in the exercise of those activities of interpretation or assessment.

With regard to the limitation of state liability solely to cases of intentional fault and serious misconduct on the part of the court, the Court of Justice pointed out that **state liability for damage caused to individuals by reason of an infringement of Community law attributable to a national court adjudicating at last instance may be incurred in the exceptional case where that court has manifestly infringed the applicable law.**

Such manifest infringement is to be assessed, *inter alia*, **in the light of a number of criteria, such as the degree of clarity and precision of the rule infringed, whether the error of law was excusable or inexcusable and the non-compliance by the court in question with its obligation to make a reference for a preliminary ruling. It is in any event presumed, where the decision involved is taken in manifest disregard of the case law of the Court of Justice on the subject.**

Accordingly, the Court of Justice held that **although it remains possible for national law to define the criteria relating to the nature or degree of the infringement which must be met before state liability can be incurred for an infringement of Community law attributable to a national court adjudicating at last instance, under no circumstances may such criteria impose requirements stricter than that of a manifest infringement of the applicable law.**

Consequently, the Court of Justice held that **the limitation of state liability solely to cases of intentional fault and serious misconduct on the part of the court is contrary to Community law if such a limitation were to lead to exclusion of liability of the Member State concerned in other cases where a manifest infringement of the applicable law was committed.**

Conclusion

The **Dillenkofer** and **Köbler** cases complete the post-**Francovich** case law insofar as it has established that the conditions relating to state liability are fixed no matter what the nature of the breach, thus ensuring uniform application of the principle throughout the Member States. It will be for the national court to determine whether or not the breach is, on its facts, sufficiently serious. As evidenced in the cases discussed, this may be a difficult question to answer and the factors to be taken into consideration will vary depending upon the particular circumstances of the case. In **Brasserie du Pêcheur** and **Factortame** the Court set out, at paras 56–57, some factors to be taken into account when determining this question with regard to legislative acts. However, the Court of Justice determined that fault, i.e. intention or negligence, is not in itself one of the conditions which it is necessary to satisfy in order for state liability to be established. Two other cases applying the principle of state liability are:

■ **Denkavit and Others** (Cases C–283, 291 & 292/94);

■ **Brinkmann Tabakfabriken GmbH** v Skatteministeriet (Case C–319/96).

Application of the principles of direct and indirect effect in UK Courts

Direct effect: the provisions of the EC Treaty

Under the law and practice within the UK, the EC Treaty, like any other Treaty, is effective in the UK only after it has been incorporated into the UK's legal system, and it will be effective only to the extent of its incorporation (**Blackburn** v **Attorney-General** [1971] 2 All ER 1380 at 1382; Lord Denning MR). The UK's accession to the European Community was given effect in national law by the European Communities Act 1972. The implementation of Community rights will, therefore, depend on the extent to which Community law has been fully incorporated by the Act, and the extent to which UK courts are prepared to interpret national law in conformity with Community obligations (**R** v **Secretary for Foreign and Commonwealth Office, ex parte Rees-Mogg** [1994] 1 CMLR 101 (QBD)).

Section 2(1), European Communities Act 1972 provides that only those provisions which 'in accordance with the Treaties are **without further enactment** to be given legal effect ... shall be ... enforced, allowed, and followed' in UK courts (emphasis added). Section 3(1) of the 1972 Act further provides that:

> For the purposes of all legal proceedings any question as to the meaning or effect of any of the Treaties, or as to the validity, meaning or effect of any Community instrument, shall be treated as a question of law and, if not referred to the European Court, be for determination as such in accordance with the principles laid down by and any relevant decision of the European Court or of any Court attached thereto.

Under s 2(1), UK courts have not had any difficulty in giving effect to Treaty provisions or regulations, since 'in accordance with the Treaties' both are to be given legal effect without further legislative enactment. Thus, the directly effective provisions of the former Art 119 EC Treaty (now Art 141) on equal pay were held to prevail over the Equal Pay Act 1970 in the following case:

Macarthys Ltd v *Smith* [1981] QB 180

The Court of Appeal held that it was bound to give effect to the former Art 119 because it was directly effective. Lord Denning MR expressed the position in this way:

> The provisions of Article 119 of the EEC Treaty [now Art 141 EC Treaty] take priority over anything in our English statute on equal pay which is inconsistent with Article 119. **That priority is given by our law. It is given by the European Communities Act 1972 itself.** (at 200-1) [emphasis added]

There was no difficulty where the legislation of the UK Parliament could be construed in accordance with Community law. The problem came where national law had been enacted after UK membership in a way that clearly conflicted with a directly effective Treaty provision:

Macarthys Ltd v *Smith* [1979] ICR 785

Lord Denning stated that:

> If the time should come when our Parliament deliberately passes an Act with the intention of repudi-
> ating the Treaty or any provision in it - and says so in express terms then I should have thought that
> it would be the duty of our courts to follow the statute of our Parliament. (at 789)

When the House of Lords was confronted with the Merchant Shipping Act 1988, which
had been enacted to prevent Spanish fishermen from 'quota hopping' into UK fishing
areas, the moment seemed to have arrived. It was fairly clear that these measures discriminated on grounds of nationality against the right of Spanish fishing businesses to
establish themselves in the UK in accordance with the directly effective former Arts 7 and
52 EC Treaty (now Arts 12 and 43). Following a reference to the Court of Justice, the
House of Lords was, however, prepared to hold the Act to be without effect to the extent
of the conflict. 'It is the duty of a UK court', said Lord Bridge in his speech, 'when delivering final judgment, to override any rule of national law found to be in conflict with
any directly enforceable rule of Community law' (**R** *v* **Secretary of State for Transport,
ex parte Factortame** [1991] 1 AC 603 at 659).

Direct effect: Directives

United Kingdom courts have experienced some difficulty with directly enforcing directives. As discussed above, *prima facie*, directives are not directly applicable, and so do not
fall into that category of Community provisions which, without further enactment, are
to be given legal effect under s 2(1), European Communities Act 1972. However, where
they have been held by the Court of Justice to create directly enforceable rights they have
been applied vertically against emanations of the state by UK courts, following references
to the Court of Justice, as in **Marshall** and **Foster** *v* **British Gas** (see above). However, as
discussed above, UK courts have had some difficulty in determining the scope of 'state
emanation' (see **Doughty**, **Griffin** and **NUT**).

Despite this difficulty with state emanation, where UK courts have determined that a
directive can be enforced against the state or an emanation of the state, UK courts have
complied fully with the principle. The House of Lords has gone as far as to hold that parts
of the Trade Union and Labour Relations Act 1978 were incompatible with a directly
effective directive (Directive 76/207) in **Equal Opportunities Commission** *v* **Secretary
of State for Employment** [1994] 1 All ER 910.

Indirect effect

Where legislation has been enacted to implement a directive, the courts have shown
themselves capable of creative interpretation, on the basis that Parliament would have
intended that the legislation be interpreted in conformity with the directive, even if it
had been misunderstood at the time of enactment:

Litster v *Forth Dry Dock* [1989] 2 WLR 634

The House of Lords had to consider Directive 77/187, which was intended to protect workers
dismissed in connection with a business transfer. The directive had been implemented in the
UK by the Transfer of Undertakings (Protection of Employment) Regulations 1981 (SI

1981/1794). The UK regulations protected employees who had been dismissed immediately before the transfer of the undertaking.

In this case the employees had been dismissed one hour before the transfer. On a literal interpretation of the regulations the employees were not employed immediately before the transfer, and therefore they could not rely on the regulations. However, several decisions of the Court of Justice had held that workers dismissed prior to the transfer, but for a reason connected with the transfer, would (for the purposes of the directive) be treated as having been employed by the undertaking at the time when it took place. The House of Lords decided that it was the duty of the UK court to give the UK regulations 'a construction which accords with the decisions of the European Court upon the corresponding provisions of the directive to which the regulation was intended to give effect' (Lord Keith). Accordingly, the House of Lords read into the regulations 'or would have been so employed if he had not been unfairly dismissed', and the dismissed employees were held to come within the scope of the regulations.

The House of Lords took a different line in the following case:

Duke v GEC Reliance [1988] 2 WLR 359

The case turned on the legality of different retirement ages for men and women, the same point as in **Marshall** and **Foster**, above. In this case, however, the employer was a private undertaking, and the question of vertical direct effect could not arise. The question before the court was whether it had an obligation to interpret the Sex Discrimination Act 1975 in accordance with the Equal Treatment Directive dated 9 February 1976. The House of Lords decided that it did not. Parliament had passed the Act in the belief that it was entitled to have discriminatory retirement ages even when the directive (which was then in draft) came into effect. Lord Templeman stated that:

> Of course a UK court will always be willing and anxious to conclude that UK law is consistent with Community law. Where an Act is passed for the purpose of giving effect to an obligation imposed by a directive or other instrument a British court will seldom encounter difficulty in concluding that the language of the Act is effective for the intended purpose. But the construction of a British Act of Parliament is a matter of judgment to be determined by British courts and to be derived from the language of the legislation considered in the light of the circumstances prevailing at the date of the enactment ... It would be most unfair to the respondent to distort the construction of the Sex Discrimination Act 1975 in order to accommodate the Equal Treatment Directive 1976 as construed by the European Court of Justice in the 1986 **Marshall** case.

The above decision has been criticised. Lord Slynn, a former Lord Advocate and English Lord of Appeal, has expressed the anxiety of UK judges on the issue:

> I find it difficult to say that a statute of 1870 must be interpreted in the light of a 1991 directive. If the former is in conflict with the latter, it is not for the judges to strain language but for Governments to introduce new legislation. (Slynn, 1992, p. 124)

Although this observation is consistent with UK constitutional principles, it is at odds with the judgment of the Court of Justice in **Simmenthal** (Case 106/77):

> Every national court must, in a case within its jurisdiction, apply Community law in its entirety and protect rights which the latter confers on individuals and must accordingly set

aside any provision of national law which may conflict with it, whether prior or subsequent to the Community rule.

The application of the principle by the UK, post-**Marleasing**, is usefully illustrated by the approach adopted by the House of Lords in the following case:

Webb v *EMO Cargo (UK) Ltd* [1995] IRLR 647

Ms Webb was employed to cover for Ms Stewart while she was on maternity leave. Ms Webb later discovered that she herself was pregnant and that she would not be able to provide the requisite cover during Ms Stewart's maternity leave. EMO Cargo dismissed Ms Webb who subsequently made a complaint that she had been discriminated against on grounds of sex. Section 1(1), Sex Discrimination Act 1975 ('the 1975 Act') states that:

> A person discriminates against a woman in any circumstances relevant for the purposes of . . . this Act if –
> (a) on the ground of her sex he treats her less favourably than he treats or would treat a man . . .

Section 5 of the 1975 Act provides that:

> (3) A comparison of the cases of persons of different sex or marital status under sections 1(1) or 3(1) . . . must be such that the relevant circumstances in the one case are the same, or not materially different, in the other.

Section 6(2) further provides that:

> It is unlawful for a person, in the case of a woman employed by him at an establishment in Great Britain, to discriminate against her –
>
> . . .
> (b) by dismissing her, or subjecting her to any other detriment.

An employment tribunal dismissed her complaint. It held that the correct approach was to compare the treatment of Ms Webb with that which would have been accorded to a man in comparable circumstances. If a man had told his employer that he would be absent from work for a similar period, there is very little doubt that likewise he would have been dismissed. Accordingly, Ms Webb's dismissal was not on the ground of her sex (under s 1(1) of the 1975 Act) and she was not treated less favourably than EMO Cargo would have treated a man.

The Employment Appeal Tribunal ([1990] IRLR 124) dismissed Ms Webb's appeal, as did the Court of Appeal ([1992] IRLR 116). The Court of Appeal stated that it was necessary to determine whether a man with a condition as nearly comparable to that of Ms Webb (i.e. pregnancy) which had the same practical effect upon his ability to do the job would, or would not, have been dismissed; this was an application of s 5(3) of the 1975 Act.

On appeal to the House of Lords ([1993] IRLR 27), Lord Keith of Kinkel held (at para 8) that there was no direct application of a gender-based criterion:

> If [Ms Webb's] expected date of confinement had not been so very close to that of Valerie Stewart she would not have been dismissed. It was her expected non-availability during the period when she was needed to cover for Valerie Stewart which was the critical factor.

Lord Keith discussed the application of s 5(3) of the 1975 Act to ascertain whether it was legitimate to compare the non-availability of a man for medical reasons. He concluded that the relevant circumstance for the purpose of s 5(3) was the expected unavailability at the material time. The precise reason (i.e. pregnancy) was not relevant, nor was it relevant that this reason was a condition only capable of affecting women, therefore (at para 11):

... on a proper construction of the relevant provisions of the 1975 Act the dismissal did not ... constitute direct unlawful discrimination.

However, the **Marleasing** interpretative obligation was acknowledged by Lord Keith, who stated (at para 21) that it applied:

Whether the domestic legislation came after or, as in this case, preceded the Directive.

Directive 76/207 (the Equal Treatment Directive) applies to the same area of activity, sex discrimination, as the 1975 Act. Article 2(1) provides that:

For the purposes of the following provisions, the principle of equal treatment shall mean that there shall be no discrimination whatsoever on grounds of sex either directly or indirectly by reference in particular to marital or family status.

Article 5(1) provides that:

Application of the principle of equal treatment with regard to working conditions, including the conditions governing dismissal, means that men and women shall be guaranteed the same conditions without discrimination on grounds of sex.

Lord Keith thought it was necessary to refer the matter to the Court of Justice for a preliminary ruling, pursuant to the former Art 177 EC Treaty (now Art 234), to ascertain if, on the facts of the case, there was a breach of the directive. If there was, then the House of Lords would be required to decide if the 1975 Act could be construed in such a way as to accord with the Court's decision. The Court of Justice (Case C-32/93) held (at para 29) that Ms Webb's dismissal contravened the directive:

Article 2(1) read with Article 5(1) of Directive 76/207 precludes dismissal of an employee who is recruited for an unlimited term with a view, initially, to replacing another employee during the latter's maternity leave and who cannot do so because, shortly after recruitment, she is found herself to be pregnant.

The Court of Justice was clearly influenced by the fact that Ms Webb was not simply taken on to cover for the maternity leave. She was initially employed some months prior to Ms Stewart's expected maternity leave, in order that she could be trained. It was intended to retain her following Ms Stewart's return to work. The Court of Justice decided that the contract of employment was for an unlimited duration rather than for a specific period directly related to the length of Ms Stewart's maternity leave. The case was then referred back to the House of Lords (**(No. 2)** [1995] IRLR 647), where Lord Keith observed (at para 11) that:

The ruling of the European Court proceeds on an interpretation of the broad principles dealt with in Articles 2(1) and 5(1) of the Directive 76/207/EEC. Sections 1(1)(a) and 5(3) of the Act of 1975 set out a more precise test of unlawful discrimination and the problem is how to fit the terms of that test into the ruling.

What the House of Lords was seeking to ascertain (at para 2) was whether it was:

... possible to construe the relevant provisions of the Act of 1975 so as to accord with the ruling of the European Court.

Lord Keith held (at para 11) that it was possible to interpret s 5(3) in such a fashion:

in a case where a woman is engaged for an indefinite period, the fact that the reason why she will be temporarily unavailable for work at a time when to her knowledge her services will be particularly required is pregnancy is a circumstance relevant to her case, being a circumstance which could not be present in the case of a hypothetical man.

The House of Lords held that Ms Webb's dismissal constituted direct sex discrimination contrary to the 1975 Act and remitted the case back to the employment tribunal for compensation to be assessed.

The application of **Marleasing** was possible in the above case because it did not involve *distorting* the meaning of the Act, an Act which preceded the directive. The Act was simply interpreted purposively by the House of Lords in order to accord with the wording and purpose of the directive.

Clearly, the **Duke** case and those cases subsequent to it are not in conflict with this decision. In these cases, Parliament had expressly permitted the discriminatory retirement ages complained of. To have decided otherwise would have required the court to *distort* the clear wording of the Sex Discrimination Act 1975.

Unimplemented directives: a continuing problem

The approach adopted by the Court of Justice to individuals affected by the non-implementation of directives was, as discussed above, a pragmatic response to a perceived problem of inequality between Member States. Those states which failed to implement directives on time might actually enjoy an advantage over those states which had shouldered the burden which the directive had imposed. Individuals in the non-implementing state would be deprived of the benefits which the directive was intended to confer upon them. Despite the increase in Art 226 EC Treaty proceedings, bringing defaulting Member States before the Court is a slow and only partial solution to the problem (see Chapter 7). Even if it achieves belated implementation of the directive, it cannot provide compensation to those individuals who have been deprived of its beneficial effect. The creation, in the first instance, of the doctrine of vertical direct effect, the right to enforce the directive against the defaulting Member State, and a gradual enlargement of that right by the Court so that enforcement is now possible against a whole range of state or state-sponsored bodies, has provided a valuable weapon in the hands of intended beneficiaries.

The failure of the Court of Justice to grasp the nettle and to give directives horizontal direct effect between individuals in **Marshall** and **Faccini Dori** has only partly been mitigated by the development of the interpretative obligation of indirect effect expounded in **Harz** and **Marleasing**. This approach depends very much on the willingness of national courts to engage in creative interpretation of national legislation. At the present time the Court seems reluctant, as it demonstrated in **Wagner Miret** (Case C–334/92), to be more specific in defining the nature of the national court's interpretative obligation. The Court of Justice has made it clear that it expects individuals who cannot establish the vertical direct effect of a directive, or who are unsuccessful in persuading a national court to give it interpretative effect, to claim damages against their own Member State. This will involve a direct claim against the Member State for its failure to implement, on the basis of the Court's decisions in **Brasserie du Pêcheur** and **Factortame** (Cases C–46 & 48/93). It may, as in **Faccini Dori**, require the individual to commence a whole new legal action after having failed to establish the interpretative effect of the directive against another individual.

However, a claim against a Member State cannot be regarded as a wholly satisfactory substitute for the enforcement of a directive against those who were intended to be bound by it. The Member State may have believed, in good faith, that it had taken all necessary steps to implement the directive, and it may be hard to establish that the breach was 'sufficiently serious'. Even if this can be established, damages may not constitute a satisfactory remedy for, say, the failure to set up an area of environmental protection, as required by an unimplemented directive. The losers may be the local community as a whole rather than an individual and it may be impossible to establish any causal link, as required by **Francovich**, between the failure to implement the directive and any specific loss suffered by an individual. These difficulties will probably remain unless and until the Court accepts that unimplemented directives may have horizontal as well as vertical direct effect.

Enforcement of a directive in the national courts: the correct approach

When considering a case relating to the enforcement of an EU directive in the national courts, the following issues should be considered in this order:

1. Is the directive directly enforceable (i.e. (i) has the directive's date for implementation expired; **and** (ii) is it sufficiently precise and unconditional; **and** (iii) is it being enforced against the state or an emanation of the state)? If it is not directly effective, then:

2. Is the directive indirectly effective (i.e. will the national courts comply with their **Marleasing** interpretative obligation and interpret national law in such a way as to comply with the wording and purpose of the directive)? If it is not indirectly effective, then:

3. Is it possible to claim **Francovich** damages from the state because of the state's failure to implement (or correctly implement) the directive?

Obviously it will be necessary to consider direct enforcement of the directive only if it has not been implemented by the Member State or it has been implemented incorrectly. If the directive has been correctly implemented then the national implementing legislation can be applied (in the UK this will either be through an Act of Parliament or delegated legislation). Flowcharts setting out the above approach are laid out in Figures 9.1 to 9.3.

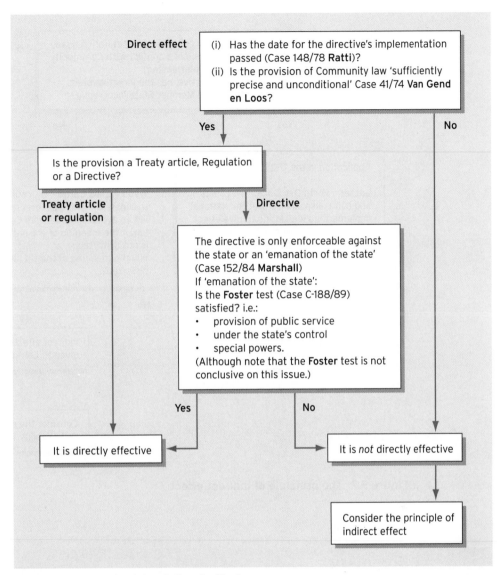

Figure 9.1 The principle of direct effect

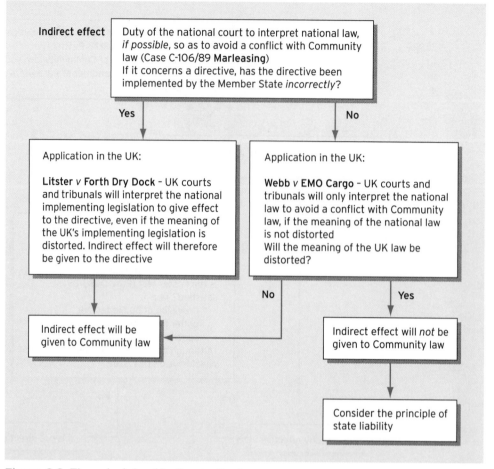

Figure 9.2 The principle of indirect effect

Summary

Now you have read this chapter you should be able to:

- Explain the concept of 'supremacy of Community law'.
- Outline what is meant by the principle of direct effect of Community law.
- Explain how the European Court of Justice determines whether a provision of Community law is capable of having direct effect.
- Evaluate the distinction between horizontal direct effect and vertical direct effect.
- Explain the rationale for the European Court of Justice's decision that directives are generally only capable of having vertical direct effect.
- Explain the concept of indirect effect, and discuss how English courts and tribunals have applied the interpretive obligation established by the European Court of Justice in its **Marleasing** judgment.

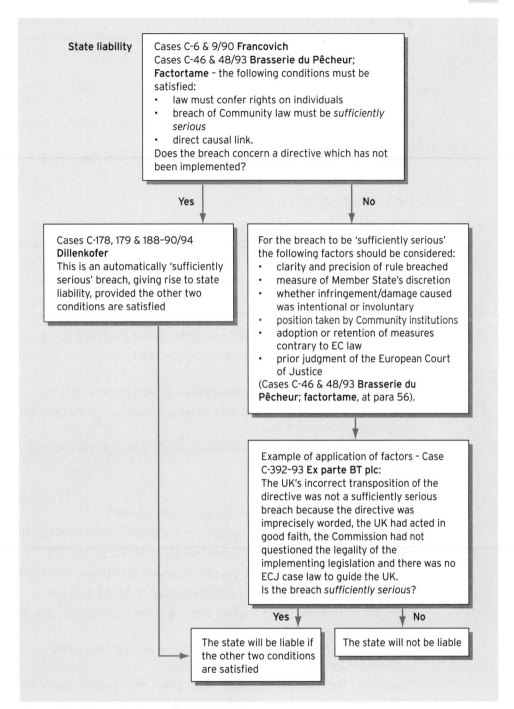

Figure 9.3 The principle of state liability

■ Evaluate the principle of state liability, established by the European Court of Justice in **Francovich**, and discuss how this principle has evolved through subsequent judgments of the Court.

References

Mancini, G.F. and Keeling, D.T., 'Democracy and the European Court of Justice' (1994) 57 MLR 175.

Slynn, G. (1992) *Introducing a New Legal Order*, Sweet & Maxwell, p. 124.

Further reading

Textbooks

Craig, P. and De Burca, G. (2003) *EU Law Text, Cases and Materials* (3rd edn), Oxford University Press, Chapters 5 to 7.

Foster, N. (2006) *Foster on EU Law* (1st edn), Oxford University Press, Chapters 4 and 5 (Sections 4.6 to 4.10, 5.3 and 5.4).

Prechal, S. (2005) *Directives in EC Law* (1st edn), Oxford University Press, Chapters 5 to 11.

Slynn, G. (1992) *Introducing a New Legal Order*, Sweet & Maxwell, p. 124.

Steiner, J., Woods, L. and Twigg-Flesner, C. (2006) *EU Law* (9th edn), Oxford University Press, Chapters 4, 5 and 8.

Storey, T. and Turner, C. (2005) *Unlocking EU Law* (1st edn), Hodder Arnold, Chapters 8 and 9.

Tillotson, J. and Foster, N. (2003) *Text, Cases and Materials on EU Law* (4th edn), Cavendish Publishing, Chapter 8.

Weatherill, S. (2006) *Cases and Materials on EU Law* (7th edn), Oxford University Press, Chapters 3, 5 and 6.

Journal articles

Bebr, G., 'Case Note on **Francovich**' (1992) 29 CML Rev 557.

De Burca, G., 'Giving Effect to European Community Directives' (1992) 55 MLR 215.

Caranta, R., 'Government Liability after **Francovich**' (1993) 52 CLJ 272.

Convery, J., 'State Liability in the UK after **Brasserie du Pêcheur**' (1997) 34 CML Rev 603.

Coppel, J., 'Rights, Duties and the End of **Marshall**' (1994) 57 MLR 859.

Craig, P.P., 'Directives: Direct, Indirect Effect and the Construction of National Legislation' (1997) 22 EL Rev 519.

Curtin, D., 'The Province of Government: Delimiting the Direct Effect of Directives in the Common Law Context' (1990) 15 EL Rev 195.

Dougan, M., 'The "Disguised" Vertical Direct Effect of Directives' (2000) 59 CLJ 586.

Drake, S., 'Twenty years after **Van Colson**: The impact of "indirect effect" on the protection of the individual's Community rights' (2005) 30 EL Rev 329.

Howells, G., 'European Directives: The Emerging Dilemmas' (1991) MLR 456.

Richards, C., 'The supremacy of Community law before the French Constitutional Court' (2006) 31 EL Rev 499.

Lenaerts, K. and Corthaut, T., 'Of birds and hedges: the role of primacy in invoking norms of EU law' (2006) 31 EL Rev 287.

Lenz, M., Tynes, D.S., and Young, L., 'Horizontal What? Back to Basics' (2000) 25 EL Rev 509.

Mancini, G.F. and Keeling, D.T., 'Democracy and the European Court of Justice' (1994) 57 MLR 175.

Mead, P., 'The Obligation to Apply European Law: Is **Duke** Dead?' (1991) 16 EL Rev 490.

Prechal, S., 'Does Direct Effect Still Matter?' (2000) 37 CML Rev 1047.

Robinson, W., 'Annotations on Case C-91/92 **Paola Faccini Dori** v **Recreb s.r.l.**' (1995) 32 CML Rev 629.

Snyder, F., 'The Effectiveness of European Community Law: Institutions, Processes, Tools and Techniques' (1993) 56 MLR 19.

Steiner, J., 'From Direct Effects of **Francovich**: Shifting Means of Enforcement of Community Law' (1993) 18 EL Rev 3.

Szyszczak, E., 'UK: Judicial Review of the Public Acts' (1998) 23 EL Rev 89.

Tridimas, T., 'Horizontal Effect of Directives: A Missed Opportunity' (1994) 19 EL Rev 621.

Van Gerven, W., 'Of Rights, Remedies and Procedures' (2000) 37 CML Rev 501.

Weatherill, S., 'Breach of Directives and Breach of Contract' (2001) 26 EL Rev 177.

10 Applying Community law in the English Courts and adapting English remedies to the requirements of Community law

Aims and objectives

At the end of this chapter you should understand:

■ How Community law is applied in English courts.

■ How English courts have adapted remedies to ensure compatibility with Community law.

The Community approach to legal remedies

Some consideration was given in Chapter 9 to the approach of English courts towards the enforcement of unimplemented directives, and that approach is complicated by the UK's unique concept of parliamentary sovereignty and the less distinctive, but equally difficult, separation of powers between legislature and judiciary. The same problems are apparent when the prospective claimant seeks an appropriate avenue for the enforcement of a right derived from Community law or the redress of a wrong resulting from its breach in the courts of England and Wales.

The effectiveness of remedies in national courts has become an increasing preoccupation of the Court of Justice, and the Court has moved from its original position on national remedies. In **Comet v Produktschap voor Siergewassen** (Case 45/76), it held that the remedy to deal with a breach of Community law should be 'no less effective' than that available to protect a right derived from national law and should not make it impossible in practice to obtain relief. This comparative standard with a very low irreducible minimum does not fully take into account the deficiencies of national legal remedies, which may place all kinds of obstacles in the path of a claimant seeking to enforce a Community right. Although the way in which national courts operate is, in theory at least, outside the competence of Community law, the practical effects of deficiencies in national legal systems have led the Court of Justice to put an increasing emphasis on the duty of cooperation in Art 10 EC Treaty, and the extent to which it binds national courts. Consequently, the Court of Justice took a stronger line in **R v Secretary of State for Transport, ex parte Factortame (No. 2)** (Case C–213/89). In this case, where the House of Lords had declared that national law did not allow an interim order against the Crown to suspend the operation of the Merchant Shipping Act 1988, the Court held that the national court must 'set aside' any national rule which precluded it from granting interim relief. In **Johnston** *v* **Chief Constable of the RUC** (Case 222/84), the Court of Justice specifically adopted Art 13 of the European Convention on Human Rights as a fundamental principle of Community law. Article 13 provides that:

> Everyone whose rights and freedoms as set forth in this Convention are violated shall have an effective remedy before a national authority notwithstanding that the violation has been committed by persons acting in an official capacity.

In the following case, the English Court of Appeal referred the case to the Court of Justice for a preliminary ruling pursuant to the former Art 177 EC Treaty (now Art 234):

Courage v *Cohan* (Case C-453/99)

The claimant had entered into a contract with the defendant. The contract was void because it was in breach of Community competition law (the former Art 85 EC Treaty (now Art 81)). The claimant was suing the defendant for breach of this contract. English law prevented a party to an illegal contract from recovering damages from the other side. However, the Court of Justice held that a party to a contract which was liable to restrict or distort competition within the meaning of the former Art 85 EC Treaty (now Art 81) was able to rely on the breach of that provision in order to obtain relief from the other contracting party. The Court further held that the former Art 85 (now Art 81) precluded the English rule under which a party to a contract was barred from claiming damages for loss caused by performance of that contract on the sole ground that the claimant was a party to that contract. However, the Court held that Community law does not preclude national law from denying a party who is found to bear *significant responsibility* for the distortion of competition the right to obtain damages from the other contracting party. Under a principle which is recognised in most of the legal systems of the Member States and which the Court has applied in the past, a litigant should not profit from his own unlawful conduct, where this is proven.

The effect of the Court's judgment in the **Factortame** case (above) is that there is now a necessary implication in Community law that 'an appropriate legal remedy must be created if one does not exist' (Advocate-General Mischo in **Francovich** *v* **Italy** (Case C–6/90)). Community legislation may also prescribe the type of remedy and the amount of damages that should be awarded (see, e.g., Directives 93/37 and 93/38 on public procurement contracts). Some directives may specify the bodies or types of bodies which should have the standing to challenge decisions infringing the directive (see, e.g., Directive 93/12 on unfair consumer contract terms). Some directives have, more recently, made specific requirements as to penalties, with a view to ensuring that national implementing legislation contains real deterrent sanctions (see, e.g., Directive 92/59 on product safety and Directive 89/592 on insider dealing). Where there is no penalty prescribed by Community law, the Court has held that national law should provide a penalty that is 'effective, proportionate and dissuasive' (**Commission** *v* **UK** (Case C–382/92)).

Public law remedies: judicial review

The obligation to implement Community law in the UK falls primarily on the government and the various agencies which it has chosen to carry out the functions of public administration. In English law, all bodies which exercise public powers, whether conferred by statute or common law, and whether public or private in origin, are subject to control and review by the courts (**Council of Civil Service Unions *v* Minister for the Civil Service** [1985] AC 374; **R *v* Panel on Takeovers and Mergers, ex parte Datafin plc** [1987] QB 815). In relation to Community law, that process of control and review extends to decisions made about the implementation of Community law. If the decision relates to the exercise of a power conferred on a subordinate body to legislate by way of delegated legislation, the court may intervene to prevent an abuse of those delegated legislative powers (**R *v* HM Treasury, ex parte Smedley** [1985] QB 657). If, on the other hand, the decision is by Parliament itself on the scope and content of primary legislation then the decision on whether or not to legislate, and in what form, is not subject to any control or review by the courts (**Blackburn *v* Attorney-General** [1971] 1 WLR 1037; **R *v* Secretary of State for Foreign and Commonwealth Affairs, ex parte Rees-Mogg** [1993] 3 CMLR 101).

It is now accepted by the English courts that they are able to rule on the compatibility of English law with Community law (**Factortame Ltd *v* Secretary of State for Transport** [1989] 2 All ER 692). The appropriate remedy in such a case is a declaration setting out the extent of the incompatibility (**R *v* Secretary of State for Employment, ex parte EOC** [1994] 2 WLR 409). Although a court in judicial review proceedings has the power to award damages, they may be awarded only where these would be available in an ordinary *private* action (e.g. breach of contract, etc.). This position has obviously been affected by the decision of the House of Lords in **R *v* Secretary of State for Transport, ex parte Factortame and Others (No. 5)** [1999] 3 WLR 1062, where the House of Lords held that the UK's breach of Community law was 'sufficiently serious', rendering the UK government liable to the claimants for all losses which flowed from the breach.

Claims in tort against the state

As discussed in Chapter 9, the Court of Justice has held on many occasions that, subject to Treaty provisions being sufficiently precise and unconditional, such provisions could create rights which were enforceable at the suit of individuals in the courts of Member States (**Van Gend en Loos** (Case 26/62)). The application of this doctrine in relation to those Treaty provisions found to be directly effective has to be worked out in the national courts according to substantive and procedural national rules. In English law, where damages are claimed, this has meant that the breach of Community law has had to be recognised either as a new tort or incorporated within the bounds of an old one.

In **Bourgoin *v* Ministry of Agriculture, Fisheries and Food (MAFF)** [1985] 3 All ER 385, the proceedings arose out of a ban imposed by the Ministry on the importation of turkeys from France in the run-up to Christmas 1981. The ban was imposed, ostensibly, on animal health grounds, but in **Commission *v* UK** (Case 40/82) the Court of Justice held that the real reason behind the ban was a desire to protect the home market from foreign competition. It was not, therefore, justified under Art 30 EC Treaty. Bourgoin was an importer who suffered considerable loss by the action of the UK government. He brought an action in damages, claiming infringement of Art 28 EC Treaty as a breach of statutory duty, breach of an innominate tort, or for misfeasance in public office. The Court of Appeal held, by a majority, that the only appropriate remedy was judicial review and that damages would not be available. Although the House of Lords had held, in **Garden Cottage Foods Ltd *v* Milk Marketing Board** [1984] AC 130, that a breach of Art 82 EC Treaty gave rise to a claim for breach of statutory duty, a breach of Art 28 by a public authority was different. Article 28 did not confer private rights, simply a right to ensure that a public duty was performed. That duty could be enforced in judicial review proceedings and, in accordance with general principles of administrative law, damages would not normally be available. Since the decision of the Court of Justice in **Brasserie du Pêcheur SA *v* Germany** ((Case 46/93), see Chapter 9) this view is no longer tenable. The question to be determined by the national court is whether or not the breach in question is 'sufficiently serious' and, if it is, whether there is a sufficient causative link between the breach and the damage suffered.

It is now clear, as a matter of English law, that a person who argues that he has suffered a loss as a result of a breach of a public law duty will not be compelled to proceed by way of judicial review, with its highly restrictive three-month time limit for the commencement of proceedings. Provided that he can show a particular loss, he does not need to prove a breach of a duty giving rise to a claim in tort, or the existence of a contract to bring a private action (**Roy *v* Kensington and Chelsea and Westminster FPC** [1992] 1 AC 624). There seems little doubt that a person who has suffered loss as a result of a breach by a public body of a Treaty provision or a legally binding act of the institutions of the Community, and who can satisfy the criteria laid down by the Court of Justice in **Brasserie du Pêcheur**, will be able to succeed in the English courts (see the view expressed *obiter* by Lord Goff in **Kirklees MBC *v* Wickes** [1993] AC 227).

Claims in tort between private individuals for breaches of Treaty provisions

Individuals who have suffered loss as the a result of a breach of a directly effective provision of the Treaty will be able to claim damages against another individual who has caused that loss. This is clearly the case in relation to Art 82 EC Treaty (**Garden Cottage Foods *v* Milk Marketing Board** [1984] AC 130). Damages may also be awarded by English courts for breach of Art 81 EC Treaty (**H.J. Banks and Co Ltd *v* British Coal Corporation** (Case C–128/92; **MTV Europe *v* BMG Records (UK) Ltd** [1995] 1 CMLR 437). Individuals are also clearly entitled to damages for discriminatory treatment at work in breach of Art 141 EC Treaty, or on grounds of nationality under Art 12 EC Treaty. An individual might, for example, wish not only to secure equal treatment, but also to obtain damages where national law precluded them. As can be seen in **Defrenne *v* SABENA** (Case 43/75), an individual may make such a claim for compensation for loss of equal pay simply on the basis of the Treaty provision (see **Macarthys Ltd *v* Smith** (Case 129/79)).

Any national limitations on the extent of compensation payable in cases of sex discrimination should not be observed where they prevent the claimant from being adequately compensated for the damage suffered. Although the decision in **Marshall *v* Southampton and South-West Hampshire Area Health Authority (No. 2)** (Case 271/91) was limited to the interpretation of Art 6, Directive 76/207 in relation to the amount of damages payable, the principles laid down are wide enough to cover other claims against the state and emanations of the state (see Woolridge and D'Sa, 1993). This view is supported by the Court of Justice's decision in the following case:

Commission v *UK* (Case C-382/92)

The Court of Justice held that the UK's implementation of Directives 77/187 (Transfer of Undertakings) and 75/129 (Consultation on Redundancy) did not provide sufficient compensation for workers affected by a breach of the rules by the employer. The Court held that the compensation payable under the Employment Protection Act 1975, which purported to implement Directive 75/129, was potentially so little as to deprive the measure of its practical effect:

> Where a Community directive does not specifically provide any penalty for an infringement or refers for that purpose to national laws, regulations and administrative provisions, Article 5 of the Treaty [now Art 10] requires the Member States to take all measures necessary to guarantee the application and effectiveness of Community law. For that purpose, while the choice of penalties remains within their discretion, **they must ensure in particular that infringements of Community law are penalised under conditions, both procedural and substantive, which are analogous to those applicable of a similar nature and which, in any event, make the penalty effective, proportionate and dissuasive.** [emphasis added]

In the above case, although the Court of Justice was speaking of 'penalties', it is clear from the circumstances of the case that it had in mind both criminal sanctions and civil damages which could, in appropriate circumstances, be punitive in nature. It is apparent from the emphasised words that the Court has now moved on from merely requiring equivalent remedies. Where the national remedy is not effective, the remedy for the breach of Community law should be 'effective, proportionate and dissuasive'. This principle will apply whether or not the defendant is the state, an emanation of the state or a private individual or undertaking.

Community law as the basis for a claim in contract, a defence in breach of contract proceedings, and for claims in quasi-contract

Community law may be used to found, or assist in, a claim for breach of contract in English courts. Under Art 141 EC Treaty, for example, discriminatory provisions in collective agreements are made unlawful and any contract, therefore, which incorporates the terms of such a discriminatory agreement will be void insofar as it offends against Art 141 (**Defrenne** *v* **SABENA** (above)). Community law may also be used as a defence to a claim for breach of contract. If an individual is sued for breach of a contract which, for example, infringes the prohibition on restrictive agreements in Art 81(1) EC Treaty, he may raise the issue of validity of the agreement under Community law as a defence (**Brasserie de Haecht** *v* **Wilkin** (Case 23/67); **Society of Lloyds** *v* **Clementson** [1995] 1 CMLR 693).

In **Amministrazione delle Finanze** *v* **San Giorgio** (Case 199/82), the Court of Justice decided that an individual was entitled to recover charges that had been levied on him contrary to a directly effective provision of Community law. The right of recovery was a necessary adjunct to the right to equal treatment. National law should, therefore, enable individuals who have been wrongly taxed or charged in this way to recover the payments which they have made. So, for example, an EU citizen in receipt of educational services must not be charged a different fee to home students (**Gravier** *v* **City of Liège** (Case

293/83)), nor may importers be levied tax at a rate which exceeds that payable in respect of home-produced goods of the same kind (Art 90 EC Treaty). When this happens, the individuals affected should be able to recover the sums overpaid.

The rule laid down by the Court of Justice in **San Giorgio** conflicted with an established rule of English law that a person who has paid money under a mistake of fact can generally recover it, but a person who has paid money under a mistake of law cannot, generally, do so (D'Sa, 1994). However, mistake of law is narrowly construed so that, for example, a payment made on the basis of a misunderstanding about a rule of foreign law is regarded as a mistake of fact. Community law is not 'foreign law', of course, since it is incorporated into English law and must be treated as a question of law and not fact (**R v Goldstein** [1983] 1 CMLR 252). In the following case, the House of Lords narrowed the rule further, so that money paid to a public body in response to an unlawful demand on the basis of a mistake of law will now be recoverable:

Woolwich Equitable Building Society v IRC [1992] 3 WLR 366

Referring to the right of recovery in relation to money wrongfully paid under Community law, Lord Goff of Chievely remarked:

> At a time when Community law is becoming increasingly important, it would be strange if the right of the citizens to recover overpaid charges were to be more restricted under domestic law than it is under Community law.

A similar extension of Community principles into the wider application of the common law followed the decision of the Court of Justice in **Factortame** that interim orders should bind the Crown, when the House of Lords subsequently held that such orders were available even in cases not involving Community law (**Re M** [1994] 1 AC 377).

Community law as a defence in criminal proceedings

Many of the landmark decisions of Community law have been made by the Court of Justice on references from national courts during the course of criminal proceedings. In **Procureur du Roi v Dassonville** (Case 8/74), the defendant was prosecuted for selling Scotch whisky without supplying purchasers with a certificate of origin. The Court held that the legislation under which he was prosecuted was incompatible with Art 28 EC Treaty and as a consequence the national court would, therefore, have been obliged to dismiss the charge against him. Similarly, the defendants in **R v Henn and Darby** (Case 34/79) were able to raise in their prosecution a potential breach of Art 28 EC Treaty, although the Court of Justice held that the UK legislation was justifiable under Art 30 EC Treaty.

In the English courts, so-called Euro-defences have been successfully raised in criminal proceedings for 'overstaying', contrary to the Immigration Act 1971. In **R v Pieck** (Case 157/79) the charge against the defendant had to be dismissed because the requirement imposed on the defendant to obtain 'leave' for his continuing residence was held to be contrary to the rights of residence conferred on him by Art 39 EC Treaty (see also **R v Kirk** (Case 63/83)). Also, where Community law provides a defence in an unimplemented directive, the defendant may rely upon it (**Pubblico Ministero v Ratti** (Case 148/78)). On the other hand, prosecutors cannot rely on an unimplemented directive to interpret the criminal law in such a way as to secure a conviction. This offends against the Community principle of legal certainty and non-retroactivity (**Officier van Justitie** *v* **Kolpinghuis Nijmegen BV** (Case 80/86)).

Euro-defences, using Art 28 EC Treaty, were relied upon by businesses prosecuted under the Shops Act 1950, until this avenue was finally closed by the Court of Justice in **Stoke-on-Trent and Norwich City Councils** *v* **B & Q** (Case C–169/91). Prosecutions are, in any event, much less likely following the liberalisation of Sunday trading in England and Wales by the Sunday Trading Act 1994. The scope for the use of Art 28 to defeat prosecutions under national laws aimed at consumer protection has also been considerably diminished by the decision of the Court of Justice to exclude from the scope of Art 28 'selling arrangements' which are unlikely to affect trade between states, in **Keck and Mithouard** (Cases C–267 & 268/91); see Chapter 18.

Summary

Now you have read this chapter you should be able to:

- Explain how Community law is applied in English courts.
- Evaluate how English courts have adapted national remedies to ensure they are compatible with the principles of Community law.

References

D'Sa, R. (1994) *European Community Law and Civil Remedies in England and Wales*, Sweet & Maxwell, Chapters 9 and 10, pp. 46–58.

Woolridge, F. and D'Sa, R. (1993) 'Damages for Breaches of Community Directives: The Decision in Marshall (No. 2)', *European Business Law Review*, Vol. 4, No. 11.

Further reading

Textbooks

Craig, P. and De Burca, G. (2003) *EU Law Text, Cases and Materials* (3rd edn), Oxford University Press, Chapters 5 to 7.

D'Sa, R. (1994) *European Community Law and Civil Remedies in England and Wales*, Sweet & Maxwell, Chapters 9 and 10, pp. 46–58.

Foster, N. (2006) *Foster on EU Law* (1st edn), Oxford University Press, Chapter 4 (Section 4.8).

Steiner, J., Woods, L. and Twigg-Flesner, C. (2006) *EU Law* (9th edn), Oxford University Press, Chapter 6.

Tettenborn, A. (2001) *Law of Restitution*, Cavendish Publishing Ltd.

Tillotson, J. and Foster, N. (2003) *Text, Cases and Materials on EU Law* (4th edn), Cavendish Publishing, Chapter 8.

Journal articles

Convery, J., 'State Liability in the UK after **Brasserie du Pêcheur**' (1997) 34 CML Rev 603.

Vincenzi, C. (1995) 'Private Initiative and Public Control in the Regulatory Process', in

Daintith, T. (ed.) *Implementing EC Law in the UK: Structures for Indirect Rule*, John Wiley & Sons.

Woolridge, F. and D'Sa, R. (1993) 'Damages for Breaches of Community Directives: The Decision in Marshall (No. 2)', *European Business Law Review*, Vol. 4, No. 11.

PART 2

The free movement of persons and services, and rights of establishment

11 European Union citizenship and free movement rights

Aims and objectives

At the end of this chapter you should understand:

■ Why Art 14(2) EC Treaty is relevant to the free movement of persons.

■ Which provisions of the EC Treaty are relevant to the free movement of workers, freedom of establishment and the free movement of services.

■ How the European Economic Area Agreement impacts upon the Community law provisions on the free movement of persons.

■ The nature of EU citizenship within the context of Art 18(1) EC Treaty.

■ Through a study of the relevant case law of the Court of Justice, how EU citizenship has, and will, impact on the Community law provisions on the free movement of persons.

■ How Directive 2004/38 has consolidated the Community law provisions relating to entry and residence.

■ What rights, other than the free movement of persons, are derived from EU citizenship.

■ The limited rights of free movement for non-EU citizens.

■ The Schengen *acquis* and the UK's participation in the Schengen arrangements.

Introduction to the free movement of persons

The free movement of persons has been a cornerstone of the European Community since its inception. That freedom was not, initially, an entitlement for citizens of Member States to move anywhere in the Community for any purpose, but was linked to a number of specific economic activities (Arts 39–42 (workers), Arts 43–48 (rights of establishment) and Arts 49–55 (services)). Each of these Treaty provisions has been elaborated by detailed secondary legislation. The rights of individuals and undertakings in the three principal categories are examined in more detail in Chapter 12 (workers) and Chapter 13 (services and establishment).

Free movement rights must be seen in the context of three important developments of recent years. The first of these are the measures taken to create the Single European Market which shall, under Art 14(2) EC Treaty, 'comprise an area without internal frontiers in which the free movement of goods, persons, services and capital is ensured'.

Although Art 14(2) creates a commitment for the Community to remove border restrictions, it is not clear whether the provision has direct effect. In **R v Secretary of State for the Home Office, ex parte Flynn** [1995] 3 CMLR 397, McCullough J held that it did not match the criteria for having direct effect. It imposed no obligation on Member States, 'let alone one which is clear and precise'. He therefore refused a claim by the applicant, an EU citizen, that he had been unlawfully detained for questioning at Dover. This decision was subsequently upheld in the Court of Appeal; although note that this was a decision of an English court and not the Court of Justice.

The second development is the European Economic Area (EEA) Agreement, which came into effect on 1 January 1994. Under the EEA Agreement all the free movement rights enjoyed under the EC Treaty were extended to the remaining states of EFTA (currently Iceland, Liechtenstein and Norway, but not including Switzerland). European Union Citizens and their families, and citizens of the participating EFTA states and their families, enjoy the full free movement rights of the Treaty and of the implementing legislation in all the territories of the EU and the participating EFTA states.

The third and most significant development is the creation of EU citizenship by the Treaty on European Union (Art 17 EC Treaty).

EU citizenship

Article 17 EC Treaty provides that:

1. **Citizenship of the Union is hereby established**. Every person holding the nationality of a Member State shall be a citizen of the Union. Citizenship of the Union shall complement and not replace national citizenship.
2. Citizens of the Union shall enjoy the rights conferred by this Treaty and shall be subject to the duties imposed thereby. [emphasis added]

Under Art 18(1) EC Treaty:

Every citizen of the Union shall have the right to move and to reside freely within the territory of the Member States, **subject to the limitations and conditions laid down in this Treaty and by the measures adopted to give it effect**. [emphasis added]

The emphasised words of Art 18(1) EC Treaty would seem to make it clear that EU citizenship does not bring any new free movement rights into being but formally attaches the existing rights, with all the qualifications and exceptions, to the new citizenship. The most that might have been said about EU citizenship and free movement is that possession of such citizenship raises a presumption of a right of entry or residence which would have to be rebutted by the host Member State if those rights were to be refused or terminated. The Treaty seemed to envisage that the existing rights would form the basis for further development, because it authorises further measures 'to strengthen or add to the rights' (Art 18(1)). The scope of EU citizenship was a central issue in the following case, which was decided by an English court, not the Court of Justice:

R v Home Secretary, ex parte Vitale and Do Amaral [1995] All ER (EC) 946

The applicants, both EU citizens, were resident in the UK and had been in receipt of income support for a number of months. They had not found work and, in the view of the Department of Employment, they were not seeking work. They were therefore asked to leave the country.

They argued that, irrespective of the truth of the allegations, they were entitled to remain simply as EU citizens. Judge J rejected this argument:

> Article 8a [EC Treaty, now Art 18(1)] provides two distinct rights, the right to move freely within the territory and the right to reside freely. Neither right is free-standing nor absolute. It is expressly and unequivocally subject to the limitations and conditions contained in the Treaty. Moreover it is clear from the provisions in Article 8a(2) [now Art 18(2)] and, more significantly, Article 8e [now Art 22], that provisions may be adopted in due course 'to strengthen or add to the rights laid down' in the part of the Treaty devoted to 'citizenship'. In effect, therefore, the existence of limitations and the potential for extending the rights of citizens are acknowledged in Article 8e as well as Article 8a. So Article 8a does not provide every citizen of the Union with an open-ended right to reside freely within every Member State.

This decision of the English Divisional Court was upheld by the Court of Appeal ([1996] All ER (EC) 461). The limited scope of Art 8a (now Art 18(1)) received some support from the Court of Justice in the following case:

Kremzow v *Austria* (Case C-299/95)

The claimant argued that, as an EU citizen, he was entitled to the protection of Community law in relation to criminal proceedings which had been brought against him. The Court of Justice held, on a reference from the national court, that the mere fact of his EU citizenship was 'not a sufficient connection with Community law to justify the application of Community provisions'.

The Court of Justice was, however, more recently prepared to hold that an EU citizen who had been *permitted* by the host state to remain there (where she had no right to remain under Community law) was entitled, as an EU citizen, to equal treatment in relation to welfare and other benefits in line with nationals of the host state. It left open the question of whether a person who is no longer exercising their free movement rights could still enjoy an independent right of residence as an EU citizen (**Sala** *v* **Freistaat Bayern** (Case C–85/96)).

One of the rights conferred by the Treaty is that contained in Art 12 EC Treaty (previously Art 6) which provides that 'Within the scope of this Treaty . . . any discrimination on grounds of nationality shall be prohibited'. In the following case, the Court of Justice applied this non-discriminatory Art 12 provision alongside the EU citizenship provisions, which enabled it to elevate the status of EU citizenship:

Grzelczyk v *Centre Public d'aide sociale d'Ottignies-Louvain-la-Neuve* (Case C-184/99)

A student of French nationality, paid his own way throughout his first three years of full-time studies at a Belgian university by taking on minor jobs and obtaining credit. At the start of his fourth and final year he applied for a Belgian social security benefit known as minimum subsistence allowance (minimex). His application was refused on the ground that under the relevant Belgian legislation a non-Belgian applicant was only eligible if *inter alia* Regulation 1612/68 applied to him. This Regulation is considered further in Chapter 12; it is applicable to 'workers' not 'students'. If he had been Belgian then he would have been entitled to the benefit, notwithstanding the fact that he was not a worker within the scope of Regulation

1612/68. The Belgian tribunal had doubts as to whether the national legislation was compatible with Arts 12 and 17 EC Treaty. The tribunal therefore referred the case to the Court of Justice for a preliminary ruling pursuant to Art 234 EC Treaty. The Court of Justice held that:

29. It is clear from the documents before the Court that a student of Belgian nationality, though not a worker within the meaning of Regulation No 1612/68, who found himself in exactly the same circumstances as Mr Grzelczyk would satisfy the conditions for obtaining the minimex. The fact that Mr Grzelczyk is not of Belgian nationality is the only bar to its being granted to him. It is not therefore in dispute that the case is one of discrimination solely on the ground of nationality.

30. Within the sphere of application of the Treaty, such discrimination is, in principle, prohibited by Article 6 [now Art 12]. In the present case, **Article 6 [now Art 12] must be read in conjunction with the provisions of the Treaty concerning citizenship of the Union in order to determine its sphere of application.**

31. **Union citizenship is destined to be the fundamental status of nationals of the Member States, enabling those who find themselves in the same situation to enjoy the same treatment in law irrespective of their nationality, subject to such exceptions as are expressly provided for.**

. . .

36. The fact that a Union citizen pursues university studies in a Member State other than the State of which he is a national cannot, of itself, deprive him of the possibility of relying on the prohibition of all discrimination on grounds of nationality laid down in Article 6 of the Treaty [now Art 12].

37. As pointed out in paragraph 30 above, in the present case that prohibition must be read in conjunction with Article 8a(1) of the Treaty [now Art 18(1)], which proclaims 'the right to move and reside freely within the territory of the Member States, subject to the limitations and conditions laid down in this Treaty and by the measures adopted to give it effect'.

38. As regards those limitations and conditions, it is clear from Article 1 of Directive 93/96 that Member States may require of students who are nationals of a different Member State and who wish to exercise the right of residence on their territory, first, that they satisfy the relevant national authority that they have sufficient resources to avoid becoming a burden on the social assistance system of the host Member State during their period of residence, next, that they be enrolled in a recognised educational establishment for the principal purpose of following a vocational training course there and, lastly, that they be covered by sickness insurance in respect of all risks in the host Member State.

39. Article 3 of Directive 93/96 makes clear that the directive does not establish any right to payment of maintenance grants by the host Member State for students who benefit from the right of residence. On the other hand, there are no provisions in the directive that preclude those to whom it applies from receiving social security benefits.

40. As regards more specifically the question of resources, Article 1 of Directive 93/96 does not require resources of any specific amount, nor that they be evidenced by specific documents. The article refers merely to a declaration, or such alternative means as are at least equivalent, which enables the student to satisfy the national authority concerned that he has, for himself and, in relevant cases, for his spouse and dependent children, sufficient resources to avoid becoming a burden on the social assistance system of the host Member State during their stay (see paragraph 44 of the judgment in Case C-424/98 **Commission** v **Italy** [2000] ECR I-4001).

. . .

46. It follows from the foregoing that Articles 6 and 8 of the Treaty [now Art 12 and Art 17] preclude entitlement to a non-contributory social benefit, such as the minimex, from being made conditional, in the case of nationals of Member States other than the host State where they are legally resident, on their falling within the scope of Regulation No 1612/68 when no such condition applies to nationals of the host Member State. [emphasis added]

In the above case, the Court of Justice stated that because it was clear that a student who was Belgian but otherwise in the same circumstances as the applicant would be entitled to minimex, the case was one of discrimination solely on the ground of nationality which, in principle, was prohibited by Art 12 EC Treaty (at paras 29–30). The Court further stated at para 30 that Art 12 had to be read in conjunction with the Treaty provisions on EU citizenship (Art 17 EC Treaty), to determine its sphere of application. The Court then went on to say that EU citizenship was destined to be the fundamental status of nationals of the Member States, enabling those who found themselves in the same situation to enjoy the same treatment in law irrespective of their nationality, subject to some exceptions as were expressly provided for (para 31).

The Court noted that Directive 93/96 requires Member States to grant a right of residence to student nationals of a Member State who satisfied certain requirements. Although Art 3 of this Directive makes clear that there is no right to payment of maintenance grants by the host Member State for students who benefit from this right of residence, it contains no provision precluding those to whom it applies from receiving social security benefits. The Court therefore held that Arts 12 and 17 EC Treaty precluded Belgium from making entitlement to minimex conditional on the applicant (Mr Grzelczyk) coming within the scope of Regulation 1612/68 (i.e. being an 'EU worker') when no such condition applied to Belgian nationals. It should be noted that Directive 93/96 has been repealed and replaced by Directive 2004/38; this directive is considered in further detail below.

The **Grzelczyk** case clearly raised the profile and status of EU citizenship. Due to the fact that the applicant had a right of residence under Community law as a student, the Court held that as an EU citizen he was entitled to be treated in the same way as a national with regard to the payment of social security benefits; an application of the non-discriminatory Art 12 EC Treaty provision. It was unclear whether this would pave the way for the Court of Justice to extend its scope to others (e.g. work-seekers). **Grzelczyk** could be distinguished from that of, for example, a work-seeker because it could be argued that a student is contributing to the economy of the host Member State whereas a work-seeker is not necessarily doing so. In any event in **Grzelczyk** the Court stated that its judgment did not prevent a Member State from (i) taking the view that a student who had recourse to social assistance was no longer fulfilling the conditions of his right of residence; or (ii) from taking measures, within the limits imposed by Community law, to either withdraw his residence permit or refuse to renew it. But in no case, the Court said, could such a measure become the automatic consequence of a student who was a national of another Member State having recourse to the host Member State's social security system (see paras 40–45). If the Court did extend this case to, for example, work-seekers, such that they were entitled to claim social security benefits under the same terms as a national, it would therefore be open to a Member State to determine that the work-seeker no longer satisfied the conditions relating to his right of residence. The right of a work-seeker to claim a social security benefit has since been considered by the Court of Justice in two cases: **Collins** (Case C–138/02) and **Ioannidis** (Case C–258/04); see below.

Directive 2004/38 (relating to the right of entry and residence) was subsequently adopted and had to be transposed into national law by 30 April 2006. Article 6(1), Directive 2004/38 provides that EU citizens shall have the right of residence in another Member State for a period of up to three months; this will therefore include work-seekers. Article 14(1), Directive 2004/38 further provides that EU citizens and their family members shall have the right of residence under Art 6, 'as long as they do not become an *unreasonable* burden on the social assistance system of the host Member State' (emphasis added). Expulsion shall not be an automatic consequence if an EU citizen or his family members have recourse to the host Member State's social assistance system (Art 14(3), Directive 2004/38).

The status of work-seekers will be considered further in Chapter 12; suffice to state here that work-seekers are afforded a reasonable period of time to seek work in the host Member State, following which, unless they can show they are actively seeking work and have a genuine chance of securing employment, their right of residence under Community law will expire. This has now been incorporated into Directive 2004/38 which provides that, other than in accordance with the provisions relating to restrictions on the right of entry and residence on grounds of public policy, security or health, an expulsion order cannot be issued against an EU citizen or his family members, if, *inter alia*, the EU citizen entered the host Member State to seek employment and he can provide evidence that he is continuing to seek work and has a genuine chance of being employed (Art 14(4), Directive 2004/38).

The principle of EU citizenship and non-discrimination developed by the Court of Justice in **Grzelczyk** has subsequently been applied by the Court in **Marie-Nathalie D'Hoop v Office national de l'emploi** (Case C–224/98) and **Garcia Avello** (Case C–148/02). European Union citizenship was also relevant in the following case:

Baumbast and R v *Secretary of State for the Home Department* (Case C-413/99)

The Court of Justice held as follows:

> A citizen of the European Union who no longer enjoys a right of residence as a migrant worker in the host Member State can, as a citizen of the Union, enjoy there a right of residence by direct application of Article 18(1) EC [Treaty]. The exercise of that right is subject to the limitations and conditions referred to in that provision, but the competent authorities and, where necessary, the national courts must ensure that those limitations and conditions are applied in compliance with the general principles of Community law and, in particular, the principle of proportionality.

In the above case the Court of Justice held that Art 18(1) EC Treaty, which provides every EU citizen with the right to move and reside freely within the territory of the Member States, grants a right of continued residence to an EU worker within the host Member State, even after the EU worker has ceased working. This right is 'subject to the limitations and conditions laid down in this Treaty' (Art 18(1) EC Treaty). Six recent cases have provided further confirmation of the increasingly important concept of EU citizenship.

In the first case, the Korkein oikeus (Supreme Court, Finland) referred a question on the interpretation of Art 18 EC Treaty to the Court of Justice for a preliminary ruling:

Pusa (Case C-224/02)

Mr Pusa, a Finnish national, was in receipt of an invalidity pension in Finland. Mr Pusa owed money to Osuuspankkien Keskinäinen Vakuutusyhtiö (OKV), and OKV sought an 'attachment' on Mr Pusa's invalidity pension to enable deductions to be made from his pension automatically; these deductions would be paid to OKV.

The case concerned the calculation of the amount which OKV should be authorised to debit from Mr Pusa's pension (i.e. the amount of the 'attachment'). The Finnish law on enforcement provides that part of remuneration is excluded from attachment, that part being calculated from the amount which remains after compulsory deduction at source of income tax in Finland. The problem in this case lay in the fact that Mr Pusa was resident in Spain and he was subject to income tax there. In accordance with the provisions of a double taxation agreement, he was not subject to any deduction at source in Finland. The part of his pension subject to attachment was therefore calculated on the basis of the gross amount of the pension, which would not have been the case if he had continued to reside in Finland.

The Finnish Supreme Court asked the Court of Justice essentially whether such a situation is compatible in particular with the freedom of movement and residence guaranteed to EU citizens by the EC Treaty.

The Court stated (as it had in previous cases), that EU citizenship is destined to be the fundamental status of nationals of the Member States and that an EU citizen must be granted in all Member States the same treatment in law as that accorded to the nationals of those Member States who find themselves in the same situation. The Court considered, first, that if the Finnish law on enforcement must be interpreted to mean that it does not in any way allow the tax paid by the person concerned in Spain to be taken into account, that difference of treatment will certainly and inevitably result in Mr Pusa being placed at a disadvantage by virtue of exercising his right to move and reside freely in the Member States, as guaranteed under Art 18 EC Treaty. The Court stated, second, that to preclude all consideration of the tax payable in the Member State of residence, when such tax has become payable and to that extent affects the actual means available to the debtor, cannot be justified in the light of the legitimate objectives pursued by such a law of preserving the creditor's right to recover the debt due to him and preserving the debtor's right to a minimum subsistence income.

Consequently, the Court held that 'Community law in principle precludes legislation of a Member State under which the attachable part of a pension paid at regular intervals in that State to a debtor is calculated by deducting from that pension the income tax pre-payment levied in that State, while the tax which the holder of such a pension must pay on it subsequently in the Member State where he resides is not taken into account at all for the purposes of calculating the attachable portion of that pension' (para 48).

However, the Court considered that 'on the other hand, **Community law does not preclude such national legislation if it provides for tax to be taken into account, where taking the tax into account is made subject to the condition that the debtor prove that he has in fact paid or is required to pay within a given period a specified amount as income tax in the Member State where he resides**'. The Court said that that is only the case 'to the extent that, first, the right of the debtor concerned to have tax taken into account is clear from that legislation; secondly, the detailed rules for taking tax into account are such as to guarantee to the interested party the right to obtain an annual adjustment of the attachable portion of his pension to the same extent as if such a tax had been deducted at source in the Member State which enacted that legislation; and, thirdly, those detailed rules do not have the effect of making it impossible or excessively difficult to exercise that right' (para 48).

The second case was quite novel, Art 18 EC Treaty being successfully relied upon to enable a Chinese national to reside in the UK on the basis that she was the carer of her newborn child who had acquired Irish nationality:

Zhu and Chen (Case C-200/02)

Mr and Mrs Chen were Chinese nationals and parents of a first child born in China. They wished to have a second child but came up against China's birth control policy, the 'one child policy', which imposes financial penalties on couples who give birth to more than one child. They therefore decided that Mrs Chen would give birth abroad. Their second child was born in September 2000 in Belfast, Northern Ireland; Northern Ireland is part of the UK. The choice of the place of birth was no accident; Irish law allows any person born in the island of Ireland (which for this purpose includes Northern Ireland) to acquire Irish nationality. The child therefore acquired Irish nationality. Because, however, she did not meet the requirements laid down by the relevant UK legislation, she did not acquire UK nationality. After the birth, Mrs Chen moved to Cardiff (Wales) with her child, and applied there for a long-term residence permit for herself and her child, which was refused. Mrs Chen appealed and the appellate authority referred a question to the Court of Justice on the lawfulness of that refusal, pointing out that the mother and child provide for their needs, they do not rely on public funds, there is no realistic possibility of their becoming so reliant, and they are insured against ill health.

The circumstance that the facts of the case concerned a young child gave the Court an occasion to state a preliminary point. The Court said that **the capacity to be the holder of rights guaranteed by the EC Treaty and by secondary law on the free movement of persons does not require that the person concerned has attained the age prescribed for the acquisition of legal capacity to exercise those rights personally.** Moreover, **the enjoyment of those rights cannot be made conditional on the attainment of a minimum age.**

As regards the child's right of residence, the Court recalled that Art 18 EC Treaty has direct effect. Purely as a national of a Member State, and therefore an EU citizen, she can rely on the right of residence laid down by that provision. Regard must be had, however, to the limitations and conditions to which that right is subject, in particular Art 1(1), Directive 90/364, which allows Member States to require that the persons concerned have sickness insurance and sufficient resources (Directive 90/364 has since been replaced by Directive 2004/38, see below). The Court found that the child had sickness insurance and sufficient resources, and therefore satisfied Art 1(1), Directive 90/364. The fact that the sufficient resources of the child were provided by her mother and she had none herself was immaterial; a requirement as to the origin of the resources cannot be added to the requirement of sufficient resources.

Finally, as regards the fact that Mrs Chen went to Ireland with the sole aim of giving her child the nationality of a Member State, in order then to secure a right of residence in the UK for herself and her child, the Court recalled that it is for each Member State to define the conditions for the acquisition and loss of nationality. A Member State may not restrict the effects of the grant of the nationality of another Member State by imposing an additional condition for the recognition of that nationality with a view to the exercise of the fundamental freedoms provided for in the Treaty.

As regards the mother's right of residence, the Court observed that Directive 90/364 recognises a right of residence for 'dependent' relatives in the ascending line of the holder of the right of residence, which assumes that material support for the family member is provided by the holder of the right of residence. In the present case, said the Court, the position was exactly the opposite. Mrs Chen could not thus be regarded as a 'dependent' relative of her child in the ascending line. On the other hand, **where a child is granted a right of residence by Art 18 EC Treaty and Directive 90/364, the parent who is the carer of the child** cannot be refused the right to reside with the child in the host Member State, as otherwise the child's right of residence would be deprived of any useful effect.

The ne. case, decided by the Court of Justice in 2005, concerned a migrant student's right to a maintenance loan at a preferential rate of interest:

Bidar (Case C-209/03)

The Court of Justice examined whether the conditions for granting student support in England and Wales complied with Community law. Student support is financial assistance granted to students by the state in the form of a loan at a preferential rate of interest to cover maintenance costs. The loan is repayable after the student completes his studies, provided he is earning in excess of a certain sum. A national of another Member State is eligible to receive such a loan if he is 'settled' in the UK and has been resident there throughout the three-year period preceding the start of the course. However, under UK law a national of another Member State cannot, in his capacity as a student, obtain the status of being settled in the UK.

Dany Bidar, a young French national, had completed the last three years of his secondary education in the UK, living as a dependent of a member of his family without ever having recourse to social assistance. He was refused financial assistance to cover his maintenance costs, which he applied for when he started a course in economics at University College London, on the grounds that he was not settled in the UK for the purposes of UK law. He brought proceedings before the English High Court, which referred three questions to the Court of Justice for a preliminary ruling.

The first of those questions sought to determine whether, as Community law currently stands, assistance such as that at issue in the present case falls outside the scope of the Treaty, in particular Art 12 EC Treaty. It should be noted that the Court held in **Lair** (Case 39/86) and **Brown** (Case 197/86) that assistance given to students for maintenance and for training falls in principle outside the scope of the Treaty for the purposes of Art 12 EC Treaty (see Chapter 12). In the present case, the Court held that Art 12 EC Treaty must be read in conjunction with the provisions on EU citizenship and noted that an EU citizen lawfully resident in the territory of the host Member State can rely on Art 12 EC Treaty in all situations which fall within the scope *ratione materiae* of Community law, in particular those involving the exercise of the right to move and reside within the territory of the Member States, as conferred by Art 18 EC Treaty. In the case of students who move to another Member State to study there, there is nothing in the text of the Treaty to suggest that they lose the rights which the Treaty confers on EU citizens. The Court added that **a national of a Member State who, as in the present case, lives in another Member State where he pursues and completes his secondary education, without it being objected that he does not have sufficient resources or sickness insurance, enjoys a right of residence on the basis of Art 18 EC Treaty and Directive 90/364** (Directive 90/364 has since been replaced by Directive 2004/38, see below). With regard to **Lair** and **Brown**, the Court stated that since judgment had been given in those cases the TEU had introduced EU citizenship and inserted a chapter devoted to education and training into the Treaty. **In the light of those factors, it had to be held that assistance such as that at issue falls within the scope of application of the Treaty for the purposes of the prohibition of discrimination laid down in Art 12 EC Treaty.**

The Court then considered whether, where the requirements for granting assistance are linked to the fact of being settled or to residence and are likely to place at a disadvantage nationals of other Member States, the difference in treatment between them and nationals of the Member State concerned can be justified. It observed that, although the Member States must, in the organisation and application of their social assistance systems, show a certain degree of financial solidarity with nationals of other Member States, it is permissible for them to ensure that the granting of that type of assistance does not become an unreasonable burden. **In the case of assistance covering the maintenance costs of students, it is thus legitimate to seek to ensure a certain degree of integration by checking that the student in question has resided in the host Member State for a certain length of time.** However, a link with the employment market, as in the case of allowances for persons seeking employment which were at issue in **D'Hoop** (Case C-224/98) and **Collins** (Case C-138/02) cannot be required.

In principle, a requirement that an applicant should be settled in the host Member State may therefore be allowed. However, in so far as it precludes any possibility for a student who is a national of another Member State to obtain the status of settled person, and hence to receive the assistance even if he has established a genuine link with the society of the host Member State, the legislation in question is incompatible with Art 12 EC Treaty.

The next two cases concerned a work-seeker's right to claim a social security benefit:

Collins (Case C-138/02)

In the UK, the grant of a 'jobseeker's allowance' to persons seeking employment is subject to a condition (i) of habitual residence or (ii) that the person is a worker for the purposes of Regulation 1612/68 or a person with a right to reside in the UK pursuant to Directive 68/360 (Directive 68/360 has since been repealed and replaced by Directive 2004/38).

Brian Collins was born in the United States and had dual American and Irish nationality. Having spent one semester in the UK in 1978 as part of his university studies and having worked for ten months in 1980 and 1981 on a part-time and casual basis in bars and the sales sector, he returned to the UK in 1998 for the purpose of seeking employment. He applied for a jobseeker's allowance but was refused on the grounds that he was not habitually resident in the UK and was not a worker for the purposes of Regulation 1612/68, nor was he entitled to reside in the UK pursuant to Directive 68/360.

Three questions were referred to the Court of Justice for a preliminary ruling in this connection, the first two of which concerned respectively the Regulation and the Directive, while the third, phrased in an open manner, asked whether there might be some provision or principle of Community law capable of assisting the applicant in his claim.

On the question of whether Mr Collins was a worker within the terms of Regulation 1612/68 (see Chapter 12), the Court took the view that, as 17 years had elapsed since he had last been engaged in an occupational activity in the UK, Mr Collins did not have a sufficiently close connection with the employment market in that Member State. The situation of Mr Collins, the Court ruled, was comparable to that of any person seeking his first employment. The Court pointed out in this regard that a distinction had to be drawn between persons looking for work in the host Member State without having previously worked there and those who have already entered the employment market in that Member State. While the former benefit from the principle of equal treatment only as regards access to employment, the latter may, on the basis of Art 7(2), Regulation 1612/68, claim the same social and tax advantages as national workers (see Chapter 12). The Court took the view that Mr Collins was not a worker in the sense in which that term covers persons who have already entered the employment market.

With regard to Directive 68/360, the Court first pointed out that the Treaty itself confers a right of residence, which may be limited in time, on nationals of Member States who are seeking employment in other Member States. The right to reside in a Member State which Directive 68/360 confers is reserved for nationals who are already employed in that Member State. Mr Collins was not in that position and he could therefore not rely on the Directive.

The Court of Justice concluded by examining the UK legislation in the light of the fundamental principle of equal treatment. Nationals of one Member State who are seeking employment in another Member State come in that regard, the Court held, within the scope of application of Art 48 EC Treaty and are thus entitled to benefit from the right to equal treatment set out in Art 48(2). However, the Court held that in principle this does not extend the right of equal treatment to benefits of a financial nature such as the jobseeker's allowance; equality of treatment in regard to social and financial benefits applies only to persons who have already entered the employment market, while others specifically benefit from it only as regards access to employment. The Court considered, however, that, **in view of the establishment of EU citizenship and the interpretation in the case law of the right to equal treatment enjoyed by EU citizens, it was no longer possible to exclude from the scope of Art 48(2) EC Treaty, which is an expression of equal treatment, a benefit of a financial nature intended to facilitate access to employment in the labour market of a Member State. In the present case, the residence condition imposed by the UK legislation was likely to be more easily satisfied by UK nationals. It could be justified only if it was based on objective considerations that were independent of the nationality of the persons concerned and proportionate to the legitimate aim of the national law. It was, the Court pointed out, legitimate for the national legislature to wish to ensure that there was a genuine link between an applicant for the allowance and the employment market, in particular by establishing that the person concerned was, for a reasonable period, in fact genuinely seeking work. However, if it is to be proportionate, a period of residence required for that purpose may not exceed what is necessary in order to enable the national authorities to be satisfied that the person concerned is genuinely seeking work.**

Ioannidis (Case C-258/04)

The Court of Justice was required to examine the case of a Greek national who arrived in Belgium in 1994 after completing his secondary education in Greece and having obtained recognition of the equivalence of his certificate of secondary education. After a three-year course of study in Liège (Belgium), he obtained a graduate diploma in physiotherapy and then registered as a jobseeker. He went to France to follow a paid training course from October 2000 to June 2001 and then returned to Belgium, where he submitted an application for a 'tideover allowance', an unemployment benefit provided for under Belgian legislation for young people seeking their first job. His application was refused because he did not fulfil the relevant requirements at that time, which were that he should have (i) completed his secondary education in Belgium; or (ii) pursued education or training of the same level and equivalent thereto in another Member State and been the dependent child of a migrant worker (for the purposes of Art 39 EC Treaty) who was residing in Belgium.

The proceedings arising out of the action brought by Mr Ioannidis against that refusal led the Cour du travail de Liège (Higher Labour Court, Liège) to refer a question to the Court of Justice regarding the compatibility of the Belgian system with Community law.

The Court observed, first of all, that nationals of a Member State seeking employment in another Member State fall within the scope of Art 39 EC Treaty and therefore enjoy the right to equal treatment laid down in Art 39(2) EC Treaty (see Chapter 12).

The remainder of the Court's answer drew on case law set out in recent judgments delivered by the Court, in particular those in **D'Hoop** (Case C-224/98) and **Collins** (Case C-138/02).

The Court of Justice observed that in **Collins** it held that, in view of the establishment of EU citizenship and the interpretation of the right to equal treatment enjoyed by EU citizens, it is no longer possible to exclude from the scope of Art 39(2) EC Treaty a benefit of a financial nature intended to facilitate access to employment in the labour market of a Member State. In addition, the Court had already found in **D'Hoop** that the tideover allowances provided for by the Belgian legislation are social benefits, the aim of which is to facilitate, for young people, the transition from education to the employment market. Mr Ioannidis was therefore justified in relying on Art 39 EC Treaty to claim that he could not be discriminated against on the basis of nationality as far as the grant of a tideover allowance was concerned. The condition that secondary education must have been completed in Belgium could be met more easily by Belgian nationals and could therefore place nationals of other Member States at a disadvantage.

As for possible justification of that difference in treatment, the Court again referred to D'Hoop, in which it held that although it is legitimate for the national legislature to wish to ensure that there is a real link between the applicant for a tideover allowance and the geographic employment market concerned, a single condition concerning the place where completion of the secondary education diploma was obtained is too general and exclusive in nature and goes beyond what is necessary to attain the objective pursued. Lastly, as regards the fact that the Belgian legislation nonetheless affords a right to a tideover allowance to an applicant if he has obtained an equivalent diploma in another Member State and if he is the dependent child of a migrant worker who is residing in Belgium, the Court considered, by converse implication, that a person who pursues higher education in a Member State and obtains a diploma there, having previously completed secondary education in another Member State, may well be in a position to establish a real link with the employment market of the first Member State, even if he is not the dependent child of a migrant worker residing in that Member State. The Court noted that, in any event, dependent children of migrant workers who are residing in Belgium derive their right to a tideover allowance from Art 7(2), Regulation 1612/68, regardless of whether there is a real link with the employment market (see Chapter 12).

The final case was decided by the Court of Justice during 2005. It provided the Court of Justice with the opportunity to clarify the limits of the material scope of the EC Treaty with regard to EU citizenship:

Schempp (Case C-403/03)

In Germany, income tax legislation provides that maintenance payments to a divorced spouse are deductible (thus reducing a person's income tax liability). That advantage is also granted where recipients (the divorced spouse in this case) have their principal or habitual residence in another Member State, provided that taxation of the recipient's maintenance payments is proved by a certificate from the tax authorities of that other Member State. Egon Schempp, a German national resident in Germany, was refused the deduction of maintenance payments made to his former spouse resident in Austria, because Austrian tax law excluded the taxation of maintenance payments.

When a question was referred to it from the Bundesfinanzhof (Federal Finance Court, Germany) for a preliminary ruling on whether the German system complied with Arts 12 and 18 EC Treaty, the Court considered first of all whether such a situation falls within the scope of Community law. The governments which had submitted observations contended that Mr Schempp had not made use of his right of free movement, and the only external factor was the fact that Mr Schempp was paying maintenance in another Member State. **The Court observed that EU citizenship is not intended to extend the material scope of the Treaty to internal situations which have no link with Community law.** However, the situation of a national of a Member State who has not made use of the right to free movement cannot, for that reason alone, be assimilated to a purely internal situation. Here, the exercise by Mr Schempp's former spouse of a right conferred under Community law to move freely to, and reside in, another Member State had an effect on his right to deduct in Germany, so **there was no question of it being an internal situation with no connection with Community law.**

The Court then considered, with regard to the principle of non-discrimination, whether Mr Schempp's situation could be compared with that of a person who was paying maintenance to a former spouse resident in Germany and was entitled to deduct the maintenance payments made to her, and it found that that was not the case. It observed that the unfavourable treatment of which Mr Schempp complained derived from the difference between the German and Austrian tax systems with regard to the taxing of maintenance payments. It is settled case law that Art 12 EC Treaty is not concerned with any disparities in treatment which may result from differences existing between the various Member States, so long as they affect all persons subject to them in accordance with objective criteria and without regard to their nationality.

As regards the application of Art 18 EC Treaty, the Court found that the German legislation did not in any way obstruct Mr Schempp's right to move to and reside in other Member States. The transfer of his former spouse's residence to Austria did entail tax consequences for him. However, the Court observed that the Treaty offers no guarantee to an EU citizen that transferring his activities to a Member State other than that in which he previously resided will be neutral as regards taxation. Given the disparities in the tax legislation of the Member States, such a transfer may be to the citizen's advantage in terms of indirect taxation or not, according to the circumstances. That principle applies *a fortiori* to a situation where the person concerned has not himself made use of his right of free movement, but claims to be the victim of a difference in treatment following the transfer of his former spouse's residence to another Member State.

The above cases demonstrate that, when determining the scope of an EU citizen's right of free movement, the Art 18(1) EC Treaty right of EU citizens to move and reside freely within the territory of the Member States and the anti-discriminatory Art 12 EC Treaty provision must be taken into consideration; in some situations these two provisions will be of fundamental importance to the outcome of the case.

An overview of the substantive Community law provisions regulating an EU citizen's right of free movement now follows.

Free movement rights

In the early days of the Community, freedom of movement was seen as the means by which labour and skills shortages in one Member State could be met out of a surplus of labour and skills in another. That approach was subsequently modified, both in later implementing legislation and by decisions of the Court of Justice. The Court has inter-preted the Treaty and the implementing provisions generously. The application of Art 39(3)(a) EC Treaty, which appears to confer a right to go to another Member State only on those able to 'accept offers of employment **actually made**' (emphasis added), to work-seekers is perhaps one of the most remarkable examples of creative interpretation (**Procureur du Roi v Royer** (Case 48/75)). Although each of the free movement rights depended until the 1990s on a specific economic activity, the Court has tended to develop a body of general principles applicable to all those exercising free movement rights. Directive 2004/38 (which replaced, *inter alia*, Directive 90/364) creates a general right of entry and residence (see below).

Most importantly, all free movement rights are directly effective and enforceable in the courts of Member States as fundamental rights. The entry or residence of those exercising them is not dependent upon any consent or leave given by the host state. Provided that an individual is engaged in an activity which confers Community rights of entry or residence, or comes within the scope of the general right of residence (for up to three months) set out in Directive 2004/38, the host state cannot terminate that right of residence (**R v Pieck** (Case 157/79)). There are exceptions to rights of entry and residence in cases where the individual constitutes a threat to public policy, public security and public health under Arts 39(3), 46(1) EC Treaty and Directive 2004/38 (which replaced, *inter alia*, Directive 64/221). These powers of Member States to derogate from individual rights of free movement have, however, been interpreted strictly by the Court (see **Adoui and Cornuaille v Belgian State** (Cases 115 and 116/81), and Chapter 15).

Since free movement rights are fundamental rights, the Court of Justice has held that they must be transparent in national legislation. Incompatible provisions of national law which, for example, exclude the employment of foreign nationals, even though they are not, in practice, applied in the case of EU citizens, must be amended to make it absol-utely clear that EU citizens enjoy equal access (**Commission v France (Re French Merchant Seamen)** (Case 167/73)). It is not sufficient that Community rights should be enjoyed by virtue of administrative concessions. Those enjoying such rights must be made aware of them and, should the need arise, be able to rely upon them before a court of law (**Commission v Germany (Re Nursing Directives)** (Case 29/84)).

Decisions affecting the exercise by an individual of free movement rights should set out the reasons for them, to enable an effective legal challenge to be made. The pro-cedures for challenging any denial of such rights, whether on the basis of public policy, public security or public health, under Directive 2004/38 (see Chapter 15), or on any other ground, should follow the Community principles of fairness and the provisions of the European Convention on Human Rights (**UNECTEF** *v* **Heylens and Others** (Case 222/86)). The provisions of the Convention are now directly applicable to the exercise of Community rights (Art 6(2) TEU). Failure to deliver those rights can give rise to a claim in damages against the Member State concerned.

Non-discrimination on grounds of nationality (Art 12 EC Treaty) is, as has been seen above, another fundamental principle of Community law that is important in the exercise of free movement rights. The detailed provisions of Regulation 1612/68 relating to equal access to employment and to other benefits enable the worker and his family to integrate into the host Member State, but there is no parallel legislation relating to the self-employed and to those providing and receiving services. Decisions of the Court of Justice relating to access to housing and the criminal process, which have been secured for workers under Regulation 1612/68 (Arts 7(2) and 9) have, however, been achieved for the self-employed and the recipients of services by a creative use of Art 12 EC Treaty (see **Commission** *v* **Italy** (Case 63/86) and **Cowan** *v* **Le Trésor Public** (Case 186/87)). Article 12 EC Treaty does, however, apply only to matters covered by the Treaty and any aspect of an individual's life which may affect his entry into or residence in another Member State as a beneficiary of Community law (unless, as discussed above, the Court applies Art 12 in conjunction with the EU citizenship provisions, to confer an independent right to be treated without discrimination in all matters).

The free movement rights will also be enhanced by measures adopted pursuant to Art 13 EC Treaty. Article 13 is the legal base for the adoption of measures to 'combat discrimination based on sex, racial or ethnic origin, religion or belief, disability, age or sexual orientation', provided such measures do not exceed the powers of the Community as conferred upon it by the EC Treaty. In other words, measures can be adopted to combat discrimination provided they are in furtherance of the existing powers of the Community.

Pursuant to Art 13 EC Treaty, the Council adopted Directive 2000/43 (OJ 2000 L 180/22) which implemented the principle of equal treatment between persons irrespective of racial or ethnic origin. The directive had to be implemented by 19 July 2003. The principle of equal treatment prohibits direct or indirect discrimination based on racial or ethnic origin (Art 1). It applies to EU and non-EU citizens and covers both public and private sectors in relation to employment, self-employment, education, social protection including social security and healthcare, social advantages, and access to and supply of goods and services (Art 3(1)). The prohibition of racial or ethnic discrimination does not, however, cover national provisions relating to the entry into and residence of third-country nationals (Art 13(2)). The directive does not, therefore, extend the free movement provisions *per se* to non-EU citizens (see below). The directive has been implemented in the UK by the following measures:

- the Race Relations Act 1976 (Amendment) Regulations 2003 SI 1626/2003;
- Race Relations Order (Amendment) Regulations (Northern Ireland) 2003 SI 341/2003.

Again pursuant to Art 13 EC Treaty, the Council adopted Directive 2000/78 (OJ 2000 L 303/16) which establishes a general framework for equal treatment in employment and occupation. The directive had to be implemented by 3 December 2003. The directive prohibits direct and indirect discrimination as regards access to employment and occupation on grounds of religion or belief, disability, age or sexual orientation. It applies to both the public and private sectors. As with Directive 2000/43, this directive applies to EU and non-EU citizens, but likewise, the prohibition does not cover national provisions relating to the entry into and residence of third-country nationals (Art 3(2)). The directive does not, therefore, extend the free movement provisions, *per se*, to non-EU citizens (see below). The directive has been implemented in the UK by a number of measures, which include the following:

- the Employment Equality (Sexual Orientation) Regulations 2003 SI 1661/2003;
- the Employment Equality (Religion or Belief) Regulations 2003 SI 1660/2003;
- the Disability Discrimination Act 1995 (Amendment) Regulations 2003 SI 1673/2003;
- the Employment Equality (Sexual Orientation) (Amendment) Regulations 2003 SI 2827/2003;
- the Employment Equality (Religion or Belief) (Amendment) Regulations 2003 SI 2828/2003;
- the Disability Discrimination Act 1995 (Pensions) Regulations 2003 SI 2770/2003;
- the Independent Schools (Employment of Teachers in Schools with a Religious Character) Regulations 2003 SI 2037/2003;
- School Standards and Framework Act 1998;
- the Industrial Tribunals (Interest on Awards in Discrimination Cases) Regulations 1996 SI 2803/1996;
- Disability Discrimination Act 1995;
- Disability Rights Commission Act 1999;
- Special Educational Needs and Disability Act 2001;
- Education (Scotland) Act 1980;
- the Fair Employment and Treatment (Northern Ireland) Order 1998 SI 3162/1998;
- Employment Equality (Sexual Orientation) Regulations (Northern Ireland) 2003 SI 497/2003;
- Industrial Tribunals (Interest on Awards in Sexual Orientation Discrimination Cases) Regulations (Northern Ireland) 2003 SI 498/2003.

Although discrimination in relation to both employment and self-employment is generally prohibited, restrictions on the employment of EU nationals in 'the public service' are permitted by Art 39(4) EC Treaty. There are similar provisions relating to the self-employed, who may be refused participation in activities which 'are connected, even occasionally, with the exercise of official authority' (Art 45 EC Treaty). There is no definition in the Treaty or the secondary legislation of either 'the public service' or 'the exercise of official authority', but both exceptions have been narrowly interpreted by the Court of Justice. The mere fact that the employer is the state is not conclusive. It is the nature of the employment which is the determining factor (**Lawrie-Blum** *v* **Land Baden-Württemberg** (Case 66/85); see Chapters 12 and 13).

To benefit from Community free movement rights, a person must be, or have been, a migrant in some sense or other. A person who has not left his own state, and does not intend to do so, cannot be a beneficiary (**Iorio** (Case 298/84)). However, this may change in relation to family reunification. Article 63(3)(a) EC Treaty, which was inserted by the Treaty of Amsterdam, enables measures to be adopted on immigration policy concerning the 'conditions of entry and residence, and standards on procedures for the issue by

Member States of long term visas and residence permits, including those for the purpose of family reunion'. Pursuant to Art 63(3)(a), a directive has been proposed to apply to EU citizens who do not exercise their free movement rights. The aim of this directive is to avoid discriminating between EU citizens who exercise their free movement rights and those who do not. In order to achieve this, it is necessary to provide for the family reuni-fication of EU citizens residing in countries of which they are nationals to be governed by the rules of Community law relating to free movement. If this directive is adopted, an EU citizen who has not exercised his free movement rights in another Member State will have the right to have specified family members installed with him. This right will over-ride any less generous national provisions. In the meantime, however, he can be a worker or a self-employed person *vis-à-vis* his own state if he works abroad for a period and then returns home. He may then enjoy the family rights of a Community migrant against his own state, which will override the more restrictive national provisions (**Morson** *v* **Netherlands** (Case 35/82); **R** *v* **IAT and Surinder Singh** (Case C–370/90)). A person who has not left his own state may still benefit from free movement rights if, for example, he has arranged employment in another Member State, or wishes to establish a business there. Subject to the public policy, public security or public health exceptions, he cannot be prevented from leaving (Art 4(1), Directive 2004/38; see below and Chapters 12, 13 and 15).

Directive 2004/38: right of entry and residence

Although the substantive provisions of the EC Treaty and secondary legislation relating to the free movement of persons will be considered in detail in subsequent chapters, Directive 2004/38 (which relates to an EU citizen's right of entry and residence in a Member State of which they are not a national) will be considered here in detail. The rationale for considering the Directive in detail at this stage is because the Directive, which had to be transposed into national law by 30 April 2006, sets out the rights of entry and residence which apply across the whole range of persons exercising their right of free movement (e.g. tourists, work-seekers, workers, the self-employed, providers and recipients of services, and retired persons). The Directive merges into a single instrument all the legislation on the right of entry and residence for EU citizens and their family members. Regulation 1612/68 has been amended (Arts 10 and 11 have been repealed), and the following nine directives have been repealed: Directives 64/221, 68/360, 72/194, 73/148, 75/34, 75/35, 90/364, 90/365 and 93/96. Regulation 1251/70 was subsequently repealed by Regulation 635/2006. The purpose of the new Directive is to simplify the law; it sets out to reduce to the bare minimum the formalities which EU citizens and their family members must complete in order to exercise their right of residence. This section provides a comprehensive review of the full range of rights of entry and residence set out within the Directive.

Scope

The Directive is designed to regulate:

(a) the conditions in which EU citizens and their families exercise their right to move and reside freely within the Member States;

(b) the right of permanent residence; and

(c) restrictions on the abovementioned rights on grounds of public policy, public security or public health.

Right of exit and entry (Articles 4 and 5)

All EU citizens have the right to leave or enter another Member State by virtue of having a valid identity card or valid passport (Arts 4(1) and 5(1)). Under no circumstances can an entry or exit visa be required (Arts 4(2) and 5(1)).

Article 3(1) provides that the Directive applies to all EU citizens exercising their right to move to, or reside in, a Member State other than that of which they are a national, and to 'family members' who accompany or join them. Article 2(2) defines 'family members' as the EU citizen's:

(a) spouse;

(b) registered partner, if the legislation of the host Member State treats registered partnerships as equivalent to marriage;

(c) direct descendants (i.e. children, grandchildren, etc.) who are under the age of 21 or who are dependants, and those of the spouse or partner as defined above;

(d) dependent direct relatives in the ascending line (i.e. parents, grandparents, etc.), and those of the spouse or partner as defined above.

This definition of 'family members' has a broader scope than the former definition set out in Art 10(1), Regulation 1612/68 (see Chapter 12).

'Family members' who do not have the nationality of a Member State (i.e. non-EU family members) may be subject to an entry visa requirement under Regulation 539/2001; residence cards will be deemed equivalent to visas (Art 5(2)).

Where the EU citizen or their family member does not have the necessary travel documents, the host Member State must afford them every facility to obtain the requisite documents or to have them sent (Art 5(4)).

In addition to family members (as defined by Art 2(2)), Art 3(2) provides that the host Member State shall, in accordance with its national legislation, 'facilitate' entry and residence for the following persons:

(a) any other family members (whether or not they are EU citizens) who are dependants or members of the household of the EU citizen having the primary right of residence, or where serious health grounds strictly require the personal care of the family member by the EU citizen;

(b) the partner with whom the EU citizen has a durable relationship, which is duly attested.

The host Member State is required to undertake an extensive examination of the personal circumstances of such persons and shall justify any denial of entry or residence (Art 3(2)).

Article 5(5) provides that the host Member State may require each person travelling to, or residing in, another Member State to register their presence in the country within a reasonable and non-discriminatory period of time. Failure to comply with this requirement may make the person liable to a proportionate and non-discriminatory sanction.

General right of residence for up to three months (Article 6)

Article 6(1) provides that EU citizens shall have the right of residence in another Member State for a period of up to three months without any conditions or formalities other than the requirement to hold a valid identity card or passport (or a valid passport in the case of non-EU family members).

Article 6(2) provides that 'family members' who do not have the nationality of a Member State (i.e. non-EU family members) enjoy the same rights as the EU citizen who they have accompanied or joined.

The host Member State may require the persons concerned to register their presence in the country within a reasonable and non-discriminatory period of time (Art 5(5), see above).

Article 14(1) provides that EU citizens and their family members shall have the right of residence under Art 6, 'as long as they do not become an *unreasonable* burden on the social assistance system of the host Member State' (emphasis added); expulsion shall not be an automatic consequence if an EU citizen or his family members have recourse to the host Member State's social assistance system (Art 14(3)). Article 14(4) further provides that (other than in accordance with the provisions relating to restrictions on the right of entry and residence on grounds of public policy, public security or public health) an expulsion order cannot be issued against an EU citizen or his family members, if:

(i)   the EU citizen is a worker or self-employed person in the host Member State; or

(ii) the EU citizen entered the host Member State to seek employment and provided he can provide evidence that he is continuing to seek work and has a genuine chance of being employed.

Right of residence for more than three months (Article 7)

The right of residence for more than three months remains subject to certain conditions. Article 7(1) provides that EU citizens have the right to reside in another Member State, for a period exceeding three months, if they:

(a)   are engaged in an economic activity in the host Member State (on an employed or self-employed basis); or

(b)   have comprehensive sickness insurance and sufficient resources for themselves and their family members to ensure that they do not become a burden on the social assistance system of the host Member State during their stay. Article 8(4) provides that Member States may not specify a minimum amount of resources which they deem sufficient, but they must take account of the personal situation of the person concerned. The amount of minimum resources cannot be higher than the threshold below which nationals of the host Member State become eligible for social assistance, or if this does not apply, higher than the minimum social security pension paid by the host Member State; or

(c)   are following a course of study, including vocational training, at a public or private institution which is accredited or financed by the host Member State. The student must have comprehensive sickness insurance and assure the Member State, by a declaration or equivalent means, that they have sufficient resources for themselves and their family members to ensure that they do not become a burden on the social assistance system of the host Member State during their stay. Article 8(3) provides that Member States may not require the declaration to refer to any specific amount of resources; or

(d) are a 'family member' of an EU citizen who falls into one of the above categories.

Article 7(2) provides that the right of residence also applies to family members who are not nationals of a Member State (i.e. non-EU family members), who are accompanying or joining an EU citizen in the host Member State, provided that such EU citizen satisfies the conditions set out in (a), (b) or (c) above.

In the case of students, there is a limitation on the family members who may accompany or join them. Article 7(4) provides that only the spouse/registered partner and dependent children shall have the right of residence as family members of the student. Dependent direct relatives in the ascending lines, and those of his spouse/registered partner shall have their entry and residence facilitated (in accordance with Art 3(2), see above).

Residence permits are abolished for EU citizens. However, Arts 8(1) and 8(2) provide that Member States may require EU citizens to register with the competent authorities within a period of not less than three months as from the date of arrival. A registration certificate will be issued immediately (Art 8(2)). For the registration certificate to be issued, Art 8(3) provides that Member States may only require the following documentation:

(a) in the case of an EU citizen to whom Art 7(1)(a) applies (i.e. a worker or self-employed person), a valid identity card or passport, and confirmation of engagement from the employer or a certificate of employment, or proof of their self-employed status;

(b) in the case of an EU citizen to whom Art 7(1)(b) applies (i.e. a citizen having sufficient resources and comprehensive sickness insurance), a valid identity card or passport, proof of comprehensive sickness insurance, and proof that they have sufficient resources for themselves and their family members not to become a burden on the social assistance system of the host Member State during their period of residence;

(c) in the case of an EU citizen to whom Art 7(1)(c) applies (i.e. a student), a valid identity card or passport, and proof of enrolment at an accredited institution, proof of comprehensive sickness insurance, and a declaration (or equivalent means) that they have sufficient resources for themselves and their family members not to become a burden on the social assistance system of the host Member State during their period of residence.

Article 8(5) provides that registration certificates will be issued to family members who are nationals of a Member State (i.e. EU family members); this is subject to the production of specified documentation. This provision also applies to other family members whose entry and residence to the host Member State shall be facilitated in accordance with Art 3(2).

Article 9 applies to family members who are not nationals of a Member State (i.e. non-EU family members). Such family members must apply for a residence card not less than three months from their date of arrival (Art 9(2)). A residence card is valid for at least five years from its date of issue, or for the envisaged period of residence of the EU citizen if this is less than five years (Art 11(1)). Article 10(2) sets out the documentation required before a residence card will be issued. This provision also applies to other family members whose entry and residence to the host Member State shall be facilitated in accordance with Art 3(2). Article 11(2) provides that the validity of a residence card shall not be affected by:

(i)   temporary absences of up to six months a year;

(ii) absences of a longer period for compulsory military service; or

(iii) one absence of up to 12 months for important reasons (e.g. pregnancy and child-birth, serious illness, study or vocational training, or a posting in another Member State or a third county).

Article 7(3) provides that an EU citizen shall retain the status of worker or self-employed person in the host Member State in the following circumstances:

(a)   he is temporarily unable to work as the result of an illness or accident;

(b)   he is in duly recorded involuntary unemployment after having been employed for more than one year and has registered as a jobseeker with the relevant employment office in the host Member State;

(c)   he is in duly recorded involuntary unemployment after completing a fixed-term employment contract of less than a year *or* after having become involuntarily unemployed during the first twelve months *and* has registered as a jobseeker with the relevant employment office in the host Member State. In this case, the status of worker shall be retained for not less than six months; or

(d)   he embarks on vocational training. Unless he is involuntarily unemployed, the retention of the status of worker shall require the training to be related to the previous employment.

Article 12(1) provides that if an EU citizen dies or departs from the host Member State, his EU family members shall not have their right of residence affected. In the case of a non-EU family member, their right of residence shall not be affected if the EU citizen dies provided that the non-EU family member has been residing in the host Member State as a family member for at least one year before the EU citizen's death (Art 12(2)).

Article 12(3) provides that if an EU citizen dies or departs from the host Member State, if his children reside in the host Member State and are enrolled at an educational establishment, then his children and the parent who has actual custody of the children (whether or not they are EU citizens) shall have the right to reside in the host Member State until the children have completed their studies.

Article 13 governs a family member's right of residence following divorce, annulment of marriage or termination of partnership. In the case of EU family members, divorce, annulment of marriage or termination of partnership does not affect the family member's right of residence (Art 13(1)). However, in the case of non-EU family members, retention of the right of residence is restricted; Art 13(2) provides that there shall be no loss of the right of residence where:

(a)   prior to the start of the divorce or annulment proceedings or termination of the registered partnership, the marriage or registered partnership had lasted at least three years, including one year in the host Member State; or

(b)   by agreement between the spouses or the registered partners, or by court order, the spouse or partner who is a non-EU national has custody of the EU citizen's children; or

(c) this is warranted by particularly difficult circumstances, such as having been a victim of domestic violence while the marriage or registered partnership was subsisting; or

(d) by agreement between the spouses or registered partners, or by court order, the spouse or partner who is a non-EU national has the right of access to a minor child, provided that the court has ruled that such access must be in the host Member State, and for as long as is required.

Article 14(2) provides that EU citizens and their family members shall have the right of residence under Arts 7, 12 and 13 'as long as they meet the conditions set out therein'; expulsion shall not be an automatic consequence if an EU citizen or his family members have recourse to the host Member State's social assistance system (Art 14(3)). Article 14(4) further provides that (other than in accordance with the provisions relating to restrictions on the right of entry and residence on grounds of public policy, public security or public health) an expulsion order cannot be issued against an EU citizen or his family members if:

(i) the EU citizen is a worker or self-employed person in the host Member State; or

(ii) the EU citizen entered the host Member State to seek employment and provided he can provide evidence that he is continuing to seek work and has a genuine chance of being employed.

Procedural safeguards (Article 15)

Article 15(1) provides that the procedures set out in Arts 30 and 31 (see below) will apply by analogy to all decisions restricting free movement of EU citizens and their family members on grounds other than public policy, public security or public health.

Expiry of the identity card or passport on the basis of which the persons concerned entered the host Member State and were issued with a registration certificate or residence card shall not constitute a ground for expulsion from the host Member State (Art 15(2)).

Right of permanent residence (Article 16)

EU citizens acquire the right of permanent residence in the host Member State after a five-year period of continuous legal residence (Art 16(1)), provided that an expulsion decision has not been enforced against them (Art 21). This right of permanent residence is no longer subject to any conditions. The same rule applies to non-EU family members who have lived with an EU citizen in the host Member State for five years (Art 16(2)), and again provided that an expulsion decision has not been enforced against them (Art 21). Article 16(3) provides that continuity of residence shall not be affected by:

(i) temporary absences not exceeding six months a year;

(ii) absences of a longer period for compulsory military service; or

(iii) one absence of up to 12 months for important reasons (e.g. pregnancy and childbirth, serious illness, study or vocational training, or a posting in another Member State or a third county).

Once granted, the right of permanent residence is lost only in the event of more than two successive years' absence from the host Member State (Arts 16(4) and 20(3)).

Article 17 recognises the right of permanent residence for EU citizens who are workers or self-employed persons and for their family members, before the five-year period of continuous residence has expired, subject to certain conditions being met. Article 17 applies to cases where the EU citizen:

(i)   has reached retirement age;

(ii) has become permanently incapable of working; or

(iii) lives in the host Member State but works in another Member State.

Article 17 also provides that the family members of an EU worker or self-employed person have the right of permanent residence if the EU worker or self-employed person dies before acquiring the right of permanent residence. This right, which applies to family members of whatever nationality, is subject to the following conditions:

(a)   the worker or self-employed person had, at the time of death, resided continuously on the territory of that Member State for two years; or

(b)   the death resulted from an accident at work or an occupational disease; or

(c)   the surviving spouse lost the nationality of that Member State following marriage to the worker or self-employed person.

Articles 12 and 13 were considered above. Of relevance to permanent residence are the following provisions.

Article 12(1) provides that if an EU citizen dies or departs from the host Member State, his family members who are nationals of a Member State shall not have their right of residence affected. However, before acquiring the right of permanent residence, the persons concerned must meet the conditions set out in Art 7(1)(a), (b), (c) or (d); see above. In the case of a non-EU family member, their right of residence shall not be affected if the EU citizen dies provided that the non-EU family member has been residing in the host Member State as a family member for at least one year before the EU citizen's death (Art 12(2)). However, before acquiring the right of permanent residence, the persons concerned must meet the conditions set out in Art 7(1)(a), (b), or (d); *note: category (c) does not apply to this situation*. Article 18 provides that the family members to whom Art 12(2) apply, who satisfy the conditions set out in Art 12(2), shall acquire the right of permanent residence after legally residing in the host Member State for a period of five consecutive years; this is without prejudice to Art 17 (see above).

Article 13 governs a family member's right of residence following divorce, annulment of marriage or termination of partnership. In the case of EU family members, divorce, annulment of marriage or termination of partnership does not affect the family member's right of residence (Art 13(1)). However, before acquiring the right of permanent residence, the persons concerned must meet the conditions set out in Art 7(1)(a), (b), (c) or (d); see above. In the case of non-EU family members, retention of the right of residence is restricted. Article 13(2) provides that there shall be no loss of the right of residence where:

(a)   prior to the start of the divorce or annulment proceedings or termination of the registered partnership, the marriage or registered partnership had lasted at least three years, including one year in the host Member State; or

(b)   by agreement between the spouses or the registered partners, or by court order, the spouse or partner who is a non-EU national has custody of the EU citizen's children; or

(c)   this is warranted by particularly difficult circumstances, such as having been a victim of domestic violence while the marriage or registered partnership was subsisting; or

(d) by agreement between the spouses or registered partners, or by court order, the spouse or partner who is a non-EU national has the right of access to a minor child, provided that the court has ruled that such access must be in the host Member State, and for as long as is required.

In this situation, however, before acquiring the right of permanent residence, the persons concerned must meet the conditions set out in Art 7(1)(a), (b), or (d). Article 18 provides that the family members to whom Art 13(2) apply, who satisfy the conditions set out in Art 13(2), shall acquire the right of permanent residence after legally residing in the host Member State for a period of five consecutive years; this is without prejudice to Art 17 (see above).

EU citizens entitled to permanent residence will be issued with a document certifying such residency (Art 19(1)). Article 20(1) provides that non-EU family members who are entitled to permanent residence will be issued with a residence card, renewable automatically every ten years. The application for a permanent residence card has to be submitted before the residence card expires (Art 20(2)); the residence card must be issued no more than six months after the application is made (Art 20(1)). Failure to apply for a permanent residence card may render the person concerned liable to proportionate and non-discriminatory sanctions (Art 20(2)).

Article 21 provides that continuity of residence may be attested by any means of proof in use in the Member State.

Common provisions on the right of residence and right of permanent residence

Article 22 provides that the right of residence and right of permanent residence shall cover the whole territory of the host Member State; territorial restrictions can only be imposed if the same restrictions apply to the host Member State's nationals. Family members, irrespective of their nationality, are entitled to engage in an economic activity on an employed or self-employed basis (Art 23).

EU citizens qualifying for the right of residence or the right of permanent residence, and the members of their family, benefit from equal treatment with host-country nationals in the areas covered by the Treaty (Art 24(1)). However, for the first three months of residence, or, while the EU citizen is exercising his right to reside while seeking work under Art 14(4)(b), the host Member State is not obliged to grant entitlement to social assistance to persons other than employed or self-employed workers and the members of their family (Art 24(2)). Equally, host Member States are not required to provide maintenance aid (i.e. student grants or student loans) to persons with a right of residence who have come to the country in question to study (Art 24(2)).

Article 25(1) provides that under no circumstances can possession of a registration certificate, etc. be made a pre-condition for the exercise of a right or the completion of an administrative formality. Entitlement to rights may be attested by any other means of proof, where such documentation is not available. Article 25(2) further provides that all the documents listed in Art 25(1) shall be issued free of charge or for a charge which does not exceed that imposed on nationals for the issuing of a similar document.

If a Member State requires their own nationals to carry an identity card, then the host Member State can require non-nationals to carry their registration certificate or residence card. The host Member State may impose the same sanction as those imposed on their own nationals if a non-national fails to comply (Art 26).

Restrictions on the right of entry and the right of residence on grounds of public policy, public security or public health

EU citizens or members of their family may be refused entry to, or expelled from, the host Member State on grounds of public policy, public security or public health (Art 27(1)). Under no circumstances may an expulsion decision be taken on economic grounds (Art 27(1)). Measures taken on the grounds of public policy or public security must comply with the principle of proportionality and must be based on the personal conduct of the individual concerned; previous criminal convictions do not automatically justify such measures (Art 27(2)). The personal conduct must represent a genuine, present and sufficiently serious threat which affects one of the fundamental interests of society (Art 27(2)).

Article 27(3) provides that in order to ascertain whether the person concerned represents a danger to public policy or public security, the host Member State, if it considers it essential, may request the Member State of origin or other Member States to provide information concerning any previous police record the person concerned may have. The request is to be made by the host Member State:

(i)   when issuing the registration certificate; or

(ii) if there is no registration system, no later than three months from the date of the person's arrival in the host Member State or date the person reported his presence in the host Member State as provided for in Art 5(5); or

(iii) when issuing the residence card.

Such enquiries must not be made as a matter of routine. The Member State consulted should provide its reply within two months.

A person who is expelled from a Member State on grounds of public policy, public security or public health shall have the right to re-enter the Member State which issued him with a passport or identity card, even if the document is no longer valid, or if the nationality of the holder is in dispute (Art 27(4)).

Article 28(1) provides that before taking an expulsion decision on grounds of public policy or public security, the host Member State must assess a number of factors such as the period for which the individual concerned has been resident, his age, state of health, family and economic situation, degree of social and cultural integration in the host Member State and the extent of his links with the country of origin. Only for serious grounds of public policy or public security can an expulsion decision be taken against an EU citizen or his family members, if the EU citizen or his family members have acquired the right of permanent residence in the host Member State (Art 28(2)). In addition, an expulsion decision may not be taken against an EU citizen or his family members who have resided in the host country for ten years or if he is a minor, unless the decision is based on imperative grounds of public security, and, in the case of a minor, provided that expulsion is necessary for the best interests of the child (Art 28(3)).

Article 29 is concerned with the restriction on the right of entry and residence on the ground of public health. The only diseases which can justify restricting the right of entry and residence are:

(i)   those with epidemic potential as defined by the relevant instruments of the World Health Organisation (WHO); and

(ii) other infectious diseases or other contagious parasitic diseases if they are subject to protection provisions applying to nationals of the host Member State (Art 29(1)).

Article 29(2) provides that diseases occurring after a three-month period from the date of arrival shall not constitute grounds for expulsion from the host Member State. A Member State can require the person concerned to undergo a medical examination, which must be provided free of charge, if there are serious indications that a medical examination is necessary; such medical examinations must not be carried out as a matter of routine (Art 29(3)). The person concerned by a decision refusing leave to enter or reside in a Member State on the ground of public policy, public security or public health must be notified in writing of that decision, in such a way that they are able to comprehend its content and the implications for them (Art 30(1)). The grounds for the decision must be given precisely and in full, unless this is contrary to the interests of state security (Art 30(2)), and the person concerned must be informed of the appeal procedures available to them (Art 30(3)). Except in cases of urgency, the subject of such decision must be allowed at least one month in which to leave the Member State (Art 30(3)).

Article 31 sets out the procedural safeguards which apply if a decision is taken against a person's right of entry and residence on the grounds of public policy, public security or public health. Article 31 provides as follows:

1. The persons concerned shall have access to judicial and, where appropriate, administrative redress procedures in the host Member State to appeal against or seek review of any decision taken against them on the grounds of public policy, public security or public health.
2. Where the application for appeal against or judicial review of the expulsion decision is accompanied by an application for an interim order to suspend enforcement of that decision, actual removal from the territory may not take place until such time as the decision on the interim order has been taken, except:
   – where the expulsion decision is based on a previous judicial decision; or
   – where the persons concerned have had previous access to judicial review; or
   – where the expulsion decision is based on imperative grounds of public security under Article 28(3).
3. The redress procedures shall allow for an examination of the legality of the decision, as well as of the facts and circumstances on which the proposed measure is based. They shall ensure that the decision is not disproportionate, particularly in view of the requirements laid down in Article 28.
4. Member States may exclude the individual concerned from their territory pending the redress procedure, but they may not prevent the individual from submitting his/her defence in person, except when his/her appearance may cause serious troubles to public policy or public security or when the appeal or judicial review concerns a denial of entry to the territory.

Persons excluded from a Member State on grounds of public policy or public security can apply for the exclusion order to be lifted after a reasonable period, and in any event after a maximum of three years, by putting forward arguments to establish that there has been a material change in the circumstances which justified the decision ordering their exclusion (Art 32(1)). The Member State concerned is required to reach a decision on such application within six months of its submission (Art 32(1)). The person applying for the lifting of the exclusion order does not have a right of entry into the Member State concerned while the application is being considered (Art 32(2)).

An expulsion order cannot be issued by a Member State as a penalty or legal consequence of a custodial penalty, unless the requirements of Arts 27–29 (see above) are complied with (Art 33(1)). Where an expulsion order is issued under this provision, and where it is enforced more than two years after it was issued, the Member State is required to check that the individual concerned is a current and genuine threat to public policy or public security, and the Member State shall assess whether there has been any material change in circumstances since the expulsion order was issued (Art 33(2)).

Other rights derived from EU citizenship

The creation of EU citizenship is part of a broader programme of enhancement of individual political and social rights in the European context. The EC Treaty and secondary legislation adopted pursuant to the Treaty confer other benefits on EU citizens in addition to the general right of residence. It is not possible to discuss these benefits in detail here, but broadly they comprise: a right to vote and stand as a candidate in local and European Parliamentary elections in other Member States where the EU citizen is resident (but this does not apply to *national* elections); a right to diplomatic representation outside the Community from any of the other Member States in territories where the citizen's own state has no consulate or embassy; a right to petition the European Parliament; a right to apply for assistance to the European Parliamentary Ombudsman; and a right of access to documents held by the Community institutions. The right to apply to the Ombudsman is not confined to EU citizens but is open to 'any natural or legal person residing or having its registered office in a Member State' (Art 195(1) EC Treaty).

As discussed above, Directive 2004/38 has established a general, but limited, right of entry and residence (for up to three months) for all those holding the nationality of a Member State. Extended rights of residence (for over three months) are, under Directive 2004/38, primarily linked to persons engaged in an economic activity. The subsequent chapters will examine the scope of those rights, identify the beneficiaries and explore the extent to which Member States are permitted to derogate from them. European Union citizenship is the primary avenue by which those rights are acquired, but Community law also confers more limited rights on those who are not EU citizens.

Free movement rights of non-EU citizens

Nationals of third states outside the Community can enjoy a number of important free movement rights under Treaties made with it. Besides the full range of free movement rights enjoyed by Iceland, Liechtenstein and Norway under the EEA Agreement discussed above, 'family members' of EU workers, the self-employed and other beneficiaries of free movement rights who are nationals of other states have the right to install themselves with the person entitled to the free movement right. Host states may demand that such individuals obtain a visa, but 'every facility' should be given to enable them to obtain one (Art 5(4), Directive 2004/38). Once installed with the principal beneficiary, the spouse or other family member is entitled to access to employment and equal treatment as if he was an EU citizen (**Gül** *v* **Regierungspräsident Düsseldorf** (Case 131/85)).

More limited rights are enjoyed by the beneficiaries of Association Agreements made with the Community. Such agreements have been held by the Court to be directly effective (**Kupferberg** (Case 104/81)). The rights in these cases are normally limited to equal treatment in employment and social security after admission, but they do not entitle the beneficiaries to enter. Such rights have been recognised in this way under the EC–Turkey Agreement (**Kus** v **Landeshauptstadt Wiesbaden** (Case C–237/91); **Eroglu** v **Baden-Württemberg** (Case C–355/93)), and under the EC–Morocco Cooperation Agreement (**Bahia Kziber** v **ONEM** (Case C–18/90); **Yousfi** v **Belgium** (Case C–58/93)). There are other agreements with *inter alia* Tunisia and Algeria, which contain provisions that could be used by nationals of those states while working in the Community.

The following case gave the Court of Justice an opportunity to rule, for the first time, on the effects of a partnership agreement between the European Community and a non-Member State:

Simutenkov (Case C-265/03)

Igor Simutenkov was a Russian national who had a residence permit and a work permit in Spain. Employed as a professional football player under an employment contract entered into with Club Deportivo Tenerife, he held a federation licence as a non-Community player issued by the Spanish Football Federation.

According to the Federation's rules, in competitions at national level clubs may field only a limited number of players from countries which do not belong to the European Economic Area. Mr Simutenkov requested that his licence be replaced by a licence as a Community player, basing his application on the EC–Russian Federation Partnership Agreement, which, in relation to working conditions, prohibits discrimination of a Russian national based on nationality. The Federation rejected Mr Simutenkov's application. The Spanish court dealing with the case referred a question to the Court of Justice for a preliminary ruling in order to ascertain whether the rules of the Spanish Football Federation were compatible with the agreement.

Having established that the principle of non-discrimination laid down by Art 23(1) of the EC–Russia Partnership Agreement could be relied on by an individual before the national courts, the Court of Justice considered the scope of that principle.

It noted, first, that **the agreement in question establishes, for the benefit of Russian workers lawfully employed in the territory of a Member State, a right to equal treatment in working conditions of the same scope as that which, in similar terms, nationals of Member States are recognised as having under the EC Treaty. That right precludes any limitation based on nationality.**

The Court went on to note that the limitation based on nationality did not relate to specific matches between teams representing their respective countries but applied to official matches between clubs and thus to the essence of the activity performed by professional players. Such a limitation was therefore not justified on sporting grounds.

The Court of Justice accordingly held that Art 23(1) of the EC–Russian Federation Partnership Agreement precluded the application to a professional sportsman of Russian nationality, who was lawfully employed by a club established in a Member State, of a rule drawn up by a sports federation of that state which provided that in competitions organised at national level, clubs could field only a limited number of players from countries which were not parties to the European Economic Area Agreement.

Other third-state nationals may benefit from Community free movement rights in a different way. Undertakings established in one Member State have the right to go to another, either to provide a service or to become established there (Arts 43, 49 EC Treaty). To enable the undertaking to carry out its activities in the host Member State it is entitled to take its workforce with it whatever their nationality. Such employees should be admitted without any requirement of a work permit in the host Member State and should be entitled to remain there until the business of the undertaking is complete. On this basis, the French immigration authorities have been obliged to allow non-EU workers employed by Portuguese and Belgian companies to work without any further restrictions than those already imposed in the state of origin of the undertaking (**Rush Portuguesa Lda** (Case C–113/89); **Van der Elst** *v* **OMI** (Case C–43/93)). This right is conferred on the undertaking rather than on the worker and if challenged should, in principle, have to be asserted by the undertaking in the courts of the Member State. Advocate-General Tesauro, in his opinion in **Van der Elst** (above), did, however, describe the workers in the **Rush Portuguesa** case as having a *derived* right in relation to entry and employment, although he did not argue that it could be asserted by them personally (p. 3813). Somewhat surprisingly, the UK's Immigration Appeal Tribunal has held that the right of the employing company in the UK can be the subject of an application for judicial review by the *employee* (**Pasha** *v* **Home Office** [1993] 2 CMLR 350).

Third-state nationals (i.e. non-EU nationals) given leave to enter any Member State may be issued with an EU visa and be able to travel anywhere in the EU for a period of up to three months. The visa may be issued by any Member State, but it is in a standard form for use in all the Member States (Art 63(3) EC Treaty, Regulation 1683/95, OJ 1995 L 164). In addition, such nationals will benefit from Directive 2000/43 prohibiting discrimination on grounds of racial or ethnic origin, and Directive 2000/78 prohibiting direct and indirect discrimination as regards access to employment and occupation on grounds of religion or belief, disability, and age or sexual orientation (see above). A more recent development for third-country nationals is provided by the Council's adoption of Directive 2003/86 (OJ 2003 L 251/12) which provides a right to family reunification for the benefit of third-country nationals who are residing lawfully within a Member State (i.e. those who hold a residence permit valid for at least one year in a Member State, and who are genuinely able to stay long term). This directive, which was adopted pursuant to Art 63(3)(a) EC Treaty, had to be implemented by 3 October 2005. The Council subsequently adopted Directive 2003/109 (OJ 2004 L 16/44), also pursuant to Art 63(3)(a) EC Treaty, which provides a right to 'long-term resident status' for third-country nationals who are long-term residents of a Member State. This directive had to be implemented by 23 January 2006.

The Schengen *acquis* and its integration into the European Union

During the 1980s, a debate opened up about the meaning of the concept of 'free movement of persons'. Some Member States felt that this should apply to EU citizens only, which would involve keeping internal border checks in order to distinguish between EU citizens and non-EU citizens. Others argued in favour of free movement for everyone, which would mean an end to internal border checks altogether. Since the Member States found it impossible to reach an agreement, France, Germany, Belgium, Luxembourg and

The Netherlands decided in 1985 to create a territory without internal borders. This became known as the 'Schengen area'. The name was taken from the name of the town in Luxembourg where the first agreements were signed. This intergovernmental cooperation expanded to include thirteen countries in 1997, following the signing of the Treaty of Amsterdam, which (on 1 May 1999) incorporated into EU law (i) the decisions taken since 1985 by Schengen group members; and (ii) the associated working structures.

Development of the Schengen area

The first agreement between the five original group members was signed on 14 June 1985. A further Convention was drafted and signed on 19 June 1990. When this Convention came into effect in 1995, it abolished the internal borders of the signatory states and created a single external border where immigration checks for the Schengen area are carried out in accordance with a single set of rules. Common rules regarding visas, asylum rights and checks at external borders were adopted to allow the free movement of persons within the signatory states without disturbing law and order.

Accordingly, in order to reconcile freedom and security, this freedom of movement was accompanied by so-called 'compensatory' measures. This involved improving coordination between the police, customs and the judiciary and taking necessary measures to combat important problems such as terrorism and organised crime. In order to make this possible, an information system known as the Schengen Information System (SIS) was set up to exchange data on people's identities and descriptions of objects which are either stolen or lost.

Little by little, the Schengen area was extended to include every Member State (excluding the UK and Ireland, and the new Member States joining the EU on 1 May 2004 and 1 January 2007, see below). Italy signed the agreement on 27 November 1990, Spain and Portugal joined on 25 June 1991, Greece followed on 6 November 1992, then Austria on 28 April 1995 and finally Denmark, Finland and Sweden on 19 December 1996.

Measures adopted by Schengen group members

Among the main measures are:

- the removal of checks at common borders, replacing them with external border checks;
- a common definition of the rules for crossing external borders and uniform rules and procedures for controls there;
- separation in air terminals and ports of people travelling within the Schengen area from those arriving from countries outside the area;
- harmonisation of the rules regarding conditions of entry and visas for short stays;
- coordination between administrations on surveillance of borders (liaison officers and harmonisation of instructions and staff training);
- the definition of the role of carriers in measures to combat illegal immigration;
- requirement for all non-EU nationals moving from one country to another to lodge a declaration;
- the drawing up of rules for asylum seekers (Dublin Convention, replaced in 2003 by the Dublin II Regulation);

- the introduction of cross-border rights of surveillance and hot pursuit for police forces in the Schengen states;

- the strengthening of legal cooperation through a faster extradition system and faster distribution of information about the implementation of criminal judgments; and

- the creation of the Schengen Information System (SIS).

These measures, together with (i) the decisions and declarations adopted by the Executive Committee set up by the 1990 Convention; (ii) the steps taken in order to implement the Convention by the authorities on whom the Executive Committee conferred decision-making powers; (iii) the agreement signed on 14 June 1985; (iv) the Convention implementing that agreement, signed on 19 June 1990; and (v) the protocols and accession agreements which followed, constitute the Schengen *acquis*.

The Schengen Information System (SIS)

An information network was set up to allow all border posts, police stations and consular agents from Schengen group Member States to access data on specific individuals or on vehicles or objects which have been lost or stolen.

Member States supply the network through national networks (N-SIS) connected to a central system (C–SIS), and this is supplemented by a network known as SIRENE (Supplementary Information Request at the National Entry).

Incorporating the Schengen Agreement into the European Union framework

A protocol attached to the Treaty of Amsterdam incorporates the developments brought about by the Schengen Agreement into the European Union framework. The Schengen area, which is the first concrete example of enhanced cooperation between thirteen Member States, is now within the legal and institutional framework of the EU and thus comes under parliamentary and judicial scrutiny and attains the objective of free movement of persons enshrined in the Single European Act 1986 while ensuring democratic Parliamentary control and giving citizens accessible legal remedies when their rights are challenged (Court of Justice and/or national courts depending on the area of law).

In order to make this integration possible, the Council of the European Union took a number of decisions. First of all, as set out in the Treaty of Amsterdam, the Council took the place of the Executive Committee created under the Schengen Agreement. On 1 May 1999 it established a procedure for incorporating the Schengen Secretariat into the General Secretariat of the Council including arrangements relating to Schengen Secretariat staff (OJ 1999 L 119). Following that, new working groups were set up to help the Council manage the work.

One of the Council's most important tasks in incorporating the Schengen area was to choose from among the provisions and measures taken by the signatory states those which formed a genuine *acquis*, i.e. a body of law which could serve as a basis for further cooperation. A list of the elements which make up the *acquis*, setting out the corresponding legal basis for each of them in the Treaties (EC Treaty or the TEU; OJ 1999 L 176 – corrigendum: OJ 2000 L 9), was adopted on 20 May 1999. Most of these acts are published in the *Official Journal*.

The Member States that joined the European Union on 1 May 2004 and 1 January 2007 are bound by the entire Schengen *acquis*, but certain provisions will apply to them only after border controls have been abolished. They will be abolished by the Council when SIS-II (see below) is operational and when those Member States have passed a test to show that they meet all the conditions required for the application of compensatory measures enabling internal border controls to be abolished. This test is new; all Schengen States have had to pass it.

As matters stand, these new Member States apply all the provisions of the Schengen *acquis* relating to police and judicial cooperation that are not directly bound up with the removal of border controls.

The participation of Denmark

Although Denmark has signed the Schengen Agreement, it can choose within the EU framework whether or not to apply any new decisions taken under Title IV EC Treaty, even those that constitute a development of the Schengen *acquis*. But Denmark is bound by certain measures under the common visa policy.

The participation of Ireland and the United Kingdom

In accordance with the protocol to the Treaty of Amsterdam, Ireland and the UK can take part in all or some of the Schengen arrangements if the thirteen Schengen group Member States and the government representative of the country in question vote unanimously in favour within the Council.

In March 1999 the UK asked to take part in some aspects of Schengen, namely police and judicial cooperation in criminal matters, the fight against drugs and the Schengen Information System (SIS). A Council Decision approving the request by the United Kingdom was adopted on 29 May 2000 (OJ 2000 L 131).

Ireland asked to take part in some aspects of Schengen, roughly corresponding to the aspects covered by the UK's request, in June 2000. The Council adopted a decision approving Ireland's request on 28 February 2002 (OJ 2002 L 64). The Commission had issued opinions on the two applications, stressing that the partial participation of the two Member States should not have the effect of reducing the consistency of the *acquis* as a whole.

After evaluating the conditions that must precede implementation of the provisions governing police and judicial cooperation, the Council decided on 22 December 2004 that this part of the Schengen *acquis* could be implemented by the UK (OJ 2004 L 395).

Relations with Iceland and Norway

Together with Sweden, Finland and Denmark, Iceland and Norway belong to the Nordic passport union, which abolished internal border checks. Sweden, Finland and Denmark became members of the Schengen group when they joined the EU. Iceland and Norway have been associated with the development of the agreements since 19 December 1996. Although they did not have voting rights on the Schengen Executive Committee, they were able to express opinions and formulate proposals.

An agreement was signed between Iceland, Norway and the EU on 18 May 1999 in order to extend that association (OJ 1999 L 176). These countries continue to participate in the drafting of new legal instruments building on the Schengen *acquis*. These acts are adopted by the EU Member States alone, but they apply to Iceland and Norway as well.

In practice, this association takes the form of a joint committee outside the EU framework made up of representatives from the Icelandic and Norwegian governments and members of the EU Council and the Commission. Procedures for notifying and accepting future measures or acts have been laid down.

An agreement approved by the Council on 28 June 1999 covers relations between Iceland and Norway, on the one hand, and Ireland and the United Kingdom, on the other, in areas of the Schengen *acquis* applying to Iceland and Norway (OJ 2000 L 15). The Community also entered into an agreement with Norway and Iceland concerning the criteria and mechanisms for establishing the state responsible for examining a request for asylum (Dublin *acquis*), which is intricately bound up with the Schengen *acquis* (OJ 2001 L 93).

On 1 December 2000 the Council decided that, as from 25 March 2001, the Schengen *acquis* arrangements would apply to the five countries of the Nordic passport union (OJ 2000 L 309). In addition, the SIS arrangements were put into effect as from 1 January 2000. In order to check whether the SIS functioned and was properly applied, the decision provided for evaluation visits to be carried out in all the Nordic states. Reports on the visits submitted to the Council in March 2001 indicated that the SIS was being properly applied and that controls at external borders (in ports and airports) met the conditions laid down.

The participation of Switzerland

The Commission began negotiations with Switzerland in 2002. They culminated in an agreement between the EU, the European Community and Switzerland on the association of Switzerland with the implementation, application and development of the Schengen *acquis* (OJ 2004 L 370).

The second-generation Schengen Information System (SI-II)

At present, the Schengen Information System (SIS) operates in thirteen Member States and two associated states (Norway and Iceland). However, the system was not designed, and therefore lacks the capacity, to operate in more than fifteen or so countries. It is therefore necessary to develop a new second-generation Schengen Information System (SIS-II) to enable the new and future Member States to use the system, and to take account of the latest developments in information technology.

On 6 December 2001 the Council accordingly adopted two instruments, making the Commission responsible for developing SIS-II and providing for the related expenditure to be covered by the general budget of the European Union:

- Council Regulation 2424/2001 on the development of the second-generation Schengen Information System (SIS-II) based on Art 66, EC Treaty;
- Council Decision 2001/866/JHA on the development of the second-generation Schengen Information System (SIS-II) based on Arts 30(1), 31 and 34, TEU.

The reason for this distinction is that the purpose of the SIS is to improve police and judicial cooperation in criminal matters (covered by Title VI TEU) and the policy on visas, immigration and the free movement of persons (covered by Title IV TEU) (OJ 2001 L 328).

On 31 May 2005 the Commission adopted three proposals for legislative instruments to replace provisions of the Schengen Convention relating to the SIS:

■ Proposal for a Regulation of the European Parliament and of the Council on the establishment, operation and use of the second-generation Schengen Information System (SIS-II) [COM (2005) 236].

■ Proposal for a Council Decision on the establishment, operation and use of the second-generation Schengen Information System (SIS-II) [COM (2005) 230 final].

■ Proposal for a Regulation of the European Parliament and of the Council regarding access to the second-generation Schengen Information System (SIS-II) by the services in the Member States responsible for issuing vehicle registration certificates [COM (2005) 237 final].

New functionalities have since been added to the SIS, some of them concerning the fight against terrorism, by Council Regulation 871/2004 (OJ 2004 L 162) and Decision 2005/211/JHA (OJ 2005 L 68).

Summary

Now you have read this chapter you should be able to:

■ Identify the key provisions of the EC Treaty which relate to the free movement of workers.

■ Evaluate how the European Court of Justice has, through its case law, defined the concept and scope of 'EU worker'.

■ Identify the secondary Community legislation which relates to the free movement of workers, and explain the rights which such legislation confers on EU workers and their families, in particular:

  – Directive 2004/38 which defines the rights of entry and residence for EU workers and their families; and

  – Regulation 1612/68 which provides for the equal treatment of migrant workers and national workers in relation to access to employment, housing, education and social rights.

■ Assess the extent to which an EU citizen is entitled to seek work in a Member State of which he is not a national, and explain whether such EU citizen is entitled (under Community law) to any social advantages in the host Member State.

■ Identify the social advantages which accrue, under Community law, to an EU worker and his family members.

■ Understand the purpose and effect of the transitional arrangements which relate to the right of free movement of an EU citizen who is a national of one of the Member States which acceded to the EU in 2004 or 2007.

Further reading

Textbooks

Barnard, C. (2004) *The Substantive Law of the EU: The four freedoms* (1st edn), Oxford University Press, Chapters 10 and 15.

Craig, P. and De Burca, G. (2003) *EU Law Text, Cases and Materials* (3rd edn), Oxford University Press, Chapter 17.

Foster, N. (2006) *Foster on EU Law* (1st edn), Oxford University Press, Chapter 9 (Sections 9.1 to 9.4, and 9.7 to 9.9).

O'Keefe, D. (1994) 'Union Citizenship', in O'Keefe, D. and Twomey, P. (eds) *Legal Issues of the Maastricht Treaty*, Wiley Chancery Laws.

O'Leary, S. (1996) *The Evolving Concept of Community Citizenship*, Kluwer.

Steiner, J., Woods, L. and Twigg-Flesner, C. (2006) *EU Law* (9th edn), Oxford University Press, Chapter 24.

Tillotson, J. and Foster, N. (2003) *Text, Cases and Materials on EU Law* (4th edn), Cavendish Publishing, Chapter 13.

Weatherill, S. (2006) *Cases and Materials on EU Law* (7th edn), Oxford University Press, Chapter 15.

Journal articles

Albors-Llorens, A. *et al.*, 'CELS (Cambridge) EC Treaty Project: Part II Citizenship of the Union' (1997) 22 EL Rev 436.

Barber, N., 'Citizenship, Nationalism and the European Union' (2002) 27 EL Rev 241.

Castro Oliveira, A., 'Workers and Other Persons: Step-by-Step from Movement to Citizenship' (2002) 39 CML Rev 77.

Closa, C., 'The Concept of Citizenship in the Treaty of European Union' (1992) 29 CML Rev 1137.

Closa, C., 'Citizenship of the Union and Nationality of Member States' (1995) 32 CML Rev 487.

Dougan, M., 'Fees, grants, loans and dole cheques: Who covers the costs of migrant education within the EU?' (2005) 42 CML Rev 943.

Hailbronner, K., 'Union citizenship and access to social benefits' (2005) 42 CML Rev 1245.

Hardy, S. and McCarthy, J. (1997) 'After Amsterdam: EU Citizenship – Myth or Reality?' *Immigration and Nationality Law and Practice*, Vol. II, No. 4, p. 118.

Jacqueson, C., 'Union Citizenship and the Court of Justice: Something new under the sun? Towards social citizenship' (2002) 27 EL Rev 260.

O'Keefe, D., 'The Free Movement of Persons in the Single Market' (1992) 13 EL Rev 3.

O'Leary, S., 'The Relationship Between Community Citizenship and the Protection of Fundamental Rights in Community Law' (1995) 32 CML Rev 487, p. 519.

O'Leary, S. (1996) *The Evolving Concept of Community Citizenship*, Kluwer.

Shaw, J., 'European Union Citizenship: The IGC and Beyond' (1997) 3 EPL, 413.

Shaw, J., 'The Many Pasts and Futures of Citizenship of the European Union' (1997) 22 EL Rev 554.

Vincenzi, C. (1995) 'European Citizenship and Free Movement Rights in the UK', *Public Law*, Summer, 1995, p. 259.

12 Free movement of workers

Aims and objectives

At the end of this chapter you should understand:

- The provisions of the EC Treaty which established the free movement of workers.

- The meaning and scope of 'EU worker' and the application of the 'employment in the public service' exception.

- The provisions of Directive 2004/38 which apply to require the abolition of restrictions to movement and residence of EU workers and their families and which provide a right for workers and their families to remain in a Member State, having been employed there.

- The provisions of Directive 2004/38 which are applicable to students and the self-sufficient.

- The provisions of Regulation 1612/68 and how they have been applied by the Court of Justice.

- How the transitional arrangements impact upon the right of free movement for EU citizens who are nationals of one of the states which became a Member State of the EU on 1 May 2004 or 1 January 2007.

Introduction to the free movement of workers

The free movement of workers is of great economic and social importance to the Community. Although the right to move to other Member States in an employed capacity was originally seen as no more than an economic function whereby a surplus of labour and skills in one part of the Community could meet a shortage in another, the worker was soon recognised in the Community's legislation, and in the decisions of the Court of Justice, as more than merely a unit of labour. The right to move under what is now Art 39 EC Treaty was seen as 'a fundamental right' which was to be 'exercised in freedom and dignity' (Preamble, Regulation 1612/68). Advocate-General Trabucchi in **Mr and Mrs F v Belgian State** (Case 7/75) stated that 'The migrant worker is not to be viewed as a mere source of labour, but as a human being'.

The exercise of the migrant worker's rights is to be facilitated in the workplace and in the broader social context of the host Member State. The implementing legislation and the jurisprudence of the Court of Justice is directed at securing the worker's departure from his state of origin and his entry, residence and integration, in the widest sense, into the economic and social fabric of the host Member State. Article 39 EC Treaty is directly effective, not only at the instance of the worker but also, the Court of Justice has held, by his employer (**Clean Car Autoservice GmbH** *v* **Landeshauptmann von Wien** (Case C–350/96)).

Consideration begins with Art 39 EC Treaty (previously Art 48) and the rights of workers:

1. Freedom of movement of workers shall be secured within the Community.
2. Such freedom of movement shall entail the abolition of any discrimination based on nationality between workers of the Member States as regards employment, remuneration and other conditions of work and employment.
3. It shall entail the right, subject to limitations justified on grounds of public policy, public security or public health:
   (a) to accept offers of employment actually made;
   (b) to move freely within the territory of Member States for this purpose;
   (c) to stay in a Member State for the purpose of employment in accordance with the provisions governing the employment of nationals of that State laid down by law, regulation or administrative action;
   (d) to remain in the territory of a Member State after having been employed in that State, subject to conditions which shall be embodied in implementing regulations to be drawn up by the Commission.
4. The provisions of this Article shall not apply to employment in the public service.

The importance of the principles of free movement and of non-discrimination have been emphasised time and again by the Court of Justice. In relation to non-discrimination, Art 39 sets out the general Art 12 EC Treaty anti-discrimination principle, but specifically in relation to workers. Article 12 EC Treaty provides that:

> Within the scope of application of this Treaty, and without prejudice to any special provisions contained therein, any discrimination on grounds of nationality shall be prohibited . . .

Secondary legislation

Article 40 EC Treaty (previously Art 49) provides for secondary legislation to be adopted to bring about the freedoms set out in Art 39:

> The Council shall . . . issue directives or make regulations setting out the measures required to bring about freedom of movement for workers, as defined in Article 39 . . .

Several directives and regulations have been adopted under the former Art 49 (now Art 40), the most important of which are discussed below.

Reverse discrimination

The rights of free movement, which are conferred on workers and their families by the above-mentioned Treaty provisions and secondary legislation, will apply only to 'EU workers'.

The provisions do not prohibit discrimination in a totally 'internal' situation: i.e. national workers cannot claim rights in their own Member State which workers who are nationals of other Member States could claim there. In **R** *v* **Saunders** (Case 175/78), the

Court of Justice held that because there was no factor connecting Saunders with any of the situations envisaged by Community law, Saunders could not rely upon the former Art 48 (now Art 39) to challenge a binding-over order which effectively excluded her from part of the national territory. There was a similar outcome in the following case:

Morson and Jhanjan v Netherlands (Cases 35 and 36/82)

Two Dutch nationals were working in their home state, The Netherlands. They wanted to bring their parents (Surinamese (i.e. non-EU) nationals) into The Netherlands to live with them. Had they been members of any other EU country, working in The Netherlands, their parents would have been covered by Directive 2004/38 (which replaced Art 10, Regulation 1612/68). Under Directive 2004/38, which is considered below, the parents would have been able to join their children. However, their children were nationals working in their own Member State, who had not exercised their right of free movement within the Community, and therefore Community law did not apply: i.e. it was a totally internal situation.

This was confirmed by the Court of Justice in **Land Nordrhein-Westfalen** *v* **Uecker; Jacquei** *v* **Land Nordrhein-Westfalen** (Cases C–64 and 65/96).

However, in the following case the facts were different, which enabled the Court of Justice to draw the opposite conclusion:

R v Immigration Appeal Tribunal and Surinder Singh, ex parte Secretary of State for the Home Department (Case C-370/90)

An Indian national married a UK national. They both worked in Germany before returning to the UK some years later. The UK argued that the spouse's right to re-enter the UK derived from national law, not Community law (i.e. it was an internal situation). The Court of Justice considered the period of work in another Member State, and stated as follows:

19. A national of a Member State might be deterred from leaving his country of origin in order to pursue an activity as an employed or self-employed person as envisaged by the Treaty in the territory of another Member State if, on returning to the Member State of which he is a national in order to pursue an activity there as an employed or self-employed person, the conditions of his entry were not at least equivalent to those which he would enjoy under the Treaty or secondary law in the territory of another Member State.
20. He would in particular be deterred from so doing if his spouse and children were not also permitted to enter and reside in the territory of his Member State of origin under conditions at least equivalent to those granted them by Community law in the territory of another Member State.

In the above case the Court of Justice held that the Community law provisions on the free movement of workers can be relied upon by a worker against the Member State of which he is a national *provided* he has resided and been employed in another Member State. This has been reconfirmed by the Court of Justice in **Terhoeve** *v* **Inspecteur van de Belastingdienst Particulieren/Ondernemingen Buitenland** (Case C–18/95).

As discussed in Chapter 11, pursuant to Art 63(3)(a) EC Treaty, a directive has been proposed to apply to EU citizens who do not exercise their free movement rights. The aim of this directive is to avoid discriminating between EU citizens who exercise their free movement rights and those who do not. In order to achieve this, it is necessary to provide for the family reunification of EU citizens residing in countries of which they are nationals to be governed by the rules of Community law relating to free movement. If this directive is adopted, an EU citizen who has not exercised his free movement rights in another Member State will have the right to have specified family members installed with him. This right will override any less generous national provisions.

Scope of the term 'worker'

As discussed above, Art 39(1) EC Treaty provides that freedom of movement for workers shall be secured within the Community. It entails the abolition of any discrimination based on nationality in relation to access to employment, remuneration and other conditions of work (Art 39(2)). As discussed in Chapter 11, two recently adopted anti-discrimination directives will have an impact on, *inter alia*, EU citizens exercising their free movement rights. Article 13 EC Treaty is the legal base for the adoption of measures to 'combat discrimination based on sex, racial or ethnic origin, religion or belief, disability, age or sexual orientation', provided such measures do not exceed the powers of the Community as conferred upon it by the EC Treaty. In other words, measures can be adopted to combat discrimination provided they are in furtherance of the existing powers of the Community.

Pursuant to Art 13 EC Treaty, the Council adopted Directive 2000/43 (OJ 2000 L 180/22) which implemented the principle of equal treatment between persons irrespective of racial or ethnic origin. The directive had to be implemented by 19 July 2003. The principle of equal treatment prohibits direct or indirect discrimination based on racial or ethnic origin (Art 1). It applies to EU and non-EU citizens and covers both public and private sectors in relation to employment, self-employment, education, social protection including social security and healthcare, social advantages, and access to and supply of goods and services (Art 3(1)). The prohibition of racial or ethnic discrimination does not, however, cover national provisions relating to the entry into and residence of third-country nationals (Art 13(2)). The directive does not, therefore, extend the free movement provisions *per se* to non-EU citizens.

Again pursuant to Art 13 EC Treaty, the Council adopted Directive 2000/78 (OJ 2000 L 303/16) which establishes a general framework for equal treatment in employment and occupation. The directive had to be implemented by 3 December 2003. The directive prohibits direct and indirect discrimination as regards access to employment and occupation on grounds of religion or belief, disability, age or sexual orientation. It applies to both the public and private sectors. As with Directive 2000/43, this directive applies to EU and non-EU citizens, but likewise, the prohibition does not cover national provisions relating to the entry into and residence of third-country nationals (Art 3(2)). The directive does not, therefore, extend the free movement provisions *per se* to non-EU citizens.

Although the exercise of workers' rights may be made subject to national rules relating to public policy, public security and public health (as limited by the provisions of Directive 2004/38, which replaced Directive 64/221; see Chapter 15), Art 39 EC Treaty provides that an EU worker should have the right to:

- accept offers of employment actually made;
- move freely within the territory of Member States for this purpose;
- stay in the Member State for the purpose of employment; and
- remain in the territory of a Member State after having been employed in that state.

Implementing legislation has given detailed effect to these provisions. Directive 2004/38 (which replaced Directive 68/360) defines the rights of workers and the obligations of the immigration authorities of Member States in relation to entry and residence. Regulation 1612/68 deals with matters relating to equal access to employment, equality of terms of employment, housing, education and social rights. Regulation 1408/71 ensures that workers who are entitled to contributory and related benefits continue to enjoy them in the host Member State and on return to their home state. Directive 2004/38 contains detailed provisions on rights of retirement in the state where the worker has been employed and confers a right of retirement on employees and the self-employed in Member States other than those where the person has been employed. All of these provisions create directly effective rights and will be considered in the context of the exercise by the worker of those rights.

The range of rights accruing under Art 39 EC Treaty and the secondary legislation is dependent upon the person coming within the scope of the term 'worker'. However, neither the EC Treaty nor the secondary legislation defines 'worker', and so the Court of Justice has been left to elaborate upon its meaning. In the following case, the Court of Justice provided some clarification:

Lawrie-Blum v *Land Baden-Württemberg* (Case 66/85)

The Court of Justice stated that:

> Objectively defined, a 'worker' is a person who is obliged to provide services for another in return for monetary reward and who is subject to the direction and control of the other person as regards the way in which the work is to be done. (para 14)

This is a classic definition and simply distinguishes an employee (i.e. a person who performs under a contract *of service*) from one who is self-employed, an independent contractor (i.e. a person who performs under a contract *for services*).

In a series of cases which have come before the Court of Justice, it has further considered the question of the scope of 'worker'. In **Hoekstra (née Unger)** v **Bestuur der Bedrijfsvereniging voor Detailhandel en Ambachten** (Case 75/63) the Court held that the activities which confer EU worker status are a matter of Community law. It is therefore for the Court to determine its meaning and scope. Had this not been the case, the result could have been an unequal application of the provisions throughout the Community: e.g. Germany's definition may not have been the same as the UK's, which may not have been the same as Greece's, etc.

In the following case, the question before the Court of Justice was whether the concept of 'worker' within the meaning of Art 39 EC Treaty includes a part-time employee who earns less than the minimum required for subsistence as defined under national law:

Levin v *Staatssecretaris van Justitie* (Case 53/81)

Mrs Levin was a British national married to a South African national. She was refused a residence permit by the Dutch authorities because it was claimed that she was not a 'worker' within the scope of the former Art 48 EC Treaty (now Art 39). She challenged the refusal before the Dutch courts, which referred the matter to the Court of Justice pursuant to the former Art 177 EC Treaty (now Art 234). The Court was asked to explain the concept of 'worker' for Community law purposes, and in particular whether it included an individual who works part-time and earns an income less than the minimum required for subsistence as defined under national law. The Court stated that there was no definition of 'worker' within the Treaty or secondary legislation and that its scope was a matter of Community law:

11. .. T]he terms 'worker' and 'activity as an employed person' may not be defined by references to the national laws of the Member States but have a Community meaning. If that were not the case, the Community rules on the free movement of workers would be frustrated, as the meaning of those terms could be fixed and modified unilaterally, without any control by the Community institutions, by national laws which would thus be able to exclude at will certain categories of persons from the benefit of the Treaty.

. . .

13. In this respect it must be stressed that these concepts define the field of application of one of the fundamental freedoms guaranteed by the Treaty and, as such, may not be interpreted restrictively.

. . .

15. An interpretation which reflects the full scope of these concepts is also in conformity with the objectives of the Treaty which include, according to Articles 2 and 3, the abolition, as between Member States, of obstacles to freedom of movement for persons, with the purpose *inter alia* of promoting throughout the Community a harmonious development of economic activities and a raising of the standard of living. Since part-time employment, although it may provide an income lower than that considered to be the minimum required for subsistence, constitutes for a large number of persons an effective means of improving their living conditions, the effectiveness of Community law would be impaired and the achievement of the objectives of the Treaty would be jeopardised if the enjoyment of rights conferred by the principle of freedom of movement for workers were reserved solely to persons engaged in full-time employment and earning, as a result, a wage at least equivalent to the guaranteed minimum wage in the sector under consideration.

. . .

17. It should however be stated that whilst part-time employment is not excluded from the field of application of the rules on freedom of movement for workers, those rules cover only the pursuit of effective and genuine activities, to the exclusion of activities on such a small scale as to be regarded as purely marginal and ancillary. It follows both from the statement of principle of freedom of movement for workers and from the place occupied by the rules relating to that principle in the system of the Treaty as a whole that those rules guarantee only the free movement of persons who pursue or are desirous of pursuing an economic activity. [emphasis added]

In the above case, as in **Hoekstra**, the Court of Justice made it clear that it is for the Court, *not* the Member States, to define the term 'worker'. The Court then went on to consider at para 15 whether or not part-time work was sufficient to bring somebody within the scope of 'EU worker' for Community law purposes. The Court stated that it was important to understand that part-time work was not only a valuable contribution to the economies of the Member States, but it also contributed to the raising of living standards for the individual employees concerned. The fact the work was part-time should not affect Mrs Levin's status as an 'EU worker'.

The Court stated at para 17 that the part-time work must constitute an 'effective and genuine' economic activity which must not be on such a small scale as to be 'purely marginal and ancillary'. This is the test to be applied to ascertain if the person is an 'EU worker'. The Court concluded by stating that the intention of the applicant was irrelevant. It was irrelevant that the applicant had taken up an economic activity in order to obtain a residence permit provided that, in the words of para 17, such economic activity was 'effective and genuine' and not on such a small scale as to be 'purely marginal and ancillary'.

This was a very important case, clarifying that part-time workers could be covered by the Community law provisions on free movement of workers. It did not matter if the worker chose to supplement his income from other sources. This was taken a step further in the following case, which involved a music teacher whose income was below the minimum level of subsistence, and who therefore claimed social security benefits to supplement her income:

Kempf v *Staatssecretaris van Justitie* (Case 139/85)

A German national was living and working in The Netherlands as a music teacher. She gave twelve lessons a week. Her application for a residence permit was refused. She challenged this refusal and the national court referred the case to the Court of Justice pursuant to the former Art 177 EC Treaty (now Art 234). It was argued by the Dutch and Danish governments that work providing an income below the minimum level of subsistence was not 'effective or genuine' if the person undertaking the work claimed social security benefits. If it was not 'effective or genuine' then the person would not come within the scope of EU worker and therefore could not benefit from the rights under the Treaty or secondary legislation. The Court of Justice held as follows:

> 14. ... In that regard, it is irrelevant whether those supplementary means of subsistence are derived from property or from the employment of a member of his family, as was the case in Levin, or whether, as in this instance, they are obtained from financial assistance drawn from the public funds of the Member State in which he resides, provided that the effective and genuine nature of his work is established. [emphasis added]

In the above case, the Court of Justice once again reiterated the test to be applied in order to ascertain whether or not a person comes within the scope of EU worker: i.e. pursuit of an economic activity which is effective and genuine, and which is not on such a small scale as to be purely marginal or ancillary.

In **Lawrie-Blum** (see above), the Court held that a trainee teacher qualified as an EU worker even though her remuneration was only nominal. The fact that the salary was less than a teacher's full salary was immaterial. What mattered was the genuinely economic nature of the work in question, and the receipt of some remuneration.

The Court of Justice has not laid down any criteria as to how much, or how little, or what kind of work, is 'effective and genuine' and not 'purely marginal and ancillary', although some guidance can be gained from the cases.

In **Steymann** *v* **Staatssecretaris van Justitie** (Case 196/87), the individual was engaged in maintenance and repair work for a religious community. He received his keep (i.e. accommodation, meals, etc.), but no wages. Despite the fact that his reward was 'in kind' rather than monetary, the Court of Justice held that he came within the scope of EU worker.

In **Bettray** *v* **Staatssecretaris van Justitie** (Case 344/87), however, the person concerned was engaged in paid work as part of a form of therapy. It was, therefore, ancillary. The Court of Justice recently gave judgment in a case which involved a socio-occupational reintegration programme:

Trojani (Case C-456/02)

A destitute French national had been given accommodation in a Salvation Army hostel in Brussels where, in return for his board and lodging and a small amount of pocket money, he performed a variety of jobs for about 30 hours per week as part of a personal socio-occupational reintegration programme. The question which arose was whether he could claim a right of residence as a worker, a self-employed worker or a person providing or receiving services within the terms of Arts 39, 43 and 49 EC Treaty respectively. If not, could he benefit from that right by direct application of Art 18 EC Treaty in his capacity merely as an EU citizen? (See Chapter 11.)

It was in fact in respect of the right of residence that the Tribunal du travail de Bruxelles (Labour Court, Brussels) questioned the Court of Justice, even though the case had been brought before it following the refusal by the Centre public d'aide sociale de Bruxelles (CPAS) to grant Mr Trojani the minimum subsistence allowance (minimex).

On the issue of the right of residence as a worker, the Court of Justice first pointed out the Community scope of the concept of EU worker. The essential feature of an employment relationship is that for a certain period of time a person performs services for and under the direction of another person in return for which he receives remuneration. Neither the *sui generis* nature of the employment relationship under national law, nor the level of productivity of the person concerned, the origin of the funds from which the remuneration is paid or the limited amount of that remuneration can have any consequence in that regard. The Court found that, in this case, the constituent elements of any paid employment relationship, that is to say, the relationship of subordination and payment of remuneration, were present: the benefits in kind and in cash which the Salvation Army provided for Mr Trojani constituted the consideration for the services which he performed for and under the direction of the hostel. However, **it remained to be determined whether those services were real and genuine or whether, on the contrary, they were on such a small scale as to be regarded as purely marginal and ancillary, with the result that the person concerned could not be classified as a worker. In that connection the Court left it to the national court to determine whether those services were real and genuine. It did, however, provide some guidelines: the national court had, in particular, to ascertain whether the services performed were capable of being treated as forming part of the normal labour market, regard being had to the status and practices of the hostel, the content of the social reintegration programme, and the nature and details of performance of the services.**

The Court also rejected the argument that the provisions governing the right of establishment might be applicable inasmuch as it had been established in the case that the activities performed were in the nature of employment. The Court likewise ruled out the applicability of the provisions on the freedom to provide services, which exclude any activity carried out on a permanent basis or, at least, without a foreseeable limit to its duration; see Chapter 13.

With regard to the right of residence of EU citizens under Art 18 EC Treaty (see Chapter 11), the Court pointed out that this provision is directly effective but stated immediately that the right to rely on it is not unconditional: it may be subject to limitations and conditions, including Art 1, Directive 90/364, which allows Member States to refuse a right of residence to citizens of the Union who do not have sufficient resources (Directive 90/364 has since been repealed and replaced by Directive 2004/38). Those limitations and conditions must, however, be applied in compliance with Community law and, in particular, in accordance with the principle of proportionality. In the present case, the Court found that it was the lack of resources which led Mr Trojani to seek the minimex, a fact which justified application of Directive 90/364 and ruled out reliance on Art 18 EC Treaty. The Court did, however, note that Mr Trojani had a residence permit. It accordingly pointed out, on its own initiative, that, with regard to a social assistance benefit such as the minimex, Mr Trojani could invoke Art 12 EC Treaty in order to secure treatment equal to that accorded to Belgian nationals.

Surprisingly small amounts of work can be regarded as sufficient to come within the scope of EU Worker. In **Raulin v Netherlands Ministry for Education and Science** (Case 357/89), the person claiming EU worker status had been on an 'on call' contract for a period of eight months. During that period she actually worked as a waitress for a total of 60 hours. Nonetheless, the Court of Justice held that the brevity of her employment period did not exclude her from coming within the scope of EU worker. This principle was reaffirmed by the Court of Justice in a more recent case: **Ninni-Orasche** (Case C–413/01).

In view of the broad scope which has been given by the Court of Justice to EU worker, some Member States have expressed concern that EU nationals from Member States with less generous welfare benefit provisions would migrate to those with more generous provisions (this is discussed further below). However, Member States have a number of options available to them in this regard. One of them, in relation to part-time workers, is to provide that benefits will only be available to national and non-national workers who are 'available for full-time work'.

Work-seekers

Not every individual wishing to go to another Member State to work will already have arranged employment. Applying a literal interpretation to Art 39(3) EC Treaty, people in this category would not seem to qualify for a right of free movement, since the beneficiaries are described as those in a position 'to accept offers of employment actually made'. However, in the following case the Court of Justice delivered a remarkably creative judgment:

Royer (Case 48/75)

The Court of Justice held that:

> ... the right of nationals of a Member State to enter the territory of another Member State and reside there for the purposes intended by the Treaty – in particular to look for or pursue an occupation or activities as employed or self-employed persons, or to rejoin their spouse or family – is a right conferred directly by the Treaty, or, as the case may be, by the provisions adopted for its implementation.

Although in the above case the Court of Justice decided that work-seekers were entitled to enter another Member State to look for work, it did not give any indication as to how long that right should continue. For a number of years it was thought that the appropriate period was three months, partly because that was the limit of the entitlement to payment of unemployment benefit under Regulation 1408/71 (see Chapter 14), and partly because the Council of Ministers had made a declaration to that effect at the time of approval of Regulation 1612/68 and the former Directive 68/360 (see the opinion of

Advocate-General Lenz in **Centre Public d'Aide Sociale *v* Lebon** (Case C–316/85)). The Court of Justice rejected both bases for limiting the rights of residence of work-seekers. In **R *v* Immigration Appeal Tribunal, ex parte Antonissen** (Case C–292/89), the Court said that there was 'no necessary link between the right to unemployment benefit in the Member State of origin and the right to stay in the host State' (para 20). The Council of Ministers' declaration had 'no legal significance', since it was not part of any binding legislative provision (para 18). The way seemed clear for an unequivocal statement by the Court of Justice on how long an individual may look for work in another Member State. The Court's response to that question only marginally clarified the issue:

R v Immigration Appeal Tribunal, ex parte Antonissen (Case C-292/89)

Antonissen was a Belgian national who came to the UK in 1984 to find work. He did not find work. In 1987 the Secretary of State decided to deport him, following his conviction and imprisonment for a drug-related offence. He sought judicial review of the decision and the case was referred to the Court of Justice. The relevant issue here concerned the length of time a person could stay in the territory of another Member State while seeking work. The Court of Justice held as follows:

16. In that regard, it must be pointed out in the first place that the effectiveness of Article 48 [now Art 39] is secured in so far as Community legislation or, in its absence, the legislation of a Member State gives persons concerned a **reasonable time in which to apprise themselves, in the territory of the Member State concerned, of offers of employment corresponding to their occupational qualifications and to take, where appropriate, the necessary steps in order to be engaged.**

    . . .

21. In the absence of a Community provision prescribing the period during which Community nationals seeking employment in a Member State may stay there, **a period of six months,** such as that laid down in the national legislation at issue in the main proceedings, **does not appear in principle to be insufficient to enable the persons concerned to apprise themselves, in the host Member State, of offers of employment** corresponding to their occupational qualifications and to take, where appropriate, the necessary steps in order to be engaged **and, therefore, does not jeopardise the effectiveness of the principle of free movement. However, if after the expiry of that period the person concerned provides evidence that he is continuing to seek employment and that he has genuine chances of being engaged, he cannot be required to leave the territory of the host Member State.** [emphasis added]

In the above case the Court of Justice held that EU nationals could enter another Member State to seek work, and that they could stay there for a *reasonable period of time* while they sought work (para 16). The Court stated that (in the context of the UK legislation existing at the material time) six months was a *reasonable period of time* to allow a person seeking work to find employment. This did not mean that a period of less than six months would not be reasonable. At the end of para 21 the Court declared that even if work has not been found at the end of this period, the EU national cannot be deported if he can show that he is still seeking work and he has genuine chances of finding work.

The Court of Justice subsequently decided, in **Commission *v* Belgium** (Case C–344/95), that the period of *three months* allocated by Belgium to EU nationals to find work is also reasonable, provided that it can be extended if the work-seeker is looking for work and has a genuine chance of finding work.

Work-seekers are entitled to entry and limited rights of residence but not the full range of benefits enjoyed by those who have full EU worker status, unless EU citizenship can be relied upon to extend the range of benefits; see Chapter 11 and below.

Directive 2004/38

Directive 2004/38 had to be transposed into national law by 30 April 2006. The Directive merges into a single document all the Community secondary legislation concerning the right of entry and residence of EU citizens and their family members.

Article 6(1) provides that EU citizens shall have the right of residence in another Member State for a period of up to three months without any conditions or formalities other than the requirement to hold a valid identity card or passport. A work-seeker would therefore be able to rely on this provision.

'Family members' who do not have the nationality of a Member State (i.e. non-EU family members) enjoy the same rights as the EU citizen who they have accompanied or joined (Art 6(2)); see below for the definition of 'family members'. Article 5(2) provides that non-EU family members may be subject to a visa requirement under Regulation 539/2001; residence cards will be deemed equivalent to short-stay visas (Art 5(2)). The host Member State may require the persons concerned to register their presence in the country within a reasonable and non-discriminatory period of time (Art 5(5)).

Article 14(1) provides that EU citizens and their family members shall have the right of residence under Art 6, 'as long as they do not become an *unreasonable* burden on the social security system of the host Member State' (emphasis added, and see below); expulsion shall not be an automatic consequence if an EU citizen or his family members have recourse to the host Member State's social assistance system (Art 14(3)). Article 14(4) further provides that (other than in accordance with the provisions relating to restrictions on the right of entry and residence on grounds of public policy, public security or public health) an expulsion order cannot be issued against an EU citizen or his family members if, *inter alia*, the EU citizen entered the host Member State to seek employment and provided he can provide evidence that he is continuing to seek work and has a genuine chance of being employed.

With regard to social assistance, Art 24(2) provides that for the first three months of residence, or while the EU citizen is exercising his right to reside while seeking work under Art 14(4)(b), the host Member State is not obliged to grant entitlement to social assistance to persons other than employed or self-employed workers and the members of their family.

EU citizens qualifying for the right of residence or the right of permanent residence and the members of their family benefit from equal treatment with host-country nationals in the areas covered by the Treaty (Art 24(1)).

The worker's family

It is not only the worker who will derive benefits from Community law, but also the family of the worker. However, the rights of the family are dependent upon the worker's status as an EU worker (see above). Although the worker has to be an EU national, the family of the worker does not. Article 10, Regulation 1612/68 defined workers' families:

1. The following shall, irrespective of their nationality, have the right to install themselves

with a worker who is a national of one Member State and who is employed in the territory of another Member State:

(a) his spouse and their descendants who are under the age of 21 or are dependants;

(b) dependent relatives in the ascending line of the worker and his spouse.

2. Member States shall facilitate the admission of any member of the family not coming within the provisions of paragraph 1 if dependent on the worker referred to above or living under his roof in the country whence he comes.

Article 10, Regulation 1612/68 was repealed by Directive 2004/38. The scope of 'family members' is now governed by Directive 2004/38. Article 3(1) provides that Directive 2004/38 applies to all EU citizens exercising their right to move to, or reside in, a Member State other than that of which they are a national, and to 'family members' who accompany or join them. Article 2(2) defines 'family members' as the EU citizen's:

(a) spouse;

(b) registered partner, if the legislation of the host Member State treats registered partnerships as equivalent to marriage;

(c) direct descendants (i.e. children, grandchildren, etc.) who are under the age of 21 or who are dependants, and those of the spouse or partner as defined above;

(d) dependent direct relatives in the ascending line (i.e. parents, grandparents, etc.), and those of the spouse or partner as defined above.

This definition of 'family members' has a broader scope than the former definition set out in Art 10(1), Regulation 1612/68 in that now registered partners come explicitly within its definition.

In addition to 'family members' (as defined by Art 2(2)), Art 3(2) provides that the host Member State shall, in accordance with its national legislation, 'facilitate' entry and residence for the following persons:

(a) any other family members (whether or not they are EU citizens) who are dependants or members of the household of the EU citizen having the primary right of residence, or where serious health grounds strictly require the personal care of the family member by the EU citizen;

(b) the partner with whom the EU citizen has a durable relationship, which is duly attested.

The host Member State is required to undertake an extensive examination of the personal circumstances of such persons and shall justify any denial of entry or residence (Art 3(2)).

Dependants

In **Centre Public d'Aide Sociale de Courcelles** *v* **Lebon** (Case 316/85) the Court of Justice held that the status of 'dependant' did not require an objective assessment as to the *need* for support, but required an assessment of the facts to ascertain whether the worker was *actually providing support* for the family member. This support could be financial or non-financial. Take the case of a child of an EU worker who is over the age of 21. If this child had sustained a disability in a motor accident and received a substantial financial settlement in subsequent civil litigation, then obviously the child would not be financially dependent upon his parents. However, if the parents provided the child with other support (e.g. arranging care), this would be sufficient to come within Art 2(2)(c), Directive 2004/38.

The Court of Justice applied Art 10(1)(a), Regulation 1612/78 in **Baumbast and R v Secretary of State for the Home Department** (Case C–413/99) and held that the right of the worker's 'spouse and their dependants who are under the age of 21 years or are dependants' to install themselves with the migrant worker must be interpreted as meaning that it is granted both to the descendants of that worker and to those of the worker's spouse. The Court said that to give a restrictive interpretation to that provision to the effect that only children common to the migrant worker and the worker's spouse have the right to install themselves would run counter to the aim of Regulation 1612/68; the aim of the Regulation being to facilitate free movement. Article 2(2), Directive 2004/38 has replaced Art 10(1), Regulation 1612/68. Article 2(2)(c), Directive 2004/38 now makes it explicitly clear that it is the direct descendants of the EU worker and also those of his spouse (or registered partner) who come within the scope of 'family members', provided those direct descendants are under the age of 21 or are dependant on the EU worker or his spouse (or registered partner).

Spouse

In **Netherlands v Reed** (Case 59/85) a UK national had travelled to The Netherlands to live with her long-term partner, who was also a UK national working in The Netherlands. The Court of Justice held that 'spouse' within Art 10(1), Regulation 1612/68 only referred to a married relationship. Article 2(2)(b), Directive 2004/38 now extends the scope of 'family members' to include the EU worker's registered partner, if the legislation of the host Member State treats registered partnerships as equivalent to marriage.

In **R v Immigration Appeal Tribunal and Surinder Singh, ex parte Secretary of State for the Home Department** (Case C–370/90), an Indian national married a UK national. They both worked in Germany, subsequently returning to the UK. Following their return to the UK they divorced. The Court of Justice held that because they were working in Germany, the EU national was an EU worker exercising her Community law free movement rights, and therefore her Indian husband could claim rights as the spouse of a Community worker. The Court did not comment on the effect of the divorce because this was not relevant to the particular factual situation; they divorced *after* they had returned to the UK. If the facts had been reversed, and they had divorced prior to their return to the UK, then the case would probably have been decided differently. The following case concerned the issue of a non-EU national residing unlawfully within a Member State when he married an EU national, and the effect that would have on the application of Art 10(1), Regulation 1612/68:

Akrich (Case C-109/01)

A Moroccan (i.e. non-EU) national, Mr Akrich, entered the UK illegally and while in the UK he married a UK national, Mrs Akrich. Mrs Akrich subsequently left the UK to work in Ireland (August 1997 to June 1998). Her husband was deported to Ireland in 1997, after the UK authorities had decided that his residency in the UK was unlawful. They both returned to the UK. The UK refused Mr Akrich entry. He claimed that as the spouse of an EU worker (his wife having been working in Ireland for 10 months), he had a right of entry into the UK under Art 10(1), Regulation 1612/68 (Art 10(1), Regulation 1612/68 has since been repealed and replaced by Directive 2004/38). The national court referred the case to the Court of Justice pursuant to Art 234 EC Treaty. The Court of Justice held that:

- In order to benefit from the right to settle with an EU national under Art 10(1), Regulation 1612/68, the spouse of the EU national must be lawfully resident in a Member State when he moves to the Member State to which the EU national is migrating. This will also apply to the EU worker's spouse or registered partner under Directive 2004/38.
- The same situation applies when an EU national who is married to a non-EU national returns to the EU national's home country, the EU national seeking to work there as an employed person. However, the home country must nonetheless take account of the right to respect for family life under Art 8 of the European Convention on Human Rights.
- In this case, the UK had argued that Mr and Mrs Akrich moved to Ireland for a temporary period for the specific purpose of being able to rely upon Community law on their return to the UK (thus evading the UK's stricter entry provisions). The Court held that in applying Art 10(1), Regulation 1612/68, the motive of the parties is irrelevant. This will also be the case under Directive 2004/38.
- Community law will not recognise marriages of convenience (i.e. sham marriages) for the purpose of Art 10(1), Regulation 1612/68. Article 35, Directive 2004/38 provides that 'Member States may adopt the necessary measures to refuse, terminate or withdraw any right conferred by this Directive in the case of abuse of rights or fraud, such as marriages of convenience ...'

Separate accommodation

In the following case, the Court of Justice was faced with the question of whether or not a spouse of an EU worker could still come within the scope of Art 10(1), Regulation 1612/68 if they separated and were no longer living together (Art 10(1), Regulation 1612/68 has since been repealed and replaced by Art 2(2), Directive 2004/38):

Diatta v Land Berlin (Case 267/83)

The applicant was a Senegalese (i.e. non-EU) national who had married a French national. Both were resident and working in Berlin (Germany). They later separated, moved into separate accommodation and she intended divorcing him. She applied for an extension to her residence permit. This was refused on the ground that she was no longer a family member of an EU worker. She challenged this refusal and the national court referred the case to the Court of Justice for a preliminary ruling pursuant to Art 177 EC Treaty (now Art 234). Article 11, Regulation 1612/68 gives the member of a Community worker's family the right to take up any activity as an employed person throughout the territory of the Member State concerned, notwithstanding her nationality (Art 11, Regulation 1612/68 has been repealed and replaced by Art 23 Directive 2004/38). The Court was asked whether a migrant worker's family must live permanently with the EU worker in order to qualify for a right of residence, or whether Art 11, Regulation 1612/68 gives a separate and independent right of residence. The Court of Justice held as follows:

18. In providing that a member of a migrant worker's family has the right to install himself with the worker, **Article 10 of the Regulation does not require that the member of the family in question must live permanently with the worker,** but, as is clear from Article 10(3), only that the accommodation which the worker has available must be such as may be considered normal for the purpose of accommodating his family. A requirement that the family must live under the same roof permanently cannot be implied.

19. In addition, such an interpretation corresponds to the spirit of Article 11 of the Regulation, which gives the member of the family the right to take up any activity as an employed person throughout the territory of the Member State concerned, even though that activity is exercised at a place some distance from the place where the migrant worker resides.

20. It must be added that the marital relationship cannot be regarded as dissolved so long as it has not been terminated by the competent authority. It is not dissolved merely because the spouses live separately, even where they intend to divorce at a later date. [emphasis added]

In the above case the Court of Justice did not decide that the family members had a separate and distinct right of residence, because the family's right to reside in the host Member State was linked to that of the EU worker. However, the Court held that there was no necessity for them to live under one roof. To decide otherwise would have conflicted with the right given to family members by Art 11, Regulation 1612/68 to work within the host Member State, notwithstanding their nationality. Article 11, Regulation 1612/68 was repealed and replaced by Art 23 Directive 2004/38. Article 23, Directive 2004/38 provides that 'irrespective of nationality, the family members of a Union citizen who have the right of residence or the right of permanent residence in a Member State shall be entitled to take up employment or self-employment there'. In **Diatta**, the EU worker was working in Berlin in Germany. If his spouse had decided to exercise her rights under Art 11, Regulation 1612/68 (now Art 23, Directive 2004/38) and work in Munich in Germany then quite clearly she would have needed to have separate accommodation because it would be practically impossible to commute between Berlin and Munich on a daily basis.

Directive 2004/38

Directive 2004/38 has made provision, for the first time, for the family members' retention of the right of residence in the event of divorce, annulment of marriage or termination of registered partnership.

In the case of EU family members, divorce, annulment of marriage or termination of partnership does not affect the family member's right of residence (Art 13(1)). However, in the case of non-EU family members, retention of the right of residence is restricted; Art 13(2) provides that there shall be no loss of the right of residence where:

(a) prior to the start of the divorce or annulment proceedings or termination of the registered partnership, the marriage or registered partnership had lasted at least three years, including one year in the host Member State; or

(b) by agreement between the spouses or the registered partners, or by court order, the spouse or partner who is a non-EU national has custody of the EU citizen's children; or

(c) this is warranted by particularly difficult circumstances, such as having been a victim of domestic violence while the marriage or registered partnership was subsisting; or

(d) by agreement between the spouses or registered partners, or by court order, the spouse or partner who is a non-EU national has the right of access to a minor child, provided that the court has ruled that such access must be in the host Member State, and for as long as is required.

The exercise of workers' rights

Directive 2004/38 has altered the legislative provisions relating to the exercise of workers' rights in relation to departure from the home state, entry into the host Member State, residence rights and residence permits, penalties for non-compliance with administrative formalities, rights of residence of work-seekers and loss of worker status on cessation of employment. The Directive repealed and replaced a number of directives, including Directive 68/360. The changes introduced by Directive 2004/38 are considered throughout this section.

Departure from the home state

A person cannot benefit from free movement rights as an EU worker until he has taken steps to leave his home state. Thus, in **Iorio** (Case 298/84), an Italian national from southern Italy, who complained of unequal treatment in relation to travel arrangements compared to local workers in the North, was held unable to rely on Community law because the matter was wholly internal to Italy. A worker cannot rely on Art 39 EC Treaty unless he has exercised the right to free movement, or is seeking to do so. The possibility that a person may do so at some time in the future is insufficient (**Moser** (Case 180/83)). However, if he wishes to go to work in another Member State, his own state is obliged to allow him to leave and to issue him with a valid identity card or passport to enable him to do so. It cannot demand that he first obtain an exit visa or equivalent document (Art 4, Directive 2004/38 (previously Art 2, Directive 68/360)). UK nationals are, therefore, entitled to be issued with a passport, and the directive will override the discretion of the Foreign Secretary under the Royal Prerogative to withhold it (**R v Secretary of State for Foreign and Commonwealth Affairs, ex parte Everett** [1989] QB 811). Limitations on departure may be imposed, however, where they are justified on grounds of public policy, public security or public health as defined by Community law (see Chapter 15).

Entry

Since the creation of the Single European Market at the beginning of 1993, national frontier controls on the movement of EU citizens and their families should have been removed (Art 14 EC Treaty). The removal of controls envisaged by Art 14 has not been realised. An attempt to challenge the remaining restrictions on the basis of Art 14 was, however, unsuccessful in the English High Court and the Court of Appeal in **R v Secretary of State for the Home Office, ex parte Flynn** (see Chapter 11). It was not intended that there would be no frontier supervision, but that routine checking of individual travel documents would be discontinued. Only where there was some basis for suspicion, justifying action on grounds of public policy, public security or public health, would the individual examination of passengers be justified. In several Member States this point has not been reached, particularly in the UK where there is anxiety about the relaxation of port controls. The permitted limitations on public policy, public security and public health are considered in Chapter 15.

Under Art 5(1), Directive 2004/38 (previously Art 3(1), Directive 68/360), EU workers and their family members (as defined in Art 2(2), Directive 2004/38 (see above)) shall be granted leave (i.e. permission) to enter a Member State 'with a valid identity card or passport'. In the case of a non-EU family member, a passport is required; an identity card will not be acceptable (Art 5(1), Directive 2004/38). No entry visa or equivalent document may be demanded save from family members who are not nationals of a Member State; such family members may be subject to an entry visa requirement under Regulation 539/2001 (Arts 5(1) and 5(2), Directive 2004/38). Directive 68/360 provided that the Member State should 'allow' the EU worker and his family members to enter, but the Court of Justice held in **R v Pieck** (Case 157/79) that beneficiaries of free movement did not require 'leave' (i.e. permission) from the host Member State, since the rights conferred by Art 39 EC Treaty are directly effective. Art 5(1), Directive 2004/38 (which repealed and replaced Directive 68/360), now stipulates that the Member States shall grant leave to enter, which seems contradictory of what the Court of Justice stated in **R v Pieck**. Notwithstanding the choice of words used in the Directive, this is undoubtedly still good law. The questioning of passengers coming to work in another Member State in relation to their ability to support themselves while there was prohibited by the former Art 3(1), Directive 68/360 (**Commission v Netherlands** (C–68/89)). As stated above, family members who are not EU citizens may have to obtain a visa, but the host Member State is expected 'to grant such persons every facility to obtain the necessary visas' (Art 5(2), Directive 2004/38 (previously Art 3(2), Directive 68/360)).

Residence rights and residence permits

The law prior to Directive 2004/38

It should be noted that the following commentary on residence rights and residence permits is based on the law prior to Directive 2004/38 coming into effect (Directive 2004/38 had to be transposed into national law by 30 April 2006). Directive 2004/38 has affected a substantial part of the law regulating residence rights and residence permits. The impact of the Directive on residence rights and residence permits is considered below.

The right of residence of a worker derived from the direct effect of Art 39 EC Treaty. It could not be subject to limitations imposed by the host Member State, other than those justified by Community law. In effect, it meant that, provided that he did nothing to warrant his expulsion, an EU worker had a right of residence for as long as he continued in employment or at least as long as he retained EU worker status. However, he was entitled to apply for a residence permit as soon as he had found work. That permit, the Court stated in **Echternach and Moritz v Netherlands Minister for Education and Science** (Cases 389 & 390/87), 'does not create the rights guaranteed by Community law and the lack of a permit cannot affect the exercise of those rights' (para 25).

Residence permits should have been issued by the host Member State in such a way as to distinguish them from other permits issued to foreign nationals. Such permits should have stated that they were issued under Directive 68/360 and Regulation 1612/68 and should have been issued free of charge, or, if there was a charge, it should not have amounted to any more than that charged to nationals of the host Member State for identity cards (Arts 4(2) and 9(1), Directive 68/360). Article 4(3), Directive 68/360 provided that a worker was entitled to be issued with a residence permit on production of:

- the document with which he entered the territory; and
- a confirmation of engagement issued by the employer.

Despite the clear words of this provision, the Court of Justice held that a worker who no longer held the original document with which he entered the country was entitled to be issued with a permit on the basis of a valid national identity card (**Giagounidis** (Case C–376/89)). Family members were entitled to be issued with a residence permit on production of the document with which they entered the territory and a document issued by the country of origin proving their relationship to the worker. In most cases these would have been marriage and birth certificates, although for remoter relations a sworn declaration may have been required. This would have been the case where there was also an issue of whether or not they were dependent on the worker (Art 4(3)(e), Directive 68/360 and Art 10(2), Regulation 1612/68).

Workers would not have had to wait until the permit was issued before they started work (Art 5, Directive 68/360). The residence permit would have been valid for the whole territory of the Member State which issued it, for a period of at least five years from the date of issue and be automatically renewable (Art 6(1), Directive 68/360). Whether or not the worker held a residence permit, he could not, in any event, have had his residence limited to any area in the Member State (**Rutili** (Case 36/75)). Workers who were to have been employed for less than a year but for more than three months, could have been issued with a permit that was valid only for the expected period of employment (Art 6(3), Directive 68/360). Residence permits could not have been withdrawn from the worker on the grounds that he was no longer in employment, either because he was involuntarily unemployed or was incapable of employment as a result of illness or accident. Whether or not an individual's unemployment was involuntary or not was a matter for the 'competent employment office' (Art 7(1), Directive 68/360).

Penalties for non-compliance with administrative formalities

The right of free movement for workers stemmed directly from Art 39 EC Treaty, and therefore a host Member State could not refuse entry to a worker or deport a worker simply because he had not obtained a residence permit. This was decided by the Court of Justice in the following case:

Royer (Case 48/75)

Royer, a French national, was working in Belgium. He was ordered to leave Belgium on the ground he was unlawfully resident there, having failed to comply with the administrative formalities requiring him to enrol on the population register. He complied with the order but subsequently returned. He was convicted of breaching the order (which prohibited his returning) and was convicted and sentenced. At a subsequent hearing the national court referred questions to the Court of Justice, asking whether the right of residence was independent of the possession of a permit, and whether failure to comply with an administrative matter regarding application for a permit could constitute grounds for deportation. The Court of Justice held as follows:

28. These provisions show that the legislative authorities of the Community were aware that, while not creating new rights in favour of persons protected by Community law, the regulation and directives concerned determined the scope and detailed rules for the exercise of rights conferred directly by the Treaty.

   . . .

33. The grant of this [residence] permit is therefore to be regarded not as a measure giving rise to rights but as a measure by a Member State serving to prove the individual position of a national of another Member State with regard to the provisions of Community law

   . . .

38. The logical consequence of the foregoing is that the mere failure by a national of a Member State to complete the legal formalities concerning access, movement and residence of aliens does not justify a decision ordering expulsion. [emphasis added]

In the above case, the Court of Justice held that Community law would not have prevented a Member State from adopting provisions to control non-nationals, which had been backed up by penalties for non-observance, but *those sanctions had to be proportionate*: i.e. they must not have imposed an excessive restriction on the free movement of workers. Accordingly, a financial penalty may have been proportionate (depending upon its level) but a term of imprisonment may not necessarily have been so. A sanction of expulsion would not have been valid because it would have completely curtailed the Treaty right of free movement.

This issue was also considered by the Court of Justice in the following case:

Commission v Germany (Case C-24/97)

German law required all residents to hold a valid identity document. However, the degree of fault and scale of fines imposed for a failure to hold the document differed according to nationality. A non-German EU national, who was exercising his free movement rights within Germany, and who *negligently* failed to obtain an identity document, would be liable to a fine of up to DM 5000; DM (i.e. Deutsche Mark) was Germany's national currency before Germany adopted the euro. In the case of a German national, an offence would be committed only if there was an *intentional or reckless disregard* to obtain an identity card, or a failure to produce it when required to do so, and the maximum fine that could generally be imposed was DM 1000. The degree of fault for a non-national (i.e. negligence) compared to that of a national (i.e. intention or reckless disregard) could be proven more easily in the case of a non-national (and therefore a non-national was more likely to be found guilty of an offence than a national). The maximum fines which could be imposed were 500 per cent greater in the case of a non-national. The Commission issued Art 169 EC Treaty (now Art 226) proceedings against Germany, and the Court of Justice held that the German law breached the free movement of workers (and establishment and services (see Chapter 13)) provisions:

13. Community law does not prevent a Member State from carrying out checks on compliance with the obligation to be able to produce a residence permit at all times, provided that it imposes the same obligation on its own nationals as regards their identity card.

14. In the event of failure to comply with that obligation, the national authorities are entitled to impose penalties comparable to those attaching to minor offences committed by their own nationals, such as those laid down in respect of failure to carry an identity card, provided that they do not impose a penalty so disproportionate that it becomes an obstacle to the free movement of workers.

15. In view of the foregoing, it must be held that, by treating nationals of other Member States residing in Germany disproportionately differently, as regards the degree of fault and the scale of fines, from German nationals when they commit a comparable infringement of the obligation to carry a valid identity document, the Federal Republic of Germany has failed to fulfil its obligation under Articles 48 [now 39], 52 [now 43] and 59 [now 49] of the Treaty, Article 4 of Directive 68/360 and Article 4 of Directive 73/148.

Article 52 EC Treaty (now Art 43), Article 59 EC Treaty (now Art 49) and Directive 73/148 applied to the freedom of establishment and the free movement of services (see Chapter 13). The above case was also relevant to administrative formalities in respect of EU nationals' residency rights under those provisions. In the above case, the Court of Justice simply affirmed the principles espoused in the **Royer** case (above). The operative part of the judgment could be summarised as follows:

- Member States could require EU nationals to produce residence permits, if nationals were under an obligation to produce their identity cards.

- A failure to comply could result in a penalty being imposed, but the penalty had to be comparable to those attaching to a minor offence committed by the state's own nationals.

- The penalty could not be so disproportionate that it became an obstacle to the free movement of workers.

Restrictive administrative formalities

Administrative formalities themselves may have infringed the free movement provisions if they were unduly restrictive. Although a Member State was permitted to require an EU worker to report to the police within a certain time period (in order to keep a record of population flow), that period had to be proportionate. This was considered by the Court of Justice in the following case:

Watson and Belmann (Case 118/75)

A British national stayed with an Italian family as an *au pair*. He failed to report his presence to the police as required under national law within three days of his arrival. The possible sanction for breach was deportation. He was charged and the Italian court referred the matter to the Court of Justice pursuant to Art 177 EC Treaty (now Art 234), seeking advice on whether the deportation provision was compatible with Community law. The Court ruled that Member States could adopt administrative provisions to ensure they had an exact knowledge of population movements. Accordingly, a requirement to report to the police did not infringe the rules on free movement of persons, but such requirements may infringe these rules if they are unduly restrictive. The Court of Justice held as follows:

> 19. In particular as regards the period within which the arrival of foreign nationals must be reported, the provisions of the Treaty are only infringed if the period fixed is unreasonable.

Directive 2004/38

Directive 2004/38 had to be transposed into national law by 30 April 2006. The following commentary relates to residence rights and residence permits under the Directive.

Right of residence for up to three months (Article 6)

Article 6(1), Directive 2004/38 provides that EU citizens shall have the right of residence in another Member State for a period of up to three months without any conditions or formalities other than the requirement to hold a valid identity card or passport.

Article 6(2) provides that 'family members' who do not have the nationality of a Member State (i.e. non-EU family members) enjoy the same rights as the EU citizen who they have accompanied or joined. Non-EU family members may be subject to a visa requirement under Regulation 539/2001; residence cards will be deemed equivalent to short-stay visas (Art 5(2)).

The host Member State may require the persons concerned to register their presence in the country within a reasonable and non-discriminatory period of time; a failure to comply with this requirement may make the person liable to proportionate and non-discriminatory sanctions (Art 5(5)).

Article 14(1) provides that EU citizens and their family members shall have the right of residence under Art 6, 'as long as they do not become an *unreasonable* burden on the social assistance system of the host Member State' (emphasis added); expulsion shall not be an automatic consequence if an EU citizen or his family members have recourse to the host Member State's social assistance system (Art 14(3)). Article 14(4) further provides that (other than in accordance with the provisions relating to restrictions on the right of entry and residence on grounds of public policy, public security or public health) an expulsion order cannot be issued against an EU citizen or his family members, if:

(i)   the EU citizen is a worker or self-employed person in the host Member State; or

(ii) the EU citizen entered the host Member State to seek employment and he can provide evidence that he is continuing to seek work and has a genuine chance of being employed.

With regard to social assistance, Article 24(2) provides that for the first three months of residence, or while the EU citizen is exercising his right to reside while seeking work under Art 14(4)(b), the host Member State is not obliged to grant entitlement to social assistance to persons other than employed or self-employed workers and the members of their family.

EU citizens qualifying for the right of residence or the right of permanent residence and the members of their family benefit from equal treatment with host-country nationals in the areas covered by the Treaty (Art 24(1)).

Right of residence for more than three months (Article 7)

The right of residence for more than three months remains subject to certain conditions. Article 7(1) provides that EU citizens have the right to reside in another Member State, for a period exceeding three months, if they are an EU worker or are a 'family member' of an EU worker.

Article 7(2) provides that the right of residence also applies to 'family members' who are not nationals of a Member State (i.e. non-EU family members), who are accompanying or joining an EU citizen in the host Member State, provided that such EU citizen is an EU worker.

Residence permits are abolished for EU citizens. However, Arts 8(1) and 8(2) provide that Member States may require EU citizens to register with the competent authorities within a period of not less than three months as from the date of arrival. A registration certificate will be issued immediately (Art 8(2)). For the registration certificate to be issued, Art 8(3) provides that Member States may only require the following documentation (in the case of an EU worker):

(i)   a valid identity card or passport; and

(ii) confirmation of engagement from the employer or a certificate of employment.

Article 8(5) provides that registration certificates will be issued to 'family members' who are nationals of a Member State (i.e. EU family members). This is subject to the production of specified documentation. This provision also applies to other family members whose entry and residence to the host Member State shall be facilitated in accordance with Art 3(2).

Article 9 applies to 'family members' who are not nationals of a Member State (i.e. non-EU family members). Such family members must apply for a residence card not less than three months from their date of arrival (Art 9(2)). A residence card is valid for at least five years from its date of issue, or for the envisaged period of residence of the EU citizen if this is less than five years (Art 11(1)). Article 10(2) sets out the documentation required before a residence card will be issued. This provision also applies to other family members whose entry and residence to the host Member State shall be facilitated in accordance with Art 3(2). Article 11(2) provides that the validity of a residence card shall not be affected by:

(i) temporary absences of up to six months a year;

(ii) absences of a longer period for compulsory military service; or

(iii) one absence of up to 12 months for important reasons (e.g. pregnancy and child-birth, serious illness, study or vocational training, or a posting in another Member State or a third county).

Article 26 provides that if a Member State requires their own nationals to carry an identity card, then the host Member State can require non-nationals to carry their registration certificate or residence card. The host Member State may impose the same sanction as those imposed on their own nationals, if a non-national fails to comply.

Loss of worker status on cessation of employment

As discussed above, a person retains EU worker status as long as he continues in employment. However, that status is not automatically lost when a person ceases to work. The provisions of the EC Treaty and the implementing legislation (prior to the adoption of Directive 2004/38) give little guidance on how long EU worker status is retained after cessation of employment. Article 39(3)(d) EC Treaty refers to the right 'to remain in the territory of a Member State after having been employed in that State, subject to conditions which shall be embodied in implementing legislation'. This was generally taken to mean the right to remain after retirement, or when the worker had become incapable of employment. Regulation 1251/70 has been made to this effect. The Court of Justice in **Lair v University of Hannover** (Case 39/86) referred to Art 39(3)(d) in more general terms, saying that 'migrant workers are granted certain rights linked to their status of worker even when they are no longer in the employment relationship'. It did not, however, indicate for how long that status might continue.

Since the right of residence is not dependent on the possession of a residence permit, it was assumed that the provisions of Art 7(1), Directive 68/360 which excluded the loss of a residence permit, except in the event of 'voluntary' unemployment, applied no less to someone who had no such permit (Directive 68/360 has been repealed and replaced by Directive 2004/38, see below). This was the view of the UK Immigration Appeal Tribunal in **Lubbersen v Secretary of State for the Home Department** [1984] 3 CMLR 77.

In the following case, the issue before the Court of Justice was whether or not EU citizenship could be relied upon to assist a migrant worker who no longer had a right of residence:

Baumbast and R v Secretary of State for the Home Department
(Case C-413/99)

The Court of Justice held that:

A citizen of the European Union who no longer enjoys a right of residence as a migrant worker in the host Member State can, as a citizen of the Union, enjoy there a right of residence by direct application of Article 18(1) EC [Treaty]. The exercise of that right is subject to the limitations and conditions referred to in that provision, but the competent authorities and, where necessary, the national courts must ensure that those limitations and conditions are applied in compliance with the general principles of Community law and, in particular, the principle of proportionality.

In the above case, the Court of Justice held that Art 18(1) EC Treaty, which provides every EU citizen with the right to move and reside freely within the territory of the Member States, grants a right of continued residence to an EU worker within the host Member State, even after the EU worker has ceased working. This right is 'subject to the limitations and conditions laid down in this Treaty' (Art 18(1) EC Treaty). It was therefore unclear as to what this right actually amounted to, but it was an important development, and built upon the recent case law of the Court of Justice relating to EU citizenship; see Chapter 11. The Court did not address the issue of whether or not the status of EU worker was retained (in addition to the right to residence).

The concept of 'voluntary' unemployment has had little attention from the Court of Justice, except in the context of the availability of 'social advantages' to those who retain EU worker status (Art 7(2), Regulation 1612/68, see below). In connection with obtaining access to educational 'social advantages', the Court has held that a worker will retain his status as an EU worker, even though he has voluntarily left that employment to take up a vocational course, provided there is a link between the course and his previous employment (**Raulin** (Case C–357/89), para 21). In **Ninni-Orasche** (Case C–413/01), the Court of Justice held that an EU worker who had been employed in the host Member State for a fixed term (which had been set at the outset) would not be considered voluntarily unemployed when that fixed term expired. In this case, the EU worker had been employed for a fixed term of two and a half months, and the worker had applied for a study grant from the host Member State when that fixed term expired.

A worker who does become voluntarily unemployed may become a work-seeker (**Tetik v Land Berlin** (Case C–171/95)).

Directive 2004/38

Directive 2004/38 now sets out the circumstances in which an EU citizen will retain the status of worker (or self-employed person). Article 7(3) provides that an EU citizen shall retain the status of worker or self-employed person in the host Member State in the following circumstances:

(a) he is temporarily unable to work as the result of an illness or accident;

(b) he is in duly recorded involuntary unemployment after having been employed for more than one year and has registered as a jobseeker with the relevant employment office in the host Member State;

(c) he is in duly recorded involuntary unemployment after completing a fixed-term employment contract of less than a year *or* after having become involuntarily unemployed during the first twelve months *and* has registered as a jobseeker with the relevant employment office in the host Member State. In this case, the status of worker shall be retained for not less than six months; or

(d) he embarks on vocational training. Unless he is involuntarily unemployed, the retention of the status of worker shall require the training to be related to the previous employment.

Article 12(1) provides that if an EU citizen dies or departs from the host Member State, his EU family members shall not have their right of residence affected. In the case of a non-EU family member, their right of residence shall not be affected if the EU citizen dies provided that the non-EU family member has been residing in the host Member State as a family member for at least one year before the EU citizen's death (Art 12(2)).

Article 12(3) provides that if an EU citizen dies or departs from the host Member State, if his children reside in the host Member State and are enrolled at an educational establishment, then his children and the parent who has actual custody of the children (whether or not they are EU citizens) shall have the right to reside in the host Member State until the children have completed their studies.

Article 13 governs a family member's right of residence following divorce, annulment of marriage or termination of partnership. In the case of EU family members, divorce, annulment of marriage or termination of partnership does not affect the family member's right of residence (Art 13(1)). However, in the case of non-EU family members, retention of the right of residence is restricted. Article 13(2) provides that there shall be no loss of the right of residence where:

(a)   prior to start of the divorce or annulment proceedings or termination of the registered partnership, the marriage or registered partnership had lasted at least three years, including one year in the host Member State; or

(b)   by agreement between the spouses or the registered partners, or by court order, the spouse or partner who is a non-EU national has custody of the EU citizen's children; or

(c)   this is warranted by particularly difficult circumstances, such as having been a victim of domestic violence while the marriage or registered partnership was subsisting; or

(d)   by agreement between the spouses or registered partners, or by court order, the spouse or partner who is a non-EU national has the right of access to a minor child, provided that the court has ruled that such access must be in the host Member State, and for as long as is required.

Article 14(2) provides that EU citizens and their family members shall have the right of residence under Arts 7, 12 and 13 'as long as they meet the conditions set out therein'; expulsion shall not be an automatic consequence if an EU citizen or his family members have recourse to the host Member State's social assistance system (Art 14(3)). Article 14(4) further provides that (other than in accordance with the provisions relating to restrictions on the right of entry and residence on grounds of public policy, public security or public health) an expulsion order cannot be issued against an EU citizen or his family members if:

(i)   the EU citizen is a worker or self-employed person in the host Member State; or

(ii) the EU citizen entered the host Member State to seek employment and provided he can provide evidence that he is continuing to seek work and has a genuine chance of being employed.

Equal access to employment, housing, education and social rights under Regulation 1612/68

Equal access to employment

Regulation 1612/68 provides a wide range of directly enforceable rights designed to enable the migrant worker to obtain employment, and to provide the means:

> ... by which the worker is guaranteed the possibility of improving his living and working conditions and promoting his social advancement. The right of freedom of movement, in order that it may be exercised by objective standards, in freedom and dignity, requires equality of treatment in fact and law in respect of all matters relating to the actual pursuit of activities as employed persons ... eligibility for housing ... the right to be joined by his family and the conditions for the integration of that family into the host country. (Preamble)

Articles 1, 3 and 4, Regulation 1612/68 require equal treatment in relation to applications for employment by those entitled to free movement rights and prohibit national quotas and other systems of limiting access to employment by foreign nationals. Where these exist, it is not sufficient for the Member State to issue instructions that they are not to be applied in relation to EU citizens. They must be repealed or amended so that EU workers are fully aware of their right to have access to that type of employment. In **Commission v France (Re French Merchant Seamen)** (Case 167/73), the Court held that a quota system excluding foreign deck officers from French ships, under the Code Maritime, was unlawful under both Arts 1–4, Regulation 1612/68 and Art 7 (now Art 12) EC Treaty. The Court refused to accept an assurance that it was not enforced against EU nationals. Individuals needed to be able to see a clear statement of their rights in the national legislation. The Court came to a similar decision in relation to the reservation of seamen's jobs for Belgian nationals (**Commission v Belgium** (Case C–37/93)). The same principle of transparency was applied by the Court in relation to nursing posts in the German health service (**Commission v Germany (Re Nursing Directives)** (Case 29/84), para 23). The only exception to this rule is the right given to Member States by Art 39(3) EC Treaty to exclude EU nationals from the public service. This exception is, however, very narrowly construed by the Court of Justice (see below). It is permissible to make a knowledge of the state's national language a precondition of appointment, provided that it is necessary for the kind of post to be filled. This may be so, even if it is a language which the applicant will not be required to use to carry out the job. In **Groener v Minister of Education** (Case 379/87), the Court of Justice held that a requirement of Irish law that teachers in vocational schools in Ireland should be able to speak Gaelic was permissible under Art 3(1), Regulation 1612/68 because of the national policy to maintain and promote the national language as a means of sustaining national education and culture.

Under Regulation 1612/68, EU work-seekers are entitled to receive the same assistance as that offered to national workers from the state's employment offices (Art 5). Recruitment should not depend on medical, vocational and other criteria which are discriminatory on grounds of nationality (Art 6). The Court of Justice has held that refusal by a government department in one Member State to take into account the employment experience of a job applicant in the government service of another Member State amounted to unlawful discrimination (**Schöning-Kougebetopoulo v Hamburg** (Case C–15/96)). Those entitled to Community free movement rights are also entitled to equal access to any form of employment on an equal basis, even that requiring official authorisation (**Gül** v **Regierungspräsident Düsseldorf** (Case 131/85)). The only exception to this is in relation to the public service under Art 39(4) EC Treaty (see below).

The general prohibition on discrimination contained in Art 39(2) EC Treaty covers not only measures that directly impact on the rights of access to employment, but any conditions which may make the engagement of EU workers more difficult or result in their employment on less favourable terms, as illustrated in the following case:

Allué and Others v *Università degli studi di Venezia* (Case 33/88)

The applicants challenged national legislation under which foreign language assistants' contracts at Italian universities were limited to one year, where no such limitation applied to other university teachers' contracts. There was evidence that about a quarter of those affected were from other Member States. On a preliminary reference under Art 177 EC Treaty (now Art 234) the Court of Justice held that, while it was permissible to adopt measures 'applying without distinction in order to ensure the sound management of universities ... such measures have to observe the principle of proportionality'. It concluded that the limitation constituted 'an insecurity factor' and was precluded by Art 39(2) EC Treaty.

Under Art 7(1) and (4), Regulation 1612/68, EU workers are entitled to the same treatment in relation to all conditions of employment, including pay, dismissal, reinstatement and re-employment, and they should benefit equally from the terms of any collective agreement negotiated with the management.

Article 7(1), Regulation 1612/68 was at issue in the following case:

Köbler (Case C-224/01)

A Member State's national legislation provided a special length-of-service increment to university professors who had carried on that role for at least 15 years with a university in that state, the universities being under state control. The national legislation did not allow periods completed at a university in other Member States to be taken into account. The Court of Justice held that such a regime was likely to impede the free movement of workers, given that it constituted a loyalty bonus. The Court of Justice stated that such a loyalty payment could be deemed compatible with Community law if it was imposed because of a pressing public interest reason which was capable of justifying the obstacle to free movement. Although the Court accepted that the objective of the bonus was to reward workers' loyalty in the context of a policy concerning research or university education, and such an objective constituted a pressing public interest reason, the Court held that the obstacle which this would have on the free movement provisions could not be justified. A loyalty bonus, which does not allow for like service within the state universities of other Member States to be taken into account, will therefore breach Art 7(1), Regulation 1612/68 and Art 39 EC Treaty.

The following case was an Art 234 EC Treaty reference to the Court of Justice by a German court:

Merida (Case C-400/02)

In Germany, the collective agreement applicable to civilians employed by foreign armed forces stationed in Germany provides, *inter alia*, for the payment by the German state of 'interim assistance' to those workers in the case where their contract of employment has been terminated. Mr Merida, a French resident who worked until 1999 for the French forces stationed in Baden-Baden, Germany, received that allowance with effect from that time.

However, the method by which it was calculated induced him to bring an action against the German state. That allowance was calculated on the basis of remuneration from which German wage tax had been notionally deducted, even where, as in Mr Merida's case, the remuneration was subject to tax in his country of residence, i.e. France, under a double taxation agreement between the two countries. The German Bundesarbeitsgericht (Federal Labour Court) asked the Court of Justice whether the method of calculation in question was compatible with Art 39 EC Treaty.

Apart from Art 39 EC Treaty, in order to reply to the question submitted, the Court of Justice referred to the prohibition of discrimination set out in Art 7(4), Regulation 1612/68. After pointing out that, unless it was objectively justified and proportionate to its aim, a provision of national law was indirectly discriminatory if it was intrinsically liable to affect migrant workers more than national workers and if there was a consequent risk that it would place the former at a particular disadvantage. The Court went on to hold that the notional deduction of German wage tax, in order to determine the basis of assessment of the interim allowance, placed frontier workers such as Mr Merida at a disadvantage. While application of that method of assessment ensured that German residents would, for the first year following the end of their contract of employment, receive an income equivalent to that of an active worker, that was not the case with regard to French residents, whose allowance, in the same way as their remuneration, was subject to tax in France.

With a view, however, to justifying the manner in which the disputed method of assessment was applied to frontier workers, the German government put forward grounds of simplified administration and limitation of financial charges. The Court unequivocally dismissed those objections, which could not in any event justify non-compliance with the obligations under the EC Treaty.

Article 7(1), Regulation 1612/68 also provides EU workers with a right to participate equally in trade unions and staff associations, and the workers should not be penalised for taking part in legitimate trade union activities (**Rutili *v* Ministre de l'Intérieur** (Case 36/75); **Association de Soutien aux Travailleurs Immigrés** (Case C–213/90)). Restrictive contractual provisions which inhibit their re-employment in other Member States may breach Art 39 EC Treaty even if they are applied by a sporting body, such as a football association, which is not an emanation of the state, and which applies the rules to all employees of that category, irrespective of nationality (**Donà *v* Mantero** (Case 13/76) and **Bosman** (Case C–415/93)).

The 'public service' exception

Although, as a general rule, Member States are not entitled to restrict access to any type of employment on grounds of nationality (Arts 12 and 39(3) EC Treaty, and Arts 1, 3, 4 and 6, Regulation 1612/68), there is one important exception. Under Art 39(4) EC Treaty, the right of equal access 'shall not apply to employment in the public service'. The term 'public service' is not defined in the Treaty or the implementing legislation. The Commission issued a notice in 1988 which indicated its view of a number of occupations in public employment which do not fall within the Art 39(4) exception. This included posts in public healthcare, teaching in state education, non-military research, and public bodies involved in the administrative services. This was a far from exhaustive list which did not have the force of law. The scope of Art 39(4) has primarily been left to the Court of Justice. The Court has sought to limit its application, in order to give the widest employment opportunities to EU workers.

In the following case, Advocate-General Mayras offered a definition in his Opinion which has largely been adopted in subsequent judgments of the Court of Justice:

Sotgiu v *Deutsche Bundespost* (Case 152/73)

Advocate-General Mayras stated as follows:

> It is clear ... that for the interpretation of Article 48(4) [now Art 39(4)] the concept of employment in the public service cannot be defined in terms of the legal status of the holder of the post. A Community interpretation which would allow a uniform application of the exception provided for by this provision requires us therefore to have resort to factual criteria based on the duties which the post held within the administration entails and the activities actually performed by the holder of the post.
>
> **The exception will only be applicable if this person possesses a power of discretion with regard to individuals or if his activity involves national interests – in particular those which are concerned with the internal or external security of the State.** [emphasis added]

In the following case, the Court of Justice elaborated on the two central criteria proposed by Advocate-General Mayras:

Commission v *Belgium* (Case 149/79)

The Court of Justice held that the former Art 48(4) EC Treaty (now Art 39(4)):

> ... removes from the ambit of Article 48 (1)–(3) [now Art 39(1)–(3)] **a series of posts which involve direct or indirect participation in the exercise of powers conferred by public law and duties designed to safeguard the general interests of the State or of other public authorities.** Such posts in fact presume on the part of those occupying them the existence of a special relationship of allegiance to the State and reciprocity of rights and duties which form the foundation of the bond of nationality. [emphasis added]

In the above case the Court of Justice adopted a somewhat looser definition than that offered by Advocate-General Mayras. Instead of the limitation applying to a person with a power of discretion over individuals, the Court held that it applied to posts participating in the exercise of such powers. In other words, all those who acted under the instructions of the person vested with the public powers would be included in the exception. On this basis, the Court seems to have accepted that the posts of head technical office supervisor, principal supervisor, works supervisor, stock controller and nightwatchman within the municipalities of Brussels and Auderghem fell within the exception. It is clear that a person with specific statutory powers, such as an environmental health officer, a registrar of births and deaths and a police officer, would all occupy posts falling within the exception relating to the exercise of public powers. In relation to national security and allegiance, appointments with the defence ministry dealing with issues relating to national defence would fall within the 'allegiance' aspect of the exception. Some posts, such as a policeman at a defence establishment, would seem to fall within both.

The essential factor is the nature of the work, not the status of the employer or of the worker, as illustrated in the following case:

Lawrie-Blum v *Land Baden-Württemberg* (Case 66/85)

The applicant was a trainee teacher employed by the Ministry of Education, with the status of a civil servant. The local state government argued that she came within the exception in Art 39(4), since she performed 'powers conferred by public law', including the preparation of lessons, the awarding of marks, and participation in the decision of whether or not pupils should move to a higher class. The Court of Justice rejected this argument. It held that the exception in Art 39(4) must be construed in such a way as to limit its scope to what is strictly necessary for safeguarding the interests which that provision allows Member States to protect.

Access to posts could not be limited simply because the host Member State designated such workers as civil servants (**Bleis** v **Ministère de l'Education Nationale** (Case C–4/91)). To allow that would be to accept the power of the Member States to determine who fell within the exception of Art 39(4). The derogation permitted by Art 39(4) applies only to access to employment; it does not apply to the terms of employment once access has been permitted. It would not therefore be permissible for national and EU citizens to be engaged in the same work but on different contractual terms or conditions (**Sotgiu** v **Deutsche Bundespost** (Case 152/73); **Allué and Coonan** v **Università di Venezia** (Case 33/88)).

The Court did not elaborate in **Lawrie-Blum** on the special qualities of public employment to which Art 39(4) is applicable, except to repeat, almost verbatim, its formulation in **Commission** v **Belgium** (above). It added that 'Those very strict conditions are not fulfilled in the case of a trainee teacher, even if he does in fact take the decisions described by the [government of] Baden-Württemberg' (para 28). Undoubtedly, senior officers in the government's Education Service would take major public policy decisions affecting education. The Court did not make it clear at what level the Art 39(4) exception would start to apply.

In the following two cases, the Court of Justice had to interpret Art 39(4) EC Treaty in relation to provisions of German and Spanish law which restricted, to nationals of the relevant Member State: (i) employment as master of a vessel used in small-scale maritime shipping; and (ii) employment as master and chief mate on merchant navy ships:

Anker and others (Case C-47/02) and *Colegio de Oficiales de la Marina Mercante Española* (Case C-405/01)

The Court of Justice stated that the concept of public service within the meaning of Art 39(4) covers posts which involve direct or indirect participation in the exercise of powers conferred by public law and duties designed to safeguard the general interests of the state or of other public authorities. This is a repeat of the formulation in **Commission** v **Belgium** (above). The Court then went on to consider the posts at issue in this case. It held that the rights conferred on those holding the posts (i.e. the master of the ship) were connected to the maintenance of safety and to the exercise of police powers. These powers go beyond the requirement merely to contribute to maintaining public safety by which any individual is bound. The master of the ship also had certain auxiliary duties in respect of the registration of births, marriages and deaths. The Court pointed out that the fact that masters are employed by a private natural or legal person is not, as such, sufficient to exclude the application of Art 39(4) because in order to perform the public functions which are delegated to them, masters act as representatives of public authority in the service of the general interests of the flag state.

The Court pointed out that the derogation must be limited to what is strictly necessary for safeguarding the general interests of the Member State concerned, which would not be imperilled if the public law rights were only exercised sporadically or even by nationals of other Member States. Therefore, the Court of Justice concluded that Art 39(4) EC Treaty must be construed as allowing a Member State to reserve the posts at issue for its own nationals only if the rights under powers conferred by public law granted to persons holding such posts are in fact exercised on a regular basis and do not represent a very minor part of their activities.

The public service in the UK

Until May 1991, all Civil Service posts in the UK were unavailable to all EU nationals, with the exception of Irish citizens who were not classified as aliens under the Aliens Employment Act 1955. The 1955 Act provided some limited exceptions, but it was far too sweeping to comply with Art 39(4), as interpreted by the Court of Justice in **Commission v Belgium** (above). The European Communities (Employment in the Civil Service) Order 1991 (SI 1991/1221) was brought into effect to enable EU citizens and their families to have access to Civil Service posts in accordance with Community law. It does not specify the posts which are to be opened up, but an internal Civil Service Circular (GC/378) listed a large number of jobs which would be open to EU citizens. The list included bookbinders, catering staff, civil researchers, cleaners, dentists, porters, plumbers, teachers, translators and typists. However, the post of curator in such museums as the National Gallery, the Tate Gallery, and the National Galleries of Scotland all remained closed to EU citizens. The Circular acknowledged that the criteria for identifying posts that came within Art 39(4) according to the concept of powers conferred by public law are difficult to apply in the UK, where the concept does not have the same meaning as in other Member States. Nevertheless, many of the posts which were still stated to be unavailable – such as that of clerical officer in the Department of Health and museum curators – were clearly not within the narrow core of state activities envisaged by the Court of Justice in **Commission v Belgium** (above). Special restrictions imposed on access by Irish nationals to the Civil Service in Northern Ireland were held by the High Court of Northern Ireland in **Re Katherine Colgan and Others** [1997] 1 CMLR 53 to be unlawful, disproportionate and not justified by what is now Art 39(4) EC Treaty.

Social advantages

Article 7(2), Regulation 1612/68 provides simply that the EU worker 'shall enjoy the same social and tax advantages as national workers'. This provision has been a fruitful source of rights for EU workers and their families. 'Social advantages' has been given the broadest of interpretations by the Court of Justice:

Ministère Public v *Even* (Case 207/78)

The Court of Justice stated that:

> 'social advantages' were all those advantages which, whether or not [they] are linked to a contract of employment, are generally granted to national workers, **primarily because of their objective status as workers or by virtue of the mere fact of their residence on the national territory** and the extension of which to workers who are nationals of other Member States therefore seems suitable to facilitate their mobility. (at p. 2034, emphasis added)

In his opinion in the following case, Advocate-General Mancini also emphasised that the equal treatment provisions of Regulation 1612/68 are not confined to the employment relationship:

Gül v *Regierungspräsident Düsseldorf* (Case 131/85)

Advocate-General Mancini stated that:

> The migrant worker is not regarded by Community law – nor is he by the internal legal systems – as a mere source of labour but is viewed as a human being. In this context the Community legislature is not concerned solely to guarantee him the right to equal pay and social benefits in connection with the employer–employee relationship, it also emphasised the need to eliminate obstacles to the mobility of the worker . . . [and see **Mr and Mrs F** v **Belgium** (Case 7/75), Opinion of A-G Trabucchi] (at p. 1579)

Adopting an approach of facilitating the removal of obstacles, and assisting the worker in the process of integrating into the social fabric of the Member State, the Court has held a very diverse range of benefits to be within the term 'social advantages', as illustrated in the following case:

Fiorinin (née Cristini) v *SNCF* (Case 32/75)

SNCF, the French railway company, offered a fare reduction to large families of French nationality. Cristini, an Italian national resident in France and the widow of an Italian national who had worked in France, was refused the reduction card on the basis of nationality. SNCF argued that Art 7(2), Regulation 1612/68 covered only advantages connected with the contract of employment. The national court made a former Art 177 EC Treaty (now Art 234) reference to the Court of Justice. It should be noted that Cristini was entitled to remain in France under Art 17(4), Directive 2004/38 (see below) as the spouse of a deceased worker. By Art 24(1), Directive 2004/38 all EU citizens residing in the territory of the host Member State 'shall enjoy equal treatment with the nationals of that Member State within the scope of the Treaty. The benefit of this right shall be extended to family members who are not nationals of a Member State and who have the right of residence or permanent residence'. The Court of Justice held as follows:

12. ... [T]he reference to 'social advantages' in Article 7(2) cannot be interpreted restrictively.
13. It therefore follows that, in view of the equality of treatment which the provision seeks to achieve, the substantive area of application must be delineated so as to include all social and tax advantages, whether or not attached to the contract of employment, such as reduction in fares for large families.
14. It then becomes necessary to examine whether such an advantage must be granted to the widow

and children after the death of the migrant worker when the national law provides that, at the request of the head of the family, each member of the family shall be issued with an identity card entitling him or her to the reduction.

15. If the widow and infant children of a national of the Member State in question are entitled to such cards provided that the request has been made by the father before his death, the same must apply where the deceased father was a migrant worker and a national of another Member State.

16. It would be contrary to the purpose and the spirit of the Community rules on freedom of movement for workers to deprive the survivors of such a benefit following the death of the worker whilst granting the same benefit to the survivors of a national.

...

19. **Accordingly the answer to the question should be that Article 7(2) of Regulation (EEC) No 1612/68 of the Council must be interpreted as meaning that the social advantages referred to by that provision include fare reduction cards issued by a national railway authority to large families and that this applies, even if the said advantage is only sought after the worker's death, to the benefit of his family remaining in the same Member State.** [emphasis added]

In the above case, the Court of Justice held that 'social advantages' under Art 7(2) do not have to be connected with the worker's contract of employment (para 13). In **Inzirillo v Caisse d'Allocations Familiales de l'Arrondissement de Lyon** (Case 63/76), the applicant was an Italian, working in France, who had been refused a disability allowance for his adult son. It was argued that Art 7(2), Regulation 1612/68 was not applicable because the allowance was not a social advantage to the worker (as provided for in Art 7(2)) but rather to his son. The Court of Justice held that offspring were covered by Art 10(1), Regulation 1612/68 (now Art 2(2)(c), Directive 2004/38) and that an allowance for handicapped adults which a Member State awarded to its own nationals constituted a social advantage to a non-national in a case like this.

In **Mutsch** (Case 137/84), the applicant was a German national working in Belgium. He was charged with a criminal offence. In that part of Belgium, German-speaking Belgian nationals were allowed to have proceedings conducted in German. Mutsch was denied this right as a non-Belgian citizen, but the Court of Justice held that he was entitled to this facility as a 'social advantage' under Art 7(2).

Netherlands v Reed (Case 59/85) was considered above with regard to family members, but it provides an interesting illustration of how Art 7(2) may come to the aid of a worker where other provisions may not assist. The case concerned a UK national who travelled to The Netherlands to live with her long-term partner, who was also a UK national working in The Netherlands. The Court of Justice held that 'spouse' within Art 10(1), Regulation 1612/68 (now Art 2(2)(a), Directive 2004/38) only referred to a married relationship. However, the problem was resolved by relying upon Art 7(2), Regulation 1612/68 on the specific facts of the case. In Dutch law, a foreigner who had a stable relationship with a working national was treated as that person's spouse. The Court held that this constituted a 'social advantage' within Art 7(2), as it would further the policy of free movement of persons. This is now covered by Art 2(2)(b), Directive 2004/38 which includes within the scope of family members a 'registered partner' if the legislation of the host Member State treats registered partnerships as equivalent to marriage.

The tax advantages referred to in Art 7(2), Regulation 1612/68 were held in **Biehl** (Case C–175/88) and **Schumacker** (Case C–279/93) to require that different rates of tax payable by residents and non-residents could not be applied to workers from other Member States.

Retaining EU worker status

The advantages to which migrant workers are entitled will continue even after they have ceased employment, provided that they retain their EU worker status. Thus, a worker who is not voluntarily unemployed can claim payments of 'social assistance' from the host Member State. He is excluded from claiming them as social security benefits under Art 4(4), Regulation 1408/71 (see Chapter 14). However, the Court held in **Scrivner v Centre Public d'Aide Sociale de Chastre** (Case 122/84) that 'a social benefit guaranteeing a minimum means of subsistence in a general manner' constituted a social advantage. In this case, the applicant was therefore entitled to the Belgian payment, minimex, on this basis, despite the fact that national rules restricted it to Belgian citizens. Similarly, a person who loses her job and takes up an educational course is entitled to an educational grant as a social advantage (**Lair v University of Hannover** (Case 39/86)). This will be the case even if the worker gives up her job voluntarily, provided that there is a link between the job and the course that is undertaken (**Raulin** (Case C–357/89), paras 18 and 22).

In the following case, the Court of Justice sought to address the issue of retention of EU worker status, following the worker's departure from the host Member State after his employment had ceased:

Ghislain Leclere, Alina Deaconescu v Caisse Nationale des Prestations Familiales (Case C-43/99)

Leclere (a Belgian national) received an invalidity pension from a Member State (Luxembourg) in which he used to work, but in which he did not reside. He was a frontier worker, living in Belgium and travelling to Luxembourg every day to work. Following an accident at work he became entitled to an invalidity pension. The pension therefore became payable while he had the status of EU worker. However, he was attempting to claim a benefit from the Luxembourg authorities for a child which he had after his employment had ended. This was refused on the ground that he no longer resided there. The Court of Justice held as follows:

> A person receiving an invalidity pension who resides in a Member State other than the State providing his pension is not a worker within the meaning of Article 7 of Regulation 1612/68/EEC and does not enjoy rights attaching to that status unless they derive from his previous professional activity.

In the above case the Court of Justice held that it does not follow that Leclere retains the status of EU worker within the meaning of Regulation 1612/68. The Court stated that he was protected by Art 39 EC Treaty and Regulation 1612/68 against any discrimination affecting rights which he had acquired during his former employment but, because he was no longer employed, and was not resident in Luxembourg, he could not claim to acquire new rights which had no links with his former occupation. This case clears up the issue of former EU workers who are no longer resident in the host Member State.

In **Ninni-Orasche** (Case C–413/01), the Court of Justice held that an EU worker who had been employed in the host Member State for a fixed term (which had been set at the outset) would not be considered voluntarily unemployed when that fixed term expired. In this case, the EU worker had been employed for a fixed term of two and a half months, and had applied for a study grant from the host Member State when that fixed term expired.

Directive 2004/38

Article 7(3), Directive 2004/38 provides that an EU citizen shall retain the status of worker or self-employed person in the host Member State in the following circumstances:

(a) he is temporarily unable to work as the result of an illness or accident;

(b) he is in duly recorded involuntary unemployment after having been employed for more than one year and has registered as a jobseeker with the relevant employment office in the host Member State;

(c) he is in duly recorded involuntary unemployment after completing a fixed-term employment contract of less than a year *or* after having become involuntarily unemployed during the first twelve months *and* has registered as a jobseeker with the relevant employment office in the host Member State. In this case, the status of worker shall be retained for no less than six months; or

(d) he embarks on vocational training. Unless he is involuntarily unemployed, the retention of the status of worker shall require the training to be related to the previous employment.

Limits of Article 7(2)

Article 7(2), Regulation 1612/68 has been held to cover all social advantages whether or not they are actually linked to the employment, and even where they are only of indirect benefit to the worker himself. But the Court of Justice has made it clear that Art 7(2) can be invoked only where the advantage is actually of some direct or indirect benefit to the worker, and not just to a family member or dependant, as illustrated in the following case:

Centre Public d'Aide Sociale de Courcelles v *Lebon* (Case 316/85)

The Court of Justice stated as follows:

> 12. However, the members of a worker's family, within the meaning of Article 10 of Regulation No 1612/68 qualify only indirectly for the equal treatment accorded to the worker himself by Article 7 of Regulation No 1612/68. Social Benefits such as the income guaranteed to old people by the legislation of a Member State (see the judgment of 12 July 1984 in Case 261/83 **Castelli** v **ONPTS** [1984] ECR 3199) or guaranteeing in general terms the minimum means of subsistence operate in favour of members of the worker's family only if such benefits may be regarded as a social advantage, within the meaning of Article 7(2) of Regulation No 1612/68, for the worker himself.

The Court of Justice was faced with a sensitive issue in the following case:

Ministère Public v *Even and ONPTS* (Case 207/78)

Even was a French national working in Belgium. He received an early retirement pension from the Belgian authorities. A percentage was deducted from the pension based upon the number of years early he had received the pension. This rule was applied to all recipients, except Belgian nationals who were in receipt of a Second World War service invalidity pension granted by an Allied nation. Even was in receipt of a French war service pension and pleaded the principle of equality of treatment between nationals and non-nationals to claim the benefit of an early retirement pension without any deduction. The national court referred the matter to the Court of Justice for a preliminary ruling under the former Art 177 EC Treaty (now Art 234). The Court of Justice held as follows:

22. It follows from all its provisions and from the objective pursued that **the advantages which this regulation extends to workers who are nationals of other Member States are all those which, whether or not linked to a contract of employment, are generally granted to national workers primarily because of their objective status as workers or by virtue of the mere fact of their residence on the national territory and the extension of which to workers who are nationals of other Member States therefore seems suitable to facilitate their mobility within the Community.**

23. ... The main reason for a benefit such as that granted by the Belgian national legislation in question to certain categories of national workers is the services which those in receipt of the benefit have rendered in wartime to their own country and its essential objective is to give those nationals an advantage by reason of the hardships suffered for that country.

24. **Such a benefit, which is based upon a scheme of national recognition, cannot therefore be considered as an advantage granted to a national worker by reason primarily of his status of worker** or resident on the national territory and for that reason does not fulfil the essential characteristics of the 'social advantages' referred to in Article 7(2) of Regulation No 1612/68. [emphasis added]

In the above case, the Court of Justice, at para 22, set out three factors to be taken into account when deciding whether a worker is entitled to a particular benefit in a host Member State under Art 7(2):

■ status as an EU worker;

■ residence on national territory;

■ suitability of the benefit in facilitating worker mobility within the Community.

In the above case, the Court held that the benefit, which was linked to wartime military service, was not suitable to facilitate the free movement of workers, and therefore did not constitute a 'social advantage' (para 24). This is not surprising given the sensitive nature of what the Court was being asked to adjudicate upon. The following case has a similar theme to that of **Ministere Public** *v* **Even and ONPTS**, and the Court of Justice reached a similar conclusion:

Baldinger (Case C-386/02)

The Austrian Law on Compensation for Prisoners of War, adopted in 2000, provides for the grant of a monthly financial benefit to former prisoners of war but which is also subject to the condition that the recipient is an Austrian national. The question referred to the Court of Justice for a preliminary ruling asked whether such legislation was compatible with the provisions governing the free movement of workers. In this case, the allowance in question had been refused to a former Austrian national who had been a prisoner of war in Russia from 1945 to 1947, but who had acquired Swedish nationality in 1967, at the same time forfeiting his Austrian nationality.

The Court successively examined the legislation in question in the light of Regulation 1408/71, Regulation 1612/68 and Art 39(2) EC Treaty.

With regard to Regulation 1408/71 (see Chapter 14), the Court stated that an allowance of this kind was excluded from its scope as it was covered by Art 4(4), which provides that the Regulation does not apply to 'benefit schemes for victims of war or its consequences'.

The Court found that the allowance in question was provided to former prisoners of war who proved that they had undergone a long period of captivity, in testimony of national gratitude for the hardships which they had endured and was thus paid as a *quid pro quo* for the service which they had rendered to their country.

The Court reasoned along identical lines with regard to Regulation 1612/68: **an allowance of the kind in issue in the case was excluded from the scope of that Regulation as it also did not come within the category of advantages granted to national workers principally because of their status as workers or national residents and, as a result, did not fulfil the essential characteristics of the 'social advantages' referred to in Art 7(2), Regulation 1612/68.**

The Court finally reached the same conclusion with regard to Art 39(2) EC Treaty, which covers conditions of employment, remuneration and other working conditions. That provision, the Court ruled, could not cover compensatory allowances linked to service rendered in wartime by citizens to their own country and the essential aim of which was to provide those citizens with a benefit because of the hardships which they had endured for that country.

In the above case, the Court of Justice held that the benefit payable to former prisoners of war did not constitute a 'social advantage' within the context of Art 7(2), Regulation 1612/68, because it did not fulfil the essential characteristics of 'social advantage'.

The following case concerned national legislation which required spouses of migrant workers who were nationals of other Member States to have resided in the territory of that Member State for four years before they became entitled to apply for indefinite leave to remain, but which required residence of only twelve months for the spouses of persons who were settled in that territory:

Kaba v *Secretary of State for the Home Department* (Case C-356/98)

Mr Kaba (K), a Yugoslav national, married a French national who found work in the UK in April 1994. In 1996 K applied for indefinite leave to remain in the UK, but was refused on the ground that paragraph 255 of the Immigration Rules 1994 was not satisfied because his wife (an EU national) had only remained in the UK as an EU worker for one year and ten months and not the required four years. After four years, K's wife could apply for indefinite leave to remain in the UK, as the spouse of an EU worker. However, K challenged this refusal maintaining that there was discrimination, contrary to Art 7(2), Regulation 1612/68. This was based upon the fact that if K's wife had been a UK citizen then he would have been eligible for indefinite leave to remain in the UK after just one year, rather than the four-year requirement which applied to the spouse of an EU worker. The national court referred the matter to the Court of Justice which held as follows:

> The relevant Community rules conferred on the spouses of migrant workers who were nationals of other Member States a right of residence co-extensive with that accorded to those workers.
>
> However, in seeking to remain in the UK, K was applying, in his capacity as the spouse of a migrant worker, for a more extensive right of residence than that conferred on the migrant worker herself.
>
> Even if such a right constituted a social advantage within Article 7(2) of Regulation 1612/68, there was still the question whether legislation such as that in issue constituted discrimination contrary to that provision.
>
> The equal treatment rule laid down in Article 7 prohibited not only overt discrimination but also all covert forms of discrimination which, by the application of other distinguishing criteria, led to the same result.
>
> It was true that where rules made the grant of an advantage subject to the requirement that the

beneficiary be present and settled in national territory, that condition was more easily met by national workers than by workers who were nationals of other Member States but, as Community law stood at present, the right of nationals of a Member State to remain in another Member State was not unconditional.

For example, Article 8a of the EC Treaty (now Article 18 EC), while granting citizens of the Union the right to move freely within the Member States, expressly referred to the limitations and conditions laid down in the Treaty and the measures adopted to give it effect. Accordingly, the Member States were entitled to rely on any objective difference there might be between their own nationals and those of other Member States, when they laid down the conditions under which leave to remain indefinitely in their territory was to be granted to the spouses of such persons.

In particular, they were entitled to require the spouses of persons who did not themselves enjoy an unconditional right of residence to be resident for a longer period than that required for the spouses of persons who already enjoyed such a right, before granting the same right to them.

Once leave to remain indefinitely had been granted, no condition could be imposed on the person to whom such leave had been granted, and therefore the authorities must be able, when the application was made, to require the applicant to have established sufficiently enduring links with the State.

In the above case the Court of Justice held that the legislation in question did not constitute discrimination contrary to Art 7(2), Regulation 1612/68. The Court therefore did not need to decide whether or not this would otherwise have been a social advantage within Art 7(2).

This case came back before the Court of Justice in **Kaba** (Case C–466/00). The Court was asked to rule on whether its reply would have been different had the Court taken into consideration the fact that the situation of those two categories of person (i.e. national worker and EU worker) were comparable in all respects under UK law, except with regard to the period of prior residence which was required for the purpose of being granted indefinite leave to remain in the UK. The Court held that this made no difference to its previous decision. The Court stated that the right of residence of an EU worker is subject to the condition that the person remains a worker or a person seeking employment, unless he or she derives that right from other provisions of Community law. An EU worker's situation is *not* comparable to that of a national who is not subject to any restriction regarding the period for which he may reside within the territory of that Member State. A national would not, during his stay, need to satisfy any condition comparable to those laid down by the provisions of Community law which grant EU workers a right of residence in another Member State. The Court held that because the rights of residence of these two categories of persons (i.e. EU worker and national worker) are not in all respects comparable, the same holds true with regard to the situation of their spouses, particularly so far as concerns the question of the duration of the residence period on completion of which they may be given indefinite leave to remain in the UK.

Article 16, Directive 2004/38 now sets out the right of permanent residence for an EU worker and his family members. EU citizens acquire the right of permanent residence in the host Member State after a five-year period of continuous legal residence (Art 16(1)), provided that an expulsion decision has not been enforced against them (Art 21). This right of permanent residence is not subject to any conditions. The same rule applies to non-EU family members who have lived with an EU citizen in the host Member State for five years (Art 16(2)), and again provided that an expulsion decision has not been enforced against them (Art 21).

Social advantages for work-seekers

Access to social advantages is conditional upon the acquisition of EU worker status. A person who has never worked in the host Member State will not be eligible, as illustrated in the following case:

Centre Public d'Aide Sociale de Courcelles v Lebon (Case 316/85)

The applicant, a French national living in Belgium, claimed minimex. She lived with her father, also French, who was a retired EU worker. She no longer satisfied the 'family member' provisions of Art 10, Regulation 1612/68 (now Art 2(2)(c), Directive 2004/38) because she was over the age of 21 and no longer dependent upon her father. She had never found employment. The Court of Justice held in this case that, since she was no longer dependent, she was not entitled to a social advantage as a member of his family, and could not claim such an advantage as a work-seeker in her own right:

> It must be pointed out that the right to equal treatment with regard to social and tax advantages applies only to workers. Those who move in search of employment qualify for equal treatment only as regards access to employment in accordance with Article 48 [now Art 39] of the EEC Treaty and Articles 2 and 5 of Regulation No 1612/68.

The following two cases concerned a work-seeker's right to claim a social security benefit:

Collins (Case C-138/02)

In the UK, the grant of a 'jobseeker's allowance' to persons seeking employment is subject to a condition (i) of habitual residence; or (ii) that the person is a worker for the purposes of Regulation 1612/68 or a person with a right to reside in the UK pursuant to Directive 68/360 (Directive 68/360 has since been repealed and replaced by Directive 2004/38).

Brian Collins was born in the United States and had dual American and Irish nationality. Having spent one semester in the UK in 1978 as part of his university studies and having worked for ten months in 1980 and 1981 on a part-time and casual basis in bars and the sales sector, he returned to the UK in 1998 for the purpose of seeking employment. He applied for a jobseeker's allowance but was refused on the grounds that he was not habitually resident in the UK and was not a worker for the purposes of Regulation 1612/68, nor was he entitled to reside in the UK pursuant to Directive 68/360.

Three questions were referred to the Court of Justice for a preliminary ruling in this connection, the first two of which concerned respectively the Regulation and the Directive, while the third, phrased in an open manner, asked whether there might be some provision or principle of Community law capable of assisting the applicant in his claim.

On the question of whether Mr Collins was a worker within the terms of Regulation 1612/68, the Court took the view that, as 17 years had elapsed since he had last been engaged in an occupational activity in the UK, Mr Collins did not have a sufficiently close connection with the employment market in that Member State. The situation of Mr Collins, the Court ruled, was comparable to that of any person seeking his first employment. The Court pointed out in this regard that a distinction had to be drawn between persons looking for work in the host Member State without having previously worked there and those who have already entered the employment market in that Member State. While the former benefit from the principle of equal treatment only as regards access to employment, the latter may, on the basis of Art 7(2), Regulation 1612/68, claim the same social and tax advantages as national workers (see Chapter 12). The Court took the view that Mr Collins was not a worker in the sense in which that term covers persons who have already entered the employment market.

With regard to Directive 68/360, the Court first pointed out that the Treaty itself confers a right of residence, which may be limited in time, on nationals of Member States who are seeking employment in other Member States. The right to reside in a Member State which Directive 68/360 confers is reserved for nationals who are already employed in that Member State. Mr Collins was not in that position and he could therefore not rely on the Directive.

The Court of Justice concluded by examining the UK legislation in the light of the fundamental principle of equal treatment. Nationals of one Member State who are seeking employment in another Member State come in that regard, the Court held, within the scope of application of Art 48 EC Treaty and are thus entitled to benefit from the right to equal treatment set out in Art 48(2). However, the Court held that in principle this does not extend the right of equal treatment to benefits of a financial nature such as the jobseeker's allowance; equality of treatment in regard to social and financial benefits applies only to persons who have already entered the employment market, while others specifically benefit from it only as regards access to employment. The Court considered, however, that, **in view of the establishment of EU citizenship and the interpretation in the case law of the right to equal treatment enjoyed by EU citizens, it was no longer possible to exclude from the scope of Art 48(2) EC Treaty, which is an expression of equal treatment, a benefit of a financial nature intended to facilitate access to employment in the labour market of a Member State. In the present case, the residence condition imposed by the UK legislation was likely to be more easily satisfied by UK nationals. It could be justified only if it was based on objective considerations that were independent of the nationality of the persons concerned and proportionate to the legitimate aim of the national law. It was, the Court pointed out, legitimate for the national legislature to wish to ensure that there was a genuine link between an applicant for the allowance and the employment market, in particular by establishing that the person concerned was, for a reasonable period, in fact genuinely seeking work. However, if it is to be proportionate, a period of residence required for that purpose may not exceed what is necessary in order to enable the national authorities to be satisfied that the person concerned is genuinely seeking work.**

Ioannidis (Case C-258/04)

The Court of Justice was required to examine the case of a Greek national who arrived in Belgium in 1994 after completing his secondary education in Greece and having obtained recognition of the equivalence of his certificate of secondary education. After a three-year course of study in Liège (Belgium), he obtained a graduate diploma in physiotherapy and then registered as a jobseeker. He went to France to follow a paid training course from October 2000 to June 2001 and then returned to Belgium, where he submitted an application for a 'tideover allowance', an unemployment benefit provided for under Belgian legislation for young people seeking their first job. His application was refused because he did not fulfil the relevant requirements at that time, which were that he should have (i) completed his secondary education in Belgium; or (ii) pursued education or training of the same level and equivalent thereto in another Member State and been the dependent child of a migrant worker (for the purposes of Art 39 EC Treaty) who was residing in Belgium.

The proceedings arising out of the action brought by Mr Ioannidis against that refusal led the Cour du travail de Liège (Higher Labour Court, Liège) to refer a question to the Court of Justice regarding the compatibility of the Belgian system with Community law.

The Court observed, first of all, that nationals of a Member State seeking employment in another Member State fall within the scope of Art 39 EC Treaty and therefore enjoy the right to equal treatment laid down in Art 39(2) EC Treaty.

The remainder of the Court's answer drew on case law set out in recent judgments delivered by the Court, in particular those in **D'Hoop** (Case C-224/98) and **Collins** (Case C-138/02).

The Court of Justice observed that in **Collins** it held that, in view of the establishment of EU citizenship and the interpretation of the right to equal treatment enjoyed by EU citizens, it is no longer possible to exclude from the scope of Art 39(2) EC Treaty a benefit of a financial nature intended to facilitate access to employment in the labour market of a Member State. In addition, the Court had already found in **D'Hoop** that the tideover allowances provided for by the Belgian legislation are social benefits, the aim of which is to facilitate, for young people, the transition from education to the employment market. Mr Ioannidis was therefore justified in relying on Art 39 EC Treaty to claim that he could not be discriminated against on the basis of nationality as far as the grant of a tideover allowance was concerned. The condition that secondary education must have been completed in Belgium could be met more easily by Belgian nationals and could therefore place nationals of other Member States at a disadvantage.

As for possible justification of that difference in treatment, the Court again referred to D'Hoop, in which it held that although it is legitimate for the national legislature to wish to ensure that there is a real link between the applicant for a tideover allowance and the geographic employment market concerned, a single condition concerning the place where completion of the secondary education diploma was obtained is too general and exclusive in nature and goes beyond what is necessary to attain the objective pursued. Lastly, as regards the fact that the Belgian legislation nonetheless affords a right to a tideover allowance to an applicant if he has obtained an equivalent diploma in another Member State and if he is the dependent child of a migrant worker who is residing in Belgium, the Court considered, by converse implication, that a person who pursues higher education in a Member State and obtains a diploma there, having previously completed secondary education in another Member State, may well be in a position to establish a real link with the employment market of the first Member State, even if he is not the dependent child of a migrant worker residing in that Member State. The Court noted that, in any event, dependent children of migrant workers who are residing in Belgium derive their right to a tideover allowance from Art 7(2), Regulation 1612/68, regardless of whether there is a real link with the employment market (see above).

Directive 2004/38

Article 14(1), Directive 2004/38 provides that EU citizens and their family members shall have the right of residence under Art 6, 'as long as they do not become an *unreasonable* burden on the social assistance system of the host Member State' (emphasis added); expulsion shall not be an automatic consequence if an EU citizen or his family members have recourse to the host Member State's social assistance system (Art 14(3)). Article 14(4) further provides that (other than in accordance with the provisions relating to restrictions on the right of entry and residence on grounds of public policy, public security or public health) an expulsion order cannot be issued against an EU citizen or his family members if, *inter alia*, the EU citizen entered the host Member State to seek employment and provided he can provide evidence that he is continuing to seek work and has a genuine chance of being employed.

With regard to social assistance, Art 24(2) provides that for the first three months of residence, or while the EU citizen is exercising his right to reside while seeking work under Art 14(4)(b), the host Member State is not obliged to grant entitlement to social assistance to persons other than employed (or self-employed) workers and the members of their family. It is not clear what impact this provision will have on the three cases decided above, which relied upon EU citizenship.

EU citizens qualifying for the right of residence or the right of permanent residence and the members of their family benefit from equal treatment with host-country nationals in the areas covered by the Treaty (Art 24(1)).

Education and vocational training

EU workers are entitled, by virtue of Art 7(3), Regulation 1612/68, to equal access to vocational schools and retraining centres. Article 12 also provides that EU workers' children are to be admitted to the host state's 'general, educational, apprenticeship and vocational training courses under the same conditions as nationals of that State'. Article 12 has received a greater degree of attention by the Court of Justice.

Neither the Treaty nor any implementing measures define the Art 12 meaning of 'vocational training', but the Court of Justice in **Gravier v City of Liège** (Case 293/83) said that 'any form of education which prepares for a qualification for a particular profession, trade or employment or which provides the necessary skills for such a profession, trade or employment is vocational training whatever the age and level of the pupil or student'. The applicant's course in **Gravier**, that of strip cartoon design, clearly fell into that category. In the following case, the Court of Justice held that whether all or part of a course was 'vocational' was for the national court to decide on the facts:

Blaizot (Case 24/86)

The Court of Justice held that academic work at university level was not excluded, provided either the final academic examination gave the required qualification for a particular trade, profession or employment, or:

> the studies in question provide specific training and skills ... [which] ... the student needs for the pursuit of a profession, trade or employment, even if no legislative or administrative provisions make the acquisition of that knowledge a prerequisite for that purpose. (para 19)

Despite the need for a course of study with at least some career-orientated skills, the Court, in **Lair v University of Hannover** (Case 39/86), did not appear to doubt that a course in Romance and Germanic languages, that had no immediate vocational orientation was, nonetheless, a 'vocational training course' (see Flynn, 1988).

The entitlement to equal access includes non-discrimination in relation to course fees (**Gravier**, above), so that, on any distinctions drawn by the host Member State between 'home' and 'foreign' students, EU citizens and their families exercising free movement rights should be classified as 'home' students. In addition, equal access applies not only to courses in the host Member State, but also to courses in other states, where the host state assists its own nationals in relation to attendance at foreign universities and colleges (**Matteucci** (Case 235/87)).

The educational rights of EU workers' children extend to a right to be admitted to the host Member State's primary and secondary schooling system, as well as to vocational courses in further and higher education (**Casagrande** (Case 9/74)).

In the following case, the Court of Justice held that the child of an EU worker had the right to go to school and pursue further education in the host Member State, and that this right, once exercised, would continue to apply to the child even if the worker had left the host state and had lost their EU worker status. This applied irrespective of whether or not the child is an EU citizen:

Baumbast and R v *Secretary of State for the Home Department* (Case C-413/99)

The Court of Justice held that:

> Children of a citizen of the European Union who have installed themselves in a Member State during the exercise by their parent of rights of residence as a migrant worker in that Member State are entitled to reside there in order to attend general educational courses there, pursuant to Article 12 of Regulation (EEC) No 1612/68 ... The fact that the parents of the children concerned have meanwhile divorced, the fact that only one parent is a citizen of the Union and that parent has ceased to be a migrant worker in the host Member State and the fact that the children are not themselves citizens of the Union are irrelevant in this regard.

Consistent with this judgment, the Court of Justice had earlier stated in **Brown** *v* **Secretary of State for Scotland** (Case 197/86) that Brown did not have any rights under Art 12, Regulation 1612/68 because he was born after his parents had ceased to work and reside in the host Member State (i.e. his parents had lost their EU worker status before Brown had been born).

In the **Baumbast** case, the Court of Justice went one step further:

Baumbast and R v *Secretary of State for the Home Department* (Case C-413/99)

The Court of Justice stated that:

> Where children have the right to reside in a host Member State in order to attend general education courses pursuant to Article 12 of Regulation No 1612/68, that provision must be interpreted as entitling the parent who is the primary carer of those children, irrespective of his nationality, to reside with them in order to facilitate the exercise of that right notwithstanding the fact that the parents have meanwhile divorced or that the parent who has the status of citizen of the European Union has ceased to be a migrant worker in the host Member State.

In the above case the Court of Justice provided that where the child was exercising the right to attend general educational courses, the parent who had primary care of the child had the right to reside with the child, even if this parent did not have EU worker status, and irrespective of whether or not this parent was an EU citizen.

The issue of access to higher education maintenance grants came before the Court of Justice in the following case. The Court of Justice held that although access to education in terms of admission fees and admission criteria was within the scope of the EC Treaty (and thus within the prohibition against discrimination under Art 12 EC Treaty), access to educational grants was not. Brown argued in the alternative that he was an EU worker and therefore had an independent right to an education grant as a social advantage under Art 7(2), Regulation 1612/68:

Brown v Secretary of State for Scotland (Case 197/86)

Brown, who was a French national of Anglo-French origin, had applied for a discretionary grant from the Scottish Education Department to attend an electrical engineering course at Cambridge. Prior to the commencement of the course, he had obtained employment with an engineering company in Edinburgh for eight months. This job was described as 'pre-university industrial training'. Although he did not qualify for a grant under the Scottish regulations, he argued that he was entitled to receive one as a social advantage in his capacity as an EU worker, under Art 7(2), Regulation 1612/68. The case was referred to the Court of Justice under what is now Art 234 EC Treaty. The Court of Justice held as follows:

> [a person who] enters into an employment relationship in the host State for a period of eight months with a view to subsequently taking up university studies there in the same field of activity ... is to be regarded as a worker within the meaning of Article 7(2) of Regulation 1612/68.

That should have concluded the issue, but the Court then added (at para 27):

> it cannot be inferred from that finding that a national of a Member State will be entitled to a grant for studies in another Member State by virtue of his status as a worker where it is established that he acquired that status exclusively as a result of his being accepted for admission to university to undertake the studies in question. In such circumstances, **the employment relationship, which is the only basis for the rights deriving from Regulation No. 1612/68, is merely ancillary to the studies to be financed by the grant.** [emphasis added]

As discussed previously, where the employment is 'ancillary' to some other purpose (e.g. 'therapy' as in the case of **Bettray** ((Case 344/87), above), the individual may not be regarded as an EU worker under either Art 39 EC Treaty or Art 7(2), Regulation 1612/68, for the purpose of social advantages. On that basis the Court of Justice, and the Advocate-General, could well have concluded that Brown was not an EU worker at all. His entitlement to social advantages would not, therefore, have arisen, as in the case of **Lebon**, above. The Court, however, decided to hold that he was both an EU worker and at the same time disentitled to the social advantages to which such workers would normally be entitled in these circumstances.

The nature of EU citizenship was considered by the Court of Justice in the following case (see Chapter 11), the outcome of which necessitates a reassessment of the **Brown** judgment:

Grzelczyk v Centre Public d'Aide Sociale d'Ottignies-Louvain-la-Neuve (Case C-184/99)

One of the rights conferred by the Treaty is that contained in Art 12 EC Treaty (previously Art 6) which provides that 'Within the scope of this Treaty ... any discrimination on grounds of nationality shall be prohibited'. In this case, a student of French nationality paid his own way throughout his first three years of full-time studies at a Belgian university by taking on minor jobs and obtaining credit. At the start of his fourth and final year he applied for a Belgian social security benefit known as minimum subsistence allowance (minimex). His application was refused on the ground that under the relevant Belgian legislation a non-Belgian applicant was only eligible if, *inter alia*, Regulation 1612/68 applied to him; it is applicable to 'workers' not 'students'. If he had been Belgian then he would have been entitled to the benefit, notwithstanding the fact that he was not a worker within the scope of Regulation 1612/68. The Belgian tribunal had doubts as to whether the national legislation was compatible with Arts 12 and 17 EC Treaty. The tribunal therefore referred the case to the Court of Justice for a preliminary ruling pursuant to Art 234 EC Treaty.

The Court of Justice stated that since it was clear that a student who was Belgian but otherwise in the same circumstances as the applicant would be entitled to minimex, the case was one of discrimination solely on the ground of nationality which, in principle, was prohibited by Art 12 EC Treaty (at paras 29–30). The Court further stated at para 30 that Art 12 had to be read in conjunction with the Treaty provisions on EU citizenship (Art 17 EC Treaty), to determine its sphere of application. The Court then went on to say that EU citizenship was destined to be the fundamental status of nationals of the Member States, enabling those who found themselves in the same situation to enjoy the same treatment in law irrespective of their nationality, subject to some exceptions as were expressly provided for (para 31).

The Court noted that Directive 93/96 required Member States to grant the right of residence to student nationals of a Member State who satisfied certain requirements (Directive 93/96 has since been repealed and replaced by Directive 2004/03). Although Art 3 of this Directive makes clear that there is no right to payment of maintenance grants by the host Member State for students who benefit from the right of residence, it contains no provision precluding those to whom it applies from receiving social security benefits. The Court therefore held that Arts 12 and 17 EC Treaty precluded Belgium from making entitlement to minimex conditional on the applicant (Mr Grzelczyk) coming within the scope of Regulation 1612/68 (i.e. being an EU worker) when no such condition applied to Belgian nationals.

Due to the fact that the applicant had a right of residence under Community law as a student, the Court held that as an EU citizen he was entitled to be treated the same as a national would be with regard to the payment of social security benefits; an application of the non-discriminatory Art 12 EC Treaty provision.

In any event the Court in this case stated that its judgment did not prevent a Member State from (i) taking the view that a student who had recourse to social assistance was no longer fulfilling the conditions of his right of residence; or (ii) from taking measures, within the limits imposed by Community law, to either withdraw his residence permit or refuse to renew it. But in no case, the Court said, could such a measure become the automatic consequence of a student who was a national of another Member State having recourse to the host Member State's social security system (see paras 40–45).

The principle of EU citizenship and non-discrimination developed by the Court of Justice in **Grzelczyk** has been subsequently applied by the Court in **Marie-Nathalie D'Hoop** *v* **Office national de l'emploi** (Case C–224/98); see Chapter 11.

In the **Brown** case, with regard to Art 7(2), Regulation 1612/68, the Court of Justice held that Brown was to be regarded as an EU worker, but because his work was linked to his studies (i.e. pre-course training) he only gained his EU worker status because of his studies and therefore he was not allowed to claim a maintenance grant under Art 7(2). Directive 93/96 expressly provided for the exclusion of maintenance grants for any student who benefited from the right of residence under the directive. However, arguably, Brown's right to residence had arisen because of his status as an EU worker rather than as a student. The Court of Justice further stated that the non-discriminatory rule in Art 12 EC Treaty did not apply to assistance to students for maintenance and training. In **Grzelczyk** the Court stated that **Brown** was decided before EU citizenship had been introduced. Although the **Grzelczyk** case may not assist students to claim maintenance grants (because of their exclusion under the former Art 3, Directive 93/96; and now excluded under Art 24(2), Directive 2004/38) this case could assist students, such as Brown, to have recourse to the host Member State social security system on the same terms as nationals.

As described above, in **Ninni-Orasche** (Case C–413/01), the Court of Justice held that an EU worker who had been employed in the host Member State for a fixed term (which had been set at the outset) would not be considered voluntarily unemployed when that fixed term expired. In this case, the EU worker had been employed for a fixed term of two and a half months, and the worker had applied for a study grant from the host Member State when that fixed term expired. Since EU worker status was retained, the right to a study grant came within the scope of Art 7(2), Regulation 1612/68.

Directive 2004/38

Article 7(1) provides that EU citizens have the right to reside in another Member State, for a period exceeding three months, if they:

> . . .
>
> (c) are following a course of study, including vocational training, at a public or private institution which is accredited or financed by the host Member State. The student must have comprehensive sickness insurance and assure the Member State, by a declaration or equivalent means, that they have sufficient resources for themselves and their family members to ensure that they do not become a burden on the social assistance system of the host Member State during their stay. Article 8(3) provides that Member States may not require the declaration to refer to any specific amount of resources; or
> (d) are a 'family member' of an EU citizen who falls into one of the above categories.

Article 7(2) provides that the right of residence also applies to family members who are not nationals of a Member State (i.e. non-EU family members), who are accompanying or joining an EU citizen in the host Member State, provided that such EU citizen satisfies the conditions set out in Art 7(1) (a), (b) or (c) above. In the case of students, there is a limitation on the family members who may accompany or join them. Article 7(4) provides that only the spouse/registered partner and dependent children shall have the right of residence as family members of the student. Dependent direct relatives in the ascending lines, and those of his spouse/registered partner shall have their entry and residence facilitated (in accordance with Art 3(2), see above).

EU citizens qualifying for the right of residence or the right of permanent residence under Directive 2004/38, and the members of such EU citizens' families, benefit from equal treatment with host-country nationals in the areas covered by the Treaty (Art 24(1)). However, for the first three months of residence, the host Member State is not obliged to grant entitlement to social assistance to persons other than employed (or self-employed) workers and the members of their family (Art 24(2)). Equally, host Member States are not required to provide maintenance aid (i.e. student grants or student loans) to persons with a right of residence who have come to the country in question to study (Art 24(2)).

Family rights

Directive 2004/38 confers extensive family rights on the EU worker. Although much of this section has been discussed above, it is useful to reconsider the basic rights relating to family members of an EU worker, now that the substantive provisions under the Treaty and secondary legislation have been examined.

An EU worker may accompanied by, or be joined by, (i) his spouse or registered partner (if the host Member State's legislation recognises registered partnerships as equivalent to marriage); (ii) their descendants who are under the age of 21 or who are dependent (this applies to the descendants of the EU worker and, separately, those of his spouse/registered partner); and (iii) his own dependent direct relatives in the ascending line and those of his spouse (Art 2(2); Art 6(2); and Art 7(1)(d)). Dependent children, grandchildren, and even great-grandchildren have the right to install themselves with the worker; the same applies to the parents and grandparents of both the EU worker and his spouse/registered partner, if dependent. Other family members not coming within the ascending or descending lines, such as aunts, uncles, nephews and nieces, should have their entry 'facilitated' if (i) they are dependent on the worker; (ii) they are members of the worker's household; or (iii) serious health grounds strictly require the worker to provide the family member with personal care; the same applies to the 'partner' of the worker provided they have a 'durable relationship' which is duly attested (Art 3(2); Art 6(2); and Art 7(1)(d)). Where a person has the right to have their entry 'facilitated', the host Member State is required to undertake an extensive examination of the personal circumstances of such persons and shall justify any denial of entry or residence (Art 3(2)). In the case of family members who are not nationals of a Member State, it is permissible that they should obtain an entry visa before being admitted, unless they have been issued with a residence card under this Directive, in which case the residence card will suffice (Art 5(2)). In cases where a visa is required, Member States should grant such persons 'every facility to obtain the necessary visas'; the visa shall be issued free of charge (Art 5(2)).

There should be no need to prove the relationship at the point of entry, although Art 5(5) provides that the host Member State may require each person travelling to, or residing in, another Member State to register their presence in the country within a reasonable and non-discriminatory period of time. Failure to comply with this requirement may make the person liable to a proportionate and non-discriminatory sanction.

If the worker is resident in the host Member State for no longer than three months, the family members will have the right of entry and residence without any conditions or formalities other than the requirement to hold a valid identity card or passport (Art 6(1)); in the case of non-EU family members only a passport will suffice (Art 6(2)).

If the worker is resident in the host Member State for longer than three months, a registration certificate will be issued to family members who are nationals of a Member State (i.e. EU family members); this is subject to the production of specified documentation (Art 8(5)). This provision also applies to other family members whose entry and residence to the host Member State is facilitated in accordance with Art 3(2), see above. In the case of family members who are not nationals of a Member State (i.e. non-EU family members), such family members must apply for a residence card not less than three months from their date of arrival (Art 9(2)). A residence card is valid for at least five years from its date of issue, or for the envisaged period of residence of the worker if this is less than five years (Art 11(1)). Article 10(2) sets out the documentation required before a residence card will be issued. This provision also applies to other non-EU family members whose entry and residence to the host Member State shall be facilitated in accordance with Art 3(2). Article 11(2) provides that the validity of a residence card shall not be affected by:

(i)   temporary absences of up to six months a year;

(ii)   absences of a longer period for compulsory military service; or

(iii) one absence of up to 12 months for important reasons (e.g. pregnancy and child-birth, serious illness, study or vocational training, or a posting in another Member State or a third county).

Much of the case law of the Court of Justice prior to Directive 2004/38 will remain relevant, but there are exceptions. While the rights of residence of spouses do not depend on their continuing cohabitation, in **Diatta v Land Berlin** (Case 267/83) the Court of Justice held that the right of residence subsisted as long as the marriage continued, irrespective of whether or not the parties to the marriage were still together. Once the marriage is dissolved, the spouse's right of residence in that capacity would appear to terminate. However, Directive 2004/38 now provides for the retention of the right of residence by family members in the event of divorce, annulment of marriage or termination of registered partnership. In the case of EU family members, divorce, annulment of marriage or termination of partnership does not affect the family member's right of residence (Art 13(1)). However, in the case of non-EU family members, retention of the right of residence is restricted. Article 13(2) provides that there shall be no loss of the right of residence where:

(a)   prior to the start of the divorce or annulment proceedings or termination of the registered partnership, the marriage or registered partnership had lasted at least three years, including one year in the host Member State; or

(b)   by agreement between the spouses or the registered partners, or by court order, the spouse or partner who is a non-EU national has custody of the EU citizen's children; or

(c)   this is warranted by particularly difficult circumstances, such as having been a victim of domestic violence while the marriage or registered partnership was subsisting; or

(d)   by agreement between the spouses or registered partners, or by court order, the spouse or partner who is a non-EU national has the right of access to a minor child, provided that the court has ruled that such access must be in the host Member State, and for as long as is required.

Article 12(1) provides that if an EU citizen dies or departs from the host Member State, his EU family members shall not have their right of residence affected. In the case of a non-EU family member, their right of residence shall not be affected if the EU citizen dies provided that the non-EU family member has been residing in the host Member State as a family member for at least one year before the EU citizen's death (Art 12(2)).

The EU worker's children have the right to be admitted to the host Member State's primary and secondary schooling system, as well as to vocational courses in further and higher education, pursuant to Art 12, Regulation 1612/68 (**Casagrande** (Case 9/74)). In **Baumbast and R v Secretary of State for the Home Department** (Case C–413/99) the Court held that the child of an EU worker had the right to go to school and pursue further education in the host Member State, and that this right, once exercised, would continue to apply to the child even if the worker had left the host state and had lost his/her EU worker status. This applied irrespective of whether or not the child is an EU citizen. The Court additionally held that where the child was exercising the right to attend general educational courses, the parent who had primary care of the child had the right to reside with the child, even if this parent did not have EU worker status, and irrespective of whether or not this parent was an EU citizen.

Family free movement rights derive directly from Community law. They apply not only to EU citizens who work in other Member States in relation to those states, but also in relation to their own state when they have returned to it after having worked abroad. In **R v Immigration Appeal Tribunal and Surinder Singh** (Case C–370/90), the Court of Justice held that a national of a Member State who has gone to another Member State in order to work there as an employed person under Art 39 EC Treaty, and returns to establish himself as a self-employed person in the territory of the Member State of which he is a national, has the right to return to that state under the same conditions as are laid down by Regulation 1612/68 or Directive 68/360 (which has been repealed and replaced by Directive 2004/38). Article 12(3), Directive 2004/38, provides that if an EU citizen dies or departs from the host Member State, if his children reside in the host Member State and are enrolled at an educational establishment, then his children and the parent who has actual custody of the children (whether or not they are EU citizens) shall have the right to reside in the host Member State until the children have completed their studies.

Members of the family have a right to work in the host Member State. Under Art 23, Directive 2004/38, all family members who have the right of residence in a Member State are entitled to take up employment or self-employment there, even if they are not nationals of any Member State (i.e. non-EU family members).

EU family members acquire the right of permanent residence in the host Member State after a five-year period of continuous legal residence (Art 16(1)), provided that an expulsion decision has not been enforced against them (Art 21). This right of permanent residence is no longer subject to any conditions. The same rule applies to non-EU family members who have lived with an EU citizen in the host Member State for five years (Art 16(2)), and again provided that an expulsion decision has not been enforced against them (Art 21).

Article 17 recognises the right of permanent residence for EU citizens who are workers or self-employed persons, and for their family members, before the five-year period of continuous residence has expired, subject to certain conditions being met (see below).

Housing provisions

The entry of family members used to be conditional upon the EU worker having available for them 'housing considered as normal for national workers in the region where he is employed' (Art 10(3), Regulation 1612/68). This condition was operative only at the time of the family's entry. An attempt by the German authorities to make access to reasonable housing provisions a precondition for the renewal of a residence permit was held by the Court of Justice in **Re Housing of Migrant Workers: EC Commission v Germany** (Case 249/86) to be unlawful. The reference to adequate housing in Art 10(3) related only to the 'installation' of the worker's family. The Court emphasised the importance of family reunion, as guaranteed by Art 8 of the European Convention on Human Rights, and the need to 'facilitate ... the integration of the worker and his family into the host Member State without any difference in treatment in relation to nationals of that State' (paras 10 and 11). Perhaps for this reason, Directive 2004/38, which repealed and replaced Art 10, Regulation 1612/68, makes no reference to a need for the EU worker to have such housing available for his family members.

The need for equal treatment in the housing field is dealt with in Art 9, Regulation 1612/68. Under this provision, the 'worker shall enjoy all the rights and benefits accorded to national workers in matters of housing, including ownership of the housing he needs'. If his family has remained in the country from where he came, they shall be considered for this purpose as residing in the region where he is working. On this basis, the EU worker is entitled to be treated, both for the purpose of applications for public housing and the purchase of a private house, as having his family with him. The Court of Justice held in **Commission** *v* **Germany** (above) that the acquisition of housing solely to secure a residence permit could be penalised if the family then moved into less suitable accommodation, but that any penalty should fall short of measures leading to expulsion (para 14).

Right of permanent residence under Directive 2004/38

Article 7, Directive 2004/38, provides a right of residence for more than three months. This provision has been considered above with regard to EU workers and students, but the right also extends to EU citizens who have comprehensive sickness insurance and sufficient resources for themselves and their family members to ensure that they do not become a burden on the social assistance system of the host Member State during their stay (Art 7(1)(a)). Article 8(4) provides that Member States may not specify a minimum amount of resources which they deem sufficient, but they must take account of the personal situation of the person concerned. The amount of minimum resources cannot be higher than the threshold below which nationals of the host Member State become eligible for social assistance, or if this does not apply, higher than the minimum social security pension paid by the host Member State. For retired persons, this right is facilitated by the fact that, under Art 10, Regulation 1408/71, recipients of invalidity or old age cash benefits, or pensions for accidents at work or occupational diseases, are entitled to continue to receive those benefits and pensions even if they reside in the territory of a Member State other than the one that pays the benefits (see Chapter 14).

EU citizens acquire the right of permanent residence in the host Member State after a five-year period of continuous legal residence (Art 16(1)), provided that an expulsion decision has not been enforced against them (Art 21). This right of permanent residence is no longer subject to any conditions. The same rule applies to non-EU family members who have lived with an EU citizen in the host Member State for five years (Art 16(2)), and again provided that an expulsion decision has not been enforced against them (Art 21). Article 16(3) provides that continuity of residence shall not be affected by:

(i)   temporary absences not exceeding six months a year;

(ii)   absences of a longer period for compulsory military service; or

(iii) one absence of up to 12 months for important reasons (e.g. pregnancy and childbirth, serious illness, study or vocational training, or a posting in another Member State or a third county).

Once granted, the right of permanent residence is lost only in the event of more than two successive years' absence from the host Member State (Arts 16(4) and 20(3)).

Article 17 recognises the right of permanent residence for EU citizens who are workers or self-employed persons, and for their family members, before the five-year period of continuous residence has expired, subject to certain conditions being met. Article 17 applies to cases where the EU citizen:

(i)   has reached retirement age;

(ii) become permanently incapable of working; or

(iii) lives in the host Member State but works in another Member State.

Article 17 also provides that the family members of an EU worker or self-employed person have the right of permanent residence if the EU worker or self-employed person dies before acquiring the right of permanent residence. This right, which applies to family members of whatever nationality, is subject to the following conditions:

(a)   the worker or self-employed person had, at the time of death, resided continuously on the territory of that Member State for two years; or

(b)   the death resulted from an accident at work or an occupational disease; or

(c)   the surviving spouse lost the nationality of that Member State following marriage to the worker or self-employed person.

Articles 12 and 13 are relevant to the right of permanent residence. Article 12(1) provides that if an EU citizen dies or departs from the host Member State, his family members who are nationals of a Member State shall not have their right of residence affected. Before acquiring the right of permanent residence, the persons concerned must meet the conditions set out in Art 7(1)(a), (b), (c) or (d); see above and Chapter 11. In the case of a non-EU family member, their right of residence shall not be affected if the EU citizen dies provided that the non-EU family member has been residing in the host Member State as a family member for at least one year before the EU citizen's death (Art 12(2)). However, before acquiring the right of permanent residence, the persons concerned must meet the conditions set out in Art 7(1)(a), (b), or (d); *note: category (c) does not apply to this situation.* Article 18 provides that the family members to whom Art 12(2) apply, who satisfy the conditions set out in Art 12(2), shall acquire the right of permanent residence after legally residing in the host Member State for a period of five consecutive years; this is without prejudice to Art 17 (see above). The families of deceased workers are entitled to all the social advantages under Art 7(2), Regulation 1612/68 that are available to the families of active and retired workers (**Cristini** *v* **SNCF** (Case 32/75) (see above))

Article 13 governs a family member's right of residence following divorce, annulment of marriage or termination of partnership. In the case of EU family members, divorce, annulment of marriage or termination of partnership does not affect the family member's right of residence (Art 13(1)). However, before acquiring the right of permanent residence, the persons concerned must meet the conditions set out in Art 7(1)(a), (b), (c) or (d); see above and Chapter 11. In the case of non-EU family members, retention of the right of residence is restricted (Art 13(2), see above).

Article 18 provides that the family members to whom Art 13(2) apply, who satisfy the conditions set out in Art 13(2), shall acquire the right of permanent residence after legally residing in the host Member State for a period of five consecutive years; this is without prejudice to Art 17 (see above).

EU citizens entitled to permanent residence will be issued with a document certifying such residency (Art 19(1)). Article 20(1) provides that non-EU family members who are entitled to permanent residence will be issued with a residence card, renewable automatically every ten years. The application for a permanent residence card has to be submitted before the residence card expires (Art 20(2)); the residence card must be issued no more

than six months after the application is made (Art 20(1)). Failure to apply for a permanent residence card may render the person concerned liable to proportionate and
non-discriminatory sanctions (Art 20(2)).

Article 21 provides that continuity of residence may be attested by any means of proof
in use in the Member State. The right of permanent residence shall cover the whole territory of the host Member State; territorial restrictions can only be imposed if the same
restrictions apply to the host Member State's nationals (Art 22). Family members, irrespective of their nationality, are entitled to engage in an economic activity on an
employed or self-employed basis (Art 23).

EU citizens qualifying for the right of permanent residence, and the members of their
family, benefit from equal treatment with host-country nationals in the areas covered by
the Treaty (Art 24(1)). Article 25(1) provides that under no circumstances can possession
of a registration certificate, etc. be made a pre-condition for the exercise of a right or the
completion of an administrative formality. Entitlement to rights may be attested by any
other means of proof where such documentation is not available. Article 25(2) further
provides that all the documents listed in Art 25(1) shall be issued free of charge or for a
charge which does not exceed that imposed on nationals for the issuing of a similar document.

If a Member State requires their own nationals to carry an identity card, then the host
Member State can require non-nationals to carry their registration certificate or residence
card. The host Member State may impose the same sanction as those imposed on their
own nationals, if a non-national fails to comply.

May 2004 enlargement – transitional arrangements

Following enlargement on 1 May 2004, transitional periods limited the free movement
of workers from the new Member States to the pre-2004 Member States. These transitional periods were set out in the Accession Treaty. Application of the transitional
arrangements to Bulgaria and Romania (which became Member States on 1 January
2007) is considered below.

For the first two years following the accession of the new Member States (i.e. until 30
April 2006), access to the labour markets of pre-2004 Member States depended on
national measures and policies, as well as bilateral agreements they may have had with
the new Member States. There was no requirement to notify the Commission formally of
the measures that were taken. From 1 May 2004, the UK decided to allow the free movement of worker provisions to apply to all EU citizens within the UK (i.e. the UK has opted
not to restrict access to its labour market). Ireland and Sweden also allowed full free movement.

At the end of the first two years the Commission was required to draft a report, which
would be the basis for a review by the Council of Ministers, of the functioning of the
transitional arrangements. The Commission's report was published on 8 February 2006
(COM (2006) 48 final).

In addition to the Council's review, Member States are required to notify the
Commission as to their intention for the next period of up to three years either to continue with national measures, or to allow free movement of workers. There should be free
movement of workers after five years, that is, by 1 May 2009. However, the possibility
does exist for a pre-2004 Member State to ask the Commission for authorisation to continue to apply national measures for a further two years, but only if it is experiencing

serious disturbances within its labour market. This requirement must be objectively justified. From 2011, seven years after accession, there will be complete freedom of movement for workers from the new Member States.

Transitional arrangements are set out in the Accession Treaty with regard to the following new Member States: Czech Republic, Estonia, Hungary, Latvia, Lithuania, Poland, Slovenia and Slovakia. For Cyprus and Malta, there are *no* restrictions on the free movement of workers, although Malta may make use of a safeguard clause (see below).

The transitional arrangements apply to citizens of the specified new Member States who seek to sign an employment contract with an employer in one of the pre-2004 Member States. It does not apply to those seeking to reside in one of the pre-2004 Member States for purposes such as study, or those who wish to establish themselves as self-employed persons, with the exception of self-employed persons providing certain services, e.g. in the construction sector in Austria and Germany.

Work-seekers are entitled to assistance from public employment services whether from a new or pre-2004 Member State. The current rules on entitlement to look for work in another Member State for up to three months also apply to nationals of the new Member States. Such work-seekers claim unemployment benefit in their own country and arrange for it to be paid in the country where they are looking for work, if they have access to the labour market of this country according to the transitional arrangements. The level of benefit is that of their home country.

If a pre-2004 Member State has stopped applying national measures and has a fully open labour market, it can ask to be authorised to re-impose restrictions, if it experiences serious labour disturbances. It is for the Commission to decide what sort of restrictions can be imposed and for how long.

A national of a new Member State who was legally working in a pre-2004 Member State on 1 May 2004 and who had a work permit or authorisation for 12 months or longer continues to have access to the labour market of that Member State. However, he does not have automatic access to the labour markets of the other pre-2004 Member States.

A national of a new Member State who moves to a pre-2004 Member State and gains legal permission to work there for 12 months or longer will have the same rights. But should he voluntarily leave that Member State, the right of access will be lost until the end of the transitional period.

Family members of a worker from a new Member State who were legally admitted to the labour market of a pre-2004 Member State for 12 months or more, and who were resident with the worker before accession (i.e. from 1 May 2004), also have access to the labour market of that Member State. If the family joined the worker after the date of accession, they only have access to the labour market of that state once they have been resident for 18 months or from the third year after accession (1 May 2007), whichever is earlier. Family members means the spouse of the worker and their children under the age of 21, or dependent.

Pre-2004 Member States cannot make access to their labour market more restrictive than it was on the date of signature of the Accession Treaty (i.e. 16 April 2003).

There are no automatic restrictions on the right of nationals of pre-2004 Member States to move to work in the new Member States. However, new Member States may choose to impose equivalent restrictions on the nationals of Member States that have themselves imposed restrictions.

In the event that any one of the pre-2004 Member States decides to apply national measures to restrict the free movement of workers, then new Member States may make use of the safeguard clause described above for nationals of the other new Member States. Malta can apply the safeguard clause even if all the pre-2004 Member States decide not to impose restrictions.

Nationals of a pre-2004 Member State seeking to work in another pre-2004 Member State are not affected by the transitional arrangements.

The Commission could not legally oblige Member States to indicate the national measures they have put in place for the first two years of the transitional period. However, in the interests of transparency, the Commission asked Member States to provide this information. Details are available on the Commission's Job Mobility Portal:

http://europa.eu.int/eures/home.jsp?lang=en

Once a worker is in a Member State, whether under a transitional arrangement or after being granted free access, he will have the full rights applicable under the rules governing the coordination of social security (Regulation 1408/71); see Chapter 14.

January 2007 enlargement – transitional arrangements

Bulgaria and Romania became Member States on 1 January 2007. The pre-2007 Member States are authorised to adopt transitional arrangements limiting the rights of Bulgarian and Romanian citizens' free movement rights for a period of up to seven years. These transitional arrangements are similar to those which apply to the states which joined the EU on 1 May 2004.

On 24 October 2006 the UK government announced that it would adopt transitional arrangements, limiting the free movement rights of Bulgarian and Romanian citizens. From 1 January 2007, the number of Bulgarian and Romanian citizens working in the UK is limited to:

- up to 20,000 seasonal agricultural and food processing workers; and
- a 'small group' of highly skilled and specialist workers.

If specific industries can demonstrate that they are suffering from labour shortages, the UK government will consider a relaxation of these transitional arrangements. There will be no restriction on the right of free movement for self-employed persons from Bulgaria and Romania.

Details of the transitional arrangements adopted by Member States will be made available through the Commission's Job Mobility Portal:

http://europa.eu.int/eures/home.jsp?lang=en

Summary

Now you have read this chapter you should be able to:

- Identify the provisions of the EC Treaty which relate to the free movement of workers.
- Evaluate how the European Court of Justice has, through its case law, defined the concept and scope of 'EU worker'.
- Understand how the 'employment in the public service' exception is applied by the European Court of Justice.
- Explain the provisions of Directive 2004/38 which relate to the abolition of restrictions to movement and residence of EU workers and their families and which provide

a right for workers and their families to remain in a Member State having been employed there.

■ Outline the provisions of Directive 2004/38 which apply to students and the self-sufficier .

■ Explain how the provisions of Regulation 1612/68 are applied by the European Court of Justice.

■ Understand the purpose and effect of the transitional arrangements which relate to the right of free movement of an EU citizen who is a national of one of the Member States which acceded to the EU in 2004 or 2007.

References

Flynn J., 'Vocational Training in Community Law and Practice' (1988) 8 YEL 59.

Schermers, H. (1991) 'Human Rights and Free Movement of Persons', in Schermers, H. (ed.) *Free Movement of Persons in Europe: Legal Problems and Experiences*, Martinus Nijhoff.

Further reading

Textbooks

Barnard, C. (2004) *The Substantive Law of the EU: The four freedoms* (1st edn), Oxford University Press, Chapter 11.

Craig, P. and De Burca, G. (2003) *EU Law Text, Cases and Materials* (3rd edn), Oxford University Press, Chapter 17.

Schermers, H. (1991) 'Human Rights and Free Movement of Persons', in Schermers, H. (ed.) *Free Movement of Persons in Europe: Legal Problems and Experiences*, Martinus Nijhoff.

Steiner, J., Woods, L. and Twigg-Flesner, C. (2006) *EU Law* (9th edn), Oxford University Press, Chapter 20.

Storey, T. and Turner, C. (2005) *Unlocking EU Law* (1st edn), Hodder Arnold, Chapter 11.

Tillotson, J. and Foster, N. (2003) *Text, Cases and Materials on EU Law* (4th edn), Cavendish Publishing, Chapter 13.

Weatherill, S. (2006) *Cases and Materials on EU Law* (7th edn), Oxford University Press, Chapter 13.

Journal articles

Adinolfi, A., 'Free movement and access to work of citizens of the new Member States: The transitional meansures' (2006) 43 CML Rev 469.

Castro Oliveira, A., 'Workers and Other Persons: Step-by-Step from Movement to Citizenship' (2002) 39 CML Rev 77.

Currie, S., 'Free movers? The post-accession experience of accession-8 migrant workers in the United Kingdom' (2006) 31 EL Rev 207.

Daniele, L., 'Non-Discriminatory Restrictions and the Free Movement of Persons' (1997) 22 EL Rev 191.

Davies, P., 'Posted Workers: Single Market or Protection of National Labour Systems?' (1997) 34 CML Rev 571.

Dougan, M., 'Fees, grants, loans and dole cheques: Who covers the costs of migrant education within the EU?' (2005) 42 CML Rev 943.

Farmer, P., 'Article 48 EC and the Taxation of Frontier Workers' (1995) 32 CML Rev 310.

Flynn J., 'Vocational Training in Community Law and Practice' (1988) 8 YEL 59.

Handoll, J., 'Article 48(4) EEC and Non-National Access to Public Employment' (1988) 13 EL Rev 223.

Peers, S., 'Dazed and Confused: Family Members' Residence Rights and the Court of Justice' (2001) 26 EL Rev 76.

Shaw, J., 'European Union Citizenship: the IGC and Beyond' (1997) 3 EPL 413.

Shaw, J., 'The Many Pasts and Futures of Citizenship in the European Union' (1997) 60 MLR 554.

Shuibine, N., 'Free Movement of Persons and the Wholly Internal Rule: Time to move on?' (2002) 39 CML Rev 731.

Stalford, H., 'Concepts of Family under EU Law – Lessons from the ECHR' (2002) *International Journal of Law, Policy and the Family* 410.

13 Freedom of establishment and the provision and receipt of services

Aims and objectives

At the end of this chapter you should understand:

■ Which provisions of the EC Treaty apply to the freedom of establishment and freedom to provide and receive services.

■ The application of Art 49 EC Treaty on the freedom to provide and receive services, and the scope for restrictions to be objectively justified.

■ The scope of Directive 2004/38 (previously Directive 90/364) with regard to the conferring of a general right of residence.

■ The provisions of Directive 2004/38 (previously Directive 73/148) on the abolition of restrictions on movement and residence.

■ The provisions of Directive 2004/38 (previously Directive 75/34) which enable a person to remain within a Member State having pursued a self-employed activity there.

■ The application of Art 12 EC Treaty and Art 24, Directive 2004/38 establishing the right of equal treatment for those exercising their Community law rights of establishment and their free movement rights as providers and recipients of services.

■ How Art 43 EC Treaty is applied in respect of qualifications and training and to analyse the impact on Art 43 of harmonisation and general directives, including changes to be made to the system of harmonisation and general directives by Directive 2005/36.

The EC Treaty and Directive 2004/38

Individuals may wish to move to another Member State to engage in a business or profession in a self-employed capacity. Article 43 EC Treaty (previously Art 52) provides for the freedom of establishment:

> Within the framework of the provisions set out below, restrictions on the freedom of establishment of nationals of a Member State in the territory of another Member State shall be prohibited. Such prohibition shall also apply to restrictions on the setting up of agencies, branches or subsidiaries by nationals of any Member State established in the territory of any Member State.

> Freedom of establishment shall include the right to take up and pursue activities as self-employed persons and to set up and manage undertakings, in particular companies or firms within the meaning of the second paragraph of Article 48, under the conditions laid down for its own nationals by the law of the country where such establishment is effected, subject to the provisions of the Chapter relating to capital.

'Establishment' is not defined in the Treaty or the implementing legislation. However, Art 43 requires the abolition of restrictions on the freedom of establishment of nationals of a Member State in the territory of another Member State. Freedom of establishment includes the right of individuals and companies to set themselves up in business in a Member State (a permanent or settled place of business). It covers the self-employed and in addition the practising of a profession or trade (e.g. lawyer, doctor, vet) on a permanent or semi-permanent basis. Naturally, a person may seek to practise a profession in another Member State in an employed capacity (i.e. as an EU worker), and therefore the Community law provisions relating to workers will apply (see Chapter 12) in addition to those of establishment which relate to recognition of the profession or trade.

Articles 49 and 50 EC Treaty (previously Arts 59 and 60) provide for the abolition of restrictions on individuals to provide services in a Member State other than that in which they are established. Article 49 provides that:

> Within the framework of the provisions set out below, restrictions on freedom to provide services within the Community shall be prohibited in respect of nationals of Member States who are established in a State of the Community other than that of the person for whom the services are intended.
>
> The Council may, acting by a qualified majority on a proposal from the Commission, extend the provisions of this Chapter to nationals of a third country who provide services and who are established within the Community.

Article 50 provides that services shall be considered to be 'services' within the meaning of the Treaty 'where they are normally provided for remuneration'. Article 50 lists such services as including activities of an industrial and commercial character, activities of craftsmen and activities of the professions. This is, however, far from being an exhaustive list. The person providing the service 'may, in order to do so, temporarily pursue his activity in the State where the service is provided'. This is 'without prejudice to the right of establishment'. There is, in fact, a close link to the right of establishment. The right to provide the service confers a right of residence as long as the service is provided.

If the service provider wishes to provide that service in the host Member State on a long-term basis then Art 43 will apply, and he may become established in that state. The crucial element that differentiates the service provider from the established business is the process of 'setting up'. This may involve anything from leasing or buying business premises, to acquiring a licence to run a company in the host Member State (see **Steinhauser v City of Biarritz** (Case 197/84) and **R v Secretary of State for Transport, ex parte Factortame** (Case C–213/89)). The Court of Justice referred to 'establishment' in the **Factortame** case as 'the actual pursuit of an economic activity through a fixed establishment for an indefinite period' (para 20).

None of the Treaty provisions confers a right to go to another Member State to *receive* services, but Directive 73/148 was more wide-ranging than Arts 43, 49 and 50 EC Treaty. It provided for the abolition of restrictions on the movement and residence of:

■ nationals of a Member State who are established or who wish to establish themselves in another Member State in order to pursue activities as self-employed persons or who wish to provide services in that state; and

■ nationals of Member States wishing to go to another Member State *as recipients of services*.

Directive 73/148 has been repealed and replaced by Directive 2004/38. Article 6, Directive 2004/38 establishes the right for all EU citizens and their family members to reside in another Member State for a period of up to three months without any conditions or formalities, other than the requirement to hold a valid identity card or passport (a passport in the case of non-EU family members). This general right of residence for up to three months will clearly be applicable to both providers and recipients of services. Article 7, Directive 2004/38 creates a right of extended residence (for more than three months) for EU citizens and their family members who, *inter alia*, are economically self-sufficient.

The scope of the Treaty provisions and the Directive in relation to (i) the providers of services; (ii) the recipients of services; and (iii) the right of establishment are now examined in turn.

Providers of services

Article 49 EC Treaty is directly effective (see, e.g., **Van Binsbergen** (Case 33/74)). However, in the following case the Court of Justice held that Art 49 will not apply to a totally internal situation:

Peter Jagerskiold v *Torolf Gustafsson* (Case C-97/98)

On 29 May 1997 Mr Gustafsson (G) fished with a spinning rod in waters belonging to Mr Jagerskiold (J) in the township of Kimoto in Finland. Two days earlier, on 27 May 1997, G had paid the fishing licence fee provided for in Finnish law, which allowed him to practise that type of fishing even in private waters.

J brought an action before the national court for a declaration that G could not, without his permission, fish with a rod in his waters, notwithstanding the fact that G had paid the fishing licence fee provided for by Finnish law. In support of his action, J argued that the Finnish law, on which the right to fish with a rod was based, was contrary to the rules of the EC Treaty concerning the free movement of goods or to those relating to the freedom to provide services. The Court held that the provisions relating to the free movement of goods did not apply, but those relating to the freedom to provide services did apply. However, the Court of Justice continued:

> ... concerning the provisions of the Treaty relating to the freedom to provide services, it is sufficient to observe that these provisions are not applicable to activities which are confined in all respects within a single Member State.
>
> **The legal proceedings pending before the Tingsratt are between two Finnish nationals, both established in Finland, concerning the right of one of them to fish in waters belonging to the other situated in Finland.**
>
> Such a situation does not present any link to one of the situations envisaged by Community law in the field of the free provision of services. [emphasis added]

Remuneration

Article 50 EC Treaty provides that services will come within the scope of the Treaty if they are 'normally provided for remuneration'. The Court of Justice considered the essential characteristic of remuneration in the following case:

Belgium v *Humbel* (Case 263/86)

The Court of Justice said that 'the essential characteristic of remuneration is that it constitutes the countervailing financial advantage for the services in question and is normally fixed between the supplier and the recipient of the service'. The Court held, on this basis, that courses of study provided in the framework of a national educational system were not provided for remuneration. The situation was not affected by the fact that students had to pay a registration fee or some other charge. By establishing and maintaining a national educational system, 'the State does not intend to engage in activities for which remuneration is received, but is fulfilling its duty to its people in the social, cultural and educational fields' (paras 17 and 18).

Education can, however, constitute a service if it is provided by a private body on a commercial basis (see **Luisi and Carbone** *v* **Ministero del Tesoro** (Case 286/83)). The services are, therefore, either of a commercial character, or they are, at least, provided in exchange for money or money's worth.

In contrast, in **Geraets-Smits** *v* **Stichting Ziekenfonds** and **Peerbooms** *v* **Stichting CZ Groep Zorgverzekeringen** (Case C–157/99), the Court of Justice held that the fact that hospital medical treatment is financed directly by sickness insurance funds on the basis of agreements and pre-set scales of fees does not remove such treatment from the sphere of services within the meaning of Art 50 EC Treaty. Article 50 EC Treaty does not require the service to be paid for by those for whom it is performed. The Court stated that the essential characteristic of remuneration lies in the fact that it constitutes consideration for the service in question.

The Court of Justice has also held that there must be an *economic* link in order to come within the provisions of the Treaty:

SPUC v *Grogan* (Case C-159/90)

Ireland had a restriction on the publication of information about the provision of abortion in other Member States (abortion was (and remains) illegal in Ireland). A Students' Union in Dublin provided information about abortion services which were lawfully available in London. This practice was challenged before the Irish Courts by the Society for the Protection of Unborn Children (SPUC). The matter was referred by the national court to the Court of Justice pursuant to the former Art 177 EC Treaty (now Art 234).

The Court of Justice held that the provision of abortion could constitute a service. However, the Court held that because the Students' Union was not distributing the information *on behalf of the economic operators* (i.e. the clinics providing the service (abortions)) Ireland could restrain its activity. The Students' Union had no economic link with the clinics – it was not being paid.

The above case may have been decided differently if the clinics themselves had been advertising their services, because clearly there would have been an *economic link*, or if the Students' Union had been acting as the agent of the clinics (and was being paid). This case was also politically sensitive given that abortion was illegal under Ireland's constitution. There could therefore have been strong policy considerations for the Court's decision.

Meaning of 'service'

The Court of Justice considered the meaning of 'service' in the following case:

Schindler (Case C-275/92)

The undertakings concerned were agents of four local state lotteries in Germany. They sent letters from The Netherlands to the UK enclosing application forms with invitations to participate in the German lotteries. The letters were confiscated by Customs and Excise on the grounds that they infringed national legislation on lotteries and gaming. The Court of Justice held that the letters were not 'goods', so the restrictions did not fall to be considered under Art 29 EC Treaty. The Court then went on to determine whether or not they were a 'service'.

The Court decided that they were a service. The services provided by the operators of the lottery enabled purchasers of tickets to participate in a game of chance with the hope of winning, by arranging for that purpose for the stakes to be collected, the draws to be organised, and the prizes for winnings to be ascertained and paid out. The services were 'normally provided for remuneration', represented by the price of the lottery ticket. They were cross-border, since they were offered in a Member State other than that in which the lottery operator was established.

The Court of Justice reached a similar conclusion in relation to the offer of financial services by telephone to potential recipients in another state (**Alpine Investments BV *v* Minister van Financiën** (Case C–384/93)), and similarly in relation to the provision of insurance (**Safir *v* Skattemyndigheten i Dalarnas Lan** (Case C–118/96); **Skandia and Ramstedt** (Case C–422/01)). As previously discussed, in **Geraets-Smits *v* Stichting Ziekenfonds** and **Peerbooms *v* Stichting CZ Groep Zorgverzekeringen** (Case C–157/99), the Court of Justice held that *medical activities* fall within the scope of Art 50 EC Treaty and there is no need to distinguish between care provided in a hospital environment and care provided outside such an environment.

In **Konsumentombudsmannen (KO) *v* Gourmet International Products AB (GIP)** (Case C–405/98) the Court of Justice held that the Treaty provisions on freedom to provide services precluded a prohibition on the advertising of alcoholic beverages because it had a particular effect on the cross-border supply of advertising space, given the international nature of the advertising market in the category of products to which the prohibition related. Such a prohibition (i.e. the *advertising* of goods) therefore constitutes a restriction on the freedom to provide services within the meaning of Art 49 EC Treaty.

The Court, however, held that such a restriction may be justified by the protection of public health, which is a ground of general interest recognised by Art 46 EC Treaty, and which is applicable to the provision of services in accordance with Art 55 EC Treaty. This is discussed further within Chapter 15.

Providers of services and their workers

Services may be provided by sole traders, companies or partnerships. If the providers are companies, they do not need to be owned or controlled by nationals of the Member State in which they are based, nor do the employees of the company providing a service in another Member State have to be EU citizens. The service provider should be able to operate in other Member States without restriction, as illustrated in the following case:

Van der Elst v *OMI* (Case C-43/93)

The claimant operated a demolition company which was established in Belgium. He employed a number of foreign workers, many of them from Morocco. They had work permits and were lawfully employed in Belgium. The company was engaged to carry out a demolition contract in France. Foreign employees were not permitted by the French authorities to work on the contract without French work permits. The national court referred the case to the Court of Justice under the former Art 177 EC Treaty (now Art 234). The Court of Justice held that the Belgian undertaking was providing a service under Arts 49 and 50 EC Treaty. The question before the Court was whether the company could transfer its workforce to France to service the demolition contract.

The Court of Justice held that where a service is being provided pursuant to Arts 49 and 50 EC Treaty, the provider of the service has the right to post its workforce in the host Member State, irrespective of the workforce's nationality. Any attempt to impose further controls on its workforce would amount to an unlawful restriction on the provision of services. The imposition of further work permit requirements would, the Court said, amount to the duplication of the procedures the company had already gone through in its home state.

Directive 96/71 has since been adopted, which concerns the posting of workers within the context of the provision of services, i.e. where an individual/undertaking provides services in another Member State, and the service provider sends his own workers to the host Member State. The following case relates to the rules which may be enacted by Member States with regard to the employment of workers posted from another Member State, in the light of Directive 96/71:

Commission v *Germany* (Case C-341/02)

The Commission brought an action against Germany for failure to fulfil its Treaty obligations, and questioning the compatibility with Directive 96/71 of the method applied by Germany for the purpose of comparing the minimum wage fixed by national German provisions with the remuneration which was actually paid by an employer established in another Member State.

In its action, the Commission criticised Germany for not recognising, as constituent elements of the minimum wage, all of the allowances and supplements paid by employers established in other Member States to their employees in the construction industry posted to Germany, with the exception of a bonus which is granted to workers in that industry. According to the Commission, the failure to take these allowances and supplements into account resulted - by reason of the different methods of calculating remuneration in other Member States - in higher wage costs for employers established in other Member States, who were thus prevented from offering their services in Germany. While the Commission acknowledged that the host Member State is allowed to determine, under Directive 96/71, the minimum rate of pay, the fact nonetheless remains that that Member State cannot, in comparing that rate and the wages paid by employers established in other Member States, impose its own payment structure.

The German government contested that argument, contending that hours worked outside the normal working hours (i.e. overtime) have a greater economic value than normal working hours and that the bonuses relating to such hours must not be taken into account in the calculation of the minimum wage.

The Court of Justice began by taking note that the parties were in agreement that, in accordance with Directive 96/71, account need not be taken, as component elements of the minimum wage, of payment for overtime, contributions to supplementary occupational retirement pension schemes, the amounts paid in respect of reimbursement of expenses actually incurred by reason of the posting and, finally, flat-rate sums calculated on a basis other than that of the hourly rate. **It is the gross amounts of wages that must be taken into account.**

The Court then stated that, in the course of the proceedings, Germany had adopted and proposed a number of amendments to its rules, which the Court considered appropriate for removing several of the inconsistencies between German law and the Directive. These included, *inter alia*, the taking into account of allowances and supplements paid by an employer which, in the calculation of the minimum wage, do not alter the relationship between the service provided by the worker and the consideration which he receives in return, and the taking into account, under certain conditions, of the bonuses in respect of the 13th and 14th salary months. However, those amendments were made after the expiry of the period laid down in the reasoned opinion, that is to say too late to be taken into consideration by the Court. Therefore, the Court had to declare that Germany had failed to fulfil its obligations.

Finally, the Court observed that it is entirely normal that, if an employer requires a worker to carry out additional work or to work under particular conditions, compensation should be provided to the worker for those additional services without it being taken into account for the purpose of calculating the minimum wage. Directive 96/71 does not require that such forms of compensation, which, if taken into account in the calculation of the minimum wage, alter the relationship between the service provided and the consideration received in return, be treated as elements of the minimum wage. The Court accordingly dismissed the Commission's action on that point.

The following case, decided by the Court of Justice in 2006, also concerned posted workers:

Commission v Germany (Case C-244/04)

Germany's Law on Aliens governs the posting of employed persons who are nationals of a non-Member State. That law provides that foreigners intending to reside for more than three months on German territory and to pursue paid employment there must be in possession of a specific residence visa. Thus, undertakings seeking to provide services in Germany must ensure that their workers from non-Member States obtain a visa from the German diplomatic representation in the Member State where the undertaking is established. As regards the detailed rules for the issue of that visa, a circular lays down that the German diplomatic representation is to satisfy itself, in advance, that, among other criteria, the worker has been employed for at least a year by the undertaking which intends to effect the posting.

The Commission brought this action against Germany pursuant to Art 226 EC Treaty, because of Germany's alleged breach of the Community law provisions on the freedom to provide services.

The Court of Justice held that a prior check may make it more difficult, or even impossible, to exercise the freedom to provide services through posted workers who are nationals of non-Member States, and thus constituted a breach of the Treaty provisions. The Court also held that the requirement of at least a year's prior employment by the undertaking effecting the posting constituted a restriction on the freedom to provide services.

Consequently, the Court of Justice concluded that Germany had infringed the provisions on the freedom to provide services.

Objective justification

As with the free movement of workers, if a restriction on the freedom to provide services is found to exist the Member State can seek to justify it on grounds of public policy, public security or public health (Art 46 EC Treaty, which is applicable by reason of Art 55). This is considered in Chapter 15.

The freedom to provide services may also be restricted by rules which are justified by overriding reasons in the general interest, provided the rules are applied to all persons and undertakings operating in the territory of the Member State where the service is provided. The restriction will not be justified if the reason for the restriction is safeguarded by the rules to which the provider of the service is subject in the Member State where he is established (see, in particular, **Commission v Italy** (Case C–180/89), and **Commission v Greece** (Case C–198/89), para 18). This objective justification defence will only apply to restrictions which are indirectly discriminatory or to those which are non-discriminatory. It is similar to the application of the '**Cassis** rule of reason' relating to the free movement of goods (see Chapter 18).

The nature of the defence was discussed by the Court of Justice in the following case, which concerned a restriction that the provider of the service must satisfy a residence requirement:

Van Binsbergen v Bestuur van de Bedrijfsvereniging voor de Metaalnijverheid (Case 33/74)

A Dutch national acted as legal adviser to the applicant in relation to legal proceedings before a Dutch court. The legal adviser moved to Belgium during the course of the proceedings and was told that he could no longer represent the applicant because under Dutch law only persons established in The Netherlands could act as legal advisers. The national court referred the matter to the Court of Justice under the former Art 177 EC Treaty (now Art 234) to determine whether or not the Dutch rule was compatible with the former Art 59 EC Treaty (now Art 49). It was undoubtedly indirectly discriminatory because it would be more difficult for a non-national to satisfy than a national. The Court of Justice held that this restriction was contrary to the former Art 59 because it was excessive. However, the Court acknowledged that not every restriction would be incompatible with the former Art 59:

12. However, taking into account the particular nature of the services to be provided, specific requirements imposed on the person providing the service cannot be considered incompatible with the
Treaty where they have as their purpose the application of professional rules justified by the
general good - in particular rules relating to the organisation, qualifications, professional ethics,
supervision and liability - which are binding upon any person established in the State in which the
service is provided, where the person providing the service would escape from the ambit of those
rules by being established in another Member State.

. . .

14. In accordance with those principles, the requirement that persons whose functions are to
assist the administration of justice must be permanently established for professional purposes within the jurisdiction of certain courts or tribunals cannot be considered incompatible
with the provisions of Articles 59 and 60 [now Arts 49 and 50], where such requirement is
objectively justified by the need to ensure observance of professional rules of conduct connected, in particular, with the administration of justice and with respect for professional
ethics.

The above case established that for an indirectly discriminatory or non-discriminatory
restriction to the provision of a service to be compatible with Art 49 (previously Art 59)
the restriction must:

1. be adopted in pursuance of a legitimate public interest, which is not incompatible
   with Community aims (some of these Community aims are set out at para 12 above
   (e.g. observance of professional ethics));

2. be equally applicable to persons established within the Member State and which
   would be avoided if the person providing the service was established in another
   Member State; and

3. be objectively justified. This involves an application of the proportionality test, i.e.:

   - is there a 'genuine need' for the restriction;

   - is the restriction appropriate to achieve the aim of such 'genuine need'; and

   - could the aim of such 'genuine need' which is being pursued by the restriction, be
     satisfied by other, less restrictive means?

In **Van Binsbergen**, the Court of Justice held that the public interest in the proper
administration of justice could be achieved by a less restrictive means (i.e. it did not
satisfy the proportionality test). Rather than a *place of residence* within the jurisdiction, an
address for service within the jurisdiction could have been imposed.

The Court of Justice further defined the scope of the objective justification defence in
the following case:

Criminal Proceedings against Webb (Case 279/80)

Webb was the manager of a company which was established in the UK and which was
licensed by the UK authorities to act as an agent for the supply of manpower. The company
was paid to recruit temporary technical staff for employment by a business located in The
Netherlands. Webb was prosecuted for having supplied workers without the necessary
licence issued by the Dutch authorities. The case was referred to the Court under the former
Art 177 EC Treaty (now Art 234) to consider the compatibility of the licence requirement with
the former Art 59 EC Treaty (now Art 49). In this case, the service being provided was the
provision of manpower (from the UK to The Netherlands). The restriction to the freedom to

provide services, which was under challenge, was the Dutch licence requirement. The Court of Justice held as follows:

> 17. In Cases 110 and 111/78 **Van Wesemael** [1979] ECR 35, the Court held that, regard being had to the particular nature of certain services, specific requirements imposed on the provider of the services cannot be considered incompatible with the Treaty where they have as their purpose the application of rules governing such activities. However, **the freedom to provide services is one of the fundamental principles of the Treaty and may be restricted only by provisions which are justified by the general good and which are imposed on all persons or undertakings operating in the said State in so far as that interest is not safeguarded by the provisions to which the provider of the service is subject in the Member State of his establishment.**
>
> ...
>
> 20. Such a measure would be excessive in relation to the aim pursued, however, if the requirements to which the issue of a licence is subject coincided with the proofs and guarantees required in the State of establishment. In order to maintain the principle of freedom to provide services **the first requirement is that in considering applications for licences and in granting them, the Member State in which the service is to be provided may not make any distinction based on the nationality of the provider of the services or the place of his establishment; the second requirement is that it must take into account the evidence and guarantees already furnished by the provider of the services for the pursuit of his activities in the Member State of his establishment.** [emphasis added]

In the above case, the Court of Justice (at para 20) set out three conditions which needed to be satisfied in order for the restriction to be objectively justified. The three conditions (similar to those established by the Court in **Van Binsbergen**) are that the restriction must:

- ■ pursue a justified aim;
- ■ be equally applicable to nationals, non-nationals and those established within and outside the Member State alike; and
- ■ not be any more restrictive or burdensome than is necessary (i.e. an application of the proportionality test).

This approach was followed by the Court of Justice in the following case:

Questore di Verona v Diego Zenatti (Case C-67/98)

Italian law made it a criminal offence to conduct or organise games of chance, and prohibited the organisation of games or betting, which were reserved to the state or to organisations holding a state concession. Betting licences were granted by the state to two organisations, which were required to serve to promote sporting activities through investments in sports facilities, especially in the poorest regions and in the peripheral areas of large cities, and to support equine sports and the breeding of horses. The restriction was intended to satisfy social policy concerns (relating to the harmful effects of gambling) and the concern to prevent fraud. These two organisations could authorise other persons and bodies who could offer appropriate safeguards.

Mr Zenatti (Z) had acted as an intermediary in Italy for the London company SSP Overseas Betting Ltd (SSP), a licensed bookmaker. Z ran an information exchange for the Italian customers of SSP in relation to bets on foreign sports events. He would send to London, by fax or Internet, forms which had been filled in by customers, together with bank transfer forms, and he would receive faxes from SSP for transmission to the same customers.

Action was taken against Z because he had not been licensed to provide such a service in Italy, and he was ordered by the national court to cease the activity. The Italian court referred the case to the Court of Justice pursuant to the former Art 177 EC Treaty (now Art 234), to consider whether the restriction was compatible with the Community law provisions on the freedom to provide services. The Court of Justice held as follows:

> The Italian legislation, inasmuch as it prohibits the taking of bets by any person or body other than those which may be licensed to do so, applies without distinction to all operators who might be interested in such an activity, whether established in Italy or in another Member State.
>
> However, such legislation constitutes an obstacle to the freedom to provide services.
>
> **The Court thus verifies whether that restriction on the freedom to provide services is permissible under the exceptions expressly provided for by the Treaty or is justified, in accordance with the case law of the Court, by overriding reasons relating to the public interest.**
>
> The legislation at issue in the main proceedings pursues objectives similar to those pursued by the UK legislation on lotteries, as identified by the Court in **Schindler**, since it seeks to prevent such gaming from being a source of private profit, to avoid risks of crime and fraud and the damaging individual and social consequences of the incitement to spend which it represents and to allow it only to the extent to which it may be socially useful as being conducive to the proper conduct of competitive sports.
>
> **Those objectives must be considered together. They concern the protection of the recipients of the service and, more generally, of consumers as well as the maintenance of order in society and have already been held to rank among those objectives which may be regarded as constituting overriding reasons relating to the public interest. Moreover, measures based on such reasons must be suitable for securing attainment of the objectives pursued and not go beyond what is necessary to attain them.**
>
> Determination of the scope of the protection which a Member State intends providing in its territory in relation to lotteries and other forms of gambling falls within the margin of appreciation which the Court recognised as being enjoyed by the national authorities. It is for those authorities to consider whether, in the context of the aim pursued, it is necessary to prohibit activities of that kind, totally or partially, or only to restrict them and lay down more or less rigorous procedures for controlling them.
>
> The provisions adopted must be assessed solely in the light of the objectives pursued by the national authorities of the Member State concerned and of the level of protection which they seek to ensure.
>
> The fact that the games in issue are not totally prohibited is not enough to show that the national legislation is not in reality intended to achieve the public-interest objectives at which it is purportedly aimed, which must be considered as a whole. Limited authorisation of gambling on the basis of special or exclusive rights granted or assigned to certain bodies, which has the advantage of confining the desire to gamble and the exploitation of gambling within controlled channels, of preventing the risk of fraud or crime in the context of such exploitation, and of using the resulting profits for public-interest purposes, likewise falls within the ambit of those objectives.
>
> **However, such a limitation is acceptable only if, from the outset, it reflects a concern to bring about a genuine diminution in gambling opportunities and if the financing of social activities through a levy on the proceeds of authorised games constitutes only an incidental beneficial consequence and not the real justification for the restrictive policy adopted. Even if it is not irrelevant that lotteries and other types of gambling may contribute significantly to the financing of benevolent or public-interest activities, that motive cannot in itself be regarded as an objective justification for restrictions on the freedom to provide services.**
>
> It is for the national court to verify whether, having regard to the specific rules governing its application, the national legislation is genuinely directed to realising the objectives which are capable of justifying it and whether the restrictions which it imposes do not appear disproportionate in the light of those objectives. [emphasis added]

In the above case, the Court of Justice held that the EC Treaty provisions on the freedom to provide services do not prevent national legislation reserving to certain bodies the right to take bets on sporting events, provided that that legislation is justified by social policy objectives which are intended to limit the harmful effects of such activities and if the restrictions which it imposes are not disproportionate in relation to those objectives. The Court further held that where a contribution is made from the profits of the autho-rised provider to benevolent activities, that should constitute only an *incidental beneficial concern*. It should not be the real justification for the restriction. The justification must be based on overriding reasons relating to the public interest (e.g. confining the desire to gamble; preventing the risk of fraud or other criminal activity).

The Court of Justice had to adjudicate on betting over the Internet in **Gambelli** (Case C–243/01). The Court held that Italian legislation, which made it punishable as a criminal offence, without a concession or licence from the state, to collect, accept, reg-ister or transmit proposed bets, particularly on sporting events via the Internet, was contrary to Arts 43 and 49 EC Treaty. However, the Court held that the restriction could be objectively justified on moral, religious and/or cultural grounds. In deciding whether or not the restriction was objectively justified, consideration could be given to the morally and financially harmful consequences for the individual and society.

The three **Van Binsbergen** conditions were applied by the Court of Justice in **Commission** *v* **France** (Case C–262/02). This case concerned a French regulation that French broadcasters could only transmit sporting events taking place in another Member State if any advertising for alcoholic beverages was removed. The French sought to justify the restriction on public health grounds. The Court of Justice held that although the French regulation was in breach of Art 59 EC Treaty (now Art 49), it was objectively jus-tified, and it was proportionate.

The **Van Binsbergen** case made it clear (at para 20) that the proportionality test requires additionally that any restrictions imposed by the Member State in which the provider is established should be taken into consideration, as it may duplicate the restric-tive measures. For example, where a licence is required, both Member States may have licensing requirements. Therefore the licence requirement of the Member State in which the service is to be provided may not be necessary. This is illustrated in the following case:

Jean-Claude Arblade, Arblade & Fils SARL; Bernard Leloup, Serge Leloup, Sofrage SARL (Cases C-369 and 376/96)

The Court of Justice had to decide whether a company established within the Community, which provided services in another Member State and posted its own workforce in the host Member State for the duration of the contract, had to comply with the host state's social legislation designed to safeguard the rights of workers (e.g. a requirement that certain social and labour documents had to be kept). The Court held that this constituted a restriction on the freedom to provide services within the meaning of Art 49 EC Treaty. However, it held that the restriction could be justified (and would therefore be compatible with the Treaty obli-gations) if it was necessary in order to safeguard, effectively and by appropriate means, the overriding public interest which the social protection of workers represents. Nevertheless, the Court stated that the national court would also have to assess whether the objective of the host state's legislation is satisfied by legislation which the service provider has to comply with in his home Member State, in which case the restriction could not be justified. The Court of Justice stated that this will be the case where:

... the undertaking is already subject, in the Member State in which it is established, to obligations which are comparable, as regards their objective of safeguarding the interests of workers, to those imposed by the legislation of the host Member State, and which relate to the same workers and the same periods of activity.

While the Court is reluctant to recognise new 'overriding interests in the general interest', it will, in exceptional circumstances, accept that such interests enable a Member State to impose a total ban on the import of the service in question, even when it is permitted, within strict limitations, in the Member State imposing the ban (**Schindler**, above).

The case of **Geraets-Smits** *v* **Stichting Ziekenfonds** and **Peerbooms** *v* **Stichting CZ Groep Zorgverzekeringen** (Case C–157/99) considered the application of objective justification in the context of recipients of services, and therefore it is considered in the next section.

Recipients of services

Article 49 EC Treaty expressly refers to the freedom to provide services but does not mention the recipient. However, secondary legislation does acknowledge the recipient: Directive 64/221 protected the position of a recipient of services who resided in or travelled to another Member State for that purpose; Art 1(b), Directive 73/148 required the abolition of restrictions on the movement and residence of nationals wishing to go to another Member State as recipients (as well as providers) of services. These two directives have been repealed and replaced by Directive 2004/38, which, as discussed above, creates a general right of entry and residence for up to three months for all EU citizens and their family members without any conditions or formalities, other than the requirement to hold a valid identity card or passport, or, in the case of non-EU family members, a passport (Art 6). Article 7, Directive 2004/38 creates a right of extended residence in excess of three months for EU citizens and their family members who, *inter alia*, are economically self-sufficient (i.e. who have sufficient resources for themselves and their family members not to become a burden on the social assistance system of the host Member State during their period of residence and have comprehensive sickness insurance cover in the host Member State).

In the following case, the Court of Justice held that the EC Treaty Articles cover the recipients of services:

Luisi and Carbone v *Ministero del Tesoro* (Cases 286/82 and 26/83)

The applicants were Italian nationals who were prosecuted for attempting to export more than the legal maximum of Italian currency for use abroad. They argued that they had exported it for use within the Community to pay for services as tourists and to purchase medical treatment. They further argued that the currency restrictions were contrary to Community law. The Court was asked whether the restrictions were covered by the rules on the payment for services covered by the former Arts 106(1), 59 and 60 EC Treaty (now Arts 107, 49 and 50 EC Treaty). The Court of Justice held as follows:

10. By virtue of Article 59 [now Art 49] of the Treaty, restrictions on freedom to provide such services are to be abolished in respect of nationals of Member States who are established in a Member

State other than that of the person for whom the service is intended. **In order to enable services to be provided, the person providing the services may go to the Member State where the person for whom it is to be provided is established or else the latter may go to the State in which the person providing the service is established. Whilst the former case is expressly mentioned in the third paragraph of Article 60 [now Art 50], which permits the person providing the service to pursue his activity temporarily in the Member State where the service is provided, the latter case is the necessary corollary thereof, which fulfils the objective of liberalising all gainful activity not covered by the free movement of goods, persons and capital**

...

16. It follows that the freedom to provide services includes the freedom, for the recipient of services, to go to another Member State in order to receive a service there, without being obstructed by restrictions, even in relation to payments and that tourists, persons receiving medical treatment and persons travelling for the purposes of education or business are to be regarded as recipients of services. [emphasis added]

In the above case, the Court of Justice held that tourism itself was a service which was covered by the former Art 59 (now Art 49). In **Cowan** *v* **Le Trésor Public** (Case 186/87), the Court of Justice declared that tourists were entitled to full equal treatment under Art 12 EC Treaty, and that equal treatment included access to the criminal process and to national provisions on criminal injuries compensation. In addition, leisure activities pursued by recipients of services from other Member States must not be subject to discriminatory treatment (**Commission** *v* **Greece** (Case C–62/96); **Commission** *v* **Spain** (Case C–45/93); **Commission** *v* **Italy** (Case C–388/01)). Equal treatment under Art 12 EC Treaty, within the context of Art 49 EC Treaty, is considered in more detail below.

Recipients of services were, like providers, entitled to remain in the host Member State only for as long as the service was received. However, given the breadth of the concept of 'services', it would seem that any EU citizen or national of an EEA state could remain in another Member State for as long as he was paying for a service. He could, for example, be paying for accommodation out of his own resources. As long as he was relying exclusively on his own resources, however modest, he was providing 'remuneration' and would seem to be entitled to remain under Arts 49 and 50 EC Treaty; and see **Belgium** *v* **Humbel** (Case 263/86). Article 7, Directive 2004/38 now makes this explicitly clear. As discussed above, Art 7 creates a right of extended residence (for more than three months) for EU citizens and their family members who, *inter alia*, are economically self-sufficient.

Objective justification

As discussed above in the context of providers of services, the freedom to provide services may be restricted by rules which are justified by overriding reasons in the general interest. The following case concerned the application of objective justification within the context of recipients of services:

Geraets-Smits v *Stichting Ziekenfonds* and *Peerbooms* v *Stichting CZ Groep Zorgverzekeringen* (Case C-157/99)

The case concerned two Dutch citizens who were resident in The Netherlands. Payment for medical treatment was made by the appropriate sickness insurance fund. The fund holder reached agreements with providers within The Netherlands for the payment of particular hospital and medical services. Although a person could go to another Member State to

receive medical services, Dutch legislation provided that this was subject to prior authorisation which would only be granted if: (i) the proposed treatment is among the benefits for
which the sickness insurance scheme assumes responsibility, which means that the treatment must be regarded as 'normal in the professional circles concerned'; and (ii) the
treatment abroad is necessary in terms of the medical condition of the person concerned,
which supposes that adequate care cannot be provided without undue delay by a care
provider which has entered into an agreement with the sickness insurance fund in The
Netherlands.

The facts of the case were that Geraets-Smits (the first applicant) left The Netherlands to
seek treatment in Germany for Parkinson's disease. Her application to the sickness insurance
fund was rejected because (i) the treatment she received was not regarded as 'normal treatment within the professional circles concerned' because the specific type of treatment she
received in Germany was not considered any better than that she would have received in The
Netherlands; and (ii) satisfactory and adequate treatment was available in The Netherlands
at an establishment which had an agreement with the sickness insurance fund.

Peerbooms (the second applicant) left The Netherlands to seek treatment in Austria when
he fell into a coma following a road accident. His application was also refused by the sickness
insurance fund on the same grounds that Geraets-Smits's application was refused.

The national court referred the case to the Court of Justice pursuant to the former Art
177 EC Treaty (now Art 234).

The Court of Justice stated that Member States have the power to organise their social
security schemes (in this case medical insurance funds) and to determine the conditions concerning the right or duty to be insured with a social security scheme. However, Member
States must comply with Community law when exercising this power.

Medical activities fall within the scope of Art 50 EC Treaty (see above). The fact that the
national legislation at issue is social security legislation does not exclude the application of
Arts 49 and 50 EC Treaty. When considering the two conditions (established by national
legislation) which were applied by the sickness insurance funds, Art 49 EC Treaty precludes
the application of any national rules which have the effect of making the provision of services between Member States more difficult than the provision of services purely within one
Member State. The Court held that the necessity to obtain prior authorisation which will only
be granted if the two conditions are satisfied deters, or even prevents, insured persons from
applying to providers of medical services established in another Member State and therefore
constitutes, both for insured persons and service providers, a barrier to the freedom to
provide services.

The Court then had to determine whether or not these conditions could be objectively justified.

The Court recognised that, as regards the objective of maintaining a balanced medical and
hospital service open to all, that objective, even if intrinsically linked to the method of
financing the social security system, may also fall within the derogations on grounds of
public health under Art 46 EC Treaty, in so far as the objective contributes to the attainment
of a high level of health protection. The Court also stated that Art 46 EC Treaty permits
Member States to restrict the freedom to provide medical and hospital services in so far as
the maintenance of treatment capacity or medical competence on national territory is essential for the public health, and even the survival, of the population.

The Court stated that it was necessary to determine whether the national legislation at
issue in these proceedings can actually be justified in the light of these overriding reasons

and, in such a case, to ensure that (i) they do not exceed what is objectively necessary for that purpose; and (ii) the same result cannot be achieved by less restrictive rules. This is an application of the proportionality test.

With regard to the prior authorisation requirement, the Court held that this does not breach Community law. However, the two conditions which are attached to the grant of such authorisation must be justified with regard to the overriding considerations considered above, and must also satisfy the requirement of proportionality.

With regard to the condition that the proposed treatment is 'normal', the Court noted that in applying this condition the Dutch sickness insurance funds only considered what was 'normal' within Dutch medical circles. Although the Court stated that it is open to a Member State to limit its costs by excluding certain products or hospital and medical treatments from reimbursement under its social security scheme, the Court held that in determining what is 'normal', consideration should be given to wider international medical views, i.e. it is necessary to consider what is normal according to the state of international medical science, and medical standards which are generally accepted at international level.

With regard to the condition concerning the 'necessity' of the proposed treatment, the Court held that this was justified provided that the condition is construed to the effect that authorisation to receive treatment in another Member State may be refused on that ground only if the same or equally effective treatment can be obtained without undue delay from an establishment with which the insured person's sickness insurance fund has contractual arrangements.

In following case, the Court of Justice confirmed its position in **Smits** and **Peerbooms**, with regard to the following two conditions: (i) making repayment of medical expenses incurred in a Member State other than that of affiliation subject to a requirement of prior authorisation; and (ii) providing that such prior authorisation will only be issued in the case of medical necessity. The Court proceeded to consider the issue of objective justification:

Müller-Fauré and van Riet (C-385/99)

In order to establish whether or not the national legislation requiring prior authorisation was objectively justified, the Court distinguished between *hospital care* and *non-hospital care*. With regard to *hospital care*, making repayment of medical expenses subject to prior acceptance of financial responsibility by the national social security system in cases where such care was provided in a Member State other than that of affiliation was, in the Court's view, a measure both reasonable and necessary. This did not compromise the planning of such care operated through the system of health service agreements (**Smits** and **Peerbooms**). That planning is designed to ensure that there is sufficient and permanent accessibility to a balanced range of high-quality hospital treatment and to control costs, preventing, as far as possible, any wastage of financial, technical and human resources. The Court did, however, go on to hold that, for the system of prior authorisation to be capable of operating, the conditions placed on the granting of such authorisation must be justified and satisfy the requirement of proportionality. Similarly, a scheme of prior administrative authorisation could not legitimise discretionary decisions taken by the national authorities which were liable to negate the effectiveness of Community law provisions on the freedom to provide services. Such a scheme therefore had to be based on objective, non-discriminatory criteria which were known in advance, in such a way as to circumscribe the exercise of the national authorities' discretion, so that it was not used arbitrarily (**Smits** and **Peerbooms**).

Finally, still following **Smits** and **Peerbooms**, the Court held that the condition which specified that treatment must be 'necessary' may be justified under Art 49 EC Treaty provided that it is interpreted as meaning that prior authorisation may be refused only where treatment which is the same or equally effective for the patient can be obtained without undue delay, within the state of affiliation, from an establishment with which the insured person's sickness insurance fund has an agreement.

With regard to *non-hospital care*, the Court held that the information in the documents brought before it for assessment did not demonstrate that removing the requirement for prior authorisation would cause cross-border movements of patients so large as to seriously undermine the financial stability of the social security system and thereby threaten the overall level of public health protection. Furthermore, such care is generally provided near to the place where the patient resides, in a cultural environment which is familiar to him and which allows him to build up a relationship of trust with the doctor treating him. Those factors were likely to limit any possible financial impact on the national social security system in question of removing the requirement for prior authorisation in respect of care provided in foreign practitioners' surgeries. Bearing in mind that it was for the Member States alone to determine the extent of the sickness cover available to insured persons, and finding that, in this case, the actual amount in respect of which reimbursement was sought was relatively small (para 106), the Court concluded that removing the requirement for prior authorisation issued by sickness funds to their insured persons, so as to enable them to benefit from such healthcare provided in a Member State other than the state of affiliation, was not likely to undermine the essential features of the sickness insurance scheme in question. The system requiring such prior authorisation for *non-hospital care* was therefore incompatible with the former Art 59 EC Treaty (now Art 49).

In the above case, the Court of Justice distinguished between hospital care and non-hospital care. In the case of hospital care, the Court held that the restrictions imposed by national legislation (requiring prior authorisation etc.) were *prima facie* compatible with Community law, provided such restrictions were necessary and proportionate. However, in the case of non-hospital care, the Court held that such restrictions were incompatible with Community law because they could not be objectively justified *per se*.

In the following case, the Court of Justice referred to its judgments in **Smits** and **Peerbooms**, and **Müller-Fauré and van Riet**, in the context of restrictions imposed on persons seeking to travel to another Member State to seek hospital treatment:

Inizan (Case C-56/01)

The Court of Justice was required to consider whether a national system established by Art 22(1)(c)(i) and (2), Regulation 1408/71 was compatible with Arts 49 and 50 EC Treaty. This system (i) required that the competent social security institution give prior authorisation before assuming financial responsibility for benefits-in-kind provided to the affiliated person on its behalf by the institution where the affiliated person was staying; and (ii) made the grant of such authorisation subject to conditions.

The Court examined the compatibility with Art 22(1)(c)(i) and (2), Regulation 1408/71 and Arts 49 EC and 50 EC Treaty, of the conditions for granting prior authorisation for the reimbursement of care costs incurred in a Member State other than the affiliated person's state of residence.

With regard to Regulation 1408/71, the Court considered the condition which stipulated that the treatment which the patient intends to undergo in a Member State other than that in which he resides must not be capable of being given to him within the time normally necessary for obtaining the treatment in question in the Member State of residence, taking account of his current state of health and the probable course of the disease. The Court held that this is not fulfilled whenever it appears that an identical course of treatment, or one with the same degree of effectiveness for the patient, may be obtained in time in the Member State of residence. In assessing whether that is the case, the competent institution is required to take into account all the circumstances of each particular case, paying due regard not only to the medical situation of the patient at the time authorisation is applied for and, where appropriate, to the degree of his pain or the nature of his handicap, which might, for example, make it impossible or excessively difficult to work, but also to his previous history (**Smits** and **Peerbooms**, and **Müller-Fauré and van Riet**).

With regard to Arts 49 and 50 EC Treaty, the Court repeated its findings in **Smits** and **Peerbooms**, and **Müller-Fauré and van Riet**. It thus held that those findings do not preclude legislation of a Member State which: (i) makes reimbursement of the cost of hospital care provided in a Member State other than that in which the insured person's sickness fund is established, conditional upon prior authorisation by that fund; and (ii) makes the grant of that authorisation subject to the condition that the insured person could not receive the treatment appropriate to his condition within the territory of the Member State where the fund is established. However, authorisation may be refused on that ground only if treatment which is the same or equally effective for the patient can be obtained without undue delay in the territory of the Member State in which he resides.

In the above case, national legislation required an 'insured person' to obtain prior authorisation prior to travelling to another Member State to receive hospital care. The national legislation stated that such authorisation would only be granted if the 'insured person' could not receive appropriate treatment within his home Member State. The Court of Justice held that authorisation could only be refused if the appropriate treatment (which must be the same or equally effective to that which the insured person was seeking in the other Member State), was available in the insured person's home Member State 'without undue delay'.

In order to facilitate the free movement of 'insured persons' seeking to exercise their Community law rights to travel to another Member State to seek medical treatment, the E112 scheme was introduced across the EU. Under the E112 scheme, the authorising Member State will issue the insured person with an E112 form; this provides proof to the medical services within the host Member State that the insured person has received the necessary authorisation. Application of the E112 scheme was one of the issues which arose in the following recent case:

R, on the application of Yvonne Watts v Bedford Primary Care Trust and the Secretary of State for Health (Case C-372/04)

Under Community law, the E112 scheme enables an application to be made for authorisation to travel abroad in order to receive treatment there. That authorisation cannot be refused where the treatment in question is normally available in the Member State of residence but cannot be provided there in the individual case without undue delay. The health insurance fund is then required to reimburse the cost of treating the patient.

Suffering from arthritis of the hips, Mrs Watts applied to the Bedford PCT (Bedford Primary Care Trust, the primary healthcare fund for Bedford, England) for authorisation to undergo surgery abroad under the E112 scheme. In that context a consultant saw her in October 2002 who classified her case as 'routine', which meant a wait of one year for surgery. The Bedford PCT refused to issue Mrs Watts with an E112 form on the ground that treatment could be provided to the patient 'within the government's NHS Plan targets' and therefore 'without undue delay'. Mrs Watts lodged an application with the High Court for judicial review of the decision refusing authorisation.

Following deterioration in her state of health, she was re-examined in January 2003 and was listed for surgery within three or four months. Bedford PCT repeated its refusal but in March 2003 Mrs Watts underwent a hip replacement operation in France for which she paid £3,900. She therefore continued with her application in the High Court, claiming in addition reimbursement of the medical fees incurred in France. The High Court dismissed the application on the ground that Mrs Watts had not had to face undue delay after the re-examination of her case in January 2003. Both Mrs Watts and the Secretary of State for Health appealed against that judgment. In those circumstances, the Court of Appeal referred to the Court of Justice questions on the scope of Regulation 1408/71 and the Treaty provisions concerning the freedom to provide services.

The scope of Regulation 1408/71 (see Chapter 14)

The Court of Justice stated that under Regulation 1408/71, the competent institution issues prior authorisation for reimbursement of the cost of the treatment provided abroad only if it cannot be provided within the time normally necessary for obtaining the treatment in question in the Member State of residence.

The Court stated that, in order to be entitled to refuse to grant authorisation on the ground of waiting time, the competent institution must establish that the waiting time, arising from objectives relating to the planning and management of the supply of hospital care, does not exceed the period which is acceptable in the light of an objective medical assessment of the clinical needs of the person concerned in the light of his medical condition and the history and probable course of his illness, the degree of pain he is in and/or the nature of his disability at the time when the authorisation is sought.

Furthermore, the setting of waiting times should be done flexibly and dynamically, so that the period initially notified to the person concerned may be reconsidered in the light of any deterioration in his state of health occurring after the first request for authorisation.

In the present case, the Court stated that it was for the referring court to determine whether the waiting time invoked by the competent body of the NHS exceeded a medically acceptable period in the light of the patient's particular condition and clinical needs.

The scope of the freedom to provide services

The Court held that a situation such as that in issue in which a person whose state of health necessitates hospital treatment goes to another Member State and there receives the treatment in question for which payment is made, falls within the scope of the provisions on freedom to provide services regardless of the way in which the national system with which that person is registered and from which reimbursement of those services is subsequently sought operates.

The Court stated that the system of prior authorisation which governs the reimbursement by the NHS of the cost of hospital treatment provided in another Member State deters or even prevents the patients concerned from applying to providers of hospital services established in another Member State and constitutes, both for those patients and for service providers, an obstacle to the freedom to provide services.

However, the Court considered that such a restriction could be justified in the light of overriding reasons. It held that, from the perspective of ensuring that there was sufficient and permanent access to high-quality hospital treatment, controlling costs and preventing, as far as possible, any wastage of financial, technical and human resources, the requirement that the assumption of costs by the national system of hospital treatment provided in another Member State be subject to prior authorisation appeared to be a measure which was both necessary and reasonable.

Nevertheless, the conditions attached to the grant of such authorisation must be justified in the light of the overriding considerations mentioned above and must satisfy the requirement of proportionality. **The regulations on the NHS do not set out the criteria for the grant or refusal of the prior authorisation necessary for reimbursement of the cost of hospital treatment provided in another Member State, and therefore do not circumscribe the exercise of the national competent authorities' discretionary power in that context. The lack of a legal framework in that regard also makes it difficult to exercise judicial review of decisions refusing to grant authorisation.**

The Court held in that regard that, where the delay arising from such waiting lists appears to exceed an acceptable period in the individual case concerned, having regard to an objective medical assessment of all the circumstances of the situation and the patient's clinical needs, **the competent institution may not refuse authorisation on the grounds of the existence of those waiting lists, an alleged distortion of the normal order of priorities linked to the relative urgency of the cases to be treated, the fact that the hospital treatment provided under the national system in question is free of charge, the duty to make available specific funds to reimburse the cost of treatment provided in another Member State and/or a comparison between the cost of that treatment and that of equivalent treatment in the Member State of residence.**

Consequently, the competent authorities of a national health service, such as the NHS, must provide mechanisms for the reimbursement of the cost of hospital treatment in another Member State to patients to whom that service is not able to provide the treatment required within a medically acceptable period.

The mechanism for reimbursement

The Court held that **the patient who was granted authorisation to receive hospital treatment in another Member State (the state of treatment), or received a refusal to authorise which was unfounded, is entitled to reimbursement by the competent institution of the cost of the treatment in accordance with the provisions of the legislation of the state of treatment, as if he was registered in that state.**

Where there is no provision for reimbursement in full, in order to place the patient in the position he would have been in had the national health service with which he is registered been able to provide him free of charge, within a medically acceptable period, with treatment equivalent to that which he received in the host Member State, the competent institution must in addition reimburse him the difference between the cost of that equivalent treatment in the state of residence up to the total amount invoiced for the treatment received in the state of treatment and the amount reimbursed by the institution of that state pursuant to the legislation of that state, where the first amount is greater than the second. Conversely, where the cost charged in the state of treatment is higher than the cost of comparable treatment in the Member State of residence, the competent institution is only required to cover the difference between the cost of the hospital treatment in the two Member States up to the cost of the same treatment in the state of residence.

As regards the travel and accommodation costs, since the obligation on the competent institution exclusively concerns the expenditure connected with the healthcare received by the patient in the Member State of treatment, they are reimbursed only to the extent that the legislation of the Member State of residence imposes a corresponding duty on its national system where the treatment is provided in a local hospital covered by that system.

Details of the E112 scheme, as applied within the UK, are available on the Department of Health's website, at:

> http://www.dh.gov.uk/PolicyAndGuidance/HealthAdviceForTravellers/GettingTreat mentAroundTheWorld/fs/en

The provision of services and rights of establishment

There is a close link between the provision of services by the self-employed and undertakings, and the establishment of businesses in another Member State: one frequently precedes the other. Thus, provisions under Arts 43–48 EC Treaty dealing with establishment, particularly the preliminaries to becoming established, will often overlap with the provision of services. Freedom of establishment includes:

> ... the right to take up and pursue activities as self-employed persons and to set up and manage undertakings, in particular companies and firms ... under the conditions laid down for its own nationals by the law of the country where such establishment is effected.
> (Art 43 EC Treaty)

'Companies and firms' means companies and firms constituted under civil or commercial law, including cooperative societies, and other legal persons governed by public or private law, except for those which are non-profit-making (Art 48). Although the inclusive term 'other legal persons' would seem to exclude the English partnership, since this has no legal personality, this is not in fact the case. The rights both to the provision of services and to establishment belong to both natural and legal persons. In practice, it does not matter whether a partnership enjoys the right to set up branches in another Member State by virtue of being a 'legal person' or a collection of 'natural persons', provided that both have their registered office, central administration or principal place of business within the EU.

Article 43 EC Treaty draws a distinction between nationals of Member States and those already established in the territory of a Member State. Each state defines its own nationals, thereby affording them with the benefits enjoyed by EU citizenship (see Chapter 11). However, an undertaking which does not have its principal office in the EU can set up agencies and branches in other Member States, provided it is established in one of the Member States.

Obstacles to establishment

Article 54 EC Treaty (now Art 44) provided for the drawing up of a general programme for the abolition of restrictions on freedom of establishment within the Community. The Council and Commission sought to give priority treatment to activities where freedom of establishment made a particularly valuable contribution to the development of production and trade, abolish administrative procedures and practices forming obstacles to establishment, and enable nationals of Member States to acquire and use land and buildings. Existing necessary safeguards for the operation of businesses and the professions would be harmonised and coordinated.

The General Programme made under Art 54 (now Art 44) was approved in December 1961. Title III of the Programme called for the abolition of discriminatory measures which could impair access to non-wage-earning activities of Community nationals. The measures to be abolished included the following:

- Provisions which made access to a non-wage-earning activity conditional upon the issue of an official authorisation or the issue of a document, such as a foreign merchant's card or a foreign professional's card.

- The imposition of taxes or other charges which would make access to a business or profession in another Member State more difficult and costly. In **Hayes** *v* **Kronenberger** (Case C–323/95), for example, the Court of Justice held that a requirement that foreign litigants from other Member States pay a sum as security for costs in court proceedings, in circumstances where local nationals were not required to do so, was discriminatory and was liable to have an adverse effect on trade in goods and services between Member States.

- Provisions which barred or limited membership in companies, particularly with regard to the activities of their members.

- Restrictions imposed on foreign nationals in relation to entry into various commercial and other contracts, the right to tender or participate in public works contracts, to borrow and have access to various forms of credit and to have access to loans and grants provided by state agencies.

To give effect to the programme, the Commission drew up a wide range of directives which were intended to facilitate access to a great variety of activities, including itinerant traders, film producers, hairdressers and the providers of gas, water and electricity services. Some of these required specific periods of academic training and practical experience, while others simply required a period of self-employment and a certificate of good character (compare the provisions in Directive 86/653 on self-employed commercial agents with Directive 87/540 on carriers of goods by waterway). It was thought, initially, that until an appropriate directive was in place, national measures would continue to apply and, in many cases, would have the effect of excluding Community nationals from participating in the relevant business or occupation. The right to equality of opportunity provided in Art 43 EC Treaty in relation to establishment and Art 50 EC Treaty in relation to the provision of services relates to the conditions for establishment and self-employment in the host Member State. These may, in many instances, be more difficult for Community nationals to satisfy, despite their overt application to local nationals and Community nationals on the same terms.

In the following case, the Court of Justice held that, like Art 39, Art 43 EC Treaty was directly effective. The fact that Art 43 was to be given effect over a period did not affect the right of the beneficiaries to enjoy immediate protection:

Reyners v *Belgian State* (Case 2/74)

The Court of Justice held that:

> Article 52 [now Art 43] . . . imposes an obligation to attain a precise result, the fulfilment of which had to be made easier by, but not made dependent on, the implementation of a programme of progressive measures. The fact that this progression has not been adhered to leaves the obligation itself intact beyond the end of the period provided for its fulfilment. (paras 26 and 27)

The above case concerned a Dutchman who had been born and educated in Belgium. He was resident in Belgium, and held a doctorate in Belgian law. He was excluded from legal practice in Belgium because he was not a Belgian. The Court of Justice held that this restriction was incompatible with Arts 12 and 43 EC Treaty.

The right of establishment and the right to provide services have been described by the Court of Justice as 'fundamental rights', and the Court has been active in asserting that businesses and the self-employed should have access to activities in Member States without hindrance, or direct or indirect discrimination, even where there were no implementing Community measures. The difficulty, in many of these cases, is that perfectly proper national measures to protect consumers and users of professional services, or to achieve other legitimate objectives have, in the same way as they have in the national context, been used by practitioners to exclude competitors from other Member States. The Court has often had to judge whether a national measure could be objectively justified, or whether it operated as an unlawful restriction. In **Commission** *v* **Italy (Re Freedom of Establishment)** (Case 168/85), the Court of Justice held that national provisions on tourism, the operation of pharmacies and access to the occupation of journalism, which denied access to those not holding Italian nationality, were incompatible with Arts 39, 43 and 49 EC Treaty. It was not sufficient that instructions should be issued disapplying them to EU citizens. They had to be repealed.

In the following case, a UK court referred questions to the Court of Justice for a preliminary ruling in relation to the interpretation of Arts 43 and 48 EC Treaty, and the question of objective justification:

Marks & Spencer (Case C-446/03)

Marks & Spencer, a company resident in the UK, is the principal trading company of a retail group specialising in the sale of off-the-peg clothing, food, homeware and financial services. It had subsidiaries in the UK and in a number of other Member States, including Germany, Belgium and France. In 2001 it ceased trading in continental Europe because of losses incurred from the mid-1990s. On 31 December 2001 the French subsidiary was sold to a third party, while the German and Belgian subsidiaries ceased operating.

In 2000 and 2001, Marks & Spencer submitted claims to the UK tax authorities for group tax relief in respect of the losses incurred by the German, Belgian and French subsidiaries. United Kingdom tax legislation (the Income and Corporation Taxes Act 1988 (ICTA)) allows the parent company of a group, under certain circumstances, to effect an off-set between its profits and losses incurred by its subsidiaries. However, those claims were rejected on the ground that the rules governing group relief do not apply to subsidiaries not resident or trading in the UK. Marks & Spencer appealed against that refusal to the Special Commissioners of Income Tax, which dismissed the appeal. Marks & Spencer then brought an appeal before the English High Court, which decided to stay proceedings and to refer questions to the Court of Justice for a preliminary ruling. The national court was uncertain whether the UK provisions, which prevent a UK-resident parent company from deducting from its taxable profits the losses it has incurred in other Member States by its subsidiaries established there, although they allow it to deduct losses incurred by a resident subsidiary, were compatible with Arts 43 and 48 EC Treaty on the freedom of establishment.

The Court of Justice recalled that, although direct taxation falls within the competence of Member States, national authorities must nonetheless exercise that competence consistently with Community law.

The Court held that the UK legislation constituted a restriction on freedom of establishment, in breach of Arts 43 and 48 EC Treaty, in that it applies different treatment for tax purposes to losses incurred by a resident subsidiary from that applied to losses incurred by a non-resident subsidiary. This would deter parent companies from setting up subsidiaries in other Member States.

However, **the Court acknowledged that such a restriction might be permitted if it pursues a legitimate objective compatible with the Treaty and is justified by imperative reasons in the public interest** (i.e. the restriction may be objectively justified). It is necessary, in such a case, that its application be appropriate to ensuring the attainment of the objective thus pursued and not go beyond what is necessary to attain it.

The Court set out the relevant objective criteria relied upon by Member States and analysed whether the UK legislation justifies the differing treatment applied by it. The criteria put forward were (i) protection of a balanced allocation of the power to impose taxation between the various Member States concerned, so that profits and losses are treated symmetrically in the same tax system; (ii) the fact that the legislation provides for avoidance of the risk of double use of losses which would exist if the losses were taken into account in the Member State of the parent company and in the Member State of the subsidiaries; and (iii) escaping the risk of tax avoidance which would exist if the losses were not taken into account in the Member State where the subsidiary was established, because otherwise the losses which accrue to a group of companies might be transferred to the companies established in the Member States which apply the highest rates of taxation and in which the tax value of the losses is the highest.

The Court held in the light of those criteria that the UK legislation pursues legitimate objectives which are compatible with the EC Treaty and constitute overriding reasons in the public interest.

However, the Court held that the UK legislation does not comply with the principle of proportionality and goes beyond what is necessary to attain the objectives pursued where (i) the non-resident subsidiary has exhausted the possibilities available in the Member State where it is established of having the losses taken into account for the accounting period concerned by the claim for relief and also for previous accounting periods; and (ii) there is no possibility for the foreign subsidiary's losses to be taken into account in the Member State where it is established for future periods either by the subsidiary itself or by a third party, in particular where the subsidiary has been sold to that third party.

Consequently, the Court of Justice held that where, in one Member State, the resident parent company demonstrates to the tax authorities that those conditions are fulfilled, it is contrary to the freedom of establishment to preclude the possibility for the parent company to deduct from its taxable profits in that Member State the losses incurred by its non-resident subsidiary.

Provisions which are less direct than national restrictions may also infringe the rights conferred by Arts 43, 49 and 50 EC Treaty. In a series of cases brought by the Commission under Art 226 EC Treaty, local restrictions on the operation of insurance services were challenged in the Court of Justice. In each of the four Member States concerned, insurance undertakings were required to conduct their business in those states through individuals already established and authorised to practise there (**Commission v Denmark** (Case 252/83); **Commission v France** (Case 220/83); **Commission v Germany** (Case 205/84); **Commission v Ireland** (Case 206/84)). The Court accepted that, in the state of Community law prevailing at the time, the authorisation and licensing of insurance services was still a matter of the law of the host Member State. However, in operating its national system, the host Member State could not duplicate equivalent statutory conditions which have already been satisfied in the Member State where the business has originally been established. Until such time as national rules on company taxation are harmonised throughout the Community, it is permissible for a Member State to impose a restriction on companies, so that they cannot move their principal place of business without the consent of the national tax authorities (**R v HM Treasury, ex parte Daily Mail and General Trust plc** (Case 81/87)). The retention of national company taxation rules should not, however, allow Member States to operate discriminatory tax rules which operate as a barrier to the establishment of branches of foreign undertakings in their territories (**R v IRC, ex parte Commerzbank AG** (Case C330/91)). A similar principle applies, pending the adoption of a common visa policy, in the case of companies which operate in other Member States and employ third-country nationals (**Van der Elst** (Case C–43/93)). Although such national rules may be accepted by the Court of Justice, they will be acceptable only if they meet the qualifications laid down by the Court in the **Gebhard** case (Case C–55/94). National measures liable to hinder or make less attractive the exercise of the fundamental freedoms guaranteed by the Treaty must fulfil four conditions:

1. they must be applied in a non-discriminatory manner;

2. they must be justified by imperative requirements in the general interest;

3. they must be suitable for securing attainment of the objective which they pursue; and

4. they must not go beyond what is necessary to attain the objective.

The Treaty of Amsterdam emphasised the presumption in favour of freedom of establishment and the right to provide services in other Member States by stating that 'the Community and the Member States . . . shall take care that such services operate on the basis of principles and conditions which enable them to fulfil their missions' (Art 16 EC Treaty).

Rights of entry and residence

The former Directive 73/148 was adopted under Title II of the General Programme for the abolition of restrictions on the right of establishment and the provision of services. Its provisions were similar to the former Directive 68/360 in relation to the entry and residence of workers. The Court of Justice does not, in fact, always draw a clear distinction between the rights of entry and residence enjoyed on the basis of being a provider or recipient of services, or being a worker (**Royer** (Case 48/75); **Watson and Belmann** (Case 118/75)). Indeed, where a person enters another Member State, he may not immediately know whether he will set up in business, provide a service or enter into employment. The last status has, however, some distinct benefits, particularly in the area of social advantages, which are not enjoyed by the self-employed (under Art 7(2), Regulation 1612/68 (see Chapter 12)).

Directive 2004/38

Directives 68/360 and 73/148 have been repealed by Directive 2004/38. Directive 2004/38 had to be transposed into national law by 30 April 2006. The directive concerns the right of EU citizens to move and reside freely within the Member States. The provisions of the directive which are relevant to the freedom of establishment, and the free movement of providers and recipients of services, are considered below.

Rights of exit and entry (Articles 4 and 5)

All EU citizens and their family members have the right to leave or enter another Member State by virtue of having a valid identity card or valid passport; in the case of non-EU family members a valid passport is required (Arts 4(1) and 5(1)). Under no circumstances can an entry or exit visa be required (Arts 4(2) and 5(1)).

Article 3(1) provides that the Directive applies to all EU citizens exercising their right to move to, or reside in, a Member State other than that of which they are a national, and to 'family members' who accompany or join them.

Article 2(2) defines 'family members' as the EU citizen's:

(a) spouse;

(b) registered partner, if the legislation of the host Member State treats registered partnerships as equivalent to marriage;

(c) direct descendants (i.e. children, grandchildren, etc.) who are under the age of 21 or who are dependants, and those of the spouse or partner as defined above;

(d) dependent direct relatives in the ascending line (i.e. parents, grandparents, etc.), and those of the spouse or partner as defined above.

This definition of 'family members' has a broader scope than the former definition set out in Art 10(1), Regulation 1612/68 (see Chapter 12). 'Family members' who do not have the nationality of a Member State (i.e. non-EU family members) may be subject to an entry visa requirement under Regulation 539/2001; residence cards will be deemed equivalent to visas (Art 5(2)).

Where the EU citizen or family member does not have the necessary travel documents, the host Member State must afford them every facility to obtain the requisite documents or to have them sent (Art 5(4)).

In addition to family members (as defined by Art 2(2)), Art 3(2) provides that the host Member State shall, in accordance with its national legislation, 'facilitate' entry and residence for the following persons:

(a) any other family members (whether or not they are EU citizens) who are dependants or members of the household of the EU citizen having the primary right of residence, or where serious health grounds strictly require the personal care of the family member by the EU citizen;

(b) the partner with whom the EU citizen has a durable relationship, which is duly attested.

The host Member State is required to undertake an extensive examination of the personal circumstances of such persons and shall justify any denial of entry or residence (Art 3(2)).

Article 5(5) provides that the host Member State may require each person travelling to or residing in another Member State to register their presence in the country within a reasonable and non-discriminatory period of time. Failure to comply with this requirement may make the person liable to a proportionate and non-discriminatory sanction.

General right of residence for a period up to three months (Article 6)

Article 6(1) provides that EU citizens shall have the right of residence in another Member State for a period of up to three months without any conditions or formalities other than the requirement to hold a valid identity card or passport (or a valid passport in the case of non-EU family members).

Article 6(2) provides that 'family members' who do not have the nationality of a Member State (i.e. non-EU family members) enjoy the same rights as the EU citizen who they have accompanied or joined.

The host Member State may require the persons concerned to register their presence in the country within a reasonable and non-discriminatory period of time (Art 5(5), see above).

Article 14(1) provides that EU citizens and their family members shall have the right of residence under Art 6, 'as long as they do not become an *unreasonable* burden on the social assistance system of the host Member State' (emphasis added); expulsion shall not be an automatic consequence if an EU citizen or his family members have recourse to the host Member State's social assistance system (Art 14(3)). Article 14(4) further provides that (other than in accordance with the provisions relating to restrictions on the right of entry and residence on grounds of public policy, public security or public health) an expulsion order cannot be issued against an EU citizen or his family members, if:

(i) the EU citizen is a worker or self-employed person in the host Member State; or

(ii) the EU citizen entered the host Member State to seek employment and provided he can provide evidence that he is continuing to seek work and has a genuine chance of being employed.

This general right of residence will be of particular relevance to those exercising the Community law rights to provide and receive services, whereas the extended right of residence provided by Art 7 (see below) will be of particular relevance to those exercising their Community law rights of establishment. The extended right of residence will also be of relevant to those exercising their Community law rights to receive services, because such residence will apply to the economically self-sufficient (Art 7(1)(b)).

Right of residence for more than three months (Article 7)

The right of residence for more than three months remains subject to certain conditions. Article 7(1) provides that EU citizens have the right to reside in another Member State, for a period exceeding three months, if they:

(a) are engaged in an economic activity in the host Member State (on an employed or self-employed basis); or

(b) have comprehensive sickness insurance and sufficient resources for themselves and their family members to ensure that they do not become a burden on the social assistance system of the host Member State during their stay. Article 8(4) provides that Member States may not specify a minimum amount of resources which they deem sufficient, but they must take account of the personal situation of the person concerned. The amount of minimum resources cannot be higher than the threshold below which nationals of the host Member State become eligible for social assistance, or if this does not apply, higher than the minimum social security pension paid by the host Member State; or

. . .

(d) are a 'family member' of an EU citizen who falls into one of the above categories.

Article 7(2) provides that the right of residence also applies to family members who are not nationals of a Member State (i.e. non-EU family members), who are accompanying or joining an EU citizen in the host Member State, provided that such EU citizen satisfies the conditions set out in (a) or (b) above.

Residence permits are abolished for EU citizens. However, Arts 8(1) and 8(2) provide that Member States may require EU citizens to register with the competent authorities within a period of not less than three months as from the date of arrival. A registration certificate will be issued immediately (Art 8(2)). For the registration certificate to be issued, Art 8(3) provides that Member States may only require the following documentation:

(a) in the case of an EU citizen to whom Art 7(1)(a) applies (i.e. a worker or self-employed person), a valid identity card or passport, and confirmation of engagement from the employer or a certificate of employment, or proof of their self-employed status;

(b) in the case of an EU citizen to whom Art 7(1)(b) applies (i.e. a citizen having sufficient resources and comprehensive sickness insurance), a valid identity card or passport, and proof of comprehensive sickness insurance, and proof that they have sufficient resources for themselves and their family members not to become a burden on the social assistance system of the host Member State during their period of residence.

Article 8(5) provides that registration certificates will be issued to family members who are nationals of a Member State (i.e. EU family members); this is subject to the production of specified documentation. This provision also applies to other family members whose entry and residence to the host Member State shall be facilitated in accordance with Art 3(2).

Article 9 applies to family members who are not nationals of a Member State (i.e. non-EU family members). Such family members must apply for a residence card not less than three months from their date of arrival (Art 9(2)). A residence card is valid for at least five years from its date of issue, or for the envisaged period of residence of the EU citizen if this is less than five years (Art 11(1)). Article 10(2) sets out the documentation required before a residence card will be issued. This provision also applies to other family members whose entry and residence to the host Member State shall be facilitated in accordance with Art 3(2). Article 11(2) provides that the validity of a residence card shall not be affected by:

(i)   temporary absences of up to six months a year;

(ii) absences of a longer period for compulsory military service; or

(iii) one absence of up to 12 months for important reasons (e.g. pregnancy and child-birth, serious illness, study or vocational training, or a posting in another Member State or a third county).

Article 7(3) provides that an EU citizen shall retain the status of worker or self-employed person in the host Member State in the following circumstances:

(a)   he is temporarily unable to work as the result of an illness or accident;

(b)   he is in duly recorded involuntary unemployment after having been employed for more than one year and has registered as a jobseeker with the relevant employment office in the host Member State;

(c)   he is in duly recorded involuntary unemployment after completing a fixed-term employment contract of less than a year *or* after having become involuntarily unemployed during the first twelve months *and* has registered as a jobseeker with the relevant employment office in the host Member State. In this case, the status of worker shall be retained for not less than six months;

(d)   he embarks on vocational training. Unless he is involuntarily unemployed, the retention of the status of worker shall require the training to be related to the previous employment.

Article 12(1) provides that if an EU citizen dies or departs from the host Member State, his EU family members shall not have their right of residence affected. In the case of a non-EU family member, their right of residence shall not be affected if the EU citizen dies provided that the non-EU family member has been residing in the host Member State as a family member for at least one year before the EU citizen's death (Art 12(2)).

Article 12(3) provides that if an EU citizen dies or departs from the host Member State, if his children reside in the host Member State and are enrolled at an educational establishment, then his children and the parent who has actual custody of the children (whether or not they are EU citizens) shall have the right to reside in the host Member State until the children have completed their studies.

Article 13 governs a family member's right of residence following divorce, annulment of marriage or termination of partnership. In the case of EU family members, divorce, annulment of marriage or termination of partnership does not affect the family member's right of residence (Art 13(1)). However, in the case of non-EU family members, retention of the right of residence is restricted; Art 13(2) provides that there shall be no loss of the right of residence where:

(a) prior to the start of the divorce or annulment proceedings or termination of the registered partnership, the marriage or registered partnership had lasted at least three years, including one year in the host Member State; or

(b) by agreement between the spouses or the registered partners, or by court order, the spouse or partner who is a non-EU national has custody of the EU citizen's children; or

(c) this is warranted by particularly difficult circumstances, such as having been a victim of domestic violence while the marriage or registered partnership was subsisting; or

(d) by agreement between the spouses or registered partners, or by court order, the spouse or partner who is a non-EU national has the right of access to a minor child, provided that the court has ruled that such access must be in the host Member State, and for as long as is required.

Article 14(2) provides that EU citizens and their family members shall have the right of residence under Arts 7, 12 and 13 'as long as they meet the conditions set out therein'; expulsion shall not be an automatic consequence if an EU citizen or his family members have recourse to the host Member State's social assistance system (Art 14(3)). Article 14(4) further provides that (other than in accordance with the provisions relating to restrictions on the right of entry and residence on grounds of public policy, public security or public health), an expulsion order cannot be issued against an EU citizen or his family members, if:

(i) the EU citizen is a worker or self-employed person in the host Member State; or

(ii) the EU citizen entered the host Member State to seek employment and provided he can provide evidence that he is continuing to seek work and has a genuine chance of being employed.

Right of permanent residence (Article 16)

EU citizens acquire the right of permanent residence in the host Member State after a five-year period of continuous legal residence (Art 16(1)), provided that an expulsion decision has not been enforced against them (Art 21). This right of permanent residence is no longer subject to any conditions. The same rule applies to non-EU family members who have lived with an EU citizen in the host Member State for five years (Art 16(2)), and again provided that an expulsion decision has not been enforced against them (Art 21). Article 16(3) provides that continuity of residence shall not be affected by:

(i) temporary absences not exceeding six months a year;

(ii) absences of a longer period for compulsory military service; or

(iii) one absence of up to 12 months for important reasons (e.g. pregnancy and childbirth, serious illness, study or vocational training, or a posting in another Member State or a third county).

Once granted, the right of permanent residence is lost only in the event of more than two successive years' absence from the host Member State (Arts 16(4) and 20(3)).

Article 17 recognises the right of permanent residence for EU citizens who are workers or self-employed persons, and for their family members, before the five-year period of continuous residence has expired, subject to certain conditions being met. Article 17 applies to cases where the EU citizen:

(i)   has reached retirement age;

(ii) has become permanently incapable of working; or

(iii) lives in the host Member State but works in another Member State.

Article 7 also provides that the family members of an EU worker or self-employed person have the right of permanent residence if the EU worker or self-employed person dies before acquiring the right of permanent residence. This right, which applies to family members of whatever nationality, is subject to the following conditions:

(a)   the worker or self-employed person had, at the time of death, resided continuously on the territory of that Member State for two years; or

(b)   the death resulted from an accident at work or an occupational disease; or

(c)   the surviving spouse lost the nationality of that Member State following marriage to the worker or self-employed person.

Article 12(1) provides that if an EU citizen dies or departs from the host Member State, his family members who are nationals of a Member State shall not have their right of residence affected. However, before acquiring the right of permanent residence, the persons concerned must meet the conditions set out in Art 7(1)(a), (b) or (d); see above. In the case of a non-EU family member, their right of residence shall not be affected if the EU citizen dies provided that the non-EU family member has been residing in the host Member State as a family member for at least one year before the EU citizen's death (Art 12(2)). However, before acquiring the right of permanent residence, the persons concerned must meet the conditions set out in Art 7(1)(a), (b), or (d). Article 18 provides that the family members to whom Art 12(2) apply, who satisfy the conditions set out in Art 12(2), shall acquire the right of permanent residence after legally residing in the host Member State for a period of five consecutive years; this is without prejudice to Art 17 (see above).

Article 13 governs a family member's right of residence following divorce, annulment of marriage or termination of partnership. In the case of EU family members, divorce, annulment of marriage or termination of partnership does not affect the family member's right of residence (Art 13(1)). However, before acquiring the right of permanent residence, the persons concerned must meet the conditions set out in Art 7(1)(a), (b) or (d); see above. In the case of non-EU family members, retention of the right of residence is restricted. Article 13(2) provides that there shall be no loss of the right of residence where:

(a)   prior to the start of the divorce or annulment proceedings or termination of the registered partnership, the marriage or registered partnership had lasted at least three years, including one year in the host Member State; or

(b)   by agreement between the spouses or the registered partners, or by court order, the spouse or partner who is a non-EU national has custody of the EU citizen's children; or

(c)   this is warranted by particularly difficult circumstances, such as having been a victim of domestic violence while the marriage or registered partnership was subsisting; or

(d)   by agreement between the spouses or registered partners, or by court order, the spouse or partner who is a non-EU national has the right of access to a minor child, provided that the court has ruled that such access must be in the host Member State, and for as long as is required.

In this situation, however, before acquiring the right of permanent residence, the persons concerned must meet the conditions set out in Art 7(1)(a), (b), or (d). Article 18 provides that the family members to whom Art 13(2) apply, who satisfy the conditions set out in Art 13(2), shall acquire the right of permanent residence after legally residing in the host Member State for a period of five consecutive years; this is without prejudice to Art 17 (see above).

EU citizens entitled to permanent residence will be issued with a document certifying such residency (Art 19(1)). Article 20(1) provides that non-EU family members who are entitled to permanent residence will be issued with a residence card, renewable automatically every ten years. The application for a permanent residence card has to be submitted before the residence card expires (Art 20(2)); the residence card must be issued no more than six months after the application is made (Art 20(1)). Failure to apply for a permanent residence card may render the person concerned liable to proportionate and non-discriminatory sanctions (Art 20(2)).

Article 21 provides that continuity of residence may be attested by any means of proof in use in the Member State.

Common provisions on the right of residence and the right of permanent residence

Article 22 provides that the right of residence and the right of permanent residence shall cover the whole territory of the host Member State; territorial restrictions can only be imposed if the same restrictions apply to the host Member State's nationals. Family members, irrespective of their nationality, are entitled to engage in an economic activity on an employed or self-employed basis (Art 23).

EU citizens qualifying for the right of residence or the right of permanent residence, and the members of their family, benefit from equal treatment with host-country nationals in the areas covered by the Treaty (Art 24(1)). However, for the first three months of residence, or while the EU citizen is exercising his right to reside while seeking work under Art 14(4)(b), the host Member State is not obliged to grant entitlement to social assistance to persons other than employed or self-employed workers and the members of their family (Art 24(2)).

Article 25(1) provides that under no circumstances can possession of a registration certificate, etc. be made a pre-condition for the exercise of a right or the completion of an administrative formality. Entitlement to rights may be attested by any other means of proof where such documentation is not available. Article 25(2) further provides that all the documents listed in Art 25(1) shall be issued free of charge or for a charge which does not exceed that imposed on nationals for the issuing of a similar document.

If a Member State requires their own nationals to carry an identity card, then the host Member State can require non-nationals to carry their registration certificate or residence card. The host Member State may impose the same sanction as those imposed on their own nationals, if a non-national fails to comply (Art 26).

The EC Treaty

In the following case, the Court of Justice considered the right of residence of a spouse who was a non-EU citizen, married to a national of a Member State established in his host Member State, but who provided services to persons established in other Member

States. The non-EU citizen had to rely directly on the EC Treaty provisions because the relevant directives did not apply to this situation (and arguably Directive 2004/38 does not apply):

Mary Carpenter v *Secretary of State for the Home Department* (Case C-60/00)

Mary Carpenter was a national of the Philippines (i.e. a non-EU national). She was given leave to enter the UK as a visitor for six months. She overstayed that leave and failed to apply for an extension of her stay, as she was required to do under UK law. She later married a UK national (Peter Carpenter). Mr Carpenter ran a business selling advertising space in journals and offered various services to the editors of those journals. His business was established in the UK, but a large proportion of the business was conducted with advertisers in other Member States. Mr Carpenter travelled to those other Member States for the purpose of his business. Mrs Carpenter applied for leave to remain as the spouse of a UK national but her application was refused. A deportation order was made against her.

Mrs Carpenter appealed. She argued that she had a right under Community law to remain in the UK. She argued that because her husband's business required him to travel around the EU, providing and receiving services, her presence within the UK made it easier for him to do this because she could look after his children from his first marriage. If she was deported she argued that it would restrict Mr Carpenter's right to provide and receive services under Art 49 EC Treaty. The appeal tribunal referred the case to the Court of Justice, for a preliminary ruling pursuant to Art 234 EC Treaty. The Court of Justice held as follows:

> Article 49 EC [Treaty] read in the light of the fundamental right to respect for family life, is to be inter-preted as precluding, in certain circumstances such as those in the main proceedings, a refusal, by the Member State of origin of a provider of services established in that Member State, who provides services to recipients established in other Member States, of the right to reside in its territory to that provider's spouse, who is a national of a third country.

In the above case, the Court of Justice held that there was a Community dimension because Mr Carpenter was providing services within other Member States. The provision of services was a fundamental right and was to be interpreted and applied in accordance with the rights set out within the European Convention for the Protection of Human Rights. The Court held that if Mrs Carpenter was deported, then this would interfere with the exercise by Mr Carpenter of his right to provide services under Art 49 EC Treaty because his right to respect for his family life within the meaning of Art 8 of the European Convention on Human Rights would have been infringed. The Court therefore held that Art 49 EC Treaty prevented Mrs Carpenter's deportation.

Equal treatment

The self-employed, and the providers and recipients of services, do not have the benefit of Art 7(2), Regulation 1612/68 (social advantages) because the regulation applies only to workers. On the face of it, this is an important difference, since social advantages have played an important part in the jurisprudence of the Court in relation to the integration of workers and their families into the host Member State (see Chapter 12). There are no equivalent provisions in Directive 2004/38 (which repealed and replaced Directive 73/148), and its beneficiaries are obliged to look to Art 12 EC Treaty to be put on an equal footing with nationals. The Court has considerably mitigated the difference by a creative application of Art 12, as is illustrated in the following cases.

In **Commission *v* Italy (Re Housing Aid)** (Case 63/86), the Court of Justice held that Italian law contravened Art 12 EC Treaty, where the law in question confined a discounted mortgage facility to Italian nationals.

The following case subsequently came before the Court of Justice:

Cowan v *Le Trésor Public* (Case 186/87)

Mr Cowan, a British citizen, was visiting Paris as a tourist (i.e. the recipient of services (see above)) when he was assaulted in the exit of a Metro station. He was held to be entitled to the same rights in relation to criminal injuries compensation as a French national. The Court of Justice confined itself to considering the availability of the compensation scheme to non-French nationals. On the same basis that it had decided that equal access to the criminal process was a necessary precondition to the vindication of the rights of the worker in the criminal process (and could thus be seen to be a 'social advantage') in **Mutsch** (Case 137/84), the Court decided that the criminal injuries scheme should be similarly available to Mr Cowan.

Presumably the Court of Justice would have come to the same conclusion in the above case if his attackers had been identified and his application had been for legal aid to bring proceedings against them for assault.

In **Commission *v* Spain** (Case C–45/93), the Court of Justice held that the principle of equal treatment extended to the right of visitors from other EU states to free admission to museums, where this facility was available to Spanish nationals (see also **Commission *v* Italy** (Case C–388/01)). In this case, the visitors could rely upon Art 12 EC Treaty, because while visiting other EU states they were considered to be the recipients of services (see above), thus coming within the scope of Art 49 EC Treaty.

In **Gravier *v* City of Liège** (Case 293/83), the Court of Justice held that Ms Gravier was exercising a right to receive education under what was then Art 128 EC Treaty. In the course of exercising such a right, she was entitled to benefit from Art 7 EC Treaty (now Art 12). On that basis she should receive equal treatment in relation to payment of the university admission fee, the *minerval*, so that she would have to pay only the same amount as 'home' students (see also **Commission *v* Belgium (Re University Fees)** (Case C–47/93)).

Although the Court of Justice has enthusiastically applied Art 12 EC Treaty to enable an individual to overcome obstacles, either overt or covert, to the exercise of rights conferred by Arts 43, 49 and 50 EC Treaty, it has been more reluctant to do so when the obstacle relates to the individual's shortage of resources. The Court held that the right to equal treatment in relation to access to vocational education did not extend to financial assistance to enable an individual to go to another Member State and receive a grant to support himself while at a vocational school or on a vocational course. Such a right did not exist under what was then Art 128 EC Treaty, nor under Art 12 EC Treaty (**Lair *v* University of Hannover** (Case 39/86)). Indeed, the right to receive education as a 'service' under Art 49 EC Treaty depended on the individual providing 'remuneration' for it (**Humbel** (Case 263/86), paras 8–13). With regard to equal treatment, Art 24(1), Directive 2004/38 provides that EU citizens qualifying for the right of residence or the right of permanent residence and the members of their family benefit from equal treatment with host-country nationals in the areas covered by the Treaty.

The 'official authority' exception

As with Art 39 EC Treaty, the rights of entry and residence of those entering to provide and receive services are subject to the right of the host Member State to derogate on grounds of public policy, public security and public health (Arts 46(1) and 55 EC Treaty). The scope of these provisions will be examined in Chapter 15. In addition, the rights enjoyed by virtue of Arts 43, 49 and 50 EC Treaty 'shall not apply . . . to activities . . . connected, even occasionally, with the exercise of official authority' (Art 45 EC Treaty). Like the public service exception in Art 39(4), 'the exercise of official authority' is not defined in the Treaty, but its scope was considered by the Court of Justice in the following case:

Reyners v *Belgian State* (Case 2/74)

Reyners, the defendant, argued that the profession of *avocat* (i.e. lawyer) was exempted from the chapter of the Treaty on rights of establishment because it sometimes involved the exercise of official authority. The Court of Justice rejected the idea that an *avocat*, despite his occasional official duties, was necessarily concerned with the exercise of official authority:

> An extension of the exception allowed by Article 55 [now Art 45] to a whole profession would be possible only in cases where such activities were linked with that profession in such a way that freedom of establishment would result in imposing on the Member State concerned the obligation to allow the exercise, even occasionally, by nationals of functions appertaining to official authority. This extension is on the other hand not possible when, within the framework of an independent profession, the activities connected with the exercise of official authority are separable from the professional activity in question taken as a whole. (paras 46 and 47)

The 'exercise of official authority' would seem to be analogous to the exercise of 'public service' under Art 39(4) EC Treaty (**Commission** v **Belgium** (Case 149/79); see above, Chapter 12), and will be just as narrowly construed by the Court of Justice (see, for example, **Commission** v **Greece** (Case C306/89) in which road traffic experts were held not to come within the Art 45 exception; and **Commission** v **Italy** (Case C–272/91) where the provision of computer services for the state lottery was likewise held not to come within the Art 45 exception).

Professional qualifications

Freedom of establishment includes the right of individuals to practise a profession or trade (e.g. lawyer, doctor, vet) on a permanent or semi-permanent basis. Naturally, a person may seek to practise a profession in another Member State in an employed capacity (i.e. as an EU worker), and therefore the Community law provisions relating to workers will apply (see Chapter 12) in addition to those of establishment which relate to recognition of the profession or trade. Freedom of establishment with regard to professional qualifications has been addressed by the Community through (i) specific harmonising directives; (ii) Directive 89/48 (the Mutual Recognition of Diplomas Directive); (iii) Directive 92/51 (the Recognition of Diplomas for other Professional Activities); and (iv) case law of the Court of Justice.

Specific harmonising directives

The lack of common qualifications in the Community, and an unwillingness to recognise diplomas and other qualifications from other Member States, proved a major obstacle to the exercise of free movement rights, especially for those with specialist skills. The problem was addressed by the General Programme, which resulted in the production of a whole range of harmonising directives relating to a wide range of activities (e.g. GPs, nurses, vets). The harmonising directives provide that if the professional satisfies the conditions set out within the directive, then recognition of the profession is guaranteed throughout the Community.

Directive 89/48: mutual recognition of diplomas

Little progress was made in relation to other traditional professions. It is generally accepted that in professions such as law, accountancy, banking and insurance the public needs to be protected against those who might misrepresent their skills and qualifications. To protect both public and professionals, many such professions are regulated by law. Regulation will cover matters such as education and training, professional conduct and disciplinary proceedings. In some Member States the regulatory process is entirely in the hands of government. In the UK and Ireland it is largely in the hands of professional bodies, operating within a statutory framework. Individuals and undertakings providing financial services will also work within a framework of self-regulation and state regulation, the trend in the UK during the 1980s and 1990s being towards self-regulation and deregulation. From the point of view of the consuming public, the self-regulation process by professionals has sometimes been seen to be as much concerned with the protection of professionals from competition as with protection of the public from abuse. It could also be perceived in a single market as a covert form of protectionism in relation to the delivery of professional services by citizens of other Member States.

The reluctance of national professional bodies to agree harmonised standards for particular occupations led the Commission to adopt a new approach in 1985, following publication of the White Paper on the single market. That approach acknowledged the need:

> ... to provide a rapid response to the expectations of nationals of Community countries who hold higher-education diplomas awarded on completion of professional education and training issued in a Member State other than that in which they wish to pursue their profession. (preamble to Directive 89/48)

The new approach involved both general educational criteria and the mutual recognition of educational diplomas and relevant practical experience. Directive 89/48 opened the way for entry into professional practice in other Member States for a whole new range of activities. In the UK these occupations include: actuaries, auditors, barristers, chiropodists, dieticians, physiotherapists, optometrists, civil engineers, marine architects, town planners, solicitors and teachers. There are more than 30 regulated professions listed in the UK's Schedule 1 of the UK's implementing regulations: the European Communities (Recognition of Professional Qualifications) (First General System) Regulations 2005 (SI 2005/18).

Directive 89/48 (which was amended by Directive 2001/19) is essentially a 'residual' directive, in the sense that it does not apply to professions which are the subject of a separate harmonising directive establishing arrangements for the mutual recognition of diplomas by Member States (Art 2). It applies to 'regulated professional activity', that is, 'a professional activity, in so far as the taking up or pursuit of such an activity or one of its modes of pursuit in a Member State is subject, directly or indirectly by virtue of laws, regulations or administrative provisions, to the possession of a diploma' (Art 1). Beneficiaries of the directive are those who can show the following:

1. possession of a diploma indicating that the holder has the professional qualifications required for the taking up or pursuit of a regulated profession in one of the Member States in a self-employed capacity or as an employed person;

2. completion of a post-secondary course of at least three years' duration, or of an equivalent duration part-time, at a university or establishment of higher education or another establishment of similar level; and

3. where appropriate, that the holder of the diploma has successfully completed the professional training required in addition to the post-secondary course.

The host Member State may also require the holder of the diploma to provide evidence of professional experience of not more than four years where the period of education and training falls short by more than one year compared to that required in the host Member State. Where the education and training received by the individual in his home state differ substantially from those required in the host Member State, or where there is a substantial mismatch between the regulated activities in the home and host Member States, the host Member State can require the holder of the diploma either to complete an adaptation period of not more than three years, or to take an aptitude test. Except in those cases where the holder would need a precise knowledge of the law of the host Member State to carry on the profession, the choice of whether to undergo an adaptation period or an aptitude test belongs to the diploma holder.

Directive 89/48 was considered by the Court of Justice in the following case:

Burbaud (Case C-285/01)

A Portuguese national was refused admission to the hospital managers' corps of the French civil service on the ground that it was first necessary to pass the entrance examination of the École Nationale de la Santé Publique (the French National School of Public Health, the ENSP). The Court of Justice first analysed whether the duties performed by the members of the corps fell within the scope of Directive 89/48. The Court held that confirmation of passing the ENSP final examination can be regarded as a diploma. Its equivalence to the qualification awarded to Burbaud by a Lisbon school must, therefore, be ascertained by the national court. The Court held that if it transpires that the diplomas are awarded on completion of equivalent education or training, the Directive precludes the French authorities from making the access of a Portuguese national to the profession of manager in a public hospital subject to the condition that she complete the ENSP course and pass its final examination. A method of recruitment which does not allow for account to be taken of specific qualifications in the field of hospital management of candidates who are nationals of other Member States places them at a disadvantage which is liable to dissuade them from exercising their rights, as workers, to freedom of movement. While such an obstacle to a fundamental freedom guaranteed by the EC Treaty may be justified by an objective in the general interest, such as selection of the best candidates in the most objective conditions possible, it is a further condition that that restriction does not go beyond what is necessary to achieve that objective. The Court held that requiring candidates who are properly qualified to pass the ENSP entrance examination has the effect of downgrading them, which is not necessary to achieve the objective pursued and which cannot therefore be justified in the light of the Treaty provisions. The Court therefore concluded that such an examination was incompatible with the EC Treaty.

Directive 89/48 has been implemented in the UK by the European Communities (Recognition of Professional Qualifications) (First General System) Regulations 2005 (SI 2005/18). Under the regulations, professional bodies are obliged to recognise the qualifications of other Community professionals, to provide full reasons where this is not done in individual cases, and to set up an independent appeal tribunal before which any refusal of recognition can be challenged.

With regard to the establishment of lawyers, Directive 98/5 was adopted at the end of 1997, the aim of which is to make it easier for lawyers to practise in other Member States. The directive, which had to be implemented by March 2000:

- permits EU lawyers to be established under their home title in another Member State;
- requires them to register with an appropriate regulatory body in the host state;
- gives them a right to representation within the host regulatory body;
- subjects them to the rules and regulatory regime of the host regulatory body; and
- offers them a 'fast track' to requalification as a lawyer of the host state.

Directive 98/5 has been implemented in the UK by the European Community (Lawyer's Practice) Regulations 2000 (SI 2000/1119), which came into force on 22 May 2000. These regulations have been amended by the European Community (Lawyer's Practice) (Amendment) Regulations 2001 (SI 2001/644) and the European Community (Lawyer's Practice) (Amendment) Regulations 2004 (SI 2004/1628). The following case, which concerned Directive 98/5, was recently decided by the Court of Justice:

Wilson v *Ordre des avocats du barreau du Luxembourg* and *Commission* v *Luxembourg* (Cases C-506/04 and C-193/05)

In order to practise the profession of lawyer in Luxembourg, Luxembourg law set down a condition that a lawyer must 'be proficient in the language of statutory provisions as well as the administrative and court languages', and required a prior test of that knowledge.

Mr Graham Wilson, a UK national, is a barrister. He is a member of the Bar of England and Wales and has practised the profession of lawyer in Luxembourg since 1994. In 2003, Mr Wilson refused to attend an oral hearing with the Bar Council in order to assess his linguistic knowledge. As a consequence, the Bar Council refused to register him on the register of lawyers practising under their home-country professional title.

Mr Wilson challenged that decision by bringing an action for annulment before a court in Luxembourg, which referred the case to the Court of Justice, seeking guidance on whether Directive 98/5 allowed the host Member State to make the right of a lawyer to practise his profession on a permanent basis in that Member State under his home-country professional title subject to a test of his proficiency in the languages of that Member State.

The Court of Justice stated that the directive aims to facilitate the exercise of the fundamental freedom of establishment for lawyers, and that it precludes a prior test of linguistic knowledge. Only a certificate attesting to registration with the competent authority of the home Member State is necessary in order to be registered with a Bar in the host Member

State. To compensate for the exclusion of this prior testing, rules of professional conduct exist to ensure the protection of consumers and the proper administration of justice. Therefore, subject to disciplinary sanctions, a European lawyer must respect those rules of both the home Member State and those of the host Member State. Among those obligations is the duty of a lawyer not to handle cases which require linguistic knowledge that he does not possess.

Furthermore, according to the directive, a European lawyer who wishes to join the profession of the host Member State must show that he has effectively and regularly pursued an activity for a period of at least three years in the law of that Member State.

The Court concluded that the directive precludes a national law which makes registration of a European lawyer with the Bar of the host Member State subject to a language test.

In parallel to this case, the Commission also brought an action against Luxembourg for its failure to fulfil obligations, taking the view that three national measures were contrary to the directive:

(i) Registration on the Bar register following an oral test to assess linguistic knowledge

Luxembourg relied on the proper administration of justice to justify the existence of that provision, but the Court of Justice observed, as in Mr Wilson's case, that the directive does not provide for any condition other than that the lawyer must produce a certificate attesting to registration in the home Member State, and concluded that the Luxembourg provision which makes registration of a European lawyer with the competent national authority subject to a prior test of linguistic knowledge as being contrary to the directive.

(ii) The prohibition on European lawyers accepting service on behalf of companies in Luxembourg

The Court noted the principle that European lawyers are entitled to pursue the same professional activities as lawyers practising under the professional title of the host Member State, subject to the exceptions provided for by the directive. The activity of accepting service on behalf of companies is not included in those exceptions. Member States are not authorised to provide in their national law for other exceptions to that principle.

(iii) The obligation to produce each year a certificate from the home Member State

The Court observed that that obligation is an unjustified administrative burden which is contrary to the directive, since the latter already enshrines a principle of mutual assistance, according to which the competent authority of the home Member State must notify the competent authority of the host Member State when disciplinary proceedings are initiated against a European lawyer.

On those three grounds, the Court of Justice declared that Luxembourg had failed to fulfil its Community obligations.

Directive 92/51: recognition of diplomas for other professional activities

Directive 89/48 applies only to regulated professional activities where the holder has completed at least three years in higher education. There remained a large residual category of many professional and other activities for which some further education was required, but which did not fall within the scope of Directive 89/48. A further directive was, therefore, approved in 1992. Directive 92/51 (which has subsequently been amended by Directive 2001/19) deals with the remaining areas of professional education and training and applies to holders of diplomas which show either that the holder has successfully completed a post-secondary course of at least a year or the equivalent on a part-time basis, entry to which is on the same basis as entry into university or higher education, or that the holder has been successful in completing one of the recognised education and training courses listed in the directive. In the same way as Directive 89/48, the host Member State may require the diploma holder to complete an adaptation period of not more than three years or to take an aptitude test (Art 4(1)(b)).

Directive 92/51 (as amended by Directive 2001/19) has been implemented in the UK by the European Communities (Recognition of Professional Qualifications) (Second General System) Regulations 2002 (SI 2002/2934), which came into force on 1 January 2003. These regulations have been amended by the European Communities (Recognition of Professional Qualifications) (Second General System) (Amendment) Regulations 2005 (SI 2005/882).

Other qualifications

In the case of a qualification which does not fall within the scope of one of the specific harmonising directives, or the general Directives 89/48 and 92/51, the basic rules (developed through the case law of the Court of Justice) will continue to apply with regard to the recognition and investigation of the equivalence of the qualification. In such a case, the person seeking to establish himself in another Member State is relying directly on Art 43 EC Treaty. It is therefore necessary to review the case law of the Court of Justice:

Thieffry v *Conseil de l'Ordre des Avocats à la Cour de Paris* (Case 71/76)

A Belgian national had obtained a doctorate in law in Belgium. He practised as an advocate in Brussels (Belgium) for a number of years. His qualifications were recognised by a French university as *equivalent* to a degree in French law. He obtained a certificate stating that he was academically qualified for the profession of *avocat*. However, the French Bar refused him admission to the training stage solely on the ground that he did not have a degree in French law.

The Court held that if the applicant had already obtained what was recognised (professionally and academically) as an *equivalent qualification* and had *satisfied the necessary training requirements* then the French Bar would not have been justified in excluding him from admission solely because he did not have a French law degree. The fact that no directives had been adopted under the former Art 57 EC Treaty (now Art 47) was irrelevant.

This was taken a stage further by the Court of Justice in the following case:

UNECTEF v Heylens (Case 222/86)

Heylens was a Belgian national who held a Belgian football trainer's diploma. He was taken on as the trainer of a French football team. He applied for recognition of his diploma as equivalent to the French diploma. His application was refused. He continued to practise as a trainer and was prosecuted by the French football trainers' union (UNECTEF). The French court referred the case to the Court of Justice under the former Art 177 EC Treaty (now Art 234) for a preliminary ruling, questioning the compatibility of the French system with Community law. The Court of Justice held as follows:

> 10. In the absence of harmonisation of the conditions of access to a particular occupation, the Member States are entitled to lay down the knowledge and qualifications needed in order to pursue it and to require the production of a diploma certifying that the holder has the relevant knowledge and qualifications.
>
> ...
>
> 13. Since it has to reconcile the requirement as to the qualifications necessary in order to pursue a particular occupation with the requirements of the free movement of workers, **the procedure for the recognition of equivalence must enable the national authorities to assure themselves, on an objective basis, that the foreign diploma certifies that its holder has the knowledge and qualifications which are, if not identical, at least equivalent to those certified by the national diploma. That assessment of the equivalence of the foreign diploma must be effected exclusively in the light of the level of knowledge and qualifications which its holder can be assumed to possess in the light of that diploma, having regard to the nature and duration of the studies and practical training which the diploma certifies that he has carried out.** [emphasis added]

In the above case, the Court of Justice held that the assessment of equivalence of a foreign diploma must be effected exclusively in the light of 'the level of knowledge and qualifications which its holder can be assumed to possess in the light of that diploma', having regard to 'the nature and duration of the studies and practical training which the diploma certifies that he has carried out'. This was further amplified by the Court of Justice in the following case:

Vlassopoulou v Ministerium für Justiz, Bundesund Europaangelegenheiten Baden Württemberg (Case C-340/89)

The applicant was a Greek who had obtained a Greek law degree and who had been admitted to the Athens Bar (in Greece). Most of her professional practice had been undertaken in Germany and involved the application of German law. She applied for admission to the German Bar. Her application was rejected on the ground that she lacked the necessary qualifications. The case came before the German Federal Supreme Court, who referred the matter to the Court of Justice to determine whether it was permissible to refuse admission for this reason. The Court of Justice held as follows:

> 15. It must be stated in this regard that, even if applied without any discrimination on the basis of nationality, national requirements concerning qualifications may have the effect of hindering nationals of the other Member States in the exercise of their right of establishment guaranteed to them by Article 52 [now Art 43] of the EEC Treaty. That could be the case if the national rules in question took no account of the knowledge and qualifications already acquired by the person concerned in another Member State.
>
> 16. Consequently, **a Member State which receives a request to admit a person to a profession to which access, under national law, depends upon the possession of a diploma or a professional qualification must take into consideration the diplomas, certificates and other evidence of**

> qualifications which the person concerned has acquired in order to exercise the same profession in another Member State by making comparison between the specialised knowledge and abilities concerned by those diplomas and the knowledge and qualifications required by the national rules. [emphasis added]

In the above case, the Court of Justice held that national authorities are required to consider any education or training received by that person which is indicated by the qualification, and to contrast that with the knowledge and skills required by the domestic qualification. If they are *equivalent* then the Member State *must* recognise the qualification. If they are not considered equivalent, then they must go on to consider the 'knowledge or training received by the applicant through study or experience'; this may be sufficient to make up for what was lacking in the formal qualification (paras 19–20).

A string of later cases has confirmed this approach:

Colegio Oficial de Agentes de la Propriedad Inmobiliara v Aguirre, Newman and Others (Case C-104/91)

Newman was prosecuted for practising as an estate agent in Spain without being a member of the Colegio. He had applied for membership but had received no response. He was a member of the Royal Institute of Chartered Surveyors in the UK. It should be noted that the prosecution took place before 4 January 1991, the date by which Directive 89/48 should have been implemented in Member States. The Spanish court referred to the Court of Justice the question of how far the Colegio was obliged to take into account the defendant's UK qualifications.

The Court held that, in the absence of harmonisation of the conditions of access to a particular profession, Member States are entitled to lay down the knowledge and qualifications needed in order to pursue it and to require the production of a diploma certifying that the holder has the relevant knowledge and qualifications. In this case, the Member State was required to carry out a comparative examination of professional qualifications, taking into account the differences between the national legal systems concerned.

If the comparison shows that the knowledge and qualifications correspond to the national provisions of the host Member State, then it is bound to accept their equivalence. If, on the other hand, the examination reveals only partial equivalence, the host Member State has the right to require the person concerned to demonstrate that he has acquired the additional knowledge and qualifications needed. The host Member State is under an obligation to give full reasons when it determines a lack of equivalence. This is to enable the person to take steps to remedy the deficiency or, if he disagrees with the decision, to challenge it in a court of law (**UNECTEF v Heylens** (Case 222/86); **Vlassopoulou** (Case C-340/89)).

Fernandez de Bobadilla v Museo Nacional del Prado and Others (Case C-234/97)

Ms Fernandez de Bobadilla (F) was a Spanish national. She obtained a BA in History of Art from an American university, following which she obtained a postgraduate degree in fine arts and restoration from a UK university. For the following three years, F worked for the Prado (in Madrid, Spain) as a restorer of works of art under a temporary contract. She also worked for other studios and museums.

The Prado is attached to Spain's Ministry of Culture, and a collective agreement entered into provided that the post of restorer would be available only to persons who possessed a specified qualification. This did not include the qualifications F had obtained.

F applied to have her qualifications recognised as equivalent to those specified in the collective agreement, but she was told that she would need to take additional examinations to demonstrate that she had sufficient knowledge. She did not take these examinations.

The Prado subsequently advertised a permanent vacancy as a restorer of works of art. F applied but her application was rejected because she did not possess one of the specified qualifications. F argued that this infringed her free movement rights.

The case came before the Court of Justice, and the Court stated that if the general Directives 89/48 or 92/51 did not apply then:

28. . . . Community law does not in principle preclude a public body in a Member State from restricting access to a post to candidates holding a qualification awarded by an educational establishment in that Member State or any other foreign qualification officially recognised by the competent authorities of that Member State. However, where the qualification was awarded in another Member State, the procedure for granting it official recognition must comply with the requirements of Community law.

29. The Court has already had occasion to set out, *inter alia*, in Case C-340/89 **Vlassopoulou** [1991] ECR I-2357, the conditions with which the competent authorities of a Member State must comply when they receive a request to admit a person to a profession to which entry under national law depends on the possession of a diploma or professional qualification.
    . . .

31. It is clear from paragraph 16 of the judgment in **Vlassopoulou** that the competent authorities of the host Member State must take into consideration the diplomas, certificates and other evidence of qualifications which the person concerned has acquired in order to practise that profession in another Member State by comparing the specialised knowledge and abilities certified by those diplomas with the knowledge and qualifications required by the national rules.

32. If the comparative examination of diplomas results in the finding that the knowledge and qualifications certified by the diploma awarded in another Member State correspond to those required by the national provisions, the competent authorities of the host Member State must recognise that diploma as fulfilling the requirements laid down by its national provisions. If, on the other hand, the comparison reveals that the knowledge and qualifications certified by the foreign diploma and those required by the national provisions correspond only partially, the competent authorities are entitled to require the person concerned to show that he has acquired the knowledge and qualifications which are lacking (judgment in **Vlassopoulou**, cited above, paragraph 19).

33. In that regard, the competent national authorities must assess whether the knowledge acquired by the candidate, either during a course of study or by way of practical experience, is sufficient to show possession of knowledge which is lacking (judgment in **Vlassopoulou**, cited above, paragraph 20).

34. **Where no general procedure for official recognition has been laid down at national level by the host Member State, or where that procedure does not comply with the requirements of Community law as set out in paragraphs 29-33 of this judgment, it is for the public body seeking to fill the post itself to investigate whether the diploma obtained by the candidate in another Member State, together, where appropriate, with practical experience, is to be regarded as equivalent to the qualification required.** [emphasis added]

In the above case, the Court of Justice was undecided as to whether or not the general Directives 89/48 and 92/51 (see above) applied and therefore it determined the case on the basis that these two directives did not apply. It reaffirmed its previous case law at paras 29–33 and stated at para 34 that it was the responsibility of the public body seeking to fill the vacancy to determine whether the foreign qualification and/or experience of the candidate was such as to afford equivalence to the qualifications specified (see also **Morgenbesser** (Case C–313/01)).

This line of reasoning was followed by the Court of Justice in the following case:

Hugo Fernando Hocsman v *Ministre de l'Emploi et de la Solidarité* (Case C-238/98)

Hocsman held a diploma of doctor of medicine awarded in 1976 by a university in Argentina. He acquired Spanish nationality in 1986, and became a French citizen in 1998. During 1980 the Spanish authorities recognised Hocsman's Argentine qualification as equivalent to the Spanish university degree in medicine and surgery, which allowed him to practise medicine in Spain and train there as a specialist. Due to the fact that he was not a Spanish national at the time of his specialist training, the qualification he was subsequently awarded (specialist in urology) was an academic title. When he became a Spanish national in 1986 he obtained authorisation to practise as a specialist in urology.

In 1990 he entered France and held various urology posts. He applied to be registered to practise general medicine, but in 1997 the French authorities rejected his application on the ground that his Argentine qualification did not entitle him to practise general medicine in France. Hocsman issued proceedings in a French court to have that decision annulled.

Although there was a harmonising directive which applied to medicine, Hocsman's Argentine qualification was not covered. The French court referred the case to the Court of Justice pursuant to Art 234 EC Treaty and asked, *inter alia*, whether a person could rely on Art 43 EC Treaty where there was a directive covering the relevant profession. The Court of Justice held as follows:

> The object of such [harmonising or coordinating] directives is, as appears from Article 57(1) of the Treaty [now Art 47(1)], to make it easier for persons to take up and pursue activities as self-employed persons, and hence to make the existing possibilities of taking up those activities easier for nationals of other Member States . . .
>
> The function of directives which lay down common rules and criteria for mutual recognition of diplomas is thus to introduce a system in which Member States are obliged to accept the equivalence of certain diplomas and cannot require the persons concerned to comply with requirements other than those laid down in the relevant directives.
>
> Where the requirements such as those set out in Directive 93/16 [which gives Community recognition to specified medical training diplomas] are satisfied, mutual recognition of the diplomas in question renders superfluous their recognition under the principle referred to [i.e. as the Court held in **Haim** (see below), that in order to verify whether a training period requirement prescribed by the national rules is satisfied, the competent national authorities must take into account the professional experience of the person concerned, including that which he has acquired in another Member State]. However, that principle unquestionably remains relevant in situations not covered by such directives, as in Dr Hocsman's case.

In the above case, the Court of Justice held that even though there was a harmonising directive covering medical training diplomas, Hocsman could still rely directly on Art 43 EC Treaty. In this instance, the principles espoused by the Court in its previous case law have to be applied to ascertain if Hocsman's qualifications and experience are sufficient to warrant recognition of his professional qualifications.

In the following case, the Court of Justice made it clear that where a qualification was not mentioned in one of the harmonising directives, then in accordance with the Court's previous case law, there is a requirement for a comparative examination of the education and training received by the applicant:

Conseil National de l'Ordre des Architectes v Nicholas Dreesen (Case C-31/00)

Dreesen (a Belgian national) had a German engineering diploma, and had been employed for various architect firms in Belgium for 25 years. He applied to a Provincial Council within Belgium to have his name entered on the register of that association so that he could practise as a self-employed architect. This was refused because the qualification he had was not specified in Directive 85/384 (a harmonising directive which applied to architects). The case came before the Court of Justice which held as follows:

> Article 43 EC [Treaty] is to be interpreted as meaning that where a Community national applies to the competent authorities of a Member State for authorisation to practise a profession, access to which depends, under national legislation, on the possession of a diploma or professional qualification or on periods of practical experience, those authorities are required to take into consideration all of the diplomas, certificates and other evidence of formal qualifications of the person concerned, and his relevant experience, with the knowledge and qualifications required by the national legislation, **even where a directive on the mutual recognition of diplomas has been adopted for the profession concerned, but where application of the directive does not result in automatic recognition of the applicant's qualification or qualifications.** [emphasis added]

Non-EU qualifications

As with most of the Treaty provisions on the free movement of persons, neither the specific harmonising directives nor the two general directives cover non-EU nationals. The issue of whether they apply to qualifications obtained outside the EU was the issue in the following case:

Tawil-Albertini v Ministre des Affairs Sociales (Case C-154/93)

The applicant was a French national. He obtained a dental qualification in Lebanon. This qualification was later recognised in Belgium as equivalent to the Belgian dentistry qualification. He subsequently applied to the French authorities to practise in France, but his application was refused. The qualifications listed in the specific Council Directive 78/686 on the mutual recognition of dental qualifications did not include any qualification obtained outside the EU. However, because his qualification had been recognised as equivalent to the Belgian diploma, and the Belgian diploma was included in the directive, he argued that his qualification was also covered by the directive.

The Court of Justice held that the mutual recognition of qualifications in dentistry was based upon minimum specific levels of competence agreed between all the Member States. Even though one Member State accepted a qualification as equivalent to its own standards it did not follow that this would bind all the other Member States. Only the qualifications listed in the specific directive were guaranteed equivalent. Obviously, if he had obtained work experience within Belgium then, according to the decision in **Hocsman**, above, that experience would have been required to be taken into consideration, relying directly on Art 43 EC Treaty rather than the directive.

The following case was referred to in the Court's judgment in **Hocsman** (see above):

Haim v Kassenzahnärztliche Vereinigung Nordrhein (Case C-319/92)

The applicant did not hold one of the qualifications specified in Council Directive 78/686, but had nevertheless been authorised to practise as a dentist in Germany. He applied to work on a social security scheme in Germany, but was told that he would have to complete a further two-year training period.

He argued that his experience working for eight years as a dentist in Belgium should be taken into account. The Court of Justice cited the **Vlassopoulou** case (above) and ruled in his favour:

> 28. The competent national authority, in order to verify whether the training period requirement prescribed by the national rules is met, must take into account the professional experience of the plaintiff in the main proceedings, including that which he has acquired during his appointment as a dental practitioner of a social security scheme in another Member State.

In each of the above cases, the applicants had obtained non-EU qualifications. In the **Haim** case, the Court of Justice held that experience within the EU must be taken into account if the Member State recognised the qualification which had been obtained from outside the EU. However, nationals of non-Member countries who are established in the EU have no rights of recognition or permission to practise under Community law. This is so even if they have obtained their professional qualification in one of the Member States and such qualification is listed in one of the earlier specific directives.

The **Tawil-Albertini** case (see above) can be contrasted with the following case:

Tennah-Durez (Case C-110/01)

Tennah-Durez carried out part of his doctor's training in Algeria. This training was subsequently recognised in Belgium (which awarded the diploma), and Tennah-Durez sought to have his diploma recognised in France. The Court of Justice began by stating that Directive 93/16 establishes automatic and unconditional recognition of certain diplomas, requiring Member States to acknowledge their equivalence without being able to demand that the persons concerned comply with conditions other than those laid down. It went on to draw a distinction between that system and the system laid down by Directive 89/48, where recognition is not automatic but allows Member States to require the person concerned to fulfil additional requirements, including a period of adaptation. Concerning the extent to which medical training may consist of training received in a non-member country, the Court held that the directive did not require all or any particular part of that training to be provided at a university of a Member State or under the supervision of such a university, and that neither did the general scheme of the directive preclude medical training leading to a diploma, certificate or other evidence of a medical qualification eligible for automatic recognition from being received *partly* outside the EU. According to the Court, what mattered was not where the training had been provided but whether it complied with the qualitative and quantitative training requirements laid down by Directive 93/16. Moreover, responsibility for ensuring that the training requirements, both qualitative and quantitative, laid down by Directive 93/16 were fully complied with fell wholly on the competent authority of the Member State awarding the diploma. A diploma thus awarded amounted to a 'doctor's passport' enabling the holder to work as a doctor throughout the EU, without the professional qualification attested to by the diploma being open to challenge in the host Member State except in specific circumstances laid down by Community law. Consequently, provided the competent authority in the Member State awarding the diploma was in a position to validate medical training received in a third country (i.e. non-Member State) and to conclude on that basis that the training duly complied with the training requirements laid down by Directive 93/16, that training could be taken into account in deciding whether to award a doctor's diploma. In that respect, the proportion of the training carried out in a third country, and in particular the fact that the major part of the training was received in such a country, is immaterial. In the first place, Directive 93/16 contains no reference or even allusion to such a criterion. Moreover, a requirement for training to have been received mainly within the EU would undermine legal certainty, since such a concept is open to several interpretations. The Court concluded that the training in question could consist, and even mainly consist, of training received in a third country, provided the competent authority of the Member State awarding the diploma was in a position to validate the training and to conclude on that basis that it duly served to meet the requirements for the training of doctors laid down by the directive. As for the extent to which national authorities are bound by a certificate confirming that the diploma conforms with the requirements of the directive, the Court held that the system of automatic and unconditional recognition would be seriously jeopardised if it was open to Member States at their discretion to question the merits of a decision taken by the competent institution of another Member State to award the diploma. However, where new evidence casts serious doubt on the authenticity of the diploma presented, or as to its conformity with the applicable legislation, it was legitimate for Member States to require from the competent institution of the Member State which awarded the diploma confirmation of its authenticity.

The difference between the **Tawil-Albertini** case and that of **Tennah-Durez** was that in the former case the actual qualification was obtained outside the EU, whereas in the latter case the qualification was obtained within the EU, but some training, which contributed to the qualification, had been undertaken outside the EU. The qualification in the former case did not come within the scope of Community law, whereas the qualification in the latter case did.

The internal situation

From the wording of Art 43 there would appear to be a limitation in that it cannot be relied upon by a person seeking to establish himself in the Member State of his nationality (although see **Neri** (Case C–153/02), below). One obvious way in which a national may be disadvantaged is where he obtains a qualification in another Member State and then seeks to have it recognised in his own Member State.

In **Knoors** *v* **Secretary of State for Economic Affairs** (Case 115/78) the Court of Justice held that the former Art 52 EC Treaty (now Art 43) could be relied upon in a person's home Member State in respect of a qualification he had obtained in another Member State. However, later case law of the Court suggested that there were limitations to this. It held that the existence of a directive recognising the foreign qualification was essential. The former Art 52 (now Art 43) of itself could not assist nationals established in the Member State of their nationality:

Ministère Public v *Auer* (Case 136/78)

A French citizen obtained a vet qualification in Italy. He was not permitted to practise in France, the Italian qualification not being considered to be equivalent. There was no Community directive in force at the time. The Court of Justice held as follows:

> 20. ... Article 52 [now Art 43] concerns only – and can concern only – in each Member State the nationals of other Member States, those of the host Member State coming already, by definition, under the rules in question.

Following the Court of Justice's judgment in the above case, the Council adopted Directives 78/1026 and 78/1027 which governed veterinary qualifications, thus recognising the qualification Auer had obtained. Generally, directives do not distinguish between nationals of the Member State in question. The case came before the Court of Justice for a second time, but on this occasion Auer was able to rely upon the directives (see **Auer** *v* **Ministère Public** (Case 271/82)).

Following the adoption of the general Directives 89/48 and 92/51 (which include most trade or professional qualifications, and which are not restricted to nationals establishing themselves in a Member State other than that of their nationality) most situations involving a *regulated profession* will be covered by the directives and therefore reliance solely on Art 43 EC Treaty will not be necessary. Accordingly, the national may rely upon the relevant directive in the Member State of his nationality with regard to qualifications and training obtained in another Member State.

However, in the following case, the Court of Justice has cast doubt on whether or not **Auer** (Case 136/78) was correctly decided:

Fernandez de Bobadilla v *Museo Nacional del Prado and Others* (Case C-234/97)

The facts of this case have been considered above. The Court of Justice held as follows:

> 30. In contrast to **Vlassopoulou**, this case concerns a Spanish national seeking to practise her profession in Spain. However, if a national of a Member State, owing to the fact that he has lawfully resided in the territory of another Member State and has acquired a professional qualification there, finds himself with regard to his State of origin in a situation which may be assimilated to that of a migrant worker, he must also be entitled to enjoy the rights and freedoms guaranteed by the Treaty (see, to that effect, Case C-19/92 **Kraus** [1993] ECR I-1663, paragraphs 15 and 16).

In the above case, the Court of Justice was undecided whether or not Directives 89/48 and 92/51 applied, and therefore it decided the case on the basis that they did not. It held that even if there was no directive applicable to the test of equivalence of her qualifications, she could rely upon the general principles of Community law.

The above applies only where there is some 'Community element'. In the **Bobadilla** case, the Community element is the completion of an educational course and training in another Member State. If there is no Community element present then this will constitute a wholly internal situation, and Community law will not provide a remedy (see **Nino and Others** (Cases 54 and 91/88 and 14/89)).

In the following case, the Court of Justice was faced with a different issue:

Neri (Case C-153/02)

An Italian administrative practice prevented the recognition of post-secondary university diplomas issued by a British university in circumstances where the courses were delivered in Italy by an educational establishment operating in the form of a capital company in accordance with an agreement between the two establishments. The Court of Justice held that the Italian refusal to recognise the diplomas was incompatible with Art 43 EC Treaty. In the view of the Court, Art 43 requires the elimination of restrictions on freedom of establishment, whether they prohibit the exercise of that freedom, impede it or render it less attractive. The Court stated that non-recognition in Italy of degrees likely to facilitate the access of students to the employment market is likely to deter students from attending courses and thus seriously hinder the pursuit by the educational establishment concerned of its economic activity in that Member State. Moreover, inasmuch as non-recognition of diplomas relates solely to degrees awarded to Italian nationals, it does not appear suitable for attaining the objective of ensuring high standards of university education. Similarly, precluding any examination and, consequently, any possibility of recognition of degrees does not comply with the requirement of proportionality and goes beyond what is necessary to ensure the objective pursued. It could not therefore be justified.

Directive 2005/36: the recognition of professional qualifications

Directive 2005/36 on the recognition of professional qualifications (OJ 2005 L 255/22) was adopted on 7 September 2005 and has to be transposed into national law by 20 October 2007. The provisions of the directive are considered in further detail below.

Scope

The Directive applies to all EU citizens seeking to practise a 'regulated profession' in a Member State other than that in which they obtained their professional qualifications, on either a self-employed or employed basis (Art 2(1)).

At a legislative level, the Directive forms part of the process of legislative consolidation aimed at combining the three general system directives (Directives 89/48, 95/51 and 1999/42) in a single text along with twelve sectoral directives (i.e. 93/16, 77/452, 77/453, 78/686, 78/687, 78/1026, 78/1027, 80/154, 80/155, 85/432, 85/433 and 85/384) covering the seven professions of doctor, nurse, dental practitioner, veterinary surgeon, midwife, pharmacist and architect. The consolidation of these fifteen directives will lead to their repeal on 20 October 2007 (Art 62).

The specific directives on the provision of services and establishment of lawyers (i.e. Directives 77/249 and 98/5) are not covered by this exercise, since they concern the recognition not of professional qualifications but of the authorisation to practice. Recognition of lawyers' qualifications is currently governed by Directive 89/48, and is thus covered by this Directive.

Allowing Member State nationals the freedom to provide services and the right of establishment

The recognition of professional qualifications enables beneficiaries to gain access in host Member States to the professions in which they are qualified, and to practice under the same conditions as nationals of that Member State in cases where these professions are regulated.

The directive makes a distinction between 'freedom to provide services' and 'freedom of establishment' on the basis of criteria identified by the Court of Justice: duration, frequency, regularity and continuity of the provision of services. Title II, Arts 5–9 relate to freedom to provide services, and Title III, Arts 10–52 relate to freedom of establishment.

Articles 5–9: facilitating temporary and occasional provision of cross-border services

Nationals of a Member State who are legally established in a given Member State may provide services on a temporary and occasional basis in another Member State under their original professional title without having to apply for recognition of their qualifications. However, if service providers relocate outside of their Member State of establishment in order to provide services, they must also provide evidence of two years' professional experience if the profession in question is not regulated in that Member State.

The host Member State may require the service provider to make a declaration prior to providing any services on its territory and renew it annually including the details of any insurance cover or other means of personal or collective protection with regard to professional liability. The host Member State may also require that the first application be accompanied by certain documents listed in the directive, such as proof of the nationality of the service provider, of their legal establishment, and of their professional qualifications.

If the host Member State requires *pro forma* registration with the competent professional association, this must occur automatically upon the competent authority which received the prior declaration forwarding the applicant's file to the professional organisation or body. For professions which have public health or safety implications and do not benefit from automatic recognition, the host Member State may carry out a prior check of the service provider's professional qualifications within the limits of the principle of proportionality.

In cases where the service is provided under the professional title of the Member State of establishment or under the formal qualification of the service provider, the competent authorities of the host Member State may require service providers to furnish the recipient of the service with certain information, particularly with regard to insurance coverage against the financial risks connected with any challenge to their professional liability.

The competent authorities shall ensure the exchange of all information necessary for complaints by a recipient of a service against a service provider to be correctly pursued. The host Member State may also ask the Member State of establishment for information regarding the service provider's legal establishment, good conduct, and the absence of any penalties for professional misconduct. With regard to both the temporary provision of services and permanent establishment in another Member State, the directive provides for the proactive exchange of information relating to any serious circumstances which arose when the individual in question was established on their territory and which are liable to have consequences for the pursuit of the professional activities concerned. This exchange of information must, at any rate, be carried out in compliance with existing legislation on data protection.

Articles 10–52: improving the existing systems of recognition for the purpose of permanent establishment in another Member State

On the other hand, 'freedom of establishment' is the framework which applies when a professional enjoys the effective freedom to become established in another Member State in order to conduct a professional activity there on a stable basis. With respect to establishment, the directive comprises the three existing systems of recognition:

(i) *Chapter I, Arts 10-15: general system for the recognition of professional qualifications.* This system applies as a fallback to all the professions not covered by specific rules of recognition and to certain situations where the migrant professional does not meet the conditions set out in other recognition schemes. This general system is based on the principle of mutual recognition, without prejudice to the application of compensatory measures if there are substantial differences between the training acquired by the migrant and the training required in the host Member State. The compensatory measure may take the form of an adaptation period or an aptitude test. The choice between one or other of these tests is up to the migrant unless specific derogations exist.

(ii) *Chapter II, Arts 16-20: system of automatic recognition of qualifications attested by professional experience.* The industrial, craft and commercial activities listed in the directive are subject, under the conditions stated, to the automatic recognition of qualifications attested by professional experience.

(iii) *Chapter III, Arts 21–49: system of automatic recognition of qualifications for specific professions.* The automatic recognition of training qualifications, on the basis of coordination of the minimum training conditions, covers the following professions: doctors, nurses responsible for general care, dental practitioners, specialised dental practitioners, veterinary surgeons, midwives, pharmacists and architects.

The three systems of recognition of qualifications, which are applicable in the context of establishment, are set out and examined in detail below.

Chapter I, Articles 10–15: general system for the recognition of professional qualifications

When, in a host Member State, access to, or pursuit of, a profession is regulated (i.e. subject to possession of specific professional qualifications), the competent authority in the host Member State allows access to the profession in question and pursuit thereof under the same conditions as for nationals, provided that the applicant holds a training qualification obtained in another Member State which attests to a level of training at least equivalent to the level immediately below that required in the host Member State.

When, on the other hand, in the Member State of the applicant, access to a profession is not subject to possession of specific professional qualifications, the applicant should, in order to be able to gain access to the profession in a host Member State which does regulate that profession, provide proof of two years of full-time professional experience over the preceding ten years on top of the qualification.

The directive distinguishes between five levels of professional qualification:

(i) attestation of competence which corresponds to general primary or secondary education, attesting that the holder has acquired general knowledge, or an attestation of competence issued by a competent authority in the home Member State on the basis of a training course not forming part of a certificate or diploma, or of three years' professional experience;

(ii) certificate which corresponds to training at secondary level, of a technical or professional nature or general in character, supplemented by a professional course;

(iii) diploma certifying successful completion of training at post-secondary level of a duration of at least one year, or professional training which is comparable in terms of responsibilities and functions;

(iv) diploma certifying successful completion of training at higher or university level of a duration of at least three years and less than four years; and

(v) diploma certifying successful completion of training at higher or university level of a duration of at least four years.

On an exceptional basis, other types of training can be treated as coming within one of the five levels.

The host Member State can make recognition of qualifications subject to the applicant completing a compensation measure (aptitude test or adaptation period of a maximum of three years) if:

(i) the training is one year shorter than that required by the host Member State; or

(ii) the training received covers substantially different matters to those covered by the evidence of formal training required in the host Member State; or

(iii) the profession, as defined in the host Member State, comprises one or more regulated professional activities which do not exist in the corresponding profession in the applicant's home Member State, and that difference consists of specific training which covers substantially different matters from those completed by the migrant.

The host Member State must, in principle, offer the applicant the choice between an adaptation period and an aptitude test. The host Member State can only derogate from this requirement in the cases specifically provided for, or with the Commission's authorisation.

The directive provides for representative professional associations at both national and European level to establish 'common platforms' by determining measures to compensate for the substantial differences identified between the training requirements in at least two-thirds of the Member States, and in all the Member States which regulate that profession. That is, the platform must make it possible to provide adequate guarantees as to the level of qualification. If such a platform is likely to make the recognition of professional qualifications easier, the Commission may submit it to the Member States and adopt an implementing measure. Once this implementing measure has been adopted, the Member States shall waive the imposition of compensatory measures on applicants who meet the platform's conditions.

By late 2010, three years after the directive had to be transposed by the Member States, the Commission shall submit to the European Parliament and the Council a report on the provision of the directive relating to common platforms and, if necessary, make appropriate proposals for amending it.

Chapter II, Articles 16–20: system of automatic recognition of qualifications attested by professional experience in certain industrial, craft and commercial activities

By including the classes of professional activity covered by the former 'transitional' directives (i.e. Directives 64/222, 64/427, 68/364, 68/366, 68/368, 70/523, 75/368, 75/369, 82/470 and 82/489, which had already been consolidated by Directive 1999/42) and reducing the number of types of recognition to three, this directive aims to continue the objective of simplifying the legislation which sets the key conditions for the recognition of professional experience.

The elements taken into consideration for the recognition of professional experience are the duration and form of professional experience (in a self-employed or employed capacity) in the reference sector. Previous training is also taken into consideration and may reduce the amount of professional experience required. All previous training should, however, be proven by a certificate recognised by the Member State or judged by a competent professional body to be fully valid.

The pursuit of professional activities referred to in list I of Annex IV (which refers to various sectors ranging from the textile industry through to the chemical industry, via the oil industry, printing, manufacturing industry, and construction) is subject to the following conditions:

Years of professional experience in a self-employed capacity	Years of professional experience in an employed capacity	Previous training
6	–	–
3	–	3
4	–	2
3	5	–
–	5 in an executive position (except hairdressing establishments)	3

With regard to the pursuit of the professional activities referred to in list II of Annex IV (which refers to numerous sectors ranging from the manufacture of transport equipment to activities allied to transport, postal services and telecommunications and photographic studios) the directive lays down the following conditions:

Years of professional experience in a self-employed capacity	Years of professional experience in an employed capacity	Previous training
5	–	–
3	–	3
4	–	2
3	5	–
–	5	3
–	6	2

With regard to the pursuit of the professional activities referred to in list III of Annex IV (which refers to numerous sectors ranging from restaurants and hotels to personal, community and recreation services, and others) the directive lays down the following conditions:

Years of professional experience in a self-employed capacity	Years of professional experience in an employed capacity	Previous training
3	-	-
2	-	Unspecified duration
2	3	-
-	3	Unspecified duration

Chapter III, Articles 21-49: system of automatic recognition of qualifications for the professions of doctor, nurse, dentist, veterinary surgeon, midwife, pharmacist and architect

Each Member State automatically recognises certificates of training giving access to professional activities as a doctor, nurse responsible for general care, dental practitioner, veterinary surgeon, midwife, pharmacist and architect, covered by Annex V to the directive.

The directive also adopts the principle of automatic recognition for medical and dental specialisations common to at least two Member States under existing law, but restricts future additions to the directive of new medical specialisations – eligible for automatic recognition – to those that are common to at least two-fifths of the Member States.

For the purposes of equivalence in qualifications, the directive sets minimum training conditions for the following professions:

(i) **Doctor**: basic medical training precedes specialist medical training or the training of general practitioners.

– *Basic medical training*: admission to basic medical training shall be contingent upon possession of a diploma or certificate providing access to universities or equivalent institutes which provide higher education and shall comprise a total of at least six years of study or 5,500 hours of theoretical and practical training provided by, or under the supervision of, a university.

– *Specialist medical training*: admission to specialist medical training shall be contingent upon completion of six years of study in basic medical training and comprise full-time theoretical and practical training at a university or other recognised centre for a minimum duration which is not less than the duration referred to by the directive in Annex V, point 5.1.3 (such as, for example, five years for the specialisation in general surgery).

– *Training of general practitioners*: admission to general medical training shall be contingent upon completion of six years of study in basic medical training and comprise full-time practical training in an approved hospital, for a minimum duration of two years for any training of general practitioners leading to the award of evidence of formal qualifications issued before 1 January 2006, and of three years for certificates of training issued after that date.

(ii) **Nurses responsible for general care**: admission to training for nurses responsible for general care shall be contingent upon completion of general education of ten years, as attested by a diploma or other recognised certificate, shall comprise at least three years of study or 4,600 hours of theoretical and clinical training on a full-time basis, and shall include at least the programme described in Annex V, point 5.2.1.

(iii) **Dental practitioners**: admission to training as a dental practitioner presupposes possession of a diploma or certificate giving access, for the studies in question, to universities or higher institutes of an equivalent level, and shall comprise a total of at least five years of full-time theoretical and practical study, comprising at least the programme described in Annex V, point 5.3.1.

(iv) **Veterinary surgeons**: admission to veterinary training shall be contingent upon possession of a diploma or certificate entitling the holder to enter, for the studies in question, university establishments or institutes of higher education of an equivalent level, and shall comprise a total of at least five years of full-time theoretical and practical study at a university or other recognised higher institute, covering at least the study programme referred to in Annex V, point 5.4.1.

(v) **Midwives**: access to training as a midwife shall be contingent upon the following routes:

(a) completion of at least the first ten years of general school education. In this case, it entails specific full-time training as a midwife comprising at least three years of theoretical and practical study covering at least the programme described in Annex V, point 5.5.1; or

(b) possession of evidence of formal qualifications as a nurse responsible for general care. In this case, it entails in total at least a specific full-time training as a midwife of 18 months' duration, covering at least the study programme described in Annex V, point 5.5.1.

(vi) **Pharmacist**: admission to a course of training as a pharmacist shall be contingent upon possession of a diploma or certificate giving access, for the studies in question, to universities or higher institutes of an equivalent level, and shall include training of at least five years' duration, including at least four years of full-time theoretical and practical training at a university and a six-month traineeship in a pharmacy which is open to the public or in a hospital.

(vii) **Architect**: admission to a course of training as an architect shall be contingent upon possession of a diploma or certificate giving access, for the studies in question, to universities or higher institutes of an equivalent level, and shall comprise a total of at least four years of full-time study or six years of study, at least three years of which are on a full-time basis. For certain qualifications, Germany derogates from the conditions for the training of architects.

The directive extends the possibility for Member States to authorise part-time training for all of these professions, provided that the overall duration, level and quality of such training is not lower than that of continuous full-time training.

With the exception of the professions of doctor and architect, the directive provides a minimum programme of subjects to follow, which leaves room for the Member States to draw up more detailed study programmes. These lists of subjects which appear in Annex V can be amended to the extent required to adapt them to scientific and technical progress. Following the professional training they have received, aspiring doctors, nurses, dentists, veterinary surgeons, midwives, pharmacists and architects will possess a training qualification which has been issued by the competent bodies in the Member States bearing the titles described in Annex V and will enable them to practise their profession in any Member State. Without prejudice to the provisions relating to established rights, the Member States shall make access to, and pursuit of, the professional activities of doctor, nurse, dentist, veterinary surgeon, midwife and pharmacist subject to possession of one of the qualifications listed in the corresponding annexes which give guarantees relating to the acquisition by the party concerned of the knowledge and aptitudes referred to in Arts 24, 31, 34, 38, 40 and 44.

Without prejudice to the specific established rights granted to the professions concerned, and particularly to general practitioners and architects (Annex VI), if the evidence of medical training (which provides access to the professional activities of doctors with basic training and specialised doctors, nurses responsible for general care, dental practitioners, specialised dental practitioners, veterinary surgeons, midwives and pharmacists) held by nationals of Member States do not satisfy all the training requirements described, each Member State shall recognise as sufficient proof certificates of training issued by those Member States insofar as they attest successful completion of training which began before the reference dates laid down in Annex V.

Articles 50-52: procedure for the mutual recognition of professional qualifications

Articles 50–51 provide that an individual application must be submitted to the competent authority in the host Member State, accompanied by certain documents and certificates as listed in the directive (see Annex VII). According to the directive, the competent authorities will in future have one month to acknowledge receipt of an application and to draw attention to any missing documents. A decision will have to be taken within three months of the date on which the application was received in full. Reasons will have to be given for any rejection and it will be possible for a rejection, or a failure to take a decision by the deadline, to be contested in the national courts.

Member State nationals shall be able to use the title conferred on them, and possibly an abbreviated form thereof, as well as the professional title of the corresponding host Member State. If a profession is regulated in the host Member State by an association or organisation (see Annex I), Member State nationals must be able to become members of that organisation or association in order to be able to use the title (Art 52).

Article 57: knowledge of languages

Member States may require migrants to have the knowledge of languages necessary for practising the profession. This provision must be applied proportionately, which rules out the systematic imposition of language tests before a professional activity can be practised. It should be noted that any evaluation of language skills is separate from the recognition of professional qualifications. It must take place after recognition, when actual access to the profession in question is sought (Art 53).

Articles 56–60: administrative cooperation and other provisions

In order to facilitate the application of the above provisions, the directive seeks close collaboration between the competent authorities in the host Member State and the home Member State, and the introduction of the following provisions:

(i)   each Member State shall designate a coordinator to facilitate the uniform application of the directive (Art 56);

(ii)   each Member State shall designate contact points by no later than 20 October 2007. These contact points will have the task of providing citizens with such information as is necessary concerning the recognition of professional qualifications and to assist them in enforcing their rights, particularly through contact with the competent authorities to rule on requests for recognition (Art 57);

(iii) the nomination of Member States' representatives to the Committee on the recognition of professional qualifications. This committee, which is chaired by the Commission representative, is to assist the Commission within the limits of the enforcement powers conferred on it by the directive (Art 58);

(iv)   the Commission shall consult with experts from the professional groups in an appropriate manner (Art 59).

Every two years, the Member States shall send a report to the Commission on the application of the system. If the application of one of the provisions of the directive presents major difficulties in a particular area, the Commission shall examine those difficulties in collaboration with the Member State concerned (Art 60(1)).

As from 20 October 2007, every five years the Commission will draw up a report on the implementation of the directive (Art 60(2)).

Future developments

On 13 January 2004, the Commission adopted a proposal for a new directive on services in the internal market. The proposed directive is proceeding through the legislative process and it is anticipated that it will be adopted during the first half of 2007. Once it has been adopted it will not have to be transposed by Member States for at least two years.

The proposed directive aims to maximise the benefits of the single market for citizens, consumers and businesses. For services, the single market is not yet working as well as it should. There are still barriers hindering service providers from establishing themselves in other Member States or trading across borders. This needs to be addressed because services are important to the EU: they account for 60–70 per cent of economic activity in the 27 Member States of the EU.

The proposed directive seeks to achieve the following:

1. Businesses will be able to establish themselves anywhere in the EU. Service providers will be able to obtain information and complete administrative formalities through single points of contact in each Member State. This will speed up authorisation and reduce costs. So, for example, a business wishing to build and run a hotel or a store in another Member State will no longer have to deal with several different authorities at national, regional and local level. A service provider will be able to complete all formalities to set up a business online. This will avoid the expense and inconvenience of

multiple visits to authorities in the Member State into which they intend to provide services. Authorisation schemes in Member States will be clearer, more transparent, less restrictive and non-discriminatory.

2. Businesses will find it easier to provide services across borders. Service providers will be free to provide their services across borders into other Member States, except where prohibited by Member State requirements that are non-discriminatory, proportionate and necessary for reasons relating to public policy, public security, public health and the protection of the environment.

   It will be possible to provide services in a Member State without having to establish there. Currently a business has to have a permanent presence to provide certain types of services. Removing a requirement to establish will make it possible for more businesses to offer services on a temporary or occasional basis. Activities covered by an establishment requirement in some Member States include many tourism-related services, e.g. mountain guides, yacht and sailing boat hire, ski instructors, etc.

   Businesses will no longer be required by a Member State to take on a particular legal form in order to provide services into that territory. Current examples of burdensome requirements in Member States include a requirement for real estate agencies to be 'natural persons' in order to be allowed to provide the service, which excludes real estate agencies which are companies from other Member States.

3. Consumers will be properly protected. Consumers will benefit from better information on businesses and the services they offer. They will know more about price and quality. It will not be possible to discriminate against consumers on grounds of residence or nationality. All EU citizens will enjoy the same rights wherever they live. For example, museums will not be able to charge non-residents higher prices and organisers of sports events, such as marathons, will not be allowed to charge non-residents higher participation fees.

4. Supervision will be better due to more effective cross-border cooperation between authorities. Member States will have to step up administrative cooperation between them to ensure improved and effective supervision of service providers without duplication. This will be underpinned by a new electronic system allowing for the direct and efficient exchange of information between Member States.

Information relating to the proposed directive, and details about the stage it has reached within the legislative process, is available at:

   http://ec.europa.eu/internal_market/services/services-dir/index_en.htm

Summary

Now you have read this chapter you should be able to:

■ Identify the provisions of the EC Treaty which apply to the freedom of establishment and the freedom to provide and receive services.

■ Explain how Art 49 EC Treaty on the freedom to provide and receive services is applied by the European Court of Justice, and to ascertain the circumstances in which restrictions to such freedom may be objectively justified.

■ Understand the circumstances in which Directive 2004/38 confers a general right of residence.

- Identify and explain the provisions of Directive 2004/38 which abolish restrictions on movement and residence.

- Discuss the conditions which apply pursuant to Directive 2004/38 with regard to an EU citizen who seeks to remain within a Member State having pursued a self-employed activity there.

- Explain how Art 12 EC Treaty and Art 24, Directive 2004/38 establish the right of equal treatment for persons who exercise their Community law rights of establishment.

- Understand how Art 12 EC Treaty and Art 24, Directive 2004/38 establish the right of equal treatment for persons who exercise their free movement rights as providers and recipients of services.

- Explain how Art 43 EC Treaty is applied in respect of qualifications and training.

- Assess the impact which harmonisation and general directives has had on Art 43 EC Treaty, and explain the changes which will be made to this system of harmonisation and general directives by Directive 2005/36.

Further reading

Textbooks

Barnard, C. (2004) *The Substantive Law of the EU: The four freedoms* (1st edn), Oxford University Press, Chapters 12 and 13.

Craig, P. and De Burca, G. (2003) *EU Law Text, Cases and Materials* (3rd edn), Oxford University Press, Chapter 18.

Foster, N. (2006) *Foster on EU Law* (1st edn), Oxford University Press, Chapter 9 (Section 9.5).

Steiner, J., Woods, L. and Twigg-Flesner, C. (2006) *EU Law* (9th edn), Oxford University Press, Chapters 21 and 22.

Storey, T. and Turner, C. (2005) *Unlocking EU Law* (1st edn), Hodder Arnold, Chapter 12.

Tillotson, J. and Foster, N. (2003) *Text, Cases and Materials on EU Law* (4th edn), Cavendish Publishing, Chapter 13.

Vincenzi, C. (1995) 'Welcoming the Well and Wealthy: The Implementation of Directive 90/364 in the UK', in Daintith, T. (ed.) *Implementing EC Law in the UK: Structures for Indirect Rule*, John Wiley & Sons.

Weatherill, S. (2006) *Cases and Materials on EU Law* (7th edn), Oxford University Press, Chapter 14.

Journal articles

Eidenmüller, H., 'Deregulating the Market for Legal Services in the European Community' (1990) 53 MLR 604.

Greaves, R. 'Advertising Restrictions and the Free Movement of Goods and Services' (1998) 34 EL Rev 305.

Hatzopoulos, V., 'Recent Developments of the Case Law of the ECJ in the Field of Services' (2000) 37 CML Rev 43.

Hatzopoulos, V. and Do, T.U., 'The Case Law of the ECJ Concerning the Free Provision of Services' (2006) 43 CML Rev 923.

Marenco, M., 'The Notion of Restriction on Freedom of Establishment and Provision of Services in the Case Law of the Court' (1991) 11 YEL 111.

Peers, S., 'Indirect Rights for Third-Country Service Providers Confirmed' (1995) 32 CML Rev 311.

Van der Woude, M. and Mead, P., 'Free Movement of the Tourist in Community Law' (1988) 25 CML Rev 117.

Weatherill, S., 'Note on **Cowan** v **Le Trésor Public**' (1989) 25 CML Rev 563.

Wouters, J., 'Conflict of Laws and the Single Market for Financial Services' (1997) 4 MJ 161, 284.

14 Social security

Aims and objectives

At the end of this chapter you should understand:

- How Art 42 EC Treaty, and Regulations 1408/71 and 574/72 facilitate the free movement of workers and the self-employed.
- The range of persons who come within the scope of Regulations 1408/71 and 574/72.
- How the principle of equal treatment is applied in the context of Regulation 1408/72.
- The principles of Art 42 EC Treaty as built upon by Regulation 1408/71 and the case law of the Court of Justice, in particular with regard to:

  - aggregation of contributions and periods of contribution;

  - exportability of benefits;

  - prevention of overlapping benefits;

  - the types of benefit covered; and

  - the double-function test.

- The difference between social assistance and social advantages, and the availability of such within the UK.
- The changes which will come into effect once Regulation 883/2004 comes into force.

Introduction to social security

All Member States of the Community have contributory social security systems, but they vary greatly in the quantity and quality of benefits which they provide. This is, potentially, a major barrier to the mobility of the employed and self-employed. A person moving to another Member State may suffer the double disadvantage of losing out on the contributions to his own national insurance scheme, with a consequent loss of benefits in his home state, and he may also find that he is not entitled to benefits in the host Member State because he has not contributed sufficiently or for long enough. The founders of the Community were clearly aware of this difficulty and provision was made to deal with it in what is now Art 42 EC Treaty. This facilitates the adoption of such measures in the field of social security as are necessary to provide freedom of movement for workers (and the self-employed (see below)). To this end it shall make arrangements to secure for migrant workers and their dependants:

- aggregation, for the purpose of acquiring and retaining the right to benefit and of calculating the amount of benefit, of all periods taken into account under the laws of the several Member States; and
- payment of benefits to persons resident in the territories of Member States.

Article 42 EC Treaty is thus aimed at enabling the migrant worker to take his accrued rights with him, in the sense that his contributions and period of contribution in his home state will be taken into account in the host Member State, and his contributions in the host Member State will be taken into account in calculating his level of benefits when he returns to his home state. Given the variation in level and type of contribution in each Member State, and the dissimilarity of social security schemes, this is a complex task. It must, however, be emphasised that the scheme is not intended to equalise the level of social security benefits throughout the Community. It is simply directed at ensuring that the migrant worker obtains, as far as possible, equal treatment within local social security schemes, and does not lose out in relation to entitlements due from his home state. The Court of Justice has declared that, when applying national social security law to migrant workers, the host Member State should interpret its own legislation in the light of the aims of Arts 32 to 42 EC Treaty. It should, as far as possible, avoid interpreting its own legislation in such a way as to discourage migrant workers from exercising their rights to freedom of movement (**Van Munster** (Case C–165/91)).

As a result of the large discrepancies between national social security schemes, this area of Community law has been highly productive of litigation and the case law is considerable and complicated. This chapter will do no more than outline the general principles and provide some examples of their interpretation by the Court of Justice and their application in the UK.

The current Community rules enacted to give effect to the principles laid down in Art 42 EC Treaty are to be found in Regulations 1408/71 and 574/72, as amended by Regulations 2001/83 and 1247/92. Regulation 1408/71, as amended by Regulation 2001/83, contains the substantive provisions. Regulation 574/72 deals with the procedures for the operation and interrelation of national social security schemes. The most recent important legislation, Regulation 1247/92, limits the availability of national welfare provisions, and will be considered in the context of UK legislation.

The European Commission has published a guide, 'Your Social Security Rights when moving within the European Union', which is available on its website at:

http://europa.eu.int/comm/employment_social/social-security-schemes/index_en.htm

The scope of Regulation 1408/71, as amended, is now examined.

The beneficiaries of the regulations

The regulations cover EU citizens who are employed or self-employed and who are, or who have been, subject to social security legislation in more than one of the Member States. Their families are also covered, together with any survivors of the worker or self-employed person after his death, provided that they were, at some stage, covered by the social security legislation of more than one Member State (Arts 1 and 2, Regulation

1408/71). Regulation 1408/71 also applies to refugees, stateless persons, and their families, as defined by Art 1 of the Geneva Convention on the Status of Refugees 1951 and Art 1 of the Convention on Stateless Persons 1954. It also applies to civil servants who are treated as such by national legislation. The term 'employed person' is much wider in scope than the term 'worker' under Art 39 EC Treaty, and it includes any person who is insured either voluntarily or compulsorily against one of the contingencies covered by the regulation. The fourth recital of Regulation 1408/71 refers to the wide variations in applicability of various national social security schemes, which made it desirable to establish the principle that the regulation applies to all nationals of a Member State insured under social security schemes for employed persons.

In relation to the self-employed, they are classified as such because, like the employed, they are included in a national scheme set up for the benefit of the self-employed, not because they might enjoy that status under Arts 43 and 49 EC Treaty. In the following case, the Court of Justice considered the meaning of 'self-employment' in the context of Regulation 1408/71:

Van Roosmalen (Case 300/84)

A missionary priest worked from 1955 until 1980 in what is now Zaire. He was not paid by the religious order of which he was a member but was maintained by his parishioners. The Court of Justice held that the concept of a self-employed person encompasses any person who pursues, other than under a contract of employment, the exercise of an independent trade or profession in respect of which he receives income permitting him to meet some or all of his needs. The situation is not affected by the fact that the income may be supplied by a third party – the parishioners, in this case.

The determining factor is the making of contributions to the national social security scheme. Thus, a person who goes to another Member State, not in the capacity of a worker, may still fall within the scope of the regulation. In **Hoekstra (née Unger)** (Case 75/63), a person subject to The Netherlands' social security legislation who fell ill during a visit to her parents in Germany was entitled to claim the cost of treatment received in that country on her return. Similarly, in **Hessische Knappschaft v Maison Singer et Fils** (Case 44/65), a German worker was killed in a road accident while on holiday in France. It was argued that the rights arising under Art 42 EC Treaty were intended to promote the free movement of workers, not holidaymakers, but the Court of Justice rejected this argument. It held that nothing in Art 42 required the concept of workers to be limited strictly to that of migrant workers as such. In **Brack v Insurance Officer** (Case 17/76), the Court of Justice held that the term 'employed persons' must be applied taking into account the objectives and spirit of the regulation and Arts 39 to 42 EC Treaty on which it is based. The claimant had been covered by the UK social security scheme, first as an employed person and then in a self-employed capacity. He had gone to France for health reasons, but had fallen seriously ill there. The Court held that he retained the status of an employed/self-employed person for the purposes of Art 1(a)(ii), Regulation 1408/71 during his stay in France.

Family members

Unlike the provisions relating to the exercise of free movement rights for workers and the self-employed under Directive 2004/38 (see Chapters 12 and 13), the scope of family membership is not defined by Community law but is left to the Member State. Under Art 1(f), Regulation 1408/71 a member of the family is any person defined or recognised as a member of the family or 'designated as a member of the household by the legislation under which benefits are provided ... Where the said legislations regard as a member of the family or a member of the household only a person living under the same roof as the worker, this condition shall be considered satisfied if the worker in question is mainly dependent on that worker'. Although the definition of family entitlement is left to the state concerned, where the definition could constitute a barrier to worker mobility, the Court of Justice has preferred a broader definition. In **Mr and Mrs F v Belgian State** (Case 7/75), the Belgian social security scheme provided a benefit payable to parents of handicapped children. This was payable only to parents of Belgian nationality and only until the child's age of majority. The Court of Justice held that neither condition should be applied to the child of an employed person covered by Regulation 1408/71.

An exception to the general rule has been introduced by Regulation 1247/92, amending Art 1(f), which provides a Community definition of 'family members' in the case of benefits for people with disabilities. The Court of Justice had already adopted a more liberal definition of 'family members' to include adult handicapped members who had never worked and could not do so (**Inzirillo** (Case 63/76)).

Equality of treatment

The beneficiaries of Regulation 1408/71 who are resident in the territory of one of the Member States 'shall be subject to the same obligations and enjoy the same benefits under the legislation of any Member State as the nationals of that state' except where the regulation provides otherwise (Art 3(1)). The effect of this provision is to prohibit direct or indirect discrimination. In **Commission v Belgium** (Case C–326/90), the Court of Justice held that the Belgian authorities had breached Art 3(1) by maintaining a requirement of a period of residence on Belgian territory which workers from other Member States subject to Belgian legislation had to fulfil in order to qualify for the grant of allowances for handicapped people, the guaranteed income for the elderly and the payment of the minimum subsistence allowance (minimex). An even more direct form of discrimination occurred in the following case:

Palermo (Case 237/78)

Under the French Social Security Code, an allowance was payable to French women of at least 65 years of age and without sufficient means, who were married and who had brought up at least five dependent children of French nationality during a period of at least nine years before their sixteenth birthday. The applicant, an Italian woman, submitted a claim for this allowance. The French authorities did not insist on the nationality requirement in the case of the applicant herself, but refused the benefit because five of the seven children were Italian and not French. The case came before the Court of Justice.

The Court of Justice held that payment of a benefit could not be made conditional on the nationality of the claimant or her children, provided that both she and the children held the nationality of a Member State.

Discrimination may occur in relation not only to entitlement to social security benefits but also to contributions. In **Allué and Coonan** (Case 33/88) a number of EU nationals employed as university teachers were obliged, as a consequence of Italian legislation, to pay their own social security contributions, whereas in the case of the ordinary salaried employees of the university, this burden was largely carried by the employer. The Court of Justice held that the practice violated Art 3(1), Regulation 1408/71. The Court of Justice has also said that a system of calculation of social security contributions that works less favourably in relation to trainee workers coming from another Member State in comparison to workers who come under the national educational system is unlawful because it is also discriminatory (**URSSAGF** *v* **Société à Responsabilité Limitée Hostellerie Le Manoir** (Case C–27/91)).

Another aspect of equality of treatment in the regulation is specifically dealt with in relation to mobility and receipt of benefits. Article 10(1), Regulation 1408/71 provides:

> Save as otherwise provided in this regulation, invalidity, old-age or survivors' cash benefits, pensions for accidents at work or occupational diseases and death grants acquired under the legislation of one or more Member States shall not be subject to any reduction, modification, suspension, withdrawal or confiscation by reason of the fact that the recipient resides in the territory of a Member State other than that in which the institution responsible for payment is situated.

The effect of Art 10(1) is that a worker or self-employed person who has, for example, contributed all his working life to a national insurance scheme in one Member State will be entitled to have that pension paid to him at the full rate, should he choose to retire to another Member State. It should be noted, however, that the right of equal treatment as it affects payment of social security and the mobility of the employed and self-employed applies only to those benefits specifically covered by Art 10(1): i.e. benefits which are 'exportable', in the sense that they are payable by the state where the contributions have been made, to the recipient in the Member State in which he or she now lives.

The principle of equality is also reflected in Directive 79/7, under which there is a prohibition against any kind of discrimination on the ground of sex (Art 4(1)). The principle applies in relation to access to social security schemes, the obligation to contribute and the calculation of contributions, and the calculation of benefits. This directive applies both to migrant workers and their families and to domestic claimants for social security who do not leave their own state. The equality requirement is, however, limited to schemes which relate to sickness, invalidity, old-age, accidents at work and occupational diseases, unemployment and social assistance, so far as the social assistance is intended to supplement or replace one of the schemes included. The directive does not, for example, cover housing benefits (**R** *v* **Secretary of State for Social Security, ex parte Smithson** (Case C–243/90)). However, where a benefit is linked to employment (e.g. child tax credit and working tax credit in the UK, which are intended to bring a family's wages up to a minimum level) the position is different. The Court of Justice has held that benefits of this kind are concerned with improving access to employment. They are therefore subject to the prohibitions against discrimination in employment as provided for in Directive 76/207 (**Meyers** *v* **Adjudication Officer** (Case C–116/94)).

The principles of Article 42 EC Treaty

The principles underlying Art 42 EC Treaty have been elaborated by Regulation 1408/71 and by decisions of the Court of Justice.

1. Aggregation of contributions and periods of contribution

The Court of Justice has held on a number of occasions that all the provisions of Regulation 1408/71 are to be interpreted in the light of Art 42 EC Treaty (see, for example, **Reichling** *v* **INAMI** (Case C–406/93)). The purpose of Art 42 is to facilitate freedom of movement for workers by securing for migrant workers and their dependants 'aggregation, for the purpose of acquiring and retaining the right to benefit and of calculating the amount of benefit of all periods taken into account under the laws of the several countries' (Art 42(a)).

Article 18(b), Regulation 1408/71 contains specific provisions on aggregation in relation to sickness and maternity benefits:

> The competent institution of a Member State whose legislation makes the acquisition, retention or recovery of the right to benefits conditional upon the completion of periods of insurance, employment or residence shall, to the extent necessary, take account of periods of insurance, employment or residence completed under the legislation of any other Member State as if they were periods completed under the legislation which it administers (as amended by the Act of Accession and Regulation 2864/72).

Reichling, above, for example, concerned the way in which the amount of invalidity benefit to which the claimant was entitled should be calculated under Art 46(2)(a), Regulation 1408/71. The legislation of the state where he claimed the benefit required the amount to be calculated on the basis of the amount of his remuneration which he last received in that state. He was not, in fact, working in that state when the invalidity occurred. The Court of Justice held that the competent institution of the state in which he made the claim must calculate it on the basis of the remuneration he received in the state where he last worked. In **Paraschi** *v* **Handelsversicherungsanstalt Württemberg** (Case C–349/87), the failure of the host Member State to take account of the circumstances of the claimant in the state of origin in calculating the qualifying period for a benefit was held to constitute discrimination in breach of both Art 39(2) EC Treaty and the aggregation provisions of Art 42 EC Treaty.

2. Exportability of benefits

Exportability is often more expressively described as 'the portability principle'. It requires that the right to receive a benefit, usually from the state of origin, attaches to a worker as he travels around the EU, irrespective of national boundaries. It also enables individuals to have benefits remitted to dependants who live in other Member States. It does not, however, apply to all types of benefit, but, as a general rule, only to those payable on a long-term basis. The benefits which are exportable are: unemployment, invalidity, old-age or survivors' cash benefits, pensions for accidents at work or occupational diseases, death grants and lump sum benefits granted in case of remarriage of a surviving spouse (Art 10(1), Regulation 1408/71). Unemployment benefit is, however, exportable only for three months after the individual has left the home territory (Art 69(1)(c),

Regulation 1408/71). Other benefits linked to the above may also be exportable. In **Re an Emigré to the Canary Islands** [1994] 1 CMLR 717, for example, the UK Social Security Commissioners decided that a constant attendance allowance that was payable to a recipient of an invalidity allowance should be treated in the same way, and be payable to the claimant who had emigrated from the UK to the Canary Islands.

3. Prevention of overlapping benefits

The concept of overlapping benefits is closely related to exportability. It is intended to prevent a worker or a self-employed person who has qualified for an exportable benefit from receiving it from both his country of origin and the state to which he has emigrated.

Article 12(1), Regulation 1408/71 provides that the regulation:

> Can neither confer nor maintain the right to several benefits of the same kind for one and the same period of compulsory insurance.

This provision does not, however, apply to invalidity, old-age, death or occupational disease payments which are awarded by the institutions of two or more Member States (Arts 41, 43(2) and (3), 46, 50, 51 and 60(1)(b), Regulation 1408/71).

In relation to those cases to which the rule against overlapping benefits applies, the position can be illustrated by a claim to unemployment benefit. A worker who is, for example, intermittently unemployed in the host Member State may not claim unemployment benefit as long as he is entitled to receive it from his state of origin (Art 71(2)). National legislation prohibiting the receipt of overlapping benefits is lawful, provided that it does not work more unfavourably for the claimant than Community law. Whether or not two benefits are of the same kind and do, in fact, overlap is a matter of interpretation of the national legislation by the national court (**Union Nationale des Mutualités Socialistes** *v* **Aldo Del Grosso** (Case C–325/93)).

In the case of old-age, invalidity and other benefits which may be paid on an overlapping basis, it is still permissible for the state paying the largest amount of benefit to set off against what it would normally pay, the amount which the beneficiary actually receives in the state where he is living, as illustrated in the following case:

Bogana v *UNMS* (Case C-193/92)

The claimant, an Italian national, had worked in both Italy and Belgium. When he became incapable of working, he returned to Italy, and became entitled in both states to invalidity benefits. He was paid the Belgian benefit, less the Italian benefit, on a pro rata basis. The Court of Justice accepted this as a proper course. However, it did not accept that when an increase in payment was made in Italy to compensate beneficiaries for the deterioration in value of the Italian currency, the Belgian payments could be decreased. To allow that to happen would depreciate the real value of the claimant's total pension.

4. The types of benefit covered

Article 4(1), Regulation 1408/71 provides that:

> This regulation shall apply to all legislation concerning the following branches of social security:
> (a) sickness and maternity benefits;
> (b) invalidity benefits, including those intended for the maintenance or improvement of earning capacity;
> (c) old-age benefits;
> (d) survivors' benefits;
> (e) benefits in respect of accidents at work and occupational diseases;
> (f) death grants;
> (g) unemployment benefits;
> (h) family benefits.

The terms 'benefits' (which is used throughout Art 4(1)) and 'pensions' are defined in Art 1(t) as 'all benefits and pensions ... payable out of public funds, revalorisation increases and supplementary allowances, ... and also lump sum benefits which may be paid in lieu of pensions, and payments made by way of reimbursement of contributions'.

Not all benefits are covered by the regulation. Article 4(4) expressly excludes three types:

1. social and medical assistance;

2. benefit schemes for victims of war and its consequences;

3. special schemes for civil servants and persons treated as such.

The effect of these exclusions is that migrant workers and the self-employed in other Member States will not be entitled to the benefits listed in Art 4(1), except where they are linked to other benefits to which they are entitled under the 'double-function test' (see below).

The regulation does not provide any criteria for differentiating between 'social security' and 'social assistance'. The Court of Justice has held that benefits must satisfy two tests to come within the regulation. First, the legislation granting the benefit must place claimants in a legally defined position as a result of which they have an absolute right to benefits as opposed to a conditional right dependent upon the exercise of a discretionary power in their favour. Second, the benefit must cover one of the risks referred to in Art 4(1) of the regulation. The characteristic feature of social assistance is that it is discretionary and will be payable according to some nationally defined criteria indicating need. In the UK, for example, a payment such as the contribution-based jobseeker's allowance is dependent on contributions and other qualifying criteria. Once they are established, there is, as a general rule, an entitlement to payment. Payment of income-based jobseeker's allowance will depend on an assessment of means, and may be reduced or withheld in certain circumstances, even when the criteria are satisfied (e.g. if a claimant refuses to accept suitable employment). Under Directive 2004/38, a claim for social assistance by an economically self-sufficient EU citizen will be indicative that the EU citizen no longer has a right of residence under that directive.

The Commission, reflecting the jurisprudence of the Court of Justice, has laid down the following criteria for identifying social assistance:

1. The benefit must be designed to alleviate a manifest condition of need in the person concerned, established after a proper investigation into his resources and bearing in

mind the standard of living in the country of residence. If cash benefits are concerned, the amount must be set, case by case, on the basis of the individual situation and means of livelihood of the person concerned.

2. The award of benefit should not be subject to any condition as to the length of employment or length of residence.

3. The fact that a benefit is non-contributory does not determine its nature as a social assistance benefit or exempt it from the rules laid down in Regulation 1408/71. In the same way, the fact that a benefit is linked to a means test is not sufficient in itself to give it the nature of a social assistance benefit. (Commentary on Regulation 1408/71 in *Compendium of Community Provisions on Social Security* (1980) Commission of the European Communities, para 4084, p. 235.)

Although the Court of Justice has emphasised that the list of benefits enumerated in Art 4(1) is exhaustive (see **Scrivner** *v* **Centre Public d'Aide Sociale de Chastre** (Case 122/84)), some benefits may, according to the circumstances, qualify as both social assistance and social security under the 'double-function' test.

5. The double-function test

Although the Court of Justice held in **Scrivner** that discretionary social assistance-type benefits would fall outside the scope of the regulation, as a result of the exclusion contained in Art 4(4), it has tended to be generous in its interpretation of the scope of Regulation 1408/71. The discretionary element which the Court established as the primary differentiation between social security and social assistance did not exclude many benefits, which might not, at first sight, appear to be social security benefits, from being accepted as coming within the scope of the regulation (**Inzirillo** (Case 63/76); **Vigier** (Case 70/80); **Palermo** (Case 237/78)). However, following **Scrivner**, in which the Court of Justice emphasised the exhaustive nature of the list in Art 4(1), Regulation 1408/71, the opportunities for claiming benefits not listed in Art 4(1) as social security benefits would seem to have diminished. In **Scrivner**, the Court turned to the 'social advantages' route in Art 7(2), Regulation 1612/68 as an alternative basis for entitlement (see below, and Chapter 12),

The 'double-function test', which was one aspect of the earlier case law, would seem to have survived. It remains important because, unlike 'social advantages', a benefit which can be brought within Regulation 1408/71 will be 'exportable', whereas 'social advantages' (see below) are available only in the host Member State and are open only to those who have the status of worker or members of a worker's family. The 'double-function' test was established by the Court of Justice in the following case:

Frilli (Case 1/72)

The Court of Justice held that even a means-tested discretionary payment could become 'social security' rather than 'social assistance' where it was used to *supplement* a contributory old-age benefit. Thus, a supplement which, when it stood alone, might be considered to be 'social assistance', could come within the scope of the regulation if it could be regarded as a supplement to one of the listed benefits.

In **Giletti** (Cases 379–381/85), the Court of Justice held that Community social security benefits could include supplements to inadequate old-age, widows' and invalidity pensions.

The 'double-function' aspect of welfare benefits, as developed in the jurisprudence of the Court of Justice, was recognised in subsequent Community legislation. The preamble to Regulation 1247/92 states that it is 'necessary to take account of this [case] law', and that changes are necessary which 'take account of the special characteristics of the benefits concerned . . . in order to protect the interests of migrant workers in accordance with the provisions of Article 51 [now Art 42] of the Treaty'. Social assistance-type benefits may therefore continue to be treated as social security where they are linked to a recognised benefit under Art 4(1), Regulation 1408/71. Where there is no such linkage, a person may have an entitlement to it only, if at all, as a social advantage under Art 7(2), Regulation 1612/68 in the host Member State where he works or has worked.

The problem of classification of non-contributory benefits has partly been alleviated as a result of the extension of the scope of Regulation 1247/92 to cover a wide range of non-contributory social security benefits.

Social assistance and social advantages

The exclusion of social and medical assistance from the scope of Regulation 1408/71 was, potentially, a major obstacle to social mobility, but it reflected the anxiety of Member States about 'social tourism'. Now that EU citizenship (and Directive 2004/38) confers a right to live anywhere in the Community, it would seem arguable, at least, that EU citizens, like citizens of the nation states, should be able to do so regardless of means. This argument, as H.C. Taschner (a Commission official) has observed, 'overlooks the fact that the social security systems of Member States still differ enormously, and any effort to harmonise these systems is met with formidable resistance, mainly by those Member States that have highly developed social security systems financed by their taxpayers . . . the fear of an uncontrolled flow of persons seeking residence for no other reason than to become beneficiaries of better social security than at home was, and is, completely justified' (Taschner, 1993). There is, in fact, little evidence that 'social tourism' is a major factor in the decision to move to another Member State, but in matters of political sensitivity of this kind, the perception is more important than the reality.

Although Regulation 1408/71 excluded social assistance, the narrow definition given to that term and the generous interpretation of the listed benefits, in the ways described above, did somewhat diminish the problems caused by that exclusion. Where 'social assistance' payments could not, by the double-function test, be linked to a social security benefit, the Court of Justice developed the scope of social advantages under Art 7(2), Regulation 1612/68 to plug the gap. The scope of social advantages has already been examined in some detail in Chapter 12, but something needs to be said about Art 7(2), Regulation 1612/68 in the context of social assistance.

In the following case, the Court of Justice had to consider the relationship between 'social assistance', which is excluded from the application of Regulation 1408/71 by Art 4(4), and 'social advantages' under Art 7(2), Regulation 1612/68:

Scrivner v *Centre Public d'Aide Sociale de Chastre* (Case 122/84)

Mr and Mrs Scrivner settled in Belgium in 1978 with their six children. In June 1982 Mr Scrivner left his employment 'for personal reasons'. It is not stated in the report what they were, but the Court of Justice seems to have assumed that they were not such as to make Mr Scrivner 'voluntarily unemployed' and therefore deprive him of his worker status (see **Raulin** (Case C-357/89), para 22). Mr Scrivner and his family were refused payment of minimex (a grant to provide the minimum means of subsistence) because it was available only to those who had been resident in Belgium for at least five years. The claimants argued that the benefit fell within Regulation 1408/71, and that they should, therefore, be protected from discrimination under Art 3(1) of the regulation. The question was referred to the Court of Justice under what is now Art 234 EC Treaty. The Court, on this occasion adopting a more restrictive approach, held that minimex did not fall within the scope of the regulation:

> The Court has stated in a number of decisions that the distinction between benefits which are excluded from the scope of Regulation 1408/71 and benefits which come within it rests entirely on factors relating to each benefit, in particular its purpose and the condition for its grant, and not whether the national legislation describes the benefit as a social security benefit or not. (para 11)

The list of benefits contained in Art 4(1) is exhaustive. In the above case, the Court of Justice therefore held that a branch of social security not mentioned in the list does not fall within that category 'even if it confers upon individuals a legally defined position entitling them to benefits'. Furthermore, minimex 'adopts "need" as an essential criterion for its application and *does not make any stipulations as to periods of work, contribution or affiliation to any particular social security body covering a specific risk*' (para 13, emphasis added). The Court was, however, prepared to accept that minimex was a social advantage under Art 7(2), Regulation 1612/68 and found that it could be seen to be an advantage granted to national workers 'primarily because of their objective status as workers or by virtue of the mere fact of their residence on the national territory'. In so deciding, the Court drew on the analogy of the guaranteed old people's income in **Castelli v ONPTS** (Case 261/83), which the Court had also found to be a social advantage under Art 7(2), Regulation 1612/68.

Self-employed persons are not entitled to receive subsistence payments or social assistance as a social advantage, because Regulation 1612/68 is applicable only to workers and their families. However, the distinction between having equal access to facilities to enable a person to pursue a business or a profession and equal access to benefits is not always clear. In **Commission v Italy** (Case 63/86), the Court of Justice held that denial of housing aid to a self-employed person claiming under Arts 43 and 49 EC Treaty was unlawful as an 'obstacle to the pursuit of the occupation itself' (para 16).

The scope of the benefits covered

The range of social security schemes listed in Art 4(1), Regulation 1408/71 has been the subject of extensive litigation in the Court of Justice. A selection of cases on the main benefits will give some idea of the scope of each benefit.

Sickness and maternity benefits

In **Heinze v Landesversicherungsanstalt Rheinprovinz** (Case 14/72) the Court of Justice held that 'sickness benefits' are not confined to benefits paid to a sick person when he is incapacitated. They include social security benefits which, without being related to earning capacity on the part of the insured person, are also granted to members of his family and which are designed principally for healing the sick person and protecting those around him. In **Commission v Luxembourg** (Case C–118/91), the Court of Justice held that a maternity benefit was covered by both Art 4, Regulation 1408/71 and Art 7(2), Regulation 1612/68 as a social advantage. Residence requirements breached both the principle of aggregation under Art 42 EC Treaty and the prohibition against discrimination.

Regulation 1408/71 applies to all legislation concerning branches of social security relating, *inter alia*, to sickness benefits. It does not apply, on the other hand, to the legislation of a Member State on special non-contributory benefits, listed in an annex to the Regulation, whose validity is confined to part of the state's territory. In the case of Austria, benefits granted under the legislation of the provinces for disabled persons and persons in the need of care were regarded as such special benefits. In the following case, the Court of Justice had to adjudicate on whether the inclusion of such benefit in the annex to the Regulation was conclusive of the fact that it constituted a special benefit:

Silvia Hosse v *Land Salzburg* (Case C-286/03)

Mr Hosse, of German nationality, was a frontier worker employed in Austria as a teacher in the Province of Salzburg. He paid taxes and social security contributions in Austria and was affiliated to sickness insurance in that state. He resided in Germany, near the Austrian frontier, with his daughter Silvia Hosse, who was severely disabled. In those circumstances, an application was made for a care allowance for Silvia Hosse, under a law of the Province of Salzburg. The application was refused on the ground that under that law the person reliant on care must have his main residence in the Province of Salzburg in order to receive the care allowance. An appeal was brought before the Oberster Gerichtshof (Supreme Court), which decided to refer several questions to the Court of Justice for a preliminary ruling.

The Court of Justice held, first, that the care allowance in question was indeed mentioned in the annex to the Regulation listing special non-contributory benefits. It stated, however, that **that mention on its own is not sufficient to exclude the allowance from the scope of the Regulation. Derogating provisions of the Regulation which exclude certain specific benefits from the scope of the Regulation must be interpreted strictly.** Those derogations can apply only to benefits which satisfy cumulatively the conditions for exclusion it lays down, that is, benefits which are both special and non-contributory and are laid down by legislation whose application is limited to part of the territory of a Member State.

Next, the Court concluded that **the care allowance in question does not constitute a special non-contributory benefit but a sickness benefit within the meaning of the Regulation.** It is a benefit which is granted objectively on the basis of a legally defined position and is intended to improve the state of health and life of persons reliant on care, its essential purpose being to supplement sickness insurance benefits.

Finally, the Court noted that the entitlement to care allowance under the law of the Province of Salzburg was Silvia Hosse's own right, not a right derived from her father. However, that did not prevent her from being able to benefit from that entitlement even though she resided in Germany, if she satisfied the other conditions of grant under the Regulation. The Court pointed out that the intention of the Regulation is that **the grant of sickness benefits should not be conditional on the residence of the members of the worker's family in the Member State of the place of employment, so as not to deter**

Community workers from exercising their right to freedom of movement. It would therefore be contrary to the Regulation to deprive the daughter of a worker of a benefit she would be entitled to if she was resident in that Member State.

The Court therefore concluded that, if Silvia Hosse fulfils the other conditions of grant, she can claim from the competent Austrian institution payment of a care allowance such as that at issue, in so far as she is not entitled to a similar benefit under the legislation of the state in whose territory she resides.

Invalidity benefits

Invalidity benefit normally means a long-term contributory benefit for adults who are unfit to work. The Administrative Commission set up under Community social security rules considers that the term 'invalidity benefits' must be interpreted broadly so as to include all benefits granted to a person who is an invalid (**Re Invalidity Benefits** [1988] CMLR 1). In **Biason** (Case 24/74), the Court of Justice held that the term included a supplementary allowance, paid by a national solidarity fund, which could be awarded to individuals receiving a life pension provided by virtue of an invalidity that reduced the worker's working or earning capacity by two-thirds. In **Newton v Chief Adjudication Officer** (Case C–358/89), the Court of Justice held that an allowance paid under the legislation of a Member State which is granted on the basis of objective criteria to persons suffering from physical disablement affecting their mobility, and to the grant of which the individuals concerned have a legally protected right, must be treated as an invalidity benefit.

Old-age benefits

These are pensions payable by the state in which the pensioner has been employed, according to the law of the state in which he retired and claimed a pension (Arts 44 and 45, Regulation 1408/71). There are complex rules under Arts 46 and 47, Regulation 1408/71 on the calculation of the amount payable in respect of each Member State to which the retired worker has paid contributions. An old-age benefit will normally be a personal retirement pension 'intended to ensure that a worker has an adequate income from the date on which he or she ... retires' (**Schmidt v Rijksdienst voor Pensioenen** (Case C–98/94)).

Unemployment benefits

A worker who is wholly unemployed and who satisfies the conditions of the legislation of a Member State for entitlement to benefits, and who goes to one or more Member States seeking employment, retains his right to benefit. He will, however, have had to register as unemployed in his home state, and have remained available for work there for at least four weeks (Art 69(1), Regulation 1408/71). He has to register as a person seeking work with the employment services of each of the Member States to which he goes and must subject himself to the procedures of that system. He will be entitled to benefit for three months after he last registered with the employment office of his home state (Art 69(1)(b) and (c)).

The Court of Justice held in **Kuyken** (Case 66/77) that the provisions of Arts 69 and 70, Regulation 1408/71 have no application to an unemployed person who has never been in employment and who has never been treated as an unemployed person under the relevant national legislation. However, in **Bonaffini v INPS** (Case 27/75), the Court of Justice held that:

Article 69 ... is intended solely to ensure for the migrant worker the limited and conditional preservation of the unemployment benefits of the competent State even if he goes to another Member State and this other Member State cannot, therefore, rely on mere failure to comply with the conditions prescribed under that Article to deny the worker entitlement to the benefit which he may claim under the national legislation of that State.

Future developments

On 29 April 2004, the Council and the European Parliament adopted Regulation 883/2004. Article 89, Regulation 883/2004 provides that 'A further Regulation shall lay down the procedure for implementation of this regulation'. To date, no such implementing regulation has been adopted and it is unclear when Regulation 883/2004 will be implemented.

This is a major piece of new legislation which will coordinate social security systems in the EU. The new 'user-friendly' regulation streamlines and updates the existing complex mass of rules in Regulation 1408/71. It will make it easier for workers and their families to move from one Member State to another, whether for professional or private reasons, without losing social security entitlements. The principle of equal treatment will be reinforced and the legislation will be simplified to ensure that the rules apply to all EU citizens who are insured whether they are employed or self-employed workers, pensioners, civil servants, students or non-active persons.

The new regulation will build on the current one to increase the level of protection given to migrant workers and their families in social security systems across the EU. Healthcare entitlements for all insured persons visiting another Member State will be aligned and restrictions on exporting special, non-contributory cash benefits will be based on transparent and objective criteria. It will be possible to extend the period during which a jobseeker can look for work in another Member State from the current three months to six. Non-active persons will be included in the regulation's scope, as will legal pre-retirement schemes. For example, an unemployed worker who lives in France and has paid social security contributions in Germany currently draws his or her unemployment benefit in France. In future he will be also be able to look for work in Germany as well as in France.

Citizens will also receive their benefits quicker as a result of improvements in the cooperation and mutual information between the authorities in the different Member States.

The full text of Regulation 883/2004 is available at:

http://europa.eu.int/comm/employment_social/social-security-schemes/legislation_en.htm

Social security and social assistance in the UK

The UK's Department for Work and Pensions has a website where information on social security benefits for EU citizens is available:

http://www.dwp.gov.uk

Social security

The full range of benefits falling within Art 4(1), Regulation 1408/71 is available in the UK. The terms on which these benefits are available are complicated but it is possible to match a number of contributory and non-contributory benefits which will be available to Community migrant workers, assuming that the qualifying provisions under both UK and Community law are met.

The UK benefits falling within Art 4(1) currently comprise: the contribution-based job-seeker's allowance, statutory sick pay and sickness benefit, maternity allowances, benefits relating to invalidity and disability, widows' benefits, retirement pensions, industrial injuries benefits and benefits for children. In **Re an Emigré to the Canary Islands** [1994] 1 CMLR 717, the Social Security Commissioner held that attendance allowance was equivalent to invalidity benefit, and should therefore, as a benefit payable under Regulation 1408/71, continue to be paid to a claimant after he had moved to another Member State. In **Snares** v **Adjudication Officer** (Case C–20/96), however, disability living allowance was held by the Court of Justice to have been validly refused to a UK citizen in Tenerife as a non-exportable benefit.

Social assistance

Since income support, income-based jobseeker's allowance and working families' tax credit are calculated according to need, they would appear to fall outside the social security criteria (see above). In relation to family credit (which has been replaced by working families' tax credit, and which itself was replaced by two new tax credits from April 2003: Child Tax Credit and Working Tax Credit), however, the Court of Justice has stated, in relation to the form of family credit payable in Northern Ireland, that it is a Community social security benefit (**Hughes** (Case C–78/91)). The position should now be viewed in the light of the UK's declaration annexed to Regulation 1247/92, Annex II, s III L. It will continue to be the case that inclusion of a benefit in a declaration will be conclusive evidence that a benefit is within the Community social security scheme. However, the regulation enables Member States to specify in the annex non-contributory benefits which are excluded from Community law. These exclusions by a Member State are permissible only when the validity of the benefit excluded 'is confined to part of its territory'. The UK's declaration excludes specific benefits (e.g. income support and atten-dance allowance). The declaration also lists separately the same provisions made under Northern Ireland legislation. Whether the UK's declaration is in fact in relation to only part of its territory, as required, is certainly open to argument (see Morris, Rahal and Storey (1993), p. 289). The effect of the declaration will have to be determined by the Court of Justice. It should, however, be remembered that, even if an entitlement to the above benefits does not arise as a social security benefit, there can be no doubt that all those benefits should be paid to an EU worker, under Art 7(2), Regulation 1612/68, as a social advantage in the same circumstances in which they would be payable to a UK citizen (see Chapter 12). The fact that the benefit is included in the list lodged by the UK government in relation to social security benefits will have no bearing on the availability of the benefit as a social advantage.

Income support

UK law is more generous than it is required to be in relation to income support (and income-based jobseeker's allowance). As discussed above, except where it is supplementing a social security benefit listed in Art 4(1), Regulation 1408/71, it does not have to be paid to an individual who has not yet reached EU worker status. The Court of Justice decided in **Lebon** (Case 316/85) that work-seekers, as opposed to workers, were not entitled to the social advantages conferred by Art 7(2), Regulation 1612/68. Income support (or income-based jobseeker's allowance) can be a social advantage, but only for a person who has, for example, worked but lost his job involuntarily and thus retains his EU worker status (see Chapter 12). In the UK, an EU citizen or other national of an EEA state, who arrives to look for work, can sign on in the UK. If he has paid sufficient contributions in his home state, he may qualify for contribution-based jobseeker's allowance and, under Art 69(1)(c), Regulation 1408/71, will be entitled to receive it for three months. He may, as he is entitled, remain to look for work for six months, or even longer (**R v Immigration Appeal Tribunal, ex parte Antonissen** (Case 292/89)). In the latter half of that six-month period he may be compelled to rely on income support or income-based jobseeker's allowance.

The practice in the UK is that EU citizens and EEA nationals who come to the UK to seek work and who have not previously worked in the UK are eligible for income support (or income-based jobseeker's allowance) for a period of up to six months. After that period, if in the opinion of the Employment Services Claimant Adviser they are no longer actively looking for work, they may be declared by the Home Office to be no longer lawfully present in the UK, and be required to leave. Their cases will then be referred to an adjudication officer and payment of income support (or income-based jobseeker's allowance) will cease.

Other EU citizens who come to the UK to retire, on social visits, as students or as economically self-sufficient persons will fall within the scope of Directive 2004/38 (see Chapter 11). All four categories provide the EU citizen with a right of residence on condition that they do not become an unreasonable burden on the social assistance system of the host state. In the UK, if an EU citizen or an EEA national who is living in the UK under the terms of Directive 2004/38 makes a claim for income support (or income-based jobseeker's allowance), he may be declared by the Home Office to be no longer lawfully present in the country and required to leave. However, this practice must now comply with Art 14(3), Directive 2004/38 which states that an expulsion measure 'must not be the automatic consequence of a Union citizen's or his family member's recourse to the social assistance system of the host Member State'.

In addition, since 1994, an EU citizen or an EEA national, or a member of their family, is not entitled to receive income support (or income-based jobseeker's allowance), council tax benefit or housing benefit unless he can show that he is 'ordinarily resident' in the UK. This provision does not apply to workers 'for the purposes of Regulation 1612/68' or a person with a right of residence under Directive 68/360 or Directive 73/148; now Directive 2004/38 (paras 2–4, Income-related Benefits Schemes (Miscellaneous Amendments) (No. 3) Regulations 1994 (SI 1994/1807)).

Therefore, an EU citizen will have to satisfy the residence test if he does not fall within one of the categories defined by the above Community provisions. This test will involve proof by the claimant: that his centre of interest lies in the UK; that he has stable employment; of his reasons for coming to this country; of the length and continuity of his residence outside the UK; and of his future intentions. There is some doubt as to the legality of this test under Community law. If Community nationals are to be allowed these benefits while in the UK, they should receive them on the same basis as nationals, without discrimination.

The relationship between claims to benefit and the exercise of free movement rights in the UK is examined further in Chapter 16.

Summary

Now you have read this chapter you should be able to:

- Explain how Art 42 EC Treaty and Regulations 1408/71 and 574/72 facilitate the free movement of workers and the self-employed.

- Understand the range of persons who come within the scope of Regulations 1408/71 and 574/72.

- Explain how the principle of equal treatment is applied in the context of Regulation 1408/72.

- Describe the principles of Art 42 EC Treaty (as amplified by Regulation 1408/71 and the case law of the European Court of Justice), in particular with regard to:
  - aggregation of contributions and periods of contribution;
  - exportability of benefits;
  - prevention of overlapping benefits;
  - types of benefit covered; and
  - double-function test.

- Evaluate the difference between social assistance and social advantages, and the availability of such within the UK.

- Identify the changes which will come into effect once Regulation 883/2004 comes into force.

References

Morris, P., Rahal, I. and Storey, H. (1993) *Ethnic Minorities Benefits Handbook Pt III*, Child Poverty Action Group.

Taschner, H.C. (1993) 'Free Movement of Students, Retired Persons and other European Citizens', in Schermers, H. (ed.) *Free Movement of Persons in Europe: Legal Problems and Experiences*, Martinus Nijhoff.

Further reading

Textbooks

Craig, P. and De Burca, G. (2003) *EU Law Text, Cases and Materials* (3rd edn), Oxford University Press, Chapters 17 and 18.

Morris, P., Rahal, I. and Storey, H. (1993) *Ethnic Minorities Benefits Handbook Pt III*, Child Poverty Action Group.

Taschner, H.C. (1993) 'Free Movement of Students, Retired Persons and other European Citizens', in Schermers, H. (ed.) *Free Movement of Persons in Europe: Legal Problems and Experiences*, Martinus Nijhoff.

Journal articles

Cornelissen, R., 'The Principle of Territoriality and the Community Regulations on Social Security (Regs 1408/71 and 574/72)' (1996) 33 CML Rev 439.

Moore, M., 'Freedom of Movement and Migrant Workers' Social Security: An Overview of the Court's Jurisprudence 1992-1997' (1998) 35 CML Rev 409.

Pennings, F., 'Co-ordination of social security on the basis of the State-of-employment principle: Time for an alternative?' (2005) 42 CML Rev 67.

Steiner, J., 'The Right to Welfare: Equality and Equity under Community Law' (1985) 10 EL Rev 21.

Verschueren, H., 'EC Social Security Coordination Excluding Third Country Nationals' (1997) 34 CML Rev 991.

Watson, P., 'Minimum Income Benefits: Social Security or Social Assistance?' (1985) 10 EL Rev 335.

15 Limitations on the free movement of persons

Aims and objectives

At the end of this chapter you should understand:

- The provisions of the EC Treaty and Directive 2004/38 which provide for derogations from the freedom of movement and residence provisions, on the grounds of public policy, public security and public health.

- The procedural protection afforded by Directive 2004/38 to EU citizens who are exercising their free movement rights.

The EC Treaty and Directive 2004/38

All the Treaty provisions conferring free movement rights, as discussed in Chapters 12 and 13, are subject to the power of national derogation on the grounds of public policy, public security and public health (Arts 39(3), 46(1) and 55 EC Treaty and Art 27(1), Directive 2004/38 (previously Art 10, Directive 68/360 and Art 8, Directive 73/148)).

Directives 64/221 (see below), 68/360 and 73/148 have all been repealed and replaced by Directive 2004/38. Directive 2004/38 had to be transposed into national law by 30 April 2006. The directive establishes the right of EU citizens and their family members to enter and reside freely within the Member States, subject to certain conditions, and in some cases to specified time limitations (see Chapters 11–13 for a discussion of the substantive rights of entry and residence). This is subject to Article 27(1) (previously Art 3(1), Directive 64/221), which provides that:

> Subject to the provisions of this Chapter [Chapter VI: Restrictions on the Right of Entry and the Right of Residence on Grounds of Public Policy, Public Security or Public Health], Member States may restrict the freedom of movement and residence of Union citizens and their family members, irrespective of nationality, on grounds of public policy, public security or public health. These grounds shall not be invoked to serve economic ends.

There is no Community definition of any of these three grounds, although Art 27(2) provides some guidance with regard to public policy and public security. This guidance was developed by the Court of Justice through its application of Art 27(1)'s predecessor, Art 3(1), Directive 64/221. Article 27(2), Directive 2004/38 provides that:

Measures taken on grounds of public policy or public security shall comply with the principle of proportionality and shall be based exclusively on the personal conduct of the individual concerned. Previous criminal convictions shall not in themselves constitute grounds for taking such measures.

The personal conduct of the individual concerned must represent a genuine, present and sufficiently serious threat affecting one of the fundamental interests of society. Justifications that are isolated from the particulars of the case or that rely on considerations of general prevention shall not be accepted.

Directive 2004/38 is intended, first, to limit the extent to which Member States are entitled to restrict the right of free movement and, second, to provide minimum standards of procedural protection for the individuals affected when Member States take such restrictive action. The scope of both aspects of the directive is now examined.

Public policy and public security

Directive 2004/38 does not attempt to define 'public policy'. It is a term that is also found in relation to permitted restrictions on the import and export of goods under Art 30 (see Chapter 18). Member States are free to determine the scope of public policy in their territory, which may be different in each Member State. It is, for example, permissible for Ireland to prohibit abortions on its territory, and equally acceptable under Community law for the UK to permit them. It would, however, probably not be compatible with Community law for a person to be prevented from receiving information in Ireland issued by an abortion clinic in the UK or from going to the UK to have an abortion. In the following case, the Court of Justice stated that abortion constituted a service within the scope of Art 50 EC Treaty:

Society for the Protection of the Unborn Child Ireland Ltd v *Grogan* (Case C-159/90)

The Court of Justice held that medical termination of pregnancy, performed in accordance with the law of the state where it was carried out, constituted a service within the scope of Art 50 EC Treaty.

In **Attorney-General** *v* X **and Others** [1992] 2 CMLR 277, decided by the Supreme Court of the Republic of Ireland, the Irish Court held that a woman who wished to go to the UK for an abortion had 'an unenumerated constitutional right to travel' under Irish law, and did not, therefore, need to rely on her Community right to travel to receive a service (pp. 303, 306). Different public policy requirements in different states may result in the quite lawful prohibition of cross-border services, even where they are legitimate in one of the states concerned, provided that the prohibition is proportionate to the risk and provided it is applied equally in the receiving state to local citizens and EU citizens alike (**HM Customs and Excise Commissioners** *v* **Schindler** (Case C–275/92)). 'Public policy' and 'public security' are used interchangeably, and they seem to be regarded by the Court of Justice as overlapping concepts. However, although the Court of Justice accepted in **Van Duyn** (Case 41/74) that 'the concept of public policy may vary from one country to another and from one period to another and it is, therefore, necessary . . . to allow the competent national authorities an area of discretion within the limits imposed by the

Treaty', in more recent years it has tended to emphasise the limitations imposed by Community law and the need for equality of treatment between local nationals and EU citizens and their families (**Commission** *v* **Germany, Re Housing of Migrant Workers** (Case 249/86), paras 18 and 19). An attempt to prevent an EU citizen from having access to a service relating to fertility treatment not available on policy grounds in the UK was held by the English Court of Appeal to be disproportionate and, therefore, unlawful (**R** *v* **The Human Fertilisation and Embryology Authority, ex parte DB** [1997] 2 WLR 806). It may well be that the Court of Justice would hold that, while the state has a broad discretion as to what services it controls on public policy grounds within its own frontiers, it would be disproportionate to prevent a citizen from receiving such services in other Member States where they are lawful.

Objective justification

Similar to the free movement of workers, if a restriction on the freedom to provide services is found to exist, the Member State can seek to justify it on grounds of public policy, public security or public health (Art 46 EC Treaty). The following case concerns Germany's successful argument that the restriction in question was objectively justified on grounds of public policy:

Omega (Case C-36/02)

Omega was a company established under German law. Omega operated an installation in Bonn (Germany) for the practice of a sport – 'laser sport' – inspired by the film *Star Wars* and using modern laser technology. That installation featured machine-gun-type laser targeting devices and sensory tags installed either in the firing corridors or on the jackets worn by players. As it took the view that games for entertainment featuring simulated killing were contrary to human dignity and thus constituted a danger to public order, the police authorities issued a prohibition order against the company, requiring it to cease operating equipment intended for firing on human targets. Following dismissal of its administrative complaint and appeals brought against that administrative measure of the police authorities, Omega brought an appeal on a point of law (Revision) before the Bundesverwaltungsgericht (Federal Administrative Court).

In support of its appeal Omega submitted, *inter alia*, that the contested order infringed the freedom to provide services under Art 49 EC Treaty as the installation in question had to use equipment and technology supplied by a UK company. The Bundesverwaltungsgericht acknowledged in this regard that, while the commercial exploitation of a 'killing game' did indeed, as the lower court had ruled, constitute an affront to human dignity contrary to the Grundgesetz (German Basic Law), its prohibition did, nonetheless, infringe the freedom to provide services guaranteed under Art 49 EC Treaty. It accordingly decided to ask the Court of Justice, by way of a reference under Art 234 EC Treaty, whether, *inter alia*, the prohibition of a commercial activity that was at variance with the fundamental values enshrined in the national constitution was compatible with Art 49 EC Treaty.

The Court of Justice held that, by prohibiting Omega from operating its game installation in accordance with the model developed by a UK company and lawfully marketed by that company in the UK, in particular under the franchising system, the contested order affected the freedom to provide services which Art 49 EC Treaty guarantees both to providers and to the persons receiving those services established in another Member State.

However, it continued, **as both the Community and its Member States are required to respect fundamental rights, the protection of those rights was a legitimate interest which could, in principle, justify a derogation from the obligations imposed by Community law, even under a fundamental freedom guaranteed by the Treaty such as the freedom to provide services. Measures which restricted the freedom to provide services could, however, be justified on public policy grounds only if they were necessary for the protection of the interests which they were intended to guarantee and only in so far as those objectives could not be attained by less restrictive measures.**

Nonetheless, the need for, and proportionality of, the provisions adopted could not be excluded merely because one Member State had chosen a system of protection different from that adopted by another State. In other words, Germany could prohibit that which the UK authorised if it could be established that the measure imposing the prohibition was both necessary and proportionate, which, as the Court observed, was indeed the situation in the case under examination. In the first place, the prohibition of the commercial exploitation of games involving the simulation of acts of violence against persons, in particular the representation of acts of homicide, corresponded to the level of protection of human dignity which the national constitution sought to guarantee within Germany. Second, by prohibiting only the variant of the laser game the object of which was to fire on human targets, the contested order did not go beyond what was necessary in order to attain the objective pursued. For those reasons, the Court concluded, the order could not be regarded as a measure unjustifiably undermining the freedom to provide services.

The discretion retained by Member States in identifying the areas of public policy which may result in the restriction of free movement rights has been substantially limited by the substantive provisions of Directive 2004/38 (previously Directive 64/221).

Scope of Directive 2004/38

Directive 2004/38 establishes the right of entry, residence and permanent residence for EU citizens and their family members. These provisions are considered in detail in Chapters 11–13, but to summarise:

- Article 6 provides a right of residence for a period of up to three months for all EU citizens and their family members without any conditions or formalities other than the requirement to hold a valid identity card or passport; in the case of non-EU family members, they must hold a valid passport.

- Article 7 provides a right of residence for a period exceeding three months for EU citizens and their family members, but this is limited to three categories:

  (i)   workers and the self-employed;

  (ii) the economically self-sufficient; i.e. those with sufficient resources not to become a burden on the social assistance system of the host Member State and who have comprehensive sickness insurance cover in the host Member State; and

  (iii) students who are following a course of study, including vocational training, at a public or private institution which is accredited or financed by the host Member State. The student must have comprehensive sickness insurance and assure the Member State that they have sufficient resources for themselves and their family members to ensure that they do not become a burden on the social assistance system of the host Member State during their stay.

■ Article 16 provides a right of permanent residence to EU citizens (including EU family members) who have legally resided in the host Member State for a continuous period of five years; non-EU family members also have the right to permanent residence provided they have legally resided with the EU citizen in the host Member State for a continuous period of five years.

As stated above, these rights of residence may be restricted on the grounds of public policy, public security or public health (Art 27(1), Directive 2004/38). Member States may decide, in some cases, that an individual, although an EU citizen, is not exercising the extended right of residence conferred by Art 7, Directive 2004/38. This is a decision taken on the facts of the case. The Court of Justice has, on a number of occasions (in the context of Directive 64/221, which was repealed and replaced by Directive 2004/38), declared that whether or not a person is a worker or a recipient of services is to be determined according to principles laid down by Community law (see, e.g., **Levin** v **Staatsecretaris van Justitie** (Case 53/81), para 11). In **Commission** v **The Netherlands** (Case C–68/89), the Court of Justice held that this was a decision which could not be made by the national authorities at the point of entry, but had to be determined subsequently on the basis of activities undertaken by the individual. It seems likely that a decision, say, that an individual is not economically active and is not economically self-sufficient to fall within the residual right of residence under Art 7(1)(b), Directive 2004/38, will not be a decision made on public policy or public security grounds. In any event, Art 14(3), Directive 2004/38 provides that expulsion shall not be an automatic consequence if an EU citizen or his family members have recourse to the host Member State's social assistance system. Article 14(4) further provides that (other than in accordance with the provisions relating to restrictions on the right of entry and residence on grounds of public policy, security or health) an expulsion order cannot be issued against an EU citizen or his family members if:

(i) the EU citizen is a worker or self-employed person in the host Member State; or

(ii) the EU citizen entered the host Member State to seek employment and provided he can provide evidence that he is continuing to seek work and has a genuine chance of being employed.

Article 27(2), Directive 2004/38 (previously Art 3(1), Directive 64/221) provides that 'Measures taken on grounds of public policy or public security shall comply with the principle of proportionality and shall be based exclusively on the personal conduct of the individual concerned'. Although Member States have a wide discretion in determining the type of 'personal conduct' which may form the basis for action, the Court of Justice has laid down a number of criteria (in the context of Art 3(1), Directive 64/221) by which such national restrictions must be judged. In the first place, the Court of Justice has said that the action of Member States must be assessed in the light of the European Convention on Human Rights, as illustrated in the following case:

Rutili v *Minister of the Interior* (Case 36/75)

An Italian national working in France had, following political and trade union activity, been confined by a ministerial order to certain areas of France. He challenged this restriction and the case was referred to the Court of Justice under what is now Art 234 EC Treaty. The Court of Justice held that:

> The concept of public policy must, in the Community context and where, in particular, it is used as a justification for derogating from the fundamental principles of equality of treatment and freedom of movement of workers, be interpreted strictly, so that its scope cannot be interpreted unilaterally by each Member State without being subject to control by the institutions of the Community. Accordingly, **restrictions cannot be imposed on the right of a national of any Member State to enter the territory of another Member State, to stay there and to move within it unless his presence constitutes a genuine and sufficiently serious threat to public policy** ... Nor, under Article 8 of Regulation 1612/68, which ensures equality of treatment as regards membership of trades unions and the exercise of rights attached thereto, may the reservation relating to public policy be invoked on grounds arising from the exercise of those rights. Taken as a whole, these limitations placed on the powers of Member States in respect of control of aliens are a specific manifestation of the more general principle, enshrined in Articles 8, 9, 10 and 11 of the Convention for the Protection of Human Rights ... which provide in identical terms, that no restrictions in the interests of national security or public safety shall be placed on the rights secured by the above-quoted articles other than such as are necessary for the protection of those interests 'in a democratic society'. [emphasis added]

In the above case the Court of Justice held that free movement rights entailed a right of entry and residence in the *whole* territory of the host Member State, and the restrictions imposed could not be justified in the case of EU nationals who were exercising their free movement rights unless they were also applicable in similar circumstances to nationals of the host Member State. The Court further held that the conduct must be both 'personal' and 'a genuine and serious threat' to public policy; this requirement has now been incorporated into Directive 2004/38 which provides that 'The personal conduct of the individual concerned must represent a genuine, present and sufficiently serious threat affecting one of the fundamental interests of society' (Art 27(2)). The concepts of 'personal conduct' and 'genuine and serious threat to public policy' were explored by the Court of Justice in the following case (within the context of Art 3(1), Directive 64/221):

Van Duyn v Home Office (Case 41/74)

Yvonne Van Duyn, a Dutch national, was a member of the Church of Scientology. She wished to enter the UK to work for the organisation. The UK government had decided in 1968 that membership of the church was 'socially harmful', but had not taken any steps to ban or restrict the activities which it carried on at its headquarters in East Grinstead, Sussex. Other Dutch nationals who wished to work for the organisation had, however, been excluded before the UK became a member of the EU (**Schmidt v Home Office** [1969] 2 Ch 149). Ms Van Duyn was refused entry on the grounds that her membership of the organisation constituted a threat to public policy. She challenged the refusal on the grounds that membership of an organisation could not be 'personal conduct' within Art 3(1), Directive 64/221 (now Art 7(2), Directive 2004/38). The case was referred to the Court of Justice, which held as follows:

> Although a person's past associations cannot, in general, justify a decision refusing him the right to move freely within the Community, it is nevertheless the case that **present association**, which reflects participation in the activities of the body or of the organisation as well as identification with its aims and designs, **may be considered a voluntary act of the person concerned** and, consequently, as part of his personal conduct within the meaning of the provision cited. (para 17) [emphasis added]

The Court of Justice held that membership of an organisation could constitute 'personal conduct'. As to whether such an organisation could be regarded as a threat to public policy when no action had been taken against it and when it operated without restriction in the UK, the Court of Justice stated that:

> The particular circumstances justifying recourse to the concept of public policy may vary from one country to another and from one period to another . . . It follows from the above that where the competent authorities of a Member State have clearly defined their standpoint as regards the activities of a particular organisation and where, considering it to be socially harmful, they have taken administrative measures to counteract their activities the Member State cannot be required, before it can rely on the concept of public policy, to make such activities unlawful, if recourse to such a measure is not thought appropriate in the circumstances. (paras 18 and 19)

The above decision was somewhat anomalous. At para 19, the Court of Justice stated that a Member State *may* be justified in taking action preventing an EU citizen from participating in an activity which is considered to be socially harmful, provided it has 'taken administrative measures to counteract these activities' among its own citizens. In this case, the UK government had simply made a statement in Parliament expressing strong disapproval of the activities of the Church of Scientology. It did not seek to ban the church from operating in the UK, and it declared that there was no power to do so.

This decision seemed to provide that Member States were justified in excluding or expelling EU citizens for belonging to an organisation engaged in activities which were both 'a serious threat to public policy' and, at the same time, were not thought by the host Member State to be serious enough to merit even the mildest criminal sanctions when the citizens of the host Member State were engaged in the same activities. While membership of an organisation committed to activities which clearly breach the criminal law, such as a terrorist organisation, would seem to fall squarely within the concept of 'personal conduct constituting a serious threat to public policy' (see, e.g., **Astrid Proll (No. 2)** [1988] 2 CMLR 387, IAT), membership of an organisation enjoying the full protection of the law would hardly seem to fall within the same category. Neither would such a decision seem to be compatible with the rights to freedom of thought, conscience and religion, and freedom of expression enshrined in Arts 9 and 10 of the European Convention on Human Rights, which should, as the Court of Justice made clear in **Rutili** (above), inform all decisions made by Member States in relation to the exercise of free movement rights.

The wide discretion which the Court seemed to accept that Member States enjoyed in **Van Duyn** in relation to the type of prohibited conduct was subsequently limited by the Court of Justice in the following case:

Adoui and Cornuaille v *Belgian State* (Cases 115 and 116/81)

The applicants in this case were French nationals who worked in a Belgian café with a somewhat dubious reputation (hostesses/prostitutes worked there). They were refused residency in Belgium on public policy grounds. The case was referred to the Court of Justice because 'prostitution as such is not prohibited by Belgian legislation, although the law does prohibit certain incidental activities, such as the exploitation of prostitution by third parties and various forms of incitement to debauchery' (para 6). On this occasion the Court emphasised the need for equality of treatment, as far as possible, between nationals and non-nationals exercising Community rights. Having pointed out that Member States cannot exclude or expel their own nationals, the Court of Justice stated that:

> Although that difference of treatment, which bears upon the nature of the measures available, must therefore be allowed, it must nevertheless be stressed that, in a Member State, the authority empowered to adopt [public policy/public security] measures must not base the exercise of its powers on assessment of certain conduct which would have the effect of applying an arbitrary distinction to the

detriment of nationals of other Member States ... Although Community law does not impose upon the Member States a uniform scale of values as regards the assessment of conduct which may be considered as contrary to public policy, **it should nevertheless be stated that conduct may not be considered as being of a sufficiently serious nature to justify restrictions on the admission to or residence within the territory of a Member State of a national of another Member State in a case where the former Member State does not adopt, with respect to the same conduct on the part of its own nationals, repressive measures or other genuine and effective measures intended to combat such conduct.** (paras 7 and 8) [emphasis added]

Had the above test been imposed in the **Van Duyn** case, it is unlikely that the outcome would have been the same because, although the UK government had 'clearly defined its standpoint' on the Church of Scientology, it had, in fact, taken no 'repressive or other genuine and effective measures to combat it'. This approach, reflecting both a standard of equality of treatment and proportionality of response, is also to be found in decisions of the Court of Justice in relation to measures taken by national authorities restricting the importation of goods, where reliance is placed on the 'public morality' derogation permitted by Art 30 EC Treaty (**Conegate Ltd** v **Customs and Excise Commissioners** (Case 121/85); see Chapter 18).

'Personal conduct' justifying action must relate exclusively to the individual on whom the restriction is imposed, as illustrated in the following case:

Bonsignore v Oberstadtdirektor der Stadt Köln (Case 67/74)

Bonsignore, an Italian national working in Germany, had been found guilty of causing the death of his brother by the negligent handling of a firearm. Following the conviction, he was ordered by the German Aliens Authority to be deported. It was accepted by the German Aliens Authority that there was little likelihood of the commission of further offences by the defendant. They were, however, seeking to use the deportation for its deterrent effect 'which the deportation of an alien found in illegal possession of a firearm would have in immigrant circles having regard to the resurgence of violence in large urban areas' (para 4). The matter was referred to the Court of Justice. Advocate-General Mayras emphasised, in his Opinion, that 'it is not permissible for a Community worker, even when convicted of a criminal offence, to be made into a "scapegoat" in order to deter other aliens from acting in the same way ... the concept of personal conduct must be examined not only in the light of the offences committed but also in view of the "potential criminality" of the offender'. The Court of Justice agreed with this view and held that Art 3(1), Directive 64/221 (now Art 7(2), Directive 2004/38) means that action taken against an individual on public policy or public security grounds 'cannot be justified on grounds extraneous to the individual case', and thus deportation as a deterrent or as a general preventive measure is prohibited.

In the above case, the Court of Justice held that action taken against an individual on public policy or public security grounds 'cannot be justified on grounds extraneous to the individual case', and thus deportation as a deterrent or as a general preventive measure is prohibited. This prohibition is now incorporated in Directive 2004/38 which provides that 'Justifications that are isolated from the particulars of the case or that rely on considerations of general prevention shall not be accepted'.

The effect of criminal convictions

Previous criminal convictions shall not 'in themselves constitute grounds' for exclusion or expulsion on grounds of public policy or public security (Art 3(2), Directive 64/221; now Art 7(2), Directive 2004/38). In the following case, the Court of Justice, was asked by Marlborough Street Magistrates' Court in London 'whether the wording of Art 3(2) of Directive 64/221 [now Art 7(2), Directive 2004/38], namely that previous criminal convictions shall not "in themselves" constitute grounds for the taking of measures based on public policy or public security, means that previous criminal convictions are solely relevant in so far as they manifest a present or future propensity to act in a manner contrary to public policy or public security; alternatively, the meaning to be attached to "in themselves" in Art 3(2) of Directive 64/221':

R v *Bouchereau* (Case 30/77)

In its reply to the magistrates' questions, the Court of Justice stated that Art 3(2), Directive 64/221 (now Art 7(2), Directive 2004/38):

> ... must be understood as requiring the national authorities to carry out a specific appraisal from the point of view of the interests inherent in protecting requirements of public policy which does not necessarily coincide with the appraisals which formed the basis of the criminal conviction.
>
> The existence of a previous criminal conviction can, therefore, only be taken into account in so far as the circumstances which gave rise to that conviction are evidence of personal conduct constituting a present threat to the requirements of public policy.
>
> **Although, in general, a finding that such a threat exists implies the existence in the individual concerned of a propensity to act in the same way in the future, it is possible that past conduct alone may constitute such a threat to the requirements of public policy.** [emphasis added]

It would seem from this judgment that what the national authorities making the decision relating to an EU citizen should be looking for is an indication of whether or not the person concerned is likely to be a present or future threat; i.e. is there a likelihood of reoffending? That would seem to be the purpose of the assessment, despite Advocate-General Warner having referred to 'circumstances when cases do arise, exceptionally, where the personal conduct of the alien has been such that, while not necessarily evincing any clear propensity on his part, has caused such deep revulsion that public policy requires his departure' ([1977] ECR 1999 at 2022). There is no indication, however, that the Court of Justice agreed with Advocate-General Warner in this regard, and indeed, it had agreed with Advocate-General Mayras in an earlier case when he warned against the use of deportation to mollify public opinion: 'one cannot avoid the impression that the deportation of a foreign worker, even a national of the Common Market, satisfies the feeling of hostility, sometimes verging on xenophobia, which the commission of an offence by an alien generally causes or revives in the indigenous population' (**Bonsignore**, above). As stated above, Art 27(2), Directive 2004/38 now incorporates these principles developed by the Court of Justice. Article 27(2) provides that:

> ... The personal conduct of the individual concerned must represent a genuine, present and sufficiently serious threat affecting one of the fundamental interests of society. Justifications that are isolated from the particulars of the case or that rely on considerations of general prevention shall not be accepted.

Article 27(2) therefore prohibits Member States from making a decision on the basis of public reaction to an offence. Setting aside the frequent misreporting of the circumstances of offences in the press which may well provoke a quite inappropriate response, the requirement in Art 27(2) is that decisions which are 'isolated from the particulars of the case or that rely on considerations of general prevention' shall not be acceptable. This clearly excludes Member States from taking into account such extraneous factors as the public response to the offence.

In **Bouchereau**, the Court of Justice stated that 'past conduct alone may constitute ... a threat to the requirements of public policy'. A 'threat' must indicate that something may happen. A reasonable interpretation of this exceptional circumstance in which past conduct constitutes a future threat might be where the offence itself indicates some kind of mental or other disorder importing the risk of recurrent offending. As is seen in the case below, however, the authorities will have to decide at the time when the decision is taken, by making an assessment, whether the individual still constitutes a threat at the time when the exclusion or expulsion is given effect, 'as the factors to be taken into account, particularly those concerning his conduct, are likely to change in the course of time' (**R v Secretary of State for the Home Department, ex parte Santillo** (Case 131/79), para 18).

The following case concerned an EU citizen who was expelled from another Member State for life:

Donatella Calfa (Case C-x348/96)

Ms Calfa, an Italian national, was charged with the possession and use of prohibited drugs while staying as a tourist in Crete (Greece). She was found guilty and sentenced to three months' imprisonment and ordered to be expelled for life from Greek territory, in accordance with national law. The national court was under an obligation to order her expulsion for life (unless there were compelling reasons, in particular family reasons). She would be able to return to Greece only after a period of three years, provided that the Minister of Justice exercised his discretion to grant approval.

Ms Calfa contested that the expulsion for life breached her Community law rights to travel to Greece as a tourist (i.e. as the recipient of services in accordance with Art 59 EC Treaty (now Art 49)). The Greek authorities argued that she could be expelled in accordance with the public policy derogation. The Greek court referred the case to the Court of Justice under what is now Art 234 EC Treaty, seeking guidance on whether the penalty was compatible with Community law. The Court of Justice held as follows:

17. Although in principle criminal legislation is a matter for which the Member States are responsible, the Court has consistently held that Community law sets certain limits to their power, and such legislation may not restrict the fundamental freedoms guaranteed by Community law ...

18. In the present case, the penalty of expulsion for life from the territory, which is applicable to the nationals of other Member States in the event of conviction for obtaining and being in possession of drugs for their own use, clearly constitutes an obstacle to the freedom to provide services recognised in Article 59 [now Art 49] of the Treaty, since it is the very negation of that freedom. This would also be true for the other fundamental freedoms laid down in Articles 48 [now Art 39 (free movement of workers)] and 52 [now Art 43 (right of establishment)] of the Treaty and referred to by the national court.

19. It is none the less necessary to consider whether such a penalty could be justified by the public policy exception provided for in *inter alia* Article 56 [now Art 46] of the Treaty, which is relied upon by the Member State in question.

20. Article 56 [now Art 46] permits Member States to adopt, with respect to nationals of other Member States, and in particular on the grounds of public policy, measures which they cannot apply to their own nationals, inasmuch as they have no authority to expel the latter from the territory or to deny them access thereto . . .

21. **Under the Court's case law, the concept of public policy may be relied upon in the event of a genuine and sufficiently serious threat to the requirements of public policy affecting one of the fundamental interests of society** (see Case 30/77 **Bouchereau** [1977] ECR 1999, para 35).

22. In this respect, **it must be accepted that a Member State may consider that the use of drugs constitutes a danger for society such as to justify special measures against foreign nationals who contravene its laws on drugs, in order to maintain public order.**

23. However, as the Court has repeatedly stated, the public policy exception, like all derogations from a fundamental principle of the Treaty, must be interpreted restrictively.

24. In that regard, Directive 64/221, Article 1(1) of which provides that the directive is to apply to *inter alia* any national of a Member State who travels to another Member State as a recipient of services, sets certain limits on the right of Member States to expel foreign nationals on the grounds of public policy. Article 3 of that directive states that measures taken on the grounds of public policy or of public security that have the effect of restricting the residence of a national of another Member State must be based exclusively on the personal conduct of the individual concerned. In addition, previous criminal convictions cannot in themselves constitute grounds for the taking of such measures. **It follows that the existence of a previous criminal conviction can, therefore, only be taken into account in so far as the circumstances which gave rise to that conviction are evidence of personal conduct constituting a present threat to the requirements of public policy** (Bouchereau, para 28).

25. **It follows that an expulsion order could be made against a Community national such as Ms Calfa only if, besides her having committed an offence under drugs laws, her personal conduct created a genuine and sufficiently serious threat affecting one of the fundamental interests of society.**

26. In the present case, the legislation at issue in the main proceedings requires nationals of other Member States found guilty, on the national territory in which that legislation applies, of an offence under the drugs laws, to be expelled for life from that territory, unless compelling reasons, in particular family reasons, justify the continued residence in the country. The penalty can be revoked only by a decision taken at the discretion of the Minister for Justice after a period of three years.

27. Therefore, expulsion for life automatically follows a criminal conviction, without any account being taken of the personal conduct of the offender or the danger which that person represents for the requirements of public policy.

28. It follows that the conditions for the application of the public policy exception provided for in Directive 64/221, as interpreted by the Court of Justice, are not fulfilled and that **the public policy exception cannot be successfully relied upon to justify a restriction on the freedom to provide services, such as that imposed by the legislation at issue in the main proceedings.**

29. In view of the foregoing considerations, the answer to be given to the national court's questions must be that Articles 48 [now 39], 52 [now 43] and 59 [now 49] of the Treaty and Article 3 of Directive 64/221 preclude legislation which, with certain exceptions, in particular where there are family reasons, requires a Member State's courts to order the expulsion for life from its territory of nationals of other Member States found guilty on that territory of the offences of obtaining and being in possession of drugs for their own personal use. [emphasis added]

In the above case, at paras 21 and 22 the Court of Justice reiterated the principles developed in its previous case law. At para 22, the Court accepted that in order to maintain public order a Member State could consider possession of drugs to constitute a danger to the public which could therefore justify special measures being taken against foreigners who breached its anti-drug laws. Having said that, the Court at para 25 stated that an EU citizen could only be expelled if it was shown that, in addition to breaching the anti-drug laws, their personal conduct 'created a genuine and sufficiently serious threat affecting one of the fundamental interests of society' (as stated above this is now incorporated in Art 27(2), Directive 2004/38). In any event, the Court held at para 28 that expulsion for life was not compatible with the Treaty provisions or Directive 64/221 (now, Directive 2004/38). This was the case even though there was the possibility of review of that decision after three years. A mandatory ban on readmission would therefore not be compatible with Community law, because an EU citizen could only be prevented from exercising his free movement rights if he constitutes a genuine and sufficient threat (present or future, *not past*) to one of the fundamental interests of society.

This is confirmed by Directive 2004/38 which provides that persons excluded from a Member State on grounds of public policy or public security can apply for the exclusion order to be lifted after a reasonable period, and in any event after a maximum of three years, by putting forward arguments to establish that there has been a material change in the circumstances which justified the decision ordering their exclusion (Art 32(1)). The Member State concerned is required to reach a decision on such application within six months of its submission (Art 32(1)). The person applying for the lifting of the exclusion order does not have a right of entry into the Member State concerned while the application is being considered (Art 32(2)).

The following case was decided by the English Court of Appeal, applying Directives 73/148 and 64/221 (both of which have been repealed and replaced by Directive 2004/38):

(1) Gough (2) Smith v Chief Constable of Derbyshire; Miller v Leeds Magistrates Court; Lilley v Director of Public Prosecutions [2002] EWCA Civ 351

Gough had been convicted of violent offences in 1998 and Smith in 1990. In addition, both had been the subject of a 'profile' prepared by the police that indicated repeated involvement in or near incidents of violence at or around football matches. Upon conviction, banning orders for two years were made against them under s 14A, Football Spectators Act 1989 as amended by the Football (Disorder) Act 2000. Their appeal to the Divisional Court was dismissed and they appealed to the Court of Appeal. The Court of Appeal did not exercise its discretion to refer the case to the Court of Justice pursuant to Art 234 EC Treaty.

Gough and Smith contended that, *inter alia*:

1. the banning orders derogated from the positive rights on freedom of movement and freedom to leave their home country which was conferred on them by Arts 1 and 2, Directive 73/148 because it was not permissible to justify a banning order on public policy grounds, alternatively no such grounds were made out on the evidence;
2. the Football (Disorder) Act 2000 was contrary to Community law and therefore inapplicable in so far as it imposed mandatory restrictions on free movement within the Community which were based on criteria that were not provided for or permitted by Community legislation; and
3. it was contrary to the Community law principle of proportionality to ban an individual from travelling anywhere within the Community even if the relevant match or tournament was not taking place within the Community.

The Court of Appeal held that:

1. It was entirely satisfied that there was a public policy exception to Art 2 of the directive. There was no absolute right to leave your home country.
2. Although at first glance it might appear disproportionate to ban all foreign travel, the court was satisfied that such a reaction was unsound. Banning orders were only to be imposed where there were strong grounds for concluding that the individual had a *propensity for taking part in football hooliganism*. It was proportionate that those who had shown such a propensity should be subject to a scheme that restricted their ability to indulge in it.

Accordingly the Court of Appeal upheld the banning orders and dismissed the appeal.

Directive 2004/38: additional provisions

There are a number of additional provisions within Directive 2004/38 which are of relevance to public policy and public security (and which were not included in Directive 64/221).

Article 27(3) provides that in order to ascertain whether the person concerned represents a danger to public policy or public security, the host Member State, if it considers it essential, may request the Member State of origin or other Member States to provide information concerning any previous police record the person concerned may have. The request is to be made by the host Member State:

(i)   when issuing the registration certificate; or

(ii) if there is no registration system, no later than three months from the date of the person's arrival in the host Member State or date the person reported his presence in the host Member State as provided for in Art 5(5); or

(iii) when issuing the residence card.

Such enquiries must not be made as a matter of routine. The Member State consulted should provide its reply within two months (see Chapters 11–13 for commentary on the issue of registration certificates and residence cards).

A person who is expelled from a Member State on grounds of public policy, public security or public health shall have the right to re-enter the Member State which issued him with a passport or identity card, even if the document is no longer valid, or if the nationality of the holder is in dispute (Art 27(4)).

Article 28(1) provides that before taking an expulsion decision on grounds of public policy or public security, the host Member State must assess a number of factors such as the period for which the individual concerned has been resident, his age, state of health, family and economic situation, degree of social and cultural integration in the host Member State and the extent of his links with the country of origin. Only for serious grounds of public policy or public security can an expulsion decision be taken against an EU citizen or his family members, if the EU citizen or his family members have acquired the right of permanent residence in the host Member State (Art 28(2); see Chapters 11–13 for commentary on the right of permanent residence). In addition, an expulsion decision may not be taken against an EU citizen or his family members who have resided in the host Member State for ten years or if he is a minor, unless the decision is based on imperative grounds of public security, and, in the case of a minor, provided that expulsion is necessary for the best interests of the child (Art 28(3)).

An expulsion order cannot be issued by a Member State as a penalty or legal consequence of a custodial penalty, unless the requirements of Arts 27–29 (see above) are complied with (Art 33(1)). Where an expulsion order is issued under this provision, and where it is enforced more than two years after it was issued, the Member State is required to check that the individual concerned is a current and genuine threat to public policy or public security, and the Member State shall assess whether there has been any material change in circumstances since the expulsion order was issued (Art 33(2)).

Public health

Article 4, Directive 64/221 permitted the exclusion of EU citizens and their families where they were suffering from the diseases listed in the annex to the directive. The list included diseases subject to quarantine under World Health Organisation regulations: tuberculosis in an active state, syphilis, and other infectious diseases subject to notification under the legislation of the host Member State. There was a separate category of diseases and disabilities which might threaten public policy and public security. These were: drug addiction, profound mental disturbance and manifest conditions of psychotic disturbance with agitation, delirium, hallucinations or confusion.

Article 4, Directive 64/221 has been repealed and replaced by Art 29, Directive 2004/38. Under Art 29(1), Directive 2004/38 the only diseases which can justify restricting the right of entry and residence on the ground of public health, are:

(i)   those with epidemic potential as defined by the relevant instruments of the World Health Organisation; and

(ii) other infectious diseases or other contagious parasitic diseases if they are subject to protection provisions applying to nationals of the host Member State.

It is not permissible to carry out routine medical examinations for any of these conditions, since to do so would be to impose an additional requirement on entry prohibited by Art 3(1), Directive 68/360; now Art 29(1), Directive 2004/38 (**Commission v Netherlands** (Case C–68/89)). Nor would it be open to a state to require production of medical or other certificates to confirm that individuals are free from infection, since this, too, would constitute a further restriction. A medical examination would, however, be lawful if a person was manifesting obvious symptoms of sickness which might indicate that he was suffering from one of the conditions listed in Art 29(1), Directive 2004/38. Article 29(3) provides that a Member State can require the person concerned to undergo a medical examination, which must be provided free of charge, if there are serious indications that a medical examination is necessary; such medical examinations must not be carried out as a matter of routine. Article 29(2) provides that diseases occurring after a three-month period from the date of arrival shall not constitute grounds for expulsion from the host Member State.

Although the following case is not concerned with the free movement of persons (as suggested by the title to this chapter) it is nevertheless concerned with the derogation from the Treaty provisions on the ground of public health, in relation to the free movement of services:

Konsumentombudsmannen (KO) v Gourmet International Products AB (GIP) (Case C-405/98)

The Court of Justice held that the Treaty provisions on freedom to provide services precluded a prohibition on the advertising of alcoholic beverages because it has a particular effect on the cross-border supply of advertising space, given the international nature of the advertising market in the category of products to which the prohibition relates, and thereby constitutes a restriction on the freedom to provide services within the meaning of Art 49 EC Treaty.

The Court, however, held that such a restriction may be justified by the protection of public health, which is a ground of general interest recognised by Art 46 EC Treaty, which is applicable to the provision of services in accordance with Art 55 EC Treaty. The Court stated that it is for the national court to determine whether, in the circumstances of law and fact which characterise the situation in the Member State concerned, the prohibition on advertising at issue in the main proceedings meets the condition of proportionality required in order for the derogation from the freedom to provide services to be justified.

Procedural protection

Articles 5 to 9, Directive 64/221 were intended to ensure that when action was taken against EU citizens or others exercising their Community free movement rights, such action was taken in accordance with minimum standards of due process. Articles 30–33, Directive 2004/38 have repealed and replaced Arts 5 to 9, Directive 64/221. The provisions of Arts 30–33, Directive 2004/38 are now considered.

Article 30(1) provides that the person concerned by a decision refusing leave to enter or reside in a Member State on the ground of public policy, public security or public health must be notified in writing of that decision, in such a way that they are able to comprehend its content and the implications for them. The grounds for the decision must be given precisely and in full, unless this is contrary to the interests of state security (Art 30(2)), and the person concerned must be informed of the appeal procedures available to them (Art 30(3)). Except in cases of urgency, the subject of such decision must be allowed at least one month in which to leave the Member State (Art 30(3)).

Article 31 sets out the procedural safeguards which apply if a decision is taken against a person's right of entry and residence on the grounds of public policy, public security or public health. Article 31 provides as follows:

1. The persons concerned shall have access to judicial and, where appropriate, administrative redress procedures in the host Member State to appeal against or seek review of any decision taken against them on the grounds of public policy, public security or public health.
2. Where the application for appeal against or judicial review of the expulsion decision is accompanied by an application for an interim order to suspend enforcement of that decision, actual removal from the territory may not take place until such time as the decision on the interim order has been taken, except:
   – where the expulsion decision is based on a previous judicial decision; or
   – where the persons concerned have had previous access to judicial review; or
   – where the expulsion decision is based on imperative grounds of public security under Article 28(3).

3. The redress procedures shall allow for an examination of the legality of the decision, as well as of the facts and circumstances on which the proposed measure is based. They shall ensure that the decision is not disproportionate, particularly in view of the requirements laid down in Article 28.

4. Member States may exclude the individual concerned from their territory pending the redress procedure, but they may not prevent the individual from submitting his/her defence in person, except when his/her appearance may cause serious troubles to public policy or public security or when the appeal or judicial review concerns a denial of entry to the territory.

Persons excluded from a Member State on grounds of public policy or public security can apply for the exclusion order to be lifted after a reasonable period, and in any event after a maximum of three years, by putting forward arguments to establish that there has been a material change in the circumstances which justified the decision ordering their exclusion (Art 32(1)). The Member State concerned is required to reach a decision on such application within six months of its submission (Art 32(1)). The person applying for the lifting of the exclusion order does not have a right of entry into the Member State concerned while the application is being considered (Art 32(2)).

An expulsion order cannot be issued by a Member State as a penalty or legal consequence of a custodial penalty, unless the requirements of Arts 27–29 (see above) are complied with (Art 33(1)). Where an expulsion order is issued under this provision, and where it is enforced more than two years after it was issued, the Member State is required to check that the individual concerned is a current and genuine threat to public policy or public security, and the Member State shall assess whether there has been any material change in circumstances since the expulsion order was issued (Art 33(2)).

The giving of sufficient reasons

Articles 5 and 6, Directive 64/221 provided that to enable an effective judicial challenge to be mounted, it was important that adequate reasons were given to a person who was excluded or expelled on public policy or public security grounds. The reasons would need to address the relevant aspects of public policy or public security on which the decision was based:

Rutili v *Minister of the Interior* (Case 36/75)

The Court of Justice held that:

> . . . this requirement means that the state concerned must, when notifying an individual of a restrictive measure adopted in his case, give him a precise and comprehensive statement of the grounds for the decision, to enable him to take effective steps to prepare his defence. (para 39)

As stated above, Directive 2004/38 (which has repealed and replaced Arts 5 and 6, Directive 64/221) now provides that the person concerned by a decision refusing leave to enter or reside in a Member State on the ground of public policy, public security or public health must be notified in writing of that decision, in such a way that they are able to comprehend its content and the implications for them. The grounds for the decision must be given precisely and in full, unless this is contrary to the interests of state security (Art 30(2)).

To be 'in full' (or 'comprehensive'), the statement will have to indicate the way in which a person continues to constitute a threat to public policy or public security. In determining whether or not to act against an individual, national authorities must 'carry out a specific appraisal from the point of view of the interests inherent in protecting the requirements of public policy' (**R** *v* **Bouchereau** (Case 30/77), para 27). It is the result of that appraisal that the authorities must communicate to the individual against whom they ha.e decided to act. If the communication does not meet these requirements then it will invalidate the decision (**R** *v* **Secretary of State for the Home Office, ex parte Dannenberg** [1984] 2 CMLR 456 (CA)).

Although Art 30(2), Directive 2004/38 provides that an individual need not be given the reasons for a decision if this is contrary to the interests of the security of the state involved, it would probably not satisfy the Community's principle of a minimum of effective judicial control if the authority does not at least provide some justification as to why the giving of reasons would threaten national security. The Court of Justice, in **Johnston** *v* **RUC** (Case 222/84), held that the mere issue of a certificate by the authorities to the effect that the disclosure of information would be prejudicial to national security was not sufficient without some indication of why this should be the case. Although the decision was given in the context of the need for an effective judicial process in Art 6, Directive 76/207, the Court emphasised that it was part of a broader principle of effective judicial control ([1986] ECR 1651 at p. 1663). However, the English Court of Appeal, in **R** *v* **Home Secretary, ex parte Gallagher** [1994] 3 CMLR 295, thought that a recital of the relevant section of the Prevention of Terrorism (Temporary Provisions) Act 1989 as the basis of an exclusion from the UK, without more, would meet the requirements of the former Art 6, Directive 64/221 (*per* Steyn LJ at p. 307). This case should be contrasted with that of **Tinnelly & Sons Ltd and McElduff** *v* **UK**. The European Court of Human Rights, in relation to religious discrimination in Northern Ireland, refused to accept that such an '*ipse dixit* of the Executive' would satisfy Art 6 of the European Convention on Human Rights.

The Schengen Agreement and Directive 2004/38

Where an EU citizen travels within the EU in order to exercise the rights which are conferred on him by the EC Treaty, his spouse (or registered partner under Directive 2004/38), who is a national of a third country (i.e. a non-Member State), is covered to a large extent by the regulations and directives on freedom of movement for persons.

Although Member States may require such a spouse/registered partner to have an entry visa they must accord him every facility in order to obtain it. The former Art 2, Directive 64/221 (replaced by Art 27(1), Directive 2004/38) also enables Member States to refuse entry into their territory to nationals of other Member States or their spouses, who are third country nationals, on grounds of public policy or public security.

The Treaty of Amsterdam integrated the Schengen Agreement and its implementing convention (CISA) into the framework of the EU by means of a protocol (see Chapter 11). The CISA has enabled checks at internal borders between the signatory States to be abolished and a single external border to be created. Common rules on visas, right to asylum, and control at external borders have been adopted in order to facilitate freedom of movement for persons in the signatory states without disrupting public policy. An information system (SIS) has been set up so that the national authorities may exchange data on the identity of persons and the description of wanted property.

Under the CISA, the assessment of whether circumstances exist which justify the entry of an alert in the SIS for an alien falls within the competence of the state which issued that alert, which is responsible for the data it entered into the SIS. The state which issued the alert is the only state authorised to add to, correct or delete that data. The other contracting states are obliged to refuse entry or a visa to an alien for whom an alert has been issued for the purposes of refusing him entry.

The following case considers the relationship between the CISA and Community law on the free movement of persons, which included Directive 64/221. Although Directive 64/221 has been repealed by Directive 2004/38, the following case remains relevant; Art 38(3), Directive 2004/38 stipulates that 'References made to the repealed provisions and Directives shall be construed as being made to this Directive':

Commission v Spain (Case 07/06)

This was the first time that the Court of Justice explained the relationship between the convention implementing the Schengen convention (CISA) and Community law on the free movement of persons. In this case, the European Commission brought proceedings against Spain before the Court of Justice following complaints from two Algerian nationals (i.e. non-EU citizens), Mr Farid and Mr Bouchair, who were the spouses of Spanish nationals, living in Dublin and London respectively.

The Spanish authorities had refused them entry into the Schengen Area simply because Germany had placed them on the SIS list of persons to be refused entry.

The Court of Justice explained, first of all, the relationship between the CISA and Community law on freedom of movement for persons.

It observed that **the Schengen Protocol confirms that the provisions of the Schengen *acquis* are applicable only if and in so far as they are compatible with European Union and European Community law.** Closer cooperation in the Schengen field had to be conducted within the legal and institutional framework of the EU and with respect for the Treaties.

It followed that **the compliance of an administrative practice with the provisions of the CISA may justify the conduct of the competent national authorities only in so far as the application of the relevant provisions is compatible with the Community rules governing freedom of movement for persons.**

The Court stated that the concept of public policy within the meaning of Directive 64/221 (now, Directive 2004/38) did not correspond to that in the CISA.

The directive states that measures taken on grounds of public policy or public security are to be based exclusively on the personal conduct of the individual concerned, so that previous criminal convictions are not in themselves to constitute grounds for the taking of such measures. The Court has always emphasised that the public policy exception is a derogation from the fundamental principle of freedom of movement for persons which must be interpreted strictly. Reliance by a national authority on the concept of public policy presupposes a genuine and sufficiently serious threat affecting one of the fundamental interests of society.

However, circumstances such as a penalty involving deprivation of liberty of at least one year or a measure based on a failure to comply with national regulations on the entry or residence of aliens may provide a basis for the entry of an alert in the SIS for the purpose of refusing entry on grounds of public policy, irrespective of any specific assessment of the threat represented by the person concerned. Entry into the Schengen Area or the issue of a visa for that purpose cannot, in principle, be granted to an alien for whom an alert has been issued for the purposes of refusing entry.

The Court therefore held that **a national of a third country who is the spouse of a**

Member State national, risks being deprived of the protection provided for by Directive 64/221 (now Directive 2004/38) where an alert has been issued for the purposes of refusing him entry. It observed that in a 1996 declaration the contracting states undertook not to issue an alert for the purposes of refusing entry in respect of a person covered by Community law unless the conditions required by that law are fulfilled. That means that a contracting state may issue an alert for such a person only after establishing that his presence constitutes a genuine, present and sufficiently serious threat affecting one of the fundamental interests of society within the meaning of Directive 64/221 (now Directive 2004/38).

Furthermore, **a Member State that consults the SIS must be able to establish, before refusing entry into the Schengen Area to the person concerned, that his presence in that area constitutes such a threat.** The Court recalled, in that connection, that the Schengen system had the means to answer requests for information made by national authorities faced with difficulties in enforcing an alert.

Therefore, **the Court found against Spain on the ground that the Spanish authorities refused entry to Mr Farid and Mr Bouchair without having first verified whether their presence constituted a genuine, present and sufficiently serious threat affecting one of the fundamental interests of society.**

Summary

Now you have read this chapter you should be able to:

■ Identify the provisions of the EC Treaty and Directive 2004/38 which provide for derogations from the freedom of movement and residence provisions, on the grounds of public policy, public security and public health.

■ Explain the procedural protection afforded by Directive 2004/38 to EU citizens who exercise their free movement rights.

■ Describe the relationship between the Schengen Agreement's implementing convention (CISA) and Directive 2004/38.

Further reading

Textbooks

Barnard, C. (2004) *The Substantive Law of the EU: The four freedoms* (1st edn), Oxford University Press, Chapter 14.

Craig, P. and De Burca, G. (2003) *EU Law Text, Cases and Materials* (3rd edn), Oxford University Press, Chapter 19.

Foster, N. (2006) *Foster on EU Law* (1st edn), Oxford University Press, Chapter 9 (Section 9.6).

Steiner, J., Woods, L. and Twigg-Flesner, C. (2006) *EU Law* (9th edn), Oxford University Press, Chapter 23.

Storey, T. and Turner, C. (2005) *Unlocking EU Law* (1st edn), Hodder Arnold, Chapter 11 (Section 11.8).

Tillotson, J. and Foster, N. (2003) *Text, Cases and Materials on EU Law* (4th edn), Cavendish Publishing, Chapter 13.

Weatherill, S. (2006) *Cases and Materials on EU Law* (7th edn), Oxford University Press, Chapter 13

Journal articles

Barav, A., 'Court Recommendations to Deport and the Free Movement of Workers in EEC Law' (1981) 6 EL Rev 139.

Connor, T.C., 'Migrant Community Nationals: Remedies for Refusal of Entry by Member States' (1998) 23 EL Rev 157.

O'Neill, M., 'Note on Joined Cases C-6/95 and C-111/95 **R** *v* **Secretary of State for the Home Department, ex parte Shingara and Radiom**' (1998) 23 EL Rev 157.

Vincenzi, C., 'Freedom of Movement in the Single Market: An Irish Solution?' (1990) NLJ 664.

Vincenzi, C., 'Deportation in Disarray: the Case of EC Nationals' [1994] Crim LR 163.

16 Free movement rights in the United Kingdom

Aims and objectives

At the end of this chapter you should understand:

■ How EU free movement rights have been implemented within the UK, in particular through the Immigration (European Economic Area) Regulations 2006.

The UK approach to free movement: the island problem

The maintenance of strict immigration controls at the ports and airports of the UK has characterised UK immigration policy since the First World War. Even after the effective date for the creation of the Single Market at the beginning of 1993 had passed, the UK government continued to maintain the need for strict frontier controls and nationality checks on all passengers coming from within the Community. As discussed in Chapter 11, the UK (and Ireland) did not participate in the Schengen Agreement. This was an agreement reached outside the EU between the other thirteen pre-2004 Member States, which removed most controls over individuals at the land frontiers of those states.

Successive UK governments have used the port control system to give effect to Community law and in some areas, such as registration with the police under the Immigration (Registration with the Police) Regulations 1972 (SI 1972/1758), as amended, Community nationals benefit from a more relaxed regime. Community law would permit such registration, although not as a condition of residence (**Watson and Belmann** (Case 118/75)); and now see Arts 5(5) and Art 8(1), Directive 2004/38. The more relaxed internal system reflects a less intrusive policy of internal controls when compared to mainland Europe. In most continental Member States immigration controls have, for a great many years, been of a post-entry type, involving registration and identity cards, because borders with other Member States were largely unpoliced except at road crossing points. The effect of the UK's island geography, however, has placed the emphasis on the entry process and the granting or refusing of leave (i.e. permission) at the point of entry.

The distinct position of those exercising Community free movement rights was finally addressed, more than 20 years after UK entry, by the Immigration (European Economic Area) Order 1994, which came into effect in July 1994 (SI 1994/1895). The Order was made under s 2(2), European Communities Act 1972 and was intended to implement the free movement rights conferred by all the directives relating to entry and residence, including Directives 64/221, 68/360, 73/148, 90/364, 90/365 and 93/96 (Explanatory Note to the Order). Although this was its intention, there were a number of areas where the 1994 Order was deficient.

The 1994 Order was repealed by the Immigration (European Economic Area) Order 2000 (the EEA Order 2000, SI 2000/2326). The EEA Order 2000, which came into force on 2 October 2000, re-enacted, with amendments, the provisions of the 1994 Order. It applied to workers, self-employed persons, providers and recipients of services, self-sufficient persons, retired persons (who had pursued an activity as an employed or self-employed person (Reg 3(1)(f))) and students. The EEA Order 2000 created free-standing rights of appeal which (in contrast to the position under the 1994 Order) were no longer dependent upon rights of appeal arising under the statutory provisions which applied to persons not claiming rights under Community law. The EEA Order 2000 copied out many of the provisions of the various directives and regulations and was a far better attempt than its predecessor at complying with Community law.

As discussed in Chapters 11–13, Directive 2004/38 (which relates to an EU citizen's right of entry and residence in a Member State of which they are not a national) had to be transposed into national law by 30 April 2006. This directive has amended Regulation 1612/68 (Arts 10 and 11 have been repealed), and repealed the following nine directives: Directives 64/221, 68/360, 72/194, 73/148, 75/34, 75/35, 90/364, 90/365 and 93/96. Regulation 635/2006 subsequently repealed Regulation 1251/70, because Directive 2004/38 already covered its substantive provisions. The EEA Order 2000 has been repealed and replaced by the Immigration (European Economic Area) Regulations 2006 (the EEA Regulations 2006, (SI 2006/1003)). These Regulations, which came into force on 30 April 2006, transpose Directive 2004/38 into UK law. Its provisions are discussed further below.

Scope of the Immigration (European Economic Area) Regulations 2006

Nationality of beneficiaries

The EEA Regulations 2006 apply to all 'EEA Nationals', i.e. to all nationals of states who were parties to the European Economic Area Agreement of 1992, which was incorporated into UK law by the European Economic Area Act 1993. It therefore applies to all the Member States of the EU together with Iceland, Liechtenstein and Norway, except the UK (Reg 2(1)). As with the EEA Order 2000, UK citizens are excluded, it would appear, because they already have an unqualified right of entry and residence under UK law (s 1, Immigration Act 1971). This is unfortunate because Community law confers certain rights on EU citizens which are more beneficial to UK citizens than the provisions of national law. The EEA Regulations 2006 also apply to Switzerland, even though it was not party to the European Economic Area Agreement of 1992 (Reg 2(1)). The UK's rationale for including Switzerland within the scope of the EEA Regulations 2006 is to avoid having to apply a slightly different free movement regime to Swiss nationals and their family members. Operationally, the UK government has stated that it would be very difficult to run two EEA regimes conferring very similar rights, and in any event Swiss nationals constitute a very small percentage of the Home Office's overall caseload (Explanatory Memorandum to the EEA Regulations 2006).

Other nationalities may benefit from more limited free movement rights under Community law. These include employees of companies based in other Member States which carry on economic activities here (**Van der Elst** *v* **OMI** (Case C–43/93); and see Chapter 13), and nationals of states which have association agreements with the Community (**Kziber** *v* **ONEM** (Case C–18/90); see Chapter 11). These are not covered by the EEA Regulations 2006, and the beneficiaries will have to rely upon the direct effect of the relevant provisions of the Treaties.

Family rights

Regulation 7(1) defines family members as the EEA national's:

(a) spouse or civil partner;
(b) direct descendants of his, or those of his spouse or his civil partner who are –
   (i) under 21; or
   (ii) dependants of his, his spouse or his civil partner;
(c) dependent direct relatives in his ascending line or that of his spouse or his civil partner.

This definition of family member mirrors that in Art 2(1), Directive 2004/38. Article 3(2), Directive 2004/38 extends its scope to other family members who should have their entry and residence 'facilitated'. Regulation 8(1), EEA Regulations 2006, refers to these other family members as 'extended family members', stating that '... "extended family member" means a person who is not a family member of an EEA national under Regulation 7(1)(a), (b) or (c) and who satisfies the conditions in paragraph (2), (3), (4) or (5)'; i.e.:

(2) A person satisfies the condition in this paragraph if the person is a relative of an EEA national, his spouse or his civil partner and -
   (a) the person is residing in an EEA State in which the EEA national also resides and is dependent upon the EEA national or is a member of his household;
   (b) the person satisfied the condition in paragraph (a) and is accompanying the EEA national to the United Kingdom or wishes to join him there; or
   (c) the person satisfied the condition in paragraph (a), has joined the EEA national in the United Kingdom and continues to be dependent upon him or to be a member of his household.
(3) A person satisfies the condition in this paragraph if the person is a relative of an EEA national or his spouse or his civil partner and, on serious health grounds, strictly requires the personal care of the EEA national, his spouse or his civil partner.
(4) A person satisfies the condition in this paragraph if the person is a relative of an EEA national and would meet the requirements in the immigration rules (other than those relating to entry clearance) for indefinite leave to enter or remain in the United Kingdom as a dependent relative of the EEA national were the EEA national a person present and settled in the United Kingdom.
(5) A person satisfies the condition in this paragraph if the person is the partner of an EEA national (other than a civil partner) and can prove to the decision maker that he is in a durable relationship with the EEA national.

While the directive states that such 'extended family members' should have their entry 'facilitated', the EEA Regulations 2006 provide that 'a person who is an extended family member and has been issued with an EEA family permit, a registration certificate or a residence card shall be treated as the family member of the relevant EEA national for as long as he continues to satisfy the conditions in Regulation 8(2), (3), (4) or (5) in relation to the EEA national and the permit, certificate or card has not ceased to be valid or been revoked'. Thus, under the EEA Regulations 2006, 'extended family members' will be treated exactly the same as 'family members' once they have been issued with the family permit, registration certificate or residence card. However, the permit will only be issued to extended family members if, *inter alia*, 'in all the circumstances, it appears to the entry clearance officer appropriate to issue . . .' (Reg 12(2)(c)); and in the case of certificates and permits if, *inter alia*, 'in all the circumstances, it appears to the Secretary of State appropriate to issue . . .' (Regs 16(5)(b) and 17(4)(b)). Where an application is received by an extended family member, the entry clearance officer or Secretary of State (as appropriate) shall 'undertake an extensive examination of the personal circumstances of the applicant and if he refuses the application shall give reasons justifying the refusal unless this is contrary to the interests of national security' (Regs 12(3), 16(6) and 17(5)).

The term 'spouse' in the EEA Regulations 2006 'does not include a party to a marriage of convenience' (Reg 2(1)). This exclusion, which was also included in the EEA Order 2000, takes advantage of Art 35, Directive 2004/38 which provides that:

> Member States may adopt the necessary measures to refuse, terminate or withdraw the right conferred by the Directive in the case of abuse of rights or fraud, such as marriages of convenience . . .

Entry

All UK ports and airports now have a route for UK, EU and EEA nationals (which for the purposes of the EEA Regulation 2006 includes Switzerland), and those arriving through the Channel Tunnel will be examined in transit. Examination will generally be confined to ensuring that a person is an EU citizen or a national of an EEA state, and any EU citizen or EEA national should be admitted simply on production of a valid identity card or passport issued by an EEA state (Reg 11(1)). In the case of family members who are not themselves EU citizens or EEA nationals, they will have to produce a valid passport (an identity card is not acceptable) and either an EEA family permit, a residence card or a permanent residence card (Reg 11(2)). The family permit, residence card and permanent residence card are issued pursuant to the EEA Regulations 2006 (Regs 12, 17 and 18, see below).

If the person does not produce on arrival one of the specified documents, before refusing the person admission to the UK, the immigration officer must give the person concerned every reasonable opportunity to (i) obtain the document; or (ii) have it brought to him within a reasonable period of time; or (iii) prove by other means that he has a right of entry under the Regulations (Reg 11(4)).

Regulation 19, EEA Regulations 2006 provides that a person can be denied admission (i) on grounds of public policy, public security or public health (see below); or (ii) if at the time of his arrival he is a family member of an EEA national *unless* (a) he is accompanying the EEA national or joining him in the UK; and (ii) the EEA national has the right to reside in the UK under the Regulations.

Residence

Under the EEA Regulations 2006, a person who is admitted to or acquires a right to reside in the UK under the Regulations *shall not* require 'leave' (i.e. permission) to remain in the UK under the Immigration Act 1971 during any period in which he has a right to reside under the Regulations, but any person *shall* require leave under the 1971 Act during any period in which he does not have such a right (Para 1, Schedule 2). Additionally, where a person has leave to enter or remain under the 1971 Act which is subject to conditions, and that person also has a right to reside under the Regulations, those conditions shall not have effect for as long as the person has that right to reside (Para 1, Schedule 2).

General right of residence for up to three months

As has previously been discussed in Chapters 11–13 Directive 2004/38 introduces an initial general right of residence for up to three months for EU nationals and their family members provided they have a valid identity card or passport (or a passport in the case of non-EU family members), and do not become an unreasonable burden on the social assistance system of the host Member State (Arts 6(1) and 14(1)). This is reflected in the EEA Regulations 2006 (Reg 13).

EU citizens qualifying for the right of residence or the right of permanent residence and the members of their family benefit from equal treatment with host-country nationals in the areas covered by the Treaty (Art 24(1), Directive 2004/38). However, for the first three months of residence, or while the EU citizen is exercising his right to reside while seeking work under Art 14(4)(b), Directive 2004/38, the host Member State is not obliged to grant entitlement to social assistance to persons other than employed or self-employed workers and the members of their family (Art 24(2), Directive 2004/38). The EEA Regulations 2006 do not implement Art 24, Directive 2004/38 because, the UK government has stated, the Regulations only concern the right of movement and residence of EEA nationals and their family members; other government departments may rely on this provision to adopt relevant secondary legislation with regard to all non-UK citizens (Explanatory Memorandum to the EEA Regulations 2006).

Right of residence for more than three months

Regulation 14(1), EEA Regulations 2006 implements Art 7, Directive 2004/38. Regulation 14(1) provides that a 'qualified person' is entitled to reside in the UK for so long as he remains a 'qualified person'. A family member of a qualified person residing in the UK under Reg 14(1) or the family member of an EEA national with a permanent right of residence under Reg 15 (see below) is entitled to reside in the UK for so long as he remains a family member of the qualified person or EEA national (Reg 14(2)). This extended right of residence, for a period exceeding three months, depends upon the EEA national coming within the scope of 'qualified person'. 'Qualified person' is defined by Reg 6(1) as a person who is an EEA national and in the UK as:

(a) a jobseeker;

(b) a worker;

(c) a self-employed person;

(d) a self-sufficient person; or

(e) a student.

Each of these categories of qualified person is further defined by the Regulations:

(a) work-seeker means a person who enters the UK in order to seek employment and who can provide evidence that he is seeking employment and has a genuine chance of being engaged (Reg 6(4));

(b) worker means a worker within the meaning of Art 39 EC Treaty (Reg 4(1)(a));

(c) self-employed person means a person who establishes himself in order to pursue an activity as a self-employed person in accordance with Art 43 EC Treaty (Reg 4(1)(b));

(d) self-sufficient person means a person who –

   (i) has sufficient resources not to become a burden on the social assistance system of the UK during his period of residence; and

   (ii) has comprehensive sickness insurance cover in the UK (Reg 4(1)(c));

(e) student means a person who –

   (i) is enrolled at a private or public establishment, including on the Department for Education and Skills' Register of Education and Training Providers or financed from public funds, for the principal purpose of following a course of study, including vocational training;

   (ii) has comprehensive sickness insurance cover in the UK; and

   (iii) assures the Secretary of State, by means of a declaration, or by such equivalent means as the person may choose, that he has sufficient resources not to become a burden on the social assistance system of the UK during his period of residence (Reg 4(1)(d)).

The above accurately implements the provisions of Art 7(1), Directive 2004/38 relating to those persons who have the right of extended residence. With regard to a self-sufficient person and a student, Reg 4(4) provides that their resources shall be considered to be sufficient 'if they exceed the maximum level of resources which a United Kingdom national and his family members may possess if he is to become eligible for social assistance under the United Kingdom benefit system'.

The right of extended residence applies to the EEA national and his family members (and extended family members, see above). However, in the case of a student, the right of extended residence to his family members will be limited; i.e. to the student's spouse or civil partner and to the dependent children of the student or of his spouse or civil partner (Reg 7(2)). The right of extended residence to a student's 'extended family members' is also limited by Reg 7(4).

Regulation 6(2) provides that a person who is no longer working shall be treated as a worker for the purpose of Reg 6(1)(b) if:

(a) he is temporarily unable to work as the result of an illness or accident;

(b) he is in duly recorded involuntary unemployment after having been employed in the United Kingdom, provided that he has registered as a jobseeker with the relevant employment office and -

   (i) he was employed for one year or more before becoming unemployed;

   (ii) he has been unemployed for no more than six months; or

   (iii) he can provide evidence that he is seeking employment in the United Kingdom and has a genuine chance of being engaged;

(c) he is involuntarily unemployed and has embarked on vocational training; or

(d) he has voluntarily ceased working and embarked on vocational training that is related to his previous employment.

A person who is no longer in self-employment shall not cease to be treated as a self-employed person if he is temporarily unable to pursue his activity as a self-employed person as a result of an illness or accident (Reg 6(3)).

Regulation 10 sets out the circumstances in which a family member will retain the right of residence, where the EEA national dies or leaves the UK, or where the EEA national and his spouse or civil partner terminate their marriage or civil partnership. This provision implements Arts 12–13, Directive 2004/38.

Regulation 16(1) provides for the issuing of a *registration certificate* to a qualified person on application and production of (i) a valid identity card or passport issued by an EEA state; and (ii) proof that he is a qualified person (Reg 16(1)). Regulation 16 also provides for the issuing of a *registration certificate* to EEA family members (Reg 16(3)) and to EEA extended family members (Reg 16(5)). Regulation 17 provides for the issuing of a *residence card* to non-EEA family members (Reg 17(1)) and to non-EEA extended family members (Reg 17(4)) .

EU citizens qualifying for the right of residence or the right of permanent residence and the members of their family benefit from equal treatment with host-country nationals in the areas covered by the Treaty (Art 24(1), Directive 2004/38). Host Member States are not required to provide maintenance aid (i.e. student grants or student loans) to persons with a right of residence who have come to the country in question to study (Art 24(2), Directive 2004/38). The EEA Regulations 2006 do not implement Art 24, Directive 2004/38.

Permanent right of residence

Regulation 15(1), EEA Regulations 2006 implements Art 16, Directive 2004/38. Regulation 15(1) sets out the persons who are entitled to reside in the UK permanently:

(a) an EEA national who has resided in the United Kingdom in accordance with these Regulations for a continuous period of five years;

(b) a family member of an EEA national who is not himself an EEA national but who has resided in the United Kingdom with the EEA national in accordance with these Regulations for a continuous period of five years;

(c) a worker or self-employed person who has ceased activity;

(d) the family member of a worker or self-employed person who has ceased activity;

(e) a person who was the family member of a worker or self-employed person where –

(i)   the worker or self-employed person has died;

(ii) the family member resided with him immediately before his death; and

(iii) the worker or self-employed person had resided continuously in the United Kingdom for at least the two years immediately before his death or the death was the result of an accident at work or an occupational disease;

(f) a person who –

(i)   has resided in the United Kingdom in accordance with these Regulations for a continuous period of five years; and

(ii) was, at the end of that period, a family member who has retained the right of residence.

Regulation 15(1)(c) refers to a worker or self-employed person who has 'ceased activity'. This is defined by Reg 5:

(1) In these Regulations, 'worker or self-employed person who has ceased activity' means an EEA national who satisfies the conditions in paragraph (2), (3), (4) or (5).

(2) A person satisfies the conditions in this paragraph if he –
  (a) terminates his activity as a worker or self-employed person and –
    (i) has reached the age at which he is entitled to a state pension on the date on which he terminates his activity; or
    (ii) in the case of a worker, ceases working to take early retirement;
  (b) pursued his activity as a worker or self-employed person in the United Kingdom for at least twelve months prior to the termination; and
  (c) resided in the United Kingdom continuously for more than three years prior to the termination.

(3) A person satisfies the conditions in this paragraph if –
  (a) he terminates his activity in the United Kingdom as a worker or self-employed person as a result of a permanent incapacity to work; and
  (b) either –
    (i) he resided in the United Kingdom continuously for more than two years prior to the termination; or
    (ii) the incapacity is the result of an accident at work or an occupational disease that entitles him to a pension payable in full or in part by an institution in the United Kingdom.

(4) A person satisfies the conditions in this paragraph if –
  (a) he is active as a worker or self-employed person in an EEA State but retains his place of residence in the United Kingdom, to which he returns as a rule at least once a week; and
  (b) prior to becoming so active in that EEA State, he had been continuously resident and continuously active as a worker or self-employed person in the United Kingdom for at least three years.

(5) A person who satisfies the condition in paragraph (4)(a) but not the condition in paragraph (4)(b) shall, for the purposes of paragraphs (2) and (3), be treated as being active and resident in the United Kingdom during any period in which he is working or self-employed in the EEA State.

(6) The conditions in paragraphs (2) and (3) as to length of residence and activity as a worker or self-employed person shall not apply in relation to a person whose spouse or civil partner is a United Kingdom national.

(7) For the purposes of this regulation –
  (a) periods of inactivity for reasons not of the person's own making;
  (b) periods of inactivity due to illness or accident; and
  (c) in the case of a worker, periods of involuntary unemployment duly recorded by the relevant employment office, shall be treated as periods of activity as a worker or self-employed person, as the case may be.

Regulation 3(2) provides that continuity of residence shall not be affected by:

(a) periods of absence from the United Kingdom which do not exceed six months in total in any year;
(b) periods of absence from the United Kingdom on military service; or
(c) any one absence from the United Kingdom not exceeding twelve months for an important reason such as pregnancy and childbirth, serious illness, study or vocational training or an overseas posting.

Once the right of permanent residence has been acquired, it will only be lost through absence from the UK for a period exceeding two consecutive years (Reg 15(2)). This is subject to Reg 19(3)(b), which provides for the exclusion of a person on the grounds of public policy, public security or public health. Regulation 18 provides for the issuing of a document certifying permanent residence to qualifying EAA nationals and a permanent residence card to qualifying non-EEA nationals.

EU citizens qualifying for the right of residence or the right of permanent residence and the members of their family benefit from equal treatment with host-country nationals in the areas covered by the Treaty (Art 24(1), Directive 2004/38). The EEA Regulations 2006 do not implement Art 24, Directive 2004/38.

Exclusion and removal

European Union citizens and EEA nationals may be removed from the UK on ceasing to have a right of residence as a qualified person, or if the removal is justified on public policy, public security or public health grounds (Reg 19(3)). Regulations 22 to 24 contain procedural provisions relating to persons who claim admission under the Regulations, who are refused admission, or are being removed.

The EEA Regulations 2006 accurately transpose the provisions of Directive 2004/38 relating to exclusion and removal.

The effect of claims to social assistance

Many EU citizens will, after they have worked and gained worker status, be entitled to benefits such as 'social advantages' under Art 7(2), Regulation 1612/68 or, in some cases, under Regulation 1408/71 (see Chapters 12 and 14). Expulsions on the ground of public policy, public security or public health are contrary to Art 27(1), Directive 2004/38, if they are taken 'to service economic ends'. This prohibition is reflected in Regulation 21(2), EEA Regulations 2006 which provides that decisions taken on grounds of public policy, public security or public health 'may not be taken to serve economic ends'. Nevertheless, there remains an important link between claims to public funds and the rights of residence of EU citizens. The link may operate in two separate, but related, ways: first, by denying the financial support which an EU citizen may require when he has insufficient resources to maintain himself; and, second, by providing evidence that he cannot support himself without recourse to social assistance.

Regulation 13(3)(b) provides that during the initial right of residence (i.e. for a period up to three months), an EEA national or his family members who become an unreasonable burden on the social assistance system of the UK shall cease to have the right to reside under the Regulations. However, Reg 19(4) provides that a person must not be removed as the *automatic consequence* of having recourse to the UK's social assistance system.

For the first three months of residence, or while the EU citizen is exercising his right to reside while seeking work under Art 14(4)(b), Directive 2004/38, the host Member State is not obliged to grant entitlement to social assistance to persons other than employed or self-employed workers and the members of their family (Art 24(2), Directive 2004/38). The EEA Regulations 2006 do not implement Art 24.

Prima facie, an economically self-sufficient person or student will have a right to remain as long as he satisfies the relevant requirements of Directive 2004/38. He cannot, however, look to the UK's welfare system for any kind of assistance, unless it is for contributory benefits to which he may be entitled under Regulation 1408/71 (see Chapter 14). Income support, housing benefit and council tax benefit, for example, are conditional upon proof by a claimant who is a national of an EEA state or an EU citizen that he is 'habitually resident in the UK, the Republic of Ireland, the Channel Islands or the

Isle of Man' (Income-related Benefits Schemes (Miscellaneous Amendments) (No. 3) Regulations 1994 (SI 1994/1807)). This condition is not applied to, for example, those who have EU worker status or during the first six months in which a worker is looking for work (Reg 21(3)(h), Income Support (General) Regulations 1987, SI 1987/1967), or to a person who has a right of residence as a self-employed person under Directive 2004/38.

The second way in which the social assistance system may jeopardise a person's right to remain is by providing evidence that he is no longer economically self-sufficient. The residence rights conferred on self-sufficient persons and students are conditional upon the beneficiaries not becoming a burden on the social assistance system of the host Member State. A claim to income support, housing benefit or council tax benefit, for example, is almost certain to fail because the habitual residence test is difficult to satisfy. The details of the claim would then be forwarded to the Home Office and, if the individual is not a worker or a self-employed person, or otherwise entitled to remain under the EEA Regulations 2006, then he could be required to leave under Regulation 19(3)(a) as someone who 'ceases to have a right to reside under these Regulations'.

Deportations

In the UK, deportations are carried out either by the Home Secretary on his own initiative or following a recommendation of the courts at the time when a sentence is imposed on an offender (ss 3(5) and (6)5, Immigration Act 1971). The Home Secretary has a general power to deport a foreign national where he 'deems his deportation to be conducive to the public good' (s 3(5)(b) Immigration Act 1971). It was on this basis that deportations of EU citizens have been carried out, although both the Home Secretary and the courts have been obliged to make decisions on whether or not to deport or recommend deportation within the limits laid down by Directive 2004/38. The Community criteria are much narrower than those allowed under UK immigration law, and the EEA Regulations 2006 lays down both the circumstances for removal and deportation, and the Community criteria.

In **R** v **Secretary of State for the Home Office, ex parte Marchon** [1993] 2 CMLR 132, the appellant, a Portuguese national, who had been a general practitioner, was convicted of dealing in drugs. He was sentenced to a long term of imprisonment but not recommended for deportation by the trial court. The Home Secretary, nonetheless, issued notice of an intention to deport him. The English Court of Appeal upheld the decision on the ground that 'the offence merits deportation . . . it involves a disregard of the basic or fundamental tenets of society' (Dillon LJ). Concurring, Beldam LJ added that there should be no hint that society was prepared to tolerate the importation of, and dealing in, drugs: 'I say this *not simply because refusal to do so would act as a deterrent to others but rather because it serves to emphasise the grave and present danger from this threat*' (emphasis added). The decision is surprising, not least because it is clearly not wholly based on the conduct of the offender and the likelihood of his future offending, but on a clear intention by the English court to take deterrent or general preventive action because of a concern about offences of this type. Such an approach obviously conflicts with the decision of the Court of Justice in **Bonsignore**, see Chapter 15. Now, it would also conflict with Reg 21(5), EEA Regulations 2006 which provides that a decision taken on the grounds of public policy or public security shall be taken in accordance with the following principles:

(a) the decision must comply with the principle of proportionality;

(b) the decision must be based exclusively on the personal conduct of the person concerned;

(c) the personal conduct of the person concerned must represent a genuine, present and sufficiently serious threat affecting one of the fundamental interests of society;

(d) matters isolated from the particulars of the case or which relate to considerations of general prevention do not justify the decision;

(e) a person's previous criminal convictions do not in themselves justify the decision.

Procedural safeguards

Regulations 25 to 29 and Schedule 1, EEA Regulations 2006 set out the appeal rights in relation to decisions taken under the Regulations.

Transposition of Directive 2004/38 and the EEA Regulations 2006

The following table sets out the provision of Directive 2004/38 in the first column, the objective of the provision of the Directive in the second column, and the corresponding implementing provision (if any) within the EEA Regulations 2006 in the third column:

Table 16.1 Transposition of Directive 2004/38 and the EEA Regulations 2006

Article Directive 2004/38	Objective of Article	Implementation by EEA Regulations 2006
Article 1: Subject		
1	Lays down the subject of the Directive.	*No action required*
		Unless otherwise stated, this Directive will be implemented by the Immigration (European Economic Area) Regulations 2006.
Article 2: Definitions		
2(1)	Definition of a *'Union citizen'* (referred to throughout this table as an 'EU citizen').	*Reg 2* In *Reg 2(1)* Union citizen is replaced by reference to a European Economic Area ('EEA') national (of an 'EEA State') as defined.
2(2)	Definition of a *'family member'*.	*Reg 7*
2(3)	Definition of a *'host Member State'*.	*Reg 2* The meaning has been expanded to include EEA States so that the definition is: *(a)* a Member State other than the United Kingdom; *(b)* Norway, Iceland or Liechtenstein; *(c)* Switzerland.
Article 3: Beneficiaries		
3(1)	Directive applies to all EU citizens who move to or reside in the host Member State and their family members who accompany/join them.	*Regs 2 and 7*

3(2)	Facilitate entry and residence for the following persons: *(i)* Any family members who are dependants or members of the household of the EU citizen or where health grounds require the personal care of the family member by the EU citizen. *(ii)* Partner with whom EU citizen has a durable relationship. Host Member State can deny entry or residence to these people after undertaking an extensive examination of the personal circumstances.	*Reg 8* Defined as 'extended family member' which means a person who is not a family member of an EEA national under *Reg 7*, but who satisfies certain conditions defined in *Reg 8(2) to 8(6)*. Reg 8(2) and (3) *Reg 8(5)* *Reg 12(3)*

Article 4: Right of exit

4	Right of exit	Persons seeking to leave the UK who hold a valid ID card or passport do not require an exit visa under national law. UK nationals may apply to the UK Passport Service for a passport which will be valid in all Member States. Accordingly, no legislative implementation is necessary.

Article 5: Right of entry

5(1)	To grant EU citizens leave to enter a Member State's territory with a valid ID card or passport.	*Reg 11(1)* An EEA national must be admitted to the UK if he produces on arrival a valid national identity card or passport issued by an EEA State.
	Right of non-EU family members to have leave to enter with a valid passport.	*Reg 11(2)* A person who is not an EEA national must be admitted to the UK if he is a family member of an EEA national, a family member who has retained the right of residence or a person with a permanent right of residence under *Reg 15* and produces on arrival: (a) a valid passport; and (b) an EEA family permit [a form of entry clearance], a residence card [provided for in *Reg 17*] or a permanent residence card [provided for in *Reg 18*].
5(2)	Non-EU family members need only have an entrance visa (in accordance with Reg 539/2001 or national law). Possession of valid residence card (*Art 10*) exempts family members from this requirement.	*Reg 11(2)* concerns the right of admission. See above. *Reg 12* provides for the issue of an EEA Family Permit.
	Such visas, if required, shall be granted free of charge and as soon as possible via accelerated procedures.	*Reg 12(4)* An EEA family permit issued under this regulation shall be issued free of charge and as soon as possible.
5(3)	Prohibits Member States from stamping passports of non-EU family members provided that they present a residence card (as required by *Art 10*).	*Reg 11(3)*

5(4)	To give EU citizens and family members every reasonable opportunity to obtain necessary documents within a reasonable period of time or to otherwise prove that they are covered by the right of free movement and residence.	*Reg 11(4)*
5(5)	Allows Member States to submit the person to proportionate and non-discriminatory sanctions if they do not report their presence within the Member States' territory within a reasonable and non-discriminatory period of time.	*No action required.*

Article 6: Right of residence for up to 3 months

6(1)	Gives EU citizens a right of residence for up to 3 months without any conditions or formalities other than requirement to hold an ID card/passport.	*Reg 13(1)*
6(2)	To apply Art 6(1) to non-EU family members who are accompanying or joining the EU citizen.	*Reg 13(2)*

Article 7: Right of residence for more than 3 months

7(1)	Gives the right of residence to all EU citizens for longer than 3 months if: *(a)* they are workers/self-employed in the host Member State; or *(b)* have sufficient resources to be self-sufficient and have comprehensive sickness insurance cover (for themselves and any accompanying family member); or *(c)* are enrolled at a private/public establishment accredited by host Member State, for the principal purpose of study and have satisfied *(b)*; or *(d)* are family members of EU citizens who have satisfied *(a)*, *(b)* or *(c)*.	*Reg 14(1)* with reference to *Reg 6(1)* (being the definition of qualified person). A qualified person is defined as: (a) a jobseeker; (b) a worker; (c) a self-employed person; (d) a self-sufficient person; or (e) a student. A qualified person is entitled to reside in the UK for so long as he remains a qualified person. *Reg 14(2)* and *Reg 7(1) and (2)*
7(2)	The right of residence in Art 7(1) extends to non-EU family members who accompany or join the EU citizen provided the EU citizen fulfils Art 7(1) (a), (b) or (c).	*Reg 14(2) and Reg 7(1) and (2)*
7(3)	A non-working EU citizen shall retain the status of a worker if: *(a)* he is temporarily unable to work as a result of an illness or accident; *(b)* and *(c)* he is involuntarily unemployed after having being employed for more than a year and is a registered jobseeker; *(d)* he embarks on vocational training. Unless he is involuntarily unemployed, the vocational training must be related to the previous employment.	*Reg 5*
7(4)	Only the spouse, the registered partner and dependent children shall have right of residence as long as the EU citizen meets the conditions under Art 7(1)(c) above (i.e. a student).	*Reg 7(2)*

Article 8: Administrative formalities for EU citizens

8(1)	For periods of residence longer than 3 months, the host Member State may require EU citizens to register with relevant authorities.	*No action required* The Secretary of State will not require this but a person may apply for a registration certificate (and the relevant provisions are described below).
8(2) and (3)	Deadline for registration may not be less than 3 months from date of arrival. Registration certificate (stating name, address and date) should be issued immediately. For registration certificate, Member States may only require: *1.* Article 7(1)(a) persons to present a valid ID card/passport, confirmation of working from employer/certificate of employment, or proof that they are self-employed. *2.* Article 7(1)(b) persons to present a valid ID card/passport and provide proof that they satisfy the conditions laid down therein. *3.* Article 7(1)(c) persons to present a valid ID card/passport, proof of enrolment at an accredited establishment and proof of comprehensive sickness insurance cover and a declaration as to sufficient resources.	*Reg 16(1) and (2)*
8(4)	The definition of the amount of 'sufficient resources'	*Reg 4(4)* The resources of the person concerned and, where applicable, any family members are to be regarded as sufficient if they exceed the maximum level of resources which a UK national and his family members may possess if he is to become eligible for social assistance under the UK benefit system.
8(5)	For a registration certificate for Member State family members, the following may be required where appropriate; *1.* A valid ID card or passport. *2.* Document attesting to the existence of a family relationship. *3.* The registration certificate of the person that they are joining. *4.* Proof that they are a family member. *5.* Document issued by relevant authority in the country of origin.	*Reg 16(3)*

Article 9: Administrative formalities for family members who are not nationals of a Member State

9(1)	Member States shall issue residence cards to non-EU family members where planned residence is greater than three months.	*Reg 17(1) and (2)*
9(2)	Deadline for submitting a residence card application may not be less than 3 months from date of arrival.	*No action required* The Secretary of State has not set a deadline. However, a person can only apply for such a card if he qualifies for an extended right of residence (under *Reg 14(2)*).

9(3)	Proportionate and non-discriminatory sanction for those who fail to comply with residence card requirements.	*No action required* The Secretary of State will not require such sanctions.

Article 10: Issue of residence cards

10(1)	Non-EU family members shall prove their residence with a document called *Residence Card of a family member of a Union citizen* which shall be issued no later than six months from date of submission of application. Certificate of application must be issued immediately.	*Reg 17(3)*
10(2)	To issue a residence card, Member States shall require: 1. A valid passport. 2. A document attesting family relationship. 3. A registration certificate or any other proof of residence in the host Member State of the EU citizen whom they are accompanying. 4. In cases falling under Art 2(2), documentary evidence that the criteria are met.	*Reg 17(1) and (3)*
	5. In cases falling under Art 3(2)(a), a document showing country from which they are arriving certifying they are dependants of the household of the EU citizen or proof that they require personal care of the EU citizen on serious health grounds.	*Reg 17(4) and (5)*

Article 11: Validity of residence cards

11(1)	Residence card provided (Art 10(1)) shall be valid for 5 years or for the envisaged period of residence of the EU citizen if less than 5 years.	*Reg 17(6)*
11(2)	Validity of residence card not affected by certain types of absence.	The Secretary of State has taken the approach that provisions on continuity of stay apply to the general right to reside. This has been provided for, in respect of family members, by *Reg 3 and Reg 15(1)*.

Article 12: Retention of right of residence by family members in the event of death or departure of the EU citizen

12(1)	The Union Citizen's death or departure from Member State shall not affect right of residence of his family members who are nationals of a Member State.	*Reg 10(2) and (3)*
	Before acquiring the right of permanent residence, the persons concerned must meet the conditions laid down in points (a), (b), (c) or (d) of Art 7(1).	*Reg 15(1)(f)*
12(2)	Non-EU family members of an EU citizen who subsequently dies shall not lose their right of residence as long as they were residing in the host Member State as family members for at least one year before the EU citizen's death.	*Reg 10(2)*

	Before acquiring the right of permanent residence, the persons concerned must meet the conditions laid down in points (a), (b), (c) or (d) of Art 7(1).	*Reg 15(1)(f)*
12(3)	EU citizen's death or departure from host Member State shall not entail loss of the right of residence of his children or of the parent who has actual custody of the children irrespective of nationality, if the children reside and are enrolled at an educational establishment in the host Member State for the purpose of studying there until the end of their studies.	*Reg 10(3) and (4), Reg 14(3)*

Article 13: Retention of the right of residence by family members in the event of divorce, annulment of marriage or termination of registered partnership

13(1)	Divorce, annulment of the EU citizen's marriage or termination of his registered partnership shall not affect the right of his family members who are nationals of a Member State.	*Regs 10(5) and 14(3)*
	Before acquiring the right of permanent residence, the persons concerned must meet the conditions laid down in points (a), (b), (c) or (d) of Art 7(1).	*Reg 15(1)(f)*
13(2)	Non-EU family members shall not lose their right of residence due to divorce, annulment of marriage or termination of the registered partnership where: *(a)* prior to the initiation of divorce or annulment proceedings or termination of the registered partnership, the marriage or registered partnership has lasted three years (at least one year in Member State); or *(b)* by agreement between the spouses or the partners or by court order, the spouse or partner who is not a national of a Member State has custody of the EU citizen's children; or *(c)* this is warranted by particular difficult circumstance (e.g. victim of domestic violence while marriage is subsisting); or *(d)* by agreement between the spouses or the partners or by court order, the non-EU spouse or partner has right of access to minor child, provided that the court has ruled that access must be in the Member State.	*Reg 10(5)*
	Before gaining permanent residence, the right of residence of the persons concerned shall remain subject to the requirement that they are able to show that they are workers, self-employed persons or that they have sufficient resources not to become a burden on the Member State's social assistance system. Or, that they are the family members of someone who satisfies these requirements.	*Reg 15(1)(f)*

Article 14: Retention of right of residence

14(1)	EU citizens and family members shall have right of initial residence (Art 6) as long as they do not become an unreasonable burden on the social assistance system of the host Member State.	*Reg 13(3)(b)*
14(2)	EU citizens and their family members shall retain the right of residence (under Arts 7, 12, 13) as long as they meet conditions set out therein. Only where there is a reasonable doubt whether an EU citizen or family member fulfils conditions in above Articles may a Member State verify if these conditions are fulfilled.	*Reg 14*
14(3)	A Member State shall not automatically expel an EU citizen or family member because of his recourse to the social assistance system.	*Reg 19(4)*
14(4)	An expulsion order can never be adopted against an EU citizen or his family members where the EU citizen: (i) is a worker or a self-employed person; or (ii) entered the territory to seek employment. EU citizens cannot be expelled as long as they can provide evidence that they are continuing to seek employment and have a genuine chance of being engaged.	*Reg 6* provides that *(1)(a)* a jobseeker (by reference to sub-para *(4)*); *(b)* a worker; *(c)* a self-employed person are defined as qualified persons. *Regulation 6(2) and (3)* provides the circumstances in which a person continues to be a worker or self-employed person when he is not working. While the person remains a qualified person, he has a right to reside (see *Reg 14(1)*) and may not be removed unless that right ceases (see *Reg 19(3)*). Similar provision is made in respect of family members of such qualified persons by *Regs 7, 8, 14(2) and 19(3)*.

Article 15: Procedural safeguards

15(1)	Procedures provided by Arts 30 and 31 shall apply to all decisions restricting free movement of EU citizens and their family members on grounds other than public policy, public security or public health.	*Reg 2(1)* defines an 'EEA Decision' and *Reg 26* sets out the rights of appeal for a person seeking to challenge such a decision.
15(2)	Expiry of the ID card/passport of person concerned shall not constitute a ground for expulsion if person was issued with registration certificate or residence card.	The only grounds of exclusion and removal from the United Kingdom are set out in *Reg 19.*
15(3)	Host Member State may not impose a ban on entry in the context on an expulsion decision to which Art 15(1) applies.	The only grounds of exclusion and removal from the United Kingdom are set out in *Reg 19.*

Article 16: Right of permanent residence

16(1)	EU citizens who have resided continuously for a period of 5 years in a host Member State shall have a right of permanent residence.	*Reg 15(1)(a)*

16(2)	The Art 16(1) right also applies to non-EU family members who have resided with the EU citizen in the host Member State for a continuous period of 5 years.	*Reg 15(1)(b)*
16(3)	Continuity of residence is not affected by: (a) temporary absence not exceeding 6 months; (b) longer absences due to military service; (c) one absence of a maximum of 12 consecutive months for important reasons such as pregnancy, childbirth, serious illness, study/vocational training, or posting in another Member State or third country.	*Reg 3*
16(4)	Right of permanent residence (once acquired) will only be lost after absence of over 2 years from host Member State.	*Reg 15(2)*

Article 17: Exemption for persons no longer working in the host Member State and their family members, with regard to the right to permanent residence

---

17(1)	Right of permanent residence in host Member State shall be enjoyed before continuous residence of 5 years by: (a) workers or self-employed persons who (at the time they stop working) have reached the legal retirement age for entitlement to an old age pension, or those who take early retirement but have been working in the past 12 months and have resided continuously for 3 years. If the host Member State does not grant the right to an old age pension to certain categories of self-employed persons, then age condition will be met once person turns 60.	*Regs 5(1) and 15(1)(c)*
	(b) workers or self-employed persons who have resided continuously in the host Member State for more than 2 years and stopped working as a result of permanent incapacity to work. If the incapacity is due to an incident at work or occupational disease entitling the person concerned to a benefit payable by the Member State (part or in full), no condition of length of residence will be imposed.	*Regs 5(1) and 15(1)(c)*
	(c) workers or self-employed persons who, after 3 years continuous employment and residence in host Member State, work in another Member State, but return to their place of residence in the host Member State at least once a week.	*Regs 5(1) and 15(1)(c)*
	For the purposes of rights referred to in (a) and (b), periods of employment spent in a Member State by the person concerned shall be regarded as having been spent in the host Member State.	*Reg 5(5)*

17(2)	Conditions of length of residence and employment laid down in Art 17(1)(a) and (b) shall not apply if the worker's or self-employed person's spouse or partner is a national of the host Member State and has lost their nationality of that Member State by marriage to that worker/self-employed person.	*Reg 5(6)*
17(3)	If the worker/self-employed person has acquired a permanent right of residence, then the family members of that person (who are residing with him) shall have a permanent right of residence in that Member State.	*Reg 15(1)(d)*
17(4)	If the worker/self-employed person dies while working (and not having acquired a permanent right of residence) his family members shall acquire the right of permanent residence on condition that: *(a)* the worker/self-employed person had resided continuously in the Member State for 2 years before death; or *(b)* death resulted from accident at work or occupational disease; or *(c)* the surviving spouse lost the nationality of that Member State following marriage to the worker/self-employed person.	*Reg 15(1)(e)*

Article 18: Acquisition of the right of permanent residence by certain family members who are not a national of a Member State

18	Family members of EU citizens gain permanent right of residence after residing lawfully in host Member State for 5 consecutive years.	*Reg 15(1)(f)*

Article 19: Document certifying permanent residence for EU citizens

19(1)	Upon application, Member States shall issue EU citizens entitled to permanent residence with a document certifying permanent residence after verifying the duration of residence.	*Reg 18(1)*
19(2)	The document certifying permanent residence shall be issued as soon as possible.	*Reg 18(1)*

Article 20: Permanent residence card for family members who are not nationals of a Member State

20(1)	Non-EU family members shall be issued with a permanent residence card within 6 months of the submission of their application. The card shall be renewable automatically every 10 years.	*Reg 18(2) and (3)*
20(2)	Application for a residence card shall be submitted before the residence card expires. Failure to comply may render the person to proportionate and non-discriminatory sanctions.	The Secretary of State has decided not to implement this provision.

20(3)	Interruption in residence not exceeding 2 years shall not affect the validity of the permanent residence card.	*Reg 18(5)* referring to *Reg 15* (which includes the reference to *15(2)* which provides that the right to permanent residence shall be lost through absence from the United Kingdom for a period exceeding 2 consecutive years).

Article 21: Continuity of residence

21	Continuity of residence may be shown by any means of proof in use in the host Member State. Continuity of residence is broken by any expulsion decision enforced against the person concerned.	Illustrations of the type of proof that could be provided will be set out in guidance. *Reg 3(3)* implements the second provision of Art 21.

Article 22: Territorial scope

22	Right of residence/permanent residence shall cover the whole territory of the host Member State. Member States may impose restrictions, but only if the same restriction apply to their own nationals.	*Regs 11, 13, 14 and 15* provide a right of admission (in respect of Reg 11) and various rights of residence, as set out, to the United Kingdom.

Article 23: Related rights

23	Family members who have the right of residence/permanent residence in a Member State shall be entitled to take up employment/self-employment there irrespective of nationality.	These Regulations do not implement this provision as they only concern the right of movement and residence of EEA nationals and their family members. However, other government departments may rely on this provision in making relevant instruments.

Article 24: Equal treatment

24(1)	All EU citizens residing in the host Member State shall enjoy equal treatment with the nationals of that Member State within the scope of the Treaty. This benefit extends to non-EU family members who have a right of residence/ permanent residence.	These regulations do not implement this provision as they only concern the right of movement and residence of EEA nationals and their family members. However, other government departments may rely on this provision in making relevant instruments.
24(2)	Host Member State shall not be obliged to confer entitlement to social assistance during the first 3 months of residence, or where appropriate a longer period (as provided for by Art 14(4)(b)). It shall not be obliged (prior to the acquisition of the right of permanent residence) to grant maintenance aid for studies including vocational training, consisting in student grants/loans to persons other than workers/self-employed persons or persons who retain such status and members of their families.	These Regulations do not implement this provision as they only concern the right of movement and residence of EEA nationals and their family members. However, other government departments may rely on this provision in making relevant instruments.

Article 25: General provisions concerning residence documents

25(1)	Possession of a certificate may under no circumstances be made a precondition for the exercise of a right or the completion of an administrative formality, as entitlement to rights may be attested by any other means of proof.	*Regs 14(1) and 15(1)* provide the basis of a person's entitlement to the relevant right to reside. This does not depend on the prior possession of the documents referred to in Art 25(1).

25(2)	The documents mentioned in Article 25(1) shall be issued free of charge.	*Regs 16(7), 17(7) and 18(4).*

Article 26: Checks

26	Allows Member States to carry out checks for non-EU nationals to carry their registration certificate/residence card as long the same applies to their own nationals.	*No action required*

Article 27: General principles

27(1)	Member States may restrict the freedom of movement and residence of EU citizens (and their family members) on grounds of public policy/health/security. These grounds cannot be invoked to serve economic ends.	*Regs 12(5), 13(3)(a), 14(5), 15(3), 16(8), 17(8), 18(5), 19(3)(b), 20(1) and (6), and Reg 21* (the main regulation on this area). *Reg 21(2)*
27(2)	Measures taken on grounds of public policy/ security shall be proportional and based exclusively on the conduct of the individual concerned. No previous criminal convictions can alone constitute grounds for taking such measures. Personal conduct must represent a genuine, present and sufficiently serious threat.	*Reg 21(5) and (6)*
27(3)	In order to ascertain whether the person concerned presents a danger, the host Member State may request other Member States to provide information concerning any previous police record that the person concerned may have. Such enquiries will not be made out of routine and a reply to any checks made will be given within 2 months.	*Legislation is not required*
27(4)	The Member State which issues the passport/ID card shall allow the holder who has been expelled from another Member State to re-enter its territory without any formalities.	*Legislation is not required*

Article 28: Protection against expulsion

28(1)	Before taking an expulsion decision, the host Member State shall take account of particular considerations.	*Reg 21(7)*
28(2)	The host Member State cannot expel an EU citizen or his family members who have a right of permanent residence except on serious grounds of public policy/security.	*Reg 21(3)*
28(3)	An expulsion decision cannot be taken against EU citizens, unless the decision is based on imperative grounds of public security, if they: (a) have resided in the host Member State for the past ten years; or (b) are a minor, except if the expulsion is in the best interests of the child.	*Reg 21(4)*

Article 29: Public health

29(1)	Only diseases with epidemic potential (as defined by World Health Organisation (WHO)) and other infectious diseases if they are the subject of protection provisions applying to nationals of the host Member State may justify the restriction on freedom of movement.	*Reg 21(7)(a)* In addition to the relevant WHO regulations, reference is also made to a disease to which section 38 of the Public Health (Control of Disease) Act 1984 applies (which concerns detention in hospital of a person with a notifiable disease).
29(2)	Diseases occurring three months after arrival in host Member State shall not constitute grounds for expulsion.	*Reg 21(7)(b)*
29(3)	Member States may (where there are serious indications that it is necessary), within three months from date of arrival, require persons entitled to the right of residence to undergo a free medical examination certifying that they are not suffering from any of the conditions in Art 29(1).	*Reg 22(2)(c)*

Article 30: Notification of decisions

30(1)	Persons concerned shall be notified in writing of any decision taken under Art 27(1), such that they are able to comprehend its content and implications.	Generally, see *Reg 26(7)* and *Schedule 2* for the application of s 105 of the Nationality, Immigration and Asylum Act 2002 (notice of immigration decision) and Regulations made under that section concerning the notification of decisions taken in respect of a person. Also, see *para 5 of Schedule 5 to the Regulations*, which amends the Immigration (Notices) Regulations 2003.
30(2)	Persons shall be informed of the decision with full reasons unless it is contrary to the interests of state security.	The above provisions in respect of Art 30(1) also apply here. See also *Regs 12(3), 16(6)* and *17(5)* in respect of decisions concerning extended family members as defined in the Regulations.
30(3)	The notification shall specify the court or administrative authority with which the person concerned may lodge an appeal, the time limit for the appeal and, where applicable, the time allowed for the person to leave the territory of the Member State. Save in duly substantiated cases of urgency, the time allowed to leave the territory shall be not be less than one month from the date of notification.	The same provisions in respect of Art 30(1) apply regarding the notification of appeal rights. *Reg 24(6)* provides that a person subject to removal from the United Kingdom will be allowed one month to leave before being removed except in duly substantiated cases of urgency, where the person is detained pursuant to a sentence or court order and/or has returned to the United Kingdom when a deportation order remains outstanding against him. In those circumstances the person will not be in a position to be able to leave the territory voluntarily within a month of the decision being notified to him.

Article 31: Procedural safeguards

31(1)	The persons concerned shall have access to judicial and, where appropriate, administrative redress procedures in the host Member State to appeal against or seek review of any decision taken against them on the grounds of public policy, public security or public health.	*Reg 26* provides for appeals generally and *Reg 28* provides for appeals to the Special Immigration Appeals Commission.
31(2)	Where the application for appeal against or judicial review of the expulsion decision is accompanied by an application for an interim order to suspend enforcement of that decision, actual removal from the territory may not take place until such time as the decision on the interim order has been taken, except: – where the expulsion decision is based on a previous judicial decision; or – where the persons concerned have had previous access to judicial review; or – where the expulsion decision is based on imperative grounds of public security under Art 28(3).	*Reg 27* provides which appeals are in-country and so have suspensive effect and which appeals are out of country. *Reg 29* concerns the effect of appeals.
31(3)	The redress procedures shall allow for an examination of the legality of the decision, as well as of the facts and circumstances on which the proposed measure is based. They shall ensure that the decision is not disproportionate, particularly in view of the requirements laid down in Art 28.	*Reg 26* provides for appeals generally and *Reg 28* provides for appeals to the Special Immigration Appeals Commission.
31(4)	Member States may exclude the individual concerned from their territory pending the redress procedure, but they may not prevent the individual from submitting his defence in person, except when his appearance may cause serious troubles to public policy or public security or when the appeal or judicial review concerns a denial of entry to the territory.	*Reg 27* provides which appeals are in-country and so have suspensive effect and which appeals are out of country.

Article 32: Duration of exclusion orders

32(1)	Persons excluded on grounds of public policy or public security may submit an application for lifting of the exclusion order after a reasonable period, depending on the circumstances, and in any event after 3 years from enforcement of the final exclusion order which has been validly adopted in accordance with Community law, by putting forward arguments to establish that there has been a material change in the circumstances which justified the decision ordering their exclusion. The Member State concerned shall reach a decision on this application within 6 months of its submission.	*Reg 24(3)* applies the relevant provisions of the Immigration Act 1971 (as amended) as set out concerning deportation orders. Section 5(2) of that Act provides that a person may apply at any time to have any out standing deportation order in place against him revoked.

32(2)	The persons referred to in Art 32(1) shall have no right of entry to the territory of the Member State concerned while their application is being considered.	*Reg 24(2)* provides that a person who enters or seeks to enter to the UK in breach of a deportation order shall be treated as an illegal entrant under Schedule 2 of the Immigration Act 1971.

Article 33: Expulsion as a penalty or legal consequence

33(1)	Expulsion orders may not be issued by the host Member State as a penalty or legal consequence of a custodial penalty, unless they conform to the requirements of Arts 27, 28 and 29.	Any recommendation for deportation made by a Court under s 3(6) of the Immigration Act 1971 in respect of a person to whom the Regulations apply, will be considered by the Secretary of State under *Reg 19(3)(b)* so the deportation order provisions of s 3(5)(a) of the Immigration Act 1971 will apply by virtue of *Reg 24(3)*.
33(2)	If an expulsion order, as provided for in Art 33(1), is enforced more than two years after it was issued, the Member State shall check that the individual concerned is currently and genuinely a threat to public policy or public security and shall assess whether there has been any material change in the circumstances since the expulsion order was issued.	This has been applied in respect of all deportation orders made under the Regulations – see *Reg 24(5)*.

Article 34: Publicity

34		*No legislative action required* The Secretary of State will make appropriate notification of the rights and obligations arising under the Directive and the Regulations.

Article 35: Abuse of rights

35		*Reg 2(1)* provides that the definition of 'civil partner' does not include a civil partnership of convenience; and the definition of 'spouse' does not include a party to a marriage of convenience.

Article 36: Sanctions

36		*No legislative action required*

Article 37: More favourable national provisions

37		*No legislative action required*

Article 38: Repeals

38		*No legislative action required*

Article 39: Report

39		*No legislative action required*

Article 40: Transposition

40		Bringing into force the Regulations. See the explanatory note to the Regulations.

Article 41: Entry into force

41		*No action required*

Article 42: Addressees

42		*No action required*

Summary

Now you have read this chapter you should be able to:

■ Explain how Community free movement rights have been implemented within the UK, in particular through the Immigration (European Economic Area) Regulations 2006, with a particular reference to:

– nationality of the beneficiaries;

– family rights;

– entry;

– residence (including the general right of residence for up to three months and the extended right of residence for in more than three months);

– permanent right of residence;

– exclusion and removal;

– the effect of claims to social assistance;

– deportations; and

– procedural safeguards.

Further reading

Textbooks

Macdonald, I. and Webber, F. (2005) *Macdonald's Immigration Law and Practice* (6th edn), Butterworths.

Vincenzi, C. (1995) 'Welcoming the Well and Wealthy: The Implementation of Directive 90/364 in the UK', in Daintith, T. (ed.) *Implementing EC Law in the UK: Structures for Indirect Rule*, John Wiley & Sons.

Vincenzi, C. and Marrington, M. (1992) *Immigration Law: The Rules Explained*, Sweet & Maxwell.

Journal articles

Currie, S., 'Free movers? The post-accession experience of accession-8 migrant workers in the United Kingdom' (2006) 31 EL Rev 207.

PART 3

The free movement of goods

17 Customs duties and internal taxation

Aims and objectives

At the end of this chapter you should understand:

- The different ways in which the free movement of goods can be hindered and made more difficult.
- How to differentiate between a customs duty and a charge having an equivalent effect to a customs duty and explain the provisions of the EC Treaty which regulate them.
- The provisions of the EC Treaty which apply to internal taxation.
- The different approach applied to internal taxation levied on goods which are similar compared to that where the effect of the internal tax affords an indirect protection to domestically produced goods.

Introduction to the free movement of goods

The European Community set as one of its central tasks the creation of an internal market characterised by the abolition, as between Member States, of obstacles to the free movement of goods, persons, services and capital. This necessarily involved 'the prohibition, as between Member States, of customs duties and quantitative restrictions on the import and export of goods, and all other measures having equivalent effect' (Art 3(1)(a) EC Treaty). The Community also bound itself, in Art 23 EC Treaty, to the maintenance of 'a customs union which shall cover all trade in goods and which shall involve the prohibition between Member States of customs duties on imports and exports and all charges having equivalent effect, and the adoption of a common customs tariff in their relations with third countries'; a third country is a country which is not a member of the EU (i.e. a non-Member State). The object of these provisions is to create not only an internal free trade area within the Community, where there are no duties imposed on the internal borders, but also a customs union where there is a common external tariff. Goods entering the Community from a third country (i.e. a non-Member State) are subject to the same external tariff, irrespective of where they enter it. Once goods from non-Member States have been subjected to the appropriate duties on crossing the external border of the Community, they are regarded as being in 'free circulation' and are to be treated like any other goods produced within the Community (Art 23 EC Treaty). Benefits are intended to accrue to producers in the opening up of new markets, the possibility of larger and hence cheaper product runs, and to consumers in the form of greatly increased choice in products at lower prices.

Tariff barriers between Member States have long since been removed. Border controls on goods were swept away by the Single European Act 1986. Much still remains to be done, however, to achieve a single undivided market in products, goods and services, such as exists, for example, between England, Scotland, Wales and Northern Ireland. The problems that still persist arise largely as a result of invisible barriers in the shape of different product and other standards, and a whole range of national measures aimed at consumer and environmental protection. Until these different standards are harmonised it would be very difficult for, say, a French manufacturer of a bicycle to make a product which he knows with confidence he will be allowed to sell to any one of the 480 million consumers living within the 27 Member States of the EU. In the long term, these problems are being addressed by the creation of EU-wide standards through the approval of harmonising directives for a huge range of products (see Chapter 18). Until this massive task is achieved, however, producers will have to rely upon Arts 28 and 29 EC Treaty, and the intervention of the Court of Justice, to ensure that national rules do not have the effect of excluding their products (see Chapter 18). Although it also remains one of the objectives of the EC Treaty to harmonise rates of indirect taxation (Art 93), little progress has been made in this area, and obstacles to the creation of a genuine undivided market continue to be caused by different rates of tax and other charges levied on goods by the Member States. The EC Treaty attempts to address these problems by the provisions of Arts 23 and 25 (prohibition of customs duties on imports and exports and all charges having equivalent effect) and the prohibition of discriminatory internal taxation (Art 90).

Within this Chapter, Arts 23 and 25 EC Treaty (which relate to customs duties and charges having an equivalent effect) will be considered initially, followed by Art 90 EC Treaty (which relates to discriminatory internal taxation). Articles 29–30 EC Treaty (which relate to quantitative restrictions and measures having an equivalent effect to quantitative restrictions) are considered in Chapter 18.

Articles 23 and 25 EC Treaty: the elimination of border charges and fiscal barriers

When the Treaty of Amsterdam (ToA) came into force on 1 May 1999, it repealed, amended and renumbered the EC Treaty provisions regulating customs duties and charges having an equivalent effect to a customs duty. This necessitates an explanation of the provisions of the EC Treaty *before* and *after* the coming into force of the ToA.

Prior to the ToA coming into force, Arts 9–17 EC Treaty regulated the imposition of customs duties (and charges which had an equivalent effect) on imports and exports. Most of these provisions have been renumbered, amended and/or repealed.

Article 9(1) EC Treaty set out the objective of the Community; this has been renumbered Art 23(1) by the ToA:

> The Community shall be based upon a customs union which shall cover all trade in goods and which shall involve the prohibition between Member States of customs duties on imports and exports and of all charges having an equivalent effect, and the adoption of a common customs tariff in their relations with third countries.

The other relevant articles pre-ToA were 12, 13 and 16. Article 12 prohibited *new* customs duties from being introduced; Art 13 required *existing* customs duties on *imports* to be phased out; and Art 16 required the abolition of customs duties on *existing exports* by 31 December 1961. The last two provisions were superfluous, and therefore Art 12 was amended (and renumbered) to cover all three situations. The new Art 25 EC Treaty provides that:

> Customs duties on imports and exports and charges having equivalent effect, shall be prohibited between Member States. This prohibition shall also apply to customs duties of a fiscal nature.

The Court of Justice held that the former Art 12 EC Treaty was directly effective (see, e.g., **Van Gend en Loos *v* Nederlandse Administratie der Belastingen** (Case 26/62)). There is little doubt that its mirror provision, the new Art 25 EC Treaty, will likewise have direct effect.

The case law of the Court of Justice with regard to these Treaty provisions is now considered.

Scope of the term 'goods'

The scope of the term 'goods' was explored by the Court of Justice in the following case:

Commission v Italy (Case 26/62)

Italy imposed a tax on the export of articles of an 'artistic, historical, archaeological or ethnographic nature'. The Commission took infraction proceedings against Italy pursuant to Art 169 EC Treaty (now Art 226) alleging this tax was in breach of the former Art 16 which required the abolition of duties and equivalent charges on exports by 31 December 1961; the substance of this provision is now included within Art 25. Italy argued, *inter alia*, that the tax was being levied on 'cultural articles' which were being exported and such articles should not be regarded as goods. This argument was rejected by the Court of Justice, which held as follows:

> Under Article 9 of the Treaty the Community is based on a customs union 'which shall cover all trade in goods'. By goods, within the meaning of that provision, **there must be understood products which can be valued in money and which are capable, as such, of forming the subject of commercial transactions.**
>
> The articles covered by the Italian law, whatever may be the characteristics which distinguish them from other types of merchandise, nevertheless resemble the latter, inasmuch as they can be valued in money and so be the subject of commercial transactions. That view corresponds with the scheme of the Italian law itself, which fixes the tax in question in proportion to the value of the articles concerned. [emphasis added]

In the above case, the Court of Justice held that goods, for the purpose of Arts 23 and 25 EC Treaty, will consist of 'products which can be valued in money and which are capable . . . of forming the subject of commercial transactions'. The scope of 'goods' will therefore be very wide. In the following case, the Court of Justice was faced with a more difficult question:

Jagerskiold v *Gustafsson* (Case C-97/98)

On 29 May 1997 Mr Gustafsson (G) fished with a spinning rod in waters belonging to Mr Jagerskiold (J) in the township of Kimoto in Finland. Two days earlier, on 27 May 1997, G had paid a fishing licence fee, as required by Finnish law, to enable him to practise that type of fishing even in private waters. J brought an action before the national court for a declaration that G could not, without his permission, fish with a rod in his waters, notwithstanding the fact that G had paid the fishing licence fee. In support of his action, J argued that the Finnish law, on which the right to fish with a rod was based, was contrary to the rules of the EC Treaty concerning, *inter alia*, the free movement of goods. The Court of Justice held as follows:

> The Court has already defined goods, for the purposes of Article 9 [now Art 23] of the EC Treaty . . . as products which can be valued in money and which are capable, as such, of forming the subject of commercial transactions.
>
> J contends that fishing rights and fishing permits derived from them constitute 'goods' within the meaning of that case law, in so far as they can be valued in money terms and may be transferred to other persons as it is expressly provided for by [Finnish law] . . .
>
> As is clear from Council Directive 88/361/EEC of 24 June 1998, the Treaty provisions on the free movement of capital cover, in particular, operations relating to shares, bonds and other securities which, like fishing rights or fishing permits, can be valued in money and may be the subject of market transactions.
>
> Similarly, the organisation of lotteries does not constitute an activity relating to 'goods', even if such an activity is coupled with the distribution of advertising material and lottery tickets, but must be regarded as a provision of 'services' within the meaning of the Treaty. In that activity, the provision of services in question are those provided by the lottery organiser in letting ticket buyers participate in the lottery against payment of the price of the lottery tickets.
>
> The same applies to the grant of fishing rights and the issue of fishing permits. **The activity consisting of making fishing waters available to third parties, for consideration and upon certain conditions, so that they can fish there constitutes a provision of services which is covered by Article 59 et seq. of the EC Treaty (now, after amendment, Article 49 et seq.) if it has a cross-frontier character. The fact that those rights or those permits are set down in documents which, as such, may be the subject of trade is not sufficient to bring them within the scope of the provisions of the Treaty relating to the free movement of goods.** [emphasis added]

In the above case, the Court of Justice held that the granting of fishing rights and the issuing of fishing permits could be valued in money and were capable of forming the subject of commercial transactions. However, they were not a tangible product; they constituted an intangible benefit even if those rights were set out in a document. The granting of fishing rights and the issuing of fishing permits could not therefore be considered to be 'goods', although they could constitute a service which would be regulated by what is now Art 49 EC Treaty (see Chapter 13).

Goods from third countries

Article 23(2) EC Treaty (formerly Art 9(2)) provides that:

> The provisions of Article 25 and of Chapter 2 of this Title shall apply to products originating in Member States and to products coming from third countries which are in free circulation in Member States.

Article 24 EC Treaty (formerly Art 10(1)) further provides that:

> Products coming from a third country shall be considered to be in free circulation in a Member State if the import formalities have been complied with and any customs duties or charges having equivalent effect which are payable have been levied in that Member State, and if they have not benefited from a total or partial drawback of such duties or charges.

These provisions provide that once goods have lawfully entered the common market from a third country (i.e. a non-Member State), the provisions of Art 25 will apply to such goods (and also 'Chapter 2 of this Title' (i.e. Arts 28–30, which are considered in Chapter 18)).

Duties and equivalent charges: the effect, not the purpose

Whether or not Art 25 EC Treaty (formerly Art 12) will apply depends upon the *effect* of the duty or charge. It is irrelevant *why* the Member State imposed the duty/charge (i.e. *purpose* is irrelevant). A reconsideration of the **Italian Art** case, which concerned the former Art 16 (the substance of which now comes within the remit of the new Art 25), will serve to illustrate this:

Commission v Italy (Case 7/68)

Italy imposed a tax on the export of articles of an 'artistic, historical, archaeological or ethnographic nature'. The Commission took infraction proceedings against Italy, alleging this tax was in breach of the former Art 16 EC Treaty (now Art 25). Italy argued, *inter alia*, that the purpose of the tax in question was not to raise revenue, but was designed to protect the artistic heritage of the country. This argument was rejected by the Court of Justice, which held as follows:

> In the opinion of the Commission the tax in dispute constitutes a tax having an effect equivalent to a customs duty on exports and therefore the tax should have been abolished, under Article 16 [now Art 25] of the Treaty, no later than the end of the first stage of the common market, that is to say, from 1 January 1962. The defendant argues that the disputed tax does not come within the category, as it has its own particular purpose which is to ensure the protection and safety of the artistic, historic and archaeological heritage which exists in the national territory. Consequently, the tax does not in any respect have a fiscal nature, and its contribution to the budget is insignificant.
>
> Article 16 of the Treaty prohibits the collection in dealings between Member States of any customs duty on exports and of any charge having an equivalent effect, that is to say, any charge which, by altering the price of an article exported, has the same restrictive effect on the free circulation of that article as a customs duty. **This provision makes no distinction based on the purpose of the duties and charges the abolition of which it requires.**
>
> It is not necessary to analyse the concept of the nature of fiscal systems on which the defendant bases its argument upon this point, for the provisions of the section of the Treaty concerning the elimination of customs duties between the Member States exclude the retention of customs duties and charges having equivalent effect without distinguishing between those which are and those which are not of a fiscal nature.
>
> **The disputed tax falls within Article 16 [now Art 25] by reason of the fact that export trade in the goods in question is hindered by the pecuniary burden which it imposes on the price of the exported articles.** [emphasis added]

The above case demonstrates that it is the *effect* of the tax and not its *purpose* which is of prime importance. To have decided otherwise would have considerably weakened the effect of the former Arts 9–17 (now Arts 23–25), the aim of which is to remove fiscal barriers from the borders of Member States which would otherwise hinder the free movement of goods. In the above case, Italy had argued that it had a legitimate reason for imposing the export tax (i.e. the protection of its artistic, historic, and archaeological heritage) which should be recognised by the Court as a sufficient reason for it to declare that the tax fell outside the scope of the Treaty. If the Italian argument had been accepted by the Court, then the Court would have had to adjudicate in the future on what other legitimate reasons were sufficient to take them outside the Treaty (and thus afford a defence to the otherwise defaulting Member State). In rejecting the Italian argument, and confirming that the reason for the charge is irrelevant, the Court has made a significant impact on removing the financial frontiers which could otherwise have remained in a disguised form and thus impacted upon the free movement of goods. This was made explicitly clear by the Court of Justice in the following case:

Commission v Italy (Case 24/68)

The Court of Justice held as follows:

6. ... the purpose of the abolition of customs barriers is not merely to eliminate their protective nature, as the Treaty sought on the contrary to give general scope and effect to the rule on the elimination of customs duties and charges having equivalent effect, in order to ensure the free movement of goods.
7. It follows from the system as a whole and from the general and absolute nature of the prohibition on any customs duty applicable to goods moving between Member States that customs duties are prohibited independently of any consideration of the purpose for which they were introduced and the destination of the revenue obtained therefrom.
   The justification for this prohibition is based on the fact that any pecuniary charge, however small, imposed on goods by reason of the fact that they cross a frontier constitutes an obstacle to the movement of such goods. [emphasis added]

This is further illustrated in the following case:

Sociaal Fonds voor de Diamantarbeiders v SA Ch. Brachfeld & Sons (Cases 2 and 3/69)

It was argued that a small levy imposed under Belgian law on imported diamonds could not be in breach of Art 9 (now Art 23) and Art 12 (now Art 25) because (i) it had no protectionist purpose because Belgium did not produce diamonds; and (ii) the levy's purpose was to provide social security benefits for Belgian diamond workers. The Court of Justice explained the rationale for the sweeping nature of these provisions:

In prohibiting the imposition of customs duties, the Treaty does not distinguish between goods according to whether or not they enter into competition with the products of the importing country. Thus, the purpose of the abolition of customs barriers is not merely to eliminate their protective nature, as the Treaty sought on the contrary to give general scope and effect to the rule on elimination of customs duties and charges having equivalent effect in order to ensure the free movement of goods. It follows from the system as a whole and from the general and absolute nature of the prohibition of any customs duty applicable to goods moving between Member States that customs duties are prohibited independently of any consideration of the purpose for which they were introduced and the destination of the revenue obtained therefrom. **The justification for this prohibition is based on the fact that any pecuniary charge – however small – imposed on goods by reason of the fact that they cross a frontier constitutes an obstacle to the movement of such goods.** [emphasis added]

Charges having an equivalent effect to a customs duty

Article 25 EC Treaty prohibits not only customs duties but also *charges having an equivalent effect* to a customs duty (CEEs). If this phrase had been omitted Member States could quite easily have avoided the prohibition. The scope of CEEs was considered by the Court of Justice in the following case:

Commission v Italy (Case 24/68)

Italy imposed a levy on goods which were exported to other Member States to finance the collecting of statistical data relating to trade patterns. The Commission challenged the legality of such a charge pursuant to its powers under the former Art 169 EC Treaty (now Art 226). The Court of Justice held as follows:

8.   The extension of the prohibition of customs duties to charges having an equivalent effect is intended to supplement the prohibition against obstacles to trade created by such duties by increasing its efficiency.

The use of these two complementary concepts thus tends, in trade between Member States, to avoid the imposition of any pecuniary charge on goods circulating within the Community by virtue of the fact that they cross a national border.

9.   Thus, in order to ascribe to a charge an effect equivalent to a customs duty, it is important to consider this effect in the light of the objectives of the Treaty, in the Parts, Titles and Chapters in which Articles 9, 12, 13 and 16 [now Arts 23 and 25] are to be found, particularly in relation to the free movement of goods.

Consequently, **any pecuniary charge, however small and whatever its designation and mode of application, which is imposed unilaterally on domestic or foreign goods by reason of the fact that they cross a frontier, and which is not a customs duty in the strict sense, constitutes a charge having equivalent effect within the meaning of Articles 9, 12, 13 and 16 [now Arts 23 and 25] of the Treaty, even if it is not imposed for the benefit of the State, is not discriminatory or protective in effect and if the product on which the charge is imposed is not in competition with any domestic product.**

10.   It follows from all the provisions referred to and from their relationship with the other provisions of the Treaty that the prohibition of new customs duties or charges having equivalent effect, linked to the principle of the free movement of goods, constitutes a fundamental rule which, without prejudice to the other provisions of the Treaty, does not permit of any exceptions. [emphasis added]

The above case established that a customs duty, in the strict sense, comprises two elements:

■ a tax or levy;
■ which is imposed simply because of the fact that the goods cross a frontier.

The above case also illustrates that the Treaty forbids more discrete forms of charges which are levied at the border. These are termed 'charges having an equivalent effect to a customs duty' (referred to as CEEs). This was defined broadly by the Court of Justice at para 9 of its judgment. The Court perceived customs duties and CEEs as a barrier to the notion of a single common market. Article 25 prohibits them and the Court has strictly interpreted the predecessors of Art 25 (the former Arts 12, 13 and 16), allowing very few exceptions. But are there any exceptions?

Provision of a service: exception to the general rule

In principle the Court of Justice has accepted that where the charge imposed is merely payment for a service which the Member State has rendered *directly* to the importer then the charge should not be regarded as a CEE, provided the charge levied is in proportion to the service provided. This is illustrated in the following case:

Commission v Belgium (Case 132/82)

Community rules allowed imported goods to be given customs clearance at public warehouses located inside a Member State rather than at the frontier. Belgium levied storage charges on goods which were stored temporarily at such warehouses at the request of the trader concerned. Charges were also levied on imported goods which simply attended the warehouse for customs clearance and were not in fact stored there. The Commission initiated infraction proceedings against Belgium, arguing that these charges were in breach of the former Arts 9, 12, 13 and 16 EC Treaty (now Arts 23 and 25). The Court of Justice held as follows:

8. It is appropriate to recall, in the first place, that according to the established case law of the Court, any pecuniary charge, however small and whatever its designation and mode of application, which is imposed unilaterally on the goods by reason of the fact that they cross a frontier and which is not a customs duty in the strict sense, constitutes a charge having equivalent effect within the meaning of Articles 9, 12, 13 and 16 [now Arts 23 and 25] of the Treaty, even if it is not levied by the State. **The position is different only if the charge in question is the consideration for a service actually rendered to the importer and is of an amount commensurate with that service, when the charge concerned, as in this case, is payable exclusively on imported products.**

9. The prohibition of charges having an effect equivalent to customs duties, laid down in provisions of the Treaty, is justified on the ground that pecuniary charges imposed by reason or on the occasion of the crossing of the frontier represent an obstacle to the free movement of goods.

10. It is in the light of those principles that the question whether the disputed storage charges may be classified as charges having an effect equivalent to customs duties must be assessed. It should therefore be noted, in the first place, that the placing of imported goods in temporary storage in the special stores of public warehouses clearly represents a service rendered to traders. A decision to deposit the goods there can indeed be taken only at the request of the trader concerned and then ensures their storage without payment of duties, until the trader has decided how they are to be dealt with. Moreover the Commission does not dispute that the placing of goods in temporary storage may legally give rise to the payment of charges commensurate with the service thus rendered.

11. However, it appears ... that the storage charges are payable equally when the goods are presented at the public warehouse solely for the completion of customs formalities, even though they have been exempted from storage and the importer has not requested that they be put in temporary storage.

12. Admittedly the Belgian Government claims that even in that case a service is rendered to the importer. It is always open to the latter to avoid payment of the disputed charges by choosing to have his goods cleared through customs at the frontier, where such a procedure is free. Moreover, by using a public warehouse, the importer is enabled to have the goods declared through customs near the places for which his products are bound and he is therefore relieved of the necessity of himself either having at his own disposal premises suitable for their clearance or having recourse to private premises, the use of which is more expensive than that of the public warehouses. It is therefore legitimate, in the Belgian Government's view, to impose a charge commensurate with that service.

13. That argument cannot however be accepted. Whilst it is true that the use of a public warehouse

in the interior of the country offers certain advantages to importers it seems clear first of all that such advantages are linked solely with the completion of customs formalities which, whatever the place, is always compulsory. It should moreover be noted that such advantages result from the scheme of Community transit introduced . . . in order to increase the fluidity of the movement of goods and to facilitate transport within the Community. There can therefore be no question of levying any charges for customs clearance facilities accorded in the interests of the common market.

14. It follows from the foregoing, that **when payment of storage charges is demanded solely in connection with the completion of customs formalities, it cannot be regarded as the consideration for a service actually rendered to the importer.**

15. **Consequently, it must be declared that, by levying storage charges on goods which originate in a Member State or are in free circulation, and which are imported into Belgium, and presented merely for the completion of customs formalities at a special store, the Kingdom of Belgium has failed to fulfil its obligations under Articles 9 and 12 [now Arts 23 and 25] of the Treaty.** [emphasis added]

In the above case, the Court of Justice held that the charge will not constitute a CEE 'if the charge in question is the consideration for a service actually rendered to the importer and is of an amount commensurate with that service' (para 8). Belgium made provision for customs formalities to be completed in-country as an alternative to at the border. Public warehouses were provided at the in-country customs posts. These warehouses provided temporary storage facilities for the goods while the customs formalities were completed. The importer had the option to store his goods in the warehouses for an extended period. In both instances, Belgium charged for the storage of the goods. In the first instance, Belgium was found to be in breach of the Treaty provisions, because the charge for the service was solely connected with the completion of customs formalities. It could not be regarded as the consideration for a service actually rendered to the importer. However, in the latter instance, if the importer chose to store his goods in the warehouse for an extended period, this would constitute a service actually rendered to the importer. Belgium could therefore charge for this service provided the charge did not exceed the actual costs incurred by Belgium in providing this service. It was accepted by the Court that charges levied in relation to private premises did not fall to be considered within the former Arts 9 and 12 EC Treaty (now Arts 23 and 25) (para 12); these provisions only apply to the state.

It is clear that an argument that the charge is consideration for a service actually rendered to the importer will be closely scrutinised by the Court. In its actual decisions, the Court has shown considerable reluctance in accepting that a particular charge falls outside Art 25. In **Ford Espania** v **Spain** (Case 170/88), the Court of Justice said that even if a specific benefit to the person or body paying the charge can be identified, the state imposing the charge will still fall foul of Art 25 if it cannot be shown that the sum demanded is proportionate to the cost of supplying the benefit. In this case, Ford received a demand for 0.165 per cent of the declared value of cars and other goods imported into Spain. The Spanish government maintained that the sum related to services rendered in connection with clearing the goods through customs. The Court held that, even if a specific benefit conferred on Ford could be shown, the flat-rate way in which the charge was calculated was evidently not fixed according to the cost of the alleged service and was, accordingly, a breach of Art 25.

The following case further illustrates the Court's reluctance to find that a charge falls outside the remit of Art 25:

Commission v Italy (Case 24/68)

The Italian government had argued that a charge which was imposed at the border constituted consideration for the collection of statistical information. It was argued that this information would provide importers with trade patterns and therefore give them a better competitive position in the Italian market. The Court of Justice held as follows:

15. The Italian Government further maintains that the disputed charge constitutes the consideration for a service rendered and as such cannot be designated as a charge having equivalent effect.

     According to the Italian Government the object of the statistics in question is to determine precisely the actual movements of goods and, consequently, changes in the state of the market. It claims that the exactness of the information thus supplied affords importers a better competitive position in the Italian market whilst exporters enjoy a similar advantage abroad and that the special advantages which dealers obtain from the survey justifies their paying for this public service and moreover demonstrates that the disputed charge is in the nature of a *quid pro quo*.

16. The statistical information in question is beneficial to the economy as a whole and *inter alia* to the relevant administrative authorities.

     Even if the competitive position of importers and exporters were to be particularly improved as a result, the statistics still constitute an advantage so general, and so difficult to assess, that the disputed charge cannot be regarded as the consideration for a specific benefit actually conferred.

17. It appears from the above mentioned considerations that in so far as the disputed charge is levied on exports it is contrary to Article 16 [now Art 25] of the Treaty.

In the above case, the Court of Justice held that the service (i.e. provision of statistics) was not *directly* rendered to the importers/exporters because it was 'beneficial to the economy as a whole and *inter alia* to the relevant administrative authorities' (para 16). Even where it is more direct, the Court may still be reluctant to rule that the charge is consideration for the service rendered:

Bresciani v Amministrazione Italiana delle Finanze (Case 87/75)

The Italian authorities imposed a charge for compulsory veterinary and public health inspections carried out on the importation of raw cowhides. The case was referred by the national court pursuant to the former Art 177 EC Treaty (now Art 234) for a preliminary ruling on the question of whether the charge for the inspection constituted a CEE. The Court of Justice held as follows:

6. The national court requests that the three following considerations be taken into account:

     First, the fact that the charge is proportionate to the quantity of the goods and not to their value distinguishes a duty of the type at issue from charges which fall within the prohibition under Article 13 [now Art 25] of the EEC Treaty. Second, a pecuniary charge of the type at issue is no more than the consideration required from individuals who, through their own action in importing products of animal origin, cause a service to be rendered. In the third place, although there may be differences in the method and time of its application, the duty at issue is also levied on similar products of domestic origin.

   . . .

8. The justification for the obligation progressively to abolish customs duties is based on the fact that any pecuniary charge, however small, imposed on goods by reason of the fact that they cross a frontier constitutes an obstacle to the free movement of goods.

     The obligation progressively to abolish customs duties is supplemented by the obligation to abolish charges having equivalent effect in order to prevent the fundamental principle of the free movement of goods within the common market from being circumvented by the imposition of pecuniary charges of various kinds by a Member State.

The use of these two complementary concepts thus tends, in trade between Member States, to avoid the imposition of any pecuniary charge on goods circulating within the Community by virtue of the fact that they cross a national frontier.

9. Consequently, any pecuniary charge, whatever its designation and mode of application, which is unilaterally imposed on goods imported from another Member State by reason of the fact that they cross a frontier, constitutes a charge having an effect equivalent to a customs duty. In appraising a duty of the type at issue it is, consequently, of no importance that it is proportionate to the quantity of the imported goods and not their value.

10. Nor, in determining the effects of the duty on the free movement of goods, is it of any importance that a duty of the type at issue is proportionate to the costs of a compulsory public health inspection carried out on entry of the goods. **The activity of the administration of the State intended to maintain a public health inspection system imposed in the general interest cannot be regarded as a service rendered to the importer such as to justify the imposition of a pecuniary charge. If, accordingly, public health inspections are still justified at the end of the transitional period, the costs which they occasion must be met by the general public which, as a whole, benefits from the free movement of Community goods.** [emphasis added]

In the above case, at para 10, the Court of Justice held that a public health inspection system was imposed to benefit the general public, and therefore was not a service rendered *directly* to the importer. It was there for the benefit of the general public and therefore it was the general public who would have to meet the costs incurred by the state in carrying out those inspections.

Even where EC law *permits* an inspection to be undertaken by the state, the national authorities cannot recover the cost from the importers (see **Commission v Belgium** (Case 314/82)).

However, if Community law *requires* an inspection to be carried out, the costs of such an inspection *may* be recoverable and will not be caught by the provisions of Art 25. This was decided by the Court of Justice in the following case:

Commission v Germany (Case 18/87)

German regional authorities charged certain fees on live animals when they were imported into Germany. These charges were to cover the cost of inspections undertaken pursuant to Directive 81/389. The question before the Court of Justice was whether such charges constituted CEEs and were therefore prohibited. The Court of Justice held as follows:

5. It should be observed in the first place that, as the Court has held on a number of occasions, the justification for the prohibition of customs duties and any charges having an equivalent effect lies in the fact that any pecuniary charge, however small, imposed on goods by reason of the fact that they cross a frontier, constitutes an obstacle to the movement of goods which is aggravated by the resulting administrative formalities. It follows that any pecuniary charge, whatever its designation and mode of application, which is imposed unilaterally on goods by reason of the fact that they cross a frontier and is not a customs duty in the strict sense constitutes a charge having an equivalent effect to a customs duty within the meaning of Articles 9, 12, 13 and 16 [now Arts 23 and 25] of the Treaty.

6. However, **the Court has held that such a charge escapes that classification if it relates to a general system of internal dues applied systematically and in accordance with the same criteria to domestic products and imported goods alike (judgment of 31 May 1979 in Case 132/78 Denkavit v France [1979] ECR 1923), if it constitutes payment for a service in fact rendered to the economic operator of a sum in proportion to the service (judgment of 9 November 1983 in**

Case 158/82 Commission v Denmark [1983] ECR 3573), or again, subject to certain conditions, if it attaches to inspections carried out to fulfil obligations imposed by Community law (judgment of 25 January 1977 in Case 46/76 Bauhuis v Netherlands [1977] ECR 5).

7. The contested fee, which is payable on importation and transit, cannot be regarded as relating to a general system of internal dues. Nor does it constitute payment for a service rendered to the operator, because this condition is satisfied only if the operator in question obtains a definite specific benefit (see judgment of 1 July 1969 in Case 24/68 Commission v Italy [1969] ECR 193), which is not the case if the inspection serves to guarantee, in the public interest, the health and life of animals in international transport (see judgment of 20 March 1984 in Case 314/82 Commission v Belgium [1984] ECR 1543).

8. Since the contested fee was charged in connection with inspections carried out pursuant to Community provision, it should be noted that according to the case law of the Court (judgment of 25 January 1977 in Bauhuis, cited above; judgment of 12 July 1977 Commission v Netherlands [1977] ECR 1355; judgment of 31 January 1984 in Case 1/83 IFG v Freistaat Bayern [1984] ECR 349) such fees may not be classified as charges having an equivalent effect to a customs duty if the following conditions are satisfied:

   (a) they do not exceed the actual costs of the inspections in connection with which they are charged;
   (b) the inspections in question are obligatory and uniform for all the products concerned in the Community;
   (c) they are prescribed by Community law in the general interest of the Community;
   (d) they promote the free movement of goods, in particular by neutralising obstacles which could arise from unilateral measures of inspection adopted in accordance with Article 36 [now Art 30] of the Treaty.

9. In this instance these conditions are satisfied by the contested fee. In the first place it has not been contested that it does not exceed the real cost of the inspection in connection with which it is charged.

10. Moreover, all the Member States of transit and destination are required, under, inter alia, Article 2(1) of Directive 81/389/EEC, cited above, to carry out the veterinary inspections in question when the animals are brought into their territories, and therefore the inspections are obligatory and uniform for all the animals concerned in the Community.

11. Those inspections are prescribed by Directive 81/389/EEC, which establishes the measures necessary for the implementation of Council Directive 77/489/EEC of 18 July 1977 on the protection of animals during international transport, with a view to the protection of live animals, an objective which is pursued in the general interest of the Community and not a specific interest of individual states.

12. Finally, it appears from the preambles to the two abovementioned directives that they are intended to harmonise the laws of the Member States regarding the protection of animals in international transport in order to eliminate technical barriers resulting from disparities in the national laws (see third, fourth and fifth recitals in the preamble to Directive 77/489/EEC and the third recital in the preamble to Directive 81/389/EEC). In addition, failing such harmonisation, each Member State was entitled to maintain or introduce, under the conditions laid down in Article 36 [now Art 30] of the Treaty, measures restricting trade which were justified on grounds of the protection of the health and life of animals. It follows that the standardisation of the inspections in question is such as to promote the free movement of goods.

13. The Commission has claimed, however, that the contested fee is to be regarded as a charge having equivalent effect to a customs duty because, in so far as fees of this type have not been harmonised, such harmonisation, moreover, being unattainable in practice, their negative effect on the free movement of goods could not be compensated or, consequently, justified by the positive effects of the Community standardisation of inspections.

14. In this respect, it should be noted that since the fee in question is intended solely as the financially and economically justified compensation for an obligation imposed in equal measure on all the Member States by Community law, it cannot be regarded as equivalent to a customs duty; nor,

consequently, can it fall within the ambit of the prohibition laid down in Articles 9 and 12 [now Arts 23 and 25] of the Treaty. [emphasis added]

In the above case, the Court of Justice held that an inspection fee levied on imported goods is valid under Community law, provided the four conditions laid down in para 8

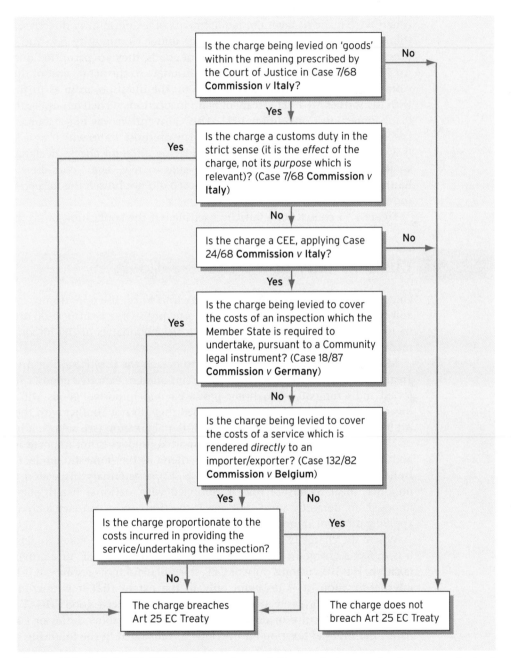

Figure 17.1 Article 25 EC Treaty: customs duties and charges having an equivalent effect

above are satisfied. Two of the four conditions which are particularly important are that (i) the inspection must be mandatory (i.e. compulsory) under Community law; and (ii) the inspection fee levied must not exceed the actual costs incurred by the Member State in carrying out the inspection. This judgment was subsequently applied by the Court in **Bauhuis** v **Netherlands** (Case 46/76), where there was a challenge to a fee imposed by the Dutch government for veterinary inspections of pigs imported into The Netherlands. Some of the checks were carried out to meet rules of national law while others were made to meet the requirements of a Community directive. The Court held that, where such checks are mandatory under Community law and are part of the process of ensuring the free movement of goods, they are permitted under what is now Art 25. The fee must, however, be proportionate to the actual cost of the inspection. In **Commission** v **Netherlands** (Case 89/76), the question arose as to the compatibility with the former Art 12 EC Treaty of plant inspections carried out under the International Plant Protection Convention 1951. This Convention was not a source of Community law, but it was binding in international law on those states which were signatories to it. It was designed to liberalise trade by replacing different checks in signatory states by a single check on which all states were able to rely. The Court drew a parallel with **Bauhuis**, and held that the charges imposed did not breach the former Art 12 EC Treaty (now Art 25).

Figure 17.1 consists of a flowchart setting out the application of Art 25 EC Treaty.

Customs duty or internal taxation?

Once the Single European Act 1986 came into force, the opportunity for border checks and charges has been much diminished. Any processing or inspection of goods that may be necessary may now take place within the boundaries of the importing state, often many miles from the frontier.

Most charges which have been held to breach the prohibition in Arts 23 and 25 EC Treaty have been those levied directly on imported or exported goods. Charges which are levied indiscriminately on home-produced *and* imported goods will not, generally, breach Art 25 and will be lawful, provided they do not conflict with the prohibition in Art 90 EC Treaty against discriminatory internal taxation (see below). A breach of Arts 23 or 25 may occur if the charge on the imported product is not imposed in the same way and determined according to the same criteria as the domestic product. In **Marimex** v **Italian Finance Administration** (Case 29/72), a veterinary inspection tax imposed on imported meat to ensure that it complied with national health standards was also imposed on domestic meat, but the inspections were conducted by different bodies applying different standards.

Where the charge is in the nature of a tax, care must be taken to determine whether it is in fact a charge in the nature of a customs duty or CEE, or a provision of internal taxation. If it is a customs duty or CEE, it is unlawful in its entirety. If it is a provision of internal taxation, it is unlawful only to the extent that it is discriminatory against imported goods or protective of domestically produced goods (**IGAV** v **ENCC** (Case 94/74)). The difficulty of distinguishing between customs duties or CEEs on the one hand, and internal taxation on the other, is illustrated in the following case:

Capolongo v Azienda Agricola (Case 77/72)

A charge ostensibly levied on both imported and domestic products was claimed to be used to promote domestic products. The Court of Justice emphasised that the same charge could not be both a customs duty or CEE, and a provision of internal taxation. It held that where a charge is levied both on imports and on domestic products, it can, nevertheless, constitute a charge equivalent to a customs duty when it is intended exclusively to support activities which specifically benefit the taxed domestic product.

In **IGAV** *v* **ENCC** (above), the Court of Justice held that this was also the case where the domestic tax was remitted on the domestic product 'wholly or in part'. The Court of Justice later modified its position in the following case:

Fratelli Cucchi (Case 77/76)

The Court of Justice held that apparent internal taxation can only constitute a charge equivalent to a customs duty (i.e. a CEE): 'if it has the sole purpose of financing activities for the specific advantage of the taxed domestic product; if the taxed product and the domestic product benefiting from it are the same; and if the charges imposed on the domestic product are made good in full'.

A much more probable conclusion is that a tax on imported and domestic products which gives a partial benefit to the taxed domestic product will constitute discriminatory internal taxation, contrary to Art 90 EC Treaty, on the basis that it indirectly imposes a heavier burden on products from other Member States than on domestic products (**Commission** *v* **Italy** (Case 73/79)).

The Court of Justice did not follow this approach in the following case:

Haahr Petroleum Ltd v Abenra Havn (Case C-90/94)

The claimant challenged a Danish law under which the port of Abenra and others charged an import surcharge of 40 per cent, which was levied in addition to duties on all imported goods loaded or unloaded within Danish commercial ports or in the deep-water approach channel to those ports. On a reference to the Court of Justice, the Court held that the charges formed part of a general system of internal taxes payable for the use of commercial ports and facilities. It had been argued by the Danish government that the charge levied was lawful under what is now Art 25 EC Treaty because it constituted a charge for a service actually rendered to traders, and could not therefore also fall foul of the prohibition against discriminatory taxation under Art 95 EC Treaty (now Art 90). Without accepting that the charge might be lawful under Art 25, the Court held that even if this was the case, it did not mean that the charge also escaped the prohibition against discriminatory taxation under Art 95 (now Art 90).

Article 90 EC Treaty: discriminatory and protectionist internal taxation

In the absence of a harmonised Community tax system, the Member States are entitled to take such measures as are necessary to make that system effective, even, it would seem, at the expense of fundamental rights under the Treaty, such as the right of establishment (**R v HM Treasury, ex parte Daily Mail** (Case 81/87)). Article 93 EC Treaty provides for the enactment of measures to harmonise legislation on turnover taxes, excise duties and other forms of indirect taxation, but because such legislation can only be adopted by the Council of Ministers acting unanimously there has been little movement. Until a fully harmonised Community tax regime is achieved, however, Member States retain their national prerogative in relation to internal taxation. This principle of national autonomy gives way to another fundamental principle, that of free movement of goods. Article 90 EC Treaty (previously Art 95) provides that:

> No Member State shall impose, directly or indirectly, on the products of other Member States any internal taxation of any kind in excess of that imposed directly or indirectly on similar domestic products.
>
> Furthermore, no Member State shall impose on the products of other Member States any internal taxation of such a nature as to afford indirect protection to other products.

The former Art 95 (and as a corollary to this, Art 90) has been held to be directly effective by the Court since 1 January 1962 (see **Alfons Lutticke GmbH v Hauptzollamt Sarrelouis** (Case 57/65)).

Since Art 90 refers to 'products of other Member States' it might well be thought that discriminatory or protectionist taxation levied on goods coming from another Member State was permissible provided those goods originated from outside the Community. Unlike the provisions relating to the free movement of goods in Part III, Title I, EC Treaty, which relate both to products originating in the Community and 'to products coming from third countries [i.e. non-Member States] which are in free circulation in Member States', there is no such application to the non-discriminatory tax rules (Art 23(2) EC Treaty). The Court therefore at first held that Member States were entitled to impose discriminatory or protectionist taxes on third-country products circulating freely in the Community, provided such taxation was compatible with any concessions made to that state in any association or other agreement (**Hansen v Hauptzollamt Flensburg** (Case 148/77)). It modified its position, however, in **Co-Frutta** (Case 193/85). In this case, which involved Italian taxation of bananas imported through other Member States, the Court of Justice accepted that the Common Customs Tariff and the Common Commercial Policy were intended to ensure a uniform treatment of goods imported from third countries and the facilitation of the free movement of such goods once they had been legitimately imported into one of the Member States.

The purpose of Art 90 EC Treaty

As discussed above, Arts 23–25 EC Treaty are designed to prevent financial measures from being imposed as a result of a product *crossing a frontier*. The financial measure does not necessarily have to be protectionist in nature; however, it often is. *Protectionist* means that the measure imposed has the effect of protecting domestic products from competition by foreign goods.

Articles 23–25 would be of little use if a Member State could impose taxes on foreign products (but not on the rival domestic product) once they were inside their territory; because the tax was not levied at the frontier it would not be caught by Arts 23–25. Article 90 seeks to prevent this where a discriminatory or protectionist charge is levied on the imported product but not on the domestic product. The purpose of Art 90 was set out by the Court of Justice in the following case:

Commission v *Denmark* (Case 171/78)

The Court of Justice held as follows:

> The ... provisions supplement, within the system of the Treaty, the provisions on the abolition of customs duties and charges having equivalent effect. **Their aim is to ensure the free movement of goods between the Member States in normal conditions of competition by the elimination of all forms of protection which result from the application of internal taxation which discriminates against products from other Member States.** As the Commission has correctly stated, Article 95 [now Art 90] must guarantee the complete neutrality of internal taxation as regards competition between domestic products and imported products. [emphasis added]

Article 90 is aimed at two distinct, but sometimes overlapping, national taxation practices: first, the taxing of the same or similar imported and home-produced products in a different way (Art 90(1)); and, second, the taxing of different but competing imported and home-produced products in such a way as to afford protection to the home-produced product (Art 90(2)). The two key concepts are therefore similarity and product competition (**Commission** *v* **France** (Case 168/78)). These two concepts are now considered further.

Article 90(1) EC Treaty: similar products

Article 90(1) is a reference to the first paragraph of Art 90, which provides that:

> No Member State shall impose, directly or indirectly, on the products of other Member States any internal taxation of any kind in excess of that imposed directly or indirectly on similar domestic products.

Article 90(1) does not require a Member State to adopt a particular system of internal taxation, just that whatever system is adopted must be applied without discrimination to similar imported products: i.e. it prohibits the imposition of internal taxes on products from other Member States which are greater than those levied on *similar* domestic products. Therefore, once the imported and domestic products are considered to be *similar*, Art 90(1) will apply.

In **Commission** *v* **France** (Case 168/78), the Court of Justice considered the concept of *similar products* in the context of Art 90(1). The Court of Justice, at para 5, stated that it was necessary to consider as *similar*, products which have:

> similar characteristics and meet the same needs from the point of view of consumers.

This has been subsequently applied by the Court of Justice in the following case:

John Walker v *Ministeriet for Skatter* (Case 243/84)

The issue before the Court of Justice was whether liqueur fruit wine was *similar* to whisky for the purposes of the former Art 95(1) (now Art 90(1)). The Court analysed the *objective characteristics* of the products, including their alcoholic contents, methods of production and consumer perceptions as to the nature of the products. The Court held that they were not similar. They had different alcohol contents and different manufacturing processes (whisky was distilled rather than fermented). Any scrutiny of the tax therefore had to be considered under the former Art 95(2) (now Art 90(2)).

The Court of Justice was required to assess the similarity of beverages in the following case:

FG Roders BV ea v *Inspecteur der Inverrechten en Accijnzen* (Joined Cases C-367 and 377/93)

Importers of French wine, Spanish sherry and Italian vermouth challenged the higher rates of excise duty that were charged on those products, as compared to fruit wines produced in the Benelux countries (i.e. Belgium, The Netherlands and Luxembourg). The Court of Justice decided that fruit wines and grape wines were similar. They are made from the same kind of agricultural products, and by the same process of natural fermentation. Both beverages possess the same kind of organoleptic properties, in particular taste and alcoholic strength, and meet the same needs of consumers, since they can be consumed for the same purposes, namely to quench thirst, to refresh, and to accompany meals.

Product similarity was also at issue in the following case:

Commission v *Italy* (Case 184/85)

The issue of product similarity related to different types of fruit. Italy levied a consumption tax on bananas which amounted to about half their import price. The tax was not levied on other fruit (e.g. apples, pears, plums). Italy produced large amounts of fruit, other than bananas which it imported from France. The Commission took action against Italy, alleging the tax infringed the former Art 95 (now Art 90). The Court of Justice first considered whether bananas and other fruit were *similar* for the purposes of the former Art 95(1) (now Art 90(1)). The Court held that they were *not* similar, taking into account the objective characteristics of the products. Any further examination of the tax had to proceed under the former Art 95(2) (now Art 90(2)), see below.

If goods are *similar* under Art 90(1) then the tax will be unlawful if it is discriminatory: this discrimination can be either direct or indirect.

Direct discrimination

Different rates and methods of taxation applied to similar imported or domestic products are usually easily recognisable. For this reason direct discrimination of this kind is rare.

In **Lutticke GmbH** *v* **Hauptzollamt Saarlouis** (Case 57/65), an internal tax was levied on imported dried milk but not on domestically produced dried milk. The tax was directly discriminatory and breached the former Art 95(1) (now Art 90(1)).

In **Bobie Getränkvertrieb** *v* **Hauptzollamt Aachen-Nord** (Case 127/75), a German beer tax imposed a sliding scale on home-produced beer, varying between DM 12 and 15 per hectolitre, according to the size of the brewery; DM (i.e. Deutsche Mark) was

Germany's national currency before Germany adopted the Euro. Imported beers had a flat-rate tax of DM 14.40 levied upon them. The Court of Justice held that the tax was discriminatory, since small foreign breweries could not avail themselves of the low rate (DM 12) available to small domestic breweries.

The method for the collection of the tax may also involve discrimination, even if the criteria for its payment do not. In **Commission** *v* **Ireland** (Case 55/79), the Court of Justice held an Irish tax incompatible with Art 95 (now Art 90). The tax was payable according to the same criteria, irrespective of the origin of the goods. However, domestic producers were permitted several weeks' grace to pay the tax, while importers had to pay immediately on importation.

Indirect discrimination

Indirectly discriminatory internal taxation will be similarly caught by Art 90(1). On the face of it an internal tax rule may not differentiate between domestic and imported goods, but the actual effect of the tax may place a greater burden on the imported goods. An example of this is illustrated in the following case:

Humblot v *Directeur des Services Fiscaux* (Case 112/84)

France imposed two different types of annual car tax. The key threshold between the two was the power rating (or fiscal horsepower) of the car. Below 16 CV the tax increased gradually in proportion to the car's fiscal horsepower, up to a maximum of 1100 francs; the franc was France's national currency before France adopted the euro. Above 16 CV a flat-rate tax of 5000 francs was imposed. The way in which the fiscal horsepower was calculated was very complicated. It took into consideration: the number of cylinders; the bore in centimetres; the stroke in centimetres; and the rotation speed in revolutions per second. The result of applying this calculation was that no French car was given a fiscal horsepower rating above 16 CV; therefore, only imported vehicles were subject to the higher flat-rate tax. The effect of the fiscal horsepower calculation was such that a foreign car of similar characteristics to a French car (e.g. same engine size, similar specifications, etc.) would fall within a higher rating and therefore attract a higher level of annual tax.

M. Humblot was charged 5000 francs on his imported car, which had been given a fiscal horsepower rating of 36 CV. He claimed the tax breached the former Art 95 (now Art 90) and sought a refund. As discussed above, the former Art 95 was directly effective and, as a corollary to this, Art 90 is also directly effective. The French court referred questions to the Court of Justice under the former Art 177 EC Treaty (now Art 234). The Court of Justice held as follows:

12. It is appropriate in the first place to stress that as Community law stands at present the Member States are at liberty to subject products such as cars to a system of road tax which increases progressively in amount depending on an objective criterion, such as the power rating for tax purposes, which may be determined in various ways.

13. Such a system of domestic taxation is, however, compatible with Article 95 [now Art 90] only in so far as it is free from any discriminatory or protective effect.

14. That is not true of a system like the one at issue in the main proceedings. Under that system there are two distinct taxes: a differential tax which increases progressively and is charged on cars not exceeding a given power rating for tax purposes and a fixed tax on cars exceeding that rating which is almost five times as high as the highest band of the differential tax. Although the system embodies no formal distinction based on the origin of the products it manifestly exhibits discriminatory or protective features contrary to Article 95 [now Art 90], since the power rating

     determining liability to the special tax has been fixed at a level such that only imported cars, in particular from other Member States, are subject to the special tax whereas all cars of domestic manufacture are liable to the distinctly more advantageous differential tax.

15. In the absence of considerations relating to the amount of the special tax, consumers seeking comparable cars as regards such matters as size, comfort, actual power, maintenance costs, durability, fuel consumption and price would naturally choose from among cars above and below the critical power rating laid down by French law. However, liability to the special tax entails a much larger increase in taxation than passing from one category of car to another in a system of progressive taxation embodying balanced differentials like the system on which the differential tax is based. **The resultant additional taxation is liable to cancel out the advantages which certain cars imported from other Member States might have in consumers' eyes over comparable cars of domestic manufacture, particularly since the special tax continues to be payable for years. In that respect the special tax reduces the amount of competition to which cars of domestic manufacture are subject and hence is contrary to the principle of neutrality with which domestic taxation must comply.**

16. In the light of the foregoing considerations the questions raised by the national court for a preliminary ruling should be answered as follows: Article 95 [now Art 90] of the EEC Treaty prohibits the charging on cars exceeding a given power rating for tax purposes of a special fixed tax the amount of which is several times the highest amount of the progressive tax payable on cars of less than the said power rating for tax purposes, where the only cars subject to the special tax are imported, in particular from other Member States. [emphasis added]

Following the above judgment, France amended its legislation, but the Court of Justice was required to adjudicate on the amended legislation's compatibility with Art 90 on numerous occasions. See, for example:

- **Feldain v Services Fiscaux du Département du Haut-Rhin** (Case 433/85);
- **Deville v Administration des Impôts** (Case 240/87);
- **Jacquier v Directeur Général des Impôts** (Case C–113/94);
- **Yves Tarantik v Direction des Services Fiscaux de Seine-et-Marne** (Case C–421/97).

A further example of indirect discrimination is illustrated in the following case:

Haahr Petroleum Ltd v Abenra Havn (Case C-90/94)

A lower rate of harbour tax was levied on goods which were unloaded in harbours which originated in inland waterways, compared to goods unloaded in harbours which originated in deep-water channels. The Court of Justice stated as follows:

> A criterion for the charging of higher taxation which by definition can never be fulfilled by similar domestic products cannot be considered to be compatible with the prohibition of discrimination laid down in Article 95 [now Art 90] of the Treaty. Such a system has the effect of excluding domestic products in advance from the heaviest taxation. Likewise, the Court has held that such differential taxation is incompatible with Community law if the products most heavily taxed are, by their very nature, imported products.

In the above case, goods unloaded at harbours in inland waterways were overwhelmingly the product of the home state, and goods unloaded at harbours originating in deep-water channels were imported. The higher taxation levied on goods unloaded at harbours originating in deep-water channels was indirectly discriminatory, and was therefore contrary to Art 90(1).

Objective justification: a defence to indirect discrimination

While direct discrimination will never be justifiable, tax rules of a Member State which tend to favour the domestic product may be held not to breach Art 90(1) if there is some *objective justification* for the conduct complained of. This objective justification must be acceptable to the Court. If accepted it will prevent Art 90(1) from being applied too harshly, as illustrated in the following case:

Chemical Farmaceutici v *DAF SpA* (Case 140/79)

Italian internal taxation of *synthetic* ethyl alcohol was higher than taxation of *fermented* ethyl alcohol. The products were interchangeable in use. Italy produced very little of the higher taxed synthetic product, and therefore the tax system had a harsher impact upon importers. The rationale for the tax policy was to encourage the manufacture of the fermented product (the raw material of which was agricultural products), thus preserving the petroleum ingredients used to make the synthetic product for other, more economically important purposes. The Court considered the legitimacy of this policy choice. The Court of Justice held as follows:

13. ... the different taxation of synthetic alcohol and of alcohol produced by fermentation in Italy is the result of an economic policy decision to favour the manufacture of alcohol from agricultural products and, correspondingly, to restrain the processing into alcohol of ethylene, a derivative of petroleum, in order to reserve that raw material for other more important economic uses. **It accordingly constitutes a legitimate choice of economic policy to which effect is given by fiscal means.** The implementation of that policy does not lead to any discrimination since although it results in discouraging imports of synthetic alcohol into Italy, it also has the consequence of hampering the development in Italy itself of production of alcohol from ethylene, that production being technically perfectly possible.

14. As the Court has stated on many occasions, particularly in the judgments cited by the Italian Government, **in its present stage of development Community law does not restrict the freedom of each Member State to lay down tax arrangements which differentiate between certain products on the basis of objective criteria, such as the nature of the raw materials used or the production processes employed. Such differentiation is compatible with Community law if it pursues economic policy objectives which are themselves compatible with the requirements of the Treaty and its secondary law and if the detailed rules are such as to avoid any form of discrimination, direct or indirect, in regard to imports from other Member States or any form of protection of competing domestic products.**

15. Differential taxation such as that which exists in Italy for denatured synthetic alcohol on the one hand and denatured alcohol obtained by fermentation on the other satisfies these requirements. It appears in fact that the system of taxation pursues an objective of legitimate industrial policy in that it is such as to promote the distillation of agricultural products as against the manufacture of alcohol from petroleum derivatives. That choice does not conflict with the rules of Community law or the requirements of a policy decided within the framework of the Community.

16. **The detailed provisions of the legislation at issue before the national court cannot be considered as discriminatory since, on the one hand, it is not disputed that imports from other Member States of alcohol obtained by fermentation qualify for the same tax treatment as Italian alcohol produced by fermentation, and on the other hand, although the rate of tax prescribed for synthetic alcohol results in restraining the importation of synthetic alcohol originating in other Member States, it has an equivalent economic effect in the national territory in that it also hampers the establishment of profitable production of the same product by Italian industry.** [emphasis added]

In the above case, the Court of Justice stated at para 16 that there was no *actual* discrimination, direct or indirect, because the tax would deter not only importers of the affected product but also national producers, even though there was very little domestic production of the affected product. The tax was applicable to both imported and domestic products, so it could only have the potential for being indirectly discriminatory (i.e. if the tax had a greater impact on the imported product than on the domestic product). If there is no actual discrimination then the tax is *per se* (i.e. automatically) outside Art 90. However, in this case the Court, in finding that there was no actual discrimination, was no doubt strongly influenced by the *reason* for the imposition of the tax (i.e. 'legitimate choice of economic policy', see para 13). It is therefore considered that this case provides scope for a defence to an internal tax that is indirectly discriminatory. The defence will apply where the measure can be objectively justified; in this case on the ground that the imposition of the tax constituted a 'legitimate choice of economic policy'. Although the Court did not expressly state it constituted a defence, it was influenced by the reason when deciding not to impose a strict application of Art 90.

Similarly, in the course of Art 226 EC Treaty proceedings brought by the Commission against France, the Court of Justice held that a more favourable tax rate applied to natural sweet wine as compared to ordinary table wine was justified. The purpose of the tax was to assist the economy of areas that were heavily reliant on such wines, which were produced in difficult circumstances (**Commission v France** (Case 196/85)). Where such tax relief is applied, it must be operated indiscriminately, even where there is a legitimate and defensible objective. Thus, it has been held that an importer of spirits into Germany was entitled to take advantage of tax relief available, *inter alia*, in respect of spirits made by small businesses and collective farms. The Court of Justice accepted that such tax concessions could meet legitimate economic and social purposes, but Art 90 required that such preferential systems must be extended without discrimination to spirits coming from other Member States (**Hansen v Hauptzollamt Flensburg** (Case 148/77)).

Articles 90(1) and (2) EC Treaty: the relationship

As discussed above, Art 90(1) prohibits the imposition of internal taxes on products from other Member States which are greater than those levied on *similar* domestic products. Therefore, once the imported and domestic products can be considered to be *similar*, Art 90(1) will apply and the taxes must be *equalised*.

Article 90(2) refers to the second paragraph of Art 90 which provides that:

> Furthermore, no Member State shall impose on the products of other Member States any internal taxation of such a nature as to afford indirect protection to other products.

Article 90(2) applies to other products which are not *similar*, but the effect of the tax is to afford *indirect protection* to some other domestic products: i.e. products which are not similar but which may otherwise be in competition with each other. For example, wine and beer may not be considered to be similar; however, they may be in competition with one another. One question which needs to be addressed when considering whether the products are in competition with one another, is whether the two products have a cross-elasticity of demand; are the products interchangeable? Having established a competitive relationship between the two products, if the tax on wine is greater than that on beer, it could deter beer drinkers from switching to wine. If the Member State which has adopted this tax policy is a major producer of beer but produces only small amounts of wine, the vast majority of it being imported, the tax policy could afford an indirect protection to its domestic beer producers.

The Court of Justice considered the scope of the former Arts 95(1) and (2) (now Art 90(1) and (2)) in the following case:

Commission v France (Case 168/78)

France had higher tax rates for spirits which were based upon grain (e.g. whisky, rum, gin, vodka) than those based upon wine or fruit (e.g. cognac, armagnac). France produced very little of the more heavily taxed grain-based spirits, but was a major producer of the wine/fruit-based spirits. The Commission took infraction proceedings against France pursuant to the former Art 169 EC Treaty (now Art 226) alleging the tax breached the former Art 95 (now Art 90). The Court of Justice held as follows:

4. [Article 95 (now Art 90) supplements] within the system of the Treaty, the provisions on the abolition of customs duties and charges having equivalent effect [i.e. Articles 9–17 (now Arts 23 and 25)]. Their aim is to ensure free movement of goods between the Member States in normal conditions of competition by the elimination of all forms of protection which result from the application of internal taxation which discriminates against products from other Member States. As the Commission has correctly stated, Article 95 [now Art 90] must guarantee the complete neutrality of internal taxation as regards competition between domestic products and imported products.

5. **The first paragraph of Article 95 [now Art 90], which is based on a comparison of the tax burdens imposed on domestic products and imported products which may be classified as 'similar', is the basic rule in this respect.** This provision, as the Court has had occasion to emphasise in its judgment of 10 October 1978 in Case 148/77, **H Hansenjun & O. C. Balle GmbH & Co.** *v* **Hauptzollamt Flensburg** [1978] ECR 1787, must be interpreted widely so as to cover all taxation procedures which conflict with the principle of the equality of treatment of domestic products and imported products; it is therefore necessary to interpret the concept of 'similar products' with sufficient flexibility. **The Court specified in the judgment of 17 February 1976 in the REWE case (Case 45/75 [1976] ECR 181) that it is necessary to consider as similar products which have 'similar characteristics and meet the same needs from the point of view of consumers'. It is therefore necessary to determine the scope of the first paragraph of Article 95 [now Art 90] on the basis not of the criterion of the strictly identical nature of the products but on that of their similar and comparable use.**

6. **The function of the second paragraph of Article 95 [now Art 90] is to cover, in addition, all forms of indirect tax protection in the case of products which, without being similar within the meaning of the first paragraph, are nevertheless in competition, even partial, indirect or potential, with certain products of the importing country.** The Court has already emphasised certain aspects of that provision in its judgment of 4 April 1978 in Case 27/77 **Firma Fink-Frucht GmbH** *v* **Hauptzollamt München-Landsbergerstrasse** [1978] ECR 223, in which it stated that for the purposes of the application of the second paragraph of Article 95 [now Art 90] it is sufficient for the imported product to be in competition with the protected domestic production by reason of one of several economic uses to which it may be put, even though the condition of similarity for the purposes of the first paragraph of Article 95 [now Art 90] is not fulfilled.

7. Whilst the criterion indicated in the first paragraph of Article 95 [now Art 90] consists in the comparison of tax burdens, whether in terms of the rate, the mode of assessment or other detailed rules for the application thereof, in view of the difficulty of making sufficiently precise comparisons between the products in question, the second paragraph of that article is based upon a more general criterion, in other words the protective nature of the system on internal taxation. [emphasis added]

The above case was decided on the basis that there had been an infringement of the former

Art 95 (now Art 90) without a detailed examination of the paragraphs separately. The reason why the Court of Justice was not unduly worried whether the infringement was based on the first or second paragraph of the former Art 95 (now Art 90) was explained by the Court as follows:

12. Two conclusions follow from this analysis of the market in spirits. First, there is, in the case of spirits considered as a whole, an indeterminate number of beverages which must be classified as 'similar products' within the meaning of the first paragraph of Article 95 [now Art 90], although it may be difficult to decide this in specific cases, in view of the nature of the factors implied by distinguishing criteria such as flavour and consumer habits. Secondly, even in cases in which it is impossible to recognise a sufficient degree of similarity between the products concerned, there are nevertheless, in the case of all spirits, common characteristics which are sufficiently pronounced to accept that in all cases there is at least partial or potential competition. It follows that the application of the second paragraph of Article 95 [now Art 90] may come into consideration in cases in which the relationship of similarity between the specific varieties of spirits remains doubtful or contested.

13. It appears from the foregoing that Article 95 [now Art 90], taken as a whole, may apply without distinction to all the products concerned. It is sufficient therefore to examine whether the application of a given national tax system is discriminatory or, as the case may be, protective, in other words whether there is a difference in the rate or the detailed rules for levying the tax and whether that difference is likely to favour a given national production.

. . .

39. The Court deems it unnecessary for the purposes of solving this dispute to give a ruling on the question whether or not the spirituous beverages concerned are wholly or partially similar products within the meaning of the first paragraph of Article 95 [now Art 90] when it is impossible reasonably to contest that without exception they are in at least partial competition with the domestic products to which the application refers and that it is impossible to deny the protective nature of the French tax system within the second paragraph of Article 95 [now Art 90].

40. In fact, as indicated above, spirits obtained from cereals have, as products obtained from distillation, sufficient characteristics in common with other spirits to constitute at least in certain circumstances an alternative choice for consumers . . .

41. As the competitive and substitution relationships between the beverages in question are such, the protective nature of the tax system criticised by the Commission is clear. A characteristic of that system is in fact that an essential part of domestic production, . . . spirits obtained from wine and fruit, come within the most favourable tax category whereas at least two types of product, almost all of which are imported from other Member States, are subject to higher taxation under the 'manufacturing tax'.

In the above case, the Court of Justice considered that classification into the first or second paragraph of the former Art 95 (now Art 90) was difficult (para 12). It also stated that the end result would be the same. At para 39 the Court concluded that the tax would fail, notwithstanding that the spirits were not similar, because they were to some degree in competition with one another and the tax was protective. The Court therefore got around the problem of classification.

However, this failure by the Court creates a problem for the defaulting Member State which will need to take remedial action to remedy the breach. If the tax is in breach of Art 90(1), the tax must be equalised. However, if the tax is in breach of Art 90(2), the *protective effect* must be eliminated; this does not necessarily require the tax to be equalised. The concept of *protective effect* is considered below, but suffice to note at this stage that in its later judgments the Court has distinguished between the two paragraphs.

Article 90(2): protective effect

One of the early 'alcohol' cases brought by the Commission was against the UK for the discriminatory taxation of wine in comparison with beer (**Commission** *v* **UK** (Case 170/78)). There is quite clearly a greater difference between the objective characteristics of beer and wine than there is between two spirits. Beer and wine were not considered to be Art 95(1) (now Art 90(1)) *similar* and therefore the Court of Justice proceeded under the former Art 95(2) (now Art 90(2)). This case provides an insight into how the Court of Justice approaches the application of the former Art 95(2) (now Art 90(2)):

Commission v UK (Case 170/78)

The UK levied a tax on certain wines, which was about five times that levied on beer in terms of 'volume'. The tax on wine represented about 38 per cent of its sale price compared to 25 per cent for beer. The UK produced vast amounts of beer, but very little wine. The Commission took infraction proceedings against the UK pursuant to the former Art 169 EC Treaty (now Art 226) claiming the differential UK tax breached the former Art 95(2) (now Art 90(2)). Following an adjournment while further evidence was gathered relating to the competitive relationship between beer and wine, the Court held as follows:

8.   As regards the question of competition between wine and beer, the Court considered that, to a certain extent at least, the two beverages in question were capable of meeting identical needs, so that it had to be acknowledged that there was a degree of substitution for one another. It pointed out that, for the purpose of measuring the possible degree of substitution, attention should not be confined to consumer habits in a Member State or in a given region. Those habits, which were essentially variable in time and space, could not be considered immutable; the tax policy of a Member State must not therefore crystallise given consumer habits so as to consolidate an advantage acquired by national industries concerned to respond to them.

9.   The Court nonetheless recognised that, in view of the substantial differences between wine and beer, it was difficult to compare the manufacturing processes and the natural properties of those beverages, as the Government of the UK had rightly observed. For that reason, the Court requested the parties to provide additional information with a view to dispelling the doubts which existed concerning the nature of the competitive relationship between the two products.

  . . .

11.   The Italian Government contended in that connection that it was inappropriate to compare beer with wines of average alcoholic strength or, a fortiori, with wines of greater alcoholic strength. In its opinion, it was the lightest wines with an alcoholic strength in the region of 9, that is to say the most popular and cheapest wines, which were genuinely in competition with beer. It therefore took the view that those wines should be chosen for purposes of comparison where it was a question of measuring the incidence of taxation on the basis of either alcoholic strength or the price of the products.

12.   The Court considers that observation by the Italian Government to be pertinent. **In view of the substantial differences in the quality and, therefore, in the price of wines, the decisive competitive relationship between beer, a popular and widely consumed beverage, and wine must be established by reference to those wines which are the most accessible to the public at large, that is to say, generally speaking the lightest and cheapest varieties. Accordingly, that is the appropriate basis for making fiscal comparisons by reference to the alcoholic strength or to the price of the two beverages.**

  . . .

19.   It is not disputed that comparison of the taxation of beer and wine by reference to the volume of the two beverages reveals that wine is taxed more heavily than beer in both relative and real terms. Not only was the taxation of wine increased substantially in relation to the taxation of beer

when the UK replaced customs duty with excise duty ... but it is also clear that during the years to which those proceedings relate, namely 1976 and 1977, the taxation of wine was, on average, five times higher, by reference to volume, than the taxation of beer; in other words wine was subject to an additional tax of 400% in round figures.

20. As regards the criterion for comparison based on alcoholic strength ...

21. In the light of the indices which the Court has already accepted, it is clear that in the UK during the period in question wine bore a tax burden which, by reference to alcoholic strength, was more than twice as heavy as that borne by beer, that is to say an additional tax burden of at least 100%.

22. As regards the criterion of the incidence of taxation on the price net of tax, the Court experienced considerable difficulty in forming an opinion, in view of the disparate nature of the information provided by the parties.

    ...

26. After considering the information provided by the parties, the Court has come to the conclusion that, if a comparison is made on the basis of those wines which are cheaper than the types of wine selected by the UK and of which several varieties are sold in significant quantities on the UK market, it becomes apparent that precisely those wines which, in view of their price, are most directly in competition with domestic beer production are subject to a considerably higher tax burden.

27. **It is clear, therefore, following the detailed inquiry conducted by the Court – whatever criterion for comparison is used, there being no need to express a preference for one or the other – that the UK's tax system has the effect of subjecting wine imported from other Member States to an additional burden so as to afford protection to domestic beer production, inasmuch as beer production constitutes the most relevant reference criterion from the point of view of competition.** Since such protection is most marked in the case of the most popular wines, the effect of the UK tax system is to stamp wine with the hallmarks of a luxury product which, in view of the tax burden which it bears, can scarcely constitute in the eyes of the consumer a genuine alternative to the typically produced domestic beverage.

28. It follows from the foregoing considerations that, by levying excise duty on still light wines made from fresh grapes at a higher rate, in relative terms, than on beer, the UK has failed to fulfil its obligations under the second paragraph of Article 95 [now Art 90] of the EEC Treaty. [emphasis added]

In the above case, the Court of Justice carried out a two-stage process in determining whether the UK had breached the former Art 95(2) (now Art 90(1)):

1. The Court sought to establish some competitive relationship between the two products to ascertain if the former Art 95(2) (now Art 90(2)) could be applicable at all (paras 8–12). In considering this issue, the Court took account of the extent to which the goods were substitutable for each other: i.e. whether they had a high or low degree of cross-elasticity.

   In considering whether or not the goods are substitutable the Court will ignore current consumer perceptions, because such perceptions can change over a period of time. Indeed the consumer may be affected because of the differential tax on the two products. This may deter the consumer from purchasing the more heavily taxed product. At para 27, the Court declared that the UK's taxation of cheap wine was to stamp it with the hallmark of a luxury product.

   If there is a competitive relationship between the two products the Court will also examine the nature of this competition. In this case the nature of the competition was held to be between beer and the cheaper, lighter wines (rather than the more expensive, heavier wines).

2. Having established a competitive relationship between the two products, the Court will ascertain whether the tax system is in fact protective of beer.

In this case it was quite clear that the differential rates had a protective effect on beer. Tax on wine was (a) 500 per cent by reference to 'volume' and (b) 100 per cent by reference to 'alcoholic strength', greater than that levied on beer.

However, the difference in the level of taxation may not be that great. The Court may therefore be faced with a much more difficult task. Much will depend on the degree of cross-elasticity between the two products. If this is low then a small tax differential will probably make no difference, whereas if it is high, the level of taxation may be of critical importance to the consumer.

Alternatively, although the differential rate of tax between the two products may be high in percentage terms, it may only be a very low proportion of the final selling price.

For example, in the UK beer and wine case, if the tax on beer had been 2p per litre compared to 10p per litre on wine then, by volume, the tax on wine is 500 per cent greater than that on beer. However, the level of tax is low with respect to the final selling price of the products and therefore the level of taxation is unlikely to have a protective effect on domestic beer producers (i.e. the tax difference alone would be unlikely to deter a beer drinker from switching to wine).

This two-stage process can be seen in the following two cases:

FG Roders BV ea v *Inspecteur der Inverrechten en Accijnzen* (Joined Cases C-367-377/93)

The Court of Justice conceded that fruit wine produced in the Benelux countries was not similar to imported sherry, madeira, vermouth and champagne. However, the Court recognised that these products might, nevertheless, be in competition with the fruit wine, and the differential tax structure might, therefore, favour the home-produced fruit wine. The Court observed that the existence of a competitive relationship between the products had to be considered to establish whether or not there was a breach of the second paragraph of Art 90. The essential question was whether the charge imposed was of such a kind as to have the effect, on the market in question, of reducing potential consumption of the imported products. The national court that has to make the final decision must have regard to the difference between the selling prices of the products in question and the impact of that difference on the consumer's choice, as well as to changes in the consumption of those products.

Commission v *Italy* (Case 184/85)

The facts of this case were considered above. The Court of Justice decided that bananas were *not* similar to other fruit and therefore Art 90(1) did not apply. However, the Court decided that there was a competitive relationship between bananas and other fruit, and went on to consider whether the Italian consumption tax levied on bananas, but not on other, home-grown fruit, had a protective effect. It held that it did have a protective effect, because the tax levied on bananas was almost half their import price, while no tax was levied on almost all Italian grown fruit. This was clear evidence of protectionism.

However, as stated above, the fact that there is a tax differential between domestic and imported goods will not automatically result in protectionism being established, as illustrated in the following case:

Commission v Belgium (Case 356/85)

Belgium levied a tax on beer which was produced in Belgium, and a tax on wine which was mostly imported. There was a 6 per cent difference in the tax levied, wine being taxed more heavily. The Court of Justice held that this did not have a protective effect because the cost of the two products differed substantially, and therefore a relatively minor difference in the tax rates would not serve to protect the Belgian beer producers.

The fact that tax is imposed on a product which is not produced in the importing state and for which there is no domestic equivalent may well mean that there is no breach of Art 90, since there will be no similar product in relation to which discrimination can be alleged or home market to be protected (**Fink-Frucht v HZA München-Landsbergerstrasse** (Case 27/67)).

Figure 17.2 consists of a flowchart setting out the application of Art 90 EC Treaty.

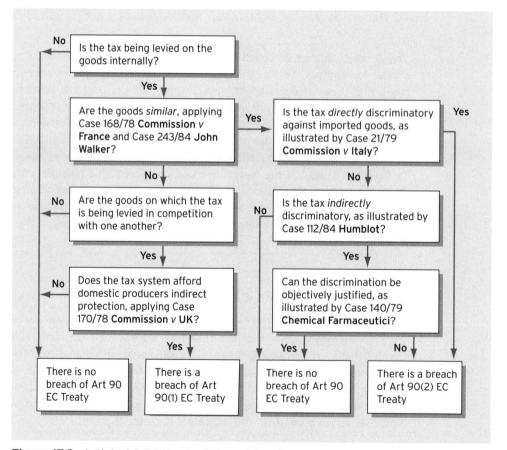

Figure 17.2 Article 90 EC Treaty: internal taxation

Summary

Now you have read this chapter you should be able to:

- Identify the ways in which the free movement of goods can be hindered and made more difficult.

- Understand how to differentiate between a customs duty and a charge having an equivalent effect to a customs duty and explain the provisions of Arts 23 and 25 EC Treaty which regulate such duties and charges.

- Explain the provisions of Art 90 EC Treaty which apply to internal taxation.

- Understand how internal taxation which is levied on goods which are similar (pursuant to Art 90(1) EC Treaty) is treated differently to the situation where the effect of the internal taxation affords an indirect protection to domestically produced goods (pursuant to Art 90(2) EC Treaty).

Further reading

Textbooks

Barnard, C. (2004) *The Substantive Law of the EU: The four freedoms* (1st edn), Oxford University Press, Chapters 2 to 4.

Craig, P. and De Burca, G. (2003) *EU Law Text, Cases and Materials* (3rd edn), Oxford University Press, Chapter 14.

Foster, N. (2006) *Foster on EU Law* (1st edn), Oxford University Press, Chapter 7 (Sections 7.4 and 7.5).

Steiner, J., Woods, L. and Twigg-Flesner, C. (2006) *EU Law* (9th edn), Oxford University Press, Chapters 14 to 17.

Storey, T. and Turner, C. (2005) *Unlocking EU Law* (1st edn), Hodder Arnold, Chapter 14.

Tillotson, J. and Foster, N. (2003) *Text, Cases and Materials on EU Law* (4th edn), Cavendish Publishing, Chapters 11 and 12.

Wallace, H., Wallace, W. and Pollack, M.A. (2005) *Policy Making in the European Union* (5th edn), Chapter 4.

Weatherill, S. (2006) *Cases and Materials on EU Law* (7th edn), Oxford University Press, Chapters 9 and 10.

Journal articles

Danusso, M. and Denton, R., 'Does the European Court of Justice Look for a Protectionist Motive under Article 95?' (1991) 1 LIEI 67.

Kuyper, P.J., 'Booze and Fast Cars: Tax Discrimination under GATT and the EC' [1996] LIEI 129.

Usher, J., 'The Single Market and Goods Imported from Third Countries' (1986) YEL 159, 167.

18 The elimination of quantitative restrictions and measures having an equivalent effect

Aims and objectives

At the end of this chapter you should understand:

- The purpose and effect of Arts 28-30 EC Treaty.
- How to distinguish between a quantitative restriction and a measure having an effect equivalent to a quantitative restriction.
- The difference between a distinctly applicable measure and an indistinctly applicable measure.
- How the law relating to indistinctly applicable measures is applied, how to differentiate between rules of dual-burden and those of equal-burden, and how to explain the impact of the **Keck** judgment.
- The circumstances in which a Member State may rely upon Art 30 EC Treaty to defend a distinctly or indistinctly applicable measure.
- How the **Cassis** rule of reason can be relied upon by a Member State to justify an indistinctly applicable measure.

An introduction to Articles 28-30 EC Treaty

The elimination of any restrictions on the free movement of goods is central to the creation of an internal market in the Member States of the Community, and this is one of the main objectives of the Community (Art 3(1)(a) EC Treaty). Article 28 (previously Art 30) EC Treaty provides that:

> Quantitative restrictions on *imports* and all measures having equivalent effect shall be *prohibited* between Member States. [emphasis added]

The prohibition of restrictions on *imports* in Art 28 is reflected by a matching prohibition on *export* restrictions in Art 29 EC Treaty (previously Art 34). Both prohibitions are, however, qualified by the right of Member States to impose limited restrictions on trade, if they can *justify* them under the criteria laid down in Art 30 EC Treaty (previously Art 36), or in some cases under the **Cassis** rule of reason (see below). Articles 28–30 EC Treaty attempt to strike a balance between achieving a genuine free and competitive market in goods on the one hand, and the recognition of the need, in some circumstances, to protect essential public interests on the other. The process of harmonising national standards of consumer and environmental protection, through a programme of standardising directives for goods throughout the Community, is part of a programme to reduce the need for such national exceptions to the general Community right of free movement of goods. Much of the jurisprudence of the Court of Justice has been devoted to consideration of the extent to which such national measures infringe the relevant provisions of the Treaty or fall within the permitted derogations.

Articles 28 and 29 EC Treaty adopt the same approach as has been adopted for the prohibitions set out in Arts 23 and 25 EC Treaty (see Chapter 17). They are aimed at measures which are clearly directed at imports and exports to and from other Member States, but they also prohibit measures which have the same effect as such restrictions, even though there may be no intention by the Member State imposing them to have that effect. Articles 28 and 29 are directly effective. Any state measure breaching them can give rise to a claim in damages against the Member State concerned, provided that the criteria laid down by the Court of Justice in **Brasserie du Pêcheur** (Case C–46/93) in relation to imports and **R v Ministry of Fisheries and Food, ex parte Hedley Lomas Ireland Ltd** (Case C–5/94) in relation to exports can be met (see Chapter 9). Articles 28 and 29 are directed at the state, therefore they cannot be used by private individuals against each other. They may, however, be used by individuals as a defence in civil proceedings where the national law is alleged to breach Arts 28 or 29 (**Vereinigte Familiapress Zeitungsverlags und Vertriebs GmbH v Heinrich Bauer Verlag** (Case C–368/95)).

The prohibition on restrictions affects all kinds of products, including agricultural produce, and it applies not only to goods which originate in the Member States but also to goods which come from third countries (i.e. non-Member States) and which are in free circulation in a Member State. Such goods are in free circulation when they have crossed the Common External Tariff wall, with all import formalities complied with and duties and charges paid (Art 24 EC Treaty; see Chapter 17).

For the purposes of Arts 28–30, the Court of Justice has held that 'goods' are 'manufactured material objects' (**Cinéthèque** (Cases 60 & 61/84)). The term is wide enough to include not only plants, vegetables, fruit and livestock and a whole variety of animal products (**Société Civile Agricole** (Case C–323/93)), but also even covers generated electricity (**Commission v Netherlands** (Case C–157/94)). The context in which an item is applied may, however, result in it being regarded not as a product in itself subject to the provisions of Arts 28–30, but as an incident to the provision of a service, and thus subject to Art 49 EC Treaty (**HM Customs and Excise Commissioners v Schindler** (Case C–275/92), para 23)). Coins and banknotes or bearer cheques are not 'goods', as their transfer is subject to the rules on transfer of capital under Art 56 EC Treaty (**Aldo Bordessa and Others** (Joined Cases C–358 & 416/93)). However, in **R v Thompson** (Case 7/78), the Court of Justice held that old gold coins were 'goods' because they were not a normal means of payment.

Articles 28–30 EC Treaty are considered in greater detail throughout the remainder of this chapter.

State measures

Articles 28 and 29 are directed at the governments of Member States; they apply only to measures adopted by the state and not measures taken by private parties. However, the provisions of Art 28 have also been held by the Court of Justice to be binding on the institutions of the Community, and the Court has expressed the view that it would have been prepared to strike down a Council Regulation requiring Member States to gather information from importers and exporters, had it been satisfied that the regulation imposed a disproportionately heavy burden on the free movement of goods (**Rene Kieffer and Romain Thill** (Case C–114/96)).

The prohibition of customs duties and discriminatory internal taxes imposed by Member States have already been considered in Chapter 17. Articles 28–30 form part of a larger strategy to free up trade and to prevent Member States from adopting both overt and covert protectionist policies. The same strategy also includes the regulation of state monopolies of a commercial character under Art 31 EC Treaty and state aids to national-ised industries under Arts 87–88 EC Treaty (see Chapter 19). It underlies Community legislation on public procurement, which is intended to prevent the governments of Member States from favouring national contractors in the award of public works con-tracts. For that reason, attempts by a private undertaking to persuade consumers to buy national products in, say, a 'Buy UK' advertising campaign will not breach Art 28 EC Treaty, although such a campaign would infringe Art 28 if promoted by a public, or pub-licly sponsored, body (**Apple and Pear Development Council** v **K.J. Lewis Ltd** (Case 222/82), see below).

So what exactly constitutes a *state* measure for the purposes of Arts 28 and 29? This question was considered by the Court of Justice in the following case:

Commission v *Ireland* (Case 249/81)

The Irish government embarked upon a 'Buy Irish' campaign. In 1978 the Irish government introduced a three-year programme to help promote Irish products. The campaign was launched by a speech delivered by the Irish Minister for Industry, Commerce and Energy. A number of measures were adopted, of which two were carried out: (i) the encouragement of the use of a 'Buy Irish' symbol for goods made in Ireland and (ii) the organisation of a pub-licity campaign by the Irish Goods Council in favour of Irish products, designed to encourage consumers to buy Irish products.

The Commission brought former Art 169 EC Treaty (now Art 226) proceedings against the Irish Government, alleging the campaign was a measure equivalent to a quantitative restric-tion and therefore in breach of the former Art 30 EC Treaty (now Art 28). Ireland defended the action on the ground it had never adopted 'measures' for the purpose of the former Art 30; it was the Irish Goods Council. It argued that any financial assistance it had given to the Council should be judged under the former Arts 92-93 EC Treaty (aids granted by states, now Arts 87-88) and not under the former Art 30 (now Art 28). The members of the Irish Goods Council were appointed by the Irish Government and it was funded in proportions of 6:1 by the government and private industry respectively. The initial question to be considered by the Court of Justice was whether or not the campaign constituted a *measure* undertaken *by the state*. The Court of Justice held as follows:

15. It is thus apparent that the Irish Government appoints the members of the Management Committee of the Irish Goods Council, grants it public subsidies which cover the greater part of its expenses and, finally, defines the aims and the broad outline of the campaign conducted by that institution to promote the sale and purchase of Irish products. In the circumstances the Irish Government cannot rely on the fact that the campaign was conducted by a private company in order to escape any liability it may have under the provisions of the Treaty.

   . . .

21. The Irish Government maintains that the prohibition against measures having an effect equiv-

alent to quantitative restrictions in Article 30 [now Art 28] is concerned only with 'measures', that is to say, binding provisions emanating from a public authority. However, no such provision has been adopted by the Irish Government, which has confined itself to giving moral support and financial aid to the activities pursued by the Irish industries.

..

23. ... the campaign is a reflection of the Irish Government's considered intention to substitute domestic products for imported products on the Irish market and thereby check the flow of imports from other Member States.

24. It must be remembered here that a representative of the Irish Government stated when the campaign was launched that it was a carefully thought-out set of initiatives constituting an integrated programme for promoting domestic products; that the Irish Goods Council was set up at the initiative of the Irish Government a few months later; and that the task of implementing the integrated programme as it was envisaged by the Government was entrusted, or left, to that Council.

...

28. Such a practice cannot escape the prohibition laid down by Article 30 [now Art 28] of the Treaty solely because it is not based on decisions which are binding upon undertakings. Even measures adopted by the government of a Member State which do not have binding effect may be capable of influencing the conduct of traders and consumers in that state and thus of frustrating the aims of the Community as set out in Article 2 and enlarged upon in Article 3 of the Treaty.

In the above case, the Court of Justice considered the involvement of the Irish government with the Irish Goods Council at para 15. At paras 21 and 28 the Court rebutted the Irish argument that only formally binding measures are caught by the former Art 30 (now Art 28).

The principle established in the above case was developed further by the Court of Justice in the following case:

Apple and Pear Development Council v K.J. Lewis Ltd (Case 222/82)

There was a statutory obligation on the growers of fruit to pay a levy to the Development Council. This statutory underpinning was sufficient to bring it within the scope of a state entity for Art 28 purposes. As the Court of Justice stated:

... a body such as the Development Council, which is set up by the government of a Member State and is financed by a charge imposed on growers, cannot under Community law enjoy the same freedom as regards the methods of advertising used as that enjoyed by producers themselves or producers' associations of a voluntary character.

The Court of Justice stated that Art 28 imposed on the Development Council 'a duty not to engage in any advertising intended to discourage the purchase of products from other Member States or to disparage those products in the eyes of consumers. Nor must it advise consumers to purchase domestic products solely by reason of their national origin' (para 18).

Similarly, in the following case:

R v The Pharmaceutical Society, ex parte API (Cases 266 and 267/87)

The Pharmaceutical Society was an independent body which had the responsibility for the regulation of standards among UK pharmacists. In order to practise, a pharmacist had to appear on the Society's register. The Society had certain statutory functions under the Pharmacy Act 1954. The Court of Justice held that the Society had a sufficient measure of state support or 'statutory underpinning' to constitute it a state entity for the purposes of Art 28. Accordingly, the Society was bound by Art 28. The Court therefore held that rules of the society which required pharmacists to supply, under a prescription, only a named branded drug were *prima facie* in breach of Art 28.

It is, of course, not only the state and public bodies which may, either directly or indirectly, seek to exclude foreign competition. Articles 28–30 EC Treaty must also be considered in the light of Arts 81 and 82 EC Treaty, which play an important part in preventing national cartels and national monopolies from using private economic power to keep goods from other Member States from entering national markets (see Chapters 20 and 21). Where the private body enjoys a monopoly conferred on it by the state, which enables it to restrict the import of foreign products by virtue of that monopoly, there may be an overlap between Arts 28 and 82. In such circumstances, the state may be liable for maintaining a situation which has the effect of excluding products from other Member States in breach of Art 28, or an unlawful state monopoly in breach of Art 31 (**Harry Franzen** (Case C–189/95) and **Société Civile Agricole** *v* **Coopérative d'Elevage de la Mayenne** (Case C–323/93), and see also Chapter 19).

If the measure has been adopted by the state, the next issue to be determined, within the context of Art 28 EC Treaty, is whether the measure constitutes a quantitative restriction (QR) or a measure having equivalent effect to a quantitative restriction (MEQR).

Quantitative restrictions (QRs)

Direct restrictions, such as quotas and bans on certain products of other Member States, were abolished or phased out in the early days of the Community and during transitional periods following the admission of new Member States. The concept of 'quantitative restrictions' (QR) is straightforward enough: in **Geddo** *v* **Ente Nazionale Risi** (Case 2/73), the Court of Justice stated that:

> The prohibition on quantitative restrictions covers measures which amount to a total or partial restraint of, according to the circumstances, imports, exports, or goods in transit.

The concept of quantitative restriction therefore applies to an outright ban (e.g. a French ban on UK beef) or the imposition of a quota (e.g. a numerical restriction on the number of vehicles which can be imported into Spain each year from Germany).

Some national prohibitions do survive, such as the prohibition on the importation of obscene materials into the UK under the Customs Consolidation Act 1876. It was argued by the UK government in **R** *v* **Henn and Darby** (Case 34/79) that a ban on the import of pornographic material under the Act was not a quantitative restriction under Art 28. The Court of Justice, in an Art 234 EC Treaty reference, disagreed. It held that Art 28 'includes such a prohibition on imports in as much as this is the most extreme form of restriction'. The reference in Art 28 to 'quantitative restrictions' was to be read in the light of Art 30, which referred also to 'prohibitions' on imports. In the event, the Court held that the prohibition in this case was justified under Art 30. That aspect of the case is discussed below. Although a quantitative restriction is readily recognisable, measures having an equivalent effect to quantitative restrictions on imports have proved much more elusive and have resulted in a large, and growing, jurisprudence on the subject by the Court of Justice.

Measures having equivalent effect to quantitative restrictions (MEQRs)

The Dassonville formula

In addition to prohibiting quantitative restrictions, Art 28 EC Treaty also prohibits 'measures having [an] equivalent effect' to quantitative restrictions (MEQRs). In the following case, the Court of Justice considered the scope of what is now Art 28 in relation to MEQRs, and provided a very useful definition (referred to as the **Dassonville** formula) of exactly what constitutes an MEQR:

Procureur du Roi v *Dassonville* (Case 8/74)

A Belgian importer of Scotch whisky was prosecuted for selling whisky with false certificates of origin. He had imported the whisky from France and it had been difficult to obtain the certificates from the producers. He argued that the Belgian law infringed Art 30 (now Art 28), in that it made the importation of whisky from anywhere other than the state of origin more difficult. The Belgian court referred the case to the Court of Justice under the former Art 177 EC Treaty (now Art 234). The Court of Justice held as follows:

2. By the first question it is asked whether a national provision prohibiting the import of goods bearing a designation of origin where such goods are not accompanied by an official document issued by the government of the exporting country certifying their right to such designation constitutes a measure having an effect equivalent to a quantitative restriction within the meaning of Article 30 [now Art 28] of the Treaty.
3. This question was raised within the context of criminal proceedings instituted in Belgium against traders who duly acquired a consignment of Scotch whisky in free circulation in France and imported it into Belgium without being in possession of a certificate of origin from the UK customs authorities, thereby infringing Belgian rules.
4. It emerges from the file and from the oral proceedings that a trader, wishing to import into Belgium Scotch whisky which is already in free circulation in France, can obtain such a certificate only with great difficulty, unlike the importer who imports directly from the producer country.
5. **All trading rules enacted by Member States which are capable of hindering, directly or indirectly, actually or potentially, intra-Community trade are to be considered as measures having an effect equivalent to quantitative restrictions.**
   . . .
9. Consequently, the requirement by a Member State of a certificate of authenticity which is less easily obtainable by importers of an authentic product which has been put into free circulation in a regular manner in another Member State than by importers of the same product coming directly from the country of origin constitutes a measure having an effect equivalent to a quantitative restriction as prohibited by the Treaty. [emphasis added]

It is clear from the Court of Justice's definition of an MEQR in para 5 of the above case that the crucial element in proving the existence of an MEQR is its *effect;* a discriminatory *intent* is not required. This is a very broad definition (the **Dassonville** formula) which, as is discussed below, indicates a determination by the Court of Justice to ensure that very few measures will be permitted to hinder the free movement of goods between Member States.

Directive 70/50

Directive 70/50, issued in December 1969, was intended to provide guidance on the kind of acts and activities which constituted 'measures' infringing Art 28 EC Treaty, and which were in existence when the EC Treaty came into force. It was formally only of application during the Member States' transitional period, yet it has been very influential in representing the Commission's view of the scope of Art 28. It is still on occasion referred to by the Court of Justice. Although many measures will have been made since that time, and will be outside the directive's scope, it still has value in identifying prohibited acts or conduct.

Article 2, Directive 70/50 covers measures 'other than those applicable equally to domestic or imported products, which hinder imports which could otherwise take place, including measures which make importation more difficult or costly than the disposal of domestic products'. Article 2 is thus concerned with national measures which apply specifically to, or affect only, imported goods. These are often referred to as 'distinctly applicable measures', because they explicitly *distinguish* between imported and domestically produced goods (see below). Article 2, Directive 70/50 contains a non-exhaustive list of the sort of measures applied to imported goods which would constitute MEQRs. They include:

- the laying down of minimum and maximum sale prices;
- the fixing of less favourable prices for imported than for domestically produced goods;
- the exclusion of prices for imported goods which reflect importation costs;
- the making of access to markets in the importing state dependent upon having an agent there;
- the laying down of conditions of payment in respect of imported products only, or the subjection of imported goods to conditions which are different from those laid down for domestic products and are more difficult to satisfy;
- requiring, for imported goods only, the giving of guarantees or the making of payment on account;
- subjecting only imported products to conditions in respect of shape, size, weight, composition, presentation and identification, or subjecting imported products to conditions which are different from those for domestic products and more difficult to satisfy;
- hindering the purchase by individuals of imported products only, or encouraging, requiring or giving preference to the purchase of domestic products only;
- the total or partial preclusion of the use of national facilities or equipment in respect of imported products only, or the total or partial confinement of such facilities to national producers;
- the prohibition or limitation of publicity in respect of imported products only, or the total or partial restriction of publicity to home-produced products.

The above list is indicative of the sort of national measures which will constitute MEQRs, but the ability of Member States to introduce measures which are either intended to protect, or will have the effect of protecting, domestically produced goods can neither be anticipated nor underestimated. The Court has laid down a number of general principles about measures which specifically affect imported goods and which constitute MEQRs. Each national measure will have to be assessed against these principles as and when the measure comes before a national court or the Court of Justice. Article 3, Directive 70/50 also refers to measures which are applied to both domestic and imported goods which may, nonetheless, have the effect of impeding imports. These are referred to as 'indistinctly applicable measures' (see below).

Distinctly applicable measures are now considered in further detail, followed by indistinctly applicable measures.

Distinctly applicable measures

Distinctly applicable measures, as stated above, are measures which are applied only to imported or exported goods; the measure is not applied to domestically produced goods. Hence the reason for them being referred to as 'distinctly applicable measures', i.e. measures which explicitly *distinguish* between domestic and foreign goods.

There are many examples where the Court of Justice has struck down national rules which apply only to imported or exported goods. Some specific categories are now considered further.

Import and export restrictions

In **International Fruit Company *v* Produktschap voor Groenten en Fruit (No. 2)** (Cases 51–54/71), the Court of Justice held that import or export licences are caught by the former Arts 30 and 34 EC Treaty (now Arts 28 and 29) because, applying **Dassonville**, such a measure is 'capable of hindering, directly or indirectly, actually or potentially, intra-Community trade'. The necessity to apply for a licence before goods can be imported into a Member State, or exported out of a Member State, has a threefold impact: (i) until the licence application has been processed, goods cannot be imported or exported (and therefore this in effect constitutes a ban); (ii) the application could be rejected; and (iii) the very fact of having to apply for a licence will require additional paperwork to be completed by the importer or exporter. Completing the paperwork will cost time and money, and this additional cost will have to be accounted for when determining the price of the goods. Increasing the cost of the goods could decrease their competitiveness with domestically produced goods, and therefore the measure is capable of affecting trade within the Community.

In **Commission *v* Italy** (Case 154/85), Italy had procedures and data requirements which applied only to the importation of cars, which meant that their registration was longer, more complicated and more expensive, compared to the registration of domestic cars. The Court of Justice held that such procedures and requirements were prohibited under the former Art 30 (now Art 28).

In **Rewe-Zentralfinanz *v* Landwirtschaftskammer** (Case 4/75), phyto-sanitary inspections on imported apples contravened the former Art 30 (now Art 28) because there were no similar inspections of domestically grown apples. The Court of Justice stressed the fact that border inspections made imports more difficult and costly.

In **Procureur de la République Besacon *v* Bouhelier** (Case 53/76), the same approach was applied to discriminatory export rules. This case concerned a French rule which imposed quality checks on watches for export, but there was no similar inspection of those intended for the domestic market. The Court of Justice held such inspections contravened the former Art 34 (now Art 29).

In the following case, the Court of Justice held that a *failure to act* by a Member State could constitute an infringement of the former Art 30 (now Art 28):

Commission v *France* (Case C-265/95)

Fruit and vegetables imported into France from other Member States were targeted by French farmers, who would obstruct their passage, preventing them from reaching their final destination. For more than a decade the Commission had received complaints concerning the inactivity of the French authorities in the face of violent acts by the French farmers. From April to July 1993 that campaign was directed particularly at strawberries originating in Spain. In August and September 1993 tomatoes from Belgium were treated in the same way. In 1994 the same type of action, involving threats against shopping centres and destruction of goods and means of transport, was directed against Spanish strawberries in particular. On 20 April 1995 further serious incidents occurred in the south-west of France, in the course of which agricultural products from Spain were destroyed. On 3 June 1995 three lorries transporting fruit and vegetables from Spain were the subject of acts of violence in the south of France, without any intervention by the police.

At the beginning of July 1995 Italian and Spanish fruit were once again destroyed by French farmers. Further serious incidents of the same type occurred in 1996 and 1997. It was not denied by France that when such incidents occurred the French police were either not present on the spot, despite the fact that in certain cases the competent authorities had been warned of the imminence of demonstration by the French farmers, or they simply failed to intervene, even where the police far outnumbered the French farmers. As regards the numerous acts of vandalism committed between April and August 1993, the French authorities could cite only a single case of criminal prosecution.

The Commission took action against France, arguing that its failure to act impeded the free movement of goods imported from other Member States and constituted a breach of the former Art 30 EC Treaty (now Art 28). The Court of Justice held as follows:

> In the light of all the foregoing factors, the Court, while not discounting the difficulties faced by the competent authorities in dealing with situations of the type in question in this case, cannot but find that, having regard to the frequency and seriousness of the incidents cited by the Commission, the measures adopted by the French Government were manifestly inadequate to ensure freedom of intra-Community trade in agricultural products on its territory by preventing and effectively dissuading the perpetrators of the offences in question from committing and repeating them.
>
> Although it is not impossible that the threat of serious disruption to public order may, in appropriate cases, justify non-intervention by the police, that argument can, on any view, be put forward only with respect to a specific incident and not, as in this case, in a general way covering all the incidents cited by the Commission . . .
>
> It must be concluded that in the present case the French Government has manifestly and persistently abstained from adopting appropriate and adequate measures to put an end to the acts of vandalism which jeopardise the free movement on its territory of certain agricultural products originating in other Member States and to prevent the recurrence of such acts . . .
>
> By failing to adopt all necessary and proportionate measures in order to prevent the free movement of fruit and vegetables from being obstructed by actions by private individuals, the French Republic has failed to fulfil its obligations under Article 30 [now Art 28] of the EC Treaty.

The above case can be contrasted with that of the following:

Schmidberger (Case C-112/00)

A demonstration in Austria resulted in the complete closure of a major transit route for a continuous period of almost 30 hours. The Court of Justice stated that a failure to ban such a demonstration is capable of restricting intra-Community trade in goods and must therefore be regarded as constituting a measure of equivalent effect to a quantitative restriction which is *prima facie* incompatible with the obligations arising from Arts 28 and 29 EC Treaty, read together with Art 10 EC Treaty, unless that failure to ban can be objectively justified.

The above case can be distinguished from that of **Commission v France** (see above) in that **Schmidberger** concerned an indistinctly applicable measure (because the demonstration would affect both domestic and imported goods), whereas **Commission v France** concerned a distinctly applicable measure (because only imported goods were being targeted). **Schmidberger** will be considered below in the context of indistinctly applicable measures, but suffice to note here that the Court of Justice held that the failure to ban the demonstration was objectively justified (primarily to respect the fundamental rights of the demonstrators' freedom of expression and freedom of assembly, which are enshrined in and guaranteed by the European Convention on Human Rights and the Austrian Constitution). Of interest is the fact that the Court of Justice pointed out differences between the facts of **Schmidberger** and those of **Commission v France**. The Court stated that in the latter case, France had failed to adopt all necessary and proportionate measures in order to prevent the free movement of fruit and vegetables from being obstructed by the actions of private individuals, such as the interception of lorries and the destruction of their loads, violence against lorry drivers and other threats. The Court found that in **Schmidberger**, unlike in **Commission v France**, (i) the demonstration at issue took place following authorisation; (ii) the obstacle to the free movement of goods resulting from that demonstration was limited; (iii) the purpose of that public demonstration was not to restrict trade in goods of a particular type or from a particular source; (iv) various administrative and supporting measures were taken by the competent authorities in order to limit as far as possible the disruption to road traffic; (v) the isolated incident in question did not give rise to a general climate of insecurity such as to have a dissuasive effect on intra-Community trade flows as a whole; and (vi) taking account of the Member States' wide margin of discretion, in the present case the competent national authorities were entitled to consider that an outright ban on the demonstration at issue would have constituted unacceptable interference with the fundamental rights of the demonstrators to gather and express peacefully their opinion in public.

Promotion of domestic goods

A Member State may promote or favour a domestic product to the detriment of competing imports, but this may be caught by Art 28. An obvious example of this is where a Member State engages in a campaign to persuade consumers to purchase domestic rather than imported products. This is illustrated in the following case:

Commission v Ireland (Case 249/81)

The Irish government (through the Irish Goods Council) embarked upon a 'Buy Irish' campaign. The aim of the campaign was to achieve 'a switch from imports to Irish products equivalent to 3 per cent of total consumer spending'. The campaign was 'a carefully thought out set of initiatives that add up to an integrated programme for promoting Irish goods, with specific proposals to involve the producer, distributor and consumer'. A number of measures were adopted, of which two were carried out: (i) the encouragement of the use of a 'Buy Irish' symbol for goods made in Ireland; and (ii) the organisation of a publicity campaign by the Irish Goods Council in favour of Irish products, designed to encourage consumers to buy Irish products. The Commission brought former Art 169 EC Treaty (now Art 226) proceedings against the Irish Government, alleging the campaign was an MEQR. The Court of Justice held as follows:

22. The Irish Government goes on to emphasise that the campaign has had no restrictive effect on imports since the proportion of Irish goods to all goods sold on the Irish market fell from 49.2 per cent in 1977 to 43.4 per cent in 1980.

 . . .

25. Whilst it may be true that the two elements of the programme which have continued in effect, namely the advertising campaign and the use of the 'Guaranteed Irish' symbol, have not had any significant success in winning over the Irish market to domestic products, it is not possible to overlook the fact that, regardless of their efficacy, those two activities form part of a government programme which is designed to achieve the substitution of domestic products for imported products and is liable to affect the volume of trade between Member States.

 . . .

27. In the circumstances the two activities in question amount to the establishment of a national practice, introduced by the Irish Government and prosecuted with its assistance, the potential effect of which on imports from other Member States is comparable to that resulting from government measures of a binding nature.

 . . .

29. That is the case where, as in this instance, such a restrictive practice represents the implementation of a programme defined by the government which affects the national economy as a whole and which is intended to check the flow of trade between Member States by encouraging the purchase of domestic products, by means of an advertising campaign on a national scale and the organisation of special procedures applicable solely to domestic products, and where those activities are attributed as a whole to the government and are pursued in an organised fashion throughout the national territory.

30. Ireland has therefore failed to fulfil its obligations under the Treaty by organising a campaign to promote the sale and purchase of Irish goods within its territory.

The Court of Justice's reasoning in the above case illustrates that in so far as the former Art 30 EC Treaty (now Art 28) is concerned, it is more interested in *substance* than in *form*. At para 25, the Court rejected the argument that because the campaign appeared to fail Community law should be unconcerned with it. There is no need to prove that trade between Member States has *actually* been affected by the measure. Applying the **Dassonville** formula, all that is necessary is for there to be the *possibility* of such an effect.

The Court of Justice remains very ready to assume that different treatment of imported goods may result in a reduced volume of sales. In **Lucien Ortscheit GmbH *v* Eurim-Pharm GmbH** (Case C–320/93), a German law prohibiting the advertising of foreign medicinal products which had not been authorised for sale in Germany but which could, nonetheless, still be imported into Germany, was held necessarily to fall within the scope of Art 28, since it did not have the same effect on the marketing of medicinal products from other Member States as on the marketing of national medicinal products. The Court added that the prohibition of advertising might restrict the volume of imports of medicinal products not authorised in Germany, because it deprived pharmacists and doctors of a source of information on the existence and availability of such products. It was, therefore, equivalent to a quantitative restriction.

In **Commission v Germany** (Case 12/74), the Court of Justice stated that it may be possible for origin-marking to be acceptable, where it implies a certain quality in the goods, that they were made from certain materials or by a particular form of manufacturing, or where the origin indicates a special place in the folklore or tradition of the particular region in question. However, this exception will be treated with caution by the Court, as illustrated in the following case:

Commission v Ireland (Case 113/80)

This case concerned Irish legislation which required imported articles of jewellery depicting motifs or possessing characteristics which suggested they were souvenirs of Ireland (e.g. an Irish character, event or scene; a wolfhound; a round tower or a shamrock) to bear an indication of their country of origin or the word 'foreign'. The Court of Justice held as follows:

1. By an application lodged at the Court Registry on 28 April 1980, the Commission instituted proceedings under Article 169 [now Art 226] of the EEC Treaty, for a declaration that Ireland had failed to fulfil its obligations under Article 30 [now Art 28] of the EEC Treaty by requiring that the imported goods falling within the scope of the Merchandise Marks (Restrictions on Sale of Imported Jewellery) Order 1971 (SI No 306) ... and the Merchandise Marks (Restriction on Importation of Jewellery) Order 1971 (SI No 307) ... bear an indication of origin or the word 'foreign'.

2. According to the explanatory notes thereto, SI No 306 (hereinafter referred to as 'the Sale Order') prohibits the sale or exposure for sale of imported articles of jewellery depicting motifs or possessing characteristics which suggest that they are souvenirs of Ireland, for example an Irish character, event or scene, wolfhound, round tower, shamrock etc. and SI No 307 (hereinafter referred to as 'the Importation Order') prohibits the importation of such articles unless, in either case, they bear an indication of their country of origin or the word 'foreign'.

3. The articles concerned are listed in a schedule to each order. However, in order to come within the scope of the orders the article must be made of precious metal or rolled precious metal or of base metal, including polished or plated articles suitable for setting.

4. In the Commission's opinion, the restrictions on the free movement of the goods covered by the two orders constitute measures having an effect equivalent to quantitative restrictions on imports, contrary to the provisions of Article 30 [now Art 28] of the EEC Treaty; it also observes that according to Article 2(3)(f) of Directive 70/50/EEC ... 'measures which lower the value of an imported product, in particular by causing a reduction in its intrinsic value, or increase its costs' must be regarded as measures having an effect equivalent to quantitative restrictions, contrary to Article 30 [now Art 28] of the EEC Treaty.

    ...

17. Thus by granting souvenirs imported from other Member States access to the domestic market solely on condition that they bear a statement of origin, whilst no such statement is required in the case of domestic products, the provisions contained in the Sale Order and the Importation Order indisputably constitute a discriminatory measure.

18. The conclusion to be drawn therefore is that by requiring all souvenirs and articles of jewellery imported from other Member States which are covered by the Sale Order and the Importation Order to bear an indication of origin or the word 'foreign', the Irish rules constitute a measure

having equivalent effect within the meaning of Article 30 [now Art 28] of the EEC Treaty. Ireland has consequently failed to fulfil its obligations under the article. [emphasis added]

However, not all measures which promote domestic goods will be caught by Art 28 EC Treaty, as illustrated in the following case:

Apple and Pear Development Council v K. J. Lewis Ltd (Case 222/82)

The Apple and Pear Development Council was set up by the UK government. It was financed by a mandatory charge imposed on UK fruit growers (the charge was calculated as a sum per hectare of land). Part of the Council's role was to market the goods. It brought actions against certain fruit growers who refused to pay the charge. The actions were defended on the basis that the charges were contrary to the former Art 30 EC Treaty (now Art 28). The Court of Justice reiterated its decision in the above case, and then continued as follows:

18. ... such a body [as the Council] is under a duty not to engage in any advertising intended to discourage the purchase of products of other Member States or to disparage those products in the eyes of consumers. Nor must it advise consumers to purchase domestic products solely by reason of their national origin.

19. On the other hand, Article 30 [now Art 28] does not prevent such a body from drawing attention, in its publicity, to the specific qualities of fruit grown in the Member State in question or from organising campaigns to promote the sale of certain varieties, mentioning their particular properties, even if those varieties are typical of national production.

The above case provides that it is permissible for the government of a Member State to promote, for example, varieties of apples. The French may promote Golden Delicious apples, and may draw attention to the particular qualities of the apples. However, such promotion may overstep the boundary if the advertising is intended to discourage the purchase of imported products. This will be a fine line to draw in practice.

Two forms of national favour have been considered: a national campaign to purchase domestic goods and origin-marking. A third form, towards which the Court of Justice is equally harsh, occurs in the field of public procurement (i.e. public service contracts). In the following case, the Court of Justice held that a Member State which reserved a proportion of its public supplies to products which were made in a particular depressed region of the country automatically contravened the former Art 30 (now Art 28) because the measure impeded imports:

Du Pont de Nemours Italiana SpA v Unità Sanitaria Locale No. 2 Di Cascara (Case C-21/88)

The Court of Justice held as follows:

11. It must be pointed out ... that such a system, which favours goods processed in a particular region of a Member State, prevents the authorities and public bodies concerned from procuring some of the supplies they need from undertakings situated in other Member States. Accordingly, it must be held that products originating in other Member States suffer discrimination in comparison with products manufactured in the Member State in question, with the result that the normal course of intra-Community trade is hindered.

12. That conclusion is not affected by the fact that the restrictive effects of a preferential system of the kind at issue are borne in the same measure both by products manufactured by undertakings

from the Member State in question which are not situated in the region covered by the preferential system and by products manufactured by undertakings established in other Member States.

13. ... the fact remains that all the products benefiting by the preferential system are domestic products.

Similarly, in **Campus Oil Ltd** *v* **Minister for Industry and Energy** (Case 72/83), Ireland had placed an obligation on importers to buy a certain proportion of their oil supplies (35 per cent) from Ireland's only state-owned refinery at prices fixed by the government. The Court of Justice held this was clearly discriminatory and breached the former Art 30 (now Art 28).

Price-fixing regulations

Another way in which a Member State can treat imports less favourably than domestic products is by fixing prices to make it more difficult for an importer to market his goods within that Member State. If price fixing is applied only to the imported product, then clearly it will be caught by Art 28 (e.g. minimum price for imported apples £10 per kg).

Indistinctly applicable measures

Article 3, Directive 70/50 (see above) covers measures which affect both home-produced and imported products, but which have a harsher impact on imported products. The measures do not explicitly distinguish between goods according to their origin, and are therefore referred to as 'indistinctly applicable measures'. Specifically, Art 3 refers to measures relating to the marketing of products dealing with shape, size, weight, composition, presentation or identification 'which are equally applicable to domestic and imported products where the restrictive effect of such measures on the free movement of goods exceeds the effects intrinsic to trade rules'. This will be the case where the restrictive effects on the free movement of goods are out of proportion to their purpose and where the same objective can be attained by other means which are less of a hindrance to trade (an application of the 'proportionality test'). These criteria have been crucial in the development of the jurisprudence of the Court of Justice in relation to national measures which appear, at least, to apply indiscriminately to both imported and home-produced goods.

In the following case, the Court of Justice laid down an important principle on whether such national provisions could constitute MEQRs:

Rewe-Zentrale AG v *Bundesmonopolverwaltung für Branntwein* (Case 120/78)

The applicant wished to import the liqueur 'Cassis de Dijon' into Germany from France; for this reason the case is usually referred to as 'the **Cassis** Case'. The relevant German authorities refused to allow the importation because the French liqueur was not of sufficient alcoholic strength to be marketed in Germany. Under German law liqueurs had to have an alcoholic strength of 25 per cent, whereas that of the French liqueur was between 15 per cent and 20 per cent. The importer challenged the decision on the basis that the rule infringed the former Art 30 (now Art 28). The case was referred to the Court of Justice under the former Art 177 EC Treaty (now Art 234). The Court accepted that, in the absence of any common rules in the Community relating to the production and marketing of alcohol, it was up to Member States to regulate these activities in their own territories. However, the Court held as follows:

> 14. ... It ... appears that the unilateral requirement imposed by the rules of a Member State of a minimum alcohol content for the purposes of the sale of alcoholic beverages constitutes an obstacle to trade which is incompatible with the provisions of Article 30 [now Art 28] of the Treaty.
>
> **There is therefore no valid reason why, provided that they have been lawfully produced and marketed in one of the Member States, alcoholic beverages should not be introduced into any other Member State**; the sale of such products may not be subject to a legal prohibition on the marketing of beverages with an alcohol content lower than the limits set by national rules. [emphasis added]

The above case reaffirms para 5 of the Court's judgment in **Dassonville** (see above]. It is made clear that the former Art 30 EC Treaty (now Art 28) can apply to indistinctly applicable rules which apply equally to domestic and imported goods, but which nevertheless inhibit trade between Member States because the rules applied are different from those which apply in the product's country of origin. This imposes a dual burden on the foreign producer. The domestic producer will already comply with domestic laws and will therefore not be further disadvantaged, whereas the foreign producer will have to change the method of production to comply with the laws of the importing Member State, thus inhibiting intra-Community trade. In this case the German producers of Cassis would already be complying with the German law requiring the alcoholic content to be at least 25 per cent. In contrast, the French producers would have had to change their manufacturing processes in order to satisfy this requirement, thus increasing their costs and decreasing any competitive (e.g. financial) advantage French Cassis might otherwise have had over German liqueurs. An additional point to be aware of is that other Member States could have different regulations: e.g. Denmark could have had a law requiring liqueurs to have a maximum alcoholic content of 10 per cent. France in this case would have had to employ different manufacturing processes for the respective Member States.

The rule of mutual recognition

The first **Cassis** principle, referred to as 'the rule of mutual recognition', is set out by the Court of Justice at para 14: once goods have been lawfully marketed in one Member State, they should be free to be marketed in any other Member State without restriction. Derogations from this general principle are considered below.

Examples of indistinctly applicable measures

Following **Cassis**, there have been a number of cases applying the rule of mutual recognition to a wide variety of different measures. Some examples follow:

Origin-marking

Commission v UK (Case 207/83)

UK legislation required that certain goods which were sold in retail markets had to be marked with their country of origin. The Commission took infraction proceedings against the UK under the former Art 169 EC Treaty (now Art 226), claiming this requirement was in breach of the former Art 30 EC Treaty (now Art 28) in that it constituted an MEQR. French manufacturers had complained that goods for the UK market had to be specially origin-marked, which increased production costs. The Commission also argued that such origin-marking encouraged consumers to exercise their prejudices in favour of national products and was likely to reduce the sale of Community-produced goods. The UK government defended the origin-marking order on the grounds that the origin details gave important information to the consumer about the nature and quality of the product, and that the requirement of origin-marking was non-discriminatory because it applied to both domestic and imported products. Considering the second of the UK's arguments (i.e. that the measure applied equally to imported and national products), the Court of Justice stated as follows:

17.   … it has to be recognised that **the purpose of indications of origin or origin-marking is to enable consumers to distinguish between domestic and imported products and this enables them to assert any prejudices which they may have against foreign products.** As the Court has had occasion to emphasise in various contexts, the Treaty, by establishing a common market and progressively approximating the economic policies of the Member States, seeks to unite national markets in a single market, the origin-marking requirement not only makes the marketing in a Member State of goods produced in other Member States in the sectors in question more difficult; it also has the effect of slowing down economic interpenetration in the Community by handicapping the sale of goods produced as a result of a division of labour between Member States.

18.   It follows from those considerations that the UK provisions in question are liable to have the effect of increasing the production costs of imported goods and making it more difficult to sell them on the UK market. [emphasis added]

In the above case, the Court of Justice was not persuaded that origin-marking was a necessary consumer protection measure. It agreed with the Commission that it encouraged the exercise of national prejudices and therefore, applying the **Dassonville** formula, the measure was capable of affecting intra-Community trade. Any distinctive national quality of the goods could be highlighted by individual retailers, but should not be the subject of national legislation.

National quality standard

Commission v Ireland (Case 45/87)

The Commission brought an action under the former Art 169 EC Treaty (now Art 226) against the Irish government for allowing a specification relating to a water supply contract in Dundalk which, it alleged, breached the former Art 30 (now Art 28). The specification stipulated that pipes had to be certified as complying with Irish Standard 188. Only one manufacturer, located in Ireland, made pipes which complied with this standard. This was an indistinctly applicable measure because the requirement applied to all pipes whether Irish or imported. One of the bids was based on the use of pipes not conforming to this standard, although it did comply with international standards. Dundalk Council refused to consider the bid for that reason. The question before the Court of Justice was whether this specification constituted a barrier to the importation of pipes for this contract. The Court held as follows:

19.   … it must first be pointed out that the inclusion of such a clause (as 4.29) in an invitation to tender may cause economic operators who produce or utilise pipes equivalent to pipes certified with Irish standards to refrain from tendering.

20. It further appears from the documents in the case that only one undertaking has been certified by the IRIS to IS 188:1975 to apply the Irish Standard Mark to pipes of the type required for the purposes of the public works contract at issue. That undertaking is located in Ireland. Consequently, the inclusion of Clause 4.29 had the effect of restricting the supply of the pipes needed for the Dundalk scheme to Irish manufacturers alone.

21. The Irish Government maintains that it is necessary to specify the standards to which materials must be manufactured, particularly in a case such as this where the pipes utilised must suit the existing network. Compliance with another standard, even an international standard such as ISO 160:1980, would not suffice to eliminate technical difficulties.

22. That technical argument cannot be accepted. The Commission's complaint does not relate to compliance with technical requirements but the refusal of the Irish authorities to verify whether those requirements are satisfied where the manufacturer of the materials has not been certified by the IRIS to IS 188. By incorporating in the notice in question the words 'or equivalent' after the reference to the Irish standard, as provided for by Directive 71/305 where it is applicable, the Irish authorities could have verified compliance with the technical conditions without from the outset restricting the contract to tenderers proposing to utilise Irish materials.

In the above case, the Court of Justice held that while it was perfectly reasonable to specify the quality of pipes to be used for the transmission of drinking water, the attainment of that object could as well have been achieved by allowing the use of pipes which had been produced abroad to a standard which was *equivalent* to the Irish standard.

In the above cases, the Court of Justice considers the *effect* of the national practice, rather than its legal form. This is quite clear in the following category:

Administrative practices

Commission v France (Case 21/84)

The Commission alleged that France had violated Art 30 EC Treaty (now Art 28) by delaying a request to approve postal franking machines from other Member States. This was an indistinctly applicable measure because approval was required for both the domestic and imported machines. However, administrative practices resulted in the approval of foreign machines being delayed. A UK manufacturer had failed to secure the approval of the French authorities, despite repeated applications, and even after France had repealed an earlier law which explicitly stated a preference for domestic machines. The Court of Justice held as follows:

11. The fact that a law or regulation such as that requiring prior approval for the marketing of postal franking machines conforms in formal terms to Article 30 [now Art 28] of the EEC Treaty is not sufficient to discharge a Member State of its obligation under that provision. Under the cloak of a general provision permitting the approval of machines imported from other Member States, the administration might very well adopt a systematically unfavourable attitude towards imported machines, either by allowing considerable delay in replying to applications for approval or in carrying out the examination procedure, or by refusing approval on the grounds of various alleged technical faults for which no detailed explanations are given or which prove to be inaccurate.

12. The prohibition on measures having an effect equivalent to quantitative restrictions would lose much of its useful effect if it did not cover protectionist or discriminatory practices of that type.

13. It must however be noted that for an administrative practice to constitute a measure prohibited under Article 30 [now Art 28] that practice must show a certain degree of consistency and generality. That generality must be assessed differently according to whether the market concerned is one on which there are numerous traders or whether it is a market, such as that in postal

franking machines, on which only a few undertakings are active. In the latter case, a national administration's treatment of a single undertaking may constitute a measure incompatible with Article 30 [now Art 28].

14. In the light of those principles it is clear from the facts of the case that the conduct of the French postal administration constitutes an impediment to imports contrary to Article 30 [now Art 28] of the EEC Treaty.

15. It must therefore be concluded that by refusing without proper justification to approve postal franking machines from another Member State, the French Republic has failed to fulfil its obligations under Article 30 [now Art 28] of the EEC Treaty.

In the above case, the Court of Justice held that a law which on the face of it does not breach Art 28, could result in a breach if the method of its application results in imported goods being treated more harshly.

Price-fixing regulations

Article 28 can also prohibit price-fixing regulations which apply to both imported and domestic goods, as was declared by the Court of Justice in the following case:

Openbaar Ministerie v *Van Tiggele* (Case 82/77)

Dutch legislation provided for minimum selling prices for certain spirits. A seller sold spirits for less than this minimum and was prosecuted. In his defence he argued that the legislation breached the former Art 30 EC Treaty (now Art 28) and should therefore be inapplicable. The question referred to the Court of Justice was whether this minimum price constituted an MEQR within the former Art 30 (now Art 28). The Court of Justice held as follows:

12. For the purposes of this prohibition it is sufficient that the measures in question are likely to hinder, directly or indirectly, actually or potentially, imports between Member States.

13. Whilst national price-control rules applicable without distinction to domestic products and imported products cannot in general produce such an effect they may do so in certain specific cases.

14. Thus imports may be impeded in particular when a national authority fixes prices or profit margins at such a level that imported products are placed at a disadvantage in relation to identical domestic products either because they cannot profitably be marketed in the conditions laid down or because the competitive advantage conferred by lower cost prices is cancelled out.

In the above case, the Court of Justice held that on the facts the Dutch law did contravene the former Art 30 (now Art 28). As a matter of Community law, price-fixing schemes must give the importer the opportunity to benefit from any competitive advantage the imported goods may possess (e.g. by the setting of a lower price than the competing domestic product), or to take account of any disadvantage they may possess (e.g. by setting a higher price). Schemes which exclude the importer's ability to achieve such flexibility are capable of violating Art 28 (although see the **Keck** case below).

Differentiation between dual-burden and equal-burden rules

Cassis, and many cases after it, concerned dual-burden rules. This would be the case where, for example, one Member State imposed certain rules relating to the manufacture of goods (e.g. margarine must be packaged in cube-shaped containers) and these rules applied equally to domestic and imported goods, even though the exporting producer would have had to comply with the relevant trade rules of his own Member State. This is said to put a dual burden on the exporting producer. **Cassis** would render such rules incompatible with Art 28 EC Treaty unless they could be saved by one of the mandatory requirements (or Art 30 EC Treaty, see below).

Equal-burden rules, by contrast, again apply to all goods (domestic and imported); they regulate trade in some manner, but do not have a protectionist effect. Even though they may have an impact on the overall volume of trade, the impact is equal as between the sale of domestic products and imported products.

Whereas dual-burden rules have been held to fall within Art 28, there was some confusion as to whether equal-burden rules should also fall within Art 28, subject to the *rule of reason* defence (and Art 30, see below).

Equal-burden rules: outside Art 28 EC Treaty

In a number of cases the Court of Justice held that rules which did not relate to the *characteristics* of the product and did not impose a dual burden on the importer, but only concerned the *conditions* under which the product was to be sold, were outside the remit of Art 28 (see, e.g., **Oebel** (Case 155/80), which concerned a national rule prohibiting the delivery of bakery products to consumers and retailers during the night, and **Quietlynn Ltd** *v* **Southend-on-Sea Borough Council** (Case C–23/89), which concerned a UK law restricting the sale of lawful sex products to shops that had been licensed by the local authority).

Equal-burden rules: within Art 28 EC Treaty

In other cases, however, the Court of Justice held that such rules would fall within Art 28. The Court would then seek to exclude them from the effect of Art 28 by applying the *rule of reason* or Art 30 defences (see below). In **Cinéthèque SA** *v* **Fédération Nationale des Cinémas Français** (Cases 60 & 61/84), French legislation prohibited the selling or hiring of film videos during the first year of the film receiving its performance certificate. The objective was to encourage people to go and watch the film at the cinema. The effect was that both domestic and imported films could not be sold during that first year. A distributor of videos relied on the former Art 30 (now Art 28) before French courts to challenge the law as a trade barrier. The Court of Justice held that although 'its effect is not to favour national production as against the production of other Member States . . . the application of such a system may create barriers to intra-Community trade in video-cassettes'. In those circumstances it held that there was a *prima facie* breach of the former Art 30 (now Art 28).

The difficult question of whether equal-burden cases fell within the former Art 30 (now Art 28) was the issue in a series of UK **Sunday Trading** cases which came before the Court of Justice. In **Torfaen Borough Council** *v* **B&Q plc** (Case 145/88), B&Q was prosecuted for violation of Sunday trading laws which prohibited retail shops from selling goods on Sundays, subject to certain exceptions. B&Q claimed that these laws constituted an MEQR. The effect of the laws was to reduce turnover, but imported goods were in the same position as domestic goods; the reduction in turnover affected all goods equally. Nevertheless, the Court of Justice held that this constituted a *prima facie* breach of Art 28.

The *Keck* judgment

This confused state of affairs was totally unhelpful. The Court of Justice was inconsistent in its approach in dealing with equal-burden rules. In the following case, the Court recognised that it was time to clear up some of the confusion and to adopt a *general rule* which would apply in these circumstances:

Criminal Proceedings against Keck and Mithouard (Cases C-267 and 268/91)

The defendants (Keck and Mithouard) were prosecuted in a French court for having resold goods at a loss, a practice which was forbidden under French law. In their defence they pleaded, *inter alia*, that this rule constituted an MEQR and was unlawful under the former Art 30 (now Art 28). The case was referred to the Court of Justice under the former Art 177 EC Treaty (now Art 234). The Court of Justice held as follows:

11. By virtue of Article 30 [now Art 28], quantitative restrictions on imports and all measures having equivalent effect are prohibited between Member States. The Court has consistently held that any measure which is capable of directly or indirectly, actually or potentially, hindering intra-Community trade constitutes a measure having equivalent effect to a quantitative restriction.

12. It is not the purpose of national legislation imposing a general prohibition on resales at a loss to regulate trade in goods between Member States.

13. Such legislation may, admittedly, restrict the volume of sales, and hence the volume of sales of products from other Member States, in so far as it deprives traders of a method of sales promotion. But the question remains whether such a possibility is sufficient to characterise the legislation in question as a measure having equivalent effect to a quantitative restriction on imports.

14. In view of the increasing tendency of traders to invoke Article 30 [now Art 28] of the Treaty as a means of challenging any rules whose effect is to limit commercial freedom even where such rules are not aimed at products from other Member States, **the Court considers it necessary to re-examine and clarify its case law on this matter.**

15. In '**Cassis de Dijon**' . . . it was held that, in the absence of harmonisation of legislation, measures of equivalent effect prohibited by Article 30 [now Art 28] include obstacles to the free movement of goods where they are the consequence of applying rules that lay down requirements to be met by such goods (such as requirements as to designation, form, size, weight, composition, presentation, labelling, packaging) to goods from other Member States where they are lawfully manufactured and marketed, even if those rules apply without distinction to all products unless their application can be justified by a public-interest objective taking precedence over the free movement of goods.

16. **However, contrary to what has previously been decided, the application to products from other Member States of national provisions restricting or prohibiting certain selling arrangements is not such as to hinder directly or indirectly, actually or potentially, trade between Member States within the meaning of the *Dassonville* judgment . . . provided that those provisions apply to all affected traders operating within the national territory and provided that they affect in the same manner, in law and fact, the marketing of domestic products and of those from other Member States.**

17. Where those conditions are fulfilled, the application of such rules to the sale of products from another Member State is not by nature such as to prevent their access to the market or to impede access any more than it impedes the access of domestic products. Such rules therefore fall outside the scope of Article 30 [now Art 28] of the Treaty.

18. Accordingly, the reply to be given to the national court is that Article 30 [now Art 28] of the EEC Treaty is to be interpreted as not applying to legislation of a Member State imposing a general prohibition on resale at a loss. [emphasis added]

In the above case, the Court of Justice established a general rule to be applied in all cases involving equal-burden rules. The Court distinguished between *rules which relate to the goods themselves* in terms of packaging, composition, size, etc. (para 15) which clearly fall within the **Cassis** doctrine, and *rules relating to selling arrangements* (para 16) which do not fall within Art 28 *provided* the conditions set out in the second part of para 16 are met.

The reason why rules which fall within para 16 are outside Art 28 is that their *purpose* is not to regulate trade as such (para 12) and because their *effect and nature* do not prevent access to the market, or at least they do not make it any more difficult for importers to penetrate the market than national traders (para 17). They impose an equal burden on both domestic producers and importers. However, if the conditions set out in para 16 are not met, then the rule would fall within Art 28. The para 16 conditions are:

- the provisions of the rule apply to all traders operating within the national territory; and
- they affect in the same manner, in law and in fact, the marketing of domestic goods and imports.

Provided these two conditions are met, then a rule which relates to selling arrangements will not come within the scope of Art 28.

Commenting on the Court's judgment in **Keck**, Advocate-General Jacobs has observed:

> It seems to me . . . that the **Dassonville** formula was indeed too broad – and illustrates the dangers in taking as a starting point a very broad proposition which subsequently has to be whittled down – but that the main body of the Court's case law on Art 30 [Art 28] was wholly satisfactory and that to introduce at this stage a notion of discrimination may raise more problems than it solves. (*The European Advocate* (1994/1995) 2, 4)

Post-*Keck* case law

'Selling arrangements' will not breach Art 28 at all, provided they are non-discriminatory. This means that they must affect, in the same way, in law and in fact, domestic goods and goods from other Member States. If they do not affect domestically produced and imported goods in the same way and are liable substantially to restrict access to the national market, then they will breach Art 28. 'Selling arrangements' can cover a multiplicity of activities. The expression includes price restrictions, as in **Keck** itself, or any other national rules which govern the way products or services are sold or advertised.

The rule in **Keck** has been applied to a number of cases relating to the marketing of goods:

Criminal Proceedings against Tankstationt' Heukske vof v *JBE Boermans* (Cases C-401 and 402/92)

National rules provided for the compulsory closure of petrol stations. The Court of Justice applied the **Keck** general rule and held that the rules did not fall within the former Art 30 (now Art 28) because they related to selling arrangements which applied equally to all traders without distinguishing between origin. It was an equal-burden rule, affecting domestic traders and importers equally. The Court stated as follows:

> Those conditions [in **Keck**] are fulfilled [in this case]. The rules in question relate to the times and places at which the goods in question may be sold to consumers. However, they apply to all relevant traders without distinguishing between the origin of the products in question and do not affect the marketing of products from other Member States in a manner different from that in which they affect domestic products.

In **Hunermund** (Case C–292/92) there was a prohibition by the German pharmacists' association, preventing its members from advertising popular medicines outside their premises. The Court of Justice ruled that this was a 'selling arrangement' within the meaning of **Keck**, and consequently Art 28 did not apply. Two years later, in **Leclerc-Siplec** (Case C–412/93), the Court of Justice considered a French law which prevented Leclerc-Siplec from advertising unleaded petrol imported by them and sold in their supermarkets. The law applied to all advertisers, irrespective of the source of their product. The Court acknowledged that 'the prohibition may . . . restrict the volume of sales, and hence of products from other Member States, in so far as it deprives distributors of a particular form of advertising for their goods'. It held that this was a 'selling arrangement' which affected the sale of all such goods equally, and Art 28 did not therefore apply.

In **Morellato** (Case C–416/00), Italian legislation prohibited the sale of bread which had been prepared by completing the baking of partly baked bread, if that bread had not been packaged by the retailer prior to its sale. In considering the question, the Court of Justice first had to determine whether such requirements constituted 'selling arrangements' which are not likely to hinder trade between Member States within the meaning of its judgment in **Keck**. The Court held that in this case the requirement for prior packaging laid down in the legislation at issue did not make it necessary to alter the product because it only related to the marketing of the bread which resulted from the final baking of pre-baked bread. The Court held that in principle such a requirement would fall outside the scope of Art 28 EC Treaty provided that it did not in reality constitute discrimination against imported products.

In the following two cases, the Court of Justice held that the measures in question imposed a dual burden on the manufacturer and were therefore, *prima facie*, in breach of Art 28 EC Treaty:

Mars (Case C–470/93)

The manufacturers challenged a national law in Germany which prohibited the selling of Mars bars marked '110 per cent' (as part of a Europe-wide selling campaign). The Court of Justice held that these requirements related to the presentation, labelling and packaging of the product lawfully manufactured and marketed in another Member State. The prohibition imposed a dual burden on the manufacturer and was therefore, *prima facie*, in breach of what is now Art 28 EC Treaty.

Vereinigte Familiapresse (Case C–368/95)

A German newspaper publisher was selling newspapers in the German and Austrian markets in which readers were offered the opportunity to take part in games with prizes. This practice breached the Austrian Unfair Competition Act 1992. A competitor tried to stop the imported German papers and the case was referred to the Court of Justice. The Court rejected the Austrian argument that this was merely a 'selling arrangement', since it affected the content of the newspaper and its access to the Austrian market. Potentially, therefore, it breached Art 30 (now Art 28). The Court of Justice held as follows:

11.   The Court finds that, even though the relevant national legislation is directed against a method of sales promotion, in this case it bears on the actual content of the products, in so far as the competitions in question form an integral part of the magazine in which they appear. As a result, the national legislation in question as applied to the facts of the case is not concerned with a selling arrangement within the meaning of the judgment in **Keck** . . .

12. Moreover, since it requires traders established in other Member States to alter the contents of the periodical, the prohibition at issue impairs access of the products concerned to the market of the Member State of importation and consequently hinders free movement of goods. It therefore constitutes in principle a measure having equivalent effect within the meaning of Article 30 [now Art 28] of the Treaty.

As discussed above, in the **Keck** case one of the conditions which has to be satisfied in order to remove a rule relating to 'selling arrangements' from the scope of Art 28 EC Treaty is that the rule affects in the same manner, in law and in fact, the marketing of domestic goods and imports. This was considered by the Court of Justice in the following case:

Konsumentombudsmannen (KO) v Gourmet International Products AB (GIP) (Case C-405/98)

A Swedish law prohibited the advertising of alcoholic beverages in periodicals. It was argued that this breached Art 28 EC Treaty. The Court of Justice stated that, if national provisions restricting or prohibiting certain selling arrangements are to avoid being caught by Art 28 EC Treaty, they must not be of such a kind as to prevent access to the market by products from another Member State or to impede access any more than they impede the access of domestic products. The Court held that, in the case of products like alcoholic beverages, the consumption of which is linked to traditional social practices and to local habits and customs, a prohibition of all advertising directed at consumers in the form of advertisements in the press is liable to impede access to the market by products from other Member States more than it impedes access by domestic products. Hence the Court held that the prohibition came within the scope of Art 28 EC Treaty, despite being concerned with selling arrangements. This was because the **Keck** condition that 'the rule affected in the same manner, in law and in fact, the marketing of domestic goods and imports' was not satisfied.

This condition was also the issue in the following case:

Deutscher Apothekerverband (C-322/01)

Germany prohibited the import and retail sale of medicinal products by mail order or over the Internet. As regards medicinal products which had received authorisation under the provisions of Directive 65/65, the Court of Justice considered the relevance of the actual or potential effect of the German restriction on intra-Community trade to assess whether it was consistent with those provisions. The Court held that the requirement that it must affect in the same manner, in law and in fact, the marketing of both domestic products and those from other Member States, was not fulfilled here. The prohibition at issue was more of an obstacle to pharmacies outside Germany than to those within it. Although there was little doubt that, as a result of the prohibition, pharmacies in Germany did not use the extra or alternative method of gaining access to the German market consisting of end consumers of medicinal products, they were still able to sell the products in their dispensaries. However, for pharmacies not established in Germany, mail order and the Internet would provide a more significant way to gain direct access to the German market. The prohibition would therefore have a greater impact on pharmacies established outside German territory and could impede access to the market for products from other Member States more than it impedes access for domestic products. The Court of Justice therefore held that the prohibition was a measure having an effect equivalent to a quantitative restriction, in breach of Art 28 EC Treaty.

Article 29 EC Treaty: exports

Most of the cases considered so far have involved national restrictions, or measures equivalent to restrictions, on *imports*. As discussed above, Art 29 EC Treaty (previously Art 34) applies in much the same way as Art 28, in that it prohibits quantitative restrictions and MEQRs, but in relation to *exports* rather than *imports*. The principles applicable to restrictions on exports are, broadly, the same. The more limited case law on measures affecting exports matches that for imports. **Procureur de la République *v* Bouhelier** (Case 53/76) provides an example of a case involving the application of Art 29. In this case, a quality control charge was only imposed on exports and not on goods sold on the domestic market. The Court of Justice held that this was a measure equivalent to a quantitative restriction on exports. However, the Court of Justice appears to look for some element of discrimination, either formal or material, in the case of exports. It emphasised that aspect in the following case:

Groenveld (Case 15/79)

The Court of Justice held as follows:

> [Article 29(1)] concerns national measures which have as their specific object or effect the restrictions of patterns of exports and thereby the establishment of a difference in treatment between the domestic trade of a Member State and its export trade in such a way as to provide a particular advantage for national production of the domestic market of the state in question at the expense of the production or of the trade of other Member States. This is not so in the case of a prohibition like that in question which is applied objectively to the production of goods of a certain kind without drawing a distinction depending on whether such goods are intended for the national market or for export. (para 7)

Whether or not there is discrimination is a matter of both national law and practice. Clearly, therefore, a national law requiring producers to deliver poultry offal to their local authority has been held, necessarily, to involve a ban on exports (**Nertsvoederfabriek Nederland** (Case 118/86)). However, legislation applied to all producers of cheese in The Netherlands, affecting its content and quality, which put Dutch producers at a disadvantage in comparison to foreign producers who did not have to produce their cheese to the same standards, was held by the Court of Justice not to be a measure equivalent to a quantitative restriction on exports, although it made exporting more difficult for Dutch producers (**Jongeneel Kaas BV *v* Netherlands** (Case 237/82)). In this case the Court demonstrated its willingness to tolerate measures which, although not actually discriminating against exports, had an adverse effect on domestic producers, which it would not have been prepared to tolerate in relation to imports.

Article 30 EC Treaty: defences to distinctly and indistinctly applicable measures

Article 30 EC Treaty (formerly Art 36) permits Member States to derogate from their obligation to ensure the free movement of goods. It provides that:

> The provisions of Articles 28 and 29 shall not preclude prohibitions or restrictions on imports, exports or goods in transit justified on grounds of public morality, public policy or public security; the protection of health and life of humans, animals and plants; the protection of national treasures possessing artistic, historic or archaeological value; or the protection of industrial and commercial property. Such prohibitions or restrictions shall not, however, constitute a means of arbitrary discrimination or a disguised restriction on trade between Member States.

These derogations comprise an *exhaustive* list and are interpreted strictly by the Court of Justice. Article 30 is most often pleaded by Member States in defence of distinctly applicable measures (**Commission** *v* **Ireland** (Case 113/80)). Article 30 is, however, equally applicable to indistinctly applicable measures, as decided by the Court of Justice in the following case:

Wurmser (Case 25/88)

The Court of Justice held as follows:

> A measure which, in regard both to domestic products and imported products, imposes an obligation to verify conformity [with the rules in force on that market] on the person who first places the product on the market is, in principle, applicable without distinction to both categories of products. It may, therefore, be justified under Article 36 [now Art 30] and under Article 30 [now Art 28] as interpreted by the Court [in the **Cassis** case].

Since the exceptions contained in Art 30 are treated as exhaustive, national measures not falling clearly within its terms are rejected by the Court.

The Art 30 exceptions can be advanced to justify national measures only in the absence of any relevant Community-wide provisions aimed at harmonising the legislation protecting the interest which the national measure seeks to protect:

Lucien Ortscheit GmbH v *Eurim-Pharm GmbH* (Case C-320/93)

German legislation prohibited the advertising of foreign drugs which had not been authorised for use in the German market, but which could, under certain conditions, be imported into Germany. The Court of Justice was in no doubt that the measure was distinctly applicable and equivalent to a quantitative restriction. It noted, however, that the health and life of humans ranks foremost among the interests protected by Art 30, and at the present stage of harmonisation there was no procedure for Community authorisation or mutual recognition of national authorisations. In those circumstances, it was for Member States, within the limits imposed by the Treaty, to decide what degree of protection they intend to ensure. In the circumstances, the Court was satisfied that the German measures were justified under Art 30.

However, if there is relevant Community legislation, there will be no scope for national measures that are incompatible with it, and Art 30 cannot be relied upon to justify the measure. The Court reiterated its position in the following case:

R v Ministry of Agriculture, Fisheries and Food, ex parte Compassion in World Farming Ltd (Case C-1/96)

The applicants had attempted to argue that the Minister was entitled to ignore the effect of a new Council directive on the treatment of farm animals in transit, and stop the export of live animals in reliance on Art 36 (now Art 30), since the directive did not conform to an international convention on the humane treatment of animals. The Court of Justice rejected this argument, insisting that Art 36 (now Art 30) could not be used to justify a national prohibition, because the directive was intended to deal exhaustively with the situation.

Similarly in the following case:

Société Agricole de la Crespelle (Case C-323/93)

French rules conferred a monopoly on a number of regional bovine insemination centres and, effectively, created a restrictive regime for the importation of bovine semen from other Member States. The Court of Justice was satisfied that the restrictive regime amounted to an MEQR, but could it be justified under the former Art 36 (now Art 30)? The Court decided that it could not be:

> The Court has consistently held that where, in application of Article 100 [now Art 94] of the EEC Treaty, Community Directives provide for the harmonisation of the measures necessary to ensure, *inter alia*, the protection of animal and human health and established Community procedures to check that they were observed, invoking Article 36 [now Art 30] is no longer justified and the appropriate checks have to be carried out and protective measures adopted within the framework of the directive.

The above rule applies where the Community has introduced a consistent and exhaustive set of measures to cover the type of importation in question (**Commission *v* Italy (Re Authorisation for Importation of Plants)** (Case C–296/92)). However, it does not preclude restrictions on imports where these are specifically authorised by the directive (**The State *v* Vitaret and Chambron** [1995] 1 CMLR 185 (this case was decided by the French Cour de Cassation, *not* the Court of Justice)).

Where Art 30 can be advanced as a justification for national measures, it is for the national government relying on it to provide evidence to support the grounds justifying its actions. This principle of casting the evidential burden upon the Member State taking the action applies not only in relation to the national measure itself, but also in relation to individual cases in which that national measure is applied. This is illustrated in the following case:

Officier van Justitie v Sandoz BV (Case 174/82)

Sandoz wished to sell confectionery in The Netherlands to which vitamin supplements had been added. The confectionery was freely sold in Belgium and Germany. The Dutch authorities refused permission for it to be sold, on the grounds that the vitamins were a risk to health. The case was referred to the Court of Justice under Art 177 EC Treaty (now Art 234).

The Court was in no doubt that the measure breached the former Art 30 (now Art 28), but in the absence of Community harmonising measures on the kinds of additives which were acceptable, it was permissible under the former Art 36 (now Art 30) for the Member State to determine the kind and extent of protection to be given. However, the Court of Justice held that the state had first to establish the existence of a risk:

> In as much as the question arises as to where the onus of proof lies when there is a request for autho-risation [to market a foodstuff] ... it must be remembered that Article 36 [now Art 30] of the Treaty creates an exception, which must be strictly interpreted, to the rule of free movement of goods within the Community which is one of the fundamental principles of the Common Market. **It is therefore for the national authorities who rely on that provision in order to adopt a measure restricting intra-Community trade to check in each instance that the measure contemplated satisfies the criteria of that provision ... Community law does not permit national rules which subject authorisation to market to proof by the importer that the product in question is not harmful to health.** (paras 22, 24) [emphasis added]

Where action may be justified under Art 30, measures taken by Member States will still have to meet two fundamental Community criteria: (i) there must be no arbitrary dis-crimination between imported and domestic products; and (ii) any national measures must be proportionate to any risk and must not restrict trade any more than is necessary to protect the legitimate public interests recognised by Art 30. The operation of these principles is discussed further below in the context of case law of the Court of Justice relating to the specific Art 30 exceptions.

Public morality

The concept of public morality will vary widely from state to state and is not elaborated in Art 30 or in any secondary legislation. The Court has, for example, refused to rule that termination of pregnancy is intrinsically immoral and cannot, therefore, constitute a service under Art 49 EC Treaty, because it is, in fact, lawfully carried out in several Member States (**Society for the Protection of the Unborn Child** *v* **Grogan** (Case C–159/90)). In **HM Customs and Excise Commissioners** *v* **Schindler and Others** (Case C–275/92) the Court of Justice observed, with regard to gambling, that 'Even if the morality of lotteries is at least questionable, it is not for the Court to substitute its assess-ment for that of the legislature where that activity is practised legally' (para 32). The Court may, however, have to assess whether or not national rules are applied proportion-ately and without discrimination (see Chapter 13). The issue first came before the Court of Justice in relation to Art 30 in a former Art 177 EC Treaty (now Art 234) reference from the UK's House of Lords:

R v *Henn and Darby* (Case 34/79)

The defendants were convicted of being 'knowingly concerned in the fraudulent evasion of the prohibition of the importation of indecent or obscene articles' contrary to s 42, Customs Consolidation Act 1876 and s 304, Customs and Excise Act 1952. The articles involved in the charges formed part of a consignment of several boxes of obscene films and magazines which had been brought into the UK in 1975 on a lorry travelling on a ferry from Rotterdam (Holland). The six films and magazines referred to in the charges were all of Danish origin.

The House of Lords referred a number of questions to the Court of Justice. The first question related to whether a law of a Member State prohibiting the importation of pornographic articles is a quantitative restriction. The Court was in no doubt that it was, since a prohibition on imports is 'the most extreme form of restriction' (para 12). However, the Court of Justice emphasised that Member States were free to take such action in appropriate circumstances:

> In principle, it is for each Member State to determine in accordance with its own scale of values and in the form selected by it the requirements of public morality in its territory. In any event, it cannot be disputed that the statutory provisions applied by the UK in regard to the importation of articles having an indecent or obscene character come within the powers reserved to the Member States by the first sentence of Article 36 [now Art 30].

The House of Lords was also concerned to know whether the fact that the prohibition imposed on the importation of pornography was different in scope from that imposed by the criminal law on the possession and publication of such material in the UK constituted a means of arbitrary discrimination or a disguised restriction on trade between Member States. In particular, there were differences in treatment of the possession and publication of pornography in different parts of the UK, and there were circumstances in which, under the Obscene Publications Act 1959, possession and publication may not be a criminal offence. The defences available in those circumstances had no application to the Customs and Excise Acts under which the defendants were prosecuted. The Court of Justice was satisfied that the differences, such as they were, were not significant:

> Whatever may be the differences between the laws on this subject in force in the different constituent parts of the UK, and notwithstanding the fact that they contain certain exceptions of limited scope, these laws, taken as a whole, have as their purpose the prohibition, or at least the restraining, of the manufacture and marketing of publications or articles of an indecent or obscene character. **In these circumstances it is permissible to conclude, on a comprehensive view, that there is no lawful trade in such goods in the UK**. A prohibition on imports which may in certain respects be more strict than some of the laws applied within the UK cannot, therefore, be regarded as amounting to a measure designed to give indirect protection to some national product or aimed at creating arbitrary discrimination. (para 21) [emphasis added]

In the above case, the Court of Justice held that although there were 'certain exceptions' with regard to the trade of pornographic material in the UK, these exceptions were 'of limited scope'. The Court therefore concluded that 'there is no lawful trade in such goods in the UK'. This is similar to the application of the *de minimus* rule in English law, the Court in this case deciding that because the degree of regulation within the UK was so high, the incidental trade of pornographic goods within the UK was on such a small scale that it could be ignored.

The following case is another example of goods being seized by HM Customs and Excise under s 42, Customs Consolidation Act 1976:

Conegate Ltd v HM Customs and Excise (Case 121/85)

The seized goods consisted of inflatable sex dolls and other erotic articles. The importers argued that the situation was different to that in **Henn and Darby** because sex dolls, although not permitted to be publicly displayed, could be lawfully sold throughout the UK. The Court of Justice agreed:

15. . . . Although Community law leaves the Member States free to make their own assessments of the indecent or obscene character of certain articles, it must be pointed out that the fact that the goods cause offence cannot be regarded as sufficiently serious to justify restrictions on the free movement of goods where the Member State concerned does not adopt, with respect to the same goods manufactured or marketed within its territory, penal measures or other serious or effective measures intended to prevent the distribution of such goods in its territory.

16. **It follows that a Member State may not rely on grounds of public morality in order to prohibit the importation of goods from other Member States when its legislation contains no prohibition on the manufacture or marketing of the same goods in its territory.** [emphasis added]

There is a striking similarity in the language used by the Court of Justice in the above case to that employed by it, with regard to the free movement of workers, in **Adoui and Cornuaille** v **Belgium** (Cases 115 and 116/81) (see Chapter 15). That case concerned the scope of the public policy exception in Art 39(3) EC Treaty. In **Adoui**, the Court of Justice held that a Member State could not take action under the public policy exception against an EU citizen unless it took some kind of 'repressive measures' against its own nationals for engaging in the same conduct on which the exclusion is based. A similar concept of equality of treatment underlies the requirement that the Member State excluding the goods on the ground of public morality must take 'penal measures or other serious or effective measures' in relation to the same kind of goods produced on its own territory.

Public policy and public security

Very few attempts have been made by national governments to justify restrictive measures on these grounds. Public policy was, however, successfully advanced by the UK government in the following case:

R v Thompson and Others (Case 7/78)

The defendants traded in coins, some of which were old UK gold coins that were no longer legal tender. They were convicted in England of being knowingly concerned in the fraudulent evasion of the prohibition on importation of gold coins into the UK. They argued, on appeal, that the provisions under which they had been convicted breached Arts 28–29 EC Treaty. The UK government defended the legislation on the ground that it was an important aspect of public policy to protect the national coinage and the Court of Justice agreed. It held that a ban on destroying old coinage with a view to it being melted down or destroyed in another Member State was justified on grounds of public policy under Art 30 because it was based on the need to protect the right to mint coinage which is traditionally regarded as involving the fundamental interests of the state.

In the following case, the French government argued before the Court of Justice that national rules fixing retail selling prices for fuel was justified on grounds of public order and public security which would arise in relation to retailers affected by unrestrained competition:

Cullet (Case 231/83)

The Advocate-General warned against the dangers of responding to public agitation:

> The acceptance of civil disturbance as a justification for encroachments upon the free movement of goods would ... have unacceptably drastic consequences. If road-blocks and other effective weapons of interest groups which feel threatened by the importation and sale at competitive prices of certain cheap products or services, or by immigrant workers or foreign businesses, were accepted as justification, the existence of the four freedoms of the Treaty could no longer be relied upon. Private interest groups would then, in the place of the Treaty and Community (and, within the limits laid down in the Treaty), determine the scope of those freedoms. In such cases, the concept of public policy requires, rather, effective action on the part of the authorities to deal with the disturbances. (para 5.3)

The Court of Justice was equally sceptical about the incapacity of the French authorities in the face of rampaging fuel retailers on the streets of France. It remarked:

> In that regard, it is sufficient to state that the French Government has not shown that it would be unable, using the means at its disposal, to deal with the consequences which an amendment of the rules in question ... would have upon public order and security. (paras 32, 33)

In response to attempts by animal welfare groups to block the export of live animals, the issue was seen by Simon Brown LJ, expressly adopting the Advocate-General's Opinion in **Cullet**, above, as a straightforward issue of the rule of law, both Community and national (**R** *v* **Coventry City Council, ex parte Phoenix Aviation** [1995] 3 All ER 37 at 67; and see also **R** *v* **Chief Constable of Sussex, ex parte International Trader's Ferry Ltd** [1995] 4 All ER 364). Although the English Court of Appeal did not uphold the decision of the Divisional Court, the Court of Justice has since reiterated that Member States cannot prevent the import or export of products because of the 'views or behaviour of a section of the Community'. A failure to act, where persistent obstruction by private groups has been drawn to the attention of the authorities, will represent a breach of the Member State's obligation to uphold the law of the Community and will not be justified by Art 30 (**Commission** *v* **France** (Case C–265/95)).

The Irish government had more success with the public security argument in the following case:

Campus Oil v *Ministry for Industry and Energy* (Case 72/83)

Irish legislation required importers of petroleum products to purchase up to 35 per cent of their requirements from Ireland's state-owned refinery at prices fixed by the Minister. There was no doubt that the requirement breached the former Art 30 (now Art 28). The government, however, argued that the measure was necessary on the ground that the importance of oil for the maintenance of the life of the country made it essential to maintain fuel capacity in Ireland. The system it had adopted was the only means by which a fuel reserve could be built up. The Court of Justice agreed that petroleum products were of fundamental importance to the country's existence, since they were needed for the country's institutions, vital services and the survival of its inhabitants. The Court therefore accepted the public security justification. It did, however, warn the Irish government that the purchasing obligation could be continued only if there was no less restrictive measure which was capable of achieving the same objective; nor should the quantities covered by the scheme exceed the minimum supply requirements without which the public security of the state would be affected. The scheme had, in other words, to be proportionate to the antici-pated risk.

Public health

The same principle of proportionality has been prominent in the many decisions of the Court of Justice in which Member States have sought to rely on the exception relating to the health of humans, animals and plants. In this context, Art 30 attempts to strike a balance between the interests involved in the creation of a single market and the protec-tion of health, and the Court is particularly careful to determine whether or not a measure is, in fact, a disguised form of protectionism. To be capable of justification as a health measure, it must form part of 'a seriously considered health policy'.

This was lacking in the following case:

Commission v UK (Re Imports of Poultry Meat) (Case 40/82)

In September 1981, the UK banned the import of turkeys from France (and some other Member States). There was evidence before the Court of Justice that, in the two years before the ban there had been a steep rise in turkey imports for the Christmas market from France and other Member States. This had been followed by a chorus of complaints about unfair competition from UK poultry producers. The imposition of a sudden ban on the import of French turkeys was, ostensibly, because of the risk of the outbreak of Newcastle Disease, a serious poultry infection. There had, however, been no recent outbreak in France, and the main object of the UK government's ostensible concern was imports of turkeys into France from Eastern European countries where there was a more serious risk. The Court was uncon-vinced by the UK justification:

> Certain established facts suggest that the real aim of the 1981 measure was to block, for commercial and economic reasons, imports of poultry products from other Member States, in particular from France. The UK government had been subject to pressure from UK poultry producers to block these imports. It hurriedly introduced its new policy with the result that French Christmas turkeys were excluded from the UK market for the 1981 season ... The deduction must be made that the 1981 measures did not form part of a seriously considered health policy.
>
> Taken together, these facts are sufficient to establish that the 1981 measures constitute a dis-guised restriction on imports of poultry products from other Member States, in particular from France, unless it can be shown that, for reasons of animal health, the only possibility open to the UK was to apply the strict measures which are at issue in this case and that, therefore, the methods pre-scribed by the 1981 measures ... were not more restrictive than was necessary for the protection of poultry flocks in Great Britain.

In the above case, the Court of Justice was satisfied that, on the evidence, there were much less restrictive methods available that were appropriate to the degree of risk. The UK had, therefore, breached Art 28. Subsequently, this successful action by the Commission led to a claim in the UK courts by an importer affected by the ban (**Bourgoin *v* Ministry of Agriculture, Fisheries and Food (MAFF)** [1986] QB 716; see Chapter 10).

Many of the cases in which the health exception is raised turn on whether there is, in fact, any risk at all. The perception of risk may, quite genuinely, be different in different

Member States. The Court of Justice will have to assess on the best available scientific evidence, first, whether there is a risk to health and, second, if there is, whether the Member State taking the restrictive measures has responded appropriately. In **Commission v France** (Case 216/84), for example, French legislation prohibited the marketing of milk substitutes. The French government attempted to justify the prohibition on the ground, first, that milk substitutes had a lower nutritional value and, second, that they were harmful to some people. The Court of Justice rejected both arguments. The fact that milk substitutes had a lower nutritional value than milk products hardly constituted a health risk when consumers had so many other food products to choose from. Milk products themselves could pose a risk to some individuals with certain allergies or suffering from certain diseases. Labelling would provide consumers with the necessary information to enable them to make a properly informed choice.

Milk also figured in **Commission v UK (Re UHT Milk)** (Case 124/81). In this case, the Commission brought Art 226 EC Treaty proceedings against the UK for imposing a requirement that UHT milk should be marketed only by approved dairies or distributors. The government argued that this was necessary to ensure that milk was free from bacterial or viral infections. The effect of the restriction was that all imported milk had to be repackaged and re-treated. The Court of Justice rejected these measures as inappropriate and unnecessary. There was evidence that milk in all Member States was of similar quality and subject to equivalent controls. The restriction was, therefore, unjustified. The Court of Justice has also held that German legislation, which prohibited the import from other Member States of meat products manufactured from meat not coming from the country of manufacture of the finished product, could not be justified on health grounds since there was no reason to believe that the risk of contamination increased simply because the fresh meat crossed a Community frontier (**Commission v Germany** (Case 153/78)).

Although the Court of Justice has held that the fact that testing has occurred in the country of origin should give rise to a presumption that the imported goods are safe to use, this is not the universal rule (**De Peijper** (Case 104/75); **Frans-Nederlandse** (Case 272/80)). In particular, differences in approach to food additives or medical products may justify additional testing by the importing Member State before authorisation to market the goods is given, as illustrated in the following case:

Officier van Justitie v Sandoz BV (Case 174/82)

There was uncertainty about the point at which a large intake of vitamin additives in food could become harmful. The Court of Justice held that the importing Member State was entitled to carry out tests on the food before it was put on the market:

> Community law permits national rules prohibiting without prior authorisation the marketing of foodstuffs lawfully marketed in another Member State to which vitamins have been added, provided that the marketing is authorised when the addition of vitamins meets a real need, especially a technical or nutritional one. (para 20)

The position is similar for medical products. The Court of Justice has held that Member States are entitled, at the present stage of harmonisation and in the absence of a procedure for Community authorisation or mutual recognition of national authorisation, to exclude from other Member States medical products which have not been authorised by the competent national authorities (**Lucien Ortscheit GmbH v Eurim-Pharm GmbH**

(Case C–320/93)). See also the cases below, discussed under the 'Public health' subsection of 'The mandatory requirement defence: the rule of reason'.

Protection of industrial and commercial property

Industrial and commercial property rights are valuable rights relating to the protection and distribution of goods and services. Such rights are protected by patents, trade marks, copyrights and similar devices. Each Member State has devised its own system for protecting the investment, creativity and innovation which has gone into a new product or system. The period of protection may vary widely between Member States and between different kinds of industrial property rights. In the UK, for example, the exclusive rights enjoyed under a patent endure for 20 years, indefinitely for trade marks, and the author's lifetime plus 70 years for copyright. Since each form of industrial property is defined under national law, it would seem *prima facie* not to be a matter within Community competence and, indeed, Art 295 EC Treaty appears to emphasise the exclusive competence of each Member State in this matter:

> This Treaty shall in no way prejudice the rules in Member States governing the system of property ownership.

However, it is clear that a restrictive approach taken by the owners of industrial property rights could have a very significant effect on the free movement of goods. The different national rules on such property rights could be used, effectively, to partition the market for those products on a national basis, and prevent the achievement of one of the Community's primary aims. The Court of Justice has, therefore, drawn a distinction between rules affecting the ownership of such rights and their exercise. It has declared that the protection given to the different systems of property ownership in different Member States by Art 295 EC Treaty does not allow national legislatures to adopt measures relating to industrial and commercial property which would adversely affect the principle of free movement of goods within the common market (**Spain *v* Council** (Case C–350/92)). It has also emphasised that this Art 30 exception cannot 'constitute a means of arbitrary discrimination or a disguised restriction on trade between Member States'. National rules protecting patents and copyrights must therefore operate without discrimination. This is illustrated in the following case:

Collins v Imtrat (Case C-92/92)

The performer Phil Collins attempted to bring proceedings to stop the distribution in Germany of pirated tapes and illegal recordings taken at his concerts. Under German law, such relief was available only to German nationals. The Court of Justice held that, although Member States were still free to determine the nature and extent of protection provided by national copyright rules, such rules should be applied indiscriminately.

On this basis it has also held that there is a breach of Art 28 when national rules require that a patent be exploited only on the territory where the patent is granted and which prohibit or restrict its development elsewhere, so that the patented goods may not be manufactured elsewhere and imported into the patent-granting Member State (**Commission *v* Italy** (Case C–235/89); **Commission *v* UK** (Case C–30/90)). There is a parallel here to the prohibition of discrimination in the acquisition of real property rights by those attempting to establish themselves under Art 43 EC Treaty (**Steinhauser** *v* **City of Biarritz** (Case 197/84); **Commission** *v* **Italy (Re Housing Aid)** (Case 63/86); see Chapter 13).

The Court has tried to allow the property exception to operate only in relation to the essential core of property rights, although what those are in each case is sometimes difficult to determine. The following case illustrates the Court of Justice's approach in the case of a patent:

Centrafarm v *Winthrop BV* (Cases 15 and 16/74)

The Court of Justice stated that:

> Article 36 [now Art 30] in fact only admits of derogations from the free movement of goods where such derogations are justified for the purpose of safeguarding rights which constitute the specific subject matter of this property. In relation to patents, the specific subject matter of the industrial property is the guarantee that the patentee, to reward the creative effort of the inventor, has the exclusive right to use an invention with a view to manufacturing industrial products and putting them into circulation for the first time, either directly or by the grant of licences to third parties, as well as the right to oppose infringements.

This exclusive right is enjoyed in the Member State in which the goods are patented. The patentee, under the Art 30 exception, can exclude goods which breach his patent. However, once the patented goods are circulated in another Member State, either by him or with his consent, his right to exclude those goods as the patentee is then said to be exhausted. This principle is demonstrated in the following case:

Centrafarm v *Winthrop BV* (Cases 15 and 16/74)

Sterling Drug Inc. held UK and Dutch patents relating to a drug called Negram. In both countries the drug was marketed either by Sterling Drug itself, or by companies which it had licensed to do so. Centrafarm, an independent Dutch company, bought supplies of the drug in both the UK and Germany, where it was much cheaper, and resold it in The Netherlands. Sterling Drug and its subsidiaries invoked their respective patent and trade mark rights before the Dutch courts to prevent Negram being marketed in The Netherlands by Centrafarm. The Dutch court referred a number of questions to the Court of Justice under the former Art 177 EC Treaty (now Art 234). The Court described the limits of national patent rights in this context:

> An obstacle to the free movement of goods may arise out of the existence, within national legislation concerning industrial and commercial property, of provisions laying down that a patentee's right is not exhausted when the product protected by the patent is marketed in another Member State, with the result that the patentee can prevent importation of the product into his own Member State when it has been marketed in another Member State. Whereas an obstacle to the free movement of goods of this kind may be justified on the ground of the protection of industrial property where such protection is invoked against a product coming from a Member State where it is not patentable and has been manufactured by third parties without the consent of the patentee and in cases where there exist patents, the original proprietors of which are legally and economically independent, a derogation from the principle of the free movement of goods is not, however, justified where the product has been put onto the market in a legal manner, by the patentee himself or with his consent, in the Member State from which it has been imported, in particular in the case of a proprietor of parallel patents. (paras 10 and 11)

The 'exhaustion of rights' principle has been applied by the Court of Justice with regard not only to patent rights, but also to trade marks, copyright and industrial design. It defined the proprietorial interest in relation to trade marks in the following case:

Centrafarm v Winthrop BV (Cases 15 and 16/74)

The Court of Justice stated that:

> The specific subject matter of the industrial property is the guarantee that the owner of the trade mark has the exclusive right to use that trade mark for the purpose of putting products protected by the trade mark into circulation for the first time, and is therefore intended to protect him against any competitor wishing to take advantage of the status and reputation of the trade mark by selling products illegally bearing the trade mark.

Crucial to the application of the 'exhaustion of rights' principle is the meaning of 'consent' in this context. Consent is assumed where the owner markets the goods himself, where he does so through a subsidiary company or where the owner and the undertaking responsible for the first marketing are under common control. The limits of consent were explored in the following case:

Pharmon BV v Hoechst AG (Case 19/84):

Hoechst owned a patent in Germany for the manufacture of a drug called Frusemide. Hoechst also owned parallel patents in The Netherlands and the UK. Although Frusemide was not manufactured by Hoechst or any of its subsidiaries in the UK, it was manufactured there by an independent company called DDSA under a compulsory licence granted under UK legislation. A compulsory licence does not require the consent of the owner of the patent, but royalties on sales are paid to him. The litigation in this case arose out of imports from the UK being placed on the Dutch market by Pharmon. Because UK prices for the drug were much lower, Pharmon stood to make a considerable profit at Hoechst BV's expense. Could Hoechst resist Pharmon's marketing in The Netherlands? The question turned on whether the compulsory licensing and payment of royalties to Hoechst amounted to 'consent'. The Court of Justice, in a former Art 177 EC Treaty (now Art 234) reference, did not think that it did:

> It is necessary to point out that where, as in this instance, the competent authorities of a Member State grant a third party a compulsory licence which allows him to carry out manufacturing and marketing operations which the patentee would normally have the right to prevent, the patentee cannot be deemed to have consented to the operation of that third party. Such a measure deprives the patent proprietor of his right to determine freely the conditions under which he markets his products. (para 25)

The Court of Justice went further in the following case:

IHT Internationale Heiztechnik GmbH v Ideal-Standard GmbH (Case C-11/93)

The Court of Justice held that action by an assignee under contract (as opposed to a subsidiary in another Member State) could not be regarded as carried out with 'consent' of the assignor in relation to the use of a trade mark on goods imported into another Member State, and the import could be restrained under the property justification in Art 30.

The above decision is surprising because it could be said that the assignment itself included a right to deal generally with the trade mark and the assignment would therefore exhaust the rights of the assignor. The Court of Justice, however, stressed that the free movement of the goods would undermine the essential function of the trade mark. Consumers would no longer be able to identify, for certain, the origin of the marked goods, and the proprietor of the trade mark could be held responsible for the poor quality of the goods for which he is in no way accountable. In this case, at least, the Court's concern for the proprietorial interest of the patentee seems to have outweighed its concern to secure the free movement of goods.

The importance of consent can be seen in two apparently similar cases involving copyright. In **Musik Vertrieb Membran GmbH** *v* **GEMA** (Case 55/80) the Court of Justice held that the performing rights society GEMA could not rely on its German copyright in sound recordings to prevent parallel imports of records from the UK which had been put on the market there with its consent. In **EMI Electrola** *v* **Patricia** (Case 341/87), the claimants owned the production and distribution rights in Germany of the musical works of Cliff Richard. The defendants sold records of Cliff Richard's songs in Germany which had been imported from Denmark, where the copyright protection had expired. The claimants applied for an order from the German courts to exclude these imports. The defendants resisted on the ground that such an order would breach Art 28, since the records were in lawful circulation within Denmark. The Court of Justice, in an Art 234 EC Treaty reference, did not agree. Lawful circulation was not equivalent to consent. The Court distinguished the **GEMA** case on the ground that the marketing in Denmark was due to the expiry of the protection period in another Member State, and not to the consent of the copyright owner or his licensee. This was an aspect of ownership and the different rights of copyright owners in different Member States. The problems caused by these difficulties would continue unless these rules were harmonised for the whole Community.

Harmonisation of industrial property rights

The Commission has two principal aims in this field. The first is that each Member State should employ, as far as possible, the same substantive industrial property rules. The second is that intellectual property monopolies should run the length and breadth of the Community, irrespective of the country of their origin. Some progress has been made towards both these aims. There are broadly similar rules in Member States governing criteria for patentability and the patent term. Registration is, however, undertaken according to different rules in different states. A Community Patent Convention, which would provide for a single (unitary) patent covering the entire territory of the Community, where the Community would be treated as one state under the existing rules of the European Patent Convention, still awaits implementation. In the meantime, some specific measures have been approved, or are being considered, to give some protection in a few areas which are regarded as particularly important in the context of the Single Market. So, for example, a regulation has been approved to extend existing protection for pharmaceutical products (Regulation 1768/92), and a Community Plant Variety Regulation has been adopted to protect the rights of plant breeders (Regulation 2100/94). A harmonising directive on copyright (Directive 2001/29) was adopted on 22 May 2001, with an implementation date of 22 December 2002.

The area of industrial property law where there has been the most progress is in relation to trade marks and designs. The Trade Mark Approximation Directive 1988 laid down principles common to the Community's national or regional trade mark systems

(Directive 89/104). In addition, the Community Trade Mark Regulation provides for a single standard of registrability for a trade mark which will grant protection to its proprietor throughout the Community (Regulation 40/94). Both were implemented in the UK by the Trade Marks Act 1994. The relationship between the Trade Mark Directive and the Court's existing case law on the protection of intellectual property rights and the scope of Art 30 was considered by the Court in **Bristol Myers Squibb** (Joined Cases C–427, 429 & 436/93). This case concernd the repackaging of goods, but the principles involved covered a much wider area of intellectual property law. Repackaging of trade marked products presents a particular problem in reconciling the fundamental principle of free movement of goods with the EC Treaty's guarantee of protection of intellectual property rights. The problem of repackaging is particularly acute in relation to pharmaceutical products, where prices vary widely throughout the Community. The wide price differentials are, largely, because the pricing of medical products in each Member State is regulated through state health service provisions. Traders can exploit the price differentials by buying goods in a low-price state and then selling them in a high-price market for a figure which undercuts the recommended retail price in that state. The usual practice, in these cases, is for the goods to be repackaged to meet the requirements of the importing Member State. The manufacturer will frequently attempt to prevent these parallel imports on the basis that the repackaging infringes its trade mark. The Court of Justice was quite early in rejecting these attempts at restraining imports and effectively partitioning the market. In **Hoffman La Roche v Centrafarm** (Case 102/77), the Court declared that the trade mark owner could not resist repackaging if (i) his marketing system contributed to the artificial partitioning of the market; (ii) the repackaging could not adversely affect the original condition of the product; (iii) he received prior notice of the marketing of the repackaged product; and (iv) the identity of the repackager was stated on the new packaging. The issue in **Bristol Myers Squibb** (Cases C–427, 429 & 436/93) was, essentially, whether, and if so, how far, the existing case law was still relevant after the coming into effect of the Trade Mark Directive 89/104. Article 7, Directive 89/104 gives legislative recognition to the idea of exhaustion of rights which, as was seen in relation to all intellectual property rights, prevents the owners of a trade mark or patent from developing separate markets for their products in each Member State (see **Centrafarm v Winthrop BV** (Cases 15 and 16/74), above). The Court stressed that, since Directive 89/104 was a harmonising measure, it had to be interpreted in the light of the EC Treaty rules on the free movement of goods. On that basis, it specifically reiterated the four conditions set out in **Hoffman La Roche** (above) and affirmed that they continued to apply. However, although the directive had to be read in the light of the former Art 36 (now Art 30), it did not allow the repackager to treat the goods (including the way they were advertised) in such a way as to damage their market 'image'. In **Parfums Christian Dior SA v Evora BV** (Case C–337/95), the subject matter of the repackaging was high-prestige perfume. The Court held that Art 7, Directive 89/104 allowed the owner of the trade mark to take steps to ensure that the presentation and advertising 'did not affect the value of the trade mark by detracting from the allure and prestigious image of the goods in question and from their aura of luxury'.

Community legislation on intellectual property rights is likely never to be exhaustive, as modern technology continues to develop new products which raise new issues. There is an inevitable time lag between the evolution of the new product and the Community's response. The exception covering intellectual property rights in Art 30, and the Court's jurisprudence on the subject, will therefore continue to be important.

Article 30 EC Treaty and the UK's implementation of the free movement of goods

The implementation of Arts 28 and 29 EC Treaty and the Community's harmonising measures in the UK has involved a major legislative programme to give effect to the Community directives that were intended to complete the Single Market by 1 January 1993. In terms of primary legislation, this involved measures of a general kind, such as the Customs and Excise Management Act 1979, which imposed a general obligation on the UK customs authorities 'for the purpose of implementing Community obligations ... [to] co-operate with other customs services ... to give effect ... to any Community requirement or practice as to the movement of goods between countries'. More specific Acts of Parliament were passed to implement major directives, such as the Product Liability Directive 85/374, which was put into effect by the Consumer Protection Act 1987. Other specific legislation was enacted to put decisions of the Court of Justice into effect. For example, the Importation of Milk Act 1983 was enacted to comply with the judgment in **Commission** *v* **UK (Re UHT Milk)** (Case 124/81) (above). In implementing the law relating to the free movement of goods, as with other Community provisions, the UK has, essentially, four options:

- where the requirements of a directive are already met in national law, no specific action may be necessary;
- where there is existing UK legislation, by creating the power to make appropriate national regulations;
- by delegated legislation under s 2(2), European Communities Act 1972; and
- through primary legislation.

Where legislation is enacted to implement a directive, it must give precise effect to the directive. It was thought by many writers that the Product Liability Directive, which created liability for the manufacturers of defective goods, had not been effectively implemented by the Consumer Protection Act 1987, and the Commission brought proceedings against the UK before the Court of Justice. This was because the Act provided a defence to manufacturers based on the state of knowledge existing at the time the goods were put into circulation in circumstances in which, the Commission argued, a manufacturer might escape liability by demonstrating that he had not been negligent if he was unaware of any potential risk. The directive itself imposed strict liability. The Court of Justice refused to accept the Commission's interpretation of the Act, and noted that there was 'nothing ... to suggest that the courts of the UK, if called upon to interpret [the Consumer Protection Act] would not do so in the light of the wording and the purposes of the Directive' (**Commission** *v* **UK** (Case C–300/95)).

The *Cassis* rule of reason: defences to indistinctly applicable measures

The **Cassis** case was considered above; the Court of Justice held that Art 28 EC Treaty applies to indistinctly applicable measures (i.e. measures which apply to *both* imported and domestic products) which impact upon the free movement of intra-Community trade. The first **Cassis** principle (the rule of mutual recognition) was discussed, which provides that once goods have been lawfully marketed in one Member State they should be free to be marketed in any other Member State without restriction. However, this is subject to the second principle, the 'rule of reason', or the 'mandatory requirements defence':

Rewe-Zentrale AG v *Bundesmonopolverwaltung für Branntwein* (Case 120/78)

In the **Cassis** case, the applicant wished to import the liqueur 'Cassis de Dijon' into Germany from France. The relevant German authorities refused to allow the importation because the French liqueur was not of sufficient alcoholic strength to be marketed in Germany. Under German law liqueurs had to have an alcoholic strength of 25 per cent, whereas that of the French liqueur was between 15 per cent and 20 per cent. The applicant argued that this rule was an MEQR, since it prevented the French version of the drink being marketed in Germany. The Court of Justice held as follows:

8. In the absence of common rules relating to the production and marketing of alcohol ... it is for the Member States to regulate all matters relating to the production and marketing of alcohol and alcoholic beverages on their own territory.

   Obstacles to movement within the Community resulting from disparities between the national laws relating to the marketing of the products in question must be accepted in so far as those provisions may be recognised as being necessary in order to satisfy mandatory requirements relating in particular to the effectiveness of fiscal supervision, the protection of public health, the fairness of commercial transactions and the defence of the consumer.

9. The Government of the Federal Republic of Germany, intervening in the proceedings, put forward various arguments which, in its view, justify the application of the provisions relating to the minimum alcohol content of alcoholic beverages, adducing considerations relating on the one hand to the protection of public health and on the other to the protection of the consumer against unfair commercial practices.

10. As regards the protection of public health the German Government states that the purpose of the fixing of minimum alcohol contents by national legislation is to avoid the proliferation of alcoholic beverages with a low alcohol content, since, in its view, such products may more easily induce a tolerance towards alcohol than more highly alcoholic beverages.

11. Such considerations are not decisive since the consumer can obtain on the market an extremely wide range of weakly or moderately alcoholic products and furthermore a large proportion of alcoholic beverages with a high alcohol content freely sold on the German market is generally consumed in diluted form.

12. The German Government also claims that the fixing of a lower limit for the alcohol content of certain liqueurs is designed to protect the consumer against unfair practices on the part of producers and distributors of alcoholic beverages.

    This argument is based on the consideration that the lowering of the alcohol content secures a competitive advantage in relation to beverages with a higher alcohol content, since alcohol constitutes by far the most expensive constituent of beverages by reason of the high rate of tax to which it is subject.

    Furthermore, according to the German Government, to allow alcoholic products into free circulation wherever, as regards their alcohol content, they comply with the rules laid down in the country of production would have the effect of imposing as a common standard within the Community the lowest alcohol content permitted in any of the Member States, and even of rendering any requirements in this field inoperative since a lower limit of this nature is foreign to the rules of several Member States.

13. As the Commission rightly observed, the fixing of limits to the alcohol content of beverages may lead to the standardisation of products placed on the market and of their designations, in the interests of a greater transparency of commercial transactions and offers for sale to the public.

However, this line of argument cannot be taken so far as to regard the mandatory fixing of minimum alcohol contents as being an essential guarantee of the fairness of commercial transactions, since **it is a simple matter to ensure that suitable information is conveyed to the purchaser by requiring the display of an indication of origin and of the alcohol content on the packaging of products.**

14. It is clear from the foregoing that the requirements relating to the minimum alcohol content of alcoholic beverages do not serve a purpose which is in the general interest and such as to take precedence over the requirements of the free movement of goods, which constitutes one of the fundamental rules of the Community.

In practice, the principal effect of requirements of this nature is to promote alcoholic beverages having a high alcohol content by excluding from the national market products of other Member States which do not answer that description.

It therefore appears that the unilateral requirement imposed by the rules of a Member State of a minimum alcohol content for the purposes of the sale of alcoholic beverages constitutes an obstacle to trade which is incompatible with the provisions of Article 30 [now Art 28] of the Treaty.

There is therefore no valid reason why, provided that they have been lawfully produced and marketed in one of the Member States, alcoholic beverages should not be introduced into any other Member State; the sale of such products may not be subject to a legal prohibition on the marketing of beverages with an alcohol content lower than the limits set by national rules. [emphasis added]

Paragraph 8 of the above judgment contains the second **Cassis** principle, which is commonly referred to as the 'rule of reason':

... Obstacles to movement within the Community resulting from disparities between the national laws relating to the marketing of the products in question must be accepted in so far as those provisions may be recognised as being necessary in order to satisfy mandatory requirements relating in particular to the effectiveness of fiscal supervision, the protection of public health, the fairness of commercial transactions and the defence of the consumer.

There are four grounds listed which may prevent a rule from being caught by Art 28:

■ fiscal supervision;

■ public health;

■ fairness of commercial transactions; and

■ protection of the consumer.

This list is not exhaustive (i.e. it can be expanded by the Court of Justice in subsequent cases, see below). Any measure which satisfies the *rule of reason* will not be caught by Art 28. This is separate and distinct from the Art 30 derogations (considered above).

The Member State is placed upon the defensive. After asserting the right of the state to regulate, the Court provides that such indistinct rules which interfere with the free movement of goods will be lawful only in so far as they are justified under one of the heads of the rule of reason.

The mandatory requirement defence: 'the rule of reason'

As discussed above, Art 30 provides a defence to rules otherwise caught by Art 28. Although this defence can apply to both distinctly and indistinctly applicable measures, the Court has applied Art 30 very strictly so that a Member State cannot breach the principle of free movement of goods very easily. However, the Court has recognised that an indistinctly applicable rule which in some way restricts trade may be defended under the **Cassis** rule of reason.

The fact that the rule of reason applies only to an indistinctly applicable measure has been made clear by the Court of Justice on a number of occasions (see, for example, **Italian State** *v* **Gilli and Andres** (Case 788/79)). The Court held that it was only where national rules applied without distinction to both national and imported products that they could be justified using the mandatory requirements derived from **Cassis**.

In the following case, the Court of Justice held that the rule of reason applied only to indistinctly applicable measures:

Commission v Ireland (Case 113/80)

When considering the nature of a distinctly applicable measure, the Irish government, as part of its defence, argued that the distinctly applicable measure could be saved because it satisfied the **Cassis** rule of reason. This was rejected by the Court of Justice which held as follows:

5.   The Irish Government does not dispute the restrictive effects of these orders on the free movement of goods. However, it contends that the disputed measures are justified in the interests of consumer protection and of fairness in commercial transactions between producers

      . . .

10. In this respect, the Court has repeatedly affirmed (in the judgments of 20 February 1979 in Case 120/78 **REWE** [1979] ECR 649, 26 June 1980 in Case 788/79 **Gilli and Andres** [1980] ECR 2071, 19 February 1981 in Case 130/80 **Kelderman** [1981] ECR 527) that 'in the absence of common rules relating to the production and marketing of the product in question it is for Member States to regulate all matters relating to its production, distribution and consumption on their own territory subject, however, to the condition that those rules do not present an obstacle ... to intra-Community trade' and that '**it is only where national rules, which apply without discrimination to both domestic and imported products, may be justified as being necessary in order to satisfy imperative requirements relating in particular to ... the fairness of commercial transactions and the defence of the consumer that they may constitute an exception to the requirements arising under Article 30 [now 28]'**.

11. **The orders concerned in the present case are not measures which are applicable to domestic products and to imported products without distinction but rather a set of rules which apply only to imported products and are therefore discriminatory in nature, with the result that the measures in issue are not covered by the decisions cited above which relate exclusively to provisions that regulate in a uniform manner the marketing of domestic products and imported products.** [emphasis added]

As discussed above, the Court of Justice set out a list of mandatory requirements in the **Cassis** case:

8. . . . Obstacles to movement within the Community resulting from disparities between the national laws relating to the marketing of the products in question must be accepted in so far as those provisions may be recognised as being necessary in order to satisfy mandatory requirements **relating in particular to the effectiveness of fiscal supervision, the protection of public health, the fairness of commercial transactions and the defence of the consumer.** [emphasis added]

This list is not exhaustive (note the use of the words 'relating in particular to . . .'). The Court has added others to that list. Some of the specific mandatory requirements are now considered.

Consumer protection

Commission v *Germany* (Case 178/84)

The Commission instituted former Art 169 EC Treaty (now Art 226) proceedings against Germany, alleging a breach of the former Art 30 (now Art 28). Germany prohibited the marketing on its territory of beer lawfully produced and marketed in other Member States if the beer failed to comply with the provisions of the *Biersteuergesetz* of 1952 (Beer Duty Act 1952). There were two provisions which the Commission wished to challenge. The first one was that the name 'Bier' could only be used for products brewed using malted barley, hops, yeast and water alone. The use of other ingredients such as maize did not prohibit the product being marketed, but it could not be called 'Bier'. The German government sought to defend its law on the basis that it was necessary to protect the German consumer who associated the label 'Bier' with beverages made exclusively from the stated ingredients. The Court of Justice ruled that the law was a barrier to free trade and then considered whether it was necessary to protect consumers:

31. The German Government's argument that section 10 of the Biersteuergesetz is essential in order to protect German consumers because, in their minds, the designation 'Bier' is inseparably linked to the beverage manufactured solely from the ingredients laid down in section 9 of the Biersteuergesetz must be rejected.

32. Firstly, consumers' conceptions which vary from one Member State to the other are also likely to evolve in the course of time within a Member State. The establishment of the Common Market is, it should be added, one of the factors that may play a major contributory role in that development. Whereas rules protecting consumers against misleading practices enable such a development to be taken into account, legislation of the kind contained in section 10 of the Biersteuergesetz prevents it from taking place. As the Court has already held in another context (Case 170/78 **Commission** v **UK**), the legislation of a Member State must not 'crystallise given consumer habits so as to consolidate an advantage acquired by national industries concerned to comply with them'.

33. Secondly, in the other Member States of the Community the designations corresponding to the German designation 'Bier' are generic designations for a fermented beverage manufactured from barley, whether malted barley on its own or with the addition of rice or maize. The same approach is taken in Community law as can be seen from heading 22.03 of the Common Customs Tariff. The German legislature itself utilises the designation 'Bier' in that way in section 9(7) and (8) of the Biersteuergesetz in order to refer to beverages not complying with the manufacturing rules laid down in section 9(1) and (2).

34. The German designation 'Bier' and its equivalents in the languages of the other Member States may therefore not be restricted to beers manufactured in accordance with the rules in force in the Federal Republic of Germany.

35. **It is admittedly legitimate to seek to enable consumers who attribute specific qualities to beers manufactured from particular raw materials to make their choice in the light of that consideration. However, as the Court has already emphasised (Case 193/80 Commission v Italy) that possibility may be ensured by means which do not prevent the importation of products which have been lawfully manufactured and marketed in other Member States and, in particular, 'by the compulsory affixing of suitable labels giving the nature of the product sold'.** By indicating the raw materials utilised in the manufacture of beer 'such a course would enable the consumer to make his choice in full knowledge of the facts and would guarantee transparency in trading and in offers to the public'. It must be added that such a system of mandatory consumer information must not entail negative assessments for beers not complying with the requirements of section 9 of the Biersteuergesetz. [emphasis added]

In the above case, the Court of Justice held that the German law breached the former Art 30 (now Art 28). Although there were some arguments in favour of Germany's 'consumer protection' claim, the Court looked at whether the action taken was necessary, or whether action which was less restrictive of intra-Community trade could have been taken (an application of the proportionality test). At para 35 the Court held that consumer interests could be met through better labelling rather than an outright ban.

Other cases have followed this approach. In **De Kikvorsch Groothandel-Import-Export BV** (Case 94/82), the Court of Justice again rejected a restrictive rule which was a barrier to free movement on the ground that better labelling could achieve the objective sought – protection of the consumer. A similar result was achieved in the following case:

Ministère Public v *Deserbais* (Case 286/86)

French legislation restricted the use of the name 'Edam' to cheese with a minimum fat content of 40 per cent. Mr Deserbais imported cheese into France from Germany, where it was lawfully produced with a fat content of 34.3 per cent. He marketed the cheese in France as 'Edam' cheese and was prosecuted. In his defence he argued that French law was not applicable because it contravened the former Art 30 (now Art 28). The matter was referred to the Court of Justice under the former Art 177 EC Treaty (now Art 234) for a preliminary ruling. The Court held as follows:

10. The national court starts from the premise that the cheese in question, containing 34 per cent fat, has been lawfully and traditionally produced in the Federal Republic of Germany under the name 'Edam' in accordance with the laws and regulations applicable to it there, and that consumers' attention is adequately drawn to that fact by the labelling.

11. It must also be stated that at the present stage of development of Community law there are no common rules governing the various types of cheeses in the Community. Accordingly, it cannot be stated in principle that a Member State may not lay down rules making the use by national producers of a name for a cheese subject to the observance of a traditional minimum fat content.

12. However, it would be incompatible with Article 30 [now Art 28] of the Treaty and the objectives of a common market to apply such rules to imported cheeses of the same type where those cheeses have been lawfully produced and marketed in another Member State under the same generic name but with a different minimum fat content. **The Member State into which they are imported cannot prevent the importation and marketing of such cheeses where adequate information for the consumer is ensured.**

13. The question may arise whether the same rule must be applied where a product presented under a particular name is so different, as regards its composition or production, from the products generally known by that name in the Community that it cannot be regarded as falling within the same category. However, no situation of that kind arises in the circumstances described by the national court in this case . . .

    Article 30 [now Art 28] *et seq.* of the Treaty must be interpreted as precluding a Member State from applying national legislation making the right to use the trade name of a type of cheese subject to the observance of a minimum fat content to products of the same type imported from another Member State when those products have been lawfully manufactured and marketed under that name in that Member State and consumers are provided with proper information. [emphasis added]

In the above case, the Court of Justice held that France's indistinctly applicable rule was a restriction on trade in relation to cheese which had been lawfully produced and marketed in Germany. It was therefore in breach of the former Art 30 (now Art 28), unless the rule could be justified under one of the heads of the rule of reason (in this case, defence of the consumer). The Court held that the consumer could be provided with adequate information on the fat content of the different 'Edam' cheeses and therefore the rule was not justified under the rule of reason. However, the Court acknowledged in para 13 that a product may be so different (as regards composition or production) from products generally known by that name in the importing country that it could not be considered to fall within the same category.

A similar issue relating to a restriction on the use of a particular name for certain goods was considered by the Court of Justice in the following case:

Commission v *Spain* (Case C-12/00) and *Commission* v *Italy* (Case C-14/00)

Spanish and Italian legislation prohibited cocoa and chocolate products to which vegetable fats other than cocoa butter had been added from being marketed under the name 'chocolate', and required them to be marketed using the term 'chocolate substitute'. As regards the applicability of Art 28 EC Treaty to the prohibition laid down by the legislation at issue, the Court of Justice observed that such legislation was likely to impede trade between Member States. It compelled the traders concerned to adjust the presentation of their products according to the place where they were to be marketed and consequently to incur additional packaging costs and adversely affect the consumer's perception of the products. The inclusion in the label of a neutral and objective statement informing consumers of the presence in the product of vegetable fats other than cocoa butter would be sufficient to ensure that consumers are given correct information. The Court concluded that the Spanish and Italian legislation which required the sales name of those products to be changed did not appear to be necessary to satisfy the overriding requirement of consumer protection and that the legislation at issue was incompatible with Art 28 EC Treaty.

The proportionality test was once again applied by the Court of Justice in the following case, resulting in Italy being prevented from relying on the 'consumer protection' defence:

Italian State v *Gilli and Andres* (Case 788/79)

Italian law required that vinegar had to be made from the fermentation of wine. Importers of apple vinegar from Germany into Italy were prosecuted for fraud. The importers relied on the former Art 30 (now Art 28) as a defence. There were no Community harmonisation rules on the issue. The Court of Justice adopted the **Cassis** reasoning and said that in the absence of harmonisation measures, a Member State could regulate the production and marketing of products within its territory, provided that such regulation did not constitute an obstacle, actually or potentially, to the free movement of intra-Community trade. This rule did hinder the free movement of goods and therefore it could be saved only if it could be justified under one of the heads of the rule of reason. The Court held that it could not be justified because once again the consumer could be protected by proper labelling of the products and in this case there was no danger to health.

The same approach was adopted by the Court of Justice in the following case:

Walter Rau Lebensmittelwerke v de Smedt PvbA (Case 261/81)

The claimants manufactured margarine and complained that a Belgian law, under which margarine had to be sold in Belgium in cube-shaped packs to distinguish it from butter, infringed the former Art 30 (now Art 28). The Court of Justice, in an Art 177 EC Treaty (now Art 234) reference, agreed. Although the rule applied to all margarine sold in Belgium, foreign manufacturers wishing to import margarine into Belgium would have to establish a special production and packaging line for the Belgian market, which would increase their production costs. There was no consumer protection reason for the packaging requirement. The true nature of the product could just as well be conveyed to the consumer by effective labelling.

The EC Treaty, as amended by the ToA, now specifically requires Community harmonising measures on the free movement of goods to contain provisions giving a right to information to consumers about matters relating to their health, safety and economic interests (Art 153). National measures should also always rely upon such information where possible, rather than on an outright prohibition against sale. However, even labelling requirements themselves may not escape Art 28, as illustrated in the following case:

Fietje (Case 27/80)

The Court of Justice stated:

10. Although the extension to imported products of an obligation to use a certain name on the label does not wholly preclude the importation into the Member State concerned of products originating in other Member States or in free circulation in those States it may nonetheless make their marketing more difficult, especially in the case of parallel imports. As the Netherlands Government itself admits in its observations, such an extension of that obligation is thus capable of impeding, at least indirectly, trade between Member States. It is therefore necessary to consider whether it may be justified on the ground of public interest in consumer protection which, according to observations of the Netherlands Government and according to 'Warenwet', underlies the rules in question.

11. If the national rules relating to a given product include the obligation to use a description that is sufficiently precise to inform the purchaser of the nature of the product and to enable it to be distinguished from products with which it may be confused, it may well be necessary, in order to give consumers effective protection, to extend this obligation to imported products also, even in such a way as to make necessary the alteration of the original labels of some of these products. At the level of Community legislation, this possibility is recognised in several directives on the approximation of the laws of the Member States relating to certain foodstuffs as well as by Council Directive 79/112/EEC of 18 December 1978 on the approximation of the laws of the Member States relating to the labelling, presentation and advertising of foodstuffs for sale to the ultimate consumer (Official Journal 1979, L33, p.1).

12. However, **there is no longer any need for such protection if the details given on the original label of the imported product have as their content information on the nature of the product and that content includes at least the same information, and is just as capable of being understood by consumers in the importing State, as the description prescribed by the rules of that State.** In the context of Article 177 [now Art 234] of the EEC Treaty, the making of findings of fact necessary in order to establish whether there is such equivalence is a matter for the national court. [emphasis added]

In the above case, the Court of Justice held that a labelling requirement (that a specific name had to appear on the label) may render it more difficult for an importer to market goods in another Member State and therefore it would fall within the former Art 30 (now Art 28) unless justified (e.g. on the ground of consumer protection). The Court held the labelling requirement would not be justified if the necessary information required by the Member State of import was included on the original label (but not the specific name) and this was just as capable of being understood by consumers. This theme was continued in the following case:

Neeltje v *Houtwipper* (Case C-293/93)

The issue in this case concerned the compatibility with Art 28 of national legislation requiring the hallmarking of precious metals which are offered for sale. All such metals in The Netherlands, both domestic and imported, had to be hallmarked to show the content of precious metals. The measure thus appeared to be indistinctly applicable, but in practice it meant that it rendered the import of precious metals into The Netherlands more difficult and costly, because importers would have to have their products reassayed and date-stamped to indicate the year of manufacture in accordance with the Dutch hallmarking law. In practice, therefore, the importers of precious metals were at a disadvantage. Although the Court of Justice accepted that hallmarking of precious metals was a mandatory requirement designed to ensure effective protection of consumers and the promotion of fair trading, it held that the way in which the system operated breached Art 28:

> A Member State cannot require a fresh hallmark be affixed to products imported from another Member State in which they have been lawfully marketed and hallmarked in accordance with the legislation of that state, where the information provided by that hallmark, in whatever form, is equivalent to that prescribed by the Member State of importation and intelligible to consumers of that state.

Fairness of commercial transactions

This overlaps with the previous mandatory requirement, and both may be pleaded in the alternative. In the **Cassis** case, Germany argued, *inter alia*, that the rule that liqueurs must contain a minimum alcohol content of 25 per cent was justified under the rule of reason on the ground of fairness of commercial transactions. It was argued that French Cassis, with a lower alcohol content, gained an unfair competitive advantage because tax on alcohol content constituted the greatest proportion of the cost of the product. A liqueur with a lower alcohol content would be taxed at a lower rate and therefore its selling price would be less than those liqueurs with a higher alcohol content (which would be subjected to a higher level of taxation). This argument was rejected by the Court of Justice.

Public health

Public health is included in both Art 30 and the list of mandatory requirements. When faced with a rule which is being defended by the imposing Member State on the ground of public health, the Court may not be overly concerned with whether it falls to be considered under Art 30 or the **Cassis** rule of reason:

Commission v *Germany* (Case 178/84)

This case, which has been considered above, concerned a German rule which banned using the name 'Bier' unless the beverage in question was made from certain prescribed ingredients. The Commission was also concerned with a provision under the German Foodstuffs Act

1974, which banned the marketing of beer which contained additives. It was accepted that this indistinctly applicable rule constituted a barrier to intra-Community trade, because it banned beer which was lawfully produced and marketed in other Member States where such beer contained additives. The question before the Court of Justice was whether this rule could be justified under the former Art 36 (now Art 30) on public health grounds:

41. The Court has consistently held (in particular in Case 174/82 **Criminal Proceedings Against Sandoz BV)** that 'in so far as there are uncertainties at the present state of scientific research it is for the Member States, in the absence of harmonisation, to decide what degree of protection of the health and life of humans they intend to assure, having regard to the requirements of the free movement of goods within the Community'.

42. As may also be seen from the decision of the Court (and especially the **Sandoz** case, cited above, in Case 247/84, **Motte,** and in Case 308/84, **Ministère Public v Muller**), in such circumstances Community law does not preclude the adoption by Member States of legislation whereby the use of additives is subjected to prior authorisation granted by a measure of general application for specific additives, in respect of all products, for certain products only or for certain uses. Such legislation meets a genuine need of health policy, namely that of restricting the uncontrolled consumption of food additives.

43. However, the application to imported products of prohibitions on marketing products containing additives which are authorised in the Member State of production but prohibited in the Member State of importation is permissible only in so far as it complies with the requirements of Article 36 [now Art 30] of the Treaty as it has been interpreted by the Court.

44. **It must be borne in mind, in the first place, that in its judgments in Sandoz, Motte and Muller, the Court inferred from the principle of proportionality underlying the last sentence of Article 36 [now Art 30] of the Treaty that prohibitions on the marketing of products containing additives authorised in the Member State of production but prohibited in the Member State of importation must be restricted to what is actually necessary to secure the protection of public health. The Court also concluded that the use of a specific additive which is authorised in another Member State must be authorised in the case of a product imported from that Member State where, in view, on the one hand, of the findings of international scientific research, and in particular the work of the Community's Scientific Committee for Food, the Codex Alimentarius Committee of the Food and Agriculture Organisation of the United Nations (FAO) and the World Health Organisation and, on the other, of the eating habits prevailing in the importing Member State, the additive in question does not present a risk to public health and meets a real need, especially a technical one.**

45. Secondly, it should be remembered that, as the Court held in Muller, by virtue of the principle of proportionality, traders must also be able to apply, under a procedure which is easily accessible to them and can be concluded within a reasonable time, for the use of specific additives to be authorised by a measure of general application . . . [emphasis added]

The Court of Justice proceeded to state that the German rule prohibited all additives and there was no procedure whereby a trader could obtain authorisation to use a specific additive. Additives were allowed in other beverages. It was argued by the German government that if the beer was manufactured in accordance with German law (i.e. s 9 of the Biersteuergesetz) additives would not be needed. The Court continued:

51. It must be emphasised that the mere reference to the fact that beer can be manufactured without additives if it is made from only the raw materials prescribed in the Federal Republic of Germany does not suffice to preclude the possibility that some additives may meet a technological need. Such an interpretation of the concept of technological need, which results in favouring national production methods, constitutes a disguised means of restricting trade between Member States.

52. The concept of technological need must be assessed in the light of the raw materials utilised and bearing in mind the assessment made by the authorities of the Member States where the product

was lawfully manufactured and marketed. Account must also be taken of the findings of international scientific research and in particular the work of the Community's Scientific Committee
for Food, the Codex Alimentarius Committee of the FAO and the World Health Organisation.

53. Consequently, in so far as the German rules on additives in beer entail a general ban on additives,
their application to beers imported from other Member States is contrary to the requirements of
Community law as laid down in the case law of the Court, since that prohibition is contrary to the
principle of proportionality and is therefore not covered by Article 36 [now Art 30] of the EEC
Treaty.

In the above case, the Court of Justice held that the German law breached the former Art
30 (now Art 28) because it was not proportionate. Although individual Member States
have a margin of discretion in deciding what level of protection to provide to consumers,
the Court, in determining whether such national measures are proportionate, will take
into account the extent of current knowledge, particularly when assessing national provisions to protect the health of consumers, as illustrated in the following case:

Proceedings against M Debus (Cases C-13 and 113/91)

The defendant was prosecuted for importing and marketing in Italy, beer containing sulphur
dioxide in a quantity permitted by the relevant French legislation but higher than that permitted in Italy. The defendant contested the prosecution on the basis that the Italian
legislation breached the former Art 30 (now Art 28). The case was referred to the Court of
Justice under the former Art 177 EC Treaty (now Art 234). The Court had little difficulty in
finding that the Italian rules led to 'a general and absolute prohibition of all beers containing
more than 20 mg of sulphur dioxide per litre without any exception whatsoever'. There was
uncontested evidence that the level of sulphur dioxide prohibited was far less than that found
to constitute a risk by the World Health Organisation. It was an indistinctly applicable
measure. The Court did not accept that, since there were other methods of preserving beer,
the importing Member State was entitled to determine the method to be used, 'since such an
interpretation of the concept of technological requirement, which leads to preference for
domestic production methods, constituted a means of imposing a disguised restriction on
trade between Member States' (see also **Sandoz BV** (Case 174/82); **Deserbais** (Case 286/86)).

In the following case, the Court of Justice was required to address the issue of prior
authorisation in the context of application of the public health mandatory requirement
(although the Court considered the defence issue under Art 30 EC Treaty rather than the
Cassis rule of reason, although the principle is exactly the same):

Greenham v Abel (Case C-95/01)

The question before the Court of Justice concerned whether Arts 28 and 30 EC Treaty must
be interpreted as meaning that they preclude a Member State from prohibiting the marketing
(without prior authorisation) of foodstuffs which have been lawfully marketed in another
Member State, if nutrients such as vitamins or minerals have been added to the foodstuff,
other than those whose use has been declared lawful in the first Member State. The Court
held that Arts 28 and 30 EC Treaty do not preclude a Member State from prohibiting the marketing of such foodstuffs, but this is subject to the following conditions:

- the prior authorisation procedure must be readily accessible and capable of being completed within a reasonable time;
- if an application for prior authorisation is refused, there must be a right to challenge this refusal before the courts; and
- a refusal to authorise marketing must be based on a detailed assessment of the risk to public health, based on the most reliable scientific data available and the most recent results of international research.

Applying these conditions in **Commission** v **France** (Case C–24/00), the Court of Justice held that France was unable to rely on the public health defence and was in breach of Art 28 EC Treaty. France had failed either to provide for a procedure for including nutrients on the list of authorised substances which was accessible, transparent, and could be completed within a reasonable time or to justify refusals on the basis of a detailed assessment of the genuine risk to public health.

The following two cases concerned the automatic classification as medicinal products of food supplements which contained certain vitamins and/or minerals:

Commission v *Germany* (Case C-387/99) and *Commission* v *Austria* (Case C-150/00)

The Commission had received a number of complaints against the administrative practice in Germany and Austria of automatically classifying as medicinal products, preparations based on certain vitamins and/or minerals lawfully marketed as food supplements in the Member State from which they were imported, where those substances are present in amounts exceeding the recommended daily intake (Case C-150/00) or exceed it by three times (Case C-387/99). The Commission brought action before the Court of Justice against Germany and Austria for infringement of Art 28 EC Treaty.

In support of those actions, the Commission argued essentially that the classification of each vitamin or mineral as a medicinal product must be carried out case-by-case, having regard to the pharmacological properties that it was recognised as having in the present state of scientific knowledge. The harmfulness of vitamins and minerals varied.

The Commission argued that a single general and abstract approach for all those substances went beyond what was necessary for achieving the objective of the protection of health laid down in Art 30 EC Treaty, so that that approach was not proportionate. The barrier to the free movement of goods resulting from the contested practices could not therefore be justified, even though it pursued a legitimate aim.

The Court of Justice, upholding the Commission's argument, held that, to determine whether vitamin preparations or preparations containing minerals should be classified as medicinal products within the meaning of Directive 65/65 on proprietary medicinal products, the national authorities, acting under the control of the Court, must work on a case-by-case basis, having regard to the characteristics of those preparations, in particular their composition, their pharmacological properties, the manner in which they are used, the extent of their distribution, their familiarity to consumers and the risks which their use may entail. Classification as a medicinal product of a vitamin preparation or a preparation containing minerals which is based solely on the recommended daily amount of the nutrient it contains does not fully satisfy the requirement for a classification on the basis of the pharmacological properties of each preparation. Even though it is true that the concentration of vitamins or minerals above which a preparation is classified as a medicinal product varies according to the vitamin or mineral in question, it does not necessarily follow that all preparations containing more than once, or three times, the recommended daily intake of one of those substances come within the definition of a medicinal product for the purposes of Directive 65/65.

The Court stated that in those circumstances it was clear that the contested practices create a barrier to trade, since such preparations lawfully marketed or produced in other Member States as food supplements cannot be marketed in Germany or Austria until they have been subject to the marketing authorisation procedure for medicinal products.

The Court held that this barrier could not be justified on the basis of Art 30 EC Treaty. While Member States are afforded a certain discretion with regard to the protection of public health, the means used must be proportionate to the objective pursued, which it must not be possible to attain by measures less restrictive of intra-Community trade. In this respect, stated the Court, the systematic nature of the contested practices does not make it possible to identify and assess a real risk to public health, which requires a detailed assessment on a case-by-case basis of the effects which the addition of the vitamins and minerals in question could entail. A preparation that would not pose a real risk to public health thus also requires a marketing authorisation as a medicinal product. In the light of those considerations, the Court held that Germany and Austria had failed to fulfil their obligations under Art 28 EC Treaty.

The above two cases involved indistinctly applicable measures, because the restrictions applied to both domestic and imported goods. The Court of Justice decided the cases with reference to the Art 30 EC Treaty derogation rather than under the **Cassis** rule of reason. The end result is nevertheless the same.

The following case concerned Germany's prohibition on the import and retail sale of medicinal products by mail order or over the Internet:

Deutscher Apothekerverband (C-322/01)

The Court of Justice held that the prohibition was a measure having an effect equivalent to a quantitative restriction for the purposes of Art 28 EC Treaty, because although it related to selling arrangements within the context of the Court's **Keck** judgment, the prohibition did not affect in the same manner, in law and in fact, the marketing of both domestic products and those from other Member States (see above). The Court then considered whether the prohibition could be justified under Art 30 EC Treaty (as with the last case, it is irrelevant that it was considered under Art 30 rather than under the mandatory requirements defence). The Court held that the only plausible arguments are those relating to the need to provide individual advice to the customer and to ensure his protection when he is supplied with medicines, and the need to check that prescriptions are genuine and to guarantee that medicinal products are widely available and sufficient to meet requirements. None of those reasons could provide a valid basis for the absolute prohibition on the sale by mail order of non-prescription medicines, because the 'virtual' pharmacy provides customers with an identical or better level of service than traditional pharmacies. On the other hand, for prescription medicines, such control could be justified in view of the greater risks which those medicines may present and the system of fixed prices which applies to them and which forms part of the German health system. The need to be able to check effectively and respon-

608 PART 3 THE FREE MOVEMENT OF GOODS

sibly the authenticity of doctors' prescriptions and to ensure that the medicine is handed over either to the customer himself, or to a person to whom its collection has been entrusted by the customer, is such as to justify a prohibition on mail order sales. Article 30 EC Treaty may, therefore, be relied on to justify such a prohibition. The Court stated that the same arguments apply where medicinal products are imported into a Member State in which they are authorised, having been previously obtained by a pharmacy in another Member State from a wholesaler in the importing Member State.

As regards the compatibility with Community law of prohibitions on advertising of medicines sold by mail order, the Court declared that such prohibitions cannot be justified for medicines which can only be supplied by pharmacies but which are not subject to prescription.

Other mandatory requirements

As stated above, the **Cassis** list is not exhaustive. The list was left open so that it could be added to by the Court of Justice as its case law developed. The Court has accepted a wide range of national measures, many of them going well beyond either those which are designed to protect consumers or the specific exceptions permitted to Member States under Art 30:

Commission v Denmark (Case 302/86)

The Commission challenged a Danish law under which all containers for beer and soft drinks must be returnable. This constituted a *prima facie* barrier because foreign manufacturers would not be geared up to selling drinks in such containers and would have to take special steps to do so, in order to supply the Danish market. Citing the case of **Walter Rau** (above), the Court of Justice recognised that the rule constituted an obstacle to trade. Was it, however, a mandatory requirement? The Court accepted that protection of the environment is one of the Community's 'essential objectives', which may justify certain limitations to the principle of the free movement of goods (see, now, Art 2 EC Treaty, as amended by the ToA). Those limitations must not, however, 'go beyond the inevitable restrictions which are justified by the pursuit of the objective of environmental protection'. It was therefore necessary to examine whether all the restrictions which the contested rules imposed on the free movement of goods were necessary to achieve the objectives pursued by those rules.

In **Commission v Germany** (Case C–463/01) and **Radlberger Getränke and S. Spitz** (Case C–309/02), the Court of Justice reconfirmed that indistinctly applicable measures could be justified on environmental protection grounds, provided that the measures taken are proportionate to the objective pursued. The following case concerned an indistinctly applicable measure which the Member State in question (Austria) sought to justify on environmental grounds (protection of the health of humans, animals and plants):

Commission v Austria (Case C-320/03)

A regulation adopted by the First Minister of the Tyrol on 27 May 2003 limited transport on the A12 motorway in the Inn valley (sectoral prohibition on road transport). That regulation prohibited lorries of more than 7.5 tonnes carrying certain goods, such as waste, stone, soil, motor vehicles, timber and cereals, from being driven on a 46 km section of the A12 motorway in the Inn valley. The aim of the contested regulation was to improve air quality so as to ensure lasting protection of human, animal and plant health.

The Court of Justice, hearing an infringement action brought by the Commission, found that by adopting the contested regulation Austria had failed to fulfil its obligations under Arts 28 and 29 EC Treaty.

The sectoral prohibition on road transport obstructed the free movement of goods, in particular their free transit, and was therefore to be regarded as constituting a measure having equivalent effect to quantitative restrictions which was incompatible with Arts 28 and 29 EC Treaty and which could not moreover be justified by overriding requirements relating to protection of the environment because it was disproportionate.

The Court held that before adopting a measure so radical as a ban, the Austrian authorities were under a duty to examine carefully the possibility of using measures less restrictive to the free movement of goods, and discount them only if their inadequacy, in relation to the objective pursued, was clearly established. More particularly, given the declared objective of transferring transportation of the goods concerned from road to rail, those authorities were required to ensure that there was sufficient and appropriate rail capacity to allow such a transfer before deciding to implement a measure such as that laid down by the Tyrolean regulation. The Court observed that it had not been conclusively established that the Austrian authorities, in preparing the contested regulation, sufficiently studied the question whether the aim of reducing pollutant emissions could be achieved by other means less restrictive to the free movement of goods and whether there actually was a realistic alternative for the transportation of the affected goods by other means of transport or by other road routes. Moreover, the Court considered that a transition period of only two months between the date on which the contested regulation was adopted and the date fixed by the Austrian authorities for implementation of the sectoral-traffic ban was clearly insufficient to reasonably allow the operators concerned to adapt to the new circumstances.

The Court of Justice has shown a willingness to accept that restrictions aimed at protecting national, cultural and social values could constitute a mandatory requirement, as illustrated in the following case:

Cinéthèque (Cases 60 and 61/84)

The Court of Justice upheld a non-discriminatory French rule prohibiting the sale or hire of videos of films within a year of their first showing at a cinema. Although the rule had the effect of restricting the import of videos from other Member States, the Court held that the restriction was justified and not, therefore, in breach of Art 28. The Court accepted that the protection of the French cinema was a legitimate objective, presumably (although it was not stated) as a means of protecting national culture.

The above case can, perhaps, be compared to a case involving the free movement of workers, **Groener *v* Minister for Education** (Case 379/87), in which the Court of Justice accepted a requirement of a knowledge of the Irish language imposed on a Dutch teacher seeking employment in Ireland, although it was not needed for the subject she was to teach. The Court did so in recognition of the clear national policy of maintaining and promoting the language as a means of promoting national identity and culture (see Chapter 12).

In the following case, the Court of Justice accepted as a mandatory requirement national rules intended to protect the character of Sunday, and the limitation of workers' hours on that day, provided that national legislation did not go further than was necessary to achieve those legitimate aims:

Torfaen Borough Council v *B & Q plc* (Case 145/88)

The Court of Justice laid down some general principles applicable to national restrictions on activities of this kind:

> It is therefore necessary in a case such as this to consider first of all whether the rules such as those at issue pursue an aim which is justified with regard to Community law. As far as that question is concerned, the Court has already stated in its judgment of 14 July 1981 in **Oebel** (Case 155/80) that national rules governing hours of work, delivery and sale in the bread and confectionery industry constitute a legitimate part of economic and social policy, consistent with the objectives of public interest pursued by the Treaty.
>
> The same consideration must apply as regards national rules governing the opening hours of retail premises. Such rules reflect certain political and economic choices in so far as their purpose is to ensure that working and non-working hours are so arranged as to accord with national or regional socio-cultural characteristics, and that, in the present state of Community law, is a matter for the Member States. Furthermore, such rules are not designed to govern the patterns of trade between Member States.

It should be noted that **Cinéthèque** and **Torfaen Borough Council** have been overturned following the Court's judgment in **Keck** (see above) because they would be outside Art 28 *per se*, with no necessity to rely upon the defence of objective justification. However, this aspect of these two judgments is undoubtedly still good law.

In **Schmidberger** (Case C–112/00), considered below, Austria had failed to ban a demonstration which resulted in the complete closure of a major transit route for almost 30 hours on end. The Court of Justice stated that a failure to ban such a demonstration is capable of restricting intra-Community trade in goods and must therefore be regarded as constituting a measure of equivalent effect to a quantitative restriction. Such a measure is *prima facie* incompatible with the obligations arising from Arts 28 and 29 EC Treaty, read together with Art 10 EC Treaty, unless that failure to ban can be objectively justified. This case differed to that of **Commission** v **France** (C–265/95), see above, in that the present case concerned an indistinctly applicable measure (because the demonstration would affect both domestic and imported goods), whereas **Commission** v **France** concerned a distinctly applicable measure (because only imported goods were being targeted). The Court of Justice was then required to determine whether Austria could objectively justify its failure to ban the demonstration:

Schmidberger (Case C-112/00)

In assessing whether there was any objective justification, the Court of Justice took account of the objective pursued by the Austrian authorities in authorising the demonstration in question and held that it was to respect the fundamental rights of the demonstrators to freedom of expression and freedom of assembly, which are enshrined in and guaranteed by the European Convention on Human Rights and the Austrian Constitution. Given that fundamental rights form an integral part of the general principles of law which the Court ensures are observed, their protection is a legitimate interest which, in principle, justifies a restriction of the obligations imposed by Community law. This is the case even under a fundamental freedom guaranteed by the Treaty such as the free movement of goods. The Court went on to say that the question of whether the facts before the referring court are consistent with respect for fundamental rights raises the question of the need to reconcile the requirements of the protection of fundamental rights in the Community with those arising from a fundamental freedom enshrined in the Treaty; i.e. the question of the respective scope of the freedom of expression and freedom of assembly and of the free movement of goods, given that they are both subject to restrictions justified by public interest objectives. In considering whether the restrictions on intra-Community trade are proportionate in the light of the objective pursued, that is the protection of fundamental rights, the Court pointed out differences between the facts of this case and those of **Commission v France**. In the latter case, the Court of Justice held that France had failed to fulfil its obligations under Art 28 EC Treaty by failing to adopt all necessary and proportionate measures in order to prevent the free movement of fruit and vegetables from being obstructed by actions of private individuals, such as the interception of lorries transporting such products and the destruction of their loads, violence against lorry drivers and other threats. The Court of Justice found that, in the present case, unlike in **Commission v France**, (i) the demonstration at issue took place following authorisation; (ii) the obstacle to the free movement of goods resulting from that demonstration was limited; (iii) the purpose of that public demonstration was not to restrict trade in goods of a particular type or from a particular source; (iv) various administrative and supporting measures were taken by the competent authorities in order to limit as far as possible the disruption to road traffic; (v) the isolated incident in question did not give rise to a general climate of insecurity such as to have a dissuasive effect on intra-Community trade flows as a whole; and (vi) taking account of the Member States' wide margin of discretion, in this case the competent national authorities were entitled to consider that an outright ban on the demonstration at issue would have constituted unacceptable interference with the fundamental rights of the demonstrators to gather and express peacefully their opinion in public. The imposition of stricter conditions concerning both the site and the duration of the demonstration in question could have been perceived as an excessive restriction, depriving the action of a substantial part of its scope. According to the Court, although an action of that type usually entails inconvenience for non-participants, such inconvenience may in principle be tolerated provided that the objective pursued is essentially the public and lawful demonstration of an opinion.

The Court concluded that the fact that the Austrian authorities did not, in the circumstances, ban the demonstration was not such as to render the failure incompatible with Arts 28 and 29 EC Treaty. In so deciding, the Court decided that the fundamental rights of the demonstrators to freedom of expression and freedom of assembly, which are enshrined in and guaranteed by the European Convention on Human Rights, was a legitimate interest which, in principle, justified a restriction of the obligations imposed by Community law.

Overcoming barriers created by differing national standards

The relationship between harmonising directives and Articles 28–30 EC Treaty

Much of the jurisprudence of the Court of Justice relating to MEQRs concerns national measures enacted, ostensibly at least, for the protection of consumers or to promote other national concerns. It was apparent from the inception of the Community that such national provisions, including an enormously diverse range of standards, could be effectively tackled only by creating a Community-wide minimum standard binding on all Member States. In that way producers could have the advantage of large product runs, without having to go to the additional expense of having to tailor their products to the standards set in each Member State. Consumers could have a wider range of products at a lower cost. Article 94 was included in the Treaty specifically for this purpose. To facilitate the approximation of national legislation on a whole range of issues affecting the development of a common market, it enables the Commission, for example, on the advice of expert advisory committees, to draft directives on Community-wide standards on the safety of specific products, to be approved *unanimously* by the Council of Ministers.

Considerable difficulties were encountered in this harmonising process, not least because some Member States, not unnaturally, wished to ensure that their own high national standards were reflected in the Community standard. Member States were unwilling to accept a standard that represented the lowest common denominator. Procedures for agreeing common standards were time-consuming and cumbersome, and since approval had to be unanimous, the opportunity for procrastination was great. The standards adopted were, in some cases, technically obsolete by the time they came into effect and the cost, in terms of lost intra-Community trade, was high.

Where, however, a common standard has been reached and the appropriate directive adopted, there is no further scope for national measures in the same field, and attempts to justify them either as mandatory requirements or under the specific exceptions in Art 30 will be rejected. In **Commission v Germany (Re Compound Feedingstuffs)** (Case 28/84), the Commission brought proceedings against the German government because, the Commission contended, Council directives adopted in 1970, 1974 and 1979 constituted a complete and exhaustive set of rules covering the whole field of production and marketing of compound animal feedstuffs. The Court of Justice agreed and consequently held that German rules on the minimum and maximum levels of certain ingredients could not apply (see also **Société Civile Agricole v Coopérative d'Elevage du Département de la Mayenne** (Case C–323/93)).

The current approach to harmonisation

The **Cassis** case gave a new impetus to the harmonisation process. It led to a declaration by the Commission that it would concentrate on steps for the harmonisation of national laws which could still affect inter-Community trade and which would have to be justified, in the absence of harmonisation, if at all, as mandatory requirements under the first **Cassis** principle or under one of the specific exceptions provided for in Art 30 EC Treaty. It also led to a Council Resolution of 7 May 1985 on a different approach to technical harmonisation and standards. The resolution established four fundamental principles on which this approach would be based:

1. Legislative harmonisation is limited to adoption, by means of directives based on Art 100 EC Treaty (now Art 94), of the essential safety requirements (or other requirements in the general interest) with which products put on the market must conform, and which should therefore enjoy free movement throughout the Community.

2. The task of drawing up the technical specifications needed for the production and placing on the market of products conforming to the essential requirements established by the directives, while taking into account the current stage of technology, is entrusted to organisations competent in the standardisation area.

3. These technical specifications are not mandatory and maintain their status of voluntary standards.

4. National authorities are obliged to recognise that products manufactured in conformity with harmonised standards (or, provisionally, with national standards) are presumed to conform to the 'essential requirements' established by the directive. This signifies that the producer has the choice of not manufacturing in conformity with the standards, but that in this event he has an obligation to prove that his products conform to the essential requirements of the directive. In order that this system may operate it is necessary to ensure:

   ■ on the one hand that the standards offer a guarantee of quality with regard to the 'essential requirements' established by the directives; and

   ■ on the other hand that the public authorities keep intact their responsibility for the protection of safety (or other requirements envisaged) on their territory.

There is a clear link between the resolution and the **Cassis** principles, which is most apparent in the four fundamental principles, above. This approach established a clear break with the past. Instead of attempting to create a detailed technical specification for a 'Europroduct', which was a difficult and lengthy task, new directives would only set minimum safety and other standards which could be satisfied in a number of different ways in Member States, including different manufacturing methods. The emphasis was now on broad performance standards rather than compliance with detailed technical specifications. Once a Community directive is adopted under this approach, and after the date for implementation has passed, performance is verified at Community level under a process monitored by the Commission. Where a directive has been adopted, Member States are obliged to assume that products purporting to conform to the essential requirements do, in fact, do so. Until new directives are adopted establishing Community-wide standards in other products, Member States should recognise (under the **Cassis** 'mutual recognition' principle) that those products meet appropriate essential requirements, unless there are indications that they do not.

Besides the adoption of a broader approach to essential requirements, agreement between Community institutions was further facilitated by the addition of Art 95 EC Treaty by the Single European Act. Under Art 95, the Council now needs only to agree on a *qualified majority* basis 'codes of essential requirements' for broad, homogeneous product areas or types of risk. This leaves manufacturers with greater flexibility in meeting such requirements. Proof of conformity with essential requirements is satisfied by conformity with standards set by Europe-wide standards bodies, such as the European Committee for Standardisation (CEN) and the European Committee for Electrotechnical Standardisation (CENELEC). Products marked with the appropriate standards mark are presumed to conform. To satisfy those Member States who were concerned about the lowering of general product standards and the effect on specific products, in exceptional circumstances Member States may adopt higher standards than those laid down in the essential requirements. Article 95 EC Treaty (as amended by the ToA) provides as follows:

(4) If, after the adoption by the Council or by the Commission of a harmonisation measure a Member State deems it necessary to apply national provisions on grounds of major needs referred to in Article 30, or relating to protection of the environment or the working environment, it shall notify the Commission of these provisions as well as the grounds for maintaining them.

...

(6) The Commission shall, within six months of the notification as referred to [above], approve or reject the national provisions involved after having verified whether or not they are a means of arbitrary discrimination or a disguised restriction on trade between Member States and whether or not they shall constitute an obstacle to the functioning of the internal market.

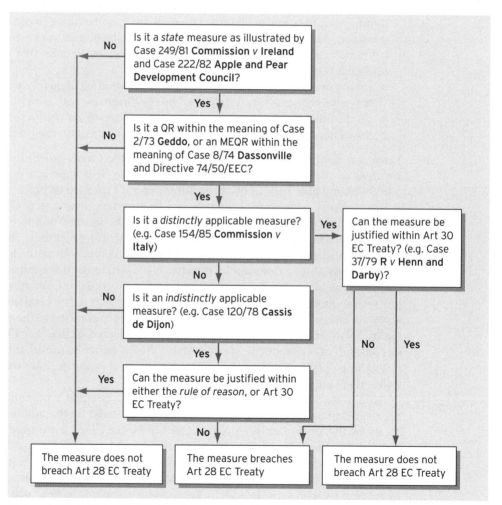

Figure 18.1 Article 28 EC Treaty: quantitative restrictions and measures having an equivalent effect

. . .

(9) By way of derogation from the procedures laid down in Articles 226 and 227, the Commission or any Member State may bring the matter directly before the Court of Justice if it considers that another Member State is making improper use of the powers provided for in this Article.

Between 1984 and 1990 over 800 European product standards were adopted, which was three times as many as in the previous 20 years. Since 1986, when a target of more than 300 directives was set to lay the foundations for the Single Market on 1 January 1993, very few national provisions were approved under the exception contained in Art 95. It remains, however, a valuable safety valve to deal with national concerns over specific products. Overall, the new approach is widely regarded as having had considerable success in reducing national legal and technical barriers and in moving the Community towards a genuine Single Market.

Figure 18.1 consists of a flowchart setting out the application of Arts 28 and 30 EC Treaty.

Summary

Now you have read this chapter you should be able to:

- Explain the purpose and effect of Arts 28–30 EC Treaty which relate to the elimination of quantitative restrictions and measures having an effect equivalent to a quantitative restriction.

- Distinguish between a quantitative restriction and a measure having an effect equivalent to a quantitative restriction.

- Explain the difference between a distinctly applicable measure and an indistinctly applicable measure.

- Understand how the law relating to indistinctly applicable measures is applied by the European Court of Justice

- Explain how to differentiate between rules of dual-burden from those of equal-burden, and assess the impact of the European Court of Justice's **Keck** judgment.

- Explain the circumstances in which a Member State may rely upon Art 30 EC Treaty to justify a distinctly or indistinctly applicable measure.

- Understand how the **Cassis** rule of reason (established by the European Court of Justice) can be relied upon by a Member State to justify an indistinctly applicable measure.

Further reading

Textbooks

Barnard, C. (2004) *The Substantive Law of the EU: The four freedoms* (1st edn), Oxford University Press, Chapters 5 to 7.

Craig, P. and De Burca, G. (2003) *EU Law Text, Cases and Materials* (3rd edn), Oxford University Press, Chapter 15.

Foster, N. (2006) *Foster on EU Law* (1st edn), Oxford University Press, Chapter 7 (Sections 7.7 to 7.11).

Steiner, J., Woods, L. and Twigg-Flesner, C. (2006) *EU Law* (9th edn), Oxford University Press, Chapters 18 to 19.

Storey, T. and Turner, C. (2005) *Unlocking EU Law* (1st edn), Hodder Arnold, Chapter 13.

Tillotson, J. and Foster, N. (2003) *Text, Cases and Materials on EU Law* (4th edn), Cavendish Publishing, Chapter 12.

Weatherill, S. (2006) *Cases and Materials on EU Law* (7th edn), Oxford University Press, Chapters 11 and 12.

Journal articles

Alexander, W., 'IP and the Free Movement of Goods – 1996 Case law of the ECJ' (1998) 29 IIC 16.

Bentley, L. and Burrell, R., 'Copyright and the Information Society in Europe: A Matter of Timing as well as Content' (1997) 34 CML Rev 1197.

Biondi, A., 'The Merchant, the Thief and the Citizen: The Circulation of Works of Art within the European Union' (1997) 34 CML Rev 1173.

Burrows, N., 'Harmonisation of Technical Standards' (1990) 53 MLR 597.

Davies, J., 'Can selling arrangements be harmonised?' (2005) 30 EL Rev 370.

Ehlermann, C., 'The Internal Market Following the Single European Act' (1987) 24 CML Rev 361.

Koutrakos, P., 'On Groceries, Alcohol and Olive Oil: More on free movement of goods after **Keck**' (2001) 26 EL Rev 391.

McGee, A. and Weatherill, S., 'The Evolution of the Single Market – Harmonization or Liberalization?' (1990) 53 MLR 578.

Millet, T., 'Free Movement of Goods and Public Morality' (1987) NLJ 39.

Mortelmans, K., 'Article 30 of the EEC Treaty and Legislation Relating to Market Circumstances: Time to Consider a New Definition?' (1991) 28 CML Rev 115.

Oliver, P., 'Some Further Reflections on the scope of Articles 28-30 (ex 30-36) EC' (1999) 36 CML Rev 783.

Reich, N., 'The November Revolution: **Keck, Meng, Audi** Revisited' (1994) 31 CML Rev 749.

Seville, C., 'Notes on Joined Cases C-427, 429 and 436/93 **Bristol-Myers Squibb and Others v Paranova A/S**' (1997) 34 CML Rev 1039.

Slot, P.J., 'Harmonisation' (1996) 21 EL Rev 378.

Steiner, J., 'Drawing the Line: Uses and Abuses of Article 30 EEC' (1992) 29 CML Rev 749.

Vicien, C.F., 'Why Parallel Imports of Pharmaceutical Products should be Forbidden' (1996) 17 ECLR 219.

Weatherill, S., 'After **Keck**: Some Thoughts on How to Clarify the Clarification' (1996) 33 CML Rev 885.

Wils, W., 'The Search for the Rule in Art 30 EEC: Much Ado About Nothing?' (1993) 18 EL Rev 475.

PART 4

Competition law

19 State monopolies and state aid

At the end of this chapter you should understand:

- How Arts 31, 82 and 86 EC Treaty are applied by the Commission, Court of Justice and Court of First Instance (CFI) to regulate state monopolies.
- How Arts 87 and 88 EC Treaty are applied by the Commission, Court of Justice and CFI to regulate state aid.
- The nature and scope of the block exemption regulations adopted pursuant to Art 89 EC Treaty, which concern the application of Arts 87 and 88 EC Treaty.
- The provisions of Regulations 659/1999 and 794/2004 which lay down the general procedural rules relating to state aid and the application of Art 88 EC Treaty.

Introduction to state monopolies and state aid

When the Community was formed, state ownership of major utilities played an important part in the economic and social policies of the founding states. It continues to do so, although state ownership is now less favoured, and subsidies and direct or indirect regulation of private undertakings providing important services have become more common. In the UK during the 1980s (while Margaret Thatcher was Prime Minister) state ownership of gas, electricity, water and the telecommunications was abandoned in favour of private ownership. State intervention will continue to provide a safety net to industries in decline or facing sudden crises, and to support undertakings providing important public services (such as gas, electricity, water, etc.). Although intervention in these activities by the state may well breach the Community's commitment to a Single Market, in which goods and services compete on an equal basis, the Community's own support for agriculture and agricultural products and its regional and social funds demonstrate an equal commitment to social, educational, health and cultural objectives supported by Community intervention. This support was continued and expanded by the Treaty on European Union, the Treaty of Amsterdam and the Treaty of Nice (Arts 136–152 EC Treaty). The EC Treaty seeks to strike a balance between state intervention and the operation of the market. In Member States, the position of public ownership is, like private ownership, protected by Art 295 EC Treaty. The balance between public and private ownership is a matter for national policy, but state ownership is subject to similar constraints as private ownership. The title to that ownership is a matter of state policy, but the exercise of ownership rights, if it affects trade between Member States, is governed by the law of the Community. The Court of Justice has increasingly seen state intervention as a process that is *prima facie* likely to interfere with the creation and operation of a Single Market in the Community, and has shown a tendency to interpret provisions of Community law allowing state monopolies and subsidies (i.e. state aid) in a restrictive manner, accepting only those seen as necessary to achieve certain clearly defined aims.

The provisions of Community law regulating state monopolies is considered first, followed by the law regulating state aid.

State monopolies

The position with regard to state monopolies is dealt with by Art 31 EC Treaty (previously Art 37):

> Member States shall adjust any state monopolies of a commercial character so as to ensure that no discrimination regarding the conditions under which goods are procured and marketed exists between nationals of Member States.
>
> The provisions of this Article shall apply to any body through which a Member State, in law or in fact, either directly or indirectly supervises, determines or appreciably influences imports or exports between Member States. These provisions shall likewise apply to monopolies delegated by the state to others.

Article 31 must be read in conjunction with Art 86 EC Treaty (previously Art 90). Article 31 is concerned with the procurement and marketing of goods while Art 86 is concerned with services. Article 86 provides:

1. In the case of public undertakings and undertakings to which Member States grant special or exclusive rights, Member States shall neither enact nor maintain in force any measure contrary to the rules contained in this Treaty, in particular to those rules provided for in Article 12 and Articles 81–89.
2. Undertakings entrusted with the operation of services of general economic interest or having the character of a revenue-producing monopoly shall be subject to the rules contained in this Treaty, in particular to the rules on competition, in so far as the application of such rules does not obstruct the performance, in law or in fact, of the particular tasks assigned to them. The development of trade must not be affected to such an extent as would be contrary to the interests of the Community.

Article 86(3) EC Treaty requires the Commission to enforce this Article by addressing, where necessary, appropriate directives or decisions to Member States.

State monopolies of a commercial character

The nature of 'state monopolies of a commercial character' referred to in Art 31 was considered by the Court of Justice in the following case:

Costa v *ENEL* (Case 6/64)

This case concerned the compatibility with Community law of the nationalisation of the Italian electricity industry. The Court of Justice held that:

> One must consider ... carefully paragraph (1) of Article 37 [now Art 31]. This prevents the creation not indeed of all national monopolies but only of those that present 'a commercial character' and even of these, insofar as they tend to introduce the discrimination aforesaid. It follows, therefore, that **to come within the terms of the prohibition of this Article, national monopolies and bodies must on the one hand have as objects transactions in commercial products capable of competition and exchanges between Member States; and on the other hand play a leading part in such exchanges.** [emphasis added]

Whether or not a state monopoly exists is a matter of law and fact.

Article 31 EC Treaty: directly effective

A claimant who proves the existence of a breach of Art 31 and loss caused by that breach may obtain an award of damages, since the provision is directly effective (**Hansen** *v* **Hauptzollamt Flensburg** (Case 91/78)).

Compatibility with Community law

The operation of a body enjoying a state monopoly may involve (i) potential restrictions on the importation of goods into a Member State, thus breaching Art 28 EC Treaty; (ii) discrimination by such a body in relation to the provision of such goods and services; and (iii) the abuse of a monopoly position. An example of the interplay of these provisions was considered by the Court of Justice in the following case:

Société Civile Agricole de la Crespelle v *Coopérative d'Elevage de la Mayenne* (Case C-323/93)

Under French law certain approved bovine insemination centres were granted exclusive rights within a defined area. Breeders established in those areas were, effectively, obliged to use their services. Such licensed centres enjoyed what the Court of Justice described as 'a contiguous series of monopolies territorially limited but together covering the entire territory of a Member State'.

The Court held, first, that the mere creation of such a dominant position by the granting of an exclusive right within the meaning of Art 86(1) EC Treaty was not as such incompatible with Art 82 EC Treaty (see Chapter 21). A Member State contravened the prohibitions contained in those two provisions only if, in merely exercising the exclusive right granted to it, the undertaking in question could not avoid abusing its dominant position. An undertaking abused its dominant position where it had an administrative monopoly and charged fees for its services which were disproportionate to the economic value of the services provided. Secondly, the Court held that national rules, which required importers of bovine semen from a Member State to deliver it only to an approved insemination or production centre, were in breach of Art 28 EC Treaty, but were in the circumstances saved by Art 30 EC Treaty as necessary for the protection of animal health (see Chapter 18).

Although the point was not specifically dealt with in this case, the Court of Justice has held that an exclusive right, *inter alia*, to import particular goods falls within the scope of Art 31 EC Treaty (**Manghera** (Case 59/75)).

In the following case, the Court of Justice had to consider the extent to which the German state alcohol monopoly was compatible with Art 31 EC Treaty:

Hansen v Hauptzollamt Flensburg (Case 91/78)

The Court of Justice held, first, that Art 31 remained applicable wherever the exercise by a state monopoly of its exclusive rights entailed a discrimination or restriction prohibited by that article. Secondly, that Art 31 prohibited a monopoly's right to purchase and resell national alcohol from being exercised so as to undercut imported products with publicly subsidised domestic products.

While Art 86(2) EC Treaty recognises that publicly owned undertakings can carry on revenue-producing economic activities, it specifically prohibits their operation in a way which would constitute an abuse of a monopoly position or which would distort the operation of the market. However, the public body is allowed to derogate from these rules, insofar as it is actually necessary to carry out the tasks assigned to it. The Court of First Instance (CFI) has considered the position of the French Post Office, with regard to this issue, in the following case:

FFSA and Others v Commission (Case T-106/96)

The 'task', in this case, was the maintenance of uneconomic postal services in rural areas. A body of insurers had unsuccessfully complained to the European Commission that the French Post Office was being unlawfully subsidised, contrary to Art 87(1) EC Treaty (previously Art 92(1)). The CFI upheld the Commission's decision. Following the decision of the Court of Justice in **Corbeau** (Case 320/91), the CFI held that the postal monopoly was necessary to enable the Post Office to subsidise the regional development of the postal service. It was only lawful, however, if 'the *sole* purpose of the aid was to offset the additional costs incurred' and 'the grant of the aid is necessary for the undertaking to perform its public service obligations under conditions of economic equilibrium'.

The following case concerned a dispute between an undertaking and a German administrative body, relating to a refusal by the German administrative body to renew authorisation for the provision of patient transport services by ambulance:

Ambulanz Glöckner (Case C-475/99)

The German court was uncertain whether reasons which related to the pursuit of a task of general economic interest were sufficient to justify the exclusion of all competition for that type of service. The German court referred a series of questions to the Court of Justice pursuant to Art 234 EC Treaty.

The Court of Justice found that the German legislation conferred on medical aid organisations a special or exclusive right within the meaning of Art 86(1) EC Treaty, which was therefore applicable in this case. With regard to Art 86(1) EC Treaty, in conjunction with Art 82 EC Treaty (see Chapter 21), the Court found, in its analysis of the relevant market, that patient transport was a service which was distinct from that of emergency transport, and that the *Land* of Rhineland-Palatinate (Germany) constituted a substantial part of the common market, given its surface area and population. The Court nevertheless left it to the national court to determine the geographical extent of the market and to determine whether a dominant position was being occupied. According to the Court, there was potentially an abuse of a dominant position in that the legislation of the *Land* reserved to certain medical aid organisations an ancillary transport activity which could be carried on by independent operators. Finally, the Court concluded that such legislation could be justified under Art 86(2) EC Treaty if the legislation did not bar the grant of an authorisation to independent operators, where the authorised medical aid organisations were unable to satisfy demand existing in the area of medical transport services.

In the following case, the Court of Justice dismissed an action brought by Portugal for annulment of a Commission decision relating to Art 86 EC Treaty:

Portugal v *Commission* (Case C-163/99)

In the contested decision, the Commission had found that the Portuguese legislation which provided for a system of discounts on landing charges that were applied according to the origin of the flight was incompatible with Art 86(1) EC Treaty, in conjunction with Art 82 EC Treaty (see Chapter 21). Portugal pleaded, *inter alia*, breach of the principle of proportionality. However, the Court of Justice held that the decision was not disproportionate, having regard to the wide discretion enjoyed by the Commission under Art 86(3). Portugal also contended that there had been no abuse of a dominant position with regard to discounts granted on the basis of the number of landings. The Court stated, however, that the system of discounts appeared to favour certain airlines, in the present case the national airlines.

The following case concerned an action brought by a trade association of companies offering express courier services, against a Commission decision declaring that the logistical and commercial assistance given by the French Post Office (La Poste) to a private company to which it had entrusted the management of its express courier service did not constitute state aid:

Chronopost, La Poste and French Republic (Joined Cases C-83/01 P, C-93/01 P and C-94/01 P)

In its judgment in **Ufex and Others** (Case T-613/97), the CFI had annulled the Commission's decision that the assistance given by the French Post Office did not constitute state aid, on the ground that the Commission should have examined whether the 'full costs' took account of the factors which an undertaking acting under normal market conditions should have taken into consideration when fixing the remuneration for the services provided.

Hearing the case on appeal, the Court of Justice considered at the outset that the assessment by the CFI had failed to take account of the fact that an undertaking such as La Poste was in a situation very different from that of a private undertaking acting under normal market conditions. La Poste had to acquire substantial infrastructures and resources to enable it to carry out its task of providing a service of general economic interest within the meaning of Art 86 EC Treaty, even in sparsely populated areas where the tariffs did not cover the cost of providing the service in question. The creation and maintenance of the basic postal network were not in line with a purely commercial approach. The Court held that the provision of logistical and commercial assistance was inseparably linked to that network, because it consisted precisely in making available that network which had no equivalent on the market.

The Court of Justice therefore concluded that, in the absence of any possibility of comparing the situation of La Poste with that of a private group of undertakings not operating in a reserved sector, 'normal market conditions', which are necessarily hypothetical, allowing it to be determined whether the provision by a public undertaking of logistical and commercial assistance to its private-law subsidiary was capable of constituting state aid, had to be assessed by reference to the objective and verifiable elements which were available. The costs borne by La Poste in providing such assistance could constitute such objective and verifiable elements. On that basis, there could be no question of state aid to the subsidiary if: (1) it was established that the price charged properly covered all the additional variable costs incurred in providing the logistical and commercial assistance, an appropriate contribution to the fixed costs arising from use of the postal network and an adequate return on the capital investment in so far as it was used for the subsidiary's competitive activity; and (2) there was nothing to suggest that those factors had been underestimated or fixed in an arbitrary fashion.

State undertakings and the need for transparency

Where an undertaking is state owned, or directly or indirectly controlled by the state, it is subject to the provisions of Directive 80/723. This directive (the Transparency Directive) was made under Art 86(3) EC Treaty and requires that financial relations between public authorities and public undertakings are transparent. 'Transparency' in this context means transparency to the Commission (Art 5, Directive 80/723). The particular matters requiring disclosure are the amount of public funds made available directly by public authorities to the public undertakings concerned, or through intermediaries, and the uses to which such public funds are put (Art 1, Directive 80/723). The extent and nature of such support may well be of concern to the Commission in determining whether or not unlawful state aids have been provided.

Directive 80/723 was amended by Directive 2000/52, the substance of which had an implementation date of 31 July 2001. The aim of the amending directive is to achieve the basic objective of transparency by laying down rules requiring specified undertakings to maintain separate accounts relating to the different activities which they carry on. This is considered to be 'the most efficient means by which fair and effective application of the rules on competition to [public and private undertakings granted special or exclusive rights or entrusted with the operation of services of general economic interest . . .] can be assured' (Preamble, Directive 2000/52). The obligation of maintaining separate accounts does not apply to undertakings whose activities are limited to the provision of services of general economic interest and which do not operate activities outside the scope of services of general economic interest, unless such undertakings receive state aid (see below).

Directive 80/723 was further amended by Directive 2005/81, which had an implementation date of 19 December 2006. The purpose of this amendment was due to the Court of Justice deciding in **Altmark Trans GmbH and Regierungspräsidium Magdeburg** v **Nahverkehrsgesellschaft Altmark GmbH** (Case C–280/00) that, under certain conditions, public service compensation does not constitute state aid within the meaning of Art 87(1) EC Treaty. This case, which is considered below, would have had an impact with regard to an undertaking's requirement to maintain separate accounts where state aid is granted to an undertaking providing services of general economic interest and which do not operate activities outside the scope of such services. The amendments made by Directive 2005/81 provide that irrespective of the legal classification of public service compensation in the light of Art 87(1) EC Treaty, the obligation to maintain separate accounts applies to all undertakings receiving such compensation that also carry on activities outside the scope of the service of general economic interest (Art 1, Directive 2005/81). It is only by maintaining separate accounts that the costs imputable to the service of general economic interest can be identified and the correct amount of compensation calculated (Preamble, Directive 2005/81).

State aid

There is no absolute prohibition of state aid in the Treaty. Rather, that the prohibitions are directed against the use of state aid in ways that are 'incompatible with the common market'.

Article 87(1) EC Treaty (previously Art 92(1)) provides that:

> Save as otherwise provided in this Treaty, any aid granted by a Member State or through state resources in any form whatsoever which distorts or threatens to distort competition by favouring certain undertakings or the production of certain goods shall, in so far as it affects trade between Member States, be incompatible with the common market.

Article 87(1) is not concerned with how state aid is granted. It is directed at aid granted by the state or derived from state resources, which either distorts or may distort competition, by favouring undertakings resulting in an impact on trade between Member States.

The scope of 'state aid'

'State aid' has a wide scope including, but not confined to, state subsidies, as determined by the Court of Justice in the following case:

Steenkolenmijnen v HA (Case 30/59)

The Court of Justice held that:

> The concept of an aid is . . . wider than that of a subsidy because it embraces not only positive benefits, such as subsidies themselves, but also interventions which, in various forms, mitigate the charges which are normally included in the budget of an undertaking and which would without, therefore, being subsidies in the strict sense of the word, be similar in character and have the same effect.

State aid may come in a large number of different guises and has been held to include: exemption from duties and taxes; exemption from parafiscal charges; preferential interest rates; guarantees of loans on especially favourable terms; making land or buildings available either for nothing or on especially favourable terms; provision of goods, services or personnel on preferential terms; indemnities against operating losses; and the purchase of a company's shares which is in financial difficulties (**Intermills *v* Commission** (Case 323/82); **Spain *v* Commission** (Joined Cases C–278–280/92); **Commission *v* Sytraval** (Case C–367/95)).

Despite the wide scope of state aid favoured by the Commission, the Court has tended to insist that if it is to be regarded as state aid it must constitute a government measure 'involving a charge on the public account' of the state concerned (**Sloman Neptun** (Case C–72/91); **Kirsammer Hack** (Case C–189/91)). This was not, however, the view of the Advocates-General in both cases. Both decisions have been the subject of criticism for allowing too much scope for states to give unfair competitive advantages to undertakings in their territories by such devices as relaxing environmental and planning controls, or by making various beneficial administrative concessions (Slotboom, 1995).

The following case related to the free movement of goods, but also had a state aid dimension:

Preussen Elektra (Case C-379/98)

A German court was unsure as to the compatibility with Community law of German legislation which obliged electricity supply undertakings to purchase the electricity produced in their area of supply from renewable energy sources, and to pay for it in accordance with a statutory minimum price. The national court sought a preliminary ruling on the interpretation of Arts 28 and 87 EC Treaty. The Court of Justice held that there was no breach of Art 28 EC Treaty (relating to the free movement of goods (see Chapter 18)).

From the point of view of state aid, the main issue was whether legislation such as the German legislation could be categorised as state aid. The Court of Justice pointed out that the concept of state aid has been defined by it as covering 'advantages granted directly or indirectly through state resources'. It then stated that 'the distinction made in [Art 87(1) EC Treaty] between "aid granted by a Member State" and aid granted "through state resources" does not signify that all advantages granted by a state, whether financed through state resources or not, constitute aid but is intended merely to bring within that definition both advantages which are granted directly by the state and those granted by a public or private body designated or established by the state' (para 58). In the case in point, the Court found that the obligation imposed on private electricity supply undertakings to purchase electricity produced from renewable energy sources at fixed minimum prices, did not involve any direct or indirect transfer of state resources to undertakings which produce that type of electricity. Accordingly, there was no state aid for the purposes of Art 87 EC Treaty. The Court also rejected the Commission's argument, put forward in the alternative, that in order to preserve the effectiveness of the state aid rules, read in conjunction with Art 10 EC Treaty (i.e. the Member States' duty to ensure that the obligations set out within the Treaty are fulfilled), it is necessary for the concept of state aid to be interpreted in such a way as to include support measures which are decided upon by the state but which are financed by private undertakings. The Court held that the Treaty articles concerning state aid refer directly to measures emanating from the Member States. Article 10 cannot be used to extend the scope of Art 87 to include conduct by states which does not fall within it.

The following case concerned the question of whether state aid covers public subsidies to allow the operation of regular urban, suburban or regional transport services:

Altmark Trans and Regierungspräsidium Magdeburg (Case C-280/00)

The Court of Justice first examined whether the condition that trade between Member States had to be affected was met. The Court emphasised that the latter did not depend on the local or regional character of the transport services supplied or on the scale of the field of activity concerned. Referring to its case law describing state aid as an advantage granted to a beneficiary undertaking which the latter would not have obtained under normal market conditions, the Court emphasised that public subsidies such as those referred to above are not caught by Art 87(1) EC Treaty where such subsidies are to be regarded as compensation for the services provided by the recipient undertakings in order to discharge public service obligations.

The Court of Justice set out four conditions which had to be met for such compensation to be regarded as being present:

1. the recipient undertaking must be actually required to discharge public service obligations and those obligations must have been clearly defined;
2. the parameters on the basis of which the compensation is calculated must have been established beforehand in an objective and transparent manner;
3. the compensation must not exceed what is necessary to cover all or part of the costs incurred in discharging the public service obligations, taking into account the relevant receipts and a reasonable profit for discharging those obligations; and
4. where the undertaking which is to discharge public service obligations is not chosen in a public procurement procedure, the level of compensation needed must have been determined on the basis of an analysis of the costs which a typical undertaking, well run and adequately provided with means of transport so as to be able to meet the necessary public service requirements, would have incurred in discharging those obligations, taking into account the relevant receipts and a reasonable profit for discharging the obligations.

State aid which is *per se* compatible under Article 87(2) EC Treaty

Some types of aid are, *per se*, deemed to be compatible under Art 87(2) EC Treaty:

The following shall be compatible with the common market:
(a) aid having a social character, granted to individual consumers, provided that such aid is granted without discrimination related to the origin of the products concerned;
(b) aid to make good the damage caused by natural disasters or exceptional occurrences;
(c) aid granted to the economy of certain areas of the Federal Republic of Germany affected by the division of Germany, in so far as such aid is required in order to compensate for the economic disadvantages caused by that division.

An example of aid of the kind referred to in (a) would be sales of basic food products such as bread, pasta and butter at a low, fixed price. In these cases the wholesaler might be compensated by the state for the loss of his profit. The proviso would, however, require that such support would be equally available to imported and home-produced products. The aid referred to in (b) is self-explanatory, and the aid to which Germany was entitled under (c) is now seen by the Commission as no longer necessary. However, it could be argued that the very considerable difficulties suffered by the Eastern territories of the Federal Republic of Germany on reunification were consequent upon the original division, and justified state subsidies to the Eastern industries to bring them up to Western standards, provided that the aid given was no more than necessary to achieve that purpose.

 **State aid which is potentially justifiable under Article 87(3) EC Treaty**

Other types of aid are seen as potentially justifiable. Under Art 87(3), there are five categories of aid. Before a Member State commences or alters any of the aid projects falling within categories (a) to (e) below, it must inform the Commission in sufficient time to enable it to submit its comments (Art 88(3)). The Commission has the power to block the project or require its amendment (Arts 88(2) and (3)). The categories are:

(a) aid to promote the economic development of areas where the standard of living is normally low or where there is serious underemployment;

(b) aid to promote the execution of an important project of common European interest or to remedy a serious disturbance in the economy of a Member State;

(c) aid to facilitate the development of certain economic activities or of certain economic areas, where such aid does not adversely affect trading conditions to an extent contrary to the common interest;

(d) aid to promote culture and heritage conservation, where such aid does not affect trading conditions and competition in the Community to an extent that is contrary to the common interest; and

(e) such other categories of aid as may be specified by decisions of the Council acting by a qualified majority on a proposal from the Commission.

Each of these five categories is now considered.

The promotion of economic development of areas of low income or high underemployment (Article 87(3)(a))

The Commission's criteria to determine whether or not an aid scheme should be approved received the support of the Court of Justice in the following case:

Philip Morris v Commission (Case 730/79)

The Court of Justice held that, first, the aid must promote or further a project that is in the Community interest as a whole. Aid which therefore promotes a national interest is unacceptable. Second, the aid must be necessary for promoting the first objective. Last, the way in which the aid is provided must be proportional to the legitimate object, and must not be likely to affect trade between Member States and distort competition.

In this case, The Netherlands government proposed to grant the applicant capital assistance to enable it to increase cigarette production so that it would account for nearly 50 per cent of cigarette production in The Netherlands. Eighty per cent of that production would be exported to other Member States. There was the possibility that aid could have an effect, therefore, on trade between Member States. Philip Morris argued that Art 87(3) only required that the investment plan be compatible with the objectives set out in paragraphs (a), (b) and (c). It did not have to be shown that the aid would contribute to the attainment of one of those legitimate objectives. The development of cigarette manufacture was to take place in Bergen-op-Zoom, where underemployment was high and the *per capita* income was lower than the national average in the rest of The Netherlands. The company maintained that the Commission had been wrong to compare underemployment and income, not with that prevailing elsewhere in The Netherlands, but with that elsewhere in the Community.

The Court of Justice rejected the argument that trade with other Member States was not likely to be distorted:

When State financial aid strengthens the position of an undertaking compared with other undertakings competing in intra-Community trade, the latter must be regarded as affected by that aid. In this case the aid which the Netherlands government proposed to grant was for an undertaking organised for international trade and this is proved by the high percentage of its production which it intends to export to other Member States. The aid in question was to help enlarge its production capacity and consequently to increase its capacity to maintain the flow of trade including that between Member States. On the other hand the aid is said to have reduced the cost of converting the production facilities and has thereby given the applicant a competitive advantage over manufacturers who have completed or intend to complete at their own expense a similar increase in the productive capacity of their plant.

The Court also refused to accept the company's argument that it was legitimate to look at underemployment and income levels only in The Netherlands, and that the Commission had been wrong to take a broader view of all the circumstances:

These arguments put forward by the applicant cannot be upheld. It should be borne in mind that the Commission has a discretion the exercise of which involves economic and social assessments which must be made in a Community context. That is the context in which the Commission has with good reason assessed the standard of living and serious underemployment in the Bergen-op-Zoom area, not with reference to the national average in the Netherlands but in relation to the Community level ... The Commission could very well take the view, as it did, that the investment to be effected in this case was not 'an important project of Common European interest' ... since the proposed aid would have permitted the transfer to the Netherlands of an investment which could be effected in other Member States in a less favourable economic situation than that of the Netherlands, where the national level of unemployment is one of the lowest in the Community.

Although the Court of Justice has held that decisions of the kind in the above case involve the making of complicated economic assessments with which the Court will not readily interfere, when the Commission purports to be acting according to a stated economic policy, its decisions must be compatible with that policy (**Spain v Commission** (above)).

The Commission issued guidelines on national regional aid outlining the circumstances in which aid would be considered to be in the interest of the Community (OJ 1998 C 74/9, as amended in OJ 2000 C 258/5). These guidelines covered the period 2000 to 2006. Further guidelines were issued in 2002 governing regional aid for large investment projects (OJ 2002 C 70/8, as amended in OJ 2003 C 263/3).

In view of important political and economic developments within the EU since the initial guidelines were issued in 1998 (including EU enlargement on 1 May 2004, the accession of Bulgaria and Romania on 1 January 2007 and the accelerated process of integration following the introduction of the single currency) a comprehensive review of national regional aid was undertaken. As a result of this review, new guidelines on national regional aid have been issued to cover the period 2007 to 2013 (OJ 2006 C 54/8). Although these guidelines do not have legal force, they will undoubtedly be taken into account by the Court of Justice.

The promotion of the execution of a project of common European interest or to remedy a serious economic disturbance (Article 87(3)(b))

The sort of projects which have been approved by the Commission under this head are mostly ones in which there is cross-Community cooperation in some technological or environmental project. In this connection, see for example the following case:

Exécutif Régional Wallon and Glaverbel v Commission (Case 62/87)

The Court of Justice held that there will be no common European interest in a scheme 'unless it forms part of a transnational European programme supported jointly by a number of governments of the Member States, or arises from concerted action by a number of Member States to combat a common threat such as environmental pollution'. As a result, the Court found that a scheme under which modernisation aid was granted to Glaverbel, who were manufacturers of glass in Belgium, was not an important project of European interest, because it was not part of a transnational programme.

Aid to facilitate the development of certain economic activities or certain economic areas (Article 87(3)(c))

In its *First Report on State Aids in the European Community* published in 1989, the Commission reported a very large increase in the preceding ten years of cases notified and investigated under the former Art 92 EC Treaty (now Art 87). A survey in the report indicated that over 108 billion Ecus were given in aid each year over that period, the majority of which went to manufacturing companies pursuant to the former Art 92(3)(c). In its *18th Report on Competition Policy*, published the same year, the Commission described its approach to applications made by Member States for approval of state aids in relation to the regional aspect of the former Art 92(3)(c) (now Art 87(3)(c)):

> Regions falling under Art 92(3) [now Art 87(3)(c)] are those with more general development problems in relation to the national as well as the Community situation. Often they suffer from the decline of traditional industries and are frequently located in the more central prosperous parts of the Community. In its Art 92(3)(c) method, the Commission has established a system which takes account of national regional problems and places them into a Community context.

The Commission has, in the context of Art 87(3)(c), operated on the basis of two primary indicators. The first is income (as measured by gross domestic product or gross value added) and the second is structural unemployment. In this context (unlike that with regard to the criteria applicable to Art 87(3)(a), above), the assessment of conditions is made in the national and the Community context. The better the position of the Member State in which the region is located in relation to the Community as a whole, the wider must be the disparity between the region concerned and the state as a whole, in order to justify the aid. Broadly, regions seeking aid must, in relative terms, be worse off than regions in poorer Member States before aid is approved by the Commission. In addition, for approval of the Commission to be secured, any aid proposal must be linked to a major restructuring of the sector of the industry concerned. It should not be used either simply to 'prop up' an ailing concern, or to allow an undertaking to gain an unfair competitive advantage (**Spain v Commission** (Case C–42/93)). In 1998, the Commission approved a research and development grant to Rolls-Royce by the UK government to develop a new generation of aero engines in Derby. The grant was authorised under Art 87(3)(c) and what is now Art 158 (reduction of disparities between different regions); but it also took account of the need to enable the Community to compete in the worldwide aviation market (*Competition Policy Newsletter* (1998) No. 2, p. 85).

The promotion of heritage conservation (Art 87(3)(d))

This provision was added by the Treaty on European Union, and must be read in the light of Art 151(2) EC Treaty. Article 151(2) provides that:

> Action by the Community shall be aimed at encouraging cooperation between Member States and, if necessary, supporting and supplementing their action in . . . conservation and safeguarding of cultural heritage of European significance.

Heritage conservation is closely linked to the promotion of tourism, the right of access to which is a primary service under Art 49 EC Treaty (**Luisi and Carbone** (Case 286/82); see Chapter 13), and to the obligation of the Community, in Title XII EC Treaty, to contribute to 'the flowering of the cultures of the Member States'. The Treaty of Amsterdam added the obligation of the Community 'to respect and promote the cultural diversity' of its members (Art 151(4) EC Treaty). This addition is intended to provide specific authorisation for the kind of aid approved by the Commission in the past to sustain the Greek film industry (Decision 89/441, OJ 1989 L 208/3).

Specific state aids approved by the Council (Article 87(3)(e))

A number of directives have been made under Art 87(3)(e), including Directive 90/684 on state aid to shipbuilding. Under the directive, state aid could be deemed to be compatible with the common market if it related to shipbuilding and ship conversion which was granted as development assistance to a developing country. The Commission had to verify the development content of the proposal in accordance with criteria laid down by an OECD Working Party. In October 1991 the German government notified the Commission of its intention to grant aid to mainland China in the form of aid credit for three container vessels to be operated by a state-owned Chinese trading company, Cosco. The Commission informed Germany that the proposed aid could not be regarded as 'genuine development aid . . . and is therefore incompatible with the common market'. It declared that it was not satisfied that the aid was any more than 'an operating aid to the German shipyards . . . rather than a genuine aid to a developing country'. This decision was challenged by the German government in an action to annul the decision under the former Art 173 EC Treaty (now Art 230).

The Court of Justice upheld the Commission's decision. The directive conferred a discretion on the Commission which was required to satisfy itself that the aid complied with the OECD criteria. It also had to verify the particular development content of the project. It decided that Cosco was not a company which needed development aid in order to contribute to the general development of China. It was entitled to come to that decision and was well within its discretion to do so.

Block exemptions

Under Art 89 EC Treaty the Council, acting by a qualified majority and having consulted with the European Parliament, can adopt regulations proposed by the Commission concerning the application of Arts 87 and 88 EC Treaty. Pursuant to Art 89, during 1998 the Council adopted Regulation 994/98, the purpose of which is to facilitate the operation of the state aid system. It provides for a block exemption system to be used for certain categories of aid. Pursuant to this regulation, on 21 January 2001 the Commission adopted three regulations for block exemptions as follows:

- Regulation 68/2001 (as amended by Regulation 363/2004) on the application of Arts 87 and 88 EC Treaty to training aid;

- Regulation 69/2001 on the application of Arts 87 and 88 EC Treaty to *de minimus* aid;

- Regulation 70/2001 (as amended by Regulation 364/2004) on the application of Arts 87 and 88 EC Treaty to state aid to small and medium-sized enterprises.

Regulation 2204/2002 on the application of Arts 87 and 88 EC Treaty to state aid for employment was adopted during 2002.

The four regulations (and the two amending regulations) are available in full-text format at:

> http://ec.europa.eu/comm/competition/state_aid/legislation/block.html

The Commission's role of monitoring the grant of state aid

The Commission has a general obligation to keep all systems of state aid under review, both those which are *prima facie* lawful under Art 87(2) and those which have been approved under the Commission's discretionary powers under Art 87(3), to ensure that both continue to be operated in a way that is compatible with the Single Market. It is the Commission which has to decide whether any kind of state aid is compatible with Community law, except for those types of aid which have been given specific clearance by the Council under Art 87(3)(e).

To enable it to assess whether or not any new aid scheme is permitted under Art 87, there is a clearance procedure which must be followed by Member States. Under Art 88(3) EC Treaty (previously Art 93(3)):

> The Commission shall be informed, in sufficient time to enable it to submit its comments, of any plans to grant or alter aid. If it considers that any such plan is not compatible with the common market having regard to Article 87, it shall without delay initiate the procedure provided for in paragraph 2. The Member State concerned shall not put its proposed measures into effect until this procedure has resulted in a final decision.

The Commission is required to decide relatively quickly if a proposed measure is justified under Art 87. In **Germany v Commission** (Case 84/82), the Court declared that two months should suffice for this purpose. If at the end of that time the Commission has not defined its attitude towards the proposal, the Member State that has made the proposal could go ahead with it, but should notify the Commission of its intention to do so.

If the Commission decides that the proposed state aid is incompatible with the Treaty, or if aid which has previously been approved by it is being misused, it can inform the state concerned that the aid scheme should be abolished or altered within a timescale fixed by the Commission, and that the aid, together with interest, should be recovered by the state (**Commission v Italy** (Case C–348/93)). Failure to comply could result in that state being brought before the Court of Justice (Art 88(2)). This occurred in the following case which was decided by the Court of Justice during 2005:

Commission v Greece (Case C-415/03)

The Court of Justice observed that the only defence available to a Member State in opposing an application by the Commission under Art 88(2) EC Treaty for a declaration that it has

failed to fulfil its Treaty obligations is to plead that it was absolutely impossible for it properly to implement the decision ordering recovery of the aid in question. The condition that it
is absolutely impossible to implement a decision is not fulfilled where the defendant government merely informs the Commission of the legal, political or practical difficulties involved in
implementing the decision, without taking any real step to recover the aid from the undertakings concerned, and without proposing to the Commission any alternative arrangements
for implementing the decision which could enable those difficulties to be overcome. Where
the implementation of such a decision encounters no more than a number of difficulties at
national level, the Commission and the Member State concerned must respect the principle
underlying Art 10 EC Treaty, which imposes a duty of genuine cooperation on the Member
States and the Community institutions to work together in good faith with a view to over-
coming difficulties while fully observing the Treaty provisions, in particular the provisions on
state aid.

The Court also stated that, in an action concerning the failure to implement a decision on
state aid which has not been referred to the Court by the Member State to which it was
addressed, the latter is not justified in challenging the lawfulness of that decision.

The Court also observed that no provision of Community law requires the Commission,
when ordering the recovery of aid declared incompatible with the common market, to fix the
exact amount of the aid to be recovered. It is sufficient for the Commission's decision to
include information enabling its recipient to work out itself, without overmuch difficulty, that
amount.

The Commission may confine itself to declaring that there is an obligation to repay the aid
in question and leave it to the national authorities to calculate the exact amounts to be repaid.
The operative part of a Commission decision on state aid is inextricably linked to the statement
of reasons for it. When the decision has to be interpreted, account must be taken of the
reasons which led to its adoption. Therefore, the amounts to be repaid pursuant to the decision
can be established by reading its operative part in conjunction with the relevant grounds.

Although it is not specifically provided for in Art 87, the Court of Justice has accepted
that any aid which has been unlawfully paid may also be recovered by the Commission
(**Commission** *v* **Germany** (Case 70/72)).

Even though the aid may have been accepted by an undertaking in good faith,
without any reason to believe that it had been paid in breach of Community law, that
innocent receipt cannot found a legitimate expectation that the aid may be retained. The
effect of doing so could be fatal to the effective operation of Arts 87 and 88, as the Court
of Justice stated in the following case:

Commission v *Germany* (Case C-5/89)

The Court of Justice held as follows:

> A Member State whose authorities have granted aid contrary to the procedural rules laid down in
> Article 93 [now Art 88] may not rely on the legitimate expectations of recipients in order to justify a
> failure to comply with the obligation to take the steps necessary to implement a Commission decision
> instructing it to recover the aid. If it could do so, Articles 92 and 93 [now Arts 87 and 88] of the Treaty
> would be set at nought, since national authorities would thus be able to rely on their own unlawful
> conduct in order to deprive decisions taken by the Commission under provisions of the Treaty of their
> effectiveness.

In **Land Rheinland-Pfalz** *v* **Alcan Deutschland GmbH** (Case C–24/95) the Court of Justice also made it clear that repayment had to be made even if it would be unlawful under state time-limit rules.

The obligation to recover aid declared incompatible with the common market was examined by the CFI in **ESF Elbe-Stahlwerke Feralpi** *v* **Commission** (Case T–6/99). In this case, the CFI held that the principle of legitimate expectation precluded the Commission from ordering the recovery of aid when, according to information from third parties, it considered its compatibility with the common market in coal and steel *several years after approval of the aid concerned*, and held it incompatible with that market.

It is not only the Commission which will have an interest in the payment of state aids. Rival companies may also feel threatened by the actual or proposed distribution of state support and may wish to challenge a decision of the Commission approving it:

ASPEC and AAC v *Commission* (Case T-435/93)

Aid had been approved by the Commission under Arts 87 and 88 in relation to the production of starch in the *mezzogiorno* area of Italy. This would have had the consequence of increasing production by 7 per cent at Community level and of establishing a production level in Italy alone which would have exceeded the previous total production capacity of that country. The challengers would have been seriously affected by the decision and the CFI recognised that they had a sufficient interest to mount a challenge under the former Art 173 EC Treaty (now Art 230) (see Chapter 8).

Although the Court has previously held that the Commission enjoys a wide discretion in granting approval, its reasoning must be consistent with its declared policy, and it must adopt proper procedures when adopting its decision (see **Spain** *v* **Commission** (above)). In **ASPEC and AAC**, the decision had never actually been taken by the full Commission but, in breach of its own procedures, had been delegated to Ray MacSharry, the then Agriculture Commissioner, on the eve of the Commission's annual holiday. The decision to approve the aid was, accordingly, annulled by the Court.

Lastly, it should be noted that damages can be awarded against the government of a Member State that has granted competition-distorting state aids without having notified these to the Commission for review (**Fédération Nationale du Commerce** *v* **France** (Case 354/90)).

Regulation 659/1999

Regulation 659/1999 was adopted by the Council on 22 March 1999 and lays down detailed rules for the application of Art 88 EC Treaty. The aim of the regulation is to improve transparency and legal certainty by codifying and clarifying the procedural rules relating to state aid. This regulation will therefore take the place of the procedural matters discussed above but, as stated, its purpose is to codify and clarify these matters rather than to replace them. The regulation sets out procedures regarding the following:

- notified aid;
- unlawful aid;
- misuse of aid; and
- existing aid schemes.

It also sets out the rights of interested parties and codifies monitoring mechanisms through a system of annual reports and on-site monitoring. This regulation has been implemented by Regulation 794/2004.

Regulations 659/1999 and 794/2004 are available in full-text format at: http://ec.europa.eu/comm/competition/state_aid/legislation/rules.html

Summary

Now you have read this chapter you should be able to:

- Explain how Arts 31, 82 and 86 EC Treaty are applied by the Commission, European Court of Justice and Court of First Instance (CFI) to regulate state monopolies.

- Outline the provisions of Directive 80/723 (the transparency Directive) which requires transparency of financial relations between public authorities and undertakings.

- Explain how Arts 87 and 88 EC Treaty are applied by the Commission, European Court of Justice and CFI to regulate state aid.

- Outline the types of aid which are per se compatible with Art 87(1) EC Treaty.

- Understand and describe the types of aid which may be potentially justifiable pursuant to Art 87(3) EC Treaty.

- Describe and evaluate the nature and scope of the block exemption regulations adopted pursuant to Art 89 EC Treaty, which concern the application of Arts 87 and 88 EC Treaty.

- Outline the provisions of Regulations 659/1999 and 794/2004 which lay down the general procedural rules relating to state aid and the application of Art 88 EC Treaty.

References

Slotboom, M., 'State Aids in Community Law: A Broad or a Narrow Definition?' (1995) 20 EL Rev 289.

Further reading

Textbooks

Craig, P. and De Burca, G. (2003) *EU Law Text, Cases* and *Materials* (3rd edn), Oxford University Press, Chapter 24.

Steiner, J., Woods, L. and Twigg-Flesner, C. (2006) *EU Law* (9th edn), Oxford University Press, Chapters 26 and 30.

Wallace, H., Wallace, W. and Pollack, M.A. (2005) *Policy Making in the European Union* (5th edn), Chapter 5.

Journal articles

Abbamonte, G., 'Competitors' Right to Challenge Illegally Granted Aid and the Problem of the Conflicting Decisions in the field of Competition Law' [1997] ECLR 87.

Abbamonte, G. and Rabassa, V., 'Foreclosure and Vertical Mergers' [2001] ECLR 214.

Bishop, B. and Caffarra, C., 'Merger Control in "New Markets"' [2001] ECLR 31.

Evans, A., 'Privatisation and State Aid Control under EC Law' (1997) 18 ECLR 259.

Evans, A. and Martin, M., 'Socially Acceptable Distortions of Competition: Community Policy on State Aid' (1991) 16 EL Rev 79.

Frazer, T., 'The New Structural Funds, State Aids and Interventions in the Single European Market' (1995) 32 CML Rev 3.

Motta, M., 'EC Merger Policy and the Airtours Case' [2000] ECLR 199.

Ross, M., 'State Aids and National Courts: Definition and other problems – a case of premature emancipation?' (2000) 37 CMLR 401.

Schütte, M. and Hix, J.P., 'The Application of the EC State Aid Rule to Privatisations: The East German Example' (1995) 32 CML Rev 215.

Sinnaeve, E., 'Block Exemptions for State Aid: More scope for state aid control of Member States and competitors' (2001) 38 CML Rev 1479.

Slotboom, M., 'State Aids in Community Law: A Broad or a Narrow Definition?' (1995) 20 EL Rev 289.

Stuart, E.G., 'Recent Developments in EU Law and Policy on State Aids' (1996) 17 ECLR 226.

Völcker, S.B., 'Developments in EC competition law in 2004: An overview' (2005) 42 CML Rev 1691.

20 Cartels and restrictive agreements: Article 81 EC Treaty

Aims and objectives

At the end of this chapter you should understand:

- The scope of Community competition law and policy.
- The scope of Art 81(1) EC Treaty which prohibits agreements which restrict competition.
- How to apply the Art 81(3) EC Treaty criteria which provide exemption from the prohibition under Art 81(1) EC Treaty.
- The procedural changes made to the application of Art 81(3) EC Treaty by Regulation 1/2003.

Competition law and policy

In its *First Report on Competition Policy* the Commission emphasised the value of effective competition in the Community. Competition is the best stimulant of economic activity, since it guarantees the widest possible freedom of action to all. An active competition policy, pursued in accordance with the provisions of the Treaties establishing the Communities, makes it easier for the supply and demand structures continually to adjust to technological development. Through the interplay of decentralised decision-making machinery, competition enables enterprises continuously to improve their efficiency, which is essential for the steady improvement of living standards and employment prospects within the countries of the Community. From this point of view, competition policy is an essential means for satisfying to a great extent the individual and collective needs of society.

Competition is not, however, regarded as an end in itself. It is one of the most important means by which a genuinely integrated market is achieved. Articles 81 and 82 EC Treaty (previously Arts 85 and 86) match Arts 28 and 29 EC Treaty (previously Arts 30 and 34), in the sense that the latter are aimed at measures taken by Member State governments which have the effect of restricting the free movement of goods (see Chapter 18), while the former are concerned with restrictive and abusive practices by undertakings which have the effect of excluding or restricting goods or services from Member States. The distinction between state and private undertaking in this context is not, of course, absolute. States may run commercial monopolies and private undertakings, and may secure an unfair competitive advantage by injections of state capital and other state aids. Both practices are subject to restriction under the Treaty and have been considered in Chapter 19. Large private business corporations, some of which have a bigger annual turnover than the gross domestic product of many small states, dominate major sectors of the EU's economy. Abusive practices by such businesses may have more impact on cross-border trade than the actions of smaller Member State governments. Paradoxically, to create a genuinely free and competitive market, some restrictions are essential to ensure that the largest actors in the market place do not distort the working of the market to their own advantage and to the disadvantage of competitors and consumers. The primary objective, therefore, of EU competition policy has been market integration. A secondary one has been a form of equity or equality of competition, an aspect of 'the level playing field' to which many businesses aspire in the Community. The third aspect of competition policy is that espoused by the Commission in its First Report – the promotion of efficiency. Increasingly, this is viewed in the wider trading context of North and South America, the Pacific rim, China and India.

Competition law, more than any other area of Community law, is informed by economic factors. Conduct which may be lawful in one context may be unlawful in another. The behaviour of business actors will have to be assessed in the light of prevailing economic circumstances, and the way in which particular markets may react. The pricing policy of a company which has a monopoly will be the subject of acute interest to consumers, whereas overpricing by a company in a highly competitive market will rapidly be corrected by the effect on that company of consumers taking their custom elsewhere. The behaviour of business undertakings in relation to competition law and policy must always, therefore, be viewed in the context of such matters as degrees of concentration and the relevance of market power, the importance of entry barriers, and actual and potential competition.

Community competition policy, taking the objectives discussed above into account, is directed towards three kinds of anti-competitive activity:

1. restrictive trading agreements between otherwise independent business undertakings which may affect trade between Member States and which distort competition within the common market (Art 81 EC Treaty); considered further within this chapter;

2. abusive, anti-competitive practices of large undertakings which dominate markets for goods or services which affect trade between Member States (Art 82 EC Treaty); considered further within Chapter 21;

3. major mergers of undertakings resulting in positions of market dominance in the Community (EC Merger Regulation 139/2004, which replaced Regulation 4064/89); considered further within Chapter 21.

Each of these kinds of anti-competitive practice is subject to regulation and control by the Commission, and the national competition authorities and courts of the Member States. The powers of the Commission, and the national competition authorities and courts of the Member States, and the way in which these powers are interpreted and applied, are considered in Chapter 22. The primary law on which the regulation of anti-competitive practices is based is considered within this chapter and the next.

Over the past few years there have been major changes to the regulation and control of these anti-competitive practices. These changes have been implemented primarily through secondary Community instruments. In addition, in some instances, the Commission has issued guidelines on the application of the anti-competitive measures.

The aim of these guidelines is to assist industry in making the regulation and control processes more transparent. These changes are discussed throughout this and the next two chapters, where relevant.

The Commission's competition website contains current primary and secondary legislation, together with proposals for the future. It also includes the full texts of non-binding guidelines. See:

> http://ec.europa.eu/comm/competition/index_en.html

Article 81 EC Treaty

Article 81 EC Treaty (previously Art 85) is directed against cooperation between companies that operate in an anti-competitive way. Article 81(1) prohibits:

> ... all agreements between undertakings, decisions by associations of undertakings and concerted practices which may affect trade between Member States and which have as their object or effect the prevention, restriction or distortion of competition within the common market.

A number of examples of the type of agreements covered by Art 81(1) are provided in Art 81(1)(a)–(e), i.e. those which:

(a) directly or indirectly fix purchase or selling prices or any other trading conditions (Art 81(1)(a));

(b) limit or control production, markets, technical development, or investment (Art 81(1)(b));

(c) share markets or sources of supply (Art 81(1)(c));

(d) apply dissimilar conditions to equivalent transactions with other trading parties, thereby placing them at a competitive disadvantage (Art 81(1)(d));

(e) make the conclusion of contracts subject to acceptance by the other parties of supplementary obligations which, by their nature or according to commercial use, have no connection with the subject of such contracts (Art 81(1)(e)).

Article 81(2) provides that any agreement or decision prohibited by Art 81(1) shall be automatically void. Although the list in Art 81(1) is not exhaustive, it is indicative of the kind of practices which will breach the prohibition. It is primarily aimed at 'horizontal' cooperation between nominally competing companies; the classic cartel. It is also designed to deal with restrictive agreements between manufacturers, wholesalers and retailers (i.e. vertical agreements) which also affect the availability of goods and services, and the terms on which they are supplied. The Commission remains free to identify other agreements or practices which are operated in an anti-competitive way. There are, in addition, a number of agreements, decisions and practices which may be declared not to breach the prohibition in Art 81(1). These are listed in Art 81(3):

> The provisions of paragraph 1 may, however, be declared inapplicable in the case of:
> – any agreement or category of agreements between undertakings;
> – any decision or category of decisions by associations of undertakings;
> – any concerted practice or category of concerted practices
> which contributes to improving the production or distribution of goods or to promoting technical or economic progress, while allowing consumers a fair share of the resulting benefit, and which does not:

(a) impose on the undertakings concerned restrictions which are not indispensable to the attainment of these objectives;

(b) afford such undertakings the possibility of eliminating competition in respect of a substantial part of the products in question.

Prior to 1 May 2004, the Commission was solely empowered to apply Art 81(3); however, Regulation 1/2003 now provides that Art 81(3) can be applied by the national competition authorities and the courts of the Member States (Arts 5 and 6, Regulation 1/2003; see below and Chapter 22).

Undertakings

The term 'undertaking' includes every kind of natural or legal person engaged in economic or commercial activity; it must be established in order to make a profit. The Court has often had to consider the nature of 'undertakings' to which Arts 81 and 82 are applicable, as illustrated in the following four cases:

Poucet v Assurances Générales de France (Case C-159/91)

Complaints had been made alleging anti-competitive restrictions on market access for 'consumers' of social insurance 'services'. The Court of Justice decided that regional social security organisations were not 'undertakings'. The Court distinguished between bodies pursuing economic activities as such and those activities which are based upon a principle of solidarity and which are pursued entirely without an intention to make a profit.

AOK Bundesverband and Others (Joined Cases C-264/01, C-306/01, C-354/01 and C-355-01)

Several questions on the interpretation of Arts 81, 82 and 86 EC Treaty were referred to the Court of Justice for a preliminary ruling by the Oberlandesgericht Düsseldorf (Higher Regional Court, Düsseldorf, Germany) and the Bundesgerichtshof (Federal Court of Justice, Germany). The cases concerned disputes between (i) associations of sickness and health insurance funds; and (ii) pharmaceutical companies, concerning the fixed maximum amounts payable by sickness funds towards the cost of medicinal products and treatment materials which had been established by the German legislature.

The Oberlandesgericht Düsseldorf and the Bundesgerichtshof essentially asked the Court of Justice whether the competition rules laid down by the EC Treaty precluded groups of sickness funds, such as the fund associations, from determining fixed maximum amounts corresponding to the upper limit of the price of medicinal products whose cost is borne by the sickness funds.

The Court adopted the solution set out in its **Poucet** case law, to the effect that the concept of an undertaking, within the context of Community competition law, does not cover bodies entrusted with the management of statutory health insurance and old-age insurance schemes which pursue an exclusively social objective and do not engage in economic activity. The Court took the view in **Poucet** that this was the position with regard to sickness funds, which, even though the legislature had given them a degree of latitude in setting contribution rates in order to promote sound management, were compelled by law to offer to their members essentially identical obligatory benefits which do not depend on the amount of the contributions. The Court of Justice accordingly ruled in the present cases that 'in determining the fixed maximum amounts, the fund associations merely perform a task for management of the German social security system which is imposed upon them by legislation a ⁻ᵈ they do not act as undertakings engaging in economic activity' (para 64). Articles 81 and 82 EC Treaty were therefore not applicable to such measures.

SAT v *Eurocontrol* (Case C-364/92)

The Court of Justice concluded that Eurocontrol, a body set up by treaty to recover fees payable by airlines for traffic control services, was not an 'undertaking'. It undertook the tasks assigned to it in the public interest with a view to assuring the maintenance and improvement of air transport. There was not a sufficient economic element in the work of Eurocontrol, which could not be held responsible for the amounts which it collected. The fees payable had been established by the states which were parties to the treaty by which it was established.

Diego Cali v *SEPG* (Case C-343/95)

The Court of Justice held that a body established under national law to collect harbour dues in the port of Genoa (intended to cover the cost of anti-pollution measures) was not an 'undertaking' within the meaning of Arts 81 and 82. The body performed 'a task in the public interest which forms part of the essential functions of the states as regards protection of the environment in maritime areas'.

However, the fact that a body is state-owned or state-financed and provides a service usually provided by the state does not prevent it from being an 'undertaking' within Arts 81 and 82 if it is providing services 'of general economic interest' (**Job Centre Coop** (Case C–55/96)).

Rules of professional conduct

The issue before the Court of First Instance (CFI) in the following case was whether the rules which regulate the exercise of a liberal profession fall within the scope of Art 81 EC Treaty:

Institut des mandataires agréés v *Commission* (Case T-144/99)

The CFI decided that rules which regulate the exercise of a liberal profession cannot be considered to fall as a matter of principle outside the scope of Art 81(1) merely because they are classified as 'rules of professional conduct' by the competent bodies. It follows that an examination on a case-by-case basis is essential in order to assess the validity of such rules under that provision of the Treaty, in particular by taking account of their impact on the freedom of action of the members of the profession and on its organisation and also on the recipients of the services in question. In this case that approach yielded real results because the CFI confirmed, on one point, the Commission's finding that a simple prohibition, under a code of conduct, of comparative advertising between professional representatives restricts competition in that it limits the ability of more efficient professional representatives to develop their

services. This has the consequence, *inter alia*, that the clientele of each professional representative is crystallised within a national market.

In **Wouters and others** *v* **Algemene Raad van de Nederlandse Orde van Advocaten**
(Case C–309/99) the Court of Justice held that a regulation concerning partnerships
between members of the Bar and other professionals, adopted by a body such as the Bar
of The Netherlands, was to be treated as a decision adopted by an association of undertakings within the meaning of Art 81(1) EC Treaty. The Court of Justice further held that
the regulation in question did not breach Art 81(1) because although its effect was to
restrict competition, the Bar of The Netherlands could reasonably have considered that
the regulation was necessary for the proper practice of the legal profession within The
Netherlands.

Sporting bodies

The following case concerned the issue of whether or not a sporting body (in this case
the International Olympic Committee (IOC)) was subject to Community competition
law. With regard the free movement of workers and freedom to provide services, the
Court of Justice has previously held that sport is subject to Community law only in so far
as it constitutes an economic activity. Therefore, for example, rules which limit the
number of professional players who are nationals of other Member States are in breach
of the provisions relating to the free movement of workers (see, for example, **Bosman**
(Case C–415/93), and Chapter 11). In the following case, the CFI extended this rationale
to Community competition law and decided that because the IOC was not engaged in
an economic activity, with regard to the rules in question, it was not subject to
Community competition law. However, the Court of Justice (delivering its judgment
during 2006) decided otherwise:

Meca-Medina and Majcen v *Commission* (Case C-519/04P)

The two applicants were athletes who competed in long-distance swimming events. They had
been suspended under the Olympic Movement's Anti-Doping Code after testing positive for
Nandrolone. They had claimed before the Commission that the IOC's anti-doping rules
infringed the Community rules on competition (and the free movement of services). They
lodged a complaint with the Commission. The Commission rejected the complaint and the
two athletes made an application to the CFI for the Commission's decision to be annulled. The
CFI upheld the decision (in Case T-313/02).

The CFI stated that, according to the settled case law of the Court of Justice, sport is
subject to Community law only in so far as it constitutes an economic activity within the
meaning of Art 2 EC Treaty. The provisions of the EC Treaty on free movement of workers
and services apply to the rules adopted in the field of sport which concern the economic
aspect which sporting activity can present. That applies, in particular, to the rules providing
for the payment of fees for the transfer of professional players between clubs (transfer
clauses) or limiting the number of professional players who are nationals of other Member
States which those clubs may field in matches. On the other hand, Community law does not
extend to what are purely sporting rules which for that reason have nothing to do with economic activity, like the rules on the composition of national teams or rules fixing, for example,
the length of matches or the number of players on the field.

After noting that the Court of Justice had not, in cases concerning Art 39 EC Treaty (free movement of workers) and Art 49 EC Treaty (freedom to provide services), had to rule on whether sporting rules are subject to the Treaty provisions on competition, the CFI considered that the principles identified in respect of free movement of workers and services are equally valid as regards the provisions of the EC Treaty relating to competition and that the opposite is also true. According to the CFI, it followed that purely sporting legislation did not come under either the Community provisions on free movement of persons and services or the provisions on competition.

The applicants appealed to the Court of Justice, seeking (i) the setting aside of the CFI's judgment; and (ii) annulment of the Commission's decision.

The Court of Justice reiterated that sport is subject to Community law in so far as it constitutes an economic activity, but that the provisions of the Treaty on freedom of movement for persons and freedom to provide services do not affect rules concerning questions which are of purely sporting interest and, as such, have nothing to do with economic activity.

The Court of Justice stated that if, by contrast, those rules do not constitute restrictions on freedom of movement because they concern questions of purely sporting interest and, as such, have nothing to do with economic activity, that fact means neither that the sporting activity in question necessarily falls outside the scope of the provisions of Community competition law nor that the rules do not satisfy the specific requirements of those provisions.

By adopting the opposite approach, without first determining whether those rules fulfilled the specific requirements of Community competition law, the Court of Justice held that the CFI erred in law. The Court of Justice set aside the judgment of the CFI.

The Court of Justice then went on to rule on the application for annulment of the Commission's decision. As regards the compatibility of the rules at issue, with the rules on competition, the Court of Justice stated that the penal nature of the rules at issue and the magnitude of the penalties applicable if they are breached, are capable of producing adverse effects on competition. In order to escape the prohibition on distortion of competition laid down by the Treaty, the restrictions imposed by those rules must be limited to what is necessary to ensure the proper conduct of competitive sport.

Rules of that kind could indeed prove excessive as a result of (i) the way in which the dividing line between circumstances which amount to doping in respect of which penalties may be imposed and those which do not is drawn; and (ii) the severity of those penalties. The Court stated that it did not appear that the restrictions which the threshold beyond which the presence of Nandrolone in an athlete's body indicated doping went beyond what was necessary in order to ensure that sporting events took place and functioned properly.

Since the applicants had not pleaded that the penalties that were applicable and were imposed in the present case were excessive, the Court of Justice held that it had not been established that the anti-doping rules at issue were disproportionate. Consequently, the Court of Justice dismissed the action for annulment of the Commission's decision.

The following case was decided by the CFI during 2005, prior to the Court of Justice's judgment in the above case:

Piau v *Commission* (Case T-193/02 (under appeal, Case C-171/05P))

The CFI once again made it clear that the competition rules can, in certain circumstances, apply in the area of sport. In this case, the Commission had rejected, on grounds of lack of Community interest, a complaint by the applicant challenging the Fédération internationale de football association (FIFA) Players' Agents Regulations. In its judgment, the CFI held that football clubs and the national associations grouping them together are undertakings and associations of undertakings respectively, within the meaning of Community competition law. Consequently, FIFA, which brings together national associations, itself constitutes an association of undertakings within the meaning of Art 81 EC Treaty. On the basis of that initial finding, the CFI held that the Players' Agents Regulations constituted a decision by an association of undertakings. The purpose of the occupation of players' agent was to introduce, on a regular basis, and for a fee, a player to a club with a view to employment, or to introduce two clubs to one another with a view to concluding a transfer contract. It was therefore an economic activity involving the provision of services, which did not fall within the scope of the specific nature of sport, as defined by the case law.

While the CFI's approach may be inconsistent with that of the Court of Justice in **Meca-Medina and Majcen** *v* **Commission**, the CFI's decision (that FIFA's Players' Agents Regulations come within the scope of Community competition law) is probably correct. The case has been appealed to the Court of Justice.

Agreements, decisions and concerted practices

Article 81 is applicable only if there is an 'agreement', a 'decision by an association of undertakings' or a 'concerted practice'.

Agreement

Agreements are not confined to binding contracts of whatever kind, but include understandings and 'gentlemen's agreements' (**ACF Chemiefarma** *v* **Commission** (Case 41/69)). The type of loose arrangement that may fall foul of Art 81(1) is demonstrated by the facts of the following case:

BMW Belgium v *Commission* (Case 32/78)

An attempt was made by BMW's subsidiary in Belgium to discourage car dealers there from selling BMW cars to other Member States. BMW dealers in Belgium had received a circular from BMW Belgium urging them not to engage in such sales. They were asked to indicate assent to this policy by signing and returning a copy of the circular. It was made clear that this was not a contractual document, but the Court nonetheless held that it was an 'agreement' under Art 81(1).

The scope of 'agreement' was considered by the CFI in the following case:

Tréfilenrope SARL v *Commission* (Case T-148/89)

The CFI declared that:

For there to be an agreement within the meaning of Article 85(1) [now Art 81(1)] of the Treaty, it is sufficient for the undertakings in question to have expressed their joint intention to conduct themselves in the market in a particular way.

In **Volkswagen** *v* **Commission** (Case T–62/98), the CFI partially dismissed the action for annulment of the Commission's decision imposing a fine on Volkswagen for infringement of Art 81 EC Treaty. Volkswagen appealed the CFI's decision to the Court of Justice:

Volkswagen v *Commission* (Case C-338/00)

The Court of Justice considered that the CFI had correctly applied the case law whereby 'a call by a motor vehicle manufacturer to its authorised dealers is not a unilateral act which falls outside the scope of Art 81(1) but is an agreement within the meaning of that provision if it forms part of a set of continuous business relations governed by a general agreement drawn up in advance'. The implementation of a policy of supply quotas by a motor manufacturer on dealers with a view to blocking re-exports, constitutes not a unilateral measure but an agreement within the meaning of that provision. In this case, in order to impose that policy, the manufacturer used clauses of the dealership agreement, such as that enabling supplies to dealers to be limited, and thereby influenced the commercial conduct of those dealers.

The 'agreement' does not have to be voluntary. In **The Community** *v* **Volkswagen AG and Others** (Case IV/35.733), the Commission concluded that there existed an 'agreement' between Volkswagen and its dealers in Italy where they complied with instructions (reinforced by heavy pressure from Volkswagen) not to sell to purchasers from outside Italy.

Decision by an association of undertakings

The commonest kind of decision at which Art 81(1) is aimed is that of a trade association which lays down standards for the activities of its members. Standardisation of pricing or the way in which a service may be supplied may well fall foul of the provisions of Art 81. Even an agreement to supply information about sales by competitors, although it is concerned with neither prices nor any anti-competitive arrangement, has been held to fall within Art 81, since it could enable the dominant suppliers to adopt strategies to resist market penetration by those competitors (**Fiatagri UK Ltd** *v* **Commission** (Case T–34/92)). The body concerned does not, however, have to be engaged in commercial activity itself, as illustrated in the following case:

NV IAZ International Belgium and Others v *Commission* (Case 96/82)

Two Belgian Royal Decrees provided that washing machines and dishwashers could be connected to the main water supply only if they satisfied Belgian standards. For the purpose of monitoring the conformity of washing machines or dishwashers with those Belgian standards, the manufacturers and sole importers of electrical appliances affiliated to certain trade organisations made an agreement with the national association of water suppliers (the ANSEAU-NAVEWA agreement). Under this agreement, all appliances put into commercial distribution had to bear a label issued by a designated trade organisation. The Commission made a decision that certain provisions of the agreement infringed Art 81(1). In its view, the offending provisions excluded the possibility for importers other than the sole importers to obtain a conformity check for the washing machines and dishwashers which they imported into Belgium under conditions which did not discriminate against them. ANSEAU attempted to argue that the agreement did not fall within Art 81(1) as its member undertakings were not legally bound by the agreement and since ANSEAU did not itself carry on any kind of economic activity. The Court of Justice rejected both arguments:

> Article [81(1)] of the Treaty also applies to associations of undertakings in so far as their own activities or those of the undertakings affiliated to them are calculated to produce the results which it aims to suppress ... A recommendation, even if it has no binding effect, cannot escape Article [81(1)] where compliance with the recommendation by the undertakings to which it is addressed has an appreciable influence in the market in question.

However, the Court of Justice has recognised a limit to the application of Art 81 where the nominees of trade organisations concerned with the fixing of prices were genuinely independent of their parent bodies:

Germany v *Delta Schiffahrts und Speditionsgesellschaft GmbH* (Case C-153/93)

Representatives of shippers and inland waterway ship operators were both represented on freight commissions which fixed inland waterway freight charges. These commissions set the relevant charges which were approved by the Federal Minister of Transport and were then compulsory. A shipper challenged these charges as being contrary to Art 81 and the case was referred to the Court of Justice under Art 234 EC Treaty. The Court held that Art 81 did not preclude rules of a Member State from providing that tariffs for commercial inland waterways traffic might be fixed by the freight commissions comprised of individuals recommended by the businesses concerned, provided that they were genuinely independent of those businesses and provided that the public authority retained a power to override their decisions.

Concerted practice

'Concerted practice' refers to some kind of coordinated action which, although it may fall short of an agreement, knowingly substitutes practical cooperation for competition. This is illustrated in the following case:

ICI v *Commission* (Case 48/69)

ICI was among a number of businesses producing aniline dyestuffs in Italy. It was the first to impose a price increase, but was shortly followed by other producers of similar products, accounting for more than 80 per cent of the market. A similar pattern of price increases had taken place among the ten major producers of aniline dyestuffs who dominated the dyestuffs market in the Community. The Commission concluded from the circumstances that there had been a 'concerted practice' between the undertakings, and imposed fines on them. The undertakings challenged the Commission's decision, arguing that the price increases merely reflected parallel behaviour in an oligopolistic market where each producer followed the price leader. An oligopoly is a market in which a small number of suppliers supply the preponderant portion of demand (for a discussion on oligopolies, see Green, Hartley and Usher, 1991, Chapter 15). The Court of Justice considered the circumstances and the nature of a concerted practice in the context of Art 81:

Article 85 [now Art 81] draws a distinction between the concept of 'concerted practices' and that of 'agreements between undertakings' or of 'decisions of associations'; the object is to bring within the prohibition of that Article a form of coordination between undertakings which, without having reached the stage where an agreement properly so called has been concluded, knowingly substitutes practical cooperation between them for the risks of competition.

By its very nature, then, a concerted practice does not have all the elements of a contract but may *inter alia* arise out of coordination which becomes apparent from the behaviour of the participants. Although parallel behaviour may not by itself be identified with a concerted practice, it may, however, amount to strong evidence of such a practice if it leads to conditions of competition which do not correspond to the normal conditions of the market, having regard to the nature of the products, the size and number of the undertakings and the volume of the said market. (paras 64 to 66)

In the above case, the Court of Justice went on to decide that there was evidence of a concerted practice that breached Art 81. Concertation is difficult to prove, and the mere fact of parallel price increases is not conclusive. There must be 'a firm, precise and consistent body of evidence' on concertation to justify such a finding (**Åhlström Osakeyhito** *v* **Commission** (Joined Cases C–89, 104, 114, 116, 117 & 125–129/85)).

An agreement between undertakings

As discussed above, the concept of an 'undertaking' is wide, and it includes all legal and natural persons involved in economic or commercial activity, such as companies, sole traders and state-owned public utilities. Undertakings may be engaged in the manufacture, sale or distribution of products or the provision of services and may comprise several companies which are owned or controlled by another one. There must be an agreement or concerted practice by two or more such undertakings, as stated by the Court of Justice in the following case:

Viho Europe BV v *Commission* (Case T-102/92)

The Court of Justice stated that there will be no agreement between 'undertakings' where it is within:

... one economic unit within which subsidiaries do not enjoy real autonomy in determining their course of action in the market. Where, as in this case, the subsidiary, although having a separate legal personality, does not freely determine its conduct on the market but carries out instructions given to it directly or indirectly by the parent company by which it is wholly controlled, Article 85(1) [now Art 81(1)] does not apply to the relationship between the subsidiary and the parent company with which it forms an economic unit.

The substantive requirements of Article 81 EC Treaty

Having established the kind of agreement or arrangement which, potentially, may breach Art 81, what is the content of such a deal that will infringe Art 81? Not all agreements that affect trading relations between undertakings will breach Art 81. Clearly, the exemption provided under Art 81(3) recognises that the potentially restrictive effect of some agreements may be outweighed by their beneficial effect. Before an assessment can be made of the grounds for exemption, however, it is necessary to isolate the constituent elements in Art 81 which will enable an offending agreement to be identified.

An agreement which may affect trade between Member States

Article 81(1)(a)–(e) (see above) provides a non-exhaustive list of the sort of agreements which will *prima facie* breach Art 81, but they must be set within a Community context. The kind of conduct at which Art 81 is primarily aimed is the conclusion of agreements or concerted practices between apparently competing producers or distributors who agree to give each other a 'free run' in specific national territories. Such horizontal agreements (e.g. between producer and producer; or between distributor and distributor) clearly continue to partition what should be a single market on a national basis, and attempt to defeat one of the primary aims of the Community. In **Suiker Unie *v* Commission** (Case 40/73), for example, sugar producers agreed to keep out of one another's territories; and in **ACF Chemiefarma *v* Commission** (Case 41/69) the undertakings concerned agreed (in a 'gentlemen's agreement') to share out domestic markets and to fix common prices of synthetic quinidine. Clearly, in these cases trade is affected and the effect of these horizontal agreements is to deny consumers the benefit of competitive products from other Member States.

The possible effect on trade between Member States received careful examination by the Court of Justice in relation to a vertical agreement (e.g. between producer and distributor) in the following landmark case:

Consten and Grundig v Commission (Case 56/64)

As part of its international distribution network, the German manufacturer of electrical equipment (Grundig) came to an agreement with the French distributor (Consten) by which Consten was appointed as Grundig's sole representative in France, Corsica and the Saarland. This is referred to as 'absolute territorial protection'; Grundig products could only be distributed in these three countries by Consten. Under that agreement Consten was authorised to use Grundig's name and trade mark, and Consten duly registered the Grundig trade mark 'GINT' in France. Consten then brought proceedings for infringement of a trade mark against a French company, UNEF, which had attempted to sell Grundig products in France which it had bought in Germany. Such goods are referred to as 'parallel imports' (i.e. goods which are purchased in one Member State and imported into another Member State). The Commission, after an investigation, decided that the Consten-Grundig agreement breached Art 81, and Grundig and Consten applied to the Court of Justice for annulment of that decision under Art 230(2) EC Treaty. The applicants argued that the Commission had relied on a mistaken interpretation of the concept of an agreement which may affect trade between Member States, and had not shown that such trade would have been greater without the disputed agreement. The Court of Justice rejected the argument:

> The concept of an agreement 'which may affect trade between Member States' is intended to define, in the law governing cartels, the boundary between the areas respectively covered by Community law and national law. It is only to the extent to which the agreement may affect trade between Member States that the deterioration in competition caused by the agreement falls under the prohibition of Community law contained in Article 85 [now Art 81]; otherwise it escapes the prohibition. In this connection, what is particularly important is whether the agreement is capable of constituting a threat, either direct or indirect, actual or potential, to freedom of trade between Member States in a manner which might harm the attainment of the objectives of a single market between States. Thus the fact that an agreement encourages an increase, even a large one, in the volume of trade between states is not sufficient to exclude the possibility that the agreement may 'affect' such trade in the above mentioned manner. In the present case, the contract between Grundig and Consten, on the one hand by preventing undertakings other than Consten from importing Grundig products into France, and on

the other hand by prohibiting Consten from re-exporting those products to other countries of the common market, indisputably affects trade between Member States.

In the above case, the Court of Justice stated that it was not necessary to wait to see if trade was in fact affected by the way in which the agreement was intended to operate. The Court said that 'there is no need to take into account the concrete effects of an agreement *once it appears that it has as its object the prevention, restriction or distortion of competition*' (emphasis added).

The effect of the **Consten and Grundig** decision is that Art 81 applies not only to competing undertakings on a horizontal level, but also to vertical agreements between companies which are not themselves competing with each other but which aim to exclude competitors from the market (as stated above, this provides the competitor with 'absolute territorial protection'), provided that the agreement is one that affects trade between Member States. Article 81 can catch such vertical supply agreements as affecting trade between Member States, even if they are not in any way concerned to affect trade outside one Member State. Trade may, however, in fact be affected if the agreement, taken in the context of trading conditions in that state, is likely to affect trade into that state. This situation is most likely to occur in relation to 'sole supply' agreements between producers and retailers, as illustrated in the following case:

Brasserie de Haecht SA v *Wilkin (No. 1)* (Case 23/67)

The proprietor of a café in Belgium obtained a loan from a Belgian brewery on the basis that he would obtain supplies of beverages exclusively from the brewery. The legality of the agreement in the context of Art 81(1) was raised in subsequent proceedings and referred by the Belgian court to the Court of Justice under Art 234 EC Treaty. The Court held that the validity of the agreement under Art 81 had to take into account not only the scope and effect of the agreement itself, but also the trading conditions in the state in which it was made. The agreement, when viewed in isolation, as Advocate-General Roemer observed in the case, did not 'seem to be prejudicial to the common market in any way … On the other hand it is possible for such an effect to occur as the result of the combined operation of all the beer distribution agreements in a Member State'. The Court agreed, and said:

> Article 85(1) [now Art 81(1)] implies that regard must be had to such effects in the context in which they occur, that is to say in the economic and legal context of such agreements, decisions and practices and where they might combine with others to have a cumulative effect on competition. In fact, it would be pointless to consider an agreement, decision or practice by reason of its effects if those effects were to be taken distinct from the market in which they are seen to operate and could only be examined apart from the body of effects, whether convergent or not surrounding their implementation.

The problem of restrictions of competition generated by the cumulative effect of similar vertical agreements was dealt with in depth by the CFI in the following case:

Roberts v *Commission* (Case T-25/99)

The operators of a pub in the UK complained to the Commission that the lease used by the local brewery, Greene King, from which, as tenants, they were subject to an obligation to obtain beer, was contrary to Art 81(1). The Commission rejected their complaint on the ground that the standard lease used by Greene King did not fall within the scope of Art 81. The action which they brought before the CFI sought the annulment of that decision. The CFI stated that the contested decision correctly defined the relevant market as that of the distribution of beer in establishments selling alcoholic beverages for consumption on the premises. The CFI then considered whether the Commission was right to find that Greene King's network of agreements, consisting of leases with a purchasing obligation concluded between that brewery and its tenants, did not make a significant contribution to the foreclosure of the relevant market, so that the agreements were not caught by the prohibition in Art 81(1). The CFI endorsed the Commission's conclusion.

In that connection the CFI stated, first, that in order to assess whether a standard beer supply agreement contributes to the cumulative effect of closing off the market produced by all such agreements, it is necessary to take into consideration the position of the contracting parties in the market. The contribution also depends on the duration of the agreements. If it is manifestly excessive in relation to the average duration of agreements generally concluded in the relevant market, the individual agreement falls under the prohibition laid down in Art 81(1). A brewery holding a relatively small share of the market which ties its sales outlets for many years may contribute to foreclosure (i.e. closing off) of the market as significantly as a brewery with a comparatively strong position in the market which regularly frees its outlets at frequent intervals. In this case neither the market share of the brewer nor the duration of the beer supply contracts were held to contribute significantly to the foreclosure of the market.

The CFI then went on to consider whether a network of agreements of a wholesaling brewery, here Greene King, which does not in itself significantly contribute to the foreclosure of the market, may be linked to networks of agreements of supplying breweries, which do contribute significantly to such foreclosure, and may thus fall within the scope of Art 81(1). Two conditions must be satisfied in that regard:

■ First, it must be considered whether the beer supply agreements concluded between the wholesaling brewery and the supplying breweries, known as 'upstream' agreements, may be regarded as forming part of the supplying breweries' networks of agreements. That condition is satisfied if the upstream agreements contain terms which may be analysed as a purchasing obligation (commitment to purchase minimum quantities, stocking obligations or non-competition obligations).

■ Second, for not only the 'upstream' agreements but also the agreements concluded between the wholesaling brewery and the establishments tied to it (the 'downstream' agreements) to be attributed to the supplying breweries' networks of agreements, it is also necessary for the agreements between the supplying breweries and the wholesaling brewery to be so restrictive that access to the wholesaling brewery's network of 'downstream' agreements is no longer possible, or at least very difficult, for other breweries. If the restrictive effect of the 'upstream' agreements is limited, other breweries are able to conclude supply agreements with the wholesaling brewery and so enter the latter's network of 'downstream' agreements. They are therefore in a position to have access to all the establishments in that network without it being necessary to conclude separate agreements with each outlet. The existence of a network of 'downstream' agreements thus constitutes a factor which can promote penetration of the market by other breweries.

Concluding its analysis, the CFI held that the Commission did not make a manifest error of assessment in concluding in the contested decision (point 106) that Greene King's network of 'downstream' agreements could not be attributed to those of the supplying breweries which had concluded beer supply agreements with Greene King.

In the following case, the CFI considered whether Art 81(1) EC Treaty was breached where an organisation set recommended prices for equipment hire, and also prohibited the hiring of such equipment to non-members:

Stichting Certificatie Kraanhuurbedrijf (SCK) and FNK and Another v *Commission* (Joined Cases T-213/95 and T-18/96)

FNK, an organisation of crane owners and hirers in The Netherlands which purported to maintain the quality of cranes hired out, published recommended prices for hire and prohibited members from hiring cranes from anyone except its members. The Commission declared that these practices were in breach of Art 85(1) (now Art 81(1)). SCK challenged the decision, arguing that, because its membership covered only 37 per cent of the market, the system of recommended hiring charges and restrictions on hiring could not affect trade between Member States. The CFI rejected this argument, stating that:

> ... even if the market share of FNK members was 'only' 37 per cent or 40 per cent of The Netherlands market, the applicants were large enough and had sufficient economic power for their practices ... to be capable of having an appreciable effect on trade between Member States.

The 'context within Member States' may also have to take account of the actions of undertakings outside the Community, where those actions have an effect within Member States. This is illustrated in the following case:

Åhlström Osakeyhito v *Commission (Re Wood Pulp)* (Joined Cases C-89, 104, 116, 117 and 125-129/85)

Concerted action by forestry undertakings in Finland, Sweden and Canada was said to have had an effect on wood pulp prices in the Community. At the time, Finland and Sweden were not members of the EU. The undertakings submitted that Art 81 did not extend to regulate conduct restricting competition outside the Community merely because it had economic repercussions within it. The Court disagreed, holding that where wood pulp producers established outside the Community sell directly to purchasers established in the Community and engage in price competition in order to win orders from those customers, that constitutes competition within the common market. Where those producers concert on the prices to be charged to their customers in the Community and put that concertation into effect by selling at prices which are actually coordinated, they are taking part in concertation which has the object and effect of restricting competition within the common market within the meaning of Art 81 EC Treaty.

Commission notices: horizontal and vertical anti-competitive activities

As stated above, Art 81(1) applies to both horizontal and vertical anti-competitive activities. The Commission has issued two notices providing non-binding guidelines concerning (1) vertical restraints; and (2) horizontal cooperation agreements.

The Guidelines on Vertical Restraints (OJ 2000 C 291/01) are stated to be 'without prejudice to the interpretation that may be given by the Court of First Instance and the Court of Justice of the European Communities in relation to the application of Article 81 to vertical agreements' (para 1(4)). The Commission's aim in issuing these guidelines is to 'help companies to make their own assessment of vertical agreements under the EC competition rules' (para 1(3)). The guidelines are structured as follows:

- Section II describes vertical agreements which generally fall outside Art 81(1).

- Section III comments on the application of the Block Exemption Regulation 2790/99 on the application of Art 81(3) EC Treaty to categories of vertical agreements and concerted practices (see below).

- Section IV describes the principles concerning the withdrawal of the block exemption and the disapplication of the Block Exemption Regulation.

- Section V addresses market definition and market share calculation issues, primarily as regards the application of the *de minimis* rule as set out in the 1997 *de minimis* notice (OJ 1997 C 372/13 which has subsequently been replaced by OJ 2001 C 368/13, see below).

- Section VI describes the general framework of analysis and the enforcement policy of the Commission in individual cases concerning vertical agreements (see below and Chapter 22).

The Guidelines on Horizontal Cooperation Agreements (OJ 2001 C 3/02) are, like the vertical restraint guidelines, stated to be 'without prejudice to the interpretation that may be given by the Court of First Instance or the Court of Justice' in relation to the application of Art 81 to such agreements (para 16). The purpose of the guidelines is to 'provide an analytical framework for the most common types of horizontal cooperation', although it is recognised that 'given the enormous variety in types and combinations of horizontal cooperation and market circumstances in which they operate, it is impossible to provide specific answers for every possible scenario' (para 7). Chapters 2 to 7 of the guidelines are concerned with specific types of agreement. Practical examples are included of situations where Art 81 would apply and where it would not. The specific types of agreement covered are as follows:

- agreements on research and development (Chapter 2, paras 39–77);

- production agreements, including specialisation agreements (Chapter 3, paras 78–114);

- purchasing agreements (Chapter 4, paras 115–138);

- commercialisation agreements (Chapter 5, paras 139–158);

- agreement on standards (Chapter 6, paras 159–178);

- environmental agreements (Chapter 7, paras 179–198).

Both sets of guidelines are available on the Commission's website at:

  http://ec.europa.eu/comm/competition/antitrust/legislation/entente3_en.html

The object or effect of distorting competition

Article 81 prohibits both conduct which is *intended* to affect trade between Member States, and conduct which, although not based upon any such intention, in fact has, or is *likely* to have, such an effect. There is no need for both elements to be present; they are alternative, not cumulative (**Ferriere Nord SpA *v* Commission** (Case C–219/ 95P)). As seen in **Consten and Grundig** (above), there will be a breach of Art 81 even if an agreement is likely to increase trade between Member States. Unlike Art 28 EC Treaty, Art 81 is not aimed at restrictions on trade between Member States as such, but at the use of restrictive agreements to partition markets and to distort the flow of trade which would normally take place in a genuinely open market. The Court of Justice stated the underlying principle of Art 81 in the following case:

Züchner v *Bayerische Vereinsbank AG* (Case 172/80)

The Court of Justice held that:

> A basic principle of the EEC competition rules is that each trader must determine independently the policy which he intends to adopt on the common market and the conditions which he intends to offer to his customers. This does not prevent the traders adapting themselves intelligently to the existing or anticipated conduct of their competitors; it does, however, strictly preclude any direct or indirect contact between such traders the object or effect of which is to create conditions of competition which do not correspond to the normal conditions of the relevant market, in the light of the nature of the products or services offered, the size and number of the undertakings and the size of the market.

In cases where there is an attempt to rig the market by price-fixing and market-sharing agreements there is no problem in concluding that the object of any agreement or concerted action is the prevention, restriction or distortion of competition. Difficulties arise in identifying situations where, although there is no such attempt at market distortion, the effect of an agreement may have the same, probably unintended, outcome. The intention of a sole-supply agreement may, for example, be that the supplier is repaid money that he may have lent the retailer and, at the same time, is guaranteed an outlet for his goods. A network of such sole-supply agreements across a Member State, even if concluded between a large number of different suppliers and retailers, may have the effect of denying penetration of that market to producers in other Member States of the goods which are subject to the agreements. This was the basis of the Court's reasoning in the **Brasserie de Haecht** case in relation to 'tied-houses' supplied by breweries in Belgium (see above).

In analysing the object and effect of an agreement the Court will look first to its content and then to its effect. Even if its terms do not indicate an intention to restrict or distort competition, its operation may have that effect. Factors such as the percentage of the market affected, and the duration and terms of the agreements will all have to be assessed, as illustrated in the following case:

Langnese-Iglo GmbH v *Commission* (Case T-7/93)

The CFI found that the applicant held more than 30 per cent of the market share of ice-cream sold through shops. These outlets were protected by a series of exclusive purchasing agreements under which the retailers bound themselves to sell only the applicant's ice-cream for two-and-a-half years and to use the freezer cabinets supplied by the applicant only for the applicant's products. The CFI concluded that, in view of the strong position occupied by the applicant in the relevant market and, in particular, its market share, the agreements contributed significantly to the closing-off of the market.

A network of sole-supply agreements across a Member State will, however, not automatically be regarded as providing an insurmountable barrier to market penetration from other Member States. In **Stergios Delimitis** *v* **Henninger Bräu** (Case C–234/89) the Court of Justice emphasised that it was important to look at the state of the market in question to determine 'whether there are real concrete possibilities for a new competitor to penetrate the bundle of contracts' (para 21). An exclusive supply agreement may even, in some circumstances, assist in opening up competition:

Société Technique Minière v *Maschinenbau Ulm GmbH* (Case 56/65)

Maschinenbau Ulm (MU) granted Société Technique Minière (STM) the exclusive right to sell its earth-moving equipment in France, on condition that STM did not sell competing machinery. The validity of the agreement was disputed in a French court, which referred the issue to the Court of Justice for a preliminary ruling. The Commission argued in the proceedings that the agreement in question breached Art 81. The Court did not agree. It described the two stages through which it was necessary to go to determine whether or not Art 81 was infringed. 'Object or effect' in this context are alternative, not cumulative. It was first necessary to look at the precise purpose of the agreement, in the economic context in which it was to be applied. An intention to interfere with competition in the way prohibited by Art 81 was to be deduced, if at all, from the clauses of the agreement itself. If those clauses indicated an *intention* to restrict competition, the fact that the involvement of one of the participants had a negligible effect on competition was irrelevant (**Usines Gustave Boël SA** *v* **Commission** (Case T-142/89)). If the agreement disclosed no such intention, or an effect on competition that was not 'sufficiently deleterious', the consequences of the agreement would then have to be considered. A consideration of those consequences would include, in the case of an exclusive sale agreement: (i) the nature and quantity, limited or otherwise, of the products covered by the agreement; (ii) the position and importance of the grantor and the concessionaire on the market for the product concerned; (iii) the isolated nature of the disputed agreement or, alternatively, its position in a series of agreements; and (iv) the severity of the clauses intended to protect the exclusive dealership or, alternatively, the opportunities allowed for other commercial competitors in the same products by way of parallel re-exportation and importation. In this case the Court also took into account the fact that there was an attempt at market penetration in another Member State, and it doubted whether there was an interference with competition if the agreement 'was really necessary for the penetration of a new area by an undertaking'.

The **Société Technique Minière** case can be distinguished from the **Consten and Grundig** case (see above) because in the latter case the agreement prohibited parallel imports (i.e. Consten had the sole right to distribute Grundig products in the specified Member State) whereas in the former case, the agreement did **not** prohibit parallel imports. The Consten and Grundig agreement was, *prima facie*, more restrictive of competition than the Société Technique Minière agreement.

The **Société Technique Minière** case not only defined the relationship between the intention and the consequences of an agreement, but also introduced the concept of *de minimis* in the context of promoting the desirable objective of market penetration (see below). In other words, a distributor of a new product in another Member State may need some protection in order to launch the product in that state. Essentially, the Court recognised that a balance needs to be struck between the legal control of agreements which appear, on their face, to be restrictive of competition, but which may, in fact, assist in promoting market integration, and product distribution. Thus, the limited restrictive effect of an agreement may be outweighed by its more beneficial long-term consequences. This has been described as a 'rule of reason'. As long as an agreement does not have as its object the restriction of competition, its anti-competitive effect may be outweighed by its ultimate competitive advantages. The apparently conflicting priorities contained within this rule of reason were considered by the Court of Justice in the following case:

Nungesser v Commission (Case 258/78)

Within a written agreement there was an attempt to protect techniques of cultivating new types of maize. The agreement conferring exclusive rights to the technique on Nungesser was challenged by the Commission, which concluded that its terms must, inevitably, breach Art 81. The Court of Justice disagreed with the Commission's approach. It decided that some protection for the licensee of the new technique for hybrid maize seeds was a necessary precondition for penetration of the German market by INRA, the developers of the technique:

> The exclusive licence which forms the subject-matter of the contested decision concerns the cultivation and marketing of hybrid maize seeds which were developed by INRA after years of research and experimentation and were unknown to German farmers at the time when the cooperation between INRA and the applicants was taking shape ... In the case of a licence of breeders' rights over hybrid maize seeds newly developed in one Member State, an undertaking established in another Member State which was not certain that it would encounter competition from other licensees for the territory granted to it, or from the owner of the right himself, might be deterred from accepting the risk of cultivating and marketing that product; such a result would be damaging to the dissemination of new technology and would prejudice competition in the Community between the new product and similar existing products. (paras 55 and 56)

Given that the launching of the new seed and cultivation technique called for some protection for the licensee, did that mean that total protection of the production and distribution of the seed was justified? The Court of Justice would not go so far, citing its view in **Consten and Grundig** that absolute territorial protection, granted to a licensee in order to enable parallel imports to be controlled and prevented, results in the artificial maintenance of separate national markets, in breach of the Treaty. It would, however, countenance the grant of an open exclusive licence, under which the grantor himself would not compete with the licensee in Germany and would not license anyone else there to do so. Such a licence should not, however, contain an assurance by the grantor that he would protect the licensee from parallel imports, by preventing licensees in other Member States from exporting to Germany.

A limited approval by the Court of Justice has also been given to apparently restrictive franchise agreements, provided that the restrictions are no more than those which are strictly necessary to ensure that the know-how and assistance provided by the franchisee do not benefit competitors, or which establish the control necessary for maintaining the identity and reputation of the network identified by the common name or symbol. However, provisions which share markets between the franchisor and the franchisee, or between franchisees, do breach Art 81 (**Pronuptia de Paris GmbH** *v* **Pronuptia de Paris Irmgaard Schillgalis** (Case 161/84)).

Despite what appeared to be the emergence of a 'rule of reason', such a rule has been firmly rejected by the CFI. In the following case, an action for annulment of a Commission decision, the applicant companies submitted that the application of a 'rule of reason' would have shown that Art 81(1) EC Treaty did not apply to an exclusivity clause and to a clause relating to the special-interest channels agreed on when Télévision par satellite (TPS) was set up, with the result that those two clauses should not have been examined under Art 81(1):

M6 and Others v Commission (Case T–112/99)

The existence of a 'rule of reason' in the application of Art 81(1) could not be upheld. The CFI took the view that an interpretation of Art 81(1) requiring, in accordance with a rule of reason, the pro and anti-competitive effects of an agreement to be weighed in order to determine whether it is caught by the prohibition laid down in Art 81(1), would be difficult to reconcile with the rules prescribed by Art 81. Article 81(3) expressly provides for the possibility of exempting agreements that restrict competition if they satisfy a number of conditions, in particular if they are indispensable to the attainment of certain objectives and do not afford undertakings the possibility of eliminating competition in respect of a substantial part of the products in question. It is only in the precise framework of that provision that the pro and anti-competitive aspects of a restriction may be weighed. Otherwise Art 81(3) would lose much of its effectiveness.

Citing certain judgments in which the Court of Justice and the CFI favoured a more flexible interpretation of the prohibition laid down in Art 81(1), the CFI nonetheless took the view that those judgments could not be interpreted as establishing the existence of a rule of reason in Community competition law. They are part of a broader trend in the case law according to which it is not necessary to hold, wholly abstractly and without drawing any distinction, that any agreement restricting the freedom of action of one or more of the parties is necessarily caught by the prohibition laid down in Art 81(1). In assessing the applicability of that article to an agreement, account should be taken of the actual conditions in which it functions, in particular the economic and legal context in which the undertakings operate, the nature of the products or services covered by the agreement and the actual operation and structure of the market concerned.

Commission guidelines on the 'effect on trade concept' contained in Articles 81 and 82 EC Treaty

Guidelines on the 'effect on trade concept' which is contained in Arts 81 and 82 EC Treaty (OJ 2004 C 101/81) were adopted by the Commission on 30 March 2004 (as part of the 'Modernisation Package' which included the adoption of Regulation 1/2003, see above and Chapter 22). The guidelines are available at:

> http://ec.europa.eu/comm/competition/antitrust/legislation/

De minimis presumption

There is a *de minimis* presumption by the Commission, which was originally contained in a notice issued in 1986 and which was amended in 1994 (Notice on Agreements of Minor Importance (OJ 1986 C 231/2, as amended by OJ 1994 C 368/20)). In the notice (as amended), the Commission stated that in its opinion, agreements between undertakings engaged in the production or distribution of goods or in the provision of services generally would not fall within the prohibition of Art 81 if the goods and services which were subject to the agreement, together with other related goods and services of the participants, did not altogether represent more than 5 per cent of the total market for such goods or services in the area of the common market affected by the agreement. In addition, to come within this exception the undertakings must not have an aggregate turnover of more than 300 million ECUs. The notice raised only a presumption. It did not alter the law, and therefore it could be rebutted by evidence to the contrary. In **Distillers Company Ltd** *v* **Commission** (Case 30/78) the presumption was held to have been di placed by evidence of a distribution agreement of a product, the entire production of hich was in the hands of a large undertaking.

The amended 1984 notice was replaced by the Commission in 1997 with a new Notice on Agreements of Minor Importance (OJ 1997 C 372/13). Under this new notice, an agreement would come within the exception if the total market share of all undertakings involved was not more than 5 per cent in the case of a horizontal agreement or 10 per cent in the case of a vertical agreement. Paragraph 19 of the notice provided that small and medium-sized enterprises (as defined in Recommendation 96/280 (OJ 1996 L 107/4)) would be treated as coming within the exception even if they exceeded the above market share thresholds. Once again, the notice raised only a presumption, which could be rebutted.

This notice was itself replaced by the Commission in 2001 by a new Notice on Agreements of Minor Importance (OJ 2001 C 368/13). The Commission issued a press release on 7 January 2002 (IP/02/13) to explain the effect of this new notice. The press release stated:

> The European Commission has adopted a new Notice on agreements of minor importance which do not appreciably restrict competition under Article 81(1) of the EC Treaty ('de minimis Notice'). The new Notice replaces the previous Notice of 1997. The revision of the 'de minimis' notice is part of the Commission's review of the EC competition rules. By defining when agreements between companies are not prohibited by the Treaty, the Notice will reduce the compliance burden for companies, especially smaller companies. At the same time the Commission will be better able to avoid examining cases which have no interest from a competition policy point of view and will thus be able to concentrate on more problematic agreements.
>
> Article 81(1) of the EC Treaty prohibits agreements which may affect trade between Member States and which have as their object or effect the prevention, restriction or distortion of competition within the common market. The Court of Justice of the European Communities has clarified that this provision is not applicable where the impact of the agreement on intra-community trade or on competition is not appreciable. In the new Notice the Commission quantifies, with the help of market share thresholds, what is *not* an appreciable restriction of competition i.e. what is 'de minimis' and is thus not prohibited by Article 81(1).
>
> The new Notice reflects an economic approach and has the following key features:
>
> The 'de minimis' thresholds are raised to 10 per cent market share for agreements between competitors and to 15 per cent for agreements between non-competitors.
>
> The previous Notice had fixed the 'de minimis' thresholds at respectively 5 per cent and 10 per cent market share. The new Notice raises these thresholds to respectively 10 per cent and 15 per cent. Competition concerns can in general not be expected when companies do not have a minimum degree of market power. The new thresholds take account of this while at the same time staying low enough to be applicable whatever the overall market structure looks like.
>
> The difference between the two thresholds takes into account, as before, that agreements between competitors in general lead more easily to anti-competitive effects than agreements between non-competitors.
>
> It specifies for the first time a market share threshold for networks of agreements producing a cumulative anti-competitive effect.

The previous de minimis Notice excluded from its benefit agreements operated on a market where 'competition is restricted by the cumulative effects of parallel networks of similar agreements established by several manufacturers or dealers'. This meant in practice that firms operating in sectors like the beer and petrol sector could usually not benefit from the de minimis Notice. The new Notice introduces a special 'de minimis' market share threshold of 5 per cent for markets where there exist such parallel networks of similar agreements.

It contains the same list of hardcore restrictions as in the horizontal and vertical Block Exemption Regulations.

The new Notice defines in a clearer and more consistent way the hardcore restrictions, i.e. those restrictions, such as price fixing and market sharing, which are normally always prohibited irrespective of the market shares of the companies concerned. Hardcore restrictions cannot benefit from the de minimis Notice. For agreements between non-competitors the new Notice has taken over the hardcore restrictions set out in Block Exemption Regulation 2790/1999 for vertical agreements. For agreements between competitors the new Notice has taken over the hardcore restrictions set out in Block Exemption Regulation 2658/2000 for specialisation agreements.

Agreements between small and medium sized enterprises are in general 'de minimis'.

The new Notice states that agreements between small and medium sized enterprises (SMEs) are rarely capable of appreciably affecting trade between Member States. Agreements between SMEs therefore generally fall outside the scope of Article 81(1).

In cases covered by the new Notice, the Commission will not institute proceedings either upon application or on its own initiative. Where companies assume in good faith that an agreement is covered by the Notice, the Commission will not impose fines. Although not binding on them, the Notice also intends to give guidance to the courts and authorities of the Member States in their application of Article 81.

Both the notice and the press release are available on the EU's competition website at:

http://ec.europa.eu/comm/competition/antitrust/deminimis/

The list of agreements likely to breach Article 81(1)

Article 81(1) contains a list, in paragraphs (a) to (e), of the kind of agreements which will be prohibited (see above). The cases examined so far range far beyond those described in that list, and it provides no more than a guide as to the sort of agreements which will fall foul of the prohibition. However, with the help of the list and the case law of the Court of Justice, it is possible to draw some conclusions as to the type of agreement which may breach Art 81. A list indicative of the types of offending agreements could include:

- exclusive distribution agreements;
- exclusive purchasing agreements;
- exclusive licences of intellectual property rights (such as patents, copyright and trade marks);
- selective distribution agreements;
- franchise agreements;
- research and development agreements;
- joint ventures on development;
- joint sale and buying agencies;
- information-sharing agreements.

Each of these types of agreement has been held at some time or other to be actually or potentially in breach of Art 81. If they are found to breach Art 81(1), they are, by Art 81(2), automatically void. The effect of this finding is that they cannot, for example, form the basis of a claim or a defence in contract in national courts. Article 81 was used in this way in both the **Brasserie de Haecht** and the **Société Technique Minière** cases (see above). In many cases, the Court is obliged to give an indication, on the basis of the facts in the relevant market (as found by the Commission), and after weighing up all the relevant circumstances, of whether the agreement actually breaches the prohibition. If it does breach Art 81(1), there always remains the possibility that it may be exempt under Art 81(3).

Exemption under Article 81(3)

The object of Art 81(3), set out at the beginning of this chapter, is to provide criteria for exemption from the prohibition under Art 81(1) on agreements which restrict competition. Essentially, exemption may apply in cases where the anti-competitive effects of an agreement or concerted practice are outweighed by the economic benefit to consumers or the public at large. Prior to 1 May 2004, exemption could result either from an individual decision of the Commission pursuant to Regulation 17/62, or as a consequence of an agreement falling within a type to which a block or group exemption had been granted (see below). In order to obtain an exemption, undertakings which entered into restrictive agreements had to either make a formal application to the Commission pursuant to Regulation 17/62, or draft their agreements to comply with one of the block or group exemption regulations which had been specifically drawn up by the Commission. In the latter instance, if the agreement complied with one of the regulations, it would automatically obtain exemption without the necessity for a formal application to the Commission.

On 1 May 2004, Regulation 1/2003 came into force, replacing Regulation 17/62 which was repealed. The new regulation is considered in detail in Chapter 22. Article 1(2), Regulation 1/2003 provides that:

> Agreements, decisions and concerted practices caught by Article 81(1) of the Treaty which satisfy the conditions of Article 81(3) of the Treaty shall not be prohibited, **no prior decision to that effect being required**. [emphasis added]

This is a major change. While the block or group exemption regulations will continue to apply, undertakings which cannot take advantage of such a regulation no longer need the prior approval of the Commission in order to be able to rely upon the Art 81(3) exemption. The rationale for this change is set out in the preamble to Regulation 1/2003:

> (2) . . . there is a need to rethink the arrangements for applying the exception from the prohibition on agreements, which restrict competition, laid down in Article 81(3) of the Treaty. Under Article 83(2)(b) of the Treaty, account must be taken in this regard of the need to ensure effective supervision, on the one hand, and to simplify administration to the greatest possible extent, on the other.
>
> (3) The centralised scheme set up by Regulation No 17 no longer secures a balance between those two objectives. It hampers application of the Community competition rules by the courts and competition authorities of the Member States, and the system of notification it involves prevents the Commission from concentrating its resources on curbing the most serious infringements. It also imposes considerable costs on undertakings.

From 1 May 2004, not only is the Commission empowered to apply Art 81(3), but also the national competition authorities and the courts of the Member States are likewise empowered (Arts 5 and 6, Regulation 1/2003).

Comfort letters and guidance letters

As stated above, prior to 1 May 2004 each agreement had to be notified to the Commission and exemption obtained under the procedure established for that purpose under Arts 4, 19 and 21, Regulation 17/62. Exemptions would only be granted for specific periods, and conditions could be attached; the exemption could be renewed or revoked. Delays of two or three years could ensue following an application, hence the need for reform. The Commission was required to give a fully reasoned decision in each case, and therefore the Commission tended to try to avoid formal decisions, which were normally reserved for what were considered to be important cases. In other cases a 'comfort letter' was issued after informal meetings with the parties concerned stating that, in the Commission's view, the agreement which had been notified did not infringe Art 81(1) at all or was of a type which fell within an exempt category. The file would then be closed, although it could be reopened if the legal, material or factual circumstances changed. The parties were then entitled to rely upon the letter and enjoy a legitimate expectation that the Commission would take no further action. Comfort letters only had a limited legal status and, because they were not 'decisions', they could not be challenged in Art 230 EC Treaty proceedings before the Court of Justice (**SA Lancôme** v **ETOS BV ('Perfumes')** (Case 99/79)). Nor were opinions expressed in such letters 'binding on the national courts but constitute a factor which the latter may take into account in examining whether or not the agreements are in accordance with the provisions of Article 85 [now Art 81]'. The reliance which the parties could place on a comfort letter depended very much on the circumstances in which the letter was issued remaining the same. Any change in those circumstances, or any misrepresentation, could result in the reopening of the file (**Langnese-Iglo** v **Commission** (Case T–7/93)).

From 1 May 2004 the Commission will no longer issue comfort letters, because from that date there is no longer a requirement to notify the Commission of an agreement in order for the Commission to decide whether or not the exemption set out in Art 81(3) applies. However, in very limited circumstances the Commission is empowered to issue a 'guidance letter'. To support the new procedural regime brought in by Regulation 1/2003, the Commission has issued a non-legally enforceable Notice: 'Informal Guidance relating to novel questions concerning Arts 81 and 82 EC Treaty that arise in individual cases (guidance letters)' (OJ 2004 C 101/78). In cases which give rise to genuine uncertainty because they present novel or unresolved questions for the application of Arts 81 and 82 EC Treaty, individual undertakings may seek informal guidance from the Commission (para 5 of the Guidance). If it is considered appropriate, the Commission may provide such guidance in a written statement, referred to as a 'guidance letter'. However, a guidance letter may only be issued by the Commission if the following cumulative conditions apply:

(a) The substantive assessment of an agreement or practice with regard to Articles 81 and/or 82 of the Treaty, poses a question of application of the law for which there is no clarification in the existing EC legal framework including the case law of the Community Courts, nor publicly available general guidance or precedent in decision-making practice or previous guidance letters.

(b) A *prima facie* evaluation of the specificities and background of the case suggests that the clarification of the novel question through a guidance letter is useful, taking into account the following elements:
  - the economic importance from the point of view of the consumer of the goods or services concerned by the agreement or practice; and/or
  - the extent to which the agreement or practice corresponds or is liable to correspond to more widely spread economic usage in the marketplace; and/or
  - the extent of the investments linked to the transaction in relation to the size of the companies concerned and the extent to which the transaction relates to a structural operation such as the creation of a non-full function joint venture.
(c) It is possible to issue a guidance letter on the basis of the information provided, i.e. no further fact-finding is required. (para 8 of the Guidance)

Furthermore, the Commission will not consider a request for a guidance letter in either of the following circumstances:

  - the questions raised in the request are identical or similar to issues raised in a case pending before the European Court of First Instance or the European Court of Justice; or
  - the agreement or practice to which the request refers is subject to proceedings pending with the Commission, a Member State court or Member State competition authority. (para 9 of the Guidance)

Paragraph 10 of the Guidance provides that the Commission will not consider hypothetical questions and 'will not issue guidance letters on agreements or practices that are no longer being implemented by the parties. Undertakings may however present a request for a guidance letter to the Commission in relation to questions raised by an agreement or practice that they envisage, i.e. before the implementation of that agreement or practice. In this case the transaction must have reached a sufficiently advanced stage for a request to be considered'.

Article 81(3): the four conditions

Whether the Art 81(3) exemption can be relied upon will depend on four conditions being satisfied:

1. The agreement must contribute to the improvement of the production or distribution of goods, or the promotion of technical or economic progress.

2. The agreement must allow consumers a fair share of the resulting benefit.

3. The agreement must not impose upon the undertakings concerned restrictions which are not indispensable to the attainment of the above objects.

4. The agreement should not provide the undertakings with the possibility of eliminating competition in respect of a substantial part of the product in question.

These are all linked conditions which must, in each case, be satisfied (Commission Decision 73/323 **Prym-Werke**).

Besides meeting the formal requirements as set out in the four conditions above, application of Art 81(3) will also be examined in the light of the Commission's broader policy objectives in relation to agreements between undertakings. The Commission's aim is to encourage those agreements which favour the introduction of new technology resulting in better production methods, economies of scale, the faster or more effective development of new products or the process of change in older industries. Agreements which are highly unlikely to secure exemption are price-fixing agreements, agreements limiting production or controlling markets, or agreements which are aimed at retaining dominance in a national market. An example of an application that met both the specific and general criteria can be seen in **Prym-Werke** [1973] CMLR D250, [1981] 2 CMLR 217 (see also the **ACEC/Berliet** decision [1968] CMLR D35; **Re Vacuum Interrupters (No. 2)** [1981] 2 CMLR 217):

Prym-Werke [1973] CMLR D250, [1981] 2 CMLR 217

Prym agreed to give up making needles and instead to buy them from Beka, who agreed to supply Prym. Beka could then specialise in needle production. The Commission explained the approach it had adopted in its decision:

> The concentration of manufacturing agreed on by Prym and Beka has, from the point of view of the improvement of production, favourable effects analogous to those of specialisation; it causes an increase of at least 50 per cent in the quantity of needles to be manufactured at the European factory, which makes it possible to make more intensive use of the existing plant and to introduce production-line manufacture.

The following case, which was considered above, concerned regulations which had been adopted by the Fédération internationale de football association (FIFA) to regulate the agents of professional football players (the 'Players' Agents Regulations'). FIFA brings together national football associations from throughout the world. Regulations adopted by FIFA are applied by all the national football associations:

Piau v Commission (Case T-193/02 (under appeal, Case C-171/05P))

The FIFA Players' Agents Regulations required agents to hold a licence. The Commission had held that the compulsory nature of this licence requirement might be justified under Art 81(3) EC Treaty. In its judgment, the CFI pointed out that the requirement to hold a licence in order to carry on the occupation of players' agent was a barrier to access to that economic activity and affected competition. Accordingly, it could be accepted only insofar as the conditions set out in Art 81(3) EC Treaty were met. The CFI found that the Commission had not made a manifest error of assessment in taking the view that the restrictions stemming from the compulsory nature of the licence might benefit from such an exemption. First, the need to raise professional and ethical standards for the occupation of players' agent in order to protect players; second, the fact that competition was not eliminated by the licence system; third, the virtual absence of any national rules; and fourth, the lack of any collective organisation for players' agents were all circumstances which justified the action taken by FIFA.

The sort of agreement which will not be exempt under Art 81(3) was considered by the CFI in the following case:

SPO v Commission (Case T-29/92)

The applicants were a group of associations of building contractors in The Netherlands. Since 1952 they had adopted a body of rules which concerned the organisation of competition. The rules were intended to 'promote and administer orderly competition, to prevent improper conduct in price tendering and to promote the formation of economically justified prices'. From 1980, these rules became binding on all contractors belonging to the member associations of the SPO. In 1988 the SPO notified its amended rules with a view, *inter alia*, to obtain an exemption under Art 81(3). The Commission rejected the application for exemption and found the SPO rules in breach of Art 81(1). The CFI upheld this decision. It had no hesitation in finding that the provision of information to SPO by contractors submitting tenders for contracts which enabled other contractors to adjust their commercial behaviour and their prices amounted to unlawful concertation in The Netherlands' building market, affecting not just Dutch contractors but contractors wishing to tender from other Member States. It therefore breached Art 81(1). The CFI, applying the four conditions for exemption, also found the rules wanting. The applicants had argued that an open tendering system would necessarily lead to ruinous competition which would ultimately have adverse repercussions on contract awarders. The CFI observed dryly that it was impossible to distinguish between normal competition and ruinous competition as, potentially, any competition is ruinous for the least efficient undertakings. That is why, by taking action to counteract what they regard as ruinous competition, the applicants necessarily restrict competition and therefore deprive consumers of its benefits.

Commission guidelines on the application of Article 81(3)

Guidelines on the application of Art 81(3) (OJ 2004 C 101/97) were adopted by the Commission on 30 March 2004 (as part of the 'Modernisation Package' which included the adoption of Regulation 1/2003; see above and Chapter 22). In order to promote coherent application and provide guidance to businesses, the detailed guidelines set out the methodology for the application of Art 81(3). These guidelines do not replace, but complement, the guidance already available in Commission guidelines on particular types of agreements, in particular the guidelines on horizontal cooperation agreements and the guidelines on vertical restraints (see above). The guidelines are available at:

http://ec.europa.eu/comm/competition/antitrust/legislation/

Block exemptions

The four conditions for exemption (see above) are reflected in the Block Exemption Regulations. Block exemptions came about as a result of the huge burden placed on the Commission by the requirement in Regulation 17/62 to investigate each application before delivering a decision. As discussed above, this requirement no longer applies following the adoption of Regulation 1/2003 and the repeal of Regulation 17/62. While the Block Exemption Regulations will remain, Art 29, Regulation 1/2003 provides that they may be withdrawn in a particular case by the Commission or a national competition authority. Article 29, Regulation 1/2003 provides as follows:

1. Where the Commission, empowered by a Council Regulation, such as Regulations 19/65/EEC, (EEC) No 2821/71, (EEC) No 3976/87, (EEC) No 1534/91 or (EEC) No 479/92, to apply Article 81(3) of the Treaty by regulation, has declared Article 81(1) of the Treaty inapplicable to certain categories of agreements, decisions by associations of undertakings or concerted practices, it may, acting on its own initiative or on a complaint, withdraw the benefit of such an exemption Regulation when it finds that in any particular case an agreement, decision or concerted practice to which the exemption Regulation applies has certain effects which are incompatible with Article 81(3) of the Treaty.

2. Where, in any particular case, agreements, decisions by associations of undertakings or

concerted practices to which a Commission Regulation referred to in paragraph 1 applies have effects which are incompatible with Article 81(3) of the Treaty in the territory of a Member State, or in a part thereof, which has all the characteristics of a distinct geographic market, the competition authority of that Member State may withdraw the benefit of the Regulation in question in respect of that territory.

The value of block exemptions is that undertakings can make their own assessment as to whether or not the agreement to which they are a party falls within the terms of an apparently relevant block exemption regulation. If the agreement is clearly within it, they may treat it as *prima facie* valid and enforceable. The Commission (and the national competition authorities and courts of the Member States) remain free to decide that agreements which purport to fall within an existing block exemption do in fact fall outside it, and to take the necessary action against the participants.

A number of block exemption regulations have been issued since 1983, some of which have been amended or replaced by subsequent regulations. Examples of block exemption regulations include:

- Technology Transfer Regulation 240/96 (OJ 1996 L 31/2), which replaced the Patent Licensing Block Exemption Regulation 2349/84 (OJ 1984 L 219/15) and the Know-how Licensing Block Exemption Regulation 556/89 (OJ 1989 L 61/1).

- Vertical Restraints Regulation 2790/99 (OJ 1999 L 326/21), which replaced the block exemptions for exclusive distribution agreements (Regulation 1983/83 (OJ 1983 L 173/1)), exclusive purchasing agreements (Regulation 1984/83 (OJ 1983 L 173/15)) and franchising agreements (Regulation 4078/88 (OJ 1988 L 359/46)).

- Specialisation Agreements Regulation 2658/2000 (OJ 2000 L 304/3), which replaced Regulation 417/85 (OJ 1985 L 53/1), the latter having expired on 31 December 2000.

- Research and Development Agreements Regulation 2659/2000 (OJ 2000 L 304/7), which replaced Regulation 418/85 (OJ 1985 L 53/5), the latter having expired on 31 December 2000.

The pattern of block exemption regulations is similar. They reflect both the content of Art 81(3) and the decisions of the Court of Justice in relation to individual applications concerning the activities covered by the regulation. However, the last two regulations in particular have moved away from the approach of listing clauses in an agreement which would be exempted from Art 81(1), and instead place a greater emphasis on defining the categories of agreements which are exempted up to a certain level of market power and on specifying the restrictions or clauses which are not to be contained in such agreements.

The fact that an agreement falls within the terms of a block exemption regulation does not confer immunity under Art 81(1) on everything purported to be done under that agreement. If, for example, the operation of the agreement in practice excludes parallel imports, the effect of the agreement would still be to restrict competition (**P Automobiles Peugeot SA *v* Commission** (Case C–322/93)). On this basis, the Commission decided that Regulation 123/85 (block exemption regulation on selective distribution in the motor vehicle sector) did not allow Volkswagen to prohibit its dealers in Italy from selling to consumers and motor agencies outside Italy (**The Community *v* Volkswagen AG and Others** (Case IV/35.733) (1998)). The decision demonstrates the way in which an agreement, ostensibly lawful as within the block exemption, can work to the disadvantage of customers and lead to the partitioning of the market.

Summary

Now you have read this chapter you should be able to:

- Outline the scope of Community competition law and policy.

- Understand and describe how Art 81(1) EC Treaty operates to prohibit agreements which restrict competition.

- Explain the conditions which apply whereby agreements, decisions and practices which come within the scope of Art 81(3) EC Treaty may be exempted from the prohibition under Art 81(1) EC Treaty.

- Outline and evaluate the procedural changes made to the application of Art 81(3) EC Treaty by Regulation 1/2003.

References

Green, N., Hartley, T.C. and Usher, J.A. (1991) *The Legal Foundations of the Single Market, Pt III*, Oxford University Press.

Further reading

Textbooks

Craig, P. and De Burca, G. (2003) *EU Law Text, Cases and Materials* (3rd edn), Oxford University Press, Chapters 21 and 22.

Foster, N. (2006) *Foster on EU Law* (1st edn), Oxford University Press, Chapter 8 (Sections 8.1 to 8.5).

Goyder, D.G. (2003) *EC Competition Law* (4th edn), Oxford University Press.

Steiner, J., Woods, L. and Twigg-Flesner, C. (2006) *EU Law* (9th edn), Oxford University Press, Chapter 27.

Storey, T. and Turner, C. (2005) *Unlocking EU Law* (1st edn), Hodder Arnold, Chapter 15 (Sections 15.1 and 15.2).

Tillotson, J. and Foster, N. (2003) *Text, Cases and Materials on EU Law* (4th edn), Cavendish Publishing, Chapter 15.

Weatherill, S. (2006) *Cases and Materials on EU Law* (7th edn), Oxford University Press, Chapter 16.

Journal articles

Barr, F., 'The New Commission Notice on Agreements of Minor Importance: Is Appreciability a Useful Measure?' [1997] ECLR 207.

Bishop, S. and Ridyard, D., 'EC Vertical Restraint Guidelines: Effect-based or *per se* policy?' [2002] ECLR 35.

Ehlermann, C.D., 'The Contribution of EC Competition Policy to the Single Market' (1992) 29 CML Rev 257.

Frazer, T., 'Competition Policy after 1992: The Next Step' (1990) 53 MLR 609.

Griffiths, M., 'A Glorification of De Minimus – The Regulation on Vertical Agreements' [2000] ECLR 241.

Harding, C. and Gibbs, A., 'Why go to Europe? An analysis of cartel appeals 1995-2004' (2005) 30 EL Rev 349.

Kallaugher, J. and Weitbrecht, A., 'Developments under Articles 81 and 82 EC – the Year 2005 in review' [2006] ECLR 137.

Kirkbride, J. and Tao Xiong, 'The European Control of Joint Ventures: An Historic Opportunity or a Mere Continuation of Existing Practice?' (1998) 23 EL Rev 37.

Lever, J. and Neubauer, S., 'Vertical Restraints, Their Motivation and Justification' [2000] ECLR 7.

Lidgard, H.H., 'Unilateral Refusal to Supply: An Agreement in Disguise?' [1997] ECLR 352.

Manzini, P., 'The European Rule of Reason – crossing the sea of doubt' [2002] ECLR 392.

Nazzini, R., 'Article 81 EC between time present and time past: A normative critique of "restriction of competition" in EU law' (2006) 43 CML Rev 497.

21 Abuse of a dominant position and mergers: Article 82 EC Treaty

Aims and objectives

At the end of this chapter you should understand:

- How Art 82 EC Treaty is applied to prevent the abuse of a dominant position.
- The relationship between Arts 81(1) and 82 EC Treaty with regard to collective dominance.
- How Art 82 EC Treaty and Regulation 139/2004 are applied to regulate mergers which may produce a degree of market control and distortion of competition which is detrimental to the effective operation of the common market.

Introduction

Article 82 EC Treaty (previously article 86) provides that:

> Any abuse by one or more undertakings of a dominant position within the common market or in a substantial part of it shall be prohibited as incompatible with the common market in so far as it may affect trade between Member States. Such abuse may, in particular, consist in:
> (a) directly or indirectly imposing unfair purchase or selling prices or other unfair trading conditions;
> (b) limiting production, markets or technical development to the prejudice of consumers;
> (c) applying dissimilar conditions to equivalent transactions with other trading parties, thereby placing them at a competitive disadvantage;
> (d) making the conclusion of contracts subject to acceptance by the other parties of supplementary obligations which, by their nature or according to commercial usage, have no connection with the subject of such contracts.

There are three key elements in Art 82. There must be:

1. a dominant position;
2. an abuse of that position; and
3. the abuse must affect trade between Member States.

Whereas Art 81 is directed at cooperation between nominally competing businesses, which has the effect of diminishing or distorting competition (see Chapter 20), Art 82 is aimed at the position and conduct of one undertaking. Essentially, Art 82 is not concerned with the *fact* of monopoly power in the Community, but with *abuse* of that monopoly or dominant position. To determine whether or not that has occurred, each of the key elements mentioned will be analysed and applied to the relevant circumstances.

A dominant position

The concept of dominance must be viewed in the context of the relevant market for the goods or services produced or distributed by the undertaking, the conduct of which is in question. In the following case, the Court of Justice defined 'a dominant position':

United Brands Co v *Commission* (Case 27/76)

The Court of Justice stated that a dominant position, within the context of Art 82 EC Treaty, is:

> A position of economic strength enjoyed by an undertaking which enables it to hinder the maintenance of effective competition on the relevant market by allowing it to behave to an appreciable extent independently of its competitors and customers and ultimately of consumers. (para 65)

To determine whether or not an undertaking is 'dominant' it is necessary to look at the relevant product market. The following case is a useful example for this exercise:

United Brands Co v *Commission* (Case 27/76)

United Brands Co (UBC), at the time of the Commission's investigation, was a conglomerate which handled 40 per cent of the EU's banana trade. In some Member States (the Benelux countries, Germany, Denmark and Ireland) its share of the banana market was much greater. The Commission accordingly concluded that it enjoyed a dominant position in the banana market which, on the facts, it was abusing. UBC challenged the decision on a number of grounds. It argued that it did not enjoy a dominant position in the *fruit market*, and that this was the proper context for the examination of its position. To support this argument, UBC stated that bananas compete with other fresh fruit in the same shops, on the same shelves, at prices which can be compared and satisfying the same needs (i.e. consumption as a dessert or between meals). On the other hand, the Commission contended that there is a demand for bananas which is distinct from the demand for other fresh fruit, especially as the banana is a very important part of the diet of certain sections of the Community, especially the very young and the very old. The specific qualities of the banana influence customer preference and induce him not readily to accept other fruits as a substitute. The Court of Justice accepted the Commission's argument that the relevant market was in bananas, and not in fruit generally:

> For the banana to be regarded as forming a market which is sufficiently differentiated from other fruit markets, it must be possible for it to be singled out by such special features distinguishing it from other fruits that it is only to a limited extent exchangeable with them and is only exposed to their competition in a way that is hardly perceptible.
>
> The ripening of bananas takes place the whole year round without any season having to be taken into account. Throughout the year production exceeds demand and can satisfy it at any time. Owing

to this particular feature the banana is a privileged fruit and its production and marketing can be adapted to the seasonal fluctuations of other fresh fruit which are known and can be computed. There is no unavoidable seasonal substitution since the consumer can obtain this fruit all the year round ... It follows from these considerations that a very large number of consumers having a constant need for bananas are not noticeably or even appreciably enticed away from the consumption of this product by the arrival of other fresh fruit on the market and that even the seasonal peak periods only affect it for a limited period of time and to a very limited extent from the point of view of substitutability.

Consequently the banana market is a market which is sufficiently distinct from the other fresh fruit markets. (paras 22–26, and 34–35)

In the above case, the most noticeable feature of this part of the judgment is the way in which the Court focused on *product substitution* as a primary determinant in isolating bananas as a separate market. There are two kinds of substitutability: (1) demand-side substitutability; and (2) supply-side substitutability.

Demand-side substitutability

Demand-side substitutability determines which products compete with each other from the perspective of the consumer. The Commission normally refers to the criteria of price, quality and intended use as the determining factors. In the **UBC** case the relatively constant price and lack of seasonal variation, and the suitability and intended use for children and the elderly meant that other fruits could not be readily substituted for bananas. This test can result in a very narrow market definition, as illustrated in the following case:

Hugin Kassaregister AB v Commission (Case 22/78)

The Commission found Hugin to be in breach of Art 82 because of its refusal to supply spare parts for Hugin cash registers to Liptons. It defined the relevant product market as consisting of spare parts for Hugin machines required by independent repairers. Hugin rejected this finding as too narrow. It insisted that the relevant market was the very competitive cash register market. The Court of Justice, however, accepted the Commission's market definition in relation to the independent repairers of Hugin machines:

The role of those undertakings [the repairers] on the market is that of businesses which require spare parts for their various activities. They need such parts in order to provide services for cash register users in the form of maintenance and repairs and for the reconditioning of used machines intended for re-sale or renting out ... It is, moreover, established that there is a specific demand for Hugin spare parts, since those spare parts are not interchangeable with spare parts for cash registers of other makes. (para 7)

The Court of Justice has accepted that there was dominance in an equally narrow market of information on the content of BBC and RTE television programmes in **RTE and ITP** *v* **Commission** (Cases C–241/91 & C–242/91P). Subsequently, in **Deutsche Bahn AG** *v* **Commission** (Case T–229/94), the Court of First Instance (CFI) held that there was a *distinct sub-market* in the carriage of maritime containers by rail and, in assessing dominance, the Commission was justified in not taking into account other services provided by rail transport operators, road hauliers and inland waterway operators.

Supply-side substitutability

Supply-side substitutability is concerned with the ability of a manufacturer to switch his production system from product A to product B, and therefore constitutes a test of whether the manufacturer of product A is a rival to the manufacturer of product B:

Tetra-Pak International SA v Commission (Case T-83/91)

The Court of Justice rejected Tetra-Pak's argument that there were separate markets for (i) aseptic cartons and the related packing machinery; and (ii) non-aseptic cartons and packaging machinery, because of the relative ease with which the manufacturer could switch from one to the other.

Europemballage and Continental Can v Commission (Case 6/72)

The issue involved packaging containers and the scope of the market. The Court of Justice held that, in order to be regarded as constituting a distinct market, the products must be individualised, not only by the mere fact that they are used in packing certain products, but also by the peculiar characteristics of production which make them specifically suitable for this purpose:

> Consequently, a dominant position on the market for light metal containers for fish and meat cannot be decisive, as long as it has not been proved that competitors from other sectors of the market for light metal containers are not in a position to enter this market, by a simple adaptation, with sufficient strength to create a serious counterweight.

Whether or not supply-side substitutability exists is a matter of fact to be investigated by the Commission, as illustrated in the following case:

Istituto Chemioterapico Italiano SpA and Commercial Solvents Corporation v Commission (Cases 6 and 7/73)

An American company, CSC, and its Italian subsidiary cut off supplies of aminobutanol to another Italian company, Zoja. Aminobutanol is an effective and cheap raw material used in the production of ethambutol, a drug used for treating tuberculosis. The Commission alleged that CSC had an almost worldwide monopoly in aminobutanol, and was considering manufacturing ethambutol in Italy, through its subsidiary there. There were other drugs for the treatment of tuberculosis, which were based on different but less effective raw materials. The Court of Justice decided that the relevant product market was the supply of aminobutanol, and not the production of ethambutol. It could not accept that Zoja could readily adapt its production facilities to other raw materials for the manufacture of ethambutol. Only if other materials could be substituted without difficulty could they be regarded as acceptable substitutes.

The geographical market

In order to decide whether or not the dominant position is held in a substantial part of the common market, it is necessary to look not only at the geographical extent of the market in question but also at: (i) the economic importance of the area as defined; (ii) the pattern and volume of the production and consumption of the relevant product; and (iii) the habits of producers and consumers in that area. An area can be defined by factors which promote its geographical isolation. Factors tending to emphasise that isolation might be lack of transport facilities, or the cost of transportation relative to the value of a product, giving an unchallengeable advantage to local producers. The transport cost factor was held in **Suiker Unie** *v* **Commission** (Case 40/73) to be very significant in defining the geographical market. Conversely, in **Tetra-Pak International SA** *v* **Commission** (Case T–83/91) the CFI supported the Commission's finding that the geographical market consisted of the whole of the Community because, *inter alia*, the very low cost of transport for cartons and machines meant that they could be easily and readily transported between states. Sometimes the geographical market can be readily identified as lying within the borders of a Member State. In **NV Nederlandsche Banden-Industrie Michelin** *v* **Commission** (Case 322/81) the Court of Justice found that tyre companies operated in the Dutch market through local subsidiaries, to which local dealers looked for their supplies. It therefore upheld the decision of the Commission to regard The Netherlands as the area in which the competition facing NBIM was located.

Another factor identifying a separate geographical market is its homogeneity. Article 9(7) of the EC Merger Regulation 139/2004 (which replaced Regulation 4064/89) recognises this factor:

> The geographical reference market shall consist of the area in which the undertakings concerned are involved in the supply and demand of products and services, in which the conditions of competition are sufficiently homogenous and which can be distinguished from neighbouring areas because, in particular, conditions of competition are appreciably different in those areas. This assessment should take account in particular of the nature and characteristics of the products or services concerned, of the existence of entry barriers or of consumer preferences, of appreciable differences of the undertakings' market shares between the area concerned and neighbouring areas or of substantial price differences.

These features were significant in the **United Brands** case when the Court of Justice considered the geographical market:

United Brands Co v Commission (Case 27/76)

With regard to the banana market throughout the Community, the Commission identified three states which had distinctive rules for the import and sale of bananas: Italy, which operated a national system of quota restrictions; the UK, which had a system of Commonwealth preference; and France, which had a similar preferential system favouring the African francophone states. Only the then remaining six Member States had a completely free market in bananas. The Commission therefore excluded France, Italy and the UK from the analysis and the other six states were identified as the relevant geographical market. The Court of Justice supported this finding on the basis that 'although the applicable tariff provisions and transport costs are of necessity different but not discriminatory ... and ... the conditions of competition are the same for all ... [t]hese six states form an area which is sufficiently homogenous to be considered in its entirety' (paras 52 and 53).

The Court of Justice went so far, in a case involving the application of Regulation 4064/89 (which was replaced in 2004 by the EC Merger Regulation 139/2004), as to hold that, for the purposes of the production of potash and rocksalt, the whole Community, apart from Germany, was 'sufficiently homogenous to be regarded overall as a separate geographical market' (**France *v* Commission** (Joined Cases C–68/94 and C–30/95)).

Dominance in fact

Besides the ability to operate independently of its rivals, another indicator of dominance is the extent of market share. The larger this is, the more likely, and well-founded, will be an acceptance of dominance. In **Hoffman La Roche *v* Commission** (Case 85/76), the company's market shares over a three-year period of 75 per cent to 87 per cent were held to be so large that they were, in themselves, evidence of a dominant position. Similarly, in **Tetra-Pak** the company's 90 per cent share of the market in aseptic cartons and the relevant packaging machines made it 'an inevitable partner for packers and guaranteed it the freedom of conduct characteristic of a dominant position'. However, in **United Brands**, a market share of between 40 per cent and 45 per cent did not 'permit the conclusion that UBC automatically controls the market'.

Besides market share, there are a number of other factors indicative of actual dominance of the market. These will include ownership of, or ready access to, massive financial resources. In addition, a firm's ability to establish and maintain a lead in product development or technical services may well contribute to the maintenance of a dominant position. The process of using financial resources or a technical advantage to maintain a dominant position could also constitute an abuse of that position.

Abuse of a dominant position

Article 82(a)–(d) provides a non-exhaustive list of the sort of conduct which will constitute an abuse of a dominant position, primarily concerned with unfair trading practices (such as imposing unfair purchase or selling prices), restricting production to create an artificial shortage, and discriminating unfairly between different trading partners. It was originally thought that Art 82 applied exclusively to practices which constituted an abuse of market power, rather than to activities intended to gain or maintain dominance. However, in **Continental Can** (see above), the Court of Justice rejected such a narrow interpretation of Art 82 and declared that 'the provision is not only aimed at practices which may cause damage to consumers directly, but also at those which are detrimental to them through their impact on an effective competitive structure, such as is mentioned in Article 3(f) of the Treaty'. Article 3(f) EC Treaty (now Art 3(g)) speaks of 'a system ensuring that competition in the internal market is not distorted':

> Abuse may therefore occur if an undertaking in a dominant position **strengthens such position in such a way that the degree of dominance reached substantially fetters competition** i.e., that only undertakings remain in the market whose behaviour depends on the dominant one. [emphasis added]

In the **Continental Can** case, the conduct complained of was an agreement by Continental Can to buy a competitor in the food packaging market that would, in the Commission's view, have enabled it to achieve absolute dominance in its sector of the market. The Court of Justice accepted, in principle, that this sort of conduct could breach Art 82, but decided, on the facts of the case, that the Commission had chosen the wrong relevant product market.

It should, however, be noted that gaining or maintaining dominance is not *per se* in breach of Art 82, as illustrated in the following case:

Gottrub Klim Grovvareforening v *Dansk Landbrugs Grovvaresel* (Case C-250/92)

The Court of Justice held that the conduct of a cooperative of growers that dominated the market of purchasers for certain agricultural supplies was not in breach of Art 82. The cooperative had strengthened its own statutes to reduce competition from members who had left the cooperative. The Court held that 'neither the creation nor the strengthening of a dominant position is in itself contrary to Article 86 EC Treaty [now Art 82] ... The activities of cooperative purchasing organisations may actually encourage more effective competition on some markets, provided that the rules binding members do no more than is necessary to ensure that the cooperative functions properly and maintains its contractual power in relation to producers'.

What is important is the effect of achieving or maintaining dominance. The Court of Justice explored this concept further in the following case:

Hoffman La Roche v *Commission* (Case 85/76)

The Court of Justice stated that:

> The concept of abuse is an objective concept relating to the behaviour of an undertaking in a dominant position where, as a result of the very presence of the undertaking in question, the degree of competition is weakened and which, through recourse to methods different from those which condition normal competition in products and services on the basis of the transactions of commercial operators, has the effect of hindering the maintenance of the degree of competition still existing in the market or the growth of that competition.

Specific abuses

Article 82 contains a number of examples of the type of conduct by an undertaking in a dominant position which constitutes an abuse. The list is indicative and not exhaustive, but it provides a useful starting point for an examination of abusive practices.

The imposition of unfair purchase or selling prices

The most obvious abuse by a supplier in a monopoly position is the imposition of extortionate prices on consumers. There is an element of subjectivity in any assessment of what is a fair price, but in **United Brands** the Court of Justice declared that a price is excessive if 'it has no reasonable relation to the economic value of the product supplied'. In determining the economic value, it is necessary to take into account the difference between the costs actually incurred and the price charged. A price may also be excessive if it is not attributable to ordinary market conditions. In **Tetra-Pak**, the CFI found that the very great disparity in charges between the prices paid by Italian purchasers and those paid elsewhere in the Community could not be explained by additional market or transport costs in Italy, but were derived simply from Tetra-Pak's dominance in that country. The prices charged in Italy were, essentially, discriminatory.

In relation to prices for services, an undertaking would be abusing its dominant position if it charged fees which were disproportionate to the economic value of the service provided. In **Société Civile Agricole de la Crespelle** v **Coopérative d'Elevage de la Mayenne** (Case C–323/93), artificial insemination centres providing bovine semen which enjoyed a virtual monopoly under national legislation in each region of France were held by the Court of Justice to be abusing their position if they were to charge additional costs over and above those actually incurred in obtaining and conserving semen imported from other Member States. The Commission has applied this decision to price-fixing for dock-work in a series of local port monopolies established by national law throughout Italy (**Re Italian Ports Employment Policy: The Italian Community** v **Italy** (Case 97/94)).

Unnaturally low prices may also amount to an abuse, where they are intended to drive an actual or potential competitor from the market. This practice is normally called 'predatory pricing', and was the issue in the following case:

AKZO Chemie BV v Commission (Case C-62/86)

The Commission found that AKZO occupied a dominant position in the market for flour additives and for organic peroxides used in the making of plastics. Another company, ECS, which was already in the flour additives market, was seeking to enter the peroxide for plastics market in the UK. The Commission found that AKZO had made direct threats to ECS, had systematically offered and supplied flour additives to ECS's customers at abnormally low prices and had also offered them products at below cost price which it did not normally supply. The Court of Justice repeated its previously stated position that Art 82 prohibits a dominant undertaking from eliminating a competitor and thus reinforcing its position by means other than competition on merit. In that sense, not all price competition can be regarded as legitimate:

> Prices lower than the average total costs by which a dominant undertaking seeks to eliminate a competitor must be regarded as an abuse. A dominant undertaking has no interest in offering such prices except to eliminate its competitors in order then to raise its prices again on the basis of its monopolistic position, since every sale involves it in a loss, namely all the fixed costs and at least a part of the variable costs relating to the unit produced.

Exclusive supply

It is not uncommon for suppliers to give discounts to customers who place large orders with them, and indeed there is nothing wrong, in principle, with such arrangements. But if the discount is tied to a requirement that the trader purchase all or a very large part of his supplies from the dominant undertaking, the arrangement may very well fall foul of Art 82:

Hoffman La Roche (Case 85/76)

The investigation by the Commission revealed that the company, which was the largest producer of pharmaceuticals in the world, occupied a dominant position in markets for a number of vitamin products. It sold these products on the basis that customers were bound by an exclusive or preferential purchasing commitment in favour of the company for all or a large proportion of their requirements. This was achieved either by an express exclusive purchase agreement, or as a result of 'fidelity rebates'. The Court of Justice rejected these arrangements, since the discounts did not reflect any real cost saving as a result of a bulk purchase (i.e. transport, storage, etc.) but were a direct attempt to 'buy' the exclusive custom of the purchaser.

Michelin v *Commission* (Case 322/81)

Michelin gave target bonuses to its dealers according to their marketing efforts. Dealers were not given a clear indication of the basis on which such bonuses were calculated. The Commission found that the system had the effect of ensuring that the dealers remained attached to Michelin in the hope of receiving the often unknown, but hoped-for, bonuses. The Court of Justice accepted the Commission's finding and ruled that discounts had to be justified by a benefit conferred on the supplier which reduced the supplier's costs and enabled the supplier to pass on the benefit in terms of reduced prices. Across-the-board discounts on a range of products are also an abuse, because they make it more difficult for other suppliers who may not have a similar range of products to compete for an opportunity to supply.

Tied sales

Article 82(d) prohibits 'making the conclusion of contracts subject to acceptance by the other parties of supplementary obligations which, by their nature or according to commercial usage, have no connection with the subject of such contracts'. Typically, this applies to an arrangement under which the supplier requires the trader to purchase its requirements of a second product (the 'tied' product) as a condition of being able to buy a first product (the 'tying' product):

Tetra-Pak (Case T-83/91)

The Commission had found that Tetra-Pak held approximately 90 per cent of, *inter alia*, the market of machines for making aseptic cartons for liquids. Purchasers of such machines were required to obtain their supplies of cartons exclusively from Tetra-Pak or from a supplier designated by it. The CFI declared:

> It is clear that the tied-sale clauses [in the agreements with purchasers] ... went beyond their ostensible purpose and are intended to strengthen Tetra-Pak's dominant position by reinforcing its customers' economic dependence on it. Those clauses are therefore wholly unreasonable in the context of protecting public health and also go beyond the recognised right of an undertaking in a dominant position to protect its commercial interests. Whether considered in isolation or together, they were unfair.

Refusal to supply

Whether or not a dominant undertaking's refusal to supply another undertaking is an abuse or not will be very much a matter of fact, depending on the circumstances of the refusal and the previous dealings of the parties:

Commercial Solvents Corporation v *Commission* (Cases 6 and 7/73)

The Corporation had decided to discontinue sales of aminobutanol to another manufacturer, Zoja, because it had decided to manufacture its derivative, ethambutol, itself. The Court of Justice held that the decision to manufacture ethambutol itself did not justify a refusal to supply the raw material to a potential rival. To do so would effectively eliminate one of the principal manufacturers of ethambutanol in the Community. There may, however, be objectively justifiable reasons for not supplying a commodity.

BP v *Commission* (Case 77/77)

BP refused to sell oil to an intermittent purchaser during the oil crisis in the early 1970s. There was, effectively, an oil embargo of Western Europe and BP had drawn up a list of regular customers whom it would continue to supply, and others whom it would not, or would supply only as and when it was able. The Court of Justice held that, in such a supply crisis, a refusal to supply was justified. There must, however, be an objective justification for a refusal.

In the following case, the issue was the nature of the banana market and a number of alleged abuses by UBC (see above):

United Brands v *Commission* (Case 27/76)

One of the alleged abuses was a refusal to supply certain, hitherto regular, customers. One of these, Olesen, had participated in an advertising campaign run by one of UBC's rivals, and it was this participation that UBC sought to 'punish'. The Court of Justice rejected this attempted justification of a refusal to supply:

> Although it is true, as the applicant points out, that the fact that an undertaking is in a dominant position cannot disentitle it from protecting its own commercial interests if they are attacked, and that such an undertaking must be conceded the right to take such reasonable steps as it deems appropriate to protect its said interests, such behaviour cannot be countenanced if its actual purpose is to strengthen this dominant position and abuse it.
>
> Even if the possibility of a counter-attack is acceptable, that attack must still be proportionate to the threat taking into account the economic strength of the undertakings confronting each other.
>
> The sanction consisting of a refusal to supply by an undertaking in a dominant position was in excess of what might, if such a situation were to arise, reasonably be contemplated as a sanction for conduct similar to that for which UBC blamed Olesen.

Another example of a refusal to supply being used to retain dominance in a market occurred in the following case (the Commission's decision was not challenged before the Court of Justice):

British Brass Band Instruments v *Boosey and Hawkes* [1988] 4 CMLR 67

Boosey and Hawkes produced and sold brass band instruments within the UK. The Commission found that they dominated 90 per cent of the UK's brass band instrument market. The BBBI wished to import and distribute brass band instruments originating in other parts of the Community. Boosey and Hawkes refused to continue to supply the BBBI with UK instruments until it desisted in its importation and sale of Continental brass band instruments. The Commission found that the discontinuance of supply was abusive.

The following case, decided by the Court of Justice during 2004, concerned the refusal by an undertaking in a dominant position to grant a licence (i.e. permission) to use a piece of computer software (referred to as a 'brick structure') which was protected by an intellectual property right:

IMS Health (Case C-418/01)

The case involved a dispute between two companies specialising in market studies in the pharmaceutical products and healthcare sectors, which centered on the claim by one of them that it was entitled to use a 'brick structure' developed by the other for the provision of data on regional sales of pharmaceutical products in Germany. The Court of Justice held that:

30.   ... for the purposes of examining whether the refusal by an undertaking in a dominant position to grant a licence for a brick structure protected by an intellectual property right which it owns is abusive, the degree of participation by users in the development of that structure and the outlay, particularly in terms of cost, on the part of potential users in order to purchase studies on regional sales of pharmaceutical products presented on the basis of an alternative structure are factors which must be taken into consideration in order to determine whether the protected structure is indispensable to the marketing of studies of that kind

   ...

52.   ... the refusal by an undertaking which holds a dominant position and owns an intellectual property right in a brick structure indispensable to the presentation of regional sales data on pharmaceutical products in a Member State to grant a licence to use that structure to another undertaking which also wishes to provide such data in the same Member State, constitutes an abuse of a dominant position within the meaning of Art 82 EC Treaty where the following conditions are fulfilled:
   (i)   the undertaking which requested the licence intends to offer, on the market for the supply of the data in question, new products or services not offered by the owner of the intellectual property right and for which there is a potential consumer demand;
   (ii)   the refusal is not justified by objective considerations;
   (iii) the refusal is such as to reserve to the owner of the intellectual property right the market for the supply of data on sales of pharmaceutical products in the Member State concerned by eliminating all competition on that market. (emphasis added)

Where an undertaking has a monopoly of information, a refusal to supply that information to a potential publisher of television programmes can constitute a refusal to supply under Art 82(b) (**RTE & ITP** *v* **Commission** (Cases C–241/91P and C–242/91P)).

Other abusive practices

The ingenuity of undertakings seeking to extend their dominance and to exclude competitors makes it impossible to provide a full account of abusive practices. The following case provides some examples of practices which have been deemed to be abusive:

Tetra-Pak International SA v Commission (Case T-83/91)

Besides the tying agreements and excessive and predatory pricing which have already been considered, Tetra-Pak was also found by the Commission to have engaged in the following abusive practices: buying back competitors' machines with a view to withdrawing them from the market; obtaining an undertaking from one of the dairies with which it did business not to use two machines it had acquired from competitors of Tetra-Pak; eliminating in Italy all Resolvo aseptic packaging machines developed by a rival company; and finally, appropriating advertising media by obtaining an exclusive rights agreement with an Italian milk industry journal under which Tetra-Pak's rivals would not be allowed to advertise in the journal.

Affecting trade between Member States

As with Art 81, there must be some effect on trade between Member States for Art 82 to apply. To satisfy this condition, it is not necessary that the effect on trade should be of a particular kind. Typically, it would meet the requirement if the effect of the conduct would be to partition markets in the Community. This is illustrated in the following case:

Greenwich Film Production v *SACEM* (Case 22/79)

SACEM was an association formed to collect royalties arising out of the performance of artistic and other works in France and elsewhere. SACEM demanded payment of royalties arising out of the performance of music in films distributed in France. Greenwich argued that SACEM effectively had a monopoly of such rights in France and was abusing its position. SACEM contended, *inter alia*, that even if this was so, it did not affect trade between Member States. The Court of Justice, however, accepted that there might be some effect. It recognised that in certain Member States organisations such as SACEM were entrusted by composers to supervise performances of their work and to collect royalties. It held that it is possible in those circumstances that 'the activities of such associations may be conducted in such a way that their effect is to partition the common market and thereby restrict the freedom to provide services which constitutes one of the objectives of the Treaty'.

This partitioning of the common market will not arise where the activities are exclusively directed at part of a Member State:

Hugin v *Commission* (Case 22/78)

The Commission had found that Hugin, the Swedish manufacturers of cash registers, had refused to supply spare parts of their machines to a London-based firm, Liptons. Liptons serviced, repaired and reconditioned such machines. Their business was essentially local, and they did no work outside the UK. The Court of Justice concluded that the abuse did not have the effect of preventing Liptons from carrying out their servicing in other Member States or affect the trade in parts between Member States, because those requiring the parts would normally obtain them direct from the manufacturers in Sweden. At the time Sweden was in neither the European Community nor the European Economic Area.

Commission guidelines on the 'effect on trade concept' contained in Articles 81 and 82 EC Treaty

Guidelines on the 'effect on trade concept' which is contained in Arts 81 and 82 EC Treaty (OJ 2004 C 101/81) were adopted by the Commission on 30 March 2004 (as part of the 'Modernisation Package' which included the adoption of Regulation 1/2003, see Chapter 22). The guidelines are available at:

http://ec.europa.eu/comm/competition/antitrust/legislation/

Relationship between Articles 81(1) and 82: collective dominance?

It is clear that many undertakings in a dominant position will endeavour to reinforce that position by various kinds of loyalty, tying and other agreements. Such agreements in themselves may infringe Art 81(1), or they may also constitute forms of abusive behaviour which breach Art 82. On the other hand, agreements between undertakings and subsidiaries may not breach Art 81 simply because they are subsidiaries, and their action is seen as the action of one and the same entity (**VIHO Europe BV** *v* **Commission** (C–73/95P)). In such circumstances, the agreement between a parent company and subsidiaries may, however, where it is intended to drive or exclude a competitor from the market, constitute an abuse of a dominant position. In **Istituto Chemioterapico Italiano and Commercial Solvents Corporation** *v* **Commission** (Cases 6 and 7/73), see above, it was CSC, the controlling company, which had instructed its subsidiary ICI not to supply aminobutanol to Zoja.

An agreement between several undertakings, each of which has a powerful position in a particular market, may come close to creating dominance which may then be subject to abuse by them. Article 82, indeed, refers to abuse by 'one or more undertakings'. However, the undertakings involved are more likely to be penalised for a breach of Art 81(1) than a breach of Art 82 (Commission decision on **Italian Flat Glass** [1990] 4 CMLR 535). The nearest the Court has come to accepting a breach of Art 82 where there is a linkage of several undertakings was in the case of an actual or proposed merger of those undertakings (see, e.g., **Continental Can** (Case 6/72)). Tacit collusion between major undertakings comprising, in effect, a tight oligopoly, may be difficult for the Commission to deal with:

Hoffman La Roche (Case 85/76)

The Court of Justice declared (in response to Advocate-General Lenz's observation that there was a problem in knowing where a collective monopoly ends and an oligopoly begins):

> A dominant position must also be distinguished from parallel courses of conduct which are peculiar to oligopolies in that in an oligopoly the courses of conduct interact, while in the case of an undertaking occupying a dominant position the conduct of the undertaking which derives profits from that position is to a great extent determined unilaterally.

In the absence of clear evidence, a concerted practice breaching Art 81(1) may not be demonstrable. If that is the case then, *a fortiori*, an abuse by connected undertakings cannot be shown to breach Art 82. Evidence of some judicial movement in relation to the concept of collective dominance came first when the CFI considered the Commission's decision in **Italian Flat Glass (SIV** *v* **Commission** (Joined Cases T–68, 77 and 78/89)). The CFI held that the former Art 86 (now Art 82) was capable of applying to independent firms which, because of the economic links between them, held a collective dominant position on the relevant market. Nevertheless, on the facts of the case, it decided that there was insufficient evidence to support a finding of collective dominance. However, in **Compagnie Maritime Belge** (Joined Cases T–24–26 and 28/93), the CFI held that the members of a shipping conference had abused the collective dominant position they held as a result of close relations between them. The Court of Justice had already, by then, accepted in principle that the former Art 86 (now Art 82) was capable of applying to collective dominance (**DIP and Others** *v* **Comune di Bassano del Grappa** (Joined Cases C–140–142/94)). The basis of these decisions is the fact that Art 82 applies to 'one or more undertakings'. Originally, this may have been intended to refer only to a primary undertaking and its subsidiaries, as in **VIHO** *v* **Commission** (Case C–73/95P), but the difficulty of proving the existence of a concerted practice in Art 81(1) seems to have led the Court to take a more sympathetic view of collective dominance, in order to bring the activities within Art 82, and to bridge the apparent gap between Arts 81 and 82.

Mergers

A merger takes place when two or more undertakings which were formerly independent are brought under common control. As a result of the decision of the Court of Justice in **Continental Can** (see above), it was clear that a merger between undertakings could, in appropriate circumstances, breach Art 82. What those circumstances were became the subject, after prolonged discussions, of a Council regulation on mergers (Council Regulation 4064/89 on the control of concentrations between undertakings). Under the regulation, the Commission was given sole competence to take decisions with regard to 'concentrations with a Community dimension'. Regulation 4064/89 was replaced in 2004 by the EC Merger Regulation 139/2004.

Such concentrations may be viewed from two perspectives. On the one hand, the combined economic strengths of fully merged undertakings, or the cooperation between undertakings which have partly merged, may produce a degree of market control and distortion of competition that is detrimental to the effective operation of the market. On the other hand, the merger may produce economies of scale, and result in the creation of an undertaking whose size and strength may enable it to compete effectively on world markets. In considering the effect of a merger under the EC Merger Regulation 139/2004, the Commission has to strike a balance between competing objectives.

Article 2(1), Regulation 139/2004 requires the Commission to make an appraisal of the proposed merger, taking into account:

(a) the need to maintain and develop effective competition within the common market in view of, among other things, the structure of all the markets concerned and the actual or potential competition from undertakings located either within or outwith the Community;

(b) the market position of the undertakings concerned and their economic and financial power, the alternatives available to suppliers and users, their access to suppliers or markets, any legal and other barriers to entry, supply and demand trends for the relevant goods and services, the interests of the intermediate and ultimate consumers, and the development of technical and economic progress provided that it is to the consumers' advantage and does not form an obstacle to competition.

Article 2(2), Regulation 139/2004 provides that a concentration which '*would not* significantly impede effective competition in the common market or in a substantial part of it, in particular as a result of the creation or strengthening of a dominant position shall be declared *compatible* with the common market' (emphasis added). Article 2(3), Regulation 139/2004 contains the corollary provision that a concentration which '*would* significantly impede effective competition in the common market or in a substantial part of it, in particular as a result of the creation or strengthening of a dominant position shall be declared *incompatible* with the common market' (emphasis added). The declaration of compatibility or incompatibility is made by the Commission in the form of a decision (Art 8, Regulation 139/2004).

The Community dimension of a merger is achieved when the aggregate worldwide turnover of all the undertakings concerned is more than €5,000 million and the aggregate Community-wide turnover of each of at least two of the undertakings involved is more than €250 million, unless each of the undertakings concerned achieves more than two-thirds of its aggregate Community-wide turnover in one and the same Member State (Art 1(2), Regulation 139/2004).

Regulation 139/2004 provides that where a concentration does not meet the above thresholds, it will still have a Community dimension where:

(a) the combined aggregate worldwide turnover of all the undertakings concerned is more than 2,500 million euros;

(b) in each of at least three Member States, the combined aggregate turnover of all the undertakings concerned is more than 100 million euros;

(c) in each of at least three Member States included for the purpose of point (b), the aggregate turnover of each of at least two of the undertakings concerned is more than 25 million euros; and

(d) the aggregate Community-wide turnover of each of at least two of the undertakings concerned is more than 100 million euros;

unless each of the undertakings concerned achieves more than two-thirds of its aggregate Community-wide turnover within one and the same Member State.

Regulation 139/2004, and more relevantly its predecessor Regulation 4064/89, have not, to date, constituted much of a barrier to mergers. The vast majority of mergers notified to the Commission have obtained clearance. The Commission seems to see mergers as a way of reducing national control of undertakings and promoting the strength of large Community undertakings on the world market. Less attention appears to be paid to the possible adverse effects on consumers in the Community. One case where the Commission denied clearance, **Aérospatiale-Alenia/de Haviland** [1992] 4 CMLR M2, on the grounds that the merger would have had an unacceptable impact on customers' freedom of choice and the balance of competition in the Community, was widely criticised by governments, many with clear political interests in a different outcome than that resulting from the decision.

In **France v Commission** (Cases C–68/94 & C–30/95), the Court of Justice gave the previous Merger Regulation 4064/89 a new cutting edge, holding that it applied to a situation of collective dominance which fell short of an actual merger (see Editorial (1998) 23 EL Rev 199, 'Collective dominance: Trump card or joker?'). Under the new EC Merger Regulation 139/2004, cooperative aspects of joint ventures by undertakings which fall within the turnover threshold will have to be notified to the Commission and assessed for compatibility with Arts 81(1) and 81(3) EC Treaty (Art 2(4), Regulation 139/2004).

The CFI gave a ground-breaking judgment when it overturned the Commission's decision to block the takeover of UK holiday company First Choice by Airtours:

Airtours plc v Commission (Case T-342/99)

It was the first time that the CFI had overturned a Commission decision to block a takeover. In its reasoning, the CFI concluded that the Commission had failed to prove satisfactorily that the proposed merger would establish a position of collective dominance. According to Art 2(3), Regulation 4064/89 (as amended), a concentration that 'creates or reinforces a dominant position as a result of which effective competition would be significantly impeded in the common market or in a substantial part of it' is to be declared incompatible with the common market. This had not been shown in this particular case and the Commission's decision was annulled.

Article 2(3), Regulation 139/2004 has substantially re-enacted Art 2(3), Regulation 4064/89. The CFI could therefore have reached a similar decision in the **Airtours** case if it had been required to apply Art 2(3), Regulation 139/2004 rather than Art 2(3) of the earlier regulation.

In the following case, decided by the CFI during 2006, the CFI annulled the Commission's decision authorising a proposed concentration between Bertelsmann and Sony, whereby the two companies would merge their global recorded music activities (with the exclusion of Sony's activities in Japan) into three new companies operated together under the name Sony BMG:

Independent Music Publishers and Labels Association (Impala) v *Commission* (Case T-464/04)

On 24 May 2004, the Commission informed the notifying parties that it had reached the provisional conclusion that the concentration was incompatible with Community law, since, in particular, it would reinforce a collective dominant position on the market for recorded music. However, after hearing the parties, the Commission on 18 July 2004 declared the concentration to be compatible with the common market.

On 3 December 2004, Impala, an international association whose members are 2,500 independent music production companies and which had participated in the procedure before the Commission, applied to the CFI for annulment of that decision.

The CFI observed that, according to the Commission's decision, the absence of a collective dominant position on the market for recorded music might be inferred from the heterogeneity of the product concerned, from the lack of transparency of the market and from the absence of retaliatory measures between the five largest companies.

However, the CFI found that the theory that promotional discounts have the effect of reducing the transparency of the market to the point of preventing the existence of a collective dominant position was not supported by a statement of reasons of the requisite legal standard and was vitiated by a manifest error of assessment. The elements on which that argument was founded were incomplete and did not include all the relevant data that ought to have been taken into account by the Commission. They were therefore not capable of supporting the conclusions drawn from them.

The CFI further pointed out that the Commission relied on the absence of evidence that retaliatory measures had been used in the past, whereas, according to case law, the mere existence of effective deterrent mechanisms is sufficient, since where the companies comply with the common policy there is no need to have recourse to sanctions. In that context, the CFI stated that the decision and the case file revealed that such credible and effective deterrent measures appeared to exist, in particular the possibility of sanctioning a deviating record company by excluding it from compilations. In addition, even if the appropriate test in that regard was to consist of determining whether retaliatory measures had been exercised in the past, the Commission's examination was inadequate. At the hearing it was not in a position to indicate the slightest step that it had completed or undertaken for that purpose.

As those two grounds constituted the essential grounds on which the Commission concluded that there was no collective dominant position, each of those errors would in itself constitute sufficient reason to annul the decision.

Furthermore, as regards the possible creation of a collective dominant position after the concentration, the CFI criticised the Commission for having carried out an extremely cursory examination and for having presented in the decision only a few superficial and formal observations on that point.

The CFI considered that the Commission could not rely, without making an error, on the lack of transparency of the market or on the absence of evidence that retaliatory measures had been used in the past in order to conclude that the concentration did not entail a risk that a collective dominant position would be created.

Summary

Now you have read this chapter you should be able to:

- Explain how Art 82 EC Treaty operates to prevent the abuse of a dominant position, describing:
  - what is meant by a dominant position (distinguishing between demand-side substitutability and supply-side substitutability);
  - in what circumstances such a dominant position will be deemed to be abused; and
  - how such abuse must affect trade between Member States.
- Describe and evaluate the relationship between Arts 81(1) and 82 EC Treaty with regard to collective dominance.
- Understand and explain how Art 82 EC Treaty and Regulation 139/2004 are applied to regulate mergers which may produce a degree of market control and distortion of competition which is detrimental to the effective operation of the common market.

References

Editorial, 'Collective dominance: Trump card or joker?' (1998) 23 EL Rev 199.

Further reading

Textbooks

Craig, P. and De Burca, G. (2003) *EU Law Text, Cases and Materials* (3rd edn), Oxford University Press, Chapter 23.

Foster, N. (2006) *Foster on EU Law* (1st edn), Oxford University Press, Chapter 8 (Sections 8.5, 8.7 and 8.10).

Goyder, D.G. (2003) *EC Competition Law* (4th edn), Oxford University Press.

Steiner, J., Woods, L. and Twigg-Flesner, C. (2006) *EU Law* (9th edn), Oxford University Press, Chapter 28.

Storey, T. and Turner, C. (2005) *Unlocking EU Law* (1st edn), Hodder Arnold, Chapter 15 (Sections 15.3 and 15.4).

Tillotson, J. and Foster, N. (2003) *Text, Cases and Materials on EU Law* (4th edn), Cavendish Publishing, Chapter 16.

Weatherill, S. (2006) *Cases and Materials on EC Law* (7th edn), Oxford University Press, Chapter 17.

Journal articles

Andrews, P., 'Is Meeting Competition a Defence to Predatory Pricing? The Irish Sugar Decision Suggests a New Approach' [1998] ECLR 49.

Art, J.Y. and van Liederkerke, D., 'Developments in EC Competition Law in 1996 – An Overview' (1997) 34 CML Rev 895.

Baxter, S. and Dethmers, F., 'Collective dominance under EC merger control – after Airtours and the introduction of unilateral effects is there still a future for collective dominance?' [2006] ECLR 148.

Brittan, Sir Leon, 'The Law and Policy of Merger Control in the EEC' (1990) 15 EL Rev 351.

Brown, A., 'Distinguishing Between Concentrative and Cooperative Ventures: Is it getting any easier?' (1996) 17 ECLR 240.

Doherty, B., 'Just What are Essential Facilities?' (2001) 38 CML Rev 397.

Eilmansberger, T., 'How to distinguish food from bad competition under Article 82 EC: In search of clearer and more coherent standards for anti-competitive abuses' (2005) 42 CML Rev 129.

Kallaugher, J. and Weitbrecht, A., 'Developments under Articles 81 and 82 EC – the Year 2005 in review' [2006] ECLR 137.

Monti, G., 'The Scope of Collective Dominance under Article 82' (2001) 38 CML Rev 131.

Niels, G., 'Collective Dominance – More than just Oligopolistic Independence' [2001] ECLR 168.

Soames, T., 'An Analysis of the Principles of Concerted Dominance: A Distinction Without a Difference?' [1996] ECLR 24.

Withers, C. and Jephcott, M., 'Where to Now for EC Oligopoly Control?' [2001] ECLR 295.

22 Enforcement of competition law: powers and procedures

Aims and objectives

At the end of this chapter you should understand:

- How the rules of Community competition law, which were previously implemented primarily by Regulation 17/62, have (from 1 May 2004) been implemented by Regulation 1/2003 and Regulation 773/2004.
- The nature and scope of the six Commission Notices issued to support Regulation 1/2003 and Regulation 773/2004.
- The Commission's role in initiating an action for an apparent breach of Arts 81 or 82 EC Treaty.
- What applications (if any) can be made by a party to a possible infringement of Arts 81 or 82 EC Treaty.
- The nature and scope of the Commission's powers of investigation and a party's right to a hearing.
- The nature and scope of the Commission's powers to make decisions, and the power to levy fines and periodic penalty payments.
- The relationship between the Commission, and the national competition authorities and courts of the Member States.
- The role of national competition authorities and courts of the Member States in the enforcement of Arts 81 and 82 EC Treaty.
- The relationship between Community and national competition law.
- How Community competition law is implemented in the UK.

Introduction

The European Commission has a general duty, imposed on it by Art 85(1) EC Treaty (previously Art 89(1)), 'to ensure the application of the principles laid down in Articles 81 and 82'. Article 85(1) requires that:

> On application by a Member State or on its own initiative, and in co-operation with the competent authorities in the Member States, who shall give it their assistance, the

Commission shall investigate cases of suspected infringement of these principles. If it finds that there has been an infringement, it shall propose appropriate measures to bring it to an end.

Under Art 85(2) EC Treaty, if the infringement is not brought to an end, the Commission is required to record details of the infringement in a reasoned decision and to authorise Member States to take the necessary measures to remedy the situation.

Article 85 EC Treaty enables the Commission to make the appropriate decision, but it does not confer specific investigative powers, define the investigative process or prescribe any means of enforcement by the Commission. These powers and duties were conferred on the Commission by Regulation 17/62 and, with the exception of transport (which was subject to a special process under Regulation 141/62), they applied to all investigations by the Commission.

Regulation 1/2003

On 1 May 2004, the same day the EU was enlarged from 15 to 25 Member States, Regulation 17/62 was replaced by Regulation 1/2003 (OJ 2003 L 1/1). This new Regulation creates the conditions for a greater involvement of national competition authorities and courts by making Arts 81 and 82 (previously Arts 85 and 86) directly applicable in their entirety (see Chapters 20 and 21). The Regulation also covers transport and therefore Regulation 141/62 has been repealed. One further regulation has been adopted:

- Regulation 773/2004 relates to the conduct of proceedings by the Commission pursuant to Arts 81 and 82 EC Treaty (OJ 2004 L 123/18).

The Commission has also issued seven notices (which are not legally binding):

- Commission Notice on cooperation within the Network of Competition Authorities (OJ 2004 C 101/43).
- Commission Notice on the cooperation between the Commission and the courts of the EU Member States in the application of Arts 81 and 82 EC Treaty (OJ 2004 C 101/54).
- Commission Notice on the handling of complaints by the Commission under Arts 81 and 82 EC Treaty (OJ 2004 C 101/65).
- Commission Notice on informal guidance relating to novel questions concerning Arts 81 and 82 EC Treaty that arise in individual cases (guidance letters) (OJ 2004 C 101/78); see Chapter 20.
- Commission Notice: Guidelines on the effect on trade concept contained in Arts 81 and 82 EC Treaty (OJ 2004 C 101/81); see Chapters 20 and 21.
- Commission Notice: Guidelines on the application of Art 81(3) EC Treaty (OJ 2004 C 101/118); see Chapter 20.
- Commission Notice on the rules for access to the Commission file in cases pursuant to Arts 81 and 82 EC Treaty, Arts 53, 54 and 57 EEA Agreement, and Regulation 773/2004 (OJ 2005 C 325/7).

The two regulations and seven notices are available in full-text format at:
http://ec.europa.eu/comm/competition/antitrust/legislation/

In the sections that follow, there is a discussion of the application of Community competition law under Regulation 17/62 as well as under Regulation 1/2003.

Initiating action by the Commission and the Member States

Where an apparent breach of Arts 81 or 82 EC Treaty has come to the notice of the Commission through, for example, a question by a member of the European Parliament, or a report in the press, the Commission can, under the general power conferred on it by Art 85, commence an investigation. Article 17, Regulation 1/2003 sets out the powers of the Commission to investigate a particular sector of the economy or particular type of agreement across various sectors 'where the trend of trade between Member States, the rigidity of prices or other circumstances suggest that competition may be restricted or distorted within the common market'. Article 5, Regulation 1/2003 empowers the competition authorities of the Member States to apply Arts 81 and 82 EC Treaty in individual cases, and the national laws relating to investigation will apply. While the competition authorities of the Member States had previously had the power to apply Arts 81(1) and 82 EC Treaty, for the first time they are empowered to apply the exception from the prohibition on agreements which restrict competition as laid down in Art 81(3) EC Treaty (see Chapter 20).

Complaints by a natural or legal person

Regulation 17/62

Article 3, Regulation 17/62 provided that Member States and 'natural and legal persons who claim a legitimate interest' could apply to the Commission to decide whether or not there had been an infringement. Since, however, the Commission has its own residual power to commence such an investigation, even a person who did not have a claim to a legitimate interest could bring details of a possible breach of Arts 81 or 82 EC Treaty to the attention of the Commission with an expectation that it would be investigated (see Hunnings, 1987; **Hoffman La Roche** (Case 85/76); **Adams** v **Commission** (Case 145/83)).

In the following two cases, the Court of Justice dismissed IECC's appeal against the judgment of the Court of First Instance (CFI):

IECC v *Commission* (Case C-449/98P) and *IECC* v *Commission* (Case C-450/98P)

IECC maintained, *inter alia*, that the CFI had committed an error of law with regard to the scope, the definition and the application of Art 3, Regulation 17/62 and the legal concept of Community interest.

The Court of Justice upheld the judgment of the CFI. It stated that, in the context of competition policy, the Commission was entitled to give differing degrees of priority to the complaints brought before it. The discretion which it thus enjoyed in that regard did not depend on the more or less advanced stage of the investigation of a case, which was only one of the circumstances that the Commission was required to take into consideration. The Court of Justice stated, however, that the CFI did not confer *unlimited* discretion on the Commission, because the CFI drew attention to the existence and scope of the review of the legality of a decision rejecting a complaint. The Court found that the Commission, in the exercise of its discretion, had to take into consideration all the relevant matters of law and fact in order to decide what action to take in response to a complaint, particularly those which the complainant brought to its attention. The number of criteria of assessment should not be limited, nor should the Commission be required to have recourse exclusively to certain criteria.

Although the Commission was not obliged to investigate every complaint it received, when it decided to open an inquiry it had to do so 'with the required care, seriousness and diligence in order to evaluate, in full knowledge, the elements of fact and law submitted for its assessment' (**Asia Motor France v Commission (No. 2)** (Case T–7/92)). The element of care involved showing proper regard for the interests of both the complainant and the respondent in the proceedings. A growing number of decisions made by the Commission were struck down by the Court of Justice and the CFI because proper procedural requirements had not been met. This had occurred partly because Regulation 17/62 was not at all specific as to how the rights of the parties should be respected during consideration of a complaint and the subsequent investigation. The Regulation was, therefore, 'fleshed out' by the Court, drawing on a variety of sources, including the European Convention on Human Rights, the International Covenant of Civil and Political Rights and the domestic constitutional systems of Member States (**National Panasonic v Commission** (Case 136/79); **Orkem v Commission** (Case 374/87)). The Commission had to learn by a process of trial and error as to whether its procedures met the evolving standards of the Court. Regulation 1/2003 which replaced Regulation 17/62 on 1 May 2004 (see above) specifically provides that it 'respects the fundamental rights and observes the principles recognised in particular by the Charter of Fundamental Rights of the European Union. Accordingly, this Regulation should be interpreted and applied with respect to those rights and principles' (Preamble, para 37). The other reason for the failure of the Commission to meet the Court's procedural requirements was the chronic shortage of resources which had, on occasion, compelled it to take shortcuts in the process, and to rely increasingly on national anti-trust agencies and national courts to deal with infringements of competition law where there was both a national and a Community dimension (see Shaw, 1995). If the Commission decided to reject a complaint, it was required by Art 253 EC Treaty to give reasons for that decision.

In **Tremblay and Others v Syndicat des Exploitants de Lieux de Loisirs (SELL)** (Case T–5/93), the Commission had received a number of complaints against the Société des Auteurs, Compositeurs et Editeurs de Musique (SACEM). The complainants, who ran discotheques throughout France, alleged that SACEM, which managed copyright in musical works in France, had infringed Arts 81 and 82. In response to the complaints, the Commission undertook an investigation and subsequently informed the complainants that its investigation provided no basis 'for concluding that the conditions for the application of Article 86 [now Art 82] are fulfilled with regard to the level of tariffs at present applied by SACEM'. In relation to Art 81, the Commission told the complainants that the practices of which they complained were essentially national, there was no Community interest involved and the issues raised were, in any event, already being considered by a number of French courts. The CFI found that the Commission had not provided the complainants with the grounds for rejecting their complaint as to the alleged partitioning of national markets by reciprocal representation contracts made between various copyright management societies in different Member States. It rejected the challenge to the Commission's finding of a lack of a sufficient Community interest and held that the fact that a national court or national competition authority was already dealing with a case concerning the compatibility of an agreement or practice with Arts 81 or 82 was a factor which the Commission could take into account in evaluating the extent to which a case displayed a Community interest (see **Automec Srl v Commission (Automec No. 2)** (Case T–24/90); Shaw, 1993; Friend, 1994).

A complainant had no right to insist that the Commission adopt a final decision as to the existence or otherwise of an alleged infringement. Where the Commission did not propose to initiate infringement proceedings, it was required by Art 6, Regulation 99/63 to inform any complainants of its reasons and to fix a time limit within which they could submit further comments in writing. In such a case, if the Commission then decided that further investigation was unwarranted or unnecessary, it should provide a sufficiently reasoned decision to the complainant to enable its legality to be challenged in judicial review proceedings under Art 230 EC Treaty (**Ladbroke Racing (Deutschland) GmbH v Commission** (Case T–74/92)).

The following joined cases, decided by the CFI during 2006, concerned a complainant's right of access to the Commission's statement of objections:

Österreichische Postsparkasse AG v Commission and Bank für Arbeit und Wirtschaft AG v Commission (Joined Cases T-213/01 and T-214/01)

The applicants, Österreichische Postsparkasse AG (Case T-213/01) and Bank für Arbeit und Wirtschaft AG (Case T-214/01), are Austrian credit institutions.

In 1997 the Commission became aware of a document entitled 'Lombard 8.5' and, in the light of that document and acting on its own initiative, initiated proceedings for infringement of the competition rules against the applicants and six other Austrian banks. Two months later an Austrian political party, the Freiheitliche Partei Österreichs (the FPÖ), sent the Lombard 8.5 document to the Commission and asked it to initiate an investigation with a view to making a finding that such an infringement had taken place.

In September 1999 the Commission sent the applicants a 'statement of objections', in which it alleged that they had concluded anti-competitive agreements with other Austrian banks relating to the fees and conditions applicable to their customers. In November 2000 the Commission notified to the applicants a supplementary statement of objections in which it alleged that they had concluded agreements relating to bank fees for national currency/euro exchange transactions.

During the administrative procedure, the FPÖ requested the Commission to send it the two statements of objections. The FPÖ maintained that it was a customer of the banks under investigation and that it had suffered economic harm as a result of the impugned practices.

Following that request, the Commission informed the applicants that it intended to forward the non-confidential versions of the statements in question to the FPÖ, in accordance with Regulation 2842/98. The applicants objected to the statements being sent to the FPÖ because, in their contention, the FPÖ could not be regarded as a complainant with a 'legitimate interest' within the meaning of Art 3(2), Regulation 17/61. In the alternative, the applicants requested the Commission to remove certain information from the non-confidential versions of the statements of objections.

In July and August 2001 the hearing officer conducting the proceedings adopted two decisions relating to the transmission of the non-confidential versions of the statements to the FPÖ and settling the applicants' requests concerning the information to be removed from them.

In September 2001 the applicants brought two actions before the CFI for annulment of those two decisions of the hearing officer and also two applications for interim relief in the form of suspension of operation of the decisions. The applications for interim relief were dismissed and in January 2002 the Commission sent the FPÖ the non-confidential versions of the statements of objections. The Governor of the *Land* of Carinthia, Mr J. Haider, then disclosed the contents of the statements to the press.

In the present cases, the applicants claimed, in substance, that the hearing officer's decisions to forward the statements to the FPÖ were adopted in breach of Regulations 17/61 and 2842/98 and also in breach of the principles of procedural economy and legitimate expectations and of the rights of the defence.

They also maintained that the statements of objections sent to the FPÖ contained business secrets and other confidential information.

The CFI rejected all the pleas in law raised by the applicants. The CFI observed that the Community legislature has established a scale according to which the degree of participation in competition proceedings is determined by the intensity of the harm caused to the interests of the person concerned, a distinction being drawn between (i) an applicant or complainant who has shown a legitimate interest; (ii) a third party showing sufficient interest; and (iii) other third parties. The CFI noted that any applicant or complainant who has shown a legitimate interest is entitled to receive a non-confidential version of the statement of objections.

The CFI considered that a final customer who shows that he has sustained or is likely to sustain harm to his economic interests owing to the restriction of competition in question has a legitimate interest for the purposes of Art 3, Regulation 17/61 in lodging an application or a complaint with the aim of securing a finding by the Commission that there has been an infringement of Arts 81 or 82 EC Treaty. As the ultimate purpose of the rules which seek to ensure that competition is not distorted in the internal market is to enhance the welfare of consumers, the recognition that such final customers who purchase goods or services have a legitimate interest in securing a finding by the Commission that there has been an infringement of Arts 81 or 82 EC Treaty helps to achieve the objectives of competition law.

The CFI concluded that natural or legal persons who show a legitimate interest in securing a finding by the Commission of an infringement of the competition rules may submit a request or a complaint to that effect even after the initial investigation stage of the infringement proceedings has been opened, either upon the Commission's own initiative or upon application by another person.

Regulation 1/2003

Under Regulation 1/2003, a complaint may be lodged with either the Commission (Art 7) or the competition authorities of the Member States (Art 5). National courts are also required to safeguard the rights of individuals through an application of Arts 81 and 82 (Art 6). Article 13 provides for the suspension or termination of proceedings:

1. Where competition authorities of two or more Member States have received a complaint or are acting on their own initiative under Article 81 or Article 82 of the Treaty against the same agreement, decision of an association or practice, the fact that one authority is dealing with the case shall be sufficient grounds for the others to suspend the proceedings before them or to reject the complaint. The Commission may likewise reject a complaint on the ground that a competition authority of a Member State is dealing with the case.

2. Where a competition authority of a Member State or the Commission has received a

complaint against an agreement, decision of an association or practice which has already been dealt with by another competition authority, it may reject it.

Regulation 773/2004

Article 33, Regulation 1/2003 specifically empowers the Commission to adopt measures relating to, *inter alia*, 'the form, content, and other details of complaints lodged pursuant to Article 7 and the procedure for rejecting complaints'. Pursuant to this power, Regulation 773/2004 was adopted. Chapter IV of this Regulation deals with the handling of complaints:

CHAPTER IV
HANDLING OF COMPLAINTS
Article 5
Admissibility of complaints

1. Natural and legal persons shall show a legitimate interest in order to be entitled to lodge a complaint for the purposes of Article 7 of Regulation (EC) No 1/2003. Such complaints shall contain the information required by Form C, as set out in the Annex. The Commission may dispense with this obligation as regards part of the information, including documents, required by Form C.
2. Three paper copies as well as, if possible, an electronic copy of the complaint shall be submitted to the Commission. The complainant shall also submit a non-confidential version of the complaint, if confidentiality is claimed for any part of the complaint.
3. Complaints shall be submitted in one of the official languages of the Community.

Article 6
Participation of complainants in proceedings

1. Where the Commission issues a statement of objections relating to a matter in respect of which it has received a complaint, it shall provide the complainant with a copy of the non-confidential version of the statement of objections and set a time-limit within which the complainant may make known its views in writing.
2. The Commission may, where appropriate, afford complainants the opportunity of expressing their views at the oral hearing of the parties to which a statement of objections has been issued, if complainants so request in their written comments.

Article 7
Rejection of complaints

1. Where the Commission considers that on the basis of the information in its possession there are insufficient grounds for acting on a complaint, it shall inform the complainant of its reasons and set a time-limit within which the complainant may make known its views in writing. The Commission shall not be obliged to take into account any further written submission received after the expiry of that time-limit.
2. If the complainant makes known its views within the time-limit set by the Commission and the written submissions made by the complainant do not lead to a different assessment of the complaint, the Commission shall reject the complaint by decision.
3. If the complainant fails to make known its views within the time-limit set by the Commission, the complaint shall be deemed to have been withdrawn.

Article 8
Access to information

1. Where the Commission has informed the complainant of its intention to reject a complaint pursuant to Article 7(1) the complainant may request access to the documents on which the Commission bases its provisional assessment. For this purpose, the com-

plainant may however not have access to business secrets and other confidential information belonging to other parties involved in the proceedings.

2. The documents to which the complainant has had access in the context of proceedings conducted by the Commission under Articles 81 and 82 of the Treaty may only be used by the complainant for the purposes of judicial or administrative proceedings for the application of those Treaty provisions.

Article 9
Rejections of complaints pursuant to Article 13 of Regulation (EC) No 1/2003
Where the Commission rejects a complaint pursuant to Article 13 of Regulation (EC) No 1/2003, it shall inform the complainant without delay of the national competition authority which is dealing or has already dealt with the case.

Article 5(1), Regulation 773/2004 provides that natural and legal persons who can show a legitimate interest are entitled to lodge a complaint. As discussed above, this is similar to the provision in Regulation 17/62. However, under the new Regulation, the complaint must be submitted in a standard format using a specific form (Art 5(1)). Following a complaint being submitted, if the Commission issues a 'statement of objections' to the party being complained about, the Commission will provide the complainant with a copy of the non-confidential version of the statement, and invite the complainant to submit written comments within a specified time limit (Art 6(1)). There will subsequently be an oral hearing of the party against which a statement of objections has been issued. If the complainant requested, in his written comments, to express his views at this hearing, then he will be allowed to do so (Art 6(2)).

The Commission is entitled to reject a complaint if, on the basis of information in its possession, it considers there are insufficient grounds for acting on a complaint. In this instance, before rejecting the complaint, the Commission will inform the complainant of its view, and invite the complainant to submit written comments within the specified time limit (Art 7(1)). If the complainant submits such written comments within the time limit, and these comments do not lead to the Commission coming to a different conclusion, then the Commission will reject the complaint (Art 7(2)). If the complainant fails to submit any written comments then the complaint will be deemed to have been withdrawn (Art 7(3)). Under Art 8, if the Commission informs the complainant of its intention to reject a complaint, the complainant has a limited right of access to documents (Art 9).

If the Commission rejects a complaint pursuant to Art 13, Regulation 1/2003 (see above), the Commission will inform the complainant, without delay, of the national competition authority which is dealing with the case (Art 9).

Commission notice on the handling of complaints by the Commission under Articles 81 and 82 of the EC Treaty

As stated above, during 2004 the Commission issued a detailed notice on the handling of complaints by the Commission under Arts 81 and 82 EC Treaty (OJ 2004 C 101/65). This notice is divided into three sections:

- introduction and subject matter of the notice;
- different possibilities for lodging complaints about suspected infringements of Arts 81 or 82 EC Treaty;
- the Commission's handling of complaints pursuant to Art 7(2), Regulation 1/2003.

The notice recognises that Regulation 1/2003 establishes a system of parallel competence for the application of Arts 81 and 82 EC Treaty by the Commission, and the national competition authorities and courts of the Member States (para 1). It further recognises that the Commission's action can be focused on the investigation of serious infringements of Arts 81 and 82 EC Treaty (para 2). There are two ways in which a complaint can be made to the Commission: (i) formally, pursuant to Art 7(2), Regulation 1/2003 (see above); or (ii) informally, for example, through the Commission's website (para 4). Part II of the notice (paras 7–25) 'gives indications about the choice between complaining to the Commission or bringing a lawsuit before a national court. Moreover, it recalls the principles related to the work-sharing between the Commission and the national competition authorities in the enforcement system established by Regulation 1/2003 that are explained in the Notice on cooperation within the network of competition authorities'.

Part III of the notice (paras 26–81) contains detailed provisions relating to:

- making a complaint pursuant to Art 7(2), Regulation 1/2003;

- assessment of complaints by the Commission;

- the Commission's procedures when dealing with complaints.

Part III is particularly informative and therefore it is set out in full (although the footnotes have been omitted):

III. THE COMMISSION'S HANDLING OF COMPLAINTS PURSUANT TO ARTICLE 7(2) OF REGULATION 1/2003

A. GENERAL

26. According to Article 7(2) of Regulation 1/2003 natural or legal persons that can show a legitimate interest are entitled to lodge a complaint to ask the Commission to find an infringement of Articles 81 and 82 EC and to require that the infringement be brought to an end in accordance with Article 7(1) of Regulation 1/2003. The present part of this Notice explains the requirements applicable to complaints based on Article 7(2) of Regulation 1/2003, their assessment and the procedure followed by the Commission.

27. The Commission, unlike civil courts, whose task is to safeguard the individual rights of private persons, is an administrative authority that must act in the public interest. It is an inherent feature of the Commission's task as public enforcer that it has a margin of discretion to set priorities in its enforcement activity.

28. The Commission is entitled to give different degrees of priority to complaints made to it and may refer to the Community interest presented by a case as a criterion of priority. The Commission may reject a complaint when it considers that the case does not display a sufficient Community interest to justify further investigation. Where the Commission rejects a complaint, the complainant is entitled to a decision of the Commission without prejudice to Article 7(3) of Regulation 773/2004.

MAKING A COMPLAINT PURSUANT TO ARTICLE 7(2) OF REGULATION 1/2003

(a) Complaint form

29. A complaint pursuant to Article 7(2) of Regulation 1/2003 can only be made about an alleged infringement of Articles 81 or 82 with a view to the Commission taking action under Article 7(1) of Regulation 1/2003. A complaint under Article 7(2) of Regulation 1/2003 has to comply with Form C mentioned in Article 5(1) of Regulation 773/2004 and annexed to that Regulation.

30. Form C is available at http://europa.eu.int/dgcomp/complaints-form [now http://ec.europa.eu/comm/competition/antitrust/others/] and is also annexed to this Notice. The complaint must be submitted in three paper copies as well as, if possible,

an electronic copy. In addition, the complainant must provide a non-confidential version of the complaint (Article 5(2) of Regulation 773/2004). Electronic transmission to the Commission is possible via the website indicated, the paper copies should be sent to the following address:

Commission Européenne/Europese Commissie
Competition DG
B–1049 Bruxelles/Brussels

31. Form C requires complainants to submit comprehensive information in relation to their complaint. They should also provide copies of relevant supporting documentation reasonably available to them and, to the extent possible, provide indications as to where relevant information and documents that are unavailable to them could be obtained by the Commission. In particular cases, the Commission may dispense with the obligation to provide information in relation to part of the information required by Form C (Article 5(1) of Regulation 773/2004). The Commission holds the view that this possibility can in particular play a role to facilitate complaints by consumer associations where they, in the context of an otherwise substantiated complaint, do not have access to specific pieces of information from the sphere of the undertakings complained of.

32. Correspondence to the Commission that does not comply with the requirements of Article 5 of Regulation 773/2004 and therefore does not constitute a complaint within the meaning of Article 7(2) of Regulation 1/2003 will be considered by the Commission as general information that, where it is useful, may lead to an own-initiative investigation (cf. point 4 above).

(b) Legitimate interest

33. The status of formal complainant under Article 7(2) of Regulation 1/2003 is reserved to legal and natural persons who can show a legitimate interest. Member States are deemed to have a legitimate interest for all complaints they choose to lodge.

34. In the past practice of the Commission, the condition of legitimate interest was not often a matter of doubt as most complainants were in a position of being directly and adversely affected by the alleged infringement. However, there are situations where the condition of a 'legitimate interest' in Article 7(2) requires further analysis to conclude that it is fulfilled. Useful guidance can best be provided by a non-exhaustive set of examples.

35. The Court of First Instance has held that an association of undertakings may claim a legitimate interest in lodging a complaint regarding conduct concerning its members, even if it is not directly concerned, as an undertaking operating in the relevant market, by the conduct complained of, provided that, first, it is entitled to represent the interests of its members and secondly, the conduct complained of is liable to adversely affect the interests of its members. Conversely, the Commission has been found to be entitled not to pursue the complaint of an association of undertakings whose members were not involved in the type of business transactions complained of.

36. From this case law, it can be inferred that undertakings (themselves or through associations that are entitled to represent their interests) can claim a legitimate interest where they are operating in the relevant market or where the conduct complained of is liable to directly and adversely affect their interests. This confirms the established practice of the Commission which has accepted that a legitimate interest can, for instance, be claimed by the parties to the agreement or practice which is the subject of the complaint, by competitors whose interests have allegedly been damaged by the behaviour complained of or by undertakings excluded from a distribution system.

37. Consumer associations can equally lodge complaints with the Commission. The

Commission moreover holds the view that individual consumers whose economic interests are directly and adversely affected insofar as they are the buyers of goods or services that are the object of an infringement can be in a position to show a legitimate interest.

38. However, the Commission does not consider as a legitimate interest within the meaning of Article 7(2) the interest of persons or organisations that wish to come forward on general interest considerations without showing that they or their members are liable to be directly and adversely affected by the infringement (*pro bono publico*).

39. Local or regional public authorities may be able to show a legitimate interest in their capacity as buyers or users of goods or services affected by the conduct complained of. Conversely, they cannot be considered as showing a legitimate interest within the meaning of Article 7(2) of Regulation 1/2003 to the extent that they bring to the attention of the Commission alleged infringements *pro bono publico*.

40. Complainants have to demonstrate their legitimate interest. Where a natural or legal person lodging a complaint is unable to demonstrate a legitimate interest, the Commission is entitled, without prejudice to its right to initiate proceedings of its own initiative, not to pursue the complaint. The Commission may ascertain whether this condition is met at any stage of the investigation.

C.   ASSESSMENT OF COMPLAINTS
(a)   Community interest

41. Under the settled case law of the Community Courts, the Commission is not required to conduct an investigation in each case or, *a fortiori*, to take a decision within the meaning of Article 249 EC on the existence or non-existence of an infringement of Articles 81 or 82, but is entitled to give differing degrees of priority to the complaints brought before it and refer to the Community interest in order to determine the degree of priority to be applied to the various complaints it receives. The position is different only if the complaint falls within the exclusive competence of the Commission.

42. The Commission must however examine carefully the factual and legal elements brought to its attention by the complainant in order to assess the Community interest in further investigation of a case.

43. The assessment of the Community interest raised by a complaint depends on the circumstances of each individual case. Accordingly, the number of criteria of assessment to which the Commission may refer is not limited, nor is the Commission required to have recourse exclusively to certain criteria. As the factual and legal circumstances may differ considerably from case to case, it is permissible to apply new criteria which had not before been considered. Where appropriate, the Commission may give priority to a single criterion for assessing the Community interest.

44. Among the criteria which have been held relevant in the case law for the assessment of the Community interest in the (further) investigation of a case are the following:
    - The Commission can reject a complaint on the ground that the complainant can bring an action to assert its rights before national courts.
    - The Commission may not regard certain situations as excluded in principle from its purview under the task entrusted to it by the Treaty but is required to assess in each case how serious the alleged infringements are and how persistent their consequences are. This means in particular that it must take into account the duration and the extent of the infringements complained of and their effect on the competition situation in the Community.
    - The Commission may have to balance the significance of the alleged infringement as regards the functioning of the common market, the probability of establishing

the existence of the infringement and the scope of the investigation required in order to fulfil its task of ensuring that Articles 81 and 82 of the Treaty are complied with.

– While the Commission's discretion does not depend on how advanced the investigation of a case is, the stage of the investigation forms part of the circumstances of the case which the Commission may have to take into consideration.

– The Commission may decide that it is not appropriate to investigate a complaint where the practices in question have ceased. However, for this purpose, the Commission will have to ascertain whether anticompetitive effects persist and if the seriousness of the infringements or the persistence of their effects does not give the complaint a Community interest.

– The Commission may also decide that it is not appropriate to investigate a complaint where the undertakings concerned agree to change their conduct in such a way that it can consider that there is no longer a sufficient Community interest to intervene.

45. Where it forms the view that a case does not display sufficient Community interest to justify (further) investigation, the Commission may reject the complaint on that ground. Such a decision can be taken either before commencing an investigation or after taking investigative measures. However, the Commission is not obliged to set aside a complaint for lack of Community interest.

(b) Assessment under Articles 81 and 82

46. The examination of a complaint under Articles 81 and 82 involves two aspects, one relating to the facts to be established to prove an infringement of Articles 81 or 82 and the other relating to the legal assessment of the conduct complained of.

47. Where the complaint, while complying with the requirements of Article 5 of Regulation 773/2004 and Form C, does not sufficiently substantiate the allegations put forward, it may be rejected on that ground. In order to reject a complaint on the ground that the conduct complained of does not infringe the EC competition rules or does not fall within their scope of application, the Commission is not obliged to take into account circumstances that have not been brought to its attention by the complainant and that it could only have uncovered by the investigation of the case.

48. The criteria for the legal assessment of agreements or practices under Articles 81 and 82 cannot be dealt with exhaustively in the present Notice. However, potential complainants should refer to the extensive guidance available from the Commission, in addition to other sources and in particular the case law of the Community Courts and the case practice of the Commission. Four specific issues are mentioned in the following points with indications on where to find further guidance.

49. Agreements and practices fall within the scope of application of Articles 81 and 82 where they are capable of affecting trade between Member States. Where an agreement or practice does not fulfil this condition, national competition law may apply, but not EC competition law. Extensive guidance on this subject can be found in the Notice on the effect on trade concept.

50. Agreements falling within the scope of Article 81 may be agreements of minor importance which are deemed not to restrict competition appreciably. Guidance on this issue can be found in the Commission's *de minimis* Notice.

51. Agreements that fulfil the conditions of a block exemption regulation are deemed to satisfy the conditions of Article 81(3). For the Commission to withdraw the benefit of the block exemption pursuant to Article 29 of Regulation 1/2003, it must find that upon individual assessment an agreement to which the exemption regulation applies has certain effects which are incompatible with Article 81(3).

52. Agreements that restrict competition within the meaning of Article 81(1) EC may fulfil the conditions of Article 81(3) EC. Pursuant to Article 1(2) of Regulation 1/2003 and without a prior administrative decision being required, such agreements are not prohibited. Guidance on the conditions to be fulfilled by an agreement pursuant to Article 81(3) can be found in the Notice on Article 81(3).

D. THE COMMISSION'S PROCEDURES WHEN DEALING WITH COMPLAINTS

(a) Overview

53. As recalled above, the Commission is not obliged to carry out an investigation on the basis of every complaint submitted with a view to establishing whether an infringement has been committed. However, the Commission is under a duty to consider carefully the factual and legal issues brought to its attention by the complainant, in order to assess whether those issues indicate conduct which is liable to infringe Articles 81 and 82.

54. In the Commission's procedure for dealing with complaints, different stages can be distinguished.

55. During the first stage, following the submission of the complaint, the Commission examines the complaint and may collect further information in order to decide what action it will take on the complaint. That stage may include an informal exchange of views between the Commission and the complainant with a view to clarifying the factual and legal issues with which the complaint is concerned. In this stage, the Commission may give an initial reaction to the complainant allowing the complainant an opportunity to expand on his allegations in the light of that initial reaction.

56. In the second stage, the Commission may investigate the case further with a view to initiating proceedings pursuant to Article 7(1) of Regulation 1/2003 against the undertakings complained of. Where the Commission considers that there are insufficient grounds for acting on the complaint, it will inform the complainant of its reasons and offer the complainant the opportunity to submit any further comments within a time-limit which it fixes (Article 7(1) of Regulation 773/2004).

57. If the complainant fails to make known its views within the time-limit set by the Commission, the complaint is deemed to have been withdrawn (Article 7(3) of Regulation 773/2004). In all other cases, in the third stage of the procedure, the Commission takes cognisance of the observations submitted by the complainant and either initiates a procedure against the subject of the complaint or adopts a decision rejecting the complaint.

58. Where the Commission rejects a complaint pursuant to Article 13 of Regulation 1/2003 on the grounds that another authority is dealing or has dealt with the case, the Commission proceeds in accordance with Article 9 of Regulation 773/2004.

59. Throughout the procedure, complainants benefit from a range of rights as provided in particular in Articles 6 to 8 of Regulation 773/2004. However, proceedings of the Commission in competition cases do not constitute adversarial proceedings between the complainant on the one hand and the companies which are the subject of the investigation on the other hand. Accordingly, the procedural rights of complainants are less far-reaching than the right to a fair hearing of the companies which are the subject of an infringement procedure.

(b) Indicative time-limit for informing the complainant of the Commission's proposed action

60. The Commission is under an obligation to decide on complaints within a reasonable time. What is a reasonable duration depends on the circumstances of each case and in particular, its context, the various procedural steps followed by the Commission, the conduct of the parties in the course of the procedure, the complexity of the case and its importance for the various parties involved.

61. The Commission will in principle endeavour to inform complainants of the action that it proposes to take on a complaint within an indicative time frame of four months from the reception of the complaint. Thus, subject to the circumstances of the individual case and in particular the possible need to request complementary information from the complainant or third parties, the Commission will in principle inform the complainant within four months whether or not it intends to investigate its case further. This time-limit does not constitute a binding statutory term.

62. Accordingly, within this four-month period, the Commission may communicate its proposed course of action to the complainant as an initial reaction within the first phase of the procedure (see point 55 above). The Commission may also, where the examination of the complaint has progressed to the second stage (see point 56 above), directly proceed to informing the complainant about its provisional assessment by a letter pursuant to Article 7(1) of Regulation 773/2004.

63. To ensure the most expeditious treatment of their complaint, it is desirable that complainants cooperate diligently in the procedures, for example by informing the Commission of new developments.

(c) Procedural rights of the complainant

64. Where the Commission addresses a statement of objections to the companies complained of pursuant to Article 10(1) of Regulation 773/2004, the complainant is entitled to receive a copy of this document from which business secrets and other confidential information of the companies concerned have been removed (non-confidential version of the statement of objections; cf. Article 6(1) of Regulation 773/2004). The complainant is invited to comment in writing on the statement of objections. A time-limit will be set for such written comments.

65. Furthermore, the Commission may, where appropriate, afford complainants the opportunity of expressing their views at the oral hearing of the parties to which a statement of objections has been addressed, if the complainants so request in their written comments.

66. Complainants may submit, of their own initiative or following a request by the Commission, documents that contain business secrets or other confidential information. Confidential information will be protected by the Commission. Under Article 16 of Regulation 773/2004, complainants are obliged to identify confidential information, give reasons why the information is considered confidential and submit a separate non-confidential version when they make their views known pursuant to Article 6(1) and 7(1) of Regulation 773/2004, as well as when they subsequently submit further information in the course of the same procedure. Moreover, the Commission may, in all other cases, request complainants which produce documents or statements to identify the documents or parts of the documents or statements which they consider to be confidential. It may in particular set a deadline for the complainant to specify why it considers a piece of information to be confidential and to provide a non-confidential version, including a concise description or non-confidential version of each piece of information deleted.

67. The qualification of information as confidential does not prevent the Commission from disclosing and using information where that is necessary to prove an infringement of Articles 81 or 82. Where business secrets and confidential information are necessary to prove an infringement, the Commission must assess for each individual document whether the need to disclose is greater than the harm which might result from disclosure.

68. Where the Commission takes the view that a complaint should not be further examined, because there is no sufficient Community interest in pursuing the case further or

on other grounds, it will inform the complainant in the form of a letter which indicates its legal basis (Article 7(1) of Regulation 773/2004), sets out the reasons that have led the Commission to provisionally conclude in the sense indicated and provides the complainant with the opportunity to submit supplementary information or observations within a time-limit set by the Commission. The Commission will also indicate the consequences of not replying pursuant to Article 7(3) of Regulation 773/2004, as explained below.

69. Pursuant to Article 8(1) of Regulation 773/2004, the complainant has the right to access the information on which the Commission bases its preliminary view. Such access is normally provided by annexing to the letter a copy of the relevant documents.

70. The time-limit for observations by the complainant on the letter pursuant to Article 7(1) of Regulation 773/2004 will be set in accordance with the circumstances of the case. It will not be shorter than four weeks (Article 17(2) of Regulation 773/2004). If the complainant does not respond within the time-limit set, the complaint is deemed to have been withdrawn pursuant to Article 7(3) of Regulation 773/2004. Complainants are also entitled to withdraw their complaint at any time if they so wish.

71. The complainant may request an extension of the time-limit for the provision of comments. Depending on the circumstances of the case, the Commission may grant such an extension.

72. In that case, where the complainant submits supplementary observations, the Commission takes cognisance of those observations. Where they are of such a nature as to make the Commission change its previous course of action, it may initiate a procedure against the companies complained of. In this procedure, the complainant has the procedural rights explained above.

73. Where the observations of the complainant do not alter the Commission's proposed course of action, it rejects the complaint by decision.

(d) The Commission decision rejecting a complaint

74. Where the Commission rejects a complaint by decision pursuant to Article 7(2) of Regulation 773/2004, it must state the reasons in accordance with Article 253 EC, i.e. in a way that is appropriate to the act at issue and takes into account the circumstances of each case.

75. The statement of reasons must disclose in a clear and unequivocal fashion the reasoning followed by the Commission in such a way as to enable the complainant to ascertain the reasons for the decision and to enable the competent Community Court to exercise its power of review. However, the Commission is not obliged to adopt a position on all the arguments relied on by the complainant in support of its complaint. It only needs to set out the facts and legal considerations which are of decisive importance in the context of the decision.

76. Where the Commission rejects a complaint in a case that also gives rise to a decision pursuant to Article 10 of Regulation 1/2003 (Finding of inapplicability of Articles 81 or 82) or Article 9 of Regulation 1/2003 (Commitments), the decision rejecting a complaint may refer to that other decision adopted on the basis of the provisions mentioned.

77. A decision to reject a complaint is subject to appeal before the Community Courts.

78. A decision rejecting a complaint prevents complainants from requiring the reopening of the investigation unless they put forward significant new evidence. Accordingly, further correspondence on the same alleged infringement by former complainants cannot be regarded as a new complaint unless significant new evidence is brought to the attention of the Commission. However, the Commission may re-open a file under appropriate circumstances.

79. A decision to reject a complaint does not definitively rule on the question of whether or not there is an infringement of Articles 81 or 82, even where the Commission has assessed the facts on the basis of Articles 81 and 82. The assessments made by the Commission in a decision rejecting a complaint therefore do not prevent a Member State court or competition authority from applying Articles 81 and 82 to agreements and practices brought before it. The assessments made by the Commission in a decision rejecting a complaint constitute facts which Member States' courts or competition authorities may take into account in examining whether the agreements or conduct in question are in conformity with Articles 81 and 82.

(e) Specific situations

80. According to Article 8 of Regulation 1/2003 the Commission may on its own initiative order interim measures where there is the risk of serious and irreparable damage to competition. Article 8 of Regulation 1/2003 makes it clear that interim measures cannot be applied for by complainants under Article 7(2) of Regulation 1/2003. Requests for interim measures by undertakings can be brought before Member States' courts which are well placed to decide on such measures.

81. Some persons may wish to inform the Commission about suspected infringements of Articles 81 or 82 without having their identity revealed to the undertakings concerned by the allegations. These persons are welcome to contact the Commission. The Commission is bound to respect an informant's request for anonymity, unless the request to remain anonymous is manifestly unjustified.

Applications by parties to a possible infringement

Regulation 17/62

Article 2, Regulation 17/62 enabled undertakings concerned with agreements which may breach Art 81(1) or Art 82 to apply to the Commission for negative clearance. This could be followed by a formal grant of clearance. This consisted of a decision by the Commission certifying that, on the basis of the facts in its possession, there were no grounds for action to be taken in respect of the agreement or conduct in question. The chief advantage of obtaining clearance was that the activity could continue under an agreement or practice until the Commission made a decision (Art 15(5), Regulation 17/62). If clearance was obtained, it provided a bar to action by the Commission while it was still in existence. The full facts had to be disclosed to the Commission. Failure to disclose them could have resulted in revocation of the clearance and the imposition of a fine on the defaulting undertaking (Art 15(1)(a), Regulation 17/62).

Article 4, Regulation 17/62 provided for the notification to the Commission of agreements, decisions and concerted practices defined by Art 81(1) EC Treaty and for which the parties sought a declaration under Art 81(3) that the agreement or practice was not subject to Art 81(1). A decision of this kind would have been for a fixed period, but it could be renewed if the requirements of Art 81(3) continued to be satisfied (see Chapter 20). The Commission could revoke or amend its decision, or prohibit certain acts by the parties where there had been any change in the facts which formed the basis of the decision, where the parties breached a condition attached to the decision, where the decision was based on incorrect information or was induced by deceit, or where the parties abused the exemption conferred on them by the decision (Art 8(3), Regulation 17/62).

The effect of application for negative clearance or for exemption under Art 81(3) could have resulted in refusal of clearance or the granting of an exemption by the Commission, or precipitated a demand for more information or even a full investigation.

Regulation 1/2003

The Commission was spending a disproportionate amount of time in dealing with applications for negative clearance (with regard to Arts 81(1) and 82 EC Treaty) and applications for exemption (with regard to Art 81(3) EC Treaty). Regulation 1/2003 changed this dramatically, and undertakings are no longer able to make such applications to the Commission. The Commission is empowered to make a 'finding of inapplicability' pursuant to Art 10, Regulation 1/2003:

> Where the Community public interest relating to the application of Articles 81 and 82 of the Treaty so requires, the Commission, acting on its own initiative, may by decision find that Article 81 of the Treaty is not applicable to an agreement, a decision by an association of undertakings or a concerted practice, either because the conditions of Article 81(1) of the Treaty are not fulfilled, or because the conditions of Article 81(3) of the Treaty are satisfied.
>
> The Commission may likewise make such a finding with reference to Article 82 of the Treaty.

Guidance letters

However, in very limited circumstances the Commission is empowered to issue a guidance letter. To support the new procedural regime brought in by Regulation 1/2003, the Commission has issued a non-legally enforceable notice: 'Informal Guidance relating to novel questions concerning Arts 81 and 82 EC Treaty that arise in individual cases (guidance letters)' (OJ 2004 C 101/78). In cases which give rise to genuine uncertainty because they present novel or unresolved questions for the application of Arts 81 and 82 EC Treaty, individual undertakings may seek informal guidance from the Commission (para 5 of the Guidance). If it is considered appropriate, the Commission may provide such guidance in a written statement, referred to as a 'guidance letter'. However, a guidance letter may only be issued by the Commission if the following cumulative conditions apply:

(a) The substantive assessment of an agreement or practice with regard to Articles 81 and/or 82 of the Treaty, poses a question of application of the law for which there is no clarification in the existing EC legal framework including the case law of the Community Courts, nor publicly available general guidance or precedent in decision-making practice or previous guidance letters.

(b) A *prima facie* evaluation of the specificities and background of the case suggests that the clarification of the novel question through a guidance letter is useful, taking into account the following elements:
   - the economic importance from the point of view of the consumer of the goods or services concerned by the agreement or practice; and/or
   - the extent to which the agreement or practice corresponds or is liable to correspond to more widely spread economic usage in the marketplace; and/or
   - the extent of the investments linked to the transaction in relation to the size of the companies concerned and the extent to which the transaction relates to a structural operation such as the creation of a non-full function joint venture.

(c) It is possible to issue a guidance letter on the basis of the information provided, i.e. no further fact-finding is required. (para 8 of the Guidance)

Furthermore, the Commission will not consider a request for a guidance letter in either of the following circumstances:

- the questions raised in the request are identical or similar to issues raised in a case pending before the European Court of First Instance or the European Court of Justice;
- the agreement or practice to which the request refers is subject to proceedings pending with the Commission, a Member State court or Member State competition authority. (para 9 of the Guidance)

Paragraph 10 of the Guidance provides that the Commission will not consider hypothetical questions and 'will not issue guidance letters on agreements or practices that are no longer being implemented by the parties. Undertakings may however present a request for a guidance letter to the Commission in relation to questions raised by an agreement or practice that they envisage, i.e. before the implementation of that agreement or practice. In this case the transaction must have reached a sufficiently advanced stage for a request to be considered'.

The provision of information

Regulation 17/62

Article 11, Regulation 17/62 was intended to assist the Commission in obtaining the information necessary to investigate a suspected infringement. Under this provision the Commission could obtain all necessary information from the governments of the Member States and from undertakings and associated undertakings (Art 11(1)). The Commission was required, when making a request for information, to state the legal basis and the purpose of the request and also the penalties under Art 15(1)(b) for supplying incorrect information. The undertakings were under a legal obligation to supply the full information required, with a penalty for failure to do so (Arts 11(4) and (5), 15(1)(b) and 16(1)(c)). Non-cooperation in the supply of information could take the form of unhelpful replies to questions as well as an outright refusal to answer them. In **Scottish Football Association v Commission** (Case T–46/92), the CFI held that the Commission was under no obligation either to pursue lengthy informal correspondence or to engage in oral discussions with the applicant, who had provided only half the information requested. It could simply, as it had done in this case, demand the information on the basis of Art 11(5), subject to a penalty of 500 ECUs per day for non-disclosure.

The request for information had to specify the kind of anti-competitive practice to which it related, and details of the request had to be sent to the government of the Member State in which the principal office of the undertaking was based (Art 11(2) and (3)):

Société Générale v Commission (Case T-34/93)

The Commission was making inquiries into the operation of the so-called Helsinki Agreement which fixed a differential system of charges made to payees of Eurocheques. This followed an investigation which had already resulted in the imposition by the Commission of heavy fines on other parties to the agreement and the abandonment of the agreement by French banks: Commission Decision 92/212 OJ 1992 195/50 (**Groupement Bancaire and Europay v Commission ('Eurocheques')**). It sent a letter to Société Générale requesting information about an apparently discriminatory charge imposed on a private payee and about the operation of another inter-bank agreement called the Package Deal Agreement. Société Générale refused to supply the information, even after the Commission had explained how it related to its investigation, and argued that a reply on the application of the Package Deal would infringe its rights as a defendant. The CFI rejected both arguments, accepting that the Commission had adequately explained its purpose in requiring the information on charging practices. It held that the answers requested were purely factual and could not be regarded as capable of requiring the Société Générale to admit an infringement of the rules on competition.

The obligation to cooperate with the Commission in its inquiries extended to the provision of all relevant information, even that which could support a finding of an infringement. However, informants were not obliged to incriminate themselves. The issue of possible self-incrimination was raised in the following two cases:

Solvay v *Commission* (Case 27/88) and *Orkem* v *Commission* (Case 374/87)

The applicants in these two cases argued that the Commission decisions requiring them to provide information under Art 11 sought to force them to incriminate themselves. The Court of Justice noted that Regulation 17/62 recognised no such right of non-self-incrimination, but instead called for active cooperation from the party investigated. The Court did, however, look at the issue in the context of the fundamental rights to which all Community law is subject. It decided that there was no such right in relation to legal persons (companies) where infringements of economic law were in issue.

The distinction made by the Court of Justice in its judgment, above, was criticised by the European Court of Human Rights in **Funke** *v* **France** (Case A/256–A), in relation to the application of Art 6(1) of the European Convention on Human Rights (ECHR); see also **Société Stenuit** *v* **France** (1992) 14 EHRR 509 (a decision of the Human Rights Commission that fines imposed by the European Commission for breaches of competition law were of a criminal nature).

In the following case, the applicant claimed that a Commission decision taken pursuant to Art 11(5), Regulation 17/62 requiring it to reply to certain questions within the period prescribed, subject to a fine if it failed to reply, infringed its rights of defence:

Mannesmannröhren-Werke v *Commission* (Case T-112/98)

Mannesmannröhren-Werke brought an action before the CFI for annulment of the Commission decision, claiming that the decision infringed its rights of defence.

In its judgment, the CFI partially upheld that claim, basing its findings on the reasoning of the Court of Justice in **Orkem**. In so ruling, the CFI asserted that there was no absolute right to silence in Community competition proceedings but confirmed that 'an undertaking to which a decision requesting information is addressed has the right to refuse to give replies in which it would be forced to admit the existence of an infringement'. In this case, the CFI partially annulled the Commission decision in so far as it contained questions calling upon the undertaking to describe the purpose of certain meetings and the decisions adopted during them.

As regards the arguments to the effect that Art 6(1) and (2) of the ECHR enabled a person in receipt of a request for information to refrain from answering the questions asked, even if they were purely factual in nature, and to refuse to produce documents to the Commission, the CFI pointed out that the applicant could not directly invoke the ECHR before the Community court.

However, the CFI emphasised that Community law recognised as fundamental principles both the rights of defence and the right to fair legal process, offering protection which was equivalent to that guaranteed by Art 6 of the ECHR. The Court of Justice and the CFI have consistently held that the recipient of requests sent by the Commission pursuant to Article 11(5), Regulation 17/62 was entitled to confine himself to answering questions of a purely factual nature and to produce only the pre-existing documents and materials sought and, moreover, was so entitled as from the very first stage of an investigation initiated by the Commission. It added that the fact of being obliged to answer purely factual questions put by the Commission and to comply with its requests for the production of documents already in existence could not constitute a breach of the principle of respect for the rights of defence or impair the right to fair legal process. There was nothing to prevent the addressee of such questions or requests from showing, whether later during the administrative procedure or in proceedings before the Community courts, when exercising his rights of defence, that the facts set out in his replies or the documents produced by him had a different meaning from that ascribed to them by the Commission.

As regards the possible impact of the Charter of Fundamental Rights of the European Union (OJ 2000 C 364/1; see Chapters 2 and 5), which was cited by the applicant, the CFI confined itself to observing that the Charter had not yet been proclaimed on the date of the adoption of the contested decision (15 May 1998) and could therefore have no implications for the legality of that decision.

Regulation 1/2003

Regulation 1/2003 has sought to refine the procedural rules relating to the gathering of information, and to ensure that such rules are compliant with the case law of the Court of Justice and CFI considered above.

Article 18(6), Regulation 1/2003 provides the Commission with the power to request all necessary information from the governments and competition authorities of the Member States. The Commission may also, by simple request or decision, require undertakings or associations of undertakings to provide all necessary information (Art 18(1)). A copy will be sent to the relevant national competition authority (Art 18(5)). If the Commission seeks the information from an undertaking or association of undertakings by *simple request*, then the Commission shall:

- state the legal basis and the purpose of the request;
- specify what information is required;
- specify the time limit within which the information must be provided; and
- indicate the penalties provided for in Art 23, Regulation 1/2003 if incorrect or misleading information is supplied. (Art 18(2), Regulation 1/2003)

If the Commission seeks the information from an undertaking or association of undertakings by *decision*, then in addition to the above, the Commission shall (i) indicate or impose the penalties provided for in Art 24, Regulation 1/2003 (i.e. periodic penalty payments); and (ii) indicate the right to have the decision reviewed by the Court of Justice.

The preamble to Regulation 1/2003 provides that:

The Commission should be empowered throughout the Community to require such information to be supplied as is necessary to detect any agreement, decision or concerted practice prohibited by Article 81 of the Treaty or any abuse of a dominant position prohibited by Article 82 of the Treaty. When complying with a decision of the Commission, **undertakings cannot be forced to admit that they have committed an infringement, but they are in any event obliged to answer factual questions and to provide documents, even if this information may be used to establish against them or against another undertaking the existence of an infringement.** (para 23) [emphasis added]

The emphasised words, although they do not appear in the main body of the Regulation, embrace the decisions of the Court of Justice and CFI considered above.

Powers of investigation

Regulation 17/62

The Commission could take a more proactive role in the conduct of its inquiries by carrying out investigations in the territory of Member States. Under Art 14, Regulation 17/62 the Commission was authorised to undertake all necessary investigations of undertakings and associations of undertakings. To this end the officials authorised by the Commission were empowered to:

1. examine the books and other business records;
2. take copies of, or extracts from, the books and business records;
3. ask for oral explanations on the spot; and
4. enter any premises, land, and means of transport of undertakings. (Art 14(1))

Officials who were authorised by the Commission to act in relation to these powers were entitled to exercise them on production of an authorisation in writing, specifying the subject matter and purpose of the investigation and the penalties for not supplying or for supplying incomplete books and other business records. Undertakings were obliged to submit to investigations ordered by a decision of the Commission. In good time before the investigation, the Commission had to inform the relevant authority in the host Member State and identify the officials concerned (Art 14(2) and (3)). Before the decision to conduct an investigation of this kind was made, the Commission had to consult the relevant authority in the host Member State. That authority was bound to give every assistance to the Commission officials, especially where the undertaking concerned was opposing the investigation (Art 14(4), (5) and (6)):

Hoechst v Commission (Case 46/87)

Two Commission investigators conducted a 'dawn raid' on the offices of Hoechst in Germany, armed with the necessary decision under Art 14(3), for the purpose of investigating various suspected infringements relating to price fixing and market sharing in the market for PVC and polyethylene. Hoechst refused to submit to the investigation, on the grounds that it was a search which was illegal in the absence of a judicial warrant. Two days later the investigators tried again, accompanied by two officials of the Federal Cartel Office and two policemen.

Hoechst again refused to submit, for the same reason. A third attempt also failed. The Commission eventually obtained access following the issue of a search warrant to the Commission by a German Court. A year later the Commission imposed a fine of 55,000 ECUs on Hoechst for its refusal to submit to the investigation. Hoechst appealed to the Court of Justice.

The Court reaffirmed its earlier rulings that fundamental rights, and the ECHR in particular, were part of the general principles of law. In interpreting Art 14, Regulation 17/62 particular regard had to be given to the rights of the defence. It held that some rights of the defence, especially those relating to legal representation and the privileged nature of correspondence between solicitor and client, had to be recognised from the preliminary inquiry stage of an investigation. Having said that, the Court emphasised the importance of the Commission's investigative powers, and the need to secure access where its inquiries were thwarted:

> That right of access would serve no useful purpose if the Commission's officials could do no more than ask for documents or files which they could identify precisely in advance. On the contrary, such a right implies the power to search for various items of information which are not already known or fully identified. Without such a power, it would be impossible for the Commission to obtain the information necessary to carry out the investigation if the undertakings concerned refused to cooperate or adopted an obstructive attitude.

The Court made it clear that, where the Commission's entry was opposed, Commission officials could not force an entry without first seeking the assistance of national courts. Those courts had to ensure that the Commission's actions were effective, and could not substitute their own assessment of whether or not the investigation ordered by the Commission was necessary, since that function was the exclusive prerogative of the Commission, subject only to review by the Court of Justice itself. In those circumstances, therefore, the Commission needed a national warrant but the national courts were more or less obliged to grant it.

The decision in the above case was, in many ways, an uncomfortable compromise between fundamental principles of national law and the need for effective Commission powers. In such cases there was an inevitable conflict between the need to give adequate notice to the person or body concerned of the purpose of the search (under Art 14(3)) on the one hand and, on the other, the difficulty of knowing precisely what was in the hands of the suspected undertaking and ensuring that it remained there when the officials arrived (for comment, see Forrester and Norall, 1989; for parallel problems in English law, see **IRC v Rossminster** [1980] AC 952 (*per* Lord Wilberforce)).

Information obtained in the course of an investigation could only be used for the purpose of the relevant request or investigation. The Commission was bound to publish its decisions, but it had to make sure that it took into account the legitimate interest of undertakings in the protection of their business secrets (Arts 20 and 21, Regulation 17/62). Although the Commission had a general obligation to send copies of the most important documents to Member States, where an undertaking had expressly raised the confidentiality of a particular document containing business secrets with the Commission, the Commission could decide not to send a particular document or set of documents to the relevant Member State (**Samenwerkende Elektriciteits-produktiebedrijven NV v Commission** (Case C–36/92P)). The obligation of secrecy was owed not only to undertakings under investigation, but also to informants and complainants (**Adams v Commission** (Case 145/83)).

Regulation 1/2003

Regulation 1/2003 provides greater clarification of the Commission's powers of inspection, and also the role of the national competition authorities and courts of the Member States with regard to inspections.

The Regulation empowers the Commission to undertake such inspections as are necessary to detect any agreement, decision or concerted practice prohibited by Art 81 EC Treaty or any abuse of a dominant position prohibited by Art 82 EC Treaty. Article 20(1), Regulation 1/2003 provides that, in order to carry out the duties assigned to it by the Regulation, the Commission 'may conduct all necessary inspections of undertakings and associations of undertakings'. The competition authorities of the Member States are required to actively assist the Commission in the exercise of these powers, if the Commission makes a request for assistance (Art 20(5)). In addition, if an undertaking opposes an inspection 'the Member State concerned shall afford them [i.e. the inspectors] the necessary assistance, requesting where appropriate the assistance of the police or of an equivalent enforcement authority, so as to enable them to conduct their inspection' (Art 20(6)). Article 20(7) provides that if this assistance requires authorisation from a national court, then such authorisation must be applied for, and in any event authorisation may be applied for as a precautionary measure. Article 20(8) sets out the role of the national court when considering an application for authorisation under Art 20(7):

> Where authorisation as referred to in paragraph 7 is applied for, the national judicial authority shall control that the Commission decision is authentic and that the coercive measures envisaged are neither arbitrary nor excessive having regard to the subject matter of the inspection. In its control of the proportionality of the coercive measures, the national judicial authority may ask the Commission, directly or through the Member State competition authority, for detailed explanations in particular on the grounds the Commission has for suspecting infringement of Articles 81 and 82 of the Treaty, as well as on the seriousness of the suspected infringement and on the nature of the involvement of the undertaking concerned. However, the national judicial authority may not call into question the necessity for the inspection nor demand that it be provided with the information in the Commission's file. The lawfulness of the Commission decision shall be subject to review only by the Court of Justice.

Detection of infringements of the competition rules is difficult, and, in order to protect competition effectively, the Commission's powers of investigation have been supplemented. In addition to the powers contained in the former Art 14(1), Regulation 17/62 (see above), Art 20(2), Regulation 1/2003 empowers the Commission to interview any representative or member of staff of the relevant undertaking 'for explanations on facts or documents relating to the subject-matter and purpose of the inspection and to record the answers'. In addition, Art 20(2) also provides that in the course of an inspection, officials authorised by the Commission are empowered to affix seals to any business premises and books or records 'for the period and to the extent necessary for the inspection'.

Similar to the provisions contained in Regulation 17/62, officials authorised by the Commission to act in relation to these powers of inspection are entitled to exercise them on production of an authorisation in writing, specifying the subject matter and purpose of the investigation and the penalties (under Art 23) for supplying incomplete books and other business records or where the answers to questions asked under Art 20(2) are incorrect or misleading (Art 20(3)). Undertakings are obliged to submit to investigations ordered by a decision of the Commission (Art 20(4)). In addition to the above information, the undertaking must also be informed of the date of the inspection, an indication of the periodical penalty payments which may be applied under Art 24, and of the undertaking's right to have the decision reviewed by the Court of Justice. In good time before the investigation the Commission has to inform the relevant authority in the host Member State (Art 20(3) and (4)).

In the past there have been cases where business records were kept in the homes of directors or other people working for an undertaking. In order to safeguard the effectiveness of inspections, Art 21 empowers officials and other persons authorised by the Commission to enter any premises where business records may be kept, including private homes. However, the exercise of this power is subject to the Commission adopting a decision, and the prior authorisation of the national court. There was no such power in Regulation 17/62. Article 21, Regulation 1/2003 provides as follows:

1. If a reasonable suspicion exists that books or other records related to the business and to the subject matter of the inspection, which may be relevant to prove a serious violation of Article 81 or Article 82 of the Treaty, are being kept in any other premises, land and means of transport, including the homes of directors, managers and other members of staff of the undertakings and associations of undertakings concerned, the Commission can by decision order an inspection to be conducted in such other premises, land and means of transport.

2. The decision shall specify the subject matter and purpose of the inspection, appoint the date on which it is to begin and indicate the right to have the decision reviewed by the Court of Justice. It shall in particular state the reasons that have led the Commission to conclude that a suspicion in the sense of paragraph 1 exists. The Commission shall take such decisions after consulting the competition authority of the Member State in whose territory the inspection is to be conducted.

3. A decision adopted pursuant to paragraph 1 cannot be executed without prior authorisation from the national judicial authority of the Member State concerned. The national judicial authority shall control that the Commission decision is authentic and that the coercive measures envisaged are neither arbitrary nor excessive having regard in particular to the seriousness of the suspected infringement, to the importance of the evidence sought, to the involvement of the undertaking concerned and to the reasonable likelihood that business books and records relating to the subject matter of the inspection are kept in the premises for which the authorisation is requested. The national judicial authority may ask the Commission, directly or through the Member State competition authority, for detailed explanations on those elements which are necessary to allow its control of the proportionality of the coercive measures envisaged. However, the national judicial authority may not call into question the necessity for the inspection nor demand that it be provided with information in the Commission's file. The lawfulness of the Commission decision shall be subject to review only by the Court of Justice.

4. The officials and other accompanying persons authorised by the Commission to conduct an inspection ordered in accordance with paragraph 1 of this Article shall have the powers set out in Article 20(2)(a), (b) and (c). Article 20(5) and (6) shall apply *mutatis mutandis*.

In order to assist the competition authorities of the Member States to apply Arts 81 and 82 EC Treaty effectively, it was considered expedient to enable them to support one another (and the Commission) by carrying out inspections and other fact-finding measures. Article 22 provides as follows:

1. The competition authority of a Member State may in its own territory carry out any inspection or other fact-finding measure under its national law on behalf and for the account of the competition authority of another Member State in order to establish whether there has been an infringement of Article 81 or Article 82 of the Treaty. Any exchange and use of the information collected shall be carried out in accordance with Article 12.
2. At the request of the Commission, the competition authorities of the Member States shall undertake the inspections which the Commission considers to be necessary under Article 20(1) or which it has ordered by decision pursuant to Article 20(4). The officials of the competition authorities of the Member States who are responsible for conducting these inspections as well as those authorised or appointed by them shall exercise their powers in accordance with their national law.

   If so requested by the Commission or by the competition authority of the Member State in whose territory the inspection is to be conducted, officials and other accompanying persons authorised by the Commission may assist the officials of the authority concerned.

Similar to Regulation 17/62, there is an obligation that information obtained during the course of an investigation shall only be used for the purpose for which it was acquired (Art 28(1), Regulation 1/2003). Article 28(2), Regulation 1/2003 sets out the undertaking's right to professional secrecy.

Regulation 773/2004

Article 33(1), Regulation 1/2003 specifically empowers the Commission to adopt measures 'as may be appropriate in order to apply this Regulation'. As discussed above, Regulation 773/2004 was adopted pursuant to this power. Chapter III of this Regulation deals with investigations by the Commission, with regard to the power to take statements (Art 3) and ask questions during inspections (Art 4). The power to take statements is set out in Art 19, Regulation 1/2003:

1. In order to carry out the duties assigned to it by this Regulation, the Commission may interview any natural or legal person who consents to be interviewed for the purpose of collecting information relating to the subject-matter of an investigation.
2. Where an interview pursuant to paragraph 1 is conducted in the premises of an undertaking, the Commission shall inform the competition authority of the Member State in whose territory the interview takes place. If so requested by the competition authority of that Member State, its officials may assist the officials and other accompanying persons authorised by the Commission to conduct the interview.

With regard to the power to take statements, Art 3, Regulation 773/2004 provides that:

1. Where the Commission interviews a person with his consent in accordance with Article 19 of Regulation (EC) No 1/2003, it shall, at the beginning of the interview, state the legal basis and the purpose of the interview, and recall its voluntary nature. It shall also inform the person interviewed of its intention to make a record of the interview.
2. The interview may be conducted by any means including by telephone or electronic means.
3. The Commission may record the statements made by the persons interviewed in any form. A copy of any recording shall be made available to the person interviewed for approval. Where necessary, the Commission shall set a time-limit within which the person interviewed may communicate to it any correction to be made to the statement.

With regard to the power to ask questions, Art 4, Regulation 773/2004 provides that:

1. When, pursuant to Article 20(2)(e) of Regulation (EC) No 1/2003, officials or other accompanying persons authorised by the Commission ask representatives or members of staff of an undertaking or of an association of undertakings for explanations, the explanations given may be recorded in any form.
2. A copy of any recording made pursuant to paragraph 1 shall be made available to the undertaking or association of undertakings concerned after the inspection.
3. In cases where a member of staff of an undertaking or of an association of undertakings who is not or was not authorised by the undertaking or by the association of undertakings to provide explanations on behalf of the undertaking or association of undertakings has been asked for explanations, the Commission shall set a time-limit within which the undertaking or the association of undertakings may communicate to the Commission any rectification, amendment or supplement to the explanations given by such member of staff. The rectification, amendment or supplement shall be added to the explanations as recorded pursuant to paragraph 1.

The right to a hearing

Regulation 17/62

Before it adopted a decision applying Arts 81 or 82 EC Treaty, the Commission was required, under Art 19, Regulation 17/62, to give the undertakings concerned the opportunity of being heard on the matters to which the Commission had taken objection. If the Commission or the relevant authorities in the Member States considered it necessary, they could also hear representations from other legal or natural persons, provided they could show a sufficient interest. Under Regulation 99/63 such representations would normally be in writing, although under Art 7, Regulation 99/63 undertakings could, if they had requested it in their written submissions, or if the Commission proposed to impose a fine on them or a periodic penalty, put forward their arguments orally.

To enable undertakings to exercise their right to make representations effectively, they had to be informed of the facts and considerations on the basis of which the Commission was minded to act (Art 2(1), Regulation 99/63; **NTN Toyo Bearing Company and Others** *v* **Council and Commission (Ballbearings)** (Case 113/77) (Advocate-General Warner)).

In **Hoffman La Roche** *v* **Commission** (Case 85/76), the Court of Justice ruled that undertakings had to be afforded 'the opportunity during the administrative procedure to make known their views on the truth and relevance of the facts and circumstances alleged and on the documents used by the Commission to support its claim that there has been an infringement'.

The duty of disclosure was not, however, absolute. There was a *class* of documents, including correspondence with Member States and purely internal Commission documents, which were regarded as confidential and which did not have to be disclosed. Other documents, such as correspondence with third-party undertakings, could also have been legitimately withheld where disclosure could have led to retaliation against those third parties by the undertaking involved in the proceedings (**BPB Industries plc and British Gypsum Ltd** *v* **Commission** (Case C–310/93P)). Previous practice was formalised by Commission Decision 94/90, incorporating its Code of Conduct of 6 December 1993.

Regulation 1049/2001

The Treaty of Amsterdam amended the EC Treaty to include a new Art 255 which provides for access to European Parliament, Council of Ministers and Commission documents. Pursuant to Art 255, Regulation 1049/2001 was adopted by the Council of Ministers and this Regulation replaced Decision 94/90 with effect from 3 December 2001. This Regulation is still in force. Refusal to grant access must be based on one of the exceptions provided for in the Regulation and must be justified on the grounds that disclosure of the document would be harmful. Article 4, Regulation 1049/2001 sets out the exceptions, for example:

1. The institutions shall refuse access to a document where disclosure would undermine the protection of:
   (a) the public interest, as regards:
      - public security
      - defence and military matters
      - international relations
      - the financial, monetary or economic policy of the Community or a Member State
   (b) privacy and the integrity of the individual, in particular in accordance with Community legislation regarding the protection of personal data.

2. The institutions shall refuse access to a document where disclosure would undermine the protection of:
   - commercial interests of a natural or legal person, including intellectual property
   - court proceedings and legal advice
   - the purpose of inspections, investigations and audits unless there is an overriding public interest in disclosure.

This Regulation is considered in more detail in Chapter 3.

Regulation 1/2003

Article 27, Regulation 1/2003 concerns the hearing of the parties, complainants and others. Article 27(1) provides that before the Commission makes a decision pursuant to: (i) Art 7 in relation to an infringement of Arts 81 or 82 EC Treaty; (ii) Art 8 in relation to interim measures; (iii) Art 23 in relation to fines; or (iv) Art 24(2) in relation to periodic penalty payments, the undertakings which are the subject of the proceedings shall be given the opportunity of being heard on the matters to which the Commission has taken objection. The rights of defence of the parties shall be fully respected in the proceedings (Art 27(2)). The parties will be entitled to have access to the Commission's file, subject to the 'legitimate interest of undertakings in the protection of their business secrets'; however, this right of access will not extend to confidential information and internal documents of either the Commission or the national competition authorities of the Member States (Art 27(2)). The Commission has issued a notice, clarifying both the extent and the exercise of the right of access to the Commission's file: Commission Notice on the rules for access to the Commission file in cases pursuant to Arts 81 and 82 EC Treaty, Arts 53, 54 and 57 EEA Agreement, and Regulation 773/2004 (OJ 2005 C 325/7).

The Commission has the right to hear any other natural or legal person, provided such a person shows a sufficient interest (Art 27(3)). The national competition authorities of the Member States may request the Commission to hear other natural or legal persons (Art 27(3)).

If the Commission intends adopting a decision pursuant to: (i) Art 9 with regard to commitments made by an undertaking, or (ii) Art 10 in relation to a finding of inapplicability, the Commission will publish a concise summary of the case and the main content of the commitments or the proposed course of action (Art 27(4)).

Regulation 773/2004

Chapter V (Arts 10–14), Regulation 773/2004 concerns the exercise of the right to be heard. Chapter V provides as follows:

CHAPTER V
EXERCISE OF THE RIGHT TO BE HEARD
Article 10
Statement of objections and reply
1. The Commission shall inform the parties concerned in writing of the objections raised against them. The statement of objections shall be notified to each of them.
2. The Commission shall, when notifying the statement of objections to the parties concerned, set a time-limit within which these parties may inform it in writing of their views. The Commission shall not be obliged to take into account written submissions received after the expiry of that time-limit.
3. The parties may, in their written submissions, set out all facts known to them which are relevant to their defence against the objections raised by the Commission. They shall attach any relevant documents as proof of the facts set out. They shall provide a paper original as well as an electronic copy or, where they do not provide an electronic copy, 28 paper copies of their submission and of the documents attached to it. They may propose that the Commission hear persons who may corroborate the facts set out in their submission.

Article 11
Right to be heard
1. The Commission shall give the parties to whom it has addressed a statement of objections the opportunity to be heard before consulting the Advisory Committee referred to in Article 14(1) of Regulation (EC) No 1/2003.
2. The Commission shall, in its decisions, deal only with objections in respect of which the parties referred to in paragraph 1 have been able to comment.

Article 12
Right to an oral hearing
The Commission shall give the parties to whom it has addressed a statement of objections the opportunity to develop their arguments at an oral hearing, if they so request in their written submissions.

Article 13
Hearing of other persons
1. If natural or legal persons other than those referred to in Articles 5 and 11 apply to be heard and show a sufficient interest, the Commission shall inform them in writing of the nature and subject matter of the procedure and shall set a time-limit within which they may make known their views in writing.
2. The Commission may, where appropriate, invite persons referred to in paragraph 1 to develop their arguments at the oral hearing of the parties to whom a statement of objections has been addressed, if the persons referred to in paragraph 1 so request in their written comments.
3. The Commission may invite any other person to express its views in writing and to

attend the oral hearing of the parties to whom a statement of objections has been addressed. The Commission may also invite such persons to express their views at that oral hearing.

Article 14
Conduct of oral hearings
1. Hearings shall be conducted by a Hearing Officer in full independence.
2. The Commission shall invite the persons to be heard to attend the oral hearing on such date as it shall determine.
3. The Commission shall invite the competition authorities of the Member States to take part in the oral hearing. It may likewise invite officials and civil servants of other authorities of the Member States.
4. Persons invited to attend shall either appear in person or be represented by legal representatives or by representatives authorised by their constitution as appropriate. Undertakings and associations of undertakings may also be represented by a duly authorised agent appointed from among their permanent staff.
5. Persons heard by the Commission may be assisted by their lawyers or other qualified persons admitted by the Hearing Officer.
6. Oral hearings shall not be public. Each person may be heard separately or in the presence of other persons invited to attend, having regard to the legitimate interest of the undertakings in the protection of their business secrets and other confidential information.
7. The Hearing Officer may allow the parties to whom a statement of objections has been addressed, the complainants, other persons invited to the hearing, the Commission services and the authorities of the Member States to ask questions during the hearing.
8. The statements made by each person heard shall be recorded. Upon request, the recording of the hearing shall be made available to the persons who attended the hearing. Regard shall be had to the legitimate interest of the parties in the protection of their business secrets and other confidential information.

The decision

There is a general principle of Community law contained in Art 253 EC Treaty that 'decisions shall state the reasons on which they are based'. They should also be made by the Commission according to the proper procedure and according to the proper form. Failure to observe these principles may render the decision a nullity from the start:

Commission v BASF AG and Others (Case C-137/92P)

The CFI had declared a Commission decision non-existent. The decision had declared that the applicants and others had infringed Art 81 in relation to the production of PVC (Commission Decision 89/190/EEC of 21 December 1988). The CFI had found that the original decision had been altered after it had been adopted by the Commissioners 'by persons who were clearly not Commissioners'. The CFI also found that the contested decision had been adopted only in its English, German and French versions, leaving it to the Commissioner then responsible for competition, Mr Sutherland, to adopt the text of the decision in the other official languages of the Community. The CFI noted that Mr Sutherland had no competence to do this and held that the measure was 'vitiated by particularly serious and manifest defects rendering it non-existent in law'.

The Commission appealed against this decision, and the appeal was allowed by the Court of Justice. The Court pointed out that, as a general rule, acts of the Community institutions are presumed to be lawful and productive of legal effects even if affected by irregularities, until such time as they are annulled or withdrawn. There was, however, an exception to that rule in relation to acts:

> ...tainted by an irregularity whose gravity is so obvious that it cannot be tolerated by the Community legal order. [Such acts] ... must be treated as having no legal effect, even provisional, that is to say that they must be regarded as legally non-existent. The purpose of this exception is to maintain a balance between two fundamental, but sometimes conflicting, requirements with which a legal order must comply, namely stability of legal relations and respect for legality.

The Court of Justice emphasised the collegiate nature of the Commission's decision-making process. It rejected the Commission's argument that in the decision-making process the college of Commissioners can confine itself to making clear its intention without having to become involved in the drafting and finalisation of the act giving effect to its intention. After the final form of the decision had been approved by the Commissioners as a body, only simple corrections of spelling and grammar could be made to the text. In the event, however, the Court of Justice thought that the CFI had gone too far in holding the decision to be non-existent. It was, however, annulled on the same procedural grounds on which the CFI decision had been based.

If the Commission decided that there had been an infringement of Arts 81 or 82, the Commission was empowered under Art 3(1), Regulation 17/62 to adopt a decision ordering that the infringement be brought to an end. The same applies under Regulation 1/2003 (Art 7(1)). Article 16, Regulation 17/62 empowered the Commission to impose a periodic penalty payment of 50 to 1,000 units of account per day, from the date of the decision until the infringement was brought to an end. It could also impose fines on the undertakings concerned. Likewise, under Regulation 1/2003 the Commission has the power to impose a periodic penalty payment, but this amount is now stated to be 'not exceeding 5% of the average daily turnover in the preceding business year per day and calculated from the date appointed by the decision' (Art 24(1)). Fines can also be imposed on the undertaking (Art 23).

Judicial review of Commission decisions

Like any other legal act of the institutions, decisions made by the Commission in relation to alleged infringements, including findings of infringements and the imposition of fines and periodic penalty payment, are subject to judicial review. The CFI may review such acts under Art 230 EC Treaty (see Chapter 8). There is an appeal on a point of law to the Court of Justice itself in relation to decisions of the CFI. The CFI, when reviewing the legality of the decision of the Commission, has the power not only to quash any decision, but also to reduce or increase any fine or periodic penalty payment imposed by the Commission (Art 229 EC Treaty; Art 31, Regulation 1/2003 (previously Art 17, Regulation 17/62)).

Regulation 1/2003: interim measures, commitments and finding of inapplicability

Regulation 1/2003 provides for three other type of decisions to be taken by the Commission. Article 8 empowers the Commission to adopt a decision ordering interim measures, provided it is an urgent case where there is a risk of 'serious and irreparable damage to competition' and provided that there is a *prima facie* finding of infringement. Article 9 provides that if the Commission intends to adopt a decision relating to an infringement of Arts 81 or 82 EC Treaty, and the undertaking(s) concerned offer commitments to meet the Commission's concerns, then the Commission is empowered to adopt a decision making those commitments binding on the undertaking(s). Article 10 provides that if the Community public interest relating to the application of Arts 81 and 82 EC Treaty so requires, the Commission may adopt a decision finding that Art 81 is not applicable to a particular agreement, either because the Art 81(1) conditions are not fulfilled or because the conditions of Art 81(3) are satisfied. The Commission can also make such a decision with reference to Art 82.

Fines and periodic penalty payments

Regulation 17/62

The Commission had the power under Art 15(1), Regulation 17/62 to impose fines, by the adoption of a decision, for intentionally or negligently supplying incorrect or misleading information, or for refusing to submit to an investigation. In cases where the Commission found a breach of Arts 81 or 82, it could, by decision, impose on an undertaking or association of undertakings fines from 1,000 to 1,000,000 units of account, or a sum in excess of that figure, provided that this was no more than 10 per cent of the turnover in the preceding year of each of the undertakings participating in the infringement. Fines could be imposed only where the undertakings had acted intentionally or negligently. The Court held that the criteria for the appropriate level of fine should take into account the nature of the restrictions on competition, the number and size of the undertakings concerned, the relative proportions of the market controlled by them and the situation in the market where the infringement was committed (**ACF Chemiefarma** *v* **Commission** (Case 41/69)).

The Commission's policy on fines was at issue in **Welded Steel Mesh** (OJ 1989 L 260/1). In this case 14 companies in France, the three Benelux countries, Germany and Italy shared markets between themselves, fixed prices and volumes, and took action to enforce their cartel. The activities of the participants amounted to 'a sustained effort, carried on for a long period covering at least five years . . . to frustrate . . . one of the main aims of the Treaty, namely the creation of a common market, by interference in the price mechanism, restrictions on import penetration of one another's domestic markets, quantity restrictions and market sharing'. Mitigating factors were taken into account: namely, the parties sometimes had not respected the price and quota regime they had established; the welded mesh sector had not been profitable; welded mesh had been subject to competition from reinforced bars, which exercised price restraint on the cartel; some companies had suffered from financial problems; one company had given the Commission some assistance in its investigations. The Commission decided not to impose 'very large' fines, and to set the fines 'considerably below the level which would normally be justified'. The fines imposed ranged from 1,375,000 ECUs to 13,000 ECUs. One of the companies in the **Welded Steel Mesh** cartel was, however, successful in obtaining a reduction of the fine imposed on it, on the basis that the Commission had by its conduct given the appellant cause to believe that the agreement was not unlawful (**Baustahlgewebe GmbH** *v* **Commission** (Case T–145/89)).

In January 1998 the Commission imposed a fine of 102 million ECUs on Volkswagen for preventing its dealers in Italy from selling its vehicles to consumers and agencies in other Member States. The conduct of Volkswagen was regarded as having been aggravated by its failure to respond to repeated warnings by the Commission, and by the fact that the breaches had continued over a period of more than ten years (**The Community** *v* **Volkswagen AG and Others** (Case IV/35.733)). In the same month, the Commission published a notice laying down a new method of determining the amount of fines (OJ 1998 C 9/3). The fines notice set out clear rules regarding the level of fines: the greater the negative impact on the single market, the larger the fine. There was agreement between the Member States that for serious infringements of the competition rules extremely high fines would be justified, no matter the size and nationality of the firm. Even minor infringements could attract a fine as high as 1,000,000 ECUs.

Regulation 1/2003

Article 23, Regulation 1/2003 is concerned with the Commission's power to impose fines, and Art 24 with the power to impose periodic penalty payments. Article 23 provides that:

1. The Commission may by decision impose on undertakings and associations of undertakings fines not exceeding 1 per cent of the total turnover in the preceding business year where, intentionally or negligently:
   (a) they supply incorrect or misleading information in response to a request made pursuant to Article 17 or Article 18(2);
   (b) in response to a request made by decision adopted pursuant to Article 17 or Article 18(3), they supply incorrect, incomplete or misleading information or do not supply information within the required time-limit;
   (c) they produce the required books or other records related to the business in incomplete form during inspections under Article 20 or refuse to submit to inspections ordered by a decision adopted pursuant to Article 20(4);
   (d) in response to a question asked in accordance with Article 20(2)(e),
      – they give an incorrect or misleading answer,
      – they fail to rectify within a time-limit set by the Commission an incorrect, incomplete or misleading answer given by a member of staff, or
      – they fail or refuse to provide a complete answer on facts relating to the subject-matter and purpose of an inspection ordered by a decision adopted pursuant to Article 20(4);
   (e) seals affixed in accordance with Article 20(2)(d) by officials or other accompanying persons authorised by the Commission have been broken.

2. The Commission may by decision impose fines on undertakings and associations of undertakings where, either intentionally or negligently:
   (a) they infringe Article 81 or Article 82 of the Treaty; or
   (b) they contravene a decision ordering interim measures under Article 8; or
   (c) they fail to comply with a commitment made binding by a decision pursuant to Article 9.

For each undertaking and association of undertakings participating in the infringement, the fine shall not exceed 10 per cent of its total turnover in the preceding business year.

Where the infringement of an association relates to the activities of its members, the fine shall not exceed 10 per cent of the sum of the total turnover of each member active on the market affected by the infringement of the association.

3. In fixing the amount of the fine, regard shall be had both to the gravity and to the duration of the infringement.

4. When a fine is imposed on an association of undertakings taking account of the turnover of its members and the association is not solvent, the association is obliged to call for contributions from its members to cover the amount of the fine.

   ·Where such contributions have not been made to the association within a time-limit fixed by the Commission, the Commission may require payment of the fine directly by any of the undertakings whose representatives were members of the decision-making bodies concerned of the association.

   After the Commission has required payment under the second subparagraph, where necessary to ensure full payment of the fine, the Commission may require payment of the balance by any of the members of the association which were active on the market on which the infringement occurred.

   However, the Commission shall not require payment under the second or the third subparagraph from undertakings which show that they have not implemented the infringing decision of the association and either were not aware of its existence or have actively distanced themselves from it before the Commission started investigating the case.

   The financial liability of each undertaking in respect of the payment of the fine shall not exceed 10 per cent of its total turnover in the preceding business year.

5. Decisions taken pursuant to paragraphs 1 and 2 shall not be of a criminal law nature.

Article 24 provides that:

1. The Commission may, by decision, impose on undertakings or associations of undertakings periodic penalty payments not exceeding 5 per cent of the average daily turnover in the preceding business year per day and calculated from the date appointed by the decision, in order to compel them:
   (a) to put an end to an infringement of Article 81 or Article 82 of the Treaty, in accordance with a decision taken pursuant to Article 7;
   (b) to comply with a decision ordering interim measures taken pursuant to Article 8;
   (c) to comply with a commitment made binding by a decision pursuant to Article 9;
   (d) to supply complete and correct information which it has requested by decision taken pursuant to Article 17 or Article 18(3);
   (e) to submit to an inspection which it has ordered by decision taken pursuant to Article 20(4).

2. Where the undertakings or associations of undertakings have satisfied the obligation which the periodic penalty payment was intended to enforce, the Commission may fix the definitive amount of the periodic penalty payment at a figure lower than that which would arise under the original decision. Article 23(4) shall apply correspondingly.

Relationship between the Commission, and the competition authorities and courts of the Member States

Regulation 17/62

Under Art 10, Regulation 17/62 the Commission was obliged to transmit to the authorities responsible for competition policy in the Member States copies of any applications made to the Commission about the conduct of undertakings or, for example, for exemption under Art 81(3) EC Treaty in relation to agreements or concerted practices. The Commission was assisted by an Advisory Committee on Restrictive Practices and Monopolies composed of officials, drawn from a number of Member States, competent in restrictive practices and monopolies. The Commission was under an obligation to carry out its procedures in close cooperation with the competent authorities in the Member States. Those authorities had the right to express an opinion about the procedures adopted by the Commission during the course of an investigation (Art 10, Regulation 17/62).

The competition authorities in Member States could also be asked by the Commission to assist in the carrying out of investigations initiated by the Commission. Under Art 13, Regulation 17/62, national officials could be called upon to gather information on behalf of the Commission under Art 14, and could be assisted by Commission officials while doing so, if the Commission so requested. There was a general assumption that national authorities would cooperate with the Commission in the enforcement of competition law. National courts were also expected to cooperate with the Commission, as the Court of Justice explained in the following case:

Stergios Delimitis v *Henninger Brau* (Case C-234/89)

The Court of Justice stated that:

> It should be noted in this context that it is always open to a national court, within the limits of the applicable national procedural rules and subject to Article 214 [now Art 287] of the Treaty [prohibiting the disclosure of confidential business information], to seek information from the Commission on the state of any procedure which the Commission may have set in motion and as to the likelihood of its giving an official ruling on the agreement in issue pursuant to Regulation 17. Under the same conditions, the national court may contact the Commission where the concrete application of Article 85(1) or Article 86 [now Art 81(1) or Art 82] raises particular difficulties, in order to obtain the economic and legal information which the institution can supply to it. Under Article 5 [now Art 10] of the Treaty, the Commission is bound by a duty of sincere co-operation with the judicial authorities of the Member State, who are responsible for ensuring that Community law is applied and respected in the national legal system. (para 53)

In a Commission Notice issued in 1993 on cooperation between national courts and the Commission in applying Arts 81 and 82 of the EC Treaty (OJ 1993 C 39/5), the Commission expressed the view that, by encouraging more effective participation by national courts in the day-to-day application of Community competition law, the Commission would have more time to 'perform its administrative task, namely to steer competition policy in the Community' (para 34). Although the Commission accepted that national courts could not grant exemptions under Art 81(3), it envisaged that where an agreement or concerted practice was apparently in breach of Art 81(1), but could nonetheless attract exemption under Art 81(3), or fall within some existing block exemption regulation, the national court could stay the proceedings to enable the Commission to reach a decision. It was not clear how this process of cooperation was intended to work in practice. In 1997, a further Commission notice was issued (Final version of the Notice OJ 1997 C 313/3, 15 October 1997). As with all such measures, the notice was not legally binding. The division of competence between national courts and the Commission, and the criteria which had to be applied in deciding whether or not a national court should refer a case to the Commission, were considered by the Court of Justice in the following case:

Fonderies Roubaix-Wattrelos (Case 63/75)

The Court of Justice held that:

> The direct applicability of those provisions [Arts 81 and 82 EC Treaty] may not, however, lead the national courts to modify the scope of the exemption regulations by extending their sphere of application to agreements not covered by them. Any such extension, whatever its scope, would affect the manner in which the Commission exercises its legislative competence.
>
> ... It now falls to examine the consequences of that division of competence as regards the specific application of the Community competition rules by national courts. Account should here be taken of the risk of national courts taking decisions which conflict with those taken or envisaged by the Commission in the implementation of Articles 85(1) [Art 81(1)] and 86 [Art 82] and also of Article 85(3) [Art 81(3)]. Such conflicting decisions would be contrary to the general principles of legal certainty and must, therefore, be avoided when national courts give decisions on agreements or practices which may subsequently be the subject of a decision by the Commission. [para 47]
>
> ... The national court may have regard to the following considerations in applying Article 85. If the conditions for the application of Article 85(1) are clearly not satisfied and there is, consequently, scarcely any risk of the Commission taking a different decision, the national court may continue the proceedings and rule on the agreement in issue. It may do the same if the agreement's incompatibility with Article 85(1) is beyond doubt and, regard being had to the exemption regulations and the Commission's previous decisions, the agreement may on no account be the subject of an exemption decision under Article 85(3). [para 50]

The question of whether or not to stay proceedings (i.e. to put the proceedings on hold) in an English court when an application had been made to the Commission for an exemption under Art 81(3) could raise difficulties for the national court, as illustrated in the following case:

MTV Europe v BMG Records (UK) Ltd [1995] 1 CMLR 437

The claimant brought an action in damages for breach of Art 81 EC Treaty. Although the agreement in issue had been notified to the Commission, no decision had yet been delivered on whether it attracted exemption under Art 81(3), and one was not likely for some time. The Commission's decision would be retrospective to the extent that the agreement could be validated from the date of notification, but that validation could not be effective *prior* to notification. There was still a prospect that the claimant could recover damages in relation to that time. The national court (Evans-Lombe J), in interlocutory proceedings, decided to continue with the case, despite the involvement of the Commission. It decided that the proceedings should continue until they reached the point of setting down for trial. If that point was reached before the Commission's decision, proceedings should at that point be stayed (i.e. put on hold), and the stay should remain in effect until one month after the Commission's decision.

The Commission thought that, although it could retain its overall function in competition law, and would cooperate with national courts and national authorities in supplying both factual and advisory information, individual claims which alleged breaches of Community law by those who had suffered loss would increasingly be dealt with by national courts, and would, in its view, be better served by them. The reasons for preferring national courts (besides the lessening of the Commission's investigative burden) were:

1. The Commission could not award compensation for loss suffered as a result of an infringement of Arts 81 or 82 EC Treaty. Such claims could only be brought before national courts. Companies were more likely to avoid infringements of the Community competition rules if they risked having to pay damages or interest in such an event.

2. National courts could usually issue interim orders to stop the infringement more quickly than the Commission.

3. Claims for breaches of Community law in national courts could usually be coupled with claims for breaches of national law. This could not be done in procedures before the Commission.

4. In those Member States where the successful party was awarded costs, these could be awarded in a claim for breach of Community law. A successful complainant in administrative procedures before the Commission had no such right, although if the proceedings were taken to the CFI, costs could be awarded in relation to the proceedings before that Court.

The above has been reflected in the provisions of Regulation 1/2003.

Regulation 1/2003

As discussed above and in Chapters 20 and 21, Regulation 1/2003 changed the role of the Commission, and the competition authorities and courts of the Member States with regard to the application of Arts 81 and 82 EC Treaty. Article 5, Regulation 1/2003 empowers the competition authorities of the Member States to apply Arts 81 and 82 in their entirety; Art 6 provides the same power to the courts of the Member States. This will have the most profound impact with regard to the application of Art 81(3) (see above and Chapter 20).

Article 35, Regulation 1/2003 provides that Member States will designate the competition authority or authorities (which could include the courts) responsible for the application of Arts 81 and 82. The competition authorities must be able to effectively comply with the Regulation. Articles 11 and 12, Regulation 1/2003 are particularly relevant to the interaction between the Commission and national competition authorities. Article 11 provides as follows:

Cooperation between the Commission and the competition authorities of the Member States
1. The Commission and the competition authorities of the Member States shall apply the Community competition rules in close cooperation.

2. The Commission shall transmit to the competition authorities of the Member States copies of the most important documents it has collected with a view to applying Articles 7, 8, 9, 10 and Article 29(1). At the request of the competition authority of a Member State, the Commission shall provide it with a copy of other existing documents necessary for the assessment of the case.

3. The competition authorities of the Member States shall, when acting under Article 81 or Article 82 of the Treaty, inform the Commission in writing before or without delay after commencing the first formal investigative measure. This information may also be made available to the competition authorities of the other Member States.

4. No later than 30 days before the adoption of a decision requiring that an infringement be brought to an end, accepting commitments or withdrawing the benefit of a block exemption Regulation, the competition authorities of the Member States shall inform the Commission. To that effect, they shall provide the Commission with a summary of the case, the envisaged decision or, in the absence thereof, any other document indicating the proposed course of action. This information may also be made available to the competition authorities of the other Member States. At the request of the Commission, the acting competition authority shall make available to the Commission other documents it holds which are necessary for the assessment of the case. The information supplied to the Commission may be made available to the competition authorities of the other Member States. National competition authorities may also exchange between themselves information necessary for the assessment of a case that they are dealing with under Article 81 or Article 82 of the Treaty.

5. The competition authorities of the Member States may consult the Commission on any case involving the application of Community law.

6. The initiation by the Commission of proceedings for the adoption of a decision under Chapter III shall relieve the competition authorities of the Member States of their competence to apply Articles 81 and 82 of the Treaty. If a competition authority of a Member State is already acting on a case, the Commission shall only initiate proceedings after consulting with that national competition authority.

Article 12 provides as follows:

Exchange of information

1. For the purpose of applying Articles 81 and 82 of the Treaty the Commission and the competition authorities of the Member States shall have the power to provide one another with and use in evidence any matter of fact or of law, including confidential information.

2. Information exchanged shall only be used in evidence for the purpose of applying Article 81 or Article 82 of the Treaty and in respect of the subject-matter for which it was collected by the transmitting authority. However, where national competition law is applied in the same case and in parallel to Community competition law and does not lead to a different outcome, information exchanged under this Article may also be used for the application of national competition law.

3. Information exchanged pursuant to paragraph 1 can only be used in evidence to impose sanctions on natural persons where:
   - the law of the transmitting authority foresees sanctions of a similar kind in relation to an infringement of Article 81 or Article 82 of the Treaty or, in the absence thereof,
   - the information has been collected in a way which respects the same level of protection of the rights of defence of natural persons as provided for under the national rules of the receiving authority. However, in this case, the information exchanged cannot be used by the receiving authority to impose custodial sanctions.

Similar to the regime under Regulation 17/62, the new Regulation likewise provides for the Commission to be assisted by an Advisory Committee. Article 14, Regulation 1/2003 establishes the Advisory Committee on Restrictive Practices and Dominant Positions, which the Commission is required to consult prior to the taking of any decision pursuant to:

- Art 7 in relation to an infringement of Arts 81 or 82 EC Treaty;
- Art 8 in relation to interim measures;
- Art 9 in relation to commitments;
- Art 10 in relation to findings of inapplicability;
- Art 23 in relation to fines;
- Art 24(2) in relation to periodic penalty payments; and
- Art 29(1) in relation to the withdrawal of an exemption regulation in a particular case (Art 14(1)).

The Committee is composed of representatives of the competition authorities of the Member States (Art 14(2)). There is provision for the consultation to take place by written procedure, subject to the right of any Member State requesting a meeting, in which case the Commission will convene a meeting (Art 14(4)). Article 14(5) provides that 'the Commission shall take the utmost account of the opinion delivered by the Advisory Committee. It shall advise the Committee of the manner in which its opinion has been taken into account'. A competition authority of a Member State can request the Commission to include on the agenda of the Advisory Committee a case that is being dealt with by another competition authority under Arts 81 and 82 EC Treaty. If a request is made then the Commission is obliged to put the case on the agenda, and it may also do so on its own initiative (Art 14(7)). The Advisory Committee does not issue an opinion with regard to such cases. The Committee can also discuss general issues of Community competition law (Art 14(7)).

Article 15, Regulation 1/2003 covers cooperation between the Commission and national courts. In a case before a national court which concerns the application of Arts 81 or 82, the court can request the Commission to provide it with any information which is in the Commission's possession, and can also ask the Commission for an opinion on the application of Community competition law (Art 15(1)). This is additional to the power (or duty in some cases) to make an Art 234 EC Treaty referral to the Court of Justice (see Chapter 6).

Member States are required to send the Commission without delay a copy of the written judgment of a national court which decides on the application of Arts 81 or 82. A competition authority of a Member State can submit written observations to national courts of *their* Member State on issues relating to the application of Arts 81 and 82, and they may also submit oral observations if the national court grants it permission (Art 15(3)). The same applies to the Commission with regard to the national courts of *all* the Member States (Art 15(3)).

The Commission has issued a non-legally binding notice on the cooperation between the Commission and the courts of the EU Member States in the application of Arts 81 and 82 EC Treaty (OJ 2004 C 101/54). This notice replaces the earlier versions (discussed above). It is available at:

> http://ec.europa.eu/comm/competition/antitrust/legislation/

The role of national competition authorities and courts in the enforcement of Community competition law

In the following case, the CFI demonstrated some sympathy for the Commission's attempt to leave individual complaints which had a largely national dimension, although potentially affecting trade between Member States, to the courts of the state most affected:

Automec and Asia Motor France v *Commission* (Cases T-24 and 28/90)

Where the national court would be able to rule on the compatibility of a national distribution agreement for cars under Art 81(1) EC Treaty and provide the appropriate remedies if there was a breach, there was no need for Commission intervention. The CFI therefore held that the Commission was not under an obligation to commence proceedings to determine whether or not a violation of Community law had occurred.

Similarly in the following case:

Tremblay v *Commission* (Case T-5/93)

The Commission had declined to investigate an alleged abuse of a monopoly position enjoyed by the Société des Auteurs, Compositeurs et Editeurs de Musique (SACEM) in relation to musical copyrights on the grounds, *inter alia*, that the effects of the alleged infringements outside France were limited and that several cases raising the same issues were pending before the French courts. The CFI supported this approach:

> The fact that a national court or national competition authority is already dealing with a case concerning the compatibility of an agreement or practice with Articles 85 and 86 [now Arts 81 and 82] of the Treaty is a factor which the Commission may take into account in evaluating the extent to which a case displays a Community interest ... The Court considers that where the effects of the infringement alleged in a complaint are essentially confined to the territory of one Member State and where proceedings have been brought before the courts and competent administrative authorities of that Member State by the complainant against the body against which the complaint was made, the Commission is entitled to reject the complaint through lack of any sufficient Community interest, provided however that the rights of the complainant or its members can be adequately safeguarded, in particular by the national courts.

Articles 81(1) and 82 EC Treaty are both directly effective in national courts and can be used both offensively and defensively. As discussed above, Art 81(3) can now be applied by the national courts. The availability of remedies for private parties in national courts on the basis of Community competition rules arose from the decision of the Court of Justice in **BRT** v **SABAM** (Case 127/73). In this case, the Court held that a party could claim that an agreement was void under Art 81(2), that an injunction should be granted to enforce the competition rules, and that damages were payable for breach of Arts 81 or 82.

The following case, which came before the Court of Justice, concerned the question of whether a party to a contract which was contrary to Art 81 EC Treaty could rely on the breach of that provision before a national court to obtain compensation for any losses which resulted from the unlawful contractual clause:

Courage and Crehan (Case C-453/99)

The Court of Justice founded its judgment on its case law relating to the nature and effect of Community law, recalling **Van Gend en Loos** (Case 26/62), **Costa** (Case 6/64) and **Francovich and Others** (Joined Cases C-6/90 and C-9/90) (see Chapter 9), and on the basis that Art 81 constitutes 'a fundamental provision which is essential for the accomplishment of the tasks entrusted to the Community and, in particular, for the functioning of the internal market' (para 20).

The Court deduced from the nature of the Community legal order, the particularly important position of the competition rules in that order, and other more specific considerations that 'any individual can rely on a breach of Article 81(1) EC Treaty before a national court even where he is a party to a contract that is liable to restrict or distort competition within the meaning of that provision' (para 24). That right entailed, *inter alia*, the right to seek compensation for the loss caused. Accordingly, there could not be any absolute bar to an action for damages being brought by one of the parties to a contract which violated Art 81(1). Moreover, the bringing of such actions strengthened the working of the Community competition rules and discouraged agreements or practices, which were frequently covert, that were liable to restrict or distort competition. However, if it was established that the party relying on the breach of Art 81 was significantly responsible for the distortion of competition, Community law would not preclude a rule of national law barring him from relying on his own unlawful actions to obtain damages.

Regulation 1/2003

As previously discussed, Regulation 1/2003 has dramatically changed the way in which Arts 81 and 82 EC Treaty will be applied in the future, now that the national competition authorities and courts of the Member States are empowered to apply the two articles in their entirety.

The Commission has issued a notice on cooperation within the Network of Competition Authorities (OJ 2004 C 101/43). This notice is divided into five sections:

- Introduction.
- Division of work (which includes the principles of allocating cases to: a single competition authority, several competition authorities acting in parallel, or the Commission; mechanisms of cooperation for the purpose of case allocation and assistance; and the position of undertakings).
- Consistent application of EC competition rules.
- The role and functioning of the Advisory Committee in the new system.
- Final remarks.

The notice is available at:

http://ec.europa.eu/comm/competition/antitrust/legislation/

Relationship between Community and national competition law

The potential for conflict between national competition rules and those of the Community was addressed by the Court of Justice in the following case, which related to a dyestuffs cartel:

Walt Wilhelm v *Bundeskartellamt* (Case 14/68)

The Court of Justice held that, since their objectives were different, national competition rules could be applied in parallel with those of the Community, but not so as to prejudice the uniform application of Community rules throughout the common market. In practice, this meant that there had to be a set-off between any fines which were imposed by the national courts and the Commission, so that the later sanctions took account of earlier ones:

> The case-law of the Court of Justice has accepted the possibility of concurrent sanctions resulting from two parallel procedures pursuing different ends, the acceptability thereof deriving from the special system of sharing jurisdiction between the Community and the Member States with regard to cartels. However, the Court of Justice has established that, by virtue of a general requirement of natural justice, the Commission must take account of penalties which have already been borne by the same undertaking for the same conduct, where they have been imposed for the infringement of the cartel law of a Member State and, consequently, have been committed on the Community territory. (**Sotralenz SA** v **Commission** (Case T-149/89))

Conduct which infringed Arts 81 or 82, but which did not infringe national law, could not be held to be lawful in that state. However, there could be situations where an agreement or prohibited conduct did not infringe Arts 81 or 82 because it did not affect trade between states, but it could still breach national competition law, and an agreement or concerted practice which had been exempted by the Commission under Art 81(3) could be lawful, even if it breached national competition rules.

Regulation 1/2003

Article 3, Regulation 1/2003 addresses the issue of the relationship between Arts 81 and 82 EC Treaty and national competition laws. Article 3 provides that:

1. Where the competition authorities of the Member States or national courts apply national competition law to agreements, decisions by associations of undertakings or concerted practices within the meaning of Article 81(1) of the Treaty which may affect trade between Member States within the meaning of that provision, they shall also apply Article 81 of the Treaty to such agreements, decisions or concerted practices. Where the competition authorities of the Member States or national courts apply national competition law to any abuse prohibited by Article 82 of the Treaty, they shall also apply Article 82 of the Treaty.

2. The application of national competition law may not lead to the prohibition of agreements, decisions by associations of undertakings or concerted practices which may affect trade between Member States but which do not restrict competition within the meaning of Article 81(1) of the Treaty, or which fulfil the conditions of Article 81(3) of the Treaty or which are covered by a Regulation for the application of Article 81(3) of the Treaty. Member States shall not under this Regulation be precluded from adopting and applying

on their territory stricter national laws which prohibit or sanction unilateral conduct engaged in by undertakings.

3. Without prejudice to general principles and other provisions of Community law, paragraphs 1 and 2 do not apply when the competition authorities and the courts of the Member States apply national merger control laws nor do they preclude the application of provisions of national law that predominantly pursue an objective different from that pursued by Articles 81 and 82 of the Treaty.

Article 16, Regulation 1/2003 provides that when national courts (or competition authorities) rule on agreements, decisions or practices under Arts 81 or 82 which are already the subject of a Commission decision, they cannot take decisions which run counter to the Commission's decision. National courts must also avoid giving decisions which would conflict with a decision contemplated by the Commission in proceedings it has initiated. In the latter situation, the national court could stay the proceedings until the Commission has reached its decision.

Implementing Community competition law in UK courts

Article 81 EC Treaty is directly effective and therefore it may be used in UK courts both as a defence to a claim for breach of contract and, for example, as the basis for a claim that an unlawful agreement between competitors has damaged an undertaking that is not a party to that agreement (**MTV Europe v BMG Records (UK) Ltd** (above); **Society of Lloyds v Clementson** [1995] 1 CMLR 693). The following case illustrates this point:

Cutsworth v Mansfield Inns [1986] 1 CMLR 1

Pursuant to an agreement, the claimants had for many years supplied coin-operated amusement machines to the tenants of more than 50 public houses. The public houses were taken over by Mansfield Inns (the defendants) in 1985 and, not long after this, the defendants gave their tenants a list of suppliers of amusement machines from whom tenants were permitted to purchase. The claimants (who were not on that list) applied for an injunction to restrain the defendants from restricting their tenants from buying from them. They claimed that there was a seriously arguable case that the covenant in the licensees' tenancy agreement had the object or effect of distorting competition and potentially affected trade between Member States, contrary to Art 81(1) EC Treaty. This argument was accepted by the national court and the injunction was granted (see also **Holleran and Evans v Daniel Thwaites plc** [1989] 2 CMLR 917).

It now seems clear that a declaration that an agreement breached Art 81(1) would not be sufficient. Under Community law, the national court would have to make an award of damages (**H.J. Banks and Co Ltd v British Coal Corporation** (Case C–128/92)). Article 81 can also be used defensively. In **Société Technique Minière v Maschinenbau Ulm** (Case 56/65), the defendant distributors were held to be able to plead the invalidity of the distribution agreement in the national courts as a defence to a breach of contract (see also **Brasserie de Haecht v Wilkin (No. 1)** (Case 23/67)).

Article 82 can provide the basis for a claim for damages in the English courts as illustrated in the following case:

Garden Cottage Foods Ltd v *Milk Marketing Board* [1984] AC 130

An application was made for an interlocutory injunction to restrain the defendants from refusing to supply milk to the claimants. The refusal to supply was alleged by the claimants to be an abuse of a dominant position by the board, and much of the case was concerned with whether or not it was appropriate, in the circumstances, to grant an interlocutory injunction. In determining this point, the House of Lords had to consider whether or not an award of damages would be available if the claimants were successful in the substantive proceedings. Lord Diplock, who delivered the principal speech, thought that damages could be awarded under English law for a breach of Art 82 EC Treaty:

> This article of the Treaty of Rome (the EEC Treaty) was held by the European Court of Justice in **Belgische Radio en Televisie** v **SV SABAM** (Case 127/73) to produce direct effects in relations between individuals and to create direct rights in respect of the individuals concerned which the national courts must protect. This decision of the European Court of Justice is to the effect that Art 86 [Art 82] is one which s 3(1) of the European Communities Act 1972 requires your lordships to follow. The rights which the article confers upon citizens in the UK accordingly fall within s 2(1) of the Act. They are without further enactment to be given legal effect in the UK and enforced accordingly. A breach of the duty imposed by Art 86 [Art 82] not to abuse a dominant position in the common market or in a substantial part of it, can thus be categorised in English law as a breach of statutory duty that is imposed not only for the purpose of promoting the general economic prosperity of the common market but also for the benefit of private individuals to whom loss or damage is caused by breach of that duty.

There is little case law on successful claims for damages for breach of Art 82 as a breach of statutory duty, but the principle has been applied in the English Divisional Court and affirmed in the Court of Appeal. In **An Bord Bainne Co-operative Limited (The Irish Dairy Board)** v **The Milk Marketing Board** [1984] 2 CMLR 584 CA, Neill J declared that the speeches of their Lordships in the **Garden Cottage** case provided 'compelling support for the proposition that contraventions of EEC regulations which have "direct effects" create rights in private law which national courts must protect'. Article 82 could also provide a defence to an action that, for example, an exclusive supply agreement was entered into by one party while being subject to abuse of a dominant position by another undertaking. Thus, the UK purchasers of Tetra-Pak drinks packaging machines who were required to buy only Tetra-Pak cartons for use in those machines would be free to buy other cartons and could use the breaches of Arts 81 and 82 found by the CFI as a defence to any action for breach of contract in UK courts (**Tetra-Pak International SA** v **Commission** (Case T–83/91)).

Summary

Now you have read this chapter you should be able to:

- Explain how the rules of Community competition law are implemented by Regulations 1/2003 and 773/2004.

- Outline and describe the nature and scope of the seven Commission Notices which have been issued to support Regulations 1/2003 and 773/2004.

- Understand and evaluate the role of the Commission when it initiates an action for an alleged breach of Arts 81 or 82 EC Treaty.

- Outline the provisions of Regulation 1/2003 which provide for a complaint to be lodged with either the Commission or the competition authority of a Member State.
- Explain what applications can be made by a party where it is unclear whether the party is in breach of Arts 81 or 82 EC Treaty, specifically explaining the legal status of a guidance letter.
- Discuss the nature and scope of the Commission's powers of investigation and a party's right to a hearing.
- Understand and describe the nature and scope of the Commission's powers to make decisions, and the power to levy fines and periodic penalty payments.
- Explain and evaluate the relationship between the Commission on the one hand, and the national competition authorities and courts of the Member States on the other.
- Compare and contrast the respective enforcement roles undertaken by national competition authorities and the courts of the Member States pursuant to Arts 81 and 82 EC Treaty.
- Analyse the relationship between Community and national competition law.
- Explain how Community competition law is implemented in the UK.

References

Friend, M. 'Rights of Complainants in EC Competition Proceedings' (1994) 110 LQR 209.

Hunnings, N.M., 'The Stanley Adams Affair or the Biter Bit' (1987) 24 CML Rev 65.

Shaw, J., 'Competition Complaints: A Comprehensive System of Remedies?' (1993) 18 EL Rev 427.

Shaw, J., 'A Review of Recent Cases on Articles 85 and 86 EC: Procedural Issues' (1995) EL Rev 83.

Further reading

Textbooks

Craig, P. and De Burca, G. (2003) *EU Law Text, Cases and Materials* (3rd edn), Oxford University Press, Chapter 25.

Foster, N. (2006) *Foster on EU Law* (1st edn), Oxford University Press, Chapter 8 (Sections 8.8 and 8.9).

Goyder, D.G. (2003) *EC Competition Law* (4th edn), Oxford University Press.

Steiner, J., Woods, L. and Twigg-Flesner, C. (2006) *EU Law* (9th edn), Oxford University Press, Chapter 29.

Storey, T. and Turner, C. (2005) *Unlocking EU Law* (1st edn), Hodder Arnold, Chapter 15 (Section 15.5).

Tillotson, J. and Foster, N. (2003) *Text, Cases and Materials on EU Law* (4th edn), Cavendish Publishing, Chapter 17.

Weatherill, S. (2006) *Cases and Materials on EU Law* (7th edn), Oxford University Press, Chapter 18.

Journal articles

Andreangeli, A., 'The impact of the Modernisation Regulation on the guarantees of due process in competition proceedings' (2006) 31 EL Rev 342.

Bourgeois, J. and Humpe, C., 'The Commission's Draft "New Regulation 17"' [2002] ECLR 43.

Brammer, S., 'Concurrent jurisdiction under Regulation 1/2003 and the issue of case allocation' (2005) 42 CML Rev 1383.

Burnside, A. and Crosslet, H., 'Co-operation in competition: A new era' (2005) 30 EL Rev 234.

Chiti, E., 'The Right of Access to Community Information under the Code of Practice' (1996) 2 EPL 363.

Davidson, J., 'Action for Damages in the English Courts for Breach of EEC Competition Law' (1985) 34 ICLQ 178.

Ehlermann, C.D., 'The Modernisation of EC Antitrust Policy: A Legal and Cultural Revolution' (2000) CML Rev 537.

Forrester, I.S. and Norall, C., 'Competition Law' (1989) 9 YEL 271, 286, 300.

Friend, M., 'Rights of Complainants in EC Competition Proceedings' (1994) 110 LQR 209.

Harris, B., 'Problems of Procedure in EEC Competition Law' (1989) NLJ 1452.

Hunnings, N.M., 'The Stanley Adams Affair or the Biter Bit' (1987) 24 CML Rev 65.

Kerse, C., 'Enforcing Community Competition Policy under Arts 8 and 89 of the EC Treaty – New Powers for UK Competition Authorities' [1997] ECLR 17.

Kingston, S., 'A "New Division of Responsibilities" in the Proposed Regulation to Modernise the Rules Implementing Articles 81 and 82 EC? A Warning Call?' [2001] ECLR 340.

Lang, J.T., 'Duties of National Authorities under Community Constitutional Law' (1998) 23 EL Rev 109.

Marsden, P.B., 'Inducing Member States' Enforcement of European Competition Law: A Competition Policy Approach to Anti-trust Federalism' [1997] 18 ECLR 234.

Nordsjo, A., 'Regulation 1/2003: Power of the Commission to adopt interim measures' [2006] ECLR 299.

Perrin, B., 'Challenges facing the EU Network of Competition Authorities: Insights from a comparative criminal law perspective' (2006) 31 EL Rev 540.

Riley, A.J., 'More Radicalism, Please. The Notice on Cooperation between National Courts and the Commission: Applying Articles 85 and 86 of the EEC Treaty' [1993] 3 ECLR 91.

Rodger, B., 'Competition law litigation in the UK courts: A study of all cases to 2004 – Part I' [2006] ECLR 241.

Rodger, B., 'Competition law litigation in the UK courts: A study of all cases to 2004 – Part II' [2006] ECLR 279.

Rodger, B., 'Competition law litigation in the UK courts: A study of all cases to 2004 – Part III' [2006] ECLR 341.

Shaw, J., 'Competition Complaints: A Comprehensive System of Remedies?' (1993) 18 EL Rev 427.

Shaw, J., 'A Review of Recent Cases on Articles 85 and 86 EC: Procedural Issues' (1995) EL Rev 83.

Van der Woude, M., 'Hearing Officers and EC Anti-trust Procedures: The Art of Making Subjective Procedures More Objective' (1996) 33 CML Rev 531.

Wesserling, R., 'The Draft Regulations Modernising the Competition Rules: The Commission is married to one idea' (2001) 26 EL Rev 357.

Wils, W.P.J., 'The Commission's New Method for Calculating Fines in Antitrust Cases' (1997) 22 EL Rev 125.

Glossary

a fortiori Latin phrase which literally means 'from the stronger', but which is more often used to mean 'even more so' or 'with even stronger reason'.

ab initio Latin phrase which means 'from the beginning'. In a legal context it refers to something being the situation from the start, rather than from when the court declared it so.

Absolute territorial protection Where a manufacturer of goods grants a business undertaking (e.g. a wholesaler or retailer) a sole licence for the sale/distribution of such goods within a particular Member State. Often this is in an attempt to prevent parallel imports. *See also* PARALLEL IMPORTS.

Abuse of a dominant position A business undertaking which has a monopoly position in the market place, and uses that position (i.e. dominance) to affect trade between the Member States is referred to as the 'abuse of a dominant position'. Article 82 European Community (EC) Treaty prohibits the use (abuse) of a dominant position in this way. *See also* MONOPOLY.

acquis Derived from French, *acquis* (or *acquis communautaire*) is used in European Union (EU) law to refer to the total body of EU Law accumulated so far. The term is also used to refer to the laws adopted under the Schengen Agreement. In this context it is referred to as the *Schengen acquis*. *See also* SCHENGEN AGREEMENT.

Acts of the Community institutions Article 249 EC Treaty empowers the Community institutions to make regulations, issue directives, take decisions, make recommendations or deliver opinions. These instruments are referred to as 'acts of the Community institutions'.

Advocate-General The Court of Justice is assisted by eight Advocates-General (Art 222 EC Treaty). The principal role of an Advocate-General is to assist the Court of Justice reach its judgment by delivering an Opinion in open court. The Opinion is not binding on the Court, although the Court usually follows the Opinion when reaching its judgment.

Aggregation of contributions Article 42 EC Treaty facilitates the European Union's policy of free movement of workers by providing EU workers with the right to have their social security contributions and period of contribution in their home state recognised in the host Member State, and their contributions and length of service in the host Member State recognised in their home state when they return. This is referred to as 'aggregation of contributions'. *See also* DOUBLE-FUNCTION TEST; EXPORTABILITY OF BENEFITS.

Benelux Agreement In 1948, Belgium, The Netherlands and Luxembourg established the Benelux customs union, which removed customs barriers between the three countries and also imposed a common customs tariff on goods entering the three countries from outside their national boundaries. In 1954 the free movement of capital was permitted between these three countries, followed by the free movement of labour in

1956. The agreement establishing these provisions is referred to as the 'Benelux Agreement'. *See also* BENELUX CUSTOMS UNION.

Benelux countries   Comprises of Belgium, Holland (also referred to as The Netherlands) and Luxembourg. *See also* BENELUX AGREEMENT; BENELUX CUSTOMS UNION.

Benelux customs union   The Benelux customs union established the free movement of goods between the three Benelux countries (Belgium, The Netherlands and Luxembourg) from 1 January 1948. Customs barriers were removed and a common customs tariff was introduced for goods entering the customs union from outside the customs union. This developed in 1954 to include the free movement of capital, and developed further in 1956 to include the free movement of labour. *See also* BENELUX AGREEMENT.

Cartel   An agreement between otherwise independent business undertakings the aim of which is to protect their market share.

CEE   CEE is the acronym for 'charge having an equivalent effect to a customs duty'. Articles 23 and 25 EC Treaty prohibit customs duties and CEEs. *See also* COMMON EXTERNAL TARIFF; CUSTOMS DUTY; CUSTOMS UNION.

CFSP   *See* COMMON FOREIGN AND SECURITY POLICY.

CISA   *See* CONVENTION FOR THE IMPLEMENTATION OF THE SCHENGEN AGREEMENT.

Co-decision procedure   The founding treaties excluded the European Parliament from direct involvement in the legislative process. The European Parliament's greatest level of involvement in the legislative process was a right to be consulted, in a few policy areas. Following the introduction of direct elections to the European Parliament in 1979 there was a call for the European Parliament to have a greater involvement in the legislative process. The cooperation procedure, set out in Art 252 EC Treaty, was introduced by the Single European Act (SEA). It empowers the European Parliament, in certain specified policy areas, to propose amendments to a legislative proposal. Following amendments to the founding treaties by subsequent treaties (e.g. Treaty on European Union [TEU], Treaty of Nice [ToN], Treaty of Amsterdam [ToA]), the cooperation procedure is now rarely used; the co-decision procedure is more commonly used. The co-decision procedure, which is set out in Art 251 EC Treaty, provides the European Parliament with a greater involvement in the legislative process. The co-decision procedure empowers the Parliament, in certain specified policy areas, to propose amendments and ultimately to veto the proposal. The legal base determines the legislative procedure which has to be used for the adoption of a particular instrument. *See also* COOPERATION PROCEDURE; LEGAL BASE.

Committee of Permanent Representatives (COREPER)   The Committee of Permanent Representatives, known by its French acronym (COREPER), comprises of senior national officials from the Member States of the EU, who are based in Brussels. The role of the Committee is to provide continuity during the inevitable absences of relevant ministers from the Council of Ministers. *See also* COUNCIL OF MINISTERS; COUNCIL OF THE EUROPEAN UNION.

Committee of the Regions   The Committee of the Regions was established by the TEU as an advisory body. It is not a formal Community institution. The members of the Committee are representatives of regional and local bodies who either hold a regional or local authority electoral mandate or are politically accountable to an elected assembly (Art 263 EC Treaty). Its main role is to deliver opinions on proposed legislation when consulted by the Council of Ministers and to issue own-initiative opinions in appropriate cases. In a few policy areas (e.g. culture (Art 151(5) EC Treaty)), the legal base for a legislative proposal stipulates that the Committee must be consulted in relation to proposed legislation. *See also* LEGAL BASE.

Common external tariff A customs union comprises an association of countries which prohibits customs duties and charges having an equivalent effect from being levied on goods as they cross the borders of the countries within the association. A common external tariff (i.e. a fixed customs duty) is applied to goods entering the customs union from a non-member country. *See also* CEE; CUSTOMS DUTY; CUSTOMS UNION.

Common Foreign and Security Policy (CFSP) The Common Foreign and Security Policy (CFSP) was established by the TEU. The TEU established the European Union, which is founded upon three pillars. The CFSP constitutes the second of the three pillars of the EU. *See also* COOPERATION IN THE FIELDS OF JUSTICE AND HOME AFFAIRS; JUSTICE AND HOME AFFAIRS; POLICE AND JUDICIAL COOPERATION IN CRIMINAL MATTERS; THREE PILLARS OF THE EUROPEAN UNION.

Common market The common market was established by the European Economic Community (EEC) Treaty (subsequently renamed the European Community (EC) Treaty). It is a free trade area founded upon the free movement of goods, labour, capital and services. *See also* EUROPEAN COMMUNITIES; EUROPEAN COMMUNITY.

Complainant Complainant refers to a person who makes a complaint. It may also refer to a person who makes a claim in a court or tribunal against another person (also referred to as the applicant or plaintiff).

Concerted practice Within the context of Art 81 EC Treaty, a concerted practice refers to some kind of coordinated action which, although it may fall short of an agreement, knowingly substitutes practical cooperation for competition. *See also* RESTRICTIVE AGREEMENT.

Conglomerate One large business undertaking which consists of divisions of (quite often unrelated) businesses.

Constitutional Treaty The (proposed) Constitutional Treaty was adopted by the Member States of the EU in 2004. This Treaty would have replaced all the existing EU treaties (e.g. EC Treaty, TEU). Before it could come into force it had to be ratified (i.e. approved) by each Member State, according to each Member State's constitutional requirements. In some Member States their constitution required approval by the electorate in a referendum. This was the situation in both France and The Netherlands, both of which rejected the Treaty in 2005. As a result, the (proposed) Constitutional Treaty has not come into force, and its future is uncertain.

Contextual interpretation Contextual interpretation is used by courts to interpret legislation. If this method is employed, the provision being interpreted is placed within its context and interpreted in relation to the provisions of the legislation in question. This method of legislative interpretation, together with teleological interpretation, are extensively used by the Court of Justice and the Court of First Instance. *See also* HISTORICAL INTERPRETATION; LITERAL INTERPRETATION; TELEOLOGICAL INTERPRETATION.

contra legem Latin phrase which means 'against the law'.

Convention for the Implementation of the Schengen Agreement (CISA) CISA is, as its title implies, the convention which implemented the Schengen Agreement. *See also* SCHENGEN AGREEMENT.

Cooperation in the fields of Justice and Home Affairs   Cooperation in the fields of Justice and Home Affairs (JHA) was established by the TEU. The TEU also established the European Union, which is founded upon three pillars. The JHA constituted the third of the three pillars of the EU. However, following amendments to the TEU and EC Treaty by the ToA, this third pillar was renamed Police and Judicial Cooperation in Criminal Matters. *See also* COMMON FOREIGN AND SECURITY POLICY; POLICE AND JUDICIAL COOPERATION IN CRIMINAL MATTERS; JUSTICE AND HOME AFFAIRS; THREE PILLARS OF THE EUROPEAN UNION.

Cooperation procedure   The founding treaties excluded the European Parliament from direct involvement in the legislative process. The European Parliament's greatest level of involvement in the legislative process was a right to be consulted, in a few policy areas. Following the introduction of direct elections to the European Parliament in 1979 there was a call for the European Parliament to have a greater involvement in the legislative process. The cooperation procedure, set out in Art 252 EC Treaty, was introduced by the SEA. It empowers the European Parliament, in certain specified policy areas, to propose amendments to a legislative proposal. Following amendments to the founding treaties by subsequent treaties (e.g. the TEU, ToN, ToA), the cooperation procedure is now rarely used; the co-decision procedure is more commonly used. The legal base determines the legislative procedure which has to be used for the adoption of a particular instrument. *See also* CO-DECISION PROCEDURE; LEGAL BASE.

COREPER   *See* COMMITTEE OF PERMANENT REPRESENTATIVES.

Corrigendum   Derived from Latin, a corrigendum is an error in printing. From time-to-time a corrigendum is published in the *Official Journal of the European Union* to correct errors in a previous edition of the journal.

Council of Ministers   The Council of Ministers is one of the Community institutions. It is also referred to as the Council of the EU (this is its official title), or simply the Council. The Council consists of a representative from each of the 27 Member States at ministerial level, who is authorised to bind the government of their Member State. *See also* COMMITTEE OF PERMANENT REPRESENTATIVES; COUNCIL OF THE EUROPEAN UNION.

Council of the European Union   The Council of the European Union is the official title of the Council of Ministers (which is also referred to as the Council) and is one of the Community institutions. The Council consists of a representative from each of the 27 Member States at ministerial level, who is authorised to bind the government of their Member State. *See also* COMMITTEE OF PERMANENT REPRESENTATIVES; COUNCIL OF MINISTERS.

Court of Auditors   The Court of Auditors is not, strictly speaking, a court. Article 7 EC Treaty classifies the Court as a Community institution. It is responsible for the external audit of the general budget of the European Communities.

Cross-elasticity   Within the context of Art 90(2) EC Treaty, cross-elasticity refers to the degree to which goods are substitutable for each other (i.e. the readiness to which a consumer will switch between two competing products).

Customs duty   A customs duty is a state levy charged on goods at the border. Articles 23 and 25 EC Treaty prohibit customs duties. *See also* CEE; COMMON EXTERNAL TARIFF; CUSTOMS UNION.

Customs union   A customs union is an association of countries which prohibits customs duties and charges having an equivalent effect from being levied on goods as they cross the borders of the countries within the association. A common external tariff (i.e.

a fixed customs duty) is applied to goods entering the customs union from a non-member country. Article 23 EC Treaty establishes a customs union between the 27 Member States of the EU. *See also* CEE; CUSTOMS DUTY; COMMON EXTERNAL TARIFF.

de minimis   Latin phrase which, in a legal context, means matters which are not worthy of the law's attention. *See also* DE MINIMUS PRESUMPTION.

de minimis presumption   In EU competition law, there are a number of formalised de minimis presumptions, set out in Commission Notices. For example, the Notice on Agreements of Minor Importance (OJ 2001 C 386/13) stipulates the circumstances in which agreements between companies (particularly smaller companies) will not be in breach of Art 81 EC Treaty. *See also* DE MINIMIS.

Decision   A decision is a legally effective Community instrument. Article 249 EC Treaty provides that a decision shall be binding in its entirety upon those to whom it is addressed.

Demand-side substitution   Demand-side substitutability determines which products compete with each other from the perspective of the consumer (e.g. whether a consumer will switch from purchasing one product, e.g. apples, to another, e.g. bananas).

Democratic deficit   When the European Communities were first founded, the legislative process primarily only involved the European Commission (which initiated/proposed the legislation) and the Council of Ministers which adopted the proposed legislation. The European Parliament's greatest level of involvement in the legislative process was a right to be consulted, in a few policy areas. When the Members of the European Parliament (MEPs) were directly elected for the first time in 1979, it was argued that its role within the legislative process should be enhanced. There was a 'democratic deficit' because the only directly elected Community institution had little or no involvement in the legislative process. Subsequent treaties (e.g. the SEA, TEU, ToN, ToA) amended the founding treaties to enhance the legislative role of the European Parliament, but ultimately the European Commission and the Council of Ministers continue to dominate the legislative process. *See also* CO-DECISION PROCEDURE; COOPERATION PROCEDURE.

Derogation   A derogation is an exception to the general rule.

Deutsche Mark   The Deutsche Mark (DM) was Germany's national currency before Germany adopted the euro. *See also* EURO.

Direct effect   If a provision of Community law has direct effect, it can be enforced in national courts and tribunals overriding any inconsistent national provisions. In order to be capable of having direct effect, the provision of Community law must be sufficiently precise and unconditional (Case 26/62 **Van Gend en Loos**). *See also* HORIZONTAL DIRECT EFFECT; VERTICAL DIRECT EFFECT.

Directive   A directive is a legally effective Community instrument. Article 249 EC Treaty provides that a directive shall be binding, as to the result to be achieved, upon each Member State to which it is addressed, but shall leave to the national authorities the choice of form and methods. This requires a Member State to adopt implementing legislation to incorporate the directive into the national legal system.

Distinctly applicable measure   Within the context of Arts 28 and 29 EC Treaty, a distinctly applicable measure is a quantitative restriction (QR) or measure having an equivalent effect to a quantitative restriction (MEQR) which is applied only to imported or exported goods; i.e. the restriction is not applied to domestically produced goods. *See also* INDISTINCTLY APPLICABLE MEASURE; MEASURE HAVING AN EQUIVALENT EFFECT TO A QUANTITATIVE RESTRICTION; QUANTITATIVE RESTRICTION.

DM   *See* DEUTSCHE MARK.

Double-function test   Article 42 EC Treaty facilitates the European Union's policy of free movement of workers by providing EU workers with the right to have their social security contributions and period of contribution in their home state recognised in the host Member State, and their contributions and length of service in the host Member State recognised in their home State when they return. Article 4(4), Regulation 1408/71 excludes discretionary social-assistance-type benefits. However, the double-function test, established by the Court of Justice in Case 1/72 **Frilli**, provides that even a means-tested discretionary payment could constitute 'social security' rather than 'social assistance', and thus come within the scope of the Regulation, if it could be regarded as a supplement to one of the benefits listed in Art 4(1), Regulation 1408/71. *See also* AGGREGATION OF CONTRIBUTIONS; EXPORTABILITY OF BENEFITS.

Dual-burden rule   Within the context of Arts 28 and 29 EC Treaty, a dual-burden rule is one which imposes an additional burden on foreign producers and goods. *See also* EQUAL-BURDEN RULE.

EC   *See* EUROPEAN COMMUNITY.

ECB   *See* EUROPEAN CENTRAL BANK.

ECHR   *See* EUROPEAN CONVENTION ON HUMAN RIGHTS.

Economic and Monetary Union (EMU)   Economic and Monetary Union was established by the EC Treaty, following amendments made to it by the TEU. A timetable for the adoption of the single currency (the euro) was set out. The euro became legal tender in 12 of the 15 pre-2004 Member States on 1 January 2002. The UK, Denmark and Sweden opted out of the single currency. On 1 January 2007 Slovenia adopted the euro. The euro has therefore replaced the national currency in 13 of the current 27 Member States. *See also* EURO; SINGLE EUROPEAN CURRENCY.

Economic and Social Committee (ECOSOC)   The Economic and Social Committee, known by its French acronym ECOSOC, was established by the TEU as an advisory body. It is not a formal Community institution. The members of the Committee are representatives of the various economic and social components of organised civil society, and in particular representatives of producers, farmers, carriers, workers, dealers, craftsmen, professional occupations, consumers and the general public (Art 257 EC Treaty). Its main role is to deliver opinions on proposed legislation when consulted by the Council of Ministers and to issue own-initiative opinions in appropriate cases. In a few policy areas (e.g. employment (Art 128(2) EC Treaty)), the legal base for a legislative proposal stipulates that the Committee must be consulted in relation to proposed legislation. *See also* LEGAL BASE.

Economically self-sufficient   An economically self-sufficient person is one who has sufficient financial resources not to be a burden on others. In the context of the European Union's free movement of persons' policy, an economically self-sufficient person is one who does not have recourse to a state's social assistance scheme.

ECOSOC   *See* ECONOMIC AND SOCIAL COMMITTEE.

ECSC   *See* EUROPEAN COAL AND STEEL COMMUNITY.

ECU   *See* EUROPEAN CURRENCY UNIT.

EEA   *See* EUROPEAN ECONOMIC AREA.

EEC   *See* EUROPEAN ECONOMIC COMMUNITY.

effet utile   French phrase which means 'useful effect'.

EFTA   *See* EUROPEAN FREE TRADE ASSOCIATION.

EIB   *See* EUROPEAN INVESTMENT BANK.

ejusdem generis rule   Latin phrase which is applied in the English legal system as an aid to legislative interpretation. The rule provides that if specific categories are followed by general words, then the general words are limited to the context of the specific categories. For example, if a UK Act of Parliament provided that a person had to apply for a licence if he owned a 'dog, cat or other animal', the rule would operate to limit the general words 'or other animal' to the context of the categories 'dog and cat'. The court could legitimately decide that 'or other animals' was limited to domestic pets.

EMU   *See* ECONOMIC AND MONETARY UNION.

Equal-burden rule   Within the context of Arts 28 and 29 EC Treaty, an equal-burden rule is a rule which applies equally to domestic and foreign producers (and goods). *See also* DUAL-BURDEN RULE.

Equitable doctrine of estoppel   To deny the assertion of a right. *See also* ESTOPPEL.

Estoppel   To deny the assertion of a right. *See also* EQUITABLE DOCTRINE OF ESTOPPEL.

EU   *See* EUROPEAN UNION.

Euratom   *See* EUROPEAN ATOMIC ENERGY COMMUNITY.

Euro   Following amendments made to the EC Treaty by the TEU, a timetable for the adoption of the Single European Currency (the euro) was established. The euro became legal tender in 12 of the 15 pre-2004 Member States on 1 January 2002. The UK, Denmark and Sweden opted out of the single currency. On 1 January 2007 Slovenia adopted the euro. The euro has therefore replaced the national currency in 13 of the current 27 Member States. *See also* ECONOMIC AND MONETARY UNION; SINGLE EUROPEAN CURRENCY.

European Atomic Energy Community (Euratom)   The European Atomic Energy Community came into force on 1 July 1958; it is one of the current two European Communities. Euratom covers the research and development of nuclear energy within the EU. *See also* EUROPEAN COAL AND STEEL COMMUNITY; EUROPEAN COMMUNITIES; EUROPEAN COMMUNITY; EUROPEAN ECONOMIC COMMUNITY; EUROPEAN UNION; TREATY ON EUROPEAN UNION.

European Central Bank (ECB)   The European Central Bank was established by Art 8 EC Treaty. It is not a Community institution within the scope of Art 7 EC Treaty. The ECB was set up as part of the progression towards the single European currency (the euro). *See also* EURO.

European Coal and Steel Community (ECSC)   The ECSC came into force on 23 July 1952 and ended on 23 July 2002. It was the first of the three European Communities to be established (the other two being the EEC (later renamed the EC) and Euratom) and regulated the control and production of coal and steel. *See also* EUROPEAN ATOMIC ENERGY COMMUNITY; EUROPEAN COMMUNITIES; EUROPEAN COMMUNITY; EUROPEAN ECONOMIC COMMUNITY; EUROPEAN UNION; TREATY ON EUROPEAN UNION.

European Commission   The European Commission is one of the Community institutions. There are 27 Commissioners (one from each of the 27 Member States). The

Commission initiates/proposes EU legislation, acts as the watchdog of the EU to ensure EU Law is being complied with, and has limited direct legislative powers.

European Communities   Initially, the European Communities collectively comprised the following three Communities: European Coal and Steel Community (ECSC), European Economic Community (EEC) (later renamed EC) and European Atomic Energy Community (Euratom). The ECSC ended on 23 July 2002 and therefore the European Communities now consists of the EC and Euratom. *See also* EUROPEAN ATOMIC ENERGY COMMUNITY; EUROPEAN COAL AND STEEL COMMUNITY; EUROPEAN COMMUNITY; EUROPEAN ECONOMIC COMMUNITY; EUROPEAN UNION; TREATY ON EUROPEAN UNION.

European Community (EC)   In 1957 the Treaty Establishing the European Economic Community (EEC Treaty) was adopted. The EEC Treaty came into force on 1 July 1958. Following subsequent amendments to the EEC Treaty, the EEC increasingly became concerned with, *inter alia*, social policy and political issues, and was not solely concerned with economic issues. For this reason, the TEU renamed the EEC Treaty. This Treaty is now titled the Treaty Establishing the European Community (EC Treaty). The European Community is the new title for the former European Economic Community. This change came into effect on 1 November 1993 when the TEU came into force. *See also* EUROPEAN ATOMIC ENERGY COMMUNITY; EUROPEAN COAL AND STEEL COMMUNITY; EUROPEAN COMMUNITIES; EUROPEAN ECONOMIC COMMUNITY; EUROPEAN UNION; TREATY ON EUROPEAN UNION.

European Convention on Human Rights (ECHR)   The European Convention on Human Rights (ECHR) is a treaty which has been entered into by a number of European countries. All 27 Member States of the EU have signed up to the ECHR. The ECHR requires signatory states to protect the human rights set out in the Convention (e.g. Art 8 ECHR protects family life, home and family correspondence). Although the ECHR is separate and distinct from the EU, Art 6(2) TEU provides that the EU will protect the fundamental rights as guaranteed by the ECHR, as general principles of Community Law. *See also* EUROPEAN COURT OF HUMAN RIGHTS.

European Council   The European Council consists of the heads of government of the 27 Member States. Its role is to provide the EU with the necessary impetus for its development and to define its general political guidelines (Art 4 TEU). The European Council meets at least twice a year, at meetings often referred to as 'European Summits'.

European Court of Human Rights   An aggrieved person whose human rights have been infringed by a state which is a signatory to the European Convention of Human Rights (ECHR) has a right to bring the case before the European Court of Human Rights. Decisions made by this court are not binding on national courts. This court is not a Community institution. *See also* EUROPEAN CONVENTION ON HUMAN RIGHTS.

European Currency Unit (ECU)   The European Currency Unit was used by the Member States for their internal accounting purposes, prior to the adoption of the euro. *See also* EURO.

European Economic Community (EEC)   The European Economic Community was created by the Treaty Establishing the European Economic Community. This Treaty (which is often referred to as the Treaty of Rome, because it was signed in Rome) came into force on 1 July 1958. The EEC created, *inter alia*, the common market. The EEC was renamed the European Community (EC) on 1 November 1993 by the Treaty on European Union (TEU). *See also* EUROPEAN ATOMIC ENERGY COMMUNITY; EUROPEAN COAL

AND STEEL COMMUNITY; EUROPEAN COMMUNITIES; EUROPEAN COMMUNITY; EUROPEAN UNION; TREATY ON EUROPEAN UNION.

European Free Trade Association (EFTA)   The European Free Trade Association was set up by non-Member States as an alternative to EU membership. EFTA established a free-trade area between the participating states (currently Iceland, Liechtenstein, Norway and Switzerland). *See also* EUROPEAN ECONOMIC AREA.

European Investment Bank (EIB)   The European Investment Bank (EIB) was established by Art 9 EC Treaty. It is not a Community institution within the scope of Art 7 EC Treaty. The EIB is the European Union's long-term lending bank and the regional development bank for Europe. It makes grants and loans to projects which affect more than one Member State, where they cannot be funded sufficiently from within those Member States.

European Parliament   The European Parliament is one of the Community institutions. Members of the European Parliament (MEPs) are directly elected to the Parliament. Direct elections took place for the first time in 1979.

European Union (EU)   The European Union was established by the Treaty on European Union (TEU). The EU comprises of three pillars: (i) the European Communities; (ii) Common Foreign and Security Policy; and (iii) Police and Judicial Cooperation in Criminal Matters. *See also* EUROPEAN ATOMIC ENERGY COMMUNITY; EUROPEAN COAL AND STEEL COMMUNITY; EUROPEAN COMMUNITIES; EUROPEAN COMMUNITY; EUROPEAN ECONOMIC COMMUNITY; TREATY ON EUROPEAN UNION.

European Union (EU) worker   A worker who comes within the scope of the provisions of EU Law relating to the free movement of workers is referred to as an 'EU worker'. An EU worker is defined as one who is engaged in a genuine and effective economic activity which is not on such a small scale as to be marginal or ancillary (Case 53/81 **Levin**). The EU law provisions only apply to an EU citizen who is working in a Member State other than that of his nationality.

Exportability of benefits   Within the context of Art 42 EC Treaty and Regulation 1408/71 (which establishes social security rights for EU workers), the right to receive a social security benefit, usually from the state of origin, attaches to an EU worker as he travels around the EU, irrespective of national boundaries. This is referred to as the 'exportability of benefits' and is also known as 'the portability principle'. *See also* AGGREGATION OF CONTRIBUTIONS; DOUBLE-FUNCTION TEST.

fait accompli   French phrase which means 'an accomplished and presumably irreversible deed or fact'.

Foreclosure   Closing off the market.

Franc   The franc was France's national currency before France adopted the euro. *See also* EURO.

Francovich damages   Francovich damages, also referred to as the principle of state liability, were established by the Court of Justice in Case C-6 and 9/90 **Francovich**. This principle provides that if a person suffers damage because of a Member State's breach of Community law, the Member State is liable to the aggrieved person if: (i) the rule of Community law infringed is intended to confer rights on individuals; (ii) the breach is sufficiently serious; and (iii) there is a direct causal link between the breach of the rule and the damage sustained by the person (Cases C-46 and 49/93 **Brasserie du Pêcheur** and **Factortame**). *See also* STATE LIABILITY.

Fundamental rights   Fundamental rights are those which the Court of Justice has deemed are central to the European Union's policies. For example, the rights established by the free movement provisions of the EC Treaty have been classified by the Court of Justice as fundamental rights. Fundamental rights will be protected by the Court of Justice from interference, unless such interference is permitted by the Treaty.

Harmonising directive   A harmonising directive is one which establishes a set of common laws which apply throughout the Member States. In the context of the recognition of professional qualifications (which forms part of the European Union's right to the freedom of establishment), a series of harmonising directives were adopted (relating to specified professions such as GPs, nurses, vets). If the professional satisfies the conditions set out in the directive, recognition of the profession is guaranteed throughout the EU. *See also* MUTUAL RECOGNITION.

Historical interpretation   Historical interpretation is used by courts to interpret legislation. If this method is employed, there is a consideration of the subjective intention of the author of the text of the legislation. This method may be equated with the English mischief rule of legislative interpretation, where the judge seeks to establish the legislative intent. This method of legislative interpretation is occasionally used by the Court of Justice and the Court of First Instance. *See also* CONTEXTUAL INTERPRETATION; LITERAL INTERPRETATION; TELEOLOGICAL INTERPRETATION.

Horizontal direct effect   A provision of Community law which is enforceable in national courts or tribunals against natural and legal persons, overriding any inconsistent national provisions, is said to have horizontal direct effect (Case C 152/84 **Marshall** *v* **Southampton** AHA). Treaty articles and regulations are capable of having horizontal direct effect if the provision is sufficiently precise and unconditional (Case 26/62 **Van Gend en Loos**). Directives cannot have horizontal direct effect (Case C 152/84 **Marshall** *v* **Southampton AHA**). *See also* DIRECT EFFECT; VERTICAL DIRECT EFFECT.

Horizontal restrictive agreement   A horizontal restrictive agreement is one where the parties to the agreement are competitors (e.g. an agreement between producers of a particular commodity).

in camera   Latin phrase which means 'in the chamber' but more commonly used to mean 'in secret'.

Indirect effect   If a provision of Community law is not directly effective (i.e. the provision cannot be enforced in national courts and tribunals), national courts and tribunals are under an obligation to interpret national law in such a way that it avoids a conflict with Community law, if that is possible (Case C-106/89 **Marleasing**). This is referred to as the principle of indirect effect. *See also* DIRECT EFFECT; INTERPRETATIVE OBLIGATION; MARLEASING INTERPRETATIVE OBLIGATION.

Indistinctly applicable measure   Within the context of Arts 28 and 29 EC Treaty, an indistinctly applicable measure is a QR or MEQR which is applied to all goods without distinction; i.e. the restriction is applied to both home-produced and foreign goods. *See also* DISTINCTLY APPLICABLE MEASURE; MEASURE HAVING AN EQUIVALENT EFFECT TO A QUANTITATIVE RESTRICTION; QUANTITATIVE RESTRICTION.

Infraction proceedings   Article 226 EC Treaty empowers the Commission to take action against a Member State which is in breach of Community Law. If the Member State fails to remedy the breach, ultimately the Commission can bring proceedings against the defaulting Member State before the Court of Justice. Such proceedings are referred to as infraction proceedings.

Intellectual property right Intellectual property rights concern the product of one person's work (by hand or brain) against unauthorised use or exploitation by another. Such rights are protected by laws relating to, *inter alia*, copyright, patents and trade marks.

inter alia Latin phrase which means 'among other things'.

inter partes Latin phrase which means 'between the parties'.

Intergovernmental Intergovernmental refers to non-legally binding cooperation between two or more countries.

Intergovernmental conference (IGC) An intergovernmental conference is the title given to a meeting of the European Council which is primarily concerned with drafting a Treaty to amend the founding treaties (i.e. EC, Euratom and TEU).

Interlocutory proceedings When court or tribunal proceedings have been initiated, sometimes the court will need to make an order (for example) before it finally determines the case. Such an order is referred to as an interim order. Interlocutory proceedings occur during the course of the action (i.e. before the case is finally determined), when, for example, an interim order is required.

Internal market The internal market is 'an area without internal frontiers in which the free movement of goods, persons, services and capital is ensured' (Art 14 EC Treaty). One of the aims of the SEA was to complete the European Union's internal market by 1 January 1993.

Interpretative obligation If a provision of Community law is not directly effective (i.e. the provision cannot be enforced in national courts and tribunals), national courts and tribunals are under an obligation to interpret national law in such a way that it avoids a conflict with Community law, if that is possible (Case C-106/89 **Marleasing**). This is known as the principle of indirect effect (and is also referred to as the national court's interpretative obligation). *See also* Direct effect; Indirect effect; Marleasing interpretative obligation.

Ioannina Declaration Under a declaration made in March 1994 at the Ioannina Summit of the European Council, it was provided that where a decision is to be taken by a qualified majority, if a minority of Member States (which do not have sufficient votes to block the decision being adopted) indicate their intention to oppose the decision, the Council of Ministers is required to do all in its power to reach, within a reasonable period of time, a satisfactory solution. This declaration is referred to as the Ioannina Declaration. *See also* Qualified majority.

ipse dixit Latin phrase which means 'he himself said it', or, in a general context to emphasise that some assertion comes from some authority.

Justice and Home Affairs (JHA) Cooperation in the fields of Justice and Home Affairs was established by the TEU. The TEU also established the European Union, which was founded upon three pillars. The JHA constituted the third of the three pillars of the EU. However, following amendments to the TEU and EC Treaty by the ToA, this third pillar was renamed Police and Judicial Cooperation in Criminal Matters. *See also* Common Foreign and Security Policy; Cooperation in the fields of Justice and Home Affairs; Police and Judicial Cooperation in Criminal Matters; three pillars of the European Union.

Judge-Rapporteur In EU Law and politics, Rapporteur refers to a person who is appointed by a deliberative body to investigate a particular issue, and to report back to that body. When a case is heard by the Court of Justice, a Judge-Rapporteur is appointed. The Court of Justice delivers a single judgment for each case (rather than each judge delivering separate judgments). It is the responsibility of the Judge-Rapporteur to draft the judgment which will inform the discussions of all the other judges assigned to that case. A single judgment will then be agreed by the judges acting by simple majority.

Jurisdiction   Jurisdiction is normally used to refer to the power of a court or tribunal to hear a case. With regard to the Court of Justice and the Court of First Instance, their jurisdiction (i.e. power) to hear cases derives from the treaties.

jus cogens   Latin phrase which means 'fundamental rights of the human person'.

Legal base   The Treaty article under which a legislative instrument (e.g. regulation, directive or decision) is proposed is often referred to as the legal base (or legal basis). The legal base will set out the legislative procedure which must be followed for the proposed instrument to be adopted. *See also* LEGAL BASIS.

Legal basis   The Treaty article under which a legislative instrument (e.g. regulation, directive or decision) is proposed is often referred to as the legal base (or legal basis). The legal base will set out the legislative procedure which must be followed for the proposed instrument to be adopted. *See also* LEGAL BASE.

Legal certainty   In Case 70/81 **Kloppenburg**, the Court of Justice stated that Community legislation must be unequivocal and its application must be predictable for those who are subject to it. This is referred to as the principle of legal certainty. *See also* NON-RETROACTIVITY.

Legitimate expectation   The principle of legitimate expectation provides that assurances relied on in good faith should be honoured (Case 169/73 **Compagnie Continentale *v* Council**).

Literal interpretation   Literal interpretation is used by courts to interpret legislation. If this method is employed, words are given their natural, plain meaning. This method of legislative interpretation is widely used by courts in the English legal system, but it is rarely used by the Court of Justice or the Court of First Instance. *See also* CONTEXTUAL INTERPRETATION; HISTORICAL INTERPRETATION; TELEOLOGICAL INTERPRETATION.

locus standi   Latin phrase which means 'a place of standing'. In a legal context it refers to an individual's right to be heard in a court or tribunal.

Luxembourg Accords   The Luxembourg Accords were the result of an impasse between France and the other Member States of the EU during 1965. France refused to attend meetings of the Council of Ministers resulting in important decision-making within the Community grinding to a halt. The Luxembourg Accords were negotiated. The Accords are not legally enforceable and are rarely (if ever) relied on.

Mandatory requirements defence   In the context of Arts 28 and 29 EC Treaty, the second **Cassis** principle (Case 120/78) established a rule of reason (also referred to as the 'mandatory requirements defence') which provides that obstacles to the free movement of goods within the Community resulting from disparities between the national laws relating to the marketing of the products in question, must be accepted in so far as those provisions may be recognised as being necessary in order to satisfy mandatory requirements relating to, in particular, the effectiveness of fiscal supervision, the protection of public health, the fairness of commercial transactions and the defence of the consumer. *See also* PROPORTIONALITY TEST; RULE OF MUTUAL RECOGNITION; RULE OF REASON.

Marleasing interpretative obligation   If a provision of Community law is not directly effective (i.e. the provision cannot be enforced in national courts and tribunals), national courts and tribunals are under an obligation to interpret national law in such a way that it avoids a conflict with Community law, if that is possible (Case C-106/89 **Marleasing**). This is known as the principle of indirect effect (and is also referred to as the national court's **Marleasing** interpretative obligation). *See also* DIRECT EFFECT; INDIRECT EFFECT; INTERPRETATIVE OBLIGATION.

Marshall Plan   Following the end of the Second World War, the USA provided financial assistance to Western European states to aid economic recovery. This aid was referred to as the Marshall Plan.

Measure having an equivalent effect to a quantitative restriction (MEQR)   In the context of Arts 28 and 29 EC Treaty, a measure having an equivalent effect to a quantitative restriction includes 'all trading rules enacted by Member States which are capable of hindering, directly or indirectly, actually or potentially, intra-Community trade' (Case 8/74 **Procureur du Roi** *v* **Dassonville**). This is also referred to as the **Dassonville** formula. *See also* DISTINCTLY APPLICABLE MEASURE; INDISTINCTLY APPLICABLE MEASURE; QUANTITATIVE RESTRICTION.

MEQR   *See* MEASURE HAVING AN EQUIVALENT EFFECT TO A QUANTITATIVE RESTRICTION.

MEP   Member of the European Parliament. *See* also EUROPEAN PARLIAMENT.

Merger   A merger occurs when two or more business undertakings join together to form one business undertaking.

Mischief rule   The mischief rule is a method of legislative interpretation, sometimes used by courts in the English legal system. When applying this rule, the judge seeks to establish the legislative intent.

Monopoly   A monopoly exists if a commodity or service is controlled solely (or primarily) by one business undertaking or the state. *See also* STATE MONOPOLY.

mutatis mutandis   Latin phrase which means 'with those things changed which need to be changed' or 'with the appropriate changes'.

NATO   *See* NORTH ATLANTIC TREATY ORGANISATION.

Natural justice   Concept derived into EU Law from the English Legal System, and is closely linked to the USA's 'due process'. The Court of Justice often refers to it as a duty to act fairly (Case 222/86 **UNECTEF** *v* **Heylens**).

Non-retroactivity   Non-retroactivity means that any changes to the law (through legislation or case law) should not be applied retrospectively. To do otherwise would conflict with the principle of legal certainty. In EU Law this principle is applied in particular with regard to legal provisions which impose criminal sanctions. *See also* LEGAL CERTAINTY.

North Atlantic Treaty Organisation (NATO)   NATO was founded in 1949, following the end of the Second World War. It is a defence organisation for North America and Europe.

obiter dictum   Latin phrase which means 'a thing said in passing'. In a legal context it refers to an observation by a judge on a point of law which is not directly relevant to the case before the court. The point of law is neither required by the judge's decision nor does it serve as a precedent. However, it may be of persuasive authority.

Objective justification   Objective justification (or the rule of reason) is a common concept throughout much of EU substantive law. It is based on the premise that a restriction, which might otherwise breach EU Law, will be permissible provided (i) the reason for the restriction is for a legitimate public interest; and (ii) the restriction is proportionate (i.e. it does not go beyond what is necessary to protect the legitimate public interest). *See also* PROPORTIONALITY TEST; RULE OF REASON.

OECD   *See* ORGANISATION FOR ECONOMIC COOPERATION AND DEVELOPMENT (OECD).

Oligopoly   An oligopoly is a market in which a small number of suppliers supply the vast majority of demand.

Opinion   Article 249 EC Treaty provides that an opinion is a non-legally enforceable Community instrument. It may have a persuasive element (i.e. it may be taken into account by the Court of Justice or Court of First Instance when determining a case).

Organisation for Economic Cooperation and Development (OECD)   The OECD is a group of 30 member countries which share a commitment to democratic government and the market economy. It has active relationships with 70 other countries and economies, non-governmental organisations (NGOs) and civil society. It is not a Community institution.

Parallel imports   Parallel imports refers to the situation where goods which are sold in one Member State, are purchased at a lower cost in another Member State, and imported (for sale) into the first Member State.

per   Latin word which means 'by means of' or 'according to'.

Pillars   The Treaty on European Union (TEU) established the European Union. Article A TEU provided that 'the Union shall be founded on the European Communities, supplemented by the policies and forms of cooperation established by this Treaty'. It followed from this that the EU was to be founded upon three pillars: (i) the European Communities (i.e. the EC, Euratom and ECSC (the ECSC expired on 23 July 2002)); (ii) Common Foreign and Security Policy (CFSP); and (iii) Cooperation in the fields of Justice and Home Affairs (JHA). Article A TEU was amended by the ToA (and renumbered Art 1 TEU). The three pillars now comprise of: (i) the European Communities (i.e. the EC and Euratom); (ii) Common Foreign and Security Policy (CFSP); and (iii) Police and Judicial Cooperation in Criminal Matters. *See also* COMMON FOREIGN AND SECURITY POLICY; COOPERATION IN THE FIELDS OF JUSTICE AND HOME AFFAIRS; JUSTICE AND HOME AFFAIRS; POLICE AND JUDICIAL COOPERATION IN CRIMINAL MATTERS; THREE PILLARS OF THE EUROPEAN UNION.

Police and Judicial Cooperation in Criminal Matters   Police and Judicial Cooperation in Criminal Matters is one of the three pillars of the European Union. Article A TEU, which established the European Union, provided that 'the Union shall be founded on the European Communities, supplemented by the policies and forms of cooperation established by this Treaty'. It followed from this that the EU was to by founded upon three pillars: (i) the European Communities (i.e. the EC, Euratom and ECSC (the ECSC expired on 23 July 2002)); (ii) Common Foreign and Security Policy (CFS); and (iii) Cooperation in the fields of Justice and Home Affairs (JHA). Article A TEU was amended by the ToA (and renumbered Art 1 TEU). The three pillars now comprise of: (i) the European Communities (i.e. the EC and Euratom); (ii) Common Foreign and Security Policy (CFS); and (iii) Police and Judicial Cooperation in Criminal Matters. *See also* COMMON FOREIGN AND SECURITY POLICY; COOPERATION IN THE FIELDS OF JUSTICE AND HOME AFFAIRS; JUSTICE AND HOME AFFAIRS; THREE PILLARS OF THE EUROPEAN UNION.

Posted workers   A business undertaking employing workers in one Member State, may send their workers to another Member State. Such workers are referred to as posted workers (i.e. a worker 'posted' from one Member State to another).

Precedent   The doctrine of precedent (*stare decisis*; a Latin phrase which means 'let the decision stand'), provides that courts and tribunals are bound by points of law decided by courts higher up in the hierarchy, and sometimes they are bound by their own previous decisions. The doctrine does not apply to the Court of Justice. However, the Court of Justice normally follows its own previous decisions for the sake of legal certainty. *See also* RATIO DECIDENDI.

Preliminary ruling   Pursuant to Art 234 EC Treaty, a national court or tribunal may (and in certain circumstances it must) refer a case to the Court of Justice if the national court or tribunal considers such a referral is necessary in order for it to reach its decision. The national court or tribunal asks the Court of Justice questions relating to interpretation of the Treaties, or the interpretation or validity of Regulations, Directives or Decisions. The Court of Justice answers those questions and sends the case back to the referring court or tribunal for it to give judgment. This procedure is referred to as the 'preliminary ruling' procedure.

prima facie   Latin phrase which means 'at first sight'. In a legal context, '*prima facie* case' refers to evidence which will suffice to support the allegation, unless there is evidence which rebuts the allegation.

pro forma   Latin phrase which means 'for form' or 'as a matter of form', i.e. prescribing a set form or procedure.

Procedural *ultra vires*   When a decision maker, who is exercising a power or discretion, fails to follow an essential procedural requirement (quite often set out in the enabling legislation), this is referred to as 'procedural ultra vires'. The exercise of the power or discretion in such circumstances is unlawful. *See also* SUBSTANTIVE *ULTRA VIRES; ULTRA VIRES*.

Product substitution   Product substitution determines which products compete with each other. *See also* DEMAND-SIDE SUBSTITUTION; SUPPLY-SIDE SUBSTITUTION.

Proportionality test   The proportionality test is imported into EU Law from the German legal system. The test is applied to ensure that interference with EU Law principles, rights, prohibitions, etc. must be no more than is necessary to achieve the stated objective, which itself must be justifiable in the public interest. *See also* OBJECTIVE JUSTIFICATION; RULE OF REASON.

Protectionism   A rule imposed by the State or a regulatory body, the aim of which is to protect domestic traders from competition by foreign traders, is referred to as 'protectionism'.

Protocol   Protocols are often annexed (i.e. attached) to EU treaties. With regard to the protocols annexed to the EC Treaty, Art 311 EC Treaty states that 'The protocols annexed to this Treaty ... shall be an integral part thereof'. The United Kingdom's opt-out from the single European currency is set out in a protocol annexed to the EC Treaty.

QR   *See* QUANTITATIVE RESTRICTION.

Qualified majority   The legal base determines the legislative procedure which has to be used for the adoption of a particular instrument. If the legal base provides for the instrument to be adopted by the Council of Ministers acting by a 'qualified majority', the votes are weighted according to the population size of the Member States. There are a total of 345 votes. If the Commission has proposed the legislation, the Council of Ministers requires 255 votes out of 345 to approve the proposal. If the Commission has not proposed the legislation, in order to approve the legislation the Council of Ministers requires 255 votes out of 345, which must additionally be cast by at least two-thirds of the Member States.

Quantitative restriction (QR)   In the context of Arts 28 and 29 EC Treaty, a quantitative restriction (QR) relates to measures which amount to a total or partial restraint of imports, exports or goods in transit (Case 2/73 **Geddo**). *See also* DISTINCTLY APPLICABLE MEASURE; INDISTINCTLY APPLICABLE MEASURE; MEASURE HAVING AN EQUIVALENT EFFECT TO A QUANTITATIVE RESTRICTION.

Rapporteur   In EU Law and politics, Rapporteur refers to a person who is appointed by a deliberative body (e.g. the European Parliament) to investigate a particular issue, and to report back to that body.

Ratification   Ratification means 'approval'.

ratio decidendi   Latin phrase which means the legal reason (or ground) for a judicial decision. It is the *ratio decidendi* (or ratio) of a case which will bind later courts under the system of precedent. *See also* PRECEDENT.

Recommendation   Article 249 EC Treaty provides that a recommendation is a non-legally enforceable Community instrument. It may have a persuasive element (i.e. it may be taken into account by the Court of Justice or Court of First Instance when determining a case).

Regulation   A regulation is a legally effective Community instrument. Article 249 EC Treaty provides that a regulation shall be directly applicable. This means it is incorporated automatically into the national legal systems of the Member States.

Respondent   A respondent is the person against whom a claim is made in a court or tribunal (also referred to as a defendant).

Restrictive agreement   A restrictive agreement is an agreement between otherwise independent business undertakings the aim of which is to protect their market share, which may affect trade between the Member States, and which distorts competition within the common market. Such agreements are prohibited by Art 81 EC Treaty.

Rule of mutual recognition   The first **Cassis** principle (Case 120/78), referred to as the 'rule of mutual recognition', provides that once goods have been lawfully marketed in one Member State, they should be free to be marketed in any other Member State without restriction.

Rule of reason   The rule of reason (or objective justification) is a common concept throughout much of EU substantive law. It is based on the premise that a restriction, which might otherwise breach EU Law, will be permissible provided (i) the reason for the restriction is for a legitimate public interest; and (ii) the restriction is proportionate (i.e. it does not go beyond what is necessary to protect the legitimate public interest). In the context of Arts 28 and 29 EC Treaty, the second **Cassis** principle (Case 120/78) established a rule of reason which provides that obstacles to the free movement of goods within the Community resulting from disparities between the national laws relating to the marketing of the products in question must be accepted in so far as those provisions may be recognised as being necessary in order to satisfy mandatory requirements relating to, in particular, the effectiveness of fiscal supervision, the protection of public health, the fairness of commercial transactions and the defence of the consumer. *See also* Mandatory requirements defence; Objective justification; Proportionality test; Rule of mutual recognition.

Schengen Agreement The Schengen Agreement abolished the internal borders of the signatory states and created a single external border where immigration checks for the Schengen area are carried out in accordance with a single set of rules. Common rules regarding visas, asylum rights and checks at external borders were adopted to allow the free movement of persons within the signatory states without disturbing law and order. The Schengen area includes every Member State excluding (i) the UK and Ireland, and (ii) the new Member States which joined the EU on 1 May 2004 and 1 January 2007. *See also* Schengen Information System.

Schengen Information System (SIS) The SIS is an information network which was set up to allow all border posts, police stations and consular agents from Schengen group Member States to access data on specific individuals or on vehicles or objects which have been lost or stolen. Member States supply the network through national networks (N-SIS) connected to a central system (C-SIS), and this is supplemented by a network known as SIRENE (Supplementary Information Request at the National Entry). *See also* Schengen Agreement.

SEA *See* Single European Act.

Secondary legislation In EU Law, secondary legislation refers to Community instruments which are adopted by the Community institutions, pursuant to powers contained within the treaties. Article 249 EC Treaty provides that such instruments shall be in the form of regulations, directives or decisions.

Single European currency Following amendments made to the EC Treaty by the TEU, a timetable for the adoption of the single European currency (the euro) was established. The euro became legal tender in 12 of the 15 pre-2004 Member States on 1 January 2002. The UK, Denmark and Sweden opted out of the single currency. On 1 January 2007 Slovenia adopted the euro. The euro has therefore replaced the national currency in 13 of the current 27 Member States. *See also* Economic and Monetary Union; Euro.

Single European Act (SEA) The SEA came into force on 1 July 1987 and amended the founding treaties (in particular the EC Treaty).

SIS *See* Schengen Information System.

Social Chapter The Social Chapter was annexed to the TEU as a protocol, applying to all of the then Member States except the UK. The Social Chapter covers, *inter alia*, employee protection rights. Following the election of a Labour government in the UK on 1 May 1997, the UK no longer objected to the Social Chapter and therefore it was incorporated into the EC Treaty when the Treaty was amended by the ToA on 1 May 1999.

Soft law Non-legally enforceable instruments which may aid the interpretation and/or application of Community law are referred to as 'soft law'. Soft law, in the EU context, includes recommendations and opinion.

stare decisis Latin phrase which means 'let the decision stand'. In a legal context it refers to the doctrine of precedent. *See also* Precedent.

State aid State aid is aid (financial or non-financial) which is granted by the state to a business undertaking. The compatibility of State aid with the common market is governed by Art 87(1) EC Treaty.

State liability   The principle of state liability, established by the Court of Justice in Case C-6 and 9/90 **Francovich**, provides that if a person suffers damage because of a Member State's breach of Community law, the Member State is liable to the aggrieved person if: (i) the rule of Community law infringed is intended to confer rights on individuals; (ii) the breach is sufficiently serious; and (iii) there is a direct causal link between the breach of the rule and the damage sustained by the person (Cases C-46 and 49/93 **Brasserie du Pêcheur** and **Factortame**). *See also* Francovich damages.

State monopoly   A state monopoly exists where a commodity or service is controlled solely by the state (e.g. nationalised utilities: gas, electricity, water, etc.). Article 31 EC Treaty regulates state monopolies. *See also* Monopoly.

Subsidiarity   Article 5 EC Treaty provides that in areas which do not fall within the Community's exclusive competence, the Community shall only take action if action cannot be sufficiently achieved by the Member States, each acting individually. This is referred to as the principle of subsidiarity.

Substantive *ultra vires*   When a decision maker, who exercises a power or discretion, has no competence to exercise such power or direction, this is referred to as 'substantive *ultra vires*'. The exercise of the power or discretion in such circumstances is unlawful. *See also* Procedural *ultra vires*; *ultra vires*.

sui generis   Latin phrase which means 'of its own kind' or 'in a class of its own'.

Supply-side substitution   Supply-side substitutability is concerned with the ability of a manufacturer to switch production from one product to another.

Teleological interpretation   Teleological interpretation is used by courts to interpret legislation. If this method is employed when interpreting EU Law, the provision will be interpreted in furtherance of the aims and objectives of the Community and the European Union as a whole. This method of legislative interpretation, together with contextual interpretation, is extensively used by the Court of Justice and the Court of First Instance. See *also* Contextual interpretation; Historical interpretation; Literal interpretation.

TEU   *See* Treaty on European Union.

Third country   Within EU Law, third-country is used to refer to a country which is not a member of the EU (i.e. a non-Member State).

Three pillars of the European Union   The Treaty on European Union (TEU) established the European Union. Article A TEU provided that 'the Union shall be founded on the European Communities, supplemented by the policies and forms of cooperation established by this Treaty'. It followed from this that the EU was to be founded upon three pillars: (i) the European Communities (i.e. the EC, Euratom and ECSC (the ECSC expired on 23 July 2002)); (ii) Common Foreign and Security Policy (CFS); and (iii) Cooperation in the fields of Justice and Home Affairs (JHA). Article A TEU was amended by the ToA (and renumbered Art 1 TEU). The three pillars now comprise of: (i) the European Communities (i.e. the EC and Euratom); (ii) Common Foreign and Security Policy (CFS); and (iii) Police and Judicial Cooperation in Criminal Matters. *See also* Common Foreign and Security Policy; Cooperation in the fields of Justice and Home Affairs; Justice and Home Affairs; Police and Judicial Cooperation in Criminal Matters.

ToA   *See* Treaty of Amsterdam.

ToN   *See* Treaty of Nice.

Treaty   A Treaty is an agreement between two or more countries. A treaty will not be legally enforceable unless this is provided for within the treaty. The treaties establishing the European Communities and the European Union incorporated enforcement mechanisms to ensure Member States complied with their EU Law obligations. In addition, Community institutions were established to develop EU Law through the adoption of Community instruments. A Court of Justice and Court of First Instance were established to ensure uniform application of EU Law throughout the Member States.

Treaty of Accession   A Treaty of Accession is adopted by the Member States to provide for enlargement of the European Union. There was a Treaty of Accession to provide for Bulgaria and Romania's entry to the EU on 1 January 2007.

Treaty of Amsterdam (ToA)   The Treaty of Amsterdam came into force on 1 May 1999 and amended the EC Treaty and the TEU.

Treaty on European Union (TEU)   The Treaty on European Union came into force on 1 November 1993. The TEU amended the founding treaties, and also established the European Union. The TEU renamed the EEC the EC. *See also* EUROPEAN ATOMIC ENERGY COMMUNITY; EUROPEAN COAL AND STEEL COMMUNITY; EUROPEAN COMMUNITIES; EUROPEAN COMMUNITY; EUROPEAN ECONOMIC COMMUNITY; EUROPEAN UNION.

Treaty of Nice (ToN)   The Treaty of Nice came into force on 1 February 2003 and amended the EC Treaty and the TEU.

Treaty of Rome   The EC Treaty is often referred to as the Treaty of Rome because it was signed in Rome on 25 March 1957. However, the Euratom Treaty was also signed in Rome at the same time. The EC Treaty's official title is 'The Treaty Establishing the European Community', not the Treaty of Rome.

ultra vires   Latin phrase which means 'beyond the power' or 'without authority'. In a legal context it means an act which is in excess of that authorised by law, thus rendering the act invalid. *See also* PROCEDURAL *ULTRA VIRES*; SUBSTANTIVE *ULTRA VIRES*.

Undertaking   An undertaking is a business. In the English legal system this could refer to a sole trader, a partnership, or a company.

Vertical direct effect   A provision of Community law which is enforceable in national courts or tribunals against the state or emanation of the state, overriding any inconsistent national provisions, is said to have vertical direct effect (Case C-188/89 **Foster v British Gas**). Treaty articles, regulations and directives are capable of having vertical direct effect if the provision is sufficiently precise and unconditional (Case 26/62 **Van Gend en Loos**). *See also* DIRECT EFFECT; HORIZONTAL DIRECT EFFECT.

Vertical restrictive agreement   A vertical restrictive agreement refers to an agreement where the parties to the agreement are not in direct competition with each another (e.g. an agreement between manufacturers, wholesalers and retailers).

vis-à-vis   French phrase which means 'in comparison with' or 'in relation to'.

Index